INTERNATIONAL FINANCE

Conventional wisdom has treated international trade as the motive force behind international financial flows. However, the last quarter of this century has witnessed an upsurge in the volume of international financial flows which have gained a momentum of their own, thus dwarfing the role of international trade. This increase in volume is generated by the large size of the international financial market systems, which are more closely integrated today than ever before.

Dilip K. Das demonstrates through the work of highly acclaimed contributors, who are leading authorities in the field of international finance, that the development of a whole range of financial instruments is one of the key forces behind greater integration of financial markets.

International Finance provides students of economics, finance and business management with medium-level discussion on international finance issues which are neither introductory nor over-specialized in nature. Six themes are developed which encompass some of the most practical and useful facets of international finance. Beginning with a description of the new size and shape of the financial markets, the first chapter focuses on how international mobile capital has become, and looks at the nature and operation of the principal international financial institutions. The role of European monetary union forms the second section where key issues in monetary policy and the central banking system are analysed. Part III evaluates world equity markets using Asia as an example, with Part IV providing papers relating to foreign exchange markets. International debt issues are discussed in Part V taking examples from the USA which is the largest debtor economy in the world. The final section deals with the currency aspect of international finance looking specifically at the deutsche mark, the yen and the internationalization of the Korean capital market.

Professor Dilip K. Das presently holds a visiting position at INSEAD, Fontainebleau, France. He has previously taught at the Indian Institute of Management, ESSEC in Paris, Webster College in Geneva and the Australian National University in Canberra. Having written extensively, his current areas of interest include international trade, international finance and the Asia–Pacific economies.

INTERNATIONAL FINANCE

Contemporary issues

Edited by
Dilip K. Das

London and New York

First published 1993
by Routledge
11 New Fetter Lane, London EC4P 4EE

Simultaneously published in the USA and Canada
by Routledge
29 West 35th Street, New York, NY 10001

Typeset in 10pt September by
Leaper & Gard Ltd, Bristol
Printed in Great Britain by
Clays Ltd, St. Ives PLC

British Library Cataloguing in Publication Data
A catalogue reference for this book is available from the British Library

ISBN 0-415-09280-9 (hbk)
0-415-09281-7

Library of Congress Cataloging in Publication Data
has been applied for

ISBN 0-415-09280-9 (hbk)
0-415-09281-7

FOR MY LITTLE FAMILY,
VASANTI, TANUSHREE AND SIDDHARTH,
FOR THEIR GOOD HUMOURED SUPPORT AND TOLERATION

CONTENTS

FIGURES

TABLES

CONTRIBUTORS

Roy Ageloff	University of Rhode Island
Philippe Aghion	The European Bank for Reconstruction and Development
Hiroya Akiba	Niigata University
Robert Z. Aliber	University of Chicago
Robin Burgess	Oxford University
Stanley W. Black	University of North Carolina, Chapel Hill
Jorge R. Calderón-Rossell	The World Bank
Rosita P. Chang	University of Rhode Island
W. Max Corden	The Johns Hopkins University
Dilip K. Das	INSEAD
Directorate-General for Economic and Financial Affairs	Commission of the European Communities
Norman S. Fieleke	Federal Reserve Bank of Boston
André Fourçans	ESSEC
Jeffrey A. Frankel	University of California, Berkeley
Jacob A. Frenkel	The International Monetary Fund
Maxwell J. Fry	University of Birmingham
Alberto Giovannini	Columbia University
Morris Goldstein	The International Monetary Fund
Gabriel Hawawini	INSEAD
Takatoshi Ito	Hitotsubashi University
Peter B. Kenen	Princeton University
Mohsin S. Khan	The International Monetary Fund
Donald R. Lessard	Massachusetts Institute of Technology
Walter Mahler	The International Monetary Fund
Ronald McKinnon	Stanford University
Karl Otto Pöhl	Bundesbank
Kenichi Ohno	The International Monetary Fund
S. Ghone Rhee	University of Rhode Island
Ibrahim F. I. Shihata	The World Bank (ICSID)
George S. Tavlas	The International Monetary Fund
Niels Thygesen	University of Copenhagen
Tomoki Waragai	Waseda University

PREFATORY AND INTRODUCTORY COMMENTS

In the last quarter century the volume of international financial flows has expanded enormously and dwarfed international trade. While at the end of 1991 world trade touched the $3.5 trillion mark, the cross-border financial flows were fifty times as much. The *World Financial Markets* data show that they rose close to $200 trillion. Conventional wisdom had treated international trade as the motive force behind international financial flows. Apparently this relationship did not hold and the international financial markets had picked up their own momentum. At present the large volume of international financial flows is generated by the large size of the international financial market system. To name one indicator, by the end of the 1980s the total volume of the Eurocurrency market was in the vicinity of $5 trillion.

The major financial markets are more closely integrated today than they ever were in the past. One of the rationales behind greater integration is the development of a whole new range of financial instruments. The decade of the 1980s has seen the evolution of greater numbers of such instruments than any such period in the past. The principal ones, *à la* Aliber, are bank deposits denominated in all the SDR currencies plus the Swiss franc, Eurobonds in several currencies, interest rate swaps, futures contracts in foreign exchange, foreign exchange swaps, zero-coupon bonds and bonds with interest payable in one currency that are convertible into another currency. Deregulation and liberalization of different financial markets gave an immense impetus to financial integration. Although the pace, scope and direction of deregu-

lation of individual markets varied, progress made on this count was indeed substantial and so was its impact. For instance, the deregulation of Japanese financial markets helped to make Japan the largest creditor country in the world in the mid-1980s. Market liberalization affected interest rate ceilings, reserve requirements and barriers to geographical expansion, which in turn stimulated free international movement of capital. Another development that led to closer integration was 'cross-penetration' of foreign ownership which is visible in the sharp increase in the number of foreign banks and security firms in all the major financial centres of the world.

The *raison d'être* of this volume is to fill a gap in the teaching of international finance. There are some good introductory textbooks and Eitman and Stonehill's book is very popular with instructors and students, although its current edition is long overdue for a thorough revision. However, when a student tries to go beyond this set of books, he is likely to be a trifle flustered because he is generally referred to journal articles or books which are either too technical or over-specialized or both. There is hardly any book to cover the intermediate ground at a medium technical level. Besides, some issues are incompletely covered by standard textbook treatments. The highly motivated students indeed make forays in the literature and sporadically locate what they need but this endeavour tends to be time consuming and frustrating. Covering the middle ground and covering issues not generally covered in standard textbooks, therefore, became the logic of selection of papers for this collection. The papers have been so chosen as not to become too technical or over-specialized and are accessible to a master's level student in economics and an MBA student. To be sure, an ambitious undergraduate, a researcher and a professional will also find the volume worth while. As much care as possible has been taken in selecting the papers. Only the most valuable ones have been chosen to serve the objective of this collection and to enhance its shelf life.

I have chosen six themes and accordingly divided the volume in as many parts. These themes relate to some of the most practical and useful facets of international finance. The six parts have been ordered in the following manner. The volume tees off with the description of the new size and shape of the financial markets and focuses on how internationally mobile capital has become. The first part also deals with the vicissitudes in the nature and operation of the principal international financial institutions. The second part relates to European monetary union and the related central banking issues. There are well-reasoned and useful discussions about monetary policy as well as currency. Part III looks at the world equity markets. It provides an overview as well as delving into the market efficiency aspect. Literature is wide and extensive on foreign exchange markets. Part IV provides some sample papers relating to some of the highly germane and exciting topics in this area. Part V has some insightful papers regarding the debt issues and contains two complementary papers on US debt. The latter issue is often ignored by many, although the USA is the largest debtor economy in the world. The final section essentially deals with the currency aspect of international finance. The collection, thus, has six cohesive segments.

The foregoing paragraphs reveal the logic of the collection, the logic of the selection process and the logic of the ordering process as well as explaining the need for the book. Every section is preceded by an introductory essay which emphasizes the highlights and salient features of each paper and fills up minor gaps. In some places some updating has also been attempted. Despite the variety and complexity of the issues, I expect the collection to be a substantive pedagogic aid and managerial problem-solving tool.

Dilip K. Das

ACKNOWLEDGEMENTS

In attempting a venture of this kind one accumulates a great debt of gratitude and I am no exception. I express my sincere thanks to the journals and organizations that not only granted permission to reprint previously published work but also did so promptly. In alphabetical order they were the *American Economic Review*, the Directorate-General for Economic and Financial Affairs, the European Economic Community, Dow Jones-Irwin Inc., the *Journal of Economic Perspectives*, Japan Center for International Finance, Kluwer Academic Publishers, *IMF Staff Papers*, the International Monetary Fund, Princeton University, International Finance Section, and the World Bank. I also thank the Brookings Institution for granting a 50 per cent reduction in the royalty fee for using Alberto Giovannini's paper. Professor Takatoshi Ito and Professor Ronald I. McKinnon took personal initiative and helped me in getting copyright permission from the original publishers of their papers. Nell Millist handled all the word-processing with her usual aplomb and efficacy. I would be remiss if I did not thank my little family, particularly my wife Vasanti, for putting up with me while I was at this strenuous and taxing job.

Dilip K. Das
INSEAD

ABOUT THE EDITOR

Professor Dilip K. Das is currently holding a visiting position at the European Institute of Business Administration (INSEAD), Fontaine-bleau, France. He has previously taught at the Webster College, Geneva, and the Indian Institute of Management where he was professor and area chairman of economics. He was also a visiting professor at ESSEC in Paris and the Australian National University. He has worked as consultant to international organizations like the World Bank and the World Commission on Development and Environment as well as the US Agency for International Development.

He was educated at St John's College, Agra, India, and the Institut Universitaire des Hautes Etudes Internationale, Geneva, where he did his MPhil and PhD. His areas of current interest include international trade, international finance and the Pacific economies. Professor Das has written extensively and contributed several papers to international professional journals and so far has written eight books, all published by world class publishers. His last two books were entitled *Korean Economic Dynamism* (1991) and *The Yen Appreciation and the International Economy* (1992). He is at present working on a book on external financial flows to developing countries, to be published by Cambridge University Press. He is fluent in French.

ABBREVIATIONS

ADB   Asian Development Bank
AfDB   African Development Bank
AIC   Akaike's information criterion
AMEX   American Stock Exchange
AMV   aggregate market value
ANIEs   Asian newly industrializing economies
APT   arbitrage pricing theory
AR   autoregressive
ARMA   autoregressive moving-average
ASEAN   Association of South East Asian Nations

BA   banker's acceptance
BEA   Bureau of Economic Analysis
BIS   Bank for International Settlements

CAPM   capital asset pricing model
CD   certificate of deposit
CIS   Commonwealth of Independent States
CME   Chicago Mercantile Exchange
CMEA   Council for Mutual Economic Aid
CPI   consumer price index

DCE   domestic credit expansion
DRLC   debt relief Laffer curve

EBRD   European Bank for Reconstruction and Development
EC   European Community
ECOFIN   Council of Economic and Finance Ministers
ECU   European currency unit
EESU   Eastern Europe and the former Soviet Union
EMCF   European Monetary Corporation Fund
EMF   European Monetary Fund
EMH   efficient market hypothesis
EMI   European Monetary Institute

EMS	European Monetary System
EMU	economic and monetary union
ERM	exchange rate mechanism
ESAF	Enhanced Structural Adjustment Facility
ESCB	European System of Central Banks
EST	eastern standard time
FDI	foreign direct investment
FEER	fundamental equilibrium exchange rate
FIAS	Foreign Investment Advisory Service
FIRA	Foreign Investment Review Act
FOMC	Federal Open Market Committee
FRN	floating rate note
FY	fiscal year
G5	Group of Five
G7	Group of Seven
G10	Group of Ten
GATT	General Agreement on Tariffs and Trade
GDP	gross domestic product
GEMSU	German Economic, Monetary and Social Union
GNP	gross national product
HKI	Hong Kong Stock Exchange
IBS	International Banking Statistics
ICSID	International Centre for Settlement of Investment Disputes
IDA	International Development Association
IDDC	International Debt Discount Corporation
IFC	International Finance Corporation
IFI	international financial institution
IMF	International Monetary Fund
IOSCO	International Organization of Securities Commissions
ISDA	International Swap Dealers Association
IS–LM	investment–savings and liquidity–money
JCIF	Japan Center for International Finance
LBO	leveraged buyout
LDCs	less developed countries
LIBOR	London Inter-Bank Offered Rate
LIFFE	London International Financial Futures Exchange
LSE	London Stock Exchange
M&A	mergers and acquisitions
MAIC	minimization of Akaike's information criterion

MDB	multilateral development bank
MIGA	Multilateral Investment Guarantee Agency
MMS	Money Market Service
MNC	multinational corporation
MOFA	majority-owned foreign affiliate
NBER	National Bureau of Economic Research
NEP	National Energy Policy
NYSE	New York Stock Exchange
OECD	Organization for Economic Cooperation and Development
OPEC	Organization of Petroleum Exporting Countries
OPIC	Overseas Private Investment Corporation
OTC	over the counter
PHLIX	Philadelphia Stock Exchange
PPP	purchasing power parity
P/E ratio	price–earnings ratio
SAF	Structural Adjustment Facility
SDR	special drawing rights
SEC	Securities and Exchange Commission
SIMEX	Singapore International Monetary Exchange
SML	security market line
SPA	State Property Agency
TOPIX	Tokyo Stock Price Index
TSE	Tokyo Stock Exchange
VAT	value-added tax

Part I

INTERNATIONAL FINANCE AND MULTILATERAL FINANCIAL INSTITUTIONS

In the first chapter the new size and shape of international capital markets are examined, along with contemporary trends in these markets. Although international trade in goods and services grew at an impressive pace through the 1980s, the external imbalances among the major industrial countries were large and were primarily responsible for enhanced international capital flows during these years. After the Plaza Accord in 1985, the yen and the other SDR currencies began to appreciate *vis-à-vis* the dollar at varying rates. The international bank lendings, which are dominated by the industrialized countries, expanded sharply over the period 1985–7 and then moderated. The same trend was observed in interbank activity. There were several reasons behind the slack, principal among them being the new capital adequacy requirements decreed by the BIS and a relatively flat yield curve. As the yen's appreciation began, the new international bond issues moved away from the dollar and towards the yen, the Swiss franc and the pound sterling. But this trend was not sustained. Over the 1980s, an integration process between different market sectors, between institutions, between maturities and between instruments had gained momentum. The cause underpinning it was the liberalization and deregulation of the domestic financial markets in all the major industrialized economies. The equity markets expanded rapidly all the world over and

there was a concomitant increase in international trade in them. Portfolio managers tried to reduce risk through international portfolio diversification and to cash in on the international arbitrage opportunities, which in turn made international equity markets more independent and efficient. In October 1987, they crashed and because of increased market interdependence the shock wave spread from one market to another at an incredible pace. Derivative products were developed for hedging against interest rates and currency value fluctuations. Their utility and popularity was high and trading expanded not only in terms of the variety of instruments offered but also in terms of trading volume. Somewhat ironically the derivative products were blamed – although only partly – for the equity market crash.

The world-wide trend of integration of financial markets, noted above, all but eliminated short-term interest rate differentials for major industrialized countries before the end of the 1980s (see Chapter 2). This should be taken to mean that the country premium was eliminated. The real and nominal exchange rate variability still remained, and, in fact, was larger in the 1980s than in the 1970s. The outcome, therefore, was that a currency premium remained, consisting of an exchange risk premium plus the expected real currency depreciation.

In Chapter 3 the distinction between the

developing and industrialized economies is discussed with respect to current account imbalances and their correcting mechanism. While a long-term self-correcting relationship exists in industrialized economies between the cumulative current account or net stock of these countries' foreign assets or liabilities and other economic variables, nothing of this sort was found in the developing economies. Without a deliberate adjustment in the macroeconomic policies, their current account imbalances may continue to grow. Fry provides an explanation for this dichotomy.

The challenge facing the World Bank group during the remaining years of the century will decline if world poverty is taken as a measure of the challenge (Chapter 4). Yet, it will be a big challenge for the World Bank and its affiliate organizations because the international economy will be larger and more complex and economies will be more closely intertwined with each other. In the mid-1990s, a third general capital increase is on the cards. This will be in addition to periodic IDA replenishments and IFC and MIGA capital increases and should enable the World Bank group to meet its growing challenge. The Bank's sister organization across the road, the International Monetary Fund, will continue to face its own challenge in endeavouring to attain balance-of-payments viability, price stability and development of productive resources of its member countries (Chapter 5). This does not mean that the Fund will limit itself to the task of demand management. Eliminating internal and external imbalances, in principle, can be brought about by a whole range of policy packages, some of which stimulate growth while others do not. A long-lasting adjustment is only feasible if the productive capacity of the economy is expanding. The Fund, therefore, has to remain committed to the policies that enhance the possibility of economic growth. One cannot lose sight of the fact that mere macroeconomic balance is in no way a sufficient condition for growth if resources are poorly allocated. Therefore, the Fund is obliged to press for elimination of distortions no matter where they originate. Yet, the fundamental fact remains that

without macroeconomic stability economic growth can falter and will not be sustainable. Economic growth has higher probability under macroeconomic stability, which makes the Fund's role pivotal for the international economy.

The last chapter in this section addresses the financing needs in Eastern Europe and the former Soviet Union (EESU) and the role of a new multilateral financial institution, namely, the European Bank for Reconstruction and Development (EBRD). There are myriad market failures and imperfections in EESU countries, most conspicuous being the absence of sound banking and credit institutions. These market failures provide a rationale for intervention by multilateral institutions like the EBRD, which can play a meaningful role in helping EESU's transition to market economies. The EBRD was established in 1991 with a mandate to establish a framework of market economy and catalyse private sector investment. Its statutes require the majority of its lending to go to the private sector on commercial terms and only if private sector finances cannot do the job alone. The role of the merchant banking division of the EBRD is totally commercial. It has attracted strong equity partners like Nestle, General Motors and GEC-Alsthom in Eastern Europe. At the end of the first year, capital commitment by EBRD, combined with commitments made by foreign investors, totalled ECU 2.1 billion. The EBRD also has a development wing with a different, long-term perspective. It concentrates on developing the infrastructure in the EESU countries so that it brings the environmental, transport and energy policies of Eastern Europe closer to those of Western Europe. To be sure, this will be a long-term and complicated process. During the first year, the EBRD has approved about twenty projects and committed ECU 260 million. During its first annual meeting in April 1992, a move was afoot to set up a special restructuring facility that could make 'soft loans' like other multilateral financial institutions to finance the conversion of the defence industries to non-military production. The proposal received short shrift from the Bank's Western shareholders.

2

1

CONTEMPORARY TRENDS IN THE INTERNATIONAL CAPITAL MARKETS

Dilip K. Das

INTRODUCTION

In this chapter we intend to scrutinize closely the salient features of the contemporary international capital markets. The chapter is an overall inclusive generalized study of developments in the second quinquennium of the 1980s. We review trends in the main market segments and seek to analyse the principal forces behind these developments, in particular investor and borrower behaviour under changing macroeconomic environment and market conditions. The study also includes an examination of the financing of current account imbalances among the major industrialized countries and a review of recent developments affecting capital market financing of the developing countries. Some of the important related issues such as efforts to promote an efficient and stable system of capital markets, increased utility and popularity of the derivative instruments and recent successes in resolving the developing country debt dilemma are also investigated. The exposition is based on the statistics and information that the IMF routinely compiles.

MACROECONOMIC ENVIRONMENT

Over the last two decades investors in the surplus countries have become more selective about the kind of claims they wish to acquire in the deficit countries, resulting in a change in the nature of financial intermediation. The trend in capital market liberalization, the spread of innovative techniques and the development of derivative products have facilitated better matching of investors' preferences and debtors' needs. Yet, the developments of the mid-1980s, that culminated in the equity market crash of October 1987, delineated the significance of macroeconomic policies that create market confidence and promote intermediation through international capital markets. Lapses on this count can lead to adverse consequences for exchange and interest rates as well as abrupt and unwelcome shifts in financial flows. They can also weaken the market confidence and lead to situations like that seen in 1987.

International trade in goods and services recorded impressive increases in the 1980s. The volume of world trade increased by 50 per cent, while in value terms it increased by three-quarters. During the mid-1980s, the external imbalances among the major industrialized countries were large and reached $168 billion in 1986 and $183 billion in 1987 (Table 1.1). The current account deficits of the developing countries, which had declined from their high level of 1982, registered a tiny surplus in the overall current account balances in 1987 before moving into the red in 1988. These imbalances are important because they are considered to be an indicator of the required net movement of capital through the financial system. Coupled with progress in financial market liberalization, the imbalances were to a great extent responsible for capital flows during these years. The macroeconomic environment in which these flows took place was characterized by a good deal of financial uncertainty associated with an upswing in interest rates in 1987, renewed concern

Table 1.1 Selected economic indicators, 1982–9 (in billions of US dollars or per cent)

	1982	1983	1984	1985	1986	1987	1988	1989 (estimate)
Total of current account deficits[a]	176	158	192	198	246	234	259	281
Industrial countries	60	69	125	138	164	183	199	223
Of which:								
Seven major countries	25	49	107	118	141	162	170	185
Developing countries	116	89	67	60	82	51	60	58
Total of fiscal balances for seven major industrial countries								
Central government	−308	−378	−370	−384	−406	−367	−347	−317
General government	−263	−287	−243	−256	−298	−238	−183	−161
Overall current account balances of developing countries[b]	−77	−58	−27	−22	−41	4	−9	−16
Reserve accumulation of developing countries (accumulation +)	−35.8	2.5	11.0	18.4	4.2	55.1	–	22.5
Growth rate in value of world trade	−6.0	−2.0	5.9	0.7	9.7	17.4	14.2	10.5
Growth rate of real GNP of industrial countries	−0.3	2.7	4.9	3.4	2.6	3.5	4.4	3.5
Inflation rate of industrial countries (GNP deflators)	7.5	5.2	4.5	3.6	3.4	3.0	3.2	4.1
Interest rates (six-month Euro-dollar deposit rate)[c]	13.6	9.9	11.3	8.6	6.8	7.3	8.1	9.3

Sources: IMF (1989); IMF *International Financial Statistics*; and Fund staff estimates
Notes: [a] Sum of all current account deficits, which includes official transfers.
[b] Sum of all current account deficits and surpluses, which includes official transfers.
[c] Period averages in per cent a year.

about inflation, and sizeable official market interventions that followed the Plaza Agreement of 22 September 1985. Interest rates, that had started falling during late 1982, began to firm up in 1987. At the beginning of the year, they were at their lowest levels since the late 1970s in the USA, Japan, Canada and Italy. However, in late 1987 they began to rise in most of the major industrial economies except Japan, a trend that was to continue during the following year. The LIBOR on six-month dollar deposits increased from 6.4 per cent in the first half of 1987 to 9.4 per cent in December 1988. In Japan, in the aftermath of the Plaza Agreement, interest rates kept on declining until the discount rate reached its lowest ever level in 1989. Some commentators of the international financial scene argued that rising long-term interest

rates in the industrial countries, especially in the USA, reflected the changing expectations regarding the stability of exchange rates among the major currencies. In fact, the depreciation of the dollar during this period was accompanied by an increase in the premium in dollar interest rates over interest rates on instruments denominated in the yen or deutsche mark. The continued depreciation of the dollar against other SDR currencies during this period was in accordance with the Plaza Agreement between the G5 countries.

A falling dollar led investors to avoid the somewhat illiquid securities of the Eurobond market in favour of the domestic bond markets. The Eurobond investors became reluctant to acquire dollar-denominated debt. The international securities markets also remained depressed during 1987, particularly during the third and fourth quarters. At the beginning of 1988, the dollar started to recover against the other SDR currencies and in the second quarter the exchange rate movement between the dollar, yen and deutsche mark became much less volatile. The subdued volatility partly reflected the public commitment made by the G5 countries to promote exchange rate stability.

There was a marked improvement in world trade and economic activity in 1988. The output growth in most industrial countries was strong and inflation remained moderate. The growth rate of real GNP in the industrial countries was 4.4 per cent which was the second highest in the 1980s (Table 1.1). The stable macroeconomic conditions in 1988 and 1989 brought about a rebound in the capital markets from their previous somewhat depressed levels. The Eurobond market recovered faster than expected. The buoyant activity level reflected settled market conditions, market resilience and generally higher expectations of stability in the main economic variables. Some of the favourable developments in the international economy were a reduction in the fiscal deficits in major industrial economies during 1988 and 1989, a reduction in claims on developing countries, a high level of investment activity leading to strong economic expansion in most industrial countries and an environment of relatively stable prices and exchange rates. In the aftermath of the Plaza Agreement, a period of exchange rate stability began, although the Agreement was not wholly responsible for it (Table 1.2). Therefore, nominal interest rate differentials started having a greater influence on the financial flows. The apprehension that inflation might come back made the industrial economies take a tight monetary stand which was reflected in a widespread increase in short-term interest rates in 1988. As opposed to this, the longer-term interest rates by and large remained stable. Their yield curve flattened and even became inverted, partly reflecting the confidence in inflation control measures as well as anti-inflationary commitments of the governments. During this period the interest rate differentials gradually widened in favour of the dollar, in particular *vis-à-*

Table 1.2 Exchange rate volatility of major currencies with respect to the US dollar, 1984–9 (in per cent)

	1984	1985	1986	1987	1988	1989
Pound sterling	2.40	4.14	1.67	2.56	3.06	2.53
Deutsche mark	3.08	3.60	1.86	2.80	2.60	3.19
French franc	2.95	3.52	2.13	2.33	2.50	3.07
Yen	1.95	3.25	3.30	3.19	2.51	2.16

Source: IMF, *International Financial Statistics*
Note: Volatility is defined as the standard deviation of the monthly proportionate changes in average exchange rates over the period indicated.

vis the yen. But from the second quarter of 1989 the inflationary pressures began to recede in the USA, leading to a fall in the US interest rates and a reversal of interest rate differentials against other currencies.

The recovery in the nominal value of the US dollar against the other major SDR currencies during the period 1988–9 had started after three years of decline. Because of relatively stable exchange markets, official intervention was not necessary after 1988 and financing of the imbalances was more or less autonomous through capital accounts. The stability of the international currency markets inspired private capital flows to respond to interest rate differentials more strongly than in 1987. Before this point in time, large-scale intervention by central banks was needed to do the same job. At the end of the decade, intervention played a minor role in the major industrialized countries, with the notable exception of the UK. The return to autonomous financing was made possible by sharp increases in net direct investment and net financing through international bond markets. The former was partly associated with the high level of merger and acquisition (M&A) activity. Such outflows were particularly high in the case of Japan, with a good deal of these flows directed to the USA, which was the major deficit country. It saw a significant increase in inward capital flows with respect to direct investment as well as through bond markets. Both of these are private-sector-dominated channels. Similar large surges were also recorded in outflows from Germany (the FRG) and the UK.

THE GENERAL MARKET AND SECTOR TRENDS

The noteworthy developments of the mid-1980s included the collapse of the perpetual FRN market which was largely due to the concern of investors about the liquidity of the instruments. These concerns were heightened by the equity market crash and for a few months thereafter there was a virtual halt in the issue of new equity-linked bonds. An increase in awareness of the systemic risk was natural and logical. A strong recovery in the international bond markets was observed after the crash and the gross issuance of fixed rate bonds during 1988 began to rise, with the issuance of equity-related fixed rate bonds also reaching a high level. Likewise the bond markets perked up and large net inflows were recorded for the USA, particularly through purchases of US Treasury bonds. Japan and the FRG continued to record net outflows. The portfolio investment in corporate equities played less of a role in the financing of current account imbalances during 1988 and 1989 than in the past. Also, there was a major change in the direction of investment, i.e. both the UK and the USA shifted from being net importers of capital through the equity markets in 1987 to net exporters in 1988 and 1989. As for lending through the banking system, net inflows in the USA and Japan declined substantially after reaching record levels in 1987. This reversal was the counterpart of the reduced reliance on official intervention noted above. The reduction lowered the need for banks to readjust their positions through interbank activities. The other causes included the impact of the new Basle ratios regarding capital adequacy and flat or inverted yield curves.

The structure of the bond market was considerably influenced by changing currency valuations and interest rate variations during the mid-1980s. The international bond market activity expanded in 1988-9 with the help of swaps. In this case, the flat yield curve and the relative stability of exchange rates served to stimulate growth in fixed rate bond investments. Investors had a clear preference for currencies with high nominal interest rates, particularly the US dollar. The need for official intervention in support of the dollar declined in 1988-9 because, first, there was a decline in the US current account deficit and, second, foreign direct investment rose significantly. Accordingly, the acquisition of liabilities by foreign monetary authorities declined substantially. During these years, net capital inflows into the USA through portfolio investments in securities markets rose moderately, although there were variations in the performance of the different market segments. For instance, owing to the interest rate differential in favour of the USA and the relative strength of the dollar, net purchases of public sector bonds by foreigners, particularly German and Japanese investors, increased substantially. Despite the inward direct investment surge, the acquisition of corporate equity in the USA dwindled over 1988-9. Net inflows through the banking sector also declined because the short-term borrowings of the US banks fell. This was partly because of the withdrawal of dollar deposits from the Eurodollar market by foreign monetary authorities.

In Japan, the current account surpluses and foreign exchange reserves were rising. Net foreign exchange reserves increased by $39 billion in 1987, which corresponded to 45 per cent of the current account surplus; in 1986, such reserve accumulation had accounted for only 18 per cent of the current account surplus. During 1988, foreign exchange reserves expanded more slowly, at a rate of $16 billion, or 20 per cent of the Japanese current account surplus. Japan's current account surpluses, net of direct investment outflows, declined significantly in 1989 and the rate of accumulation of the official reserves was also reduced, while net financing to the rest of the world through financial markets did not rise. However, there was a change in the composition of such financing, i.e. outflows through the securities markets declined and the net flow through the banking system rose. For the reasons given in the preceding paragraph, Japan was a big purchaser of US Treasury bonds and its net capital outflows through bond markets rose dramatically. These outflows were more than offset by equally dramatic inflows through the stock market. In 1988, foreigners switched to heavy purchasing of Japanese stocks which was opposite to the past trend. The stock market had also rebounded to its pre-crash levels, reflecting confidence of the investors in the Japanese economy. The banking sector in Japan experienced a large amount of inflows because the Japanese investors tried to cover their long-term investment by short-term borrowing. The inflows of short-term capital increased considerably in 1987, which mainly reflected the borrowing of the Japanese banks. But Japan continued to be a net lender of long-term capital and a net borrower of short-term capital.

Germany, like Japan, recorded a large increase in the long-term outflows of capital through securities markets. This was the net result of reduced purchases of domestic securities by foreigners and a sharp increase in purchase of foreign bonds by German investors. The cause behind these outflows is the same, namely, widening of interest differentials in favour of the dollar. Despite large surpluses, the central bank had to intervene to support the deutsche mark because of strong outflows. Between 1987 and 1988, net flows of private capital doubled, partly reflecting a sharp decline in foreign purchases of German securities. This development is partly associated with changes in the exchange rate expectations and partly with investors' concerns about a new German tax on interest income. The banking sector witnessed a net inflow of long-term capital over 1988 and 1989 which occurred because of the German banks' issuance of bonds and placing of the proceeds on long-term deposits in German banks, thereby taking advantage of the lower interest rates on foreign bonds. With respect to short-term capital, there was a small net increase which corresponded to the purchases by the Bundesbank of deutsche marks in the exchange market and to an increase in the net interbank claims of German banks.

In recent years, the UK has become a major source of external finance to the USA. Of late, substantial capital outflows have taken place through security markets. The increased demand for foreign securities by British investors was directed towards both bond and corporate securities. This was a reversal of the disinvestment trend of the final months of 1987. Also, while short-term interest rates provided a significant premium on sterling assets, the long-term picture was less favourable. It was because of the former that the current account deficit of the UK was largely financed through a massive increase in net inflows of funds through the banking system. These inflows were supported by official intervention.

International bank lendings

International bank lendings are overwhelmingly dominated by borrowers in the industrial countries. International bank claims on these countries expanded from $210 billion in 1985 to $547 billion in 1987. After this spurt, the flows moderated substantially (Table 1.3). This sector is dominated by interbank activities, i.e. interbank loans and interbank deposits account for three-quarters or more of flows. The 1988 slowdown in the activities of the banks extended to non-banks as well. Bank claims on non-bank entities in industrial countries, which had more than doubled between 1985 and 1986 and had again risen in 1987, plunged sharply in 1988 (Table 1.4). The reasons for contraction in interbank lending include new capital adequacy requirements by the BIS which forced the banks to slow the expansion of their balance sheets, particularly in activities with low profit margins relative to their risk weighting. Second, these flows swelled in 1987 as a result of the opening of the Japan Offshore Market in December 1986. Third, the relatively flat yield curve mentioned earlier reduced the incentives for financing medium- and long-term investment through short-term interbank borrowing. As opposed to this, bank lendings to non-bank entities in the industrialized economies went ahead with the same pace as in the past and

Table 1.3 Changes in cross-border bank claims and liabilities, 1983–1989.III[a] (in billions of US dollars)

	1983	1984	1985	1986	1987	1988	1988	1989
							First three quarters	
Total change in claims[b]	170	181	276	536	795	552	466	514
Industrial countries	115	127	210	413	547	475	405	390
Of which:								
USA	40	36	55	94	106	109	74	43
Japan	10	20	40	154	223	203	184	129
Developing countries[c]	31	11	3	2	21	−9	−13	5
Offshore centres[d]	12	28	28	86	164	83	74	82
Other transactors[e]	8	6	11	−7	20	8	15	30
Unallocated (non-banks)[f]	5	8	24	41	43	−5	−14	7
Memorandum items								
Capital importing developing countries[c,g]	26	12	5	3	20	−13	−16	3
Non-oil developing countries[c,h]	24	14	3	2	20	−14	−16	6
Fifteen heavily indebted countries	11	5	−6	−1	2	−16	−12	−2
Total change in liabilities[i]	166	185	300	592	751	532	430	497
Industrial countries	99	114	196	431	493	376	316	374
Of which:								
USA	35	7	22	82	57	85	50	11
Japan	15	12	42	114	147	149	132	120
Developing countries[c]	21	23	22	−7	49	36	31	28
Offshore centres[d]	34	24	46	130	145	99	87	50
Other transactors[e]	10	2	9	−7	17	6	6	16
Unallocated (non-banks)[f]	3	22	28	45	47	14	−9	29
Memorandum items								
Capital importing developing countries[c,g]	27	24	20	8	38	24	19	25
Non-oil developing countries[c,h]	26	22	15	16	38	24	19	22
Fifteen heavily indebted countries	10	14	5	−4	10	5	6	9
Change in total net claims[j]	4	−4	−24	−57	44	20	36	17
Industrial countries	16	13	14	−17	54	99	90	16
Of which:								
USA	5	29	32	12	49	24	24	32
Japan	−5	8	−2	40	76	55	52	9
Developing countries[c]	10	−12	−19	9	−29	−44	−44	−23
Offshore centres[d]	−22	5	−17	−45	20	−16	−13	32
Other transactors[e]	−2	4	2	1	3	2	9	14
Unallocated (non-banks)	2	−15	−4	−4	−4	−20	−6	−22
Memorandum items								
Capital importing developing countries[c,g]	–	−12	−15	−5	−18	−37	−35	−22
Non-oil developing countries[c,h]	−2	−8	−12	−14	−18	−38	−35	−17
Fifteen heavily indebted countries	1	−8	−10	3	−7	−21	−18	−11

Sources: IMF, *International Financial Statistics* (*IFS*), and Fund staff estimates

Notes: [a] Data on changes in bank claims and liabilities are derived from stock data on the reporting countries' liabilities and assets, excluding changes attributed to exchange rate movements.

[b] As measured by differences in the outstanding liabilities of borrowing countries defined as cross-border interbank accounts by residence of borrowing bank plus international bank credits to non-banks by residence of borrower.

picked up somewhat in 1989. Fourth, investor interest in the international bond market was rekindled by somewhat reduced uncertainty regarding the behaviour of exchange rates and bond yields. The same uncertainty benefited the international banking activity in 1987 because banks provided suitable instruments and investors were led to borrow from them in order to finance purchases of hedging instruments.

An interesting change was observed in long-term bank credit commitments which rose sharply in 1988 due to high merger-related lending. It represented over 30 per cent of new syndicated Eurocredits. Corporate borrowings for debt consolidation was also heavy. However, lending to sovereign borrowers remained subdued because the creditworthy developing country borrowers were able to raise funds more cheaply through swap-related Eurobond issues.

International bond markets

In the aftermath of the Plaza Agreement, the new bond issues moved away from bonds denominated in dollars towards those denominated in yen, Swiss francs and pounds sterling. The dollar-denominated bonds declined from 55 per cent of the total in 1986 to 37 per cent in 1987 and subsequently stabilized around this level. Since the yen's strong appreciation was expected, the share of bonds denominated in yen increased from 10 per cent in 1986 to 15 per cent in 1987. Because of low interest rates in Japan and high interest rates in the UK and the USA, this trend did not continue. Over the period 1984–7, several significant changes took place in the type of instruments used for new bond issues. While the issuance of fixed interest rate bonds accounted for a growing share of total international bonds issued during this period, the relative importance of FRNs and equity-related bonds varied sharply. FRNs, which accounted for about 35 per cent of total international bond issues in 1984–5, declined sharply to only 7 per cent in 1986–7. At the same time, issuance of equity-related bonds, which accounted for about 9 per cent of total international bond issues in 1984–5, rose sharply to reach 24 per cent of total issues in 1987. The reduction in the use of FRNs reflected liquidity problems resulting from the collapse of the market for perpetual FRNs, which has been noted earlier, in December 1986. As opposed to this, on a number of national markets the equity-related bonds expanded during the first nine months of 1987, when equity prices were rising. In 1988, despite increasing competition from Euro-commercial paper and fixed rate note swaps, the issuance of FRNs started to recover fast. This was largely due to rising interest rates, which made floating rates more attractive for investors. The fixed interest rate bonds declined after several years of sustained growth. Despite the equity market crash of 1979, the issuance of equity-

Table 1.4 Change in interbank claims and liabilities, 1983–1990.III[a] (in billions of US dollars)

	1983	1984	1985	1986	1987	1988	1989	1989	1990
								First three quarters	
Total change in claims[b]	127	153	219	451	663	475	637	458	276
Industrial countries	97	117	186	377	468	391	436	323	256
Of which:									
USA	39	25	33	69	83	69	59	33	11
Japan	8	22	40	149	192	185	136	94	31
Developing countries[c]	14	5	7	4	15	−5	–	−2	−4
Offshore centres[d]	10	26	19	81	164	80	171	109	36
Other transactors[e]	5	5	8	−10	16	9	30	27	−13
Memorandum items									
Capital importing developing countries[c,f]	12	6	7	4	13	−9	−2	−1	–
Non-oil developing countries[c,g]	13	7	5	4	13	−12	−3	−2	−2
Fifteen heavily indebted countries	9	1	–	−1	2	−10	−3	−2	−10
Total change in liabilities[h]	108	151	213	472	626	439	643	448	255
Industrial countries	71	109	168	370	438	323	458	340	266
Of which:									
USA	19	14	8	56	35	63	60	38	−27
Japan	15	11	40	111	145	147	125	108	32
Developing countries[c]	3	22	–	−9	34	17	38	17	25
Offshore centres[d]	26	18	37	117	138	94	135	76	−20
Other transactors[e]	8	2	8	−6	16	5	12	15	−16
Memorandum items									
Capital importing developing countries[c,f]	11	22	4	3	26	11	36	17	35
Non-oil developing countries[c,g]	11	21	1	11	26	12	33	16	32
Fifteen heavily indebted countries	–	11	−3	−6	5	−1	7	5	9
Change in total net claims[i]	19	2	5	−21	37	37	−6	10	21
Industrial countries	26	8	17	7	30	68	−22	−17	−9
Of which:									
USA	20	11	25	13	48	6	−2	−5	38
Japan	−7	11	−1	37	47	39	12	−14	−1
Developing countries[c]	11	−17	6	13	−19	−22	−39	−19	−29
Offshore centres[d]	−16	9	−18	−36	26	−14	37	33	57
Other transactors[e]	−2	3	–	−4	–	5	18	13	3
Memorandum items									
Capital importing developing countries[c,f]	2	−16	3	1	−13	−20	−39	−18	−34
Non-oil developing countries[c,g]	2	−14	4	−7	−14	−24	−37	−17	−34
Fifteen heavily indebted countries	9	−10	3	6	−3	−9	−10	−7	−19
Net errors and omissions[j]	−19	−2	−5	21	−37	−37	6	−10	−21

Sources: IMF, *International Financial Statistics* (*IFS*); and Fund staff estimates.

Notes: [a] Data on changes in claims and liabilities are derived from stock data on the reporting countries' liabilities and assets, excluding changes attributed to exchange rate movements.

[b] As measured by differences in the outstanding liabilities of borrowing countries, defined as cross-border interbank accounts by residence of borrowing bank.

[c] Excluding offshore centres.

[d] Consisting of The Bahamas, Bahrain, the Cayman Islands, Hong Kong, the Netherlands Antilles, Panama and Singapore.

ᵉ Transactors included in *IFS* measures for the world, to enhance global symmetry, but excluded from *IFS* measures for 'All countries'. The data comprise changes in the accounts of the BIS with banks other than central banks and changes in identified cross-border interbank accounts of centrally planned economies (excluding Fund members).

ᶠ Consisting of all developing countries except the eight Middle Eastern oil exporters (the Islamic Republic of Iran, Iraq, Kuwait, the Libyan Arab Jamahiriya, Oman, Qatar, Saudi Arabia and the United Arab Emirates) for which external debt statistics are either not available or are small in relation to external assets.

ᵍ Consisting of all developing countries except the eight Middle Eastern oil exporters (listed in note f), Algeria, Indonesia, Nigeria and Venezuela.

ʰ As measured by differences in the outstanding assets of depositing countries, defined as cross-border interbank accounts by residence of lending banks.

ⁱ Difference between changes in claims and liabilities.

ʲ Calculated as the difference between global measures of cross-border changes in interbank claims and liabilities.

related bonds – convertibles and bonds with equity warrants attached – expanded sharply during 1987. This was due to large issuance activity in the first three-quarters of the year. The activity encompassed both a fall in the sales of convertible bonds and an increase in the use of bonds with equity warrants (see Tables 1.5, 1.6 and 1.7).

After a contraction, the international bond markets sharply expanded in 1988. They recovered to their former peak level activity which was reached in 1986. Their recovery was assisted by strong expansion in the swap market and continued during 1989 when the Japanese borrowers issued equity warrants. Other market segments remained subdued because of the flattening of the yield curve for several currencies which has been alluded to earlier (Table 1.8). Besides, liquidity in the secondary markets for international bonds has increasingly been viewed as limited. The investors showed a preference for the bonds issued by top-quality sovereign borrowers where the risk was rated as low. Little wonder that these issues were dominated by industrial countries. In 1988 and 1989, their issues accounted for 87 per cent of the total issues of international bonds. The share of the developing countries was miniscule – 4 per cent of the total in 1988 and 2 per cent in 1989.

Early repayment of bonds, which had become a market style, slowed down in 1989 (Table 1.9). Rising interest rates prevented many borrowers from refinancing the existing debt. As regards the currency composition, the scene continued to change and the share of dollar-denominated bonds which was 37 per cent during 1987 and 1988 went up to 50 per cent the following year. The dollar's

gaining strength and declining interest rate were the reasons behind this development. Bonds denominated in yen fell from 15 to 10 per cent of the total between 1987 and 1989, owing to uncertainties about the exchange rate as well as movements in differentials between Japanese and US interest rates. Fears about the depreciation of the deutsche mark and the Swiss franc also led to low issuance of bonds denominated in these currencies. The types of instruments used in the international bond markets further underwent a significant change. Issues in fixed rate bonds increased by 32 per cent in 1988 due to the credibility of anti-inflationary programmes. The favourable terms available in the swap markets also assisted the growth. Markets dampened in 1989 because of the flattening of the yield curve, which reduced the demand for medium-term bonds *vis-à-vis* short-term bonds. Borrowers from the USA and the UK were the most important in this market segment. Although the use of floating rate instruments had declined in 1987, it later picked up a little because of borrowing by the mortgage institutions and building societies from the UK.

The equity-related bond issues, after a moderate decline in 1988, rose again in 1989. These market segments were overwhelmingly dominated by the Japanese issuers who accounted for 87 per cent of the new issues in 1988 and 96 per cent the following year. The issues were the bonds denominated in US dollars with equity warrants. The investors were attracted to them because of the profit opportunities provided by the strong performance of the Tokyo stock market.

A noteworthy development of 1989 was the

Table 1.5 Market for fixed rate bonds, 1985–9 (in billions of US dollars)

	1985	1986	1987	1988	1989
Borrowers, total	94.8	141.5	121.3	160.2	153.7
Industrial countries	77.3	122.8	100.8	136.6	126.6
Of which:					
Australia	5.1	5.4	4.6	6.6	5.5
Austria	2.0	3.2	4.6	6.3	4.4
Belgium	0.7	2.3	3.6	2.8	2.0
Canada	7.5	13.4	8.3	12.8	12.2
Denmark	2.2	7.2	3.9	3.9	2.9
Finland	0.9	2.8	2.6	4.3	4.7
France	4.8	8.6	7.7	12.2	12.1
Germany, Federal Republic of	1.6	7.7	8.4	10.5	8.3
Italy	0.8	2.0	4.9	7.3	9.5
Japan	11.4	15.7	13.4	14.2	20.2
Netherlands	1.2	2.5	2.8	3.6	3.5
New Zealand	1.3	3.0	2.4	1.8	1.6
Norway	1.4	4.3	3.7	5.0	2.5
Sweden	3.9	5.5	4.4	8.1	5.8
UK	2.5	5.1	6.2	14.0	13.6
USA	26.2	29.0	14.5	14.6	12.4
Developing countries	2.3	2.6	3.3	5.5	4.5
Other, including international organizations	15.2	16.1	17.2	18.1	22.6
Currency distribution, total	94.8	141.5	121.3	160.2	153.7
US dollar	45.1	64.1	30.9	46.7	54.9
Japanese yen	11.3	21.9	22.6	19.9	22.2
Swiss franc	10.5	16.4	16.9	17.7	5.9
Deutsche mark	6.7	11.6	12.7	21.4	11.3
ECU	6.0	5.8	7.0	10.8	13.0
Pound sterling	3.1	4.7	8.9	12.3	12.7
Australian dollar	3.1	3.2	7.5	7.3	6.4
Canadian dollar	2.2	5.3	5.9	13.0	10.7
Netherlands guilder	1.6	2.5	1.9	2.5	1.6
Other	5.2	6.0	7.0	8.6	15.0

Source: OECD, *Financial Market Trends*

successful issue by the World Bank of the first global bond which was launched simultaneously in Europe and the USA. We shall see in the next section that liberalization and elimination of controls in a number of markets has blurred the line between the domestic markets and Euromarkets. The market segmentation is made mainly by divergent market traditions and practices. The global bond of the World Bank was an attempt to reconcile these practices and overcome the differences because, if they could be overcome, the borrower would have simultaneous access to a large pool of investors, thus reducing his cost. Another advantage that the Bank expected to have was to tap the most liquid market segments in the USA by being classified with the US government agencies.

FUNDAMENTAL CHANGES IN MARKET TRENDS

The developments and changes that have taken place in financial markets in the recent past have been influenced by two fundamental processes:

12

Table 1.6 Market for floating rate issues, 1985–9 (in billions of US dollars)

	1985	1986	1987	1988	1989
Borrowers, total	58.7	51.2	13.0	22.3	17.4
Industrial countries	48.5	47.3	11.3	20.2	16.4
Of which:					
Belgium	1.8	1.6	0.1	–	0.6
Canada	2.1	3.0	0.1	0.1	0.1
Denmark	0.6	1.2	–	0.2	0.5
France	6.5	4.2	0.7	2.9	–
Italy	4.4	2.0	2.0	0.2	0.7
Japan	2.3	1.8	2.2	0.7	0.5
Sweden	2.2	0.1	–	0.2	–
UK	12.2	12.8	2.4	11.4	6.9
USA	10.5	10.1	2.0	1.6	1.8
Developing countries	6.2	2.1	1.4	1.8	0.7
Other, including international organizations	4.0	1.8	0.3	0.3	0.3
Currency distribution, total	58.7	51.2	13.0	22.3	17.4
US dollar	50.5	41.1	4.6	8.4	7.0
Pound sterling	3.4	5.7	2.0	9.9	5.8
Deutsche mark	3.2	1.6	0.4	1.4	2.5
ECU	1.0	1.0	0.2	–	2.0
Other	0.6	1.8	5.8	2.6	2.0

Source: OECD, *Financial Market Trends*

Table 1.7 Market for equity-related bonds, 1985–9 (in billions of US dollars)

	1985	1986	1987	1988	1989
Borrowers, total	11.3	26.9	43.0	41.0	80.1
Japan	5.9	14.9	28.0	35.6	76.6
USA	3.2	3.4	4.7	0.6	0.4
UK	0.7	1.5	4.0	0.9	0.6
Germany, Federal Republic of	1.0	1.7	1.5	0.6	0.6
Switzerland	0.1	1.2	0.4	–	–
Other OECD countries	0.4	4.2	4.4	3.2	1.6
Other borrowers	–	–	–	0.1	0.4
Currency distribution, total	11.3	26.9	43.0	41.0	80.1
US dollar	5.3	16.4	29.2	28.8	64.0
Swiss franc	3.9	6.5	6.8	8.1	12.3
Deutsche mark	1.3	2.8	2.0	0.9	2.6
Other	0.8	1.2	5.0	3.2	1.2

Source: OECD, *Financial Market Trends*

first, the strengthening of the linkages between the individual markets which tended to integrate national economies and provide a deeper market for instruments of different kinds; second, in so far as the market participants operate with increasing freedom in the various segments of the international financial system, the international financial markets are globalized – the decision-maker can increasingly think of them as an integrated whole. We focus on these two factors separately below.

Table 1.8 Gross international bond issues and placements by groups of borrowers, 1985–9[a]
(in millions of US dollars)

	1985	1986	1987	1988	1989
Foreign bonds	31,229	39,359	40,252	48,273	41,964
Industrial countries	19,736	29,161	30,990	37,111	30,576
Developing countries	1,815	1,790	1,480	2,185	1,795
International organizations	9,350	8,360	7,461	8,307	8,249
Other	327	48	320	670	1,343
Eurobonds	136,543	187,747	140,535	178,869	212,004
Industrial countries	118,194	172,020	125,293	161,190	191,142
Developing countries	6,681	2,989	2,459	4,074	2,887
International organizations	8,543	10,488	11,320	11,393	13,362
Other	3,124	2,250	1,463	2,213	4,613
International bonds	167,772	227,106	180,786	227,143	253,967
Industrial countries	137,931	201,181	156,283	198,301	221,719
Developing countries	8,497	4,779	3,939	6,259[b]	4,682
International organizations	17,893	18,848	18,781	19,700	21,611
Other	3,450	2,298	1,783	2,883	5,955

Source: OECD, *Financial Statistics Monthly*
Notes: [a] The country classifications are those used by the Fund. Excludes special issues by development institutions placed
directly with governments or central banks and, from October 1984, issues specifically targeted to foreigners.
[b] Excludes issue of collateralized Mexican bonds related to the Mexican debt exchange concluded in February 1988.

Market integration

An integration process between countries, between different market sectors, between institutions, between maturities and between instruments gained momentum during the 1980s. It brought the capital markets closer together and linked them, enabling the intermediation process between saving and investment to become more efficient and thereby reducing the cost of capital to firms and increasing returns to savers. Better integrated markets facilitate the reallocation of a broadening spectrum of risks, thus enhancing the scope and efficiency of international and intertemporal resource allocation. The flip-side of this coin is that this process may be creating new risks that are not fully understood as yet.

The integration of capital markets followed the policy initiatives to liberalize restrictions and deregulate the domestic markets in all the major industrialized economies. For instance, in the US financial markets the dividing line between banking and the securities business has become increasingly nebulous. Several restrictions have been eliminated between Eurocurrency markets in Germany and the UK, encouraging the merging of domestic and offshore capital markets. The most recent steps in this direction were taken by the Japanese authorities who have freed interest rates through a reduction in the minimum size of deposits bearing full market rates. Steps to liberalize Euro-yen lending and encourage the development of domestic money markets are also under way. Dismantling of restrictions on the entry of foreign banks and financial institutions in domestic markets stimulated the market integration process. Since the foreign banks lack the base of retail business, they do most of their business with other customers and other banks, yet they do make the domestic markets more competitive. In this context, it should be noted that the OECD has a code regarding the freedom of capital movement and the industrial countries are party to this code. However, some industrial countries are still opposed to the idea of allowing the takeover of large domestic banks and securities houses by non-residents.

Table 1.9 Early repayments of international bonds, 1985–9 (in billions of US dollars)

	1985	1986	1987	1988	1989
Total (by currency of denomination)	18.7	41.1	41.5	42.1	31.7
US dollar	17.3	34.5	24.3	23.9	17.3
Deutsche mark	0.5	2.3	3.9	2.5	2.0
Swiss franc	0.3	1.5	6.2	7.1	1.5
Japanese yen	0.3	1.6	4.7	5.2	5.9
Pound sterling	0.1	0.2	0.7	1.5	2.3
Other	0.2	1.0	1.7	1.9	2.7
Total (by type of security)	18.7	41.1	41.5	42.1	31.7
Fixed rate bonds	6.3	18.0	26.1	25.2	17.7
Floating rate notes	11.3	19.7	10.8	14.5	10.8
Convertibles	0.5	1.8	3.0	1.8	3.0
Floating rate certificates of deposit	0.6	1.6	1.6	0.6	0.2
Total (by country of issuer)	18.7	41.0	41.5	42.1	31.7
Australia	0.1	1.4	2.2	0.7	2.3
Canada	0.7	2.5	2.6	3.0	2.5
Denmark	1.0	1.8	1.0	1.9	0.9
France	4.0	6.7	4.6	4.2	2.8
Italy	–	2.0	0.5	2.5	0.9
Japan	1.1	3.1	3.4	2.3	1.0
Sweden	3.4	4.0	2.3	4.1	1.0
UK	0.8	2.4	1.5	3.8	2.2
USA	3.4	6.6	7.6	5.0	7.9
International organizations	2.3	3.6	2.4	2.4	2.5
Other	1.9	6.9	13.4	12.2	7.7

Source: OECD, *Financial Market Trends*

An economic integration process in the EC is at present under way and several dramatic strides have been made towards the integration of financial markets. Likewise, under the US–Canada Free Trade Agreement similar efforts are under way in North America. In the EC, the Second Banking Directive allows a Community bank to perform throughout the Community all the functions it is authorized to perform in its home country. Since several important measures have already been taken and there is a high degree of commitment to integrating financial services in the Community, the remaining restrictions will fizzle away gradually. In addition, the freedom of capital movements will pressurize the authorities to harmonize taxes and other regulations.

The blurring of distinctions between different instruments is another characteristic feature of the current capital markets. Although the distinction between syndicated loans and bonds exists, syndicate banks are becoming more like underwriters because they tend to sell off almost all the loan participation to other banks and financial institutions. The note issuing programmes adopted by corporate borrowers used to be a prerogative of banks in the past. The integration process in the financial markets has been assisted by growth and expansion of the derivative products. They have managed to increase the efficiency of the financial markets at both national and international levels. Integration of the international financial markets leads to globalization of investor and borrower behaviour. Let us look at that now.

Globalization

Over the 1980s, large institutional investors dominated the assets issued on international capital markets. A large proportion of assets were issued by insurance companies, pension funds, mutual funds and other investment trusts. The institutional investors have a markedly different behavioural pattern from that of individual investors which, in turn, has important implications for the development of capital markets. They are under intense competitive pressure and are better placed to use the derivative products to adjust their portfolios than individual investors are. They also respond more rapidly to market developments and their moves are well researched, which implies that the institutional investors have a shorter time horizon than the individual investors.

There has been a strong tendency among institutional investors to turn to foreign assets to reduce the volatility of their returns and steady their earnings. For instance, the share of foreign equities and bonds in the total portfolio of UK pension funds rose from 5 per cent in 1979 to 20 per cent in 1988. The foreign securities in total securities holdings of life insurance companies rose from 15 per cent in 1981 to 31 per cent in 1988. However, most countries for prudential reasons regulate and limit the amount of foreign assets that can be acquired, although these regulations are now dwindling.

The globalization trend in the financial markets was assisted by the advances in financial information and telecommunications technology and the emergence of the derivative products markets. Together they changed their roles of institutional investors and financial intermediaries. The large market power of these investors increased the scope and reduced the cost of financial engineering, i.e. the creation of customized products for both borrowers and investors. At present, in many markets large institutional investors can obtain tailor-made assets that are not available to the general public. The telecommunications technology now also allows these investors to circumvent the middleman function of the securities houses and have a direct real-time access to capital markets and bid on securities directly as they are issued. In fact, 'disintermediation' became a buzz word of the late 1980s.

INTERNATIONAL EQUITY MARKETS

During the 1980s, the equity markets expanded rapidly all over the world and there was a concomitant increase in international trade in them, i.e. transactions in domestic stocks involving non-residents soared. The international equity issues entail underwriting and distribution of equity securities to investors in one or more markets outside the issuers' home country by national or international underwriting syndicates, e.g. Canadian fund managers investing in Japanese stock or British investment trusts selling Germany equity. The growth in international trading in equities suffered in 1987 and fell in 1988 (Table 1.10), yet the annual average growth rate for the period 1979–88 was 18 per cent. The average annual growth of share prices was 16 per cent during this period. By 1988, international equity trading amounted to over $1.2 trillion and, in one out of every nine equity tradings, the buyer or the seller was a non-resident. The reason behind such a brisk growth in international equity markets was an attempt by portfolio managers to reduce risk through international portfolio diversification. It also reflected a tendency to cash in on international arbitrage opportunities emerging from changing macroeconomic and regulatory environments. The portfolio diversification trend was facilitated by a reduction in barriers to both international capital movements and international provision of financial services. Towards the end of the decade, about 10 per cent of investment portfolios in the large industrial countries consisted of foreign assets.

With expansion in trade in international equities, the international stock markets have grown more interdependent. This is reflected in an increase in correlation between the price movements in different market centres. The correlation coefficient between stock price indices in the USA and other industrialized countries increased, on average, from 0.35 in 1975–9 to 0.62 in 1985–8. The greater interdependence reflects greater market efficiency, i.e. funds can freely flow from

Table 1.10 Gross international equity flows, 1986–1989.I[a] (in billions of US dollars)

	1986	1987	1988	1988	1989
				First quarter	
Investor from:					
USA	101.5	189.3	150.8	35.7	50.7
Japan	34.8	125.0	150.1	38.4	35.6
UK	173.6	232.9	224.1	37.1[b]	46.0[b]
Continental Europe	258.3	369.9	332.6	–	–
Of which:					
Germany, Federal Republic of [c]	42.9	59.4	42.3	10.1	14.1
Rest of world[d]	232.6	427.4	355.0	–	–
Equity:					
USA	277.5	481.9	363.8	95.3	91.8
Japan	189.6	354.5	327.1	74.4	114.5
UK	84.3	144.1	120.8	–	–
Continental Europe	185.5	208.9	244.2	–	–
Of which:					
Germany, Federal Republic of	77.9	76.8	60.7	13.7	17.7
Rest of world	60.9	155.0	156.7	–	–
Total	800.8	1,344.5	1,212.6	–	–

Source: Howell and Cozzini 1989

Notes: [a] Gross flows are defined as the sum of equity purchases and sales associated with international portfolio investment.
[b] Including only pension funds, insurance companies and open- and closed-ended mutual funds.
[c] Excluding investment certificates.
[d] Includes US Employee Retirement Income Security Act (ERISA) funds.

markets where assets are overvalued to those where they are undervalued. Eventually, the stock prices tend to be based on risk–return criteria, making the most productive use of resources feasible. The flip-side of this coin is that interdependence makes market shocks easily transferable. The incidents of October 1987, as we shall see, demonstrated the speed with which adverse market developments can spread through equity markets almost all over the world. As stated, the expansionary trend in international equity trading was interrupted by the events of October 1987 and the value of trading dropped by 10 per cent in 1988. The number of traded shares showed a more precipitous fall of 26 per cent. However, these flows recovered strongly in 1989. The gross international equity investment from the FRG, Japan, the UK and the USA reached an annualized flow of $584 billion in the first quarter of 1989, compared with $485 billion in the previous year and $546 billion in 1987.

Although the equity market crash of 1987 has been factually, if somewhat euphemistically, referred to in the preceding paragraphs, we need to dwell on it further to bring out its real and comparative dimensions. The severity of this shock has been compared with the collapse of equity prices in October 1929. What was unique about the October 1987 decline in equity prices was not the scale of decline but the speed with which it took place and spread from one market to another – the panic selling was almost global in nature. Countries with short settlement periods reported exceptional pressure from foreign market participants seeking to utilize the liquidity of their markets to meet obligations elsewhere. It was observed that the effect of trading halts or price limits in one market spilled over into other

17

markets. With the multiple listings of stocks and instruments on a number of exchanges, such phenomena are not surprising. There were several reasons behind the collapse, many of which lay in the macroeconomic factors and the structural characteristics of equity markets. Large and persistent external payments and fiscal imbalances in some of the large industrial countries have been viewed by many analysts as being incompatible with stable financial and foreign exchange market conditions. Although these imbalances created pressures on financial and foreign exchange markets, the short-term developments in equity markets in the months preceding the crash were viewed as most directly affected by (a) the interest and exchange rate movements and (b) perceived policy conflicts between the authorities in some of the major industrialized countries.

The new or primary international equity issues, other than equity-linked bonds, soared from $300 million in 1984 to $18 billion in 1987. The interruption of 1987 was squarely reflected by a sharp decrease in new international issues of equity to $7.7 billion in 1988 (Table 1.11). The decline was particularly sharp in the issues of Euroequities and issues related to privatizations. Although the Euroequities dominate the international equity market, privatization-related issues have also grown large in volume. Judged by the 1988 performance, investors in the UK were the most active in international equity markets. The value of their trade was estimated at $224 billion, or 18 per

cent of the total value of international equity trade. The USA and Japan came next each with 12 per cent of the total value of the international equity market transactions, while investors from Europe accounted for 27 per cent. Among the Europeans, the Swiss investors were the most active and accounted for 11 per cent of global equity turnover. As for the benefits of these flows, the USA was the largest recipient of international equity investment. Europe has been of increasing importance, partly as a result of the corporate restructuring that has taken place in relation to the planned establishment of a unified European market by 1992. International interest in Japan has been strong and it has been estimated that non-residents own as much as 4 per cent of the Japanese equity securities.

M&As were a significant source of cross-border equity flows. In 1988, they generated about $125 billion in cross-border flows through 2,500 international M&A deals. Again, firms in the UK were the most aggressive in this arena, acquiring foreign firms with a total value of $44 billion, three-quarters of which were accounted for by the acquisition of US firms. The value of international acquisitions by the European companies was $37 billion, almost half of it involving acquisitions of US firms. The M&As in the USA remained the most attractive target for international portfolio investors in other industrialized economies.

DEVELOPMENT AND GROWTH IN DERIVATIVE PRODUCTS

Exchange rates and interest rates remained highly volatile during the 1970s and the early 1980s and created a need for hedging instruments which in turn stimulated the search for new products and techniques to transform and reallocate financial risks. The environment of financial liberalization, market innovation and relaxation of controls in the industrial countries made this search easier. Consequently, the interest rate and currency fluctuation hedging instruments came into being and their use expanded rapidly. A significant development was the use of exchange-traded contracts as opposed to

Table 1.11 International equity market – primary issues, 1984–8 (in billions of US dollars)

	1984	1985	1986	1987	1988
Total[a]	0.3	2.7	11.7	18.2	7.7
Euro-equities	0.3	2.2	6.2	8.0	3.1
Privatizations	–	0.1	1.8	7.5	1.4
Other	–	0.4	3.7	2.7	3.2
Memorandum item					
Equity-linked bonds	11.2	14.0	38.6	61.2	46.6

Source: Howell and Cozzini 1989
Note: [a] Excluding equity-linked bonds.

over the counter (OTC) contracts. These contracts had the advantage that their associated secondary markets were far more liquid. Since the exchange acted as counterparty in such contracts and the margin requirements had to be maintained on a daily basis, exchange-traded instruments had much less credit risk than the OTC instruments. On exchanges around the world, this trading activity continued to expand vigorously not only in terms of the variety of instruments offered but also in terms of trading volume.

The Euro-dollar interest rate future contracts began life on the Chicago Mercantile Exchange (CME) in 1981 and expanded rapidly. By 1987, the average monthly trading volume at the CME had risen by 88 per cent to 1.8 million contracts having a face value of $1.8 billion, and the expansion continued. Of late, the LIFFE and SIMEX also expanded their trading in the Euro-dollar interest rate futures but the volumes traded on these exchanges were modest compared with those on the CME. Likewise, trading in Euro-dollar options contracts, which began in 1985 at the CME and the LIFFE, also expanded sharply. The SIMEX Euro-dollar options, however, have shown limited growth because of excessive premia. The interest rate futures and options contracts have also traded actively on the major exchanges. For instance, the volume of futures contracts on US Treasury bonds on the LIFFE recorded a dramatic increase from a monthly average of 23,628 contracts in 1984 to 127,360 contracts in 1987 and has continued to expand. In August 1987, the LIFFE also began futures contracts on Japanese government bonds which began strongly but the market stabilized thereafter at a moderate level of about 11,000 contracts a month. The volume of trading of futures contracts on ninety-day US Treasury bills has also been large at CME but the average volumes have contracted recently. The same trend has been observed in options contracts on US Treasury bills.

The trading activity in currency futures has been concentrated in the CME and other exchanges in the USA, as noted in the preceding paragraph, and has expanded considerably. Of late, trading in yen futures experienced the highest growth rate.

Similarly, trading currency options began in 1982 on the Philadelphia Stock Exchange (PHLX) and it has remained the most active centre for currency options. The trading volumes in the yen and the deutsche mark have recorded the highest expansion rates.

Since the early 1980s, an important OTC hedging instrument hs emerged and its use has grown in significance and volume. It is the medium-term swap which is used to arbitrage differences in borrowing costs across financial markets and to reallocate the interest rate and exchange rate risks contained in medium-term financial transactions. The access to swaps is limited by creditworthiness considerations. Borrowers in industrial countries use interest rate swap markets to convert their floating interest rate debt into the equivalent of fixed interest rate debts, both measured on the same notional principal amount and the same maturity. The interest rate and currency swaps have been among the fastest growing financial instruments of the 1980s. By the end of 1987, the total amount of outstanding swap transactions reached the $1.1 trillion mark. Interest rate swaps account for 80 per cent of the total outstanding swap transactions while currency swaps account for the remaining 20 per cent. A large part of the latter involves the dollar and the yen swaps. A study of the International Swap Dealers Association (ISDA), New York, revealed a very low incidence of losses. Of the seventy-one major firms covered, only eleven had any losses to report, which reflects the general creditworthiness of counterparties engaged in swaps. The expansion of OTC markets for derivative products has continued and by the end of 1988 the market volume for interest rate and currency swaps reached $1.3 trillion. Of this, about $1.0 trillion were the interest rate swaps and $317 million were currency swaps. The annual report of the ISDA revealed that, at the end of 1988, 72 per cent of the interest rate swaps were in dollars and 8 per cent in yen. For currency swaps, 86 per cent involved dollars and 42 per cent yen. It should be noted that the percentage of swaps denominated in all currencies total 200 per cent because each currency swap involves two currencies. Other OTC derivative products, namely interest rate caps, floors, collars and 'swaptions', accounted for $327 billion of notional principal at the end of 1988.

DEVELOPING COUNTRIES IN THE CAPITAL MARKETS

When measured in terms of net or gross capital flows, the degree of integration of developing countries in the international financial system was less at the end of the 1980s than at the beginning. This was the result of the development of the debt crisis and the resultant reappraisal of the risks involved in the bank lending to the public sectors of the highly indebted LDCs. The spontaneous flows have declined and remained limited to the developing countries that have not restructured their debt in the recent past. The bond markets experienced the same and the volume of bonds issued by LDCs declined dramatically. As opposed to this, foreign direct investment in these countries rose, which was partly a consequence of debt–equity conversion schemes. Interest in the LDC portfolio investment also rose and several invest-ment funds were established. The Asian newly industrializing economies (ANIEs) expanded their links with the international financial markets as both users and suppliers of capital, and integrated themselves better than most other LDCs.

A clear polarization can be observed in recent trends in bank claims. LDCs without debt-servicing problems recorded increases in bank claims as well as bond issues, whereas the claims on fifteen heavily indebted countries witnessed a decline. According to the Fund's *International Banking Statistics* (IBS), the estimated cash flow from banks to the latter group of LDCs during 1985–8 was $14 billion compared with a net repayment of $15 billion, measured by the exchange-rate-adjusted change in stocks. During the first three quarters of 1988, despite minor increases in disbursements, bank claims on this group of LDCs declined by an estimated $11.3 billion. Total disbursements under the concerted lending arrangements during 1988 were $6.0

billion, marginally above the 1987 level of $5.7 billion. Attempts to resolve the LDC debt riddle continued and the terms of rescheduling were relatively more favourable to LDCs in 1988 when the average maturities extended up to eighteen years and the average spreads above the LIBOR contracted to 83 points. The use of exit bonds also increased substantially. The banks found them more acceptable in the case of Brazil than they had in the past for Argentina. More attractive pricing was the main reason behind it. Several Latin American debtors made special efforts to reduce their debt.

In their eagerness to bring down the exposure to debt-ridden LDCs, banks accelerated the rate of disposing of claims on them in 1988. The US banks' claims declined by $12.7 billion in 1988, which followed a decline of $10 billion the year before. The smaller and regional US banks accounted for a major part of this decline. Banks in other countries, except Germany and Japan, bent with the wind and reduced their LDC exposures as well. Coupled with the strengthening of bank capital bases, this trend improves the ratio of LDC debt to bank capital in all major banking systems. Likewise, the nine US money-centre banks strengthened their capital bases considerably, although it should be noted that their levels of exposure in relation to capital were generally among the highest in the world. The trend in making provisions against LDC exposure con-tinued in 1988, but it was much smaller than in the past. Japan was a late starter in this respect and the Japanese banks were allowed to raise their pro-visioning levels from 5 per cent to 15 per cent only in early 1989. Canada also raised the mandatory provisioning standards. However, in the USA and Japan, the mandatory provisioning standards remained at the lowest level in the world.

The debt of LDCs with servicing problems tended to be traded at a discount to its face value and gradually a secondary market developed in LDC debt. The exact size of the secondary market is not known but the 1988 transactions were in the vicinity of $40 billion, far above the $5 billion mark reached in 1985. Although there was a decline in turnover in the first two months of 1989 to about one-half of the 1988 level, the announcement of the Brady Plan in March 1989 by the US Treasury caused the turnover to recover strongly. The participating banks anticipated more debt-restructuring agreements and the resumption of a debt–equity programme. Two kinds of transactions dominate the secondary market: (a) debt swaps, which help banks restructure their LDC loan portfolios to their advantage, and (b) cash transactions, which include purchases by countries of their own debt at a discount and conversion of debt into equity. Such transactions have grown in importance with the increase in debt conversion schemes.

The secondary market prices of LDC debt had a declining trend in the latter half of the 1980s, and they fell further sharply between July 1988 and March 1989. The weighted average price for the debt of fifteen heavily indebted LDCs came down to 33 cents per dollar of the face value. The 1985 level was 70 per cent of the face value (Figure 1.1). In 1986 and 1987 the declines were largely due to the combination of the introduction of a moratorium by Brazil and the provisioning decision by Citibank. The recent fall reflected the market's tendency to respond sharply to changes in perceptions of the general outlook of the debt strategy

– possibly a sign of a thin market. The short-term movements in the secondary market prices were fuelled essentially by opportunities for debt–equity transactions. The non-bank financial institutions have not shown a great deal of interest in LDC debt and efforts to repackage LDC loans as marketable securities have so far met little success. According to the estimates of the IMF, the total volume of debt conversion under officially recognized schemes was as low as $4.6 billion in 1987 and $8.2 billion in 1988.

It took about five years after the eruption of the LDC debt crisis for the capital market to evolve its strategy towards the secondary LDC debt market. Since this market has increased considerably in volume, banks now recognize that the secondary market prices contain a certain amount of information and that at these prices some of their claims could be liquidated. They have also become more aware of the possibilities that the secondary market offers them for reorganizing and streamlining their portfolios. That the secondary debt market is the market-oriented solution of a long-festering debt crisis is more widely accepted in the international capital market and several large banks have reorganized their LDC debt operations to merge with their asset-trading operations. These banks are actively reducing their LDC debt exposures through the secondary market.

In order to integrate themselves better with the international capital markets, LDCs will need to ensure that their policies foster and encourage an attractive financial environment for investors. Besides, domestic savers and investors can benefit from a more global outlook and the investment opportunities abroad. We have seen that the international capital movements have become easier because of financial liberalization and technological developments; therefore, there is an all the more pressing need to improve the standards of the domestic financial markets in LDCs. If this does not happen, capital flight will increase. In addition, to attract capital from both residents and foreign investors, well-functioning domestic financial systems are indispensable. Since the rates of return on many investment projects in LDCs are high, if

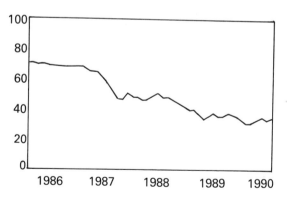

Figure 1.1 Secondary market prices for developing country loans, 1986–April 1990 (in per cent of face value)

Source: IMF 1990

their financial markets are integrated with those in the rest of the world many LDCs stand a reasonably good chance of attracting the much needed capital. The only conditional clause here is that these LDCs have to see that their country risk factor does not offset the high return factor.

The emerging stock markets

The emerging stock markets in India, Indonesia, Korea, Malaysia, Taiwan, Thailand, Brazil, Chile and Mexico performed well over the 1980s, the bulk of gains coming since 1985. The stock markets in these LDCs have come to be known as the emerging stock markets. Low oil prices, the booming world trade and relatively successful economic policies in the key emerging market developing countries helped share prices rise strongly. With the exception of Brazil, where large devaluations against the US dollar more than eroded gains in the local market, other emerging markets did extraordinarily well over the 1985–9 period. In Taiwan, the market recorded outstanding growth and roughly doubled each year (Figure 1.2). The majority of the key emerging stock markets are in outward-oriented economies which prospered faster on the back of sustained

export growth, particularly in manufacturing. In Asia, for instance, Taiwan, Korea, Thailand and Malaysia were highly successful on the export front throughout the 1980s. Indonesia saw no growth in the dollar value of its exports between 1980 and 1989 but this conceals a 40 per cent increase in exports since the halving of oil prices in 1986. The Latin American three, Brazil, Chile and Mexico, showed less impressive growth during the 1980s than those in Asia but could still be judged to be exporting successes. India is not considered to be an export success.

Two factors, namely higher rates of share price appreciation and prospects of gains from diversification, make a strong case for investing in the emerging markets. The IFC data suggest that a portfolio with a mix of emerging and developed market securities will show lower variability than one with only the latter. Some investors and fund managers see emerging markets as a growth area that cannot be ignored. An indicator of potential growth is that their market capitalization in aggregate is only about 5 per cent of world stock market capitalization, despite a 12 per cent share in the world GDP. However, fund managers believe that they need to be cautious in buying because company valuations in the embryonic

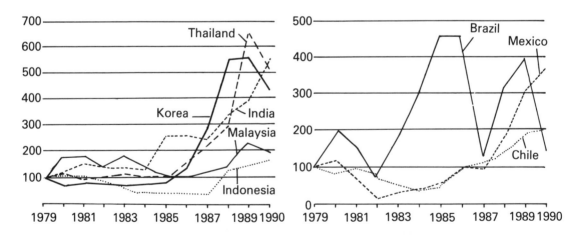

Figure 1.2 Asian and Latin American stock markets in dollar terms (1979 = 100)

Source: The Amex Bank 1990

markets may not fairly reflect the best forecast on earnings growth. Their emphasis is not to be on buying the market as a whole but on picking the specific stocks.

After several good years, 1990 has been a difficult period for these markets and by October 1990 market capitalization was down by an average of 39 per cent on their end 1989 levels (weighted by market capitalization). The relatively poor performance is also visible in the market prices of traded country funds. With only a few exceptions, their quoted prices fell during 1992. Some of the declines can be explained as being market corrections after rapid rises over the past few years had taken prices to unsustainable levels.

RISK MANAGEMENT IN THE INTERNATIONAL FINANCIAL INSTITUTIONS

Inasmuch as competitive pressure in the international financial markets has increased as a result of a dynamic growth in innovative products and the use of derivative instruments and the advancement in telecommunications technology, the general level of risk has *pari passu* soared. Apparently, it is necessary to control it and keep it within prudent limits. To be sure, increased competition and market liberalization have had a favourable effect on the market efficiency because competition is considered as value creating. However, along with that the financial markets should remain sound and supportive of growth in the real economy and confidence in them must not waiver. Therefore, supervisory authorities in a number of countries are reassessing the adequacy of prudential arrangements, at both national and international levels.

There are two principal kinds of risks: credit risk and liquidity risk. The former implies that a counterparty is not able to reimburse the bank when an obligation falls due. The general perception is that the credit risk in the international banking system has been increasing and that banks have stumbled into riskier areas in search of higher rates of return on assets so that stock prices and

capital can be raised. Second, there is evidence that liquidity risk has also increased. It refers to the inability of the banks to have, or to be able to raise, enough liquid assets to meet current needs. Some of the innovative products have turned out to be less liquid than initially believed. Besides, banks have moved into securities business and changes in securities market conditions can suddenly transform short-term credits into illiquid assets. This tendency has forced banks to examine each other's credit rating a little more carefully and look for new mechanisms for limiting exposure. Third, due to a gradual elimination of interest rate controls and a reduction in the sources of low cost funding, banks could become more exposed to interest rate risk if their interest rate in liabilities is not matched with that in assets. Funding raised on floating rates and lending on a similar basis reduces interest risk to an extent but effectively converts it into increased credit risk. A mismatch of currency composition in assets and liabilities can create an additional risk which exposes banks to the possibility of adverse changes in exchange rates. Lastly, although the derivative products were designed to control risk through various hedging techniques, these new instruments as alluded to earlier are not without their own risk characteristics. It is difficult to know what they are until sufficient experience has been gained regarding how they function, and in particular how they function during an economic downturn. With so many banks and financial institutions using innovative products, it is felt that the risk involved is at times inadequately appreciated. It is partly due to the arcane nature of some of the new instruments and computerized strategies that often drive their use. The Basle capital adequacy standards have begun to take such multiple exposures into account. The newest standards for banks, in fact, have been designed to achieve three objectives: (a) to harmonize the competitive conditions under which international banks operate, (b) to bring indirect financial commitments within a general prudential framework, and (c) to inject more capital into the banking system. We shall return to this issue a little later.

The securities houses are not being left out of supervision and relative responsibilities of the parent company and of branches are being defined. Having uniform standards for securities houses is difficult because there are considerable differences in the structures of securities businesses in different countries. In addition, the focuses and objectives of securities market regulations differ from country to country. With financial markets becoming more fully integrated, the need for an internationally consistent supervision approach is greater than it was in the past. Deliberations are under way in the International Organization of Securities Commissions (IOSCO), the OECD and other fora on these and related aspects. Attention is also being paid to the safety and efficiency of the securities transactions.

The work of the regulatory authorities has become increasingly difficult with the gradual breakdown of functional barriers within the financial services industry. While the most apparent trend is in the integration of banking and securities businesses, there is also a gradual trend towards the integration of banking, insurance and other financial services. Regulating and supervising diversified financial conglomerates is therefore onerous but necessary because a problem in one area can quickly spread from one financial sector to another. Therefore, functional rather than institutional supervision is becoming more relevant. This approach was taken by the Financial Services Act of the UK which regulates specific lines of business, ignoring the fact of whether it is a bank or a security house that is involved.

In the ultimate analysis, the supervisory authorities have to establish a level of regulation that maximizes market competition without jeopardizing safety and soundness. With deepening market integration, the problem of striking a balance between the two prime objectives is becoming more complex. The over-arching challenge for the supervisory authorities lies in finding the appropriate level of prudential supervision in a liberalized regulatory environment.

The latest measures taken by the BIS and endorsed by the G10 in July 1988 were rather significant. They fixed a minimum capital base for international banks at 8 per cent of risk-weighted assets and off-balance-sheet commitments. These are the minimum capital requirements but national authorities are free to impose more stringent requirements. The general reaction of the banks was (a) to raise more capital, (b) to shed or restructure assets and (c) to endeavour to generate higher returns by improvising margins. The first measure has already led banks all over the world to increase their primary and secondary capital. The shedding of LDC debt or reducing their LDC exposure has been favourably received by the financial market. The pressure for higher capital ratios has led many banks either to securitize their claims or to sell to non-bank financial institutions and investors. It has also led some banks to rein in the growth of their assets. Many international banks have adjusted their balance sheets to switch the relative weight of capital-absorbing assets in favour of those with low-risk weights. The need to raise returns on assets and generate more funds has encouraged banks to move towards earning more fee income. This movement has been necessitated by a squeeze in margins in regular banking business due to an excess capacity in the industry.

SUMMING UP

The macroeconomic environment is an important influence over the international capital markets. Although international trade in goods and services grew at an impressive pace over the 1980s, the external imbalances among the major industrial countries were large and were responsible for international capital flows during these years. The interest rates, which had had a declining trend since late 1982, began to firm up in late 1987. After the Plaza Agreement in September 1985, the yen and other SDR currencies began to appreciate vis-à-vis the dollar at varying rates. The exchange rate volatility was reduced – although the Agreement was not wholly responsible for it – and nominal interest rate differentials began to exert greater influence over the financial flows. After three years of decline, the dollar began to recover in 1988. Because of the relative stability of the exchange markets, official intervention was not necessary after 1988 and financing of imbalances was more or less autonomous through the capital accounts.

The international bank lendings, which are dominated by the industrialized countries, expanded sharply over 1985–7 and then moderated. The same trend was observed in interbank activity. There were several reasons behind the moderation, principal among them being the new capital adequacy requirements decreed by the BIS and a relatively flat yield curve. The long-term bank credit commitments rose sharply after 1988 because of high M&A-related lendings.

After the Plaza Agreement, the yen's appreciation began and the new international bond issues moved away from the dollar and towards the yen, the Swiss franc and the pound sterling, although this trend was not sustained for long. The type of instruments in use in this market segment also underwent a change. The issuance of fixed interest rate bonds accounted for a growing share of total international bonds issued, and the relative importance of FRNs and equity-related bonds varied sharply. After a contraction in 1987, the markets expanded in 1988 to reach their former 1986 peak level. This recovery was supported by expansion in the swap markets. An important development of 1989 was the World Bank's global bond which was launched simultaneously in the USA and Europe.

An integration process between countries, between different market sectors, between institutions, between maturities and between instruments gained momentum during the 1980s. It followed the policy initiatives to liberalize restrictions and deregulate the domestic markets in all the major industrialized economies. Institutional investors dominated the international capital markets and there was a strong tendency among them to turn to foreign assets to reduce the volatility of their returns and steady their earnings, which in turn promoted a globalization trend. It was supported by advances in financial information and telecommunications technology as well as the emerg-

ence of the derivative products markets. This trend also facilitated financial engineering. The telecommunications technology now allows institutional investors to circumvent the middleman function of securities houses and have a direct real-time access to capital markets and bid on securities directly as they are issued. In fact, 'disintermediation' became a buzz word of the late 1980s.

The equity markets expanded rapidly all over the world and there was a concomitant increase in international trade in them. Portfolio managers wanted to reduce risk through international portfolio diversification and cash in on the international arbitrage opportunities. This made international stock markets more interdependent and efficient. In October 1987, they crashed and because of increased interdependence the shock wave spread from one market to another at an incredible pace. The collapse is partly explained by the macroeconomic factors and the structural characteristics of the equity markets. In addition, there were several short-term developments that actually brought about the fall.

Derivative products were developed for hedging against interest rate and currency value fluctuations. Their utility and popularity were high and trading expanded not only in terms of the variety of instruments offered but also in terms of trading volume. Interest rate futures and currency futures continued to expand. The medium-term swaps, i.e. interest rate and currency swaps, have been among the fastest growing financial instruments of the 1980s. The general creditworthiness of counterparties engaged in swap operations was high and losses were extremely low.

The debt crisis took its toll and developing countries were less integrated in the international financial system at the end of the 1980s than they were at the beginning. While the spontaneous flows to highly indebted countries have remained limited, the Asian newly industrializing economies expanded their links with the international financial markets both as users and suppliers of capital. They are better integrated than most other developing countries and are fast developing into a noteworthy segment of the international capital markets. Many banks accelerated the rate of disposing of claims on developing countries and scaled down their exposure to them. The banks also continued to make provisions against their LDC exposure and strengthened their capital bases considerably. The Japanese banks were the last to do so because of domestic regulations. A secondary market in LDC debts has now developed. Two kinds of transactions dominated this market, namely, debt swaps and cash transactions. This market offered a market-oriented solution to the long-festering LDC debt dilemma.

In several developing countries, namely India, Indonesia, Korea, Malaysia, Taiwan, Thailand, Brazil, Chile and Mexico, stock markets performed impressively over the 1980s, especially after 1985. The international economic climate supported this brisk growth. The majority of these markets were in the outward-oriented economies which prospered faster on the back of sustained export growth. Two factors, i.e. high rates of share price appreciation and prospects of gains from diversification, made a strong case for investing in these emerging markets. After several good years, 1990 turned out to be a moderate year for these stock markets.

The general level of risk in the international capital markets has soared because of brisk growth in the use of derivative instruments, increased competitive pressure and the application of telecommunications technology to the financial markets. Therefore, supervisory authorities in a number of countries are reassessing the adequacy of prudential arrangements, both at national and international levels. The securities houses are not being left out of supervision. The work of the regulatory authorities has become increasingly difficult because of integration and globalization trends in financial services. The most recent measures taken by the BIS have a great deal of significance in this regard. According to their norm, the minimum capital base for international banks has to be 8 per cent of the risk-weighted assets and off-balance-sheet commitments. In order to meet this norm, banks have raised more capital, shed or restructured assets and tried to generate higher returns by improving margins. After October 1987, there has been a heightened concern among the national and multilateral supervisory authorities for containing the risk and keeping it within prudent limits.

REFERENCES

Howell, M. and Cozzini, A. (1989) *International Equity Flows – 1989 Edition: Are International Equities Ex-Growth?*, London: Salomon Brothers.

IMF (1989) *World Economic Outlook, October 1989: A Survey by the Staff of the International Monetary Fund*, World Economic and Financial Surveys, Washington, DC: IMF.

IMF (1990) *Annual Report 1990*, Washington, DC: IMF, August, p. 32.

The Amex Bank (1990) *The Amex Bank Review*, December.

2

QUANTIFYING INTERNATIONAL CAPITAL MOBILITY IN THE 1980s

Jeffrey A. Frankel

Feldstein and Horioka upset conventional wisdom in 1980 when they concluded that changes in countries' rates of national saving had a very large effect on their rates of investment, and interpreted this finding as evidence of low capital mobility. Although their regressions have been subject to a great variety of criticisms, their basic finding seems to hold up. But does it imply imperfect capital mobility?

Let us begin by asking why we would ever expect a shortfall in one country's national saving *not* to reduce the overall availability of funds and thereby crowd out investment projects that might otherwise be undertaken in that country. After all, national saving and investment are linked through an identity. (The variable that completes the identity is, of course, the current account balance.)

The aggregation together of all forms of 'capital' has caused more than the usual amount of confusion in the literature on international capital mobility. Nobody ever claimed that international flows of foreign direct investment were large enough that a typical investment project in the domestic country would costlessly be undertaken directly by a foreign company when there was a shortfall in domestic saving.[1] Rather, the argument was that the typical American corporation could borrow at the going interest rate in order to finance its investment projects and, if the degree of capital mobility were sufficiently high, the going interest rate would be tied down to the world interest rate by international flows of *portfolio* capital. If portfolio capital were a perfect substitute for physical capital, then the difference would be immaterial; but the two types of capital are probably not in fact perfect substitutes.

In this chapter a number of alternative ways of quantifying the degree of international capital mobility are examined. One conclusion is that the barriers to cross-border flows are low enough that, by 1989, financial markets can be said to be virtually completely integrated among the large industrial countries (and among some smaller countries as well). But this is a different proposition from saying that real interest rates are equalized across countries, which is still different from saying that investment projects in a country are unaffected by a shortfall in national saving. We shall see that there are several crucial links that can, and probably do, fail to hold.

In many cases, notably the UK and Japan (and perhaps now Italy and France as well), the finding of high integration with world financial markets is a relatively new one, attributable to liberalization programmes over the last ten years. Even in the case of financial markets in the USA, integration with the Euromarkets appears to have been incomplete as recently as 1982.[2] An important conclusion of this chapter for the USA is that the current account deficits of the 1980s have been large enough, and by now have lasted long enough, to reduce estimates of the correlation between saving and investment significantly. The increased degree of world-wide financial integration since 1979 is identified as one likely factor that has allowed such large capital flows to take place over the past decade. But even if US interest rates are now viewed as tied to world interest rates,[3] there are still other weak links in the chain. The implication is that crowding out of domestic investment can still take place.

FOUR ALTERNATIVE DEFINITIONS OF INTERNATIONAL CAPITAL MOBILITY

By the second half of the 1970s, international economists had come to speak of the world financial system as characterized by perfect capital mobility. In many ways, this was 'jumping the gun'. It is true that financial integration had been greatly enhanced after 1973 by the removal of capital controls on the part of the USA, Germany, Canada, Switzerland and the Netherlands; by the steady process of technical and institutional innovation, particularly in the Euromarkets; and by the recycling of OPEC surpluses to developing countries. But almost all developing countries retained extensive restrictions on international capital flows, as did a majority of industrialized countries. Even among the five major countries without capital controls, capital was not perfectly mobile by some definitions.

There are at least four distinct definitions of perfect capital mobility that are in widespread use.

1 The *Feldstein–Horioka definition*: exogenous changes in national saving (i.e. in either private savings or government budgets) can be easily financed by borrowing from abroad at the going real interest rate, and thus need not crowd out investment in the originating country (except perhaps to the extent that the country is large in world financial markets).
2 *Real interest parity*: international capital flows equalize real interest rates across countries.
3 *Uncovered interest parity*: capital flows equalize expected rates of return on countries' bonds, despite exposure to exchange risk.
4 *Closed interest parity*: capital flows equalize interest rates across countries when contracted in a common currency.

These four possible definitions are in ascending order of specificity. Only the last condition is an unalloyed criterion for capital mobility in the sense of the degree of financial market integration across national boundaries.[4]

As we shall see, each of the first three conditions, if it is to hold, requires an auxiliary assumption in addition to the condition that follows it. Uncovered interest parity requires not only closed (or covered) interest parity, but also the condition that the exchange risk premium is zero. Real interest parity requires not only uncovered interest parity, but also the condition that expected real depreciation is zero. The Feldstein–Horioka condition requires not only real interest parity, but also a certain condition on the determinants of investment. But even though the relevance to the degree of integration of financial markets decreases as auxiliary conditions are added, the relevance to questions regarding the origin of international payments imbalances increases. We begin our consideration of the various criteria of capital mobility with the Feldstein–Horioka definition.

FELDSTEIN–HORIOKA TESTS

The Feldstein–Horioka definition requires that the country's real interest rate is tied to the world real interest rate by criterion (2); it is, after all, the real interest rate rather than the nominal interest rate on which saving and investment in theory depend. But for criterion (1) to hold, it is also necessary that any and all determinants of a country's rate of investment *other* than its real interest rate be uncorrelated with its rate of national saving. Let the investment rate be given by

$$\left(\frac{I}{Y}\right)_i = a - br_i + u_i \qquad (2.1)$$

where I is the level of capital formation, Y is national output, r is the domestic real interest rate and u represents all other factors, whether quantifiable or not, that determine the rate of investment. Feldstein and Horioka (1980) regressed the investment rate against the national saving rate,

$$\left(\frac{I}{Y}\right)_i = A + B\left(\frac{NS}{Y}\right)_i + v_i \qquad (2.1)'$$

where NS is private saving minus the budget deficit. To get the zero coefficient B that they were looking for requires not only real interest parity, i.e.

$$r_i - r^* = 0 \qquad (2.2)$$

(with the world interest rate r^* exogenous or in any other way uncorrelated with $(NS/Y)_i$, but also a zero correlation between u_i and $(NS/Y)_i$.

The saving–investment literature

Feldstein and Horioka's finding that the coefficient B is in fact closer to unity than to zero has been reproduced many times. Most authors have not been willing, however, to follow them in drawing the inference that financial markets are not highly integrated. There have been many econometric critiques, falling into two general categories.

The point most commonly made is that national saving is endogenous, or in our terms is correlated with u_i. This will be the case if national saving and investment are both procyclical, as they are in fact known to be, or if they both respond to the population or productivity growth rates.[5] It will also be the case if governments respond endogenously to incipient current account imbalances with policies to change public (or private) saving in such a way as to reduce the imbalances. This 'policy reaction' argument has been made by Fieleke (1982), Tobin (1983), Westphal (1983), Caprio and Howard (1984), Summers (1988), Roubini (1988) and Bayoumi (1990). But Feldstein and Horioka made an effort to handle the econometric endogeneity of national saving, more so than have some of their critics. To handle the cyclical endogeneity, they computed averages over a sufficiently long period of time that business cycles could be argued to wash out. To handle other sources of endogeneity, they used demographic variables as instrumental variables for the saving rate.

The other econometric critique is that, if the domestic country is large in world financial markets, r^* will not be exogenous with respect to $(NS/Y)_i$, and therefore, even if $r = r^*$, r and in turn $(I/Y)_i$ will be correlated with $(NS/Y)_i$. In other words, a shortfall in domestic savings will drive up the world interest rate and thus crowd out investment in the domestic country as well as abroad. This 'large-country' argument has been made by Murphy (1984) and Tobin (1983). An insufficiently appreciated point is that the large-country argument does not create a problem in cross-section studies, because all countries share the same world interest rate r^*. Since r^* simply goes into the constant term in a cross-section regression, it cannot be the source of any correlation with the right-hand-side variable. The large-country problem cannot explain why the countries that are high-saving relative to the average tend to coincide with the countries that are high-investing relative to the average.[6]

If the regressions of saving and investment rates were a good test for barriers to financial market integration, one would expect to see the coefficient falling over time. Until now, the evidence has if anything showed the coefficient rising over time. This finding has emerged both from cross-section studies, which typically report pre- and post-1973 results (Feldstein 1983; Penati and Dooley 1984; Dooley et al. 1987), and from pure time-series studies (Obstfeld 1986, 1989[7]; Frankel 1986) for the USA. The econometric endogeneity of national saving does not appear to be the explanation for this finding, because it holds equally well when instrumental variables are used.[8]

The easy explanation for the finding is that, econometric problems aside, real interest parity – criterion (2) above – has not held any better in recent years than it did in the past. Mishkin (1984a: 1352), for example, found even more significant rejections of real interest parity among major industrialized countries for the floating rate period after 1973.II than he did for his entire 1967.II–1979.II sample period. Caramazza et al. (1986: 43–7) also found that some of the major industrialized countries in the 1980s (1980.1–

1985.6) moved farther from real interest parity than they had been in the 1970s (1973.7–1979.12).[9] In the early 1980s, the real interest rate in the USA, in particular, rose far above the real interest rate of its major trading partners, by any of a variety of measures.[10] If the domestic real interest rate is not tied to the foreign real interest rate, then there is no reason to expect a zero coefficient in the saving–investment regression. We discuss in a later section the factors underlying real interest differentials.

The US saving–investment regression updated

Since 1980 the massive fiscal experiment carried out under the Reagan Administration has been rapidly undermining the statistical finding of a high saving–investment correlation for the case of the USA. The increase in the structural budget deficit, which was neither accommodated by monetary policy nor financed by an increase in private saving, reduced the national saving rate by 3 per cent of GNP relative to the 1970s. The investment rate – which, like the saving rate, initially fell in the 1981–2 recession – in the late 1980s approximately re-attained its 1980 level at best.[11] The saving shortfall was made up, necessarily, by a flood of borrowing from abroad equal to more than 3 per cent of GNP – hence the current account deficit of $161 billion in 1987. (By

contrast, the US current account balance was on average equal to zero in the 1970s.)

By now, the divergence between US national saving and investment has been sufficiently large and long lasting to show up in longer-term regressions of the Feldstein–Horioka type. If one seeks to isolate the degree of capital mobility or crowding out for the USA in particular, and how it has changed over time, then time-series regression is necessary (whereas if one is concerned with such measures world-wide, then cross-section regressions of the sort performed by Feldstein and Horioka are better). Table 2.1 reports instrumental variables regressions of investment against national saving for the USA from 1870 to 1987.[12] The data are illustrated in Figure 2.1. Decade averages are used for each variable, which removes some of the cyclical variation but gives us only twelve observations. (Yearly data are not in any case available before 1930.) This is one more observation than was available in Frankel (1986: Table 2.2), whose data only went up to the 1970s.

As before, the coefficient is statistically greater than zero and is not statistically different from unity, suggesting a high degree of crowding out (or, in Feldstein and Horioka's terms, a low degree of capital mobility). But the point estimate of the coefficient (when correcting for possible serial correlation) drops from 0.91 in the earlier study to 0.79 in the longer sample. We can allow for a time

Table 2.1 The Feldstein–Horioka coefficient by decades, 1869–1987: instrumental variables regression of US investment against national saving (as shares of GNP)

Constant	Coefficient	Time trend in coefficient	Durbin–Watson statistic	Autoregressive parameter	R^2
0.411 (1.340)	0.976 (0.086)		1.45		0.96
3.324 (1.842)	0.785 (0.118)			0.46 (0.33)	0.97
3.291 (6.176)	0.854 (0.279)	−0.011 (0.21)	0.73		0.92
1.061 (1.507)	0.924 (0.093)	0.001 (0.005)		0.03 (0.08)	0.96

Note: Instrumental variables: dependence ratio and military expenditure/GNP.

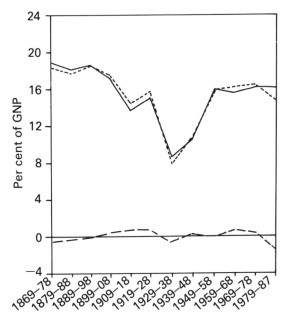

Figure 2.1 US national saving (private saving plus government budget surplus), investment and current account; ten-year averages: ———, investment/GNP; — — , current account/GNP; ------, national saving/GNP

trend in the coefficient; it drops from *plus* 0.01 a year in the earlier study to *minus* 0.01 a year (or plus 0.001, when correcting for serial correlation) in the longer sample. Thus the additional years 1980–7 do show up as anticipated: as exhibiting a lower US degree of crowding out, even if the change is small. (The trend is not statistically significant, but this is not surprising given the small number of observations.)

A data set that begins later would seem more promising than the twelve decade averages. Table 2.2 reports regressions for yearly data beginning in 1930. Much of the variation in the yearly data is cyclical, so Table 2.3 uses saving and investment rates that have been cyclically adjusted for a sample period that begins in 1955. These data are shown in Figure 2.2. (The cyclical adjustment of each is accomplished by first regressing it on the GNP gap, defined as the percentage deviation from the Bureau of Economic Analysis's 'middle expansion trend' of GNP, and then taking the residuals.)

In previous work with a sample period of 1956–84, the coefficient in a regression of cyclically adjusted saving and investment rates was estimated at 0.80, statistically indistinguishable from unity (Frankel 1986: 43–4). But now the

Table 2.2 The Feldstein–Horioka coefficient by years, 1929–87: instrumental variables regression of US investment against national saving (as shares of GNP) (comparing regressions before and after 1980)

	Constant	Coefficient	Durbin–Watson statistic	Autoregressive parameter	R^2
1929–87	2.99 (0.88)	0.79 (0.06)	0.64		0.94
1930–87	4.85 (2.61)	0.67 (0.19)		0.77 (0.09)	0.89
1929–79	1.89 (0.61)	0.86 (0.04)	1.31		0.97
1930–79	2.00 (0.66)	0.85 (0.05)		0.38 (0.13)	0.95
1980–7	13.73 (3.85)	0.15 (0.27)	2.09		
1981–7	−0.36 (0.56)	0.03 (0.02)		−0.37 Not converged	0.00

Table 2.3 The Feldstein–Horioka coefficient by years, 1955–87: instrumental variables regression of US investment against national saving (as shares of GNP and cyclically adjusted)

	Constant	Coefficient	Durbin–Watson statistic	Autoregressive parameter	R^2
1929–87	0.00[a]	−0.06	0.96		0.25
		(0.25)			
1930–87	0.00[a]	0.03		0.50	0.42
		(0.26)		(0.15)	
1929–79	−0.68	1.37	1.61		0.73
	(0.17)	(0.23)			
1930–79	−0.57	1.05		0.35	0.70
	(0.18)	(0.19)		(0.20)	
1980–7	0.39	0.13	2.46		0.30
	(0.36)	(0.17)			
1981–7	0.58	0.22		−0.13	0.34
	(0.37)	(0.16)		(0.41)	

Note: [a] Constant term is automatically zero because cyclically adjusted rates are residuals from a 1955–87 regression against the GNP gap.

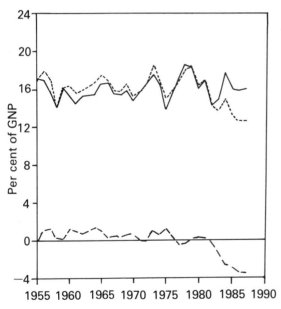

Figure 2.2 US national saving, investment and current account: ———, investment/GNP; — —, current account/GNP; – – – –, national saving/GNP

coefficient has dropped essentially to zero, suggesting a zero degree of crowding out, or a zero degree of 'saving-retention' (or, in the Feldstein–Horioka terminology, 'perfect capital mobility'). This finding is the result of the addition to the sample of another three years (1985–7) of record current account deficits, a period also in which the cyclically adjusted national saving rate was historically low. When the equation is estimated with an allowance for a time trend in the coefficient, the trend is negative (though statistically insignificant), whereas the earlier sample that stopped in 1984 showed a time trend that was positive (and insignificant).

To verify that the 1980s experience is indeed the source of the precipitous fall in the saving–investment coefficient,[13] the sample period is split at 1980. For the period 1955–79, not only is the coefficient statistically indistinguishable from unity, but the point estimate is slightly *greater* than unity.[14] It is clearly the unprecedented developments of the present decade that have overturned the hitherto-robust saving–investment relationship for the case of the USA. It is likely that financial liberalization in Japan, the UK and other countries, and continued innovation in the Euromarkets (and perhaps the 1984 repeal of the US withholding tax on borrowing from abroad), have resulted in a higher degree of capital mobility, and thereby facilitated the record flow of capital to the USA in the 1980s. But the magnitude of the inflow is in the first instance attributable to the unprecedented magnitude of the decline in national saving.[15]

DIFFERENTIALS IN EXPECTED RATES OF RETURN, AND EXPECTED REAL DEPRECIATION

If the goal is to measure the degree of integration of capital markets, rather than the degree to which decreases in national saving have crowded out investment, then it is better to look at differences in rates of return across countries rather than looking at saving–investment correlations.[16] But measuring *real* interest differentials will not do the trick. An international investor, when deciding which country's assets to buy, will not compare the interest rates in different countries each expressed in terms of expected purchasing power over that country's goods. When he or she thinks to evaluate assets in terms of purchasing power, all assets will be evaluated in terms of the same basket, the one consumed by that particular investor. The expected inflation rate then drops out of differentials in expected rates of return among assets.

The differential in expected rates of return on two countries' bonds is the uncovered interest differential, the nominal interest differential minus the expected change in the exchange rate: $i - i^* - (Ds^e)$. If asset demands are highly sensitive to expected rates of return, then the differential will be zero, which gives us uncovered interest parity:

$$I - i^* - (Ds^e) = 0. \qquad (2.3)$$

To distinguish this parity condition, which is criterion (3) above, from the other definitions, it has often been designated 'perfect substitutability': not only is there little in the manner of transactions costs or government-imposed controls to separate national markets, but also domestic-currency and foreign-currency bonds are perfect substitutes in investors' portfolios.

Just as criterion (1) is considerably stronger than criterion (2), so is criterion (2) considerably stronger than criterion (3). For real interest parity to hold, one must have not only uncovered interest parity, but an additional condition as well, which is sometimes called *ex ante* relative PPP:

$$Ds^e = Dp^e - Dp^{e*}. \qquad (2.2)'$$

Equation (2.2)′ and equation (2.3) together imply equation (2.2). If goods markets are perfectly integrated, meaning not only that there is little in the manner of transportation costs or government-imposed barriers to separate national markets, but also that domestic and foreign goods are perfect substitutes in consumers' utility functions, then PPP holds. PPP in turn implies (2.2)′. But as is well known by now, goods markets are not in fact perfectly integrated. Because of the possibility of expected real depreciation, real interest parity can fail even if criterion (3) holds perfectly. The remainder of this section considers the question of whether *ex ante* relative PPP – equation (2.2)′ – holds.

The enormous real appreciation of the dollar in the early 1980s and the subsequent real depreciation have by now convinced the remaining doubters, but abundant statistical evidence against PPP was there all along. Krugman (1978: 406), for example, computed for the floating rate period from July 1973 to December 1976 standard deviations of the (logarithmic) real exchange rate equal to 6.0 per cent for the pound–dollar rate and 8.4 per cent for the mark–dollar rate. He also computed serial correlation coefficients for PPP deviations of 0.897 and 0.854, respectively, on a monthly basis, equal to 0.271 and 0.150 on an annual basis. The serial correlation coefficient is of interest because it is equal to one minus the speed of adjustment to PPP. It may be best not to rely exclusively on the standard deviation of the real exchange rate as a summary statistic for the degree of integration of goods markets, because it in part reflects the magnitude of monetary disturbances during the period.[17]

Table 2.4 shows updated annual statistics on the real exchange rate between the USA and Great Britain. The real pound–dollar rate is illustrated in Figure 2.3. During the floating rate period 1973–87, though there is no significant time trend, there is a large standard error of 15.6 per cent. The serial correlation in the deviations from PPP is estimated at 0.687, with a standard error of 0.208. This means that the estimated speed of adjustment to PPP is 0.313 per year and that one can easily reject the hypothesis of instantaneous adjustment.

From the ashes of absolute PPP, a phoenix has risen. In response to findings such as those reported here, some authors have swung from one extreme, the proposition that the tendency of the real exchange rate to return to a constant is complete and instantaneous, to the opposite extreme, that there is no such tendency at all. The hypothesis that the real exchange rate follows a random walk is just as good as the hypothesis of absolute PPP for implying *ex ante* relative PPP. But there is even less of an *a priori* case why PPP should hold in rate-of-change form rather than in the level form.

Even though *ex ante* relative PPP has little basis in theory, it does appear to have some empirical support. Typically, the estimated speeds of adjustment during the floating rate period, 0.31 in Table

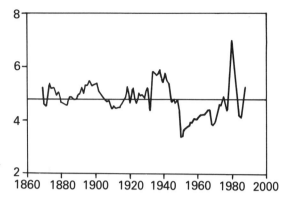

Figure 2.3 Dollar–pound real exchange rate 1869–1987, with period average (dollars per pound at 1929 prices)

2.4 (1973–87), while not so low as to be implausible as point estimates, are nevertheless low enough that one statistically cannot reject the hypothesis that they are zero. In other words, one cannot reject the random walk hypothesis that the autoregression coefficient is unity.

A 95 per cent confidence interval on the autoregressive coefficient AR covers the range 0.27–1.10. If the null hypothesis is an autoregressive coefficient of unity, one cannot legitimately use the standard t test derived from a regression where the right-hand side variable is the level of the real exchange rate, because under the null hypothesis the variance is infinite. There are a number of ways of

Table 2.4 Purchasing power parity between the USA and the UK: the real exchange rate

	1973–87	1945–72	1945–87	1869–87
Statistics on percentage deviation from mean				
Mean absolute deviation	0.120	0.074	0.110	0.093
Standard deviation	0.156	0.091	0.156	0.121
Time trend	0.001	−0.001	0.006*	−0.001*
	(0.010)	(0.002)	(0.002)	(0.000)
Autoregressions	0.687*	0.722*	0.830*	0.844*
	(0.208)	(0.130)	(0.092)	(0.050)

Notes: Standard errors are reported in parentheses.
 *Significant at the 95 per cent level.

dealing with this non-stationarity problem. Here one simply applies the corrected Dickey–Fuller 95 per cent significance level, 3.00. The 0.31 estimate for the floating rate period is insignificantly different from zero.

This failure to reject a random walk in the real exchange rate is the same result as found by Roll (1979), Frenkel (1981: 699), Adler and Lehman (1983), Darby (1981), Mishkin (1984a: 1351–3) and Piggott and Sweeney (1985). Most of these studies used monthly data. On the one hand, the greater abundance of data reduces the standard error of the estimate but, on the other hand, one is no longer testing whether AR = 0.69 is different from unity but rather whether 0.97 (= $AR^{1/12}$) is different from unity, so that it may not be much easier to reject. Another problem is that one does not know that the nature of the true autoregressive process is truly first order on a monthly (or continuous-time) basis. In any case, the monthly data in the studies cited were generally not powerful enough to reject the random walk.[18]

A more promising alternative is to choose a longer time sample to get a more powerful estimate. Table 2.4 also reports statistics for the entire post-war period 1945–87. PPP held better for the Bretton Woods years than it did after 1973, as measured either by the mean absolute deviation and standard deviation of the real exchange rate or by the ability to reject the hypothesis of zero auto-correlation. But, despite the longer time sample, one is only at the borderline of being able to reject the random walk. The 95 per cent confidence interval for AR runs from 0.64 to 1.02 and the t ratio of 1.85 falls short of the Dickey–Fuller 95 per cent significance level of 2.93.

The asymptotic standard error of an estimate of AR is approximately the square root of $(1-AR^2)/N$. So if the true speed of adjustment is of the order of 30 per cent a year (AR = 0.7), a simple calculation suggests that we might require at least forty-nine years of data $(2.93^2(1 - 0.7^2)/(1 - 0.7)^2 = 48.6)$ to be able to reject the null hypothesis of AR = 1. It is not very surprising that forty-three years of data are not enough, much less the fifteen years of data used in most studies.[19] (Econometricians

consider the asymptotic standard error on which this calculation is based to be a bad approximation in small samples. But the correct power calculation suggests that, if anything, the sample required to reject a random walk would be even larger than forty-nine.)[20]

The last column of Table 2.4 presents an entire 119 years of US–UK data. With a time sample this long, the standard error is reduced considerably. The rejection of no serial correlation in the real exchange rate is even stronger than in the shorter time samples. More importantly, one is finally able to detect a statistically significant tendency for the real exchange rate to regress to PPP, at a rate of 16 per cent a year. The confidence interval for AR runs from 0.75 to 0.94, safely less than unity, and the t ratio of 3.12 exceeds the Dickey–Fuller significance level of 2.89.[21]

The motivation for looking at PPP in this section has been to obtain insight into the expected rate of real depreciation, because that is the variable that can give rise to real interest differentials even in the presence of uncovered interest parity.[22] In rejecting the random walk description of the real exchange rate, one has rejected the claim that the rationally expected rate of real depreciation is zero.[23] To take an example, in 1983–4, when the dollar had appreciated some 30 per cent above its PPP value, survey data show expected future real depreciation of 4.3 per cent per year. It is thus not difficult to explain the existence of the US real interest differential, even without appealing to any sort of risk premium. There is little excuse for authors such as Koraczyk (1985: 350) and Darby (1986: 420) ruling out the possibility of expected real depreciation *a priori* and thereby concluding that real interest differentials *necessarily* constitute risk premia.

If the failure of *ex ante* relative PPP could, in itself, explain the failure of real interest parity, then it could also, by itself, explain the failure of saving and investment to be uncorrelated. In the recent US context, a fall in national saving could cause an increase in the real interest differential and therefore a fall in investment, even if financial markets are perfectly integrated and even if the fall in saving is truly exogenous, provided that the real interest differential is associated with expected real depreciation of the dollar.

Demonstrating that the failure of *ex ante* relative PPP is *capable* of producing a correlation between saving and investment is, of course, not the same thing as asserting that this in fact is the explanation for the observed correlation. Plenty of other competing explanations have been proposed. But some support for the idea that the existence of expected real depreciation *is* key to the observed correlation comes from Cardia (1988). She simulates saving and investment rates in a sequence of models featuring shocks to fiscal spending, money growth and productivity, in order to see which models are capable, for empirically relevant magnitudes of the parameters, of producing saving–investment correlations as high as those observed. To get at some of the explanations that have been most prominently proposed, she constructs models both with and without PPP, both with and without endogenous response of fiscal policy to current account imbalances and both with and without the small-country assumption. The finding is that the model that allows for deviations from PPP is able to explain saving–investment correlations as high as unity, while the various models that impose PPP are generally not able to do so.[24]

Further empirical support for the idea that the Feldstein–Horioka results may in fact be due to imperfect integration of goods markets, rather than imperfect integration of financial markets, is provided by a test by Bayoumi and Rose (1991). They compute the correlation of saving and investment across regions within the UK, reasoning that these regions – unlike nations – are highly integrated with respect to their goods markets, and find no positive correlation.

A DECOMPOSITION OF REAL INTEREST DIFFERENTIALS FOR TWENTY-FIVE COUNTRIES

Because there are so many competing definitions of the degree of international capital mobility, it would be worth knowing if the sort of countries that register high by one criterion are also the sort that register high by the others. In this section we look at rates of return in the 1980s across a sample of twenty-five countries. We begin with the broadest measure of barriers to international capital mobility, the differential in real interest rates, defined as

$$r - r^* = (i - \mathrm{D}p^e) - (i^* - \mathrm{D}p^{e*}). \quad (2.5)$$

Subsequently we shall decompose the real interest differential into a component due to 'political' or country factors and a component due to currency factors:

$$r - r^* = (i - i^* - \mathrm{fd}) - (\mathrm{fd} - \mathrm{D}p^e \\ + \mathrm{D}p^{e*}) \quad (2.6)$$

where i is the domestic nominal interest rate, i^* is the foreign nominal interest rate and fd is the forward discount on the domestic currency. The first term $(i - i^* - \mathrm{fd})$ is the covered interest differential. We call it the political or country premium because it captures all barriers to integration of financial markets across national boundaries: transactions costs, information costs, capital controls, tax laws that discriminate by country of residence, default risk and risk of future capital controls. The second term could be described as the real forward discount. We call it the currency premium because it captures differences in assets according to the currency in which they are denominated, rather than in terms of the political jurisdiction in which they are issued. As we shall see, the currency premium can in turn be decomposed into two factors, the exchange risk premium and expected real depreciation.

The decomposition of the real interest differential would not be possible without the use of data on forward exchange rates. Many previous studies have used forward rate data to test covered interest parity, but only for a few countries. The present study uses forward rate data for a panel of twenty-five countries, which as far as I know is the largest set ever examined. The set of twenty-five includes countries both large and small, industrialized and developing, Atlantic and Pacific. The forward rate data for most of the countries come from Barclays Bank in London, via Data Resources Inc.[25]

Real interest differentials

Table 2.5 reports statistics on three-month real interest differentials for the twenty-five countries, expressed in each case as the local interest rate measured relative to the Eurodollar interest rate. For local interest rates we use the interbank market rate or, where no market rate exists, the most flexibly determined interest rate available.[26]. We use, to begin with, the realized inflation rates during the *ex post* three-month period. The first column reports the mean real interest differential during the sample period, September 1982 to January 1988. (In this and subsequent tables the statistics go up to April 1988 because the *ex post* data run three months behind the *ex ante* expectations.) The numbers are negative for a majority of countries, averaging −1.74 across all twenty-five, which reflects the high level of real dollar interest rates during this period.

The countries are classified into five groups chosen on *a priori* grounds. The group with real interest rates farthest below the world rate includes Bahrain, Greece, Mexico, Portugal and South Africa. These five (very diverse) countries bear the burden of representing a wide class of LDCs in our sample. Altogether there are eight countries classified as LDCs that happen to have forward rate data available, and thereby appear in our sample; three of these are East Asian countries (Hong Kong, Singapore and Malaysia) that are thought to have open financial markets in the 1980s and so are here classified separately.

One might object that the large negative real interest differentials in the group of five reflect administered local interest rates that are kept artificially low by 'financial repression'. But countries cannot maintain artificially low interest rates without barriers to capital outflow. These statistics reflect a low degree of capital mobility precisely as we want them to. In this respect our group of five is typical of LDCs. A number of

studies, including much larger LDC samples than are available here, have shown the extremes to which real interest rates can go, particularly some very negative levels in the 1970s.

As with the other measures of interest rate differentials that we shall be considering below, the mean is not always the most useful statistic. A small mean over a particular sample period may hide fluctuations in both directions. Even if a mean is statistically significant,[27] it is useful to know in addition the variability of the differential. The standard deviation is reported in the second column of Table 2.5. We also report the root mean squared error in the third column. (This would be a superior measure of how closely the rates are tied together if, for example, we are worried about the possibility of a large differential that is fairly constant over time because of government administration of interest rates.) Finally we report in the fourth column how big a band would be needed to encompass 95 per cent of the deviations from real interest parity.

Country-group comparisons of the measures of real interest differential variability in some respects suit *a priori* expectations: the five closed LDCs constitute the group with the highest variability and the five open Atlantic countries the group with the lowest.[28] But there are some results that are anomalous if the real interest differential is taken as a measure of financial market integration. France, for example, had stringent capital controls in place during our sample period (at least until the latter part) and yet appears, by the criterion of real interest differential variability, to have a *higher* degree of capital mobility than Japan, which announced liberalization of its capital controls before our sample period (1979–80). One might conceivably argue that the Japanese liberalization must not have been genuine. But the French real interest differential is smaller and less variable even than those of the Netherlands and Switzerland, major countries that are known to be virtually free of capital controls. Only Canada shows a smaller and less variable real interest differential than France.

Because the realized inflation rates could not

Table 2.5 Real interest differentials (local minus Euro-dollar; three-month rates): interest differential less realized inflation differential, September 1982–January 1988

	Number of observations	Mean	Standard error	Series standard deviation	Root mean squared error	95% band
Open Atlantic developed countries						
Canada	63	0.09	0.38	2.09	2.09	3.96
Germany	63	−1.29	0.65	2.77	3.06	5.95
Netherlands	62	−0.71	0.86	3.91	3.97	7.63
Switzerland	62	−2.72	0.81	3.39	4.36	8.43
UK	63	0.46	0.79	3.45	3.48	5.69
Group	313	−0.83	0.66	3.16	3.46	
Liberalizing Pacific						
Hong Kong	62	−2.89	0.94	4.80	5.62	11.61
Malaysia	62	0.83	1.00	4.61	4.68	8.19
Singapore	61	0.08	0.68	3.33	3.34	6.71
Group	185	−0.67	0.82	4.28	4.62	
Closed less developed countries						
Bahrain	60	2.19	1.46	7.10	7.44	12.93
Greece	56	−9.22	1.91	9.36	13.19	21.77
Mexico	62	−20.28	9.43	21.19	29.45	52.13
Portugal	61	−3.90	2.97	11.28	11.95	23.62
South Africa	61	−4.84	1.17	4.85	6.88	11.16
Group	300	−7.25	1.30	12.16	16.06	
Closed European developed countries						
Austria	64	−2.20	0.83	3.84	4.43	7.32
Belgium	63	0.53	0.68	2.90	2.95	4.99
Denmark	61	−3.42	0.90	4.34	5.54	9.64
France	64	−0.48	0.72	2.94	2.98	5.54
Ireland	61	1.53	1.03	3.95	4.24	7.13
Italy	61	1.01	0.86	3.62	3.76	5.83
Norway	50	−0.64	0.84	3.23	3.29	6.83
Spain	63	0.53	1.44	5.92	5.95	11.90
Sweden	63	−0.21	1.07	4.52	4.53	8.28
Group	550	−0.37	0.81	4.00	4.29	
Liberalizing Pacific developed countries						
Australia	60	1.16	0.90	3.69	3.87	7.43
Japan	63	−0.58	0.62	3.41	3.46	6.03
New Zealand	60	1.04	1.83	7.15	7.23	11.36
Group	183	0.52	0.73	5.00	5.09	
All countries	1,531	−1.74		6.47	8.07	

have been precisely known *a priori*, it is necessary to project them onto contemporaneously known variables. Three such variables were used: the forward discount, the nominal interest differential and the lagged inflation differential. (The results are reported in NBER Working Paper 2856, but are omitted here to save space.) In a majority of cases, a statistically significant amount of the variation in the real interest differential turned out to be forecastable.[29] The standard deviation of the projected differential gives us our final measure of variability. The results for the *ex ante* real interest differential are mostly similar to those for the *ex post* data. France, for example, still shows a lower degree of variability than the Netherlands.

Covered interest differentials: the country premium

We now use the Barclays forward rate data to decompose the real interest differential into one part due to country factors and another part due to currency factors, as in equation (2.5). The first component, the covered interest differential, encompasses all factors related to the political jurisdiction in which the asset is issued. Its size and variability measures barriers to international capital mobility in the most narrow and proper definition of the term.

The first column of Table 2.6 reports the mean of the covered interest differential for each of our twenty-five countries. A good rule of thumb, when the absolute magnitude of the mean or the variability of the differential indicates the existence of significant barriers, is as follows: a negative differential *vis-à-vis* the Eurocurrency market indicates that, to the extent that barriers exist, there are capital controls or transactions costs currently operating to discourage capital from flowing out of the country. Investors would not settle for a lower return domestically if they were free to earn abroad the higher return covered to eliminate exchange risk. This is the case for all the LDCs in the sample with the exception of Hong Kong and for all of the traditionally 'closed' European countries with the exceptions of Austria and Belgium (which should

by now probably be classified with the 'open' countries). The negative differential that existed for the UK before Margaret Thatcher removed capital controls in 1979 is now extremely small (see Figure 2.4; also Artis and Taylor 1990). Similarly, Canada's differential is effectively zero.[30]

The fourth column, the size of the band wide enough to encompass 95 per cent of deviations from international covered interest parity, can be compared with the approach of Frenkel and Levich (1977). They tested a larger band which was meant to represent transactions costs between pound and dollar securities. They found (1977: 1217), for the case of the UK, that a smaller percentage of deviations (87.6–89.7 per cent) fell within the band. This confirms that capital mobility has increased since the 1970s.

Germany and several other neighbouring European countries (Switzerland, the Netherlands, Austria and Belgium) show higher interest rates locally than offshore, which suggests some barriers discouraging capital *inflow*: investors would not settle for a lower mark return in the Euromarket if they were free to get the higher return in Germany. But the magnitude is quite small, as it has been observed to be ever since Germany removed most of its controls on capital inflow in 1974. Figure 2.5 shows the evidence of the 1974 liberalization (see also Dooley and Isard 1980; Giavazzi and Pagano 1985: 27).

Japan has a covered differential that by all measures is smaller and less variable than those of Switzerland and Germany, let alone France and most of the other countries. This might come as a surprise to those accustomed to thinking of Japanese financial markets in terms of the large barriers to capital inflow that were in place in the 1970s. The liberalization of Japanese markets, which has been documented elsewhere, continued during our sample period (Figure 2.6; see also Otani 1983; Frankel 1984). Australia and New Zealand, while lagging well behind Japan, also show signs of liberalization during the course of our sample period.[31]

The covered interest differential for France is much larger and more variable than that for the

Table 2.6 Country premia or covered interest differentials (local minus Euro-dollar; three-month rates): interest differential less forward discount, September 1982–April 1988

	Number of observations	Mean	Standard error	Series standard deviation	Root mean squared error	95% band
Open Atlantic developed countries						
Canada	68	−0.10	0.03	0.21	0.24	0.44
Germany	68	0.35	0.03	0.24	0.42	0.75
Netherlands	68	0.21	0.02	0.13	0.25	0.45
Switzerland	68	0.42	0.03	0.23	0.48	0.79
UK	68	−0.14	0.02	0.20	0.25	0.41
Group	340	0.14	0.01	0.21	0.34	
Liberalizing Pacific						
Hong Kong	68	0.13	0.03	0.28	0.31	0.60
Malaysia	63	−1.46	0.16	1.28	1.95	3.73
Singapore	64	−0.30	0.04	0.31	0.43	0.73
Group	195	−0.52	0.05	0.76	1.14	
Closed less developed countries						
Bahrain	64	−2.15	0.13	1.06	2.41	4.17
Greece	58	−9.39	0.80	6.08	11.26	20.39
Mexico	43	−16.47	1.83	12.01	20.54	28.86
Portugal	61	−7.93	1.23	9.59	12.49	27.83
South Africa	67	−1.07	1.17	9.55	9.61	2.68
Group	293	−6.64	0.48	8.23	11.82	
Closed European developed countries						
Austria	65	0.13	0.05	0.39	0.41	0.39
Belgium	68	0.12	0.03	0.26	0.29	0.59
Denmark	68	−3.53	0.19	1.57	3.89	6.63
France	68	−1.74	0.32	2.68	3.20	7.18
Ireland	66	−0.79	0.51	4.17	4.24	7.80
Italy	68	−0.40	0.23	1.92	1.96	4.11
Norway	50	−1.03	0.11	0.76	1.29	2.10
Spain	67	−2.40	0.45	3.66	4.39	7.95
Sweden	68	−0.23	0.06	0.45	0.51	0.81
Group	588	−1.10	0.09	2.25	2.77	
Liberalizing Pacific developed countries						
Australia	68	−0.75	0.23	1.94	2.08	2.59
Japan	68	0.09	0.03	0.21	0.23	0.43
New Zealand	68	−1.63	0.29	2.42	2.92	5.24
Group	204	−0.76	0.12	1.78	2.06	
All countries	1,620	−1.73	0.09	3.81	5.36	

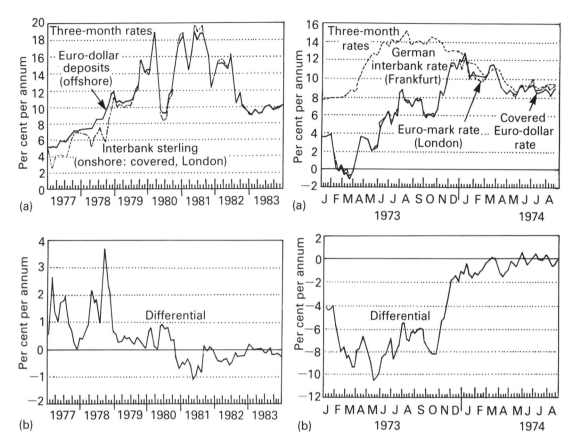

Figure 2.4 Financial liberalization in the UK: UK and Euro-dollar interest rates. Data are monthly averages of weekly (Wednesday) observations. The covered interbank sterling rate is calculated using the three-month forward premium on the sterling–dollar exchange rate. Positive values in part (b) indicate a differential in favour of offshore assets

Figure 2.5 Financial liberalization in Germany: German and Eurocurrency interest rates. Data are Wednesday quotations. The covered Euro-dollar rate is calculated using the three-month forward premium for the deutsche mark–dollar exchange rate. Positive values in part (b) indicate a differential in favour of offshore assets

other major industrialized countries known to be free of capital controls. This is the reverse of the finding from the criterion of real interest differentials in Table 2.5. It supports the value of the criterion of covered interest differentials as the proper test of financial market integration. The differential, with its negative sign signifying controls on French capital outflows, has been previously studied, especially its tendency to shoot up shortly before devaluations of the franc.[32] Our data indicate that the last major occurrence of this phenomenon was February 1986; since then the differential has been close to zero.

Similarly, the same phenomenon for Italy, which has also been previously studied (e.g. Giavazzi and Pagano 1985), appears to have ended after the February 1986 realignment. France and Italy apparently dismantled their capital controls quickly enough to meet a 1990 deadline for liberalization set by the EC Twelve (*The Economist* 1988). Of four countries that required a later deadline, Spain and Portugal have by our measures

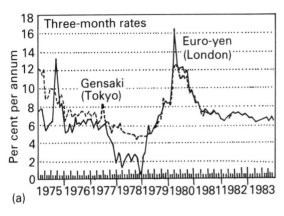

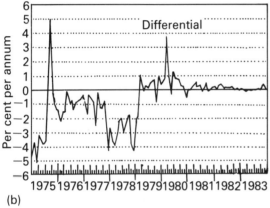

Figure 2.6 Financial liberalization in Japan: Japanese and Euro-yen interest rates. Data are month-end figures. Positive values in part (b) indicate a differential in favour of offshore assets

already been liberalizing (plots show that the magnitude of the covered interest differential fell sharply in 1987 for these two countries), but Greece and Ireland have not. Sweden is one non-EC European country that appears to have moved toward liberalization during our sample period, while Norway does not. All of these European countries show up with negative mean differentials, which implies that the remaining controls act to discourage capital outflow rather than inflow. For the EC countries, this finding supports records of the European Commission which report more freedom for short-term inflows than short-term outflows.[33]

Registering impressively open financial markets are our three East Asian LDCs (which, especially in the case of Singapore, have rapidly outgrown the appellation 'less developed'). Hong Kong and Singapore show even smaller covered differentials than some open European countries like Germany. Malaysia's differential has been considerably higher, particularly in 1986, but still compares favourably with some European countries.

Not surprisingly, our remaining LDCs (Mexico, Greece, Portugal, Bahrain and South Africa) show by far the largest and most variable covered interest differentials.[34] Again, the results are precisely what one would expect if covered interest differentials are the proper criterion for capital mobility, but the reverse of what the saving–investment criterion shows.

Why does the covered differential criterion give such different answers from the saving–investment criterion, which shows a high degree of saving retention among industrialized countries? Feldstein and Horioka argue that financial markets are less well integrated at longer-term maturities, as compared with the three-month maturities used in tests of covered interest parity such as those reported above:

> It is clear from the yields on short-term securities in the Eurocurrency market and the forward prices of those currencies that liquid financial capital moves very rapidly to arbitrage such short-term differentials.... There are however reasons to be sceptical about the extent of such long-term arbitrage.
>
> (1980: 315)

Studies of international interest parity have been restricted by a lack of forward exchange rates at horizons going out much further than one year.[35] But even without the use of forward rate data, there are ways of getting around the problem of exchange risk. Data on currency swap rates can be used in place of forward exchange rates to test the long-term version of interest rate parity. Popper (1990) finds that the swap-covered return differential on five-year US government bonds versus Japanese bonds averaged only 1.7 basis points from 3 October 1985 to 10 July 1986, and that the differential on seven-year bonds averaged only 5.3 basis points. The means mask some variation in the differential. But a band of 46 basis points is large enough to encompass 95 per cent of the observations for the five-year bonds. The band is 34 basis points for the seven-year bonds. The means on five-year bonds for some other major countries are as follows: Canada, 15.9; Switzerland, 18.7; UK 51.1; and Germany, 28.4.

The magnitude of these long-term differentials compares favourably with the magnitude of the short-term differentials. The implication is that Feldstein and Horioka are wrong in their conjecture that there is a term-structure wedge separating national capital markets.[36] The most relevant distinction appears to be not long term versus short term, but rather real versus nominal.

'Real forward discounts': the currency premium

Even for those countries that exhibit no substantial country premium, as reflected in covered interest parity ($fd - (i - i^*) = 0$), there may still be a substantial currency premium that drives real interest differentials ($(i - Dp^e) - (i^* - Dp^{e*})$) away from zero. If real interest differentials are not arbitraged to zero, then there is in turn no reason to expect saving–investment correlations to be zero. Table 2.7 reports the statistics for the currency premium, as measured by the 'real forward discount':

$$fd - (Dp^e - Dp^{e*}).$$

Germany, Switzerland, the Netherlands, Austria and Japan, for example, all have substantial real forward discounts (or – more precisely – real forward premia) which constitute approximately the entirety of their real interest differentials. These are countries with currencies that have experienced a lot of exchange rate variability, both nominal and real, vis-à-vis the dollar since 1973 and especially since 1980. As a consequence, some combination of exchange risk premia and expected real depreciation – factors pertaining to the

currency, not to the political jurisdiction – produces the gap in real interest rates. For these five financially open industrialized countries, and for Hong Kong as well, the currency factors produce a *negative* real interest differential, while the covered interest differential (though small) is *positive*: the small regulations or frictions that remain in these countries are, if anything, working to resist capital inflow (at least at the short end of the maturity spectrum) and not outflow as one would mistakenly conclude from the real interest differential criterion. The other countries all have highly variable currency premia as well. Indeed the real forward discount (currency premium) is more variable than the covered interest differential (country premium) for all but three of our twenty-five countries (Greece, Mexico and France). The last rows of Tables 2.6 and 2.7 show that the average variability across all countries is higher for the currency premium than for the country premium.

We can project the real forward discount on the same three variables as we did for the real interest differential (the forward discount, nominal interest differential and lagged inflation differential) to get an *ex ante* measure.[37] Its standard deviation now shows six countries for whom the currency premium is less variable than the country premium (Greece, Mexico, Portugal, France, Italy and Spain). But the currency premium remains the major obstacle to real interest parity for most countries.

Further decomposition into exchange risk premium and expected real depreciation

Our decomposition so far has lumped together two terms, the exchange risk premium and expected real depreciation, into the currency premium:

$$fd - Dp^e + Dp^{e*} = (fd - Ds^e) + (Ds^e - Dp^e + Dp^{e*}).$$

In this section we attempt to complete the decomposition by separating these two terms. To do so requires a measure or model of expected depreci-

Table 2.7 Currency premia or real forward discounts: forward discount less realized inflation differential, September 1982–January 1988

	Number of observations	Mean	Standard error	Series standard deviation	Root mean squared error	95% band
Open Atlantic developed countries						
Canada	63	0.18	0.38	2.08	2.09	4.02
Germany	63	−1.66	0.69	2.89	3.34	6.57
Netherlands	62	−0.92	0.88	3.98	4.09	7.52
Switzerland	62	−3.15	0.84	3.49	4.72	8.79
UK	63	0.61	0.83	3.56	3.61	5.97
Group	313	−0.98	0.69	3.24	3.65	
Liberalizing Pacific						
Hong Kong	62	−2.99	0.93	4.79	5.66	11.76
Malaysia	62	2.29	1.14	5.06	5.56	10.17
Singapore	62	0.40	0.67	0.32	3.35	6.86
Group	186	−0.10	0.82	4.43	4.95	
Closed less developed countries						
Bahrain	60	4.37	1.52	7.27	8.51	16.18
Greece	60	0.83	1.67	9.98	10.01	18.77
Mexico	43	0.03	3.58	15.23	15.23	22.08
Portugal	59	4.94	2.13	11.73	12.74	21.56
South Africa	62	−3.82	1.81	11.36	11.99	14.75
Group	284	1.29	1.37	11.05	11.60	
Closed European developed countries						
Austria	62	−2.25	0.88	3.94	4.55	7.68
Belgium	63	0.42	0.69	2.95	2.98	5.05
Denmark	61	0.14	1.01	4.63	4.63	7.13
France	64	1.35	0.54	2.50	2.85	4.82
Ireland	59	2.14	1.40	6.41	6.76	13.85
Italy	61	1.42	0.72	3.15	3.46	5.52
Norway	64	1.07	0.75	3.25	3.43	5.91
Spain	63	3.12	1.26	5.53	6.36	11.08
Sweden	63	0.04	1.07	4.57	4.57	8.29
Group	560	0.83	0.67	4.23	4.54	
Liberalizing Pacific developed countries						
Australia	60	1.97	0.88	4.06	4.52	7.85
Japan	63	−0.69	0.64	3.48	3.55	6.32
New Zealand	60	2.82	1.98	7.96	8.46	14.11
Group	183	1.33	0.79	5.48	5.84	
All countries	1,526	0.49		6.11	6.50	

ation. The usual approach is to use the *ex post* changes in the spot rate (Ds) as a measure of *ex ante* expectations (Ds^e), and to argue that under rational expectations the expectational error ($e \equiv Ds - Ds^e$) should be random (uncorrelated with information currently available at time t).

The first column of Table 2.8 reports the mean value of fd − Ds for each of our countries. Most of the means are positive, showing that the weak dollar period (1985–8) dominates over the strong dollar period (1982–5).[38] But only three currencies have mean risk premia, of either sign, that are statistically significant.[39] Furthermore, in a majority of cases (sixteen out of twenty-five), the sign of the mean return differential is the *opposite* of the sign of the mean real interest differential during the same period (Table 2.5, first column). So this measure of the exchange risk premium does not explain any positive part of the real interest differential.

The measures of the variability of fd − Ds show up very large in the second, third and fourth columns. These are measures of the variability of *ex post* return differentials and not *ex ante* return differentials. They tell us little about the variability of the exchange risk premium. But the high variability of the exchange rate does tell us two things. First, it provides an obvious explanation – low power – of why the first moments might not be statistically significant. On the other hand, the existence of substantial uncertainty regarding the future spot rate suggests, via the theory of optimal portfolio diversification, that a non-zero exchange risk premium must exist to reward risk-averse investors for holding currencies that are perceived as risky or that are in oversupply.

To estimate the *ex ante* exchange risk premium, we can project fd − depr onto our same three variables: the forward discount, the interest differential and the inflation differential.[40] The regression is statistically significant for a majority of currencies, as many others have found.[41] The standard deviation shows that the most variable exchange risk premia belong to Mexico and New Zealand, but the UK, the Netherlands, Austria, Germany and Switzerland follow close behind.

In Table 2.9 we report the statistics for the other component of the currency premium, expected real depreciation. As noted earlier, given the widely accepted failure of PPP on levels, there is no theoretical reason to expect it necessarily to hold in terms of expected rates of change, the hypothesis sometimes known as *ex ante* relative PPP. Table 2.9 reports the statistics for *ex post* real depreciation. The means in the first column are negative, indicating real appreciation of the currency against the dollar, for all European countries and for most other countries as well. The only five exceptions, countries that experienced real depreciation against the dollar, were our three East Asian developing countries, Australia and Bahrain. Bahrain was the only one, of either sign, that was statistically significant.

We already know, from the results reported above for the 119 years of US–UK data, that we cannot expect to reject *ex ante* relative PPP on just a few years of data: new disturbances to the real exchange rate are so large that one needs a much longer time sample to find evidence of systematic movement. But the signs of the mean real depreciations are usually (in twenty out of twenty-five cases) the same as the signs of the mean real interest differentials given in Table 2.5, suggesting a high correlation of the real interest differential and expected real depreciation across countries.[42]

To estimate *ex ante* expected real depreciation, we project *ex post* real depreciation, again, on the same three contemporaneous variables.[43] The standard deviations for the various currencies are quite similar to those for the projected exchange risk premium.[44] In most cases (eighteen out of twenty-five) the projected exchange risk premium is slightly more variable than projected real depreciation.

CONCLUSION

We can sum up with four conclusions.

1 Capital controls and other barriers to the movement of capital across national borders remained for such countries as the UK and Japan until as recently as 1979, and for France

Table 2.8 Return to forward exchange speculation: forward discount less realized exchange depreciation, September 1982–January 1988

	Number of observations	Mean	Standard error	Series standard deviation	Root mean squared error	95% band
Open Atlantic developed countries						
Canada	65	1.04	2.03	9.15	9.21	16.95
Germany	65	4.11	5.92	25.85	26.18	44.23
Netherlands	65	4.35	6.09	26.32	26.68	44.91
Switzerland	65	3.98	6.22	27.74	28.02	46.77
UK	65	3.77	6.21	27.72	27.98	42.95
Group	325	3.45	5.36	24.27	24.55	
Liberalizing Pacific						
Hong Kong	65	−3.78	2.22	10.76	11.41	24.43
Malaysia	65	−0.74	2.31	10.31	10.34	18.92
Singapore	65	−0.35	2.01	9.64	9.65	18.07
Group	195	−1.62	1.71	10.19	10.44	
Closed less developed countries						
Greece	65	3.64	5.32	25.84	25.10	46.22
Mexico	43	6.04	12.29	50.74	51.10	89.44
Portugal	61	11.27	5.07	22.53	25.23	41.80
Saudi Arabia	65	−1.49	0.52	2.82	3.19	5.55
South Africa	65	−4.83	9.19	42.50	42.77	83.90
Group	299	2.59	3.83	31.59	32.21	
Closed European developed countries						
Austria	63	5.38	6.00	26.27	26.82	46.00
Belgium	65	7.51	5.40	23.77	24.94	44.75
Denmark	65	7.50	5.51	24.27	25.42	43.91
France	65	7.47	5.54	24.23	25.37	42.98
Ireland	63	7.27	5.75	24.67	25.73	45.05
Italy	65	8.77	5.33	23.20	24.82	40.91
Norway	65	7.20	4.73	21.10	22.31	38.55
Spain	65	8.98	5.04	22.28	24.05	45.08
Sweden	65	6.20	4.47	20.21	21.15	39.05
Group	581	7.37	5.82	23.22	24.39	
Liberalizing Pacific developed countries						
Australia	65	1.09	6.55	32.41	32.43	61.46
Japan	65	10.98	5.57	25.12	27.45	53.50
New Zealand	65	8.81	8.42	36.98	38.03	73.92
Group	195	6.96	5.59	31.72	32.75	
All countries	1,595	4.53		25.25	26.01	

Table 2.9 Real depreciation of currency: realized exchange depreciation less realized inflation differential, September 1982–January 1988

	Number of observations	Mean	Standard error	Series standard deviation	Root mean squared error	95% band
Open Atlantic developed countries						
Canada	63	−0.27	1.81	8.45	8.46	15.17
Germany	63	−6.35	5.75	25.10	25.90	44.21
Netherlands	62	−6.11	5.90	25.14	25.88	43.78
Switzerland	62	−8.35	6.11	26.78	28.07	45.67
UK	63	−2.84	6.06	27.29	27.44	47.88
Group	313	−4.77	5.24	23.48	24.13	
Liberalizing Pacific						
Hong Kong	62	0.62	2.23	10.61	10.63	22.57
Malaysia	62	2.44	2.46	10.60	10.88	19.74
Singapore	62	0.63	2.39	10.86	10.88	19.23
Group	186	1.23	2.11	10.63	10.74	
Closed less developed countries						
Bahrain	60	5.92	1.62	7.94	9.94	21.24
Greece	60	−1.82	4.99	25.08	25.15	46.41
Mexico	62	−3.32	9.31	47.96	48.96	89.57
Portugal	57	−8.12	4.73	22.63	24.06	46.25
South Africa	62	−0.27	10.74	47.16	47.16	78.62
Group	301	−1.46	4.27	33.93	34.26	
Closed European developed countries						
Austria	64	−7.30	5.64	25.16	26.21	44.92
Belgium	63	−7.69	5.09	22.61	23.90	44.90
Denmark	61	−7.94	5.60	24.05	25.35	41.85
France	64	−6.26	5.39	24.87	24.87	42.24
Ireland	61	−5.85	5.56	24.12	24.84	43.47
Italy	61	−8.01	5.44	23.24	24.60	41.38
Norway	64	−5.92	4.64	21.05	21.88	37.90
Spain	63	−6.01	5.25	22.67	23.47	39.51
Sweden	63	−6.23	3.95	18.36	19.41	33.17
Group	564	−6.79	5.76	22.73	23.74	
Liberalizing Pacific developed countries						
Australia	60	2.38	6.78	33.00	33.09	70.90
Japan	63	−12.13	5.63	25.30	28.10	52.98
New Zealand	60	−4.77	8.49	37.00	37.31	82.32
Group	183	−4.96	5.63	31.86	32.79	
All countries	1,547	−4.16		25.61	26.28	

and Italy until as recently as 1986. But a continuing world-wide trend of integration of financial markets in the 1980s had all but eliminated short-term interest differentials for major industrialized countries by 1988.

2   Only the *country premium* has been eliminated; this means that only *covered* interest differentials are small. Real and nominal exchange rate variabilities remain, and indeed were larger in the 1980s than in the 1970s.[46] The result is that a *currency premium* remains, consisting of an exchange risk premium plus an expected real currency depreciation. This means that, even with the equalization of covered interest rates, large differentials in *real* interest rates remain.

3   The USA in the 1980s began to borrow on such a massive scale internationally that the traditional Feldstein–Horioka finding of a near-unit correlation between national saving and investment has broken down. The process of liberalization in Japan and other major countries was probably one factor behind this massive flow of capital to the USA.

4   In addition to the gaps that distinguish covered interest parity from real interest parity, there is a further gap that separates real interest parity from the proposition that changes in national saving do not crowd out investment because they are readily financed by borrowing from abroad. Bonds are not perfect substitutes for equities and equities are not perfect substitutes for plant and equipment. Thus, at each stage, there are good reasons to think that shortfalls in national saving continue to be capable of crowding out investment, even if to a smaller extent than before 1980.

NOTES

1   Despite the increased attention to inward foreign direct investment in the USA in recent years, it continues to be a smaller component of the capital inflow than portfolio investment. As of the end of 1987, foreign direct investment accounted for only 17 per cent of the total stock of foreign-held assets in the USA.

2   There were relatively large differentials separating US interest rates from the Eurodollar rates; at the long-term end of the spectrum, well-known US corporations could borrow more cheaply in the Euromarket than they could domestically. These differentials fell steadily toward zero between 1982 and 1986, probably as a result of the innovation that occurred in the Euromarkets – partly in response to these differentials – making it easier for US corporations to borrow there. Much of this innovation went under the name of securitization. See Frankel (1988a) for documentation and further references. (It appears that the securitization trend suffered a set-back in 1987 and 1988, in part associated with the October 1987 stock-market crash; it is now said to be slightly *more* costly for US corporations to include bonds in the Euromarket than domestically. It remains to be seen whether this reversal of the trend toward perfect integration is serious or lasting.)

3   And even if this relationship does not break down in the future under pressure from fears of international creditors that US indebtedness is becoming excessive.

4   There is a fifth possible – yet more narrowly defined – criterion for the degree of integration of financial markets: the size of transactions costs as measured directly by the bid–ask spread in, for example, the foreign exchange market. Surprisingly, the covered interest differential does not appear to be statistically related to the bid–ask spread (MacArthur 1988).

5   Obstfeld (1986) and Summers (1988) argue that the saving–investment correlation may be due to the common influence of growth rates.

6   Obstfeld (1986, 1989) makes the large-country point in a time-series context, where it properly belongs. But even in a time-series regression for a single country such as the USA, one can correct for the large-country problem by expressing saving and investment rates as deviations from the rest-of-world rates of saving and investment, respectively. Under the null hypothesis, an exogenous fall in the US saving rate may drive up the world real interest rate and crowd out investment, but there is no evident reason for the crowding-out to be reflected in US investment to any greater extent than in rest-of-world investment. In Frankel (1986: 44–5), I found that the close correspondence between US saving and investment for 1970–85 remains, even with this adjustment.

7   Obstfeld (1986) finds that the coefficient fell after 1973, in time-series correlations for most of his

countries, but he (1989) finds that it has risen over time (1967–84 against 1956–66), with the USA showing the highest correlation of any.

8   In a US time-series context, Frankel (1986) used two instrumental variables: the fraction of the population over 65 years of age and the ratio of military expenditure to GNP. The former is considered a determinant of private saving and the latter of public saving, and both have some claim to exogeneity. In the context of cross-sections of developing and industrialized countries, Dooley *et al.* (1987) used the dependency ratio and, again, the military expenditure variable.

9   Other studies that reject real interest parity for major industrialized countries include Mishkin (1984a, b), Cumby and Obstfeld (1984), Mark (1985) and Cumby and Mishkin (1986). Glick (1987) examines real interest differentials for six Pacific Basin countries *vis-à-vis* the USA.

10 The ten-year real interest differential *vis-à-vis* a weighted average of G5 countries was about 3 per cent in 1984, whether expected inflation is measured by a distributed lag, by OECD forecasts or by Data Resources Incorporated forecasts. In 1980, by contrast, the differential was about −2 per cent (Frankel 1986: 35–6).

11 Gross investment was 16.0 per cent of GNP in 1980, which was itself considered a low number (down 0.5 per cent from 1971–80).

12 The instrumental variables used are the dependency ratio (the sum of those older than 64 and those younger than 21, divided by the working-age population in between), which is a determinant of private saving, and military expenditure as a share of GNP, which is a determinant of the federal budget deficit. A data appendix is available (NBER Working Paper 2856, February 1989) for details on these and the other variables.

13 There are two other potential sources of differences from the results in Frankel (1986): the Commerce Department (Bureau of Economic Analysis, *Survey of Current Business*) released revised national accounts data for the entire period in 1986, and we now use the dependency ratio as the demographic instrumental variable in place of the ratio of the over-65 to the over-20 population. But the years 1985–7 are indeed the source of the fall in the coefficient; when these three years are omitted the coefficient is greater than unity (as when the 1980s are omitted in Table 2.2).

14 If the 1956–87 sample is split at 1974, when the USA and Germany removed capital controls, rather than at 1979, there is still a precipitous decline in the cyclically adjusted saving–investment coefficient over time: from 0.87 (statistically no different from unity) to 0.31 (borderline difference from zero). (Table 3a in NBER Working Paper 2856, February 1989). If the 1930–87 sample is split at 1958, when many European countries restored currency convertibility, there is a small increase in the coefficient over time: from 0.83 (statistically different from unity) to 1.14 (no difference from unity) (Table 2a in NBER Working Paper 2856, February 1989). But this is no doubt because the saving and investment rates are not cyclically adjusted for this period (the BEA series is not available back to 1930). Only when expressed on a cyclically adjusted basis is the US national saving rate of 1985–90 especially low.

15 Feldstein and Bacchetta (1989) find a similar drop in the saving–investment coefficient in the 1980s for a cross-section of industrialized countries (though they do not use instrumental variables, and are thus liable to the econometric criticisms that others have raised concerning the endogeneity of national saving).

16 Measuring barriers to integration by differences in rates of return has the problem that a given degree of integration can appear smaller or larger depending on the disturbances to saving (or to other variables) during the sample period in question. For example, the greater degree of variability in the US real interest differential in the 1980s, as compared to the 1970s or 1960s, could be attributed to the greater swings in variables such as the structural budget deficit, rather than to a lower degree of capital mobility. All we can say for sure is that if the barriers to integration are essentially zero (the degree of capital mobility is essentially perfect), then differentials in rates of return should be essentially zero.

17 For example, Krugman found that the standard deviation for the real mark–dollar exchange rate during the German hyperinflation, from February 1920 to December 1923, was much larger (20.8 per cent) than during the 1970s, even though the serial correlation was no higher (0.765).

18 Cumby and Obstfeld (1984: 146) used a Q statistic to test for higher-order serial correlation in monthly real exchange rate changes and found none. However, they also found that expected inflation differentials were unrelated to expected exchange rate changes, rejecting the random walk characterization of the real exchange rate. Huizinga (1987) was also able to reject the random walk in some cases.

19 As already noted, an AR of 0.7 on a yearly basis corresponds to an AR of 0.97 on a monthly basis ($0.97^{12} = 0.70$). Thus it might take 564 months of data ($2.93^2(1 - 0.97^2)/(1 - 0.97)^2 = 563.7$) to be

able to reject the null hypothesis of AR = 1. This is forty-seven years, very little gain in efficiency over the test on yearly data. Summers (1988) demonstrates the low power of random walk tests in the context of stock-market prices.

20 DeJong *et al.* (1988: Table II) offer power tables for the Dickey–Fuller test which show that, when the true AR parameter is 0.8, even a sample size of 100 is only sufficient to reject a random walk about 65 per cent of the time.

21 As the sample period covers a number of changes in exchange rate regime, it would be desirable to allow for shifts in the coefficient (and in the variance of the disturbance term). But many of the proponents of a random walk in the real exchange rate claim it as evidence in favour of an 'equilibrium' hypothesis, under which fluctuations in the real exchange rate are caused only by real, as opposed to monetary, factors. Under this null hypothesis, changes in regime should not matter for the real exchange rate. Thus our statistical test is a valid rejection of the null hypothesis, even though it lumps together all 119 years of observations.

22 Sticky goods prices are only one of a number of possible sources of deviations from *ex ante* relative PPP. Another is the existence of the prices of non-traded goods in the relevant price index. Dornbusch (1983) shows how movement in the relative price of non-traded goods affects the real interest rate, saving, and borrowing from abroad, while Engel and Kletzer (1987) show specifically how such movement can give rise to the Feldstein–Horioka finding. Bovenberg (1989) too shows how imperfect substitutability of goods can give rise to the finding.

23 The rationally expected rate of real depreciation estimated from a specific time-series process is not necessarily the same as the actual expectation of real depreciation held by investors. Frankel (1986: 58–9) used survey data on expectations of exchange rate changes (collected by the *Economist*-affiliated *Financial Report*) and forecasts of price level changes (by Data Resources Incorporated) to compute a direct measure of expected real depreciation for the dollar against five currencies. The numbers showed an expectation that the real exchange rate tends to regress back toward PPP at a statistically significant rate of 8–12 per cent a year.

24 Obstfeld (1986) shows, in a life-cycle model of saving with actual OECD data on the functional distribution of income and on population growth, that the coefficient in an investment regression can be similar to those estimated by Feldstein and Horioka. (Similar claims based on models of intertemporal optimization are made by Ghosh (1988),

Roubini (1988), Tesar (1988) and Leiderman and Razin (1989).) But Feldstein and Bacchetta (1989) argue that the growth rate is not in fact responsible for the observed coefficient.

25 Some of these data were also analysed in Frankel and MacArthur (1988). Some forward rate observations for Italy, Austria and Belgium in the Barclays' data looked suspicious. In addition, Barclays does not quote a rate for Portugal. For this study, forward exchange rates for Italy and Belgium are taken from the Bank of America (also obtained via DRI), and for Austria and Portugal from the *Financial Times*. The Barclays' data for Ireland also appear suspect (1986–8).

26 The data appendix to NBER Working Paper 2309 gives details.

27 The standard errors for individual country means are usable, indeed are conservative, despite the use of overlapping observations, because they are calculated as if there were $T/3$ observations rather than the actual T observations used.

28 Saving–investment regressions, by contrast, show the counterintuitive result: coefficients for LDCs that are lower (suggesting higher capital mobility, in Feldstein and Horioka's terms) than for industrialized countries. See Fieleke (1982), Dooley *et al.* (1987) and Summers (1988).

29 It is possible that, for some countries, seasonal variation constitutes one forecastable component.

30 As shown, for example, by Boothe *et al.* (1985: 112).

31 The frequently large negative covered differential that had been observed for Australia up to mid-1983 (see, for example, Argy 1987) largely vanished thereafter.

32 Claassen and Wyplosz (1982), Giavazzi and Pagano (1985: 27–8), Frankel (1982) and Wyplosz (1986), among others.

33 For France, Italy, Ireland, Spain and Greece (as reported in *World Financial Markets* (9 September 1988: 5)). Denmark's covered differential remains quite high in our sample. The country has been reported to have no capital controls left (*The Economist* 1988), but this evidently applies only to securities: the European Commission reports that deposits and other short-term transactions remain subject to authorization in Denmark as of 1988.

34 Bahrain shows a smaller differential than the others, and even than some of the European countries with controls, like Spain and Ireland. (It should be noted that the forward rate quoted by Barclays applies to the Saudi Arabian riyal; we match it up with the Bahraini interest rate because no local interest rate is available for Saudi Arabia and the two countries are said to be closely tied

financially. The riyal is classified by the IMF under the same exchange rate arrangement as Bahrain's currency, the dinar, which would suggest that the same forward rate could be applied to both. But the riyal exchange rate does in fact vary somewhat, so that our measured covered interest differential is not entirely legitimate.)

35 Taylor (1988) is one of the most recent of many studies of covered interest parity within the London Euromarket. Such studies do not get at the degree of financial market integration across national boundaries. When authors find deviations from covered interest parity in such data (e.g. Mishkin 1984a: 1350), it is often due to the low quality of the data, for example, inexact timing. With high-quality data, Taylor finds that covered interest parity held extremely well in 1985, that it held less well in the 1970s, particularly during 'turbulent' periods, that the differential had mostly vanished by 1979 and that the differentials that do exist are slightly larger in the longer-term maturities than in the shorter-term maturities. But, like other studies, Taylor has no data on maturities longer than one year.

36 It is still quite likely, however, that there is a wedge in each country separating the long-term interest rate from the after-tax cost of capital facing firms. Such a wedge could be due either to the corporate income tax system or to imperfect substitutability between bonds and capital. Hatsopoulos *et al.* (1988) argue that the cost of capital facing US corporations is higher than that facing Japanese corporations even when real interest rates are equal, because US companies rely more heavily on equity financing, which is more expensive than debt financing. See also Feldstein (1987).

37 The results are reported in NBER Working Paper 2856, but are omitted here to save space.

38 The five exceptions, currencies that depreciated against the dollar at a rate more rapid than predicted by the forward discount, were the Hong Kong dollar, Malaysian ringgit, Singapore dollar, Saudi Arabian riyal and South African rand.

39 The currencies are the Saudi Arabian riyal and two that appreciated strongly against the dollar relative to the forward rate: the Japanese yen and the Portuguese escudo.

40 Again, the results are reported in NBER Working Paper 2856 (February 1989) but are omitted here.

41 Many others have found a highly significant predictable component of fd-exp depr, often when regressing against fd, and particularly in-sample. It is possible that such findings are not due to a time-varying premium, as the rational expectations approach would have it, but rather to a time-

varying model of spot rate determination (together with insufficiently long sample periods) and learning by investors. Such speculations go outside the scope of this chapter (see Frankel and Froot 1988; Froot and Frankel 1989).

42 The second to fourth columns show very high variability in real depreciation, but again this tells us little about the variation of *ex ante* expected depreciation, beyond the observation that the high level of variability implies low power in our tests of *ex ante* relative PPP.

43 Once again, the results are reported in NBER Working Paper 2856 (February 1989), but are omitted here.

44 It seems that in both cases an apparently predictable component of the spot rate changes constitutes most of the variation (as opposed to variation in the forward discount or inflation differential, respectively): the significant coefficients on the forward discount, interest differential and *ex post* inflation differential when $Ds - Dp - Dp^*$ is the dependent variable are always of opposite sign and similar magnitude to the coefficients when $fd - Ds$ is the dependent variable.

45 One view is that the high degree of integration of financial markets is one of the *causes* of the high degree of volatility of exchange rates. The issue is discussed, and further references given, in Frankel (1988b).

REFERENCES

Adler, M. and Lehman, B. (1983) 'Deviations from purchasing power parity in the long run', *Journal of Finance* 39 (5): 1471–8.

Argy, V. (1987) 'International financial liberalisation – the Australian and Japanese experiences compared', *Bank of Japan Monetary and Economic Studies* 5 (1): 105–68.

Artis, M. and Taylor, M. (1990) 'Abolishing exchange control: the UK experience', in A. S. Courakis and M. P. Taylor (eds) *Private Behaviour and Government Policy in Interdependent Economies*, Oxford: Clarendon Press, pp. 129–58.

Bayoumi, T. (1990) 'Saving–investment correlations: immobile capital, government policy, or endogenous behavior', *IMF Staff Papers* 37: 360–87.

Bayoumi, T. and Rose, A. (1991) 'Domestic saving and intra-national capital flows', *European Economic Review*, forthcoming.

Boothe, P., Clinton, K., Cote, A. and Longworth, D. (1985) *International Asset Substitutability: Theory and Evidence for Canada*, Ottawa: Bank of Canada.

Bovenberg, A.L. (1989) 'The effects of capital income

taxation on international competitiveness and trade flows', *American Economic Review* 79 (5): 1045–64.

Caprio, G. and Howard, D. (1984) 'Domestic saving, current accounts, and international capital mobility', International Finance Discussion Paper 244, Washington, DC: Federal Reserve Board.

Caramazza, F., Clinton, K., Cote, A. and Longworth, D. (1986) 'International capital mobility and asset substitutability: some theory and evidence on recent structural changes', Technical Report 44, Bank of Canada.

Cardia, E. (1988) 'Crowding out in open economies', Cahier 8823, Université de Montréal, June.

Claassen, E. and Wyplosz, C. (1982) 'Capital controls: some principles and the French experience', *Annales de l'INSEE* 47–8: 237–67.

Cumby, R. and Mishkin, F. (1986) 'The international linkage of real interest rates: the European–U.S. connection', *Journal of International Money and Finance* 5: 5–24.

Cumby, R. and Obstfeld, M. (1984) 'International interest rate and price level linkages under flexible exchange rates: a review of recent evidence', in J. Bilson and R. Marston (eds) *Exchange Rate Theory and Practice*, Chicago, IL: University of Chicago Press.

Darby, M. (1981) 'Does purchasing power parity work?', *Proceedings of the Fifth West Coast Academic/Federal Reserve Economic Research Seminar*, Federal Reserve Bank of San Francisco.

—— (1986) 'The internationalization of American banking and finance: structure, risk and world interest rates', *Journal of International Money and Finance* 5 (4): 403–28.

DeJong, D. Nankervis, J., Savin, N. E. and Whiteman, C. (1988) 'Integration versus trend stationarity in macroeconomic time series', Department of Economics Working Paper 88-27a, University of Iowa, December.

Dooley, M. and Isard, P. (1980) 'Capital controls, political risk and deviations from interest-rate parity', *Journal of Political Economy* 88 (2): 370–84.

Dooley, M., Frankel, J. and Mathieson, D. (1987) 'International capital mobility: what do saving–investment correlations tell us?', *International Monetary Fund Staff Papers* 34 (3): 503–30.

Dornbusch, R. (1983) 'Real interest rates, home goods and optimal external borrowing', *Journal of Political Economy* 90 (1): 141–53.

The Economist (1988) 'Capitalism', 21 May: 95.

Engel, C. and Kletzer, K. (1987) 'Saving and investment in an open economy with non-traded goods', NBER Working Paper 2141, February; *International Economic Review*, forthcoming.

Feldstein, M. (1983) 'Domestic saving and international capital movements in the long run and the short run', *European Economic Review* 21: 139–51.

—— (ed.) (1987) *The Effects of Taxation on Capital Accumulation*, Chicago, IL: University of Chicago Press.

Feldstein, M. and Bacchetta, P. (1989) 'National savings and international investment', in D. Bernheim and J. Shoven (eds) (1991) *National Saving and Economic Performance*, NBER Conference on Saving.

Feldstein, M. and Horioka, C. (1980) 'Domestic saving and international capital flows', *Economic Journal* 90: 314–29.

Fieleke, N. (1982) 'National saving and international investment', in *Saving and Government Policy*, Conference Series 25, Federal Reserve Bank of Boston.

Frankel, J. (1982) 'On the franc', *Annales de l'INSEE* 47–8: 185–221.

—— (1984) 'The yen/dollar agreement: liberalizing Japanese capital markets', Policy Analyses in International Economics 9, Washington, DC: Institute for International Economics.

—— (1986) 'International capital mobility and crowding-out in the U.S. economy: imperfect integration of financial markets or of goods markets?', in R. Hafer (ed.) *How Open is the U.S. Economy?*, Lexington, MA: Lexington Books, pp. 33–67.

—— (1988a) 'International capital flows and domestic economic policies', in M. Feldstein (ed.) *The United States in the World Economy*, Chicago, IL: University of Chicago Press.

—— (1988b) 'International capital mobility and exchange rate variability', in N. Fieleke (ed.) *International Payments Imbalances in the 1980's*, Bald Peak, NH: Federal Reserve Bank of Boston.

Frankel, J. and Froot, K. (1988) 'Chartists, fundamentalists, and the demand for dollars', *Greek Economic Review* 10 (1). Also forthcoming in A. Courakis and M. Taylor (eds) *Policy Issues for Interdependent Economies*, Oxford: Oxford University Press.

Frankel, J. and MacArthur, A. (1988) 'Political vs. currency premia in international real interest differentials: a study of forward rates for 24 countries', *European Economic Review* 32: 1083–121. Reprinted in R. MacDonald and M. Taylor (eds) (1992) *Exchange Rate Economics*, vol. II, International Library of Critical Writings in Economics, Cheltenham: Edward Elgar.

Frenkel, J. (1981) 'Flexible exchange rates, prices and the role of "news": lessons from the 1970s', *Journal of Political Economy* 89 (4): 665–705.

Frenkel, J. and Levich, R. (1977) 'Transaction costs and interest arbitrage: tranquil versus turbulent periods', *Journal of Political Economy* 85 (6): 1209–26.

Froot, K. and Frankel, J. (1989) 'Forward discount bias: is it an exchange risk premium?', *Quarterly Journal of Economics* 104 (1): 139–61.

Ghosh, A. R. (1988) 'How mobile is capital? Some simple tests', Harvard University.

Giavazzi, F. and Pagano, M. (1985) 'Capital controls and the European Monetary System', in *Capital Controls and Foreign Exchange Legislation*, occasional paper, Milano: Euromobiliare.

Glick, R. (1987) 'Interest rate linkages in the Pacific Basin', *Economic Review* 3: 31–42.

Huizinga, J. (1987) 'An empirical investigation of the long run behavior of real exchange rates', in K. Brunner and A. Meltzer (eds) *Empirical Studies of Velocity, Real Exchange Rates, Unemployment and Productivity*, Carnegie–Rochester Conference Series on Public Policy, vol. 27, pp. 149–214.

Koraczyk, R. (1985) 'The pricing of forward contracts for foreign exchange', *Journal of Political Economy* 93 (2): 346–68.

Krugman, P. (1978) 'Purchasing power parity and exchange rates: another look at the evidence', *Journal of International Economics* 8 (3): 397–407.

Leiderman, L. and Razin, A. (1989) *The Saving–Investment Balance: An Empirical Investigation*, Washington, DC: IMF, June.

MacArthur, A. (1988) 'International financial market integration: empirical analysis with data from forward and futures currency markets', Ph.D. thesis, University of California, Berkeley.

Mark, N. (1985) 'Some evidence on the international inequality of real interest rates', *Journal of International Money and Finance* 4: 189–208.

Mishkin, F. (1984a) 'Are real interest rates equal across countries? An empirical investigation of international parity conditions', *Journal of Finance* 39: 1345–58.

—— (1984b) 'The real interest rate: a multi-country empirical study', *Canadian Journal of Economics* 17 (2): 283–311.

Murphy, R. (1984) 'Capital mobility and the relationship between saving and investment in OECD countries', *Journal of International Money and Finance* 3: 327–42.

Obstfeld, M. (1986a) 'Capital mobility in the world economy: theory and measurement', *Carnegie-Rochester Conference Series on Public Policy* 31: 1–24.

—— (1989) 'How integrated are world capital markets? Some new tests', NBER Working Paper 2075. Also forthcoming in R. Findlay *et al.* (eds) *Debt, Stabilization and Development: Essays in Memory of Carlos Diaz-Alejandro*, Oxford: Basil Blackwell.

Otani, I. (1983) 'Exchange rate instability and capital controls: the Japanese experience 1978–81', in D. Bigman and T. Taya (eds) *Exchange Rate and Trade Instability: Causes, Consequences and Remedies*, Cambridge, MA: Ballinger.

Penati, A. and Dooley, M. (1984) 'Current account imbalances and capital formation in industrial countries, 1949–1981', *IMF Staff Papers* 31: 1–24.

Pigott, C. and Sweeney, R. (1985) in S. Arndt, R. Sweeney and T. Willett (eds) *Exchange Rates, Trade and the U.S. Economy*, Washington, DC: American Enterprise Institute.

Popper, H. (1990) 'International capital mobility: direct evidence from long-term currency swaps', *International Finance Discussion Papers 386*, Washington, DC: Federal Reserve Board, September.

Roll, R. (1979) 'Violations of purchasing power parity and their implications for efficient international commodity markets', in M. Sarnat and G. Szego (eds) *International Finance and Trade*, vol. 1, Cambridge, MA: Ballinger.

Roubini, N. (1988) 'Current account and budget deficits in an intertemporal model of consumption and taxation smoothing: a solution to the "Feldstein–Horioka puzzle"?', Yale University, October.

Summers, L. (1988) 'Tax policy and international competitiveness', in J. Frenkel (ed.) *International Aspects of Fiscal Policies*, Chicago, IL: University of Chicago Press for the National Bureau of Economic Research.

Taylor, M. (1988) 'Covered interest arbitrage and market turbulence: an empirical analysis', Centre for Economic Policy Research Discussion Paper 236.

Tesar, L. (1988) 'Savings, investment and international capital flows', Working Paper 154, University of Rochester, August.

Tobin, J. (1983) '"Domestic saving and international capital movements in the long run and the short run," by M. Feldstein: comment', *European Economic Review* 21: 153–6.

Westphal, U. (1983) 'Comments on domestic saving and international capital movements in the long run and the short run', *European Economic Review* 21: 157–9.

Wyplosz, C. (1986) 'Capital flows liberalization and the EMS: a French perspective', INSEAD Working Papers 86/40; *European Economy*, European Economic Community, June 1988.

3

UNSTABLE CURRENT ACCOUNT BEHAVIOUR AND CAPITAL FLOWS IN DEVELOPING COUNTRIES

Maxwell J. Fry

INTRODUCTION

Prompted by reports from such international organizations as the IMF, the Western press has bombarded its readers with stories of the US massive current account deficits and the equally enormous surpluses enjoyed by Germany and Japan. Even in the unemotional language of an international bureaucracy, the IMF refers to these current account imbalances as 'large' (*World Economic Outlook 1986*: 7; *World Economic Outlook 1987*: 9; *World Economic Outlook 1988*: 1; *World Economic Outlook 1989*: 1; *World Economic Outlook 1990*: 2). As a percentage of GDP, however, Table 3.1 shows that these imbalances are relatively modest compared with those experienced by some of the developing countries over the period 1972–89.

The 'large' current account imbalances in the three largest industrial countries 'have raised concerns about sustainability and possible adverse reactions in financial markets' (*World Economic Outlook 1990*: 2). A current account imbalance produces a change in a country's net stock of foreign assets or liabilities (hereafter referred to as net foreign claims). One important question, therefore, is whether or not stabilizing forces prevent continued increases in these net foreign claim positions and ensure a smooth adjustment to a long-run equilibrium. If no such mechanisms exist, adjustment may be forced through financial crisis.

Jocelyn Horne, Jeroen Kremers and Paul Masson (1989) analyse the current account imbalances of Germany, Japan and the USA using cointegration to test for the existence of long-run equilibrium relationships between the net stock of foreign claims and other variables. They find that the ratio of net foreign claims to GNP, FY, is cointegrated with the ratio of government debt to GNP and population dependence ratios relative to those in the rest of the world. They also detect short-run feedback effects from the stock of net foreign claims to variables such as domestic absorption, real exchange rates and real interest rates which act as stabilizers to ensure an eventual return to long-run equilibrium (Horne *et al.* 1989: 22).

Population dependence ratios are clearly bounded and have specific values for steady-state demographic equilibrium. A rational government would necessarily keep its indebtedness within some bounds too. Hence, cointegration of the net foreign claim ratio with these two variables implies that it too has some long-run steady-state value. In this steady state, the current account would ensure that net foreign claims changed exactly in proportion to GNP. Such a current account imbalance would be sustainable indefinitely, since it would not change the ratio of net foreign claims to GNP.

The Horne–Kremers–Masson paper ends with a statement on the related issue of saving–investment correlations: 'A shock to either saving or investment, by leading to an accumulation of foreign assets or liabilities, will bring about forces that tend to feed back onto absorption and output, in such a way that over time the effect of the shock is reversed. The faster these mechanisms operate,

Table 3.1 Current account imbalances in selected countries, 1972–89

Country	Year	Current account as percentage of GDP
Saudi Arabia	1974	82.3
Iran	1974	26.8
Iraq	1974	22.9
Taiwan	1986	22.7
Venezuela	1974	22.0
Nigeria	1974	16.4
Syria	1973	13.0
Germany	1989	4.7
Japan	1986	4.4
USA	1987	−3.2
Pakistan	1974	−10.4
Korea	1974	−10.8
Peru	1975	−11.2
Egypt	1974	−12.3
Kenya	1980	−12.5
Algeria	1978	−13.5
Portugal	1982	−14.0
Chile	1981	−14.5
Venezuela	1978	−14.6
Sri Lanka	1980	−16.3
Morocco	1977	−16.8
Madagascar	1980	−17.1
Côte d'Ivoire	1980	−17.9
Zambia	1981	−18.5
Zaire	1977	−31.4

Source: IMF, *International Financial Statistics: 1990 Yearbook*, pp. 154–5
Note: This table records current account imbalances in selected countries with populations of at least 5 million.

the net foreign claim positions of three developing countries – Korea, Sri Lanka and Taiwan (Fry 1991; Fry *et al.* 1991). Korea recorded a sizeable current account deficit of 10.8 per cent of GDP in 1974 and Korea's total foreign debt fluctuated around 50 per cent of GNP between 1980 and 1985 (World Bank 1990).[1] In 1985, the IMF classified Korea as one of seven 'major borrowers' (*World Economic Outlook 1985*: 199). From 1986, however, Korea ran large current account surpluses and virtually eliminated its net international indebtedness by 1989.

Sri Lanka and Taiwan represent countries near the extremes of the observations in Table 3.1. Sri Lanka recorded a current account deficit of 16.3 per cent of GDP in 1980 and, except in 1984, has continued to run substantial current account deficits. Consequently, Sri Lanka's total foreign debt has risen from 46 per cent of GNP in 1980 to 75 per cent in 1988 (World Bank 1990). Almost at the other extreme, Taiwan recorded a current account surplus of 22.7 per cent of GDP in 1986. Except in 1980, Taiwan has posted current account surpluses since 1976. Cumulating current account positions since the early 1950s suggest that Taiwan became a net international creditor in 1977.

Figures 3.1 and 3.2 compare the somewhat volatile current account ratios of Korea, Sri Lanka

the less likely is the emergence of large current account surplus or deficit positions' (Horne *et al.* 1989: 24). In essence, policy concern over the balance of payments is a concern not so much over a current account imbalance but rather over an inexorable accumulation of net foreign claims. The Horne–Kremers–Masson paper suggests that macroeconomic forces pull the current account imbalances in Germany, Japan and the USA towards sustainable long-run steady states. Hence, policy concern is unwarranted and no specific policy actions are required for this outcome.

Elsewhere I conclude that no such comforting conclusion can be derived from similar analysis of

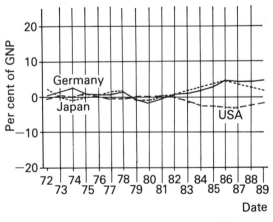

Figure 3.1 Current account imbalances in Germany, Japan and USA

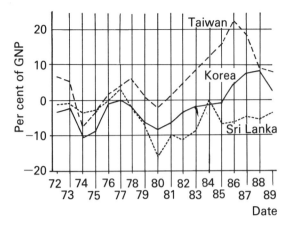

Figure 3.2 Current account imbalances in Korea, Sri Lanka and Taiwan

and Taiwan with those of the three largest industrial economies over the period 1972–89. In relation to GDP, current account imbalances have been far larger in the three developing countries than in the three large industrial countries. This chapter addresses the general issue of large current account imbalances in developing countries. The subsequent section of this chapter presents a small-scale macroeconomic model designed to explain how current accounts can be stable in industrial countries but unstable in developing countries. Estimates of versions of this model for a sample of developing countries are discussed in the third section. The final section examines the implications of estimates of current account ratios and monetary policy reaction functions for long-run stability of the current accounts in Korea, Sri Lanka and Taiwan.

A SMALL-SCALE MACROECONOMIC MODEL OF A REPRESENTATIVE DEVELOPING ECONOMY

The extent and financing of a balance-of-payments deficit on current account depend both on a country's desire to spend more than its income and on the willingness of the rest of the world to finance the deficit. In other words, the current

account deficit is determined simultaneously by both the demand for and the supply of foreign saving. The model developed here attempts to capture the essential determinants of this interactive process.

This small-scale macroeconomic model of a representative developing economy specifies saving and investment functions as well as export and import equations. An important feature of the model is that it permits the accumulated current account position or ratio of foreign debt to real GNP to converge to a constant and hence sustainable steady state. A steady state exists if higher foreign indebtedness reduces investment by more than it reduces saving, or raises investment by less than it raises saving. The model also specifies the rate of economic growth, which is itself influenced by the level of foreign debt through both the volume and productivity of investment.

Capital inflows allow investment to exceed national saving; domestic investment equals national saving plus the current account deficit or foreign saving. Capital inflows, therefore, can increase investment and GNP in real terms. Figure 3.3 echoes Lloyd Metzler (1968) in viewing the current account deficit as the difference between domestic investment and national saving. In Figure 3.3, I represents domestic investment or the marginal efficiency of investment curve; there is more investment at lower interest rates. The line Sn

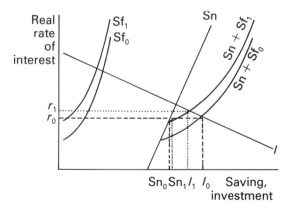

Figure 3.3 Domestic investment, national saving and the current account deficit

represents national saving; here it is shown as a rather steep curve indicating that national saving does not vary greatly with changes in the domestic real interest rate. Most developing countries face an upward-sloping supply curve of foreign saving Sf_0. However, the effective cost at which foreign saving begins to be supplied in any particular year depends on the country's debt position inherited from past borrowing. At some point, the foreign saving supply curve may become vertical, reflecting complete credit rationing.

At the effective cost of foreign borrowing r_0, domestic investment I_0 exceeds national saving Sn_0. Hence, the inflow of foreign saving is positive and the country runs a current account deficit on its balance of payments equal to $I_0 - Sn_0$. The accumulation of debt resulting from the current account deficit in year 0 raises the foreign saving function to Sf_1, producing an effective cost of foreign borrowing of r_1 in year 1. In this case, foreign debt accumulation reduces domestic investment and raises national saving through a higher country-specific risk premium; the current account deficit declines until it reaches a steady-state equilibrium with a constant debt–GNP ratio. Here then is a theoretical explanation for the negative effect of net foreign claims on the current account in the three largest OECD countries; a more negative value of net foreign claims could be expected to improve the current account in these countries.

Figure 3.3 conceals three important additional links in this model between saving, investment and the current account deficit in the case of developing countries where much of foreign debt takes the form of government and government-guaranteed foreign debt. First and second, the level of this type of foreign debt accumulated from past current account deficits may itself affect the positions of both the saving and investment functions in Figure 3.3, for reasons explained below. Third, capital inflows may affect the investment function. Capital inflows appreciate the real exchange rate, thus making imports cheaper. Cheaper imports of capital equipment may stimulate domestic investment.

The main problem in estimating the model sketched in Figure 3.3 is that effective costs of foreign borrowing or domestic shadow interest rates, r_0 and r_1 in Figure 3.3, are unobservable. As Vassilis Hajivassiliou (1987: 205) points out: 'The spread over the London interbank offer rate (LIBOR) does not perform the key role of clearing the market for international loans. Instead allocation of scarce credit among third world countries is fundamentally carried out through quantity offers and requests.' To overcome this difficulty, a reduced-form equation for r can be derived from simple demand and supply functions for foreign saving. The demand for foreign saving equals the saving–investment gap, which depends on all the determinants of national saving and domestic investment, including the effective cost of foreign borrowing: $Sf^d = \xi(\overset{-}{r})$.

The supply of foreign saving is determined by the world real interest rate RW plus a country-specific risk premium, the effective premium which produces the effective cost of foreign borrowing and hence the domestic shadow interest rate. This premium is determined by previous debt buildup DETY (Dooley 1986; Edwards 1986) and the ratio of public sector credit to total domestic credit DCGR. The variable DCGR is a proxy for fiscal performance (Harberger 1981: 40). This ratio may also indicate the general state of macroeconomic management. A government that extracts high seigniorage from the banking system may well be following a variety of other growth-inhibiting macroeconomic policies. Foreign lenders are doubly deterred from lending to countries whose governments exhibit weak fiscal discipline (so eroding confidence in their guarantees) and poor macroeconomic management, which stalls the growth process. Hence, the supply function is $Sf^s = \zeta(\overset{+}{r}, R\overline{W}, DE\overline{T}Y, DC\overline{G}R)$. Equating demand and supply provides a reduced-form expression for the domestic shadow interest rate or the effective cost of foreign borrowing: $r = \varphi(R\overset{+}{W}, DE\overset{+}{T}Y, DC\overset{+}{G}R)$. With RW, DETY and DCGR substituted for r, the quasi-reduced form macroeconomic model of a representative developing economy is presented in Table 3.1.[2]

Saving

The saving function SNY expressed as the ratio of national saving to GNP (both in current prices) estimated here is based on a life-cycle model (Mason 1987). The standard life-cycle saving model has young, income-earning households saving to finance consumption when they become old, non-earning households. Figure 3.4 illustrates these life-cycle patterns of income and consumption. Income $E(a)$ and consumption $C(a)$ of a household aged a are expressed as a fraction of lifetime income. The simplest life-cycle model assumes that each household consumes all its resources over its lifetime. In this case, the level of household consumption L over its lifetime

$$L = \int C(a)\mathrm{d}a \qquad (3.1)$$

is equal to unity.

Even if no household saves over its lifetime, aggregate saving can still be positive provided that there is positive growth in aggregate real income. The aggregate saving rate is determined by the age profile of the average household's saving $S(a) = E(a) - C(a)$ and by the lifetime resources that each age group can mobilize. If $V(a)$ is the ratio of lifetime resources of all households aged a to

aggregate real income, then $V(a)S(a)$ is the total saving of age group a as a fraction of aggregate real income. The aggregate saving rate s is derived by summing across all age groups:

$$s = \int V(a)S(a)\mathrm{d}a. \qquad (3.2)$$

With steady-state growth, $V(a)$ is independent of time and given by

$$V(a) = V(0)\mathrm{e}^{-ga}, \qquad (3.3)$$

where $V(0)$ is the ratio of lifetime resources of newly formed households to aggregate real income and g is the rate of growth in aggregate real income. If g is zero

$$s = V(0)(1 - L) = 0. \qquad (3.4)$$

All aggregate real income is consumed because $V(a)$ is a constant, L equals 1 and $\int S(a)\mathrm{d}a$ is $1 - L$. With positive growth in aggregate real income, however, the lifetime resources $V(a)$ of young savers exceed those of old dissavers and there will be positive aggregate saving. This is the rate-of-growth effect.

Once bequests are introduced into the life-cycle saving model, the level of a household's saving over its lifetime L may be less than unity and aggregate saving can occur even in a static economy. The level of saving can be influenced by a vector of independent variables z and the saving function can be written

$$s \approx \alpha z + \beta g. \qquad (3.5)$$

The rate-of-growth effect in the life-cycle model refers to the rate of growth in aggregate real income. Invariably, empirical tests have been carried out using the rate of growth in aggregate real output – real GNP or real GDP – defined here as YG. In an open economy, however, the rate of growth in income differs from the rate of growth in output due to terms-of-trade changes. Aggregate real income can be defined as $y + x(P_x/P_m - 1)$, where y is real GNP, x is exports measured at

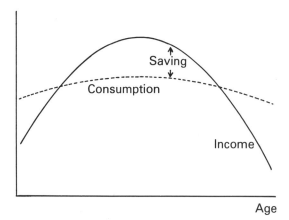

Figure 3.4 Life-cycle patterns of income, comsumption and saving

constant prices and P_x/P_m is the price of exports divided by the price of imports or the gross barter terms of trade. The terms-of-trade variable TTG used here is defined as the rate of change in real income attributable to terms-of-trade changes.

The real rate of interest determines the price of future consumption and bequests relative to current consumption. Economic theory indicates that saving can be influenced either positively or negatively by a rise in the interest rate. If the substitution effect outweighs the income effect, then the saving ratio rises with an increase in the domestic real shadow interest rate r, for which one can substitute φ(RW, DETY, DCGR).

The world real interest rate RW is proxied by the six-month LIBOR dollar deposit rate minus wholesale price inflation in the USA (both continuously compounded). The world real interest rate is a determinant both of the domestic real shadow interest rate and the return on foreign financial assets. The effect of a rise in the world real interest rate on the national saving ratio is ambiguous, since the income effect can outweigh the substitution effect.

Most developing countries prohibit capital outflows. Hence, capital flight has to take place through over-invoicing imports and under-invoicing exports.[3] Indeed, in most developing countries, a large proportion of capital outflows does take place illegally through under-invoicing exports and over-invoicing imports (Khan and Haque 1985; Cuddington 1986: 38; Dooley 1986; Watson *et al.* 1986). This method of removing capital from a country reduces measured national saving, even in the unlikely event that the true level of saving remains constant. Hence, a rise in RW could reduce recorded national saving, even if the substitution effect does outweigh the income effect. In such a case, the effect of a rise in the world real interest rate on the measured national saving ratio is doubly ambiguous.

Higher domestic debt incurred by the government, proxied here by the ratio of public or government credit to total domestic credit DCGR, raises the probability of increased asset taxation in the future and so encourages capital flight (Plosser 1982; King and Plosser 1985; Hamilton and Flavin 1986). When the government extracts higher seigniorage from the banking system by raising DCGR, at least part of the implicit tax falls on depositors/savers (Fry 1988: ch. 5). Both these effects deter the accumulation of domestic financial assets and hence are likely to reduce measured national saving. However, this leftward shift in the saving function could be countered by a movement up the curve, because an increase in DCGR also raises r.

Governments in many developing countries guarantee the repayment of foreign loans acquired by the private sector. Presumably, the modern Ricardian equivalence view would hold that, if households expect the existence of government-guaranteed foreign loans to necessitate government expenditure and hence higher taxation in the future, private saving would rise as more guarantees were extended. Hence, the Ricardian equivalence hypothesis suggests that more government-guaranteed foreign debt could actually raise the national saving ratio, since this future contingent government liability does not reduce the current level of government saving.

As households notice foreign debt rising, however, they may well anticipate higher future tax burdens for its servicing (Eaton 1987). They will therefore have an increasing incentive to transfer assets abroad, as foreseen by David Ricardo:

> A country which has accumulated a large debt, is placed in a most artificial situation; and although the amount of taxes, and the increased price of labour, may not, and I believe does not, place it under any other disadvantage with respect to foreign countries, except the unavoidable one of paying those taxes, yet it becomes the interest of every contributor to withdraw his shoulder from the burthen, and to shift this payment from himself to another; and the temptation to remove himself and his capital to another country, where he will be exempted from such burthens, becomes at last irresistible,

and overcomes the natural reluctance which every man feels to quit the place of his birth, and the scene of his early associations. A country which has involved itself in the difficulties attending this artificial system, would act wisely by ransoming itself from them, at the sacrifice of any portion of its property which might be necessary to redeem its debt.

(1821: 247–8)

Savers could also perceive that a high and rising foreign debt ratio may goad the government into stimulating exports, which would involve a devaluation in the real exchange rate. In this case, the gross real returns on assets held abroad could be higher than the gross real returns on domestic assets. Hence, one might expect a higher value of government plus government-guaranteed foreign debt to reduce measured national saving, implying a leftward shift of the saving function in Figure 3.3.

The magnitude of capital flight caused by a buildup of this type of foreign debt can be, and in several developing countries has been, destabilizing. Instead of the rising foreign debt reducing domestic investment and increasing national saving and so closing the current account deficit by raising the domestic real interest rate, the foreign debt buildup shifts the national saving function leftwards so rapidly that the current account deficit *increases*. Real interest rates can reach, and in several developing countries have reached, astronomical levels without reducing the current account deficit. The end result is financial and economic paralysis. This then is the theoretical case for a positive effect of net foreign claims on the current account; a more negative value of net foreign claims can worsen the current account, if net foreign claims consist mainly of government and government-guaranteed foreign debt. Hence, whether the foreign claim ratio has a positive or negative effect on the current account is an empirical question.

The variable used here for developing country analysis is DETY, defined as the beginning-of-year stock of government plus government-guaranteed foreign debt divided by the previous year's GNP.[4] The variable DETY also determines the domestic real shadow interest rate. A higher debt ratio produces a higher domestic interest rate and hence a movement up the saving function in Figure 3.3. The financial or interest rate effect on saving could be opposite to the fiscal effect outlined above. To allow for these conflicting and possibly non-linear influences of debt on saving, the debt–GNP ratio can be entered in quadratic form; the debt ratio and the square of the debt ratio are included in the saving function.

The population dependence ratio DEPR could be expected to exert a negative effect on the national saving ratio, since a larger number of children in a household generally raises consumption in relation to income (Fry and Mason 1982).

To the extent that some households are liquidity constrained, credit conditions could affect consumption and saving behaviour. In this case, the change in domestic credit scaled by nominal GNP, DDCY, is used as a proxy for credit availability. An alternative variable that could be used is the real change in private sector credit as a proportion of real GNP, DCPY. Finally, equation (1) (Table 3.2) includes the government budget balance; budget deficits are likely to reduce the national saving ratio.

In effect, equation (1) is the private sector saving function Snp/Y to which the government saving ratio Sng/Y has been added; Snp is private national saving, Sng is government sector national saving and Y is GNP, all measured at current prices. Unfortunately, disaggregated saving data are unavailable.[5] In any case, inflation badly distorts the measurement of disaggregated private and public saving because of the failure to account correctly for the inflation tax revenue. Fortunately, however, including components of public saving that are not substitutes for private saving affects only the intercept, provided they are independent of the explanatory variables (Fry and Mason 1982: 433).

Investment

The investment function IKY specified here as the ratio of investment to GNP (both in constant prices) is based on the flexible accelerator model. Mario Blejer and Mohsin Khan (1984: 382–3) describe some of the difficulties of estimating neo-classical investment functions for developing countries. In particular, there are no readily available measures of the capital stock or its rate of return. There is therefore little choice in practice but to use some version of the accelerator model, particularly for pooled time-series analysis on data from several developing countries (Fry 1986: 62–4).

The accelerator model has the desired capital stock K^* proportional to real output y:

$$K^* = \alpha y. \qquad (3.6)$$

This can be expressed in terms of a desired ratio of investment to output $(I/Y)^*$:

$$\left(\frac{I}{Y}\right)^* = \alpha\gamma, \qquad (3.7)$$

where γ is the rate of growth in output.

The partial adjustment mechanism specified for the investment ratio is somewhat more complicated than the equivalent mechanism for the level of investment. Specifically, there could be a lag in achieving the same investment ratio this year as last year if output rose rapidly last year; this year's desired investment level will be higher than last year's, despite a constant desired ratio of investment to output. To incorporate this adjustment lag, last year's growth rate γ_{t-1} can be included as an additional explanatory variable.

The remaining adjustment mechanism allows the actual investment rate to adjust partially in any one period to the difference between the desired investment rate and the investment rate in the previous period:

$$\Delta\left(\frac{I}{Y}\right) = \lambda\left[\left(\frac{I}{Y}\right)^* - \left(\frac{I}{Y}\right)_{t-1}\right] \qquad (3.8)$$

or

$$\frac{I}{Y} = \lambda\left(\frac{I}{Y}\right)^* + (1-\lambda)\left(\frac{I}{Y}\right)_{t-1}, \qquad (3.9)$$

where λ is the coefficient of adjustment.

The flexible accelerator model allows economic conditions to influence the adjustment coefficient λ. Specifically,

$$\lambda = \beta_0 + \left[\frac{\beta_1 z_1 + \beta_2 z_2 + \beta_3 z_3 + \ldots}{(I/Y)^* - (I/Y)_{t-1}}\right] \qquad (3.10)$$

where z_i are the variables (including an intercept term for the depreciation rate) that affect λ. The speed of adjustment in the flexible accelerator investment function is determined here by the world real interest rate RW, the terms of trade TT, the real exchange rate REX, the government budget balance GBY, the ratio of foreign debt to lagged GNP DETY, the ratio of public sector credit to total domestic credit DCGR and credit availability – DCPY or DDCY.

Domestic costs of borrowing are extraordinarily difficult to measure in almost all developing countries because of selective credit policies and disequilibrium institutional interest rates. The domestic investment ratio, however, would be affected negatively by the world real interest rate RW provided there were some international capital mobility. As argued above, RW has a positive effect on the domestic real shadow interest rate r.

Torsten Persson and Lars Svensson (1985) show that an unanticipated permanent improvement in the terms of trade raises the investment ratio in their model by increasing the return to capital. It is important to test whether current or lagged improvements in the terms of trade TT_{t-1} raise the investment ratio in the developing countries examined here.

The price of intermediate imports may affect the profitability of investment projects in these developing countries. Hence, the real exchange rate REX is included as a proxy for the price of non-tradeable goods in relation to import prices. A higher value of REX implies a lower relative price of imports. By appreciating the real exchange rate, therefore, capital inflows may stimulate investment.

Fiscal policy could affect the investment ratio, although its impact is ambiguous. Expansionary fiscal policy proxied by the government budget balance GBY scaled by nominal GNP could crowd out or complement investment (Sundararajan and Thakur 1980).

Alain Ize and Guillermo Ortiz (1987) argue that foreign indebtedness deters domestic investment because it raises the probability of higher taxes on domestic assets in the future. This would cause a leftward shift in the investment function in Figure 3.3. Anne Krueger (1987: 163) suggests that debt-servicing obligations constitute a public finance problem: 'When debt-service obligations are high, increasing public resources to service debt will be likely to reduce incentives and resources available to the private sector sufficiently to preclude the necessary investment response.' Jeffrey Sachs (1986: 416–18; 1989; 1990) documents the deleterious effects of the foreign debt buildup on investment in Latin America.

The foreign debt ratio could also be a proxy for the country-specific risk premium or the intensity of non-price credit rationing imposed by foreign lenders. In such a case, the foreign debt ratio may affect the investment ratio negatively because it reflects a higher cost (possibly infinite in the case of rationing) of investible funds, implying a movement up the investment function in Figure 3.3. Empirically, it is impossible to distinguish between a shift in as opposed to a movement along the investment function caused by an increase in foreign debt without a full-blown structural model that requires data which are unavailable.

It is possible that, in its early stages, debt buildup could actually stimulate investment. Profitable investment opportunities in export activities may be perceived as debt service mounts and the drive to raise foreign exchange earnings is intensified. Conflicting and possibly non-linear effects of debt on investment are incorporated by including the debt ratio DETY in quadratic form, exactly the same specification used in the saving function.

Higher domestic debt incurred by the government, again proxied by DCGR, deters domestic investment for the same reasons that it deters saving. As suggested earlier, this ratio may also proxy for the general state of macroeconomic management, which could affect the investment climate negatively. These two effects produce a leftward shift in the investment function shown in Figure 3.3. In addition, a higher DCGR ratio deters foreign saving and so raises r, producing a movement up the investment curve in Figure 3.3. All three effects, of course, imply that a rise in DCGR reduces domestic investment.

The availability of institutional credit can be an important determinant of the investment ratio, for the reasons discussed by Alan Blinder and Joseph Stiglitz (1983, Fry (1980) and Peter Keller (1980). Banks specialize in acquiring information on default risk. Such information is highly specific to each client and difficult to sell. Hence, the market for bank loans is a customer market, in which borrowers and lenders are very imperfect substitutes. A credit squeeze rations out some bank borrowers who may be unable to find loans elsewhere and so be unable to finance their investment projects (Blinder and Stiglitz 1983: 300). Here, therefore, the investment ratio IKY is influenced by the change in the real volume of private sector domestic credit $\Delta(DCp/P)/y_{t-1}$ scaled by lagged real GNP, where P is the GNP deflator and y is real GNP. Blejer and Khan (1984: 389) use the change in real private sector domestic credit $\Delta(DCp/P)$ in their investment function. This is equivalent to $\Delta(DCp/P)/y_{t-1}$, denoted DCPY, in a model using the investment ratio as the dependent variable. The private sector domestic credit variable is treated as exogenous in this model, given the administered institutional interest rate setting arrangements that existed in most of the sample countries over virtually the entire observation period for the empirical analysis (Fry 1981, 1982).[6] The change in total domestic credit DDCY scaled by GNP could be tested as an alternative to DCPY.

Economic growth

The growth rate function specified here as the continuously compounded rate of growth in real GNP, YG, is a reduced-form equation derived from a modified production function and aggregate demand conditions. The first explanatory variable is the rate of growth in the capital stock KG, and the second explanatory variable is the rate of growth in the labour force LG.[7] There is no alternative to assuming that the unemployment rate remains constant, since employment data are unavailable for all but a handful of developing countries.

The ratio of foreign debt to GNP may affect growth not only through the investment ratio but also by affecting the efficiency of investment. For example, the proportion of government or public sector investment in total domestic investment may rise as the foreign debt ratio increases. If public investment is less efficient than private investment, a higher foreign debt ratio will reduce the average return to investment and hence lower the rate of economic growth. If public investment is more efficient than private investment, more foreign debt will have the opposite effect on the growth rate. In either case, DETY should be entered interactively with KG in the growth rate function.

Gershon Feder (1982) argues that there are two channels – higher marginal productivities and externalities – through which rapid export growth can affect the rate of economic growth in excess of the contribution of net export growth to GNP. If exports affect the production of non-exports with a constant elasticity θ, the rate of growth in gross exports at constant prices XKG captures solely the externality effect, while the rate of growth in exports scaled by the lagged export–GNP ratio XGY picks up both the differential marginal productivity δ and the externality effects: $YG = \alpha \text{IKY} + \beta \text{LG} + [\delta/(1+\delta) - \theta]\text{XGY} + \theta\text{XKG}$ (Feder 1982: 67). If only XKG is significant, this would imply that $\delta/(1+\delta) = \theta$.

Constantine Glezakos (1978), Axel Leijonhufvud (1981) and others show that greater uncertainty with respect to the future price level reduces

output growth. Hence, the growth rate may be affected negatively by the variance of money growth shocks VM, as measured by the variance of innovations to the time-series process of money growth. The innovations are residuals of country-specific regressions of the money growth rate on its own lagged value and a constant. Fry and David Lilien (1986) find that VM has a negative effect on the rate of economic growth in pooled time-series analysis of fifty-five developed and developing countries.

Finally, growth of the OECD economies YGW, the real six-month LIBOR deposit rate RW, and oil price inflation OILINF are included to capture external demand effects on growth not picked up by export growth (Callier 1984).

Trade equations

The import demand equation IMKY is expressed as the ratio of imports to GNP (both in constant prices). Each of the sample developing countries faces an infinitely elastic supply of imports. Hence, its import volume is determined solely by its own demand. This demand is affected by the prices of exports, imports and non-tradeable goods. The price variables actually used here are the real exchange rate REX, as a proxy for the relative price of non-traded goods to imports, and the terms of trade TT, which is of course the ratio of export to import prices.

The income elasticity of import demand is unitary,[8] but the composition of GNP affects imports. Specifically, investment is more import intensive than consumption. Hence, the ratio of imports to GNP is determined in part by the ratio IKY of investment to GNP.

Adjustment to the desired level of imports may be constrained by the availability of foreign exchange earned by exporters. Many developing countries impose quantitative restrictions on imports of consumer goods. Typically, licences to import these restricted items are rationed not on the basis of total foreign exchange availability but rather on the availability of non-borrowed foreign exchange or foreign exchange earned by exporters.

The ratio of nominal exports to nominal GNP, XY, is used to proxy this rationing constraint. Since export earnings must also be used to service foreign debt, quantitative restrictions on imports may also be tightened as debt service obligations rise. For this reason, the ratio IDETY of interest cost of foreign debt to GNP is included as another explanatory variable in the import demand function. Finally, import demand may be constrained by credit availability. Hence, domestic credit expansion DDCY scaled by nominal GNP or the change in the real volume of private sector domestic credit DCPY scaled by lagged real GNP can be included as the final determinant of the import ratio.

The volume of exports in this model is determined by both demand and supply (Schadler 1986: Sundararajan 1986). Export supply XY^s, expressed as the ratio of exports to GNP (both in constant prices), is determined by relative costs of production proxied here by the unit labour cost real exchange rate REXULC. The demand for the developing countries' exports XY^d is determined by income growth YGW in the OECD countries, as well as export and import prices TT.

Monetary policy reaction function

The monetary policy reaction function, specified as the change in domestic credit DDCY scaled by GNP, is designed to discover whether or not developing countries have pursued monetary policies aimed at affecting their current account positions. Specifically, the monetary authorities might tighten monetary policy when the current account deficit CAY is large or when foreign indebtedness DETY is high. The reaction function also includes the change in net foreign assets of the banking system DNFAY scaled by GNP to detect any systematic 'sterilization' of the effects of such asset acquisition on the money supply and other economic variables to which the monetary authorities might have reacted. In particular, the monetary authorities might have squeezed domestic credit when domestic inflation INF or oil price inflation OILINF was high. The gap between domestic inflation and inflation in the USA INFGAP could be substituted for INF, since the monetary authorities might have been more concerned with the relative than the absolute rate of inflation.

Finally, the monetary authorities might squeeze domestic credit to the private sector when the credit requirements of the government, as measured by the change in net domestic credit to the government DNDCGY scaled by GNP, increase. A complete neutralization of the public sector's credit requirements would imply a coefficient of zero for DNDCGY. A partial offset would produce a coefficient greater than zero but less than unity.

THE SMALL-SCALE MACROECONOMIC MODEL AND CURRENT ACCOUNT BEHAVIOUR IN DEVELOPING COUNTRIES

The model presented in the previous section has been estimated using 502 observations pooled from twenty-eight developing countries heavily indebted to the World Bank and separately for Korea (1961–89) and Taiwan (1963–87) (Fry 1989, 1990b, 1991).[9] Quasi-reduced-form models of the current account and monetary policy reaction functions have also been estimated for Korea (1961–89), Sri Lanka (1951–88) and Taiwan (1952–89) (Fry 1991; Fry et al. 1991).

The pooled time-series estimates indicate that capital inflows raise economic growth by allowing investment to exceed saving and by stimulating investment indirectly through the real exchange rate effect. However, a rising ratio of foreign debt to GNP eventually has three negative impacts on growth: it reduces the saving ratio, it deters domestic investment and it lowers the efficiency of investment. These negative effects of debt stock start to outweigh the positive effects of debt flow when the debt–GNP ratio reaches about 0.5.[10] In fact, debt–GNP ratios ranged from 0.02 to 1.28 in the sample countries. The problem arises from the lack of any automatic deterrent to continued debt accumulation after its effects turn malign.

Figure 3.5 shows the direct and indirect effects of increasing foreign debt on the national saving and domestic investment ratios. These are short-run equilibrium effects, since the values of all lagged endogenous variables are held constant while DETY is increased from 0 to 2.[11] The gap between the saving ratio and the investment ratio increases monotonically, so widening the current account deficit, as the debt ratio rises. The same result occurs whether the foreign debt ratio is entered linearly or to the third or fourth power with beginning or end-of-year values in both the saving and investment ratio equations. Whether entered linearly or in quadratic form, the debt–export ratio also produces the same result but has a somewhat lower explanatory power than the debt–GNP ratio in both the saving and investment functions.[12]

For dynamic simulations, the small-scale macroeconomic model presented in the previous section is closed with the two current account identities expressed in current prices:

$$CAY = XY - IMY + NFIY, \qquad (3.11)$$

$$CAY = SNY - IY, \qquad (3.12)$$

where CAY is the balance of payments on current account divided by nominal GNP, XY is the nominal export ratio, IMY is the nominal import ratio, NFIY is the exogenously determined ratio of net factor income from abroad to nominal GNP, SNY is the nominal saving ratio and IY is the nominal investment ratio. This definition of the current account ratio is derived from the national income rather than the balance-of-payments accounts. It excludes unrequited transfers and hence differs from the balance-of-payments definition used in the first section.

The eight equations of the macroeconomic model (equations (1)–(6) in Table 3.2 and equations (3.11) and (3.12)) can be transformed to explain the saving, investment, export and import ratios, the rate of economic growth, the current account ratio, the real exchange rate and the terms of trade. The import demand function is inverted so that the real exchange rate becomes the dependent variable, the export demand function is also inverted to give the terms of trade as the dependent variable and equation (3.11) is rearranged to determine the import ratio. Some additional identities are required to run the in-sample dynamic simulations of the model to produce the simulated current account ratios for Korea and Taiwan shown in Figures 3.6 and 3.7.[13] The simulated current account ratio explains 83 per cent of the variance in the actual current account ratio for Korea and 97 per cent for Taiwan.

CURRENT ACCOUNT BEHAVIOUR AND MONETARY POLICY REACTION FUNCTIONS

The monetary policy reaction function, equation (7) of the model presented in Table 3.2, has been estimated together with a quasi-reduced-form current account equation for Korea, Sri Lanka and Taiwan (Fry 1991; Fry et al. 1991). The current account equations include the relevant variables from the estimates of the small-scale macroeconomic model presented in the second section that yielded significant coefficients in the current account estimates together with the lagged cumulative current account position or net foreign claim ratio FY_{t-1}. In a broad sense, therefore, this

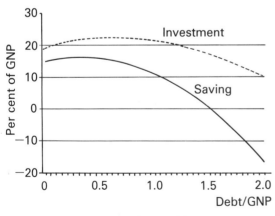

Figure 3.5 Effect of rising foreign debt ratio on saving and investment ratios

Table 3.2 Small-scale macroeconomic model of a representative developing economy

$$SNY = a_{10} + \overset{+}{a}_{11}\hat{YG} + \overset{+}{a}_{12}\hat{TTG} + \overset{?}{a}_{13}RW + \overset{-}{a}_{14}DCGR + \overset{?}{a}_{15}DETY$$

$$+ \overset{?}{a}_{16}DETY^2 + \overset{-}{a}_{17}DEPR + \overset{-}{a}_{18}\hat{DDCY} + \overset{-}{a}_{19}GBY + \overset{+}{a}_{20}SNY_{t-1} \tag{1}$$

$$IKY = a_{30} + \overset{+}{a}_{31}\hat{YG} + \overset{-}{a}_{32}RW + \overset{+}{a}_{33}\hat{TT} + \overset{+}{a}_{34}\hat{REX} + \overset{?}{a}_{35}GBY$$

$$+ \overset{?}{a}_{36}DETY + \overset{?}{a}_{37}DETY^2 + \overset{-}{a}_{38}DCGR + \overset{-}{a}_{39}DCPY + \overset{+}{a}_{40}IKY_{t-1} \tag{2}$$

$$YG = a_{50} + \overset{+}{a}_{51}\hat{KG} + \overset{+}{a}_{52}LG + \overset{?}{a}_{53}(\hat{KG \cdot DETY}) + \overset{+}{a}_{54}\hat{XKG}$$

$$+ \overset{-}{a}_{55}VM + \overset{+}{a}_{56}YGW + \overset{-}{a}_{57}RW + \overset{-}{a}_{58}OILINF + \overset{+}{a}_{59}YG_{t-1} \tag{3}$$

$$IMKY = a_{60} + \overset{+}{a}_{61}\hat{REX} + \overset{+}{a}_{62}\hat{TT} + \overset{+}{a}_{63}\hat{IKY} + \overset{+}{a}_{64}\hat{XY} + \overset{-}{a}_{65}IDETY + \overset{+}{a}_{66}\hat{DDCY} + \overset{+}{a}_{67}IMKY_{t-1} \tag{4}$$

$$XKY^3 = a_{70} + \overset{-}{a}_{71}\hat{REXULC} + \overset{+}{a}_{72}XKY_{t-1} \tag{5}$$

$$XKY^d = a_{80} + \overset{-}{a}_{81}\hat{TT} + \overset{+}{a}_{82}YGW + \overset{+}{a}_{83}XKY_{t-1} \tag{6}$$

$$DDCY = a_{90} + \overset{+}{a}_{91}\hat{CAY} + \overset{-}{a}_{92}DETY + \overset{-}{a}_{93}\hat{DNFAY} + \overset{?}{a}_{94}OILINF + \overset{-}{a}_{95}INFGAP + \overset{?}{a}_{96}DNDCGY \tag{7}$$

Endogenous variables

SNY	gross national saving/GNP (current prices)
YG	rate of growth in GNP (constant prices, continuously compounded)
TT	terms of trade (export price index/import price index)
TTG	rate of growth in aggregate income attributable to terms-of-trade improvements (constant prices, continuously compounded) (*TT* is the terms-of-trade index):

$$TTG \equiv \log\{[(\hat{TT} - TT_{t-1})/TT_{t-1}]\, XY_{t-1} + 1\}$$

IKY	gross domestic investment/GNP (constant prices)
KG	rate of change in the capital stock (constant prices, continuously compounded)
REX	real exchange rate ((domestic GNP deflator/US wholesale price index)/domestic currency per US dollar)
REXULC	unit labour cost real exchange rate ((domestic unit labour cost index/US unit labour cost index)/domestic currency per US dollar)
XKG	rate of growth in exports (constant prices, continuously compounded)
IMKY	imports/GNP (constant prices)
XY	exports/GNP (current prices)
XKY	exports/GNP (constant prices)
DDCY	change in domestic credit/GNP (current prices)
CAY	balance of payments on current account/GNP (current prices)
DNFAY	change in banking system's net foreign assets/GNP (current prices)

Exogenous or predetermined variables

DEPR	population dependence ratio (population under 15 and over 64 divided by total population)
GBY	government budget balance/GNP (current prices)
RW	world real interest rate (six-month LIBOR deposit rate minus US inflation, continuously compounded)
DCGR	net domestic credit to government/domestic credit (average of beginning and end-of-year figures, current prices)
DETY	beginning-of-year government plus government-guaranteed foreign debt/lagged GNP (current prices)
DCPY	change in real domestic credit to private sector/GNP (constant prices)
LG	rate of growth in population aged 15 to 64
VM	country-specific variance in money growth shocks

YGW   rate of growth in OECD output (constant prices, continuously compounded)
IDETY   interest cost of foreign debt/GNP (current prices)
OILINF   rate of change in oil price (continuously compounded dollar price)
INFGAP   domestic inflation rate minus US inflation rate
DNDCGY   change in domestic credit to the government sector/GNP (current prices)

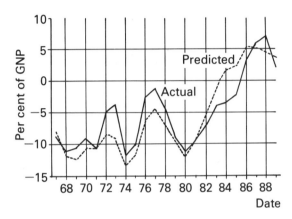

Figure 3.6 Actual and simulated current account ratios
in Korea, 1967–89

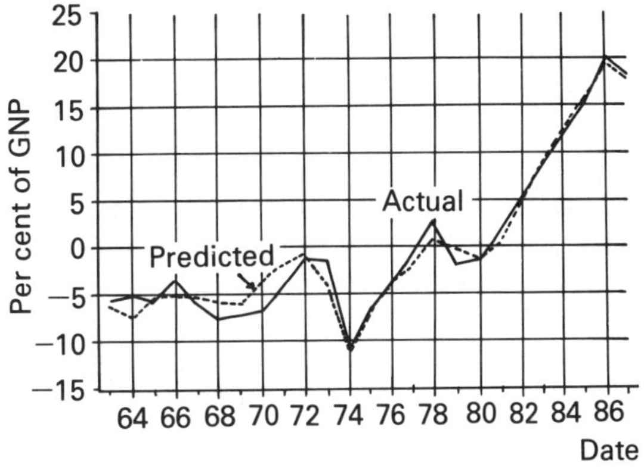

Figure 3.7 Actual and simulated current account ratios
in Taiwan, 1963–87

current account equation is an error correction model. In all three current account estimates, the coefficient of DDCY is negative and significant.

The estimates suggest that Korea's current account is stable, while those of Sri Lanka and Taiwan are unstable. Specifically, the coefficient of the net foreign claim ratio FY_{t-1} is significantly negative in the estimated current account equation for Korea.[14] This implies that changes in Korea's net stock of foreign claims produced forces to reduce or reverse the flows that created the stocks over time. In other words, this negative effect of a stock variable on the flow generating it is stabilizing or error correcting.

Neither Korea's lagged net foreign claim position nor the net foreign claim ratio interacted with a post-1982 dummy was significant at any confidence level in the monetary policy reaction function. In other words, the Korean monetary authorities do not appear to have pursued any systematic monetary policy to reverse current

account deficits leading to a buildup in international debt (or, conversely, to reverse current account surpluses leading to an inexorable accumulation of foreign assets).

The coefficient of FY_{t-1} in the current account equation for both Sri Lanka and Taiwan is significantly positive. The positive effect of FY_{t-1} implies that changes in the net stock of foreign assets in these two countries produce forces which stimulate further the flows that create the stocks. In other words, this positive effect of a stock variable on the flow that generates it is destabilizing or error compounding. However, the reaction function estimates show that Taiwan's central bank has increased domestic credit significantly when net foreign assets have been higher; the coefficient of FY_{t-1} is also positive in the domestic credit estimate. This produces a stabilizing effect on the buildup of net foreign assets, since domestic credit expansion reduces Taiwan's current account surplus. In contrast, the coefficient of FY_{t-1} in Sri

Lanka's monetary policy reaction function is negative. Sri Lanka's central bank increased domestic credit, so worsening the current account, when foreign indebtedness increased. This, of course, was a destabilizing policy reaction.

The current account and monetary policy equations estimated in Fry (1991) and Fry *et al.* (1991) can be used to simulate the future course of the current account ratios in Korea, Sri Lanka and Taiwan. These simulations use average values of the exogenous explanatory variables over the period 1985–9 and assume that the average annual growth rates in real GNP over the decade 1979–89 continue in the future. The variables CAY_{t-1}, FY_{t-1} and $DDCY_{t-1}$ take their 1989 values. The simulations are shown in Figures 3.8 and 3.9.

Figure 3.8 shows that, from a current account surplus of 2 per cent of GNP in 1989, Korea's current account falls to −3 per cent of GNP in 1994 before converging to −1 per cent of GNP by the end of the century. Given the relatively high return on Korea's capital stock, running a current account deficit of this magnitude hardly seems inappropriate. Since the current account ratio is well below the rate of economic growth, Korea's ratio of net foreign claims to GNP necessarily converges to a long-run steady-state value, in this particular case equalling −13 per cent of GNP.

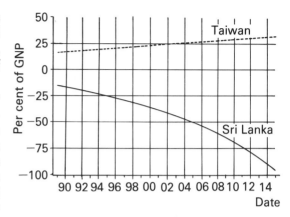

Figure 3.9 Forecast current account ratios for Sri Lanka and Taiwan, 1989–2015

In contrast, the current account simulations for Sri Lanka and Taiwan shown in Figure 3.9 suggest that, without deliberate policy changes, current account imbalances will continue to widen. Hence, Sri Lanka's foreign debt ratio and Taiwan's net foreign asset ratio will continue to increase indefinitely. Taiwan's central bank does appear to have expanded domestic credit in response to a rise in net foreign assets. Over the estimation period, however, this response has been insufficient to reverse Taiwan's buildup of foreign assets.

These findings by no means imply that Sri Lanka and Taiwan are doomed to unstable current accounts in the future. All the estimates discussed here indicate that monetary policy has had a significant influence on Korea's current account. If the monetary authorities wished to pursue a net foreign claim target or to stabilize fluctuations in the current account positions, there is little doubt that monetary policy could be effective in achieving such objectives.

CONCLUSION

In this chapter we have examined current account imbalances and concomitant net capital flows in a sample of developing countries. A small-scale macroeconomic model performed well in tracking current account ratios, while error-correction

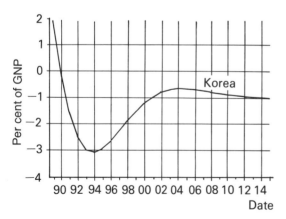

Figure 3.8 Forecast current account ratio for Korea, 1989–2015

mechanisms indicate that current accounts in developing countries can be unstable. Dynamic simulations suggest that Korea's current account might find a steady state with a deficit of less than 1 per cent of GNP. However, similar simulations for Sri Lanka and Taiwan indicate that, without deliberate changes in macroeconomic policies, their current account imbalances could continue to grow.

NOTES

1   This definition of foreign debt includes long-term and short-term public and private foreign debt, including private foreign debt not guaranteed by the government.

2   The circumflexes denote the endogenous explanatory variables. Lagged dependent variables are included in the first six equations to allow for adjustment lags.

3   An exporter submits an invoice for a smaller sum than that actually received for the exports when surrendering foreign exchange to the central bank; the difference can then be deposited in the exporter's bank account abroad. Conversely, an importer submits an invoice for an amount exceeding the true cost of the imports in order to siphon the difference into his foreign bank account.

4   The debt data are measured at the end of each year. Debt at the end of one year is the same as debt at the beginning of the next year. Empirical results can be tested to determine whether they are dependent on the choice of beginning-of-year versus end-of-year debt or lagged versus current GNP.

5   Indeed, not even government deficit or government revenue and consumption expenditure data are available for many developing countries.

6   One prediction of the financial repression hypothesis is that a rise in the deposit rate towards its free-market equilibrium level will increase the availability of private sector domestic credit in real terms and hence stimulate investment (Blejer and Khan 1984: 386). When the real deposit rate is substituted for the private sector domestic credit variable in a similar investment function applied to fourteen Asian developing countries, its estimated coefficient is indeed positive and significant (Fry 1986: 67).

7   For empirical purposes, the capital stock can be estimated roughly by assuming an average capital–GNP ratio of 2.5 during the first few years of the observation period and cumulating gross real investment annually after depreciating the previous

year's capital stock by 5 per cent. In fact, capital stock estimates are available for Korea and Taiwan (Pyo 1988; Fry 1990a). Where labour force data are unavailable, the labour force can be estimated as the population multiplied by (1 − the population dependence ratio), where the population dependence ratio is defined as the population under 15 and over 64 divided by the total population.

8   The validity of this assumption can be tested by including, in turn, the logarithm of per capita real GNP, the reciprocal of the logarithm of per capita real GNP and the rate of economic growth in both the import demand and the export supply functions. The assumption of unitary income elasticity would be supported if the coefficients of all these alternative income measures were insignificant.

9   In the pooled time-series estimate, the regression period is 1967–85, but there are less than nineteen observations for some countries. The country sample (dates given when not 1967–85) is as follows: Algeria, Argentina (1970–84), Bangladesh (1976–85), Brazil, Cameroon (1967–84), Chile (1974–84), Colombia, Egypt, India, Indonesia, Ivory Coast, Jamaica, Kenya (1970–85), Korea, Malaysia, Mexico (1967–84), Morocco (1967–84), Nigeria (1967–84), Pakistan, Peru, Philippines, Portugal (1967–84), Sudan (1967–84), Thailand, Tunisia, Turkey, Yugoslavia and Zambia.

10   This corresponds to a debt–export ratio of about 2.4 for this sample of countries.

11   All the current-period endogenous variables, however, are allowed to find their equilibrium levels for each value of the beginning-of-year debt stock.

12   The gap between the national saving ratio and the domestic investment ratio equals the current account–GNP ratio. The simple correlation between the current account ratio CAY and DETY for individual countries is significantly negative in fourteen cases and significantly positive in four (India, Korea, Mexico and Yugoslavia). When the regression period is truncated at 1981 instead of 1985 in recognition of the substantial adjustment in Korea and Mexico over the period 1982–5, the relationship is significantly positive only for India and Yugoslavia. In India's case, however, the coefficient of DETY is smaller in the saving function than it is in the investment function. The pooled results with respect to the debt effect are therefore corroborated by these simple individual-country regressions. Truncating the observations of all the sample countries at 1981 for the pooled time-series estimates makes very little difference; the absolute values of all the debt coefficients in the

saving and investment equations are somewhat larger.

13 For example, the investment and import ratios have to be adjusted to current prices. The appropriate price deflators are taken to be exogenous in this simulation. An additional estimated equation is used to explain the unit labour cost real exchange rate as a function of the standard real exchange rate and a time trend.

14 Net stocks of foreign claims are calculated here by cumulating the dollar value of the current account position, defined as exports of goods and services plus net unrequited transfers minus imports of goods and services, from 1950. I assume that the value of net foreign claims was zero in 1949.

REFERENCES

Blejer, M. I. and Khan, M. S. (1984) 'Government policy and private investment in developing countries', *International Monetary Fund Staff Papers* 31 (2): 379–403.

Blinder, A. S. and Stiglitz, J. E. (1983) 'Money, credit constraints, and economic activity', *American Economic Review* 73 (2): 297–302.

Callier, P. (1984) 'Growth of developing countries and world interest rates', *Journal of Macroeconomics* 6 (4): 465–71.

Cuddington, J. T. (1986) 'Capital flight: estimates, issues, and explanations', *Princeton Studies in International Finance* 58, December.

Dooley, M. P. (1986) 'Country-specific risk premiums, capital flight and net investment income payments in selected developing countries', Department Memorandum DM/86/17, Washington, DC: International Monetary Fund, March.

Eaton, J. (1987) 'Public debt guarantees and private capital flight', *World Bank Economic Review* 1 (3): 377–95.

Edwards, S. (1986) 'The pricing of bonds and bank loans in international markets: an empirical analysis of developing countries' foreign borrowing', *European Economic Review* 30 (3): 565–89.

Feder, G. (1982) 'On exports and economic growth', *Journal of Development Economics* 12 (1): 59–73.

Fry, M. J. (1980) 'Money, interest, inflation and growth in Turkey', *Journal of Monetary Economics* 6 (4): 535–45.

—— (1981) 'Inflation and economic growth in Pacific Basin developing economies', *Federal Reserve Bank of San Francisco Economic Review*, Fall: 8–18.

—— (1982) 'Analysing disequilibrium interest-rate systems in developing countries', *World Development* 10(12): 1049–57.

—— (1986) 'Terms-of-trade dynamics in Asia: an analysis of national saving and domestic investment responses to terms-of-trade changes in 14 Asian LDCs', *Journal of International Money and Finance* 5 (1): 57–73.

—— (1988) *Money, Interest, and Banking in Economic Development*, Baltimore, MD: Johns Hopkins University Press.

—— (1989) 'Foreign debt instability: an analysis of national saving and domestic investment responses to foreign debt accumulation in 28 developing countries', *Journal of International Money and Finance* 8 (3): 315–44.

—— (1990a) 'The rate of return to Taiwan's capital stock, 1961–87', *Hong Kong Economic Papers* (20): 17–30.

—— (1990b) 'Taiwan's current account surplus: incipient Dutch disease?', *International Economic Journal* 4 (3): 93–112.

—— (1991) 'Long-run and short-run behavior of Korea's current account', *International Economic Journal*, forthcoming.

Fry, M. J. and Lilien, D. M. (1986) 'Monetary policy responses to exogenous shocks', *American Economic Review* 76 (2): 79–83.

Fry, M. J. and Mason, A. (1982) 'The variable rate-of-growth effect in the life cycle saving model: children, capital inflows, interest and growth in a new specification of the life-cycle model applied to seven Asian developing countries', *Economic Inquiry* 20 (3): 426–42.

Fry, M. J., Sosvilla-Rivero, S. and Burridge, P. (1991) 'Current account imbalances in Sri Lanka and Taiwan: long-run adjustment mechanisms and policy reaction functions', Birmingham: University of Birmingham, International Finance Group, January.

Glezakos, C. (1978) 'Inflation and growth: a reconsideration of the evidence from LDCs', *Journal of Developing Areas* 12 (2): 171–82.

Hajivassiliou, V. A. (1987) 'The external debt repayments problems of LDCs: an econometric model based on panel data', *Journal of Econometrics* 36 (1–2): 205–30.

Hamilton, J. D. and Flavin, M. A. (1986) 'On the limitations of government borrowing: a framework for empirical testing', *American Economic Review* 76 (4): 808–19.

Harberger, A. C. (1981) 'In step and out of step with the world inflation: a summary history of countries, 1952–1976', in J. Flanders and A. Razin (eds) *Development in an Inflationary World*, New York: Academic Press, pp. 35–46.

Horne, J., Kremers, J. and Masson, P. (1989) 'Net foreign assets and international adjustment in the United States, Japan and the Federal Republic of Germany', Working Paper WP/89/22, Washington,

DC: International Monetary Fund, March.

Ize, A. and Ortiz, G. (1987) 'Fiscal rigidities, public debt, and capital flight', *International Monetary Fund Staff Papers* 34 (2): 311–32.

Keller, P. M. (1980) 'Implications of credit policies for output and the balance of payments', *International Monetary Fund Staff Papers* 27 (3): 451–77.

Khan, M. S. and Haque, N. U. (1985) 'Foreign borrowing and capital flight: a formal analysis', *International Monetary Fund Staff Papers* 32 (4): 606–28.

King, R. C. and Plosser, C. I. (1985) 'Money, deficits, and inflation', *Carnegie–Rochester Conference Series on Public Policy* 22 (Spring): 147–95.

Krueger, A. O. (1987) 'Debt, capital flows, and LDC growth', *American Economic Review* 77 (2): 159–64.

Leijonhufvud, A. (1981) 'Costs and consequences of inflation', in A. Leijonhufvud (ed.) *Information and Coordination: Essays in Macroeconomic Theory*, New York: Oxford University Press, pp. 227–69.

Mason, A. (1987) 'National saving rates and population growth: a new model and new evidence', in D. G. Johnson and R. D. Lee (eds) *Population Growth and Economic Development: Issues and Evidence*, Madison, WI: University of Wisconsin Press for the National Academy of Sciences, pp. 523–60.

Metzler, L. A. (1968) 'The process of international adjustment under conditions of full employment: a Keynesian view', in R. E. Caves and H. G. Johnson (eds) *Readings in International Economics*, Homewood, IL: Richard D. Irwin for the American Economic Association, pp. 465–86.

Persson, R. and Svensson, L. E. O. (1985) 'Current account dynamics and the terms of trade: Harberger–Laursen–Metzler two generations later', *Journal of Political Economy* 93 (1): 43–65.

Plosser, C. I. (1982) 'Government financial decisions and asset returns', *Journal of Monetary Economics* 9 (3): 325–52.

Pyo, H.-K. (1988) 'Estimates of capital stock and capital/output coefficients by industries for the Republic of Korea (1953–1986)', Working Paper 8810, Seoul: Korea Development Institute, September.

Ricardo, D. (1821) *On the Principles of Political Economy and Taxation*, 3rd edn, ed. by Piero Sraffa, London: Cambridge University Press, 1951.

Sachs, J. D. (1986) 'Managing the LDC debt crisis', *Brookings Papers on Economic Activity* (2): 397–431.

—— (ed.) (1989) *Developing Country Debt and the World Economy*, Chicago, IL: University of Chicago Press for the National Bureau of Economic Research.

—— (ed.) (1990) *Developing Country Debt and Economic Performance*, vols 1–3, Chicago, IL: University of Chicago Press for the National Bureau of Economic Research.

Schadler, S. M. (1986) 'Effect of a slowdown in industrial economies on selected Asian countries', *International Monetary Fund Staff Papers* 33 (2): 345–72.

Sundararajan, V. (1986) 'Exchange rate versus credit policy: analysis with a monetary model of trade and inflation in India', *Journal of Development Economics* 20 (1): 75–105.

Sundararajan, V. and Thakur, S. (1980) 'Public investment, crowding out, and growth: a dynamic model applied to India and Korea', *International Monetary Fund Staff Papers* 27 (4): 814–55.

Watson, C. M., Kincaid, G. R., Atkinson, C., Kalter, E. and Folkerts-Landau, D. (1986) *International Capital Markets: Developments and Prospects*, Washington, DC: International Monetary Fund, World Economic and Financial Surveys, December.

World Bank (1990) *World Tables 1989–90: Socio-economic Time-series Access and Retrieval System, Version 1.0*, Washington, DC: World Bank, March.

4

THE WORLD BANK IN THE 1990s

Ibrahim F.I. Shihata

INTRODUCTION

In this chapter (written as a basis for a lecture delivered before the Law Asia Energy Section International Conference, Melbourne, Australia, on 3 October 1990) we discuss the challenges that the World Bank Group may be expected to face in the remaining years of this century. Considering the dramatic events which are at present evolving in the Middle East, this assessment is all the more relevant in a world community which needs, perhaps more than ever before, the full co-operation of its members and increasing ingenuity and dedication from its multilateral institutions.

The World Bank Group consists not only of the IBRD, but also of four other institutions that the IBRD has helped to create to undertake activities complementary to its own. The IDA extends highly concessional credits for projects and programmes in the less developed poorer member countries, the IBRD's lending being confined to the more creditworthy members. The IFC promotes and provides financing, through loans, guarantees and equity participations, to *private* enterprises in its member countries, the IBRD being unable to extend financing to such enterprises without a government guarantee. The newly established MIGA is the only globally operating intergovernmental organization which specializes in providing investment insurance against political risks. Finally, the International Centre for Settlement of Investment Disputes (ICSID), the only non-financial organization within the World Bank Group, provides facilities for the conciliation and

arbitration of disputes between governments and foreign investors.

Though each of these five institutions has distinct functions, they share a common objective: the encouragement of the transfer of resources for productive purposes to their developing member countries. The combined authorized capital resources of the IBRD, the IDA, the IFC and the MIGA now stand at over $242 billion.[1] The IBRD's authorized capital accounts for most of this amount ($171.4 billion (*World Bank Annual Report* 1990: 77), of which $128.6 billion had been subscribed by 1 September 1990[2]). Only some 7.2 per cent of the IBRD's subscribed capital is paid in, mostly (90 per cent) in the local currency of each member; the rest is 'callable capital' supporting IBRD borrowing from the market.[3] This is the so-called guarantee capital which may be called only if the IBRD is unable otherwise to meet its obligations towards its creditors (including the beneficiaries of its guarantees). This guarantee capital has never been called nor is it expected to be ever called, as the Bank makes sure that it can always meet its obligations without resorting to this capital. Borrowing on the strength of the IBRD's capital resources has cumulatively exceeded $166.5 billion over the years and stands at about $11.5 billion per year[4] at present.

In recent years, the IFC has joined the IBRD in borrowing increasing amounts from the market (more than half a billion annually). The IDA, which relies on periodic contributions from its members and recently has started to rely also on the repayments or 'reflows' of its credits, has just completed a Ninth Replenishment of its resources ($15.5 billion) (*World Bank Annual Report* 1990: 39) for operations in the coming three years alone. Together, the IBRD and the IDA (which I shall refer to here together as the Bank) administer, in addition, numerous trust funds on behalf of other donors (some $2.4 billion in commitments by mid-1990) (World Bank internal reports, unpublished).

In the last fiscal year the IBRD committed from its own resources $15.2 billion and disbursed $14 billion (*World Bank Annual Report* 1990: 13). IDA committed $5.5 billion and disbursed $3.9 billion (*World Bank Annual Report* 1990) during the same year, while the IFC committed and disbursed little less than $1.0 billion.[5] The overall operations of the World Bank Group in the last fiscal year amounted to $21.8 billion in commitments in addition to $242.1 million in trust funds and facilities administered by them.

From its establishment to the end of the last fiscal year (30 June 1990), the IBRD approved loans in an aggregate amount exceeding $189 billion for 106 countries.[6] The IDA's cumulative operations totalled $58.2 billion for eighty-eight countries (*World Bank Annual Report* 1962–90) and the IFC's $9.7 billion for ninety-four countries (*IFC Annual Report* 1956–90).

In addition to such material resources, the institutions have highly qualified and motivated multinational staffs, a global perspective, an impressive economic research capability, a growing knowledge in policy-based operations and probably the most extensive world-wide experience in project preparation, finance and supervision. As a result, they have established a credible capacity to mobilize financial resources both from capital markets and concessional sources to back up their lending operations, advice and technical assistance. It is no exaggeration to state therefore that the World Bank Group represents to date a major centre for finance, research and advisory services for the development of developing countries. This is not to boast about the achievements of these institutions but to emphasize their relevance in the years to come as well as the importance of the role they can play in co-operation with other sources of finance and expertise in meeting the increased demands of the 1990s.

THE PERFORMANCE OF THE DEVELOPING COUNTRIES – RECORD AND OUTLOOK

The role and activities of the World Bank Group in the 1990s will be moulded, on the one hand, by the future needs of its borrowing member countries and, on the other, by the degree of industrial countries' willingness and ability to meet these needs. Such roles and activities will also be greatly affected by the capacity of the Group for innovation and intellectual leadership in the development field. This capacity was successfully tested in the 1980s when the Bank managed to enlarge the scope of its work and greatly diversify its activities, without introducing for this purpose amendments to its Articles of Agreement. Any assessment of further prospects must naturally take into account the historical record and the current situation out of which the future will grow.

Post-Second World War

The post-Second World War period has witnessed a tremendous rise in the living standards in developing countries as a whole. In the period from 1965 to 1985, the countries with a per capita income of less than $6,000 per year (in 1987 dollars)[7] increased their share in world real GDP from 16 per cent to 21 per cent and their share of world manufactures exports volumes from 11 per cent to 13 per cent.[8] Although such percentage shares of world production and trade remain modest, these countries have realized remarkable improvements in their basic infrastructures, in life expectancies, nutritional standards and educational attainments. Some countries have made especially impressive progress. Life expectancy in China, which has more than one-fourth of the developing countries' total population, reached 70 years by 1988. Indonesia cut down the incidence of poverty from 60 per cent to 20 per cent of its population within two decades.[9] The infrastructure in some oil-exporting Arab countries has attained the best world standards. The growth of manufactures in certain Southeast Asian countries has reached record levels. And many countries have achieved high per capita incomes which led to their graduation from Bank borrowing.

From 1965 to 1980, each of the major regions of the developing world on average sustained impressive positive rates of growth in real per capita income (World Bank 1990a: 11, Table 1.2). Strong commodity prices and ready access among middle-income countries in particular to a then highly liquid private banking system helped many such countries to weather the economic storms of the 1970s with continued increases or, in a few cases, modest reductions in growth. Between 1965 and 1985 consumption per capita in real terms increased in developing countries by almost 70 per cent, life expectancy went up from 51 to 62 years and the net enrolment rate in primary education increased from 73 to 84 per cent (World Bank 1990a: 39, Figure 3.1).[10] Meanwhile, the share of manufactured goods in total exports greatly increased in these countries, reaching 40 per cent in 1989 (after a low of 20 per cent in 1965) (World Bank 1987: Tables 4, 11 and 27).

Record of the 1980s

The last decade, however, represents a mixed and in many respects disappointing picture. No wonder it has been depicted as a 'lost decade' for many countries and the growth experienced in it as a 'two-track development' process (World Bank 1990a: 7; *World Bank Annual Report* 1990: 23).

In East and South Asia, where over 70 per cent of the world's poor live, the 1980s were a period of continued progress. Indeed in South Asia real per capita incomes by the end of the decade averaged more than one-third above their level in 1980 (World Bank 1990a: 11, Table 1.2). And in East Asia living standards rose at a remarkable rate of 6.7 per cent in the 1980s (World Bank 1990a).

However, large parts of the developing world did not share in this progress. In Latin America, real per capita income growth turned negative during the decade (World Bank 1990a); for several countries in the region, living standards fell back to those of the early 1970s. Worse still is the position of Sub-Saharan Africa where real per capita growth rates, already stagnating in the 1970s, dropped precipitously in the 1980s (World Bank 1990a). In that region living standards are now no higher than those of the 1960s. And in the Middle East and North Africa, real per capita growth rates, though remaining positive, fell by over a third compared with the 3.9 per cent average annual gain registered during the fifteen years up to 1980. More severe declines in real per capita income growth rates were witnessed in Eastern Europe (World Bank 1990a).

Several factors account for these pervasive declines. The prices of many developing country commodities, which were strong in the 1970s, fell to their lowest post-war levels in the 1980s. Average non-oil commodity prices, in real terms, dropped by more than one-third across the 1980s (World Bank 1990a: 13), while oil prices declined to their lowest real levels since the price rises of 1973.

Falling terms of trade were accompanied by rises in real interest rates in the early 1980s after a period when large government deficits and investment expansion had been financed through foreign indebtedness, domestic borrowing and printing money. These movements, subsequently coupled with sharp declines in export proceeds, led to debt service difficulties which in turn prompted a virtual cut-off in voluntary commercial lending to heavily indebted developing countries, particularly in Latin America. The total debt stock of developing countries reached $1.3 trillion in 1989, and is expected to exceed that figure by the end of 1990, from the level of $649 billion in 1980 (World Bank 1989–90: 2, Table 1). Over 60 per cent of this debt is owed to commercial banks. The debt service payments of such countries started to outpace new borrowings in the 1980s, contributing to the phenomenon of net resources moving not from rich to poor countries but from poor to rich.

Debt burden and transfer of resources

Overall, net transfers from the small group of severely indebted middle-income countries to their private creditors during 1982–9 totalled $150 billion (World Bank 1989–90: 112). The overall negative net transfers, including capital flight, have of course been much larger during the decade. The low-income developing countries in Sub-Saharan Africa have faced a debt crisis that is of a smaller magnitude in absolute terms – the 1988 debt stock of the severely indebted among them was $103 billion (World Bank 1990a: 126), less than a fifth of the $516 billion accumulated debt of the middle-income group (World Bank 1990a). Yet the debt of low-income countries is in relative terms more onerous, amounting to 111 per cent of their combined GNP in 1988 compared with 54 per cent for the middle-income countries as a whole (World Bank 1990a). (However, the interest payment to GNP ratio in the severely indebted countries reached 4 per cent for the middle-income countries and 2.8 per cent for the low-income countries in the same year (World Bank 1989–90: Supplement I, 18, 20).) With their weak financial and infrastructural positions, narrow export bases, low nutritional and educational standards and rapid population growth, the prospects that the low-income countries may naturally 'grow out' of their debt burdens seems dim (World Bank 1990a: 126). In contrast to the higher–middle-income countries, the major proportion of the low-income group's stock of foreign debt – nearly 70 per cent – is official, reflecting their poverty and general inability to borrow from private markets. With aid levels having registered only modest increases, debt service due payments of many low-income countries have in recent years represented a very high proportion of their receipts of official development assistance; and for some such countries total debt service has exceeded gross aid disbursements. Even after international debt reduction initiatives, it is estimated that debt service will continue to cost the low-income countries an average of 5 per cent of GDP during the 1990s. The situation is not much better in most of the lower–middle-income countries (defined in the World Bank as those with 1988 per capita GNP between $546 and $2,200).

Foreign direct investment flows to developing countries also declined during most of the 1980s (see World Bank 1989a: 2ff.; 1990b: 4–5), despite its impressive increase on a world-wide basis. Such investment continues to be heavily concentrated in a small number of countries, with some notable expansion during the 1980s in China and other Southeast Asian countries. The recent growth of aggregate foreign direct investment, in current dollars, since 1988 cannot compensate for the fall of the massive foreign lending practised in the 1970s. Furthermore, a good portion of such recent foreign direct investment, as well as of external official flows, has been linked to efforts to reduce existing debt rather than to finance flows of goods and services needed for new investment. The decline in domestic savings and investment experienced in several countries in the 1980s has added to the predicament of the affected countries. Most of the latter decline was accounted for by a sharp drop in domestic private investment, which on a net basis appears to have fallen to zero or even below in some countries. Public investment has also declined in many developing countries, especially those which followed stabilization and adjustment measures. The opening up of Eastern European countries and the anticipation of a large unified market in post-1992 Europe raise new questions about the potential diversion of investment flows which might otherwise have gone to the less developed regions.

Domestic and external factors

While failed domestic policies have contributed to such declines, no measure of good policies in developing countries could, in my view, have fully overcome the sharp decline in terms of trade for the commodity exporters. Nor could it stop the surge in protectionism in developed countries' markets or reduce interest rates in creditor countries to the benefit of the indebted ones. It would therefore be wrong to place the blame entirely on developing countries. This is not to under-estimate the importance of appropriate domestic policies and the essential need for efficient and honest government. Inadequate or negative domestic action in response to highly disruptive outside events has frequently deepened economic crises in a vicious circle. Thus, for example, many governments resorted increasingly to printing money to finance large deficits that had in large measure been funded by borrowings before the cut-off in commercial bank lending. The severe inflation that this has fuelled has undermined investor confidence, reduced investment levels and provoked further capital flight. The over-regulation of investment and the inefficient implementation of such regulations, characteristic of many developing countries, have also stifled investment or driven it into the informal sector, thus further increasing governmental deficits by impairing revenue collection. In a large number of developing countries, such deficits, which themselves also serve to add to investors' lack of confidence, have been exacerbated by continuous subventions to inefficient state enterprises. Resource constraints have in turn imposed cuts in spending on infrastructure and social services, adding further to economic downgrading and to the suffering of the poor. Currency overvaluation has also been a particular problem in the poorly performing regions of Latin America and Sub-Saharan Africa.

The complexity of the domestic circumstances under which external difficulties are being faced in developing countries also promises to increase. There seems to be a general and growing realization that the role of government in economic activities has reached its peak and may well be reversed in future. Such a role was greatly expanded in the 1970s, fuelled by increased income and borrowing in the oil-exporting countries and by easy credit in the others. In several countries, public expenditure as a percentage of GDP increased dramatically with serious implications for management efficiency and financing of governments.

Many developing countries are also experienc-ing democratization processes. Others are still struggling with domestic pressures combined, in some cases, with occasional but increasing break-downs in the system of governance and administration. The desperation of the world's poor in the context of mass urbanization movements poses particular threats in this context. Concern for human rights is simultaneously building up on a world-wide scale. In addition, the diversity of situations among developing countries continues to grow with, as noted earlier, some registering significant economic success and many others suffering increasing decline and isolation from world trade and finance.

While these domestic factors must be acknowledged and corrected, the effects of external factors beyond the control of these countries should not be under-estimated. Nor should the above-mentioned facts be allowed to justify reductions of the much needed external assistance to developing countries in the future.

The domestic developments of the 1980s took place in the context of major international changes. The most important developments in the latter part of the decade have been those occurring in the Soviet Union and Eastern Europe, with the resulting changes in East–West relations. Along with the growing economic strength of Japan and Germany, greater integration in Europe and the strong economic performance of India, China and Southeast Asian countries, an economically multi-polar world has emerged. In such a world, and with the possible continued relative decline of the US economy, the strategic rationales that have in the past been offered to support development assistance may come increasingly into question in the 1990s. With aid flows being also channelled to the 'transforming' economies of Eastern Europe, the possibility of significant real increases in the total level (let alone in terms of percentage of the donors' GNP) of official development assistance to the traditional developing countries, especially to the 'aid-dependent' ones, seems to be slim indeed. Recent experience further indicates that the prospects are bleak for significant new commercial lending to overcome the resource constraints which limit the ability of the poorer developing countries to invest enough to regenerate growth in the 1990s. More recently, the unfortunate developments in the Middle East seem to have complicated the situation further and to have created additional constraints on the growth prospects in industrial and developing countries alike.

The already noted 'two-track' feature of world development now seems likely to be strengthened, with trade and growth increasingly being concentrated among relatively small numbers of mostly industrialized countries. The ongoing scientific revolution with its impact on rapid technological changes and, in certain industries, on decreasing reliance on labour and/or primary commodities is also confined to a large extent to this group of countries. As a result, developing countries may increasingly lose the comparative advantages they have traditionally enjoyed in terms of less costly labour and abundant raw materials. Increasing deterioration of physical capital and of the quality of education adds to the disadvantages that many of these countries face in competing in world markets. The trend towards the formation of strong economic blocs among groups of developed countries could also add to the marginalization of developing countries, especially if post-1992 Europe concentrates on its internal trade. Meanwhile, the degradation of the global environment, caused for the most part by activities in the industrial world, continues to the detriment of all. Fortunately, however, a growing awareness of the interdependence of development and the environment is taking hold with the realization that economic growth, in the absence of sound environmental policies, depletes the earth's natural resources and places growing pressures on the earth's assimilative capacity (World Bank 1990c: 9).

If the growth patterns that characterized the 1980s were repeated in the 1990s, the highly indebted countries (both low- and middle-income) would find themselves with at least an additional 165 million people and with real per capita incomes lower than today (World Bank 1990a: 16), in many cases much lower than the near subsistence levels that are now widespread. Most of the 850 million people expected to be born in developing countries during the new decade would find themselves in poverty (World Bank 1990a: 138). The challenge of this decade is to reverse this trend.

Some positive signs

The economic prospects for the 1990s may thus be daunting and have been made more so by recent events. However, they are not without hope. While the 1980s may have been a 'lost decade' for many developing countries, large numbers of them have improved on, or at least not lost, the gains of the 1970s and previous years. Countries of Southeast Asia provide the most striking example in this regard. The debt crisis of the middle-income countries, though by no means completely resolved, no longer poses a vital threat to the principal commercial banks and may thus be more susceptible now to orderly solutions. There also seems to be a growing consensus that further action is needed among the Paris Club creditors to develop new options in addressing the mounting official debt of lower–middle-income countries, as evidenced by the declaration of the Economic Summit of Industrialized Nations held in Houston on 9–11 July 1990 and in the individual actions of some official creditors. The official debt of Sub-Saharan low-income countries is also being forgiven. The recession of the early 1980s has been followed by one of the longest periods of peace-time expansion in industrial countries which may hold on despite recent doubts. Western financial markets (including Japan's) are evolving into a global financial market and efforts are under way in the Uruguay Round of the GATT and other fora to liberalize international trade (*World Bank Annual Report* 1990: 35–7). According to World Bank staff estimates, industrialized countries were expected, before the recent Middle East events, to maintain strong real growth in the 1990s (at about 3 per cent a year); world real interest rates were also expected to ease and commodity prices to rise gradually (World Bank 1990a: 16). Such positive developments may now be in some doubt but they promise to benefit developing countries, especially if the trade restrictions that were widely imposed in the 1980s are also eased. Average real growth for developing countries in the 1990s was estimated in the 1990 World Development Report at 5.1 per cent a year (World Bank 1990a: 16, Table 1.3) compared with 4.3 per cent in the 1980s (World Bank 1990a), though this would be due in large measure to continued strong performances by East Asian countries in particular. Such high expectations may have to be revised, however, in view of the latest developments.

The changes in East–West relations should, however, provide new opportunities to generate greater effectiveness in co-operative problem solving and, eventually, a reduction in world-wide military expenditures. If such a 'peace dividend' is achieved at all, it may release for development purposes part of the huge sums – some $900 billion in 1989 alone – spent by NATO and Warsaw Pact countries for military purposes.[11] However, in the light of recent developments in the Gulf area, it is not clear again whether this hope will have a serious chance of being fulfilled.

PROSPECTS FOR THE WORLD BANK GROUP

Objectives and priorities

Against the backdrop of such rapidly changing and uncertain circumstances, the World Bank (including its affiliated institutions) will be guided by its fundamental and long-standing development mission of promoting economic growth with a view to reducing poverty and improving the standards of living world-wide. To achieve this objective, the Bank must in the first place remain a viable financial institution able to mobilize resources in the international capital markets and in the donor community at the most appropriate terms and in the amounts required to support developing country efforts. The overall mission of such a financially strong institution requires progress towards a number of broad strategic

objectives which were defined in a Bank staff report prepared in 1989 in terms of five inter-related elements:

1   to mobilize adequate external resources to meet the investment needs of developing countries;
2   to devise cost-effective and environmentally sustainable means of reducing poverty and bringing poor people into the mainstream of economic growth;
3   to sustain and extend policy reforms which enhance equitable and efficient growth;
4   to develop human resources and institutional capacity in member countries; and
5   to strengthen developing countries' credit-worthiness and access to global financial markets and to a range of efficient financial services.

Such objectives may be simply summed up in one purpose: to foster economic growth which is sustainable and equitable and which reduces poverty the most.

Meeting such long-term objectives while making the best use of the Bank's comparative advantage requires changes in priorities which have already started to be reflected in Bank Group operations. These priorities shall be addressed within the framework of the Bank's mandate as expressed in its Articles of Agreement and taking into consideration the historical context of the Bank's operations and the fact that long-term planning and projections are always subject to variables which may be impossible to predict. It is possible, however, to state with some degree of certainty that the Bank's main concern will continue to be poverty alleviation through economic growth and that this will require greater attention to human resource development, expansion of income-earning opportunities and the extension of basic social services to the poor. Sustainable economic growth will also require a strong role in addressing the debt problem and in ensuring that growth will sustain rather than undermine the environment. Given prevailing trends in the Bank's member countries, such growth is likely to be generated more through private sector development than through the further expansion of state enterprises.

In pursuing these objectives the Bank is likely to take into consideration not only the appropriateness of the economic policies pursued by its borrowing members, but also the way the borrowing members' economies are actually being managed. This issue, increasingly referred to as 'good government', has proved to be of vital importance both for developing countries and for the external sources of development finance. The Bank's efforts in this respect are likely to concentrate on the effectiveness of its assistance, the strengthening of relevant government institutions and the streamlining of their rules and procedures, rather than on the broader political considerations which the Bank is prohibited under its Articles from taking into account.[12] In other words, the Bank is called upon to ensure that the funds it provides or administers on behalf of other donors are put to good use and that the assisted economy as a whole is managed according to rational policies and objective rules which are actually applied to all the persons and situations addressed by them. This is basically the 'rule of law' concept which assumes a government characterized by the integrity and competence of its public service and based on rules which are followed in practice under a system of accountability.

Types and sectoral distribution of loans

Although, since the Bank's reorganization in 1986, Bank operations have become more focused on the borrowing country's overall needs and policies than merely on individual projects, investment lending, mostly for specific project purposes, accounted for over two-thirds (66.3 per cent) of total operations throughout the 1980s. This emphasis is consistent with the Bank's basic mandate and the explicit requirements of its charter. Lending in support of policy reform, the so-called structural and sectoral adjustment loans, and other non-project lending accounted for 17.5 per cent. The remaining 16.2 per cent were accounted for by lending to financial intermedi-

aries, technical assistance and supplemental loans. Only one operation was approved, at the end of calendar year 1989, for the purpose of reducing the debt burden of a member country (*World Bank Annual Report* 1982–9).

In the sectoral distribution of loans, agriculture and rural development accounted in the 1980s for the largest share of commitments (23.7 per cent), followed by energy and power (19.7 per cent), telecommunications and transportation (13.3 per cent), urban public services (9.6 per cent), development finance companies (9.1 per cent), industry (6.1 per cent), education (4.5 per cent), small-scale enterprises (2.8 per cent), population, health and nutrition (1.3 per cent), technical assistance (0.7 per cent) and public sector management (0.4 per cent). Non-project loans, other than sectoral adjustment loans, accounted for the remaining 8.8 per cent (*World Bank Annual Report* 1982–9).

While any forecast of the *magnitude and types of future operations* over the 1990s may be difficult to make with certainty, some trends may readily be ascertained, especially for the early years of the decade. The country focus is likely to be further emphasized in the Bank's operations. This is a process which involves an assessment of the country's development challenges and needs and the formulation of Bank assistance programmes accordingly. Volume expansion in Bank operations is also planned for most borrowing members, barring unforeseen downrisks. The actual level of lending in FY89 was $16.4 billion for the IBRD and $4.9 billion for the IDA (*World Bank Annual Report* 1989: 11). In FY90 the level reached $15.2 billion and $5.5 billion respectively (*World Bank Annual Report* 1990: 13), despite higher projected figures. It is now expected to reach $54 billion for the IBRD (World Bank 1990e: 4) and $17.7 billion for the IDA (World Bank 1990e: 6) over the subsequent three years FY91–3 on the basis of presently available capital resources. Actual levels may of course reach lower or higher figures depending mainly on the prospects of growth in recipient countries, on the degree of their readiness to adopt economic reforms and, of course, on whether new borrowing members are added to the present list.

In this expansionary context, *adjustment lending* (World Bank 1990d: 1ff.), i.e. lending to finance the phased reduction of a country's balance-of-payments deficit in order to facilitate implementation of agreed policy reforms, is likely to continue in most of the 1990s above the average level achieved in the 1980s, which was 18 per cent of total lending by the IBRD and 12 per cent by the IDA. This average reflects a modest start (8 per cent and 4 per cent respectively in 1980–2) with a generally steady growth during the decade to levels of 17.5 per cent in adjustment lending commitments for the IBRD and 23.8 per cent for the IDA in FY90 (*World Bank Annual Report* 1990: 13, 55). At present, adjustment lending is planned to account for 20 per cent of total commitments in FY90–2 but a reduction of this share is envisaged for subsequent years.

Lending for commercial debt and debt service reduction, so far extended to the Philippines and Mexico and now envisaged for Venezuela and Morocco, may expand further to cover the overall share planned for this new type of lending under the Bank's debt strategy inspired by the Brady initiative. Such a share may reach the level of 7 per cent of overall Bank lending this year. It may grow later to the agreed level of about 25 per cent of a country's adjustment lending programme or 10 per cent of its overall lending programme over a three-year period, and possibly, where justified, up to 15 per cent of this programme. Lending for this purpose, however, may be constrained by a number of factors including the fact that it should not materialize in the absence of an adequate financing plan for the country over the medium term or if the debt reduction involved fails to meet the materiality test (i.e. if in the Bank's judgement it will not have a significant positive impact on the investment prospects in the country).

Bank *lending to financial intermediaries* may experience some contraction due to financial difficulties facing such intermediaries in many countries and an emerging more disciplined Bank policy in their regard. Lending for this purpose, however, later on in the decade is likely to increase consistently with the Bank's emphasis on private

sector development unless a new division of labour between the Bank and the IFC causes the Bank to give the IFC a primary role in financing such intermediaries.

Investment lending, both for specific projects and for investment sectors and subsectors, is expected to continue to account throughout the 1990s for about two-thirds of total lending, especially in the latter part of the decade when adjustment lending begins to subside. So-called hybrid loans (having investment and policy components) may expand in this context. The scope of free-standing operations for poverty alleviation, for enhancing women's access to economic opportunities and for reconstruction efforts following wars and other emergencies is also expected to be further enlarged.

These overall trends may not, of course, materialize for every country. A large share of the lending to certain countries, especially those which are yet to start or are just starting their adjustment programmes, is likely to be for quick disbursement purposes in the form of balance-of-payments support and debt reduction. The share of adjustment lending to Sub-Saharan African countries may also continue above the general Bank's norm.

The sectoral distribution of investment loans is also likely to change in the 1990s to reflect a greater emphasis on certain sectors and issues. While agriculture may continue to be the largest single beneficiary with added emphasis on projects designed to support the poorer segments and women, human resource development, infrastructure and the protection of the environment are likely to figure more prominently in Bank lending in the 1990s, all within the broader framework of poverty alleviation. The Bank is now planning to double lending for education (to more than $1.5 billion annually (*World Bank Annual Report* 1990: 59)) and to increase its lending for population to some $800 million in FY90–2 alone (*World Bank Annual Report* 1990: 60). It is also intensifying its concern for such issues as women in development, health and nutrition (*World Bank Annual Report* 1990: 59–63). The great concern being attached to environmental issues will be reflected in the design and financing of projects with environmental impact as well as in free-standing loans for environmental preservation and improvement (*World Bank Annual Report* 1990: 63–7). Such a trend would certainly be strengthened further if the discussed initiative under discussion at present of establishing, under the Bank's auspices, a special facility for global environment projects is implemented.

Given these trends and the fact that expansion of lending for certain purposes may decrease lending for other purposes, the share of certain sectors may have to decline. This has been the case for the energy sector. The trend may continue in the 1990s unless reversed by heightened interest in this sector in the light of the recent events in the Middle East. Higher oil prices may well lead once again to such a result. However, this is an area where long-term trends and not temporary developments should have guided our members' and the Bank's actions. Recent developments may only point to the shortsightedness of not giving this sector its due attention in the last few years. At present it is impossible to predict the development of oil prices in the immediate future. Iraq and Kuwait, which are now out of production, produced over the first half of 1990 some 5 million barrels a day or about 20 per cent of OPEC output. This is being largely replaced now by other producers. In mid-1990, global petroleum stocks on land and sea amounted to 5.5 billion barrels, equivalent to one hundred days of world consumption. While these facts should restrain abrupt rises in oil prices, the tension surrounding the Gulf region and the fact that military action has not been excluded are causing nervousness in the spot market which keeps the prices at their present level. Meanwhile, the trajectory of oil prices in the near future remains unpredictable. World Bank staff can only envisage different scenarios under those circumstances. One scenario assumes a fairly rapid return to normalcy in the oil markets. A second scenario assumes a period of uncertainty extending to over a year and then a gradual return to fundamentals in the market. A third envisages a prolonged period of uncertainty extending over

several years. And a fourth speculates on the outcome for world oil markets in the event of a major military conflict. Projected prices naturally differ sharply under each scenario. While this introduces complications and confusion in planning for the near future, it is clear that at least for the remainder of 1990, and perhaps for the following year or two, there will be a significant adverse impact on low-income oil importers which have no access to commercial financial markets as well as on middle-income oil importers which are exposed both to oil price rises and to the risk of higher interest rates on their external borrowings. Some marginal oil exporters may also face large net losses as a result of disruption in their exports, reduction in remittances of workers in the Gulf region and a drop in tourism as well as higher interest rates and other factors. Such unfortunate events should at least revive interest in long-term solutions for world energy problems – solutions that do not falter once prices temporarily fall.

Another area where Bank financing is declining is public sector industrial development. A decline in lending to public enterprises will be consistent with a general trend in the Bank, as well as in its member countries, towards a greater emphasis on the private sector.

Promotion of the private sector is likely in fact to be a hallmark of Bank Group activities in the 1990s (*World Bank Annual Report* 1990: 68), because of increased concern with efficiency and flexibility as well as a concerted policy direction advocated by the Bank's major shareholders. Part of this will be reflected in the Bank's expanding research work. Another will be seen in the policy reforms required under adjustment loans, including legal reforms and support for the financial sector in particular. A third aspect will be the support for privatization and restructuring of public sector enterprises and possibly the reform of the civil service.[13] Entrepreneurial development and increasing the private sector's access to appropriate technology may receive particular attention in this respect.

The above projections of the amounts and types of Bank lending in the 1990s were made before the recent Gulf crisis arose. They still represent projected Bank activities with two possible additions. The Bank is now planning to provide emergency loans for purposes such as housing, settlement and job creation in the countries immediately affected by this crisis which have to absorb large numbers of returning workers. The Bank is also envisaging an expansion in its quick disbursing adjustment lending to these and other developing countries likely to be affected by the oil price rise, should the rise continue at its present level or exceed it. Efforts have in fact started in the Bank to co-ordinate aid to the immediately affected countries and to accelerate disbursement of Bank loans generally; such efforts may well expand if the adverse effects of the crisis prove to be of greater scope or longer duration than expected at present.

Increased disbursement by the IBRD in the 1980s, due to increasing loan commitments and a continued rise in fast disbursing loans, has over time increased the amount of repayments and debt service of IBRD loans. As a result, *net* disbursement by the IBRD to its borrowers became relatively modest, in spite of generally rising loan commitment levels. In fiscal years 1989 and 1990, net disbursement has averaged $3.8 billion while the average lending during these years has been $15.8 billion. This does not necessarily mean a diminishing role for the Bank with regard to the countries it assists; rather, it emphasizes the increasing importance of the other aspects of Bank activities, especially policy advice on economic reform and technical assistance. These activities have been consistently on the rise and are certain to remain so in the 1990s.

One important lesson drawn from the Bank's adjustment lending in the 1980s has been the need for increased investment in the context of stabilization and other adjustment measures. Lower investment levels have had their toll in terms of lower growth rates and other social costs to the poor. Reversing this trend requires increased external financing, where the Bank is only one actor, and alleviation of the debt overhang, where the main action depends on other actors. These factors, along with the limitations on the countries' abilities to increase their domestic savings under prevailing circumstances, add to the challenges ahead.

Membership and eligibility

In addition to the changes in the types and sectoral distribution of Bank loans, changes are taking place in the composition of Bank members and borrowers. With one possible exception, no major borrower is expected to graduate in the immediate future from IBRD lending (i.e. to reach such high per capita income, $4,080 in 1989 dollars, as to trigger its ineligibility for IBRD loans). However, some countries where per capita income was slightly above the IDA operational cut-off ($700 in 1989 dollars) are experiencing declines in per capita income to below that limit which would make them operationally eligible for IDA credits. This might invite some, perhaps modest, future changes in the present allocation of IDA resources. In addition, with the accession of new members such as Poland, Czechoslovakia and Bulgaria and the change of policy in Romania regarding borrowing from the Bank, an increasing portion of Bank operations will be directed to Eastern Europe. The level of lending to China (which has declined substantially since the events of 1989) is likely to depend for some time on the economic programme of that country and the extent to which other Bank members are likely to support such a programme. Switzerland is expected to join the Bank and will of course be a non-borrowing member. This will further strengthen the Bank's capital.

One important question the Bank will face in the 1990s is whether the Soviet Union will join the Bank as a member and whether it will be borrowing from the Bank (Feinberg 1990: 1ff.). While there are indications of some interest in this matter, it may take some time before the Soviet Union meets requirements for membership in the IMF which is a prerequisite for Bank membership. It should not be difficult to predict, however, that such a development could take place in the first half of the 1990s. Should this materialize, the Bank's capital would increase accordingly and the Soviet Union would probably become a borrower in increasing volumes, both in support of the transformation of its huge economy towards a market economy and in order to finance the modernization and expansion of its productive facilities. The admission of the Soviet Union would then complete the universality of the World Bank.

IFC operations, which have grown by an average of 25 per cent per year since FY85, amounted at the end of FY90 to some $9.7 billion in approved investments, 16 per cent more than in FY89 (*IFC Annual Report* 1990: 3). The IFC has also played a catalytic role, mobilizing funds from other sources in excess of its own. For instance, in FY90 alone it approved $1.5 billion in investments and in doing so mobilized about $8.0 billion from other sources – about $5.0 for every dollar invested by it (*IFC Annual Report* 1990: 3). By pioneering in the formation of 'developing country funds', of which many are now operating successfully, and by supporting capital market development programmes in developing countries, the IFC is also helping in the expansion of portfolio equity investment and more generally in the process of capital accumulation for investment. A doubling of IFC's capital to $2.6 billion is at present in an advanced stage of discussion. With its several innovative initiatives, such an increase should enable the IFC to play an even larger role in the 1990s.

The MIGA's activities are also growing fast despite its present modest number of operations. Over 220 applications for its insurance cover have been received, 116 have been registered of which five have been approved and sixteen are in an advanced stage of processing (MIGA 1990: 14; *World Bank Annual Report* 1990: 103). Its promotional activities have also been initiated and it is co-operating with the IFC in assisting interested governments in attracting foreign investment through a joint facility known as the Foreign Investment Advisory Service (FIAS). Although it is premature to judge MIGA's performance at this early stage, expansion of both its guarantee and

advisory roles is strongly expected in the years to come. MIGA's business plan for FY90–3 envisages approvals of some forty operations exceeding $1.3 billion.

Finally, the ICSID, which has strengthened its research and information activities in the 1980s, is expected to maintain its position as the world's foremost source of data on foreign investment law and to continue to perform its useful role in the settlement of legal disputes involving foreign investment through offering credible and effective arbitration and conciliation facilities (ICSID 1990).

CONCLUSION

Under the favourable assumptions worked out by the World Bank staff in 1990, the incidence of world poverty is expected to decline in the 1990s and the number of poor people to fall from 1.1 billion in 1985 to 825 million in 2000 (World Bank 1990a: 5). This will be a major achievement, given the expected drastic increase in total world population. Less optimistic figures appear, however, in the Human Development Report published this year by the UNDP.[14]

Even with the lower figures of the World Bank, one-sixth of humanity will still be living with a minimum income and under bare nutritional adequacy. And, most unfortunately, in some regions the number of the poor is likely to increase, raising the share of Sub-Saharan Africa to 32 per cent from its 1985 level of 16 per cent (while Asia's share is expected to drop from 72 per cent to 53 per cent). The rapid population growth will also cut annual real GDP growth per capita to much lower levels than the projected overall growth rates mentioned earlier (from 5.1 per cent overall to 3.2 per cent per capita in the 1990s; in Sub-Saharan Africa from a 3.7 per cent real rate of GDP growth to a mere 0.5 per cent per capita rate).

The level of world poverty will of course be much higher if the global economy performs less favourably than the Bank staff expected at the time of this writing (October 1990), which, unfortunately, seems to be likely now. In either case, the

Bank Group is called upon to perform an increasingly complex and important task as its member nations become more closely intertwined with each other and with the rest of the world. A third general capital increase is expected for the IBRD in the second half of the 1990s. This, in addition to periodic IDA replenishments and IFC (and perhaps MIGA) capital increases, should enable the Group to meet, albeit partially, this growing challenge.

In meeting its responsibilities, the Bank realizes that development is a long haul process which comprises in particular human development, institutional development, maintenance of an appropriate framework of policies and increased investment for productive purposes. Such aspects are planned to be actively pursued with the overall objective of sustaining growth while reducing poverty and protecting the environment. This is basically the objective of our member countries. The role of the World Bank Group is to assist them in the challenge of meeting this objective under the world's difficult and rapidly changing conditions. This important role is likely to be enhanced in the 1990s where continued reforms, reduced indebtedness and increased external financing remain essential requirements for most developing countries in a global economic context characterized by extreme volatility. Such requirements call for strong international co-operative efforts. Fortunately, present day international relations seem to be more conducive to such co-operative efforts than at any time since the Bank's establishment.

NOTES

1 The IBRD's authorized capital accounts for $171.4 billion, the IFC's for $1.3 billion and the MIGA's for $1.082 billion. The IDA's capital resources received in the form of pledged contributions total $68.6 billion. Unless otherwise indicated these and the following figures are based on data at nominal prices.

2 The World Bank Annual Report (1990) mentions the figure $125.3 billion for subscribed capital on 30 June 1990. France's subscription increased effective 30 August 1990, which accounts for the figure in the text.

3 The unit of payment of members' subscriptions

defined in the IBRD Articles of Agreement is 'gold or United States dollars' for the 2 per cent portion of the price of each share to be initially paid (Article II, Section 7(i) and Section 8(a) IBRD); 'the currency of the member' for the 18 per cent portion 'subject to call' (Article II, Section 7(i) IBRD) and 'gold, United States dollars or the currency required to discharge the obligation of the Bank' for payments made under the remaining 80 per cent as may be needed to meet the obligations of the Bank (Article II, Section 7(ii) IBRD). Actual paid-in portions of subsequent capital increases were much less than the initially envisaged percentages. Also, the gold US dollar of 30 July 1944, the standard of value of the IBRD capital, is now interpreted to mean the 1974 US dollar ($1.20635) (see Shihata 1989).

4 Total IBRD borrowing reached $9.3 billion in FY89 (*World Bank Annual Report* 1989: 11) and $11.7 billion in FY90 (*World Bank Annual Report* 1990: 76 and Table 4.1).

5 *IFC Annual Report* (1990: 13–14); these figures include the IFC African Enterprise Facility whose commitments were $1.94 million and whose disbursements amounted to $1.58 million.

6 World Bank Information Statement dated 10 September 1990 (p. 10).

7 This is the criterion often used for covering 'developing countries' (comprising low-, low–middle- and high–middle-income countries) in present World Bank documents.

8 World Bank (1987: Tables 2 and 3); World Bank (1990a: Tables 2 and 3); GATT International Trade, various publications. Adjustments have been made to the published figures shown in these sources to convert nominal values to volumes at 1980 prices and exchange rates and to provide estimates for some East European and Asian countries not reported in these sources; compare figures in Sewell (1990).

9 See the Speech of the President of the World Bank before the 1990 Bank–Fund Annual Meetings (p. 4).

10 See also the Speech of the President of the World Bank before the 1990 Bank–Fund Annual Meetings (p. 3).

11 According to World Bank sources military expenditures of NATO for 1989 accounted for $500 billion and those of Warsaw Pact countries for about $400 billion. For an outlook on defence expenditures in the 1990s, see World Bank (1990a: 17, Box 1.3).

12 See Article IV, Section 10; Article V, Section 5(c) and Article III, Section 5(b) IBRD. Similar provisions appear in the charters of the IFC, the IDA and the MIGA.

13 *World Bank Annual Report* (1990: 87ff.); for more

details see World Bank (1989b).

14 See UNDP (1990: 61) where it is envisaged that 1.5 billion people will be living in poverty by the end of the century.

REFERENCES

Feinberg, R. E. (1990) *The Soviet Union and the Bretton Woods Institutions: Risk and Rewards of Membership*, Public Policy Papers, Institute for East–West Security Studies.

ICSID (International Centre for Settlement of Investment Disputes) (1990) *Annual Report*, Washington, DC: World Bank.

IFC Annual Report (1956–90) Washington, DC: World Bank.

MIGA (Multilateral Investment Guarantee Agency) (1990) *Annual Report*, Washington, DC: World Bank.

Sewell, J. W. (1990) 'The metamorphosis of the Third World: US interest in the 1990's', in W. R. Brock and R. D. Hormats (eds) *The Global Economy: America's Role in the Decade Ahead*, New York: W. W. Norton, ch. 5.

Shihata, I. F. I. (1989) 'The "gold dollar" as a measure of capital valuation after termination of the par value system: the case of the IBRD capital', *German Yearbook of International Law* 32: 55–86.

UNDP (United Nations Development Programme) (1990) *Human Development Report*, Washington, DC: United Nations.

World Bank (1987) *World Development Report: World Development Indicators*, Washington, DC: World Bank.

World Bank (1989–90) *World Debt Tables*, vol. 1, Washington, DC: World Bank.

World Bank (1989a) *The Role of Foreign Direct Investment in Financing Developing Countries*, Washington, DC: World Bank, 24 July, sec. M89-998.

World Bank (1989b) *Developing the Private Sector – A Challenge for the World Bank*, Washington, DC: World Bank.

World Bank (1990a) *World Development Report: World Development Indicators*, Washington, DC: World Bank.

World Bank (1990b) *The Developing Countries and the Short-term Outlook for the Global Economy*, Washington, DC: World Bank, 3 August, sec. M90-1039 (limited circulation).

World Bank (1990c) 'The World Bank and the environment', *First Annual Report Fiscal*, Washington, DC: World Bank.

World Bank (1990d) *Adjustment Lending Policies for Sustainable Growth*, Policy and Research Series 14.

World Bank (1990e) Internal report on the IBRD/IDA programmes and budgets for the fiscal year ending 30 June 1991, sec. M90-1049, IDA/sec. M90-305, 6 August (limited circulation).

World Bank Annual Report (1962–90) Washington, DC: World Bank.

5

THE INTERNATIONAL MONETARY FUND'S ADJUSTMENT POLICIES AND ECONOMIC DEVELOPMENT

Jacob A. Frenkel and Mohsin S. Khan

INTRODUCTION

The Articles of Agreement of the IMF (hereafter the Fund) state that the promotion of trade, the increasing of levels of employment and real income and the development of productive resources are to be the primary objectives of economic policy (Article I). While the Fund's major area of concern may in practice be balance-of-payments disequilibrium, the policies it recommends to reduce the degree and duration of external and internal imbalances must be set within the context of achieving and maintaining satisfactory rates of economic growth. In general, therefore, the Fund aims at assisting its member countries to establish conditions that would yield balance-of-payments viability, price stability and a growth rate that would support a steady improvement in living standards.

In analysing Fund policies designed to achieve these multiple objectives, it is useful first to consider the circumstances in which the Fund is called in to assist in designing an adjustment programme and to provide financial support for it. Definitionally the need for a stabilization programme, whether supported by the Fund or otherwise, arises when a country experiences a persisting imbalance between aggregate domestic demand (absorption) and aggregate supply, which is reflected in a worsening of its external payments position. This imbalance may be due to external factors – such as an exogenous deterioration of the terms of trade or an increase in foreign interest

rates – or to inappropriate domestic policies that expand aggregate domestic demand too rapidly relative to the productive potential of the economy. As long as foreign financing is available, the relative expansion of domestic demand can be sustained for an extended period – albeit at the cost of a persisting current account deficit, a loss of international competitiveness and distortions in relative prices owing to rapid inflation, an inefficient allocation of resources and a heavier foreign debt burden.

It is obvious that this disequilibrium cannot persist indefinitely. The country would eventually lose international creditworthiness and the cessation of foreign financing would necessitate adjustment. This forced adjustment may be abrupt and is likely to be very disruptive for the economy. The basic objective of the Fund is to press for the adoption of appropriate policies before the crisis emerges and to provide for a more orderly adjustment of the imbalance between absorption and domestic supply within a reasonable period of time.

The first order of business in these circumstances is to stabilize the economy – lower the inflation rate, restore competitiveness, reduce the current account deficit and check the loss of international reserves – by correcting the macroeconomic imbalances that gave rise to the problems. But it is clear that adjustment cannot be durable if it is not followed by satisfactory growth, so that even if the immediate aim is restoring macroeconomic stability in the economy the Fund cannot lose sight of the growth objective. Once stability is assured, then policies to expand the productive capacity of the economy and improve the efficiency with which resources are utilized are more likely to be successful. Experience and theory suggest that such a pattern of sequencing of macroeconomic and structural policies is warranted.

Although growth is a central element in the Fund's objectives, it should be stressed that the Fund is not a development agency. Its mandate is to provide temporary financial support and not development aid. Consequently, the Fund does not have a 'development paradigm' as such. Nevertheless, by establishing macroeconomic equilibrium in the economy, the Fund can be said to provide the necessary foundation on which development is based. Furthermore, the Fund has been increasingly emphasizing structural reforms in its policy advice, and while this change stems from the recognition that economic stability cannot be regained in the absence of basic institutional and economic changes, such reforms obviously have a direct bearing on long-term growth and the structural transformations that are part of the development process.

The purpose of this chapter is to outline in broad terms the policy content of Fund-supported adjustment programmes, and particularly how these policies are expected to achieve macroeconomic stability and higher growth. The discussion of policies, which include aggregate demand policies, structural policies, exchange rate policies and external debt policies, is taken up in the next section. The empirical relationship between general macroeconomic stability and long-run economic growth in a large sample of sixty-nine developing countries over the period 1973–88 is examined in the third section. The concluding section pulls together the main propositions of the chapter and the lessons that can be drawn on the role of Fund policies in economic development.

FUND ECONOMIC POLICIES

To achieve the goals of balance-of-payments viability, price stability and a sustained satisfactory rate of economic growth, the Fund helps countries to design a comprehensive package of economic policies (IMF 1987). The policy measures differ across countries, but each package has certain common features. The most important characteristic of the Fund policy package is perhaps the emphasis placed on the role of the market and relative prices in the expansion and allocation of resources. This is the reason that measures to reduce distortions created by, among others, price rigidities, monopolies and imperfect competition, taxes, subsidies, trade restrictions and other direct controls over different facets of economic activity are generally given prominence in Fund-supported adjustment programmes. Experience has shown that measures such as the decentralization of economic decisions and the use of realistic prices to guide such decisions can improve the efficiency of production and investment in a variety of political and institutional settings.[1]

However, this emphasis on 'getting prices right' is not to suggest that the Fund sees no role for the government in the economy or that it is opposed to any and all forms of government intervention. The standard economic case for government intervention, i.e. when there is evidence of obvious market failure, is well appreciated, as are the arguments that developing-country governments need to provide the basic infrastructure for development to take place. The general market orientation has implications for the type of development strategy that can be adopted, but it should be stressed that this is not why the Fund advocates the policies it does. Indeed, the Fund is neutral on development strategies[2] and its policies are geared to achieving the best possible macroeconomic outcomes under the given circumstances.

The Fund also recognizes that governments pursue a wide variety of policy objectives, and these may at times conflict. For example, as noted by Tanzi (1986), from an economic standpoint governments have allocation and distribution functions, in addition to a stabilization role. Allocation includes, *inter alia*, many non-economic functions of the government, such as defence. Even these non-economic functions, however, require budgetary expenditures and therefore play a role in economic decision-making that impinges on stabilization policy. Similarly, governments often have distributional goals, such as assisting particular sectors or groups in the economy that are deemed to be especially in need or to promote a more equitable distribution of income and wealth. Attempts to achieve such goals have often led to the establishment of complicated tax systems, subsidy schemes, licensing, price controls, selective credit and interest rate regulations and other measures. The pursuit of allocation and distributional objectives may thus impede the adoption of measures required to correct a balance-of-payments disequilibrium and liberalize the economic system. Required cuts in fiscal expenditure may be omitted because the government is unwilling to cut back on budget items reflecting its priorities in the areas of allocation and distribution; or it may be unwilling to eliminate an import and foreign exchange licensing system that is designed to channel foreign exchange to preferred activities. The Fund's position on such issues is that the ultimate decision is that of the government, provided the totality of relevant tax and expenditure decisions is consistent with the overall budget constraint.

What then are the policies that would be considered to achieve balance-of-payments viability in the context of low inflation and improved growth performance? In general, most economists would tend to subscribe to the following set of measures:

1 monetary restraint aimed at reducing the growth of absorption and the rate of inflation – however, care should be taken to prevent the private sector from being crowded out of the credit markets;

2 setting interest rates at positive real levels, but not so high as to choke off investment and possibly cause the collapse of financial institutions – thus, generally speaking, real interest rates should be positive but low;

3 reduction in the fiscal deficit through cuts in government expenditures and/or increases in taxes – account should be taken of the relationship between public and private saving and public and private investment in the method chosen to reduce the deficit; e.g. under some circumstances an increase in public saving may lead to a partially offsetting fall in private saving; also, private and public investment may be complementary, to the extent that the public sector provides the necessary infrastructure, and thus reductions in public investment may have adverse effects on private investment and growth (see Blejer and Khan 1984);

4 exchange rate action to ensure a real exchange rate that would improve international competitiveness and create the incentive to expand the production of internationally tradeable goods;

5 policies to reduce external debt if it is perceived as being currently unsustainable, or to limit foreign borrowing if it is likely to become so in the future;

6 introducing structural reforms, i.e. financial reforms, producer pricing policies, trade reforms etc., to make the economy more flexible and efficient.

In the remainder of this section we shall discuss these policies, grouping them into the following four categories: aggregate demand policies; structural policies; exchange rate policies; and external debt policies.[3]

Aggregate demand policies

In controlling aggregate demand the Fund relies primarily on monetary and fiscal restraint.[4] How these traditional policies work is, of course, very familiar. On the monetary policy side one can start with the case of a small open economy where the transmission mechanism is described in versions of the monetary approach to the balance of payments (see IMF 1977, 1987; Frenkel and Johnson 1976, 1978; Frenkel and Mussa 1985). This approach holds that, with fixed exchange rates, an expansion of the domestic component of the money stock (domestic credit) in excess of the growth of money demand induces the public to dispose of surplus money by acquiring foreign goods and securities – a worsening of the balance of payments – leaving the long-run values of domestic output and prices unaffected. When exchange rates are fully flexible, a similar expansion in domestic credit results in an increase in the money supply, a proportional depreciation of the domestic currency and a corresponding rise in the domestic price level. Once again, in the ultimate equilibrium output is unaffected.

But questions have been raised about whether such a model is applicable to most developing countries where financial markets are underdeveloped, interest rates are set below market-clearing levels by the government, a relatively free curb market operates and foreign exchange controls are in force. How does monetary policy operate under these conditions?

Assuming that exchange controls are effective, the central bank can determine the monetary base through its control over the availability of foreign exchange and its provision of credit to the government and to the banks. Starting from portfolio equilibrium, a fall in the supply of credit to the private sector will reduce absorption through wealth effects and cause borrowers to turn to the curb markets, pushing up interest rates there and causing the interest-sensitive components of aggregate demand to decline. In particular, in line with the Tobin Q mechanism, the implicit value of real assets will fall relative to their production costs, and demand for such assets will be reduced. The decline in aggregate demand will tend to improve the current account of the balance of payments and put downward pressure on inflation. Similarly, a decrease in the money supply leaves the private sector with too little money in its portfolio relative to loans and real assets. As a result, the supply of curb market loans falls, leading to a rise in curb market interest rates and a

reduction in demand. Even though the changes in the money supply may be neutral in the long run, during the adjustment process a restrictive monetary policy reduces capacity utilization and raises unemployment. The size and duration of the deflationary effect will depend on, among other things, the stickiness of prices, wage-setting behaviour, the degree of slack in the economy, the interest-sensitivity of investment decisions and the extent to which policies were anticipated when wage contracts were negotiated.

In the area of fiscal policy, the direct effects of changes in government expenditures are fairly familiar. Government spending on goods and services is itself a component of domestic expenditure, and as such it contributes directly to absorption. If government purchases are limited to non-tradeable goods, they add to domestic aggregate demand. If they are limited to tradeable goods, however, they have no direct effect on domestic aggregate demand, output or inflation; they only worsen the trade balance.

There is much controversy, however, over the indirect effects of government purchases. At issue is the extent to which an increase in government spending reduces or increases private spending, thus resulting in a rise in total spending different from the original increases in government expenditure. Private spending can be affected if the extra government expenditure is viewed as a substitute for, or a complement to, that of the private sector, or if it increases the private sector's tax liability either now or in the future. The latter is the well-known Ricardian equivalence proposition developed by Barro (1974).[5] The limited empirical evidence on rational expectations models of government and private spending does not support the extreme view of a complete offset however (see Haque and Montiel 1989).

Taxes on the private sector affect work–leisure, consumption–saving and investment choices, as well as private disposable income. The effect of a change in private disposable income on private spending is likely to depend on whether the tax is viewed as temporary or permanent; on the characteristics of the taxpayers, including demographic factors such as age and household size (since these affect the marginal propensity to save); and on the nature of the credit markets (which will affect the extent to which taxpayers are liquidity constrained). Transfers have exactly the opposite effect of taxes and should increase private absorption.

All in all, theory and empirical evidence can be used to support the proposition that in practice a reduction in the fiscal deficit tends to reduce aggregate demand. *Ceteris paribus*, this improves the balance of payments and reduces inflationary pressures in the economy.[6] Furthermore, as developing countries rely heavily on bank financing of fiscal deficits, an improvement in the budget position should reduce the amount of liquidity being injected into the system. For both these reasons – reducing the claim on resources and monetary expansion – cutting the fiscal deficit becomes an essential, if not the most critical, element of an adjustment programme.

Structural policies

Structural reforms are now part and parcel of adjustment programmes, and the basic concern of the Fund is how such reforms can help in achieving the objectives of medium-term external and internal balance. Frequently efforts to shift resources away from inefficient uses are impeded by various institutional rigidities, and in this context structural reforms to eliminate or offset these rigidities play a critical role in achieving balance-of-payments viability and in laying the basis for durable economic growth that, in turn, is necessary to sustain the adjustment effort. Thus, policies which influence aggregate demand and structural policies are to be viewed as complements. The structural reforms included in Fund policy packages vary from country to country, with the objective being to achieve the required transformation of the economy and to avoid a policy mix that places too much weight on demand-management measures that may not be able to address the deep-seated structural problems of developing countries.

Structural policies can take many forms

depending on the nature of the economy and the types of problems it faces. Broadly speaking, structural policies include measures to improve efficiency and resource allocation, as well as policies to expand the productive capacity of the economy. The former group includes all measures to reduce the distortions that drive a wedge between prices and marginal costs, while the latter includes policies that promote investment and saving. Naturally under these broad headings would fall a whole host of structural reforms. Here we shall consider only three particular ones: (a) trade reforms; (b) agricultural pricing reforms; and (c) financial sector reforms.[7]

Trade reforms

There is a large and growing literature pointing to the inefficiencies created by artificial barriers to foreign trade.[8] Tariffs, quotas and other restrictions on trade and payments reduce the volume of trade and the amount of specialization and tend to foster import-substituting industries that lack efficiency and flexibility of firms continuously exposed to international competition. Several studies – e.g. Balassa (1982) and Krueger *et al.* (1981) – have shown that countries with outward-looking strategies have generally fared better in terms of growth, employment and adjustment to external shocks than those following an inward-looking approach. The outward-oriented strategies basically call for the appropriate incentives for domestic production to shift towards exporting or competing with imports. The relative success of these policies has prompted considerable efforts to encourage developing countries to create incentives for the production of tradeables and to liberalize their trading systems (see Edwards 1989; Krueger 1985).

While the appropriate design and speed of trade liberalization will be affected by a variety of factors, such as the extent and degree of protection in the particular country, the availability of foreign financing, the existence of other structural rigidities, the commitment of the government to reforms and the implementation of other supporting macroeconomic policies, some general lessons have emerged from experience. The first step in the liberalization process is to move from quantitative restrictions to tariffs.[9] After price differentials have been established as the main instrument of protection, targets and timetables can be set for their reduction. The next step in the process is to lower effective tariff protection and reduce the dispersion of tariffs. This can be done in one step or gradually over time depending on the circumstances of the individual country. Good arguments can be made on either side, and the Fund is not wedded to one particular way. The whole idea is to get factor prices right, improve the allocation of resources and reduce the anti-export bias, thereby strengthening the balance of payments. In some cases it may be possible to move to lower tariffs across the board quickly, but in others it may be useful to introduce timetables specifying the changes to occur and the final tariff levels.[10]

Agricultural pricing reforms

Governments often fix the prices of agricultural commodities at levels below those prevailing in world markets. The purpose of such a policy is to stabilize producer prices and income and to subsidize the food consumption of the urban population. When this policy results in severe distortions of producer prices or in wide-ranging subsidization, it can have a powerful effect on the level and allocation of agriculture production and on consumption. Given the importance of the agricultural sector in many developing countries, inappropriate producer pricing policies can have a direct impact on the achievement of macro-economic stability and a sustainable balance of payments. Marketing boards, which are common-place in these countries, are the regulatory bodies administering prices and purchasing the bulk of the farmers' output. If a marketing board tries to increase its revenues (or reduce its losses) by holding prices below world levels, it is effectively taxing output. This creates disincentives to both production and exports and can increase imports

and smuggling. To the extent that the marketing board runs at a loss and requires transfers to cover these, the agricultural pricing policy can cause fiscal problems for the government.

Obviously, raising prices to world levels would be beneficial from both the production and fiscal standpoints. Empirical evidence suggests that higher producer prices will lead to an increase in output, particularly in the longer run (see Bond 1983). There is little quantitative support for the 'elasticity pessimism' view that prevails in some circles. While the ultimate aim may be to have a system where agricultural prices are freely determined in the market-place, it may be necessary to go through certain intermediate stages to prevent a disruption of existing production, marketing and institutional arrangements. The first step could be initially to set prices at the world level and then follow that up by having a procedure for maintaining the relationship between domestic and world prices. At the final stage the system could be fully liberalized, with domestic marketing and exporting being undertaken by the private sector.

Financial reforms

The importance of the financial sector in mobilizing resources to support investment and growth makes it a prime target for reform. In many developing countries the financial system is tightly controlled by the government and ceilings are placed on nominal interest rates. With inflation, such controls have resulted in strongly negative real rates of interest. Real financial savings have grown less rapidly than the real economy; and disintermediation, particularly through curb markets or capital flight, has been a serious problem. Such developments can sharply restrict the availability of credit through the financial system and thereby inhibit the level and efficiency of investment. Since available credit is often allocated to large firms and state enterprises first, finance for small firms and households can be severely rationed; as a result, uneconomic projects are often undertaken at the expense of more efficient ones.

The Fund policy prescription in this situation is to press for positive real interest rates and for policies to make the financial system more efficient. The government must be able to reassure domestic savers that they will earn real returns that are competitive with those abroad. This assurance is an essential step in promoting balance-of-payments adjustment, increasing foreign investment and preventing capital flight.

But it needs to be stressed that changes in interest rates and other financial reforms designed to improve the competitiveness and efficiency of the financial system must be co-ordinated with other measures in a programme. Experience suggests that this co-ordination is especially important during the early phases of the reform process (see World Bank 1989). In particular, certain combinations of policies can disrupt a financial system – through the emergence of very high real interest rates and the collapse of banks – that is undergoing structural change (see, for example, Diaz-Alejandro 1985; Corbo and de Melo 1985). The fiscal situation must be brought under control to avoid sharp changes in the flow of funds in and out of the financial system. And interest rate policy has to be co-ordinated with exchange rate policy to ensure that capital movements do not destabilize the financial reform. Successful liberalization can also require institutional changes – strengthening of the legal protection of property rights, changes in bank supervision procedures, expansion of private domestic banks, eased entry of foreign banks, creation of a capital market and reform of publicly owned financial institutions.

In summary, structural reforms can help in a very fundamental way in the adjustment process. Nevertheless, it is worth noting that such reforms are not without difficulties. Some of the more obvious ones are, first, that by their very nature distortions tend to be microeconomic, and microeconomic policy measures suffer from certain theoretical weaknesses. Very soon one runs up against the propositions of the theory of the second best, and it is not always clear whether removing only some distortions will produce an increase in efficiency and welfare in the economy overall.

Second, there is the issue of time lags, which is very relevant to the Fund as a short-term lender.[11] Substantial time may be needed for structural policies to show results. Major shifts in resource allocation may entail a significant rise in capital formation in expanding sectors, combined with the release of capital and labour from the contracting sectors. If capital and labour do not move easily from sector to sector, changes in relative prices and incentives may produce unemployment for a long period before adjustment can be completed. Foreign financing is essential to ensure that the adjustment is as costless as possible, and this is what the Fund attempts to arrange through its own resources, as well as by playing a catalytic role in mobilizing external funds.

Finally, if reforms cannot proceed simultaneously, in what sequence should they be implemented? Unfortunately, economic theory provides little guidance on the optimal sequence, and experience in countries that have undertaken reforms suggests that the interaction between structural policies is complex and does not permit one to generalize easily. The one lesson from experience that does emerge is that domestic goods and labour markets should be liberalized prior to trade liberalization. Artificial controls on wages or on labour mobility can undo all that the trade liberalization is designed to achieve. Similarly, it has been argued that the liberalization of the trade account of the balance of payments should precede that of the capital account, since asset markets adjust more rapidly than goods markets and the opposite sequence could result in large capital movements that could adversely affect the real exchange rate (see Frenkel 1982, 1987; Khan and Zahler 1983). There are also good theoretical and empirical reasons to suggest that macroeconomic stabilization and effective bank supervision should generally precede large-scale domestic financial sector liberalization. Other than these very broad lessons there is not much more one can deduce, and accordingly the Fund needs to proceed on a case-by-case basis on the pace and sequencing of structural reforms.

Exchange rate policies

Devaluation is often required in adjustment programmes to correct the overvaluation of the domestic currency that occurred during the period leading up to the programme. This change in the exchange rate is aimed at improving international competitiveness and increasing the incentive to produce tradeable goods, and as devaluation affects absorption and domestic supply it contains elements of both aggregate demand and structural policies.

The main theoretical aspects of devaluation have been discussed extensively (see Dornbusch 1980). Consider, for example, the textbook case of a small country that cannot affect its terms of trade. A devaluation increases foreign prices measured in domestic currency terms and thus, in the domestic economy, increases the price of tradeable goods relative to non-traded goods. On the demand side, the effect of a devaluation on absorption is negative: the rise in the overall price level reduces the real value of private sector financial assets (denominated in domestic currency) and also of those factor incomes whose nominal values do not rise proportionally with the devaluation. On the supply side, however, devaluation will boost output and cause a shift of factors to the tradeable goods sector as long as the prices of (variable) domestic factors of production rise proportionally less than the domestic currency price of final output. In other words, if devaluation succeeds in changing the real exchange rate, regarded by many as the most important relative price in the economy, then it will have structural consequences.

The above analysis is quite straightforward, but it highlights the importance of getting the 'right' real exchange rate. But this is no easy task. Two particular issues arise in this context: (a) What is the appropriate change in the nominal exchange rate in order to achieve a target real exchange rate? (b) What are the effects of a change in the real exchange rate?

Size of exchange rate adjustment

The issue of choosing a target value for the real exchange rate and thus the size of the devaluation needed to achieve this target is an extremely complex one. In theory one can work out the real exchange rate that would yield a pattern of consumption and production such that there would be steady improvement in the balance of payments. But this would require a general equilibrium model that would specify the relevant relationships between the exchange rate, imports, exports, capital flows, inflation etc. Needless to say, for most developing countries this type of model does not exist and the absence of data often precludes the construction of such models.

Therefore, it has become common practice in developing countries to employ various versions of PPP calculations, such as indices of real exchange rates based on some combination of export and import weights, to assess the extent of the overvaluation. These indices are quite useful when prices at home are rising considerably faster than abroad; in those circumstances, judgements about the size of the devaluation that is needed can be reasonably accurate. All one has to do is assume that a particular real exchange rate was 'right' at some base period and use that as the target. Obviously this approach can be subject to considerable error but, in the absence of a full-blown model, one has to cut corners and use what is available. What should be stressed is that this index, and indeed any index, has only a limited value and should only be used with caution and with as much additional information on trade flows, capital movements, the exchange rate in the parallel market etc. as possible.

Once a target for the real exchange rate has been set, policies to achieve it must be chosen. In principle, it would be possible to keep the nominal exchange rate constant and apply deflationary policies to bring down prices and wages. This would probably cause substantial falls in output and employment, at least in the short run. Nor would a nominal devaluation be enough on its own. Without supporting policies that limit the increase in domestic prices, a nominal devaluation would have only a transitory effect on the real exchange rate. In the long run domestic prices would rise by the full amount of the devaluation, returning the real exchange rate to its original level. The extent to which a nominal devaluation affects the real exchange rate – and for how long – depends, among other things, on the sizes of the substitution elasticities between tradeable and non-tradeable goods in production and consumption and on the share of tradeable goods in total expenditure (see Khan and Lizondo 1987) as well as directly on the supporting measures – fiscal, monetary, trade and wage policies – that are implemented. Basically, the size of the devaluation cannot be determined in isolation.

Effects of devaluation

There is some controversy in the literature regarding the effects and effectiveness of devaluation. There are those who have argued that devaluation does not improve the trade balance, increases inflation and creates a recession in the process (see Krugman and Taylor 1978; Hanson 1983). On the other hand, there is the view that as long as devaluation alters the real exchange rate by raising product prices in domestic currency relative to factor incomes, it will raise output to the extent that the short-run marginal cost curves of the tradeable goods industries are upward sloping. The longer a real depreciation persists, the greater the benefits.[12] This rise in output and fall in absorption should dampen inflationary pressures and improve the current account. While there is only a limited amount of empirical evidence on the subject, what there is supports the view that devaluation will work in the direction of improving competitiveness and the balance of payments. How long the improvement lasts will again depend on other policies that are in place.

Finally, on the exchange rate policy issue it should be noted that devaluation – i.e. a move from one particular exchange rate to another – is not the only option. Free floating is another polar option, and in between there are variants of crawling pegs. Very few developing countries, however, operate a freely floating exchange rate; most either maintain fixed parities or follow some type of crawling peg rule. Although there may be advantages in fixing the rate, with imposed discipline being one of the major arguments for doing so, there are also disadvantages which have been described in the literature.[13] Furthermore, exchange rate rules, particularly those that attempt to maintain a constant real exchange rate, are not ideal either as they can increase unwarranted fluctuations in output, prevent equilibrating changes in relative prices and resource allocation or increase inflation (see, for example, Frenkel 1981; Dornbusch 1982; Adams and Gros 1986).

External debt policies

The well-known theory of 'growth with debt' argues that a country can and should borrow from abroad as long as the proceeds from such loans produce a return to cover the cost of the borrowing (see McDonald 1982). In that case the borrower is increasing capacity with the aid of foreign savings.

Historically the Fund's external debt policies have been guided by this principle, and considerable emphasis has been placed on the intertemporal budget constraint of the government. Borrowing now to finance spending should be matched by repayments to be made in the future. This rule defines the limits to foreign financing from the demand side, and therefore the degree of adjustment that needs to be undertaken.

While calculation of a sustainable level of borrowing is possible in theory, in practice it is a nearly impossible task. As such, one has to resort to indicators such as debt service or debt to GNP ratios to provide some clues. But the equilibrium levels of such ratios will vary from country to country and for a given country over time, so that one cannot be too confident about the information content of these types of indicators. Perhaps the chief practical value of the indicators is that they give warning of when debt might grow explosively. A sharp increase in the debt service ratio may trigger a more thorough look at the debt situation to see whether the country is using foreign borrowing efficiently, and if it is not then appropriate steps need to be taken to bring the ratio down.

In the 1980s the debt issue became an overriding problem for a number of developing countries – middle and low income alike.[14] The sharp decline in the supply of foreign capital created severe adjustment difficulties for these countries, forcing them to try and achieve external balance much faster than they would have preferred. There was a need for a sharp reduction in absorption, but the debt situation adversely affected investment and growth as well.

Aside from the credit rationing effect on investment, foreign debt may affect investment through what has come to be known as the 'debt overhang' channel. The debt overhang disincentive to investment can arise in a situation in which the debtor country benefits very little from the return to any additional investment because of debt service obligations. When a country is unable to service its debt in full, so actual payments are determined by some negotiation process between the debtor country and the creditor, the amount of debt payments usually becomes linked to the economic performance of the debtor country. The debtor country may need to increase taxation of various sources of income, and this has the consequence that at least part of the return to investment will go to the creditors rather than to the investor. The uncertain outlook and the prospects of taxation necessary to service the debt weaken the incentive to invest in the domestic economy. Similarly, by reducing the necessary domestic political support, the debt overhang is also likely to discourage government efforts to undertake adjustment policies and, through actual or expected economic policies, it is likely to spread to the private sector, affecting its incentives to accumulate domestic assets. The rationale for voluntary debt reduction is based on the supposition that the disincentive effect of foreign debt may be so strong that a reduction in the debt stock would generate such a strong improvement in the debtor's economy that debt repayments would actually rise.[15]

To assist countries that find themselves in a debt crisis situation the Fund has undertaken a number of steps: providing additional financing from its own resources; facilitating rescheduling of the existing stock of debt; encouraging additional lending from both official and private sources; and participating in market-based debt reduction schemes. All these efforts are made with the idea of eventually having these countries return to normal borrowing relations. In general, external debt policies in Fund-supported programmes are aimed at easing the liquidity problems of countries and helping them maintain their long-run growth path.

EMPIRICAL ASPECTS OF FUND ECONOMIC POLICIES

The natural questions to consider next are to what extent Fund policies achieve their objectives of an improvement in external and internal balance – i.e. macroeconomic stability – and whether macroeconomic stability is associated with higher long-term economic growth. Since the Fund's role in the development process hinges on these two questions, it is obviously essential to gauge their empirical validity.

Starting with the first of these questions, there is now a substantial literature concerned with the macroeconomic effects of Fund-supported adjustment programmes.[16] The estimates provided by Khan (1990) for a sample of sixty-nine of a total of seventy-six countries that had upper credit tranche arrangements with the Fund during 1973–88 are the most recent and probably the most reliable of those available.[17] These estimates show that the implementation of a programme leads on average to (i) an improvement in the overall balance of payments; (ii) an improvement in the current account balance; and (iii) a reduction in the rate of inflation. But as is almost always the case with stabilization efforts, this improvement in the external position and in the inflation picture is achieved with some short-term cost, namely a decline in the growth of real GDP.[18] Over time, however, this cost is reduced and the positive effects of programmes are strengthened. Thus the empirical evidence confirms the hypothesis that the adoption of a Fund-supported adjustment programme will generally lead to a more stable macroeconomic situation.

Establishing that Fund programmes are conducive to macroeconomic stability is not the end of the story, since we need to show how macroeconomic stability is related to long-run growth and development. But linking macroeconomic stability to long-run growth is no easy task. In the first place, the economics profession lacks a fully satisfactory theory that directly relates macroeconomic policies and structural reforms to growth, other than via changes in the rate of capital formation. Therefore, macroeconomic policies are judged by the effects they have on investment, with the argument being that policies that have a favourable effect on investment are good for growth. But growth is a multi-faceted process involving many factors other than physical investment. In general, growth of output will depend, *inter alia*, on growth of the labour force, changes in the efficiency of investment, changes in human capital (education, skills and health), and technological developments.[19] We do not know as yet how precisely economic policies of the type contained in Fund programmes will affect these other determinants.[20] There is a presumption, supported by limited empirical evidence, that policies to achieve macroeconomic stability will affect growth in a positive fashion because they create a climate which is conducive to investment, increased domestic savings and a larger flow of foreign financing, all of which will tend to raise the growth rate (see Fischer 1987; Dornbusch and Reynoso 1989). Beyond these generalities, however, there is not much.

In the absence of a suitable theory, we conducted a purely statistical analysis of the relationship between long-run growth and macroeconomic stability. Our aim was a limited one of trying to determine whether the generally held view that macroeconomic stability and growth performance go hand in hand has any degree of empirical support. To this end we ran simple regressions using cross-section data for sixty-nine

developing countries averaged over the period 1973–88 relating the growth of real GDP to various indicators of macroeconomic stability. These indicators, chosen arbitrarily since there is no generally accepted measure of macroeconomic stability, included the following alternatives: inflation, the fiscal balance (as a percentage of GDP) and the percentage change in the real exchange rate.

The results of these alternative regressions are shown in Table 5.1.[21] It should be emphasized that these equations are not intended to explain growth and accordingly should only be interpreted as simple tests of association.[22] With regard to the relationships themselves one can note that there is uniform support for the hypothesis that growth and alternative measures of macroeconomic stability are positively related in our large sample of developing countries. The countries with higher average growth rates over the period 1973–88 also tend to have had

1 lower average rates of inflation,[23]
2 better average fiscal positions,
3 larger average depreciations of the real effective exchange rate.[24]

Taken at face value, the regressions confirm the view that countries that have adopted appropriate

Table 5.1 Cross-section estimates of growth and macroeconomic stability relationships[a]

Constant	Inflation	Fiscal balance[b]	Real exchange rate[c]	R^2
3.239 (12.73)	−0.003 (1.83)			0.100 (1.97)
3.763 (10.03)		0.112 (2.35)		0.100 (1.95)
3.154 (2.90)			−0.112 (2.90)	0.113 (1.91)

Notes: Standard errors in parentheses.
[a] All data are averages for the period 1973–88. The dependent variable is the average growth of real GDP.
[b] As a percentage of GDP.
[c] Percentage change in the real effective exchange rate.

policies – keeping the inflation rate low, not allowing overvaluation of the currency, maintaining fiscal responsibility – have also managed to attain higher long-run growth rates. How exactly the mechanisms work may be unclear, but the stylized facts bear out the relationship between macroeconomic policies and growth. One could therefore argue that, to the extent that Fund policies succeed in their objectives of establishing macroeconomic balance in the economy, they play a positive role in the long-term growth process.

CONCLUSIONS

In this chapter we have attempted to show that the Fund employs a variety of policy measures to attain the multiple objectives defined by its Articles of Agreement – balance-of-payments viability, price stability and development of the productive resources of its member countries. This description should dispel the notion that the Fund is exclusively concerned with the balance of payments and that it relies solely on demand restraint, supplemented by devaluation of the domestic currency, towards this end. Eliminating internal or external imbalances can in principle be brought about by a whole range of policy packages; some of these packages stimulate economic growth and some do not. The Fund recognizes that strong and long-lasting adjustment is only feasible if the productive capacity of the economy is expanding, and thus it is committed to favouring those policies that enhance the possibility of higher growth. However, it is important to note that the choice of policies and the nature of the policy mix in Fund-supported programmes result from extensive negotiations between the Fund and the country authorities. Ultimately the final package reflects the views of both the Fund and the government, as well as prevailing circumstances in the country and in international goods and credit markets.

As stabilization is a primary objective of the Fund, measures to restrain the growth of aggregate demand naturally figure prominently in the policy package. The establishment of a stable macroeconomic environment is a *sine qua non* for increased savings, investment and foreign inflows – all of which are central to the growth process. But macroeconomic balance is by no means a sufficient condition for growth if resources are poorly utilized. Therefore, the Fund presses for structural reforms to make the economy more flexible and efficient. The elimination of distortions – irrespective of their origin – is now as frequent a component of Fund-supported programmes as is the elimination of macroeconomic imbalances. This is why in programmes one can see trade liberalization, market pricing in the agricultural and other sectors of the economy and financial sector reforms generally accompanying fiscal and monetary restraint and exchange rate action. To support this policy package the Fund provides financial resources, arranges for additional foreign financing from both official and private sources and devises ways of reducing the debt burden of the country.

Do Fund programmes succeed in achieving macroeconomic stability? This is, of course, a very difficult question that involves a great deal of subjective judgement, especially when it comes to comparing the effects of a programme on macroeconomic outcomes with what would have been observed in the absence of the programme. The available empirical evidence on the issue indicates that Fund-supported adjustment programmes have had beneficial effects in terms of reducing external and internal imbalances – i.e. programmes have been associated with improvement in the balance of payments and the current account balance and with a reduction in the rate of inflation. In other words, Fund programmes lead to a better macroeconomic environment. Furthermore, there is some empirical evidence demonstrating a link between macroeconomic stability and higher long-term economic growth. Therefore, to the extent that the Fund is able to promote macroeconomic stability, its policy recommendations contribute to long-run growth and development.

In conclusion, the main lesson that emerges from experience as well as from the analysis in this chapter can be summarized as follows: without macroeconomic stability economic growth can falter and not be sustained. Furthermore, without broad-based economic growth the basic structural and social transformations which make up the process of development will not occur, and the other objectives of development policy, such as a more equitable distribution of resources and income, providing employment, improving living standards and the quality of life, and the alleviation of poverty, are unlikely to be met. This does not mean that adequate growth will automatically follow if countries are able to achieve macroeconomic stability. But the chances are greatly improved. In this sense Fund policies can be thought of as improving these chances and thus the basic conditions for economic development.

NOTES

1   Including the centrally planned economies. See, for example, Wolf (1985).
2   For a discussion of alternative development strategies, see Sen (1983). A strongly market-oriented approach to development is the one taken by Lal (1983).
3   This categorization was suggested in IMF (1987).
4   The demand side effects of exchange rate policy are taken up later in this section.
5   The open economy variant of this proposition is developed in Frenkel and Razin (1987). See Corden (1985) for a discussion of this effect in the context of developing countries.
6   The extent to which these effects occur depends on how the fiscal deficit is reduced. For a discussion see Frenkel and Razin (1988) and Khan and Lizondo (1987).
7   Other structural reforms include, for example, tax reforms, elimination of controls in the goods and labour markets and the reform of public enterprises.
8   See, for example, the survey by Edwards (1989) and Krueger et al. (1981).
9   Simplification of quantitative restrictions – e.g. replacement of positive lists by negative lists etc. – may well precede their elimination.
10   This is particularly relevant where tariffs constitute a major source of revenue; a gradual programme of tariff reduction may be called for while other sources of revenue are being tapped.
11   Of course, the new Structural Adjustment Facility (SAF) and the Enhanced Structural Adjustment Facility (ESAF) that provide financing to low-income countries have significantly lengthened the maturity period.
12   See Lizondo and Montiel (1989) for a survey of the contractionary devaluation arguments.
13   One is that a fixed rate is vulnerable to speculative attacks; see Blanco and Garber (1986).
14   See the papers in Frenkel et al. (1989) for an analysis of the theoretical and empirical aspects of the debt crisis.
15   For analytical arguments along these lines see, for example, Helpman (1989) and Krugman (1989).
16   See the survey by Khan (1990).
17   This is because they are based on a relatively new methodology that avoids some of the conceptual and econometric shortcomings of the statistical approaches utilized in previous studies. For a discussion of these shortcomings and ways to overcome them see Goldstein and Montiel (1986) and Khan (1990).
18   This result is consistent with other empirical evidence on the short-run growth effects of Fund programmes; see Khan and Knight (1985).
19   See, for example, Fischer (1987) for a recent discussion of the factors that are important in the determination of growth.
20   Available empirical studies indicate that these factors could account for more than 50 per cent of the changes in growth rates in developing countries.
21   The data for these tests were obtained from IMF, *International Financial Statistics*, and the *World Economic Outlook* database.
22   They could be viewed as a formalization of scatter diagrams. As such one should not be overly concerned about the lack of goodness-of-fit that one observes in all the equations in Table 5.1. The R^2 can be improved by adding other variables such as the investment–income ratio into the regression, as was done by Dornbusch and Reynoso (1989). However, it is obvious that one of the channels through which macroeconomic stability affects growth is the investment–income ratio itself.
23   A similar negative relationship between growth and inflation is obtained by Dornbusch and Reynoso (1989).
24   Note that the exchange rate is defined as units of foreign currency per unit of domestic currency. A depreciation therefore implies a fall in the index.

REFERENCES

Adams, C. F. and Gros, D. (1986) 'The consequences of real exchange rate rules for inflation', *IMF Staff Papers*, September: 439–76.

Balassa, B. (1982) 'Structural adjustment policies in developing economies', *World Development*, January: 23–38.

Barro, R. J. (1974) 'Are government bonds net wealth?', *Journal of Political Economy*, November–December: 1095–117.

Blanco, H. and Garber, P. M. (1986) 'Recurrent devaluation and speculative attacks on the Mexican peso', *Journal of Political Economy*, February: 148–66.

Blejer, M. I. and Khan, M. S. (1984) 'Government policy and private investment in developing countries', *IMF Staff Papers*, June: 379–403.

Bond, M. E. (1983) 'Agricultural responses to prices in sub-Saharan African countries', *IMF Staff Papers*, December: 703–26.

Corbo, V. and de Melo, J. (1985) 'Overview and summary', *World Development*, August: 863–9.

Corden, M. (1985) 'The relevance for developing countries of recent developments in macroeconomic theory', Harvard University, unpublished.

Diaz-Alejandro, C. F. (1985) 'Good-by financial repression, hello financial crash', *Journal of Development Economics*, September–October: 1–24.

Dornbusch, R. (1980) *Open Economy Macroeconomics*, New York: Basic Books.

—— (1982) 'PPP exchange rate rules and macroeconomic stability', *Journal of Political Economy*, February: 158–65,

Dornbusch, R. and Reynoso, A. (1989) 'Financial factors in economic development', *American Economic Review*, May: 204–9.

Edwards, S. (1989) 'The sequencing of structural reforms', NBER Working Paper 3138, October.

Fischer, S. (1987) 'Economic growth and economic policy', in V. Corbo, M. Goldstein and M. Khan (eds) *Growth-Oriented Adjustment Programs*, Washington, DC: IMF and the World Bank, pp. 151–78.

Frenkel, J. A. (1981) 'Flexible exchange rates, prices and the role of "news": lessons from the 1970s', *Journal of Political Economy*, August: 665–705.

—— (1982) 'The order of economic liberalization: discussion', in K. Brunner and A. Metzler (eds) *Economic Policy in a World of Change*, vol. 17, Carnegie-Rochester Series.

—— (1987) 'Comments on economic growth and economic policy', in V. Corbo, M. Goldstein and M. Khan (eds) *Growth Oriented Adjustment Programs*, Washington, DC: IMF and the World Bank, pp. 226–36.

Frenkel, J. A. and Johnson, H. G. (eds) (1976) *The Monetary Approach to the Balance of Payments*, London: Allen & Unwin.

—— and —— (1978) *The Economics of Exchange Rates*, Reading, MA: Addison-Wesley.

Frenkel, J. A. and Mussa, M. (1985) 'Asset markets, exchange rates, and the balance of payments', in R. W. Jones and P. B. Kenen (eds) *Handbook of International Economics*, vol. II, Amsterdam: North–Holland; New York: Elsevier, pp. 679–747.

Frenkel, J. A. and Razin, A. (1987) *Fiscal Policies and the World Economy*, Cambridge, MA: MIT Press.

—— and —— (1988) *Spending, Taxes and Deficits: International Intertemporal Approach*, Princeton Studies in International Finance 63, International Finance Section, December.

Frenkel, J. A., Dooley, M. P. and Wickham, P. (eds) (1989) *Analytical Issues in Debt*, Washington, DC: IMF.

Goldstein, M. and Montiel, P. J. (1986) 'Evaluating Fund stabilization programs with multicountry data: some methodological pitfalls', *IMF Staff Papers*, June: 304–44.

Hanson, J. A. (1983) 'Contractionary devaluation, substitution in production and consumption, and the role of the labor market', *Journal of International Economics*, February: 178–89.

Haque, N. U. and Montiel, P. J. (1989) 'Consumption in developing countries: tests for liquidity constraints and finite horizons', *Review of Economics and Statistics*, August: 408–15.

Helpman, E. (1989) 'Voluntary debt reduction: incentives and welfare', in J.A. Frenkel, M.P. Dooley and P. Wickham (eds) *Analytical Issues in Debt*, Washington, DC: IMF, pp. 279–310.

IMF (International Monetary Fund) (1977) *The Monetary Approach to the Balance of Payments*, Washington, DC: IMF.

—— (1987) *Theoretical Aspects of the Design of Fund-Supported Adjustment Programs*, IMF Occasional Paper 55, September.

Khan, M. S. (1990) 'The macroeconomic effects of IMF-supported adjustment programs: an empirical assessment', *IMF Staff Papers*, June: 195–231.

Khan, M. S. and Knight, M. D. (1985) *Fund-Supported Adjustment Programs and Economic Growth*, IMF Occasional Paper 41, November.

Khan, M. S. and Lizondo, J. S. (1987) 'Devaluation, fiscal deficits, and the real exchange rate', *World Bank Economic Review*, January: 357–74.

Khan, M. S. and Zahler, R. (1983) 'The macroeconomic effects of changes in barriers to trade and capital flows: a simulation analysis', *IMF Staff Papers*, June: 223–82.

Krueger, A. O. (1985) 'How to liberalize a small, open economy', in M. Connolly and J. McDermott (eds) *The Economics of the Caribbean Basin*, New York: Praeger, pp. 12–23.

Krueger, A. O., Lary, H. B., Monson, T. and Akrasanee, N. (eds) (1981) *Trade and Employment in Developing Countries*, Chicago, IL: Chicago University Press.

Krugman, P. (1989) 'Market based debt-reduction schemes', in J. A. Frenkel, M. P. Dooley and P. Wickham (eds) *Analytical Issues in Debt*, Washington, DC: IMF, pp. 258–78.

Krugman, P. and Taylor, L. (1978) 'Contractionary effects of devaluation', *Journal of International Economics*, August: 445–56.

Lal, D. (1983) *The Poverty of Development Economics*, London: Institute of Economic Affairs.

Lizondo, J. S. and Montiel, P. J. (1989) 'Contractionary devaluation in developing countries: an analytical overview', *IMF Staff Papers*, March: 182–227.

McDonald, D. C. (1982) 'Debt capacity and developing country borrowing: a survey of the literature', *IMF Staff Papers*, December: 603–46.

Sen, A. K. (1983) 'Development: which way now?', *Economic Journal*, December: 745–62.

Tanzi, V. (1986) 'The growth of public expenditure in industrial countries: an international and historical perspective', IMF, unpublished, February.

Wolf, T. A. (1985) 'Economic stabilization in planned economies: toward an analytical framework', *IMF Staff Papers*, March: 78–131.

World Bank (1989) *World Development Report 1989*, Washington, DC: World Bank.

6

FINANCING IN EASTERN EUROPE AND THE FORMER SOVIET UNION
Issues and institutional support

Philippe Aghion and Robin Burgess

INTRODUCTION

As the citizens of Eastern Europe and the former Soviet Union (EESU) are rapidly discovering, transition involves a good deal more than adherence to the dogma of privatization and market forces: increases in personal freedom have not been accompanied by spectacular increases in standard of living. Instead there is a recession in the region: demand has fallen, intra-EESU trade has collapsed, unemployment is rising and fiscal deficits, debt and inflation have become problems. The challenge is to build on the new freedoms of economic agents to generate welfare improvements and growth in EESU countries.

The recent experience of Poland, Czechoslovakia and Hungary has shown that macro stabilization, price liberalization and a minimum degree of convertibility can be achieved rapidly. The more complex and fundamental issues of restructuring and privatization have yet to be properly addressed. These two processes in many ways define transition. The scope of the challenge is unprecedented in history and the costs of making these deep adjustments will be very large. Success in *maintaining* stability in the macro sphere and in pushing the overall reform process forward, however, depends on advances in these areas. Microeconomic reform now represents the central challenge of transition in EESU.

Our focus in this chapter is on privatization, restructuring and foreign direct investments in EESU countries. These are likely to be slowed down by numerous market failures and imperfections, most notably the absence of sound banking and credit institutions; the inadequacy of physical infrastructures such as telecommunications, transport and energy; the absence of a market for corporate control and management skills; and the lack of access to international capital markets.

We shall argue that each of these market failures provides a rationale for intervention by multilateral institutions (like the EBRD) who can help the transition to market economies through involvement in privatization and restructuring and through the creation and/or modernization of infrastructures and institutions necessary for private sector development.

In the following section we start the chapter by setting out the financing constraints facing EESU countries and by showing how multilateral institutions can be effective at easing these constraints. The central contribution of the chapter is contained in the third and fourth sections which are devoted, respectively, to privatization and restructuring. In each of these sections, we first try to carefully define the issues and problems associated with these two fundamental aspects of market transformation and then we examine how international institutions can support these processes. The bulk of the examples are drawn from the experience of the EBRD.[1] In the fifth section we offer some concluding remarks.

101

THE FINANCING GAP

A natural way to approach the financing problem is to ask how much money is actually needed to rebuild EESU and to compare this with how much is available. Assuming that domestic variables remain constant, Collins and Rodrik (1991) note that about $1.5 trillion a year in foreign capital will be needed to raise the amount of productive capital per worker in EESU to that which would be required to achieve 7 per cent per annum growth which is compatible with reaching a Western capital–output ratio after a ten-year period.[2] If one compares these figures with actual and projected capital inflows, one realizes that what can be expected is less by more than a whole order of magnitude. Collins and Rodrik (1991), for example, estimate likely capital inflows based on empirical data on current and future likely commitments of foreign (public and private) creditors and obtain a median figure of $55 billion per annum for EESU. This figure is in the region of a Marshall Plan, i.e. one which would contribute a modest 2 per cent of recipient GNP per annum, corresponding to a flow of $48 billion per annum (see Collins and Rodrik 1991).

Recent empirical estimates of the total amount of credits pledged to EESU in 1991 are small (e.g. approximately $37 billion; see Economic Commission for Europe 1991; Handler *et al.* 1991). A large part of these funds have not yet been disbursed. At this early stage of transition, roughly two-thirds of this total represents commitments by multinational institutions including the EBRD, IMF, World Bank and EC.

From the private side, capital inflows have (so far) been limited. While the level of interest among potential industrial investors is high, the actual flows are disappointingly low. As of October 1991, it is estimated that the aggregate foreign direct investment earmarked for EESU as recorded in registered joint venture and investment proposals had reached approximately $13 billion, representing over 30 thousand investment projects.[3] The actual dollars disbursed and the number of ventures which are operational,

however, are at best 40 per cent of the recorded figures. A few small countries with favourable investment environments have been relatively successful. Hungary, for example, attracted foreign direct investment in excess of $1 billion in 1991 alone. Increasingly, Czechoslovakia is attracting investors.

Foreign direct investment should play a strategic role in central Europe and EESU countries which goes beyond the flow of capital. The operational commitment on the part of trade investors also brings a transfer of technology and managerial skills, helps introduce new standards of product quality and operational efficiency and can open access to new markets. Much still needs to be done by the host countries to create a more attractive environment for investments.

The difference between required and committed capital, which we term the 'financing gap', is thus very large indeed. So large, in fact, that it would be naive to depend solely on capital inflows to finance development in the region. One should not be too discouraged by such a clear conclusion. In the first place, in EESU one can *de facto* reject the assumption of constancy in domestic variables. Indeed, the expectation would be that transition involves, in the long term, a shift from a low-efficiency command economy to a market economy. These efficiency effects are likely to be of much greater importance than the pure financial effects associated with capital inflows and they point to the importance of the domestic reform process for growth creation in the region. Indeed what falls out of this crude analysis is the finding that capital *will and will have to* come in large part from domestic sources.[4]

Another point to notice is that the current low contribution of private financing is largely a reflection of considerable political and economic uncertainty in the region and of the unpreparedness of the large bulk of domestic firms to absorb and effectively utilize foreign credit. Private flows, however, can be expected to increase significantly as uncertainty is reduced and firms become more creditworthy and responsive to market signals. These flows will heavily dominate official flows in the medium and long term. Much of the increased contribution of private flows will be effected through an expansion of East–West trade (see Aghion and Burgess 1991). Indeed, the attraction of foreign direct investment to finance export expansion is considered to be critical for the development of the region. Export expansion will itself depend on access to foreign markets and this is an area where Western market economies can play a role in easing the financing constraint of EESU (see Messerlin 1991). Another element is debt relief to encourage and support the restructuring efforts of the governments of EESU.

The above discussion suggests that a substantial financial gap will remain in EESU countries for the next five to ten years. In this context, international financial institutions (IFIs) like the World Bank or the EBRD might still play a significant role in fostering investments and growth in EESU, even though they can only provide a moderate financial contribution. First, the high debt rating (AAA)[5] enjoyed by these institutions allows them to borrow on international credit markets at preferential rates of interest. This in turn would allow the EBRD, say, to make public or private loans at market rates of interest without imposing on its East European counterpart as high a collateral requirement as private lenders would. The difference in terms of East European enterprises' access to credit would be non-negligible. Second, both the reputational effect of the AAA rating and the preferred creditor status enjoyed by international financial institutions (EBRD, World Bank, IFC etc.) create a considerable scope for co-investments with private (Western) partners. In particular, the preferred creditor status,[6] which makes IFIs the most senior creditors in any public loan to EESU institutions or enterprises, is automatically transmitted to the IFI's (private) co-lenders. Thus, directly and indirectly, multilateral institutions can both ease the EESU's access to international credit and stimulate foreign direct investments into these countries.

The fact that IFIs can mobilize considerable financial resources (e.g. through co-investment) and that these are targeted at critical bottlenecks to

structural reform implies that the overall impact on EESU growth may be large relative to the original financial contribution of these institutions.

PRIVATIZATION

The concentration of economic activity in the public sector under central planning is marked. For example, in 1986 in Czechoslovakia, 97 per cent of value added was in the state sector and in 1985 in the USSR the corresponding figure was 96 per cent (see Fischer 1991). No country in EESU has a share of public sector in value added which falls below 60 per cent, whilst the OECD countries all have shares below 20 per cent. These observations have led to calls for rapid or immediate privatization of a large fraction of state-owned enterprises.

Aside from decreasing the size of the public sector, privatization was widely perceived as the most effective procedure whereby to salvage and restructure state enterprises, and at the same time improve the efficiency of EESU economies (in the sense both of better resource allocations and of a decoupling between production and political decision-making processes). This, in turn, motivated the setting up of mass privatization programmes the scale and speed of which were well in excess of any historic privatization episode.

At the onset of transition the discussion of what to do with existing firms seemed clear cut. Non-viable firms would be declared bankrupt and eliminated. Viable firms would be privatized and this act would lead to the introduction of a correct set of incentives for market production. Both processes would be quick. In practice neither of these has occurred to any significant extent though there has been some success in the privatization of very small enterprises (less than a hundred employees). A richer and broader theory and discussion has followed on the heels of these empirical observations where both the potential and importance of privatization in the short run is de-emphasized. The focus is being reoriented toward industrial restructuring with emphasis on incentives within the firm, management and technology transfers, vertical disintegration, demonopolization, containment of adjustment costs, finance and banking, infrastructure and the correction of market failures. These measures are increasingly seen as necessary to rationalize production, improve market functioning, facilitate privatization and contain the social costs of adjustments.

The emergence of a large and well-functioning private sector is critical to a successful transition to a market economy.[7] If one examines the total population of firms in transition economies, four well-defined and complementary sets of industrial policies suggest themselves. First, there is a lower strata of existing public firms which are non-viable in the long term and require policies to break them up or bankrupt them. Second, there is a large number of small enterprises and a smaller number of large viable state enterprises which can be quickly sold to domestic or foreign trade investors. Third, there is a large middle ground of large semi-viable public firms which require restructuring policies prior to their privatization, i.e. prior to finding potential purchasers. Finally, there is a fast-growing population of new private enterprises which would benefit from improved infrastructures and also from institutional support including an improved access to credit. Our focus in this section is on the narrow issue of rapid mass privatization; other aspects of industrial policy are covered in the fourth section.

Implementation problems

Most countries in EESU have established or are in the process of establishing an administrative framework for privatization. The procedures adopted tend to be different for small and large enterprises.

Small enterprises and other small economic units can be privatized relatively quickly through a simple decentralized mechanism (e.g. auctions). The bulk of the task of restructuring and rationalizing production can be left to the new owners. In many cases profits can be expected within a relatively short period. Sales of small economic assets are also often attractive to the governments as they generate a short-term source of revenue

and divest overstrained governments of responsibility for administration. These conditions set them apart from the situation in large enterprises and the experience reflects these differences. Newly privatized small enterprises and economic units along with new enterprises form the bed-rock of private initiative in transition economies.

The privatization of small public enterprises and state-owned economic units (e.g. retail networks, services) has to some extent been both rapid and successful. In Czechoslovakia over 15,000 small units were auctioned in 1991. In Poland approximately 60,000 small units were leased or sold to the private sector in 1990 and 1991 and 70 per cent of retail trade is now in the private sector. In Hungary a similar auction process is under way. Bulgaria is making some progress in privatization of small units in trade, services and tourism. In Romania the process for divesting small assets of commercial companies, such as small shops and restaurants, has been started under the supervision of the National Agency of Privatization. In Russia laws have been proposed for the auction of most small assets and some auctions have taken place in St Petersburg. In Moscow the local authorities favour direct sales to minimize the displacement of the existing workforce; the situation with respect to the Russian authorities still requires clarification. Other nations and republics including Latvia, Russia and Kazakhstan are making progress in selling small assets.

The experience to date tends to argue in favour of sales auctions over other methods (e.g. direct sales or free distribution) for privatizing small enterprises. Auctions for small companies are best organized at a local level and they require simple and clear procedures set up by the state.[8] The particular auction mechanism that seems to perform most efficiently in a wide range of circumstances in the so-called English auction, whereby the price is publicly announced and then repeatedly raised by the auctioneer until only one bidder remains (see Maskin (1992) for a formal analysis). In general, auctions have several advantages over other schemes: first, they are relatively simple to implement; second, they provide a rough valuation of the firm and can allocate assets in the absence of sound equity market institutions; and third, they can be relatively fair in the sense that no particular interest may be *a priori* protected or favoured (e.g. anyone can bid).

The absence of efficient financial markets in EESU, however, may qualify this last proposition: in the EESU context, indeed, initial wealth may override efficiency considerations in determining how the small privatized firms will be allocated among new private owners. As a way to reduce the extent to which limited access to borrowing could prevent the most efficient bidders from missing the auctions, a multi-part pricing scheme could be instituted whereby a bidder would be liable both to a down payment at the auction stage and to a debt repayment out of future cash revenues (see Maskin 1992). The down payment would constitute the bidder's initial equity share of the privatized firm, while the auctioneer's (government's) claim would constitute the firm's initial debt. In the case where the government's claims were not met, the firm's ownership and control would be transferred back to the state agency which would then organize a second auction. The procedure just described can be reinterpreted as a variant of leasing-rights auctions where the successful bidder would have the option to acquire full ownership of the firm after a prespecified time period and at a prespecified exercise price.[9]

The 'debt–equity' ratio in multi-part auctions should be set sufficiently high that initial wealth constraints do not prevent efficient bidders from participating in the auctions, but not too high for moral hazard reasons.[10] Too high a debt–equity ratio may indeed discourage successful bidders from investing the required effort or from choosing the adequate level of risks in managing the firm's assets.[11] (See Appendix 2 for the sketch of a formal proof.)

The main problems in organizing auctions are, first, the lack of entrepreneurs able to run the newly privatized firms and, second, the lack of public agents to administer the process. This in turn explains why the auctioning of small firms is best accomplished at a local level but within a coherent national framework, and if possible with international advice. Their great strength is that they can effectively and quickly transfer activities (e.g. small-scale production, retail, services) in which the state clearly has no comparative advantage to the private sector.

The privatization of large state-owned companies is proceeding more slowly than initially expected. Indeed in many industries, despite the existence of privatization plans, there is a virtual standstill in the enactment of these plans. This appears to be related, *inter alia*, to ill-defined property rights (including restitution); administrative bottlenecks (including uncertainty over areas of competence); high restructuring costs involving enterprise balance sheets, labour reorganization and operational restructuring; the low level of domestic savings; and a scarcity of management resources. The weaknesses which underlie many privatization plans are further compounded by legal and political complications which delay privatization.

With the purpose of speeding up the privatization process for large and medium size enterprises, a number of Western economists have advocated mass give-away schemes working through voucher systems (see Blanchard *et al.* 1991; Frydman and Rapaczynski 1990).

Both Czechoslovakia and Poland have adopted such schemes, with Czechoslovakia using vouchers as a vehicle for direct distribution of enterprise shares to the population, whereas Poland is adopting a two-step approach whereby citizens can use their voucher endowments to acquire ownership in privatization funds managed by professional fund managers which in turn have the responsibility of restructuring and/or selling off the enterprises that have been allocated to them.[12] There are reasons to remain sceptical about these voucher schemes. One reason is that the schemes appear to be complicated and also costly to implement. For example, in Poland we have estimated that the registration cost for voucher claims would amount to $2.50–4.00 per person (i.e. up to $80 million in total if we assume that half of the Polish population would be entitled to voucher endowment).

More importantly, the schemes are not immune either from excessive transfers of enterprise ownership to wealthier or better organized private groups of individuals as is already the case in Czechoslovakia,[13] or to governance problems associated with the high degree of ownership dispersion in the enterprises or, in the Polish case, in the privatization intermediaries. In particular the separation between ownership (by all Polish citizens) and management (entrusted to a limited number of fund managers) of the Polish privatization funds raises a serious incentive issue (see Frydman and Rapaczynski 1990). On the other hand, the Polish 'solution' to this problem, which consists of the setting up of Supervisory Boards elected by the Fund's shareholders, is conducive to excessive and arbitrary state intervention as long as these new private shareholders remain dispersed.

More generally the excessive emphasis on building up an administrative machinery to operate grand schemes such as the Polish one has led to long and difficult legislative processes for each major transaction.

Potential buyers are often put off by the complexity and uncertainty of these legislative processes, which are due not only to administrative problems and bureaucratic difficulties but also to the long rounds of mutual concessions and requests emanating from the various interested constituencies.

Efficient decentralized procedures might thus appear more appropriate. Such procedures would typically involve one of a small number of privatization agencies responsible for restructuring and selling off large state-owned enterprises. The best seem to be state bodies such as the Treuhandanstalt in Germany, operating on a decentralized basis with experts in the various sectors of industry and managed by (or with) specialized Western fund managers whose reputation would be put at stake. Such agencies would encourage large privatizations to be initiated and processed by the enterprises themselves and by prospective trade investors. Efficient privatization agencies would require a large number of experts and also a substantial amount of financial capital to assist new investors in modernizing the enterprise they acquire and/or to protect the labour force against the adverse consequences of necessary restructuring and thereby avoid major social conflicts. A natural source for such financial capital should be the proceeds of the privatization itself. In the absence of appropriate taxation systems or of external financing sources such as that provided by West German citizens in Germany, (multi-part) auction mechanisms such as the one suggested above would substantially contribute to the finances of privatization agencies. Extending these mechanisms from small to large state-owned companies, however, involves a number of theoretical difficulties. In particular, the lack of domestic savings, together with the moral hazard problems involved in having debt–equity ratios which are too large, may constitute a case for piecewise auctioning procedures. Similar procedures might also be recommended in the case where governments are relatively more risk averse than private investors and the uncertainty about the future profitability of the company is to be resolved progressively over time. The flip-side of piecemeal auctioning procedures, however, is the risk that control rights might be diluted over too large a number of successful bidders. Here is a trade-off that should be carefully evaluated. In any case, the need for governments to seek out 'stable cores' of investors is widely recognized as a priority in the privatization of large state-owned enterprises, even in the context of the various share distribution schemes where the governments would remain pivotal (minority) shareholders (see Fischer 1991).

Having argued that voucher schemes are likely to be complicated, that they do not properly address valuation and restructuring issues and that they turn out to slow down the privatization process compared with more pragmatic and traditional approaches (such as direct sales and auctions), is there still a justification for this type of scheme? There may be one such justification, based essentially on political considerations and the reduction of incentive barriers to privatization. Free distribution of vouchers to employees or citizens can appeal to perceptions of wealth sharing and thus add to political popularity. Political and to some extent efficiency considerations (see Fischer 1991) may also argue in favour of a conciliatory attitude towards incumbent managers (the so-called 'nomenklatura'); these managers need to be given some incentive to participate in the privatization for otherwise they can act as a significant barrier to the process. However, the above requirements can be met through direct distribution of shares to managers and employees which should not affect more than 20 per cent and 30 per cent, respectively, of total state ownership in large state-owned enterprises so as to preserve corporate governance.[14]

Shleifer and Vishny (1992) in the case of Russia suggest that a better compromise between stakeholder incentives, corporate governance and political considerations might be achieved through direct distribution of voting shares to incumbent managers and workers and of non-voting shares to local government.[15]

Should there be one or several privatization agencies operating in each country? Having one central privatization agency run by the state but decentralized both by regions and sectors has a number of advantages which become increasingly apparent in view of the German or the Hungarian experiences.[16] A single agency also has the advantage of being able to establish clear and coherent guidelines for privatization. In addition the managers or management funds in charge of a unique agency (or a small number of agencies) are more visible and can be held responsible for the programme outcome. On the other hand, having a large number of agencies operate in parallel might improve incentives in each of them by having agencies' managers rewarded on a relative performance basis. The performance criterion could be an aggregate indicator of consumer and producer surplus generaed by privatizations rather than sales revenues alone. Indeed, using sales revenues as the unique managerial compensation criterion might deter the privatization agencies from engaging in the demonopolization of large state-owned enterprises before auctioning them.

As concerns the financing of the privatization process, as we have already argued above, significant financial resources will be needed. Part of these resources will be in the form of foreign direct investment (including the repurchasing of part of the enterprises' debt by foreign investors) but most of the resources for privatization will have to be generated domestically through (i) funding from domestic banks, (ii) debt–equity swaps by the creditors of state enterprises, including banks, to finance additional equity investments, and (iii) the reform of enterprise taxation and the broadening of the tax system. Allocating shares in privatized enterprises to banks will also contribute to their recapitalization, whilst their bad loans to state enterprises will be written off – i.e. removed from their balance sheets.[17] Also, allocating shares to banks would increase their incentive to monitor the performance of the firm, even in a situation of solvency. Such a monitoring role may prove to be particularly important in the early stages of the transition process when, on the one hand, holding companies and their subsidiaries will not yet have acquired a self-sustaining reputation and, on the other hand, the disciplinary role of the stock market will not be substantial as it is nowadays in countries like the UK and USA where, in any case, the efficiency of the takeover mechanism for this purpose is widely questioned.

Support by international institutions

What is the role of international institutions in supporting the privatization process in EESU? Two main areas of activity may be recognized: financial support and technical assistance.

As concerns viable enterprises, international institutions like the EBRD can act as a catalyst to privatization, either by helping to arrange direct sales to a foreign trade partner or by encouraging investment. These measures not only dilute state ownership and recapitalize enterprises; they also embody transfers of technology and management ability which are essential for modernization and the rationalization of production. Co-investment by an international institution can also help to attract investment by domestic or foreign partners (see Appendix 1) which may be instrumental in turning around semi-viable companies.

However, the main way in which international institutions can assist governments in organizing and implementing mass privatization programmes is through technical advice and assistance. Given empirical developments in EESU, this assistance should be based on experience at the firm level.

In the city of Moscow, for example, the EBRD is assisting in the formulation and implementation of a privatization programme for roughly 16,000 small businesses and 700 medium to large enterprises, controlled by the city. The experience gained from the immediate processing of 'pilot transactions' is now being applied to designing an overall scheme that can deal with the large numbers of enterprises involved in a realistic and workable way. At the request of the Mayor of St Petersburg, a short-term technical assistance project based on a similar approach has been started there.

The European Bank and the World Bank Group are jointly organizing a large-scale privatization advisory project for the Russian republic, and the European Bank has already been able to bring the Moscow and St Petersburg experience to bear on a better definition of various elements of the overall Russian programme. A project management unit, to be situated within the Russian State Committee for the Management of State Property, is currently being staffed to launch this project.

There is also increasing focus on restructuring to make firms attractive to investors and tenable for privatization. In Hungary, for example, the European Bank is helping to assess the viability and define the business plan of a 'turnaround company', which will buy potentially viable businesses from the state which are in need of restructuring and investment in order to become attractive to buyers.

In EESU empirical developments relating to privatization have run ahead of the capability of policy or theory to address them. This led to the emergence of an 'empirical' or pragmatic approach to privatization amongst international institutions.

This approach, based on experience, is the most realistic way in which to proceed. Four lessons emerge in this context.

1   For large enterprises restructuring cannot be divorced from privatization. Macro reform and the act of privatization do not in themselves guarantee the existence of an appropriate set of incentives. Similarly, without proper attention for restructuring at the firm level, privatization may not itself proceed.

2   Governments require advice on what needs to be done institutionally to facilitate implementation of the large volume of transactions inherent in mass privatization.

3   Greater attention needs to be paid to the management structure within firms. Direct foreign assistance in this area can be helpful, but there is also a role for international institutions in attracting foreign investment which will serve a similar role.

4   The multi-track approach to privatization which confronts the various boundaries for privatization is the most appropriate. Single elaborate plans for privatization are inappropriate and foreign assistance should address different economic levels and be based on the specifics of a given country.

RESTRUCTURING

The transformation of economic structure that is taking place in EESU is unprecedented in scope. It is generally acknowledged that the move from a command to a market economy will improve economic efficiency and welfare. In the long run, however, there is a great deal of debate on how such a transition should be accomplished, and at what speed, in order to keep close to what could be considered as a Pareto-improving path (see Flemming 1990).[18]

Context

At least three distinct sets of arguments suggest that interventions to provide restructuring may be advisable and that complete reliance on privatization and the operation of market forces may be an untenable strategy.

1 State enterprises are largely obsolete in terms of

   (a) their trade structures which relied heavily on the command Comecon system;
   (b) their domestic markets which also relied on planned interfirm trade flows;
   (c) technological processes; and
   (d) their management systems and management culture.

   Most state managers are still unable to respond to consumer demand or behave in a production-oriented manner. Time is needed to turn these enterprises around to make them both viable and saleable.

2 Conflicting ownership and control claims of stakeholders in state enterprises need to be addressed. At present each stakeholder (e.g. government, managers, workers) has extensive veto power over changes and the standard way of resolving disagreements is to maintain the status quo, thus blocking privatization and restructuring.

3 Trade and price liberalization, especially if implemented in a non-gradual way, will impose substantial adjustment costs in the east in the form of a rapid decumulation of capital in non-competitive (industrial) sectors. These sectors used to benefit from preferential market access mutually granted under CMEA rules, hence producing and exporting goods for which they had no or little comparative advantage (in particular in manufacturing, as shown by the large mismatch between Eastern European exports to OECD countries and to other Eastern European countries in the late 1980s). The large-scale phasing out of obsolete activities caused by trade liberalization can only be *gradually* offset by the emergence of new activities and sectors and the entry of new firms into these sectors. This 'stock–flow' problem, in turn, should induce high rates of unemployment and therefore

substantial wastes in human capital resources in the short (and medium) terms.[19] Containment of social costs associated with industrial reorganization is an essential part of restructuring and is critical to the transition process as a whole.

Industrial restructuring and the rationalization of production in the process of transition toward a market economy should involve three major elements: measures to bankrupt or break up non-viable state enterprises and to enforce hard budget constraints; measures to restructure semi-viable large state enterprises prior to privatization; and measures to encourage the emergence of new private firms. In this section of the chapter we shall concentrate on some issues and principles underlying each of these important areas of restructuring policy and then turn to the role of multilateral institutions in supporting the overall process.

Bankruptcy

A number of enterprises and sectors in EESU have no competitive advantage and would be producing negative value added if input prices were fully costed. Despite strong macroeconomic pressures, the clear redundancy of some industries and the enaction of new bankruptcy law in several EESU countries, very few bankruptcies have actually occurred.

Mitchell (1990) argues that a major part of the explanation for this phenomenon lies in the rapid expansion of interfirm credits. This expansion has been based on the rational belief of creditors that the government would eventually bail out any debtor firm in financial distress. The belief has been found to be well founded and relies on the high costs to the government of dismantling large failing companies in EESU. As Mitchell (1990) points out,

the extent of political costs entailed in liquidations is in part a function of inadequate development of capital markets that would facilitate the sale of a firm's assets. They are also likely attributable to the role of enterprises in providing social services to their employees. Housing, pensions, medical benefits and daycare are often provided through the workplace. Dissolving a firm may extinguish a worker's right to several of these benefits, especially housing.[20]

Other political costs include the increased burdens on safety-net systems and fiscal revenue generated by mass unemployment. In addition, there is the danger that the bankruptcy of one firm might prove contagious and spread to other firms, given the high degree of technical and financial interdependence across firms and sectors.

These considerations imply that no credible enforcement of bankruptcy laws and hard budget constraints can seriously be expected in these countries until the political and social costs associated with liquidation have been substantially reduced, e.g. through the establishment of a generalized social security system, unemployment compensation and so on.

In addition, for bankruptcy and restructuring to be enforceable the industrial sector needs to be demonopolized and the branch ministries dismantled to avoid situations where the creditor-supplier would not insist on recovering its claims either because it is controlled by the same branch ministry as the debtor firm or because the debtor firm is a monopsonist. It is necessary to increase the independence of banks *vis-à-vis* both the central government and the firms they invest in. This implies the commercialization or privatization of banks.

At a more fundamental level, how one ascertains the viability of a particular firm is problematic in the context of EESU countries. As long as prices are not market determined, it is hard to evaluate which firms should survive and which should be liquidated. It is especially hard to distinguish between idiosyncratic and macroeconomic causes of financial distress. The absence of capital markets makes it difficult to determine the survival value of a firm in transition economies. Indeed, in a market economy, a standard way to determine whether a firm should survive or not is whether the firm's value is greater in continuation or in liquid-

ation. Continuation value, however, is best estimated by the value of the outstanding equity and debt when secondary markets exist for both types of claim. In theory, the stock market price reflects the available information on a firm's future stream of income; however, the development of stock markets in EESU in the near future seems unlikely.[21]

In advising governments in EESU (in particular Russia) on bankruptcy reform, one needs to take into account the risk of excessive (or too rapid) liquidation arising both from the high systemic risks inherent in the monopolistic structure of EESU production and from the high degree of capital market imperfections. Aside from complicating the asset valuation problem, these market imperfections may also prevent more junior creditors or shareholders (who would most favour reorganization over liquidation) from borrowing the required funds to buy out the more senior creditors for control of the firm's assets (in the case where the net present value of the firm exceeds its liquidation value).

Turnaround

There is a large middle ground of semi-viable state enterprises in transition economies which require restructuring to achieve financial viability and become privatizable. In this section we draw out some clear lessons about what can be done to this important class of firms. We structure the discussion around three themes:

1 vertical disintegration;
2 incentives and commercialization; and
3 management and technology transfers.

The basic premise of this section is that, where markets cannot operate, institutions are needed that can organize transfers of control from the state to domestic residents.[22] The above discussions of the various legal, political, incentive and practical barriers to privatization made it clear indeed that in many countries in EESU there will be a prolonged interim period in which the state will continue to own a considerable part of the enterprise sector. Restructuring measures can achieve a certain degree of marketization of state enterprises, thus bringing them close to competitive functioning and privatization. This intermediate stage of industrial organization between central planning and private ownership which might be termed commercialization has so far received insufficient attention.

Vertical disintegration and financial restructuring

Enterprises under central planning pursue different objectives from those in capitalist economies. In particular many enterprises have a level of vertical integration which may imply excessive input costs in a market environment and the distraction of management from core economic activities.[23] Enterprise reform then must consist of concentrating resources on upgrading activities in areas where firms have a comparative advantage (i.e. production) and eliminating activities where the firm has no comparative advantage (e.g. social security, housing).

Vertical disintegration must consist first of breaking off and eliminating loss-making activities. This may arise at the instigation of managers seeking profits but the process may also be co-ordinated and facilitated by the involvement of government agencies. For example, the experience of East Germany has shown that the existing management is often pivotal in proposing reorganization plans to be implemented by the Treuhand. These involve plant closures, redundancies and the disposal of existing assets, as well as market expansion and the development of alliances with Western companies (Carlin and Mayer 1992).

Second, there is a need to break up systems of integrated component supply. Inputs may continue to be provided through integrated systems only if these meet the criterion of being competitive relative to other sources.

Third, enterprises need to be absolved from their responsibilities to provide social services, in particular social security benefits and housing. These services will have to be provided by an alternative source (e.g. local and/or government),

however, for otherwise workers facing unemployment risks will display strong resistance to restructuring measures.

Fourth, it is important to try and break up highly integrated combinats which are not natural monopolies before privatization takes place in the corresponding sectors. It may indeed become harder to demonopolize and deconcentrate an industrial sector *after* such a sector has been privatized. New private monopolies will not spontaneously engage in demonopolization because this would reduce their profits. 'As western experience shows, it would be much harder to rely on prospective anti-trust legislation and institutions to break-up private monopolies' (Tirole 1991). The role of foreign competition in limiting monopolistic price distortions should not be over-emphasized either. The extent to which free trade can substitute for internal demonopolization of EESU economies depends first on the relative size of these economies compared with the rest of the world, second on the relative size of the tradeable goods sectors and third on the average income level in any country in EESU compared with other (Western) countries. In particular, if the average income per capita is low in a given EESU country, high quality producers in richer countries may prefer to sell at higher prices and concentrate on their domestic customers rather than penetrate EESU markets by lowering their price for the same products to take into account the lower purchasing power in the region.[24] In that case, the opening of EESU to free trade does not necessarily threaten the local monopoly power of (low quality) domestic producers in that country.

Another major impediment to the marketization and restructuring of state enterprises is the large amount of debt inherited from the socialist system. These debts are often of a magnitude sufficient to prevent enterprises from gaining a competitive footing in the domestic or world markets. It is clear that the restructuring of historic debt and current operational restructuring of enterprises should be kept separate. As the government is both the creditor (through state banks or state-owned enterprises) and the owner of the state enterprises, the writing off of inherited debt is easy to accomplish while the company is in state hands. In this case indeed, writing off debt involves shifting resources within the government budget. On the other hand, a complete writing off of the debt may create moral hazard problems as regards future borrowing. Instead in most EESU countries a more gradual approach has been adopted whereby the government buys up historic debt through the commercial banks, thus recapitalizing them. In both the case of the Treuhand in East Germany and in Czechoslovakia the necessary funds to do this were derived from the privatization funds so as not to threaten the normal tax-financed budget. These funds can be used both to write off old enterprise debt and to provide a direct capital injection to the banks. Direct debt–equity swaps would recapitalize banks further and provide banks with a shareholding interest in enterprise. Also, allocating shares to banks would increase their incentive to monitor the performance of the firm, even in a situation of solvency. Such a monitoring role may prove to be particularly important in the early stages of the transition process when, on the one hand, holding companies and their subsidiaries will not yet have acquired a self-sustaining reputation and, on the other hand, the disciplinary role of the stock market will not be substantial as it is nowadays in countries like the UK and the USA where, in any case, the efficiency of the takeover mechanism for this purpose is widely questioned.

Incentives and commercialization

Different stakeholders in large public enterprises need to be provided with incentives to engage in restructuring and privatization. Many of the current stakeholders, such as incumbent managers and local government, may indeed be satisfied with the status quo as it grants them substantial control rights. Where managers do want to engage in reform their efforts may be blocked by workers' councils and unions whose priority is to maintain employment for their members. Restructuring may thus come to a standstill as each of the stake-

holders has sufficient effective control to veto any changes. This means no layoffs, no wage restraint, no plant closures and no management changes until a way of resolving conflict between stakeholders is found. There are two complementary strategies that offer some solutions to these incentives and governance problems. First, stakeholders need to receive strong command and financial incentives (e.g. the form of stock options on the future privatized firm) both to preserve the assets of the corporations today and to prepare for their privatization at a later date. Second, enterprises should be commercialized so that they are separated from the government and their formal governance structure becomes more clearly established (see Shleifer and Vishny 1992).

Commercialization or corporatization of public enterprises is often seen as an intermediate and necessary step to turnaround and full marketization. In essence, the introduction of competition and market-oriented behaviour by management and worker is at this early stage of transition more important than a nominal change in ownership. This problem has not yet been systematically addressed in any of the EESU countries.

Carlin and Mayer (1992) list the six central functions of the Treuhand as follows. It establishes the social value of firms; it disposes of uneconomic activities; it creates supervisory boards; it finds prospective buyers; it imposes investment and employment conditions; and it evaluates firms in a creditworthy sense. These functions help firms to restructure and ready themselves for privatization but also help achieve social objectives concerning employment, regional and industrial policy.[25] The creation of supervisory boards and the training of East German managers is gradually permitting the evolution of self-sufficient enterprises that can raise debt finance externally while retaining control over operations.

For Russia, Shleifer and Vishny (1992) have advocated mandatory commercialization (or corporatization) of all the enterprises. They suggest that, within six months, all large state enterprises should be converted into joint stock companies with publicly traded shares and boards of directors. Initially, all the shares would be held by the central government, but over time, as the privatization proceeds, they would be given away or sold to the various stakeholders and investors in order to remove incentive barriers and solve the corporate governance problem. The board of directors would initially consist of the representatives of the national privatization agency, the managers, the representatives of the workers, bankers and others involved with the corporation. The idea is to realign intrafirm incentives and make the state companies resemble private companies from the start. Such mandatory extensive commercialization has also been advocated by Lipton and Sachs (1990) for Poland and by the IMF *et al.* (1991) for the (former) Soviet Union.

In the case of Hungary, the new law on economic transformation transfers state-owned enterprises from the jurisdiction of enterprise councils to a company status, under the control of the State Property Agency (SPA). Corporatization involves such measures as the introduction of a board of directors and audited balance sheets. The state is made the legal owner, at least for the period up to privatization. Supervision of enterprise managements is partly subcontracted to approved advisory agencies which act as the agents of the SPA.

In Poland managers, who have pushed strongly for restructuring, often find themselves in a position of tension with the workers councils. Commercialization is then envisaged as an important intermediate step to protect the manager from the control of the workers council as it gives them some independence and a stronger profit incentive. Also the managers' emphasis on profitability would be best guaranteed by means of appropriate management compensations, involving long-term profit-sharing or stock options (see Tirole 1991).

Based on the argument that only new owners know what is good for the firm, the Czechoslovak government seems to be taking the view that speedy privatization is the only solution to governance and control problems. As a result, no systematic thought has been given to the control of the middle stratum of semi-viable enterprises which may not be privatizable in the short term. Ignoring the problem, or leaving it to the market, is not helpful as regional unemployment problems and recession imply that there is mounting pressure to give subsidies or cheap credit to existing state enterprises.

In summary, the view that state enterprises which cannot be rapidly privatized should be eliminated is unlikely to make economic sense from a medium-term point of view as a non-negligible fraction of industrial production could be made marketable after marginal investments in physical and human capital. A central question which remains open is how such investment should be co-ordinated and encouraged. Moreover, from a political viewpoint, the huge potential unemployment problem would make the elimination solution unviable in the short term.

Management and technology transfers

The bulk of enterprises in EESU require technical assistance as regards management practice, pricing and costing, accounting, marketing and research and development. Central privatization and restructuring agencies can have a pivotal role in co-ordinating transfers of technical assistance (e.g. Treuhand in East Germany – see Carlin and Mayer 1992).

At this stage in the restructuring process, heavy emphasis should also be put on projects involving strong foreign strategic partners, whether in minority or majority positions. The significance of foreign partners lies in their ability to compensate for the physical and commercial obsolescence of many enterprises in EESU and, through their commitment to provide technical, marketing and managerial know-how, to accelerate the transformation of these enterprises into modern businesses. These businesses will then be more able to attract capital.

Whilst in East Germany enterprises are able to draw upon both the expertise and resources of West German managers (Carlin and Mayer 1992), the shortage of both foreign direct investment and technical assistance in other countries of EESU points to a significant role for multilateral institutions to act as foreign partners during the early stages of restructuring.

Labour reallocation and the role of new private firms

Recent studies (e.g. Burda 1991; Hare and Hughes 1991) have emphasized the extent to which the (potentially loss-making) heavy industries and agriculture have absorbed an excessive share of the labour force at the expense of the service and light-industry sectors which are potentially more profitable in net present value terms. The expansion of employment in these disregarded sectors will have to take place within new small and medium-sized enterprises.

The implied employment reallocation that should take place in EESU is quite substantial. For example, the *A Study of the Soviet Economy* (IMF *et al.* 1991)[26] shows that if one only considers a downward readjustment of Soviet overmanned agriculture and manufacturing sectors together with an upward readjustment of the undermanned wholesale–retail trade, financial and insurance sectors (so as to coincide with the average Western shares of employment in those sectors), then this would already amount to a labour reallocation of over 21 million Soviet workers, which corresponds to over 14 per cent of the total labour force (assuming that the labour force remains stationary in the next few years).[27]

The natural sectors for expansion are consumer services, retail distribution,[28] construction and repair services, transportation and shipping activities and the financial sector, all of which are underdeveloped by Western standards. Although private employment has expanded rapidly in these areas, especially in countries like Poland, Hungary and, to a smaller extent, the Soviet Union, massive growth in new small (private) businesses is still necessary to absorb a significant share of the large-scale layoffs from the traditional state industrial strongholds.

However, the scope for increasing the size and number of enterprises in these new sectors is limited by the current lack of financial resources and the unavailability of credit. In Czechoslovakia, for example, only 4.7 per cent of all outstanding credit is to the private sector and this credit tends to be provided on less favourable terms. More importantly, as a legacy of the central planning system, most of the (public) banks in the region are unable to operate on a commercial basis. In particular, they do not have a concept of credit risk and creditworthiness, their main functions having been for more than forty years to collect deposits and allocate funds within the overall state budget without regard to the laws of supply and demand. In most EESU countries, local enterprises, private or public, find it nearly impossible to do such simple transactions as collect payments on exports, transfer funds, pay for imports, obtain letters of credit, open pay-roll accounts, pay local bills by cheque or wire or enquire about account balances. Borrowers, on the other hand, are unaccustomed to normal debt service and co-operation with their creditors. These represent serious constraints to the emergence of market activity. The strengthening of financial institutions and the development of private financial intermediaries represent an area where foreign expertise can be critical. The role of banks in transition economies needs to be completely redefined and they should be set up as institutions independent of government and run along commercial lines. Establishing a legislative framework in which property rights are well defined and contracts adhered to is another priority.

Another source of inertia in reallocating labour to light-industry and service sectors is the inappropriate qualification and training of the labour force. Burda (1991) stresses that there is a mismatch between job vacancies and worker's skills. There is excess supply of university graduates on the one hand and of blue collar labour on the other hand. Technical assistance to assist with training and labour reallocation becomes crucial at this stage.

A third important source of inertia in employment reallocation is housing. Privatization of housing should therefore play a crucial role in speeding up the restructuring process in EESU countries. Unfortunately, as pointed out by Fischer (1991), little attention has been devoted to the problems involved in privatizing the housing sector, in particular the unavailability of credit markets which is likely to slow down the sale of housing process substantially.

The implication then is that the growth of new small and medium-sized enterprises will be the major factor in the growth of a large private sector in EESU. This process will take time and during the period of labour reallocation complementary measures need to be designed to contain the number of liquidations and the ensuing flow of workers into unemployment to within 'reasonable' limits. These will be critical at least in the short run, so that the disbursal of unemployment benefits, necessary to prevent major social unrest, would not cause such a drain on fiscal resources so as to threaten macrostability. Such measures include temporary employment subsidies (see Flemming 1990) that would automatically accrue to firms or sectors that experienced negative quasi-rents as a consequence of dramatic changes in relative prices, for example as a result of a rise in the price of inputs relative to that of output, opening of trade or price liberalization. Such subsidies could be financed through a uniform profit or VAT tax. Temporary trade tariffs or state subsidies that would temporarily protect some sectors in the process of catching up in order that they become competitive with Western markets may also help (see Aghion and Burgess 1991).

International institutional support

Market failures and missing markets characterize all EESU countries at the current stage of the transition process. Advice and essential investments are needed to provide an environment conducive to industrial restructuring and private enterprise. There is a substantial need for international institutional support to improve market functioning and foster private sector activity through helping to build infrastructure and provide a regulatory and legislative framework which allows competition to work effectively.

Market failure arguments are particularly persuasive as concerns infrastructural investments where increasing returns, public goods and externalities can all be of considerable importance. Investments to improve transport, energy usage and telecommunications can have large positive effects on market development for all types of firms. Infrastructural investment will also have a key role to play in the redevelopment of regions which have suffered extensive environmental contamination or which will suffer major contractions in employment. These projects may be co-ordinated through EESU governments but should also attract foreign investment.

As we have shown, foreign direct investment and foreign partners can play a critical role in restructuring. However, the vast bulk of enterprises in Central and Eastern Europe will have to be restructured without the assistance of foreign strategic partners. International institutional support to assist this process should take a number of forms:

1 support for investment funds, including restructuring funds;
2 technical assistance for the restructuring of certain selected industries or enterprises, where this currently assists the management of key enterprises to take action;
3 bridge-to-sale finance for enterprises which require restructuring in order to complement their privatization plan and which can provide adequate security (which may include government guarantees).

Severe capital market imperfections impair the transactions of all types of firms but credit constraints act as a major barrier to entry for small and medium-size enterprises. This type of market failure explains why institutions like EBRD concentrate on providing lines of credit or equity resources to financial intermediaries (like the Dutch bank NMB in Poland or the Czechoslovakia Investment Corporation Inc. in Czechoslovakia) which, themselves, are dedicated to assisting small and medium-sized enterprises in these countries.

CONCLUDING REMARKS

The subject of this chapter has been microeconomic reform in EESU countries. A number of questions remain open, the answers to which are critical to the future course of transition. First, there is the issue of corporate governance and incentives. How should the various stakeholders in existing large state-owned companies be compensated so as to be amenable to and if possible promote restructuring and/or privatization policies, and what are the implications of this question for the design of efficient privatization methods? For example, what is the role of stock options and management buy-outs within the privatization process?

Another critical issue is the extent to which central institutions (e.g. Treuhand) can co-ordinate efforts to overcome the various governance and incentive patterns. There is also the question of the optimal design of such institutions given the specialities of different countries. The magnitude of the labour reallocation expected in EESU also raises the question as to what should be the trade-off of responsibilities between enterprises and the government for the social costs of transition.

A further issue is that of legal reform and enforcement, for example in the area of bankruptcy. In particular, what can be expected from the enactment of new laws in relation to the existing institutional framework as regards enforcement? For example, should bankruptcy laws be directly borrowed from Western economies or do they need to be progressively adapted as market structures and institutions emerge in EESU, or is there room for legal innovation?

Banking regulation is another area that has received very little attention. Yet the absence of a well-functioning commercial banking system in EESU remains a major barrier to the emergence of market activity. There is the question of what should be done with state banks in the interim period. For example, to what extent should

government or state bank credit be maintained to public enterprises? More importantly, there is the issue of how to provide financial support for new small and medium-sized enterprises and to allow them to compete on an equal credit footing with firms within the public sector credit system.

Finally, there is the issue of how to design international financial institutions to best assist the transition process. More exactly, how should the operations and priorities of these institutions be structured and how should different institutions interact? The unique position and special needs of transition economies suggest that some rethinking in this area is required (see Appendix 1). One might also ask how the financing policies of these multilateral institutions should reflect the structure of risks in the countries of operations. In this respect, as regards co-investment, the maintenance of creditworthiness (through conservative financial strategies) is of paramount importance.

APPENDIX 1: THE ROLE AND FINANCING POLICY OF THE EUROPEAN BANK FOR RECONSTRUCTION AND DEVELOPMENT

The European Bank for Reconstruction and Development mandate

The European Bank's economic mandate is to foster the transition to market economies through the promotion of private sector investment, through its involvement in privatization and through the creation and/or modernization of infrastructures and institutions (including financial intermediaries) necessary for private sector development. In short, the EBRD is primarily a market-based 'transition' bank. This is in contrast to MDBs like the IBRD and the IFC (or the ADB and the AfDB) whose charters emphasize growth and development as primary objectives but do not refer to the transition from one system to another or to the privatization of existing state-owned enterprises.[29]

To make the Bank's commitment to privatization a credible private sector development, its founding charter imposes that 60 per cent of the Bank's committed loans and equity participations be devoted to private sector investments and privatization activities (this is the 'merchant bank' half of the Bank), with only 40 per cent of total commitment being devoted to public infrastructure (this is the 'development bank' branch).

The rationale for this dual approach (merchant bank/development bank) stems from the conviction that development banks (e.g. the IBRD) over the last forty to fifty years have placed too much emphasis on public sector lending and planning. This tendency arose partly because of the observed efficiency of central planning during the Second World War, in particular in the USA and the UK (see Little 1982). In the World Bank group a shift in emphasis was signalled by those setting up a separate institution (the IFC) for operations with the private sector. However, the two entities have rarely moved along the same strategic path, thus making for a less effective use of total resources. By combining the two approaches under the same roof, the EBRD stresses the interdependence between private demand for and public supply of essential services and institutions necessary for the growth of private entrepreneurship in EESU. An example of this combination between 'bottom-up' (merchant banking) and 'top-down' (development banking) activities can be gleaned from the so-called 'pilot-privatization' programmes in Moscow and St Petersburg. The European Bank uses detailed empirical studies of a small number of medium-sized 'pilot enterprises' (e.g. the plastic manufacturer Diapason and the stone-processor MKK in Moscow) to identify the various obstacles (financial and legal) that constrain the privatization process as a whole.

The 'top-down' (or development banking) activities of the Bank are then aimed at removing such obstacles whilst assisting in building up the legal, regulatory, physical and financial infrastructures needed by new private enterprises to operate under normal conditions. The 'bottom-up' (or merchant banking) activities of the Bank, in turn, directly support and assist enterprises in order to foster the growth of the private sector.

In summary the role and concept of the EBRD differs significantly from other MDBs. Unlike the IMF it is not involved in national monetary policy or macro stabilization. Unlike the IBRD and the IMF its emphasis is not on the provision of direct financial assistance to governments and loans are restricted to viable projects mainly in the private sector. It does share with the IFC a policy of making investments in the equity of private sector companies[30] both to absorb risk and ease credit constraints; however, it has a much stronger commitment to privatization. Technical assistance constitutes a significant part of EBRD activities and is normally provided directly to public and private sector firms and institutions rather than through government channels which has been the standard approach (e.g. IBRD). The concept is to assist and support the domestic reform process rather than finance it.

The EBRD approach stems both from observations about the past problems and constraints of development banks[31] and from the conviction that the transition problem is in many respects distinct from the classical economic development problem. The former involves a *change* in economic systems (involving a reduction in state ownership of physical assets and state control over economic activity), whereas classical development theory usually deals with growth and welfare improvements within a *given* economic system. This distinction helps explain the Bank's emphasis on restructuring and privatization. This is also in line with a change of thinking within development economics that emphasizes the role of the state not in planning or production but rather in the provision of infrastructure, social services and a legislative, financial and regulatory framework conducive to private enterprise (see Stern 1991).[32] The main focus of the EBRD is on private sector development; however, the development banking/merchant banking structure of the EBRD aims to capitalize on public–private complementarities such as these.

Financing policy of the European Bank for Reconstruction and Development

Like the IFC and the IBRD, the Bank can make loans (but only project loans, i.e. not policy loans); like the IFC it can invest in the equity capital of private sector enterprises or public enterprises in the process of being privatized. Like the IBRD and the IFC, the EBRD can guarantee securities in which it has invested to facilitate their sale if enterprises have failed to sell them on the primary markets. It can also, unlike these other institutions, underwrite securities issued by private (or public) enterprises. In addition the Bank can provide technical assistance and training. The European Bank's total capital amounts to ECU 10 billion ($12 billion), 30 per cent of which will be paid in within four years (see Table 6A.1). The subscribed capital of the IBRD is $140 billion, out of which 18.8 billion is paid in. The total callable capital of the IFC is $3.5 billion, out of which 2.5 billion is paid in.

Before examining the operations of the Bank, let us briefly describe its capital structure and financing policy. In doing this we will try to answer the question: how did the Bank obtain an AAA debt rating by *Standard and Poor* in spite of the high credit risk and sovereign risk concentrations in EESU countries?

Compared with other MDBs, the EBRD benefits from a high proportion of paid-in capital and within both paid-in and callable capital there is a high proportion originating from AAA-rated countries. In the case of the EBRD, the total share of AAA member countries is above 66 per cent (the figure for the IBRD is about 55 per cent and, for the IFC, 61 per cent).

Lending by the European Bank is fully collateralized and therefore the Bank could only default on its borrowings if both its customers and its shareholders defaulted.

It follows from the above that the total disbursed loans, equity investments, guarantees and underwritings of the Bank cannot exceed the sum of callable capital and reserves. This brings us to the asset side of the Bank's balance sheet.

In theory (i.e. according to the founding agreements), we just split the 'asset' side of the balance sheet between our various ordinary operations (in disbursed terms rather than in committed terms) (Table 6A.2).

The founding agreements limit total disbursed equity investments to paid-in capital and reserves. This in turn makes it less likely that the repayment of the Bank's credits will depend on the uncalled capital of borrowing member countries.[33] The IFC has already introduced the same limit for similar reasons. This additional limit on equity

Table 6A.1 European Bank for Reconstruction and Development financial structure: liabilities

Assets	Liabilities
	Paid-in capital (+ reserves and surplus) 30%
	(IFC: 32%, IBRD: 7.2% only)
	Borrowings (70%)
	Total liabilities equivalent to 10 billion ECU ($12 billion)

Table 6A.2 European Bank for Reconstruction and Development balance sheet

Equity investment	Paid-in capital 30%	
Loans and guarantees		
	Borrowings 70%	Equivalent to callable capital
Liquidity		
Assets	Liabilities	

investments implies roughly that the Bank's ordinary operations might eventually be split in the ratio 4:3:3 – 40 per cent of public sector loans, 30 per cent of private sector loans, 30 per cent of private sector equity investments.

Also contributing to the Bank's management policy of not to resort to calling the uncalled callable capital is the liquidity level which, as in the World Bank, is set at a minimum level of 45 per cent of the next three years' cash requirements.[34] At this level the bank expects to cover all committed but undisbursed lending and investment during the same time period.

As concerns the terms of the Bank's operations, they are meant to be profitable overall (although profit maximization is not the primary criterion of the Bank's investment policy) while covering the various risks, especially the credit risk and the country risk.[35]

There is a strict policy to ensure that the risk of the Bank's operations remain manageable.

1 Specific limits are established on lending and equity financing by type of project, by country and by industry (this is the so-called risk-management matrix).

2 Loans are priced according to the credit risk class.

3 Credit and country risks are diversified by imposing a maximum exposure to individual projects, and/or individual borrowers, and individual countries. For example, no single borrower can be eligible for more than 5 per cent of total paid-in capital plus reserves. Also, the maximum equity exposure in each individual project is 3 per cent as in the IFC.

4 The EBRD share in any project financing should not exceed 50 per cent of total project cost for public sector loans and 35 per cent of total project cost for private sector loans or equity participation. This in turn guarantees that the credit risks will be shared with co-financiers. The upper limit for public sector loans is relatively larger owing to the following:

(a) the preferred creditor status of the Bank

regarding public sector loans (i.e. no debt obligations of the recipient country can be senior to those of the Bank);

(b) the fact that (all) public sector loans are backed by a guarantee from the borrowing member country.

5 Defaulting borrowers will be submitted to sanctions similar to those imposed by the IBRD: all further disbursements to a country will be suspended if a public borrower in that country is more than thirty days overdue on its repayments and no new commitment will be made when arrears exceed sixty days. For a private borrower, the suspension of disbursements will occur if the overdue period exceeds sixty days.

6 The Bank is exempt from any official action restricting the transferability of payments such as in the case of the repatriation of dividends. Any restriction such as foreign exchange control or remittance of capital gains on equity investments will be considered as a default by the country concerned.

All these precautionary provisions will clearly not completely eliminate the credit risks faced by the Bank. In order to meet its founding charter's requirements without having to resort to uncalled subscribed capital, the Bank is required to maintain adequate provisions against possible losses (on loans, equity investments, underwritings) and to charge such losses primarily to a general loss provision fund which for the moment covers only private sector activities.[36] This fund will be supplied automatically with 4 per cent of all new loans' disbursement and with 6 per cent of all equity disbursements at the time these disbursements are made. (The corresponding figures are 2.5 per cent for IBRD loans and 2 per cent for IFC loans or equity investments.) This loss provision fund will later be supplemented by transfers from retained earnings so as eventually to cover 10 per cent of disbursed loans and 25 per cent of disbursed equity. To be more precise, the Bank's founding charter requires that the EBRD transfer all retained earnings to a statutory reserve until these targets are reached. Also, the statutory reserve must represent 10 per cent of the authorized capital before the Bank will be able to pay out dividends and/or make transfer to other special funds. These measures further enhance the creditworthiness of the EBRD in the face of considerable EESU risk.

To be complete, we must indicate that 'special operations' such as technical assistance and training activities will be financed through a special fund which is both supplied and managed separately from the above. The supplies consist essentially of special grants from member countries' governments in addition to the callable capital of the Bank.

APPENDIX 2: THE TRADE-OFF BETWEEN CASH CONSTRAINTS AND MORAL HAZARD IN AUCTIONS: AN EXAMPLE

We restrict our attention to first-price auctions, although the argument would clearly carry over to other types of auctions (e.g. second-price or English auctions).

The government chooses in advance the proportions $(\alpha, 1 - \alpha)$ for the firm it privatizes, where α (respectively $1 - \alpha$) is the share of the bid price paid in period 1, i.e. equity (respectively in period 2, i.e. debt). Then, if b_i and B_i denote period 1 and period 2 parts of bidder i's bid, $i \in \{1, \ldots, n\}$, we must have

$$b_i = \alpha(b_i + B_i), \qquad \text{i.e. } b_i = \frac{\alpha B_i}{1 - \alpha}. \qquad (6A.1)$$

Let us first consider the simplest case without moral hazard or cash constraints. The revenue generated by bidder i is simply his valuation a_i which is privately known by bidder i. From the point of view of the other bidders $j \neq i$, a_i is *uniformly* distributed on the interval $[0, 1]$, so that $\text{prob}(a_i \leq a) = F(a) \equiv a, \forall a$.

Consider the decision of bidder i whose valuation is a_i. Given (6A.1) above, his two-part bid $(b_i,$

$B_i)$ is entirely determined by the second-period bid B_i since the debt–equity ratio $(1 - \alpha)/\alpha$ is already fixed by the government.

The Nash equilibrium (or more precisely the Bayesian equilibrium) of the first-price auction, whereby the highest bidder gets the firm at his (highest) bid price, is defined as follows. Bidder i predicts that all other bidders are bidding according to the same bidding function $B(a_j)$. Then, if bidder i bids a second-period price B_i, he will earn a surplus equal to

$$a_i - (b_i + B_i) = a_i - \frac{B_i}{1 - \alpha}$$

if he wins and a surplus of zero if he loses. The probability of winning with a bid B_i is the probability that all the other $n - 1$ bidders have valuations a_j such that $B(a_j) < a_i$ and this probability is equal to $[B^{-1}(B_i)]^{n-1}$. Then, bidder i chooses his bid B_i to maximize his expected surplus:

$$\pi_i = \left(a_i - \frac{B_i}{1 - \alpha}\right)[B^{-1}(B_i)]^{n-1}.$$

Now the Nash requirement imposes that the rivals' use of the decision rule B be consistent with their own maximization behaviour. Hence the symmetric Nash equilibrium of the first-price auction is defined by the bidding function $B(a)$ such that

$$B(a_i) = \text{argmax}\left\{\left(a_i - \frac{B_i}{1 - \alpha}\right)[B^{-1}(B_i)]^{n-1}\right\}. \qquad (6A.2)$$

Then we get[37]

$$B(a_i) = (1 - \alpha)\frac{n - 1}{n}a_i. \qquad (6A.3)$$

Therefore, in the absence of wealth constraints and moral hazard, the government obtains the same total payment $\forall \alpha$, equal to

$$\frac{B(\bar{a})}{1-\alpha} = \frac{n-1}{n}\bar{a}, \qquad \text{where } \bar{a} = \max_i a_i.$$

Introducing wealth constraints $b_i \leq m_i$, we get

$$B(a_i) = (1-\alpha)\min\left(\frac{n-1}{n}a_i, \frac{m_i}{\alpha}\right),$$

so that the government's revenue is given by

$$\frac{\bar{B}}{1-\alpha} = \min\left(\frac{n-1}{n}a_i, \frac{m_i}{\alpha}\right),$$

where i is the winning bidder defined by argmax $B(a_j) = i$. Clearly, the government's revenue is maximized when $\alpha = 0$, i.e. when an 'all-debt' structure is first set up.

To obtain a 'trade-off', i.e. an interior solution in α, let us introduce moral hazard considerations by means of the following example. We assume that bidder i can realize his valuation a_i only if the enterprise is successful, which in turn depends upon bidder i's effort once he has acquired the firm. Formally, if y_i denotes the revenue generated by bidder i in period 2 through his management of the privatized enterprise, we assume that

$$y_i = \begin{cases} a_i \text{ with probability } P \\ 0 \text{ with probability } 1 - P \end{cases}$$

where P is the effort and $C(P) = P^2/2A$ is the quadratic cost of effort.

First, let us assume wealth constraints away. Then, given $(\alpha, 1-\alpha)$ chosen by the government and given his winning bid offer B_i, bidder i chooses effort P so as to maximize

$$\max_P [P(a_i - B_i) - C(P)]$$

which implies first-order conditions

$$a_i - B_i = \frac{P}{A}$$

giving

$$P = A(a_i - B_i)$$

which we assume to be strictly less than unity. (More generally, $P = \min[1, A(a_i - B_i)]$.)

Anticipating this choice of effort, bidder i will choose B_i so as to maximize

$$\max_{B_i}\left\{(a_i - B_i)\left(a_i - \frac{B_i}{1-\alpha}\right)[B^{-1}(B_i)]^{n-1}\right\}$$

$$= \max_{B_i} II_i. \tag{6A.4}$$

First-order conditions are

$$\frac{\partial II_i}{\partial a_i} = \left(a_i - \frac{B_i}{1-\alpha} + a_i - B_i\right)a_i^{n-1} \tag{6A.5}$$

Let $B_i = \hat{B}a_i$. We have (integrating (6A.5))

$$II_i = \frac{2a_i^{n+1}}{n+1} - \frac{\hat{B}a_i^{n+1}}{(1-\alpha)(n+1)} - \frac{\hat{B}a_i^{n+1}}{n+1}. \tag{6A.6}$$

Equations (6A.5) and (6A.6) imply that $\hat{B}$ is a solution to the equation

$$\frac{\hat{B}^2}{1-\alpha} - \frac{n}{n+1}\left(1 + \frac{1}{1-\alpha}\right)\hat{B} + 1 - \frac{2}{n+1} = 0.$$

When $n \to +\infty$, the solution $\hat{\varsigma}$ converges to $1 - \alpha$.

The corresponding effort level is given by

$$P(a_i) = Aa_i[1 - (1-\alpha)] = \alpha Aa_i.$$

In particular, the higher α is (i.e. the lower the debt–equity ratio), the higher is the effort of bidder i. We thus obtain the trade-off we were looking for once wealth constraints are reintroduced.

Assuming that the government chooses α *ex ante* so as to maximize its expected sales revenue, one should generally end up with an interior solution α^*. The following remarks should be noted.

1 The precise derivation of α^* requires further assumptions on the distribution of valuations and wealth endowments; under these assumptions, *ex ante* efficiency maximization would also generally lead to an interior solution α^{**}.

2 As mentioned in the text, if bankruptcy involved substantial costs for the bidder-manager, the optimal debt–equity ratio would correspond to $\alpha^* = 0$.

NOTES

1 Appendix 1 provides a description of the role and financing policy of the EBRD.

2 Handler *et al.* (1991) independently and using a Harrod–Domar approach obtain a similar figure of $1.0–1.1 trillion for the cumulated capital requirement of the EESU region in the year 2000.

3 EBRD estimates.

4 This is in keeping with the history of economic development in both industrial and developing nations. Mobilization of savings is critical – on this aspect in EESU see Tanzi (1991).

5 See Appendix 1 for a definition of these ratings.

6 Note that the preferred creditor status, which grants absolute seniority of debt claims to the IFI which beneficiates from this status, may also have the negative second-order effect of crowding out subsequent loans to the public sector that would by definition be junior to the IFI's loans.

7 See Williamson (1991) for an interesting discussion of this issue.

8 Note that though the bulk of this discussion is couched in terms of enterprises, the arguments cited apply equally well to other types of small economic assets (e.g. retail outlets, services).

9 The leasing out of a state enterprise's assets to new private company(ies), sometimes confusingly called 'liquidation', has proved to be very popular in Poland for the privatization of smaller companies. Of 143 liquidated as at June 1991, forty-eight were privatized through sale of assets and ninety-five through the leasing of assets. Leasing of small enterprises has also been an integral part of the industrial reforms in China.

10 This idea emerged from fruitful conversations with John Flemming and John Vickers. A similar multi-part auction approach is also developed by Bolton and Roland (1992).

11 However, as Grossman and Hart (1982) point out, if bankruptcy involved substantial (private) costs for the bidder-manager, then a higher debt–equity ratio would induce more effort from him.

12 Romania has developed a similar programme, but with a smaller number of funds and a greater reliance on state-administered trade sales. Amongst the other CIS republics, the Ukraine and Kazakhstan are considering vouchers.

13 The emergence of 'funds' (e.g. the Harvard Fund) which offer a sum in excess of a voucher price in return for ownership of the voucher when it becomes tradeable is an example of this process.

14 For example, in Poland the government conserves 30 per cent of the shares in large state-owned enterprises undergoing mass privatization. In Romania, where a voucher scheme is also being promoted, the government conserves 70 per cent of the shares of large state-owned enterprises in the first stage of their privatization.

15 Giving *voting* shares to local governments 'would make them large shareholders with a substantial interest in active control. While workers' shares are dispersed, local government shares are concentrated. In many cases, local governments would use their ownership rights to deal with privatization and to continue managing the state firms ...'.

16 'Concentration of powers in a single agency responsible only to the highest level of government has made it easier to develop a privatization programme, particularly when the agency is given direct powers to divest assets. With such a centralisation of powers, and because of the size of the privatization task, it has often been easier to implement privatizations if there is some decentralisation of operations to local or regional branches, possibly coupled with a delegation of authority to enterprises for enterprise-led privatizations' (Sasson 1991).

17 To recapitalize banks further, the state can also issue government bonds and exchange them against non-performing loans to enterprises. Shares received by state banks in the privatization of enterprises could later be sold to repay the government loans.

18 In particular, adherence to such a Pareto-improving path might not be achieved through a reform package that would involve industrial dislocation, mass unemployment and a deep recession in the short run.

19 Adjustment costs due to short-downs and labour reallocation across firms and sectors are magnified by short-term factors affecting companies: reduced domestic demand, the collapse of intra-EESU trade, vertical disintegration and high debts, interest payments and taxes.

20 The same considerations become relevant when addressing the privatization issue: to prevent

workers' councils from blocking privatizations (as they have already done so in several EESU countries), social compensations for layoffs should be paid by the privatized company with financial help from the privatization agency.

21 See Aghion *et al.* (1992) for a bankruptcy procedure which overcomes this valuation issue.

22 In this context the experience of central privatization agencies such as the Treuhand in East Germany are of considerable interest (see Carlin and Mayer 1992).

23 In addtion, excessive vertical integration may induce inefficient (over)investment incentives and market foreclosure outcomes that, in the EESU context, would jeopardize the emergence and development of new private businesses.

24 This type of argument may help to explain the empirical finding of a concentration of trade in high quality products amongst the rich industrial nations. The argument can be formalized using a Shaked–Sutton (1982) type of model; see Aghion and Burgess (1991) for a technical discussion of trade and growth in the EESU setting.

25 Note that central government agrees to have a much greater ability to internalize social costs than private firms.

26 Prepared by the World Bank, the OECD, the EBRD and the IMF.

27 Given that the total Soviet labour force is around 148 million people, the volume of total current employment in agriculture and manufacturing is about 64.8 million workers. This figure should be brought down to 47.4 million in order to meet the average Western proportions. On the other hand, total current employment in the wholesale–retail trade is about 9.8 million workers. This volume should increase to 38.5 million so as to meet Western standards. The corresponding aggregate turnover is at least equal to the minimum of these two labour flows, i.e. over 21 million workers (the maximum of the two flows is 27 million workers).

28 Although the existing state-owned retail shops are often considered as being overmanned by Western standards, in the sense that the productivity of labour on each individual transaction is much lower than in the West. There is nonetheless considerable scope for increasing the amount of retail transactions, both within existing retail units and through the multiplication of new retail shops and services throughout the countries. Such spreading out of retail units may involve some new inefficiency, e.g. of having shops unvisited during most of the working day; on the other hand, it eliminates the great economic inefficiency involved in the persistence of queues.

29 For example, the IFC's official mandate is to further economic development by encouraging the growth of private enterprises in member countries.

30 The provision by EBRD of lines of credit and equity investments in the Dutch bank NMB and in the Czechoslovakia Investment Corporation Inc. which provide critical financing for small and medium-sized enterprises in Poland and Czechoslovakia is a good example of this approach.

31 The poor financial and repayment performance of loans to the public sector in developing countries is a major consideration. The perceived inefficiency of the state in promoting private enterprise in these countries is another.

32 In a transition setting the implication is that the role of the state will change significantly; however, it will still remain important to the process. Indeed, given the great need for infrastructure, social support, co-ordination and the establishment of clear guidelines for economic activity, it would seem unwise to adopt a minimalist view of the state during transition.

33 The management policy of the Bank is also restricting the total volume of committed operations to less than 90 per cent of total callable capital and reserves, so that the repayment of the Bank's creditors should never depend on the callable capital of EESU countries.

34 The IFC has adopted a still more conservative policy with liquid assets covering over 90 per cent of the next three years' estimated cash requirements.

35 The latter embodies political risks, risks arising due to low foreign-currency earnings and risks related to foreign debt policy. There is also the foreign exchange risks, which the Bank will eliminate on its lending operations by imposing that its loans be repaid in the same hard currency (ECU, US$, yen …) as the one they are being billed in. Equity investments will present a special risk in this respect since they will largely be denominated in non-convertible currencies. In that case, the exchange rate risk will be borne by the Bank. Finally, interest rate risk will be issued by having interest rates set at the time of the loan disbursement, while the loan margin will be set at the time the loan is committed!

36 Losses on loans, equity investments and under-writings will be charged in the following order:

1 'automatic' provisions against losses;
2 statutory reserves (retained earnings);
3 unimposed paid-in capital;
4 uncalled subscribed capital.

No provision is made regarding losses arising in

'special operations' such as technical assistance, which are covered by a special fund.

$$37 \quad \frac{\partial II_i}{\partial a_i} = \frac{dII_i}{da_i} = [B^{-1}(B_i)]^{n-1} = a_i^{n-1}$$

(by the envelope theorem). Hence

$$II_i = \frac{a_i^n}{n} = \left(a_i - \frac{B_i}{1-\alpha}\right)a_i^{n-1}$$

which yields (6A.3).

BIBLIOGRAPHY

Aghion, P. and Burgess, R. (1991) 'Trade and growth in Eastern Europe and the Soviet Union', mimeo, London: EBRD.

Aghion, P., Hart, O. and Moore, J. (1992) 'The economics of bankruptcy reform', paper presented at the NBER Conference on Transition in Eastern Europe, Cambridge, MA.

Blanchard, O., Dornbusch, R., Layard, R. and Summers, L. (1991) *Reform in Eastern Europe*, Cambridge, MA: MIT Press.

Bolton, P. and Rolland, C. (1992) 'The economics of mass-privatization', *Economic Policy*, forthcoming.

Burda, M. (1991) 'Labour and product markets in Czechoslovakia and the ex-GDR: a twin study', *European Economy*, Special Edition No. 2, Brussels.

Carlin, W. and Mayer, C. (1992) 'The Treuhandanstalt: privatization by state and market', paper presented at the NBER Conference on Transition in Eastern Europe, Cambridge, MA.

Collins, S. and Rodrik, D. (1991) 'Eastern Europe and the Soviet Union in the world economy', in *Policy Analysis in International Economics No. 32*, Washington, DC: Institute for International Economics.

Economic Commission for Europe (1991) *Economic Survey of Europe, 1991–92*, New York: United Nations.

Fischer, S. (1991) 'Privatization in Eastern European transformation', Working Paper, Washington, DC: Institute for Policy Reform.

Flemming, J. (1990) 'Gradualism and shock treatment for tax and structural reform', *Fiscal Studies* 11 (3): 12–26.

Frydman, R. and Rapaczynski, A. (1990) 'Markets and institutions in large scale privatizations', mimeo, New York University.

Grossman, S. and Hart, O. (1982) 'Corporate financial structure and managerial incentives', in J. McCall (ed.) *The Economics of Information and Uncertainty*, Chicago, IL: University of Chicago Press.

Handler, H., Kramer, A. and Stankovsky, J. (1991) *Debt, Capital Requirements and Training of the Eastern Countries*, Austrian Institute of Economic Research.

Hare, P. and Hughes, G. (1991) 'Competitiveness and industrial restructuring in Czechoslovakia, Hungary and Poland', *European Economy*, Special Edition No. 2, Brussels.

IMF, World Bank, OECD, EBRD (1991) *A Study of the Soviet Economy*.

Lipton, D. and Sachs, J. (1990) 'Creating a market economy in Eastern Europe: the case of Poland', *Brookings Papers on Economic Activity* 1.

Little, I. M. D. (1982) *Economic Development*, New York: Basic Books.

Maskin, E. (1992) 'Auctions and privatization, mimeo, Harvard University.

Messerlin, P. A. (1991) *Trade between OECD Countries and Central and Eastern European Countries*, Institut d'Etudes Politiques de Paris.

Mitchell, J. (1990) 'The economics of bankruptcy in reforming socialist economies', mimeo, Cornell University.

Sasson, H. (1991) 'The privatization experience in Western Europe', mimeo, EBRD, London.

Shaked, A. and Sutton, J. (1982) 'Relaxing price competition through product differentiation', *Review of Economic Studies* 49: 3–13.

Shleifer, A. and Vishny, R. W. (1992) 'Privatization in Russia: first steps', paper presented at the NBER Conference on Transition in Eastern Europe, Cambridge, MA.

Stern, N. (1991) 'Public policy and the economics of development', *European Economic Review* 35: 241–71.

Tanzi, V. (1991) 'Mobilisation of savings in Eastern European countries: the role of the state', in A. B. Atkinson and R. Brunetta (eds) *Economics for the New Europe*, London: International Economic Association.

Tirole, J. (1991) 'Privatization in Eastern Europe: incentives and the economics of transition', mimeo, Massachusetts Institute of Technology.

Williamson, O. (1991) 'Private ownership and the capital market', paper presented at a conference on privatization at the Kiel Institute of World Economics.

Part II

THE EUROPEAN MONETARY UNION

The Delors Committee report, entitled *Economic and Monetary Union in the European Community* (Committee for the Study of Economic and Monetary Union, Brussels, June 1990), focused on the main features of an economic and monetary union among members of the EC and how to achieve it. Interested readers are recommended to read it. The report emphasized that economic and monetary union must be achieved together. It indicated three basic characteristics of a monetary union: (1) total and irreversible convertibility of currencies, (2) complete freedom of capital movements in fully integrated financial markets and (3) irrevocably fixed exchange rates with no fluctuation margin between members' currencies. The basic elements of an economic union are a single market within which goods, services, capital and labour can move freely, a joint competition policy to strengthen market mechanisms, common structural and regional policies and sufficient co-ordination of macroeconomic policies, including binding rules for budgetary policies. The Delors report envisaged the creation of a union as a gradual – if not evolutionary – process. It saw no need to set deadlines for the completion of any stage. It insisted, however, on stage one beginning no later than 1 July 1990, when full liberalization of capital movements was to become effective for most of the EC countries. In this stage, the emphasis was to be on strengthening the economic and monetary policy co-ordination needed to secure greater convergence of economic performance in all key sectors. The second stage was envisioned to focus on institutional reforms, i.e. the European System of Central Banks (ESCB) had to be evolved, established and made functional. The difficult and sensitive task of transferring decision-making power from the national authorities to the ESCB was to be attained towards the end of this stage. Again, no timetable was set. The third and final stage was to attain the irrevocable locking of exchange rates and the complete transfer of essential powers to the Community institutions. The ESCB, at this stage, was to be fully operational and its Council would control exchange market interventions in third currencies, in line with the exchange rate policy adopted by the Community. The transition to a single community currency was to be carried out at this stage.

To be sure, economic and monetary union will have a far-reaching impact. It is expected to improve the microeconomic efficiency of the economy. The flip-side is that the union will also have macroeconomic aspects, affecting both inflation and the real economy. As for efficiency gains, a single currency will eliminate currency transaction costs and exchange rate uncertainty completely. The intra-EC transaction costs amount to around $15–20 billion annually which is a little under 0.5 per cent of the GDP of the community. Market integration will result in further efficiency gains. The various microeconomic and static efficiency gains will combine to improve the macroeconomic dynamics. Any efforts that improve the risk-adjusted rate of return on investment will eventually stimulate a higher investment effort which, in turn, will stimulate medium- and long-term growth.

A gradual consensus has emerged in the EC that the future central bank, which would be styled after the Bundesbank in terms of institutional structure and independence, must devote maximum attention to the maintenance of price stability. The economies in the Community, which have been lax in this respect, can minimize the transitional costs of disinflation by association with institutions enjoying a reputation of stability. Thus, the Community can benefit from building its monetary union around the most stable currencies of the EMS. In addition, when the ECU emerges as a major industrial currency, it will have its own benefits. Principal among them are lower transaction costs for the EC's external trade; advantages for EC banks which might gain in market share in international portfolio transactions; a lesser need for external reserves held by the EC central banks; and some international seigniorage gains from ECU bank notes.

The Economic and Monetary Union has taken a big step forward with the treaty of Maastricht (December 1991). The treaty has laid down the main element and determined the course of economic and monetary union for years ahead. A three-stage approach to monetary union has been proposed under the treaty. These stages are equivalent to what the Delors report proposed. The treaty visualizes that initially the member states are to work towards convergence of economic performance. To this end, four indicators are to be used: inflation differentials, exchange rate stability, interest rate differentials and sustainable fiscal deficits and debt. In the first stage, policy changes are to be initiated by member states to improve policy co-ordination. In the following stage, the surveillance of progress towards meeting these criteria will be intensified. In the final stage, member states that meet the specified economic conditions will irrevocably fix their exchange rates and form a monetary union. The treaty suggests time boundaries: if a majority of states are able to achieve the necessary conditions in 1996, stage three could begin in 1997; if not, it would begin in January 1999.

The conditions prescribed for participation in the economic and monetary union are indubitably stringent: (1) the inflation rate must not exceed by more than 1.5 percentage points the inflation rates of the three best-performing member states; (2) long-term interest rates must not be more than 2 percentage points above those in the three member states with lowest inflation; (3) the exchange rate must have been held for two years within the narrow band of fluctuation of the exchange rate mechanism of the EMS without a devaluation at the member state's own initiative; (4) the general government deficit, which includes the consolidated deficit of the central, state and local governments and the social security funds, must not exceed 3 per cent of GDP; and (5) the ratio of public debt to GDP should be no higher than 60 per cent. From January 1994, which is when the second stage begins, member states will be required to implement their plans for enabling them to meet the convergence criteria. Public sector deficits and debt will be monitored and the lagging member states will receive policy recommendations from the EC Council of Ministers. The member states will also be expected to make necessary adjustments in their national central banking and financial markets. Also, all the barriers on the movement of capital will need to be dismantled.

A new institute called the European Monetary Institute (EMI) will be created. It will comprise the national central bank governors and will replace the EMCF. The EMI will not only take over the tasks of the EMCF but also strengthen co-operation among central banks, monitor developments in the EMS and lay the technical groundwork for the establishment of the ESCB. Additionally, the EMI may manage foreign exchange reserves as an agent for national central banks. A summit meeting of the heads of the states in 1996 will decide whether a majority of member states fulfil the necessary conditions for the adoption of a single currency and whether it is appropriate for the EC to enter the third and final phase. After determining the time for entering the final stage, the ESCB will be established. Also, at this time the member states that are adjudged as ready to participate in the union will transfer authority over monetary and exchange rate policy to the ESCB.

The first chapter in this section traces the recent progress made, comments on alternative possibilities and gropes towards the future path for the European monetary union. For the Delors plan to be successful, the twin conditions needed are (1) the convergence of inflationary expectations and (2) the stability of exchange rates. The second chapter, by Giovannini, discusses the problems of achieving and sustaining these twin objectives. It also addresses the extent to which inflationary expectations have converged among France, Germany and Italy and what this implies for monetary reform.

The third chapter, by Frenkel and Goldstein, goes a step ahead and discusses the key issues relating to the design and implementation of monetary policy in the emerging economic and monetary union. It goes on to explore the inter-relationships between price stability, current account equilibrium and exchange rate stability. Turning to the implementation of monetary policy, the issues addressed include co-ordination versus autonomy, rules versus discretion and the role of sterilized official intervention. Thygesen, a member of the Delors Committee, dwells on identical issues

in the fourth chapter. He briefly reviews some analytical and operational issues arising at an advanced stage of monetary integration. He raises the question of whether an intermediate set of objectives can be helpful in underpinning the attainment of the final targets. Towards the end of this chapter he also goes into the possible instruments by which the ESCB and the participating national central banks might discharge and divide their responsibilities for monetary policy.

The fifth chapter in this section goes intensively into the economics of economic and monetary union and tries to assess its costs and benefits. It compares the costs and benefits of three pure regimes, namely financial market autarky, free float and economic and monetary union. It also clarifies several economic concepts used in the context of economic and monetary union. Finally, the sixth chapter first studies the conceptual background of a one-currency-Europe and concludes that despite some limitations a single currency would be a great help in creating economic integration as well as monetary stability as long as certain conditions are fulfilled. This chapter also deals with the institutional propositions as well as the role of the ECU in the process of European monetary union.

7

THE EUROPEAN MONETARY SYSTEM AND ITS FUTURE PROSPECTS

Karl Otto Pöhl

INTRODUCTION

The member countries of the EC have made considerable progress in recent years in their efforts to achieve greater convergence in their economic policies and economic development. Stability of the value of money as the prime objective at the national level and exchange rate stability as the common goal within the EMS have been achieved to a higher degree than ever before. The generally favourable economic and monetary situation provides sound prerequisites for achieving the objective of creating a single European market by 1992. This would fulfil essential preconditions for an *economic union*.

With the planned creation of an integrated financial market with free movement of capital, a basic component of a future *monetary union* would also exist. An additional basic element, namely firmly fixed exchange rates, is admittedly not in prospect within the foreseeable future because setbacks in co-ordinating economic policy can no more be excluded than can disturbances in the financial markets and the real economy, which can make exchange rate adjustments necessary. Also, corrections in exchange rates will remain a necessary safety valve for the foreseeable future within the EMS in order to reduce any tensions that may arise without incurring excessive damage to individual economies or the Community as a whole. Even the unification of the markets to form a single European market does not necessarily presuppose the existence of a monetary union or a common currency.

The time may nevertheless have come to develop some concrete ideas about the process of integration which can lead to a monetary union.

A number of recent proposals seek to anticipate the emergence of new conflicts between the common objective of exchange rate stability and national notions of price stability through a quantum leap, by coupling the commitment to achieve a single European market and an integrated financial space with freedom of capital movements by 1992 with the creation of a European central bank. From the German point of view it is essential to ensure, in the discussions about the future design of a European monetary order, that monetary and credit policy is not geared to stability to a lesser extent in an economically united Europe than is the case at present in the Federal Republic of Germany. Apart from this, it should be made clear that monetary integration cannot move ahead of general economic integration, since otherwise the whole process of integration would be burdened with considerable economic and social tensions. Moreover, examples from history demonstrate that new nations did not confer a uniform monetary order on themselves until after the process of unification was concluded. Any durable attempt to fix exchange rates within the Community and finally to replace national currencies by a European currency would be doomed to failure so long as a minimum of policy-shaping and decision-making in the field of economic and fiscal policy does not take place at the Community level. Without this prerequisite being met, a common European monetary policy cannot ensure monetary stability on its own. Above all, it cannot paper over the problems in the Community arising from differing economic and fiscal policies.

The following considerations begin with the basic elements of an economic and monetary union. The thread cannot simply be picked up from the ideas contained in the Werner report as long ago as 1970, namely to move towards this goal via a multi-stage plan. Experience has been gained with the 'snake' and the EMS, and with the progress in economic and monetary policy co-operation evidence has been found which suggests the need for a new start. In this context, it must be ensured from the outset that agreement exists between the governments and the Community institutions for which they are responsible with respect to the basic issues of economic policy. Above all, agreement must exist that stability of the value of money is the indispensable pre-requisite for the achievement of other goals. Particular importance should therefore be attached to the principles on which a European monetary order should be based.

Drawing partially on preliminary work conducted within the Community on the second stage of the EMS, three models of monetary integration are then presented and examined with respect to their compatibility with the demands of a future monetary union. The models that have been selected take ideas into account that play a role in political discussions or could play a role in them at any time. Since it can be assumed that the goal of monetary union cannot be reached in a quantum jump but only as the result of a process of integration encompassing economic and monetary policy, individual conceivable stages of integration with their political implications are taken into consideration. The problems arising from the differing speed of integration on the part of individual countries as well as from the institutional and legal aspects of integration are also discussed.

THE FINAL OBJECTIVE OF MONETARY INTEGRATION

Economic and monetary integration

The characteristics of a monetary union

The final objective of monetary union was defined as long ago as 1970 in the Werner report in a formulation that still applies today: '*A monetary union* implies inside its boundaries the total and irreversible convertibility of currencies, the elimination of margins of fluctuation in exchange rates, the irrevocable fixing of parity rates and the complete liberation of movements of capital.' *The decisive criteria for a monetary union are thus the irrevocable fixing of exchange rates and movements of capital within the single monetary area that are free from restrictions. The monetary union is the 'monetary superstructure' of the economic union* in which the 'four freedoms' have been realized, namely the free movements of goods, services, labour and capital. Within the common single market, economic activity is to be based on a free market system of competition. Besides agreement on regulative policy, an economic union demands a far-reaching harmonization of government regulations in order to bring about equal competitive conditions and uniform markets. Although structural and regional differences between the member countries (especially differences in income and productivity) are compatible with an economic union, the structural and regional policy of the Community must take them into account.

In principle, national currencies can be retained in the monetary union. However, the introduction of a uniform monetary symbol would give the union a 'monetary identity', eliminate the residual risk of parity changes among the national currencies and hence assure the continuing existence of a single monetary area. The replacement of national currencies by a common currency would indeed be the 'crowning act' of the process of monetary integration.

Above and beyond the integration effects of a single European market, a monetary union provides a number of additional economic advantages. First, the irrevocable fixing of parities means that the exchange rate risk associated with the intra-Community exchange of goods, services and capital is eliminated. This will foster, in particular, the integration of the financial markets and the strengthening of competition. Second, there will be a saving in transaction costs since market participants will be increasingly willing to accept partner currencies or the common currency without taking recourse to hedging operations and to hold them as a means of payment or investment in the place of national currencies. Third, the creation of a monetary area with a greater weight internationally entails advantages in transactions with third countries since the international acceptance of the Community will grow, the Community will become less susceptible to external shocks and it will be able to represent its monetary policy interests more effectively at the international level. The introduction of a common currency would allow full advantage to be drawn from these benefits.

Implications for economic policy

Within the monetary union, economic policy must be directed towards eliminating causes of tension that could jeopardize its cohesion and towards preventing new tensions from arising. The irrevocable fixing of parity rates is possible only on the basis of exchange rates at which differences in rates of price increase, in balance-of-payments positions and in the field of public finances have been eliminated to a large extent. With fixed exchange rates, insufficient convergence in these three fields would give rise to adjustment constraints in the real economy that would endanger the cohesion of the monetary union or would ultimately bring about adjustments in parities forcefully. The harmonization of rates of inflation at the lowest possible level is necessary since any shifts that may arise in terms of price competitiveness can no longer be offset by realignments. Countries with an above-average rate of inflation would suffer competitive losses; conversely, tendencies towards excess demand

would be triggered in countries with cost advantages.

When parity relationships are irrevocably fixed, the external positions of the partner countries must be compatible with each other since the competitive weaknesses of one partner would burden the aggregate balance-of-payments position of the monetary union *vis-à-vis* the rest of the world. Even if the current account position of the monetary union were in balance as a whole it would not be possible for a single country within the Community to rely on capital inflows and the corresponding growth of indebtedness indefinitely. Finally, there would have to be a large degree of convergence in the field of public finance. Considerable, or even unlimited, recourse by a member state (or the central authority) to central bank credit would make monetary control throughout the monetary area difficult, if not impossible, and – no matter how they are financed – excessive national budget deficits would burden the overall current account position of the monetary union.

Securing convergence within the monetary union – with the retention of national currencies initially – will imply losses in independence in terms of national economic policy, i.e. a shift of responsibilities from the national to the Community level. This applies both to fiscal, economic, social and wages policy as well as – to a particularly marked extent – to monetary policy: ideally, within the monetary union national currencies are 'perfect substitutes', i.e. market participants are indifferent as regards the various existing currencies. The irrevocable fixing of parity rates under conditions of complete freedom of capital movements implies that national interest rate levels must converge (apart from minor differences arising from market imperfections). It will thus no longer be possible to conduct an independent national monetary policy that is geared to a national standard.

The basic stance of monetary policy must be laid down by a co-ordinating body at the Community level. National central banks will then only be executive organs for the Community's monetary policy. To the extent that they are able to achieve the operational objectives laid down by the Community, the harmonization of their instruments will not be necessary initially. This will in any case be possible only within limits in the preliminary stages since there are wide differences in existing structures of national money, credit and capital markets that will not disappear immediately even after the complete liberalization of capital movements. However, owing to differing national transmission mechanisms of monetary policy as well as structural differences in the demand for money, it will be possible to achieve a uniform policy for monetary growth that is geared to a monetary target for the Community only gradually. Thus, as far as its practical application is concerned, national differences will persist. The creation of a uniform European money market which the central authority responsible for monetary policy can manage with instruments of its own, however, will be necessary at the latest when a common currency is introduced.

Monetary policy co-ordination needs to be complemented by the transfer of responsibility for monetary relationships with the rest of the world to the Community level since the exchange rates of the partner currencies must develop uniformly. Exchange rate policy *vis-à-vis* third countries must therefore be laid down at the Community level, interventions on the foreign exchange market must be decided jointly (with intervention operations perhaps being centralized at a national central bank or a common fund for reasons of expediency) and monetary reserves must be pooled. In the field of international monetary policy the Community would act as a single entity. Instead of individual countries, it would then also need to be a member of the IMF.

Whereas the national states would necessarily lose their monetary policy independence in a monetary union, they can quite easily retain certain responsibilities in the field of fiscal and economic policy, as is the case in every federation of states. However, in order to exclude any doubts about the cohesion of the monetary union from the outset and at the same time avoid an overburdening of monetary policy, it must be ensured that there is

sufficient conformity of action in fiscal and economic policy within the Community. This is because any lack of convergence that could give rise to expectations of parity changes would need to be 'bridged' through interventions and interest rate measures on the national money markets in order to ensure the continuing existence of the monetary or exchange rate union. Over time it will thus be necessary to allow for the necessary transfer of economic and fiscal policy responsibilities from national authorities to Community organs.

In order to optimize economic policy as a whole the overall economic objectives for the monetary area should be laid down at the Community level. Broad agreement would also need to be reached on the policy mix, i.e. the combination of fiscal and monetary policy appropriate for achieving the overall economic objectives. This would provide a basic guideline for each country's fiscal policy. Moreover, together with the creation of the single European market, a far-reaching – but not necessarily complete – harmonization of indirect taxes would be necessary in order to avoid competitive distortions. Although, given the existing low degree of mobility of income earners, direct taxes do not need to be harmonized to the same extent, with unchanged shares of expenditure by the public sector in GNP, the harmonization of indirect taxes will also create a need to adjust direct taxes as well as the overall burden of levies.

In the light of existing structural imbalances within the Community, when parity rates are irrevocably fixed it will be necessary to put in place a system of 'fiscal compensation' through a Community organ in favour of the structurally weak member countries. Transfer payments would compensate the weaker members for the burdens of adjustment associated with the definitive renouncement of devaluations as a means of maintaining their competitiveness. Thus, within the monetary union, balance-of-payments policy is replaced by regional policy, with the latter helping to finance interregional differences in current account imbalances through transfer payments. The differences in the level of economic development of individual member countries of the Community suggest that extremely large funds would be needed to finance the necessary fiscal compensation. Only through a very effective regional policy could these differences perhaps be reduced to an extent that would be compatible with the existence of a monetary union.

Incomes policy must also take the fixing of parity rates within the monetary union into account. Divergences in regional developments (such as differing rates of increase in productivity or shifts in demand, for instance) require a correspondingly differentiated development of wages in so far as they are not offset by fiscal adjustment within the Community. Although regional imbalances can be offset through the mobility of the factors of production, this kind of adjustment would be associated with a shifting of capital and finally also of labour out of the less competitive regions that would be undesirable in terms of regional policy (and which, owing to the far lesser degree of mobility of labour, would not occur without friction). Thus, given diverging developments in competitiveness, renouncing exchange rate adjustments will require a differentiated wages policy, which would also need to cover ancillary wage costs. In branches of industry that manufacture their products under widely similar conditions a harmonization of nominal wage developments is to be expected within the monetary union in the absence of which diverging rates of inflation could arise. For this reason, even before the inception of the monetary union the basic willingness of both sides of industry to pursue a wages and incomes policy geared to the operating conditions of such a union must exist, especially bearing in mind that an increasing orientation of wage demands towards the highest level in the Community is to be expected within the monetary union. However, given the independent right to conclude collective wage agreements that is appropriate in an economic union based on the rules of free competition, the scope for economic policy to affect the development of wages and salaries directly is very restricted. Everything will therefore ultimately depend on a credible and

rigorously pursued monetary policy that limits the scope for passing on cost increases and hence prevents excessive increases in nominal wages from occurring.

The economic policy implications of a monetary union can be summed up as follows. A monetary union presupposes considerable shifts in the responsibility for economic policy to a central authority and hence a far-reaching reshaping of the Community in political and institutional terms in the direction of a broader union. Although complete political union is not absolutely necessary for the establishment of a monetary union, the loss of national sovereignty in economic and monetary policy associated with it is so serious that it would probably be bearable only in the context of extremely close and irrevocable political integration. At all events, within a monetary union, monetary policy can only be conducted at a Community level. A substantial transfer of authority will also be necessary in the field of fiscal policy.

Principles of a European monetary order

Eschewing technical institutional and monetary details, the following section outlines the decisive principles that absolutely must be taken into account when setting up a European central bank system. (For simplicity, the point of departure is the final stage of monetary integration, namely the transition to a common European currency. However, the following criteria must also be fulfilled already at the stage when the monetary union is created, i.e. the irrevocable fixing of the parity rates of national currencies.) The following principles appear to be indispensable.

1   The mandate of the central bank must be to maintain stability of the value of money as the prime objective of European monetary policy. While fulfilling this task, the central bank has to support general economic policy as laid down at the Community level. Domestic stability of the value of money must take precedence over exchange rate stability. This

does not exclude the possibility that depreciation *vis-à-vis* third currencies and the associated import of inflation be counteracted by appropriate monetary policy measures. In the event of the establishment of an international monetary system with limited exchange rate flexibility *vis-à-vis* third currencies, the central bank would need to be given at least the right to participate in discussions on parity changes.

2   The overriding commitment to maintaining the stability of the value of money must be safeguarded through the central bank's independence of instructions from national governments and Community authorities. This simultaneously requires the personal independence of the members of the respective organs, assured by their being appointed to office for a period of at least eight to ten years without the possibility of their being removed from office for political reasons.

3   All the member countries would need to be represented in the monetary policy decision-making body, with voting power being weighted in the light of the economic importance of the member countries.

4   A federal structure of the central bank system – according to the pattern of the Federal Reserve System, for instance – would correspond best to the existing state of national sovereignty and would additionally strengthen the independence of the central bank. (Before the final stage involving the introduction of a uniform currency, only a federally structured central bank system is conceivable in any case.)

5   The financing of public sector deficits by the central bank (apart from occasional cash advances) makes effective monetary control impossible over the long term. For a European central bank to be able to fulfil its mandate to ensure monetary stability, strict limitations must be imposed on its granting credit to public authorities of all kinds (including Community authorities). This also applies to indirect government financing through the granting of credit to any central banks of the member countries that continue to exist.

6   The European central bank must be equipped with the monetary policy instruments to enable it to manage the money supply effectively without recourse to quantitative controls (or other forms of direct intervention in the workings of the financial markets). Interest rate and liquidity policy instruments must be available both for the general management and for the fine-tuning of the European money market.

7   The European central bank should be given the right to take part in the establishment of general regulations in the field of banking supervision. Moreover, owing to its expertise, deriving in particular from its business relations with credit institutions, the central bank should be closely involved in day-to-day banking supervisory activities.

MODELS OF MONETARY INTEGRATION

European Monetary Fund

The further development of the EMCF to form a European Monetary Fund (EMF) as a kind of 'regional IMF' probably comes closest to the concept the architects of the EMS had in mind, seeing that in accordance with the Resolution of the European Council of 5 December 1978 the final system was to be characterized by 'the creation of the European Monetary Fund as well as the full utilization of the ECU as a reserve asset and a means of settlement'. In addition, the 'existing credit mechanisms' would be consolidated 'into a single fund'. Moreover, in conjunction with the conclusions relating to monetary policy reached at the meeting of the European Council in Bremen on 6–7 July 1978, besides US dollars and gold, 'member currencies in an amount of a comparable order of magnitude' were to be brought into the Fund. In the discussions in the years 1981–2 about the entry of the EMS into the final stage it was assumed that this could also involve a final transfer of reserves.

A regional Reserve Fund with functions similar to those of the IMF would put this institution in a position to become involved in the process of balance-of-payments adjustment and financing on the part of its members. In this way, it could help to avoid recourse being taken to measures that disturb or delay the process of integration in the event of balance-of-payments difficulties. In the opinion of the proponents of such a Fund solution, the use of such balance-of-payments assistance as well as the resources made available by the Fund for the specific purpose of financing interventions could at the same time also help to stabilize exchange rate relationships within the EMS. If, in the course of monetary integration, it should come about that national external payments balances cease to exist and there is only a Community external payments balance instead, then the Fund would have to support the process of adjustment and financing of the balance of payments with its resources.

In the case of a Fund along the lines of a 'regional IMF' whose policy would be primarily directed towards safeguarding the external balance of the Community member countries as well as exchange rate stability, the question arises as to the extent to which such a policy would also foster convergence within the Community on the basis of price stability. This possibility only exists in the case of conditional balance-of-payments credits being granted, i.e. when the consequences of insufficient convergence have already become evident. At stages prior to this, especially when providing resources for intervention purposes without any conditions attached, it could not impose any convergence constraints in the direction of non-inflationary growth in the Community. The danger that within the EMS the orientation towards domestic stability would be pushed into the background in favour of external stability is obvious. Since the general thrust and co-ordination of economic, fiscal and monetary policy would play a role in this model of a Fund only at the margin (when conditional credits are granted) the stability-oriented monetary policy of the hard currency countries could be undermined. More-

over, mixing central bank functions together with areas of government responsibility within a single Fund bars the way to a European central bank with a decision-making body that is independent of governments, and is thus to be rejected.

A European parallel currency

1 As an alternative to the gradual development towards a European monetary union – on the basis of greater economic policy convergence, close co-ordination of monetary policy and diminishing recourse to exchange rate realignments – the concept of a parallel currency has been under discussion since the mid-1970s. According to this concept, the driving force behind the process of integration should be the market, not initiatives taken by national governments or Community authorities.

Alongside national currencies, an additional Community currency would be put into circulation which can fulfil all the functions of money (a means of payment, a unit of account and a store of value) as far as possible. The parallel currency would be designed in such a way that – without being given preferential treatment – it would be able not only to maintain its position alongside the national currencies but also gradually to crowd out the individual national currencies in line with the generally accepted pace of integration. With the growing importance of the parallel currency, the national central banks would increasingly lose their scope for autonomous monetary policy action in favour of a Community central banking institu-tion since a growing proportion of the money in circulation in each country would no longer be under national control. Thus, there would be a *de facto* loss of independence in the sphere of national monetary policy without the need for any explicit shift in responsibilities to the Community level. This process would end with the abolition of the national currencies through a special sovereign act and the introduction of a single European currency.

Compared with the well-known difficulties of progressively restricting national responsibility for economic policy through political acts, the idea of a parallel currency may appear to be quite 'elegant' at first sight. It would meet with the desire to undertake politically effective and symbolic steps (such as introducing a European currency, including the issuing of banknotes and coins, and setting up a European central bank) without a major need to relinquish sovereignty rights at the outset. However, on closer inspection it becomes evident that this approach also requires an immediate and far-reaching need for changes in institutional terms if the 'currency competition' that is set in motion is to proceed in a way that is acceptable for all the member countries. In this context, a large number of open and very complex questions arise. Agreement can be expressed with a recent study on the EMS, which states that 'the full logical implications of this approach were never drawn up at the official level' (Gros and Thygesen 1988).

2 Currency competition between the national currencies and a parallel currency can arise only if the latter is placed on an equal footing with all national currencies with respect to their relevant functions. Besides the envisaged complete liberalization of capital movements, i.e. the free use of each national currency and a parallel currency in external transactions, there would have to be equality of status for each national currency within the domestic economy as well. In order to ensure a sufficient degree of acceptance of the parallel currency as a means of payment its utilization would have to be permissible for domestic transactions also; however, its full recognition as legal tender wold not appear to be necessary. A harmonization of exchange rate regulations would be required beforehand in order that an undesirable uneven distribution of the parallel currency did not come about from the start.

3 The economic effects of the introduction of a parallel currency depend on the concrete aspects of its design. On the basis of the existing European monetary unit, the ECU, a large number of parallel currency concepts with, in part, widely differing implications can be conceived of depending in each case on the criteria that are decisive – an independent status for the ECU as opposed to a basket definition, exchange rate regulations and the role to be played by central banks. As points of reference, two 'interim solutions' of practical relevance constituting, on the one hand, the issuing of ECUs at the national level and, on the other hand, their being issued at the Community level are presented below: in the first case, the ECU is defined, as at present, as a basket of currencies with a fixed but adjustable exchange rate (type 1); in the second case, the ECU is an independently defined unit which would be put into circulation as an additional currency with a fixed but adjustable exchange rate (type 2).

By contrast, the 'present state' (a basket ECU with a fixed but adjustable exchange rate[1] without the systematic involvement of central banks in the private creation of ECUs) as well as the 'final state' of a *de facto* monetary union (basket ECU or independently defined ECU with an absolutely fixed exchange rate) are not analysed in detail.[2] As far as the 'present state' is concerned, on the basis of experience the purely private circulation of ECUs (which is only possible on the basis of a basket ECU) is of limited significance and such a restricted role of the ECU will not contribute towards monetary integration. We have already dealt extensively in the previous section with the final state. In the case of immutably fixed exchange rates *vis-à-vis* the national currencies, the ECU would not be a parallel currency but a dual currency; monetary union would then not be an objective still to be attained by means of the parallel currency but would already exist. The difference between an independently defined ECU and a basket ECU would be meaningless in the final state so that this case does not need to be discussed any further.

4 As already mentioned above, the parallel currency approach seeks to approach the final state of monetary union over the longer term through currencies competing with each other and with the ECU.[3] In order for the parallel currency to have a

chance in this competition among currencies it must be attractive from the point of view of individual economic agents as an investment currency (i.e. the net yield from the development of interest rates and exchange rates must be able to compete with the net yield obtainable on assets invested in a national currency) and should not be inferior to the national currency as a transaction currency (i.e. the transaction costs and the exchange rate risk involved in cash management must be as low as possible). To the extent that a crowding out of the national currency occurs, this process must operate in the right direction, i.e. 'good money' must not be replaced by 'bad money' (Gresham's law) if price stability is to be maintained. How competition between the individual currencies actually develops and what monetary policy implications can be associated with it depends crucially on the way the parallel currency is designed in each case.

The basket ECU as a parallel currency (type 1)

As things stand today, the use of the basket ECU as a parallel currency while retaining fixed but adjustable rates *vis-à-vis* the individual national currencies appears to be the most obvious approach. The decisive step towards the introduction of such a parallel currency would consist of making it possible for ECUs to be created by the national central banks (in accordance with uniform directives) or by a Community monetary authority. The basket ECU would then be created not only by the private bundling together of the individual components – as is currently the case – but also through the granting of credit or intervention operations by the central banks or a Community monetary authority.

Under the conditions described above, apart from third currencies, twelve national EC currencies and the basket ECU as an investment and external transaction currency together with two domestic transaction and accounting units would in this case be available to the citizens of the EC. With fixed but adjustable exchange rates, the use of the basket ECU would depend on the risk and yield preferences of investors; although the basket

ECU would be suitable as a diversification instrument, being the weighted average of the national currencies, it cannot be superior to all other individual currencies or mixtures of currencies. With freedom of capital movements and persistent divergences within the EMS it is quite possible that for a number of reasons the German mark will be generally preferred as an investment currency and will crowd out both the ECU and other national currencies. Although with an increasing degree of convergence between the EC currencies the German mark will lose some of its relatively greater attractiveness for non-residents, the diversification motive for ECU-denominated investments will lose importance at the same time. Investments denominated in other Community currencies would tend to be less profitable in the eyes of investors in each country so that in both cases little argues in favour of investments denominated in ECUs.

The ability of the ECU as a transaction currency to crowd out national currencies within the domestic economy cannot be judged in much more positive terms either. Especially in the case of foreseeable divergences, the exchange rate risk involved would impair the use of the ECU for day-to-day transactions, for example through the constant need to determine exchange rates, irritating conversion rates and greater difficulty in agreeing prices between domestic contractual partners who would have to take possible exchange risks into account if the contract is denominated in ECUs. Even in the event of greater convergence, habits, the acquired 'memory of prices' in national currency and similar factors tend to argue against the spread of the ECU. Thus, on balance, the best that can be expected is that the ECU would be increasingly used in intra-Community trade as a 'compromise currency', whereby, however, the crucial factor would probably not least be the negotiating position of the business partners concerned.

As a weighted average of national currencies, a basket ECU cannot therefore exert any durable and especially any symmetrical pressure in the direction of crowding out national currencies and hence cannot be seen as an additional instrument for bringing about integration either. Precisely with respect to the fact that the attractiveness of a basket ECU is not assured as far as individual economic agents are concerned, it can be assumed that the EC central banks would be obliged to stabilize the exchange rate of such an ECU through unlimited purchases in order to foster the use of the ECU.[4] Should ECUs circulate on a relatively large scale, such an intervention obligation would have important consequences for monetary policy; in the final analysis, it would be tantamount to undertaking unlimited purchases of partner currencies without settlement and bringing about the integration of the circulation of official and private ECUs. If the market wanted to exchange ECUs for national currency then this would depress the exchange rate of the ECU against the currency in question. Through purchases to support the ECU the desired national currency will then be made available. As a result, ECU holdings would accumulate with the central banks whose currencies are in stronger demand than the currencies of its partners (or the ECU) whereas the central banks responsible for issuing the currencies that are less in demand would have to issue ECUs by purchasing their own currency. On the assumption that divergences exist within the EMS, a *de facto* asymmetrical crowding out of the national currencies concerned within Europe would come about. The national stability policy of the hard currency countries would be undermined. National price objectives would necessarily have to be sacrificed to the average rate of inflation in Europe. For these reasons, such a concept alone requires management of the money supply at the European level in order to ensure an equal rate of money creation (ECU plus national currency). Only in this way would it be possible to avoid a 'dual coverage' of GDP in Europe through the circulation of ECUs and national currencies.

Moreover, redesigning the existing ECU to form a parallel currency would make it difficult to record the national money supply statistically if ECU banknotes were to be issued.[5] Although it would be known how many ECU banknotes had been issued in all, it would not be known how many of them are actually held in the Federal Republic of Germany or any other country. In addition, there would be exchange-rate-induced fluctuations in the national money supply expressed in terms of national currency. Finally, account would also need to be taken of the general possibility that already exists today of shifting funds into offshore centres; this might possibly play an even greater role for holdings of ECUs than is the case with respect to national currencies. These reservations apply in equal measure to the independently defined ECU that is discussed in the following section.

An independently defined ECU as a parallel currency (type 2)

In the case of an independently defined ECU with a fixed but adjustable exchange rate *vis-à-vis* the Community currencies, the development of the value of the parallel currency would be divorced from the development of the components forming the basket as it exists today but would depend on the frequency and extent of future realignments within the EMS. In principle, two possibilities exist as far as the exchange rate regulations governing an independently defined ECU are concerned.

On the one hand, the ECU can be made 'superior' to all EMS currencies by laying down the parities and intervention points of the national currencies *vis-à-vis* the ECU as the focal point of the system. Their bilateral central rates would then be derived from the ECU parity of each national currency with the consequence that the bilateral margin of fluctuation between two national currencies would be twice as large as it is *vis-à-vis* the ECU (for example, a band of $\pm$ 1⅛ per cent *vis-à-vis* the ECU would result in a bilateral band of $\pm$ 2¼ per cent). Thus, as a regional pivotal currency in the Community, the ECU would play a similar role in formal terms as the US dollar did in the former Bretton Woods system (without, however, having its own currency area as a base).

On the other hand, the independently defined ECU could be placed on the same footing as the national currencies: in this case, it would be treated as the currency of a thirteenth member country and would correspondingly have the same margin of fluctuation as the national currencies (whereby it could nevertheless be the focal point of the parity grid for computational purposes). Although the first variant would be of greater symbolic importance in the field of European politics and would foster the acceptance of the ECU as a parallel currency owing to its narrower margin of fluctuation, in principle both variants raise the same problems to a large extent.

As far as the ability of the ECU to crowd out other currencies is concerned, its being defined as an independent entity could potentially have both advantages and disadvantages because the new ECU could develop *a priori* more strongly than the strongest Community currency but could also develop more weakly than the weakest Community currency. In the absence of additional assumptions, such as equipping the parallel currency with a 'value guarantee' (whereby, of course, only its use as an investment instrument and not as a borrowing instrument would be fostered) or assuring its usability world-wide, the ability of an independently defined ECU to crowd out other currencies as an investment instrument cannot be assessed conclusively. Ultimately, the decisive factor for the development of its value would be the extent to which ECUs are created by a Community authority (or by the national central banks of the Community member countries in accordance with uniform Community directives) in relation to the monetary demand for ECUs, which in turn would depend on the degree of acceptance of the ECU inside and outside the Community.

As is the case with a national currency, independently defined ECUs would be put into circulation through credits granted by the issuing authority to banks or public sector entities as well as through purchases of partner currencies or third currencies via interventions on the foreign exchange markets. In the final analysis, the governing factor in this process would need to be the monetary demand for ECUs which results from the use of the ECU as a currency in cash transactions, settlement opera-

tions and other payment transactions as well as for investment purposes in competition with each individual national currency.

It is, of course, difficult to assess according to which criteria such a monetary demand for ECUs would emerge. This would not least depend on how great the risk of a change in the value of ECU cash holdings is assessed to be in relation to holdings in national currency. Holding ECUs for transaction purposes would probably be a more attractive proposition in countries with a weak currency than in countries whose currencies tend to appreciate *vis-à-vis* the ECU. Economic agents in countries with a strong currency will at best hold ECUs for transaction purposes to the extent that they have to conclude and also settle contracts denominated in ECUs in intra-Community trade and payment transactions for competitive reasons. The wide use of the ECU by residents as an investment and reserve currency both inside and outside the Community would presuppose wide and deep markets, as well as the willingness of bodies inside (and outside) the Community that enjoy confidence to incur debt in the ECU as currency in a form and on conditions that appear advantageous to investors. However, a sufficient degree of acceptance on the part of investors – both inside and outside the Community – is to be expected only if the creation of the ECU as an independent currency is carefully limited by the central bank(s) responsible for this task.

The granting of an excessive amount of ECU credits to the national or Community fiscal authorities (for example for transfer payments within the Community) in particular could lead to an oversupply of ECUs and ultimately to a deterioration in the value of the ECU *vis-à-vis* national currencies in the Community. This would not only impair the competitive position of the ECU in relation to the national currencies; owing to the obligations of the national central banks to intervene against the ECU, excess ECUs would also need to be taken out of the market by the central banks against national currency, which would make it difficult – if not impossible – for the countries concerned to conduct a monetary policy geared to stability.

These risks to monetary policy would need to be assessed all the more carefully the more strongly the creation of ECUs were to be subject to political influences and the less flexible the exchange rate of the ECU were to be.

5 In the final analysis, a parallel currency strategy presupposes that the process whereby other currencies are crowded out through the free play of market forces actually does work. The requisite symmetrical substitution of all Community currencies by the parallel currency would come about only if the parallel currency

1 were given the same domestic status as every other Community currency;
2 could compete even with the strongest Community currency, taking interest rate and exchange rate developments into account;
3 involved minimum costs as a transaction currency, which would practically be the case only if it were pegged to the national currencies sufficiently firmly.

However, this more or less amounts to a definition of the final stage to which the parallel currency is supposed to lead. The interim solutions, comprising a basket ECU or an independently defined ECU with fixed but adjustable exchange rates, do not provide sufficient assurance that the process of integration would be free of tensions. On the contrary, they would involve the risk that national monetary policy would no longer be able to fulfil its mandate to ensure stability owing to larger-scale central bank interventions. In weighing up the costs and benefits of a parallel currency strategy it also needs to be taken into account that for day-to-day payment operations (cash transactions, settlement operations by machine, cashless payment transactions) a parallel currency would be entirely impractical. Ultimately, this leads to the conclusion that little would be gained politically by introducing a parallel currency but that much would be placed at risk in terms of stability policy.

A European monetary authority on the way to a single currency

If the concept of a 'regional IMF' that was behind the original plans to create the EMS appears to be obsolete in the meantime and a European parallel currency is not an approach towards monetary union that deserves support, then it appears appropriate to prepare the prerequisites for introducing a single European currency at a later date by gradually harmonizing the national currencies in qualitative terms. Such a development could be brought about by extending the role of the EC Committee of Governors. In this context, it is not absolutely necessary for it to become the management body of an EC monetary authority equipped with operational tools immediately; it could also exercise the function of a central decision-making body within a Community central bank system comprising the Committee and the national central banks involved.

The Committee of Governors is particularly suitable for an extension of its functions because (in contrast, for example, to the Administrative Council of the EMCF) it is *de jure* free from instructions. However, taking part in this Committee does not automatically annul the *de facto* dependence on instructions of individual Governors that exists under national law. It would therefore be desirable if this dependence could be gradually eliminated as the functions of the Committee are further extended and could be replaced by increasing independence. As in the case of all other models, its mandate (maintaining the stability of money) and its status (freedom from instructions) should be assured at the outset.

Since the process of integration is to be seen as an evolutionary process, before decision-making responsibilities are transferred to supranational institutions, the question should be examined as to whether additional possibilities to extend co-ordination exist and in which direction they lie. Above all, further steps appear conceivable and would also be useful where the present forms of co-operation are based mainly on an *ex post* exchange of information (policy *vis-à-vis* third currencies, changes in the field of supervision, laying down the interim objectives of monetary policy etc.). They could gradually be developed into an *ex ante* exchange of information, such as is already occasionally practised on an informal basis.

In principle, the activity of the Committee of Governors (the title of which could be changed in the course of this process to 'European Central Bank Council', for instance, in order to emphasize its importance) would be directed towards co-ordinating national objectives, individual decisions and the employment of monetary instruments. Based on current procedures, the degree of co-ordination could be gradually increased in the direction of obligatory advance consultations to the level of a kind of right to issue general directives.

In this way, the scope for national monetary policy action would be gradually reduced. It would, for example, encompass the pursuit of intermediate objectives adopted in the process of co-ordination or set later as part of the power to issue directives. The scope for action would remain greatest in choosing appropriate instruments for achieving the objectives, but here again the Committee would gain increasing influence over the course of time with the aim of gradually harmonizing the criteria on which the employment of certain instruments is based, extending to the creation of as uniform a set of instruments as possible.

As a kind of natural continuation of the tasks already undertaken by the Committee at present with respect to the exchange rates of the Community currencies in relation to each other and *vis-à-vis* third currencies, it would have to co-ordinate the intervention policy of the EC central banks with respect to the internal and external relationships of the Community, with a sufficient degree of exchange rate flexibility *vis-à-vis* third currencies being assured. In this context, account would need to be taken of the differing weights of the currencies within the EMS as well as their international role. Exchange rate policy *vis-à-vis* the rest of the world would have to take into consideration the fact that the third countries

concerned (the USA and Japan) play a major part in determining the various exchange rate relationships. At a later stage, the Committee could assume the responsibility for influencing exchange rates that is still a national preserve, so that in the event of any foreign exchange market interventions the national central banks would progressively operate in the framework of 'their administering a mandate'. The responsibility for determining central rates could also be transferred from the member governments to the Committee. In this way, there would be a greater scope for relevant decisions to be asserted regardless of political expediency.

A Committee of Governors with scope to influence exchange rate policy and monetary policy in the member countries could make an effective contribution to convergence that would foster integration. The objective behind the basic thrust of its policy would need to be to influence monetary policy in each member country in such a way that a symmetrical development is brought about on the basis of as great a degree of price stability as possible. The success of such an undertaking is indivisibly associated with comparable progress in terms of integration being achieved in fiscal policy and other areas relevant to economic policy.

TRANSITIONAL PROBLEMS

Legal basis

Competence in the field of economic and monetary policy has not yet been transferred to the EC. The member states continue to be responsible for these spheres of policy; however, they do have the commitment to co-ordinate their policies (Sections 2, 104, 105 and 145 of the Treaty of Rome) in order to achieve their common objectives, to maintain a high level of employment and stability of the price level, to ensure equilibrium in the overall balance of payments and to maintain confidence in their currencies (Section 104 of the Treaty of Rome). A certain restriction for the member countries through Community law is to be seen in the fact that they should consider their exchange rate policies as a matter of common interest (Section 107 of the Treaty of Rome).

Restrictions that go further result from the rules governing the EMS. Leaving aside two Council directives relating to the EMCF and the ECU, they are based on multilaterally agreed acts of self-restriction on the part of the central banks concerned and hence are not part of the legislation of the Community proper. In accordance with a regulation in respect of the Treaty (Section 102(a) of the Treaty of Rome) introduced together with the Single European Act of 1986, institutional changes in the field of economic and monetary policy undertaken in the course of further developments require the conclusion of a new Treaty under international law in accordance with Section 236 of the Treaty of Rome. How far an international treaty is necessary in individual cases depends on the scope that each central bank has in extending economic policy co-operation under its basis in law. This probably differs from country to country since the central banks in the individual member countries have a differing status in law.

[No definitive catalogue can be drawn up for Germany indicating what acts of legislation would be required in each case for measures that are designed to develop the EMS further. In abstract terms, the following guidelines can be set forth.

1   In the Federal Republic of Germany, under Section 24 of the Basic Law, the transfer of sovereign rights to international institutions requires an Act of Parliament. This requirement of constitutional law is to be interpreted strictly (Federal Constitutional Law 58, p. 1ff., and especially p. 35).

2   The Deutsche Bundesbank is able to participate in closer monetary policy co-operation through greater co-operation among central banks only within certain limits. A limit would be reached if the Bundesbank were to accept decisions by an external body – such as the Committee of Governors – with respect to monetary policy measures which it is its duty to decide upon autonomously. In doing so, it would relinquish the exercise of the authority

it has under the Bundesbank Act. German public and administrative law assumes that a body that has been entrusted with tasks and responsibilities exercises these responsibilities directly; delegating them to another body is only possible if it is empowered to do so by law. It is also not permissible for such a body to link the decisions entrusted to it to the agreement of other bodies. In contrast, mutual agreements and concertations are and remain possible.

3   The Deutsche Bundesbank is not able to establish a joint institution together with other central banks and grant it powers in the field of monetary policy either: for this, owing to the lack of the necessary authorization, it does not have the power of organization required under public law.

4   Finally, on the basis of existing law, the Deutsche Bundesbank cannot transfer parts or all of its monetary reserves permanently and irrevocably to a common fund; such a transfer would go beyond the scope of the 'operations' that the Bank is empowered to conduct.]

Before national responsibilities are transferred to the Community, sufficient clarity should exist as to the distributions of responsibilities at the Community level. The point behind this is to ensure that the principles of a European monetary order as described above have been put into effect at least in basic terms at every stage of integration. With respect to the position of the Community monetary authorities this means that no rights of any kind to issue instructions are granted to the political level and that an influence on national central banks does not accrue to the national political authorities to which they do not have a right under national law. This would speak in favour of making the Committee of EC Central Bank Governors, which is free from political instructions both at the national and the Community level, the starting point for further development in institutional terms. The members of this Committee would need to enjoy personal independence from the bodies that appoint them, which admittedly also presupposes corresponding independence in their functions at the national level. In contrast, the EMCF, which is tied to directives issued by the EC Council of Ministers and hence is subject to political instructions, is not suitable as a monetary authority for the Community.

Integration in stages

Whether responsibilities in the field of monetary policy can be transferred to the Community level in several steps or in a single act of law depends on the concept on which the integration process is based. In principle, preference should be given to a global concept of integration with a clearly formulated final objective, as described above, with the individual steps being geared to this objective. A process of integration determined only by pragmatic considerations would not offer any guarantee that the final objective will actually be attained. It would be in accordance with this global concept of integration if the necessary authorization were not to be restricted to individual steps in the process of integration but were to relate to the stage-by-stage plan as a whole, or at least to its major components. The member countries applied this procedure successfully in bringing about the customs union in the first decade of the Community's existence. However, experience with the plan of 1970 to achieve economic and monetary union in stages argues against setting a rigid timetable for the process of integration. Rather, institutional changes, which also include extensions in the spheres of competence of existing Community institutions, should be made dependent on qualitative progress towards convergence in the field of economic and monetary policy. The member countries would, of course, need to agree on a common procedure to determine whether the prerequisites have been fulfilled for the next stage towards economic and monetary union to be put into effect.

From a legal point of view, the establishment of an economic and monetary union in the Community does not depend on the existence of a political union. Rather, it is an accepted fact that the member countries of the Community can separate certain tasks from the multitude of responsibilities they have and transfer them to a supranational institution. They nevertheless continue to exist as states. They continue to pursue their own policies in major fields and have the necessary executive power to do so (territorial and individual sovereignty). To this extent, the jointly created supranational entity – in this case, the EC – exists as an 'association for the specific purpose of integrating certain functions'.

As was already stated in the Werner Report of 1970, a lasting economic and monetary union requires the transfer of far-reaching responsibilities of national authorities to the Community plane above and beyond the direct field of monetary policy. An 'association for the specific purpose of integrating certain functions' would therefore probably only be able to survive if it is supported by a far-reaching reshaping of the Community in political and institutional terms in the direction of a more comprehensive union. To this extent, progress towards economic, monetary and general political union is mutually interdependent and thus sets the framework in which progress in institutional terms appears possible.

Partial integration versus comprehensive integration

Important political considerations can also plead against integration by stages where individual groups of countries move towards integration at varying speeds. Endeavours should therefore be made to include all the Community member countries in the process of monetary integration. So long as considerable differentials exist within the Community in terms of prosperity and productivity that are not offset to a large extent and in good time through corresponding transfers of resources in the context of fiscal compensation within the union, movements in the factors of production between the various regions can occur as internal market conditions are brought about. The more developed regions will be given impulses to growth at the expense of the periphery. To the extent that they do not prefer to allow themselves to be guided by general political considerations, this risk will probably deter a number of member countries of the Community from joining a monetary union. In contrast, a core group of countries, such as those comprising the members of the present EMS exchange rate system, appear to be quite strong enough in economic terms to agree to closer and closer ties with corresponding consequences in the field of economic policy.

The concept of integration by stages was practised under the 'snake' system and is practised *de facto* within the EMS. Since monetary policy coordination largely took place in these systems up to now on a co-operative basis the coexistence of differing rights and obligations in various countries did not impair co-operation. If, however, substantial progress towards integration is tied to major institutional bonds, individual countries, by exercising their veto, could bring about a situation where such progress is made only on the basis of the lowest common denominator. The countries capable of integrating could escape this situation by agreeing on more rapid steps towards integration among themselves. In this case, the countries at the lower level of integration would no longer be able to participate in the monetary policy decision-making bodies of the Community on an equal basis as is the case at the present level of co-operation by means of a gentlemen's agreement. Only the countries prepared to subject themselves to its standards could have a claim to participate fully in the monetary union.

Integration by stages would be tantamount to dividing the Community into two parts which would not remain restricted to the monetary sphere as integration progressed but would also lead to the individual member countries of the Community having different rights and obligations. Although such a system of differing rights and obligations in individual spheres would not be considered to be incompatible with the Treaty of Rome, independent bodies of the monetary union would need to be created alongside the organs of the Community in order to meet the demands of the final objective. In the light of the present state of development of the European Community, not only would this division between the level of co-operation and the level of integration raise serious problems of a practical nature but the unification of Europe would gain a new quality through the partial integration of a number of core member countries compared with the approach to integration adopted in the past. New hurdles would be raised for the countries on the periphery that would be increasingly difficult to take. The proponents of faster integration of the core member countries see this primarily as a transitional problem: they argue that, with the system being open to a corresponding extent, the countries initially excluded from this process could catch up with the train of integration later on when the economic prerequisites to do so have been created. However, the danger must not be dismissed that ultimately the differences between the member countries in economic terms will become cemented with the division of Europe into two parts in the field of monetary policy and in the related institutions. Although the pull of an incipient monetary union would be strong for the countries on the periphery, the high barriers of access to it might possibly frustrate their joining it in the long run. If the unification of Europe as a whole is also being striven for, then two-speed integration in the monetary sphere would tend to be an obstacle.

Integration under the Treaty of Rome or outside it

The stage-by-stage plan together with the description of the individual steps up to the final stage could be decided upon in a single package and used to extend the Treaty of Rome by the dimension comprising economic and monetary union. This 'package solution' would have the advantage that the member countries would only have to form a political opinion once and that it would not be necessary to negotiate the union several times over in 'small coin' before the national legislative bodies, apart from the imponderables of the procedure as arose with the ratification of the Single European Act.

Through a 'package solution' of this nature, not only would the objectives be laid down in contractual form but the requisite responsibilities of the Community would also be established. As a result, the issuing of 'regulations in unforeseen circumstances' under Section 235 of the Treaty of Rome would no longer be necessary. Disagreements would be excluded on the issue, for instance, as to when 'institutional changes' occur (see Section 102(a)) or whether a measure in the field of monetary policy is still accessible to – extensive – interpretation under Section 235.

If, in the context of such an extended Treaty, a decision-making body decides to conclude one stage of integration and initiates the next step in monetary policy co-operation, then the question arises as to which body should be granted this responsibility. Several solutions to this question are conceivable. The Treaty already entrusts the Council with the authority to take decisions on such determinations in other cases (see, for example, the determination of the Council with respect to the transitional period: Section 8 of the Treaty of Rome). In principle, the Commission could also be entrusted with making such a determination. As regards the technical expertise involved, however, the Committee of Central Bank Governors could also be considered for this task. A mixed body is conceivable as well.

However, if it is assumed that not all the member countries enter the integrational stage in the field of monetary policy at the same time, it will hardly be possible to grant these member countries the right to participate in its design. The countries engaged in the process of integration will not want to expose themselves to the risk of being partly governed by outsiders and will expect that only those countries take part which expose themselves to the same risk. For this reason, it could prove necessary to lay down the corresponding rules among the active participants outside the Treaty of Rome initially. Basically speaking this route was taken with the inception of the EMS. It would avoid the 'systematics' of the Treaty of Rome and make monetary integration within the framework of the Committee of Governors

possible, which corresponds to the basic features of a European monetary order described above. At a later stage, ways would need to be discussed on how to harmonize the new set of rules with the Treaty of Rome.

The objection could be raised against bringing about monetary integration outside the Treaty of Rome that this approach would not correspond to the final objective of creating an economic and monetary union within the Community. Under Section 102(a), it could be argued, member countries have undertaken a mandatory commitment to adopt the procedure laid down in Section 236 of the Treaty of Rome when they enter the institutional stage. They would have to refrain from all measures that could jeopardize the achievement of the objectives laid down in the Treaty of Rome (Section 5, Subsection 2). The Commission will also have a considerable interest in incorporating the monetary policy institutions in the Treaty of Rome.

If the route prescribed under Section 236 of the Treaty of Rome is taken then the entry into force of changes in the Treaty is made dependent on their being ratified by all the member countries. An individual member country would then be in a position to prevent the institutionalization of co-operation, or at least to delay it considerably.

CONCLUDING REMARKS

Since the inception of the EMS considerable progress has been made in the Community in the field of monetary policy co-operation. In conjunction with the latest measures to establish an integrated financial area and the planned establishment of the single European market, the perspective of an economic and monetary union now appears in a favourable light again. Economic and monetary union would mark the end of a development which, despite all the considerable progress that has been made, will still take some time to achieve. Not all the member countries of the Community participate in the exchange rate mechanism of the EMS, and not all the participating countries subject themselves to the same conditions. The economic prerequisites for a monetary union that is characterized by immutably fixed exchange rates between the participating countries will probably not exist for the foreseeable future. Even among the members who form the nucleus of the exchange rate system, tensions must repeatedly be expected for the foreseeable future owing to differing economic policy preferences and constraints as well as the resultant divergences in their economic development, which will make realignments in the central rates of their currencies necessary. Even within a common single market these problems will not simply disappear, especially since this market will trigger additional structural adjustment constraints, the extent of which cannot as yet be fully assessed. For this reason, too, it will not be possible to do without occasional realignments in central rates for the foreseeable future. This indicates the necessity for further progress in the direction of greater convergence in a large number of macroeconomic as well as structural fields.

The existing EC Committee of Central Bank Governors offers itself as the basic unit in organizational terms of an EC monetary authority which does not threaten to run counter to the demands of the final stage at the outset. Competence in the field of monetary policy could be increasingly transferred to it over the course of time. In the initial stage it would direct its activities towards co-ordinating national monetary policy objectives, individual decisions and the employment of monetary policy instruments. Parallel to this, it would ensure an increasingly greater degree of harmonization of the exchange rate policies of the member countries. Working from this basis, its responsibilities could gradually be extended in the direction of obligatory advance consultations and go as far as having the right to issue directives on questions of monetary and exchange rate policy. A major factor in co-ordinating monetary policy at the Community level is the centralized process of shaping policy, which could be undertaken by the national central banks as the constituent parts of a European central bank system. In organizational terms, the Committee of Governors could be supported by its own enlarged secretariat.

Developing its own activities in the money and foreign exchange markets on the part of an EC monetary authority equipped with technical resources and staff as well as monetary policy instruments would not appear to be necessary until the national currencies have been abolished and a single European currency has been introduced. The step-by-step transition from a national to a Community monetary policy should take place on a legal basis that does not relate to individual steps in the process of integration but to this process as a whole. As far as possible, all the member countries of the Community should embark jointly on the path towards economic and monetary union in order not to handicap the integration of Europe as a whole at a later date.

If only a few Community member countries were to spur forward this would have serious economic and political consequences. Ultimately, the danger would exist of Western Europe being permanently divided into two parts if the barriers to access to the smaller system were to become too high. However, to the extent that separate action in Europe were politically desired, the door would have to be left open for the countries excluded in the initial stages to join later. But these countries could not be granted any right to participate in the affairs of the monetary union. Besides institutional arrangements of this nature, however, it is of outstanding importance for the success of monetary integration for the gradual transfer of monetary policy to the Community level to be accompanied by sufficient progress in the integration of economic and fiscal policy. Isolated steps in the monetary field would overburden monetary policy in political terms and jeopardize the credibility of the process of unification in the longer run.

NOTES

1 Ignoring the special role of the lira, sterling and the drachma.
2 The independently defined ECU with a flexible exchange rate (type 3) propagated in scientific circles is also not examined because, although it is a

model with theoretical advantages, it cannot be considered a realistic alternative.

3   It appears doubtful whether all member countries would be prepared to engage in unrestricted competition among currencies with all its consequences, including large-scale crowding out of the national currency! It can probably be realistically assumed that national monetary authorities do not want to risk their currencies being crowded out of circulation in the domestic economy and will therefore keep the extent to which the parallel currency spreads under control by restricting its use in one way or another.

4   If, as is assumed, all the basket currencies are part of a system of fixed but adjustable exchange rates, then intervention points for the basket ECU *vis-à-vis* each individual national currency can be derived from their bilateral intervention points.

5   If an ECU parallel currency were introduced, ECU banknotes would probably be issued even if the ECU were not to be declared legal tender.

REFERENCE

Gros, D. and Thygesen, N. (1988) *The EMS: Achievements, Current Issues and Directions for the Future*, Brussels: Centre for European Policy Studies.

8

EUROPEAN MONETARY REFORM
Progress and prospects
Alberto Giovannini

In the past two years, a new plan for monetary union in Europe has gained widespread popularity. The plan has also invigorated the initiative to build a single currency area among EC countries – an initiative that has been a recurrent feature of the debate on European monetary policy throughout the post-war period. Indeed, many observers now believe that the achievement of a monetary union is highly likely: C. Fred Bergsten states that Western Europe is '*almost certain* to go beyond "completion of the internal market" to an Economic and Monetary Union, or EMU' (Bergsten 1990: 97, my italics).

The policy problems related to monetary reform are determined by the approach taken to reform. In the late 1960s, two alternative strategies were much debated; surprisingly, they have received little attention recently. The first programme, known as the gradualist strategy (the supporters of which have been labelled 'economists'), relies on progressive removal of trade barriers, convergence of inflation rates, progressive stability of exchange rates and parallel modification of monetary policies and institutions. The second strategy involves a sudden currency reform (its supporters have been labelled 'monetarists'). This strategy amounts to either the irrevocable locking of exchange rates, with the elimination of target zones, or the replacement of national currencies with a single currency. Both possibilities would require a common central bank to manage the system.

The current plan for monetary union, the so-called Delors plan, largely reflects the view of the 'economists'.[1] Significantly, the Delors plan does not set deadlines for monetary union, nor does it demand that certain criteria be met in order to move from one stage to the next in the institutional reform. As a result, and despite an early show of support, it is not clear how much commitment exists for this plan, even among the continental governments that are members of the EMS.

How might the current plan for monetary union become successful? In the absence of new institutional developments, the convergence of inflationary expectations and the stability of exchange rates are necessary conditions for the success of the gradualist strategy. This chapter discusses the problem of achieving and sustaining these twin objectives and, more broadly, the Delors plan's chance for success. I consider the historical and institutional background for European monetary union: the monetary arrangements of the post-war period, the early attempts at achieving monetary cohesion and the characteristics of the Delors plan. I also address the extent to which inflationary expectations have converged among France, Germany and Italy, and what this implies for monetary reform.

Western European countries have been talking about monetary union for three decades now. An understanding of the historical developments surrounding monetary union reveals much about the nature and potential success of the current initiative. I deal with these issues in the first section of the chapter. In the second section, I focus on the experiences of the three largest countries involved in the debate on monetary union – France,

Germany and Italy. All three have been members of the EMS since its inception. This section explores the question of convergence of inflationary and exchange rate expectations, which can be gauged from the behaviour of both wages and, especially, interest rates. In the third section, I use alternative models to examine the empirical evidence presented for France, Germany and Italy. The main questions are how much does the pegging of exchange rates contribute to the convergence of inflation rates and interest rates, and how credible is a plan for monetary union that hinges on the pegging. One noticeable result of this section – a result that has potentially important implications for the theory of exchange rate regimes and optimum currency areas – is that pronouncing exchange rates to be fixed may not eliminate distortions in real interest rates and real wages. In the fourth section I discuss the current prospects for monetary union in the light of the

evidence presented and finish with some general conclusions.

Throughout the chapter, I assume that the goal of monetary union is to converge to the low level of inflation in Germany. This attitude is widely reflected in all official documents and has arguably justified the cohesion of the EMS.

RENEWED MOMENTUM TOWARD MONETARY UNION

References to economic and monetary union appear as early as the Treaty of Rome in 1957. The accelerating pace of negotiations seen in the past eighteen months should be set against the background of previous attempts at achieving monetary cohesion. Such an exercise should also help assess the prospects of the current efforts in the light of earlier failures. Exchange rate developments of the past thirty years are depicted in Figure 8.1. The

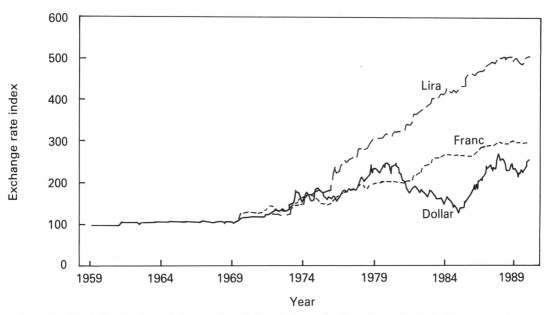

Figure 8.1 The Italian lira, French franc and US dollar relative to the deutsche mark, 1959–89 (January 1959 = 100). Exchange rates were calculated as the unit of foreign currency per deutsche mark. Ticks represent January of the year indicated

Source: IMF, *International Financial Statistics*

figure shows the real bilateral exchange rates of one deutsche mark relative to the US dollar, the French franc and the Italian lira, and summarizes the monetary arrangements of the three European countries in the past thirty years.

The Treaty of Rome advocated, together with the creation of a common market for goods, the removal of exchange controls in tandem with the liberalization of goods markets. The treaty also recommended that exchange rate changes by member countries be elevated to the status of 'matters of common interest'. These statements of principle, however, proved ineffective in practice. The exchange rate realignments of the deutsche mark in March 1961, the French franc in August 1969 and the deutsche mark again in October 1969 were unilateral decisions.[2] Except in these cases, the stability of intra-European exchange rates before 1971 was assured by pegging each currency to the dollar.

The first attempt

The response of the EC to the deutsche mark re-alignment, and to the unfolding of the crisis in the Bretton Woods regime, was a solemn statement by the heads of state at the European Summit held at The Hague in December 1969. The statement expressed the desire to see the Community develop into an economic and monetary union through the implementation of a phased plan. Some views expressed at the time have been echoed in the current debate – with the French advocating a sudden locking of parities and the elimination of fluctuation bands and the Germans preferring a gradual approach in which the convergence of macroeconomic structure and performance is a precondition for monetary union.[3]

The Summit appointed a committee, headed by Pierre Werner, Prime Minister and Finance Minister of Luxembourg, to report on practical steps for achieving economic and monetary union. The resulting Werner report argued that monetary union must occur in three stages.[4] During the first two stages, co-ordination of economic policy had to be strengthened. The process of co-ordination would combine prior consultation with follow-up monitoring. The second stage was further characterized by the creation of a 'European Fund for Monetary Co-operation', which would 'progressively manage Community reserves' and would manage intra-European balance-of-payments financing. This fund would be integrated, in the third stage, into a system of Community central banks. Parity readjustments were ruled out for the second stage. In particular, the Werner committee concluded that:

> The ultimate objective ... appears to be one that can be attained within the present decade, provided that it continues to enjoy the political support of the governments.... The adoption of a single currency could be the final stage of this union, ensuring the irreversibility of the process.[5]

The Werner report was the outcome of heated debates that saw the French government, with its strong aversion to any institutional changes that would limit national sovereignty, pitted against the five remaining countries, which favoured some transfer of power to a European institution and changes in the Treaty of Rome. In the end, the nations agreed to leave many details about intermediate stages unspecified and focus on the first stage and the final objective, which was safely in the distant future.

On 22 March 1971, the EC Council of Ministers signed a resolution adopting the Werner report and laying down a timetable for the reforms needed to enhance the integration of goods and financial markets.[6] On the policy side, the resolution advocated more power for the Monetary Committee and the Committee of Central Bank Governors. It also recommended a narrowing of fluctuation bands for exchange rates.

Two months later foreign exchange markets provided the conditions for the effective meltdown of the Werner plan. Germany called an emergency meeting of EC finance ministers to propose floating the deutsche mark. The French opposed the idea and advocated tighter capital controls. No agreement was reached at the meeting; the mark and the guilder were floated, while all other countries tightened capital controls. Ironically, some of the tax reforms called for in March 1971 – capital income taxation and corporate taxes – still have to be tackled by the EC.

Monetary initiatives of the 1970s

Figure 8.1 also shows that the collapse of the 'North Atlantic' Bretton Woods system was followed by dramatic exchange rate fluctuations, during which the franc and the lira have progressively diverged from the dollar. Neither of the currencies has regained its stability, relative to the mark, that characterized the dollar-based regime of the 1960s.

The European monetary initiatives of the rest of the 1970s are better known. From April 1972 to March 1973, the 'snake in the tunnel' strategy was in effect, the tunnel representing the bilateral fluctuation margins with the dollar (4.5 per cent) and the snake the narrower margins of intra-European rates (2.25 per cent). After March 1973, the European currencies floated freely against the dollar. After that point, the only stable members of the snake were Germany, Belgium, the Netherlands and Luxembourg. The other large EC countries, France and Italy, soon left the system – in January 1974 and February 1973 respectively. France briefly rejoined from July 1975 to March 1976.

The EMS was set up in December 1978 and became effective in March 1979. Its exchange rate mechanism included all EC members except the UK. Jacques Delors has noted that the EMS was based on intergovernmental agreement rather than on Community law (Delors 1989). While explicit references to economic and monetary union seem absent, the EMS was regarded as instrumental to further EC integration.

The purpose of the European Monetary System is to establish a greater measure of monetary stability in the Community. It should be seen as a fundamental component of a more comprehensive strategy aimed at lasting growth with stability, a progressive return to full employment, the harmonization of living standards and the lessening of regional disparities within the Community. The Monetary System will facilitate the convergence of economic development and give fresh impetus to the process of European Union.[7]

Whether the EMS actually provided that 'fresh impetus' is not clear. Its success has been mainly reflected in the fact that changes in intra-European exchange rates became a matter of truly common concern. As a result, bilateral rates in Europe have fluctuated less than the dollar, despite the differences in trends (see Figure 8.1). The success of the EMS has certainly contributed to the serious consideration being given to extending the reach and depth of the experiment. But as Marcello de Cecco and I note, the EMS, by itself, has not induced changes in monetary institutions that sustain closer co-operation: two of the EMS's technical features that were designed with that objective – the EMCF and the ECU – did not achieve the status originally envisaged by their supporters.[8]

The Delors report

The roots of the most recent project for monetary union – the Delors report – are not in the monetary area. Unlike the initiative that led to the Werner report, which could be viewed as a last-resort effort to brace against a collapsing monetary system, the Delors report grew out of the June 1985 White Paper on the completion of the internal market and the 1986 Single European Act. The former laid out the '1992' plan; the latter was the outcome of an intergovernmental conference held in Luxembourg in December 1985 to modify the Treaty of Rome. The treaty now includes a formal commitment to complete the 1992 plan and make several institutional changes to facilitate its completion. These changes include extension of qualified-majority voting to about two-thirds of the draft directives that make up the 1992 plan and increased involvement of the European Parliament. A crucial pillar of the single market programme is the liberalization of capital flows within the Community. This was achieved early with the June 1988 adoption, by the Council of Economic and Finance Ministers (ECOFIN), of a draft proposal on the creation of a European financial area. In the same month, the heads of state commissioned a study on the achievement of economic and monetary union from a group of central bankers and outside experts headed by Jacques Delors. The group presented its results at the European Council meeting in Madrid in June 1989.

The Delors report guides the current debate on monetary union. Its main feature is the concept of gradualism: monetary union is to be achieved over time so that the economies and the necessary institutions can adapt. Several reasons are given for the gradualist strategy. First, the mandate to the Delors Committee explicitly asked for a plan that would achieve the 'progressive realization of economic and monetary union'. Sudden monetary reform was politically unacceptable in the summer of 1988. Second, monetary union is seen as part of a broader plan that includes the completion of the internal market. This view is inspired by optimal-currency-area arguments: sufficient mobility of goods and factors is a precondition for monetary union. Third, monetary union needs time to create new institutions, including a European central bank.

The gradual plan proceeds in three stages. In stage I, capital movements among all countries (except Spain, Greece and Portugal) are fully liberalized. Membership in the exchange rate mechanism of the EMS is enlarged. And monetary policy co-operation is improved by giving more powers to the EC Committee of Central Bank Governors in order to facilitate so-called *ex ante* co-ordination of monetary policies. Exchange rate realignments are permitted during this first stage.

In stage II, which would take place several years in the future, the European System of Central Banks (ESCB) replaces the Committee of Central Bank Governors and the EMCF. Exchange rates are virtually fixed, with realignments allowed only under exceptional circumstances, and monetary policy is set at the Community level, with the implicit understanding that national authorities follow the guidelines. In stage III, exchange rates are irrevocably locked and the ECSB replaces the national central banks. At the end of stage III (a possible stage IV itself) a single currency would be adopted.

The Delors report also deals with a number of measures in the economic field. Most important are the completion of the internal market programme and increased macroeconomic policy co-ordination, in particular budgetary discipline achieved through 'precise quantitative guidelines'.[9]

The report does not specify deadlines although the developments of 1990 have provided some. At the European Council in June 1989, the heads of state agreed to embark on the first stage of the Delors plan. It was a significant step; as stated in the Delors report, 'Although this process is set out in stages which guide the progressive movement to the final objective, the decision to enter upon the first stage should be a decision to embark on the entire process.'[10] At the Strasbourg Summit of December 1989, it was agreed that two inter-governmental conferences would convene by December 1990 – one to prepare the changes in the Treaty of Rome needed for monetary union; the other to deal with political union. At the European Summit in Dublin in April 1990, the heads of state declared that the changes in the treaty relating to economic and monetary union must be ratified by national governments before the end of 1992. Hence, stage II of the Delors plan may begin in January 1993.

The Delors report was not motivated by an analysis of the costs and benefits of a monetary union in Europe, although subsequent studies have addressed some of these issues.[11] A study by the European Commission, entitled *One Market, One Money*, assesses the economic impact of the economic and monetary union resulting from several different policy developments, including elimination of transactions costs and foreign exchange risk premia; achievement of price stability through an independent central bank; G7 co-ordination of exchange rates and distribution of world foreign exchange reserves and seigniorage gains; concern about budgetary policy; and loss of the exchange rate instrument to offset country-specific shocks (Commission of the European Communities 1990). The study relies on a series of partial equilibrium analyses of different markets, and appropriately refrains from producing a single summary quantification of the effects of a monetary union.

Estimation of the welfare effects of a single currency, a classic question in international economics, hinges heavily on what is known about the demand for different currencies in an integrated area (McKinnon 1963; Mundell 1968; Kenen 1969; Cooper 1976). That knowledge is, at best, limited. Although this is an active area of research, a comprehensive analysis is still beyond reach.[12] In addition, political considerations play an important role in the discussion of the desirability of a monetary union, as Robert Triffin emphasized (Triffin 1960). Hence this chapter focuses on the process toward monetary union, taking the desirability of the final objective as given.

Difference between Delors and Werner reports

To an observer with no training in the language of diplomacy, the Delors report looks extremely similar to the Werner report. The latter is also made up of three stages – during the first stage policy co-ordination would be enhanced; during the second stage a 'European Monetary Fund' would be set up; and during the third stage exchange rates would be irrevocably locked. During the first two stages, exchange rate adjustments would be allowed, though they should be unnecessary by the second stage. Furthermore, the Werner report contains several economic measures including the joint setting of both the medium-term objectives for macroeconomic policies and the broad outlines of short-term policies, and common agreement on the acceptable margins for national budget totals and on the method of financing deficits. Finally, both reports discuss the need to set up a European central bank.[13]

Their marked similarities suggest several questions: Is the Delors report any 'better' than the Werner report? Why has the more recent plan for monetary reform enjoyed greater success? Have changes in the European political and economic climate made the prospects for monetary union brighter for the 1990s than they were for the 1970s?

The first question must have been raised within the Delors committee. The first of the papers published with the report addresses precisely this question (Baer and Padoa-Schioppa 1989). The authors point out a number of technical problems with the Werner report, such as a 'lack of safeguards against lapses in policy consensus', 'institutional ambiguities' and a 'lack of internal momentum'. But the differences in the two reports' respective political and economic environments, as Gunther Baer and Tommasa Padoa-Schioppa stress, must have played a major role in the weaknesses of the Werner report.

Political factors

Observers have long noted that the 1986 Single European Act, which was the culmination of the EC integration process and which put forward the 1992 programme, would have important political consequences. The political significance of the Act has been evidenced by the heated debate between the UK and the other European governments regarding the way to complete the internal market (see, for example, Wolf 1989). Until last year, though, increased economic integration of the EC had always preceded stronger political cohesion.[14]

With the events of 1989, however, political cohesion no longer takes its lead just from stronger economic ties, but has gained a strength of its own. The dismembering of the communist world has decreased the strategic significance of ties with the USA and has provided the conditions for an acceleration of European integration. An anecdote about how the 1990 intergovernmental conference was convened helps illustrate the new interplay of political and economic elements in the negotiations.[15] Up to the day before the start of the

Strasbourg Summit in December 1989, German economic officials were unwilling to see an inter-governmental conference on monetary union called during the following three years; yet, at the end of the meeting, the monetary conference was convened for December 1990. This drastic reversal was most probably obtained in exchange for the support of German unification by the Community governments.

In summary, the differences in the world strategic scenario, and in particular the difference in the political relations among European states, may provide a more favourable environment for European monetary reform than was the case in the early 1970s. The risk is that increased cross-border competition arising from the removal of controls will amplify political frictions among Western European governments and bring the integration plan to a halt. This prospect could be labelled the 'Ridley scenario'.

Economic factors

The differences between the economic conditions of the EC in the 1990s and in the 1970s derive from two phenomena. The first is economic integration. Table 8.1 reports trade data for the six original members of the EC and shows the imports and exports to Community countries as a fraction of imports and exports to the rest of the world. By 1989, the only countries for which intra-Community trade had not swamped external trade are Germany (intra-Community imports are 110 per cent of imports from the rest of the world, the same figure for exports is 120 per cent) and Italy. All six countries have experienced steady growth in intra-Community trade since the 1960s. The differences between 1970 and 1989 are not dramatic, however, except for perhaps France and Italy. Economic integration will be further boosted by completion of the internal market. Indeed, the Commission suggests that a double feedback is at work between the single market programme and monetary union, in that a single currency would help achieve more integrated markets. Yet, whether the 1990 Europe of twelve countries is a

Table 8.1 Intra-community trade relative to trade with the rest of the world, original European Community countries, 1960, 1970 and 1989[a] (per cent)

	1960	1970	1989[b]
Exports			
Belgium and Luxembourg	154.5	302.7	303.1
France	63.0	139.6	162.7
Germany	67.0	98.9	120.2
Italy	66.7	107.1	144.6
Netherlands	158.2	266.3	309.6
Imports			
Belgium and Luxembourg	131.0	196.0	239.1
France	53.5	126.7	189.0
Germany	66.3	106.3	109.8
Italy	58.1	91.3	133.3
Netherlands	118.1	172.7	158.9

Source: *European Economy*, November 1989

Notes: [a] The table reports each country's imports and exports to EC countries as a percentage of imports and exports to the rest of the world.

[b] Figures for 1989 are estimated using incomplete data.

more integrated economy than the 1970 Europe of six countries is an open question.

The second economic phenomenon that differentiates the 1990s from the 1970s is the liberalization of financial markets. Historical experience suggests that all fixed exchange rate regimes have been characterized by extensive use of capital controls (see, for example, Giovannini 1989). These controls were justified by a desire to stem speculative attacks on central banks' reserves. The complete removal of capital controls will force European countries to create a new institutional arrangement to ensure closer monetary policy co-operation, since without co-operation fixed parities would very probably collapse.[16]

In summary, there are reasons to believe that, even though the Werner report and the Delors report have many similarities, the chances for monetary reform in Europe in the 1990s are significantly better than they were in the 1970s. Yet, a monetary union is by no means guaranteed. In the following section I review the recent experience of the present monetary system and introduce

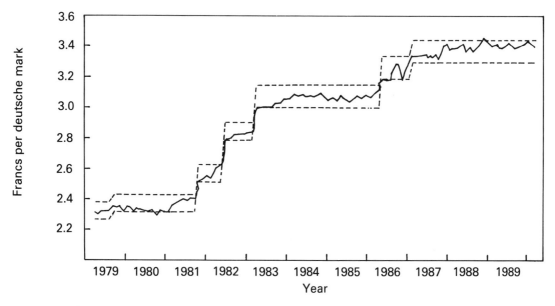

Figure 8.2 The French franc in the European Monetary System, March 1979–December 1989. The franc–mark exchange rate is shown, along with the bilateral fluctuation margins

Sources: IMF, *International Financial Statistics*; Masera 1987

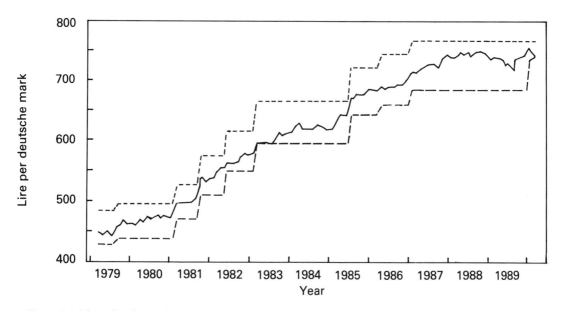

Figure 8.3 The Italian lira in the European Monetary System, March 1979–December 1989. The lira–mark exchange rate is shown, along with the bilateral fluctuation margins

Sources: IMF, *International Financial Statistics*; Masera 1987

155

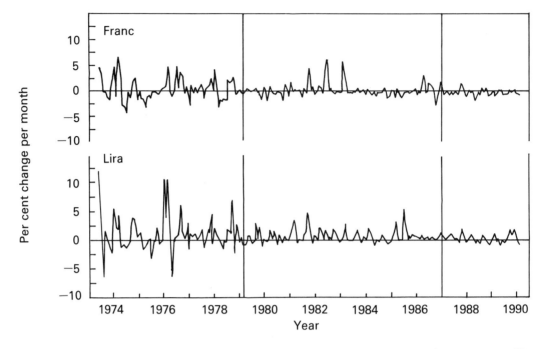

Figure 8.4 Fluctuations in the lira–mark and franc–mark exchange rates, June 1973–December 1989. Vertical lines mark changes in the exchange rate regime: March 1979 marks the start of the European Monetary System; January 1987 marks the change in exchange rate management announced by France and Italy. Ticks represent January of each year

Source: IMF, *International Financial Statistics*

economic problems raised by the gradualist project of monetary union.

REVIEW OF THE RECENT EXPERIENCE

This section presents empirical evidence on the behaviour of inflation and interest rates relative to exchange rates, with special attention to 1987–90. For several reasons, I limit the discussion to the experiences of France and Italy relative to Germany. First, these two countries are Germany's two largest trading partners and therefore carry a lot of political weight in the current negotiations on monetary reform. Second, France and Italy have participated in the exchange rate arrangement since its inception – unlike Spain and the UK, for example – and started from rather divergent initial

conditions. Third, the two are unlike the small countries, whose openness *vis-à-vis* the rest of the EC makes monetary reform less questionable. Fourth, several aspects of France and Italy's recent experience can be applied to other countries.

Figures 8.2 and 8.3 plot the French franc–deutsche mark and the Italian lira–deutsche mark exchange rates during the EMS, together with their respective bilateral fluctuation margins. The discrete movements of the bilateral fluctuation margins occur at the dates of realignment of central parities.[17] Figure 8.4 plots the monthly percentage changes in these bilateral exchange rates since June 1973.

The figures reveal a number of facts. First, the EMS period is characterized by trends in bilateral exchange rates. These trends are somewhat broken in the case of the franc, but appear largely accommodated by adjustments in bilateral parities in the case of the lira. Only in the past three years has the tendency of the franc and the lira to depreciate against the mark subsided. Correspondingly, the frequency of realignments is shown to have decreased recently.

Despite the presence of trends, especially in the early years of the EMS, Figure 8.4 highlights a second empirical regularity: the variability of bilateral exchange rates has decreased since the start of the EMS (the vertical line at March 1979 marks the start of the EMS). This impression is confirmed by statistical tests. Non-parametric tests indicate that the volatility of total and unanticipated exchange rate changes has decreased since the formation of the EMS (Giavazzi and Giovannini 1989).

Finally, the three figures suggest that both the volatility of the intra-European exchange rates and the tendency of the franc and lira to depreciate against the mark have decreased since 1987. Some observers claim that 1987 marks the beginning of a change in the EMS regime (the vertical line at January 1987 marks the beginning of this new regime) (see, in particular, Giavazzi and Spaventa 1990). Since that time, France and Italy have resolutely avoided exchange rate depreciations. The change in attitude at the Banque de France and the Banca d'Italia was especially noticeable in 1989, when both resisted pressure from the Bundesbank to devalue through the further tightening of domestic credit.

Exchange rates and inflation

Figure 8.5 reports CPI inflation rates for France, Germany and Italy since 1958. The figure shows that inflation rates in these countries began to diverge significantly after the first oil shock; the divergences have not been completely eliminated. The EMS was created just before the second oil shock, and significant reduction in and convergence of inflation rates are not observed until the second half of the 1980s. The most recent data

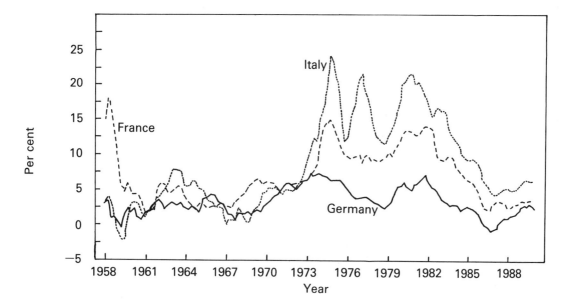

Figure 8.5 Inflation in France, Italy and Germany, January 1958–March 1989. Inflation figures are the annualized percentage changes in the monthly consumer price index. Ticks represent January of each year

Source: IMF, *International Financial Statistics*

Table 8.2 Changes in unit labour costs and in the exchange rate, France and Italy relative to Germany, 1980–9 (per cent)

| Year | France and Germany | | Italy and Germany | |
	Relative unit labour costs[a]	Exchange rate[b]	Relative unit labour costs[a]	Exchange rate[b]
1980	6.9	−0.7	12.3	2.3
1981	8.0	10.6	16.9	12.0
1982	8.3	11.0	13.4	8.3
1983	8.3	8.3	14.9	5.7
1984	5.2	−0.6	8.1	0.9
1985	2.8	0.8	6.4	10.9
1986	−0.4	8.3	2.9	2.6
1987	−0.1	1.5	4.3	5.7
1988	0.8	0.8	5.9	−0.8
1989[c]	1.5	0.2	5.9	2.0

Source: European Economy, November 1989
Note: [a] The change in relative unit labour costs is the difference between the growth rate of unit labour costs in each country and that in Germany.
[b] The change in the exchange rate is the annual rate of change of the franc–mark and lira–mark exchange rates.
[c] Figures for 1989 are estimated using incomplete data.

Table 8.3 Change in real compensation per employee, Germany, France and Italy, 1979–89[a] (per cent)

Year	Germany	France	Italy
1979	1.8	2.0	2.4
1980	1.0	1.8	1.9
1981	−0.8	1.1	3.9
1982	−0.5	2.3	0.2
1983	0.5	0.4	0.8
1984	1.0	0.5	0.0
1985	1.0	0.8	1.0
1986	4.1	1.4	1.6
1987	2.2	0.6	4.0
1988	2.0	1.1	3.8
1989[b]	0.0	0.5	2.7

Source: European Economy, November 1989
Notes: [a] The table shows annual growth rates deflated by the consumer price index.
[b] Figures for 1989 are estimated using incomplete data.

indicate almost complete convergence of French and German inflation, while Italy maintains a differential of about 3.5 per cent with its partners. The experience of most other EC countries has been similar to that of France and Italy – the exceptions being Greece and Portugal whose inflation rates exceeded 10 per cent in the past year.

Whether the EMS has significantly helped its members fight inflation is the subject of some controversy. The view I have taken elsewhere is that the statistical evidence supporting the hypothesis that the EMS has made a difference is very weak (Giavazzi and Giovannini 1989). The stochastic process governing output and wage and price inflation has shifted in France, Denmark, Germany, Ireland and Italy. The relation between output and inflation has worsened in Germany and has improved in all other countries, as the 'imported credibility' theory would predict.

However, the shift is not statistically significant, though the small sample size may account for this. Furthermore, a similar shift is observed for the UK, whose currency was floating at the time. And finally, the shift occurs after 1983 and not at the inception of the EMS. In conclusion, the 'credibility boost' of the EMS has been rather limited, though it should not be wholly dismissed.

The interaction of exchange rate changes and inflation is highlighted in Table 8.2, which reports

Table 8.4 Productivity growth, Germany, France and Italy, 1982–9[a] (per cent)

Year	Germany	France	Italy
1982	1.1	2.4	−0.3
1983	3.1	1.1	0.4
1984	2.7	2.3	2.8
1985	1.3	2.0	2.0
1986	1.3	1.9	1.9
1987	1.2	2.1	2.9
1988	3.0	2.8	2.5
1989[b]	2.3	1.8	2.6

Source: European Economy, November 1989
Notes: [a] The table reports annual growth rates in productivity, which is defined as GDP in constant market prices per person employed.
[b] Figures for 1989 are estimated using incomplete data.

the annual rates of change in unit labour costs and the annual rates of change in the franc–mark and lira–mark exchange rates. The table underscores

Table 8.5 Adjusted relative wages and terms of trade, France and Italy relative to Germany, 1979–89 (ratio)

Year	France and Germany		Italy and Germany	
	Relative wages[a]	Terms of trade[b]	Relative wages[a]	Terms of trade[b]
1979	98.6	103.0	90.5	97.4
1980	104.8	100.0	97.8	100.0
1981	108.7	101.3	106.1	98.9
1982	105.1	100.3	108.5	101.3
1983	102.8	100.2	117.4	103.4
1984	105.3	100.9	122.2	104.2
1985	109.3	103.0	123.6	104.1
1986	104.1	102.0	121.3	105.6
1987	99.7	98.4	121.4	104.3
1988	99.9	98.8	126.9	104.5
1989[c]	101.1	99.4	137.2	104.6

Source: *European Economy*, November 1989

Notes: [a] Adjusted relative wages are the ratio of adjusted wage shares (total economy) in GDP, multiplied by the (exchange-rate-adjusted) ratio of GDP deflators, for France and Italy relative to Germany.

[b] Terms of trade are the ratio of export unit values to import unit values, indexed with 1982 = 100, for France and Italy relative to Germany.

[b] Figures for 1989 are estimated using incomplete data.

the differences within the EMS during the 1980s. Until 1986, large exchange rate depreciations in France and Italy accompanied large divergences in the growth rates of unit labour costs relative to Germany. Notice that in 1981 and 1982 the rate of depreciation of the exchange rate in France exceeded the rate of change of relative labour costs, while in Italy the opposite was true. This difference probably reflects the well-known decision by Italian authorities to enter the EMS with a 'depreciated' currency. This step helped them disinflate through appreciation of the *real* exchange rate.

After 1987, exchange rates have been stable. Yet, in the case of Italy, the growth rate of unit labour costs has continued to exceed that in Germany. Table 8.3 reports the growth of real compensation per employee, measured in terms of the CPI. In the past three years, despite the persistence of inflation differentials, real wages have grown significantly in Italy, whereas French wages have remained broadly in line with German wages. Finally, Table 8.4, which reports the growth of productivity, shows that the three countries have performed similarly; adjusting for productivity growth does not significantly change the pattern of competitiveness reflected by the growth rate of relative wages.

Table 8.6 Balance of payments, Germany, France and Italy, 1983–9 (billions of US dollars)

Year	Germany		France		Italy	
	Current account[a]	Capital account[b]	Current account[a]	Capital account[b]	Current account[a]	Capital account[b]
1983	5.41	−1.24	−5.17	1.08	1.38	−5.53
1984	9.75	−7.63	−0.88	0.57	−2.50	1.58
1985	17.00	−22.64	−0.04	−5.64	−3.54	8.41
1986	40.09	−49.43	2.43	−7.29	2.91	−8.01
1987	46.12	−73.34	−4.45	2.82	−1.66	−7.67
1988	50.47	−31.08	−3.55	11.23	−5.45	10.47
1989[c]	55.58	−58.43	−4.30	5.03	−13.50	26.33

Sources: IMF, *International Financial Statistics*; The Bank of Italy

Notes: [a] The current account balance excludes exceptional financing.

[b] The capital account balance is calculated as the total change in reserves less the current account balance.

[c] The 1989 Italian data refer to the period January–October; data are from The Bank of Italy.

Table 8.7 Output growth and unemployment, Germany, France and Italy, 1983–9[a] (per cent)

Year	Germany		France		Italy	
	GDP growth	Unemployment	GDP growth	Unemployment	GDP growth	Unemployment
1983	1.5	6.9	0.7	8.2	1.1	9.0
1984	2.8	7.1	1.3	9.9	3.2	9.5
1985	2.0	7.3	1.7	10.3	2.9	9.4
1986	2.3	6.5	2.1	10.4	2.9	10.6
1987	1.9	6.4	2.2	10.5	3.1	10.1
1988	3.7	6.4	3.4	10.2	3.9	10.6
1989[b]	3.8	5.6	3.3	9.5	3.5	10.5

Source: *European Economy*, November 1989

Notes: [a] The table reports annual growth rates of GDP and unemployment as a percentage of the civilian labour force.
[b] Figures for 1989 are estimated using incomplete data.

The effects of inflation differentials on international competitiveness are summarized in Table 8.5. The table reports the levels of wages in France and Italy (relative to Germany) when adjusted for productivity, and the terms of trade of the two countries (also relative to Germany). Relative wages are adjusted by multiplying the ratio of wage shares in GDP by the relative GDP deflator. Terms of trade are export unit values divided by import unit values. The table highlights the differences between France and Italy. The former corrected its own losses in competitiveness with the devaluations of 1983 and 1986, while the latter's adjusted relative wages have increased steadily throughout the past ten years, except for a small correction in 1986. Relative terms of trade, which include the effects of fluctuations of dollar prices on the import and export baskets of these countries, broadly reflect the behaviour of relative wages.[18]

In summary, the recent and drastic stabilization of exchange rates has occurred at a time when inflation rates, in Italy especially, have not fallen to German levels. As a result, the stabilization has been accompanied – in both France and Italy – by losses in competitiveness relative to Germany. In the case of Italy, this loss in competitiveness adds to a sustained trend of real appreciations that has increased adjusted relative wages by as much as 40 per cent since 1980. The repercussions of these policies on external accounts are shown in Table 8.6, which reports current account balances and international capital flows. The French and Italian losses in competitiveness of the past three years are reflected in widening current account deficits; they are *overfinanced*, however, by capital inflows in both countries. The balance-of-payments surpluses of France and Italy in the past three years indicate that the stance of monetary (domestic credit) policies in the two countries has been tighter than in Germany. Table 8.7 reports data on output growth and unemployment and shows that since the mid-1980s the three countries have had surprisingly similar performances. Sustained growth and high unemployment characterize the recent experiences of all three countries. The large movements in relative prices have had a small impact on output growth because of strong domestic demand in Italy and France.

Exchange rates and interest rates

Relative interest rate levels are measured by nominal interest rate differentials adjusted by changes in the nominal exchange rate. Thus, both interest rates and exchange rates determine the return to investors. The realized difference in return, d, between foreign and domestic investment is given by

$$d = R - (R^* + \hat{s}), \qquad (8.1)$$

where R and R^* represent the nominal domestic and foreign rates of interest respectively, and $\hat{s}$ is the percentage change in the price of foreign currency in terms of the domestic currency.[19]

The expected rate-of-return differential r is given by

$$r = R - (R^* + \hat{s}^e), \qquad (8.2)$$

where $\hat{s}^e$ is the expected rate of depreciation of the domestic currency relative to the foreign currency. The realized return differential can be decomposed thus:

$$d = r + (\hat{s}^e - \hat{s}). \qquad (8.3)$$

That is, realized rate-of-return differentials are the sum of two components: expected rate-of-return differentials and unexpected changes in exchange rates, or exchange rate 'surprises'. The surprises are only in exchange rates because both the domestic and foreign interest rates are fully known when the investment is made. In other words, nominal interest rates are assumed to be free of default risk. In what follows, I report evidence on d and provide estimates of the decomposition in equation (8.3). The decomposition is carried out by computing plausible estimates of the expected rate-of-return differentials. Estimates of exchange rates surprises are the residuals.[20]

Realized rate-of-return differentials

Realized rate-of-return differentials are obtained by computing the net profit from two strategies in the foreign exchange market. The first strategy, taking a long position in marks, is to borrow lire or francs, buy marks spot, lend marks and then sell marks spot at maturity. The second, taking a short position in marks, is to borrow marks, buy lire or

francs spot, lend lire or francs, and then repay the mark loan by selling the lire or francs spot at maturity. Profits for both strategies are computed in dollars.

Because Italy and France imposed controls on international capital flows in the first half of the 1980s and thus effectively isolated the domestic and international money markets in their currencies, I use data on the offshore (Euro) market in French francs, deutsche marks and Italian lire. An added advantage of these data is that offshore money market instruments that are denominated in different currencies are practically identical as far as reserve, insurance and tax provisions are concerned.

The calculation of speculative profits takes explicit account of the transactions costs. Specifically, the profits on a long position in marks are

$$\tau\left[\left(1 + \frac{R_t^{*B}}{\tau}\right)\frac{S_{t+12/\tau}^{*B}}{S_t^{*A}} - \left(1 + \frac{R_t^A}{\tau}\right)\frac{S_{t+12/\tau}^A}{S_t^B}\right], \qquad (8.4)$$

where τ equals 12 or 1 depending on whether interest rates are monthly or annual (the subscript t is monthly). R^* is the mark interest rate in annual terms, R is the interest rate on franc or lira deposits, S^* is the dollar–mark exchange rate, while S is the price of one lira or one franc in dollars. The superscripts B and A denote bid and asked rates, respectively. The profits on a short position in marks are obtained by interchanging the two terms within the brackets in equation (8.4) and substituting bid rates for asked rates and asked rates for bid rates.

Figures 8.6 and 8.7 show the profits (computed using equation (8.4)) over the period January 1981–May 1990 on one-month investments. The profits from both a strategy of borrowing francs or lire and lending marks and a strategy of borrowing marks and lending francs or lire are reported. A solid line denotes the former; a broken line denotes the latter. When it is profitable to borrow francs or lire and then lend marks, the solid line falls below zero. Conversely, when the opposite strategy is profitable, the broken line rises above zero.[21] The

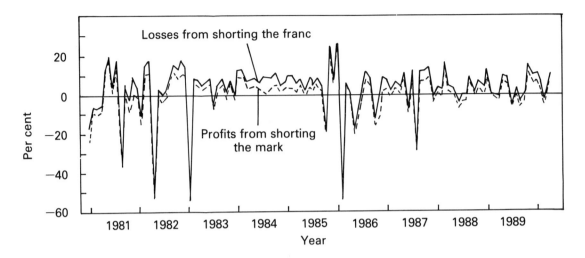

Figure 8.6 Profitability of one-month investments: the franc relative to the mark, January 1981–May 1990. The figure shows the annual percentage return on investment strategies of shorting the franc (borrowing francs to lend marks) and shorting the mark (borrowing marks to lend francs) for one-month deposits. All returns are calculated in US dollars

Source: Data Resources Incorporated data base

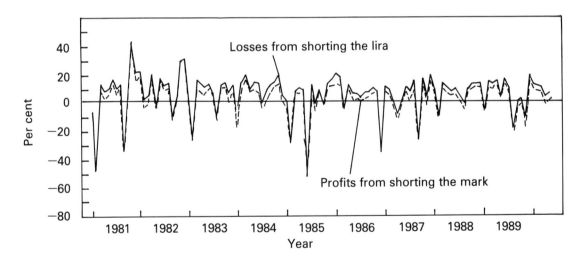

Figure 8.7 Profitability of one-month investments: the lira relative to the mark, January 1981–May 1990. The figure shows the annual percentage return on investment strategies of shorting the lira (borrowimg lire to lend marks) and shorting the mark (borrowing marks to lend lire) for one-month deposits. All returns are calculated in US dollars

Source: Data Resources Incorporated data base

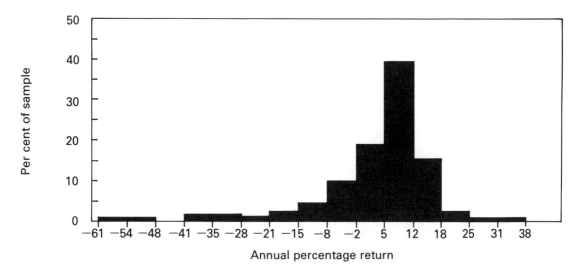

Figure 8.8 Distribution of lira returns on shorting the mark: January 1981–June 1990. The figure shows the frequency of realized returns for a strategy of borrowing marks in order to lend lire in the one-month Euro-deposits markets

Source: Data Resources Incorporated data base

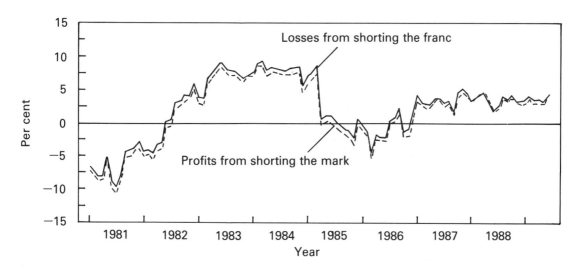

Figure 8.9 Profitability of one-year investments: the franc relative to the mark, January 1981–June 1989. The figure shows the annual percentage return on investment strategies of shorting the franc (borrowing francs in order to lend marks) and shorting the mark (borrowing marks to lend francs) for one-year deposits. All returns are calculated in US dollars

Source: Data Resources Incorporated data base

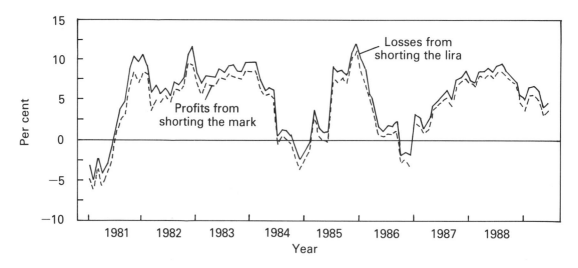

Figure 8.10 Profitability of one-year investments: the lira relative to the mark, January 1981–June 1989. The figure shows the annual percentage return of investment strategies of shorting the lira (borrowing lire in order to lend marks) and shorting the mark (borrowing marks to lend lire) for one-year deposits. All returns are calculated in US dollars

Source: Data Resources Incorporated data base

distribution of realized returns is very similar for both currencies: shorting the franc and the lira relative to the mark has been profitable less than a quarter of the time during the past ten years, and almost never since the beginning of 1988. However, when profitable, shorting the franc and lira has yielded high returns.

By contrast, the figures show that shorting the mark in favour of the franc or lira has yielded lower but much more consistent returns. Indeed, this strategy has been profitable 65 per cent of the time in the case of the franc, and 75 per cent in the case of the lira. Figure 8.8, which plots the distribution of returns from shorting the mark and lending lire, illustrates this asymmetry.[22] The distribution of lira returns is approximately the same, with the highest frequency of small positive realizations and a very low frequency of extremely negative or extremely positive realizations.

The profitability of investments in one-year deposits – shown in Figures 8.9 and 8.10 – has followed a pattern similar to, though more marked than, the one-month investments. Shorting the

franc in favour of the mark has been profitable only 30 per cent of the time, while the opposite strategy was profitable 70 per cent of the time.[23] Contrary to the evidence from one-month interest rates, the size of speculative returns is similar for both strategies. In the case of the lira, speculation against the mark has been profitable eighty-six out of the 102 months in the sample, while the opposite strategy has been profitable only thirteen out of 102 months. An investor would have made money consistently, every month from June 1981 to June 1984 and from January 1987 to June 1990, had he simply borrowed marks to invest in lire. Strikingly, the size of the 'short-mark' positive profits is much larger than that of the 'short-lira' positive profits.

Interest rate differentials and exchange rate margins

The analysis of bilateral exchange rate margins provides additional evidence relevant to the decomposition of realized rate-of-return differentials.[24] In March 1979, France and Italy declared that they would not allow their exchange rates with the mark to cross given margins without an official modification of the margins. Given this intention, suppose that the required rate-of-return differential between marks and francs were zero. If the upper bound on the franc–mark exchange rate were fully credible, the franc interest rate at time t could never exceed the following value:

$$\bar{R}_t = (1 + R^*)\frac{\bar{S}}{S_t} - 1. \tag{8.5}$$

For simplicity, I consider only interest rates on one-year investments. In the equation, $\bar{S}$ denotes the upper bound on the franc–mark exchange rate, while S_t is the spot franc–mark exchange rate at time t. Similarly, the franc interest rate can never be lower than

$$\underline{R}_t = (1 + R^*)\frac{\underline{S}}{S_t} - 1, \tag{8.6}$$

where $\underline{S}$ is the lower bound on the franc–mark exchange rate.

$\bar{R}_t$ and $\underline{R}_t$ are observable at every time t. If the franc interest rate at t is outside these two bounds, either the margins are not credible – i.e. agents expect that, over the maturity of the interest rates considered, the exchange rate can cross the margins – or the required rate-of-return differentials are non-zero.

Figures 8.11 and 8.12 compare the actual one-year franc and lira interest rates with the upper and lower 'credibility' bounds implied by the spot exchange rates, the exchange rate margins and the mark interest rates. Both the franc and lira interest rates are consistently above the upper bound, which confirms the evidence on the systematic biases of realized returns discussed previously. If risk premia are second order, Figures 8.11 and 8.12 indicate that the perceived probability of realignments is quite high, since the expected value of the exchange rate exceeds the upper bound. The highest values in the distribution of exchange rates one year ahead must significantly exceed the upper

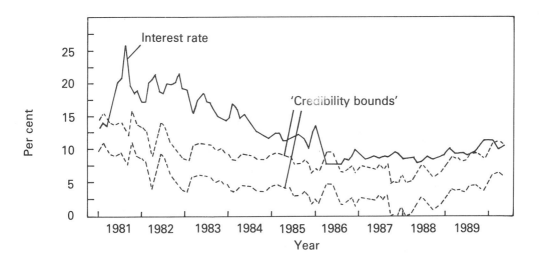

Figure 8.11 Franc interest rate and its 'credibility bounds', January 1981–June 1990: ————, the actual one-year franc interest rate; ------, the 'credibility bounds' implied from the spot exchange rates, the exchange rate margins and the mark interest rates (see equations (8.5) and (8.6))

Sources: Data Resources Incorporated data base; Masera 1987

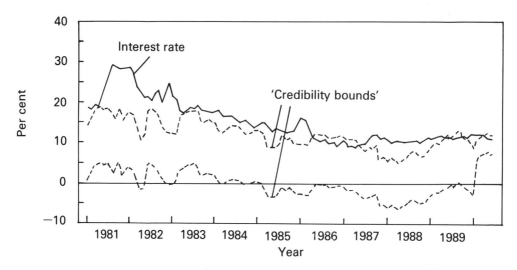

Figure 8.12 Lira interest rate and its 'credibility bounds', January 1981–April 1990: ———, the actual one-year lira interest rate; – – – – –, the 'credibility bounds' implied from the spot exchange rates, the exchange rate margins and the mark interest rates (see equations (8.5) and (8.6))

Sources: Data Resources Incorporated data base; Masera 1987

bound in order for the mean to be greater than the upper bound. Notice, however, that the divergence between the actual interest rates and the upper bounds has decreased over the last three years.

Long-term interest rates

To complete the analysis of interest rates, I report nominal long-term rates in Table 8.8. These rates are long-term government bond yields from the IMF's *International Financial Statistics*. A number of problems with the data, however, preclude the precise calculations presented above. First, the maturity of these bonds is not reported and may not be the same in each country. Second, domestic government bonds have not been as freely trade-able as Eurodeposits, especially during the first half of the 1980s.

The decomposition of return differentials on long-term interest rates is

$$\frac{1 + R_t^L}{1 + R_t^{*L}} = (1 + r^L) \left[\prod_{i=0}^{L} (1 + \hat{s}_{t+i}^e) \right]^{1/L}, \quad (8.7)$$

where L represents the maturity (in years) of the bonds; R^L and R^{*L} are the domestic and foreign rates of interest for bonds of maturity L; r^L is the risk premium and $\hat{s}_t^e$ is the expected annual rate of change in the exchange rate from year t to year $t + 1$. Equation (8.7) says that, net of the risk premium, interest rate differentials represent the *average* expected rate of depreciation of the exchange rate over the maturity of the bonds. From this perspective, the large differentials among nominal bond rates observed in January 1990 suggest rather large expectations of exchange rate adjustment. In order to verify this guess, however, it is necessary to evaluate the size of risk premia.

Alternative explanations for interest rate differentials

Equation (8.3) breaks down the realized excess returns of franc and lira assets relative to mark assets. The equation says that realized rate-of-return differentials equal the sum of expected rate-of-return differentials and exchange rate surprises. To determine whether the long sequences of large

Table 8.8 Long-term government bond yields, Germany, France and Italy, 1979–90[a] (per cent)

Period	Germany	France	Italy
1979–86	7.96	12.24	16.01
1987–9	6.34	9.09	10.19
January 1990	8.07	9.52	11.52
June 1990	8.86	9.76	11.69

Source: IMF, *International Financial Statistics*, October 1990 and *1990 Yearbook*

Note: [a] The figures are the average bond yields for the period shown.

return differentials could be a long sequence of exchange rate surprises, I discuss the determinants of the first term on the right-hand side of equation (8.3) and its plausible size. An attempt to quantify expected rates of return should consider three possible sets of determinants: transactions costs, capital market segmentations (capital controls) and the pricing of risk with perfect and imperfect capital markets.

Transactions costs

In the presence of transactions costs and uncertainty about returns on foreign-currency deposits, traders' strategies can be characterized by an 'inactivity' band, the size of which is determined by the magnitude of the transactions costs in the foreign exchange markets and the uncertainty in expected rates of return (Baldwin 1990). An increase in the expected return on lira deposits, for instance, may not be accompanied by a shift in portfolios if traders believe that the costs of adjusting the portfolios and closing out their position in the future exceed the expected return on the lira investment. Uncertainty and transactions costs therefore induce traders not to eliminate expected rate-of-return differentials unless they reach sufficiently high values, or are expected to persist.

What does this observation imply for equilibrium returns? If all market participants behave according to the same trading rules, it is possible that, even in the absence of risk aversion, expected

rate-of-return differentials will be positively autocorrelated.[25] With rational expectations, realized rate-of-return differentials would also be positively autocorrelated. Autocorrelation of returns, however, does not imply the biases that seem to characterize excess returns on lira and franc deposits. Therefore, the effects of transactions costs are not likely to explain the evidence reported in Figures 8.6–8.10.

Capital controls

The segmentation of national capital markets prevents efficient portfolio diversification and induces expected rate-of-return differentials on assets located in different countries. France and Italy used controls, at least until 1986, that prevented full arbitrage between domestic and foreign capital markets. These controls have typically generated large differentials between domestic and offshore interest rates on the same types of interbank deposits.

The evidence in Figures 8.6–8.10 is constructed using interest rates on Eurodeposits, i.e. rates on deposits denominated in francs, marks and lire but located outside the three countries. In principle, Euro-rates should simply reflect the market's assessment of risk and exchange rate changes.

Yet capital controls may also affect offshore interest rates through two channels: first, the difficulty in transferring funds from onshore to offshore may give rise to liquidity premia because of the thinness of the offshore market; second, all transfers of funds in the Euromarkets are cleared in the countries of the currencies being traded – high political risk may be reflected in an unwillingness to trade and in additional liquidity premia. Neither argument seems to apply to the currencies considered. Funds do not need to be transferred from onshore to offshore for agents to take advantage of the profit opportunities documented above. It is sufficient to purchase liras or francs in the foreign exchange market and then lend them in the Eurodeposit market. As far as political risk is concerned, restrictions that prevent the clearing of funds related to offshore transactions would be extremely severe and are unlikely to be imposed in countries like France and Italy, even after all types of transfers of funds between domestic residents and foreigners have been prohibited.

Finally, the evidence discussed previously indicates that realized return differentials have persisted well after the liberalization of capital controls in 1986. Since that time, the wedge between onshore rates and offshore rates has disappeared. In some instances domestic interest rates have been higher than offshore rates.[26]

Equilibrium pricing of foreign exchange risk

The next potential explanation of expected rate-of-return differentials is the equilibrium pricing of foreign exchange risk. To assess the importance of foreign exchange risk premia, one must rely on some version of the CAPM. However, empirical evidence has repeatedly rejected various specifications of the international CAPM, precisely because the risk premia generated by these models are significantly smaller and less volatile than empirical risk premia.[27]

The potential sources of the CAPM's empirical failure are two. First, statistical tests may have rejected the CAPM because of specification error. In particular, it may be that agents are not all alike, either because they have different attitudes toward risk or because they cannot use financial markets to diversify away certain types of risk. In both cases the 'representative agent' paradigm does not apply. As the following discussion will point out, the computation of risk premia can, to some extent, allow for these problems. Second, if the pattern of returns in the foreign exchange markets is such that large adjustments occur infrequently, standard tests of the CAPM that do not account for this peculiar distribution of returns are flawed: this is the 'peso' problem (Krasker 1980). In the presence of a peso problem, even if expectations are rational, the probability that sample averages match agents' expectations is very low in small samples, despite the fact that sample averages are unbiased estimates of population averages.

Consider the standard representative-agent CAPM. From the investor's optimization problem,

the model yields equilibrium relations between conditional expectations and conditional covariances of asset returns. As a general framework, I adopt the version of the CAPM derived by Philippe Weil and myself (Giovannini and Weil 1990). When rates of return on the assets in the portfolio and consumption growth are jointly log-normally distributed,[23] the equilibrium relations between expected returns on deposits denominated in france (f), liras (l) and marks (m) are

$$\ln\left[\frac{E(\bar{R}^{\mathrm{f}})}{E(\bar{R}^{\mathrm{m}})}\right] = \rho\,\frac{1-\gamma}{1-\rho}\,(\sigma_{\mathrm{f,c}} - \sigma_{\mathrm{m,c}})$$

$$+ \frac{\gamma-\rho}{1-\rho}\,(\sigma_{\mathrm{f,M}} - \sigma_{\mathrm{m,M}}), \qquad (8.8)$$

$$\ln\left[\frac{E(\bar{R}^{\mathrm{l}})}{E(\bar{R}^{\mathrm{m}})}\right] = \rho\,\frac{1-\gamma}{1-\rho}\,(\sigma_{\mathrm{l,c}} - \sigma_{\mathrm{m,c}})$$

$$+ \frac{\gamma-\rho}{1-\rho}\,(\sigma_{\mathrm{l,M}} - \sigma_{\mathrm{m,M}}). \qquad (8.9)$$

When deposits in currency i have a gross return, adjusted for changes in the exchange rate of $\bar{R}^i$, the term on the left-hand side is the log of the ratio of expected gross returns measured in dollars. The reciprocal of the coefficient of intertemporal substitution is ρ and γ is the coefficient of relative risk aversion. The variable $\sigma_{i,M}$ is the covariance of the log of the gross rate of return on asset i with the log of the gross return on the market portfolio, while $\sigma_{i,c}$ is the covariance of the log of the gross rate of return on asset i with the log of the gross rate of growth of consumption. The equations are defined for $\rho \neq 1$.[29]

These equations include traditional asset pricing models as special cases. For example, under logarithmic risk preferences ($\gamma = 1$) equations (8.8) and (8.9) collapse to the so-called 'static' asset pricing equations, where only the covariance of an asset with the market rate of return determines its expected return in equilibrium, while in the case where risk aversion equals intertemporal substitution ($\gamma = \rho$, the case of von Neumann preferences) the two equations reduce to the 'consumption-based' CAPM.

To obtain some rough estimates of the size of risk premia from the CAPM, I estimate average covariances of franc, lira and mark returns on one-year Eurodeposits over the 1980s (using non-overlapping data) with market and consumption indices. In Giovannini and Weil's paper, all first and second moments are conditional on information available every period. Here the calibration uses average data instead. The error-in-variables problem is negligible if the covariance between the time-varying first and second moments is second order.[30]

Calibration of the model requires a choice between the relevant consumption and market indices. Under the representative-agent assumption, the market index should be an average of national market indices and the consumption index an average of national consumptions. The indices I chose are *Capital International Perspective*'s world market index and the consumption growth of OECD countries.[31] There are reasons to believe that the representative-agent assumption does not hold, however, because individual countries' attitudes toward risk may not be the same. First, consumption is not highly correlated across countries, and second, as Michael Adler and Bernard Dumas point out, deviations from PPP and the law of one price indicate that the conditions for aggregation of national indices are not met (Adler and Dumas 1983).

Unfortunately, aggregate asset pricing equations for general models that allow heterogeneous investors are not available. For this reason, it may be helpful to explore whether the predictions of rate-of-return differentials differ significantly from one national investor to another in order to evaluate the empirical significance of specification errors. Hence, I compute equilibrium relative returns from the viewpoint of a UK investor (i.e. I use the UK stock market index and the rate of growth of UK consumption) and a Japanese investor (using the same measures for Japan).[32]

Table 8.9 reports the results of this exercise.

Table 8.9 Calibration of risk premia, for investors in selected currencies, 1981–9[a]

	World investor (US dollar)	UK investor (pound)	Japanese investor (yen)
Sample data			
Average rate-of-return differentials			
Franc	1.44	1.05	1.05
Lira	4.30	4.14	4.14
Covariance with market			
Mark	0.0200	0.0173	−0.0061
Franc	0.0192	0.0212	0.0322
Lira	0.0220	0.0211	0.0321
Covariance with consumption			
Mark	0.0005	0.0003	−0.0009
Franc	−0.0000	−0.0000	0.0010
Lira	0.0013	0.0000	0.0011
Theoretical risk premia			
Static CAPM ($\gamma = 1$)			
Franc	−0.09	0.39	3.84
Lira	0.20	0.39	3.83
Consumption CAPM ($\gamma = \rho = 2$)			
Franc	−0.12	−0.06	0.38
Lira	0.15	−0.03	0.15
Consumption CAPM ($\gamma = \rho = 10$)			
Franc	−0.61	−0.30	1.87
Lira	0.74	−0.15	2.02
General CAPM ($\gamma = 10, \rho = 2$)			
Franc	−0.41	−0.62	−27.29
Lira	−0.23	−3.40	−27.00

Sources: Author's own calculations using equations (8.8) and (8.9) from text. The world market index comes from Morgan Guaranty; in it, national stock markets are aggregated using their relative capitalizations as weights. The consumption growth measure comes from the OECD's *Main Economic Indicators*

Note: [a] The table reports results for investments in French francs, Italian lire and deutsche marks.

The top section of the table contains the average relative returns (the terms on the left-hand side of equations (8.8) and (8.9) expressed as percentages) as measured from the data, together with the relevant average covariances, also from the data. The bottom section contains the implied relative expected returns from the model under a small set of parameter combinations – the case of the static

CAPM ($\gamma = 1$), the case of the consumption CAPM ($\gamma = \rho = 2$ and 10, respectively) and a general case that combines high risk aversion ($\gamma = 10$) with the coefficient of intertemporal substitution equal to 0.5 ($\rho = 2$). The three units in the columns are, respectively, dollars, pounds and yen.[33]

Except for the case of the Japanese investor, the table indicates that the average risk premia consistent with asset pricing models tend to be smaller than those observed in the data. The models often predict higher expected returns on mark assets than on franc or lira assets. In the case of the Japanese investor, the static CAPM produces risk premia that resemble the observed data, but a change in parameters generates very large differences between the data and the model's predictions.

I now turn to the second reason why asset pricing models are rejected: peso problems. The potential of large and rare devaluations might explain the evidence from Table 8.9. The table suggests that risk premia do not seem to account for the average rate-of-return differentials between marks, francs and lire. Yet this evidence is not necessarily inconsistent with rational expectations. It could indicate that investors had been expecting exchange rate changes that never occurred, but that, given policy-makers' objectives and constraints and the distribution of exogenous shocks to Germany, France and Italy, changes are not to be ruled out. The presence of a 'peso problem' should not significantly bias risk premia because it should not affect covariances with the market and consumption. The occurrence of large exchange rate changes can significantly change the covariances in equations (8.8) and (8.9) if those exchange rate changes are associated with large changes in either consumption, market return, or both. This is unlikely to occur if the world portfolio and the representative investor's consumption, both on which the asset pricing equation is based, are well diversified. Errors can occur in small samples, however, if the large realizations of exchange rate changes are either over-represented or under-represented in the sample. Since my inter-

pretation of the evidence is that, if anything, these large exchange rate changes are under-represented in the sample used for my computations, and since population covariances should be unaffected by their potential occurrence, my computations should be little affected by the peso problem.

Hence, the results reported in Table 8.9 lead me to conclude that standard asset pricing models do not seem consistently to explain average excess returns on lira and franc deposits relative to deposits in marks. Theoretical risk premia appear to be small, or, more seriously, of the opposite sign than the observed average rate-of-return differentials.

Risk premia with non-marketable risk

One reason why the CAPM fails empirically might be, as pointed out above, the presence of risk that cannot be efficiently diversified away in financial markets. While in the previous section I argued that, in the presence of well-diversified international portfolios, the rare and large depreciations of the lira and the franc relative to the mark should not significantly affect covariances with the market and consumption as computed in Table 8.9, this may not occur in the presence of non-marketable risk.

To illustrate this possibility, consider the optimization problem of an individual investor maximizing expected utility. The efficiency condition is that (at every time and conditional on the information available) the expectation of the product of the gross return on asset i and the marginal rate of substitution in consumption must equal unity:

$$E(\eta \bar{R}_i) = 1, \qquad (8.10)$$

where η is the ratio of the marginal utility of consumption at the time of the pay-off of asset i to the current marginal utility of consumption. Following Weil, consider a two-period set-up where at the start of the first period all agents are identical in their endowments and risk characteristics.[34] Their total income is the sum of a marketable and a non-marketable component. The non-marketable component is distributed identi-cally across investors.[35] Given the definition of the risk-free rate of return, $R^F = 1/E(\eta)$, and the relation $E(\eta\bar{R}_i) = E(\eta)E(\bar{R}_i) + \text{cov}(\eta,\bar{R}_i)$, we obtain

$$E(\bar{R}_i) = R^F[1 - \text{cov}(\eta, \bar{R}_i)] \qquad (8.11)$$

for any i, and thus

$$\frac{E(\bar{R}_i)}{E(\bar{R}_j)} = \frac{1 - \text{cov}(\eta, \bar{R}_i)}{1 - \text{cov}(\eta, \bar{R}_j)}. \qquad (8.12)$$

The expression within the brackets in equation (8.11) is greater than unity, since $\text{cov}(\eta, \bar{R}_i)$ is negative: an increase in the rate of return on an asset in the portfolio increases future consumption and therefore decreases its marginal utility. Equations (8.11) and (8.12) are formally identical to standard asset pricing equations, like those from which equations (8.8) and (8.9) are derived. The important difference is the presence of non-marketable risk in the marginal rate of substitution η. Because of the presence of this risk, risk premia can diverge from those in the standard asset pricing model if returns on different assets have different covariances with the marginal rate of substitution.

From the analysis above, it can be shown that the size of the theoretical risk-free rate and the empirical rate-of-return differentials is such that the covariance between the marginal rate of substi-tution and the rate of return on francs and lire should be about twice the size of the covariance computed assuming perfect risk pooling. However, it is difficult to find convincing reasons why large exchange rate changes should affect the covari-ances of franc and lira assets more than that of mark assets. The most plausible forms of non-marketable risk in international financial markets are those relating to the problems of asymmetric information and those arising from legal constraints on financial intermediaries.[36] Large exchange rate changes produce potentially large transfers of wealth among financial intermediaries in the Euromarkets and can give rise to liquidity problems and bankruptcies. However, the mechanics of these liquidity crises do not depend on the specific currency composition of bank port-folios. For these reasons, the covariance of returns on lira and franc assets with the marginal utility of consumption (or with any other benchmark) should not be significantly affected by large changes in the franc–mark or lira–mark exchange rates. Therefore, the kind of non-marketable risks that characterize international financial markets should not affect expected rates of return on deposits denominated in different currencies.

REAL WAGES AND REAL INTEREST RATES

The evidence presented in the previous section can be summarized as follows. The past three years have been characterized by increased stability of exchange rates within the EMS: both volatility and trends in the franc–mark and lira–mark exchange rates have decreased noticeably. The decrease in inflation differentials among Germany, France and Italy has been achieved, especially in the case of Italy, with a substantial increase in real wages and an improvement in the terms of trade. The past three years have witnessed some worsening of the competitive position of both France and Italy. Persistent interest differentials between franc, lira and mark assets are difficult to explain by risk premia and capital market imperfections. And finally, the mirror image of high realized real interest rates and high real wages has been current account deficits and capital account surpluses (often more than offsetting the current account deficits) in Italy and France. In Germany, by contrast, there have been large current account surpluses matched by capital account deficits.

What underlies the persistence of real wage and real interest differentials at low levels of inflation well after the dramatic reduction of the inflation disparities of the mid-1980s?[37] This section reviews alternative explanations.

'Pure' wage and price stickiness

The first natural candidate is the traditional wage–price stickiness story.[38] According to this theory, high real wages and a loss in competitiveness result from the transition to credible exchange rate targeting because only a fraction of existing prices and wages in the economy are reset every period.

The first problem with this explanation is that the new regime has been in place for some time now; the transition is presumably over. Some claim that France and Italy dramatically altered their domestic policies in response to the discipline of the EMS in the mid-1980s; others regard January 1987 as the date when these two countries pledged to forgo parity changes. The persistence of real wage and real interest differentials three years after the presumed change in regime is hard to square with the standard models of overlapping wage contracts. In those models, inertia lasts only for the maximum length of wage contracts.[39] What would then be needed is some type of protracted price stickiness of the type discussed, for example, by Olivier Blanchard (1983).

Even if protracted nominal sluggishness is present, however, these models still cannot explain the persistence of interest rate differentials. If the exchange rate is credibly fixed, the increase in money demand coming from the fall in inflationary expectations due to the change in regime would automatically be accommodated by balance-of-payments surpluses. The nominal interest rate need not go up.[40] In order to explain the observed interest rate differential, one should rely on slow adjustment in international asset markets, or risk premia, a hypothesis that was ruled out earlier.

In the end, there are a number of reasons to believe that nominal stickiness may not exclusively explain the observed behaviour of real interest rates and real wages in France and Italy relative to Germany. This is not to say that nominal inertia is irrelevant, but only that additional explanations may be useful.

Credibility problems

The next possible hypothesis is that the policy change lacked credibility. In order to illustrate that hypothesis, it is useful to follow Robert Barro and David Gordon's standard model of interaction between the government and the private sector.[41]

The model incorporates several assumptions. First, unanticipated changes in nominal exchange rates have real effects. Second, monetary authorities perceive a cost in exchange rate changes, which under a managed floating regime can represent the cost of the induced higher inflation. In a regime like the EMS, the cost could represent, together with the cost of higher inflation, the political cost of exchange rate changes. Third, there are distortions in the economy that could be corrected, even if temporarily, by exchange rate changes. The best example for European countries is the monopoly power of some trade unions. Fourth, monetary authorities can respond to events faster than the aggregate private sector. And fifth, the state of the economy is represented by the realization of an exogenous disturbance that affects the real economy. In other words, slow multiperiod adjustment of prices or wages is ruled out for the sake of tractability.

The unanticipated exchange rate changes and the exogenous disturbance affect the economy as follows:

$$y = (\hat{s} - \hat{s}^e) - \varepsilon, \qquad (8.13)$$

where ε is a white noise real disturbance and y is the departure of real income from trend.

The preference of monetary authorities is represented by the following loss function:

$$L = E[\hat{s}^2 + \varphi(y - K)^2], \qquad (8.14)$$

where the first term represents the costs of exchange rate changes and the second term, with $K > 0$, represents the distortions that may be corrected by exchange rate changes.

The ability of monetary authorities to respond to events faster than the aggregate economy is captured in the assumption that monetary authorities set the rate at which the exchange rate is changed after observing ε, while the private sector forms expectations on monetary policy before the realization of ε. Under these assumptions, a regime of managed floating would be one where $\hat{s}$ is the solution of the following problem:

$$\min[\hat{s}^2 + \varphi(y - K)^2], \qquad (8.15)$$

subject to

$$y = (\hat{s} - \hat{s}^e) - \varepsilon, \qquad \text{with } \hat{s}^e \text{ given.}$$

The change in the exchange rate, the equilibrium activity and the expectations of exchange rate changes are, respectively,

$$\hat{s} = \varphi K + \frac{\varphi}{1 + \varphi}\, \varepsilon, \qquad (8.16)$$

$$y = -\frac{1}{1 + \varphi}\, \varepsilon, \qquad (8.17)$$

$$\hat{s}^e = \varphi K. \qquad (8.18)$$

These familiar results highlight the inflationary bias in a regime where the central bank is unable to commit credibly to a fixed exchange rate target.

Learning about the change in regime

Consider now the case where national monetary authorities – for reasons that are not explicit in the model (like the desire to accelerate European integration) – abandon any attempt to correct domestic distortions with the exchange rate, and stick to the fixed exchange rate parity: $\hat{s}$ is equal to zero independent of the state.

The private sector, not fully aware of or convinced by this change in regime, believes that the authorities could revert to the discretionary management of the exchange rate described above. The public assigns a probability p that the monetary authorities will not follow the fixed exchange rate rule. Every period, this probability is revised optimally on the basis of the observed behaviour of the monetary authorities, i.e. p_{t+1} is

decreased if $\hat{s}_t = 0$. The expectation of the exchange rate change is thus

$$\hat{s}^e = p\hat{s}^{e,d}, \qquad (8.19)$$

where $\hat{s}^{e,d}$ is the expectation of the depreciation of the exchange rate when the authorities follow discretionary exchange rate management. Assuming rational expectations, $\hat{s}^{e,d}$ is formed using the knowledge of the authorities' incentives, which are embodied in the first-order condition for the constrained minimization in equation (8.15). Thus,

$$E[\hat{s}^e + \varphi(\hat{s}^e - p\hat{s}^{e,d} - \varepsilon - K)] = 0. \quad (8.20)$$

This implies

$$\hat{s}^{e,d} = \frac{1}{1 - \varphi(1 - p)}\, \varphi K,$$

$$\hat{s}^e = \frac{p}{1 - \varphi(1 - p)}\, \varphi K.$$

If the authorities adhere to the exchange rate parity, p is progressively decreased until it reaches zero. The transition, however, is characterized by a series of prediction errors. This generates data resembling the phenomena described above.

Consider interest rate differentials. Equation (8.3) indicates that realized interest rate differentials could be high, even if expected real interest differentials were zero. Negative exchange rate surprises also depress economic activity:

$$y = -\hat{s}^e - \varepsilon = -\frac{p}{1 - \varphi(1 - p)}\, \varphi K - \varepsilon.$$

The intuition behind this result can be provided by the evidence on real wage differentials. Wages are set with an expectation of a positive exchange rate depreciation. If the exchange rate depreciation is not realized, the loss in competitiveness is reflected in a fall in economic activity.

The model of slow adjustment of expectations

raises two questions. The first regards the speed of adjustment of expectations. The model predicts that expectations of exchange rate changes would asymptotically converge to zero. This convergence has not occurred in countries like France and, especially, Italy. More strikingly, this convergence does not seem to occur in countries with an experience of much more stable exchange rates.

The case of Austria provides an interesting example. Until the early 1970s the schilling and the mark were tied together by the Bretton Woods system: both currencies were pegged to the dollar (hence the March 1961 revaluation of the mark was reflected in a devaluation of the schilling). With the collapse of the Bretton Woods regime, the schilling was pegged to a basket of currencies in which the mark gained an increasing weight. Finally, in 1981 the schilling was tied to the mark exclusively. The only sizeable change in the schilling–mark exchange rate occurred at the end of 1969, when the price of the mark increased progressively from about 6.5 to around 7.0 (a depreciation of 7.5 per cent). In contrast to the franc and the lira, the schilling has kept remarkably stable relative to the mark throughout the 1980s.

In the years after 1986, the period for which reliable data are available, Austrian short-term interest rates exceeded German short-term rates by an average of about 50 basis points. The experience of the Netherlands, a member of the EMS that has kept its currency and monetary policy tightly linked to Germany's, broadly matches the evidence for Austria.

Transactions costs and liquidity premia are important in explaining these small interest rate differentials; for this reason, it is more difficult to identify expectations of exchange rate changes. Yet, this evidence raises the possibility that governments' commitment to a given parity may be less than fully credible, even in the long run. After all, the fact that different currencies are maintained reflects the governments' right to change their currencies' value. Given that exchange rate changes have real effects, governments may be reluctant to give up this instrument.

Exchange rate changes as 'escape clauses'

An alternative to the 'learning' model presented above is a model where the public is aware that there will always be instances when the monetary authorities will want to use the exchange rate.[42]

Here the government's strategy is a mixture of fixing the exchange rate ($\hat{s} = 0$) and discretionary policy. For this reason, the model is labelled 'escape clause'. Discretionary policy is chosen whenever the exogenous shock ε exceeds a given range. The public fully understands this and bases its own expectations about the government's behaviour on the probability of large realizations of ε, the instances when the escape clause will be invoked. Given that ε is serially independent, these probabilities are constant.

The solution of this model is formally identical to that of the learning model, except that now p is constant and represents the probability that ε lies beyond the 'normal' range. Hence, as long as ε remains in the normal range there will be high realized real interest rates and high real wages. When the large realizations of ε occur, the government's discretionary exchange rate changes will be more effective, because the public will be more surprised than under a managed exchange rate regime. Thus, it can easily be shown that there are parameter values such that this strategy would be preferred by the government to both fixed exchange rates and managed floating (see Flood and Isard 1989; Persson and Tabellini 1990). The mixed strategy is thus credible.[43]

Extensions and implications

An important difference between these models and reality is that the state of the economy is not serially independent. Because of the sluggishness of prices and wages, and the slow response of employment to real wages, the loss in competitiveness gradually builds up. In other words, for a given stream of realizations of the exogenous disturbance, the incentives to change the exchange rate increase, since the losses in competitiveness due to past increases in prices remain. In the model discussed above, the losses in competitiveness do not linger; rather they result in an immediate fall in economic activity.

An extension of the model to deal formally with these issues is beyond the scope of this chapter. My guess is that the escape clause equilibrium, if it is at all viable, may be subject to more frequent exchange rate realignments and larger biases of realized real interest rates when the realignments do not occur. An additional, more manageable extension of the model mixes the learning and the escape clause parables. Elements of both stories seem relevant to the European experience: the public is not sure how serious the commitment is to monetary convergence and might revise its views as years go by; yet, there is always a belief that governments may use the exchange rate under extreme circumstances. Even the probability that the government might resort to exchange rate changes may be subject to revision.

An interesting feature of the above analysis extends the theory of optimum currency areas. A regime of fixed exchange rates with separate currencies is not equivalent to a single currency, because the public understands that the monetary authorities may use exchange rates to correct distortions. This awareness leads to biases on rates of return to productive factors, for which the welfare effects are estimable.

A calculation of the welfare effects of the interest rate distortions should take uncertainty into account, and in particular the fact that in the escape clause model large realizations of the exogenous shock occasionally occur. Two types of effects should be relevant in this calculation. First, the long-run rate of return might be tied down, either by a modified golden-rule condition, or, in the case of a small open economy, by the world rate of interest. In this case, the wedges discussed here may have large welfare effects, similar to those arising from taxing savings. And second, when uncertainty is accounted for, a more precise estimate of the investment distortion is possible.

TRANSITION TO MONETARY UNION

This section examines the current policy debate in the light of the evidence presented above and its possible interpretations. What follows, however, is necessarily an attempt to take only a snapshot of the diplomatic exchanges that have accelerated in the very recent past. The speed-up may be due to the December 1990 intergovernmental conference, which will seek changes in the Treaty of Rome allowing for the creation of a common European central bank.

In this section, I discuss the feasibility – and indeed the desirability – of gradualism as a strategy to achieve a monetary union. Next I turn to the perceived problems hindering further progress of the monetary union: the budgetary and debt problems and the question of a 'two-speed' economic and monetary union, with a core group of countries moving toward a single currency before the rest of the EC. Finally, I describe the likely positions of the major negotiators at the intergovernmental conference.

Can gradualism work?

I have presented evidence that exchange rate targets in the EMS are still not fully credible. This lack of credibility is the curse of gradualism. I have also shown that, if the incentives to change exchange rates remain intact, expectations of change will persist. The question then is whether the Delors plan has significantly affected the incentives for France and Italy to devalue their currencies relative to the mark. These incentives combine the real effects of surprise realignments and the political and economic costs of these realignments.

Some observers believe that the political costs of devaluations, as perceived by French and Italian authorities, are higher now than they were five years ago. This might well reflect these two countries' greater political enthusiasm for an integrated European economy with a single currency. The resistance of other EC partners, as well as problems raised by external economic shocks, may, however, lower the perceived political costs of exchange rate changes. The intrinsic dynamics of wages and prices can also lower the perceived costs of devaluation, because exchange rate misalignments build up in the absence of full convergence of inflation rates. Finally, the present institutional setting further justifies the lack of credibility of exchange rate targets. Nothing prevents monetary authorities from using changes in bilateral parities to accommodate price imbalances. Indeed, the Delors report views this strategy as acceptable – even desirable (at least according to the interpretation of this plan by German authorities) – in the transition, since it allows exchange rate realignments during stage I, and possibly even during stage II.

The model discussed previously implies that, when exchange rate targets are not fully credible, convergence can never be complete.[44] For this reason, it is unlikely that monetary authorities would be able to maintain exchange rate targets throughout the whole adjustment period. Thus, gradualism fails. The elimination of small inflation rate differentials seems a faulty criterion to guide a monetary reform. The stubbornness of small inflation differentials prevents monetary authorities from deciding when maximum inflation convergence is reached.

These observations are based on the implicit assumption that real shocks are absent. Under this assumption, and absent the non-neutralities arising from credibility problems under fixed exchange rates, all relative prices between the low- and high-inflation countries would be equal to unity. Indeed, this implicit assumption provides the benchmark for the inflation-convergence criterion. In reality, however, real shocks are present, and therefore the criterion of inflation convergence becomes even less reliable, because it requires the knowledge of equilibrium relative prices. The difficulties in computing equilibrium relative prices arise from the well-known uncertainties about the relevant economic model and its parameters, discussed, for example, by Jeffrey Frankel (1988).

In conclusion, economic theory suggests that gradualism is not an effective strategy for monetary reform. The recent increase in the price of oil will almost surely bring the weakness of gradualism into the open. First, the increase in the price of oil is a real shock and EC countries may believe it is necessary to allow intra-European real exchange rates to change. This implies giving up the twin objectives of exchange rate stability and inflation rate convergence. In addition, the increase in the price of oil will affect inflation and inflationary expectations. Calculations that I performed with Francesco Giavazzi using 1980 input–output tables show that the aggregate effect of a 10 per cent increase in the price of energy products ranges from 1.3 per cent in France to 1.9 per cent in the Netherlands when constant nominal wages are assumed and all other prices are allowed to adjust. The effect ranges from 6.6 per cent in the Netherlands to 7.2 per cent in Germany and the UK when constant real wages are assumed for all the countries (Giavazzi and Giovannini 1987). These numbers take into account the effects of intra-European input–output interactions. They indicate that the structure of production in EC countries does not necessarily disadvantage the 'high-inflation' countries. However, the large differences between constant nominal wage and constant real-wage simulations suggest that, despite the technological homogeneity of European economies, an energy shock can have large destabilizing effects if it affects price-setters' expectations unevenly.[45]

The pitfalls of the gradualist approach lend support to the alternative 'monetarist' strategy. The monetarist strategy calls for a sudden and permanent change in the monetary regime. Elsewhere I have argued that the best way to achieve a monetary union, once the common monetary authority is in place, is through currency reform (Giovannini 1990). Currency reform is a replacement of national currencies either by a single currency or by new national currencies that exchange at parity (one mark equals one franc, equals one lira and so on).[46] This reform is carried out over a specified period of time, during which residents of each country swap old banknotes for new banknotes at a prespecified rate. Bank accounts are automatically converted. As a result, the stock of money in circulation is unaffected. During the same period, all outstanding assets and liabilities in the economy have to be recalculated, requiring considerable expense: all accounting and control systems – both private and public – have to be translated.

While the two alternatives (one-to-one exchange rates versus a single currency) produce the same effect on prices (aligning nominal prices of all goods in the EC), they are not exactly equivalent for two reasons. On the one hand, some countries might be unwilling to give up their national currency's name and symbol in exchange for a single currency, perhaps the ECU. These countries may find it more desirable to change the units in which their national currencies are denominated. On the other hand, the persistence of banknotes with the old names and symbols might make the currency of those countries with previously high inflation somewhat less desirable, especially in retail transactions. A compromise solution would be to print new banknotes with the ECU name together with the names of all the currencies in the monetary union.

The advantages of currency reform are many. First, the abolition of exchange rates eliminates the distortions arising from expectations of exchange rate changes. Second, a currency reform solves unit-of-account problems by cutting down on the calculations necessary to translate prices in different currencies – with N currencies, the number of relevant bilateral exchange rates is $N^2/2 - N/2$.[47] Third, it allows final adjustments of exchange rates without inducing any changes in inflationary expectations. Finally, and most importantly, it is the only reform that is fully credible, since it does not allow reversals to the old regime.

However, a currency reform is a politically costly undertaking because it requires the full and immediate commitment of all countries that decide to join; it forces the set-up of a common European central bank and the settlement of issues related to the bank's management, accountability and tasks.[48]

Obstacles to a currency reform

The sensible strategy for monetary union is a currency reform. This proposal, however, faces two important obstacles. The first is the creation of a common central bank that is independent of national fiscal authorities and can carry out its own objectives without undue pressure or influence from national governments. The second obstacle is the question of participation in the monetary union.

One source of pressure on a European central bank that has been frequently debated in the past year is the divergent fiscal stances of the individual countries. Table 8.10 shows debt–GNP ratios for EC countries. The table highlights the nature of the divergences. Differences in debt–GNP ratios induce large differences in interest spending and, even with similar primary balances, differences in net borrowing. Thus, high-debt governments are forced to turn to financial markets both to roll over large stocks of debt and, typically, to finance larger current deficits.

The data in Table 8.10 raise two questions. Can a monetary union function without a central fiscal authority? What threats do independent fiscal authorities present to the successful functioning of a European central bank?

The first question is raised by those who regard central banks as fiscal agencies of the government, charged with managing the government debt, either by selling securities to the market or by purchasing government securities directly in exchange for high-powered money. Over the years,

Table 8.10 Debt–GNP ratios, European Community countries, 1989

Country	Debt–GNP ratio
Belgium	127
France	35
Germany	43
Italy	99
Netherlands	78
UK	44
EC12	58

Source: Estimates from Bishop 1990: 2

central banking has progressively moved away from these functions, for which the private banking sector is perfectly equipped. Now central banks are concerned about the soundness of financial intermediaries, the stability of interest rates and the exchange rate, and the control of inflation.[49] Another concern about fiscal authority regards the optimum-currency-area trade-off between monetary and fiscal policy stressed, for example, by Peter Kenen (1969). The creation of a single currency area might allow a centralized fiscal authority to redistribute income in response to region-specific shocks.[50] The current policy sentiment, especially in the EC countries, is that a centralized and permanent system of income transfers may be plagued by inefficiencies. Financial intermediaries and development banks, perhaps under the explicit direction of national governments, are probably better suited for identifying the relevant development opportunities, for selecting the most socially efficient projects and for monitoring their progress.

The second question raised by the current structure of fiscal authority and its divergent imbalances regards the spillover of national fiscal shocks into the whole Community, and the effect these spillovers have on the operations of a common central bank.[51] Three types of spillovers are relevant in this case. The first is the traditional Keynesian spillover, associated with the export of crowding out in a region characterized by integrated financial markets and a single currency. The bias in this case is expansionary and the effects are an increase in the real interest rate and an appreciation of the region's real exchange rate relative to the rest of the world. Hence, the pressure on a central bank would be to offset these biases through monetary expansion.[52] The second type of spillover comes from distortionary taxation in the presence of increased mobility of goods and factors within the area. Uncoordinated tax policies lead to tax competition and undertaxation of the mobile factors with adverse effects on national budgets. If national governments are unable either to decrease spending or to increase taxation of the immobile factors by the required amounts, tax competition

increases the net borrowing of national governments and may force the common central bank to monetize part of the deficits. In addition, higher government borrowing increases the stock of government debt. The third type of spillover is related to the dynamics of debt and deficits and to the systemic effects of funding crises of individual governments. In countries with large stocks of debt, questions are raised about the ability of the national government to adhere to its intertemporal budget constraints without debt repudiation or other forms of extraordinary taxation. The impact of these crises on financial markets may be quite significant, especially if the absolute size of the government debt is large. The common central bank may be led to inject liquidity into financial markets in order to avoid the negative effects of a systemic crisis associated with multiple collapses of financial intermediaries.

Spillovers of the first kind are not quantifiable, since the relevant transmission is the one from national saving rates to the real exchange rate and the real interest rate. As Laurence Kotlikoff convincingly argues, it is not possible to establish a reliable link between government savings, as measured by the government budget, and national savings.[53] Spillovers of the second kind deserve more careful consideration, although to date there are no reliable numbers on the impact of the single market on tax revenue (assuming no change in national tax structures and policies). At the same time, the Community has practically abandoned attempts to overhaul tax co-ordination comprehensively. Concerns about the ability of countries like Italy to stabilize their debt–GDP ratios make spillovers of the third kind the most significant and the most urgent.

The attitudes of official institutions toward the co-ordination of national fiscal authorities with the common central bank mix concerns about stability in the transition – i.e. the presence of incentives to depreciate currencies during the transition – and concerns about the operation of the monetary union. The Delors report considers convergence of fiscal deficits a crucial condition for monetary union and advocates concerted budgetary actions during stage I including the development of 'quantitative guidelines and medium-term orientations'. In the second stage, the report calls for 'precise, although not yet binding' rules that relate to the size of budget deficits and their financing. In the third stage, budgetary rules would become binding. The EC document on economic and monetary union advocates the adoption of 'binding procedures', whereby member states submit rules or guidelines for their budgetary laws during the transition, the adequacy of which would be discussed at the Community level (European Commission 1990). In the final stage, the Community proposes monitoring, adjusting and enforcing through peer pressure. Finally, the EC Monetary Committee spells out in even greater detail 'principles of sound budgetary policies', which include the elimination of governments' access to direct financing by central banks, no cross-government 'bail out' rules and the correction of excessive deficits, together with, if possible, incorporation of criteria to determine acceptable levels of budget deficits into the Treaty of Rome (EC Monetary Committee 1990).

It is not clear which specific externalities would be corrected by the proposed rules, especially the rules relating to ceilings on national budget deficits. These rules have been criticized on the grounds that budgetary ceilings may eliminate the flexibility that national governments need to offset regional shocks in the monetary union (given the loss of monetary control) (see especially Buiter and Kletzer 1990). In the case of the USA, budget rules such as Gramm–Rudman–Hollings have led to a proliferation of artificial accounting devices with little substantial deficit reduction achieved. Furthermore, it is difficult to develop credible sanctions against countries that break the rules. More importantly, none of the proposed rules directly attacks the most serious threat to the stability of a fledgling European monetary union: the occurrence of debt crises. In principle, a more satisfactory solution to the problem of ensuring the minimization of the risks of debt crises, while at the same time avoiding a slowdown of the monetary union, would have been the definition of fiscal

preconditions for countries to join the union. These preconditions could include requirements to stabilize convincingly – or at least reduce – the debt–GDP ratio before joining the union. These preconditions are politically costly, however, both for the countries 'in trouble' and for the 'virtuous' countries, which tend to resist accelerations in the progress toward monetary union. The former would have to engineer large fiscal stabilizations fast, without the option of delaying adjustment or the hope of exporting the political costs of the adjustment to the rest of Europe. The latter would have to proceed immediately to the next step of the union, either together with the countries that have completed the fiscal stabilization or without them.

These observations highlight the second important obstacle to the currency reform – the question of participation in the monetary union, or the 'two-speed' economic and monetary union. The Delors report does not impose the constraint of full participation on all stages of the monetary union, yet the importance of this reform is such that several governments have expressed uneasiness with informal proposals of having the monetary union begin with a small number of EC countries that would increase progressively. These proposals have been prompted by the observations of the sizeable inflation differentials between Germany and, say, Greece and Portugal, or the apparent difficulties that Spain and Italy are having keeping their inflation rates low without losing external competitiveness. The debate on a 'two-speed' economic and monetary union has been similar to the debate on fiscal policy problems. In both cases the concern was that the 'weak' countries would impart an inflationary bias on the union's central bank. If the cause of higher inflation is fiscal policy, the discussion above applies. By contrast, if the source of high inflation is simply the monetary authorities' lack of credibility, it is unclear that a monetary union would seriously damage the 'hard core' countries, except when the public perceives that the reputation of the new European central bank is a weighted average of the reputations of the central banks of its member countries. Concern by the low-inflation countries about these risks, as well as resistance by the high-inflation countries to any project aimed at speeding up the monetary union for only a subset of the EC, are additional reasons to delay the monetary reform.[54]

December 1990 intergovernmental conference

On 8 October, the UK government decided that the pound should join the EMS.[55] Despite a long series of official statements that the pound would join the EMS only when the UK rate of inflation converged with that of Germany (the current differential is about 6 per cent), this decision has not surprised those who expected the UK to ensure itself a crucial role at the intergovernmental conference. The entry of the UK into the active negotiations on economic and monetary union will crucially determine their outcome. The British position on economic and monetary union could become the swing factor in the collective decisions, since that country is the natural ally of neither the 'monetarists' nor the 'economists'.

The two extremes of the political spectrum toward economic and monetary union are represented by Germany – the 'economist' – and France and Italy together with Belgium – the 'monetarists'. The latter countries favour steady progress of monetary union and, with the possible exception of France, would not oppose the idea of a currency reform. They support the concept of an independent central bank modelled after the Bundesbank and the Federal Reserve System. They acknowledge the important role of the EMS in their own disinflation experience.

At the other end of the spectrum, Germany is the champion of the 'economist' view on monetary union.[56] It strongly resists initiatives that might accelerate the process. It fully believes that, with the appropriate adjustment, inflation and inflationary expectations can fully converge. It regards the convergence of inflationary expectations an absolute precondition for embarking on the next stages of the monetary union.

It is very difficult to determine where the UK fits into this picture. Britain has consistently opposed

all recent initiatives to increase economic integration in Europe, including the completion of the single market, the economic and monetary union and the intergovernmental conference. The UK rationale is well explained by the following interpretation of Prime Minister Thatcher's thought:

> But part of this function [of the Conservative Party] is 'external vigilance as a condition of our liberty,' and, as she [Thatcher] has also trenchantly indicated – the Government has not laboured arduously since 1979 to eject socialism in the UK only to find it entering through the back-door via Brussels; thus any intention that the European Commission's writ should extend to the minutiae of economic and social policies must be firmly rejected.
>
> (Minford 1989)

The position of the UK government is a blend of a vigorous antiregulation and antisocialist sentiment with a strong desire to preserve national sovereignty and national identity.[57]

The special position of the UK government makes its contributions to the discussion on economic and monetary union somewhat orthogonal to the rest of the debate. The UK Treasury presented two related proposals in 1989 and 1990. The first called for an 'evolutionary' approach to monetary union that would exploit to the maximum the virtues of competition (UK Treasury 1989). According to this proposal, the best way to manage the transition to monetary union is to remove all obstacles that prevent private agents from effectively diversifying their currency portfolios. The effects of deregulation would be to increase the pressures on 'deviating' monetary authorities and force convergence to the 'best' regime, characterized by stable purchasing power and an efficient payments system. The Treasury document suggested that the move to a single currency could happen as a result of 'natural evolution' resembling the law of the survival of the fittest.

More recently, the UK government has circulated a follow-up to the 1989 document stressing the need to give independent status to the ECU. For this reason, the latest proposal is sometimes labelled the 'hard ECU' proposal. This proposal is aimed at ensuring that, if the markets decide to adopt a single currency, it will be the ECU.[58]

Thus, on the issue of the relevant horizon for economic and monetary union, it is difficult to see the UK becoming an ally of Italy, France and Belgium given its opposition to government-directed monetary reform. It is also difficult to see the UK as an ally of Germany since that would imply an acceptance of the EMS status quo, which is characterized by a distribution of monetary sovereignty biased in favour of Germany's monetary authorities. In sum, the divergent positions of the EC governments at the start of the inter-governmental conference do not provide clear signals about its outcome. While there is always the possibility of a diplomatic breakthrough, it seems that the conference is not likely to provide much additional impetus to a monetary union among EC countries.

CONCLUDING REMARKS

In this chapter I have discussed the problem of monetary reform in Europe. The current initiative of EC countries to move toward a single currency is similar to the Werner plan, discussed and approved in 1970. That plan was quickly discarded in the face of an exogenous shock: international capital flows toward the mark in anticipation of a collapse of the Bretton Woods system. Twenty years later, a second plan for monetary union is challenged by another exogenous shock: the increase in the price of oil caused by the invasion of Kuwait and the tension in the Gulf area. The results of my analysis suggest that the gradualist strategy lacks credibility and thus may be hard to maintain.

Partly because of the oil shock, the European currency reform has now reached a deadlock. The strategy currently pursued, gradualism, can mask a lack of commitment by national governments and is therefore less than fully credible. The alternative strategy, currency reform, requires the solution of

difficult political problems that include the creation of a multinational central bank and the substitution of national currency with a new money at unfamiliar exchange rates. In the absence of strong political leadership, currency reform is unlikely in the near future. The current halfway house, characterized by complete capital mobility, tight exchange rate targets and lack of institutional co-ordination of national monetary authorities, could easily collapse.

The recurrence of similar difficulties twenty years after the failure of the Werner plan highlights the basic problem faced by European countries with respect to currency reform: they understand and seek the benefits of a single currency, but sudden reform poses considerable political difficulties and large adjustment costs. As a result, they tend to adopt gradualist strategies that are likely to be self-defeating.

NOTES

1   The study by the Committee for the Study of Economic and Monetary Union (1989) is commonly called the Delors plan or Delors report.
2   Sterling was devalued in November 1967, but at the time the UK was not a member of the EC.
3   At that time, the 'monetarist' and 'economist' labels were created to characterize these two views respectively. See Tsoukalis (1977).
4   The Werner report, officially entitled 'Resolution of the Council and of the Representatives of the Governments of the Member States of March 1971', is recorded in Monetary Committee of the European Communities (1986).
5   See the introduction to the Werner report in Monetary Committee of the European Communities (1986).
6   The first stage would start in January 1971 and last no more than three years. From 1 January 1974, VAT and excise taxes as well as taxes on dividends and interest would be harmonized. Also, the EC would work to harmonize 'those kinds of tax which are likely to have a direct influence on capital movements within the Community'. Efforts to harmonize corporate taxes would also take place.

The EC also planned the progressive liberalization of capital markets and the improved co-ordination of financial regulatory activities.
7   So concluded the Presidency of the European

Council in 1978; see de Cecco and Giovannini (1989: 2).

8 See de Cecco and Giovannini (1989). By contrast, Michael Emerson (1982) claims that the EMS has significantly affected the institutional development of the Community, in that it has 'brought a major policy function back into the Community setting, as compared to the snake mechanism that had left it. It has linked together Community monetary and public finance mechanisms, and its economic policy coordination procedure'.

9 I discuss the fiscal problems of monetary union in a later section.

10 Delors report (paragraph 39); see Committee for the Study of Economic and Monetary Union (1989: 31).

11 Padoa-Schioppa (1988) was perhaps the first public official to advocate a modification of the EMS toward a monetary union. He argued that the integration of goods and financial markets brought about by the single market programme would make the EMS too vulnerable to speculative attacks.

12 See, in particular, Bertola (1989) and Canzoneri and Rogers (1990). A wide-ranging discussion of the economic effects of economic and monetary union is given by Eichengreen (1990).

13 The respective discussions are labelled 'Community System for the Central Banks' in the Werner report and 'European System of Central Banks' in the Delors report.

14 In the 1960s the political issues tended to surface in the context of economic discussions. A good example is the defence of European monetary independence by Giscard d'Estaing (1969) and, before him, Rueff (1967), which was based on the desire to take away seigniorage from the USA.

15 This anecdote is based on discussions with members of the German delegation.

16 This argument is advanced by Padoa-Schioppa (1988).

17 In the case of the lira – appearing in Figure 8.3 – the January 1990 narrowing of the band (from 6.0 per cent to 2.25 per cent on both sides) was accomplished together with an adjustment of the central parity: the central parity was changed so that the upper bound before and after the realignment remained the same.

18 In the case of Italy, the divergences between the terms of trade and the aggregate relative wages suggest divergent behaviour of wages in the tradeable and non-tradeable sectors.

19 This relation is an approximation. It is exact for continuously compounded rates.

20 For an analysis of interest rate differentials between Spain, Portugal and Germany, see de Macedo and Torres (1989).

21 For both deposit rates and exchange rates, the source is Reuters. All series are sampled at the London close.

22 The sample distribution of returns for the franc relative to the mark is very similar.

23 I report both statistics because there could well be several instances when, because of transactions costs, neither strategy is profitable.

24 See Svensson (1990) for an application of this analysis to the Swedish krona.

25 Absence of risk aversion implies a world where expected rate-of-return differentials would be zero in the absence of transactions costs.

26 See Giavazzi and Spaventa (1990). These phenomena reflected liquidity problems, onshore rather than offshore, and restrictions on capital inflows.

27 The empirical literature on the CAPM is vast. For a critical survey of international models, see Frankel and Meese (1987).

28 This assumption can only hold approximately. Giovannini and Jorion (1989) argue that the approximation is satisfactory.

29 When $\rho = 1$ Giovannini and Weil (1990) show that covariances with consumption growth and the market rate of return are identical. Hence both the market CAPM and the consumption CAPM are true, but equations (8.8) and (8.9) are not defined.

30 From the β representation of expected returns, note that the conditional expected return on an asset is equal to the product of the conditional β times the conditional expected return on the benchmark portfolio. If the time covariance of the conditional βs and the conditional expectations of the return on the benchmark portfolio is negligible, the expectation of that product is approximately equal to the product of expectations.

31 The world market index comes from Morgan Guaranty; in it, national stock markets are aggregated using their relative capitalizations as weights. The consumption growth measure comes from the OECD's *Main Economic Indicators*.

32 Columbia Center for International Business Cycle Research provided the stock market indices. Consumption growth comes from OECD *Main Economic Indicators*.

33 While relative real returns are in principle more appropriate than nominal returns, in practice inflation uncertainty is so small relative to exchange rate uncertainty that the difference between real and nominal calibration is negligible.

34 See Weil (1990). If returns and non-marketable risk were identically and independently distributed, this model would be applicable to a multiperiod set-up.

35 When all investors are alike, they all hold the same portfolio of tradeable securities, which in equilib-

rium equals the market portfolio.

36 For problems relating to asymmetric information, see Diamond and Dybvig (1983).

37 The problem of high real interest rates in the EMS, and its relation to the credibility of exchange rate targets, is discussed in Dornbusch (forthcoming).

38 Analyses of inflation stabilization with exchange rate targeting are carried out in Cukierman (1988) and Fischer (1988). Wage and price dynamics under alternative exchange regimes are discussed in Dornbusch (1982) and Alogoskoufis (1990).

39 In addition, empirical evidence suggests that in Europe nominal wage stickiness is significantly less important than in the USA: see, for example, Sachs (1979), Branson and Rotemberg (1980) and Grubb *et al.* (1982, 1983).

40 Of course the real interest rate in terms of domestic goods would increase. This would occur because the differential between own-good interest rates is approximately equal to the expected change in the relative price of the two goods. But the relative price of the domestic good is expected to fall as the transition period draws to a close.

41 Barro and Gordon (1983a, b). In this section, I closely follow the excellent treatment of these models found in Persson and Tabellini (1990).

42 This model has recently been developed by Flood and Isard (1989). Also see Cukierman (1990) for a discussion applied to the Delors plan.

43 Another virtue of the 'escape clause' model is that it could be sustained in a multi-period setting, where this game resembles the one studied by Rotemberg and Saloner (1986).

44 The model shows that nominal interest rates will never converge. In the model, the rate of inflation does not appear, but it is reasonable to assume that price inflation is equal to $\hat{s}$, whereas wage inflation is equal to $\hat{s}^e$. Therefore price inflation converges but wage inflation does not: the result is a fall in economic activity. The general lesson is that, in the absence of exchange rate adjustments, inflation rate differentials may persist for prolonged periods before the disruptions brought to the external balance and employment lower real wages.

45 These calculations do not account for the impact of the oil price increase on wealth and aggregate demand.

46 Triffin (1960) advocated a reform that locked intra-European exchange rates at parity.

47 The advantages of a single currency are discussed in detail by Ernst & Young (1990) and Gros and Thygesen (1990).

48 For a discussion of the problems of ensuring the independence of a European central bank, see Neumann (1990).

49 See Goodhart (1988) for a historical and comparative perspective on the evolution of central banking. Goodhart stresses the role of central banks as public insurers of systemic risk, and traces it back to the birth of the Bank of England. Barro (1989) discusses the concerns of central banks with interest rate stability.

50 See Sachs and Sala y Martin (1989) for evidence on the USA.

51 See Cohen and Wyplosz (1989) and Buiter and Kletzer (forthcoming) for discussions of externalities associated with non-cooperative fiscal policies.

52 Alternatively, some central bankers would find it more appropriate to offset the aggregate spending biases by monetary contraction, which would further increase interest rates.

53 Kotlikoff (1988, 1990). A regression of national saving rates over the 1980–4 period in the EC countries over government saving rates yields a coefficient of 0.18 (standard error 0.31). The coefficient for the period 1985–9 is 0.17 (standard error 0.27).

54 The outright opposition to the idea of a 'two-speed' monetary union by the high-inflation countries (see, for example, 'Spain counts cost of joining the club', *Financial Times*, 20 June 1990) stems from the perception that the reputation cost of being left behind is very high, and its political effects might be equally serious.

55 The fluctuation bands chosen by the UK government are 6 per cent on both sides of central parities.

56 For an excellent exposition of the position of German monetary authorities, see Deutsche Bundesbank (1990).

57 Spaventa (1990) and Wolf (1989) provide two useful discussions of the political aspects of the debate on economic and monetary union.

58 UK Treasury (1990). While it is not the purpose of this section to analyse the theoretical underpinnings of the different countries' views, it might be useful to point out that the circulation of the ECU in parallel to national currencies – even with all the features that are proposed to ensure the stability of its purchasing power – does not necessarily induce its adoption as the single European currency. This question hinges on the existence of multiple equilibria in an economy of competing currencies. The 'thick market' externalities associated with the use of a widely circulating medium of exchange can generate many self-sustaining equilibria, and it is not clear what it takes to move from one to the other.

REFERENCES

Adler, M. and Dumas, B. (1983) 'International portfolio choice and corporation finance: a synthesis', *Journal of Finance* 38: 925–84.

Alogoskoufis, G. (1990) 'Exchange rate regimes and the persistence of inflation', Working Paper 390, London: Centre for Economic Policy Research.

Baer, G. D. and Padoa-Schioppa, T. (1989) 'The Werner report revisited', in Committee for the Study of Economic and Monetary Union, *Report on Economic and Monetary Union in the European Community*, Luxembourg: Office of Official Publications of the European Communities.

Baldwin, R. E. (1990) 'Hysteresis bands and market efficiency tests', Columbia University.

Barro, R. J. (1989) 'Interest-rate targeting', *Journal of Monetary Economics* 23: 3–30.

Barro, R. J. and Gordon, D. B. (1983a) 'Rules, discretion, and reputation in a model of monetary policy', *Journal of Monetary Economics* 12: 101–21.

—— and —— (1983b) 'A positive theory of monetary policy in a natural rate model', *Journal of Political Economy* 91: 589–610.

Bergsten, C. F. (1990) 'The world economy after the Cold War', *Foreign Affairs* 69: 96–112.

Bertola, G. (1989) 'Factor flexibility, uncertainty, and exchange rate regimes', in M. de Cecco and A. Giovannini (eds) *A European Central Bank? Perspectives on Monetary Union after Ten Years of the EMS*, Cambridge: Cambridge University Press.

Bishop, G. (1990) '1992 and beyond, Italian public debt at the dawn of monetary union – a foreigner's view', London: European Business Analysis, Salomon Brothers, February.

Blanchard, O. J. (1983) 'Price asynchronization and price level inertia', in R. Dornbusch and M. H. Simonsen (eds) *Inflation, Debt, and Indexation*, Cambridge, MA: MIT Press.

Branson, W. H. and Rotemberg, J. J. (1980) 'International adjustment with wage rigidity', *European Economic Review* 13: 309–22.

Buiter, W. H. and Kletzer, K. M. (1990) 'Reflections on the fiscal implications of a common currency', in A. Giovannini and C. Mayer (eds) *European Financial Integration*, New York: Cambridge University Press.

Canzoneri, M. B. and Rogers, C. A. (1990) 'Is the European community an optimal currency area? Optimal taxation versus the cost of multiple currencies', *American Economic Review* 80: 419–33.

de Cecco, M. and Giovannini, A. (1989) 'Introduction', in M. de Cecco and A. Giovannini (eds) *A European Central Bank? Perspectives on Monetary Union after Ten Years of the EMS*, Cambridge: Cambridge University Press.

Cohen, D. and Wyplosz, C. (1989) 'The European monetary union: an agnostic evaluation', in R. C. Bryant, D. A. Currie, J. A. Frenkel, P. R. Masson and R. Purtes (eds) *Macroeconomic Policies in an Interdependent World*, Washington, DC: Brookings Institution.

Commission of the European Communities (1990) *One Market, One Money: An Evaluation of the Potential Benefits and Costs of Forming an Economic and Monetary Union*, Luxembourg: Office of Official Publications of the European Communities.

Committee for the Study of Economic and Monetary Union (1989) *Report on Economic and Monetary Union in the European Community*, Luxembourg: Office of Official Publications of the European Communities.

Cooper, R. N. (1976) 'Worldwide vs. regional integration: is there an optimal size of the integrated area?', in F. Machlup (ed.) *Economic Integration: Worldwide, Regional, Sectoral, Proceedings of the Fourth Congress of the International Economic Association*, New York: Halstead Press.

Cukierman, A. (1988) 'The end of the high Israeli inflation: an experiment in heterodox stabilization', in M. Bruno, G. D. DiTella, R. Dornbusch and S. Fischer (eds) *Inflation Stabilization: The Experience of Israel, Argentina, Brazil, Bolivia, and Mexico*, Cambridge, MA: MIT Press.

—— (1990) 'Fixed parities versus a commonly managed currency and the case against "stage two"', Tel-aviv University, June.

Delors, J. (1989) 'Economic and monetary union and relaunching the construction of Europe', in Committee for the Study of Economic and Monetary Union, *Report on Economic and Monetary Union in the European Community*, Luxembourg: Office of Official Publications of the European Communities.

Deutsche Bundesbank (1990) 'Statement of the Deutsche Bundesbank on the establishment of an economic and monetary union in Europe', *Monthly Report of the Deutsche Bundesbank* 42: 40–4.

Diamond, D. W. and Dybvig, P. H. (1983) 'Bank runs, deposit insurance and liquidity', *Journal of Political Economy* 91: 401–19.

Dornbusch, R. (1982) 'PPP exchange-rate rules and macroeconomic stability', *Journal of Political Economy* 90: 158–65.

—— (forthcoming) 'Problems of European monetary integration', in A. Giovannini and C. Mayer (eds) *European Financial Integration*, New York: Cambridge University Press.

EC Monetary Committee (1990) 'Economic and monetary union beyond stage 1: orientations for the preparation of the intergovernmental conference', Brussels, March.

Eichengreen, B. (1990) 'One money for Europe? Lessons from the US currency union', *Economic Policy* 10: 117–87.

Emerson, M. (1982) 'Experience under the EMS and prospects for further progress towards EMU', in M.T. Sumner and G. Zis (eds) *European Monetary Union, Progress and Prospects*, New York: St Martin's Press.

Ernst & Young (1990) *A Strategy for the ECU*, London: Ernst & Young and National Institute of Economic and Social Research.

European Commission (1990) 'Economic and monetary union. The economic rationale and design of the system', Brussels, March.

Fischer, S. (1988) 'Real balances, the exchange rate, and indexation: real variables in disinflation', *Quarterly Journal of Economics* 103: 27–49.

Flood, R. and Isard, P. (1989) 'Simple rules, discretion and monetary policy', Working Paper 2934, Cambridge, MA: National Bureau of Economic Research, April.

Frankel, J. A. (1988) *Obstacles to International Macroeconomic Policy Coordination*, Princeton Studies in International Finance 64, Princeton, NJ: International Finance Section, Princeton University, December.

Frankel, J. A. and Meese, R. (1987) 'Are exchange rates excessively variable?', *NBER Macroeconomics Annual* 2: 117–62.

Giavazzi, F. and Giovannini, A. (1987) 'Exchange rates and prices in Europe', *Weltwirtschaftliches Archiv* 123: 592–604.

—— and —— (1989) *Limiting Exchange Rate Flexibility: The European Monetary System*, Cambridge, MA: MIT Press.

Giavazzi, F. and Spaventa, L. (1990) 'The "new" EMS', Working Paper 369, London: Centre for Economic Policy Research, January.

Giovannini, A. (1989) 'How do fixed-exchange-rates regimes work? The evidnece from the Gold Standard, Bretton Woods and the EMS', in M. Miller, B. Eichengreen and R. Portes (eds) *Blueprints for Exchange-Rate Management*, New York: Academic Press.

—— (1990) *The Transition to European Monetary Union*, Essays in International Finance 178, Princeton, NJ: International Finance Section, Princeton University, November.

Giovannini, A. and Jorion, P. (1989) 'Time-series tests of a non-expected-utility model of asset pricing', Working Paper 3195, Cambridge, MA: National Bureau of Economic Research, December.

Giovannini, A. and Weil, P. (1990) 'Risk aversion and intertemporal substitution in the capital asset pricing model', Working Paper 2824, Cambridge, MA:

National Bureau of Economic Research, January.

Giscard d'Estaing, V. (1969) 'The international monetary order', in R.A. Mundell and A.K. Swoboda (eds) *Monetary Problems of the International Economy*, Chicago, IL: University of Chicago Press.

Goodhart, C. A. E. (1989) *The Evolution of Central Banks*, Cambridge, MA: MIT Press.

Gros, D. and Thygesen, N. (1990) 'From the EMS towards EMU: how to manage in the transition?', Brussels: Centre for European Policy Studies.

Grubb, D., Jackman, R. and Layard, R. (1982) 'Causes of the current stagflation', *Review of Economic Studies* 49: 707–30.

——, —— and —— (1983) 'Wage rigidity and unemployment in OECD countries', *European Economic Review* 21: 11–39.

Kenen, P. B. (1969) 'The theory of optimum currency areas: an eclectic view', in R. A. Mundell and A. K. Swoboda (eds) *Monetary Problems of the International Economy*, Chicago, IL: University of Chicago Press.

Kotlikoff, L. J. (1988) 'The deficit is not a well-defined measure of fiscal policy', *Science* 241: 791–5.

—— (1990) 'From deficit delusion to the fiscal balance rule: looking for an economically meaningful way to assess fiscal policy', Boston University, June.

Krasker, W. S. (1980) 'The "peso problem" in testing the efficiency of forward exchange markets', *Journal of Monetary Economics* 6: 269–76.

de Macedo, J. B. and Torres, F. (1989) 'Interest differentials, financial integration and EMS shadowing: Portugal and a comparison to Spain', Commission of the European Communities.

Masera, R. S. (1987) *L'Unificazione Monetaria E Lo Sme*, Bologna: il Mulino.

McKinnon, R. I. (1963) 'Optimal currency areas', *American Economic Review* 53: 717–25.

Minford, P. (1989) *European Monetary Union and 1992*, London: Selsdon Group Special Paper, October.

Monetary Committee of the European Communities (1986) *Compendium of Community Monetary Texts*, Luxembourg: Office of Official Publications of the European Communities.

Mundell, R. A. (1968) *International Economics*, New York: Macmillan.

Neumann, M. J. M. (1990) 'Central bank independence as a prerequisite to price stability', University of Bonn.

Padoa-Schioppa, T. (1988) 'The European monetary system: a long term view', in F. Giavazzi, S. Micossi and M. Miller (eds) *The European Monetary System*, New York: Cambridge University Press.

Persson, T. and Tabellini, G. (1990) *Macroeconomic Policy, Credibility and Politics*, New York: Harwood Academic Publishers.

Rotemberg, J. J. and Saloner, G. (1986) 'A supergame-theoretic model of price wars during booms', *American Economic Review* 76: 390–407.

Rueff, J. (1967) 'The Rueff approach', in R. Hinshaw (ed.) *Monetary Reform and the Price of Gold, Alternative Approaches*, Baltimore, MD: Johns Hopkins University Press.

Sachs, J. D. (1979) 'Wages, profits, and macroeconomic adjustment: a comparative study', *Brookings Papers on Economic Activity* 2: 269–319.

Sachs, J. D. and Sala y Martin, X. (1989) 'Federal fiscal policy and optimum currency areas', Harvard University.

Spaventa, L. (1990) 'The political economy of European monetary integration', *Banca Nazionale del Lavoro Quarterly Review* 172: 3–20.

Svensson, L. E. O. (1990) 'The simplest test of target zone credibility', Working Paper 3394, Cambridge, MA: National Bureau of Economic Research, June.

Triffin, R. (1960) *Gold and the Dollar Crisis: The Future of Convertibility*, New Haven, CT: Yale University Press.

Tsoukalis, L. (1977) *The Politics and Economics of European Monetary Integration*, London: Allen & Unwin.

UK Treasury (1989) *An Evolutionary Approach to Economic and Monetary Union*, London: HM Treasury.

—— (1990) 'Economic and monetary union: beyond stage 1', Chancellor's Speech to Germany Industry Forum, London, 20 June.

Weil, P. (1990) 'Equilibrium asset pricing with undiversifiable labor income risk', Harvard University.

Wolf, M. (1989) *1992: Global Implications of the European Community's Programme for Completing the Internal Market*, New York: The Lehrman Institute.

9

MONETARY POLICY IN AN EMERGING EUROPEAN ECONOMIC AND MONETARY UNION: KEY ISSUES

Jacob A. Frenkel and Morris Goldstein

INTRODUCTION

In this chapter we discuss key issues relating to the design and implementation of monetary policy in an emerging European economic and monetary union. We neither endorse nor dismiss specific institutional proposals for transition to economic and monetary union. Instead, our purpose is to focus on broad policy issues that are of systemic interest and that need to be addressed in any serious examination of economic and monetary union.

The chapter is organized along the following lines. The second section looks at the *goals* of monetary policy. The emphasis here is on the inter-relationships among price stability, current account equilibrium and exchange rate stability. The third section turns to the *implementation* of monetary policy. The key issues in this connection revolve around co-ordination versus autonomy, rules versus discretion and the role of sterilized official intervention. Finally, the fourth section considers the implications of *fiscal policy* for the conduct of monetary policy and examines some alternative mechanisms for encouraging fiscal discipline.

GOALS OF MONETARY POLICY

Monetary union is generally taken to imply both irrevocably fixed exchange rates (or perhaps even a common currency) and full integration of financial and banking markets (Delors Committee Report 1989). From this definition, it follows that the path to economic and monetary union requires reaching a consensus among participants on the goals of monetary policy.

The goals of monetary policy are normally taken to be price stability, full employment and sustainable economic growth; in some cases, exchange rate stability and stability of the financial system are also featured. Such a listing, however, obscures an important shift in policy-making between the 1980s and the two previous decades. Control of inflation has generally been elevated above avoiding more-than-frictional unemployment, and real output targeting has given way to targeting nominal variables (Polak 1988). Price stability has come to be regarded – appropriately in our view – as a necessary (albeit not sufficient) condition for the achievement of other economic goals, including sustainable economic growth. Consistent with this theme, there would appear to be broad agreement that a European System of Central Banks, or EuroFed, should have an explicit mandate to pursue price stability. Moreover, to give 'teeth' to this commitment, some analysts have proposed giving the EuroFed substantial independence and prohibiting it from granting credit to the public sector.

What is less clear is how policy-making authorities should respond to developments in current accounts, and how they should frame their exchange rate objectives.

Historically, not all potential members of an economic and monetary union have given the same emphasis to current account balance relative to other goals. Masson and Melitz (1990) highlight

187

the instructive comparison between France and the Federal Republic of Germany. Over the 1963–88 period, the average current account imbalance relative to GNP was −0.4 per cent for France and 1.2 per cent for Germany.[1] In the years since 1986, France's current account was in virtual balance, while Germany's was in large surplus, attaining levels of about 4 per cent of GNP.[2] On the side of inflation, French and German performances have been very close since 1987, around 3 per cent per year (using GDP deflators); not so over the longer 1950–88 period, when German inflation averaged close to 4 per cent versus roughly 7 per cent for France. Further liberalization of European capital markets – by rendering it easier to finance intra-European external imbalances – could make more important any inter-country differences in the weighting of current account objectives. In this connection, Giavazzi and Spaventa (1990) document the flow of capital within the EMS over the past three years from low-inflation countries to countries with higher inflation and higher nominal interest rates (Italy and Spain). Despite significant sterilization of reserve increases, domestic demand has grown relatively rapidly in the high-inflation countries and their current account positions have deteriorated. Yet these current account deficits have been overfinanced by capital inflows.[3] There is also the matter of Europe's *aggregate* current account position, which could well be a factor influencing a future ECU–US dollar or ECU–yen exchange rate. The current account position for the industrialized countries of Europe as a group was approximately balanced last year, but there is no compelling reason for it to remain so in the future.

What then should be the attitude of authorities to current account imbalances? Several writers – ourselves included – have argued that a differentiated approach to current account imbalances is warranted (Frenkel and Goldstein 1990). Non-zero current account positions arise from a variety of sources, some of which are 'good' and require no intervention, and some of which are 'bad' and do require intervention. For example, an imbalance that arises from reversible inter-country

differences in the age distribution of the population – which in turn yield different life-cycle-induced private saving patterns – is likely to be benign. In contrast, an imbalance that reflects unsustainable borrowing abroad to finance a consumption spree should surely be placed in the malign category. We would not want to pretend that these distinctions can be measured with great precision. Nevertheless, we see merit in a framework that would consider at least the following three factors in an evaluation of current account imbalances: first, whether the fiscal position is appropriate (in terms of both the level and composition of government spending, as well as the structure of taxes and borrowing used to finance the budget);[4] second, whether increased investment associated with the external imbalance can be expected to provide a rate of return that exceeds the cost of borrowing (including externalities); and third, whether any increased consumption associated with the imbalance is temporary and desirable for purposes of intertemporal consumption smoothing.

The bottom line of this differentiated approach to current account imbalances is that one needs to know the origin of an imbalance before one can decide both *if* it needs correction and, if so, *how* to correct it. In addition, there is the question of how any increased *global* need for saving should be accounted for in individual-country or regional policy decisions about current account imbalances.

Next, consider the role that exchange rate stability should play in the design of monetary policy. This subject really merits a full paper to itself but here we are content to focus on (1) exchange rate management *vis-à-vis* non-economic-monetary-union currencies; (2) loss of the nominal exchange rate as a policy instrument; and (3) the choice between rapid and gradual approaches to economic and monetary union, with hard and soft exchange rate commitments respectively.

On other occasions, we have argued that a tri-polar exchange rate system, where exchange rate commitments are 'looser' and 'quieter' across the poles than within regional currency areas, represents a feasible and desirable evolution of the international monetary system (Frenkel *et al.* 1989). Several of the arguments for such a system are directly relevant to how an evolving economic and monetary union might react to exchange rate movements *outside* the union. In brief, the main points are as follows: (1) an exchange rate system which has as its regional nominal anchors three relatively independent central banks – each committed to price stability – is not conducive to policy 'blueprints' (of, say, the Williamson–Miller (1987) variety) that require monetary policy in the anchor countries to give first priority to keeping exchange rates within loud target zones; (2) real exchange rates across the three poles need to change to some extent anyway to reflect changes in real economic conditions over time; (3) better disciplined monetary and fiscal policy within each of the currency areas would go a long way toward establishing more disciplined exchange markets across the poles; (4) intervention to manage exchange rates across the poles – be it in the form of official statements on the desirable direction of exchange rate movements, or of concerted, steri-lized exchange market intervention, or, in the last resort, of co-ordinated adjustments in monetary policy – should be saved for cases where there is strong evidence of bubbles or large misalignments in exchange rates. In order to avoid any misunder-standing, we emphasize that this is *not* a call for return to 'benign neglect' in the management of major-currency exchange rates. On the contrary, we regard a reasonable degree of exchange rate stability for key currencies as a public good for the system. Our argument instead is that the stabiliz-ing effect of any official exchange rate commit-ment on expectations depends on its credibility. A looser commitment across the poles wherein authorities 'keep their powder dry' for large, clear-call misalignments and do not claim that the primary assignment of monetary policy is for external balance should be more credible than a (nominally) tighter and louder commitment. But the same logic also points to tight, loud exchange rate commitments *within* currency areas – one of which is an emerging economic and monetary union. Here, the incentives for stabilizing exchange

rates are greater because these economies are more open, trade flows among union members account for a large share of members' total trade, exchange rate stability is closely linked to larger, regional integration objectives, and larger gains in anti-inflationary credibility are to be had by 'tying one's hands' on monetary policy via exchange rate fixity.

So much for managing the union's exchange rate *vis-à-vis* other major currencies. What about the more pressing issue of managing exchange rates within, and on the way to, monetary union?

One key factor relates to the consequences of losing the nominal exchange rate as a policy instrument. Economic theory suggests that the types of shocks hitting an economy (monetary versus real) should be an important factor in the choice of an exchange rate regime (Aizenman and Frenkel 1982). The potential problem of a monetary union is adjusting to country-specific real shocks. Here, three questions need to be addressed. First, are the real economic shocks that typically hit European economies industry specific or country specific? If they are industry specific and if potential economic and monetary union members have a sufficiently diversified industrial structure, then it is possible that these shocks largely cancel out at the country level; this would of course make loss of the nominal exchange rate less costly. Alternatively, if shocks are predomi-nantly country specific, potential difficulties are obviously greater. A second question is whether the increased competition in goods and factors markets associated with 1992 will increase the downward flexibility of money wages and prices in Europe (Viñals 1990). If so, and we do not discount this possibility, it will be less costly to achieve needed changes in real exchange rates via changes in internal wages and prices.[5] Question three is whether a federal fiscal authority that automatically adjusted a country's tax and transfer payments in the event of country-specific real shocks could act efficiently as a cushioning device – and in a roughly budget-neutral fashion for the union as a whole. As is well known, this kind of tax and transfer system operates in the USA, where it has been estimated that it offsets roughly 40 per cent of region-specific income shocks (Sachs and Sala-i-Martin 1989). The more confident one can be that the answers to the above three questions are 'yes', the less concerned can monetary authorities afford to be in embracing greater (nominal) exchange rate fixity on the path to economic and monetary union. Suffice to say that these three questions also constitute a fertile area for further empirical research.

Assume, in keeping with the spirit of economic and monetary union, that a judgement has been made to make use of the nominal exchange rate as a policy instrument only in 'exceptional circumstances'. As recognized in the Delors report and in other studies, this still leaves unanswered the key issue of what types and 'staging' of exchange rate regimes would be desirable for the transition to economic and monetary union. For our purposes, it is sufficient to review briefly two of the possible options.

One option would be to move rapidly to economic and monetary union itself, i.e. to a common currency (e.g. the ECU) and to a central monetary authority (e.g. the EuroFed). This would carry a number of attractions. First, it gives maximum credibility to exchange rate stability by eliminating exchange rates within the union. A common currency is harder to 'undo' than a commitment to 'irrevocably fixed' exchange rates and market participants presumably know it. Second, a common currency allows economic and monetary union participants to obtain more of the efficiency gains associated with moving closer to one money than do 'softer' exchange rate options.[6] Third, a central monetary authority can in principle avoid the negative externalities associated with beggar-thy-neighbour policies taken by competing national monetary authorities. And fourth, a central monetary authority may be able to implement monetary control more effectively than individual national central banks, because the demand for money in the wider area may be more stable under open capital markets and full financial liberalization than are individual-country money demands. In this connection, Kremers and Lane (1990) have recently found (using a two-step error correction model) that a stable, aggregate demand for narrow money can be identified for the group of countries participating in the ERM; in fact, this aggregate function is more satisfactory in some respects than comparable demand-for-money functions in individual countries. The intuitive explanation which they offer for this finding is that the improved performance that comes about from capturing currency substitution and portfolio diversification effects in the aggregate equation more than makes up for the reduced performance associated with imposing the same money demand parameters on all countries.

On the negative side of the ledger, there are two concerns about a rapid move to economic and monetary union. One is that the participating countries will not be 'ready' for a common currency or a common monetary policy – be it because of inadequate convergence of economic performance (particularly of inflation), because of inadequate consensus on the goals or framework for monetary policy, or because of inadequate experience with common institutions. To some observers, this lack of readiness calls either for a 'two-track' approach, where the fast track is limited to a subset of potential members who already are ready in terms of convergence of economic performance, or for waiting together until a wider group of members is ready. A second objection is that an administrative, centralized approach to currency and monetary management will result in average – or, even worse, collusive lower-than-average – performance; in contrast, a 'competitive' approach – so the argument goes – would allow the market to converge on 'the best in the Community' (UK Treasury 1989).

A second option is to have a slower transition to economic and monetary union, characterized by (1) the coexistence of a federal monetary authority and national, central banks and (2) a looser commitment to fixed exchange rates. This option clearly provides more scope for 'learning by doing' and for making monetary policy more 'accountable' to national governments. But as critics of the gradual approach point out, such a strategy cannot escape the constraint that only two of the following three objectives can be achieved simultaneously: open capital markets, fixed exchange rates and independent monetary policy. With capital controls all but gone and with increased opportunities for diversification of currency portfolios, a commitment to truly fixed exchange rates will be credible only if monetary policy co-ordination – *ex ante* and *ex post* – is tighter than in the past. Following the arguments of Canzoneri and Diba (1990), an increase in currency substitution may not imply a need for larger adjustments in interest rates – since demands for close substitutes can be equalized with smaller price adjustments than demands for imperfect substitutes. But the very liberalization processes that give rise to increased currency substitution, along with any destabilizing speculation, will probably also call for more *frequent* recourse to co-ordinated interest rate adjustments; otherwise, national monetary control is apt to be rendered less effective. A related challenge thrown up by the coexistence of central and national monetary authorities, and by a desire to introduce more symmetry of adjustment into the system, is that the 'rules of the game' may become more difficult to define than in the existing (asymmetric) EMS. Not only does the assignment of responsibilities have to be clearly understood, but also that assignment has to respect the primacy of price stability as a goal of economic and monetary union. This need for tighter and more well-defined monetary policy co-ordination could of course be reduced by backing away from a rigid exchange rate commitment, but – so opponents argue – only at the cost of sacrificing some of the public good attributes ascribed to exchange rate stability or, even worse, of inviting repeated speculative attacks that would threaten the stability of the system itself.[7]

IMPLEMENTATION OF MONETARY POLICY

In this section, we move on to discuss three broad issues relating to the implementation of monetary policy: co-ordination versus autonomy, rules versus discretion and the role of sterilized exchange market intervention.

Neither co-ordination nor autonomy should be seen as objectives in themselves. Instead, they are better regarded as facilitating mechanisms for obtaining better policy performance. Co-ordination is essentially a mechanism for internalizing the externalities that arise from quantitatively significant 'spillover effects' of national policy actions. Autonomy, in contrast, relies on independent decentralized policy decisions at the national level to achieve policy objectives. As the post-war experience confirms, both co-ordination and autonomy are capable of producing good and bad outcomes depending on how they are used (for specific examples see Frenkel *et al.* 1989).

Having said that, we see the ongoing process of financial liberalization, innovation, globalization and securitization as strengthening the case for co-ordination on at least three counts. First, the shift away from credit rationing and quantitative restrictions on lending means that the transmission mechanism of monetary policy falls more heavily on interest rates and exchange rates – the 'competitive' variables most often the subject of beggar-thy-neighbour complaints. Co-ordination is a way of discouraging beggar-thy-neighbour practices. In this regard, it is relevant to note that the degree of conflict that exists in the transition to economic and monetary union is not irrelevant for prospects of actually achieving it. Second, and as suggested earlier, when there is a jump increase in currency substitution, it will be difficult to implement reliable monetary control at the national level without stronger co-ordination among monetary authorities. Third, the problem of *systemic risk* does not lend itself easily to an autonomous, competitive approach. We think this point is particularly relevant to Europe of 1992 and beyond. In an environment where there are increasing competitive pressures in financial services, universal banking, increased inter-country correlation of equity price movements and a desire on the part of monetary authorities to establish or to maintain anti-inflationary credibility, it would not be surprising if some financial institutions experienced difficulties. A national monetary authority might act to 'contain' such difficulties by providing emergency liquidity support or by activating official or private deposit insurance schemes. However, official 'safety nets', like other types of insurance, raise moral hazard issues – in this case, the encouragement to undertake an unduly high share of risky activities, with unfavourable consequences for the public sector's liability. This problem could be reduced if financial institutions maintained adequate capital requirements and/or if access to deposit insurance went hand-in-hand with restrictions on institutions' activities. But in a world of financial liberalization any single country's attempt to impose stiffer regulatory standards could result merely in firms fleeing to countries with more lax standards, i.e. regulatory arbitrage. A co-ordinated approach to regulation can accomplish what a competitive approach cannot.[8] The recently concluded Basle Agreement on risk-weighted capital standards for G10 commercial banks is a case in point.

This brings us to the familiar issue of *rules versus discretion*, which would need to be addressed whether a co-ordinated or a competitive approach to monetary policy was selected. Those who favour policy rules make essentially three arguments. First, rules are a viable mechanism for imposing discipline on economic policy-makers who might otherwise manipulate instruments of policy for their own objectives and to the detriment of the public. This theme is underscored in the burgeoning literature on 'time-inconsistent' policies (Kydland and Prescott 1977; Calvo 1978; Barro and Gordon 1983). This literature illustrates how in the absence of a mechanism for precommitment of policy choices (i.e. a rule), discretionary period-by-period policy choices will result in an inefficiency; in particular, when real variables depend on nominal surprises, discretionary policy will produce a higher average rate of inflation than is necessary – with no compensating increase in real output. Second, rules can reduce negotiations costs and burden-sharing conflicts. Kenen (1987), for example, has argued that if there is an excess demand for co-ordination it should be eliminated not by increasing the supply of co-ordination but

rather by reducing the demand for co-ordination via rules. Third, rules are regarded as enhancing the predictability of policy actions and thereby improving the private sector's ability to make informed resource allocation decisions.

These arguments in favour of policy rules are powerful, but their immediate operational attractiveness is blunted by two considerations, both of which are relevant to an emerging economic and monetary union. One is that rigid rules that do not adapt to major changes in the operating environment run the risk of worsening policy performance. The weakening in many countries of the link between narrow monetary aggregates and the ultimate goals of monetary policy in the face of large-scale financial innovation and institutional change is a leading case in point (Freedman 1990). In recognition of these changes in the operating environment, several prominent supporters of policy rules have incorporated trend changes in velocity into their money supply or national income rules (what we might call 'evolutionary' rules),[9] while several monetary authorities have indicated that they now employ a more 'eclectic' approach to monetary policy (where the behaviour of monetary aggregates is taken into account along with a set of other variables) (Blundell-Wignall *et al.* 1990). A second consideration is that rules will impart greater discipline to policy only to the extent that penalties for breaking the rules are significant enough to ensure that the rules are followed. The sanctions available against sovereign nations for breach of economic policy commitments should not be exaggerated.

A third key issue surrounding the implementation of monetary policy concerns the role of exchange market intervention. Controversy regarding intervention applies almost exclusively to sterilized intervention, i.e. to intervention which is not allowed to affect the monetary base. The seductive appeal of sterilized intervention – especially in a situation where capital controls are being phased out – is that, if effective, it would allow authorities to manage exchange rates while monetary policy was seeing to internal balance. This should be differentiated from using the pattern of *non*-sterilized intervention as an 'alarm bell' for making co-ordinated adjustments of monetary policies – since in this case intervention is acting as an arm of monetary policy and not as an additional policy instrument (Giovannini 1990).

Sterilized intervention is posited to affect exchange rates through two channels. One is via portfolio effects. Specifically, by altering the relative outside supplies of (imperfectly substitutable) assets denominated in domestic and foreign currency, intervention changes the risk characteristics of the market portfolio and induces changes in exchange rates (Branson and Henderson 1985). The second channel is the signalling effect. The line of argument here is that exchange rates reflect expectations of future macroeconomic policies and that monetary authorities have inside information on future monetary policy and can credibly signal future monetary policy via intervention (Mussa 1981). Intervention is said to be a good signalling device because authorities are 'putting their money where their mouth is', because (if sterilized) signals can be given without affecting the real economy and because intervention can be displayed rapidly and around the clock.[10]

The last official study of intervention, namely the Jurgensen Report (1983), concluded that sterilized intervention was a relatively weak instrument of exchange rate policy. An examination of the effectiveness of intervention over the 1985–7 period was recently made·by Obstfeld (1990).[11] His main conclusions can be summarized as follows. First, the dominant policy determinants of broad exchange rate movements of recent years have been monetary and fiscal actions, not sterilized intervention. Second, except possibly in 1987, the scale of intervention has been too small (relative to huge outstanding asset stocks) to have significant portfolio effects. Third, the signals sent by intervention have been effective only when they have been backed up by the prompt adjustment of monetary policies, or when other events (e.g. unexpected trade balance developments) have coincidentally altered market sentiment. Finally, the most convincing intervention operations have

been 'concerted' ones. This last conclusion is also consistent with the results of the only existing empirical study that had access to daily intervention data for the 1985–7 period. Specifically, Dominguez (1989) found that concerted intervention had a larger and longer-term influence on exchange rate expectations than did unilateral intervention.

From all this we conclude that while sterilized intervention may be helpful at times in calming disorderly foreign exchange markets or in signalling authorities' views about the appropriateness of market exchange rates, it is *not* likely by itself to be powerful enough to extricate monetary policy from internal–external policy dilemmas, i.e. it would not be powerful enough to stabilize exchange rates when there is little convergence in members' monetary policies. Within these limitations, one can probably maximize the impact by implementing intervention in a concerted, co-ordinated way.

THE SEARCH FOR FISCAL DISCIPLINE

While this is a chapter about the design and implementation of monetary policy, we feel compelled to offer a few remarks on fiscal policy as well. Indeed, a striking lesson of the 1980s is that when fiscal policy is undisciplined and is working in a direction opposite to that of monetary policy, efforts to promote price stability, effective external adjustment and exchange market stability will be seriously handicapped. The intensive discussion that has already gone on about the need for fiscal discipline in an emerging economic and monetary union – and on how best to get it – suggests that this issue is just as relevant to the European policy dialogue as to that in North America.

There are three potential mechanisms for encouraging greater fiscal policy discipline: (1) the exchange rate regime; (2) the market; and (3) peer group surveillance.[12]

Experience is not kind to the view that the exchange rate regime by itself can enforce discipline on fiscal policy. After more than ten years of operation, and with a clear progression toward greater fixity of exchange rates, there is little evidence of fiscal policy convergence in the EMS. Monetary policy convergence, yes – but not fiscal policy. In a similar vein, the North American experience with much greater exchange rate flexibility hardly suggests that this exchange rate regime can consistently rein-in fiscal policies. As indicated in some of our earlier work, it is not difficult to construct theoretical examples where the exchange rate regime sends either a 'false signal' or no signal at all about the need for fiscal adjustment (Frenkel and Goldstein 1986, 1988). Typically, this comes about because the higher interest rate associated with fiscal expansion induces a capital inflow that either prompts a loosening of monetary policy (to keep the exchange rate within its target) or simply makes the fiscal deficit easier to finance.

What then about the discipline imposed by 'the markets'? Such market discipline is usually said to operate via two channels. One is the higher cost of borrowing associated with consistent, fiscal imprudence – as the markets exact an increasing risk premium to reflect lower expected repayment. At some point, markets could even impose their ultimate sanction by refusing to lend altogether to the unrepentant borrower. The second channel of market discipline is via pressure for tax harmonization. In short, a government that spends a lot will eventually have to tax a lot; but high taxes, in turn, will induce firms and individuals to move to jurisdictions with lower taxes. Declining tax revenues will then force tax harmonization and, finally, a halt to excessive spending.

For market discipline to work, five conditions need to be satisfied. First, the market must have accurate and comprehensive information on the size and composition of the debtor's obligations, so that it can make a valid assessment of debt-servicing obligations relative to ability to pay. Those who feel that this is a problem that applies solely to developing-country debtors might want to examine the case of the financial crisis facing New York City in the mid-1970s. Credit-rating agencies can of course assist in this information processing task, but they need to be cautious since a rating change can become a self-fulfilling prophecy. In addition, debtors may not have incentives to reveal unfavourable information before mandated reporting dates.

A second condition is that there must not be any implicit or explicit guarantee of a bail-out. For if there is the expectation of a bail-out, then the interest rate charged will reflect the creditworthiness of the guarantor – not that of the debtor. The market's perception of a bail-out is sometimes cited as a reason why interest rate spreads on bank loans to developing countries in the 1970s were so slow to rise (Folkerts-Landau 1985). It is of course possible for the overseeing fiscal authority to issue a 'no bail-out pledge'. The problem is that it may be difficult to make this pledge credible in the absence of a history where troubled debtors were in fact not bailed out.

Condition three is that the financial system must be strong enough such that a given debtor is not regarded as 'too large to fail'; if other financial institutions are large holders of the troubled debtor's obligations, it will be harder to exercise discipline.

A fourth condition is that the borrower's debt not be monetized by central bank purchases. This is because the resulting erosion of the real value of the debt will make it difficult for the market to price it accurately.

Yet a fifth condition – which applies specifically to the tax harmonization channels – is that there must be neither high costs of mobility nor provision of public services that compensate for tax differentials (Eichengreen 1990). If mobility costs are high, individuals and firms are less likely to 'vote with their feet' when taxes are raised. If better public services are offered in high-tax districts, then high taxes do not provide an incentive to leave.

To this point, the empirical literature on market discipline is quite limited. From the viewpoint of an emerging economic and monetary union, perhaps the most relevant work is that dealing with common currency areas which have federal fiscal systems – and where there is no explicit or implicit guarantee of a bail-out for fiscal adventurism at the local level. The USA and Canada fulfil these requirements.[13] A recent analysis of the relationship between interest rate spreads and debt burdens for US states was undertaken by Eichengreen (1990). In brief, he finds a weak, positive relationship between debt burdens and the cost of borrowing; interestingly enough, there is no evidence of a non-linearity that would make the rise in borrowing costs accelerate at very high debt levels.

Even if the empirical evidence linking borrowing costs to fiscal irresponsibility were stronger than it is, this would give us only half the picture. The missing half is evidence that higher borrowing costs induce governments to correct fiscal policy excesses. To our knowledge, no tests of the latter linkage – be it in the form of government reaction functions or otherwise – are yet available.

Finally, fiscal discipline might be encouraged by peer group surveillance. As is well known, this can take a number of forms. One possibility would be a fiscal policy rule that put, say, a ceiling on each participant's fiscal deficit.[14] The main difficulty with rigid fiscal policy rules is that they may not take adequate account of relevant inter-country differences in private savings rates, in outstanding debt stocks, in the uses to which government expenditures are put, in past credit histories etc. In addition, as suggested in our earlier discussion of rules versus discretion, there may be few sanctions that can be imposed on non-complying members. For these reasons, peer group surveillance typically takes place in a voluntary, discretionary format. But this mode of operation faces its own obstacles: fiscal policy is inflexible (at least relative to monetary policy); fiscal policy can operate with long and variable lags that depend in good measure on the pace of legislative actions; and the effects of fiscal policy on macro variables of interest hinge on what kind of fiscal action is taken (taxes versus expenditures, expenditures on tradeables versus non-tradeables, taxes on saving versus taxes on investment etc.). In addition, surveillance exercises invariably employ multi-indicator methods, where the tendency of different indicators to point in different directions gives considerable scope for discretion in policy diagnosis and prescription.

The likelihood that no single mechanism can be relied upon to yield fiscal discipline means that a broad-based approach that leans both on markets and on surveillance will be called for. The transition to economic and monetary union will go a lot smoother if fiscal policy can be made to work with monetary policy in achieving the basic economic goals of economic and monetary union.

NOTES

1 Without regard to sign, the average absolute values of these imbalances for the same period were 0.8 per cent of GNP for France and 1.5 per cent for Germany.

2 German Economic, Monetary and Social Union (GEMSU) is expected to contribute to a reduced German external imbalance in the period ahead.

3 As noted by Giavazzi and Spaventa (1990), a key factor in the direction of capital flows has been the market's apparent expectation that exchange rates in the higher-inflation countries will remain fixed and will not offset the lure of higher nominal interest rates.

4 Expenditures should reflect social needs and financing should take account of optimal tax smoothing and burden sharing across generations.

5 An interesting connected question is how European trade unions and business associations will respond to greater competitive pressures.

6 Thygesen and Gros (1990) have argued that transaction costs, incentives to practise price discrimination and the need for international reserves will all be lower with a common currency than with irrevocably fixed exchange rates.

7 Giovannini (1990) emphasizes the difficulties of conducting monetary policy under open capital markets when there is no credible commitment to exchange rate fixity.

8 Key (1989) argues that a competitive approach to deregulation may be chosen precisely because it establishes incentives that lead to convergence on a minimal set of regulations; at the same time, the danger of the competitive approach is that convergence may occur at a level that is below the social optimum.

9 McCallum (1990). A key task for empirical research is to illustrate how these evolutionary

195

policy rules would have performed in a variety of models and circumstances – so that a relevant 'counter-factual' can be constructed; this counter-factual could then be employed as a standard against which historical, discretionary policy can be evaluated.

10 Some observers are sceptical about the signalling effect of intervention because they doubt whether gains and losses on official intervention operations will be subject to much public scrutiny.

11 See also the recent survey of empirical evidence on intervention by Edison (1990) which reaches similar conclusions.

12 A fourth mechanism is national, self-imposed mechanisms that differ from country to country. Gramm–Rudman–Hollings legislation in the USA is one clear example of this kind of mechanism.

13 A dissenting view is that the experience of US states and of Canadian provinces is of only limited relevance for the prospect of fiscal discipline in an economic and monetary union because these states and provinces can exert much less pressure for bailouts or monetization than would individual member countries in an economic and monetary union.

14 Such a rule on budget deficits appeared in the Delors Committee Report. A more recent EC Commission Report (1990) argues instead for voluntary co-ordination and surveillance.

REFERENCES

Aizenman, J. and Frenkel, J. A. (1982) 'Aspects of the optimal management of exchange rates', *Journal of International Economics* 13 (November): 231–56.

Barro, R. and Gordon, D. (1983) 'A positive theory of monetary policy in a natural rate model', *Journal of Political Economy* 91 (August): 589–610.

Blundell-Wignall, A., Browne, F. and Manasse, P. (1990) 'Monetary policy in the wake of financial liberalization', OECD Working Paper 77, OECD: Paris, April.

Branson, W. and Henderson, D. (1985) 'The specification and influence of asset markets', in R. Jones and P. Kenen (eds) *Handbook of International Economics*, Amsterdam: North-Holland.

Calvo, G. (1978) 'On the time consistency of optimal policy in a monetary economy', *Econometrica* 46 (November): 1411–28.

Canzoneri, M. and Diba, B. (1990) 'Currency substitution: the inflation discipline for the EC?', unpublished manuscript, Georgetown University, May.

Delors Committee Report (1989) *Report on Economic and Monetary Union in the European Community*, Committee for the Study of Economic and Monetary

Union, June, Luxembourg: Office of Official Publications of the European Communities.

Dominguez, K. (1989) 'Market responses to coordinated central bank intervention', unpublished, Harvard University, April.

EC Commission (1990) 'Economic and monetary union: the economic rationale and design of the system', March.

Edison, H. (1990) 'Foreign currency operations: an annotated bibliography', International Finance Discussion Paper 380, Board of Governors of the Federal Reserve System, May.

Eichengreen, B. (1990) 'One money for Europe? Lessons from the US currency union', *Economic Policy* 10 (April): 118–87.

Folkerts-Landau, D. (1985) 'The changing role of international bank lending in development finance', *IMF Staff Papers* 32 (June): 317–63, Washington, DC: IMF.

Freedman, C. (1990) 'Monetary policy in the 1990s: lessons and challenges', in Federal Reserve Bank of Kansas City, *Monetary Policy Issues in the 1990*, Kansas City, KS: Federal Reserve Bank of Kansas City.

Frenkel, J. A. and Goldstein, M. (1986) 'A guide to target zones', *IMF Staff Papers* 33 (December): 633–70, Washington, DC: IMF.

—— and —— (1988) 'The international monetary system: developments and prospects', paper presented to Cato Institute Conference, February 1988. Printed in *Cato Journal* 8 (Fall): 255–307.

—— and —— (1990) 'Monetary policies, capital market integration, and the exchange rate regime', *Cahiers Economiques et Monetaires* 37: 5–30.

Frenkel, J. A. and Masson, P. (1989) 'International dimensions of monetary policy: coordination versus autonomy', in Federal Reserve Bank of Kansas City, *Monetary Policy Issues in the 1990s*, Kansas City, KS: Federal Reserve Bank of Kansas City, pp. 183–232.

Giavazzi, F. and Spaventa, L. (1990) 'The "new" EMS', CEPR Discussion Paper 369, London: Centre for Economic Policy Research, January.

Giovannini, A. (1990) 'The transition to monetary union', Bank of Italy, March.

Gros, D. and Thygesen, N. (1990) 'Towards monetary union in the European Community: why and how', unpublished, Center for European Policy Studies, Brussels, May.

Kenen, P. (1987) 'Exchange rates and policy coordination', Brookings Discussion Papers in International Economics 61, Washington, DC: Brookings Institution, October.

Key, S. (1989) 'Financial integration in the European community', International Finance Discussion Paper 349, Federal Reserve Board, April.

Kremers, J. M. and Lane, T. (1990) 'Economic and

monetary integration and the aggregate demand for money in the EMS', Working Paper WP/90/23, March, Washington, DC: IMF.

Kydland, F. and Prescott, E. (1977) 'Rules rather than discretion: the inconsistency of optimal plans', *Journal of Political Economy*, June: 473–91.

Masson, P. and Melitz, J. (1990) 'Fiscal policy interdependence in a European monetary union', Working Paper WP/90/24, Washington, DC: IMF, March.

McCallum, B. (1990) 'Targets, indicators, and instruments of monetary policy', Working Paper WP/90/41, Washington, DC: IMF, April.

Mussa, M. (1981) *The Role of Official Intervention*, Occasional Paper 6, New York: Group of Thirty.

Obstfeld, M. (1990) 'The effectiveness of foreign-exchange intervention: recent experience', in W. Branson, J. Frenkel and M. Goldstein (eds) *Policy Coordination and Exchange Rate Fluctuations*, Chicago, IL: NBER and University of Chicago Press, forthcoming.

Polak, J. (1988) 'Economic policy objectives in the major industrial countries and their effects on policy-making', in W. Guth (ed.) *Economic Policy Co-ordination*, Washington, DC: IMF and HWWA.

Sachs, J. and Sala-i-Martin, X. (1989) 'Federal fiscal policy and optimum currency areas', unpublished, Harvard University.

UK Treasury (1989) *An Evolutionary Approach to Economic and Monetary Union*, London: HM Treasury.

Viñals, J. (1990) 'The EMS, Spain and macroeconomic policy', CEPR Discussion Paper 389, London: Centre for Economic Policy Research, March.

Williamson, J. and Miller, M. (1987) *Targets and Indicators: A Blueprint for the International Coordination of Economic Policy*, Washington, DC: Institute for International Economics.

10

A EUROPEAN CENTRAL BANKING SYSTEM

Some analytical and operational considerations

Niels Thygesen

INTRODUCTION

The purpose of this chapter is to review briefly some analytical and operational issues which arise at an advanced stage of monetary integration. These issues are relevant to the present rather tightly managed EMS which has developed gradually since 1983, and their resolution could be experimented with in the decentralized and pre-institutional first stage. They are essential in any effort to clarify how monetary policy might be designed and operated in the second stage if a 'gradual transfer of decision-making power from national authorities to a Community institution' has to take place (paragraph 57, the Delors Committee Report, hereafter referred to as 'the Report'). I accept that it may not be possible at the present juncture to propose a detailed blueprint for accomplishing such a transition in stage two, but the considerations in the following sections are kept in sufficiently general terms to incorporate a range of analytical and operational approaches. The chapter is also relevant to the collective management through the proposed ESCB in stage three prior to the introduction of a common currency.

The chapter contains three sections. The first asks how the ultimate objective(s) of monetary and other macroeconomic policies might be formulated to give concreteness to the general description in the Report. The second discusses to what extent intermediate objectives might be helpful in under-pinning the attainment of the ultimate objectives. Finally, the third section looks at the possible instruments by which the ESCB and the participating national central banks might discharge and divide their responsibility for monetary policy. Throughout the chapter reference will be made to Table 10.1 which lists ultimate and intermediate objectives and the main policy instruments.

All three subjects raised in this chapter obviously require further analytical work, study of empirical regularities and assessment of practical feasibility. They are treated here in a highly preliminary way, though with some confidence that the issues will have to be addressed in order to prepare properly for the second and third stages outlined in the Report.

ULTIMATE OBJECTIVES

As regards the ultimate objectives of policies in an economic and monetary union the Report states (paragraph 16) that 'these policies should be geared to price stability, balanced growth, converging standards of living, high employment and external equilibrium'.

It is difficult to assess, in the absence of additional precision on the relative weight to be given to these wide-ranging objectives, how procedures may be developed for monitoring whether policies are appropriate. The present chapter assumes that the prime contribution of monetary policy to the

Table 10.1 Ultimate and intermediate objectives of monetary and other macroeconomic policies and the instruments of monetary policy

	Collective	*National/relative*
Ultimate objectives	Maintain approximate medium-term stability of producer prices in the internal market	Keep growth in nominal private final demand close to targeted path in each country
	Maintain sustainable current account position for area *vis-à-vis* rest of the world	
Intermediate objectives	Keep growth of monetary aggregate for area as a whole within targeted interval	Keep growth in domestic credit (DCE) within targeted interval in each country
		Keep stable exchange rates *vis-à-vis* other currencies within the area
Instruments available	General (and differentiated) reserve requirements against national DCEs	Intervention rates and policy in intra-area currency band
	Lending rates of ESCB	Interest rate differentials within area
	Intervention policy *vis-à-vis* third currencies	(Small) parity realignments

attainment of ultimate policy objectives will be made if the ESCB is committed to the objective of price stability, while supporting – subject to this proviso – the general economic policy set at the Community level by the competent bodies. This is the formulation chosen in paragraph 32 of the Report which describes the mandate for the ESCB.

Implicitly this division of responsibilities implies that all the remaining objectives would, in principle, be the concern of the non-monetary authorities at the national and Community levels. Since exchange market interventions in third currencies would also be carried out 'in accordance with guidelines established by the ESCB Council' (paragraph 57 on stage two) and subsequently 'on the sole responsibility of the ESCB Council in accordance with Community exchange rate policy' (paragraph 60 on stage three) it is necessary to recall that such interventions would provide not only an additional instrument for influencing price trends in the Community, but also the objective of external equilibrium. The ESCB Council would accordingly be faced with the problem of designing guidelines for interventions which take into account both its prime objective of price stability and the need to contain the build-up of unsustainable external disequilibria, most appropriately defined as large collective current account imbalances *vis-à-vis* the rest of the world. The Report does not say explicitly that internal price stability always has to take precedence over the external value of EC currencies in terms of third currencies, but it clearly envisages no significant degree of commitment to stabilize the latter. Though it may well be in this area that the issue of designing an appropriate mix of monetary and non-monetary policies will find the clearest expression, the attainment of some degree of external equilibrium would impinge primarily on the budgetary authorities.

In view of this interpretation, the judgement on the performance of monetary policy and the fulfilment by the ESCB of its mandate would hinge on an interpretation of the objective of price stability. That objective would have to be expressible in collective terms for the Community, but it could also usefully be linked to national indicators of a nominal nature in order to monitor the compatibility of policies. There appear to be two main contenders for the role of collective objective.

The first is to use medium-term stability of average producer prices in the internal market for goods as an indicator. The increasing competition and specialization resulting from the completion of the internal market will tend to make prices for internationally traded goods more homogeneous, gradually removing the scope for price discrimination between national markets. A weighted average of national producer price indices for the participating countries, expressed in a common unit, for example ECUs, would provide an increasingly reliable indicator of a common price trend. There is evidence from earlier periods of stable exchange rates, notably the gold standard, that close convergence in producer prices is observable in an exchange rate regime of the tightness envisaged (see, for example, McKinnon and Ohno 1988).

While such an index would give expression in a meaningful way to a common price performance in the Community, it might be desirable to focus particularly on the domestic (i.e. internal to the EC) stories of inflation in producer prices for which ESCB monetary policy would be most directly accountable. A deflator of value added in the manufacturing industry calculated as a weighted average for the internal market would leave out of account the inflationary (or disinflationary) shocks such as terms-of-trade changes resulting from swings in the prices of energy, other intermediate imports or raw materials. Such external shocks generate fluctuations in the inflation rate which may in practice have to be at least in part accommodated by variations in the collective money supply. An ultimate objective expressed in terms of stability in the average of national value added deflators would not be radically different from the course followed in the Community in the 1980s; the second oil price shock led to a temporary acceleration of producer prices in Europe, even in the Federal Republic of Germany, while the 1985–6 decline in import prices for raw materials, energy and other intermediate inputs (as well as in the dollar) temporarily pushed the rate of change of producer prices

below zero in the low-inflation EMS countries.

In short, by aiming to keep the rate of inflation measured by an average of value added deflators within a narrow band close to zero, say between zero and 2 per cent, or to keep the average increase in producer prices within a slightly wider band, similarly centred around a minimal rate of inflation, the ESCB could give specific content to the notion of a stability-oriented monetary policy and simplify the monitoring of its policies.

The other main contender is a broad-based index such as a Community-wide consumer price index, widely perceived to reflect the cost of inflation to the economy. In an area as large and diverse as the Community, national price trends measured by consumer prices, however, may diverge substantially between countries even over the medium term, because the weight of non-traded goods and services in this index is substantial and price trends for these goods are less directly constrained by the process of market integration. It might be confusing to public opinion to announce a collective price objective around which substantial variation in national performances persisted.

A collective price objective formulated in terms of an essentially common indicator, such as average producer prices, may be sufficient for guiding the aggregate thrust of monetary policy. However, for the purpose of linking up with monetary instruments or with national macroeconomic objectives which will continue to have great importance throughout stage two and into stage three, the collective objective could be supplemented by criteria of national performance consistent with the common inflation objective. One possible way of doing this, broadly in line with trends in national policy-making in a number of industrial countries in the 1980s, would be to set targets for the rate of increase of some measure of nominal income for each participating country.

To be more specific, objectives for the rate of increase in private final demand (private consumption, business fixed investment and residential construction) might be thought of as the national income measure most relevant in the context of monetary policy. For each participating country, the national and Community authorities would make a judgement on the unavoidable rate of inflation in private final demand prices expressed in the national currency and a rate of increase of real demand judged feasible in the light of trend capacity growth and the initial situation. The national inflation rates thus calculated would typically on average be a bit above the collective objective for producer prices in the Community, because the broader price indices for final demand would comprise non-traded goods and services for which productivity increases are typically slower than for the sectors producig internationally traded goods in the EC market. National inflation rates in terms of final demand prices might also diverge slightly year by year, as the differentials in productivity between sectors are unlikely to be uniform across countries. Gradually goods market integration would tend to impose approximate parallelism on national price levels in this broader sense, as the range of traded goods expands and factor mobility increases.

Various forms of nominal income targeting have appeared in national policy-making in the 1980s when the confidence in monetary aggregates as intermediate targets was weakening, while a turn to objectives for the growth of real output was perceived as unrealizable and potentially inflationary. Maintaining a suitable measure of nominal income close to a steady growth path provides a framework for monitoring national economic policies and for co-ordinating them internationally, as is recognized in some of the main proposals for improving global policy co-ordination and reforming the international monetary system (see, for example, Williamson and Miller 1987).

In the present context, nominal income targeting would provide a linkage to potential intermediate objectives at the national level and through them to decisions relating to a money supply process which will remain, at least through stage two, largely national in execution if not in design. Such a framework would be suitable for the co-ordination of monetary and fiscal policies in the Community in so far as it would facilitate the identification of policy conflicts. The later would arise if the execution by the ESCB of its mandate for assuring price were to be eroded by the sum total of national fiscal policies, implying a growth rate in nominal final demand in one or more countries inconsistent with the objective for average inflation. In this way the framework would pinpoint requirements for fiscal co-ordination in an analytically more satisfactory way than by simply looking at the size of budget imbalances relative to GNP, or to national savings, as a basis for imposing 'binding rules' on such imbalances. By monitoring both the national component of ESCB monetary policy and fiscal policy in terms of the same nominal income targets, the risk of open conflicts is reduced.

INTERMEDIATE OBJECTIVES

In principle, it would be possible to gear monetary instruments directly to ultimate objectives. If the Community-wide index of producer prices were to accelerate – and information on prices could be available with a time-lag of one to two months – such an observed development would provide an indication that average interest rates in the Community should be raised to contain money creation. If the growth rate of nominal demand in a particular country were to run well ahead of the agreed national target, that would – after a somewhat longer information lag – trigger a country-specific response by the tightening of one or more monetary instruments in the country concerned. Symmetric responses could be envisaged if a deceleration of average inflation or a shortfall of nominal demand became observable. Simple feedback rules of this type could provide a stabilizing framework within which both average and nationally differentiated departures from targets were dampened.

But further attention to the way changes in monetary instruments influence the ultimate objectives of average inflation and the rate of growth of nominal demand in the participating countries through monetary and/or credit aggregates is advisable for at least two reasons. First, formu-

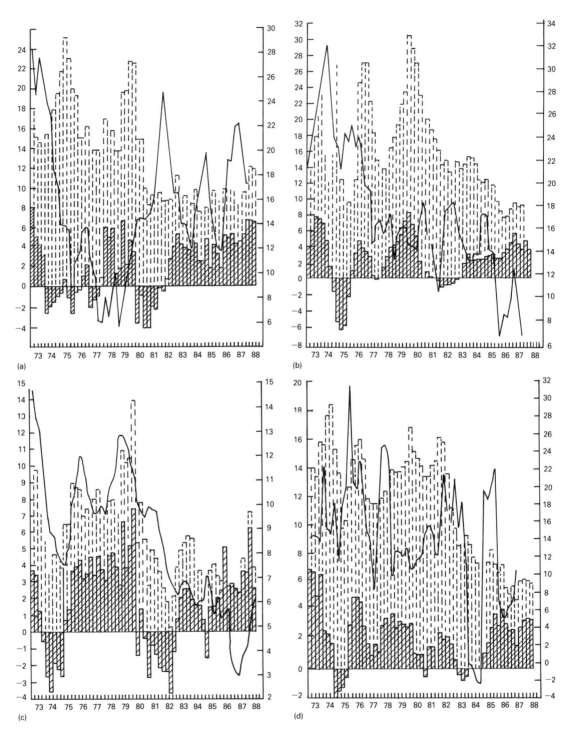

Figure 10.1 Domestic credit expansion and growth rates in nominal and real private final demand (━━━, real private demand; ━ ━ ━ ━ ━, nominal private demand; ——————, domestic credit): (a) UK; (b) Italy; (c) Germany; (d) France

Source: OECD

lating policy with respect to one or more appropriately chosen aggregate(s) will improve the understanding of monetary policy and enhance its credibility; it will become easier to monitor the actions of the ESCB than in the situation where policy performance is assessed only on the basis of the ultimate objectives over which monetary policy, within any given shorter time horizon, has only a limited influence. Second, if reserve requirements are to be applied as one of the main instruments of the ESCB, they have to be seen to work in a broadly similar way in the participating countries by relating to a monetary or credit aggregate which exerts some longer-run influence on the ultimate objectives.

A possible procedure would consist of setting a collective target for total annual money creation in the participating countries, consistent with the objective for average inflation. Abstracting temporarily from net interventions in third currencies by the participants, total additions to the broad money stock (M2 or M3) would be matched by the sum of domestic counterparts to money creation in each country, since purchases of other participating currencies by one participating central bank are offset by sales elsewhere within the system. In principle, there would be no sterilization of interventions in partner currencies. The task of controlling total money creation would then consist in applying instruments which influence, through incentives or obligations, the readiness of each central bank to keep DCE close to a targeted, and collectively agreed, rate for the country in question. Setting the latter through a collective decision-making process in the ESCB would constitute the core of the *ex ante* coordination effort. The process would assist in making mutually consistent the national objectives for the growth of nominal demand from which the national DCEs are derived. Deviations between actual and targeted DCE would in turn give some early information on deviations between actual and targeted growth in nominal demand. A procedure of this nature has been outlined in some detail by Russo and Tullio (1988).

It cannot be claimed with confidence that (1)

national DCEs can be closely controlled or that (2) they are tightly linked to nominal demand over shorter periods of time, two desirable characteristics of intermediate monetary objectives, as analysed meticulously by Bryant (1980). A recent OECD study shows a fairly weak quarter-to-quarter relationship between DCE (and different monetary aggregates) and changes in nominal demand for the four largest EC economies. On the other hand, a clear tendency for both to decelerate has been observable in Germany, France and Italy (but not in the UK) since the early 1980s (see Figure 10.1).

Despite the evidently high degree of slack in the relationship of DCE and nominal demand, using the former as intermediate objective may be justified by two considerations: (1) it provides the most direct linkage to total money creation in the area; and (2) it is an extension, in the direction of symmetry, of the present informal practice in the EMS in which most countries, with the significant exception of Germany, look to rates of DCE relative to others in the EMS as the consistent underpinning for the main intermediate objective of maintaining stable exchange rates in the EMS. For the Federal Republic of Germany the shift from the present intermediate objective (target for broad money, M3) to a DCE target, with in principle no provision for sterilization, should be acceptable, provided that overall money creation in the area were seen to be more directly subjected to stability-oriented, collectively agreed decisions and efficient instruments for implementing them, as is proposed in the main Report through the establishment of the ESCB with a mandate to pursue price stability.

Total money creation would depart from the sum of national DCEs to the extent that non-sterilized interventions *vis-à-vis* third currencies were undertaken by the ESCB directly or by one of the participating central banks. There is no presumption that such interventions would be sterilized; efforts to stem what was considered excessive depreciation of the area's currencies *vis-à-vis* the dollar through sales of dollars might well require some overall tightening of monetary conditions and higher average interest rates for the

Community as a whole, and vice versa in the case of purchases of dollars to stem overly rapid appreciation of the participating currencies. The degree of sterilization would be matter for discretionary decisions arrived at collectively through the ESCB Council. The latter would also, in consultation with the participating central banks, take a view on which currency or currencies to use in dollar interventions. One important criterion in reaching such decisions would be to maximize the cohesiveness of the currencies within the system as that finds expression in the exchange markets. Guidance would be found also in the degree of correspondence in each country between a central bank's DCE objective and the observed growth in credit including potential effects of sterilization operations linked to interventions in third currencies which the ESCB may assign to that particular central bank.

For the individual central bank, the main short-term intermediate objective would continue to be the maintenance of stable exchange rates *vis-à-vis* other participating currencies. Some *ex ante* co-ordination of DCE objectives should make that task easier on average; but in practice the DCE objective may in particular situations have to be overridden to maintain exchange rate stability.

INSTRUMENTS AVAILABLE

Even prior to the attribution of any particular instrument to the ESCB, the collecive formulation of ultimate and intermediate monetary objectives would in itself constitute a major step towards *ex ante* co-ordination desirable in stage one. Nothing would prevent the EMS central banks from keeping their present exchange of information on their respective formulation of domestic monetary policy, or from giving the reports prepared by a special group of experts for the Committee of Central Bank Governors a more deliberately common analytical framework along the above lines. Similarly, the reports prepared by another expert group on exchange market interventions could begin to be used in a more forward-looking way to formulate intervention strategies rather

than to review the past record. Closer co-ordination could begin to replicate the effects of a more advanced stage, even while the policy analysis and recommendations emerging from it remain strictly advisory, as is the case for stage one.

Yet it is unlikely that anything resembling closely a common monetary policy could be conducted merely through discussions, but without vesting in the ESCB genuine decision-making power with respect to at least some significant instruments of monetary policy. Indeed, that is the rationale of suggesting the set-up of the ESCB for stage two before the irrevocable locking of parities which makes a common monetary policy a simple necessity. But there are difficulties in determining how monetary authority might be shared between a centre – the ESCB Council and Board – and the participating national central banks. The efficiency of operations requires that there should never be any doubt in the financial markets, among national policy-makers or elsewhere, as to which body has the responsibility for taking particular decisions. Monetary authority is less easily divisible than budgetary authority where elements of decentralization and even of competitive behaviour between different levels of government, or within the same level, may be observed in national states.

Four types of policy decisions have to be considered as being at the core of any design of a workable allocation of responsibilities within an ESCB in stage two:

1 adjustment of short-term interest differentials;
2 intervention policy *vis-à-vis* third currencies;
3 changes in reserve requirements; and
4 changes in intra-area parties (realignments).

Reference is again made to Figure 10.1.

The adjustment of relative short-term interest rates is the central instrument in managing the present EMS, and a high degree of co-ordination and occasionally *de facto* joint, or at least bilateral, decisions have been observed. As Governor Godeaux explains, since the so-called Basle–Nyborg agreement of September 1987 in particular, participants have developed a flexible set of instruments for containing incipient exchange market tensions: intramarginal intervention, wider use of the fluctuation band and changes in short-term interest rate differentials. This combination has proved fairly robust in most periods of tension since September 1987. But a risk remains that the experience of earlier periods of tension will be repeated; then public criticism and mutual recrimination between Ministers for Finance occasionally intensified tensions and made monetary management very difficult. The main examples of such episodes are December 1986 to January 1987, November 1987 and – to a minor extent – April 1989. The participation of additional currencies in the EMS in the course of stage one, notably sterling, which has traditionally been managed with considerable involvement on the part of the UK Treasury and even of the Prime Minister, will make it urgent to strengthen procedures for genuine co-ordination further and to make the transition to a more joint form of management in stage two at an early stage.

While decision-making in this sensitive area would still remain in national hands in stage two, the launching of the ESCB at the beginning of stage two would in itself imply that national governments would be less likely than in the past to involve themselves directly in the management of exchange crises. In the course of stage one the Committee of Central Bank Governors will already have begun to perform more efficiently the role of a multilateral arbitrator that has been missing occasionally in the past. A common analytical framework developed around the intermediate targets will give more explicit guidance as to who should adjust to whom. If the proposal to develop a joint operational facility for exchange and money market operations, as outlined in Professor Lamfalussy's paper, is pursued that would in itself bring participating central banks into more continuous contact also with respect to their transactions in their domestic financial markets and would facilitate co-ordinated action on interest rates.

The gradual and partial upgrading of decision-making on relative interest rate adjustment from the purely national level to a Community body, in the first stage the Committee of Governors, from the second stage the ESCB Council, will not in itself assure that the average level of interest rates in the participating countries is appropriate, though it should tend to make such an outcome more likely than the present system with its occasional inefficiencies of interest rate escalations and tensions. To get a firmer grip on the average level of rates, the attribution to the ESCB of an instrument which permits a collective influence on domestic sources of money creation would be necessary. Such an instrument is described briefly below in the form of the ability for the ESCB to impose compulsory reserve requirements on domestic money creation and to develop gradually a market for a European reserve base with its own lending rate.

A second instrument for which some degree of joint management could be envisaged is foreign exchange interventions in third currencies. There are two economic arguments for such an attribution: (1) the medium-term need to contribute to the containment of major misalignments, and (2) the smoothing of short-term volatility vis-à-vis third currencies.

The former argument can hardly be assessed without making a judgement on the feasibility of a more managed global exchange rate system and the degree of commitment by other major monetary authorities, notably in the USA, to support, through interventions and domestic monetary adjustments, any understanding reached on the appropriate level of the main bilateral exchange rates. Given the experience of the period since 1977 and the major present current account imbalances, projected to persist well into the 1990s, it would be hazardous to assume that an emerging joint dollar policy of the EMS countries would be anything more than ad hoc guidelines for managing a collective appreciation of the EMS currencies as smoothly as possible. Calculations with large macroeconometric models suggest that the appreciation may have to be at least of the order of 20 per cent in real terms on average for the EMS currencies from the levels prevailing in mid-1989 if the European countries are to assume a reasonable share of the adjustment of the US current deficit to a sustainable low level (see Cline 1989). This will put the cohesion of the EMS currencies to a severe test, but it will also provide a unique opportunity, as was the case in 1985–7, for reconciling low inflation in Europe with a relatively expansionary monetary policy in the Community, hence contributing to an improved and satisfactory price performance in the crucial transition period from the present more decentralized operation towards economic and monetary union.

As regards the task of smoothing short-term volatility, it must be noted that tensions among EMS currencies have often in the past decade been triggered by financial disturbances from third currencies, notably movements in the dollar. The currencies participating in the EMS were seen by the markets as being sensitive in different degrees to such disturbances. These perceived differences had their origins in varying degrees of controls on capital movements and in expectations of the likelihood of divergent policy reactions to the external financial disturbances. For example, a depreciation of the dollar was normally expected to strengthen the German mark relative to most other EMS currencies, both because the German mark had a far larger domestic financial base and the most liberal regime for capital flows and because non-German authorities in the EMS were seen as more prone than the Bundesbank to try to avoid the contractionary effects of the appreciation of their currencies. The tensions to which these – real or perceived – differences in structure and/or behaviour gave rise were occasionally mitigated by an EMS realignment. Conversely, in periods of an appreciating dollar, outflows from Europe were observed to be particularly strong from the German mark area, reflecting primarily the closer substitutability between the US dollar and the German mark than that prevailing for other EMS currencies, but presumably also a decreasing probability of a realignment within the system. In recent years the liberalization of capital movements in France and Italy and in some smaller EMS countries, the deepening of continental European financial markets and the improved cohesion of the

EMS economies have all contributed to a weakening of the earlier negative correlation between movements in the US dollar (in effective exchange rate terms) and movements in non-German-mark currencies in the EMS vis-à-vis the mark, as shown, for example, by Giavazzi and Giovannini (1989). But the tendency for dollar movements to affect the EMS currencies differentially may be expected to persist in moderate form into stage two. The task remains in that case to avoid that such tensions, if they are unwarranted by more fundamental economic divergence within the EMS, persist and force realignments.

While this could in principle be achieved through joint guidelines for essentially decentralized interventions by the participating national central banks, a visible capacity to intervene jointly in third currencies, and to do so in ways that further the cohesion of the EMS, is potentially important. Without a presence in the major exchange markets the ESCB would lack the capacity to check the impact of external financial disturbances on EMS stability at source. Hence 'a certain amount of reserve pooling' (Report, paragraph 57) as well as ample working balances in EMS currencies would be desirable in stage two.

It is impossible to determine a priori what percentage of external official reserves would have to be pooled in order to create a credibility effect in the financial markets for an emerging joint intervention policy. Leaving the percentage low, say 10–20 per cent, would run the risk of simply complicating existing co-operative procedures without making a qualitative difference, though even with limited pooling some beneficial effects could be expected simply from the learning experience of co-ordinating interventions through the same trading floor rather than by consultations over the telephone. Governor de Larosière describes these gains relative to the present EMS.

Joint interventions in third currencies by means of pooling of part of exchange reserves did not win general favour in the Report as a proposal for the first stage; too much emphasis might be put on external considerations relative to the correction of imbalances within the Community (paragraph 54).

This argument would not apply to an ESCB capacity to intervene in stage two along with the attribution of other monetary instruments with more direct domestic implications for the participants as proposed here.

A third instrument, specifically assigned to the ESCB, would be the ability to impose variable reserve requirements on domestic money creation.

Whereas the first two instruments (and the fourth to be discussed below) are directed primarily at relative adjustments within the EMS, changes in required reserve ratios affect the overall thrust of monetary policy. International monetary agreements, including the Bretton Woods system and the EMS, have typically been more explicit on relative than on aggregate adjustment in the participating countries. The EMS procedures for relative adjustment may leave something to be desired, as explained above, and they may leave too much discretion to national monetary authorities to remove ambiguities and tensions. Yet more attention has been given to these procedures than to discussion of whether monetary policy has an appropriate aggregate thrust.

The Bretton Woods system and the early EMS did not have to face up to this issue directly, because both systems were protected by a mixture of capital controls for the short term and some scope for changing the exchange rate in the longer term. The post-1983 EMS has had more difficulty in avoiding the issue. In the absence of some aggregate monetary target for the whole system, an implicit monetary rule has emerged: monetary policy in all participating countries has tended to be determined, via the ambition to hold more rigidly fixed nominal exchange rates, mainly by that of its largest and least-inflationary participant. The practice in the EMS that reserves used for intervention in defending a weak currency have to be reconstituted within the span of a few months means that convergence – provided that exchange rates do remain fixed – will be towards the low inflation in the Federal Republic of Germany and not towards some average as would be the case if intervention credits provided a more permanent safety net. In that case efforts at sterilization would

have become more widespread in the weaker currency countries, and aggregate money creation could have drifted upwards.

By using the degree of freedom for aggregate monetary policy by implicitly attaching policies to the domestic monetary target in Germany, the EMS has succeeded since 1983 to an unexpected degree in becoming 'a zone of monetary stability' in the double sense of promoting both exchange rate *and* price stability. The challenge for stage two and stage three is to design intermediate objectives and monetary instruments so as to make likely an extension of these desirable features within the more collectively managed system marked by the transition to the ESCB.

A major reason why the past system would in any case have to be revised is that the hegemonial role of the largest country already shows signs of weakening and must be expected to be eroded further during stage one as additional currencies join the EMS and short-term capital transactions are fully liberalized. This process affects the size of potential flows in the new member countries, in those countries that undertake additional liberalization, notably France and Italy, and in Germany. The ability of the Bundesbank to keep a preferred domestic monetary target as close to a desired path as has typically been the case for the past fifteen years must be expected to weaken further. Financial integration increases the risk of policy errors and hence the incentive for all participants to modify the present paradigm. Another factor working in the same direction is the increasing ease, as the credibility of fixed exchange rates becomes more well founded, with which all non-German participants can attract inflows of capital by maintaining short-term rates only moderately above those in Germany. The improved substitutability between participating currencies inexorably pushes the thinking of all monetary authorities in the direction of more attention to aggregate money creation in the area, to the formulation of intermediate objectives for domestic money creation consistent with an aggregate target and to designing procedures whereby the latter can be kept roughly on their agreed course.

Governor Ciampi spells out in some detail how an ability for the ESCB to impose variable reserve requirements on the domestic money creation for which each national central bank is primarily responsible could be set up in stage two, and the present chapter associates itself fully with his basic ideas and the analysis of the various technical options available. The essential feature is that the ESCB should be empowered to impose – uniform or differentiated – reserve requirements on either the increase in the monetary liabilities of each national central bank or the credit extended by the member banks to their respective domestic sectors. This requirement would be met only by holding reserves with the ESCB; and the supply of reserves would be entirely controlled by the latter through allocations of a reserve asset (official ECUs) to each central bank corresponding to the demand for reserves which would arise if agreed targets for money creation or DCE were observed. Alternatively, the supply of reserves would be created by open market purchases of the ESCB. Both cost and availability considerations would provide central banks with an incentive to stay close to declared objectives. The ESCB would have to be given some discretion in extending or withdrawing reserves to provide marginal accommodation. The new system could replace the present method of creating official ECUs through temporary swaps of one-fifth of gold and dollar reserves as well as the credits extended through the very-short-term facility of the EMCF.

The system would create a monetary control mechanism analogous to that through which national central banks, who use reserve requirements, influence money and credit creation through their banking systems. It would introduce a certain hierarchy in the relationship between the ESCB and its constituent national central banks, while leaving some freedom for each national central bank in designing its domestic instruments.

The reserve requirements could also be applied directly to DCE in the total national banking system, i.e. on the domestic sources of broad money creation. The advantage of this method would be that it assigns the collective monetary

instrument more directly to a natural intermediate objective – DCE – underpinning fixed exchange rates; but it might introduce more slack in the control mechanism, as it would no longer apply to items that appear on the balance sheet of the central banks for which the latter could be regarded as more directly responsible.

In the variants of an operational framework for an integrated monetary policy described by Governor Ciampi and in the previous paragraph, the ESCB would not have any direct contact with commercial banks or with financial markets in general. Its sphere of operation would be confined to transactions with the second tier of the three-tier system, the national central banks. This would be unduly confining from the time during stage three when a common currency is introduced. To manage a common currency the ESCB would need to have direct transactions with commercial banks, as does any national central bank at present. To prepare for this during the earlier part of stage three, possibly already in stage two, it may be useful to explore in what ways the ESCB could be put into a position to have some direct influence on liquidity conditions without always relying on its ability through guidelines and incentives to exert its influence indirectly via the national central banks. In any case, since legislation enabling the ESCB to deal directly with financial markets in the final stage of economic and monetary union would also be part of a comprehensive Treaty revision, attention to the nature of such contracts is not premature.

One way to give the ESCB such influence would be to allow it to make open market operations in national markets. The ESCB might, for example, use the securities it has acquired from the national central banks for such open market transactions. One could impose, initially, limits on the total amount of purchases and sales which can be made within any given period. This would be especially important at the start, when the ESCB would be mainly purchasing securities, since its initial stock would be small. These limits could be raised over time, allowing in stage three the operations of the ESCB to become more important than those of the national central banks in their respective markets.

A different and complementary approach, more directly in extension of the reserve requirement system applied to national central banks, would be to introduce a uniform European reserve requirement on commercial bank deposits, or on increases thereof. A small fraction of such deposits would be held with the ESCB and denominated in ECU. A federal funds market, in which the ESCB as the only issuer would have strict control of the total supply, could then develop in which commercial banks would trade among themselves the reserve balances they need to satisfy the European reserve requirement. The approach would imply that the ESCB be given direct influence on a market which reflects system-wide liquidity conditions.

The approach could be implemented by giving the ESCB the authority to set, within limits set in its statutes, a compulsory reserve requirement on all deposits of Community residents with Community commercial banks. To give banks initial access to deposits with the ESCB, the latter could initially buy the appropriate amount of securities in the market; hence the system could be regarded as complementary to the idea outlined above to permit the ESCB to undertake limited open market transactions in initial periods. The securities purchased could be denominated either in ECU or in national currencies, provided that, if introduced in stage two, the proportions of the latter correspond to the weights in the ECU basket. Once the initial amount of reserves has been created and absorbed into required reserves, the ESCB could engage in additional marginal accommodation by supplying federal funds through modest discretionary open market operations. A tightening of the federal funds market would come about if required reserves were to run ahead of this process of supplying them; and a rise in the federal funds rate would induce banks to slow down the underlying deposit creation. The approach is compatible with the usual range of operating procedures for a central bank from interest rate to reserves targeting.

Different operating procedures would presumably be appropriate as the ESCB extends its authority from stage two to stage three and to the ultimate management of a single currency, but the basic mechanism would not have to be modified. In effect, the ESCB, from its beginning, could act in some respects as a true central bank, reinforcing its more indirect and orchestrating functions inherent in the way that the earlier proposals constrain it to being a bank for the central banks only.

Suggesting some form of reserve requirement as the major instrument for an emerging joint policy to influence the domestic sources of money creation – as a complement to the control over the external sources which a joint exchange rate and intervention policy *vis-à-vis* third currencies would provide – is bound to raise critical questions on the approach. Although reserve requirements have historically been the prime method by which central banks have achieved monetary control in most countries, reliance on that instrument may appear to be limited in the Community today (see, for example, the survey of Kneeshaw and Van den Bergh 1989). In most industrial countries the banking system has become indebted to the central bank to an extent that makes it dependent on the terms on which marginal accommodation of reserve needs is provided. The mechanisms suggested illustrate ways in which an analogous influence may be brought to bear through a reserve requirement system on the relationship between the ESCB and the participating central banks (the three-tier system) and gradually extended to financial markets in general. A direct contact between the central institution and the financial market would provide a smooth passage to the final stage when the ESCB is to manage a common currency.

The three instruments proposed so far – collective guidance of relative interest rate adjustments, joint interventions in third currencies with a definitively pooled part of foreign exchange reserves and the imposition of variable reserve requirements on domestic money creation – are all major examples of shifts towards the European level of decision-making authority in well-specified areas of the kind that could be considered for stage two and extended into stage three, as long as there is no single currency issued by the ESCB beyond the restricted circuit for the management of the reserves market referred to above.

It remains to consider how the one decision in the EMS which is today subject to *de facto* joint decision-making, namely realignments of central rates, could be handled in stage two. Would there be a case for vesting authority over this instrument with the ESCB as part of monetary management rather than leaving it as in the present EMS with the Ecofin Council? There are arguments for and against such a transfer.

A major purpose of setting up elements of a collective monetary authority – the ESCB – before the irrevocable locking of parities which marks the transition to the third and final stage of economic and monetary union is to constrain realignments and eliminate the need for them. A more specific objective would be to assure that the occasional and rare recourse to them will be made in sufficiently small steps to preserve continuity of market exchange rates around realignments. This has been an important feature in the containment of speculative pressures in the recent EMS experience. If financial market participants would interpret a transfer of authority for making the residual small realignments to the participating central banks part of the ESCB's task as a signal of an intended tightening of the EMS in the transition to full economic and monetary union, such a transfer could prove stabilizing and hence desirable.

Putting the question in this way, however, suggests the counter-argument, namely that governments might not succeed in conveying such a signal. They might instead feel relief at not having to bear, as in the present EMS, the political burden of visibly initiating a realignment – and without a new, more hidden, discipline inherent in membership of a union with irrevocably fixed exchange rates. The Council of the ESCB might be faced with *fait accompli* situations in which only a realignment would ease tensions and with national policy-makers blaming either private speculators or the central bankers themselves for the outcome. This would imply a deterioration relative to the recent performance of the EMS.

On balance, these arguments suggest that the decisive considerations in assigning the authority to undertake realignments are how close participants have come to meeting the prerequisites for full union. It would be dangerous, if feasible, to shift the responsibility for deciding on realignments to the ESCB in stage two if any major divergence of economic performance has persisted into that stage. But it would be desirable to shift that responsibility if the need for realignments were generally accepted as residual only and if adequate monetary instruments for underpinning fixed rates had been assigned to the ESCB along the lines proposed above. A tentative conclusion is that the authority to decide on realignments could become part of the mandate of the ESCB in stage two, but that this is less of a priority than the attribution of the other, day-to-day, instruments of an increasingly collective monetary policy.

REFERENCES

Bryant, R. C. (1980) *Money and Monetary Policy in Interdependent Nations.* Washington, DC: Brookings Institution.

Cline, W. R. (1989) *United States External Adjustment and the World Economy*, Washington, DC: Institute for International Economics.

Frenkel, J. (1989) 'A modest proposal for international nominal targeting', NBER Working Paper 2849, Cambridge, MA: National Bureau of Economic Research.

Giavazzi, F. and Giovannini, A. (1989) *Limiting Exchange-rate Flexibility: The EMS*, Cambridge, MA: MIT Press.

Kneeshaw, J. T. and Van den Bergh, P. (1989) 'Changes in central bank money market operating procedures in the 1980s', *BIS Economic Papers* 23, Bank for International Settlements, Basle.

McKinnon, R. and Ohno, K. (1988) 'Purchasing power parity as a monetary standard', unpublished, Memorandum 276, Center for Research in Economic Growth, Stanford University.

Russo, M. and Tullio, G. (1988) 'Monetary policy coordination within the European Monetary System: Is there a rule?', in F. Giavazzi, S. Micossi and M. H. Miller (eds) *The EMS*, Cambridge: Cambridge University Press, Chapter 11.

Williamson, J. and Miller, M. H. (1987) 'Targets and indicators: a blueprint for the international coordination of economic policy', *Policy Analyses in International Economics* 22, Washington, DC: Institute for International Economics.

11

THE ECONOMICS OF EMU

Directorate-General for Economic and Financial Affairs, Commission of the European Communities

EMU AND ALTERNATIVES

The basic definition of economic and monetary union (EMU) is institutional and legal. This section first discusses its economic content, which is necessary for an assessment of its costs and benefits, and then discusses the economic content of the reference cases against which the costs and benefits of EMU are assessed, namely a 'stage 1 + 1992' baseline and alternative exchange rate regimes.

The economic content of EMU

The Madrid meeting of the European Council of June 1989 endorsed the approach to EMU proposed by the report of the Committee for the Study of Economic and Monetary Union (the Delors report), and as decided by the European Council the first stage of the realization of EMU began on 1 July 1990.

The economic definition of EMU given by the Delors report is now widely accepted. For monetary union, it uses as a definition the three conditions stated in the 1970 Werner report, namely:

1 total and irreversible convertibility of currencies;
2 complete liberalization of capital transactions and full integration of banking and financial markets;
3 elimination of margins of fluctuation and irrevocable locking of exchange rate parities.

As mentioned in the report, the first two condi-

tions have already been met, or will be with the completion of the internal market programme.[1] Therefore, the decisive step towards full monetary union appears to be the irrevocable locking of exchange rates, which implies the creation of a single central bank (EuroFed). As discussed in more detail below, the adoption of a single currency would then be highly desirable. since membership in the ERM of the EMS is at present narrower than Community membership, it would be important that all its member states participate in the ERM beforehand.

The definition of economic union is less clear

Table 11.1 Major features of 1992 and economic and monetary union

	'1992'	Stage 1 EMU	Final EMU
Monetary union			
Convertibility	×	×	×
Free capital movements	×	×	×
Irrevocable parities/single currency			×
All member states in the ERM/EMU		×	×
Economic union			
Single market	×	×	×
Competition policy	P	P	E
Regional and structural policies	P	P	E
Macroeconomic co-ordination		P	E

Notes: P, partially; E, enhanced.

211

cut since it involves measures relating to different fields. It is also, by nature, more open-ended than monetary union. The Delors report describes it in terms of four basic elements:

1   the single market within which persons, goods, services and capital can move freely;
2   competition policy and other measures aimed at strengthening market mechanisms;
3   common policies aimed at structural change and regional development;
4   macroeconomic policy co-ordination, including binding rules for budgetary policies.

The precise contents and implications of these measures and policies are discussed below and analysed in various sections of this study. Table 11.1 gives a synthetic presentation of the features of EMU compared with those of the single market programme.

General principles

The above presentation makes clear that the overall conception of EMU aims at a certain balance in the progress towards monetary union on the one hand and economic union on the other. This approach is called parallelism and was stressed by the European Council meeting of Madrid. Other principles to be followed in the design of EMU are subsidiarity and the necessity to allow for specific situations.

Subsidiarity is an important criterion for assigning tasks to the different levels of government in a multi-level government system. In its most general form, it states that a task should be assigned to the lowest level of government unless welfare gains can be reaped by assigning it to a higher level.[2] It is therefore a principle which aims at the decentralization of government functions as long as this is justified on efficiency grounds. In the Community context, the application of this principle should ensure that a policy function is assigned to the Community level only when it can be performed in a more efficient way at that level than by national or local governments.

Application of the principle of subsidiarity in

Table 11.2 The economic meaning of the principle of subsidiarity: assigning tasks to the Community on efficiency grounds

Two economic criteria can be used as necessary conditions for assigning on efficiency grounds a particular policy function to the Community:

(i)   assignment of a policy function at the national level is inefficient because of the existence of cross-country spillovers giving rise to externalities; since national governments do not take fully into account the consequences of their actions on the rest of the Community, they are bound to take suboptimal decisions;

(ii)   the management of a policy function involves indivisibilities and/or economies of scale, which imply that productivity and effectiveness are improved when it is performed at a higher level.

For both criteria it is essential that externalities or economies of scale are significant at the Community level. Environmental effects (e.g. acid rain) provide classic cases of externalities; other examples can also be found in macroeconomic policy. Community-wide economies of scale are apparent in certain research and development investments (e.g. space programmes).

For the assignment to the Community level to be an adequate response, however, it is necessary that two additional conditions are met:

(a)   this assignment is demonstrated to yield net benefits after administrative costs and the balance of government versus market failures are taken into account, and

(b)   *ad hoc* co-ordination among national governments is not sufficient to correct for inefficiencies.

Other motives of assignment of tasks to the Community level can stem from distributional or citizenship considerations, which are not discussed here.

the economic field can be based on the two familiar criteria of cross-country spillovers and economies of scale as discussed in Table 11.2.

The necessity of taking into account the diversity of specific situations refers to the fact that all member states are not at present in the same economic condition, given for example different inflation rates or levels of development.

The remainder of this section analyses the

economic content of EMU and presents the related assumptions upon which this study is based.

Economic union

The economic consequences of 1992 have been evaluated in detail in the study 'The economics of 1992' (*European Economy* 1988a). Table 11.1 summarizes the elements of economic union which were not, or were only partially, part of the single market programme: mainly regional and structural policy on the one hand and macroeconomic coordination on the other.

An important issue for the analysis of EMU is the extent of the integration effects that can be expected from the completion of the internal market. Although persons, goods and services, and capital will be allowed to move freely across frontiers, this does not mean that integration will be perfect from the outset. Effective integration can be expected to lag somewhat behind *de jure* integration. However, a distinction has to be made in this respect between the mobility of capital, goods and persons.

1 Capital mobility across countries can be expected to be almost perfect once exchange controls are removed in the narrow sense that arbitrage equalizes interest rates corrected for the forward exchange discount. This condition, known as covered interest rate parity, means that it becomes theoretically equivalent to borrow in the home currency or to borrow in a foreign currency and to hedge against exchange rate variations. Covered interest rate parity already holds for countries which have removed exchange controls.

Nevertheless, this only means that agents throughout the Community have equal access to lending or borrowing in the same currency whichever currency they choose. But covered interest rate parity does not imply that either nominal or real interest rates are equalized across currencies or that capital circulates across the EC in the same way as within the USA. Without monetary union, agents would still form expectations of exchange rate changes and/or ask for risk premia when they lend in a foreign currency, with the consequence that real interest rates differ across the Community and that cross-country financing is limited by the exchange rate risk. The importance of this remaining barrier is a matter of theoretical and empirical discussion but its existence is indisputable.

Since monetary union would remove this last barrier, it can be assumed that perfect capital mobility would be achieved. Government bonds of the same maturity and risk would become perfect substitutes across the Community. However, domestic and foreign stocks would still be imperfect substitutes because of a different degree of information on domestic and foreign firms. To that extent, some segmentation of capital markets would remain even in EMU (see, for example, Artus 1990).

2 Integration of the markets for goods and services can be expected to increase in the course of the progress towards the single market. Nevertheless, this will be a lengthy process because obstacles to perfect integration not only arise from legal or technical barriers but also from habits of consumers and the behaviour of firms, especially in the service sector where so-called 'non-tradeables' account for a large part of the production. Even for typical manufactured tradeables, integration is far from complete since goods produced in two different member states are imperfect substitutes and consumption structures are still biased towards home goods.[3] This imperfect integration is apparent at the macroeconomic level as the marginal propensity to spend on home country goods is much higher than the marginal propensity to import in most member states (exceptions being the smallest, very open economies).

Imperfect integration has important consequences for the design and properties of an economic and monetary union.[4] First, goods market integration cannot be expected to arbitrage away differences in price levels as would be the case for homogeneous commodities, which means that changes in real exchange rates (i.e. price competitiveness) are still possible within the Community whatever the exchange rate regime. As documented below, the experience of existing monetary unions indicates that, although nominal exchange rates are fixed, real exchange rates can be affected by differentiated movements in domestic prices. Second, such real exchange rate changes remain a necessary component of the national adjustment to policy or non-policy shocks of a domestic or external origin. Third, country-specific shocks can arise in product markets (e.g. a fall in the demand for goods from a given country) or the effect of global shocks can differ across countries.

3 Labour mobility within the Community can also be expected to increase but is bound to remain limited, except for specific skills, owing to cultural and linguistic barriers. Even within member states or within the USA, mobility is actually far from perfect as exemplified by differences in regional unemployment rates. Therefore, at least in the decades ahead, labour market integration will remain limited and, except for certain well-established migration flows, labour mobility between countries cannot be expected to act as a significant equilibrating mechanism within EMU.

A reasonable assumption for EMU is therefore that the degree of integration of markets will be high for capital, still limited but increasing for goods and services and low for labour. This is an important characteristic which, at least in the years existing ahead, will differentiate the Community from economic and monetary unions such as the federal states, whose degree of integration is higher.

Another major difference between EMU and existing monetary unions in federal states will be the degree of centralization of public finance. In modern federal states like the USA, Canada, Australia or Germany, federal government expenditures account for at least half of total government expenditures.[5] This gives to the federal budget, first, the role of reducing automatically regional income differentials (through progressive income taxation and social transfers) and, second, enough weight to be used in aggregate macroeconomic management. Since the Community budget only

amounts to 2 per cent of total EC government expenditures, neither its interregional nor its global function can be compared with that of federal budgets. In so far as shocks affect incomes of member states in an asymmetric way, other adjustment mechanisms will have to take the place of a central budget as an automatic stabilizer. To the extent that aggregate fiscal policy measures are required, most if not all of this policy will have to be implemented through co-ordination among member states.

Monetary union with irrevocably fixed exchange rates

When a monetary union has the form of irrevocably fixed exchange rates, the logical consequences of this definition have to be made clear in order to avoid misunderstandings. 'Irrevocability' of exchange rates has to be taken literally if monetary union is to mean something other than a mere hardening of the EMS.

Three propositions can be made in order to characterize the macroeconomic effects of a monetary union.

1 Irrevocably fixed exchange rates imply nominal interest rates equalization. With perfect capital mobility, nominal interest rates on assets of the same nature, maturity and specific risk can only differ because of (a) expected depreciation and (b) exchange risk premia. Both can only arise to the extent that their irrevocability is not fully credible in the eyes of the markets. Thus, truly irrevocable exchange rates imply the same interest rates across the union.[6] This is a direct consequence of the incompatibility of fixed exchange rates, full capital mobility and autonomy of monetary policies already underlined by the Padoa-Schioppa (1987) report.

2 Irrevocably fixed exchange rates require that national currencies become almost perfect substitutes. Since interest rates are equalized and conversion rates are fixed, the only differences between holding currency x or currency

Table 11.3 Six differences between a single currency and irrevocably fixed exchange rates

---

1 *Transaction costs:* a single currency would eliminate all the costs arising to firms and individuals from conversions from one Community currency into another.

2 *Transparency of prices:* as goods and services would be priced in the same currency, this would further strengthen the pro-competitive effect of the single market.

3 *Economies of scale:* a single currency would lead markets for the same categories of financial instruments to merge, yielding benefits in terms of market depth and efficiency.

4 *Credibility:* a single currency gives from the outset maximum credibility to monetary union.

5 *Visibility:* a single currency would be for all Community agents a visible sign of the creation of EMU and would make those agents more conscious of the associated wage and price discipline.

6 *External benefits:* only with a single currency can the EMU lead to a recasting of international currencies and to a more balanced international monetary regime.

---

y are that (a) the acceptabilities of x and y for transactions differ on their respective territories (in particular owing to legal tender provisions), and (b) conversion of x into y entails transaction costs as long as par-clearing is not established. From a macroeconomic point of view, irrevocably fixed exchange rates are equivalent to a single currency except that the rate of conversion is not one for one.

3 Irrevocably fixed exchange rates imply that monetary policy is put under the control of a single institution. Exchange rates can only be deemed irrevocable if all official monetary institutions within the Community guarantee without limits the conversion of any currency of the system into another at the given rate. Indeed without this multilateral guarantee there would be no difference between monetary union and the unilateral commitments to

exchange rate fixity that are already made within the ERM, albeit whose credibility is hard to achieve and always subject to changes in the judgement of the markets. But this requires giving the responsibility for monetary policy to a single institution, since in the absence of this centralization any creation of money by a national central bank would impact throughout the union without any possibility for another member state to shelter from its consequences. Without a central institution, the system would therefore incorporate a strong incentive for countries to 'free-ride' at the expense of their neighbours, i.e. to expand money supply and seigniorage gains excessively at home without bearing the full associated inflation costs.[7] Even the 'anchor country' of the ERM would lose its monetary autonomy since irrevocably fixed exchange rates would remove all asymmetries within the system.

The macroeconomic implications of a monetary union with irrevocably fixed exchange rates are therefore the same as those of a single currency. In spite of the persistence of national monetary symbols whose denominations and values differ, these in fact become different images of the same currency. In consequence, the discipline imposed upon monetary policy is exactly the same in both cases: there is no room for decentralization and differences in the conduct of monetary policy.[8]

The above propositions are based on the assumption that all agents believe in the irrevocability of exchange rates. However, the nature of the commitments which could lead agents to rule out any possibility of parity changes is not easy to define. Exchange rate credibility can be achieved either through the building of a reputation or through commitments whose breach would be very costly in political and/or economic terms.

Experience shows that reputation building is a lengthy process, and that even long-lasting exchange rate stability does not necessarily lead to the complete disappearance of bond rate differentials. Two relevant experiences are those of the

Netherlands, which since 1983 has maintained a fixed central rate within the ERM with respect to the deutsche mark, and that of Austria which at least since 1981 has pegged its currency to the deutsche mark.[9] Although both countries benefited from particularly good starting conditions because of their size, their economic links with Germany, their inflation record and the autonomy of their central banks, the convergence of bond rates took in both cases several years to be achieved. Moreover, the option of a permanent and unilateral deutsche mark peg is not really available for larger member states like France, Italy, Spain and the UK for obvious economic and political reasons.

Credibility is a direct function of the strength of the commitment to exchange rate fixity and of the difficulty of seceding from the union: tying one's hands, in the words of Giavazzi and Pagano (1988), yields benefits to the country which makes this commitment. In an EMU, an externality is also at work since credibility is a property of the system which is shared by all its members. Commitment can never be absolute, since whatever its technicalities monetary union is the result of a treaty among sovereign states which can always be renounced. However, the institutional setting of a monetary union affects its credibility. As long as currencies as well as national money and bond markets remain distinct – which would be the case with irrevocably fixed rates but not the single currency – it is still possible to leave the system at a moderate economic cost. Moreover, since the existence of separate markets for bonds denominated in different currencies provides a measure of credibility through yield differentials for assets of the same category and risk, the irrevocability of the exchange rates can always be questioned by market forces.

Monetary union with a single currency

Since a strong and binding commitment to exchange rate fixity is a necessary condition of the success of EMU, the question arises how institutional devices could enhance the credibility of this commitment. A natural candidate is the adoption

of a single currency which would replace existing national currencies.[10] Starting with the Werner report, the choice of a single currency has been considered an alternative definition of monetary union, and it has been argued above that both definitions are macroeconomically equivalent, provided that fixed exchange rates are indeed irrevocable. However, a single currency has a number of additional advantages which are discussed throughout this report and summarized in Table 11.3. The only cost it entails, apart from the cost of introducing it, is in effect a benefit: it makes exit from the union very difficult. An early move to a single currency would therefore increase the net benefit of EMU.

The nature of this single currency has to be discussed briefly in order to avoid misunderstandings. Two major questions are first its relation to existing national currencies and second its relation to the present ECU.

As to the relation to existing national currencies, the introduction of a single currency (the ECU) would necessitate in each country a change in the unit of account. The new unit of account could be used for all bank notes and coin in the Community, which would no doubt continue to bear different national symbols (as in the Belgian

Table 11.4 Indicators of city and regional inflation divergence within Canada

Annual rates	1971.I–1979.IV	1980.I–1987.IV
Relative city-consumer prices (eight cities/Toronto)		
(i) average standard deviation	1.1	1.6
(ii) maximum standard deviation	2.2	2.2
Relative provincial GDP deflators (nine provinces/Ontario)		
(i) average	8.6	4.1
(ii) maximum	33.6	11.3

Source: Adapted from Poloz 1990
Note: Based on standard deviations of relative price levels with respect to Toronto for city-CPIs (eight cities) and to the Province of Ontario for provincial GDP deflators (nine provinces).

and Luxembourg francs, or English and Scottish pounds). Alternatively notes and coin could continue to bear their traditional names in each country but would be exchanged one to one for ECUs. Therefore, one franc would be equivalent to one lira or one mark, which would be different names for the ECU. A further alternative is that notes and coins could be denominated in ECU on one side and the national currency name on the other, so long as the same quantity was indicated. There would be no significant economic differences between these alternatives.

As to the relation between the present private ECU and future ECUs, they would be different in that the new ECU would be a full currency instead of a mere financial instrument. Its supply would be under the control of a single institution instead of being the result of separate policies governing the value of the national currencies constituting the basket ECU. Despite this difference, however, the choice of the same unit of account could ensure that at the outset of the monetary union both would have the same value. There would be no change in ECU-denominated contracts.

This study concentrates on the benefits and costs of a full EMU with a single currency. However, specific differences between the single currency and a fixed exchange rate system are discussed throughout the text.

Macroeconomic convergence in EMU

Since EMU will be characterized on the one hand by imperfect economic integration and on the other by a single monetary policy, the issue arises of what degree of price and more generally macroeconomic convergence is required for the stability of EMU.

In existing federal states, inflation can frequently diverge in the short run by a few percentage points. Table 11.4 presents aggregate evidence drawn from the Canadian experience. Because of different local conditions, consumer price inflation varies across cities, while GDP deflators exhibit large spreads across provinces because of different industrial structures (some

provinces being heavily specialized in the production of oil and raw materials). In fact, real exchange rate variability is sometimes even higher within Canada than across ERM countries (see Poloz (1990) for details).

In the long run, however, price inflation does not in general diverge by more than a fraction of a percentage point per year across states or regions. In Europe the monetary unions between Ireland and the UK, and Belgium and Luxembourg, for example, led to almost complete convergence in inflation rates over the long run. From 1950 until 1978 (when the Irish pound ceased to be linked to the UK pound and joined the EMS), the average difference in annual consumer price inflation between Ireland and the UK was less than 0.4 per cent. Similarly, between Luxembourg and Belgium the average difference over the period 1950–88 was about 0.3 per cent per annum.

However, even these small differences in rates of growth of consumer prices can lead to considerable differences in price levels. For the Ireland–UK case the cumulative difference was about 10 per cent (over twenty-eight years) and for the Belgian–

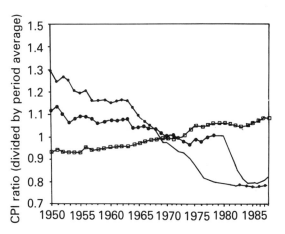

Figure 11.1 Evolution of relative consumer prices in three monetary unions, 1950–88: +, Germany/Netherlands; ◆, UK/Ireland; □, Belgium/Luxembourg. Base period average is unity. Lines with symbols represent periods with constant nominal exchange rates. Lines without symbols represent periods with variable exchange rates

Luxembourg case it was about 15 per cent (over thirty-eight years). Between Germany and the Netherlands there was even a cumulative difference of about 20 per cent for the nineteen years (from 1950 to 1969) during which the exchange rate was fixed. However, this lack of convergence, which became stronger towards the end of the period, might have led to the cut in the link after 1969 (Figure 11.1).

Long-run convergence in inflation is the result of arbitrage in tradeable goods whose price, although not equalized, cannot permanently diverge. There is no equivalent mechanism, however, to foster convergence in the price of non-tradeable goods. Movements of factors of production, i.e. capital and labour, impose some limits to divergences in the price of non-tradeables, but experience shows that this process is very slow. Real estate prices, for example, can diverge considerably inside a monetary union if local growth conditions differ. Convergence does not have to be perfect, therefore, in terms of consumer price inflation and certainly not in terms of the level of consumer prices.[11]

Inflation differentials can even arise from equi-

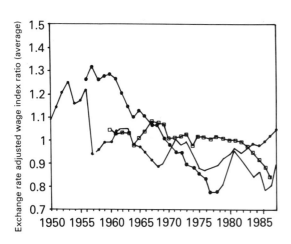

Figure 11.2 Evolution of relative wage levels in three monetary unions, 1950–88: ◇, Germany/Netherlands; +, UK/Ireland; □, Belgium/Luxembourg. Base period average is unity. Lines with symbols represent periods with constant nominal exchange rates. Lines without symbols represent periods with variable exchange rates

librating mechanisms, when the starting point is one of divergence. A well-known example of such a mechanism is the real appreciation of the exchange rate generally experienced by catching-up countries.[12] Although such figures are surrounded with considerable uncertainty, comparison of price levels indicates that in 1989 consumer prices were about 40 per cent below the Community average in Portugal and some 20 per cent below average in Spain.[13] As catching-up proceeds, this gap will narrow through higher inflation in these countries than in the rest of the EC. Assuming, for example, full catching-up and equalization of price levels in twenty years, this would mean that recorded consumer price inflation would each year be 2.5 percentage points higher in Portugal, and about 1 per cent higher in Spain than in the whole Community. It must be stressed, of course, that such differentials would only be warranted to the extent that they went hand in hand with higher productivity gains and growth.

Labour costs also require convergence. But in this area there are even more reasons for national differences in the short and long run since differences in productivity growth rates should be approximately reflected in the growth of real wages. Actually, convergence in labour costs without convergence in productivity could only lead to regional pockets of unemployment and stagnation. It is therefore of paramount importance that regional labour costs remain in line with productivity differentials.

The experience of the three European monetary unions already examined can again be used to illustrate this. The relative wage levels displayed in Figure 11.2 suggest that real wages could diverge by as much as a percentage point per year over long periods of time. This is almost three times higher than the corresponding figure for differences in consumer price inflation mentioned above. For example, wages in Ireland have increased by about 40 percentage points more than in the UK during the period 1950–78, an average difference of more than 1 per cent per annum over this twenty-eight-year period. The difference in the degree of convergence of wages and consumer prices can be seen by comparing Figures 11.1 and 11.2, showing that wages typically diverged more than consumer prices in three cases of intra-European monetary unions.

Since EMU will comprise a group of countries with large initial differences in labour productivity levels, nominal wage increases should diverge as long as productivity grows at different rates. Present GDP per employed person (a rough measure of labour productivity) is estimated to be about 50 per cent of the Community average in Portugal.[14] If this gap were closed in twenty years, real wages could rise annually by 3.5 per cent more in Portugal than in the Community as a whole. German reunification provides an even more striking example: if East German labour productivity were before reunification about 50 per cent of the West German level, a catch-up in about ten years could see wage increases by 7 per cent more each year in East Germany.

The need for convergence in public budget imbalances is more difficult to assess since in existing federal states national or regional deficits (or surpluses) do not in general converge to a common value. Moreover, member states should retain a large autonomy as regards short-run budgetary policy. However, excessive deficits that lead to exploding public debts are not compatible with EMU, essentially because the policy of price stability of the EuroFed might be jeopardized if individual member countries run up excessive public debts or deficits. Co-ordination of fiscal policies among member states would also be required.

The necessary degree of convergence in terms of external current account imbalances is also difficult to assess. Since the current account is identically equal to the difference between overall savings and investment, it is clear that a balanced current account is not always a desirable result. Economies with a low capital–labour ratio and therefore with a relatively large potential for investment would actually gain from being able to finance investment partially through foreign savings, thus running current account deficits. This implies that current account imbalances should not

be a cause for concern if they reflect patterns of this type and are financed automatically through private capital flows, which is in principle the case in a well-functioning EMU with a single currency. However, in the transitional stages current account imbalances will still remain highly visible and might at times signal the need for policy adjustments. It is difficult to decide, *a priori*, whether current accounts disappear as an issue already when capital markets are completely integrated and exchange rate fixity becomes credible, or only when there is a single currency.

A well-functioning EMU does not need only convergence in the macroeconomic performance of its member countries. An efficient management of macroeconomic policy for the union also requires that there is convergence in the policy preferences, or at least agreement on the policy objectives, and therefore on the weighting of targets and the choice of instruments of economic policy. For example, if there is a large, common, inflationary shock, such as an increase in the price of oil, member countries should have a reasonable degree of convergence regarding the desirable degree of smoothing of the consequences of the shock on output and inflation. Otherwise, some countries might, for example, decide to suppress its inflationary consequences using price controls. Ths would inevitably lead to distortions within the single market. However, the same requirement for convergence implies policy autonomy in the use of domestic (e.g. budgetary) instruments while facing asymmetric shocks.

The common goal of price stability is therefore not sufficient by itself to lead to full convergence and ensure a stable EMU. it would need to be underpinned by other fundamental ground rules, such as the 1992 rules for market competition and rules on fiscal discipline. Inside a consistent set of such ground rules (which together may be termed '*Ordnungspolitik*' in German) there would then be room for subsidiarity and competitive processes at the firm and government level. Without a common framework for economic policy, national reactions to large shocks might be fundamentally different and endanger the cohesion of the union.

Stages of EMU

The three-stage approach outlined in the Delors report provides a blueprint for the realization of EMU. Therefore, the precise economic content and implications of each of these stages has to be made explicit. Table 11.5 presents in a simplified fashion the major features of each of those stages. Since stage III is identical to monetary union as already described, the comments below concentrate on stages I and II.

The major decisions to be taken in stage I are already effective since in the economic field the internal market programme is on track, the reform of the structural Funds is in operation and the new decision governing co-ordination and surveillance was finalized in early 1990. In the monetary field capital market liberalization is effective in most member states and monetary co-ordination is being strengthened within the framework of the Committee of Central Bank Governors. The remaining aspects mainly relate to country-specific adjustments, i.e. participation in the ERM, further convergence towards low inflation and budgetary adjustments.

In contrast with stage I, which is basically defined in economic terms, stage II is mainly institutional in nature. It is meant to be a transitional stage only. The Delors report placed emphasis on the gradual transfer in stage II of responsibility for monetary policy. After discussion, the emphasis has since been placed more on the technical preparation of the EuroFed institution in stage II, on the grounds that policy responsibility must be clear cut. For this reason it is now widely considered that stage II should be quite short.

The economic logic of stage II is that of a transition between an asymmetric system where monetary policy is co-ordinated through the exchange markets and a system in which monetary policy is set at the Community level and exchange markets lose their co-ordination function. The single most important step in this process is the irrevocable fixing of parities at the outset of stage III.

The economic and monetary content of stage III has already been described. On the economic side application of the principle of subsidiarity results in an evolutionary set of policy responsibilities, with considerable room for debate and experimentation over the best regime at any one time. This concerns especially the rules and competences of national and EC budgets.

The timing of the transition through the stages is largely a matter for political choice, although

Table 11.5 Major features of the three stages of economic and monetary union

Economic	Monetary
Stage I	
Completion of the internal market	Capital market liberalization
Strengthened competition policy	Enhanced monetary and exchange rate co-ordination
Full implementation of the reform of the structural Funds	Realignments possible, but infrequent
	All EC currencies in the narrow-band ERM
Enhanced co-ordination and surveillance	Extended use of the ECU
Budgetary adjustments in high debt/deficit countries	
Stage II	
Evaluation and adaptation of stage I policies	Establishment of EuroFed
Review of national macroeconomic adjustments	Possible narrowing of EMS bands
Stage III	
Definitive budgetary co-ordination system	EuroFed in charge of monetary policy
Possible strengthening of structural and regional policies	Irrevocably fixed exchange rates or ECU as single currency

pure cost–benefit considerations tend to argue in favour of a rapid move toward full EMU. However, the speed of this convergence will depend heavily on the timing and credibility of the political commitments to move to stages II and III.

Alternatives to EMU

Against what benchmark situation should the effects of EMU be assessed? This question is less obvious than it seems at first sight since the situation of today cannot be taken as a stable point of reference for two reasons: first, decisions have been taken whose effects are not yet visible, e.g. regarding the completion of the internal market and capital market liberalization; second, commitments have been made which are not yet translated into effective decisions, e.g. the British commitment to participate in the ERM during stage I. The present situation can therefore only be viewed as a snapshot in an ongoing process. Choosing this situation as a baseline would not be satisfactory. It would in addition introduce somewhat artificial differences among member states depending on their present situation within or with respect to the ERM. This section reviews the alternative baselines against which EMU can be evaluated.

Stage I as a baseline

A natural starting point for comparisons is stage I, or an 'EMS + 1992' hypothetical baseline, which is assumed to incorporate all the effects of decisions and commitments described in the first part of Table 11.5. This is the basic hypothesis which is retained throughout this study, although comparisons are in some cases also made with alternative baselines. Given the importance of the 1992 programme in this regard, a relatively large part of economic union effects are therefore already present. Most of the additional gains from EMU would thus arise from progress in the monetary field, whose effects may be evaluated against a clear and uniform benchmark.

Since stage I is not yet observed, assumptions have to be made regarding its functioning. Major

issues regard (1) its basic monetary logic, (2) the practice of realignments and (3) the microeconomic and macroeconomic effects of capital market liberalization.

1 As to its basic monetary logic, stage I would not be very different from the EMS of the late 1980s. As in any other fixed-but-adjustable exchange rate system, one can assume that it will remain asymmetric in the sense that one particular national central bank acts as a *de facto* leader. Whether this 'anchor country' would be Germany as in the 1980s or whether a competition for the leadership might arise is an open issue. Whichever the leader, however, the logic of such a system is that overall monetary policy is set by a particular central bank, while the policy of the $N − 1$ other members is devoted to the peg of the exchange rate. Therefore, as long as central parities remain fixed, the only room for manoeuvre for autonomous monetary policies is provided by the possibility of exchange rate movements within the bands.

This relates to the monetary logic of a fixed-but-adjustable exchange rate system without capital controls. Admittedly, monetary policy coordination could become more symmetric in the perspective of EMU through informal co-operation among central banks, as a preparation for stages II and III. However, for the evaluation of EMU, stage I has to be regarded as much as possible as a steady state, setting aside features that would stem from future developments of EMU.

2 The most uncertain issue concerning the evolution of the EMS in stage I concerns the practice of realignments. Two extreme models are (a) some kind of loosely defined soft EMS, and (b) a *de facto* monetary union where realignments would become exceptional, an image of which can be provided by the present situation between Germany and the Netherlands.[15] Capital market liberalization within the context of a fixed-but-adjustable exchange rate system points in the direction of the second model: realignments would still be possible, but since anticipated realignments can give rise to potentially unlimited capital move-

ments, one cannot assume that this instrument can be used by governments systematically.

Realignments come onto the agenda when countries either are characterized by different inflation trends or are subject to country-specific shocks. Whether or not significant differences in inflation trends could still be compensated by periodic realignments in stage I is in principle an open issue. The disciplinary effect of the EMS has proved effective since the second half of the 1980s when realignments became rare and compensated only half of the inflation differentials (Table 11.6). This is widely considered to be a major factor of inflation convergence within the narrow-band ERM. This record should continue with the removal of the last capital controls, for the only way to discourage speculative attacks is (i) to make the realignments rare and randomly distributed, (ii) to offset inflation differentials only partially and (iii) to avoid discrete jumps in the market exchange rate, i.e. to realign inside the band. Since the first two are costly in terms of relative prices while the third either implies a renunciation of the EMS (if bands are so wide that the system becomes closer to a flexible rate system) or frequent realignments, these techniques cannot really accommodate large and permanent inflation

differentials. This is the reason for expecting further inflation convergence in stage I.[16] Actually, there is already a clear tendency within the core ERM towards a *de facto* narrowing of the bands of fluctuation *vis-à-vis* the deutsche mark.

An opposite strand of arguments states that capital controls, by allowing for delayed realignments and therefore real exchange rate appreciations in the more inflationary countries, were a key component of inflation discipline in the EMS. Another argument states that exchange rate credibility would lead to a decrease in nominal interest rates in inflationary countries, thereby leading to low real interest rates and a weakening of inflation discipline (see Giavazzi and Giovannini 1989; Giavazzi and Spaventa 1990). Those arguments, however, can only be considered of some validity in the short run. They do not demonstrate how large differences in trend inflation could be accommodated at low cost within a stage I EMU without leading to speculative attacks. Therefore it can be considered that, with regard to inflation discipline, the implications of stage I would not be very different from those of a full EMU.

However, realignments might still be possible in the case of country-specific shocks, provided those shocks are unexpected. A country hit, for example,

Table 11.6 Realignments in the European Monetary System, 1979–89 (*vis-à-vis* the deutsche mark)

	British pound	Danish krone	French franc	Irish pound	Italian lira	Dutch guilder	Narrow band	ERM
1979–83								
Number of realignments	5	7	4	4	5	2	22	27
Average size (per cent)	4.9	4.4	7.1	5.2	6.3	2	5.1	5.3
Average cumulated price differential	1.65	3.1	6.7	12.0	9.8	1.0	5.0	5.9
Degree of offsetting (per cent)	296.6	139.8	105.4	43.5	64.4	203.2	101.2	89.7
1984–7								
Number of realignments	2	2	2	3	3	–	9	12
Average size (per cent)	1.5	2.5	4.5	4.7	4.7	–	3.5	3.8
Average cumulated price differential	5.3	6.8	8.3	6.1	9.3	–	6.6	7.3
Degree of offsetting (per cent)	28.5	36.5	54.5	77.2	50.7	–	52.7	52.1

Source: Commission services

Note: All data refer to bilateral deutsche mark exchange rates. Cumulated price differentials (CPI, monthly data) are measured between two realignments. Offsetting of inflation differentials is measured by the ratio of central rate variation to the price differential by the time of the realignment.

by a fall in the demand for its exports (a demand shock) or a surge in nominal wages (a supply shock) could use the exchange rate instrument in order to modify its real exchange rate or to accommodate the inflationary shock. This is where stage I would retain nominal exchange rate flexibility that would be lost in the full EMU.

3 Capital market liberalization is already in effect for most countries; however, its full impact is not yet observed. It will not only affect potential short-term capital movements, but also the integration of financial markets. One can therefore expect the supply of financial products to increase, presumably providing larger hedging opportunities, and also some reduction in transaction and hedging costs because of economies of scale, technological change and greater competition (see *European Economy* 1988b; Gros 1990). Although the extent of these microeconomic effects cannot be assessed with precision, they have to be taken into account in the cost–benefit evaluation of EMU.[17]

Summing up, the following hypotheses are made regarding stage I.

1 The working of the exchange rate system will remain asymmetric, with an anchor country setting the overall monetary policy while the $N - 1$ others are co-ordinated through the exchange markets.

2 Exchange rate discipline in stage I will see further convergence towards low inflation, practically eliminating trend differences in inflation rates which do not arise from equilibrating mechanisms. However, realignments would still be an available instrument in the case of unexpected country-specific shocks.

3 The removal of capital controls will yield savings in transaction and hedging costs as well as a closer integration of capital markets, but will fall short of what a genuine EMU would bring.

The above characterization of stage I is based on the assumption that it is stable, at least as a transitional stage. However, this stability has been

questioned by a number of authors, either directly or with reference to the 'evolutionary approach to EMU', proposed in 1989 by the British government (UK Treasury 1989), which bears close resemblance to a protracted stage I. It is argued that stage I can be considered stable as long as economic policies in the member states are consistent with the constraints of the system, but that 'systemic instability' could arise from a refusal of the asymmetric character of the system or from a competition for leadership. Indeed, the stability of a stage I lasting for a few years and considered to be a transition towards full EMU and that of the same system without the prospect of moving on to the definitive EMU are two different issues: as long as governments and agents expect a new regime to be established in the near future, their behaviour is conditioned accordingly. Historically, the coexistence of fixed exchange rates and completely free capital movements never lasted for very long (see Carli 1989; Giovannini 1989). It cannot be taken for granted that a renunciation of EMU would not, sooner or later, lead some countries to opt for more exchange rate flexibility or, alternatively, to reintroduce some capital controls. Therefore, the costs and benefits of EMU have to be discussed in the wider context of the possible alternative choices of exchange rate regimes.

Alternative exchange rate regimes

The well-known inconsistency between financial integration, fixed exchange rates and monetary policy autonomy provides an appropriate starting point for the discussion of the alternatives to EMU. All three objectives are legitimate, the first two because of the economic benefits they yield and the third because policy autonomy is, *ceteris paribus*, desirable on subsidiarity grounds. A tri-dimensional trade-off is therefore at work, which can be represented by Figure 11.3 (adapted from Aglietta 1988). The three objectives are represented along the three axes of the figure. Any point within the triangle can therefore be characterized by the degree to which each of these objectives is fulfilled. The three sides of the triangle are each

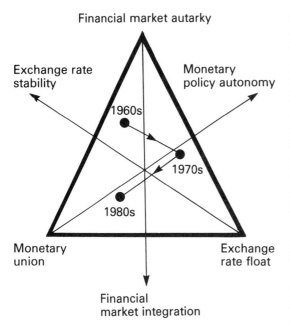

Financial market autarky

Exchange rate
stability

Monetary
policy autonomy

1960s

1970s

1980s

Monetary
union

Exchange
rate float

Financial
market integration

Figure 11.3 A graphical representation of alternative
exchange rate regimes

characterized by complete fulfilment of one particular condition. Its three corners correspond to
situations where two conditions are simultaneously fulfilled, the third being excluded:

1   financial market autarky (complete fixity of
    exchange rate and policy autonomy, but total
    control of capital movements; current account
    imbalances are settled through official bi-
    lateral capital transactions);
2   exchange rate float (complete financial inte-
    gration and autonomy, with exchange rate
    determined by the market without any unsteri-
    lized intervention);
3   monetary union (complete financial integra-
    tion and exchange rate fixity, with zero policy
    autonomy).

The evolution of the exchange rate regimes
within the Community can be illustrated on the
figure. The compromise of the 1960s was characterized by low financial integration due to widespread capital controls and high exchange rate
stability. The breakdown of the Bretton Woods

system led to greater autonomy at the expense of
exchange rate stability, and while the 1970s
witnessed to some extent greater financial integration, some countries reverted to capital controls
to prevent exchange rate crisis. The creation of the
EMS in 1979 has been a reaction to this experience
as well as a statement of preference for exchange
rate stability, and the 1980s have been characterized by both greater exchange rate fixity and
greater financial integration (at the expense of
autonomy). Stage I basically represents a continuation of this trend. This is also the case for full
EMU.

Neither financial autarky nor a clean float
represent real alternatives to EMU. It is hard to
imagine why and how European governments
would choose to renounce the benefits of a
Community-wide financial market or to abandon
their aim of exchange rate stability after the
successes of the EMS. Both moves would represent
a dramatic reversal of the historical trend.
However, the two cases are useful benchmarks for
a discussion of the costs and benefits of EMU.

The 'hard ECU' proposal

Another proposal which has been put forward in
the summer of 1990 as an alternative to the Delors
Committee approach is the 'hard ECU' of the UK
Chancellor of the Exchequer.

In this case the ECU would be developed as a
parallel currency managed by a new institution,
which could be called the EMF. As a first step, the
Chancellor proposes setting up a new institution
(the EMF) to act as a currency board and provide
ECU bank notes on demand for Community
currencies. To ensure no new money creation,
EMF ECU notes would have to be fully backed by
its own holdings of component currencies. The
ECU would remain a basket currency, with its
interest and exchange rates being determined as
now.

A further step would involve a switch from a
basket ECU to a 'hard ECU', managed by the
EMF, which would fully feature in the EMS on
equal terms with other currencies, staying within

ERM margins and never being devalued at realignments in relation to any Community currency. The EMF would issue hard ECU deposits in the Community only in return for national currencies. Any excess of national currencies held by the EMF would have to be repurchased by the central banks concerned for hard currencies. The hard ECU is intended specifically to strengthen the pressures for anti-inflationary convergence in the Community by putting it at the centre of the EMS.

The hard ECU plan represents a considerable development of the previous position expressed by the Treasury (UK Treasury 1989): it acknowledges the need for a new Community monetary institution and allows for the possibility of a single currency at the end of the process.

An assessment of the benefits and costs of the hard ECU proposal must take into account its uncertain evolution. To its proponent, this uncertainty is one of its main attractions, since it stems from the freedom of choice over whether to use the hard ECU, which is left to the markets. This means that, in relation to the existing situation, no economic agent has to undergo extra costs by using the hard ECU, since national currencies remain as alternatives. On the other hand, this uncertainty also means unpredictable currency substitution possibilities. This could have costs in terms of macroeconomic stability, with monetary control made more difficult.

As regards the hard ECU's likely economic impact, this would of course depend on whether it was actually taken up and used in macroeconomically significant amounts: clearly, if the amounts used were small, the effects would be very slight.

If, however, the hard ECU were to become widely used, its impact may be considered in terms of the effects discussed in this chapter. To the extent that the hard ECU were used for international commerce and achieved the economies of scale observed with major currencies, there could be savings in transaction costs for some users. However, these costs would not be eliminated as with a single currency. Similarly some exchange rate uncertainty would remain. While the mechanism contains an incentive in favour of stability-oriented macroeconomic policies, it is not clear that this would add to the disciplines already experienced by currencies that participate in the narrow band of the exchange rate mechanism of the EMS (or the incentive to be faced by the other Community countries when they put their currencies into the narrow band). It is likely to be in the least convergent countries that the use of the hard ECU would grow fastest. If in some countries the hard ECU acquired a significant market share in relation to the national currency, there would arise the question of what the denominator would be for domestic wage and price contracts. Presumably this transitional stage would also mean considerable uncertainty for economic agents, until the time came for the switch to a single currency. Externally, the hard ECU could take on a wider international role, but not to the extent that a single Community currency would.

THE ECONOMIC IMPACT OF EMU

The aim of the present section is to outline the costs and benefits of EMU as well as to discuss the methods and techniques of their evaluation: the following subsection reviews the theoretical aspects, and the next subsection the nature of costs and benefits, together with the more technical questions of economic evaluation and measurement.

The basic message of this investigation is that both because of the present state of the theory of monetary unification and because of the diversity of the effects involved, an overall quantitative evaluation of the gains from EMU would be both out of reach and inappropriate. The present study has accordingly the more modest aim of proposing a framework for the analysis of the economics of EMU and of providing some partial quantifications. However, qualitative conclusions can be drawn from a comprehensive approach to the costs and benefits of EMU.

Building blocks for the analysis of EMU

In contrast with the trade field, where standard

economic theory has for long offered straight-forward arguments in favour of trade liberalization and economic integration more generally, the analysis of EMU cannot be based on a simple, unified, ready-to-use theory of the benefits of monetary integration. The two issues of economic integration and monetary integration are indeed treated very differently in economic theory. The case for economic integration is based on a unified and secure microeconomic approach since, whatever the latest developments in the theory of international trade, the basic rationale for the internal market programme is still rooted in the approaches of Adam Smith and David Ricardo.[18] Monetary integration, however, immediately raises a more complex set of theoretical and empirical issues.[19]

This may seem paradoxical since, as pointed out by various authors (e.g. Krugman 1989a; Baldwin 1990), the use of a single money seems to be as essential to the unification of the US internal market as the absence of any direct or indirect trade barriers. Though the diversity of industrial structures among US states or regions is as great as among the member states of the Community, the idea of appreciating the Texas dollar when the price of oil rises, or depreciating the Michigan dollar when Detroit is outpriced by Japanese car exports, sounds as pointless as introducing custom duties inside the US market. The same applies to other federal states, which without exception have chosen to have a single currency. History also shows that monetary unification has most frequently gone hand in hand with trade integration.[20] One could therefore expect economic theory to provide the rationale for these empirical observations.

There is indeed a theory whose aim is to aid the analysis of monetary integration: the theory of optimum currency areas developed in the 1960s by Robert Mundell, Ronald McKinnon and others. The basic insight of this approach is that the adoption of a single currency involves a trade-off between, on the one hand, the benefits arising from monetary integration and, on the other hand, the costs incurred when the exchange rate is lost as an adjustment instrument. This insight remains valid

and is taken as a basis for the present study. However, a precise and comprehensive identification of those costs and benefits is not provided by the theory of optimum currency areas, since (i) some of the benefits associated with monetary unification are assumed without further investigation, while others are simply omitted, and (ii) the framework for the analysis of costs is rather limited and outdated. The most well-known conclusion of this approach, namely that labour mobility across an area is the essential criterion for deciding whether monetary union is desirable, appears to be largely overstated in early formulations of the theory, at least as regards the EC. Moreover, economic theory has evolved substantially in several relevant branches since the early 1960s (Table 11.7), but the revision of the theory of optimal currency areas has not kept up with this. Thus, the analysis of EMU does not need to be limited to this rather narrow approach.

Recent developments in several branches of economics provide elements of a comprehensive approach to the costs and benefits of EMU.

1   Although almost no recent research has been specifically devoted to the microeconomics of monetary union – except the contribution by R. Baldwin – some recent developments in the microeconomics of imperfect markets (i.e. in the presence of externalities, or adjustment and information costs) lead to a better if still incomplete understanding of the channels through which the adoption of a single currency would provide output and welfare gains (Baldwin 1990).

2   A large body of literature has been devoted to the question of the choice of an optimal exchange rate policy for a small economy in a stochastic environment, and thus in an environment of random disturbances.[21] The issue is which monetary and exchange rate policy performs best for reducing aggregate macroeconomic variability, i.e. insulates the economy better from the effects of shocks. This line of research has established (i) that the choice between exchange rate regimes not

Table 11.7 Economic and monetary union and the theory of optimum currency areas

---

The theory of optimum currency areas was developed in the 1960s in order to determine what should be the appropriate domain within which exchange rates are fixed. (Major contributions include Mundell (1961), McKinnon (1963) and Kenen (1969). For more recent surveys, see Ishiyama (1975) and Wihlborg and Willett (1990).)

The question relates to the debate at that time between the proponents of exchange rate fixity and those of floating exchange rates. The basic argument for floating was twofold: first that exchange rate changes were a less costly way of correcting current account imbalances, and more generally of adjusting relative prices between two countries when prices are sticky, and second that it would allow countries to pursue independent macroeconomic policies (e.g. to choose different inflation rates) (see, for example, Friedman 1953).

The optimum currency areas approach uses an implicit stabilization framework and introduces the issues of asymmetries and alternative adjustment channels when countries face exogenous shocks. Mundell (1961) points out that exchange rate flexibility is of no use between the USA and Canada if, due to a shock to the industrial structure, both countries are hurt by a shift in the relative economic conditions of their eastern and western parts. What is needed instead is a change in the relative prices of eastern and western products. Therefore, the right criterion for designing a currency area should be the degree of factor (capital, i.e. physical investment, and labour) mobility within the region, since a high degree of factor mobility would provide the adjustment channel which is lost in a fixed exchange rate regime. It was precisely because of a low labour mobility within Europe that Meade (1957) argued that exchange rates should remain flexible within that zone. It became conventional wisdom to say that Europe was *not* an optimum currency area.

Although the overall approach remains a useful starting point, this conclusion only holds within a specific and rather limited framework whose adequacy for today's analysis is questionable. First, the microeconomic benefits of a monetary union are simply assumed without further exploration: in Mundell's words, 'money is a convenience and this restricts the optimum number of currencies'. Second, although labour mobility across Europe remains low – but it is also limited within the USA – the mobility of both physical and especially financial capital is now much higher than in the early 1960s. As pointed out by Ingram (1959, 1973), the degree of international financial integration has to be introduced as a specific criterion and the alternative adjustment channel of cross-country financing has therefore to be taken into account. Third, Mundell's implicit framework is a world of rigid wages and prices. Although wage–price stickiness is still a fact of life, their rigidity could be less than in Mundell's framework, and the possibility of market adjustments has to be considered. Fourth, there is the implicit assumption that no inefficiencies arise from flexible exchange rates, such as because of instability in the exchange markets and non-co-operative or suboptimal policies. Obviously this can no longer be considered an acceptable hypothesis in the light of recent experience.

Fifth, the whole approach ignores policy credibility issues which have been stressed by recent macroeconomic theory. Sixth, the theory of optimum currency treats the whole area as a small country within a given world and thus it ignores the external effects of monetary integration.

The approaches of McKinnon (1963) and Kenen (1969) to this same topic are different. McKinnon points out that if exchange rate changes are used to offset the effects of domestic demand shocks on the current account, price instability is bound to increase in line with the degree of openness (or the share of tradeables in production) in a floating rates regime. This is particularly relevant within the EC and is a major reason behind the long-standing choice of a peg system by smaller open economies like the Netherlands and Belgium. Moreover, Krugman (1989a), building on this argument, argues that the costs of monetary union decrease and the benefits increase with the intensity of trade within the currency area. Kenen focuses on the degree of product diversification and argues that countries characterized by a low degree of diversification should retain exchange rate flexibility in order to offset product-specific shocks, while a high degree of product diversification, by averaging product-specific shocks, could compensate for low labour mobility. In practice EC countries typically have highly diversified industrial structures.

Summing up, the optimum currency area approach provides useful insights but cannot be considered a comprehensive framework in which the costs and benefits of EMU can be analysed. Empirical applications of this approach are scarce and hardly conclusive.

---

only depends on the pattern of shocks (domestic or foreign, real or monetary) affecting the economy but also on the degree of wage–price indexation, and that with full and instantaneous indexation there is no difference whatsoever between fixed and floating rates, and (ii) that neither fixed nor floating exchange rates are generally optimal, but rather that some country-dependent mix of the two regimes is preferable.[22]

3   Applications of game theory in the field of macroeconomic policy have led to emphasis on issues in the choice of an exchange rate regime which had for long been stressed by policy-makers but were largely ignored by the literature of the 1960s. This approach leads to questioning the standard policy autonomy argument in favour of flexible exchange rates from two different angles. First, this autonomy might not be optimal from a political economy point of view, e.g. if domestic monetary authorities suffer from low credibility.[23] In such instances, policy discipline through the pegging of the exchange rate to a hard currency can be a short cut to a long and painful reputation building. This line of research appears to be especially relevant in the European case since, for several countries, membership of the ERM has been perceived as a way to borrow the credibility of the Bundesbank.[24] Second, the risks of suboptimal outcomes when monetary policies separately aim at contradictory results have been stressed by the literature on policy co-ordination.[25]

4   Another domain of research concerns the relative performance of alternative monetary arrangements at the world level. Two decades of disappointing experience with floating exchange rates have stimulated new research on the causes of exchange rate instability and on possible remedies.[26] This research is of special relevance in the European case since the creation of EMU would bring more symmetry in the international monetary system and could therefore be a building block for wider changes in this system.

5   Last but not least, there is already a substantial and growing body of research on the economics of EMU which draws on all the above theories, and of which the papers presented in 'The economics of EMU' (*European Economy* 1990) offer an up-to-date sample.

These developments in economic research do not yet provide an integrated approach to monetary union. One might doubt they ever will, since very different fields of economic theory are involved in the analysis of EMU: microeconomic efficiency has little to do with stability in a stochastic environment or with the rules-versus-discretion debate in macroeconomic policy. Recent contributions which, in the spirit of the optimum currency area approach, attempt to isolate a trade-off in the choice for or against EMU (seigniorage versus transaction costs or insulation from shocks versus time inconsistency)[27] only highlight partial aspects of the choice problem raised by EMU. In any case, much more research has to be done before these different branches can be linked together within a unified model of the welfare effects of international money.

However, empirical analysis can obtain results from these various fields as building blocks for a comprehensive approach to EMU. As detailed below, it turns out that this approach leads to basing the case for EMU on a much broader framework of analysis than that provided by the theory of optimal currency areas.

Before turning in more detail to the nature of costs and benefits, three important methodological points have to be made.

1   A number of questions arise whose answers rely on different paradigms. The use of a single currency yields efficiency gains which are of much the same nature as those arising from the elimination of physical and technical barriers to trade. The natural framework for the analysis of these effects is the classical microeconomic paradigm of competitive markets and flexible prices. The costs of losing the exchange rate instrument, however, only

arises in a world of imperfect integration and sticky prices, i.e. within a Keynesian paradigm, since the whole macroeconomic issue of choice of an exchange rate regime is irrelevant if markets are perfectly integrated and prices fully flexible. Finally, the analysis of the credibility of EMU and of its effects for inflation discipline has to be based on a third paradigm, where considerations of political economy play an important role, together with theories of expectations and strategic behaviour. In all, therefore, one has to accept a somewhat eclectic approach.

2   In view of the present state of the theory, an attempt to make an overall quantitative evaluation of the costs and benefits of EMU would hardly be meaningful. Some of the effects that can be expected from EMU cannot be quantified yet, and others would only be evaluated with a considerable margin of uncertainty. For example, few results are available regarding the welfare costs of inflation, despite the fact that most economists and policy-makers agree on the importance of these effects. Moreover, the lack of a unified theory would raise problems of inconsistency in the aggregation of effects of a different nature. This does not preclude partial quantifications, and indeed several such assessments of specific effects are given throughout this chapter.

3   Reliance on the most recent literature has the advantage of bringing in the most recent insights of current research, but also has its cost: results can be model dependent, and are therefore less secure and widely accepted than with established theories. Empirical assessments also remain fragile and are frequently disappointing.

Costs and benefits

According to the method sketched out above, the present cost–benefit analysis of EMU is based on the combination of different approaches. The aim of this section is to present in more detail the categorization of effects and the methodology of the present study.

Direct and indirect effects of EMU

The final economic impacts of EMU will arise both directly from changes in the economic system of the Community and indirectly through policy and behavioural changes induced by the systemic changes. Although this is not a watertight distinction since any change immediately impacts on the system as a whole, it is important to sort out indirect effects from direct ones since the latter are unconditional while the former are conditional on the policy stance of EuroFed and national fiscal authorities and on the modifications in the behaviour of private agents that can be expected from both systemic and policy changes. For example, savings in transaction costs are an unconditional consequence of the adoption of a single currency which directly affects economic efficiency, while price stability is conditional on the policy of EuroFed and on wage and price discipline.

It could be argued that those effects which are conditional on the quality of economic policies should not be assessed as arising from EMU *per se*: whatever the institutional design of the system, it cannot be taken for granted that it will lead to more appropriate policies. However, as discussed above, policy discipline effects cannot be ignored as they are an integral part of the motives behind the choice of EMU. Indeed, it is well known that any exchange rate regime has disciplinary effects on economic policies, and this has for long been considered one of the prominent aspects of the choice of an exchange rate regime.

What can be expected is that an adequate design of the institutional system, notably in the statutes of EuroFed or in the framework for budgetary policies, will yield benefits either because of a greater effectiveness of Community and national policies or through a removal of the inefficiencies associated with low policy credibility, which have a strong impact on expectations and risk premia incorporated in interest rates and other

Table 11.8 Major categories of effects of economic and monetary union

	Nature of the final impact	Main channels of action	
		Direct	*Indirect*
Microeconomic efficiency	Steady-state level of output and income in the Community	Savings in transaction and hedging costs Disappearance of exchange rate uncertainty and instability	Strengthening of the internal market Integration of goods and capital markets Effects of lower uncertainty on the riskiness of investment Induced dynamic effects Seigniorage revenue losses for some member states Effects on taxation and provision of public goods
Macroeconomic stability	Steady-state rate of inflation Variability of output and inflation, with associated consequences for welfare	Loss of an adjustment instrument for asymmetric shocks Disappearance of non-cooperative exchange rate policies Greater availability of external financing	Price stability as consequence of EuroFed policy Sound, co-ordinated fiscal policies
Regional equity	Distributional effects among member states and regions	Spatial distribution of direct micro and macro gains	Differentiated impacts of EMU depending on initial macroeconomic conditions and economic policy strategies
External effects	Both micro and macro effects for the Community	Additional savings on transaction costs, revenues from international seigniorage and reduction in the need for exchange reserves	Better co-ordination internationally Changes in the international monetary system
Transitional effects	Changes in the macroeconomic transition path towards EMU	Disinflation costs Costs of fiscal adjustment	Drop in real interest rates Effects on the dollar–ECU exchange rate

financial variables. An independent EuroFed with a clear mandate to achieve price stability would inherit the reputation of the most stability-oriented central banks of the Community. As to the budgetary regime, governments should retain fiscal flexibility for stabilization and adjustment purposes, but as public debt monetization would be ruled out, the avoidance of unsustainable fiscal positions would become an absolute requirement. There would also be a strengthening of co-ordination and surveillance procedures.

Throughout this study, it has been assumed that EuroFed would fulfil its mandate to aim at price stability. Regarding budgetary policies, it is generally assumed that member states would not depart from disciplined policies. As the importance of these and of other explicit policy assumptions is highlighted when needed in the text, the reader should be able to distinguish between direct and indirect effects of EMU.

The same kind of issues arise for behavioural changes. It is well known that the behaviour of private agents cannot be supposed to remain invariant with respect to systemic or policy regime changes. Wage-bargaining and price-setting behaviours, for example, are not independent from the policy of the central bank. However, there is no sure way to identify precisely the consequences of EMU on agents' behaviour, and excessive reliance on behavioural changes could also be misleading.

In most of this chapter, behaviour has only been supposed to be affected through the impact of the exchange rate and monetary policy regime on expectations. This means, for example, that wage-setting behaviour is supposed to be changed in so far as price expectations would be modified by the exchange rate and policy regime.[28] This assumption is warranted since EMU will not be a mere unilateral commitment to exchange rate stability, but rather an institutional change whose impact should be clear for all agents (especially with the adoption of a single currency). It has also been assumed that the policy of EuroFed would be as credible to the public as the policy of the more stability-oriented central banks of the Community.

The distinction between direct and indirect effects, which refers to the channels of action, should not be mistaken for that between static and dynamic effects, which refers to the time dimension. Static effects are supposed to arise at the outset of EMU, or possibly with some lag. These are for instance savings on transaction costs or the benefits of stable prices. Dynamic effects are those which only build up progressively over time, because capital accumulation or other stock adjustments are involved. They translate into an increase in the rate of economic growth for a substantial period. This is the case for the effects of a lower riskiness of investment, but it also arises when hysteresis is at work, as for example in the emergence of the ECU as a major international currency.[29]

Costs and benefits in outline

Regarding the permanent effects of EMU, three major categories of final impacts have been distinguished which relate to microeconomic efficiency, macroeconomic stability and regional equity. In addition, EMU will give rise to important transitional effects, mainly of a macroeconomic nature. Costs and benefits of EMU, grouped in these four major categories, are summarized in Table 11.8. For clarity, external effects resulting from the consequences of EMU for the Community's relations with the rest of the world are presented separately from purely internal effects, although they have the same type of final impact.

1 Microeconomic efficiency effects are basically of the same nature as those arising from the completion of the internal market (see *European Economy* 1988a). They proceed from two microeconomic phenomena in the monetary field (the disappearance of exchange rate uncertainty and transaction costs) and one in the economic field (measures to strengthen the internal market, e.g. competition policy). Although, as detailed in Baldwin (1990), the microeconomics of monetary union raise difficult technical issues, the basic logic is straightforward: EMU yields (i) direct benefits arising from savings on transaction and hedging costs; (ii) indirect benefits due to the impact on trade, cross-border investment and capital flows of the disappearance of exchange rate barriers; and (iii) further dynamic benefits due to the impact on domestic investment decisions of an overall reduction in uncertainty (conditional on the stability gains brought by EuroFed policy).

Efficiency gains are microeconomic in nature but would obviously translate into macroeconomic effects. They can ultimately be expected to raise the level of output and real income in the Community permanently because of a higher overall factor productivity and a higher capital stock, in the same way as the completion of the internal market is expected to yield output and income gains. During the transition to this higher steady state, growth would be increased.

231

According to 'new growth models', there is even the possibility of a sustained rise in the GDP growth rate of the Community. This remains a conjecture, however (Baldwin and Lyons 1990).

As for any efficiency gains, there will also be temporary negative effects and adjustments in the short run, for example as the foreign exchange activities of banks decrease.

To a large extent, gains of this category are not conditional on macroeconomic policies. Some would nevertheless disappear if inadequate policies were to give rise to macroeconomic instability. In addition, for EMU to yield efficiency gains in the medium run, real exchange rate levels within the Community have to be consistent with economic fundamentals. Although an initial misalignment could be eventually corrected through relative price movements without changing the nominal exchange rate, it could in the meantime have severe welfare-reducing effects. It is therefore important that initial levels are in line with fundamentals. This assumption is maintained throughout this chapter.

In addition to its effects on the private sector, EMU will also affect taxation and the provision of public goods and more generally public sector efficiency.

2 Macroeconomic stability effects are of a different nature. These effects concern the variability of macroeconomic variables, both nominal and real. Variability arises as a consequence of policy and non-policy shocks of a domestic (e.g. non-permanent changes in the behaviour of private agents) or external (e.g. a change in a partner country's economic policy) origin. This is an important topic for two reasons. First, variability in macroeconomic variables like the price level, inflation,[30] GDP and employment is welfare reducing *per se* for risk-averse agents, even if their average level remains unaffected (Table 11.9). Second, aggregate variability also permanently influences the level of output, at least if it goes with greater uncertainty, because it reduces the information content of prices and leads to an increase in risk premia (Baldwin 1990).

Regarding stability, EMU yields both perma-nent costs and benefits. The net impact in terms of macroeconomic stability in EMU is therefore an empirical issue. The main costs arise from the loss of a policy instrument for stabilization. Once exchange rates are irrevocably fixed, national monetary policies can no longer be used to cushion the effects of asymmetric disturbances, either through market adjustments (as in a floating rate regime) or through discretionary exchange rate adjustments (as in the EMS). In this respect the loss of the monetary and exchange rate policy at the national level has to be considered a cost as long as wages and prices do not fully and instantaneously respond to a disequilibrium in the labour or goods markets. This is the basic optimum-currency-area argument, which obviously only applies to relativities, since the common monetary policy can be used to cushion the impact of common shocks.

In addition to the benefits already discussed resulting from the extension of price stability to all member states, significant gains would arise from the removal of inefficiencies associated with exchange rate flexibility. Exchange rate instability, i.e. that part of its variability which does not result from fundamental changes in policies or in the economy more generally, is harmful because it impacts on macroeconomic variables like inflation and output, therefore increasing their variability.[31] The removal of this market failure would be stabilizing.[32] Another effect concerns failures of governments and authorities to act in a co-operative fashion. Non-cooperative monetary and exchange rate policies are welfare reducing, for example, if each government separately aims to export the adverse consequences of a common inflationary shock through exchange rate appreci-ation. This risk would disappear in EMU. In addition, the alternative adjustment mechanism of external financing exists, and its availability is increased by exchange rate fixity.

Admittedly, the EMS already removes at least part of exchange rate instability, and reduces the risk of non-cooperative policies since realignments are not unilaterally decided but negotiated. The same would hold in stage I. This is a clear benefit,

Table 11.9 Measurement issues in the cost–benefits analysis

EMU will have three concurrent types of impact:

  (i) on the level of output in the steady state and the path towards this new equilibrium;
 (ii) on its variability in a stochastic environment (i.e. characterized by the occurrence of random economic shocks);
(iii) inflation and other macroeconomic variables are also affected in both the foregoing ways.

(i) Effects which impact on the level of output (mostly efficiency effects) can be measured either in terms of output or in terms of welfare. The output measure can be related directly to usual macroeconomic statistics (GDP), but it is 'gross', since it does not take into account the cost of forgoing present consumption in order to accumulate capital. The welfare measure, which is derived from microeconomic utility considerations, is theoretically more appropriate. However, it is less easy to grasp and rests on assumptions concerning among other things the rate of time preference. Both measures are close to each other in the case of direct, static efficiency gains, but can differ widely as soon as intertemporal issues are involved.

(ii) Variability in macroeconomic variables raises in addition the issue of risk aversion. Only for risk-neutral individuals and firms would temporary deviations from equilibrium not be welfare reducing, provided they are averaged over time. The welfare cost of variability *per se*, however, is not of the same nature as the welfare cost of, for example, a permanent income loss. Aggregation of level and variability effects could only rest on a measure of risk aversion.

(iii) Taking into account other macroeconomic variables implies relying on a weighting of these variables. Due to the non-availability of a social welfare function derived from the utility functions of individuals, economists usually use macroeconomic welfare functions that are supposed to reflect policy preferences (and the welfare of the general public, provided policy-makers express the preferences of this public). Here, also, evaluations have to rest on some rather arbitrary quantitative assumptions regarding the weighting of deviations of output and inflation from their optimal level. (A specific problem is that the weight of inflation in usual macro welfare functions (which attempts to reflect the preferences of policy-makers) cannot be based on microeconomic grounds. See Blanchard and Fisher (1989: ch. 11).)

An overall measurement of the effects of EMU would have been vulnerable to changes in technical assumptions regarding the parameters discussed above. For the partial quantifications which are given in this study, reliance is placed mostly on usual statistics, i.e. output rather than welfare, and generally to discuss the results of macroeconomic model simulations in terms of changes in familiar variables rather than on the basis of a macro welfare function.

---

but this also goes with a cost because of asymmetry in monetary policy. As long as one national central bank sets the pace for monetary policy in the Community as a whole, policy reactions to asymmetric shocks are unlikely to be optimal since the legitimate objective of the national central bank is to seek the stability of domestic prices in its national economy. For example, if the French economy were hit by an inflationary shock there would be no case for the Bundesbank to tighten its policy.[33] In EMU, the policy of EuroFed would be more symmetric and would only react to country-specific developments which affect price stability in the Community as a whole.

3 Regional equity effects concern the distribution of costs and benefits among member states and regions. Differences in industrial structure, size and level of development, or foreign trade patterns can significantly affect the balance of costs and benefits across member states. For example, the analysis of transaction costs shows that these are higher for smaller countries, which rarely use their own currency in trade invoicing and whose financial markets lack depth. Initial macroeconomic conditions are also an important factor to take into account, as differences in inflation rates or fiscal conditions can alter the extent of policy changes brought about by EMU, at least transitionally.

4 External effects originate in the large size of the Community in the world economy. Because of its size, the effects of EMU would not be limited to the Community but would also have an impact on the international monetary and economic system. First, the ECU would become one of the major world currencies alongside the dollar and the yen, and could acquire a vehicular role in trade and finance for EC residents as well as non-residents. This could bring additional savings on transaction costs, yield some revenues from international seigniorage and impact on macroeconomic stability. Second, the Community would be able to engage more effectively in international policy co-ordination and to speak with a single voice in international monetary affairs. More generally, policy co-ordination at the G7 level would be transformed as the number of large players would be basically reduced to three. This would also impact on macroeconomic stability. Finally, both moves could ultimately induce wide-ranging changes in the international monetary system.

5 Transitional effects differ from permanent ones which arise in comparing a steady-state EMU to an alternative steady state, generally assumed to be '1992 + EMS' (but alternative baselines are also discussed). Only these effects represent the durable benefits and costs of EMU. However, since the starting point may not be a steady state, and indeed is surely not such for some countries, the costs and benefits of a relatively rapid move towards EMU have to be considered compared with those which would arise from a lengthy convergence within the framework of stage I. In particular a number of member states still suffer from low exchange rate and monetary policy credibility, and therefore from relatively high real *ex post* interest rates. Although most if not all of these phenomena would disappear in due course in a steady-state stage I, experience shows that this is a lengthy process. A more prompt move towards EMU could significantly affect the balance of macroeconomic costs and benefits in the transition towards low inflation and budgetary positions. Transitional issues also arise in the external field,

as an increase in the demand for ECU assets could lead to an appreciation of the Community currency.

Methodology of evaluations

Strictly speaking, the effects of EMU should only be deemed positive or negative with respect to an explicit welfare function. Aggregation of these effects would also imply the choice of a common yardstick, which as discussed in Table 11.9 could only rest on some rather arbitrary assumptions. In practice, this has not been necessary, since no overall quantitative evaluation has been attempted. However, as several partial evaluations are given in this study, issues of comparability and relative importance arise. Table 11.10 attempts to summarize the major elements which contribute to this evaluation.

The categories of effects distinguished above relate to different fields of economic theory, and to some extent to different paradigms, as summarized in the first two columns of Table 11.10. This has consequences for the methods and instruments of evaluation that are available and on the possibility of quantifying the different effects.

1 For microeconomic efficiency effects, the natural focus is on their permanent impact on the levels of output and welfare. The associated framework of analysis is therefore the classical full employment/flexible prices model, since these assumptions are standard for the long run.[34] However, in the textbook versions of the standard microeconomic model, where transaction costs are zero and adjustments are costless and where all agents have perfect information and no aversion towards risk, exchange rate regimes are neutral. Gains from a move towards monetary union arise when these oversimplifying assumptions are relaxed, which frequently implies using recent insights from research in progress.

Evaluation techniques are diverse. Gains from the elimination of transaction costs can be directly assessed using surveys and data on bank balance sheets, provided that assumptions are made

Table 11.10 Assumptions and methods of quantitative evaluations of economic and monetary union

	Underlying theories	Main assumptions	Methods and instruments	Quantitative assessment
Microeconomic efficiency	Microeconomics of imperfect markets Growth theory ('old' and 'new')	Flexible prices and full employment (long run) Information and adjustment costs, risk aversion	Direct evaluations and surveys (transaction costs) Computations with calibrated growth models	Substantial for direct effects Partial and tentative for indirect and dynamic effects
Macroeconomic stability	Macroeconomic theory Game-theoretic approach to economic policy Political economy	Sticky prices and under-employment (short run) Imperfect credibility	Econometric techniques Deterministic simulations with macro models Stochastic simulations	Partial evaluation for analytical purposes Attempt at a synthetic quantification through stochastic simulations
Regional equity	Both micro and macro approaches Theory of economic integration	As for micro and macro	No specific instrument	No quantitative assessment for individual member states
External	International monetary economics Theory of international policy co-ordination	Relaxation of the 'small country' assumption	No specific instrument	Only for specific effects
Transitional effects	As for macro stability	As for macro stability	No specific instrument	Only for specific effects

regarding the respective effects of capital market liberalization and the adoption of a single currency. The assessment of indirect effects is more partial and tentative since, first, only some aspects are quantified, and second, evaluations with present models are bound to provide orders of magnitude, rather than precise figures. Dynamic gains are evaluated using either calibrated standard growth models or the more recent endogenous growth models.

The time horizon corresponding to these effects is short for the most direct ones, like the elimination of transaction and hedging costs. Indirect and dynamic effects can normally be expected to accrue over many years if not decades, but the experience with the internal market tends to show

that favourable expectations can lead firms to increase investment even before the policy measures are effectively implemented.

2 The basic framework of analysis for macroeconomic stability effects is that of neo-Keynesian models, which are characterized by sticky wages and prices in the short run. Only in this kind of model can the loss of the exchange rate instrument be assessed. However, this framework has to be extended to encompass policy discipline effects also.

The degree of wage–price rigidity, and the associated costs of losing the exchange rate instrument, can be evaluated using econometric techniques or the estimates incorporated in empirical macroeconomic models (Table 11.11). However, standard methods can provide only some analytical elements rather than comprehensive assessment, since (i) deterministic situations only evaluate the effects of single, specific shocks and (ii) the impact of a change in the monetary regime on the behaviour of agents is not taken into account. Both limitations can be overcome through stochastic simulations with a model incorporating forward-looking features. The results of these simulations represent the average behaviour of an economy facing randomly distributed shocks, under different exchange rate regimes. They provide therefore a synthetic assessment. But this also is not fully comprehensive as some other gains resulting from the availability of alternative adjustment mechanisms or from the elimination of non-cooperative exchange rate behaviour are not taken into account.

Generally speaking, this type of macroeconomic stability effects will arise as soon as exchange rates are irrevocably fixed. The time horizon corresponding to this category of effects can be assessed to be about five years for specific shocks since the real effects of nominal exchange rate changes do not last longer.

Policy discipline effects also concern macroeconomic stability, but instead of focusing on the availability and effectiveness of policy instruments, the approach here focuses on their possible misuses. As already mentioned, the corresponding analytical framework stresses both the nature of economic policies that monetary authorities and governments can be expected to follow within a given framework of incentives and their interaction with private agents who form expectations regarding future policies.

Quantification of such effects is difficult since (i) the effectiveness of the EMU policy framework can only be a matter of judgement, (ii) there is only a weak causal link between a given framework of incentives and the policies which are effectively followed and (iii) credibility varies over time and cannot generally be directly observed. Experience with the EMS provides a good reference since the system has evolved from merely an exchange rate stabilizing device into a very effective disciplinary device without major institutional changes. Only partial computations are therefore given (mostly as regards transitional aspects), which aim at indicating orders of magnitude; they do not represent a comprehensive assessment of the policy discipline effects of EMU. Model simulations are also provided for illustrative purposes.

It is difficult to establish which part of policy discipline effects can be expected to be reaped at the outset of stage III, and which part will only arise after the reputation of EuroFed is established and fiscal co-ordination and surveillance procedures have proven effective.

3 The evaluation of regional equity effects relies on the same approaches as microeconomic and macroeconomic evaluations, supplemented by insights from the theory of economic integration. Conclusions regarding the regional impact of EMU are drawn from this analysis, but no specific attempt at a country-by-country quantitative evaluation has been made. The time horizon for these effects is the same as for microeconomic and macroeconomic effects.

4 The analysis of external effects rests on the standard framework for the study of international monetary regimes. Data are provided to give an assessment of possible changes in the international use of currencies, but no quantitative evaluations of the associated gains are given except for very direct and specific effects like the reduction on transaction costs or the revenues from international seigniorage. Indeed, a large part of the gains one can expect in this field depends on the behaviour of third countries, since EMU will only create opportunities for change in international monetary co-operation.

A large part of the external effects of EMU can be expected to arise only in the medium to long run, because of hysteresis in the international role of currencies and of the delays required for systemic changes in international monetary relations.

Table 11.11 Macroeconomic models for simulations of economic and monetary union

Two different multi-country macroeconomic models have been used for evaluating some of the effects of EMU.

The Quest model of the Commission's services is a medium-sized quarterly model in the neo-Keynesian tradition. As a structural model, it involves a complete representation of the national economies and of their trade linkages. The 1989 version which has been used for this study incorporates individual structural models of four member states (France, Germany, Italy, UK) and the USA.[a] Exchange rates in Quest are exogenous, i.e. the exchange rate is considered as a policy instrument. This approximates to the situation within the EMS, as a country facing an adverse shock can settle upon a realignment in order to offset the impact of the shock. Simulations therefore provide some assessment of the cost of losing this instrument.

Quest, however, cannot be used for an evaluation of the macroeconomic stability properties of alternative exchange rate regimes (including float), for such an evaluation requires, first, that exchange rates are endogenous, and second that the model takes into account that a change of regime impacts on the behaviour of agents. This second requirement originates in the 'Lucas critique' of policy evaluation with econometric models, according to which changes in policy regime alter the behavioural parameters of the model (see Lucas 1976). Its theoretical relevance in the case of a regime change like EMU is indisputable, especially for the adoption of a single currency, since the nature of this change, its permanent character and the associated constraints would be highly visible for and credible to all agents. The extent of these changes in behaviour is however an empirical issue.

The Multimod model developed at the IMF responds to a large extent to these two problems.[b] The forward-looking financial block of this small annual model of the G7 economies involves an endogenous determination of exchange rates through a financial arbitrage condition (under the assumptions of perfect capital mobility, complete asset substitutability and perfect foresight), whereas the real sector incorporates in a simplified fashion both backward- and forward-looking features. When simulating the effects of shocks under different regimes, it is assumed that agents have full knowledge of the structure of the economy and therefore of the consequences of the shock.[c] However, wage–price stickiness (which can be due to multi-year contracts) and liquidity constraints imply short-term departures from equilibrium in the Keynesian tradition.

The specific features of Multimod make it a suitable instrument for an examination of macroeconomic stability in EMU, either through deterministic simulations which attempt at evaluating the effects of the same shock under alternative regimes, or through stochastic simulations whose aim is to provide an overall quantitative assessment of these regimes in an environment of random disturbances. However, Multimod has its weak points too. First, it is a highly aggregated model which sometimes rests on simplifying assumptions, especially when compared with structural models like Quest. Second, the estimation strategy followed by the IMF team has been to incorporate only significant parameter differences across countries, which is both a strength (because of the uncertainty surrounding these asymmetries) and a weakness (because the precision of individual equations is reduced). Third, as a forward-looking model Multimod tends to exhibit much less nominal rigidity than standard macro models, and more generally a stronger tendency to revert to the baseline equilibrium. Since the estimation of forward-looking models raises a number of technical difficulties, there is a certain degree of uncertainty in this field too. Fourth and conversely, although regime changes impact on behaviour through expectations, it is still possible that some genuine behavioural changes regarding, for example, investment or wage behaviours arising from EMU are ignored.

Due to the different characteristics of the two models, it has been chosen to specialize each in a certain type of simulation. The main purpose of the Quest simulations is to evaluate the cost of losing the exchange rate as an instrument in a standard target-instrument policy framework, whereas Multimod simulations are devoted to the overall assessment of the consequences of EMU for macroeconomic stability. However, results from both models can also be considered as representing the uncertainty surrounding the true model of the economy and therefore the range of possible effects of EMU.

Notes: [a] For an overall presentation of Quest, from which the version used in this study however differs in some respects, see Bekx *et al.* (1989). Models for other EC member states and Japan are under development. In the present Quest model, feedbacks from the rest of the world are, however, incorporated in a reduced form.

[b] Commission services are grateful to the IMF for providing the latest version of Multimod as well as technical support, but the simulations have been carried out under their sole responsibility. Neither the results nor possible errors should be attributed in any way to the IMF.

[c] Technically, expectations are model-consistent, which means that in deterministic simulations future values of variables and the impact on the behaviour of agents are known (obviously, this is not the case for unanticipated shocks). For a general presentation of Multimod, see Masson *et al.* (1990). The version used in this study differs from the one presented in this chapter due to minor changes introduced in the version used at the Commission.

5 Transitional effects are basically of a macro-economic nature. The same approaches have been used as for evaluating macroeconomic stability effects, especially as regards issues of credibility and policy discipline.

Costs and benefits of alternative exchange rate regimes

It has been argued early in this chapter that, for comprehensiveness, benefits and costs of EMU should not only be assessed with respect to the '1992 + EMS' baseline but also in comparison with alternative exchange rate regimes. Since this is obviously a very wide issue, only the main arguments will be given here. For this purpose, Table 11.12 gives in a schematic fashion the costs and benefits of the three 'pure' regimes of Figure 11.3: financial markets autarky, free float and EMU.

The costs of financial autarky are immediately apparent: microeconomic efficiency is bound to be low owing to a complete segmentation of capital markets; no significant external influence can be expected for the Community as priority is given to autonomy over co-ordination and collective influence building. The average macroeconomic performance can also be expected to be poor in a regime characterized by the need for each country to achieve external balance: asymmetric shocks but also symmetric ones, if policy reactions differ, would give rise to balance-of-payment crises as in the 1970s. Only for shocks that arise from exchange rate instability can this regime achieve a fair performance. Finally, policy discipline is not high in such a regime since external pressures only arise when the country experiences a current account deficit. As past experience consistently shows, this is at most a second best since current account deficits exhibit only a weak and at least delayed correlation with either monetary or fiscal mismanagement.

The arguments for free float are well known: each country has maximum policy autonomy and, provided wage–price indexation is not complete in the short run, exchange rate changes can cushion asymmetric shocks. In spite of these arguments, however, the performance of flexible exchange rates is generally considered disappointing for several reasons. First, exchange rate variability is an obstacle to microeconomic efficiency: as shown by the recent US experience, wide exchange rate swings degrade the quality of price signals and lead firms to adopt 'wait and see' attitudes;[35] moreover, exchange rate misalignments imply significant welfare losses, especially when adjustment costs are important. Second, stabilizing properties of floating exchange rates are only apparent while facing country-specific, i.e. asymmetric, real shocks; symmetric shocks, especially supply shocks, give rise to beggar-thy-neighbour exchange rate policies as each country tries to export inflation or unemployment; moreover, monetary shocks to the exchange rate itself, which arise from failures in the international financial markets, are a source of instability. Third, policy autonomy in a floating rates regime implies that no strong effects on policy discipline can be expected. Finally, individual participation of member states in a floating rates regime cannot be expected to increase the influence of the Community as a whole.

Over the whole range of effects considered in Table 11.12, the only important disadvantage of EMU concerns macroeconomic stability in the presence of asymmetric shocks. This is indeed a well-known argument and has unambiguously to be considered a cost, but one that should be weighed against the clear advantages that EMU yields in other fields.

Although for most member states neither a pure floating regime nor financial autarky are real alternatives to EMU, the qualitative framework of arguments presented points to the basic features of its costs and benefits compared with hybrid regimes that could present possible alternatives. As already discussed, an important methodological choice of the present study is to assess the costs and benefits of EMU compared with a '1992 + EMS' baseline, in spite of the rather hypothetical character of some of its features and of the diversity of present situations among member states regarding their participation in the ERM. In

Table 11.12 A schematic presentation of costs and benefits of alternative exchange rate regimes

	Financial autarky	Free float	EMU
Microeconomic efficiency	Low	Medium	High
Macroeconomic stability In the presence of shocks			
Asymmetric shocks	Low	High	Low
Symmetric shocks	Medium	Low	High
Exchange rate instability	High	Low	High
Resulting from policy discipline			
Monetary credibility	Medium	Country dependent	High
Fiscal discipline	Country dependent	Medium	Medium
External influence	Low	Low	High

so far as the risk of systemic instability in stage I could lead the system to a reversion to some kind of pre-stage I regime (i.e. some loosely defined mix of capital controls and crawling peg as in the early EMS), it is apparent that the net benefit of EMU could only be greater.

NOTES

1 Capital markets liberalization is effective in most member states. Only Spain, Portugal and Greece still maintain exchange controls and these will be progressively removed by 1992. In some cases the phasing out may be extended until 1995.

2 This definition follows Van Rompuy *et al.* (1990), to which the reader can refer for a detailed discussion of economic federalism.

3 Markets for automobiles are a good example.

4 The importance of imperfect integration of goods markets for the analysis of exchange rate regimes has been stressed by Baldwin and Krugman (1987) and Krugman (1989a) in response to the 'global monetarist' approach of McKinnon. For an attempt to measure macroeconomically this integration in the Community, see Aglietta *et al.* (1990).

5 The minimum is 45 per cent for Canada.

6 Strictly speaking, this is only true if currencies are exchanged at par since, in the presence of transaction costs, interest rate arbitrage is not perfect and short-term interest rate differentials can therefore appear.

7 This is shown, for example, by Casella (1990) and Krugman (1989a).

8 This only refers to macroeconomic policy. Other functions of central banks, like supervision, may be more decentralized, but are not discussed here.

9 The Austrian experience is analysed by Genberg (1989) and Hochreiter and Törnqvist (1990).

10 The term 'common currency' is ambiguous: it sometimes refers to a single currency, which would replace the national currencies, and sometimes to a parallel currency, which would be issued in addition to existing ones. It is therefore not used throughout this chapter. See also below on the hard ECU proposal.

11 Even prices of tradeables can exhibit wide divergence in level terms. A recent survey by Runzheiner Mitchell Europe shows that both before and after tax retail prices of typical standardized manufactured goods of the same brand name often vary by 100 per cent or more across the Community. Arguably, price transparency within EMU could reduce these variations, but some divergence would surely remain. See *The Financial Times*, 9 July 1991.

12 The standard rationale behind this phenomenon is that, as catching-up proceeds, the relative price of non-tradeables, for which productivity gains are lower, increases with respect to that of tradeables. Assuming PPP in the traded goods sector, this leads to real exchange rate appreciation. The analysis of mechanisms of this type goes back to Ricardo. For a modern restatement, see Balassa (1964).

13 Data are taken from Eurostat, *Indice des prix à la consommation*, supplément 1 (1990).

14 GDP per employed person, at standard purchasing power exchange rates. Data from Eurostat.

15 In May 1990, Belgium announced its intention to commit itself to exchange rate stability *vis-à-vis* the

deutsche mark. The French government has also repeatedly stressed its intention to rule out devaluations.

16 The requirements for a realignment rule in an EMS without capital controls are discussed by Driffill (1988) and Obstfeld (1988).

17 Other effects of the removal of capital controls concern the allocation of savings, i.e. microeconomic and macroeconomic effects of capital markets integration. Here also the removal of capital controls is expected to yield some benefits, although this is incomplete as long as exchange rate risk remains a barrier to capital mobility.

18 However, as pointed out by Ingram (1973), most estimates of the benefits of the Common Market, made in advance of the economic realities, were close to zero.

19 Paul Krugman (1989a) states: 'The economics of international money, by contrast [to those of trade integration], are not at all well understood: they hinge crucially not only on sophisticated and ambiguous issues like credibility and coordination, but on even deeper issues like transaction costs and bounded rationality.'

20 A classic example is that of the German monetary unification in the nineteenth century, which followed a few years after the trade and economic unification under the Zollverein. See Holtfrerich (1989).

21 See, for example, Marston (1985), Aizenman and Frenkel (1985). For a recent survey, see Argy (1989).

22 Another related approach stresses the relative information content of exchange rate regimes in rational expectations models. The emphasis is on the degree to which prices provide the right information to agents regarding the nature of the shocks affecting the economy under alternative exchange rate regimes. No strong result in favour of one regime or another emerges from this literature. See Wihlborg and Willett (1990) for a survey.

23 This might arise from public choice considerations, but also from the time-inconsistency argument. See Kydland and Prescott (1977) and Barro and Gordon (1983).

24 See, for example, Giavazzi and Pagano (1988) and several contributions in Giavazzi et al. (1988).

25 For a recent survey, see Currie et al. (1989).

26 See, for example, Williamson (1985), McKinnon (1988) and Krugman (1989a).

27 On the first aspect, see Canzoneri and Rogers (1990). On the second, see, for example, Van der Ploeg (1990).

28 The exact definition of a behavioural change depends on the model which is used to represent behaviours. For example, changes in the reaction of wages to an inflationary shock as a consequence of monetary union would be assessed as an exogenous change in behaviour in a model with adaptive expectations, though it would only be an endogenous reaction to the regime change in a model with forward-looking expectations.

29 There is a slight difference in terminology on this point between this study and the report on the economics of 1992 in *European Economy* (1988a).

30 Variability in prices, i.e. inflation, has to be distinguished from variability in inflation, i.e. in the change in the rate of increase of prices. Theoretically prices can be rising while the rate of inflation is stable. However, in practice inflation and its variability are correlated.

31 Exchange rate instability has to be distinguished from variability and uncertainty. Variability refers to the observed changes in exchange rates. Uncertainty refers to the unanticipated component of these changes. Instability refers to that part of variability which cannot be explained by changes in policies or other economic fundamentals.

32 Obviously, this is only true in so far as the variability of other variables (e.g. the dollar exchange rate) does not increase as a consequence of intra-Community exchange rate fixity.

33 Except for offsetting the effects of spillovers of French inflation on Germany.

34 'Full employment' does not mean that there is indeed full employment in the baseline, but only that the long run refers to the horizon where short-term unemployment effects of efficiency gains are eliminated.

35 See Baldwin (1988), Dixit (1989) and for a general discussion Krugman (1989b).

BIBLIOGRAPHY

Aglietta, M. (1988) 'Régimes monétaires, monnaie supranationale, monnaie commune', paper presented at the International Barcelona Conference on the Theory of Regulation, June.

Aglietta, M., Coudert, V. and Delessy, H. (1990) 'Politiques budgétaires et ajustements macro-économiques dans la perspective de l'intégration monétaire européenne', *Lectures critiques du rapport Delors, De Pecunia* II (2–3) Brussels, September.

Aizenman, J. and Frenkel, J. A. (1985) 'Optimal wage indexation, foreign exchange intervention, and monetary policy'. *American Economic Review* 75 (3): 402–23.

Argy, V. (1989) 'Choice of exchange rate regime for a smaller economy – a survey of some key issues', in V.

Argy and P. De Grauwe (eds) *Choosing an Exchange Rate Regime: the Challenge for Smaller Industrial Countries*, Washington, DC: CEPS/IMF.

Artus, P. (1990) 'Epargne nationale, investissement et intégration internationale', Document de travail 1990–17/T, Caisse des Dépôts et Consignations.

Backus, D. and Driffill, J. (1985) 'Inflation and reputation', *American Economic Review* 76 (3): 530–8.

Balassa, B. (1964) 'The purchasing power parity doctrine: a reappraisal', *Journal of Political Economy*, December.

Baldwin, R. (1988) 'Hysteresis in import prices: the beachhead effect', *American Economic Review* 78 (4).

—— (1990) 'On the microeconomics of EMU', in *European Economy*, 'The economics of EMU', special issue.

Baldwin, R. and Krugman, P. (1987) 'The persistence of the US trade deficit', *Brookings Papers on Economic Activity* 1.

Baldwin, R. and Lyons, R. (1990) 'External economics and European integration: the potential for self-fulfilling expectations', in *European Economy*, 'The economics of EMU', special issue.

Barro, R. J. and Gordon, D. (1983) 'A critical theory of monetary policy in a natural rate model', *Journal of Political Economy* 91 (August): 589–610.

Bekx, P., Bucher, A., Italianer, A. and Mors, M. (1989) 'The Quest model (version 1988)', *EC Economic Papers* 75 (March).

Blanchard, O. J. and Fisher, S. (1989) *Lectures on Macroeconomics*, Cambridge, MA: MIT Press.

Canzoneri, M. and Rogers, C. A. (1990) 'Is the European Community an optimal currency area? Optimal taxation versus the cost of multiple currencies', *American Economic Review* 80: 419–33.

Carli, G. (1989) *The Evolution towards Economic and Monetary Union: a Response to the HM Treasury Paper*, Ministerio del Tesoro, December.

Casella, A. (1990) 'Participation in a monetary union', NBER Working Paper 3220, January.

Currie, A., Holtham, G. and Hughes Hallett, A. (1989) 'The theory and practice of international policy coordination: does coordination pay?', in R. Bryant, D. Currie and R. Portes (eds) *Macroeconomic Policies in an Interdependent World*, Washington, DC: CEPR/The Brookings Institution/IMF.

Dixit, A. (1989) 'Entry and exit decisions under uncertainty', *Journal of Political Economy* 97: 620ff.

Driffill, J. (1988) 'The stability and sustainability of the European Monetary System with perfect capital markets', in F. Giavazzi, S. Micossi and M. Miller (eds) *The European Monetary System*, Cambridge: Cambridge University Press.

European Economy (1988a) 'The economics of 1992', Special issue 35, March.

—— (1988b) 'Creation of a European financial area', Special issue 36, May.

—— (1990) 'The economics of EMU', special issue.

Flood, R., Bhandari, J. and Horne, J. (1989) 'Evolution of exchange rate regimes', *IMF Staff Papers* 36 (4).

Friedman, M. (1953) 'The case for flexible exchange rates', in M. Friedman (ed.) *Essays in Positive Economics*, Chicago, IL: University of Chicago Press.

Genberg, H. (1989) 'In the shadow of the mark: exchange rate and monetary policy in Austria and Switzerland', in V. Argy and P. De Grauwe (eds) *Choosing an Exchange Rate Regime: the Challenge for Smaller Industrial Countries*, Washington, DC: CEPS/IMF.

Giavazzi, F. and Giovannini, A. (1989) *The European Monetary System*, Cambridge, MA: MIT Press.

Giavazzi, F. and Pagano, M. (1988) 'The advantage of tying one's hands', *European Economic Review* 32 (June): 1055–82.

Giavazzi, F. and Spaventa, L. (1990) 'The new EMS', CEPR Discussion Paper 369, January.

Giavazzi, F., Micossi, S. and Miller, M. (eds) (1988) *The European Monetary System*, Cambridge: Cambridge University Press.

Giovannini, A. (1989) 'How do fixed exchange rate regimes work? Evidence from the gold standard Bretton Woods and the EMS', in M. Miller, B. Eichengreen and R. Portes (eds) *Blueprints for Exchange-Rate Management*, New York: Academic Press.

Gros, D. (1990) 'The EMS without capital controls', *Ecu Newsletter* 30 (October): 22–6.

Hochreiter, E. and Törnqvist, A. (1990) 'Austria's monetary and exchange rate policy – some comparative remarks with respect to Sweden', *Lectures critiques du rapport Delors, De Pecunia* II (2–3), Brussels, September.

Holtfrerich, C. L. (1989) 'The monetary unification process in nineteenth-century Germany: relevance and lessons for Europe today', in M. de Cecco and A. Giovannini (eds) *A European Central Bank?*, Cambridge: Cambridge University Press.

Ingram, J. C. (1959) 'State and regional payments mechanisms', *Quarterly Journal of Economics* 73 (November): 619–32.

—— (1973) '*The Case for European Monetary Integration*', Princeton essays in international finance 98, Princeton University, April.

Ishiyama, Y. (1975) 'The theory of optimum currency areas: a survey', *IMF Staff Papers* 22.

Kenen, P. B. (1969) 'The theory of optimum currency areas: an eclectic view', in R. A. Mundell and A. K. Swoboda (eds) *Monetary Problems of the International Economy*, Chicago, IL: University of Chicago Press.

Krugman, P. (1989a) *Exchange Rate Instability*, Cambridge, MA: MIT Press.

—— (1989b) 'Policy problems of a monetary union', paper prepared for the CEPR/Bank of Greece Conference on the EMS in the 1990s.

Kydland, F. E. and Prescott, E. C. (1977) 'Rules rather than discretion: the inconsistency of optimal plans', *Journal of Political Economy* 85 (3): 473–91.

Lucas, R. E. (1976) 'Econometric policy evaluation: a critique', in K. Brunner and A. H. Meltzer (eds) *The Phillips Curve and Labor Markets*, Carnegie-Rochester Conference Series on Public Policy 1, pp. 19–46.

Marston, R. C. (1984) 'Exchange rate unions as an alternative to flexible rates: the effects of real and monetary disturbances', in J. O. Bilson and R. C. Marston (eds) *Exchange Rate Theory and Practice*, Chicago, IL: University of Chicago Press.

—— (1985) 'Stabilization policies in open economies', in R. Jones and P. Kenen (eds) *Handbook of International Economics*, vol. II, Amsterdam: Elsevier.

Masson, P., Symansky, S. and Meredith, G. (1990) 'Multimod Mark II: a revised and extended model', IMF Occasional Paper 71, July.

McKinnon, R. I. (1963) 'Optimum currency areas', *American Economic Review* 53 (September): 717–25.

—— (1988) 'Monetary and exchange rate policies for international financial stability: a proposal', *Journal of Economic Perspectives* 2 (1): 83–103.

Meade, J. E. (1957) 'The balance-of-payments problems of a European free-trade area', *Economic Journal* (September): 379–96.

Mundell, R. A. (1961) 'A theory of optimum currency areas', *American Economic Review* 51 (September): 657–65.

Obstfeld, M. (1988) 'Competitiveness, realignment, and speculation: the role of financial markets', in F. Giavazzi, S. Micossi and M. Miller (eds) *The European Monetary System*, Cambridge: Cambridge University Press.

Padoa-Schioppa, T. (1987) *Efficiency, Stability, Equity*, Oxford: Oxford University Press.

Poloz, S. (1990) 'Real exchange rate adjustment between regions in a common currency area', mimeo, Bank of Canada, February.

UK Treasury (1989) *An Evolutionary Approach to Economic and Monetary Union* London: HM Treasury, November.

Van der Ploeg, F. (1990) 'Macroeconomic policy coordination during the various phases of economic and monetary integration in Europe', in *European Economy*, 'The economics of EMU', special issue.

Van Rompuy, P., Abrahams, F. and Heremans, D. (1990) 'Economic federalism and the EMU', in *European Economy*, 'The economics of EMU', special issue.

Wihlborg, C. and Willett, T. (1990) 'Optimum currency areas revisited', mimeo, April.

Williamson (1985) *The Exchange Rate System*, Washington, DC: Institute for International Economics.

12

ONE CURRENCY FOR EUROPE
From theory to practice

André Fourçans

INTRODUCTION

Were the founding fathers of the EC planning for one currency for Europe? The Rome Treaty of 1957 made no reference at all to such an objective. It was only at the Hague conference in 1969 that monetary union was first adopted as a long-term goal of the Community. Since then, this idea has had its ups and downs over time. Today it seems to be at an all time high, especially after the Treaty adopted in Maastricht in December 1991 and signed in February 1992.

In spite of the new impetus given to monetary union the debate about the need for a single currency is still ongoing. In the following section we study the conceptual background of the question. Despite some drawbacks we conclude that a single currency would be a great help in creating economic integration as well as monetary stability, as long as some conditions are fulfilled. Counter positions to that view are also analysed: fixed exchange rates with national monies, flexible exchange rates and competitive monies.

In the third section we concentrate on European monetary union *per se*. We study the strategy adopted in Maastricht in order to create a single currency, with special emphasis on the transition period towards integration. We also discuss to what extent fiscal policy co-ordination is necessary and the role that the ECU should play in the process.

The final and concluding section sets forth the necessity for close co-ordination of monetary policies as well as the need for a European central bank, with the main measures to be adopted for achieving this.

IS THERE A NEED FOR A SINGLE CURRENCY?

The pros of a single currency

The role of money

To understand better the advantage of monetary union we must go back to the fundamental role of money. Economically, it is this conceptual background that justifies the progress towards monetary union and a single currency.[1] Such a reminder is essential in so far as many discussions on European questions seem to forget it.

The use of money diminishes information and transaction costs of trade. As a unit of account, medium of exchange and store of value, money demonstrates a high economic and social productivity. It reduces uncertainty and costs associated with economic activity by reducing resources necessary to acquire, process and stock information and to pursue production and transaction activities (Brunner and Meltzer 1971). These advantages increase with the currency domain (Mundell 1961). In other words, the *qualitative* arguments in favour of a single currency are the same as those in favour of a monetary rather than a barter economy, even though the *quantitative* gains to be expected from the transition from a multi-currency to a single-currency domain are less than those from a barter to a monetary economy.

More concretely, a single currency facilitates comparison of international prices and costs without having to generate and collect information relative to actual and future exchange rates and to different rules and regulations about exchange controls. It eliminates exchange rate uncertainties as well as transaction costs due to the exchange of monies. It suppresses the socially unproductive activities resulting from exchanging one currency for another. A multi-currency world, with (potential or real) exchange risk, constitutes an obstacle to market integration, be they financial and money markets or goods markets (Kenen 1976).

A single currency versus fixed exchange rates

A fixed exchange rate system demonstrates some, but only some, attributes of a single-currency system.

Even by supposing perfectly fixed exchange rates (i.e. without any expectations of parity changes), a single-currency system still possesses one main advantage: it eliminates the socially unproductive costs of exchanging one money for another. With this criterion in mind, there would be no reason to maintain a fixed parity system; one currency area would be more efficient.

In the real world, adjustments of parities exist within a fixed exchange rate system. Of course, a single currency eliminates these risks since exchange rates do not exist any more.[2] It also suppresses all the risks associated with the possible occurrence of exchange controls and other rules or regulations concerning the exchange of currencies. It therefore leads to a better allocation of international funds.[3]

Yet, if a single currency gets rid of *nominal* exchange rate fluctuations it does not eradicate *real* exchange rate changes due to disparities in relative prices and costs between countries.[4] But real exchange rate variations would be less than with a fixed (or flexible) but adjustable exchange system since they would not be affected by expectations about the relative stability of each currency (Lehment 1984).

Another important difference between a fixed

rate and a single-currency system resides in the type of monetary management that each implies. In the first case, monetary policy co-ordination is unavoidable so as to maintain the fixed rate system. In the second case, one, and only one, monetary policy must be conducted. If the different countries of the area agree on the policy objective, the latter is institutionally easier to achieve in a single-currency system than in a system whereby different monetary policies need to be co-ordinated (Christie and Fratianni 1978). Having said this, one should not forget that an improvement in the efficiency of monetary policy does not mean an improvement in the wisdom of that policy. If a 'bad' policy is implemented, its negative consequences are exacerbated.

An increased mobility of goods and production factors

A widening of the currency area due to a monetary union leads to a better allocation of resources. Consumer welfare is increased by a sharpening of the competition thus created, with the traditional advantages of such an occurrence (on prices, product quality and innovation). Production costs decrease as a result of more freedom in trade, economies of scale and optimal choice of investment. Hence the gains in employment and growth.[5]

The cons of a single currency

Loss of one degree of freedom: exchange rate adjustment

A single currency (or irrevocably fixed rates) would render short-run economic adjustments more difficult in so far as nominal exchange rate changes are eliminated. As nominal exchange rates are more flexible than prices and wages, it is easier to correct imbalances by a change in parities than by a change in prices and wages. This case is defendable in the short run. In the longer run, the adjustment of nominal exchange rates to eliminate fundamental imbalances in the economy could on the contrary aggravate the situation in so far as the parity variation (in a flexible or a fixed but adjustable exchange system) would be used as a substitute for the necessary change in policies (budgetary, fiscal, interest rates etc.); or in so far as the policy would be implemented too late and in a more difficult situation. History shows that such events ought not to be considered lightly.

Furthermore, a single currency diminishes the amount of adjustments implied by real shocks (productivity changes, changes in preferences in tradeable goods or in supply conditions) compared with a flexible or adjustable fixed rate system. The latter may lead to supplementary adjustments due to monetary shocks (variations in monetary growth and/or in expectations) that stimulate flows of capital (Lehment 1984).

Loss of one degree of freedom: independence of monetary policy

One single currency implies the loss of national monetary sovereignty.[6] What is raised here is the possibility for each country to determine its inflation rate and to use the inflation–unemployment trade-off if it exists.

In a currency area all countries have the same *ex post*, if not *ex ante*, inflation rate. The transition from the *ex ante* to the *ex post* inflation rate may lead to an unemployment rise if wages do not adjust in the higher inflation countries. This risk exists in any anti-inflationary process, whatever the cause of the process.[7] However, it must be added that the anti-inflationary costs have largely been paid by most of the European countries (Bailey *et al.* 1987), except for some of the 'southern countries'. The problem is therefore less acute nowadays. One must also add that as far as the establishment of a fixed exchange rate system (or a *fortiori* of a single currency) compels the most inflationary countries to change their policy, the constraint so imposed can be considered an advantage rather than a drawback (as long as the gains resulting from the inflation slow-down are superior to the costs of the unemployment increase during the adjustment period).

Furthermore, monetary independence does not automatically mean an increase in efficiency. The real efficiency constraint appears to be the degree of openness of the economy rather than the exchange rate regime *per se*, especially when financial flows are free to move (Frenkel and Goldstein 1988). And flexible exchange rates do not protect from changes in relative prices between countries. This implies internal adjustments, whether in fixed or flexible rates (or with a single currency); only the speed of adjustment can vary. If monetary policy has no long-run influence on employment and growth, it is obvious that the problem of monetary independence to achieve the goals of lasting full employment and growth becomes irrelevant.

The real question then is whether or not there is an inflation–unemployment trade-off. If this trade-off does not exist, i.e. if the Phillips curve is vertical, the problem disappears. If there is a negative short-run and a vertical long-run Phillips curve, the problem exists only during the transition period, the length of which depends on the speed of adjustment of inflation expectations and wages. If the Phillips curve remains negative even in the long run, then the problem becomes serious. But, without reviewing the (large) literature on the matter, few would nowadays defend this thesis.

Undesirable regional consequences

A currency area may entail undesirable regional consequences if compensatory measures are not taken.

'Demonstration effects', or a centralized wage-setting process whereby wages would evolve at the same pace whatever the productivity gains of each region, would lead to an increase in unemployment in the 'periphery' (Christie and Fratianni 1978). In this case, a redistributive policy could be established between the different regions (or countries), from the richer to the poorer peripheral zones.[8] The aid should be conceived so as to accelerate productivity gains in the unfavoured regions and to alleviate social costs through income redistribution.

It would also be important to decentralize wage negotiations as far as possible in order to bring them more in line with productivity gains in each part of the monetary area.

In addition there is the possibility that, through a decrease in information and transaction costs, as well as through lower banking risks, a single currency would accelerate the movements of physical capital and labour between regions. Even though the new allocation of production factors so induced would be economically efficient for the area as a whole (which is one objective of a monetary union), it would occur at the expense of some regions. Here, too, redistributive income policies and/or incentives (be they fiscal or other) could help alleviate the problem.

Is private currency competition superior to one single currency?

To be complete, it is necessary to analyse the view that competition between private currencies supplied by banks would be a superior solution to one single currency (Hayek 1978; Salin 1984).

Uncertainty information and transaction costs

The arguments in favour of 'free banking' are those associated with the advantages of competition between producers of goods and services, whatever they are. These advantages are undeniable in terms of prices, product quality and innovations. But to apply the traditional competitive analysis to the problem treated here neglects an essential fact: the role played by money to diminish uncertainty as well as information and transaction costs.

Even by supposing that private-currency competition would bring about all the benefits promised by defenders of this view,[9] it is doubtful whether such a system would lead to a monetary order providing trustable information as to the future development of the monetary environment. Such competition would introduce supplementary uncertainty in the establishment of consumption, saving and investment plans. One may also expect that short-run uncertainties about the behaviour of monetary aggregates so introduced would lead to more 'surprises' in the free banking system, and thus would lead to greater economic uncertainty than with the present monetary order (Brunner 1984).

Several competitive currencies, be they of the highest quality, can only be *inferior* to a single currency in terms of information and transaction cost minimization (on one condition though: that the single currency be of high quality, as we shall see later). Obviously, several monies would not only mean the use of resources to obtain information as to the prices of goods and services in each currency, but would also add the uncertainty associated with the exchange rates between these currencies.[10] One single currency would not have these drawbacks – and the larger the monetary domain, the stronger the argument. Furthermore, one single currency would be a superior solution in so far as its use would probably spread to a wider domain than each competitive currency in and of itself.

Stability and economic integration

Even if one accepts the high quality of each competitive currency in terms of a stable price level, they would not make it possible to obtain one fundamental goal of a monetary union in as effective a way as one single currency: the economic integration of the area (Claassen 1984), with all its favourable consequences in terms of optimal allocation of resources.[11] Competitive currencies would constitute a superior alternative to a single currency if, and only if, they demonstrated a higher quality than the single currency, an occurrence which remains to be proved (this does not imply either that the single money would automatically be well managed), in order to make up for their inferior position as far as integration is concerned.

Production of money and natural monopoly

Large fixed costs and very meagre marginal costs suggest that money production presents the characteristics of a decreasing average cost industry that leads to natural monopoly. If such is the case, only one producer in the monetary zone is economically efficient. Private production of money would lead, if not in the short run at least in the long run, to the elimination of all producers but one[12] (Klein 1974; Vaubel 1977). In other words, after a transitory (and shaky?) period, the multi-currency system would transform itself into a single-currency system. That may be the reason why history suggests that, in almost all cases, all monetary systems (in a given area) consisted of one currency or of several currencies exchangeable into a dominating single currency[13] (Klein 1977).

Private competitive currencies and the quality of money

Proponents of private competitive currencies argue that the competitive process will create and maintain high-quality currencies, whereas a single money managed by public authorities is doomed to depreciate (Salin 1984).

It is difficult to give strong arguments for or against the first assertion, and empirical or historical evidence is rather meagre. One could admit that private monies could impede durable inflation or deflation.[14] Some remain sceptical, however, about such a possibility (Friedman 1984), the reason being that there are no guaranteed stable purchasing power bonds in which banks could invest as a counterpart to their issue of a stable purchasing power money. Public authorities would have to issue such bonds, in large quantities, in order for this to happen.

The argument about the tendency of public authorities to let their currency depreciate as long as they have no constraint imposed on monetary management must, in itself, be taken seriously.[15] Yet recent history indicates that this is not an absolute fate. The quality of monetary control has improved in Europe over the last ten years.

It does remain that in order to avoid, in a lasting way, any risk of monetary mismanagement, a single-currency system should be associated with a monetary constitution, with simple and clearly defined rules, as we shall see below.

EUROPEAN MONETARY UNION IN THEORY AND PRACTICE

What strategy should be adopted in order to reach the goal of a single currency in Europe? The strategy chosen is of major importance. The various economic, institutional and political problems to be solved necessitate an approach that is vigorous enough to proceed at a reasonable pace but also flexible enough to minimize transition costs and make it politically acceptable by all the countries involved. To understand that question better, it is first necessary to establish where European monetary integration stands, i.e. to examine where the EMS stands and what its implications are.

The European monetary system more than ten years after

After more than ten years in operation, one can say that the EMS has reached its first objective reasonably well: to stabilize exchange rates between European currencies. The goal of a 'stable monetary zone' has been satisfactorily achieved, even though several adjustments of parities were implemented.

Since the beginning of the 1980s, greater convergence of the various economies of Europe is undeniable, especially as far as a lower rate of inflation is concerned. Whether or not this progress towards convergence is due to the EMS is debatable.

A majority argue that it is the German Bundesbank dominance over the EMS which explains this result (e.g. Sarcinelli 1986; Giavazzi and Giovannini 1988). Fratianni and Von Hagen (1990a, b) disagree with that view and offer empirical tests rejecting the German dominance, yet showing the Bundesbank independence in pursuing her own policy goals.

Despite these disagreements it does remain true that, via the constraint imposed by the EMS, the authorities of the various countries have learned to consult each other on their main economic and monetary policies and to take more decisions in common. Decisions on 'realignments' of exchange rates are now largely taken together. The same argument can be defended, though to a lesser extent, about short-term interest rate policies.

The EMS appears to have stabilized exchange rate expectations and thereby to have increased the credibility of (relatively) fixed parities, with its positive consequences on intra-community trade and resource allocation. Yet the reinforcement of the EMS raises several questions.

The roads to monetary integration

An 'inconsistent quartet'

With the free movements of financial capital and the elimination of non-tariff barriers to trade,[16] a challenge must be faced. The European zone must reconcile (1) full capital mobility, (2) free trade, (3) fixed exchange rates and (4) autonomous national monetary policy. Theory as well as experience suggests that this quartet is inconsistent – at least one has to give way (Padoa-Schioppa 1988).

Obviously, if the goal is to obtain a true single market with monetary union, it is the fourth factor which must give way: national monetary policy autonomy.

Via the EMS constraint, monetary policies are already close enough, be it through co-ordination or dominance of German policy. With the increasing liberalization of the flow of capital, goods, services and resources, more co-ordination will be unavoidable, and will have to be tightened when liberalization is complete (in 1993 if all goes as expected). If not, one can expect the EMS to work erratically, at least less satisfactorily than during its 'first phase'. If monetary policies are not sufficiently well co-ordinated, the third factor, i.e. fixed exchange rates, will have to give way. In other words, one can expect more frequent realignments of rates (except if the free movement of financial flows is suppressed and exchange controls are established).

The anchor and burden of adjustment questions

Some (e.g. Giavazzi and Giovannini 1988; Schinasi 1989) argue that a well-managed and well-defined nominal anchor is necessary for international monetary orders to be successful. And, as we saw, the same authors generally consider that the past success of the EMS is due to the deutsche mark role as an anchor to the system. Other countries have thus to adjust their policies to Germany's, even though these are inconsistent with their national objectives: the burden of adjustment is therefore asymmetric and falls more heavily on the weaker currency countries. If the proponents of this view are right, this means that the deutsche mark will have to keep on fulfilling that function and asymmetry is 'the price' to pay. If the Bundesbank is not the dominant player but anyway pursues its own policy goals of low inflation (as Fratianni and Von Hagen suggest) it does not make much economic difference (though it would politically speaking) to the future working of the EMS: other countries will have to follow monetary policies on the same lines in order to attain the goal of fixed exchange rates with complete liberalization within the Community.

In that case, could the deutsche mark be considered as an anchor? This seems to be a semantical question of little relevance. If one admits that the Bundesbank will never accept inflationary policies (a reasonable hypothesis in view of historical experience) and if the Community wants to maintain fixed exchange rates with free movements of funds and resources, each country's monetary policy will have to be geared toward price-level stability. In other words, there ought to be a non-ambiguous and clear agreement by each member state on the price-level stability objective, with its consequences in terms of co-ordination of (at least) their monetary policies.

Is there a need for fiscal policy co-ordination?

Does the reinforcement of integration mean some co-ordination of fiscal policies? In the final stage of a monetary union, what kind of fiscal policy co-ordination is necessary, if indeed it really is necessary at all? The answers to these questions must be balanced.

On one hand, one can argue that the stronger the monetary integration the greater the fiscal discipline will be, owing to market constraints. With fixed exchange rates and perfect capital mobility a country's budget deficit is financed by issuing debt on the capital market (money financing is assumed to be prohibited). If the deficit is too high, the country will not be able to finance it, or will only be able to finance it at a higher cost (i.e. at a higher interest rate). This cost constraint is then supposed to discipline countries in their fiscal policies, and hence lead to implicit and sufficient co-ordination (Padoa-Schioppa 1988). On the other hand, it is possible to argue that free capital mobility on a large financial market renders the financing of deficits easier, and so introduces another degree of freedom in fiscal management; this could diminish incentives to maintain budget deficits within reasonable limits.

Furthermore, if it is a large country, or a combination of countries, which follows a lax fiscal policy, there will be a flow of savings out of the other countries and an interest rate rise for the monetary zone as a whole, with its consequences on investment and growth.

In all federal states (except Australia), regional governments appear to be autonomous in their fiscal management. Yet, there exists an important difference with the institutional set-up in Europe: the 'Central Federal State' budget of the EC is almost negligible compared with the budget of each member state, whereas in traditional federal organizations (such as the USA) the central budget is very large. In this respect, unless the 'central budget' of the EC were to be very significantly increased (a doubtful possibility) it does not provide a sufficient '*marge de manoeuvre*' for an effective macro-fiscal policy for the Community as a whole (Lamfalussy 1989).

If the market cannot provide enough national budgetary discipline, some co-ordination of fiscal policies seems unavoidable. And the greater the need is for such a co-ordination the greater will be the desire to use fiscal policy as a macro-regulator for Europe as a whole.[17]

With the single market and monetary union, all the European economies will be intertwined, in terms of financial and money markets as well as in terms of goods and services. Fiscal policy in one country will have a direct impact on the other countries, especially for a large country. The efficiency of, let us say, an expansionary fiscal policy on income will be reduced in so far as there will be 'leakages' to other countries via the 'imports' thus generated. Hence, incentives to follow such national policies will diminish. A 'co-operative solution' in, say, an expansionary direction would eliminate this problem since income effects would reinforce each other. The co-operative solution would therefore be more efficient.[18] However, it could also be argued that by increasing efficiency this type of solution also increases risk since any policy error would be compounded. In other words, the absence of policy diversification, through efficiency gains, renders more important the effect of 'good' as well as 'bad' policies.

During the transition period towards monetary union it seems reasonable to establish some fiscal policy discipline so as to avoid external imbalances. A growing budget deficit in one country (especially for large countries) may entail an interest rate rise which, even if the rise does not last, may induce a flow of capital that would put pressures on exchange rates and jeopardize their fixity, i.e. one of the main objectives of monetary integration (before complete monetary union is obtained, of course).

The role played by the *amount* of government expenditure and taxes must also be mentioned. It may have an impact on productivity and/or induce flows of capital (be they financial or physical) and of labour between member states. Here, too, a minimal level of convergence, through some co-ordination, appears unavoidable. This does *not* imply, though, centralization or harmonization of the budgetary, fiscal and social security systems of each nation state.

Finally, let us say a few words about the great and important problem of an approximate harmonization of indirect taxes (value added tax and excise taxes) in order to suppress fiscal frontiers. Here, the objective is not some common EC macro-policy, but to avoid the risk of 'unfair competition' due to too great indirect tax differences between countries.

To sum up, it seems that a minimal degree of fiscal co-ordination is desirable, but without the need for strong central rules and regulations.

A CRITICAL REVIEW OF THE TREATY ON EUROPEAN MONETARY UNION

In view of the above economic background, we shall analyse the Treaty on European Monetary Union (1992) and the proposal of the Delors Committee (Delors 1989) which served as the background for the Treaty. We shall also analyse some more specific proposals such as the parallel currency approach.

The final objective: one currency for Europe

The Treaty on European Monetary Union as well as the Delors report agree on the main goal: to establish a *single currency* (the ECU) in the final stage of monetary union. This choice means that they recognize that the benefits of a single currency outweigh its costs. Yet the Delors report postponed the establishment of this currency until monetary union is completed, without the slightest hint as to the possible date for such an outcome; this strategy opened the door to unlimited delays. Fortunately, the Treaty has become more specific on that matter since a single currency will presumably be put in place by 1 January 1999 at the latest. Yet, only countries with an inflation rate generally in line with the best performers in Europe and a budget deficit contained within certain limits will be allowed to enter the union.[19] It is doubtful whether the single currency would be established if only, say, three or four countries met the test, which may appear very rough to some countries, at least rougher than would seem necessary (see below). There is therefore still some uncertainty as to this

supposedly 'deadlock' date. We must also consider the fact that Great Britain may decide, through an 'opt out' clause, not to enter the economic and monetary union. All in all, even if the union is created in 1999, it is doubtful that it will involve all European countries; therefore, one can expect it to constitute a partial union. Having said this, it should be added that, if all goes well, the currency union could be created as soon as January 1997 since leaders, by agreement based on a weighted majority vote, could initiate it with as few as seven member states who are prepared to go ahead (as long as they meet the above-mentioned economic criteria). Again the currency union would not be complete in this case.

What symmetry of adjustments and what fixity of exchange rates?

As was seen earlier, if the Bundesbank never accepts to deviate, at least in the long run, from a relatively stable price-level goal, the European system with fixed exchange rates and complete capital mobility can only function if all countries agree on the same goal. Otherwise, the 'inconsistent quartet' problem will arise. This means closer co-ordination of monetary policies, and in order to bring about such co-ordination the establishment of a European central bank (EuroFed) is of paramount importance.

An agreement on that matter also exists. The Treaty (and the Delors report) considers explicitly that the price stability goal must be the goal of the future European central bank. However, the European Monetary Institute, which should be created by 1 January 1994 (the second stage of the move to economic and monetary union), should be the beginning of the future central bank and is far from being that. Its monetary powers will be small and it resembles more the already existing Committee of Governors of the nations' central banks than a future European central bank.

A major question, avoided in the Treaty and the Delors report, must be investigated: should the current exchange rate limits be quickly narrowed or is it better to wait until a single currency exists and maintain the status quo until then?

It will be necessary for all currencies to enter the EMS and for all of them to be subjected to the same limits. However, it is difficult to say whether a *fast* narrowing (in the long run this narrowing is unavoidable and will occur at the latest on the day when the single currency is established) of exchange rate limits would ease integration or render integration more difficult.

With free capital mobility, exchange rate pressures increase and with them the risk of exchange rate fluctuations. To avoid realignments, intervention mechanisms and monetary co-operation become of paramount importance. Exchange rate limits that are too narrow could entail the need for numerous realignments and thus jeopardize the system's credibility as long as strong co-operation has not yet been established. On the other hand, in order to avoid realignments, narrower bands could induce (force?) monetary authorities to accelerate the convergence and co-ordination measures; in that case the pace towards the EuroFed and monetary union would be increased.

Fiscal and 'regional' policies

The Delors report puts emphasis on the need for strong fiscal policy co-ordination in terms of deficit financing, government expenditure and taxes. It suggests the establishment of medium-term objectives. In the final stage of monetary union, the report proposes that *binding* rules be established. The final Treaty is a little less stringent but does remain rigorous in that respect. We saw that the economic criteria for entering the union are rather strict and may block the entry of some important countries. Yet, as was discussed earlier, in terms of the prerequisite for economic and monetary union the need for fiscal policy co-ordination is probably not as strong as the impression that emerges from the Treaty.

Although the proposals for regional policies and financial redistribution are justified, the proposals appear to be overstated as far as fiscal policies are concerned. They probably reflect central bankers'

fears of having to finance budget deficits through money creation in the case of lax fiscal policies. This fear is understandable, but during the transition period it is more related to the 'policy mix' *within* each country than to the policy co-ordination problem *between* member states. When the single currency is created, this problem disappears and what is important is to severely limit, or even forbid, any monetary financing of each country's deficit by the European central bank; this constraint seems to be accepted by member states and is part of the Treaty.

The ECU and the parallel currency strategy

The Delors report and the Treaty reject the ECU parallel currency as a means of accelerating the pace of the monetary union process for two main reasons: first, because it would add another source of money creation that could jeopardize price stability; second, because it would further complicate the already difficult co-ordination of national monetary policies. The inflationary risk can easily be avoided by having the ECU created *only through substitution* with national monies (Alphandéry and Fourçans 1984a, b). There is no reason for this procedure to entail more complexity within the monetary policy co-ordinating process (see also Mayer 1986).

When the ECU basket of currencies is converted into a new fully fledged parallel currency, it is then obvious that its issue should be controlled and regulated by a European central bank (see Alphandéry and Fourçans (1984a, b) and Basevi *et al.* (1975) for parallel currency strategies).

If the Treaty's institutional approach towards union works well, *a priori*, the ECU (as a basket of currencies or as a complete currency in itself, like the 'hard ECU') as a parallel currency is not a necessary condition of the integration process. But we saw that there are still uncertainties as to the date when all countries would be part of the economic and monetary union.

The widely agreed-on date of 1999 for a fully shared single currency would be more credible if the role of the ECU was reinforced; it would constitute a force for monetary and financial integration that would help accelerate the move of all countries towards union. It is regrettable that the Treaty did not incorporate that idea.

CONCLUSION: TOWARDS A EUROPEAN CENTRAL BANK

Whatever the date when economic and monetary union is created and whatever the number of countries that enter the union, the approach chosen means more monetary co-ordination during the transition period and, at the latest when a single currency is created, the establishment of a European central bank.

From the beginning of the EMS, and especially from the start of the 1980s, monetary co-ordination has been improving. With the new capital mobility, this co-ordination must be reinforced. How? Without entering into the technical details of the process (which are not the object of this chapter), what main lines should be followed?

Two main strategies can be implemented (Guitian *et al.* 1988). First, by admitting agreement on the price stability objective, each country could set up growth objectives for its *internal* money sources in line with internal price stability and real growth, with the further agreement *not to sterilize* international reserves in order to maintain fixed exchange rates.

The second strategy could consist of fixing a money growth objective for the Community as a whole in view of the expected real growth of all the countries taken together; the monetary rule could (should?) be adjusted, for example, to velocity changes, financial innovations and structural changes in production supply.

In both strategies a common decision-making process is necessary. To ease the implementation of such a process the establishment of a common policy body, i.e. the European central bank, would be very welcome. And if one adds the desire to develop the ECU, and therefore the need to manage its issue, we have another reason for setting up such an institution.

According to the Maastricht Treaty the European central bank will only be created a few months before currency union is established. The European Monetary Institute to be set up on 1 January 1994 will have limited monetary powers; its role will be to lay the groundwork for blending the various national currencies into a single currency but it will not have any of the instruments of a central bank.

As far as the future European central bank is concerned, all the questions relating to its precise role and development, its management and its degree of independence with respect to each member state and to the European political systems must be put forward and answered (Fourçans 1989; Thygesen 1989). In that respect, a monetary constitution with simple and clear rules must be implemented and agreed upon by the different member states.

NOTES

1 *Conceptually*, the arguments in favour of one currency for Europe are also those in favour of one money for the world at large. In that respect, the efficiency of the international exchange system would be enhanced (Tower and Willet 1976).

2 With forward markets it is possible to eliminate the financial risk of exchange rate fluctuations. But for maturities beyond three months, forward markets are very thin. Even if they were greatly developed, the coverage operations would necessitate investment of resources which are freed by the existence of a single currency (Basevi *et al.* 1975).

3 These arguments in favour of a single- rather than a multi-currency area with fixed rates apply *a fortiori*, with more weight, to the comparison between a one-currency system and a flexible exchange rate system.

4 These disparities would be reduced, if not suppressed, through the market integration that would result from the existence of a single currency.

5 With the single market the Cecchini report (1988) estimates a gain of +5 per cent in GNP and 1 million to 5 million more jobs for the EC.

6 One could argue that, even without one single currency, monetary sovereignty does not really exist, especially when financial flows are completely free to move between countries (see below).

7 In other words, whether the inflation rate decrease results from the establishment of fixed exchange

rates and a single currency or from restrictive national economic policies in a flexible exchange rate system.

8   The EC has already set up a policy of this type. The amount of funds involved should be multiplied by two, in real terms, between 1989 and 1993. One might expect that these funds will be increased even more with the acceleration of monetary union.

9   High-quality monies, i.e. monies with stable purchasing power fulfilling in the best possible way their medium of exchange, unit of account and store of value functions.

10 Let us imagine the situation where it would be possible to pay for your can of coca-cola with several currencies: you would have to obtain the price in each of the currencies, then calculate the arbitrage operations between these currencies depending on the respective exchange rates; without mentioning the burden of carrying the different currencies in your wallet. A fine old mess!

11 Yet, see the previously given drawbacks in terms of regional allocation of resources.

12 Also, the 'theory of currency substitution' suggests that freely substitutable currencies would lead to monetary union. Indeed, each central bank (or private producer of money) would be forced to offer the same money quality and the exchange rates between the currencies would become fixed (Girton and Ropper 1980).

13 The only example of simultaneous monies cum flexible exchange rates, for a significantly long period of time, is the Chinese bimetallic (silver and gold) system from 1650 to 1850. The other cases are either for short periods of time or in atypical periods (during wars or just after) such as in the USA during the civil war when gold and 'greenbacks' circulated freely. An in-depth study of the 'free banking' episode in the USA before the civil war shows that the system was based on domination of a gold exchange standard, the greenbacks being labelled in gold value at a fixed exchange rate (Klein 1977).

14 Of course, during the transition period when several monies would exist, i.e. as long as competition has not led to equilibrium with a single currency, as is suggested by the natural monopoly argument and the theory of currency substitution.

15 This argument is also used in favour of the superiority, to a single-currency system, of a monetary system in which existing (not private) currencies could compete. In Europe, as long as financial and money markets remain open to the rest of the world (how could it be otherwise?), competition between a European currency and the dollar, the yen etc. will remain. Competition between existing monies will persist ... as long as a world currency does not exist (and that is a long way off!).

16 Through 'mutual recognition' of technical norms, the opening of central and local government markets and the approximate harmonization of indirect taxes – the latter objective being far from attained.

17 Cannot one expect such a desire to increase at the same time as integration does?

18 Assuming, of course, that fiscal policy *has* an effect on income. But this debate goes beyond the purpose of this chapter.

19 More precisely, a country's deficit should not exceed 3 per cent of its GNP, a country's public debt should be no more than 60 per cent of GNP, inflation should not exceed that of the three best-performing member states for the previous year by more than 1.5 percentage points and interest rates should not exceed those of the three best-performing countries in the previous year by more than 2 points. Members are admitted after a qualified majority vote. New members may be admitted every two years through the same voting rule.

REFERENCES

Alphandéry, E. and Fourçans, A. (1984a) 'L'Ecu: stratégie pour une Europe en crise', *Revue Banque*, April: 397–402.

—— and —— (1984b) 'How to create a single European currency', *The Financial Times*, 20 June.

Bailey, R. W., Bordes, C., Driscoll, M. J. and Strauss-Kahn, M. O. (1987) 'Monnaie, demande globale et inertie des rythmes d'inflation dans les principaux pays européens', *Economie Appliquée* 93: 483–538.

Basevi, G., Fratianni, M., Giersch, H., Korteweg, P., O'Mahony, O., Partin, M., Peeters, Th., Salin, P. and Thygesen, N. (1975) 'The All Saints Day manifesto for European monetary union', *The Economist*, 1 November.

de Boissieu, C. (1987) 'L'Ecu et la libéralisation financière en Europe', *Revue d'Economie Politique* 4: 435–50.

Brunner, K. (1984) 'Monetary policy and monetary order', *Aussenwirtschaft* 39.

Brunner, K. and Meltzer, A. (1971) 'The use of money: money in the theory of an exchange economy', *American Economic Review* 61: 784–805.

Cecchini, P. (1988) '1992: a New European Economy', *European Economy* 35.

Christie, H. and Fratianni, M. (1978) 'European monetary union: rehabilitation of a case and some thoughts for strategy', in M. Fratianni and T. Peeter (eds) *One Money for Europe*, London: Macmillan.

Christophersen Report (1990) 'Report on economic and monetary union: economic foundation and system conception', *European Communities*, April.

Claassen, E. M. (1984) 'Monetary integration and monetary stability: the economic criteria of the monetary constitution', in P. Salin (ed.) *Currency Competition and Monetary Union*, Dordrecht: Martinus Nijhoff.

Delors, J. (1989) 'Report on economic and monetary union in the European community', *European Communities*, Luxembourg.

Fourçans, A. (1989) 'Une banque centrale pour l'Europe', *Le Monde*, 29 June.

Fratianni, M. and Von Hagen, J. (1990a) 'The European monetary system ten years after', *Carnegie-Rochester Conference Series* 32.

—— and —— (1990b) 'German dominance in the EMS: the empirical evidence', *Open Economies Review* 1 (1): 67–88.

Frenkel, J. and Goldstein, M. (1988) 'The international monetary system: developments and prospects', Working Paper 88/45, Washington, DC: International Monetary Fund, May.

Friedman, M. (1984) 'Currency competition: a skeptical view', in P. Salin (ed.) *Currency Competition and Monetary Union*, Dordrecht: Martinus Nijhoff.

Giavazzi, F. and Giovannini, F. (1988) 'Modèles du SME: l'Europe n'est-elle qu'une zone deutsche mark?', *Revue Economique* 3 (May): 641–66.

Girton, L. and Ropper, D. (1980) 'The theory of currency substitution and monetary unification', *Economie Appliquée* 33: 155–60.

Guitian, M., Russo, M. and Tullio, G. (1988) 'Policy coordination in the European monetary system', *IMF Occasional Paper* 61, September.

Hayek, F. (1978) 'Denationalisation of money', *Hobart Paper*, 2nd edn, Institute of Economic Affairs.

Kenen, P. (1976) *Capital Mobility and Financial Integration*, Princeton Studies in International Finance 39.

Klein, B. (1974) 'The competitive supply of money', *Journal of Money, Credit and Banking* 6 (November): 423–54.

—— (1977) 'Competing monies, European monetary union, and the dollar', in M. Fratianni and T. Peeter (eds) *One Money for Europe*, London: Macmillan.

Lamfalussy, A. (1989) 'Macro-coordination of fiscal policies in an economic and monetary union in Europe', in Committee for the Study of Economic and Monetary Union, *Report on Economic and Monetary Union in the European Community*, Luxembourg: Office of Official Publications of the European Communities.

Lehment, H. (1984) 'Freely flexible exchange rates or a common currency? A new look at the issue', in P. Salin (ed.) *Currency Competition and Monetary Union*, Dordrecht: Martinus Nijhoff.

Masera, R. (1986) 'An increasing role for the Ecu: a character in search of a script', *Banca d'Italia*.

Mayer, H. (1986) 'Private Ecus potential macroeconomic policy dimensions', *BIS Economic Papers* 16, Bank for International Settlements, April.

Mundell, R. (1961) A theory of optimum currency areas', *American Economic Review*, September: 657–65.

Padoa-Schioppa, T. (1988) 'The European monetary system: a long term view', in F. Giavazzi, J. Micossi and M. Miller (eds) *The European Monetary System*, Cambridge: Cambridge University Press.

Salin, P. (1984) 'Which monetary integration?', in P. Salin (ed.) *Currency Competition and Monetary Union*, Dordrecht: Martinus Nijhoff.

Sarcinelli, M. (1986) 'The EMS and the international monetary system: towards greater stability', *Banca Nazionale del Lavoro Quarterly Review*, March: 57–84.

Schinasi, G. (1989) 'European integration, exchange rate management, and monetary reform: a review of the major issues', *International Finance Discussion Papers*, Board of Governors of the Federal Reserve System, October.

Thygesen, N. (1989) 'On the prospects for a European central bank', in M. de Cecco and A. Giovannini (eds) *A European Central Bank*, Cambridge: Cambridge University Press.

Tower, E. and Willet, T. (1976) 'The theory of optimum currency area and exchange rate flexibility', *Special Papers in International Economics* 11, Princeton University, May.

Treaty on European Monetary Union (1992) *European Communities*, Luxembourg.

Vaubel, R. (1977) 'Free currency competition', *Weltwirtschaftliches Archiv* 3: 435–61.

Part III

WORLD EQUITY MARKETS

One indicator of the changing global financial environment is interest in the across-the-border stock markets, which has increased progressively over the decades of the 1970s and 1980s. Gross equity trading in foreign stock markets by industrialized economies increased at an annual rate of over 50 per cent during the latter half of the 1980s. The intellectual interest has grown *pari passu* and so has literature on world stock markets. Going international is considered a profitable situation because of the low correlation between stock prices in different markets. Basically, gains from international diversification are similar to those that accrue within a domestic market. However, there is convincing evidence that diversification benefits are much stronger in across-the-border stock markets than within domestic markets. One of the underlying reasons is that economic disturbances are in general market specific and do not sway foreign stock markets. International diversification also lowers overall portfolio risk because international stock markets display relatively low statistical correlation. Brisker growth in economies other than the US economy in the recent past has stimulated across-the-border equity investments. It led to more rapid increases in the market value of equities in Europe and Japan than in the USA. In addition, the currencies in these areas also appreciated, raising the returns on equities in Europe and Japan. Investors in other countries increased their demand of US equities to diversify the currency mix of their portfolio holdings.

In the first chapter of this section Calderón-Rossell reviews the related literature, the bulk of which is focused on industrialized economies. The principal foci are international asset pricing, factors influencing across-the-border equity investment and its implications for economic growth. This chapter provides a good survey of what is known about international stock markets. The second chapter is more analytical and examines the international evidence regarding the validity of the efficient market hypothesis. It also investigates the validity of the capital asset pricing model and the arbitrage pricing theory as descriptors and predictors of common stock returns in various stock exchanges around the world. It concludes that there is sufficient evidence to suggest that investment strategies which attempt to exploit stock market anomalies around the world can improve global portfolio performance. There are several reasons why anomaly-based investment strategy can enhance global portfolio returns. However, it fails to answer whether the extra returns earned on anomaly-based investment strategies are a free lunch or mere fair compensation on a riskier investment.

The Asia–Pacific region has been the fastest growing economic region of the world and, along with Japan, has found the third dynamic growth pole of the international economy. Gradual opening of the capital markets in this region in the 1980s is considered a significant financial development. The combined market value of the region's common equities add up to approximately one-third of the world's total capital market volume. The last chapter, by Rhee, Chang and Ageloff, is addressed to this important segment of the international equity markets. The Asia–Pacific equity markets offer excellent long-term investment opportunities as the economies in the region are gradually introducing a series of changes in their economic policies. They are moving towards deregulation of markets and privatization of industries and services. In fact, sufficient progress in this regard has already been made. The authors predict a heightened interest by individual and institutional investors in these financial markets in the foreseeable future. The Asia–Pacific equity markets will be an alluring alternative to the matured markets in North America and Western Europe.

13

TOWARDS THE THEORY OF WORLD STOCK MARKETS

An overview

Jorge R. Calderón-Rossell

INTRODUCTION

Interest in foreign stock markets has significantly increased during the last two decades, particularly during the 1980s when international portfolio investments seem to have increased substantially.[1] Evidence of this interest is reflected in the increasing literature on the subject which is briefly reviewed in this chapter. While advances have been made in both the theory and the empirical analysis of international portfolio investments, significant and fundamental research is still needed on several fronts to advance our understanding of the establishment, functioning, growth and interaction of stock markets with the economies in which they operate. This understanding is critical in order to confidently provide policy recommendations leading to the further development of world stock markets.

Studies of international stock markets have often been born by extending the concepts and the knowledge on the functioning of domestic stock markets. Because of this, the recent domestic markets literature is also briefly discussed in this chapter. Particularly relevant contributions are those analysing the functioning of stock markets and their interaction with economic variables and policies. Different stages of economic development appear to impinge on stock market development. With this notion, a subset of the literature has focused on emerging markets, i.e. those operating in developing economies. The bulk of the sub-

stantive literature, however, has focused on developed markets, i.e. those operating in developed economies.

Stock markets, on the other hand, do not work in isolation as they form part of the financial system and arise as a consequence of the international monetary system. To the extent that they were considered relevant, studies in these areas that could throw some light on the development of international stock markets are also briefly reviewed.

Central to the study of the world stock markets is also the controversy between integration and segmentation of capital markets, which by necessity needs to be considered also.

The purpose of this chapter is to review briefly what we know so far about international stock markets, with special attention paid to identifying possible policy implications. The study does not pretend to be exhaustive. A special effort is made to highlight issues that may provoke further research which would advance our understanding of stock markets. Because of this, the chapter is basically descriptive and only attempts to be analytical on certain relevant theoretical issues. Such understanding is essential for providing policy recommendations leading to further development of international stock markets.

The following section focuses on the international asset pricing literature. The assumptions of CAPMs that have been extended to international markets are examined in detail, with special attention to possible violations of these assumptions in the case of international markets. Possible avenues for further research to develop a general international equilibrium model are briefly discussed; and some of the limitations of these models for providing policy recommendations are examined.

In the third section we review the macro-economics literature, including international monetary economics papers dealing with capital and monetary flows and the relevant determinants of such flows. Also, contributions on the inter-action of security markets with the economy are also examined. The need for disaggregating non-monetary assets in macroeconomic models and the behaviour of such assets under certain policy variables are also reviewed. It is argued that Tobin's open economy macro model provides the basis for further developing our understanding of stock markets with the economy.

Focusing more on overall financial systems and economic development in the fourth section, the possible implications for the development of stock market activities with an economic development perspective and its potential contribution to economic growth are reviewed. The impact of foreign aid in the development of domestic savings and investments is also briefly mentioned.

Extending the discussions of the fourth section, the specific literature on emerging markets is examined in the fifth section. The particular characteristics of emerging markets in contrast with those already developed is presented. The potential role that governments could play in promoting stock markets in developed economies is discussed.

The sixth section examines in particular three relevant issues of international stock markets: (i) the controversy of integration versus segmentation; (ii) foreign direct investments as an alternative to constrained portfolio investments; and (iii) the capital flight debate.

The concluding section evaluates the current knowledge of international stock markets and advocates further research aiming to identify potential policy guidelines for the development of stock markets. The underlying premise is that stock market growth would improve the allocable efficiency of resources internationally and induce further economic growth on a world-wide scale.

INTERNATIONAL ASSET PRICING AND DIVERSIFICATION

The interest in foreign stock markets since the seminal paper by Grubel (1968) has been largely motivated by the expected benefits to be accrued by investors from diversifying their portfolios in world markets.[2] Under different comparative advantages, and thus different economic structures, financial assets issued in different countries are subject to a valuation process determined by each country's economic and business cycle as well as its fiscal, financial and monetary policies. Policy differences aside, the non-synchronous economic and business cycles are the basis for internationally diversifying equity portfolios. This economic reality is the basis for selecting stocks or portfolios with weakly correlated international returns, which has been greatly emphasized in the international asset pricing models literature.

In extending domestic portfolio theory into the international arena, it is often implicitly assumed that all domestic equity markets in the world, except for the eventuality of following different business cycles, have the same attributes and similar characteristics regarding their performance and asset pricing. By further assuming that all individuals have homogeneous preferences and beliefs and that markets are complete and perfect, an optimal allocation of world wealth is determined at the theoretical level.

All the standard assumptions of CAPMs which are often applied to international markets[3] can be encompassed in the general notion of perfect, complete, homogeneous consumption, tastes and beliefs; stable, efficient and integrated capital markets whereby efficient markets include at least three different aspects, i.e. exchange or operational, production or allocable and informational efficiency.[4] Violations of these assumptions result in unbalanced non-equilibrium portfolios, or inefficient world market portfolios (see Stulz 1981a). Therefore, by extending CAPMs to the international environment where domestic markets are considered part of an integrated world market, the underlying assumptions of such models need to be re-examined.

A long list of assumptions and valuation criteria of CAPMs are still questionable in the international arena. Several financial economists and contributions in the literature suggest that in the international market, more so than within a single domestic market, participants are heterogeneous. For example, Adler and Dumas (1983) have pointed out that deviations from PPP lead to heterogeneity among international investors. Also based on the comparative advantage of their country and their individual wealth, market participants may have different tastes and perceptions, and thus different expectations and attitudes towards risks. Even from a domestic perspective, Sametz (1970) has pointed out that interpersonal differences in the perception of and the attitudes towards risk and uncertainty are perhaps the single most important factor in the forming of capital markets. The following points are also important: firms issuing securities in world markets may not be price-takers;[5] non-competitive behaviour, exclusive technologies and the limited number of firms are sources of non-optimality of stock market allocation (see Jenson and Long 1972; Merton and Subrahmanyam 1974); under economies of scale and industrial structures where economic groups have market power, particularly those in small economies, not all investors may maximize single-period expected utility based only on mean and variance returns; given the small capitalization of certain markets and companies, investors may not be able to buy or sell as much of every security without affecting prices; all investors, particularly in small countries, may not be able to borrow or lend an unlimited amount of risk-free assets; based on different rates of economic growth, the expected real return on assets may differ and the supply of securities may not be fixed, and so the relative prices of assets may be unstable thereby preventing markets reaching equilibrium condi-

tions;[6] given the small number of listed securities in several countries and their small market capitalization, investors may find it attractive to buy and sell assets outside organized markets; given capital flow restrictions, capital mobility is impaired, limiting the integration of world markets and creating additional international capital market imperfections (see, for example, Guy 1978; Stulz 1981a); other imperfections (see, for example, Samuels 1981) – such as information, transaction costs and taxes[7] – abound in world markets. Subject to different fiscal, financial and monetary policies that affect relative asset prices and their stability, world markets may not be in equilibrium and are subject to a sovereign risk which though largely ignored at the domestic level is relevant internationally. The risk of policy changes in individual markets needs to be explicitly taken into account in international investments. In addition, while violating perfect market conditions, the monopoly of firms (particularly of MNCs) may not permit the separation of production and financial decisions. Under these conditions, production and financial markets may not be Pareto optimal, and therefore the allocation of resources may not be efficient.[8]

Also, if international markets are incomplete, as discussed in Hart (1975), it would be relevant to analyse the consequences of opening new international markets. Hart (1975) presents a case where, in providing new opportunities to trade (i.e. new markets), investors do not recognize the interdependence between the gains from trade at different times, and their utilities, and thus their welfare, are reduced. In particular, it would be relevant to determine what the world-wide wealth effects are when domestic markets or partial international markets are extended to a full world capital market by introducing (or 'opening') the rest of the world market.

Besides possible violations of CAPM's assumptions, overriding questions remain open regarding the criteria to be used for valuing international assets and regarding the controversy of integration versus segmentation of world markets (see the penultimate section).

An extensive body of the literature has focused

on the valuation of assets based on domestic versus international factors; and is therefore concerned also with the foreign exchange risk faced by international investors.[9] If PPP does not hold (as in Dumas 1977; Adler and Dumas 1983), investors are subject to an exchange risk. Based on homogeneous beliefs and investors' access to home-country risk-free assets, Solnik (1977) has argued that foreign exchange risk is neutralized by holding investors' own-country risk-free assets. While Solnik's assumptions are questionable, the different but preferred consumption basket of investors may result in foreign exchange risks (see Stulz 1981b; Adler and Dumas 1983). Undoubtedly, for a better understanding of such risks there is still a need to develop an acceptable theory of foreign exchange rate determination which so far has eluded us.[10] As Adler and Dumas (1983) have pointed out, a general equilibrium model of international capital markets with heterogeneous consumption tastes would require as yet unknown procedures for computing equilibrium prices. Thus, such a general equilibrium model would also require an optimal allocation of foreign exchange risk-bearing among international investors. The rationale for such an allocation of exchange risk still needs to be worked out in the context of international asset pricing models.[11]

Given their different purchasing power, investors from different countries (unless they have decreasing absolute risk aversion, i.e. they have logarithmic utilities) will differ in identifying an efficient portfolio and therefore the measurement of returns in any single currency unit could not serve as a benchmark for valuation. Heterogeneous investors, as suggested by Adler and Dumas (1983), could value assets relative to each other but then the market portfolio becomes unobservable. Thus, resolving the problem of portfolio choice when investors' real returns differ is a necessary first step towards a truly international CAPM. Because of these limitations, as Adler and Dumas have pointed out, besides the descriptive value of the statistics, the available international CAPM 'results offer neither guidelines for the construction of optimally diversified portfolios nor

the basis for evaluating the benefits or value of such diversification' (1983: 939).

The issue of integration versus segmentation of markets still remains a controversial issue in the empirical analysis of world markets.[12] While further research is required to determine the extent of world market integration, the overriding evidence of restrictions and lack of information regarding a substantial number of individual markets suggests that they are not perfectly integrated world-wide. As in Lee and Sachdeva,

a capital market is segmented when certain groups of investors limit their investments to a subset of the universe of all possible asset claims. Such market segmentation can occur because of ignorance about the universe of possible asset claims or because of transaction costs (brokerage costs, taxes, or information acquisition costs), or because of legal impediments.

(1977: 479)

Without examining in detail other market imperfections, it is evident that very little is known about world markets. Only recently (see Calderón-Rossell 1990) has the full structure of world markets started to be analysed. On the basis of this limited information, *a priori* it is anticipated that world markets are segmented. If emerging markets are ignored, it is plausible that developed markets may be more closely related given their openness to trade and the influence of monetary and economic variables. Such interrelation, however, could be limited by different government policies and real return divergences.

So far, the advances in CAPM theory permit us to deal with incomplete markets,[13] heterogeneous investors (but with the same beliefs) and B taste parameters (the universal separation theorem). Under such assumptions the equilibrium rates of return will be determined as if the securities markets were complete (see Rubinstein 1974, 1975; Ohlson 1987) and, desite differences in wealth, utility of present consumption, rate of patience and A taste parameters (see Rubinstein 1974), the optimal portfolio of risky securities (the market portfolio) will be the same for all individuals. Nevertheless, if the universal separation theorem holds, incomplete markets are also operational (exchange) and production (allocable) efficient (see Stiglitz 1972).[14]

In addition, in markets where the universal separation theorem holds or where a composite individual can be constructed, equilibrium rates of return are insensitive to the population and to the distribution of resources among individuals (see Rubinstein 1974). This is particularly relevant for emerging markets and, if such assumptions hold in international markets, Branson's (1970) international capital flows determination as a function of wealth becomes questionable. So, if international markets are susceptible to be represented by a composite individual, this implies that investors will hold a proportion of the market capitalization of individual countries similar to the proportion that they represent in world markets, i.e. they would hold the world market portfolio. It is plausible, however, that by introducing transactions and information costs which may be high in small capitalized markets or in markets with a significant number of small firms, the revised optimal world market portfolio may not include investments in certain emerging markets. Thus, the transaction and information differential costs and their impact in world portfolio choices needs to be determined and empirically validated.[15]

Therefore, if investors hold the world market portfolio, the capitalization of individual stock markets, and particularly of emerging markets, will not increase by the flow of investments from rich countries but by increasing stock investments within their own economies. Thus, even with fully open economies, the flow of foreign investments would be mainly determined by the growth of individual domestic markets. This is a relevant empirical question[16] that could help policy-makers to determine whether fiscal, financial and monetary policies could be aimed to attract international investments (see Rubinstein 1974). If the universal separation theorem holds, however, interference by policy-makers that alters rates of return will lead to a non-optimal allocation of resources.

The main stumbling block for extending the universal separation theorem to international markets is the B taste parameter, which is expected to be different between investors from different countries. This represents what Adler and Dumas (1983) have identified as the main constraint for computing equilibrium prices. Nevertheless, if international investors have logarithmic utilities, returns measured in any currency could serve as a benchmark for valuation.

In searching for a complete international CAPM, two avenues of research become obvious. The first is theoretical and would be to search for a general equilibrium model with heterogeneity in consumption tastes. The second is empirical and would be to determine to what extent international investors have different consumption tastes or if they have logarithmic utilities. While Dumas (1977) briefly discussed studies that found similarities of consumption tastes in developed countries, such studies need to be extended to both developed and developing economies. Differences in wealth, the consumption opportunity set and stages of economic development suggest that consumption tastes between developed and developing markets may differ; this, however, remains an open issue. Assuming that markets are fully integrated, Stulz (1981b) has already developed a model dealing with temporary different consumption opportunity sets in (but not across) different countries where the real expected return on a risky asset is proportional to the covariance of that asset with changes in the world real consumption rate. If a country's real consumption closely correlates with the world real consumption, differences in consumption opportunity sets are apparently not likely to matter for studies of international asset pricing. This appears to imply that, even with different investor tastes, world markets would be integrated and therefore could be modelled on the basis of a simple international asset pricing model with returns valued in real terms. However, differences in consumption opportunity sets can create significant differences in asset holdings across countries. While violation of PPP would limit the results of this model, some premises about non-observability of foreign prices question the full integration assumption. But before examining the correlation of real asset returns in world markets, additional research is needed to determine to what extent world investors evaluate returns based on nominal versus real returns. Therefore, the empirical line of research focuses on the determination of consumption or taste differences which may still permit analysis of international asset pricing with existing models.

In contrast, if the search for a theoretical general equilibrium model with different consumption tastes is successful, it is necessary to analyse the extent to which violations of the CAPM's assumptions would affect equilibrium returns. After finding this general equilibrium model, the relaxation of assumptions (regarding imperfections, inefficiencies, segmentation, changing supply of securities etc.) could be studied following Stapleton and Subrahmanyam's (1980) approach.

Therefore, only if empirical studies support the use of existing models of international asset pricing or if new theoretical developments lead to a general equilibrium model with different consumption tastes could we be confident of existing guidelines, or of those that would be developed based on the new general equilibrium model for the construction of optimally diversified international portfolios or of the benefits of such diversification. Until further research provides support for existing guidelines and models, caution must be exercised in their application and use. As Stulz has pointed out: 'Buying the market portfolio in a foreign country might just be buying a highly inefficient portfolio for domestic investors' (1981a: 933). Users of existing models and guidelines may help the development of future research by documenting their experience so as to point out the path that could help to develop an acceptable theory of international finance. Perhaps by examining actual foreign portfolio investments in world markets,[17] investment patterns may be identified that could help explain portfolio choices and international asset pricing and that could permit testing of existing and future international asset pricing models.[18, 19]

While a complete international security pricing model would be relevant for determining the world stock market portfolio and for analysing the informational efficiency of organized world markets, such a model would have to be expanded to include other assets to study the exchange (operational) and allocable (production) efficiency of world markets. The inclusion of other financial assets and securities traded in non-organized markets in a broad and complete international CAPM would throw some light on the overall efficiency of organized world securities markets.

The development of studies aimed to determine the allocable efficiency of stock markets is particularly relevant. While financial markets could be allocable efficient (channelling resources to the economic activities with the highest expected return for a given level of risk) such financial allocations do not necessarily result in an economically efficient (Pareto optimal) allocation of resources. In addition to Fama (1972) and Jensen and Long (1972), Stiglitz (1972, 1981a, b, 1982) has presented several arguments to question the validity of the optimality of resource allocation of financial markets. Because of this, Stiglitz (1981b) calls for a quantification of the significance of the potential market failures to determine whether selective government intervention could result in an improved allocation of resources (see also Greenwald and Stiglitz 1986; Cohn and Pringle 1973). As Stiglitz (1981b) recognizes that the direct observation of allocable efficiency is virtually impossible[20] and several approaches to study the allocable efficiency of markets are limited, it is then first necessary to develop acceptable tests or to estimate the magnitude of the distortions quantitatively. Perhaps production decisions and CAPMs (such as Leland 1974) need to be integrated in the context of open economies to study the allocable efficiency of stock markets further.

While the determination of a broad and complete international asset pricing model is relevant, it still belongs to the realm of partial analysis where most variables are exogenously determined. Thus, such models would not permit an analysis of possible feedback effects of changes in the economic and financial setting and therefore they would be limited to providing recommendations or guidelines for policy-makers. These policy recommendations may come through in developing and examining general equilibrium macroeconomic models, such as those developed by Tobin (1982), where financial markets, and stock markets in particular, would be integrated into open economies. Such developments are still in their infancy and much more remains to be done to analyse international asset pricing models in the context of open economies and under changing fiscal, financial and monetary policies.

MACROECONOMIC ANALYSIS

At the macro level most of the literature has focused on the implications of capital flows (mainly long-term loans or bonds) on balance of payments, trade balances, foreign exchange rates and equalization of factors of production.[21] As Tobin and Braga de Macedo (1980) have pointed out, formal macroeconomic analysis of open economies with capital mobility began with the work of Fleming (1962) and Mundell (1961, 1963, 1964). The great contribution of the Mundell–Fleming model, as pointed out by Frenkel and Razin (1987), has been its systematic analysis of the role played by international capital mobility in determining the effectiveness of macroeconomic policies under alternative exchange rate regimes. As this model has been extensively discussed elsewhere (see Frenkel and Razin 1987), and it does not have the level of disaggregation that could be found in Tobin (as discussed below), it will not be examined further here.

Particularly influential has been the work by Branson (1970), who identified stock and flow effects in determining international capital movements. Under a partial analysis framework, Branson identified the major determinants (i.e. total wealth of home-country investors, the level of domestic and foreign interest rates, risk considerations and the level of other variables such as exports) of total assets held abroad. Of these determinants, given their relative magnitude, wealth considerations are most relevant. Under acceptable risk levels, and great discrepancies in domestic and foreign interest rates, the wealthier the country the larger would be the value of total assets held abroad by its residents.

In Branson (1970), assuming constant portfolio sizes, the movements of capital in response to changes in the differential between foreign and domestic interest rates are a consequence of pure stock adjustments. The larger the portfolio and the interest differentials, the larger the magnitude of stock adjustments and therefore of capital movements. Continued capital movements, on the other hand, are mainly ascribable to the portfolio's growth (the flow effect) which relative to stock effects is considered to be small.[22] Therefore, interest differentials would be more important than growth in explaining capital movements. But in a world of changing interest rates and growing portfolios, observed capital movements reflect the combined result of both stock and flow effects.

Branson's empirical analysis, however, did not separate equities and long-term claims on foreigners. They were lumped together and determined as a residual of total US claims on foreigners exclusive of foreign direct investment, short-term claims and long-term banking claims. Disregarding well-known differences between equities and loans, Branson's approach implies that the major determinants for movements of both types of assets are the same, or alternatively that equities and loans would be perfect substitutes. These implicit assumptions, however, are questionable and need to be validated.[23] Unless perfect substitutability of equities and loans can be proved or a clear transmission process by which interest rates determine stock prices is identified, movements of equities and loans need to be disaggregated and explained. Branson's straightforward model determines major factors affecting loan movements but his partial analysis needs to be reassessed in an open economy macroeconomic model where different types of assets are recognized.

Extending Branson's model to a general equilibrium model of financial markets in an open economy, but still ignoring foreign exchange rate fluctuations and differences in asset type, Kouri and Porter (1974) found that changes in income are highly significant in explaining capital flows. Thus, in contrast to Branson's emphasis, capital flows reflect divergent growth rates and cyclical phases between countries. Kouri and Porter further claim that the more basic sources of capital flows are fluctuations in money demand and supply.[24]

While Kouri and Porter's approach may be consistent with a dynamic international asset pricing model where stock portfolios grow with the economy in which they are held, Branson's wealth relevance for international portfolios is at odds with a truly international asset pricing model.[25] If Branson's view were applicable to stock markets, investors of wealthier countries would have a larger share of foreign stocks than those determined by the international market portfolio. A resolution of these divergent views is particularly relevant for policy-makers interested in attracting foreign capital. If Branson's views hold, policy-makers could expect a significant flow of investments from wealthier countries. But if the international asset pricing models are correct, such an inflow would be largely determined by the size and growth of the domestic market relative to world markets. Evidently the impact of monetary policies for attracting foreign capital in one case would be more relevant than in the other. So additional studies need to be made for determining the factors explaining international investments in stock markets.

Under a portfolio approach, Allen (1973) analyses the demand for financial assets (bonds and money) as determined by income, the world interest rate and wealth. Assuming perfect capital mobility and fixed exchange rates, an increase in the stock of either bonds or money will stimulate a readjustment of portfolios. Under constant portfolios, there would be no investment demand or supply of assets and thus no capital movements. In a growing economy, portfolio equilibrium would require world issuance of new assets at the rate of growth of the world economy. Zero balance of payments and zero net capital flows would be consistent with new issuance of bonds and currency in each country at the same rate as its economic growth. Thus, a different pattern of growth among countries would result in portfolio adjustments and capital flows due mainly to wealth effects.

While focusing on the determinants of the net factors income from abroad, Borts and Kopecky (1972) suggest, along the lines of Allen, that the movements of capital can be explained by the same determinants that explain the growth of an economy. As the net factors income from abroad only measures the net aggregate revenues of both investments and services from abroad, and is usually determined as a residual between GDP and GNP calculations, Borts and Kopecky's results are suspicious and not particularly illuminating.[26]

Overall, capital movements and their implications regarding equity investments in world markets[27] have been largely ignored in the open economy macroeconomics literature. While some authors claim that 'international capital flows improve the efficiency of resource allocation in the world and thereby raise world output and welfare' (Grubel 1977: 544), empirical studies to validate this hypothesis need to be developed. Dooley et al.'s (1987) study on the saving–investment correlation, by implication, casts doubts on the allocable efficiency of capital markets. They conclude that even if international financial markets are integrated so as to equalize financial expected returns, the expected returns on physical capital are not equalized. Under such segmentation between financial and physical assets it is doubtful that international financial resources are efficiently allocated, and therefore that world output and welfare are increased. At the theoretical level and with a domestic perspective, Jensen and Long (1972) have also shown that, if capital markets are somewhat less than perfect, the private allocation of investment in general is inconsistent with the social welfare and social wealth optimum allocation. In this regard, income redistribution effects of international portfolio investments need to be examined also. Therefore, substantial research is still needed to review the allocable efficiency of capital markets, and in particular that of equity markets.

Except for money and credit type instruments, other financial assets have also been largely ignored even in the closed economy macroeconomics literature.[28] Despite the implicit relationship between macroeconomic aggregates and financial markets,[29] most macroeconomic analyses focus primarily – if not exclusively – on money, and more recently on long-term financial instruments or credit aggregates (see discussions in Feltestein 1981; Friedman 1981). Perhaps, because of specialization and differences in curricula, there is a divorce between financial economists and macroeconomists which has stinted the integration of financial markets in macroeconomic models. Although empirical studies have analysed the relationship of stock prices and certain economic indicators,[30] except for Tobin's and Gavin's work briefly discussed below and a more limited model by Greenwald et al. (1984), I am not aware of a comprehensive macroeconomic model that incorporates stock markets and economic behaviour. For an increasing understanding of international capital flows within equity markets, and their impact on world-wide economic and business activities, the relationship of domestic equity markets and economic variables is of primary importance and needs clear identification. If such a relationship is established, perhaps the body of the theory of economics may be easily adapted for analysing the behaviour of financial markets.

With a domestic perspective, the best descriptive relationship of security markets and the economy, or economic aggregates, so far has been provided in an article by Davidson (1968) and more comprehensively in his book *Money and the Real World* (1978).[31] In Davidson's view, if monetary policy does not accommodate the growth of investments in real assets, *ceteris paribus*, the supply of stocks increases while the demand and stock prices drop, limiting the rate of capital accumulation and therefore reducing economic growth.[32]

Central to this view is the relationship of stock prices and money supply which remains an unre-

solved and controversial issue. Based on the informational efficiency of stock markets, it has been argued that stock prices or returns anticipate (lead) changes in money growth rates. Still recognizing that in general monetary aggregates affect stock prices, Cooper (1974), Pesando (1974), Rozeff (1974)[33] and, more recently, Davidson and Froyen (1982) found support for the efficient market hypothesis.[34] At the other extreme of this controversy, Palmer (1970), Keran (1971), Homa and Jaffee (1971) and Hamburger and Kochin (1972) found support for the notion that stock market returns lag changes in money growth rates.[35]

The relationship between stock prices and economic activity was also examined by Pearce (1983),[36] Gray (1984), Brinner (1987) and Wyss (1987). Pearce's views are based on the behaviour between the movements of stock price indices and the index of industrial production. He found that stock prices usually lead industrial production activity in the USA. However, this relationship was weaker in the UK and Canada and absent in West Germany and France; no explanation was given and no theoretical basis was provided to account for the differences. In contrast, Gray analyses the correlation of stock return risk premia over bond yields. Based on a partial model of stock prices,[37] he found a positive correlation between the expected and actual risk premia and projected stock prices and returns for the 1978 and 1988 period.[38] The analyses of Brinner (1987) and Wyss (1987), on the other hand, are based on the Data Resources Incorporated forecasting model. Along the lines of Davidson (1968, 1978), Brinner and Wyss recognize that increases in stock prices increase household wealth, which induces greater consumer spending and investments in real assets by making it cheaper to issue new securities and more expensive to acquire capacity by mergers and acquisitions.[39]

In the absence of a complete macroeconomic model explaining the interaction of macroeconomic variables and stock markets, Chen et al. (1983) applied factor analysis to search for a set of macroeconomic variables that systematically influenced stock market returns and to study the implication of this influence in asset pricing. The results of their study, however, were inconclusive. Perhaps the interaction and simultaneous determination of certain macroeconomic variables could limit the success of factor analysis for finding the correct set of variables affecting stock market behaviour. In this regard, the extension of Tobin's model discussed below may be more promising.

An extremely significant breakthrough, which apparently has been largely unrecognized, has been made by Tobin and presented in his Nobel lecture in Stockholm on 8 December 1981. Based on his previous work (Tobin 1969; Tobin and Brainard 1968), Tobin (1982) has extended the standard macro model that limits itself to two asset categories – money and everything else – by including foreign currency assets and, for the first time, equities. This is apparently the first macro model that provides the level of disaggregation necessary to study the stock market and its interaction with an open economy seriously while examining policy implications and feedbacks into other economic variables. As Tobin recognizes, an essential part of macroeconomic activity is the dynamics of flows and stocks, investment and capital, saving and wealth and the specific forms of saving and asset stocks; transactions which are the sources of variation of money stocks make a difference, particularly if such transactions alter the wealth and portfolio position of the participants in the economy. In Tobin's model it is also assumed that the initial wealth and portfolio composition of economic agents are given; otherwise they would have to be endogenously determined.[40] Tobin also recognizes that financial and capital markets are highly imperfect co-ordinators of saving and investment. This imperfection is a source of macroeconomic instability but an opportunity for macroeconomic policies of stabilization.[41]

As Tobin has pointed out, the innovation of his model is to integrate saving and portfolio decisions in a macroeconomic model. The markets which determine asset prices and interest rates co-ordinate these demand flows with the supply flows arising from real investment, the government

deficit and the external current account. Tobin's model simultaneously handles the flows arising from saving and asset accumulation and those from portfolio adjustments. Government's financing requirements immediately affect financial markets.

Aside from the general policy implication of Tobin's model regarding fiscal and monetary policies under a flexible exchange rate (see Tobin (1982: 191) for details), the foreign exchange rate is determined by markets in which demands and supplies for current and capital accounts are combined. While this approach is effective for analysing the impact of total international flows on the foreign exchange rate, it hinders the analysis for flows arising from trade and those from stock investments. By disaggregating such flows, an extension of Tobin's model could provide insights not yet available on the impact of foreign investments in domestic markets of equities (stocks). Tobin's model may also be relevant for studying the impact and determination of foreign exchange risks.

Under sticky exchange rate expectations and exchange appreciations, Tobin's analysis in his Keynesian version determines that expansionary fiscal and monetary policies are effective. In a fiscal expansion, exchange appreciation reduces the demand for money because the wealth held in foreign investments is lower while the return of such investments is higher. Again within the Keynesian version, the number of possible substitution patterns of financial assets creates ambiguities that need to be resolved. The results of the model are determined contingent on certain substitution patterns.

Under the classical variant where prices are endogenously determined, the monetary expansion is not neutral. It lowers real interest rates and shifts the composition of output from consumption to investment.

Central to Tobin's model is its own q-theory which establishes the relationship between changes in individual stocks as a function of the market value of the firm and the replacement cost of its fixed assets. While this relationship is still subject to further analysis,[42] a plausible alternative linking investments in real assets with the issuance of securities still needs to be identified. This in itself is an area that needs further investigation and which points to a weakness in investment theory. What are the determinants for enterprises to identify and undertake investments in real assets? While no theory has yet provided a satisfactory answer to this question, once a behavioural equation is developed, the financing of such undertakings could be left open to determine the composition of debt and equity as a function of cost and risk differences.[43]

Among the recommendations for extending his model, Tobin suggests including a complete foreign sector where its demands for all local assets are introduced, as opposed to specifying all foreign transactions through the balance-of-payments equation. Tobin and Braga De Macedo (1980) have already made some inroads in extending this model to the international arena. Unfortunately, equities and bonds were considered perfect substitutes, preventing focus on the equities market alone. By disaggregating equity markets, the effect of macroeconomic policies and other assets on open economies linked by trade, capital markets and floating exchange rates could be analysed. Perhaps another useful extension would be the introduction of short-term financial assets which would permit economic agents to invest in very liquid interest-earning assets as opposed to long-term financial investments in bonds or equities which are usually less liquid. This would resemble real world financial markets more. Even without these extensions, Tobin's model is rich and provides the necessary framework for carefully studying the implications of fiscal, financial and monetary policies on equity markets.

While the empirical testing of Tobin's model[44] would be practically limited by data constraints perhaps to the US economy, the richness of the model could permit theoretical extensions for increasing our understanding of the behaviour and functioning of world equity markets. Therefore, such theoretical extensions and empirical studies to test the basic model and its extensions should be encouraged.

Besides Tobin's model, Blanchard (1981) extended the IS–LM closed economy model by assuming that asset values, rather than interest rates, are the main determinants of aggregate demand and output. Assuming further that stocks and short- and long-term bonds are perfect substitutes, and that agents are satisfied with the proportion of money in their portfolios, Blanchard (1981) shows that the effect of a change either in current policy or in anticipated policy is a discrete change in the stock market due to the change in the anticipated sequence of profits and real rate of interest. Perhaps the perfect asset substitution assumption obscures the policy effects on stock markets and indirectly increases their relevance in the economy which may vary in different economies.

Gavin (1986) extended Blanchard's closed economy model to an open small economy model in which the stock market determines domestic aggregate demand. He found that if stock market effects are important enough, then a monetary expansion can result in real exchange rate appreciation, rather than depreciation. Also, Gavin's results regarding the effectiveness of fiscal expansion are similar to those of Tobin (1982). If the favourable effects on future productivity lead to strong enough stock market effects, an anticipated fiscal expansion can lead to an output expansion rather than a contraction. Similar to Blanchard and Tobin's models, Gavin's model is restricted by substitutable assets but is less disaggregated than that of Tobin and therefore more limited. Furthermore, by assuming strong stock market effects, Gavin's model may not resemble the actual relevance of stock markets in economic activity. While his model still permits the analysis of stronger influences such as the real exchange rate, the relative relevance of financial markets and their effect on economic variables may be better analysed by Tobin's model and the suggested extensions.

In addition, Asikoglu (1986) attempted to develop a general equilibrium macroeconomic model which includes stock markets. However, under certainty conditions[45] and other simplifying assumptions, including no differentials in net yields between domestic and foreign equities, and based on Tobin's q-theory, the so-called equities are redundant and are practically a mirror image of real capital accumulation, so the results and the analysis are not particularly useful.

Greenwald *et al.* (1984) and Greenwald and Stiglitz (1988) have recently suggested that informational inefficiencies, particularly of equity markets, determine macroeconomic cyclical behaviour. Their models focus primarily on the behaviour of firms regarding output. Informational inefficiencies determine large fluctuations in the cost of capital which in turn determine observed cyclical variations in firms' investments and prices. The interpretation of such models in a full macroeconomic model may shed some light on the behaviour of equity markets under certain fiscal, financial and monetary policies. Such developments, however, remain a challenge for further research.

Evidently, the analysis of the interaction between financial markets and the economy is an open field that needs to be closely explored. In this regard, Tobin's contributions provide a strong base under which future analysis could be developed. The interaction between financial markets and the economy would be helpful for determining investors' portfolio adjustments based on current and expected economic activity,[46] studying market feedback effects on the economy, asset pricing (including risks) relative to real assets, price levels, capital flows and monetary, credit and fiscal policies, as well as the functioning of different financial intermediaries and markets. By further studying the interaction of markets and the economy at the domestic level and extending such models under an open economy framework we would be better able to understand the determinants of international capital flows and their impact on the world economy.

As Tobin has pointed out:

The traditional aggregation of all non-monetary assets into a single asset with a common interest rate does not permit analysis of some important policies, institutional structures and events....

Asset disaggregation is essential for analyzing, among other phenomena, financing of capital accumulation and government deficits, details of monetary and debt management policies, international capital movements and foreign exchange markets, and financial intermediation ... what transactions are the source of variation of money stocks makes a difference, depending on how they alter the wealth and portfolio positions of economic agents.

(1982: 172, 173)

In summary, the incorporation of equities in open economy macroeconomic models could help us to understand the impact of fiscal, financial and monetary policies in the functioning, growth, asset pricing, determination of optimal portfolios, portfolio adjustments, substitution patterns with other financial assets, risks, international movements, allocable efficiency and welfare implications of equity markets,[47] their impact on other macroeconomic aggregates and their contribution to economic growth. Such an analysis is nowadays more relevant for policy-makers[48] adopting policy reforms aimed to correct economic external and internal imbalances, or to promote the development of equity markets, or to simultaneously achieve both objectives in the medium term.[49]

ECONOMIC DEVELOPMENT

A different subset of the literature has focused on the relationship of financial markets and economic development.[50] Most of this literature, including empirical studies regarding financial repression, has been recently surveyed by Kitchen (1986). Therefore, only an overview is presented below.

Except for the financial repression studies, most of these contributions are largely descriptive and inductive. Largely focusing on financial markets as a relevant mechanism for economic growth, the significance of this body of the literature lies on the analysis of the major determinants of the growth of financial markets and the introduction of concepts and measurements to characterize it. While the real rates of interest and government controls are identified as major determinants of financial market growth, the financial deepening (shallow finance) and financial repression concepts and ratio measurements have been introduced to describe the development status of financial markets in different economies. While there is consensus on the view that financial development leads to economic development, no conclusive evidence has been provided so far. Recently, Dornbusch and Reynoso (1988) have questioned the validity of such claims and suggest that financial factors are important if they are very distorted; otherwise, probably they do not make much difference to the level of per capita GNP.

The comparative analysis presented in a few studies indicates that financial markets in developing countries have a much narrower range of institutions and instruments and are much smaller with respect to the size of their economies than those of developed countries. Lacking a full macroeconomic model where most financial market variables are integrated with real economic activity, the majority of the theoretical discussions evolve around the national and flow of funds accounts with particular emphasis on savings, investments and money, and as a consequence on credit markets. Particular attention is paid to fiscal, financial and monetary policies that affect the growth of overall financial markets.[51] The most salient policy instrument determining the growth of savings and investments, and thus determining financial liberalization, is the real rate of interest.[52]

In discussing financial markets in aggregation, with limited data and smaller capital markets in relation to the total financial system,[53] the explicit role and the functioning of stock markets are practically ignored. Wai (1980: ch. 15), however, concludes that the development impact of capital markets in developing countries has been small, and that although they can play a positive and increasing role in development, their contributions would remain modest. Further studies are required to determine the benefits of well-developed equity

markets for economic development. But first, as Dornbusch and Reynoso (1988) pointed out, methods to determine how economic growth can be attributed to financial markets need to be designed.

The relatively small size of stock markets *vis-à-vis* their economies (even in the case of industrialized countries) and the limited number of market participants (see Calderón-Rossell 1990), may continue to constrain the impact of stock markets on economic growth. The relative developmental impact of stock markets in developing countries may be increased, however, by reducing market imperfections and increasing their allocable efficiency. Nevertheless, the analyses of particular imperfections and their consequences are still needed. Studies on the flow of savings into different financial markets and the effects of such flows on monetary and economic variables would also help policy-makers to adopt policies leading to the further development of financial markets, enhancement of their allocable efficiency and enhancement of their role in allocating the bearing of risks. The prospect for further increasing the stock markets' developmental impact also needs to be re-examined in the light of the growth and increasing integration and efficiency of world capital markets. Financial markets' developmental impact, however, is not expected to overshadow the relevance of sound and stable macroeconomic policies. On the contrary, the financial markets' contribution to economic growth will be determined by government policies.

The recent experience of financial liberalization and the limited success in developing more efficient financial markets is examined by Dooley and Mathieson (1987). The high specialization of developing economies and the historically excessive regulation of financial systems are identified as the main constraints for financial market development. Economic specialization limits the potential diversification for market participants and the excessive regulation of financial systems is not conducive to promoting rational and prudent credit decisions. It is implicitly suggested that excessive controls have not helped to develop the necessary experience and skills of investors and financial institutions to operate in a freer financial environment. Among other measures for the success of financial liberalization and for maintaining the stability of financial institutions, Dooley and Mathieson suggest limiting their par-value liabilities, including foreign exchange exposure, and adopting prudent regulation and supervision.

A subset of the economic development literature has also focused on the impact of capital inflows in monetary aggregates (see Mathieson 1979) and in economic growth and savings.[54] To control monetary aggregates, Mathieson (1979) suggests gradually adjusting and co-ordinating changes in exchange and interest rates while initially reducing the domestic component of base money. Gupta and Anisul (1983) on the other hand empirically examine the impact of foreign capital inflows on economic growth and domestic savings. Their study confirms that, although foreign capital makes a positive contribution to growth, domestic savings are more important. The impact of foreign capital differs by type. While the evidence is mixed, Gupta and Anisul concluded that foreign aid is more productive for economic growth than foreign private capital. Perhaps this could be explained by the conditionality usually imposed on foreign aid which is commonly provided for financing economically beneficial investments. In contrast, they found that foreign aid has a negative effect on domestic savings while the impact of foreign private capital in a few cases is positive. Gupta and Anisul suggest that the negative impact of foreign aid on savings could be a result of the recipient government relaxing its efforts to mobilize resources domestically, expecting that the foreign aid inflow would cover the savings gap.[55]

The development of a complete macroeconomic model for an open economy where disaggregated financial markets are integrated with real economic activity[56] would also help for re-examining the impact of financial markets in economic growth as well as for reviewing the effect of fiscal, financial and monetary policies on the growth of domestic savings. In addition, such a model would help in an analysis of the effect of foreign capital flows on economic and domestic savings growth. Thus the development of such a model *à la* Tobin with a complete disaggregation of financial markets (where the impact of stock markets could also be analysed) is long overdue and remains a challenge for future research. Perhaps only through this model can different policies be evaluated for confidently making policy recommendations that would help to further develop financial markets and the economies where they operate.

EMERGING MARKETS

The bulk of portfolio theory, market performance and asset pricing literature which has mostly been developed with a domestic perspective and has mainly focused on (or implicitly assumed) developed equity markets is well known and abundant.[57] In contrast, the literature examining the organization and institutional structure, the functioning and performance, the growth constraints, the savings mobilization role, its world market integration and the macroeconomic, welfare and developmental impact of emerging markets and their response to different fiscal, financial and monetary policies is extremely limited, fragmented and often of doubtful quality. Most of the limited emerging market literature is generally descriptive and usually follows a case approach which prevents the development of generalizations.[58]

Overall, the results of this literature (often focused on overall capital markets as opposed to stock markets alone) indicate that the establishment, growth and functioning of emerging markets are bound by historical circumstances, cultural factors, economic and financial development, economic and financial market structures and government policies. Because of this, generalizations about all emerging markets also need to be considered with caution and an in-depth analysis of individual emerging markets is required for providing adequate policy recommendations for their development. Furthermore, given data limitations and information of doubtful quality, most of the studies in this body of the literature have usually been qualified, often considered preliminary and tentative. Therefore, the same word of caution applies to this review.

The general view of this subset of the literature is that, with very few exceptions, securities markets in developing countries are characterized to be small relative to the economies where they operate, particularly when the representation of the industrial sector in stock markets is not proportional to its contribution to economic activity; thin, with little or no trading and with insignificant amounts of new issues by private companies and therefore with limited liquidity;[59] and less efficient and usually riskier than securities markets in developed countries.[60] Securities markets in developing countries are further characterized by having strong risk-averse investors, who lack the confidence to participate in a market subject to insider dealings and manipulations, and a limited supply of securities, in particular through organized stock exchanges.[61] Nevertheless, in a few cases and in particular instances a limited number of emerging markets have performed rather well, occasionally outperforming developed markets.[62] Beset by policies that have resulted in repressed and shallow financial markets, emerging markets are not expected to function similarly to developed markets. In this light, it is most likely that emerging markets, more so than developed markets, are incomplete and imperfect.[63] While this is still subject to further analyses, it is clear that functional differences between markets result in internationally segmented markets and as a corollary in a suboptimal allocation of wealth on a world-wide basis.

Regarding relative riskiness, perhaps due to market imperfections in the real sector and in the industrial organization of developing countries, it has been suggested that large companies in developing markets may have a smaller risk than those of developed countries. Such riskiness only focuses on the low variability of prices and not on the market power of some companies which may permit stock market manipulation, thereby representing a higher risk for investors. The market

portfolio of developed markets, on the other hand, with a wider number of investment opportunities[64] is usually less risky than the market portfolio of emerging markets. Despite the capital flights controversy, the potential for international diversification and its benefits is nevertheless also available to emerging markets.[65]

With a limited understanding on all aspects of emerging markets, an incomplete theoretical framework and scarce empirical investigations, domestic and international investors, international organizations and policy-makers practically operate in a vacuum that may prevent them achieving their objectives. The intuition that emerging markets need to be promoted in most economies, for example, still needs to be validated by rigorous and systematic studies of the underlying economic structure and policy framework under which such markets operate. With the limited understanding of the functioning of stock markets in the context of the macroeconomy, policy recommendations regarding the development, functioning, openness and control of emerging markets are suspect and need to be re-examined in the context of a general macroeconomic model which is still awaiting development (see the third section of this chapter).

A significant controversy exists about the role that governments should play in the establishment, promotion and control of stock markets. While some writers suggest that, for promoting the development of stock markets, governments should decide on the role those markets would play *vis-à-vis* other methods for financing development, others support the premise that the allocation of savings through such markets should be determined by economic forces. Generally it is recommended that the establishment of stock markets should be motivated by economic reasons rather than, as in some instances, political reasons. In practice some government officials from some developing countries have been ambivalent and indifferent in promoting stock markets and suspicious of foreign influences and controls. This may in part be explained by the expected limited impact of stock markets on economic development. Stock markets nevertheless may still increase the efficiency of allocating domestic and foreign savings. In some instances, stock markets have been used to promote the indigenization of foreign companies. Furthermore, in the 1980s they have been considered as a serious alternative in attracting foreign investments and are considered to be instrumental in the privatization of government-owned corporations and in the reduction of foreign debt through debt-to-equity conversion mechanisms. In contrast, some suggest that the promotion of stock markets is not always recommended, particularly when market imperfections abound and in the case of emerging markets as stock markets would exacerbate the uneven distribution of wealth and income in developing countries. While certain conditions should exist for developing stock markets, such as a vigorous and healthy private sector, sufficient domestic savings, a stable economic and financial environment, an adequate legal and regulatory framework and adequate fiscal, financial and monetary policies, in general it is suggested that the participation of governments in the securities market should be limited and perhaps concentrated on enhancing the protection of investors. Controls need to be in place for avoiding insider trading, manipulation and occasional speculative splurges that have ended in several cases in a crash that has eliminated the interest of market investors and thus reverted markets to a lethargic state. However, the emphasis should be on developing strong and transparent capital market organizations and institutions rather than on stringent controls and bureaucratic procedures.

Policies to increase the liquidity and yields while reducing risks of securities have been adopted in several countries. In some cases fiscal policies through tax incentives apparently yielded positive results[66] but the effects are not as positive as expected. Overall, however, systematic analysis of the effectiveness of those policies still needs to be carried out.

Again the soundness of policy recommendations can be better evaluated by using a general equilibrium open economy macroeconomic model as discussed before. Perhaps in its absence, warnings are commonly offered for the potential negative effects of policies aimed to develop capital markets further. It is usually recommended that such markets should not be developed if there is no real demand for the services they can provide and when their development may lead to an unsustainable growth, particularly in the early stages. Differences of opinion exist in terms of the speed by which policy-makers should promote securities markets. While some recommend fast policy actions with errors in judgement to be corrected with experience, others recommend a positive but gradual approach for policy actions. Undoubtedly, the preferred approach needs to be selected considering the particular characteristics of the economy and culture where those markets would operate. The limited evidence shows that errors in judgement in the developing securities markets usually do not provide, except in the long run, second chances for correcting wrong policies and decisions. As several writers suggest, the process for developing securities markets is costly and risky. Therefore, policy recommendations should be analysed in depth and when adopted they should be decisively implemented.

Other policy objectives recommended in this subset of the literature are to increase savings in the economy, to foster more even distribution of wealth and income and to eliminate barriers for the free allocation of savings.[67] A diversity of financial institutions particularly of the institutional investor type, should be promoted and encouraged to participate in the securities market.[68] The timely and adequate availability of information should be encouraged[69] and the training and sophistication of market participants needs to be increased.[70]

The fundamental development of emerging markets is a continuous process and much more remains to be done to complete their development and to exploit their potential fully. To achieve these objectives, further developments of the theory and empirical work on emerging equity markets and international capital flows needs to be encouraged.

Besides the general suggestions for further

research presented in this chapter, there are particular questions that need to be answered to understand the functioning and inherent limitations of emerging markets better. If emerging markets are thin and therefore illiquid, would they still be able to attract international investors? For this assessment, international CAPMs that take into account liquidity risks need to be developed. In the context of the standard CAPMs it is claimed that international investors are in a better position to incur additional risks than domestic investors, but such risks refer to market and not to liquidity risks. Thus, even if emerging markets could open up additional investment opportunities, their liquidity risks may be so high that international investors may not be willing to participate in such markets. Externalities in the information about the behaviour of other decision-makers, and uncertainty about the environment (see Radner 1968), generate a demand for liquidity which may be exacerbated in the case of emerging markets.

At the theoretical level, Lintner (1970) and Litzenberger and Budd (1972) have shown that the risk premium and the market price of risk, subject to the class of investors' utility functions, varies with the growth in per capita national wealth, the size of the market and the number of market participants. This would help to explain the higher risks of emerging markets which could then be reduced by increasing the number of market participants and market capitalization. Risk premium, however, may increase with per capita wealth increases, i.e. with economic growth. If so, this would limit the feasible rate of growth of the economy. In addition to the thinness and limited diversification of emerging markets, the risks determined by the stages of economic development and growth may explain why emerging markets are more volatile than developed markets. In this regard, the stability of economic policies for reducing the volatility of emerging markets is more relevant in developing than developed countries.[71] Given the limited research on emerging markets it is not surprising that the Lintner and Litzenberger and Budd theories have not been subjected to empirical testing. Besides testing these theories,

additional efforts should be made to develop the theory of stock market growth, in particular with regard to relative growth with respect to the economy.

Other aspects of emerging markets also remain open for further analysis. Are emerging markets of very small economies able to provide sufficient and increasing investment opportunities to justify relatively high information costs? Or is the supply of investment opportunities in those markets basically fixed, thereby exacerbating those costs? While international CAPMs assume a fixed number of securities, they vary in practice.[72] It is expected that the number of securities in emerging markets may be subject to change more than in the case of developed countries; thus, the effect of changes in the supply of securities on capital asset pricing and portfolio choices needs to be evaluated. If the economic growth of developing countries is higher than the growth of developed economies, are emerging markets able to provide sufficient investment opportunities and stocks commensurate with the high economic growth to attract substantial foreign portfolio investment? Or is the market capitalization of emerging markets so small that it inhibits international flows despite the higher economic growth and potential profitability? Are there minimum economy sizes and number of market participants below which stock markets are inoperative? If so, what are the alternatives for small economies for improving the allocation of resources and the exchange of assets? Given the smallness of emerging markets relative to world markets, would emerging markets provide higher average returns than large developed markets in a similar way to the small-firm size effect in developed markets? If so, could that explain potential higher returns but also higher risks?[73] Is the size effect of small companies also present within emerging markets?

With very few exceptions, the analysis of emerging markets has eluded the interest of renowned financial and macro economists. Also owing to severe information constraints, low levels of market capitalization, high volatility and unfamiliarity, emerging markets have not significantly attracted international investors and research houses of financial institutions. Only recently, as a result of the breakdown of the international financial intermediation process after 1982 and the related global debt crisis,[74] has the role of emerging markets in the reduction of debt, as a vehicle to attract financial resources and as an alternative to term lending for financing development, attracted the attention of international organizations, policy-makers and the international financial community.[75] Significant efforts are still needed to develop our understanding of emerging markets and to design adequate policies for their development.

To help in this endeavour, the development of a complete survey and statistical information of world markets on a timely basis needs to be made available on a consistent and comparable basis. Also, to study international flows further, disaggregated information on different types of capital flows, particularly on foreign portfolio investments, needs to be made available. In this regard, the IMF balance-of-payments statistics could be expanded to include disaggregated types of capital flows. The IMF financial statistics are well known and widely disseminated and thus could make this information available to both researchers and international investors.

INTEGRATION AND CAPITAL FLOWS

Central to the study of international financial systems, particularly regarding stock markets, is the controversy on the integration versus segmentation of markets. While a number of international capital asset pricing and macroeconomic models implicitly assume integrated markets, a subset of the literature specifically focuses on this controversy. Assuming that segmentation of stock markets is mainly a result of government controls, some researchers have suggested that foreign direct investments are a plausible alternative to attain the diversification benefits not available if stock markets are segmented. In the middle of the integration versus segmentation controversy lies

the study of capital flight and its economic and welfare implications. Given the relevance of these issues in the study of stock markets, specific studies on these subjects and other aspects not covered before are succinctly discussed below.

The world stock markets and segmentation

Central to the focus of this chapter is the apparent ignorance about the universe of possible asset claims in world markets. Except for a recent paper by Calderón-Rossell (1990), no study that analyses total world markets where emerging markets are taken into account is known to the author. Most studies of international markets are usually concentrated on developed markets, and so no concept of a full world stock market exists.[76] Data limitations, which include unavailability or untimeliness, inconsistent information and high cost, and the relative smallness of emerging markets may have contributed to a partial view of world markets. Under these constraints and based on this apparent ignorance, as discussed in Lee and Sachdeva (1977), world markets would be segmented.

Empirical methods so far have not successfully determined if world capital markets are segmented or integrated.[77] However, even if capital markets are perfectly integrated, the high levels of uncertainty motivated in part by untimely information may constrain the diversification of the optimal world portfolio (as in Gennotte 1986) and therefore lead to ignoring the *true* world capital market.[78] If so, asset allocation in world markets may not be efficient. The optimal asset allocation depends on the investment universe (see Solnik and Noetzlin 1982). The constrained optimal portfolio choice under incomplete information in total world markets is also an area that needs to be further developed.

Furthermore, while the absence of information resembles the absence of markets (see Ohlson 1987), particularly in limiting an optimal allocation of resources, the big difference between these scenarios is that the former may be corrected by investing in obtaining information but the latter is beyond the control of investors. Both domestic theoretical models and empirical research on portfolio choices under such constraints need to be extended to the international arena.

The determination of segmentation versus integration of capital markets, the absence of a complete world market perspective and the uncertainty due to the lack of information or other causes are relevant factors that affect a world-wide optimal allocation of wealth. Therefore, besides determining the overall efficiency of capital markets (particularly of emerging stock markets) and their role in the allocation of world wealth, policy-makers need to adopt policies that enhance the integration of equity markets (and thus develop home-country stock markets). This would permit increasing world welfare and growth.

Besides fully open economy policies, multiple listings and electronic linkages are areas that could enhance the integration of world markets and should be explored in detail. However, it appears that multiple listings face similar questions to those of MNCs in their alternative role for portfolio investments that is discussed below.[79] The existing technical advances in international communications would permit a drastic reduction in information gaps, would substantially increase the efficiency of world markets and would permit an optimal and timely allocation of world resources which are expected to increase world welfare. The electronic linkages of world markets would require a massive and tremendous effort for modernizing the policy-making process in individual markets, the development of consistent information and data analysis (including stock markets data and accounting information), new clearing procedures and controls and a complete change in the way that transactions take place. Perhaps international institutional investors and international organizations can take the lead in promoting these developments. It is possible that the integration of markets in the EC that is expected to take place in the 1990s and the introduction of Globex, a computer system for trading futures on a worldwide basis designed by the Chicago Mercantile Exchange and Reuters Holding (*The Wall Street Journal* 1989), may provide lessons to take into account for the full integration of world markets. Therefore, such experiences need to be closely watched.

For the integration of world markets and the necessary development of individual and international markets, further developments of theories and empirical work and the additional training of macroeconomists and policy-makers in these matters remain fundamental and priority tasks. Largely because of the lack of a universal understanding on how stock markets operate and the weaknesses of curricula for training economists, policies focusing on the development of stock markets have not been forthcoming. Universities and international organizations can fulfil a useful role in this regard. Supporting research in this area, strengthening curricula and transferring this knowledge and future developments to policy-makers, particularly those in emerging markets, may help to focus their attention on stock markets and on adopting policies for their development, thereby improving the allocation of resources and world welfare.

Foreign direct investment as a vehicle for portfolio investments

The role of MNCs in providing an indirect diversification vehicle in segmented international markets has been examined by Adler (1974), Ekern and Wilson (1974), Severn (1974), Adler and Dumas (1975), Lee and Sachdeva (1977) and Rugman (1977). Although foreign direct investments are more closely related to markets in real assets and corporate control, it has been claimed that they provide a diversification potential which may not otherwise be available to international investors. In its own right, at both the micro and macro level, as well as from different perspectives,[80] particular attention has been given to foreign direct investments. No attempt is made here to cover this literature.[81]

In the context of the international capital asset pricing theory, but introducing barriers for international portfolio investments in certain markets, the portfolio diversification potential through MNCs needs to be evaluated by distinguishing between international portfolio investments versus foreign direct investments. But first, significant questions regarding the market valuation of MNCs in domestic markets (see Errunza and Senbet 1981) need to be resolved. To what extent is multi-nationality reflected in the domestic the MNC's home country) market price of MNCs? Are MNC shares evaluated in the context of a pure domestic risk–return relationship or are they evaluated from an implicit but unspecified segmented inter-national risk–return relationship? Besides the effect of increasing the number of shares in the domestic market, is the market price line of pure domestic firms affected by the inclusion of MNC shares? If MNCs provide additional diversifi-cations to those available in large domestic stock markets, is such diversification recognized in domestic asset pricings? If such additional diversi-fication exists, stock markets may not be Pareto production efficient in view of the monopolistic competitiveness of MNCs. And if such larger diversification exists but is not recognized by domestic markets, the lack of Pareto production efficiency of markets would be exacerbated by informational inefficiencies. Lacking information about the relative merits of different international investment opportunities and the relative prob-abilities of events, prices would simply be random as discussed in Stiglitz (1981a). On the other hand, if MNCs' monopolistic competitive position is determined by the comparative advantages of the economic structure at home, it is unlikely that by investing abroad they can provide the same diversi-fication potential of international portfolio invest-ments. Foreign portfolios provide additional investment opportunities based on the economic structure of foreign countries. Unless we are able to answer these questions, the diversification potential of MNCs remains a moot question.

The capital flight controversy

Extraneously enough, differences in wealth between developed and emerging markets have created biases and an asymmetry in value judge-ments regarding international capital flows. The social welfare of an individual country is not necessarily the same as the world welfare. Flows arising from investors of developed markets considered as a positive development are cast in the framework of international portfolio diversifi-cations. In contrast, flows from emerging markets perceived as a negative process are commonly referred to as capital flights.[82] So investors from developed markets are *good knights* while those from emerging markets are *evil knights*. Under that perspective, international investments and diversi-fication opportunities should be available only to *good knights* but not to *evil knights*. As Cumby and Levich have remarked, 'the notion that capital flight represents a source of disutility focuses on a nationalistic measure of social utility' (1987: 31). This perspective, however, goes against the notion that open economies would lead to an increase in world output and welfare.

Focusing on controls, Dooley (1986) has proposed that capital flights should be considered as those not reported in the balance of payments. The presumption is that such flows would be illegal and perhaps motivated by tax avoidance and controls. Aside of legal considerations, atten-tion should be paid to the determinants of such unreported transactions. Perhaps they are moti-vated by the underlying perception and risk aversion of investors who are attempting to circumvent expected restrictions on wealth and capital movements and are therefore seeking to diversify their portfolios internationally. Such potential restrictions may reduce or eliminate the benefits of future investment opportunities with obvious implications on individual welfare. Are the country policies adequate? What are the income redistribution effects of capital flows? To evaluate government policies and the income redistribution effects of capital flows, improvements may be needed in the national accounts and balance-of-payments statistics for obtaining sufficiently disaggregated information on all international transactions and capital movements. After examin-ing the factors that motivate such illegal flows, adequate policies that would increase investors' confidence and market opportunities need to be adopted.

All in all, even if Dooley's classification of capital flows is adopted, unreported transactions from emerging markets may still increase investors' and developing countries' overall income and welfare. While the value of assets and income denominated in national currencies is initially reduced by the devaluation of real foreign exchange rates that usually follows capital flights, the future income stream and capital gains of assets held abroad could still be higher than the losses in national currencies. Besides increasing investors' and countries' wealth, the free flow of investments in international markets would also enhance the efficiency of markets and their role in (i) wealth allocation and (ii) the bearing of risks on a world-wide basis which may lead to an overall increase in investors' utility and welfare. The influence of relative differences in market factors and economic conditions between foreign countries needs to be further analysed by studying capital flows from emerging markets. After all, individual opportunities[83] are determined by relative market opportunities and endowments (see Ohlson 1987). This would help policy-makers to adopt adequate policies for creating the necessary framework for investors to channel their resources into local markets. In an interdependent world, this would require a world-wide co-ordination of policies. Under open economies and world-wide market opportunities it is anticipated that emerging markets will continue to increase. Thus, given the expected benefits, unless proven otherwise, such flows should be encouraged.

CONCLUSIONS

The integration of financial markets, and particularly of stock markets, into real economic activity is an area of the theory of financial economics that is still subject to fundamental research. Despite the progress made so far, there is no comprehensive theory that describes how financial markets interact with economic activity and about the impact of financial markets in economic growth.[84] In this regard, the potential contributions of stock markets have been largely ignored. While there is a generalized view that financial development leads economic development there is no conclusive evidence to support this claim. In fact there is still a need to develop methods to evaluate the impact of financial markets on economic growth. Without these methods we can say little about such an impact. Recently it has been argued that financial matters are relevant only when they are greatly distorted.

Without an acceptable financial–economic theory, the merits of developing strong and diversified financial markets and their benefit for economic activity cannot be properly assessed; particularly relevant is the question of the allocable efficiency of financial markets. It has been claimed that even if financial markets are financially allocable efficient this does not necessarily lead to an efficient economic allocation of resources. Such inefficiency would therefore hinder an optimal development of output and welfare.

If at the domestic level we still can say little about the impact of financial markets on economic activity, at the international level we know less about the interaction of world financial markets in world economic growth and welfare. However, under an open economy framework some progress has been made in analysing the relative impact of certain variables such as interest rates, capital flows and foreign exchange rates on balance of payments, trade and monetary aggregates. Nevertheless, we still know very little about the impact and interaction of world stock markets in the world economy.

Without a fundamental theory about this impact and interaction, we cannot provide policy recommendations with confidence for the establishment, growth and operation of stock markets, and are also unable to assess the merits for promoting their development. This is particularly relevant for developing economies where stock market activities are very limited. The hypothesis that the integration of world stock markets can help developing economies to attract world wealth to finance economic growth also needs to be validated. While we are still searching for an acceptable theory of financial–economic markets, we should encourage policies leading to the elimination or reduction of market imperfections. This is expected to enhance market efficiency and its developmental impact. Undoubtedly, the contributions of stock market developments are not expected to override the adoption of sound policies for economic growth.

Under a general equilibrium framework, Tobin's model on money and finance in the macroeconomic process provides the basis to develop further our understanding of how financial markets interact with economic activity. Further extensions are required to include short-term financial assets, to distinguish between current and capital accounts and to include a complete foreign sector with disaggregated foreign assets. Besides the q-theory, alternative investment theories for explaining the relationship between investment in real assets and the issuance of stocks are also needed. To understand asset exchange markets and their impact on economic activity better and to analyse capital mobility among asset markets it would also be relevant to study non-organized exchanges. Given the relative smallness of organized stock markets, non-organized markets may be more relevant. As it is anticipated that non-organized exchanges may be less efficient than organized exchanges, it is important to understand why asset exchanges may be more prevalent in non-organized than in organized markets. This may permit the development of policies leading to the growth of organized exchanges and the reduction of asset exchange market inefficiencies.

The extension of Tobin's model could also help in a re-examination of international asset pricing theory, in particular its simplifying assumptions, and to analyse international asset pricing in a dynamic setting where world markets are subject to different fiscal, financial and monetary policies. Also, such extensions could be helpful in resolving the controversies regarding integration and segmentation of world markets and capital flights.

Under a partial analysis perspective and awaiting the development of a general equilibrium model as discussed above, it is also relevant to develop international asset pricing models with heterogeneous investors. Alternatively, empirical studies need to be made to determine whether investors in world-wide markets can be characterized by logarithmic utilities or to determine whether the universal separation theorem holds in world markets. This would help in a re-examination of international asset pricing and portfolio adjustments. Also it would provide insights to determine whether adequate policies could be adopted for attracting foreign investments to develop and increase home stock markets and for financing economic growth by foreign portfolio investments. Given the limitations existing at present about the different criteria used for evaluating assets by international investors, existing international asset pricing models, the results of relative valuations of world stock markets' performance and the assessment of their potential diversification benefits need to be treated with caution.

In order to develop acceptable international general and partial equilibrium models, the relative differences between home and foreign stock markets and between developed and emerging markets in particular need to be further analysed. A significant effort needs to be made to study emerging markets further. It is particularly relevant to analyse to what extent economic specialization of certain economies hinders the development of stock markets. It would be useful to examine whether the limitations of economic specialization could be overcome by integrating certain stock markets into world markets and to what extent stock market liquidity is increased by such integration. It is possible that by trading stocks internationally or integrating individual markets into world markets their liquidity could be enhanced. The pool of international investors may provide the liquidity that domestic investors are unable to supply in certain markets.

Questions regarding the valuation of risks and their diversification potential remain open. More importantly the impact of the monopolistic power of certain firms in the allocable efficiency of stock markets needs to be examined in detail. Perhaps this would require the integration of production and financial decisions in the context of international asset pricing models that are yet to be developed.

The assessment of the benefits of diversification for investors from developing countries participating in world markets would shed some light to correct biases regarding the controversy of capital flights. It is anticipated that such flows would increase, and as they are expected to be beneficial they should also be encouraged. This may help to increase world output and welfare.

In conclusion, the theory and understanding of the functioning of stock markets and their interaction with the economies where they operate is still in its infancy. While this study attempts to review the state of the art and suggests some avenues for further research, the overriding conclusion is that such research needs to be of a very fundamental nature. The explosion of the literature focusing on very narrow aspects of stock markets, while illuminating in certain instances, has not helped to provide the basic framework to build a theory of financial–economic markets. Without this framework, policy-makers are operating in a vacuum that requires immediate attention. Tobin, however, provides the basis on which we could develop this theory further, which remains a significant challenge for future research.

NOTES

1 Between 1985 and September 1987, gross equity trading across borders in Canada, Germany, Japan and the USA increased at an annual average rate of 69.6 per cent; in the first nine months of 1987 such trading amounted to $730.7 billion equivalent.

2 See the collection of papers in Elton and Gruber (1975); a very good survey by Adler and Dumas (1983); the survey of international diversification in Reilly (1985: ch. 21); the numerous contributions by Solnik (1973, 1974a, b, c, 1977) and more recently the papers by Stulz (1981a, b, 1984); Solnik and Noetzlin (1982); Grauer and Hakanson (1987) and Eun and Resnick (1988); and the collection of related papers in Hawkins et al. (1983) to name a few.

3 For a review of standard assumptions of the basic CAPM, see Linderberg (1979) and the discussions in Logue and Rogalski (1979), Adler and Dumas (1983) and Samuels (1981); see also the critiques of Roll (1977) regarding the measurement problems of the CAPM.

4 For a detailed discussion see Rubinstein (1975) and Stiglitz (1981b).

5 The oligopolistic or monopolistic power of certain industrial sectors, particularly in international markets, is well known.

6 The covariances of returns would be unstable and the portfolio demand for given returns needs to be continuously adjusted.

7 While at the domestic level King and Leape (1984) found that taxes do not play a decisive role in explaining the difference in the portfolio composition of US households, at the international level differential taxes may have a relevant impact that needs to be examined.

8 See Errunza and Senbet (1981); at the domestic level see also Fama (1972), Jensen and Long (1972) and Stiglitz (1972).

9 See the works of Heckerman (1972), Solnik (1974a, c), Grauer et al. (1976), Stulz (1981b) and Adler and Dumas (1983); see also the empirical analysis of Calderón-Rossell (1987, 1990) and Schollhammer and Chung (1987) who in general found that the relationship between foreign exchange rate changes and domestic stock prices varies in different markets. In a simulation of the US economy, Gavin (1986) shows that a decline in interest rates leads to a stock price increase and a depreciation of the real exchange rate. Soenen and Hennigar (1987) found that the US stock market and the US dollar effective exchange rates move in opposite directions. Given the reduced survey of those studies and the different exchange rates used, the relationship between stock prices and the exchange rate needs to be further analysed.

10 Without attempting to review or even mention the complete literature on the subject, see the review of the floating exchange rate experience and deviations from fundamentals in Dornbusch and Frankel (1987), and the impact of the growing internationalization of economic decisions about real variables on the instability of exchange rates in Isard (1988).

11 For a discussion on the role of securities in the optimal allocation of risk-bearing at the domestic level, see Arrow (1963–4).

12 See the discussion in Adler and Dumas (1983) and the penultimate section of this chapter.

13 In a complete economy the marginal rate of substitution between claims on current and future

consumption is the same for all consumers; thus, unless markets are incomplete, there is no incentive for any future market activity – see Long (1972).

14 At the empirical level, however, King and Leape (1984) found that US households hold incomplete portfolios. Holdings of corporate equities in particular are mainly determined by wealth (net worth), occupation and education level of investors.

15 At the domestic level, King and Leape (1984) found that the cost of acquiring and processing information is a major factor affecting US household portfolio behaviour. Thus, it is anticipated that at the international level such costs and their effect would be more relevant.

16 That is, to determine to what extent world market participants can be characterized by the universal separation theorem or can be represented by a composite individual.

17 This would require a concerted effort by practitioners and academicians for developing and making the necessary data available for such an undertaking.

18 For an example of an empirical analysis of portfolio holdings see King and Leape (1984).

19 To better understand international portfolio investments (stock and flows) in market portfolios versus single securities, individual markets could be considered as a composite or aggregated security (i.e. equivalent to a single security representing each domestic market) as in Solnik (1973) and Lee (1969); Lee found that there is a group of investors specialized in Canadian securities as opposed to securities in various countries; in the context of an international asset pricing model this needs to be explained perhaps by international market imperfections. Lee's model also suggests that, owing to the reduction of risk, investors would invest and hold foreign securities even if expected returns are lower than for domestic securities.

20 Data determining the joint probability distribution of returns to all possible projects are not observable.

21 See the basic survey by Spitaller (1971); the more extensive survey by Bryant (1975); papers in Machlup *et al.* (1972); the work by Kenen (1976) and Makin (1974); and, more recently, the contributions by Ruffin (1984), Cuddington (1986), Frenkel and Razin (1987), Stockman and Hernández (1988) and Svensson (1988). For a brief review of the definition and a critical analysis on the empirical work regarding the measurement of capital mobility see also Obstfeld (1986a) and its accompanying comment by Stulz (1986).

22 This implies that the growth rate of wealth is always lower than unity, or 100 per cent in percentage terms.

23 On the other hand, given the small size of equities relative to loans the aggregation of assets may not significantly alter Branson's empirical results.

24 Shifts in money demand are also explained by income fluctuations.

25 Under such a model, international investors would hold the international market portfolio which is a weighted average of world stock markets.

26 Balassa (1972) also pointed out that Borts and Kopecky did not include any feedback effects from foreign investment in economic growth.

27 That is, international portfolio investments as opposed to foreign direct investment and equities as opposed to bonds.

28 For reasons why the role of money and, as a consequence, other financial assets have been largely ignored in macro analysis – despite Keynes' contribution in this regard – see Davidson (1968: 291, fn.).

29 Ultimately, securities, and stocks in particular, represent claims on future but uncertain consumption.

30 See also a brief survey of this literature in Reilly (1985: ch. 12); and the few comments provided below on the same.

31 In his book Davidson examined a few limitations not covered in his article. In general such limitations include ignoring the potential substitutability of some financial assets; a complete absence of asset risk differences; limited attributes to the role of money and equities by assuming that money holdings maintain intact the real wealth of investors; ignoring the stocks' liquidity question and the role of expectations; and further disregarding the relevance of new equity issues.

32 This is another 'liquidity trap' that restrains expansion (Davidson 1968: 317).

33 Rozeff provides also a critical analysis of the related literature of the 1960s and 1970s.

34 To the extent that changes in the monetary aggregates are unanticipated, such changes should influence stock prices as in Pesando (1974).

35 Hamburger (1968) has also studied the demand for, and the substitution among, financial assets in which he unfortunately did not include equities. He found that the demand for financial assets is mainly determined by interest rates and wealth, while the effect of income appears negligible. By finding that time and savings deposits at commercial banks are close substitutes for savings accounts at other financial institutions and marketable bonds, Hamburger found no support to extend the definition of money to include assets other than demand

deposits and currency. More than fifteen years later this view has been changed (see technical definitions of the new concept of money or monetary aggregation in the US *Federal Reserve Bulletin*, published monthly). Based on these findings, he suggests that monetary policy should be aimed at controlling not only financial intermediaries but the issuing of marketable securities as well.

36 Pearce also briefly reviewed the related theoretical and empirical literature.

37 Stock prices are determined, in Gray's opinion, by dividends and the spread between stock returns and expected growth rate which Gray considers a 'very useful indication of the way the world really works' (1984: 75).

38 With hindsight such projections apparently were higher than actual.

39 While, as in Davidson, the stock market may provide a barometer of investors' confidence, such an indicator may be occasionally incorrect, particularly given the recent experience of the October 1987 US market crash (overconfidence which has been correctly anticipated by Brinner and Wyss).

40 For a discussion of this problem in the context of aggregation see Brennan and Kraus (1978).

41 In the absence of adequate models that integrate financial and capital markets, all these are issues that seem to have been largely ignored or have not been dealt with. Simplifying assumptions regarding perfectly competitive and complete markets and instantaneous clearing conditions may limit the analysis of these issues using existing equilibrium models.

42 As there are no easily available replacement cost values, direct testing may still be on the agenda for future empirical analysis; see also the analysis of Tobin and Brainard (1977) and the discussion in Hayashi (1982); also given the volatility of market values it would be expected that q may be unstable and therefore of limited value in governing firm's investment decisions.

43 In imperfect markets, the financing decisions of the firm are not irrelevant.

44 And even more so of its extensions.

45 So in the absence of risks, as Davidson pointed out, money is not needed.

46 That is, the substitution between real and financial assets and, within the latter, the substitution among different types of security holdings.

47 Including income redistribution effects.

48 Of developing countries in particular.

49 For a discussion on the proper sequencing of the standard stabilization cum liberalization programmes aimed to correct imbalances see Lal (1987); such programmes may currently have a significant bearing on the development of international equity markets, particularly emerging markets. Apparently because of other priorities, the effects of stabilization programmes on stock market development have not been analysed by policy-makers and international organizations. Despite its potential to provide important insights regarding the effect of fiscal, financial and monetary policies on financial sector developments, and the implications for international investors, this is an area that has also eluded the interest of academicians and investors. The experience in Latin America in particular may be rich in opportunities for further studies, albeit full of lessons for policy-makers.

50 See Patrick (1966), Gurley and Shaw (1960), Goldsmith (1966, 1969), Shaw (1973), McKinnon (1973), Michalopoulos (1975), Mathieson (1979), the collective writings of Wai (1980), and more recently Drake (1980) and Dooley and Mathieson (1987).

51 That is, policies leading to financial liberalization.

52 Again, for a review of the empirical literature see Kitchen (1986).

53 Except for the writings of Wai (1980: Part IV).

54 See the survey of the literature and the contributions by Gupta and Anisul (1983), and regarding aid see Cassen (1986).

55 While a full discussion of the effect of aid on economic performance is not intended, interested readers are referred to Cassen (1986: particularly Chapter 2) and its references. I am grateful to Guy P. Pfeffermann for bringing this reference to my attention.

56 As proposed in the third section.

57 For a good collection of classical articles see Jensen (1972) and Lorie and Brealey (1978); the collection of papers in Elton and Gruber (1979), Bicksler (1981) and in Sharpe and Cootner (1982) and the references in Reilly (1985) and Krouse (1986), to name a few.

58 For a limited review of existing literature see Errunza and Rosenberg (1982), Kitchen (1986) and Sudweeks (1987); studies focusing on particular markets can be found in Gandhi *et al.* (1980), Dickie (1981), Bletsas (1982), Bruck (1982), Papaioannou (1982), Calamanti (1983), The Bank of Korea (1984), Parkinson (1984), *Pakistan & Gulf Economist* (1985), Asian Development Bank (1986) and Abdul-Hadi (1988). International capital asset pricing studies on specific emerging markets are found in Lessard (1973) and Levy and Sarnat (1975). Studies regarding the efficiency and riskiness of emerging markets have been mainly made by Errunza and Etienne (1985a, 1987) and Errunza and Rosenberg (1982). Focusing on all

long-term securities, the only comprehensive survey of stock and bonds issues in emerging markets and their characteristics, so far, has been provided by Patrick and Wai (Wai 1980: 15) which included also policy recommendations for developing capital markets in developing countries. An examination of changes in emerging capital markets (including all long-term securities) and additional policy recommendations for their development were also provided by Wai (1980: chs 16 and 17); see also his accompanying papers on all financial markets in developing countries (chs 14 and 18).

59 For some this has been one of the major constraints for further developing capital markets in developing countries.

60 Existing empirical studies directly or indirectly mainly focus on informational efficiency and not on exchange and allocable efficiency, which are extremely important properties to consider in determining asset pricing and in assessing the impact of markets in the economy.

61 This is in part due to (i) cross-shareholdings among companies, (ii) the relevance of strong economic groups, (iii) limited business opportunities in smaller markets for goods and services and (iv) modest valuation of companies with underpriced securities which do not adequately cover expected risk premia.

62 As discussed in the second section of this chapter, problems of measurement abound and so these results in particular need to be considered with caution.

63 For a discussion of incomplete markets see Haley and Schall (1979) or Ohlson (1987).

64 Thus with a larger potential for diversification.

65 The same theoretical and empirical problems as those discussed in the second section of this chapter apply to emerging markets. The development of regional markets or mutual funds comprising several countries has been suggested in order to increase the limited diversification potential of certain domestic markets and for increasing the integration of economic regions where intra-regional trading would be increased and encouraged. In certain cases, however, it was found that the diversification of such mutual funds was not better than well-diversified domestic portfolios.

66 For a discussion of the fiscal policy role in conditioning monetary policy and in influencing financial variables see Isard (1988).

67 Government policies aimed at controlling credit allocation and the portfolio of financial institutions, the excessive participation of governments that has crowded out the private sector, and fiscal biases in favour of credit versus equity have not

been conducive to the development of securities markets, in part because all of these long-term securities are often much more relevant than stocks.

68 The dominance of pure commercial banking institutions and the lack of strong institutional investors often have not fostered the growth of securities markets.

69 Information on emerging markets is usually unavailable and when accessible it is of doubtful quality and subject to manipulation, particularly regarding issues of securities from the private sector.

70 Often there is a shortage of trained and experienced professionals in financial services; perhaps this may be due in part to the low volume of trading and market activities which is not sufficient to cover the costs of trained professionals, and as a consequence the low volume of market activities is charged onerous costs which at the same time discourage market activities and their development.

71 For a discussion of the effect of certain monetary policy strategies on the instability of financial variables see Isard (1988).

72 That is, no new issues or endogenous production are allowed.

73 For discussion of these issues at the domestic level see Roll (1981) and Chan (1985).

74 For a good review see Solberg (1988).

75 In this regard, the IFC has been instrumental in (i) calling the attention of international financial institutions and policy-makers to the role that emerging markets can play in debt reduction schemes and in attracting capital for financing development (several policy papers and particular studies have been prepared and made available to the public, mainly by IFC's Capital Markets Department and, more recently, to some extent by its Foreign Investment Advisory Service Unit); (ii) collecting and disseminating information on emerging markets through the IFC's Emerging Markets Database; (iii) helping emerging markets to obtain access to international capital markets by sponsoring, co-underwriting, investing and promoting several types of international funds, including publicly offered investment funds in Korea, Thailand, Malaysia and Brazil, privately placed investment funds in Brazil and on a world-wide basis at least two emerging market funds and debt-to-equity conversion funds in the Philippines, Chile and Brazil (the IFC played different roles in most of these funds); (iv) assisting specific corporations, most notably in Mexico, to reduce their foreign debt and to restructure their finances and operations; as a result a new unit was established in the IFC to provide financial engineering advisory

services on a world-wide basis in co-ordination with the IFC's regional investment departments; and (v) further providing advice to policy-makers and corporate officers regarding the development of financial markets, and institutions, and increasing foreign direct investments.

76 With eighteen developed stock and bond markets, Ibbotson *et al.*'s (1982) survey is the most comprehensive world developed markets data analysis known to date.

77 See the discussion in Adler and Dumas (1983), the work of Solnik (1974c, 1977), Stehle (1977) and more recently the papers by Kohlhagen (1983), Errunza and Losq (1985b), Jorion and Schwartz (1986), Obstfeld (1986b) and Wheatley (1985).

78 That is, all available investment opportunities in world markets, including those in emerging markets.

79 Few studies have examined the issue of multiple listings in international markets; see, for example, Alexander (1988).

80 That span from trade theories to management science, passing through, among others, industrial organization and corporate finance perspectives.

81 For a complete review of the foreign direct investment literature see Dunning (1973), Stevens (1973), Hufbauer (1975) and Lombard (1975); more recently see also the work by Dunning (1981), Calderón-Rossell (1985), Rugman (1986) and Brander and Spencer (1987); for a discussion of the impact of fiscal policies in the allocation of physical capital in different countries see also Isard (1988).

82 For a review of definitions, related issues and a selected bibliography see Cuddington (1986), Dooley (1986) and Lessard and Williamson (1987).

83 And by implication, investments, capital flows and welfare.

84 While the focus of this study is on stock markets, given the limited knowledge we have on the understanding of overall financial markets and economic activity the discussion in this chapter is extended to all financial markets. Undoubtedly, if we have a limited knowledge about all markets the gap in our understanding of the workings of stock markets and economic activity is exacerbated. Thus, whenever financial markets are mentioned, by implication stock markets are particularly included.

BIBLIOGRAPHY

Abdul-Hadi, A. S. F. (1988) *Stock Markets of the Arab World: Trends, Problems and Prospects for Integration*, London: Routledge.

Adler, M. (1974) 'The cost of capital and valuation of a two-country firm', *Journal of Finance*, March: 119–32.

Adler, M. and Dumas, B. (1975) 'Optimal international acquisitions', *Journal of Finance*, March: 1–19.

——— and ——— (1983) 'International portfolio choice and corporation finance: a synthesis', *Journal of Finance*, June: 925–84.

Agmon, T. (1972) 'The relations among equity markets: a study of share price co-movements in the United States, United Kingdom, Germany and Japan', *Journal of Finance*, September: 839–56.

——— (1973) 'Country risk: the significance of the country factors for share price movements in the United Kingdom, Germany and Japan', *Journal of Business*, January: 24–32.

Alexander, G. J., Eun, C. S. and Janakiramanan, S. (1988) 'International listings and stock returns: some empirical evidence', *Journal of Financial and Quantitative Analysis*, June: 135–51.

Allen, P. R. (1973) 'A portfolio approach to international capital flows', *Journal of International Economics* 3: 135–60.

Arrow, K. J. (1963–4) 'The role of securities in the optimal allocation of risk bearing', *Review of Economic Studies*, April: 91–6.

Asian Development Bank (1986) *Capital Market Development in the Asia-Pacific Region, An Asian Development Bank Symposium*, Manila, Philippines: Asian Development Bank, January.

Asikoglu, M. U. (1986) 'The stock market and capital accumulation in an open economy with flexible exchange rates', Discussion Paper 632, Institute for Economic Research, Queen's University, Kingston, Ontario, February.

Balassa, B. (1972) 'Comment', in F. Machlup, W. Salant and L. Tarshis (eds) *International Mobility and Movement of Capital*, New York: Columbia University Press for the National Bureau of Economic Research.

The Bank of Korea (1984) 'Estimation of stock price quotations in Korea', *Quarterly Economics Review*, June: 33–40.

Bergstrom, G. L. (1975) 'A new route to higher returns and lower risks', *Journal of Portfolio Management*, Fall: 30–8.

Bicksler, J. L. (ed.) (1981) *Handbook of Financial Economics*, 2nd edn, Amsterdam: North-Holland.

Blanchard, O. J. (1981) 'Output, the stock market, and interest rates', *American Economic Review*, March: 132–43.

Bletsas, A. C. (1982) 'Rates of return on investments in the Athens Stock Exchange: 1955–1975', *Greek Economic Review*, August: 242–54.

Borts, G. H. and Kopecky, K. J. (1972) 'Capital movements and economic growth in developed countries', in F. Machlup, W. Salant and L. Tarshis (eds) *International Mobility and Movement of Capital*, New York: Columbia University Press for the National Bureau of Economic Research.

Brander, J. A. and Spencer, B. J. (1987) 'Foreign direct investment with unemployment and endogenous taxes and tariffs', *Journal of International Economics*, May: 257–79.

Branson, W. H. (1970) 'Monetary policy and the new view of international capital movements', *Brookings Papers on Economic Activity* 2.

Branson, W. H. and Henderson, D. W. (1985) 'The specification and influence of asset markets', in R. W. Jones and P. B. Kenen (eds) *Handbook of International Economics*, vol. 2, Amsterdam: North-Holland.

Brennan, M. J. and Kraus, A. (1978) 'Necessary conditions for aggregation in securities market', *Journal of Financial and Quantitative Analysis*, September: 407–18.

Brinner, R. E. (1987) 'Meaning of the market', in Data Resources Incorporated *Review of the U.S. Economy*, February: 1–10.

Bruce, N. and Purvis, D. D. (1985) 'The specification of goods and factor markets in open economy macroeconomic models', in R. W. Jones and P. B. Kenen (eds) *Handbook of International Economics*, vol. 2, Amsterdam: North-Holland.

Bruck, N. (ed.) (1982) *Capital Markets Under Inflation*, Buenos Aires, Argentina: Buenos Aires Stock Exchange in co-operation with the Inter-American Development Bank.

Bryant, R. C. (1975) 'Empirical research on financial capital flows', in P.B. Kenen (ed.) *International Trade and Finance, Frontiers for Research*, Cambridge: Cambridge University Press.

Calamanti, A. (1983) *The Securities Market and Underdevelopment: The Stock Exchange in the Ivory Coast – Morocco – Tunisia*, Milan: Finafrica-Cariplo and Giuffre.

Calderón-Rossell, J. R. (1985) 'Towards the theory of foreign direct investment', *Oxford Economic Papers* 37: 282–91.

—— (1987) 'The foreign exchange risk of stock returns', unpublished manuscript, IFC, September.

—— (1990) 'The structure and evolution of world stock markets', in S. Ghon Rhee and R. P. Chang (eds) *Pacific-Basin Capital Markets Research, Proceedings of the First Annual Pacific-Basin Finance Conference, Taipei, China, 13–15 March 1989*, Amsterdam: North-Holland.

Cass, R. H. (1975) 'A global approach to portfolio management', *Journal of Portfolio Management*, Winter: 40–8.

Cassen, Robert & Associates (1986) *Does Aid Work? Report to an Intergovernmental Task Force*, Oxford: Clarendon Press.

Chan, K. C., Chen, N.-F. and Hsieh, D. A. (1985) 'An exploratory investigation of the firm size effect', *Journal of Financial Economics*, September: 451–71.

Chen, N.-F., Roll, R. and Ross, S. A. (1983) 'Economic forces and the stock market: testing the APT and alternative asset pricing theories', CRSP Working Paper 119, Chicago, IL: University of Chicago, December.

Cheng, H.-S. (1980) 'Financial deepening in Pacific Basin countries', *Economic Review*, Federal Reserve Bank of San Francisco, Summer.

Cohn, R. and Pringle, J. J. (1973) 'Imperfections in international financial markets: implications for risk premia and the cost of capital to firms', *Journal of Finance*, March: 59–66.

Cooper, R. V. L. (1974) 'Efficient capital markets and the quantity theory of money', *Journal of Finance*, June: 887–908.

Cuddington, J. T. (1986) *Capital Flight: Estimates, Issues and Explanations*, Princeton Studies in International Finance 58, Princeton, NJ, International Finance Section, Department of Economics, Princeton University.

Cumby, R. and Levich, R. (1987) 'On the definition and magnitude of recent capital flight', in D. R. Lessard and J. Williamson (eds) *Capital Flight and Third World Debt*, Washington, DC: Institute for International Economics, ch. 3.

Davidson, L. S. and Froyen, R. T. (1982) 'Monetary policy and stock returns: are stock markets efficient?', *Review, Federal Reserve Bank of St Louis*, March: 3–12.

Davidson, P. (1968) 'Money, portfolio balance, capital accumulation, and economic growth', *Econometrica*, April: 291–321.

—— (1978) *Money and the Real World*, 2nd edn, London: Macmillan.

Diamond, P. A. (1967) 'The role of a stock market in a general equilibrium model with technological uncertainty', *American Economic Review*, September: 759–76.

Dickie, R. B. (1981) 'Development of Third World securities markets: an analysis of general principles and a case study of the Indonesian market', *Law and Policy in International Business* 13: 177–232.

Dooley, M. (1986) 'Country specific risk premiums, capital flight and net investment income payments in selected developing countries', Departmental Memorandum DM/86/17, IMF.

Dooley, M. and Mathieson, D. J. (1987) 'Financial liberalization and stability within developing countries', IMF Working Paper WP/87/19, 17 March.

Dooley, M., Frankel, J. and Mathieson, D. J. (1987) 'International capital mobility. What do saving–investment correlations tell us?', *IMF Staff Papers*, September.

Dornbusch, R. (1980) *Open Economy Macroeconomics*, New York: Basic Books.

Dornbusch, R. and Frankel, J. (1987) 'The flexible exchange rate system: experience and alternatives', Working Paper 2464, National Bureau of Economic Research, December.

Dornbusch, R. and Reynoso, A. (1988) 'Financial factors in economic development', paper presented at the Annual Meeting of the American Economic Association, New York, 28–30 December.

Drake, P. J. (1980) *Money, Finance and Development*, Oxford: Martin Robertson.

Dumas, B. (1977) 'Testing international asset pricing: some pessimistic views – discussion', *Journal of Finance*, May: 512–15.

Dunning, J. H. (1973) 'The determinants of international production', *Oxford Economic Papers (New series)*, November: 289–336.

—— (1981) *International Production and the Multinational Enterprise*, London: Allen & Unwin.

Ekern, S. and Wilson, R. (1974) 'On the theory of the firm in an economy with incomplete markets', *Bell Journal of Economics and Management Science*, Spring: 171–80.

Elton, E. J. and Gruber, M. J. (1975) *International Capital Markets*, Amsterdam: North-Holland.

—— and —— (1979) *Portfolio Theory, 25 Years After. Essays in Honor of Harry Markowitz*, Tims Studies in the Management Sciences, vol. II, Amsterdam: North-Holland.

Errunza, V. and Losq, E. (1985a) 'The behavior of stock prices on LDC markets', *Journal of Banking and Finance*, December: 561–75.

—— and —— (1985b) 'International asset pricing under mild segmentation: theory and test', *Journal of Finance*, March: 105–24.

—— and —— (1987) 'How risky are emerging markets?', *Journal of Portfolio Management*, Fall: 62–7.

Errunza, V. and Rosenberg, B. (1982) 'Investment in developed and less developed countries', *Journal of Financial and Quantitative Analysis*, December: 741–62.

Errunza, V. and Senbet, L. W. (1981) 'The effects of international operations on the market value of the firm: theory and evidence', *Journal of Finance*, May: 401–17.

Eun, C. S. and Resnick, B. (1988) 'Exchange rate uncertainty, forward contracts, and international portfolio selection', *Journal of Finance*, March: 197–215.

Fama, E. F. (1972) 'Perfect competition and optimal production decisions under uncertainty', *Bell Journal of Economics and Management Science*, Autumn: 509–30.

Feltenstein, A. (1981) 'Money and bonds in a disaggregated open economy', Departmental Memorandum DM/81/58, IMF, 11 August.

Fleming, J. M. (1962) 'Domestic financial policies under fixed and under floating exchange rates', *IMF Staff Papers*, November: 369–79.

Francis, J. C. (1980) *Investments, Analysis and Management*, 3rd edn, New York: McGraw-Hill.

Frankel, J. A. (1985) 'International capital mobility and crowding out in the U.S. economy: imperfect integration of financial markets or of goods markets?', Working Paper 1773, National Bureau of Economic Research, December.

Frenkel, J. A. and Razin, A. (1987) 'The Mundell–Fleming model a quarter century later: a unified exposition', *IMF Staff Papers*, December: 567–620.

Freund, W. C. (1988) 'Electronic trading and linkages in international equity markets', paper presented at the Annual Meeting of the American Economic Association, New York, 28–30 December.

Friedman, B. M. (1981) 'The roles of money and credit in macroeconomic analysis', Discussion Paper 859, Cambridge, MA: Harvard Institute of Economic Research, Harvard University, November. Also published in J. Tobin (ed.) (1983) *Essays in Memory of Arthur M. Okun*, Washington, DC: The Brookings Institution.

Gandhi, D. K., Saunders, A. and Woodward, R. S. (1980) 'Thin capital markets: a case study of the Kuwaiti Stock Market', *Applied Economics* 12: 341–9.

Gavin, M. K. (1986) 'The stock market and exchange rate dynamics', International Finance Discussion Paper 278, April.

Gennotte, G. (1986) 'Optimal portfolio choice under incomplete information', *Journal of Finance*, July: 733–46.

Goldsmith, R. W. (1966) *The Determinants of Financial Structure*, Paris: Development Centre of the Organization for Economic Co-operation and Development.

—— (1969) *Financial Structure and Development*, New Haven, CT: Yale University Press.

Grauer, F. L. A., Litzenberger, R. H. and Stehle, R. E. (1976) 'Sharing rules and equilibrium in an international capital market under certainty', *Journal of Financial Economics*, June: 233–56.

Grauer, R. R. and Hakansson, N. H. (1987) 'Gains from international diversification: 1968–85 returns on portfolios of stocks and bonds', *Journal of Finance*, July: 721–41.

Gray, W. S. (1984) 'The stock market and the economy in 1988', *Journal of Portfolio Management*, Summer: 73–80.

Greenwald, B. and Stiglitz, J. E. (1986) 'Externalities in economies with imperfect information and incomplete markets', *Quarterly Journal of Economics*, May: 229–64.

—— and —— (1988) 'Financial market imperfections and business cycles', Working Paper 2494, National Bureau of Economic Research, July.

Greenwald, B., Stiglitz, J. E. and Weiss, A. (1984) 'Informational imperfections in the capital market and macro-economic fluctuations', Working Paper 1335, National Bureau of Economic Research, April.

Grubel, H. G. (1968) 'Internationally diversified portfolio: welfare gains and capital flows', *American Economic Review*, December: 1299–314.

Grubel, H. G. and Fadner, K. (1971) 'The interdependence of international equity markets', *Journal of Finance*, March: 89–94.

—— and —— (1977) *International Economics*, Homewood, IL: Richard D. Irwin.

Gupta, K. L. and Islam, M. A. (1983) *Foreign Capital, Savings and Growth*, International Studies in Economics and Econometrics, vol. 9, Dordrecht: Reidel.

Gurley, J. G. and Shaw, E. S. (1960) *Money in a Theory of Finance*, Washington, DC: The Brookings Institution.

Guy, J. R. F. (1978) 'An examination of the effects of international diversification from the British viewpoint on both hypothetical and real portfolios', *Journal of Finance*, December: 1425–38.

Haley, C. W. and Schall, L. D. (1979) *The Theory of Financial Decisions*, 2nd edn, New York: McGraw-Hill.

Hamburger, M. J. (1968) 'Household demand for financial assets', *Econometrica*, January: 97–118.

Hamburger, M. J. and Kochin, L. A. (1972) 'Money and stock prices: the channels of influence', *Journal of Finance*, May: 231–49.

Hart, O. D. (1975) 'On the optimality of equilibrium when the market structure is incomplete', *Journal of Economic Theory*, December: 418–43.

Hawkins, R. G., Levich, R. M. and Wihlborg, C. G. (eds) *The Internationalization of Financial Markets and National Economic Policy, Research in International Business and Finance, a Research Annual*, vol. 3, Greenwich, CT: JAI Press.

Hayashi, F. (1982) 'Tobin's marginal *q* and average *q*: a neoclassical interpretation', *Econometrics*, January: 213–24.

Heckerman, D. (1972) 'On the effects of exchange risk', *Journal of International Economics*, November: 379–87.

Henning, C. N., Pigott, W. and Scott, R. H. (1975) *Financial Markets and the Economy*, Englewood Cliffs, NJ: Prentice Hall (3rd edn, 1981).

Homa, E. K. and Jaffee, D. A. (1971) 'The study of money and common stock prices', *Journal of Finance*, December: 1045–66.

Hufbauer, G. C. (1975) 'The multinational corporation and direct investment', in P. B. Kenen (ed.) *International Trade and Finance, Frontiers for Research*, Cambridge: Cambridge University Press.

Ibbotson, R. and Sinquefield, R. A. (1982) *Stocks, Bonds, Bills, and Inflation: The Past and the Future*, Charlottesville, VA: Financial Analyst Research Foundation.

Ibbotson, R. G., Carr, R. C. and Robinson, A. W. (1982) 'International equity and bond returns', *Financial Analysts Journal*, July–August: 61–83. Also reprinted in D. R. Lessard (ed.) (1985) *International Financial Management, Theory and Application*, 2nd edn, New York: Wiley.

Isard, P. (1988) 'The implication of fiscal condition and growing internationalization for monetary policies and financial market conditions', IMF Working Paper WP/88/52, 29 June.

IMF (various issues) *International Financial Statistics*, Bureau of Statistics of the International Monetary Fund.

International Finance Corporation (1986–8) *Emerging Stock Markets: Factbooks, and Quarterly Reviews*, various issues and database.

Jacquillant, B. and Solnik, B. (1978) 'Multinationals are poor tools for diversification', *Journal of Portfolio Management*, Winter: 8–12.

Jensen, M. C. (ed.) (1972) *Studies in the Theory of Capital Markets*, New York: Praeger.

Jensen, M. C. and Long, J. B. Jr. (1972) 'Corporate investment under uncertainty and Pareto optimality in the capital markets', *Bell Journal of Economics and Management Science*, Spring: 151–74.

Jorion, P. and Schwartz, E. (1986) 'Integration vs. segmentation in the Canadian stock market', *Journal of Finance*, July: 603–14.

Joy, M. O., Panton, D. B., Reilley, F. K. and Martin, S. A. (1976) 'Co-movements of major international equity markets', *Financial Review* 11: 1–20.

Kenen, P. B. (1976) *Capital Mobility and Financial Integration: A Survey*, Princeton Studies in International Finance 39, International Finance Section, Department of Economics, Princeton, NJ: Princeton University.

Keran, M. W. (1971) 'Expectations, money and the stock markets', *Review, Federal Reserve Bank of St Louis*, January: 16–31.

King, M. and Leape, J. I. (1984) 'Wealth and portfolio composition: theory and evidence', Discussion Paper 68, Economic and Social Research Council Programme, Taxation, Incentives and the Distribution of Income, September.

Kitchen, R. L. (1986) *Finance for the Developing Countries*, Chichester: Wiley.

Kohlhagen, S. W. (1983) 'Overlapping national invest-ment portfolios: evidence and implications of international integration of secondary markets for financial assets', in R. G. Hawkins, R. M. Levich and C. G. Wihlborg (eds) *Research in International Business and Finance*, vol. 3, Greenwich, CT: JAI Press, 113–37.

Kouri, P. J. K. and Porter, M. G. (1974) 'International capital flows and portfolio equilibrium', *Journal of Political Economy*, May–June: 443–67.

Krouse, C. G. (1986) *Capital Markets and Prices, Valuing Uncertain Income Streams*, Amsterdam: North-Holland.

Lal, D. (1987) 'The political economy of economic liberalization', *Economic Review, The World Bank*, January: 273–99.

Layman, T. A. (1987) 'The economics of debt for equity conversions'. Discussion Paper 87–5, International Business and Banking Institute, Graduate School of International Studies, School of Business Adminis-tration, University of Miami, July.

Lee, C. H. (1969) 'A stock-adjustment analysis of capital movements: the United States–Canadian case', *Journal of Political Economy*, July: 512–23.

Lee, W. Y. and Sachdeva, K. S. (1977) 'The role of the multinational firm in the integration of segmented capital markets', *Journal of Finance*, May: 479–92.

Leland, H. E. (1974) 'Production theory and the stock market', *Bell Journal of Economics and Management Science*, Spring: 125–44.

Lessard, D. R. (1973) 'International portfolio diversi-fication: a multivariate analysis for a group of Latin American countries', *Journal of Finance*, June: 619–33.

—— (1974) 'World, national, and industry factors in equity returns', *Journal of Finance*, May: 379–91.

—— (1976) 'World, country, and industry relation-ships in equity returns', *Financial Analysts Journal*, January–February: 32–8.

Lessard, D. R. and Williamson, J. (eds) (1987) *Capital, Flight and Third World Debt*, Washington, DC: Institute for International Economics.

Levy, H. and Sarnat, M. (1970) 'International diversi-fication of investment portfolios', *American Econ-omic Review*, September: 668–75.

—— and —— (1975) 'Devaluation risk and the portfolio analysis of international investment', in E. J. Elton and M. J. Gruber (eds) *International Capital Markets*, Amsterdam: North-Holland.

Lindenberg, E. B. (1979) 'Capital market equilibrium with price affecting institutional investors', in E. J. Elton and M. J. Gruber (eds) *Portfolio Theory, 25 Years After. Essays in Honor of Harry Markowitz*, Tims Studies in the Management Sciences, vol. 11, Amsterdam: North-Holland.

Lintner, J. (1970) 'The market price of risk, size of market and investor's risk aversion', *Review of Economic Statistics*, February: 87–99.

Litzenberger, R. H. and Budd, A. P. (1972) 'Secular trends in risk premiums', *Journal of Finance*, September: 857–64.

Logue, D. E. (1982) 'An experiment in international diversification', *Journal of Portfolio Management*, Fall: 22–7.

Logue, D. E. and Rogalski, R. J. (1979) 'Offshore alphas: should diversification begin at home?', *Journal of Portfolio Management*, Winter: 5–10.

Lombard, F. (1975) 'La théorie des investissements directs: examen crtique à la lumière des flux d'investissement européens aux Etats-Unis', *Manage-ment International Review* 15 (4–5): 35–47.

Long, J. B. Jr. (1972) 'Consumption–investment decisions and equilibrium in the securities market', in M. E. Jensen (ed.) *Studies in the Theory of Capital Markets*, New York: Praeger.

Lorie, J. and Brealey, R. (eds) (1978) *Modern Develop-ments in Investment Management. A Book of Readings*, 2nd edn, Hinsdale, IL: Dryden.

Machlup, F., Salant, W. S. and Tarshis, L. (eds) (1972) *International Mobility and Movement of Capital*, New York: Columbia University Press.

Makin, J. H. (1974) *Capital Flows and Exchange-Rate Flexibility in the Post- Bretton Woods Era*, Essays in International Finance 103, International Finance Section, Department of Economics, Princeton University, Princeton, NJ, February.

Maldonado, R. and Saunders, A. (1981) 'International portfolio diversification and the inter-temporal stability of international stock market relationships, 1957–1978', *Financial Management*, Autumn: 54–63.

Marston, R. C. (1985) 'Stabilization policies in open economies', in R. W. Jones and P. B. Kenen (eds) *Handbook of International Economics*, vol. 2, Amsterdam: North-Holland.

Mathieson, D. J. (1979) 'Financial reform and capital flows in a developing economy', Departmental Memorandum DM/79/11, IMF, 21 February.

McDonald, J. G. (1973) 'French mutual fund perform-ance: evaluation of internationally diversified port-folios', *Journal of Finance*, December: 1161–80.

McKinnon, R. I. (1973) *Money & Capital in Economic Development*, Washington, DC: The Brookings Institution.

Merton, R. C. and Subrahmanyam, M. G. (1974) 'The optimality of a competitive stock market', *Bell Journal of Economics and Management Science*, Spring: 145–70.

Michalopoulos, C. (1975) *Financing Needs of Devel-oping Countries: Proposals for International Action*,

Essays in International Finance 110, International Finance Section, Department of Economics, Princeton University, Princeton, NJ, June.

Moore, G. H. (1975) 'Stock prices and the business cycle', *Journal of Portfolio Management*, Spring: 59–64.

Mossin, J. (1973) *Theory of Financial Markets*, Englewood Cliffs, NJ: Prentice Hall.

Mundell, R. A. (1961) 'Flexible exchange rates and employment policy', *Canadian Journal of Economics and Political Science*, November: 509–17.

—— (1963) 'Capital mobility and stabilization policy under fixed and flexible exchange rates', *Canadian Journal of Economics and Political Science*, November: 475–85.

—— (1964) 'Capital mobility and size: a reply', *Canadian Journal of Economics and Political Science*, May: 421–31.

Obstfeld, M. (1986a) 'Capital mobility in the world economy: theory and measurement', in K. Brunner and A. H. Meltzer (eds) *The National Bureau Method, International Capital Mobility and Other Essays*, Carnegie-Rochester Conference Series on Public Policy, Amsterdam: North-Holland, Spring.

—— (1986b) 'How integrated are world capital markets? Some new tests', Working Paper 2075, National Bureau of Economic Research, November.

Ohlson, J. A. (1987) *The Theory of Financial Markets and Information*, New York: North-Holland.

Pakistan & Gulf Economist (1985) 'The Karachi Stock Exchange – special report', 4 January: 11–47.

Palmer, M. (1970) 'Money supply, portfolio adjustments and stock prices', *Financial Analysts Journal*, July–August: 19–22.

Papaioannou, G. J. (1982) 'Thinness and short-run price dependence in the Athens Stock Exchange', *Greek Economic Review*, December: 315–33.

Parkinson, J. M. (1984) 'The Nairobi Stock Exchange in the context of development of Kenya', *Savings and Development, Quarterly Review* 4: 363–72.

Patrick, H. T. (1966) 'Financial development and economic growth in underdeveloped countries', *Economic Development and Cultural Change*, January: 174–89.

Pearce, D. K. (1983) 'Stock prices and the economy', *Economic Review, Federal Reserve Bank of Kansas City*, November: 7–22.

Pesando, J. E. (1974) 'The supply of money and common stock prices: further observations on the econometric evidence', *Journal of Finance*, June: 909–21.

Radner, R. (1968) 'Competitive equilibrium under uncertainty', *Econometrica*, January: 31–58.

Reilly, F. K. (1985) *Investment Analysis and Portfolio Management*, 2nd edn, Chicago, IL: Dryden.

Roll, R. (1977) 'A critique of the asset pricing theory's

tests', *Journal of Financial Economics*, March: 129–76.

—— (1981) 'A possible explanation of the small firm effect', *Journal of Finance*, September: 879–88.

Rowley, A. (1987) *Asian Stock Markets, The Inside Story*, Hong Kong: Far Eastern Economic Review.

Rozeff, M. S. (1974) 'Money and stock prices: market efficiency and the lag in effect of monetary policy', *Journal of Financial Economics*, September: 245–302.

—— (1975) 'The money supply and the stock market', *Financial Analysts Journal*, September–October: 18–26.

Rubinstein, M. (1974) 'An aggregation theorem for securities markets', *Journal of Financial Economics*, September: 225–44.

—— (1975) 'Securities market efficiency in an Arrow–Debreu economy', *American Economic Review*, December: 812–24.

Ruffin, R. J. (1984) 'International factors movements', in R. W. Jones and P. B. Kenen (eds) *Handbook of International Economics*, vol. 1, Amsterdam: North-Holland.

Rugman, A. M. (1977) 'International diversification by financial and direct investment', *Journal of Economics and Business*, Fall: 31–7.

—— (1986) 'New theories of the multinational enterprise: an assessment of internationalization theory', *Bulletin of Economic Research*, May: 101–18.

Sametz, A. W. (1970) 'The capital market', in M. E. Polakoff and others (eds) *Financial Institutions and Markets*, Boston, MA: Houghton Mifflin.

—— (ed.) (1972) *Financial Development and Economic Growth, The Economic Consequences of Underdeveloped Capital Markets*, New York: New York University Press.

Samuels, J. M. (1981) 'Inefficient capital markets and their implication', in F. G. J. Derkinderen and R. C. Crum (eds) *Risk, Capital Costs, and Project Financing Decisions*, Boston, MA: Martinus Nijhoff.

Schollhammer, H. and Chung, C. Y. (1987) 'The effect of exchange rate changes on the interdependence among national equity markets: an empirical investigation of the United States, Japan, Britain and Germany', paper presented at the Annual Meeting of the Academy of International Business, Chicago, 12–15 November.

Severn, A. K. (1974) 'Investor evaluation of foreign and domestic risk', *Journal of Finance*, May: 545–50.

Sharpe, W. F. and Cootner, C. M. (eds) (1982) *Financial Economics, Essays in Honor of Paul Cootner*, Englewood Cliffs, NJ: Prentice Hall.

Shaw, E. S. (1973) *Finance Deepening in Economic Development*, New York: Oxford University Press.

Silber, W. L. (1972) 'Thinness in capital markets',

Working Paper 72-10, Graduate School of Business Administration, New York University.

Soenen, L. A. and Hennigar, E. S. (1987) 'An analysis of exchange rates and stock prices – the U.S. experience between 1980 and 1986', paper presented at the Annual Meeting of the Academy of International Business, Chicago, 12–15 November.

Solberg, R. L. (1988) *Sovereign Rescheduling Risk and Portfolio Management*, London: Unwin Hyman.

Solnik, B. H. (1973) *European Capital Markets, Towards a General Theory of International Investment*, Lexington, MA: Lexington Books.

—— (1974a) 'The international pricing of risk: an empirical investigation of the world capital markets structure', *Journal of Finance*, May: 365–78.

—— (1974b) 'Why not diversify internationally rather than domestically?', *Financial Analysts Journal*, July–August: 48–54.

—— (1974c) 'An equilibrium model of the international capital market', *Journal of Economic Theory*, August: 500–24.

—— (1977) 'Testing international asset pricing: some pessimistic views', *Journal of Finance*, May: 503–12.

Solnik, B. H. and Noetzlin, B. (1982) 'Optimal international asset allocation', *Journal of Portfolio Management*, Fall: 11–21.

Spinkel, B. W. (1964) *Money and Stock Prices*, Homewood, IL: Richard D. Irwin.

—— (1971) *Money and Markets: A Monetarist View*, Homewood, IL: Richard D. Irwin.

Spitaller, E. (1971) 'A survey of recent quantitative studies of long-term capital movements', *IMF Staff Papers*, March: 189–220.

Srinivasan, T. N. (1986) 'The costs and benefits of being a small, remote, island, landlocked or ministate economy', *Research Observer, The World Bank*, July: 205–18.

Stapleton, R. C. and Subrahmanyam, M. G. (1980) *Capital Market Equilibrium and Corporate Financial Decisions*, Greenwich, CT: JAI Press.

Stehle, R. (1977) 'An empirical test of the alternative hypotheses of national and international pricing of risky assets', *Journal of Finance*, May: 493–502.

Stevens, G. V. C. (1973) 'The multinational firm and the determinants of investment', International Finance Discussion Papers 29, 23 May.

Stiglitz, J. E. (1972) 'On the optimality of the stock market allocation of investment', *Quarterly Journal of Economics*, February: 25–60.

—— (1981a) 'Information and capital markets', Working Paper 678, National Bureau of Economic Research, May.

—— (1981b) 'Pareto optimality and competition', *Journal of Finance*, May: 235–51.

—— (1982) 'The inefficiency of the stock market equilibrium', *Review of Economic Studies*, April: 241–61.

Stockman, A. C. and Hernandez, D. A. (1988) 'Exchange controls, capital controls, and international financial assets', *American Economic Review*, June: 362–74.

Stulz, R. M. (1981a) 'On the effects of barriers to international investments', *Journal of Finance*, September: 923–34.

—— (1981b) 'A model of international asset pricing', *Journal of Financial Economics*, December: 383–406.

—— (1984) 'Pricing capital assets in an international setting: an introduction', *Journal of International Business Studies*, Winter: 55–73.

—— (1986) 'Capital mobility in the world economy: theory and measurement; a comment', in K. Brunner and A. H. Meltzer (eds) *The National Bureau Method, International Capital Mobility and Other Essays*, Carnegie-Rochester Conference Series on Public Policy, Amsterdam: North-Holland, Spring.

Sudweeks, B. L. (1987) 'Equity market development in developing countries: general principles, case studies, portfolio implications, and relevance for the People's Republic of China', Ph.D. Dissertation, The George Washington University, March.

Svensson, L. E. O. (1988) 'Trade in risky assets', *American Economic Review*, June: 375–94.

Tobin, J. (1969) 'A general equilibrium approach to monetary theory', *Journal of Money, Credit and Banking*, February: 15–29.

—— (1982) 'Money and finance in the macroeconomic process', *Journal of Money, Credit, and Banking*, May: 171–204.

Tobin, J. and Braga De Macedo, J. (1980) 'The short-run macroeconomics of floating exchange rates: an exposition', in J. S. Chipman and C. P. Kindleberger (eds) *The Flexible Exchange Rates and the Balance of Payments: Essays in Memory of Egon Sohmen*, Amsterdam: North-Holland, pp. 5–28.

Tobin, J. and Brainard, W. C. (1968) 'Pitfalls in financial model building', *American Economic Review*, May: 99–122.

—— and —— (1977) 'Asset markets and the cost of capital', in R. Nelson and B. Belassa (eds) *Economic Progress, Private Values and Public Policy: Essays in Honor of William Fellner*, Amsterdam: North-Holland.

Versluysen, E. L. (1988) 'Financial deregulation and the globalization of capital markets', World Bank PPPR Working Paper WPS40, August.

Wai, U. T. (1978) 'The optimal size and ideal structure of financial markets in developing countries', Departmental Memorandum DM/78/74, IMF.

—— (1980) *Economic Essays on Developing Countries*, Alphen aan den Rijn, The Netherlands: Sijthoff & Nordhoff.

The Wall Street Journal (1989) C1, Friday, 3 February.

Wheatley, S. (1985) 'Some tests of international equity markets integration', unpublished manuscript, Graduate School of Business, University of Washington, November.

Wyss, D. A. (1987) 'Can the stock market rally the economy?', in Data Resources Incorporated *Review of the U.S. Economy*, February: 19–22.

14

MARKET EFFICIENCY AND EQUITY PRICING
International evidence and implications for global investing
Gabriel Hawawini

INTRODUCTION

In this chapter we examine the notion of market efficiency and present a survey of the international evidence regarding the validity of the efficient market hypothesis (EMH). The focus is on the most recent evidence which is generally at odds with this hypothesis. We also investigate the validity of the CAPM and the arbitrage pricing theory as descriptors and predictors of common stock returns in various stock exchanges around the world. Throughout the chapter we examine the implications of our findings for global portfolio management.

THE EFFICIENT MARKET HYPOTHESIS

In this section we first discuss the meaning and implications of the EMH and then examine its empirical validity. In discussing the concept of market efficiency we must first distinguish between two kinds of efficiency:[1] informational (or outside) efficiency and operational (or inside) efficiency. Outside efficiency refers to the performance of a market as an information processor and a price-setter whereas inside efficiency refers to the performance of a market as an exchange system. If we want to know whether a market is informationally efficient we must ask if that market is able to process information rapidly and set the price of securities at a level that reflects all that is known about firms. If we want to know whether a market

is operationally efficient we must ask if that market offers an inexpensive and reliable trading mechanism. In other words, we wish to know what the magnitude of transaction costs (commissions, bid–ask spread, market impact of trade etc.) is, how fast orders can be executed and how long it takes to settle a trade. Note that informational efficiency and operational efficiency are related. Poor operational efficiency may delay the adjustment of prices to new information and prevent them from reaching their equilibrium value. The operational efficiency of equity markets around the world is examined elsewhere in this book. Several aspects of their informational efficiency are reviewed below.

What is an informationally efficient market?

Broadly speaking, a market is said to be informationally efficient if, at every moment in time, the current price of securities fully reflects all available and relevant information.[2] If prices do reflect all that is known about firms, then security prices should be equal to their true value defined as discounted future cash flows. This in turn implies that investors cannot use public information to earn abnormal returns. In practice, however, prices may differ from their true value because of factors such as the speed of price adjustment to new information and transaction costs. If prices adjusted instantaneously to new information and transaction costs were zero, then security prices would be equal to their true value at every moment in time.

The idea underlying the EMH is quite simple. If all information is readily available to a large number of rational profit-seeking investors, or if the trading decisions of informed investors are imitated, then arbitrage operations should drive the current price of a security to its true value. Investors who consistently do better than average in picking undervalued stocks will accumulate these stocks at the expense of those which they believe to be overvalued. This investment strategy will drive the price of securities toward their true value. Conversely, investors who consistently do worse than average in picking undervalued stocks (i.e. they end up with overvalued stocks) will carry fewer of those stocks, driving their prices down. It follows that in an efficient market, securities will trade at prices which are close to their true value and investors will be unable systematically to earn above-normal profits.

Efficiency, of course, can only be defined relative to a specific type of information. Types of information are usually classified in three distinct categories. The first type is the historical sequence of prices. The second is public knowledge of companies' past performance as well as public forecasts regarding future performance and possible actions. Finally, the third type is private or privileged information. It is only available to insiders and those who have access to companies' policies and plans. These three types of information are then used to define three forms or degrees of market efficiency. The weak form of the EMH corresponds to the first type of information. It asserts that current prices fully and instantaneously reflect all the information implied by the historical sequence of prices. The semi-strong form of the EMH corresponds to the second *and* first types of information. It asserts that current prices fully and instantaneously reflect all public information about companies, including, of course, the information implied in the historical sequence of prices. Finally, the strong form of the EMH corresponds to the first, second and third types of information. It asserts that current prices fully and instantan-

eously reflect *all* information, *public* as well as *private*. Note that when we define degrees of market efficiency from weak to strong the information set becomes wider and cumulative.

Early evidence on the validity of the efficient market hypothesis

Although rather simple to define, the EMH is quite difficult to test. One cannot say for certain whether the EMH holds true. For example, it is practically impossible to provide evidence that all possible mathematical combinations of past prices are good for predicting future prices. Also, one may not be able, for example, to conclude that a market is efficient in the semi-strong form because the information set (all publicly available information) cannot be tested exhaustively. Prices may react efficiently to a given subset of information (say earnings announcements) and inefficiently to another subset (say stock splits).

A large number of tests of the EMH in its three forms have been conducted, first with US stock market data and later with data from foreign equity markets. Tests of the weak form of efficiency concluded that changes in the price of common stocks follow a random walk, i.e. their behaviour is consistent with the notion of an efficient market in its weak form.[3] One way to test the random walk model is to find out whether the historical sequence of returns on a given security are independent of one another or whether they are related to one another. This can be done by calculating the serial correlation coefficient between the sequence of the stock's daily returns and the same sequence lagged one, two or more days.[4] If the calculated serial correlation coefficient is not significantly different from zero in a statistical sense, we can conclude that the random walk model is valid, i.e. the knowledge of the past behaviour of a stock's price movements cannot be used to predict the future behaviour of that stock's price movements. A large number of studies have tested this model on US and foreign stock prices and have shown that, with few exceptions, the random walk model cannot be refuted.[5] Significant correlations between stock returns may exist over daily return intervals but disappear with the lengthening of the time interval over which securities' returns are measured. Serial correlation coefficients, however, even when statistically significant, are generally not strong enough or sufficiently stable to enable investors to achieve above-normal profits. There may exist complex patterns of common stock returns, however, which serial correlation analysis is unable to detect. These complex patterns, if they exist, could be taken advantage of by formulating mechanical trading rules such as filter rules, point-and-figure charts, moving averages, relative strength rules and portfolio rebalancing strategies. A mechanical rule is considered successful if its systematic application to stock prices would have enabled a trader to earn a higher return than a passive buy-and-hold strategy, at the same level of risk and net of transaction costs. The evidence based on US and foreign markets indicates that none of these techniques can be used to achieve systematic and permanent superior performance.[6]

Tests of the semi-strong form of efficiency are usually performed by examining the speed with which the price of securities adjusts to the new information contained in dividend and earnings announcements, as well as announcements regarding new issues of common stocks, mergers and acquisitions, block trading and changes in accounting rules and reporting methods. If prices adjust no later than the date of the announcement, the market is informationally efficient with respect to that type of information. If price adjustments are observed *after* the date of the announcement, the market is informationally inefficient with respect to that type of information. A large number of tests based on US and foreign data concluded that markets are generally informationally efficient in the semi-strong form.[7]

In a strong-form-efficient market, all information (including inside information) is fully reflected in the price of securities. This means that individuals with monopolistic access to non-public information will be unable to earn abnormal profits. This may not be the case on the NYSE. There is evidence indicating that corporate insiders (who

must list their trading with the SEC) tend to purchase in the months prior to a price increase and sell in the months before a price decline (Jaffe 1974). No similar studies have been performed in markets outside the USA because of a lack of data on insider trading. Nevertheless, the widely held view on this matter is that trading on inside information does take place on most foreign stock exchanges and that some individuals and institutions do manage to garner abnormal profits from these activities. We must await rigorous empirical work in this area before drawing any meaningful conclusion.

An alternative test of the strong form of market efficiency is to examine the performance of professionally managed institutional portfolios. Professional portfolio managers should be able to obtain and profit from valuable investment information before it is fully reflected in the market. Several studies have shown that managers of US mutual funds were unable to beat the market consistently. There exists a small number of studies which have investigated the performance of European institutional investors (Hawawini 1984). The results are usually in line with those found on the NYSE. Professional European investors have not been able to outperform the market consistently.

Recent evidence at odds with the efficient market hypothesis

A growing number of studies have recently uncovered several phenomena that are inconsistent with the EMH in its weak and semi-strong forms (see Keim 1986; Banz and Hawawini 1987).

There is evidence of recurrent seasonality in common stock returns in the US and foreign markets. Stock market returns differ, on average, depending on which day of the week they are measured (day-of-the-week effect) or which month of the year they are calculated (month-of-the-year effect). This phenomenon is *inconsistent* with the weak form of market efficiency since investors can predict higher or lower returns for specific days of the week or months of the year. The seasonal behaviour of common stock returns and its implications for global investment management are examined in the fourth and sixth sections.

There is also evidence that portfolios constructed on the basis of firm size (market value of shares outstanding) have different average returns. Small-firm portfolios tend to outperform their larger counterparts even after returns are adjusted for the difference in the level of risk that may exist between small and large companies. This size effect is inconsistent with the semi-strong form of market efficiency since investors can predict a higher average return for a portfolio constructed on the basis of publicly available information (market capitalization). The small-firm effect, other stock market anomalies and their implications for global investment management are examined in the fifth and sixth sections.

MODELS OF EQUITY PRICING

Until the early 1980s, the CAPM was the standard tool used to describe common stock returns in an efficient market.[8] A large number of empirical studies published in the 1970s concluded that the CAPM was a good descriptor and predictor of the behaviour of common stock returns in the USA, Europe and Japan. In the late 1970s, however, the validity of the CAPM was seriously questioned, first conceptually and later empirically.[9] As this was happening, an alternative equity pricing model, known as the arbitrage pricing theory (APT), was developed in the mid-1970s to overcome some of the deficiencies of the CAPM. This model was tested in the early 1980s using US, European and Japanese data.[10] At the time of this writing, the most recent tests of equity pricing models seem to cast some doubt on the validity of the CAPM as a descriptor and predictor of common stock returns. They also indicate that the APT may provide a superior alternative to the CAPM. In what follows we provide a description of both models and a review of their empirical tests.

The capital asset pricing model

One of the fundamental principles of modern finance is that the higher the risk of an asset, the higher its expected return. If you buy a high-risk, high-expected-return portfolio and hold it over a sufficiently long period of time (say a few years), that portfolio should earn a higher actual return than the low-risk, low-expected-return portfolio.

What do we mean by risk and how is it measured? What is the relationship between a portfolio's expected return and its risk? The CAPM provides answers to these questions.

One of the building blocks of the CAPM is the principle of risk decomposition. The total risk of a security can be broken down into two independent components: a market-related component and a firm-specific component. The former is a measure of the extent to which the price of a security fluctuates in response to the general market movement. The latter is a measure of the extent to which the price of a security fluctuates in response to information unique to the firm which issued the security. We can write

total risk = [market risk] + [firm-specific risk],

where the variance of a security's returns is the measure of its total risk.[11]

It can be shown that the market risk of a security is proportional to the variance of the market as a whole:

$$[\text{market risk of security}_i] = \beta_i^2 [\text{variance of the market}],$$

where the proportionality factor β_i is called the β coefficient of security i or its *systematic* risk. It is a measure of the sensitivity of security i's return to the returns of the market. A security with a β coefficient equal to unity has as much market risk as the market as a whole. But a security with a β coefficient greater than unity has more market risk than the market as a whole. And a security with a β coefficient less than unity has less market risk than the market as a whole. In other words, high-β

stocks have higher market risk than low-β stocks. Suppose that security i has a β coefficient of 0.80 and that the variance of its returns is 0.25 per cent. Suppose, further, that the market as a whole has a variance of 0.10 per cent. According to the above equation, the market risk of security i is $(0.80)^2 \times (0.10$ per cent$) = 0.064$ per cent. And since its total risk is 0.25 per cent it follows that security i has a firm-specific or residual risk of 0.186 per cent (0.25 per cent minus 0.064 per cent). Note that 25.60 per cent (0.064 per cent divided by 0.25 per cent) of the total risk of security i is generated by the market movement (market risk) and the remaining 74.40 per cent of its total risk is generated by information unique to firm i (firm-specific risk).

The CAPM builds on the above principle of risk decomposition as well as two other basic facts. First, individuals dislike risk, i.e. they are risk averse. Second, security prices do not move in perfect unison, i.e. their returns are less than perfectly correlated. Hence, increasing the number of securities in a portfolio can reduce its total risk without changing its expected return. As a result, investors will tend to hold well-diversified portfolios. What then is the relevant measure of the risk of a security when that security is part of a well-diversified portfolio? Only the market risk of a security is relevant in a portfolio context because the firm-specific risk is diversified away. Indeed, an investor holding a well-diversified portfolio of securities only bears the market risk of the securities making up the portfolio. The firm-specific components of the risks of the securities will offset one another and approach zero as the size of the portfolio increases.

Since the firm-specific risk of a security can be eliminated by investors by simply holding the security as part of a portfolio, the CAPM claims that the firm-specific risk of a security is irrelevant in the pricing of that security. In other words, because investors can diversify away the firm-specific risk of securities, they do not have to bear that risk and hence should not be compensated for it. They should only be remunerated for bearing market risk because market risk cannot be diversi-

fied away. Thus, the expected return of a security (the remuneration for holding that security) must be related only to the market risk of that security. Securities with high β coefficients (a measure of their market risk) must have higher expected returns than securities with low β coefficients.

The CAPM gives the theoretical equilibrium relationship that must exist between an asset's expected return $E(R_i)$ and its β coefficient β_i:

$$E(R_i) = R_F + [E(R_m) - R_F]\,\beta_i\,.$$

According to the CAPM, the expected return on a risky asset is equal to the return on a risk-free asset R_F plus a risk premium which is proportional to the β coefficient of that asset. The proportionality factor (also called the market risk premium) is the difference between the expected return on the market as a whole (indicated by the subscript m) and the risk-free rate of return. If the risk-free rate is 6 per cent and the expected return on the market is 11 per cent, then, according to the CAPM, the expected return of security i is given by

$$E(R_i) = 0.06 + 0.05\beta_i\,.$$

If security i has a β coefficient of 0.80, its expected return is 10 per cent according to the CAPM, the sum of a risk-free rate of 6 per cent and a risk premium of $(0.05)(0.80) = 4.00$ per cent.

Early evidence on the validity of the capital asset pricing model

How can we test the validity of the CAPM? Note that the model is based on expected returns which are not observable. But if the relation between security returns remains relatively stable through time, then historical average returns can be used as a proxy for the unobservable expected returns. Thus, to verify the empirical validity of the model we can examine the historical relation between portfolio average returns and their corresponding estimated β coefficients. If that relation is linear with an intercept equal to the risk-free rate and a slope equal to the excess return on a broad market index, then the CAPM is a valid model of stock price behaviour. We shall have an additional test of the validity of the CAPM if we can show that firm-specific risk is unrelated to average returns. Recall that, according to the CAPM, firm-specific risk can be diversified away and, hence, should not be priced in the market. In other words, an asset's firm-specific risk should not be related to that asset's average return.

One of the first rigorous tests of the CAPM was performed on portfolios of stocks traded on the NYSE from 1935 to June 1968.[12] The estimated relationship between average *monthly* returns $\bar{R}_i$, β_i, β_i^2 and firm-specific risk over the thirty-four-year period was found to be

$$\bar{R}_i = [0.0020] + [0.0114]\,\beta_i - 0.0026\beta_i^2 + 0.0516\,(\text{firm-specific risk}),$$

where the coefficients in square brackets are the only ones that are significantly different from zero in a statistical sense. The above empirical relationship has an estimated monthly intercept of 0.20 per cent (2.4 per cent on an annual basis) and an estimated monthly β slope of 1.14 per cent (13.48 per cent on an annual basis). The intercept is not significantly different from the average risk-free rate prevailing over the period 1935–68 and the slope is not significantly different from the prevailing market premium (average market return minus average risk-free rate) over that same period. The conclusion is obvious. The CAPM, when tested over a long period of time on the NYSE, cannot be rejected. Market risk is the only factor which has a significant relationship with average returns. Firm-specific risk is irrelevant for security pricing and so is β^2, implying that average return is a positive and linear function of systematic risk.

Similar, but somewhat weaker, conclusions were reached when the CAPM was first tested on European and Japanese data. In general, the price behaviour of common stocks was found to be consistent with the CAPM in Canada, the UK, Germany, France, Spain, Belgium, Japan and Thailand.[13]

But despite the empirical evidence supporting the CAPM, it has not been universally accepted.

Criticisms range from its simplicity to the problem of how one should define the 'market'. Recently, the empirical validity of the CAPM was re-examined in the light of the size anomaly and the seasonal behaviour of stock market returns (see pages 293–4). The most recent evidence casts some doubt on the validity of this model as a descriptor and predictor of common stock returns. This evidence and its implications are examined in the seventh section following a review of stock market anomalies in the fourth, fifth and sixth sections.

The arbitrage pricing theory model

The APT is a multi-factor equilibrium pricing model which is more general than the CAPM. It assumes that the returns on securities are linearly related to a small number of common or systematic factors rather than a single factor as in the case of the CAPM. The model applies to any set of securities as long as their number is much larger than the number of common factors. The model does not require that investors hold all outstanding securities and hence the 'market', which is central to the CAPM, plays no particular role in the APT.

Suppose that there are three common factors that influence the stock market. According to the APT, the expected return of asset i is

$$E(R_i) = R_F + \lambda_1 b_{1i} + \lambda_2 b_{2i} + \lambda_3 b_{3i},$$

where λ_1, λ_2 and λ_3 are the three risk premia corresponding to the three sensitivity coefficients of asset i, b_{1i}, b_{2i} and b_{3i}. These sensitivity coefficients are similar to the β coefficient in the CAPM. The β of a stock is a measure of the sensitivity of that stock's returns to the returns of the market as a whole. Likewise, b_{1i} is a measure of the sensitivity of the returns of stock i to the returns of the first common factor etc.

Clearly, there is a *structural* similarity between the APT model and the CAPM. Assuming there is only one common or systematic factor affecting *all* securities outstanding and that this factor is the return on the market as a whole, then the APT pricing relationship collapses to the CAPM pricing relationship. In this case, the sensitivity coefficient to the unique market factor is the β coefficient and the risk premium λ_1 is equal to $E(R_m) - R_F$, the CAPM risk premium.

The APT's generality, however, is to some extent a weakness. The model indicates that an asset's expected return is a linear function of a set of sensitivity coefficients to systematic or common factors. But the number of common factors and their nature are not known. As a consequence, tests of the APT model are particularly difficult to design. Most tests of this model employ the methodology suggested by Roll and Ross (1980). This methodology, outlined below, has been recently applied to French, German and UK data.[14]

Before discussing the available European and Japanese evidence, we present a brief review of the Roll and Ross approach to testing the APT model. They used daily returns data from July 1962 through December 1972 for a sample of about 1,260 NYSE and AMEX companies. Their sample of stocks was divided into forty-two groups of thirty securities each and each group's variance–covariance matrix was estimated from the returns data. Because of limitations imposed by computer software, each group was analysed separately. By applying maximum likelihood factor analysis, they determined simultaneously the number of common factors F_j and their corresponding sensitivity coefficients b_{ij}, called factor loadings. Finally, they performed a cross-sectional test of the APT model by running a linear regression in which average stock returns is the dependent variable and the set of factor loadings b_{ij} are the independent variables. This method allows them to estimate the risk premia associated with each factor and to determine the number of factors that are 'priced' according to the APT. They found that for 75 per cent of the groups they analysed, there is a 50 per cent chance that five factors are significant and that three to four factors explain the cross-sectional variation in average stock returns. They concluded that the APT model performs well under empirical scrutiny.

The results of tests of the APT model applied to European data indicate that equity pricing is generally consistent with this model. The number of significant common factors varies across studies. In the case of France seven common factors are significant in explaining the variance of common stock returns. For German data the number of factors retained depends on the criterion employed to select those which are significant. The smallest number of factors is one and the largest forty-three. British studies suggest fifteen to twenty relevant factors for UK data.

The disparity in the number of significant common factors reported in these studies is essentially due to differences in the size of the groups analysed, the statistical technique employed to extract the factors from the data and the type of criterion adopted to select those factors which are relevant. Turning to the cross-sectional evidence, three to five factors seem to explain the cross-sectional variation of average return of French stocks. The number is about eight for German stocks and one to seven for UK stocks. What general conclusion can be drawn from these results? There is strong evidence that more than one common factor explains the variation of European stock returns and that the first factor explains 25–40 per cent of that variation. This factor, which is highly correlated with a market index, may be the return on the market as a whole.

A major weakness of the tests of the APT model described above is their inability to identify the *nature* of the common factors. We know that a few common factors are involved in the pricing of equity, but what are they? An alternative approach to testing the APT model is to prespecify a set of macroeconomic variables which are believed, *a priori*, to act as common factors and examine whether the sensitivity coefficients of stock returns to these common factors explain the cross-sectional variation of average stock returns. This approach has been applied to both US stocks and Japanese stocks.[15] The latter study is briefly described below.

A set of eight economic variables were selected as likely common factors that would affect the monthly returns of Japanese stocks traded on the

First Section of the Tokyo Stock Exchange (TSE) from January 1975 to December 1984. These are (1) the monthly growth rate in an index of industrial production; (2) changes in expected inflation; (3) unexpected inflation (expected inflation minus actual inflation); (4) unexpected changes in the risk premium with the risk premium defined as the spread between government and corporate bonds; (5) unexpected changes in the slope of the term structure of interest rates with the slope defined as the spread between the rate on long-term government bonds and the short-term risk-free rate; (6) unexpected changes in the forward yen–dollar exchange rate; (7) the growth rate in oil prices (translated in yen); and (8) the return of a market index of TSE stocks. It was found that only three of these factors have a significant effect on Japanese common stock returns. These are (1) changes in expected inflation, (2) unexpected changes in the risk premium, and (3) unexpected changes in the slope of the term structure of interest rates. Monthly growth rate in industrial production, unexpected changes in the foreign exchange and oil price changes are not priced on the TSE. More important, however, is the finding that once the three significant common factors are taken into account the market index does not have any influence on stock returns. This result should not be interpreted to mean that market index is irrelevant in pricing equity. Actually, the market index, when taken alone, does influence stock returns. But it has no *additional* effect on stock returns beyond the joint effect of the three significant common factors.

SEASONALITIES IN STOCK MARKET RETURNS

In the second section we suggested that the presence of seasonalities in stock market returns is inconsistent with the weak form of the EMH unless we can show that the higher average returns earned during specific days of the week or during particular months of the year would disappear once returns are adjusted for transaction costs and incremental risk (if any). In this section we present evidence of seasonality in the daily and monthly returns of the stock market indices of a sample of countries that includes Australia, Canada, Europe, Japan, Singapore and the USA. Of the two phenomena, we shall see that the most relevant to global investment strategies is the monthly seasonal. For this reason, the causes of monthly seasonality and the implications of this phenomenon for global portfolio mnagement are examined in separate sections.

Seasonality in stock market daily returns

Table 14.1 provides the average daily return of nine market indices for the first five days of the week. The sample covers nine countries over a sixteen-year period (January 1969 to December 1984) except for the case of Australia, Finland and Spain for which the daily mean returns are calculated over shorter periods. Framed returns are significantly different from zero in a statistical sense. These returns are computed using the closing value of the market index. For example, Monday returns are computed from Friday close to Monday close and hence include the weekend (Friday close to Monday open) as well as Monday (Monday open to Monday close). In all the countries in the sample except Japan, the exchange is closed during the weekend (Saturday and Sunday). In Japan, however, the exchange is open every second Saturday for morning trade.

Several observations can be made.

1 There is a significant 'day-of-the-week' effect in all countries. That is, average stock market returns on different days of the week are not the same (although not provided in Table 14.1, a statistical test confirms that statement for the nine countries in the sample).

2 Average daily returns during the last three days of the week (Wednesday, Thursday and Friday) are *positive* whereas average daily returns during the first two days of the week (Monday and Tuesday) are often negative.

3 Average returns are significantly negative on Monday in North America (Canada and the

Table 14.1 International evidence of daily seasonality in stock market returns

Country	Daily mean returns (per cent): 1969–84 (unless otherwise indicated)[a]				
	Monday	Tuesday	Wednesday	Thursday	Friday
Australia (1975.IV–1984)	0.044	[−0.116]	0.045	[0.198]	[0.157]
Canada	[−0.157]	−0.003	[0.073]	[0.075]	[0.094]
Finland (1977–82)	[0.086]	[0.066]	0.030	[0.070]	[0.074]
France	−0.050	[−0.157]	[0.100]	[0.152]	[0.082]
Japan	[0.090]	[−0.095]	[0.139]	0.025	0.039
Singapore	−0.036	[−0.107]	[0.079]	[0.121]	[0.100]
Spain (1979–83)	Market closed	−0.072	0.003	0.037	0.071
UK	[−0.095]	[0.106]	[0.090]	0.011	0.044
USA	[−0.134]	0.013	0.057	0.021	0.058

Sources: Australia, Ball and Bowers 1987; Finland, Berglund 1985; Spain, Santesmases 1986; all other countries from
Condoyanni *et al.* 1987
Notes: [a] Returns in square brackets are significantly different from zero at the 0.05 level. The remaining returns are not
significantly different from zero.
[b] The Finnish returns are calculated from September to May only. The Helsinki Stock Exchange is closed on Mondays
during the summer months (June to August).

USA) and the UK, a phenomenon known as the 'Monday effect'.

4   There is *no* Monday effect in the Far East (Japan and Singapore), Australia, Finland and France. Except for the case of Finland, the Monday effect is replaced by a Tuesday effect. That is, significantly negative average returns are observed on Tuesday in these countries.

Several questions immediately come to mind. Can these patterns of daily returns be explained? Why do they differ across countries (the Monday effect in Canada, the USA and the UK and the Tuesday effect in the Far East, Australia and France)? Do they violate the weak form of the EMH? Do they have any practical implications for global investing?

A partial explanation of the Monday effect in the USA and the UK is based on the settlement-delay hypothesis: the fact that there exists a delay of several days between the day a stock is traded and the day the funds are actually transferred (Lakonishok and Levi 1982). On the NYSE there is a five-business-day settlement period to which we must add a business day for cheque clearing. This means that for stocks purchased on a business day

other than Friday, the buyer will have eight *calendar* days before losing funds. For stocks purchased on Friday, he will have ten calendar days and thus two more days of interest earnings. In an efficient securities market the buyer should be willing to pay more for stocks purchased on Friday by an amount not exceeding two days of interest. Consequently, observed returns on Friday should be higher than those on other days of the week and those of Monday should be lower. A similar argument may explain the Monday effect reported on the London Stock Exchange (LSE). (Theobald and Price 1984). On that exchange trading takes place over consecutive account periods of two weeks' length beginning every other Monday. Settlement, however, is made on the second Monday after the end of the account. This means that for stocks purchased on the first Monday of the account, the buyer will have twenty-one calendar days before losing funds, whereas for stocks purchased the preceding Friday, he will have only ten calendar days. For stocks purchased on the second Monday of the account, the buyer will have fourteen calendar days but seventeen calendar days for stocks purchased the preceding Friday. According to the settlement-delay hypothesis, the first Monday returns of the account should be higher than the returns on the other days of the week and the second Monday returns should be lower. However, the fact that stocks generally go ex-dividend on the *first* Monday of the account will partly offset the rise in price and return predicted for that day by the settlement-delay hypothesis. Indeed, returns on non-ex-dividend Mondays are generally negative, whereas returns on ex-dividend Mondays are generally positive. This result is qualitatively consistent with the settlement-delay hypothesis but the magnitude of the Monday effect on the NYSE and the LSE cannot be fully explained by the settlement-delay hypothesis. At the time of this writing it remains a partial puzzle.

The Tuesday effect in Australia, France, Japan and Singapore may be the result of time-zone differences relative to New York. With the exception of France, these countries are all one day ahead of New York. Hence, the Tuesday effect in these countries may reflect the earlier Monday effect in New York, suggesting that there exist significant correlations among daily stock returns across the world's stock exchanges. These correlations are lagged by a day rather than being contemporaneous. The Tuesday effect in the French index may be explained by the fact that, contrary to the UK index, the French index is compiled *before* the US market opens.

Can these phenomena be interpreted as violations of the EMH? It is doubtful that a trader could earn abnormal returns by exploiting the Monday/Tuesday effects. It would require short selling which may not be available. And transaction costs are likely to eliminate most of the abnormal profit. What are the implications for global investing? The evidence clearly indicates that the major stock exchanges around the world are part of a global market in which the price movements of individual exchanges are closely interrelated. The linkages among the major exchanges around the world is practically instantaneous. Lags in the correlation structure of stock returns around the world seem to reflect differences in time zones. The Monday effect reported in North America and the UK is replaced by a Tuesday effect in countries outside the New York time zone. There may be some advantages to be gained from that knowledge; investors *planning* to buy stocks should do so preferably on Monday for Canadian, US and UK stocks and on Tuesday for French and Far Eastern stocks. And a stock sale should preferably be carried out on a Wednesday, Thursday or Friday.

Seasonality in stock market monthly returns

Table 14.2 provides the average monthly returns of eleven market indices for every month of the year. The sample covers nine countries over a twenty-one-year period (January 1959 to December 1979) except for the case of the Finnish stock market and the UK Financial Times All-Share Index for which the periods of analysis differ.

Several observations can be made.

1 There is a significant 'month-of-the-year' effect in all countries. That is, average stock market returns in different months of the year are not the same (although not provided in Table 14.2, a statistical test confirms that statement for the countries that make up the sample).

2 Average returns during January are always positive and generally significantly higher than during the rest of the year.

3 The 'January effect' depends on the composition of the stock market index. Broader and equally weighted indices exhibit a stronger January effect than narrower indices. The equally weighted index of all NYSE shares has a January returns of 5.08 per cent compared with 1.04 per cent for a value-weighted index. This phenomenon is a manifestation of the small-firm effect. The equally weighted index gives more weight to small firms than does the value-weighted index. And small firms are generally responsible for the January effect. This important aspect of the January effect is discussed in a following section.

The January effect raises the same set of questions as those raised by the Monday effect. How can it

Table 14.2 International evidence of monthly seasonality in stock market returns

Country	Month-to-month percentage mean returns (January 1959–December 1979)[a]												
	January	February	March	April	May	June	July	August	September	October	November	December	All months
Australia	2.65	−0.58	0.51	0.84	0.97	0.43	0.66	−0.37	−2.39	2.13	−0.85	3.99	0.67
Belgium	3.20	1.09	0.40	1.48	−1.36	−0.84	1.44	−1.17	−1.87	−0.69	0.42	−0.09	0.17
Canada	2.90	0.07	0.79	0.41	−0.96	−0.30	0.69	0.60	−0.06	−0.82	1.44	2.61	0.61
Finland	3.62	2.09	2.63	0.95	−0.02	1.55	2.53	0.97	−0.76	0.77	0.61	2.51	n.a.
France	3.72	−0.18	1.98	0.94	−0.66	−1.90	1.53	1.03	−1.21	−0.72	0.43	0.15	0.43
Japan	3.53	1.13	1.88	0.30	0.96	2.06	−0.32	−0.83	−0.13	−0.98	1.65	1.80	0.92
Spain	2.24	1.29	0.32	1.59	−1.87	0.06	0.79	1.29	−1.64	0.19	−0.44	−0.01	0.32
UK	3.40	0.69	1.25	3.13	−1.21	−1.69	−1.11	1.88	−0.24	0.80	−0.61	2.06	0.70
UK FT-A	3.06	0.79	1.15	3.57	−1.00	−0.85	−0.22	2.62	0.03	1.26	0.16	2.34	1.08
USA	1.04	−0.41	1.27	0.96	−1.38	−0.56	0.14	0.34	−0.79	0.78	1.03	1.42	0.32
US EW[b]	5.08	0.55	1.55	0.44	−1.42	−1.00	0.73	0.72	−0.42	−0.79	1.79	1.37	n.a.

Sources: Finland, Berglund 1985; UK FT-A (Financial Times All-Share Index), Levis 1985; all other data are from Gultekin and Gultekin (1983) and are based on stock market indices from *Capital International Perspective* (value-weighted indices)

Notes: n.a., not available.

[a] Except for Finland where the period covered is from January 1970 to December 1983 and UK FT-A where the period covered is from January 1958 to December 1982.

[b] Equally weighted index of NYSE shares.

be explained? Does it violate the EMH? What are its implications for portfolio management and global investing? These questions are addressed in the following four sections.

A SIZE EFFECT IN STOCK MARKETS AROUND THE WORLD

Which of two portfolios has the higher probability of achieving a higher average return in the near future? We have already pointed out in the third section that the CAPM claims that it is the portfolio with the higher systematic risk. But we have also mentioned earlier that a substantial body of empirical evidence, gathered over the last ten years, suggests that the portfolio containing the securities of firms with the smallest market capitalization outperforms, on average, the portfolio with the larger market capitalization even after adjusting returns for the difference in the level of risk that may exist between small and large firms. This is what we called 'the size effect' in equity markets.

In the second section we argued that the size effect is inconsistent with the semi-strong form of the EMH. In this section we report evidence of a size effect in most equity markets around the world. *But we show that this phenomenon is not stable over time.* It does not manifest itself over all holding periods or during every month of the year. We shall see that this aspect of the size effect has obvious implications for the design and implementation of investment strategies that seek to exploit this anomaly to improve portfolio performance. We also examine some possible explanations of the size effect and conclude with a brief survey of stock market anomalies other than the size anomaly.

International evidence of a size effect

The evidence is summarized in Table 14.3 for the Australian, Canadian, European, Japanese and American stock markets. First note the difference in size (market capitalization) between the largest and the smallest portfolio in the samples drawn

from the nine countries. In the case of Spain the largest portfolio is 228 times larger than the smallest portfolio. But in the case of Japan the largest portfolio is only twenty-five times larger than the smallest portfolio. The size premium earned by the smallest portfolio is measured by the difference between the average monthly return on the smallest portfolio of firms and the average monthly return on the largest portfolio of firms. The size premium is positive in all countries. But its magnitude varies across markets. It is most pronounced in Australia (5.73 per cent per month) and Japan (0.89 per cent per month) and least pronounced in the UK (0.40 per cent per month) and Canada (0.44 per cent per month). Note that the *annualized* size premium (monthly size premium multiplied by twelve) varies from 68.76 per cent in Australia (over the twenty-four-year test period) to only 4.75 per cent in the UK (over the twenty-five-year test period). A size effect exists in the nine countries but it is not significant in the UK and Canada. Also, because the sample periods are different across countries, we do not know whether the magnitude of the size effect is significantly different across the nine countries.

What about risk? Can differences in risk between the smallest and largest portfolios explain the size premium? The evidence is found in Table 14.3. In three European countries for which data are available (Finland, France and the UK), the market risk of the smallest firms is lower than the market risk of the largest firms. In Australia and Belgium they are the same. It is not clear why small firms in Finland, France and the UK have, on average, lower βs than large firms but the implication is clear. If we adjust for differences in risk, the size premium would be higher than the one reported in Table 14.3 in the case of these three countries (since small firms have lower βs) and about the same in Australia and Belgium (since small and large firms have, on average, roughly the same βs in these two countries). In Japan and the USA we have the opposite phenomenon: small firms have, on average, higher market risk than large firms. This is intuitively more appealing. Small firms are, on average, more risky than large

Table 14.3 International evidence of a size premium

	Australia	Belgium	Canada	Finland	France	Japan	Spain	UK	USA
Test period	1958–81	1969–83	1973–80	1970–81	1968–80	1966–83	1963–82	1958–82	1926–79
Number of securities	281 to 937	170	391	50	201	First section TSE	98 to 140	All LSE	All NYSE
Number of size portfolios	10	5	5	10	5	5	10	10	5
Market value of largest portfolio of firms divided by market value of smallest portfolio of firms[a]	n.a.	188	67	113	83	25	228	182	124
Average monthly return on the smallest portfolio of firms (per cent)[b]	6.75	1.17	1.67	1.65	1.62	2.03	0.58	1.33	1.77
Average monthly return on the largest portfolio of firms (per cent)[b]	1.02	0.65	1.23	0.89	0.97	1.14	0.02	0.93	0.93
Size premium (small minus large) (per cent)	5.73	0.52	0.44	0.76	0.65	0.89	0.56	0.40	0.84
Average risk of smallest portfolio standard β coefficient[d]	1.04	1.01	n.a.	0.36	0.42	1.12	n.a.	0.31	1.45
adjusted β coefficient[e]	n.a.	n.a.	n.a.	0.50	0.55	1.22	n.a.	0.64	1.60
Average risk of largest portfolio standard β coefficient[d]	0.95	0.98	n.a.	1.00	1.05	0.81	n.a.	1.01	0.96
adjusted β coefficient[e]	n.a.	n.a.	n.a.	0.95	1.05	0.77	n.a.	1.02	0.93

Sources: Australia, Brown et al. 1983; Belgium, Hawawini et al. 1988; Canada, Berges et al. 1984; Finland, Wahlroos and Berglund 1986; France, Hamon 1986; Japan, Nakamura and Terada 1984; Spain, Rubio 1988; UK, Levis 1985; USA, Banz 1982

Notes: TSE, Tokyo Stock Exchange; NYSE, New York Stock Exchange; LSE, London Stock Exchange; n.a., not available.
[a] The ratio is based on the average market value over the sample period, except for the USA where the ratio is calculated in 1975 and Finland where it is calculated in 1970.
[b] All returns are significantly different from zero at the 0.05 level.
[c] For Spain the average return on the small and the large portfolios are returns in excess of those predicted by the CAPM, i.e. they are risk-adjusted return.
[d] Standard β coefficients are estimated using ordinary least square regression.
[e] Adjusted βs are estimated using the Scholes and Williams (1977) method in the case of France and the Dimson (1979) method in all other cases. These two methods adjust the estimated β coefficient for the thin trading that characterizes smaller firms.

firms in Japan and the USA. But the higher market risk of small firms in these two countries does not account for the size premium. The risk-adjusted size premium is smaller than the unadjusted risk premium reported in Table 14.3 for Japan and the USA but it is still significantly different from zero.

Stationarity of the size premium and implications for investment management

Is the size premium a stable and recurrent phenomenon or does it manifest itself randomly over time? The answer to this question is important because the knowledge of the time behaviour of the size premium is crucial to the design and implementation of investment strategies that seek to exploit the size effect in order to improve portfolio performance.

The evidence suggests that the size effect is a recurrent phenomenon but there are periods of time over which large firms, on average, outperform small firms. Also, the magnitude of the size premium is not constant. For example, in the case of the USA (the country for which we have the most extensive evidence) the size premium varied between a low of −10.20 per cent over the subperiod 1926–30 and a high of 43.80 per cent over the subperiod 1931–5.

In the next section we shall show that the magnitude and the sign of the size premium are not the same, on average, during all months of the year. In most countries the size premium is usually large and positive during specific months of the year, particularly during the month of January.

The implication for investors who seek to exploit the size effect by holding portfolios of small firms is that such portfolios must be held over a period of time of sufficient length (at least ten years) to ensure a high probability of achieving superior performance (Keim 1983; Bauer and Wirick 1986). Note that the fact that the size premium manifests itself during specific months of the year can also be exploited to achieve superior performance. This is shown in the next section as well as in the eighth section.

Possible explanations of the size effect

There are basically two possible interpretations of the small-firm effect. The first is that the phenomenon does not exist; its appearance is simply the result of poor measurement procedures. If stock returns and market risk were measured properly, the size effect would disappear. The second interpretation is that the size effect is the result of an incorrect specification of the pricing model (the CAPM) that we are using to calculate the risk-adjusted size premium. If we had a 'correct' model of the risk–return relationship, which would incorporate all aspects of risk relevant for investors, then the risk-adjusted size premium would disappear.

Suppose that the market risk of small firms is systematically under-estimated and that the market risk of large firms is systematically over-estimated. In other words, the 'true' market risk of small firms is higher than their estimated market risk and the 'true' market risk of large firms is lower than their estimated market risk. If that were the case, then the 'true' risk-adjusted return on small firms would be lower than the observed return (and that of large firms would be higher) with the end result that the risk-adjusted size premium may disappear (Hawawini 1983). This outcome would be reinforced if the 'true' return on small firms were lower than those estimated from the data. This may be the case if we account, for example, for the higher costs of trading small firms. In this case the size premium measured *net* of transaction costs would be smaller if small firms have higher transaction costs than their larger counterparts (Amihud and Mendelson 1986).

But why should the estimated market risk of small firms be below its 'true' value? The estimated β coefficient of infrequently traded stocks is lower than their 'true' β coefficient, and since small firms tend to trade relatively infrequently their β coefficients are under-estimated. It is possible to adjust βs to correct for the thin trading of smaller firms. A look at Table 14.3 indicates that the adjusted βs of small firms are indeed higher than their standard βs. But even with adjusted βs, the size premium remains. Hence, adjusted βs reduce but do not eliminate the size premium.

The second possible explanation of the size effect is that the CAPM does not adequately adjust for risk and hence is not a reliable model to calculate risk-adjusted returns. This explanation is, of course, to some extent a truism. The CAPM is an incomplete model as shown in the third section. There are several kinds of risk which might be responsible for the size anomaly. Suppose that smaller firms are perceived to be riskier because investors have relatively less information about them than about larger firms. If that were the case, then the excess return earned on small firms is simply a compensation for holding riskier securities. This extra risk may not be fully captured by the β coefficient and size may simply act as a proxy for a missing risk factor introduced by differential information across firms.

Other stock market anomalies

Size is not the only characteristic of firms that could be used to earn abnormal returns. Evidence of stock market anomalies other than the size effect is limited to the US market. It is briefly surveyed below. Although similar studies have not yet been performed in other stock markets, our suspicion is that anomalies similar to those found in the US market will soon be uncovered in stock markets around the world.

There is evidence that portfolios of firms with low P/E ratios outperform portfolios of firms with high P/E ratios. The earliest study of this phenomenon examined the average annual returns, from April 1957 through March 1971, of over 750 NYSE stocks assigned to one of five portfolios on the basis of the magnitude of their year-end P/E ratio (Basu 1977). The lowest P/E portfolio earned, on average 8 percentage points more than the highest P/E portfolio after adjusting returns for the difference in risk that may exist between the lowest and the highest P/E portfolio. Is the P/E effect another anomaly or is it an indirect manifestation of the size effect? Low P/E firms are mostly small firms and the P/E effect could be just

a proxy for the size effect. Several studies concluded that once returns are controlled for differences in risk and size the P/E effect disappears. Other studies claim the opposite (Banz and Breen 1986). We do not yet know which effect is a proxy for the other or if both effects are proxies for one or more unknown risk factors (beyond systematic market risk) that generate asset returns.

Other stock market anomalies include a price-to-book-value effect, a 'neglected' firms effect, a period-of-listing effect and a dividend yield effect.[16] Firms with relatively low price-to-book-value ratios seem to outperform, on average, firms with relatively high price-to-book-value ratios. Firms which are not followed regularly by financial analysts and which are not widely held by institutional investors tend to outperform firms which are scrutinized by analysts and adopted by institutional investors. Firms listed on the NYSE for the *least* number of months earn, on average, abnormal returns. So do firms with either zero or high dividend yields. Some of these phenomena are related to the size effect (the price-to-book-value effect and the 'neglected' firms effect). Others seem to persist even after returns are adjusted for size (the period-of-listing effect and the dividend yield effect). Some exhibit seasonality. For example, the dividend yield effect manifests itself mostly in the month of January. It is most likely that these and similar anomalies will soon be uncovered in stock markets around the world.

MONTHLY SEASONALITY IN THE SIZE PREMIUM AND IMPLICATIONS FOR INVESTMENT MANAGEMENT

We have seen that a size premium exists in stock markets around the world. We have also mentioned the fact that the size premium is not stationary. It varies depending on the month of the year over which portfolio returns are measured.

In this section we present some international evidence of monthly seasonality in the size premium and show how the tax environment may provide a possible explanation of this phenomenon. We conclude with a look at the monthly risk–return performance of size portfolios on the TSE, the world's largest exchange, and the Brussels Bourse, one of the world's smallest.

International evidence of monthly seasonality in the size premium

The evidence is summarized in Table 14.4 for a subsample of the countries presented in Table 14.3. No evidence is available for the missing countries in Table 14.4. The size premium is measured as in Table 14.3 but, instead of taking all months of the year into consideration, the size premium is first measured during the month of January and then during the rest of the year (from February through December). In all countries except France and the UK the size premium is significantly larger during January than during the rest of the year. Note that the size premium is positive in all countries during the rest of the year

but its magnitude is significantly smaller than during the month of January (except again for the case of France and the UK).

How can this phenomenon be explained and what are its practical investment implications? Possible explanations are discussed below. Investment implications are discussed in the following subsection.

A clue to the monthly behaviour of the size premium may be found in the tax laws. January is the first month of the fiscal year in all countries listed in Table 14.4 except for the UK where April is the first month of the fiscal year. The seasonal behaviour of the size premium may be partly tax induced. According to this hypothesis, investors can reduce their taxes by selling the stocks on which they lost money during the year. In doing so they realize capital losses that are deductible from their taxable income. The sale of securities at the end of the fiscal year depresses their prices which

Table 14.4 International evidence of seasonality in the size premium

	Belgium	Finland	France	Japan	UK
Test period	1969–83	1970–83	1968–80	1966–83	1958–82
Number of securities	170	40	201	First section TSE	All LSE
Number of size portfolios	5	5	5	5	10
Market value of largest portfolio divided by market value of smallest portfolio	188	113	83	25	182
January return on:[a]					
Smallest portfolio (per cent)	5.4	5.9	3.7	8.3	2.3
Largest portfolio (per cent)	3.0	2.5	4.4	2.2	3.6
January size premium (per cent)[b]	2.4	3.4	−0.7	6.1	−1.3
Rest-of-the-year return on:[c]					
Smallest portfolio (per cent)	0.8	1.8	1.4	1.5	1.2
Largest portfolio (per cent)	0.4	1.0	0.7	0.8	0.7
Rest-of-the-year premium (per cent)	0.4	0.8	0.7	0.7	0.5

Sources: Belgium, Hawawini *et al.* 1988; Finland, Berglund 1985; France, Hamon 1986; Japan, Nakamura and Terada 1984; UK, Levis 1985. Note that, except for the case of Finland, the sources used are the same as those used in Table 14.3
Notes: TSE, Tokyo Stock Exchange; LSE, London Stock Exchange.
   [a] All monthly mean returns are significantly different from zero.
   [b] The January size premium is significantly different from zero only in Belgium, Finland and Japan.
   [c] Monthly mean returns are not significantly different from zero for the largest portfolios.

recover at the beginning of the next fiscal year as stocks move back to their equilibrium value. Because small-firm stocks are more volatile than large-firm stocks they are more likely to be candidates for year-end tax selling – hence the observed January size premium in Belgium, Finland and Japan and the April size premium in the UK. The evidence is far from conclusive, however. Indeed, no January size premium is reported in France, a country that taxes capital gains. But a January size premium is reported in Japan, a country that does *not* tax capital gains. Of course, the January size premium in Japan may be induced by foreign investors who pay capital gains taxes in their country. A piece of evidence in favour of the tax-induced hypothesis is that no seasonality was detected in the UK *prior* to the introduction of capital gains taxes in this country in April 1965. (Reinganum and Shapiro 1987). After that date seasonality appeared both in January and April. The April seasonal is consistent with the tax-induced hypothesis. What about the January seasonal? Well, it may be due to the trading activities of foreign investors. But, then, why did it appear after 1965? We do not know.

It is worth noting that in the UK the size premium has been shown to be the largest during the month of May when it is equal to 2.45 per cent (1.29 per cent for the smallest portfolio minus −1.16 per cent for the largest portfolio). This represents an annualized return of almost 30 per cent. Interestingly, there is an old British maxim that says 'sell in May and go away'. Obviously the maxim applies to large rather than small firms (Levis 1985).

Implications for investment management

First note that the fact that we may be able to explain the size premium (the tax-induced hypothesis, for example) does not justify its persistence in the data. If investors know that there is a January size premium in Belgium or Japan why do they not take advantage of it by simply buying small firms in December and reselling them in January? Obviously, if they did, the January size

premium would eventually disappear. Possible reasons for its continued presence are that transaction costs may be prohibitive and that the January size premium is observed *on average*. There are years when the premium is actually negative. Hence any strategy which seeks to exploit the January effect is not riskless and, as pointed out in the previous section, should be a long-term strategy. That is, investors must buy small firms in December, sell them in January (when exactly?) and do so for several years with the hope that their investment will not be wiped out as a result of a significant unexpected negative January risk premium during a particular year.

Consider the following investment strategy. At the end of every year rank a sample of securities in decreasing order of their market value. Hold either the largest or the smallest quintile portfolio only during the month of January. What would have been your realized average *monthly* return if you repeated this strategy for thirty-one years on the TSE (from January 1955 to December 1985) and for fifteen years on the Brussels Bourse (from January 1969 to December 1983)?

The average January return would have been 7.21 per cent on the Japanese small portfolio compared with 3.35 per cent on the large portfolio. And the average January return would have been 5.35 per cent on the Belgian small portfolio compared with 3.04 per cent on the large portfolio. Clearly, holding the small portfolio only during the month of January yields a higher average return. This conclusion is not altered if we adjust portfolio returns to account for the higher market risk of the Japanese small portfolio. In Belgium no adjustment is necessary since the two size portfolios have the same average market risk (see Table 14.3). The superior performance of the small portfolio, however, will be reduced by the transaction costs generated by the repeated buying and selling of small-firm securities.

We shall now show that there is a higher risk, higher reward strategy. Rank the securities in the largest and smallest quintile portfolios by the magnitude of their market risk and construct four subportfolios of approximately the same size but with different levels of market risk. The results are shown in Table 14.5. The strategy that consists of holding the portfolio containing firms that are *both* small and risky would outperform all other risk- and size-related strategies and particularly so during January. The Japanese small-size, high-risk portfolio (with a value of 5,406 million yen and a β of 1.97) would have achieved an average January return of 12.40 per cent (almost 150 per cent on an annual basis). The average January return on the corresponding Belgian portfolio (with a value of 33.5 million francs and a β of 2.42) would have been equal to 10.31 per cent (almost 125 per cent on an annual basis). It should be emphasized that

not all of these average returns are 'abnormal'. They reflect in large part the reward that compensates high-risk investment strategies.

A LOOK AT EQUITY PRICING IN THE LIGHT OF STOCK MARKET ANOMALIES

We have seen in the third section that the early tests of the CAPM indicated that the behaviour of common stock returns was consistent with equity pricing according to this model. But if there exists a seasonal size premium in equity markets, early tests of the CAPM would not capture it. The

Table 14.5 Risk and return characteristics of the largest and smallest size portfolios which have been partioned into four subportfolios ranked by decreasing magnitude of their risk (β coefficient) in Japan and Belgium

Average portfolio size (in millions)	Subportfolios ranked by risk		Average monthly return[b]	
	Risk (β)[a]	Size	All year (%)	January (%)
Japan: January 1955–December 1985				
¥164,716[c]	1.44	¥158,275	1.29	6.20
largest quintile	0.89	¥179,708	0.77	3.33
	0.57	¥160,110	0.61	2.74
	0.21	¥160,772	0.69	1.14
¥4942	1.97	¥5,406	2.02	12.40
smallest quintile	1.37	¥4,776	1.34	8.16
	0.97	¥4,710	1.35	5.75
	0.43	¥4,876	1.42	2.51
Belgium: January 1969–December 1983				
BF 6587[d]	1.75	BF 5,985	0.82	6.11[e]
largest quintile	1.11	BF 6,049	0.77	3.36[e]
	0.79	BF 8,278	0.38	2.12[e]
	0.28	BF 6,036	0.61	0.58[e]
BF 34.5	2.42	BF 33.5	2.15	10.31[e]
smallest quintile	1.19	BF 37.4	0.96	5.77[e]
	0.64	BF 34.2	0.75	3.58[e]
	−0.20	BF 32.8	0.81	1.74[e]

Sources: Japan, Hawawini 1991; Belgium, Hawawini *et al.* 1988
Notes: [a] All β coefficients are significantly different from zero at the 0.05 level.
   [b] All mean returns are significantly different from zero at the 0.05 level.
   [c] In millions of Japanese yen.
   [d] In millions of Belgian francs.
   [e] All mean values are significantly different from zero at the 0.05 level except for the all-year monthly return for the largest portfolio with a risk of 0.79.

relationship between average returns and market risk must be re-examined in light of the seasonal behaviour of the size premium.

In this section we look at the evidence regarding the validity of the CAPM as a pricing model given the existence of a size effect and the presence of seasonality in the monthly returns of common stocks. We conclude that the evidence casts some doubt on the validity of this model.

The first test of the CAPM with an explicit recognition of size as an explanatory variable was

performed using US stock market data (Banz 1981). Average returns were found to be positively related to market risk and negatively related to firm size. Later tests have shown that the relationship between average returns, market risk and firm size is unstable and seasonal (Tinic and West 1984, 1986).

We now have evidence indicating that a similar pricing structure occurs in stock markets around the world. Some of this evidence is summarized in Table 14.6 for the equity markets of Canada,

Table 14.6 Estimation of average risk premium and the average size premium based on the relationship
$$[RETURN_p]_t = \gamma_0 + \gamma_1[BETA_p]_{t-k} + \gamma_2[SIZE_p]_{t-k}$$

Country and period over which the average premium is estimated	Average risk premium (γ_1)	Average size premium[a] (γ_2)
Belgium (1/71–12/83)		
Average over all months of the year	−0.0020	[−0.0008]
Average over January months only	[0.0172]	[−0.0022]
Canada (2/64–12/82)		
Average over all months of the year	0.0074	−0.0012
Average over January months only	[0.0284]	[−0.0065]
France (1/71–12/83)		
Average over all months of the year	[−0.0093]	−0.0000
Average over January months only	0.0218	[−0.0050]
Japan (1/57–12/85)		
Average over all months of the year	[−0.0048]	[−0.0023]
Average over January months only	[0.0160]	[−0.0139]
Spain (1/78–12/82)		
Average over all months of the year	0.0061	[−0.0165]
Average over January months only	[0.0630]	–
UK (1/57–12/83)		
Average over all months of the year	−0.0032	[−0.0008]
Average over April months only	[0.0157]	[−0.0004]
Average over May months only	[−0.0150]	[−0.0025]
USA (1/59–12/82)		
Average over all months of the year	0.0073	–
Average over January months only	[0.0529]	–

Sources: Belgium, Hawawini *et al.* 1988; Canada, Calvet and Lefoll 1989; France, Hawawini and Viallet 1987; Japan, Hawawini 1991; Spain, Rubio 1988; UK, Corhay *et al.* 1987a; USA, Tinic and West 1984
Notes: Premia in square brackets have average values that are significantly different from zero at the 0.05 level. Premia not in square brackets have average values that are not significantly different from zero.
[a] In the case of Spain the size variable is measured by the market value of firms. In the cases of the UK and Canada, the size variable is measured by the logarithm of the market value of firms. In all other cases, the size variable is measured by the ratio $(V_i - V_m)/V_m$, where V_i is the firm's market value and V_m is the average market value of all firms in the sample.

Europe and Japan. The tests are designed in the following manner. Stocks are allocated to portfolios according to the magnitude of their market risk (β) *and* their year-end relative size (31 December). Actual portfolios' returns are then calculated for every month of the year following the portfolio construction year. If the CAPM is a valid pricing model then portfolio returns must be, on average, positively and linearly related to portfolio market risk and *unrelated* to portfolio size. And this relationship should hold, on average, irrespective of the month of the year. The evidence in Table 14.6 is not consistent with this statement. In all countries except France and Japan there is no relationship, on average, between return and market risk when all months of the year are considered. Note that only numbers in square brackets are significantly different from zero in a statistical sense. There is a negative relationship between returns and portfolio size, however, in all countries except Canada and France. Now if we turn to the average relationship between returns, market risk and size, only during the month of January do we find that in all countries except the UK returns are, on average, positively related to market risk and negatively related to portfolio size. In the UK, returns are, on average, positively related to market risk and negatively related to portfolio size only during the month of April. Recall that April is the first month of the fiscal year in the UK and January is the first month of the fiscal year in the other countries in the sample. Again, tax-induced trading may be responsible for this phenomenon. Note that these results are consistent with the findings summarized in Table 14.5 and discussed in the previous section. The estimated relationships reported in Table 14.6, however, provide an *explicit* test of the CAPM as a linear one-factor asset pricing model.

What conclusion can be drawn from the evidence in Table 14.6? Clearly, the CAPM is not an adequate pricing model. As mentioned earlier, this may be due to poor estimation of market risk. But it is doubtful that 'clean' βs, even if they could be obtained, would salvage the CAPM. More likely, there are other yet unknown risk factors (beyond 'clean' βs) that affect the returns on securities. One alternative to the CAPM would be a multi-factor asset pricing model such as the APT with an explicit recognition of a number of common macroeconomic factors that affect (explain) the return on securities. We have seen in the third section how such a model has been applied to Japanese common stocks with some success. Unfortunately, multi-factor pricing models, like the CAPM, seem to exhibit both seasonality and a size effect (Gultekin and Gultekin 1987). At the time of this writing, there were no equilibrium pricing models that could satisfactorily explain these two phenomena.

SOME GLOBAL INVESTMENT STRATEGIES THAT EXPLOIT STOCK MARKET ANOMALIES

Can US investors exploit the anomalous price behaviour observed in foreign stock markets in order to enhance the return on their portfolio without significantly increasing their portfolio's risk? In this section we present some preliminary results which indicate that the anomalous behaviour of US and foreign stock prices may provide an opportunity for US investors to improve their portfolio performance. We provide tentative answers to two specific questions. First, can US investors exploit the January size premium observed in foreign stock markets? Second, can US investors exploit the size effect in order to increase their potential gains from international diversification?

A strategy that captures the January size premium on the Tokyo Stock Exchange

The evidence surveyed in the preceding sections showed the presence of a size effect on the TSE. We have also seen that the size premium on the TSE is significantly larger in January than during the rest of the year. What can a US investor do to exploit this phenomenon? The investor can purchase and hold a portfolio of small Japanese firms instead of a broad portfolio of Japanese firms. What would have been the risk and return characteristics of the investor's portfolio over the ten-year period from January 1975 to December 1984 after translating all returns into US dollars? A look at Table 14.7 indicates that the annual return on a value-weighted portfolio of the smallest quintile of all shares traded on the First Section of the TSE would have been, on average, significantly larger than the annual return on a value-weighted portfolio of all shares traded on the First Section of the TSE: 28 per cent instead of 18 per cent when average returns are measured with an arithmetic mean. But the total risk of the small portfolio (measured by the standard deviation of annual returns)[17] would have been significantly higher: 38 per cent instead of 18 per cent. Recall that the risk and return of the portfolios listed in Table 14.7 include the effect of changes in the US dollar–yen exchange rate over the ten-year period. That is, they also reflect currency risk and return. Holding the small-firm portfolio increases average return but it also increases total risk.

There is an alternative strategy that may increase average return without increasing total risk. Consider the following: since the size premium is significantly larger during January, why not hold the small-firm portfolio during January and then switch to the broad portfolio during the rest of the year? This strategy should allow investors to take full advantage of the January size premium. What would have been this strategy's risk–reward trade-off for a US investor over the ten-year period from January 1975 to December 1984? A look at Table 14.7 indicates that the average (arithmetic) annual return would have been 22 per cent and the risk 14 per cent. Compared with holding the broad portfolio during the twelve months of the year, the switching strategy enhanced average returns by 4 percentage points and simultaneously *reduced* risk by 4 percentage points. Clearly, the switching strategy dominates the broad investment strategy irrespective of investors' tolerance for risk. Transaction costs, however, will reduce the average premium earned by the switching strategy. Furthermore, we did not test the alternative strategies over a sufficiently long period of time and for other stock exchanges to allow us to draw definitive conclusions. But these preliminary results are of sufficient interest to justify further investigation of the

Table 14.7 A strategy for US investors to exploit the January size premium on the Tokyo Stock Exchange (per cent)

| Investment strategies[a] | Ten-year average annual returns (1975–84) | | Risk |
	Arithmetic mean	Geometric mean	Standard deviation[e]
$TSE (all year)[b]	18	17	18
$TSE/S (all year)[c]	28	22	38
$TSE/S (January), $TSE (rest of the year)[d]	22	21	14

Notes: [a] The returns and risk characteristics of the alternative investment strategies were computed using returns compiled by Hamao 1986a.
[b] US dollar-adjusted return on a value-weighted index of all shares traded on the First Section of the Tokyo Stock Exchange if held all year.
[c] US dollar-adjusted return on a value-weighted index of the smallest quintile of all shares traded on the First Section of the Tokyo Stock Exchange if held all year.
[d] $TSE/S held in January and $TSE held from February to December.
[e] The standard deviation of returns is equal to

$$\left(\sum_{t=1}^{10} \frac{(\text{return}_t - \text{arithmetic mean return})^2}{10} \right)^{1/2}$$

311

potential for portfolio improvement offered by anomalies in the returns of foreign stocks.

The size effect and international diversification

The lower the correlation coefficient between the returns of two assets, the smaller the total risk (standard deviation of returns) of a portfolio containing the two assets. Since a change in the magnitude of the correlation coefficient does not affect the portfolio's average return, it follows that a lower correlation means less portfolio risk without a reduction in portfolio average return. Everything else being the same, the lower the correlation coefficient between the returns of two assets, the higher the gains from diversifying one's wealth between these two assets.

Suppose that one of the two assets is a portfolio of US stocks and the other is either a portfolio of UK stocks or a portfolio of Japanese stocks. In Table 14.8 we report the structure of cross-correlation coefficients between the US and UK markets and the US and Japanese markets for

combinations of large and small portfolios. The upper part of Table 14.8 gives the correlation coefficients between US and UK annual portfolio returns and the lower part gives the correlation coefficients between US and Japanese annual portfolio returns for a ten-year period from January 1977 to December 1986. Recall that all returns have been translated into US dollars.

The US large portfolio is the Standard & Poors 500, the UK large portfolio is the Financial Times All-Share Index and the Japanese large portfolio is the larger half of the First Section of the TSE. The US small portfolio is the smallest quintile of all shares traded on the NYSE and the AMEX, the UK small portfolio is the smaller half of all shares traded on the LSE and the Japanese small portfolio is the smaller half of all shares traded on the First Section of the TSE.

A look at Table 14.8 allows us to make the following three observations.

1 The highest correlations are between the returns of the large and small portfolios from

Table 14.8 Opportunities for international diversification across large and small capitalization portfolios (structure of cross correlation coefficients between the US and the UK markets and the US and Japanese markets based on ten years of annual returns from 1977 to 1986)

	USA		UK/Japan	
	Large portfolio	*Small portfolio*	*Large portfolio*	*Small portfolio*
USA vs UK				
US large portfolio	1.00			
US small portfolio	0.44	1.00		
UK large portfolio	0.31	0.24	1.00	
UK small portfolio	−0.32	0.08	0.83	1.00
USA vs Japan				
US large portfolio	1.00			
US small portfolio	0.44	1.00		
Japan large portfolio	0.28	−0.38	1.00	
Japan small portfolio	0.15	−0.12	0.81	1.00

Source: Correlation coefficients are computed using returns compiled by Dimensional Fund Advisors Inc. (1987)
Notes: US large portfolio is the Standard & Poors 500; US small portfolio is the New York Stock Exchange and American Stock Exchange smallest quintile (bottom fifth); UK large portfolio is the Financial Times All-Share Index (translated into US dollars); UK small portfolio is the smaller half of the London Stock Exchange (translated into US dollars); Japan large portfolio is the larger half of the First Section of the Tokyo Stock Exchange (translated into US dollars); Japan small portfolio is the smaller half of the First Section of the Tokyo Stock Exchange (translated into US dollars).

the same country. The returns of large and small portfolios are highly correlated in the UK and Japan (0.83 and 0.81 respectively) but less so in the USA (0.44). This result may be due to the fact that the small portfolio in the UK and Japan is defined as the smallest *half* of all stocks whereas in the USA it is the smallest *fifth* of all stocks.

2   The correlation coefficient between the returns of the small portfolios of any two countries is lower than the correlation coefficient between the large portfolios of the same two countries. The correlation coefficient between the returns of the US and the UK large portfolios is 0.31 but it is only 0.08 between the returns of the small portfolios. The correlation coefficient between the returns of the US and the Japanese large portfolios is 0.28 but it is only −0.12 between the returns of the small portfolios. The fact that the correlation coefficients between the returns of the US and the UK small portfolios and the US and the Japanese small portfolios are lower than those between the large portfolios is not surprising. We would expect, on average, a higher interdependence between the level of activity of the largest firms in the USA, the UK and Japan than between the level of activity of the smallest firms in these countries. And the higher interdependence between the level of activity of the largest firms should be translated into higher correlation coefficients between their market rates of return.

Table 14.9 Risk and return characteristics of alternative international diversification strategies across large and small portfolios over the period 1977–86 (all returns translated into US dollars)

Alternative investment strategies[a]	Average annual return (%)	Risk[b] (standard deviation) (%)
(1) US large portfolio	15	14
(2) Japan large portfolio	27	30
(3) ½(1) + ½(2)[c]	21	18
(4) US small portfolio	23	16
(5) Japan small portfolio	31	37
(6) ½(4) + ½(5)	27	19
(1) US large portfolio	15	14
(7) UK large portfolio	25	23
(8) ½(1) + ½(7)	20	15
(4) US small portfolio	23	16
(9) UK small portfolio	31	33
(10) ½(4) + ½(9)	27	19

Source: Average returns and risk are computed using raw returns compiled by Dimensional Fund Advisors, Inc. (1987)

Notes: [a] See notes to Table 14.8 for the definition of large and small portfolios in the USA, Japan and the UK.
  [b] See note e to Table 14.7 for the definition of the standard deviation of returns.
  [c] The risk or standard deviation (SD) of the combination is calculated as follows:

$$SD(3) = \{(\tfrac{1}{2})^2[SD(1)]^2 + (\tfrac{1}{2})^2[SD(2)]^2 + 2(\tfrac{1}{2})^2 COR[(1),(2)]SD(1)SD(2)\}^{\tfrac{1}{2}}$$

where COR is the correlation coefficient reported in Table 14.8.

The implication of the above is that the gains from international diversification across small portfolios should be higher than the gains from international diversification across large portfolios. This is illustrated in Table 14.9. Consider the case of the USA and Japan. A US investor who invested one-half of his wealth in each of the two countries' largest portfolios over the ten-year period from 1977 to 1986 would have realized a 21 per cent average annual return with a risk (standard deviation of portfolio returns) of 18 per cent. But an investment of one-half of the US investor's wealth in each one of the two countries' smallest portfolios over the same ten-year period would have yielded an average annual return of 27 per cent with a risk of 19 per cent. International diversification across the smallest portfolios provides, on average, 6 percentage points of additional return with an increase in risk of 1 percentage point.

Note that a similar diversification strategy with the UK would have not worked as well over the ten-year period from 1977 to 1984. The diversified small portfolio realized 27 per cent, a premium of 7 percentage points above the diversified large portfolio, but the risk of the diversified small port-folio is significantly higher than the risk of the diversified large portfolio (19 per cent versus 15 per cent).

3   Finally, note that some of the lowest corre-lation coefficients are between large and small portfolios of different countries. The correla-tion coefficient between the US large portfolio returns and the UK small portfolio returns is −0.32 and that between the Japanese large portfolio returns and the US small portfolio returns is −0.38. These negative correlations indicate that there are also potential gains from international diversification between small and large portfolios of different coun-tries.

CONCLUDING REMARKS

In this chapter we examined the validity of the EMH, the CAPM and the APT. We surveyed a large number of studies that reported anomalous empirical regularities in common stock returns. These anomalies were shown to be at odds with the EMH and generally inconsistent with equity pricing according to the CAPM. Several invest-ment strategies that attempt to exploit stock market anomalies were presented and tested with data from foreign markets.

What general conclusion can we draw from the material covered in this chapter? We believe that there is sufficient evidence to suggest that invest-ment strategies which attempt to exploit stock market anomalies around the world can improve *global* portfolio performance. There are several reasons why anomaly-based investment strategies can enhance global portfolio returns with little or no incremental risk.

1   We have seen that the correlation coefficients between the returns of small-firm portfolios from different countries are generally signifi-cantly lower than the correlation coefficients between the returns of large-firm portfolios. The implication is that the gains from inter-national diversification across small-firm port-folios are higher than the gains from international diversification across large port-folios. Although we do not have the evidence to back it up, we suspect that the above phenomenon can be generalized to portfolios constructed on the basis of anomalies other than the small-firm effect. Our suspicion is based on the conjecture that the level of activity of firms whose securities display anomalous price behaviour is more likely to be related to the domestic sector of the economy than to the international sector. And the returns of firms in the domestic sectors are less likely to be correlated across countries than the returns of firms in the international sector.

2   If the above is true it follows that there are opportunities to enhance global portfolio performance by uncovering foreign securities with anomalous price behaviour. This could be done by searching for the presence of anomalies in foreign markets similar to those already uncovered in the USA (see page 305). It is likely that stock market anomalies similar to those found in the USA do exist in foreign markets. We have seen that this is the case for the size anomaly as well as the seasonal behaviour of stock market returns. There is no reason to believe that it will not be the case for other stock market anomalies uncovered in the USA.

Note that global investment strategies that attempt to exploit the presence of recurrent anomalous price behaviour such as the size effect are more likely to succeed than global investment strategies that seek to exploit the presence, if any, of inefficient price adjust-ments to new information about foreign firms. In the latter case, foreign investors will be at a disadvantage *vis-à-vis* local investors who are expected to have access to greater, better and quicker information on firms traded in the local market. This will obviously give local investors an edge over foreign investors. Anomaly-based investment strategies, however, do not put foreign investors at a disadvantage *vis-à-vis* local investors because, in this case, continual and rapid access to new information about local firms is no longer necessary. What is required is to construct and hold a portfolio of firms that exhibit an anomalous price behaviour. With anomaly-based investment strategies, foreign investors may even outperform local investors if they uncover a stock anomaly in a local market before the local investors realize it exists and attempt to exploit it.

Anomaly-based global investment strategies, however, present as many challenges as they do opportunities. Among these we can cite the following.

1 High implementation and transaction costs: uncovering firms whose securities exhibit anomalous price behaviour, gathering and interpreting information about these firms and finally trading in them will generally result in higher than average implementation and transaction costs. Hence, anomaly-based investment strategies must be long-term, buy-and-hold strategies that minimize portfolio turnover and transaction costs.

2 Clients' resistance to adopting unconventional investment strategies: it may be difficult to convince a potential client to commit funds to an investment strategy that calls for global diversification of portfolios constructed on the basis of stock market anomalies, particularly if such strategies have not been tested extensively. But then, if extensive tests were available, the opportunity would no longer be there. To cite a well-known portfolio manager (Le Baron 1983), 'I can remember discussing market imperfections (as we called them then) with clients in the mid-70's, when investing in anything other than the Nifty Fifty was considered imprudent. Academic evidence would have helped more then … [but] inefficiencies cease to exist just where and when they are well documented to have been present.'

3 Last but not least, we should not forget that the notion of an anomaly is not absolute but relative. When we identify an anomalous price behaviour it is always *vis-à-vis* what we defined as a 'correct' price behaviour, i.e. a price behaviour that is consistent with a pricing model such as the CAPM or the APT. We call the size effect an anomaly because we are not capable of fully explaining this phenomenon with our current pricing models and their related concept of risk. Hence, the abnormal returns associated with small firms and other anomalies may disappear once their risk is properly defined and correctly measured. In other words, the fundamental question remains unanswered: is the extra return earned on anomaly-based investment strategies a free lunch or is it simply a fair compensation on a riskier investment?

NOTES

1 This distinction is suggested by West (1975).
2 The concept of informational efficiency is developed in Fama (1970) and Fama (1976).
3 On 19 October 1987, the Dow Jones Industrial Average (NYSE) dropped by a historic 22.61 per cent, its sharpest single-day fall on record. It would be tempting to interpret this break in stock prices as an irrefutable proof of the invalidity of the EMH in general and the random walk model in particular. The 19 October 1987 crash, however, does not necessarily contradict the random walk model. According to this model there is a very small probability that extremely large price changes will occur. It happened on 19 October 1987. Prices dropped dramatically and then resumed their random variations around a much lower stock price level than that prevailing before the crash. This sequence of events is not inconsistent with the random walk model.
4 The serial correlation coefficient between two sequences of returns measures the strength of the relationship between the two sequences. If the serial correlation is equal to zero, the two sequences of returns are unrelated; hence, one cannot predict tomorrow's price using the information contained in the sequence of past prices. If the serial correlation coefficient is significantly either positive or negative, in a statistical sense, then there is evidence that past behaviour of stock price movements can be used successfully to predict tomorrow's stock return.

5 See Hawawini (1984) for a survey of the US and European evidence. For some of the Asian evidence see Ang and Pohlman (1978), D'Ambrosio (1980) and Barnes (1985).

6 See Hawawini (1984) for a survey of the US and European evidence.

7 See Hawawini (1984) for a survey of the US and European evidence. Few tests of the semi-strong form of the EMH were performed with data from Asian markets. For the case of Hong Kong see Dawson (1984). For the case of the Kuala Lumpur Stock Exchange, see Dawson (1981).

8 The CAPM was developed by Sharpe (1964).

9 Conceptual limitations were pointed out by Roll (1977) and empirical deficiencies were documented by Banz (1981).

10 The APT was developed by Ross (1976) and tested on US data by Roll and Ross (1980). For the European evidence see Hawawini (1984). For the Japanese evidence see Hamao (1986b). The outcome of these studies is briefly described and discussed on pages 296–8.

11 Suppose that a security will return, over a given holding period, either 5 per cent or 15 per cent with an equal likelihood of occurrence. The security's expected return is 10 per cent (one-half of 5 per cent plus one-half of 15 per cent). Its total risk is measured by the variance of its returns as follows:

$$\text{total risk} = \tfrac{1}{2}(0.05 - 0.10)^2 + \tfrac{1}{2}(0.15 - 0.10)^2$$
$$= 0.0025 = 0.25 \text{ per cent.}$$

It is the weighted sum of the squared deviation of each outcome from their expected value where the weights are the likelihood of occurrence.

12 This test was performed by Fama and MacBeth (1973).

13 For the Canadian evidence see Calvet and Lefoll (1989). For the UK and German evidence, see Guy (1976) and Guy (1977) respectively. For the French and the Belgian evidence see Hawawini et al. (1983) and Hawawini et al. (1982) respectively. For the Spanish evidence see Palacios (1973). For the Japanese evidence see Lau et al. (1975) and for the Thai evidence see Sareewiwatthana and Malone (1985).

14 For France see Dumontier (1986); for Germany see Winkelmann (1984) and for the UK see Beenstock and Chan (1983, 1984).

15 For the US evidence see Chen et al. (1986) and for the Japanese evidence see Hamao (1986b).

16 See, respectively, Stattman (1980), Arbel and Strebel (1982), Barry and Brown (1984) and Keim (1985).

17 The standard deviation of returns is the square root of the variance of returns. See note 11 and the notes to Table 14.7.

BIBLIOGRAPHY

Amihud, Y. and Mendelson, H. (1986) 'Asset pricing and the bid–ask spread', *Journal of Financial Economics* 17 (December): 223–50.

Ang, J. and Pohlman, R. (1978) 'A note on the price behavior of Far Eastern stocks', *Journal of International Business Studies*, Spring–Summer: 103–7.

Arbel, A. and Strebel, P. (1982) 'The neglected and small-firm effects', *Financial Review* 17 (November): 201–18.

Ball, R. and Bowers, J. (1987) 'Daily seasonals in equity and fixed-interest returns: Australian evidence and tests of plausible hypotheses', in E. Dimson (ed.) *Stock Market Anomalies*, Cambridge: Cambridge University Press.

Banz, R. (1981) 'The relationship between return and market value of common stock', *Journal of Financial Economics* 9 (March): 3–18.

—— (1982) 'The small firm effect revisited', unpublished manuscript, Northwestern University, April.

Banz, R. and Breen, W. (1986) 'Sample dependent results using accounting and market data: some evidence', *Journal of Finance* 41 (September): 779–94.

Banz, R. and Hawawini, G. (1987) 'Equity pricing and stock market anomalies', *Financial Markets and Portfolio Management* 1 (3): 7–15.

Barnes, P. (1985) 'Thin trading and stock market efficiency: the case of the Kuala Lumpur stock exchange', *Journal of Business Finance and Accounting* 12 (Winter): 609–17.

Barry, C. and Brown, S. (1984) 'Differential information and the small firm effect', *Journal of Financial Economics* 13 (June): 283–94.

Basu, S. (1977) 'Investment performance of common stocks in relation to their price–earnings ratios: a test of the efficient market hypothesis', *Journal of Finance* 32 (June): 663–82.

Bauer, R. and Wirick, R. (1986) 'Investment strategies to exploit the small-firm and January anomalies', Working Paper, School of Business Administration, The University of Western Ontario, London, Ontario, October.

Beenstock, M. and Chan, K.-F. (1983) 'The factor structure of security returns in the U.K.', Working Paper, City University, Business School, London.

—— and —— (1984) 'Testing asset pricing theories in the U.K. securities market 1962–1981', Working Paper, City University Business School, London.

Berges, A., McConnell, J. and Schlarbaum, G. (1984) 'The turn of the year in Canada', *Journal of Finance* 39 (March): 185–92.

van den Bergh, W. and Wessels, R. (1985) 'Stock market seasonality and taxes: an examination of the tax-loss selling hypothesis', *Journal of Business Finance and Accounting* 12 (Winter): 515–30.

Berglund, T. (1985) 'Anomalies in stock returns in a thin security market: the case of the Helsinki Stock Exchange', Doctoral Thesis, The Swedish School of Economics and Business Administration, Helsinki, October.

Brown, P., Keim, D., Kleidon, A. and Marsh, T. (1983) 'Stock return seasonalities and the tax-loss selling hypothesis: analysis of the arguments and Australian evidence', *Journal of Financial Economics* 12 (June): 105–28.

Calvet, A. and Lefoll, J. (1989) 'Risk and return on Canadian capital markets: seasonality and size effects', *Finance* 10 (June): 21–39.

Chen, N.-F., Roll, R. and Ross, S. (1986) 'Economic forces and the stock market', *Journal of Business* 59: 383–403.

Condoyanni, L., O'Hanlon, J. and Ward, C. W. R. (1987) 'Day of the week effect on stock returns: international evidence', *Journal of Business Finance and Accounting* 14 (Summer): 159–74.

Corhay, A., Hawawini, G. and Michel, P. (1987a) 'The pricing of equity on the London Stock Exchange: seasonality and size premium', in E. Dimson (ed.) *Stock Market Anomalies*, Cambridge: Cambridge University Press.

——, —— and —— (1987b) 'Seasonality in the risk–return relationship: some international evidence', *Journal of Finance* 42 (March): 49–68.

D'Ambrosio, C. (1980) 'Random walk and the Stock Exchange of Singapore', *The Financial Review*, Spring: 1–12.

Dawson, S. (1981) 'A test of stock recommendations and market efficiency for the Kuala Lumpur Stock Exchange', *Singapore Management Review*, July: 69–72.

—— (1984) 'The trend toward efficiency for less developed stock exchanges: Hong Kong', *Journal of Business Finance and Accounting* 11 (Summer): 151–61.

Dimensional Fund Advisors (1987) 'Sixty-one years of returns: 1926–1986 matrix', London: Dimensional Fund Advisors.

Dimson, E. (1979) 'Risk measurement when shares are subject to infrequent trading', *Journal of Financial Economics* 7 (June): 197–226.

—— (1987) *Stock Market Anomalies*, Cambridge: Cambridge University Press.

Dumontier, M. (1986) 'Arbitrage pricing models: an empirical study on the Paris market', *Finance* 7 (June): 7–21 (in French).

Fama, E. (1970) 'Efficient capital markets: a review of theory and empirical work', *Journal of Finance* 25 (March): 382–417.

—— (1976) *Foundations of Finance*, New York: Basic Books.

Fama, E. and MacBeth, J. (1973) 'Risk, return and equilibrium: empirical tests', *Journal of Political Economy* 71 (May–June): 607–36.

Gultekin, M. and Gultekin, B. (1983) 'Stock market seasonality: international evidence', *Journal of Financial Economics* 12 (December): 469–82.

—— and —— (1987) 'Stock return anomalies and tests of the APT', *Journal of Finance* 42 (December): 1213–24.

Guy, J. (1976) 'The Stock Exchange, London: an empirical analysis of monthly data from 1960–1970', in R. Brealey and G. Rankine (eds) *European Finance Association 1975 Proceedings*, Amsterdam: North-Holland.

—— (1977) 'The behavior of equity securities on the German Stock Exchange', *Journal of Banking and Finance* 1: 71–93.

Hamao, Y. (1986a) 'A standard database for the analysis of Japanese security markets', Working Paper, Yale School of Management.

—— (1986b) 'An empirical examination of the arbitrage pricing theory using Japanese data', Working Paper, Yale School of Management.

Hamon, J. (1986) 'The seasonal character of monthly returns on the Paris Bourse', *Finance* 7 (June): 57–74 (in French).

Hawawini, G. (1983) 'Why beta shifts as the return interval changes', *Financial Analysts Journal* 39 (May–June): 73–7.

—— (1984) *European Equity Markets: Price Behavior and Efficiency*, Monograph Series in Finance and Economics, Salomon Brothers Center for the Study of Financial Institutions, New York University.

—— (1991) 'Stock market anomalies and the pricing of equity on the Tokyo Stock Exchange', in W. T. Ziemba, W. Bailey and Y. Hamao (eds) *Japanese Financial Market Research*, Amsterdam: North-Holland.

Hawawini, G. and Michel, P. (1982) 'The pricing of risky assets on the Belgian Stock Market', *Journal of Banking and Finance* 6 (June): 161–78.

Hawawini, G. and Viallet, C. (1987) 'Seasonality, size premium and the relationship between the risk and return of French common stocks', Working Paper, INSEAD and the Wharton School of the University of Pennsylvania.

Hawawini, G., Michel, P. and Viallet, C. (1983) 'An

assessment of the risk and return of French common stocks', *Journal of Business Finance and Accounting* 10 (Autumn): 333–50.

Hawawini, G., Michel, P. and Corhay, A. (1988) 'A look at validity of the capital asset pricing model in light of equity market anomalies: the case of Belgian common stocks', in S. J. Taylor (ed.) *A Reappraisal of the Efficiency of Financial Markets*, Berlin: Springer-Verlag.

Jaffe, J. (1974) 'Special information and insider trading', *Journal of Business* 47 (July): 410–28.

Keim, D. (1983) 'Size-related anomalies and stock return seasonality: further empirical evidence', *Journal of Financial Economics* 12 (June): 13–32.

—— (1985) 'Dividend yields and stock returns: implications of abnormal January returns', *Journal of Financial Economics* 14 (September): 473–90.

—— (1986) 'The capital asset pricing model and market anomalies', *Financial Analysts Journal* 42 (May–June): 19–34.

Lakonishok, J. and Levi, M. (1982) 'Weekend effects on stock returns: a note', *Journal of Finance* 37 (June): 569–88.

Lau, S., Quay, S. and Ramsey, C. (1975) 'The Tokyo Stock Exchange and the capital asset pricing model', *Journal of Finance* 30 (March): 507–13.

LeBaron, D. (1983) 'Reflections on market inefficiency', *Financial Analysts Journal* 39 (May–June): 16–23.

Levis, M. (1985) 'Are small firms big performers?', *The Investment Analyst* 76 (April): 21–7.

Nakamura, T. and Terada, N. (1984) 'The size effect and seasonality in Japanese stock returns', paper presented at the Institute for Quantitative Research in Finance (The Q Group).

Palacios, J. (1973) 'The stock market in Spain: tests of efficiency and capital market theory', Doctoral Thesis, Stanford University.

Reinganum, M. (1981a) 'The arbitrage pricing theory: some empirical results', *Journal of Finance* 36 (May): 313–21.

—— (1981b) 'A misspecification of capital asset pricing: empirical anomalies based on earnings yields and market values', *Journal of Financial Economics* 9 (March): 19–46.

Reinganum, M. and Shapiro, A. (1987) 'Taxes and stock return seasonality: evidence from the London Stock Exchange', *Journal of Business* 60 (2): 281–95.

Roll, R. (1977) 'A critique of the asset pricing theory's test. Part 1: On past and potential testability of the theory', *Journal of Financial Economics* 4 (March): 130–76.

—— (1983) 'The turn-of-the-year effect and the return premia of small firms', *Journal of Portfolio Management* 9 (Winter): 18–28.

Roll, R. and Ross, S. (1980) 'An empirical investigation of arbitrage pricing theory', *Journal of Finance* 35 (December): 1073–105.

Ross, S. (1976) 'The arbitrage theory of capital asset pricing', *Journal of Economic Theory* 13 (December): 341–60.

Rubio, G. (1988) 'Further evidence on asset pricing: the case of the Spanish capital market', *Journal of Banking and Finance* 12: 221–42.

Santesmases, M. (1986) 'An investigation of the Spanish stock market seasonalities', *Journal of Business Finance and Accounting* 13 (Summer): 267–76.

Sareewiwatthana, P. and Malone, P. (1985) 'Market behavior and the capital asset pricing model in the Securities Exchange of Thailand: an empirical application', *Journal of Business Finance and Accounting* 12 (Autumn): 439–52.

Scholes, M. and Williams, J. (1977) 'Estimating betas from non-synchronous data', *Journal of Financial Economics* 5 (December): 309–28.

Sharpe, W. (1964) 'Capital asset prices: a theory of market equilibrium under conditions of risk', *Journal of Finance* 19 (September): 425–42.

Stattman, D. (1980) 'Book values and expected stock returns', unpublished MBA Honors Paper, University of Chicago.

Theobald, M. and Price, V. (1984) 'Seasonality estimation in thin markets', *Journal of Finance* 39 (June): 377–92.

Tinic, S. and West, R. (1984) 'Risk and return: January versus the rest of the year', *Journal of Financial Economics* 13 (December): 561–74.

—— and —— (1986) 'Risk, return and equilibrium: a revisit', *Journal of Political Economy* 94 (February): 124–47.

Wahlroos, B. and Berglund, T. (1986) 'Anomalies and equilibrium returns in a small stock market', *Journal of Business Research* 14: 423–40.

West, R. (1975) 'Two kinds of market efficiency', *Financial Analysts Journal* 31 (November–December): 30–4.

Winkelmann, M. (1984) 'Testing APT for the German Stock Market', paper presented at the 11th Annual Meeting of the European Finance Association, Manchester.

15

AN INTRODUCTION TO ASIAN CAPITAL MARKETS

S. Ghon Rhee, Rosita P. Chang and Roy Ageloff

INTRODUCTION

The countries in the Asian Pacific region, as a group, have been enjoying the highest economic growth rate in the world. The combined market value of the region's common equities accounts for approximately one-third of the world's total capital market volume. The strategic importance of capital markets in this region for international investment decisions is well demonstrated by the increasing number of mutual funds specializing in Asian equities. It is also demonstrated by the phenomenal success of many closed-end invest- ment companies including the Asia Pacific Fund (1986), the Korea Fund (1986), the Korea–Europe Fund (1987), the Malaysia Fund (1987), the Taiwan Fund (1984) and the Thai Fund (1986) in the US and London capital markets.

One of the most significant international finan- cial developments of the 1980s has been the gradual opening of the capital markets of Asian Pacific countries to the outside world. In September 1987, the Securities Exchange of Thailand set up an Alien Board to facilitate trading of Thai securities among foreign investors as part of its effort to open the Thai market. Starting in August 1989, foreign investors are allowed to exchange their Korean convertible bonds into stocks, which will open the door for direct foreign ownership of Korean blue-chip firms such as Samsung Electronics Co., Daewoo Heavy Indus- tries Co., Yukong Ltd and Gold Star Co. (*Korea Stock Exchange* 1988). From 1991, foreign brokerage houses are allowed to join the Korea

Stock Exchange as members through establishing joint ventures with Korean firms. At the time of writing (1990), twenty-five foreign securities firms are active members of the Tokyo Stock Exchange (TSE) while trading by foreign investors of Japanese shares amounted to 17 per cent of total trading value in 1989. Beginning in 1991, foreign investors are allowed to invest directly in the Taiwan Stock Exchange but the trading volume for foreign investors is limited to $5 million per day.

In spite of their economic growth and their important role in world trade, it has only been in recent years that the Asian capital markets have received any attention from academic researchers. Most of these, however, have concentrated on Japan. The topics studied include the small-firm effect, the P/E ratio effect, the January effect and the day-of-the-week pattern of daily stock returns.[1] More recent papers move beyond addressing stock market anomalies to examine fundamental issues such as the normality of return distribution (Bailey *et al.* 1990), the return and volume variance effect (Barclay *et al.* 1988), rights offering (Kang 1990), (Kim and Lee 1990; Wethyavivorn and Koo-Smith 1991) and cross-market initial public offerings volatility (Ng *et al.* 1991). This new set of studies broadens the range of research topics and is an encouraging development in the research on Asian markets. The studies stimulate further research not only in Japan but also in other countries in the region.

This chapter examines the microstructure of the Asian equity markets. It is intended to enhance an understanding of each of the major stock exchanges in Asia by presenting their profiles and current status.

MARKET SIZE

At the end of 1989, a total of 3,836 firms were listed on the major stock exchanges of nine Asian Pacific countries: Hong Kong, Indonesia, Japan, Korea, Malaysia, the Philippines, Singapore, the Republic of China (Taiwan) and Thailand. Total market capitalization amounted to $4,829.7 billion. This amount is 2.58 times as large as the NYSE's market capitalization. As shown in Table 15.1, the market capitalization of the TSE was $4,260.4 billion, accounting for 88.21 per cent of the entire Asian equity markets. Next in order are Taiwan with 4.88 per cent, Korea with 2.91 per cent and Hong Kong with 1.61 per cent.[2]

Of the 3,836 firms listed on the Asian exchanges, 3,450 firms were domestic and the remaining 386 firms were foreign firms. The number of firms reported for Japan includes the TSE-listed firms only. There are seven other independent exchanges in Japan located in Osaka, Nagoya, Kyoto, Hiroshima, Fukuoka, Niigata and Sapporo. The TSE, the largest among the seven, has 79 per cent of all listed companies in Japan and

97 per cent of the market value. Of the 1,597 firms, 945 domestic firms were cross-listed between the TSE and the remaining seven exchanges, while 652 firms were listed only on the TSE. However, 422 firms were listed not on the TSE but on the remaining seven exchanges. Indonesia and the Philippines are the other two countries in the region which have multiple exchanges. There are two stock exchanges in Indonesia: the Jakarta Stock Exchange and the Surabaya Stock Exchange. In the Philippines there are the Manila Stock Exchange and the Makati Stock Exchange. In both countries, the securities are required to be cross-listed. The reported market capitalization for Indonesia and the Philippines represent those of the Jakarta Stock Exchange and the Manila Stock Exchange, respectively.

TRADING VALUE AND TURNOVER RATIO

In 1989, the total annual trading value of the nine Asian Pacific countries was $3,618.0 billion (see Table 15.2), which is 2.36 times that of the NYSE. The TSE accounted for 67.20 per cent of the total trading value, followed by Taiwan with 26.98 per cent and Korea with 3.34 per cent.[3] In terms of turnover ratio, Taiwan has the highest turnover

Table 15.1 Market size (as of December 1989)

Country	Number of firms listed	Domestic firms	Foreign firms	Total market capitalization (US$ billion)	
Hong Kong	298	284	14	77.6	(1.61%)
Indonesia	56	56	0	2.5	(0.04%)
Japan	1,716	1,597	119	4,260.4	(88.21%)
Korea	626	626	0	140.5	(2.91%)
Malaysia	307	251	56	39.6	(0.82%)
Philippines	144	144	0	11.6	(0.24%)
Singapore	333	136	197	35.9	(0.74%)
Taiwan	181	181	0	235.9	(4.88%)
Thailand	175	175	0	25.7	(0.53%)
Total	3,836	3,450	386	4,829.7	(100.00%)
NYSE	1,720	1,633	87	3,029.7	

Table 15.2 Trading volume (as of December 1989)

Country	Trading volume (US$ billion)		Turnover ratio (%)
Hong Kong	34.6	(0.96%)	44.61
Indonesia	0.5	(0.01%)	38.70
Japan	2,431.2	(67.20%)	61.70
Korea	120.9	(3.34%)	106.87
Malaysia	18.5	(0.51%)	17.30
Philippines	1.3	(0.04%)	16.24
Singapore	20.1	(0.56%)	39.30
Taiwan	976.2	(26.98%)	537.50
Thailand	14.7	(0.41%)	85.90
Total	3,618.0	(100.00%)	
NYSE	1,542.8		52.00

ratio of 537.50 per cent, followed by Korea with 106.87 per cent and Thailand with 85.90 per cent. It is amazing that even though the Taiwan Stock Exchange accounted for only 4.88 per cent of the combined market capitalization in the region, it had 27 per cent of the combined trading value, making the Taiwan Stock Exchange one of the busiest stock exchanges in the world.

STOCK MARKET INDICES

Table 15.3 summarizes background information concerning stock market indices computed by the stock exchanges of nine countries. All the indices are calculated using the market-value-weighted formula as defined by

$$\text{current index} = \frac{\text{current AMV}}{\text{base AMV}} \times \text{base index},$$

where AMV stands for the aggregate market value. The base index and base date vary from one exchange to another. Comparable indices in the USA are the Standard & Poor's Composite Indices and NYSE Common Stock Indices. For the purpose of maintaining the continuity of the reported index numbers, the base AMV must be adjusted for (a) new listings; (b) delistings; (c) rights offerings; (d) public offerings; (e) private placements; (f) mergers; (g) exercises of warrants; and (h) conversions of convertible securities into common stock.

Table 15.3 shows the major composite index, base date, base index value and its composition.

Table 15.3 Asian stock market indices (as of December 1989)

Country	Index name	Base date	Base index	Composition	Supplementary indices
Hong Kong	Hong Kong Index (HKI)	02/04/86	1,000	49	6 industry indices
Indonesia	Composite Share Price Index	10/08/82	100	All listed firms	None
Japan	Tokyo Stock Price Index (TOPIX)	04/01/68	100	First Section stocks	(a) Section indices (b) Indices by firm size (c) 28 industry indices
Korea	Korea Composite Stock Price Index (KCSPI)	04/01/80	100	All listed firms	(a) Section indices (b) Indices by firm size (c) 34 industry indices
Malaysia	KLSE Composite	1977	100	83	6 industry indices
Philippines	MSE Composite Price Index	02/01/85	100	25	3 industry indices
Singapore	S.E.S. All-Share Index	1975	100	All listed firms	6 industry indices
Taiwan (R.O.C.)	Weighted Stock Price Index	01/01/66	100	All listed firms	(a) 2 section indices (b) 8 industry indices
Thailand	SET Index	30/04/75	100	All listed firms	5 industry indices

The major composite index is supplemented by subindices as well as other composite indices.[4] For example, in addition to the Tokyo Stock Price Index (TOPIX), which covers 1,136 stocks listed in the First Section, the TSE computes a composite index called the Second Section Stock Price Index covering 446 stocks listed on its Second Section.[5] The TSE's First Section comprises the larger listed shares which meet the listing criteria while the Second Section shares are relatively new on the exchange and are those issued by smaller firms.[6] Additionally, the TOPIX subindices for twenty-eight industry groups and three indices for large, medium and small firms are also computed and published (TSE 1990b).[7] Another popular index in Japan is the Nikkei-Dow Average Share Price Index, which is computed on a formula similar to the Dow-Jones Industrial Average (Asia Securities Analysts Council 1982). The computation method of stock market indices of Korea, Taiwan and Thailand is identical to that of the TOPIX indices. (See Korea Stock Exchange 1990; Taiwan Stock Exchange 1990; Thailand Securities Exchange 1990.)

The Stock Exchange of Hong Kong Ltd adopted a new composite index called the Hong Kong Index (HKI) on 2 April 1986 after consolidating the Far East Stock Exchange Ltd, the Hong Kong Stock Exchange, the Kam Ngan Stock Exchange Ltd and the Kowloon Stock Exchange. The HKI is computed using forty-nine constituent blue-chip stocks selected from six representative industries in Hong Kong. Another popular index, the Hang Seng Index, is computed by the Hang Seng Bank Ltd. It is composed of thirty-three constituent stocks which include four finance stocks, six utilities, nine properties and fourteen commerce and industrials. Of the thirty-three stocks in the Hang Seng Index, thirty-one are included in the HKI.[8] (See Hang Seng Bank Ltd 1984; Hong Kong Stock Exchange 1989.)

MARKET PERFORMANCE

Table 15.4 presents summary statistics on monthly returns of market portfolios of nine Asian Pacific

Table 15.4 Summary statistics of Asian market portfolio returns (January 1980–December 1989)

Country	In local currency	In US dollars	
	Mean (%)	*Mean (%)*	*Exchange gain (%)*
Hong Kong	0.98	0.59	−0.40
Japan	1.53	1.97	0.37
Korea	1.84	1.56	−0.30
Malaysia	0.46	0.11	−0.15
Philippines	0.78	−0.12	−1.00
Singapore	0.50	0.57	0.09
Taiwan	2.39	2.66	0.25
Thailand	1.48	1.29	−0.21
Mean[a]	1.55	1.93	0.32
NYSE	–	0.99	–

Note: [a] The market capitalization weighted average.

countries. It covers the ten-year period from January 1980 to December 1989. All major stock market indices introduced in the previous section were used for computation except the Hong Kong Index. The Hang Seng Index was used for Hong Kong because the new Hong Kong Index was only established in 1984.

The performance of Asian equity markets has far exceeded that of the US market as measured by the Standard & Poor's 500 Composite Index.[9] For example, the US stock market registered an average monthly return of 0.99 per cent during the ten-year study period. Over the same period, the nine Asian equity markets yielded a market-capitalization-weighted average local currency return of 1.55 per cent per month.

The average return in US dollars of the Asian markets amounted to 1.93 per cent. Of this amount, monthly foreign exchange gain was 0.32 per cent. In terms of local currency return, the performance of the Taiwan market portfolio is the best with an average return of 2.39 per cent, followed by Korea with 1.84 per cent, Japan with 1.53 per cent and Thailand with 1.48 per cent. When measured in returns of US dollars, Taiwan,

Japan and Korea are the top three performers, with respective monthly returns of 2.66 per cent, 1.97 per cent and 1.56 per cent. The returns on Taiwan and Japanese market portfolios were augmented by respective foreign exchange gains of 0.25 per cent and 0.37 per cent per month. In contrast, Korean won depreciated against US dollars by 0.30 per cent per month and Thai baht depreciated by 0.21 per cent per month.

These phenomenally high returns have not been achieved without risk. The total risk of investments in Asian equity markets, as measured by the standard deviation of local currency returns, is on average 1.5 times greater than that of the US market. As indicated in Table 15.5, the market portfolios of Hong Kong, Malaysia, the Philippines and Taiwan have standard deviations at least twice as large as the US market portfolio. During the study period, Japan was the only country with a smaller standard deviation than the USA, 0.0413 versus 0.0480. The total risk of Asian market portfolio returns in US dollars is larger than the total risk measured using the local currency returns. For example, the total risk rises from 0.0413 to 0.0585 as the yen-denominated returns are converted into US-dollar-denominated returns. The difference between the two, 0.0172, is the contribution of currency risk. However, note from the last column that the exchange risk as measured

by the standard deviation of the rate of change in spot rates is greater than this difference. The exchange risk of Japanese yen is 0.0357. This indicates that more than half of the exchange risk is eliminated by the diversification effect. This would be true when portfolio returns in local currency have low correlations with the rates of change in spot exchange rates. Usually, the observed correlations between the two are very low, and sometimes even negative. For example, the estimated correlation between returns on the market portfolio in Japanese yen and the rates of change in the yen value is only 0.18.

Also reported in Table 15.5 are β estimates of each country's market portfolio. They are estimated using a market model in which monthly local currency returns, as well as US dollar returns, on each country's market portfolio are regressed on the US market portfolio's returns. The estimated βs when local currency returns are used range from Korea's 0.20 to Malaysia's 0.93. All the β estimates except for Korea and the Philippines are significant at the $\alpha = 1$ per cent level. The estimated βs increase slightly when the US dollar returns are used for the regressions. The results strongly indicate that the correlation between each of the Asian markets and the US market is fairly low.

Tables 15.6 and 15.7 report the correlation

Table 15.5 Summary statistics of Asian market portfolio risk (January 1980–December 1989)

Country	In local currency returns			In US dollar returns			
	Total risk	β[a]		Total risk	β[a]		Exchange risk
Hong Kong	0.1032	0.86	(4.71)[b]	0.1100	0.87	(4.48)[b]	0.0170
Japan	0.0413	0.37	(5.09)[b]	0.0585	0.32	(2.99)[b]	0.0357
Korea	0.0607	0.20	(1.73)	0.0645	0.17	(1.39)	0.0201
Malaysia	0.0915	0.93	(5.97)[b]	0.0968	0.97	(5.80)[b]	0.0142
Philippines	0.0957	0.25	(1.35)	0.1040	0.26	(1.32)	0.0460
Singapore	0.0672	0.72	(6.48)[b]	0.0710	0.75	(6.28)[b]	0.0161
Taiwan	0.1120	0.61	(2.92)[b]	0.1168	0.61	(2.82)[b]	0.0193
Thailand	0.0623	0.49	(4.38)[b]	0.0637	0.48	(4.26)[b]	0.0194
NYSE	–	–		0.0480	1.00		–

Notes: [a] Figures in parentheses are *t* values.
  [b] Statistically significant at $\alpha = 1\%$.

Table 15.6 Correlation matrix: local currency return (January 1980–December 1989)

	Japan	Korea	Malaysia	Philippines	Singapore	Taiwan	Thailand	USA
Hong Kong	0.28[a]	0.10	0.45[a]	0.19[b]	0.46[a]	0.25[a]	0.34[a]	0.40[a]
Japan		0.27[a]	0.28[a]	0.02	0.28[a]	0.32[a]	0.19[b]	0.42[a]
Korea			0.10	0.19[b]	0.12	−0.04	−0.11	0.16
Malaysia				0.08	0.97[a]	0.37[a]	0.38[a]	0.51[a]
Philippines					0.10	−0.19[b]	0.02	0.12
Singapore						0.37[a]	0.40[a]	0.53[a]
Taiwan							0.52[a]	0.26[a]
Thailand								0.37[a]

Notes: [a] Statistically significant at $\alpha = 1\%$.
[b] Statistically significant at $\alpha = 5\%$.

Table 15.7 Correlation matrix: US dollar return (January 1980–December 1989)

	Japan	Korea	Malaysia	Philippines	Singapore	Taiwan	Thailand	USA
Hong Kong	0.23[b]	0.09	0.44[a]	0.19[b]	0.46[a]	0.23[b]	0.29[a]	0.38[a]
Japan		0.27[a]	0.19	0.09	0.22[b]	0.12	0.02	0.27[a]
Korea			0.04	0.20[b]	0.07	−0.01	−0.03	0.13
Malaysia				0.15	0.97[a]	0.41[a]	0.39[a]	0.51[a]
Philippines					0.15	−0.16	0.06	0.12
Singapore						0.33[a]	0.40[a]	0.51[a]
Taiwan							0.49[a]	0.25[a]
Thailand								0.36[a]

Notes: [a] Statistically significant at $\alpha = 1\%$.
[b] Statistically significant at $\alpha = 5\%$.

between the Asian markets and the US market. Table 15.6 shows the correlation matrix when local currency returns on each of the Asian market portfolios are used. Indonesia is excluded because of an incomplete set of observations. The last column indicates the correlations between the Asian markets and the US market. The lowest correlation of 0.12 is obtained for the Philippines, while the highest correlation of 0.53 is observed for Singapore. The correlations among Asian markets are also relatively low. This implies a good potential for risk diversification. The only exception is the correlation of 0.97 observed between Singapore and Malaysia, which is not surprising in the light of the large number of cross-listed firms.

The correlations between Japan and the remaining Asian countries are surprisingly low. Thus, the percentage of common variance among the Asian markets is extremely small despite their geographical proximity.

Table 15.7 reports the correlation matrix when monthly returns in US dollars are used. In most cases, the estimated correlation coefficients are smaller than those reported in Table 15.6. Nevertheless, the relative independence of the Asian and US markets is clearly suggested by both tables. Without the market crash of October 1987, which triggered world stock markets to move together for a while, the correlations could have been much smaller than reported.[10]

PRICE–EARNINGS RATIOS AND DIVIDEND YIELDS

Table 15.8 presents P/E ratios and dividend yields for each country. In 1989, the TSE reported the highest P/E ratio of 70.60, followed by Indonesia with 63.80, Taiwan with 55.91 and Malaysia with 36.22. The P/E ratio of the NYSE-listed shares was 15.00. The lowest P/E ratio of 10.76 was reported from Hong Kong. P/E ratios of Korea and the Philippines were also relatively low.

In terms of dividend yields, Hong Kong and Thailand reported high dividend yields of 6.05 per cent and 5.30 per cent respectively. The average dividend yield of the NYSE stocks was 3.20 per cent. In contrast, low dividend yields were observed for Japan with 0.45 per cent and Taiwan with 1.58 per cent. Two reasons may be cited for this trend: (a) many Asian firms maintain a dividend policy under which a fixed percentage of the par value is paid as dividend; and (b) stock prices had been steadily going up in the past few years.

BROKERAGE FEES AND OTHER TRANSACTION COSTS

Table 15.9 summarizes brokerage fees applicable to each of the nine Asian Pacific countries. For ease of comparison, the brokerage fees in US dollars are

Table 15.8 Price–earnings ratios and dividend yields (as of December 1989)

Country	P/E ratio	Dividend yield (%)
Hong Kong	10.76	6.05
Indonesia	63.80	5.30
Japan	70.60	0.45
Korea	14.30	2.00
Malaysia	36.22	2.02
Philippines	12.50	4.78
Singapore	19.01	n.a.
Taiwan	55.91	1.58
Thailand	26.39	2.07
NYSE	15.00	3.20

Note: n.a., not applicable.

Table 15.9 Brokerage fees and other costs (as of December 1989)

Country	For investment US$10,000 (US dollars)	For investment US$100,000 (US dollars)
Hong Kong	61.40–136.60[a]	605.91–1,355.91[a]
Indonesia	100.30	1,000.30
Japan	115.78	816.96
Korea	66.30	606.30
Malaysia	140.00[b]	1,400.00[b]
Philippines	175.00	1,750.00
Singapore	100.00	2,010.00
Taiwan	15.00[c]	150.00[c]
Thailand	50.00	500.00

Notes: [a] Stockbrokers in Hong Kong may charge a fee of not less than 0.25 per cent, but not more than 1 per cent of the value of the transaction.
[b] The brokerage fee varies depending upon the price per share in Kuala Lumpur. For the convenience of illustration, it is assumed that the share is priced at M$1.00 or above.
[c] The brokerage commission rates for share transactions in Taiwan are 0.15 per cent in Taipei and 0.2 per cent in other cities. The Taipei rate is used.

estimated assuming total investments of $10,000 and $100,000, respectively. Whenever relevant information is available, other transaction costs including stamp taxes, exchange taxes, registration fees etc. are included. For an investment of $10,000, transaction costs range from $15 in Taiwan to $221 in Australia. For a larger investment of $100,000, Malaysia is the most costly while Taiwan is the least costly. Low transaction costs in Taiwan explain why the Taiwan Stock Exchange is one of the busiest in the world. Investors in Thailand and Korea also enjoy relatively low transaction costs.

TRADING HOURS AND TRADING DAYS

Based upon the trading hours summarized in Table 15.10, the following scenario can be drawn. At 7 p.m. eastern standard time (EST) in the USA, the TSE begins trading, followed by the Korea Stock Exchange at 7.40 p.m., the Taiwan Stock

325

Table 15.10 Trading hours and trading days (as of December 1989)

Country	Trading hours		Weekly trading hours	Trading days
Hong Kong	M–F:	10:00 am–12:30 pm 2:30 pm–3:30 pm	17½	246
Indonesia	M–F:	10:00 am–12:00 noon	10	247
Japan	M–F:	9:00 am–11:00 am 1:00 pm–3:00 pm	22	249
Korea	M–F: S:	9:40 am–11:40 am 1:20 pm–3:20 pm 9:40 am–11:40 am	22	289
Malaysia	M–F:	10:00 am–11:00 am 11:15 am–12:30 pm 2:30 pm–4:00 pm	18¾	244
Philippines	M–F:	9:30 am–12:00 noon	12½	244
Singapore	M–F:	10:00 am–11:00 am 11:15 am–12:30 pm 2:30 pm–4:00 pm	18¾	250
Taiwan	M–F: S:	9:00 am–12:00 noon 9:00 am–11:00 am	17	287
Thailand	M–F:	9:30 am–11:30 am	10	247
NYSE	M–F:	9:30 am–4:00 pm	32½	252

Exchange at 8 p.m. and the Manila Stock Exchange at 8.30 p.m. At 9 p.m., stock exchanges in Hong Kong, Kuala Lumpur and Singapore will be open. The Stock Exchange of Thailand and the Jakarta Stock Exchange will be the last to open at 9.30 p.m. and 10 p.m. respectively. The first ones to close are stock exchanges in Kuala Lumpur and Singapore at 3 a.m., EST. All exchanges in Asia have short trading hours, ranging from 2 hours to 3¾ hours, in contrast to 6½ hours of trading at the NYSE.

As of December 1989, the Korea Stock Exchange and the Taiwan Stock Exchange are the only two exchanges in Asia which conduct business on Saturdays. The trading days for Asian exchanges range from 289 days for Korea to 244 days in Malaysia.

FOREIGN EXCHANGE CONTROL AND FOREIGN OWNERSHIP

The accessibility of US investors to the Asian equity markets is determined by two major factors: (a) foreign exchange control and (b) limitation on foreign ownership. The nine Asian countries can be classified into four categories depending upon the degree of government control over foreign exchange and foreign ownership, as is summarized in Table 15.11 (Ernst & Whinney 1988b). These categories are as follows.

Category 1 The *laissez-faire* economy, where neither exchange control nor any limitations regarding ownership of domestic firms by foreign investors exists. Hong Kong is the only market in this category.

Category 2 The capital markets are fully liberalized except for restrictions on selec-

Table 15.11 Control of foreign exchange and foreign ownership (as of December 1989)

Country	Foreign exchange control	Restriction on foreign ownership	Category
Hong Kong	None	None	1
Indonesia	None for normal investment portfolio activities	None for 49% ownership or less	3
Japan	None	None except industries in 'national interest'	2
Korea	Yes but being liberalized	Severely restricted	4
Malaysia	None for normal investment portfolio activities	None for 15% ownership or less	3
Philippines	Yes but fairly liberal for normal investment portfolio activities	None for 40% ownership or less via 'B' class shares	3
Singapore	None	None except limits on selected domestic firms	2
Taiwan	Yes on in-bound foreign capital	Severely restricted	4
Thailand	Yes but fairly liberal	(a) None for 25% ownership or less in commercial banks (b) None for 50% ownership or less in others (c) Foreigners trade on Alien Board only	3

tive industries and/or firms in 'national interest'. Japan and Singapore may be classified in this category. Neither country has foreign exchange control and, in general, there is no limitation on the acquisition of domestic firms by foreigners except those firms/industries so designated by the government.

Category 3   The capital markets are substantially open but not completely liberalized. Australia, Indonesia, Malaysia, New Zealand, the Philippines and Thailand belong to this category. Usually, foreign exchange controls do not exist or they are minimal for normal investment portfolio activities. However, foreign ownership of domestic firms is limited to a fixed percentage of the shares outstanding or of voting rights.[11]

Category 4   The capital markets are in the process of being opened. Foreign exchange controls exist and foreign investors do not have direct access to local equity markets. Korea and Taiwan are in this category. Some foreigners do have stakes in domestic firms through joint ventures or direct foreign investment approved by the government.

Korea and Taiwan are expected to allow foreigners to invest in domestic securities in 1991. Currently, foreign investors can have indirect access to local markets only through purchase of shares issued by authorized mutual funds or closed-end investment companies. Since October 1981 the Korean government has allowed five mutual funds and two closed-end investment companies to be launched for portfolio investment in Korean securities by non-residents. Under similar arrangements, four investment companies had been introduced for foreign investors who wanted to have access to the Taiwan market. Although foreign investors have direct access to the Thai capital market, there are eight investment companies participating in the Thai market and a few more waiting for approval from government authorities.

WITHHOLDING TAX RATES FOR FOREIGN INVESTORS

Table 15.12 summarizes withholding tax rates on dividends, interest and capital gains in the nine Asian countries. Three countries have bilateral tax treaties with the USA (Ernst & Whinney 1988a). As a result, low withholding tax rates are applic-

able for US investors in Japan, Korea and the Philippines. Hong Kong, Malaysia and Singapore do not impose dividend income taxes although no bilateral tax treaties exist. Most of the Asian nations do not penalize investors, foreign as well as domestic, on capital gains from normal portfolio investment operations, except for Thailand. Among the non-tax-treaty countries, the withholding tax rate on interest is highest in Singapore at 33 per cent. Thailand comes next with a 25 per cent tax rate on interest. Indonesia and Malaysia impose a 20 per cent withholding tax.

CONCLUSION

The capital markets studied in this chapter offer solid long-term investment opportunities as each

Table 15.12 Withholding tax rates of foreign investors (as of December 1989)

Country	Dividend	Interest	Capital gain
Hong Kong	0%	(a) 0% if paid by financial institutions (b) 16.5% if paid by others	0%
Indonesia	20%	20%	Lack of information
Japan	Foreign investors: 20%	Foreign investors: 20%	Not taxable except gains derived from frequent and large transactions
	US investors: 15%	US investors: 15%	
Korea	Foreign investors:	Foreign investors:	Taxable unless exempted under tax treaty
	(a) Public corporations 10% (b) Others 25%	(a) Bank interest 10% (b) Others 25%	
	US investors: 15%	US investors: 12%	0%
Malaysia	0%	20%	0%
Philippines	Foreign investors: 35%	Foreign investors: 20%	0.25% based upon the gross selling price
	US investors: 35%	US investors: 15%	
Singapore	0%	33%	0%
Taiwan	(a) 35% (b) 20% for foreign investment by the government	(a) 20% (b) 0% on interest paid by approved banks	0%
Thailand	20%	25%	25%

country in the region is in the process of introducing a series of changes in economic policies which favour the private sector and deregulate its market. Each country has been making good progress in privatizing government-owned corporations and in the gradual deregulation of the financial sector of its economy. As a result, personal and institutional investors will have greater interest in the Asian capital markets as an alternative to mature markets in the USA and European countries. A systematic research effort is warranted for a better and comprehensive understanding of the region's capital markets.

NOTES

1 See Brown *et al.* (1983), Jaffe and Westerfield (1985), Kato and Schalheim (1985), Lee *et al.* (1989), Chou and Johnson (1990) and *Manila Stock Exchange Annual Report* (1990) among others.

2 See Ministry of Finance, Indonesia (1988a, b), Hong Kong Stock Exchange (1989), *Manila Stock Exchange Annual Report* (1989, 1990), TSE (1989, 1990a, b, c), Korea Stock Exchange (1990), NYSE (1990), Singapore Stock Exchange (1990), Taiwan Stock Exchange (1990) and Thailand Securities Exchange (1990).

3 The TSE handled 86.1 per cent of the total trading value in Japan, followed by Osaka with 10.8 per cent and Nagoya with 2.7 per cent.

4 The formula for Indonesia's Composite Share Price Index is not available to us.

5 At the TSE, foreign stocks are assigned to the Foreign Section while domestic stocks are assigned to either the First or Second Section. As of December 1989, 1,136 firms are listed on the First Section, 446 firms on the Second Section and 119 firms on the Foreign Section.

6 Assignment of listed firms to the First or Second Section depends upon multiple criteria for (a) the scale of business, (b) the liquidity of the securities, (c) trading volume, (d) business results etc.

7 It is interesting to note that the size of firms is determined by the number of shares listed:

(a) large firms have 200 million or more shares listed;

(b) medium firms have 60 million or more shares but under 200 million shares listed;

(c) small firms have less than 60 million shares listed.

8 Unfortunately, sufficient information is not available about the composite share price index of Indonesia.

9 The use of the Standard & Poor's 500 Composite Index is justified because (a) all foreign market indices are value weighted and (b) no dividend reinvestments are taken into account.

10 Bailey *et al.* (1990) suggest that significant departure from the random walk hypothesis may produce a downward bias in the estimated correlations between daily returns on Asian market portfolios and those on US market portfolios.

11 The Securities Exchange of Thailand set up the Alien Board in September 1987 to facilitate trading securities by foreigners for the issues which had reached the maximum statutory or voluntary limit of foreign ownership. The Manila Stock Exchange, on the other hand, introduced two classes of shares – class A and class B. Foreign investors are allowed to buy and sell class B shares but not class A shares. Interestingly, a price differential is observed for the same firm's issue between the Regular Board and Alien Board in Bangkok. This differential also exists in Manila between class A shares and class B shares issued by the same firm.

REFERENCES

Asian Development Bank (1985) *Capital Market Development in Selected Developing Member Countries of the Asian Development Bank*, Manila: Asian Development Bank.

——— (1986) *Capital Market Development in the Asia-Pacific Region*, summary of the proceedings and papers presented at a Symposium held on 14–16 January 1986 in Manila, Philippines, Manila: Asian Development Bank.

Asian Securities Analysts Council (1982) *Securities Markets in Asia and Oceania*, Tokyo: The Asian Securities' Analysts Council, May.

Asia Pacific Fund (1986) *Preliminary Prospectus*, September.

Bailey, W., Stulz, R. M. and Yen, S. (1990) 'Properties of daily stock returns from the Pacific Basin stock markets: evidence and implications', in S. G. Rhee and R. P. Chang (eds) *Pacific-Basin Capital Markets Research*, vol. I, Amsterdam: Elsevier, pp. 155–71.

Barclay, M. J., Litzenberger, R. H. and Warner, J. B. (1988) 'Private information, trading volume, and stock return variance', Working Paper, University of Rochester, presented at the First Annual Pacific-Basin Finance Conference.

Brown, P., Keim, D. B., Kleidon, A. W. and Marsh, T. A. (1983) 'Stock return seasonalities and the tax-loss-selling hypothesis', *Journal of Financial Economics* 12: 105–27.

Chou, S. and Johnson, K. H. (1990) 'An empirical analysis of stock market anomalies: evidence from the Republic of China in Taiwan', in S. G. Rhee and R. P. Chang (eds) *Pacific-Basin Capital Markets Research*, vol. I, Amsterdam: Elsevier, pp. 283–312.

Ernst & Whinney (1988a) *Foreign and U.S. Corporate Income and Withholding Tax Rates*, New York: Ernst & Whinney.

—— (1988b) *Foreign Exchange Rates and Restrictions*, New York: Ernst & Whinney.

Hang Seng Bank Ltd (1984) *Hang Seng Index Fact Sheet*, Economic Research Department, Hang Seng Bank Ltd, July.

Hong Kong Stock Exchange (1988) *What Do You Know About The Hong Kong Index?*, Hong Kong: The Hong Kong Stock Exchange, May.

—— (1989) *Fact Book 1989*, Hong Kong: The Stock Exchange of Hong Kong Ltd.

Jaffe, J. and Westerfield, R. (1985) 'Patterns in Japanese common stock returns: day of the week and turn of the year effects', *Journal of Financial and Quantitative Analysis* 20: 261–72.

Kang, H. (1990) 'Effects of seasoned equity offerings in Korea on shareholder's wealth', in S. G. Rhee and R. P. Chang (eds) *Pacific-Basin Capital Markets Research*, vol. I, Amsterdam: Elsevier, pp. 265–82.

Kato, K. and Schalheim, J. S. (1985) 'Seasonal and size anomalies in the Japanese stock market', *Journal of Financial and Quantitative Analysis* 20: 243–59.

Kim, E. H. and Lee, Y. K. (1990) 'Issuing stocks in Korea', in S. G. Rhee and R. P. Chang (eds) *Pacific-Basin Capital Markets Research*, vol. I, Amsterdam: Elsevier, pp. 243–53.

Korea Fund (1986) *Prospectus*, April.

Korea–Europe Fund Ltd (1987) *Prospectus*, March.

Korea Stock Exchange (1988) *Korea Stock Exchange*, Seoul: The Korea Stock Exchange, October.

—— (1990) *Fact Book*, Seoul: The Korea Stock Exchange, May.

Kuala Lumpur Stock Exchange Annual Reports (1990).

Lee, I., Pettit, R. R. and Swankoski, M. V. (1989) 'Daily return relationship among Asian stock markets', Working Paper, University of Houston, presented at the First Annual Pacific-Basin Finance Conference.

Ma, T. and Shaw, T. Y. (1989) 'The relationship between market value, P/E ratio, trading volume and the stock return of Taiwan Stock Exchange', in S. G. Rhee and R. P. Chang (eds) *Pacific-Basin Capital Markets Research*, vol. I, Amsterdam: Elsevier, pp. 313–35.

Malaysia Fund (1987) *Prospectus*, May.

Manila Stock Exchange (1988) *Investors' Information Guide*.

—— (1989) *Manila Stock Exchange Annual Report*.

—— (1990) *Manila Stock Exchange Annual Report*.

Ministry of Finance, Indonesia (1988a) *Fact Book*, Jakarta: The Indonesian Capital Market, Capital Market Executive Agency, Ministry of Finance, Republic of Indonesia.

—— (1988b) *Supplement to the Fact Book of the Indonesian Capital Market*, statistical supplement, Capital Market Executive Agency, Ministry of Finance, Republic of Indonesia.

Ng, V. K., Chang, R. P. and Chou, R. Y. (1991) 'An examination of the behavior of Pacific-Basin stock market volatility', in S. G. Rhee and R. P. Chang (eds) *Pacific-Basin Capital Markets Research*, vol. II, Amsterdam: Elsevier.

NYSE (1990) *Fact Book 1990*. New York: The New York Stock Exchange.

Rhee, S. G., Chang, R. P. and Ageloff, R. (1990) 'An overview of equity markets in Pacific-Basin countries', in S. G. Rhee and R. P. Chang (eds) *Pacific-Basin Capital Markets Research*, vol. I, Amsterdam: Elsevier, pp. 81–100.

Singapore Stock Exchange (1975–August 1988) *The SES All-Share Price Indices*, Singapore: The Stock Exchange of Singapore Ltd.

—— (1990) *Fact Book 1990*, Singapore: The Stock Exchange of Singapore.

Taiwan (R.O.C.) Fund (1984) Placing Memorandum, December.

Taiwan Stock Exchange (1990) *Fact Book 1989*, Taipei: The Taiwan Stock Exchange.

Thai Fund (1986) *Prospectus*, December.

Thailand Securities Exchange (1990) *Fact Book '90*, Bangkok: The Securities Exchange of Thailand.

TSE (1988) *TOPIX: Tokyo Stock Price Index*, Tokyo: The Tokyo Stock Exchange, June.

—— (1989) *Fact Book 1989*, Tokyo: The Tokyo Stock Exchange.

—— (1990a) *Fact Book 1990*, Tokyo: The Tokyo Stock Exchange.

—— (1990b) 'Comparative statistical table of East Asia stock exchanges', presented at IXth EASEC Meeting, Manila, December.

—— (1990c) 'Commissions and other costs of East Asian stock exchanges', presented at IXth EASEC Meeting, Manila, December.

Wethyavivorn, K. and Koo-smith, Y. (1991) 'Initial public offers in Thailand, 1988–1989: price and return patterns', in S. G. Rhee and R. P. Chang (eds) *Pacific-Basin Capital Markets Research*, vol. II, Amsterdam: Elsevier.

Part IV

FOREIGN EXCHANGE MARKETS

This section samples some of the papers on foreign exchange markets. It is widely believed that international capital mobility is close to perfect and therefore arbitrage equalizes interest rates across countries. If this equalization hypothesis is true, it will have far-reaching implications. For one thing, it will imply that domestic interest rates no longer reflect monetary policy and that the exchange rate has displaced the interest rate as the primary indicator of the easing or tightening of monetary policy. However, perfect capital mobility need not be taken as leading to international equalization of interest rates because of high exchange rate variability under the floating rate regime, which may partly be caused by high capital mobility. Frankel's chapter contends that covered interest differentials did not vary enough in the 1980s to be an important source of variation in international short-term interest differentials. It dwells on how ongoing liberalization affected the correlation of exchange rates with short- and long-term interest rates in the 1980s and suggests another alternative indicator of fluctuations in exchange rates, namely the term structure of interest rates. It ends with a proposal for international nominal targeting for the monetary authorities.

Inasmuch as rational expectations have become such an important concept in macroeconomic and financial hypotheses, Ito measures the expectations of market participants on the yen–dollar exchange rate. Using a better data set than used previously by Frankel and Froot, Ito concludes that if market participants are heterogeneous and have a constant-term basis in their expectation forma-

tion, there is also an element of 'wishful expectation' in both importers and exporters. When the useful rationality tests were applied, the unbiasedness of expectations was rejected in a small number of cases for shorter horizons and unanimously for the six-month horizon. Orthogonality was soundly rejected. The inference that emerged is that there is strong evidence against the formation of rational expectations in the Tokyo foreign exchange market. The third chapter, by Akiba and Waragai, attempts to focus on the exact point in time when significant structural changes occurred in the foreign exchange markets. It also empirically examines whether the link between the spot and the forward exchange rate is strong. That is, is the change in the future spot rate fully reflected in available information, namely the change in the forward rate? The two authors have developed a new application of Akaike's information criterion, bringing the MAIC method (minimization of Akaike's information criterion) one step further. It is an improvement over the traditional methods because of its arbitrariness-free characteristic of detecting structural change. They examined the forward foreign exchange rates of five major currencies *vis-à-vis* the dollar for the recent period 1974–86. They found that their data showed no strong link between the forward and spot rates. This conclusion is an important one.

When the floating exchange rate system was adopted, it was believed that it would provide an automatic trade adjustment mechanism, a neo-classical economist's dream. In reality, however, it was at variance and the international economy saw large swings in exchange rates during the 1980s. These swings could not be explained by macro-economic fundamentals. To make the situation worse, large trade imbalances in the industrialized economies continued. The mainstream economic and policy advisers came to believe that exchange rates need to be managed; market forces cannot be trusted. The result was the Plaza Agreement of 1985, the Louvre Accord of 1987 and the annual G7 macroeconomic policy co-ordination exercises. As exchange rate movements began to be controlled, or endeavours along these lines began, plans of how this has to be achieved began to emerge from academia. The most talked about proposal involves 'target zones' which envisage adjustable targets of exchange rate movements with the objective of balancing current account in the medium term. Ohno, in the fourth chapter in this section, has come up with an alternative proposal. He contends that stabilizing nominal exchange rates based on the normative interpretation of PPP will ensure long-term price stability. He argues that there are *a fortiori* possibilities for his proposal to succeed because the international economy is increasingly integrated. The idea is not original and, in fact, originated with McKinnon's earlier researches. Ohno begins with reviews of different interpretations of PPP and introduces and discusses the McKinnon proposal. He then goes on to discuss the need for a regime transition from a floating exchange rate system to a fixed exchange rate system and finally discusses the estimation of PPP.

In a related chapter, Ito argues that while economists debated the merits and demerits of various proposals a target zone was in place for the yen–dollar exchange rate, although its existence was hardly recognized. In the brief fifth chapter in this section, he argues that it did exist and there were five phases. He proposes his plan of a moving target zone towards the end of the chapter.

In the post Bretton Woods fixed parity system, the nature of exchange rate volatility has changed considerably. During the Bretton Woods period, the exchange rate of the dollar *vis-à-vis* the currencies of major industrial countries was fixed and whenever there was a need for adjustment exchange rates moved in discrete jumps. However, the post Bretton Woods era of floating exchange rates is governed by market forces and exchange rates adjust continuously. Monetary authorities do intervene in currency markets. The EC economies tried to control this volatility by establishing the EMS in 1979. This system forces the currencies of the member countries to keep the level of their exchange rates within a predetermined range *vis-à-vis* one another.

In the last chapter in this section, by McKinnon, the mechanism of how floating exchange rates have not worked has been traced out. It is assumed that under normal circumstances interest rates will work as shock absorbers for balancing currency risk associated with expected inflation or differential taxation. However, under a floating exchange rate regime, interest rates in each money market behave as if caught in a liquidity trap. The problem arises because the domains for national money circulation remain somewhat isolated while the bond market is generally fully integrated internationally. The national rate of interest is incapable of equilibrating the domestic money market on the one hand and the international bond market on the other. The result is an excessively high degree of exchange rate volatility that distorts the flow of international commodity trade and causes cycles of inflation and deflation in open economies.

16

INTERNATIONAL FINANCIAL INTEGRATION

Relations between interest rates and exchange rates

Jeffrey A. Frankel

Conventional wisdom holds that international capital mobility is close to perfect. It is sometimes thought that perfect capital mobility implies that arbitrage equalizes interest rates across countries, on either a nominal or a real basis. The equalization of interest rates, if valid, would have powerful implications. It would mean, for example, that the domestic interest rate would no longer be free to reflect expansionary monetary policy: in the Mundell–Fleming theory, the high degree of international financial integration would imply that the exchange rate had displaced the interest rate as the primary indicator of the easing or tightening of monetary policy.

Perfect capital mobility, in the sense of low barriers to the movement of capital across national boundaries, does not imply the international equalization of nominal or real interest rates, however. The reason is high exchange rate variability under floating exchange rates (which may itself be in part a result of high capital mobility). Countries' interest rates are expressed in their own currencies and thus may differ because of factors associated with the currencies in question rather than the national boundaries.

This chapter begins by showing how the UK and Japan in 1979 removed capital controls to join the club of countries integrated into world financial markets and how liberalization has spread to

more countries in the 1980s. It argues the possibility that covered interest differentials did not vary enough in the 1980s to be important sources of variation in international short-term interest differentials. I then consider how liberalization affected the correlations of exchange rates with short- and long-term interest rates in the 1980s.

Even if perfect capital mobility does not eliminate interest differentials completely, so that the domestic interest rate continues to be affected by monetary policy, one might think that the exchange rate would nevertheless be a very good indicator of the stance of monetary policy. But the exchange rate sometimes fluctuates sharply for reasons that are apparently unrelated to macro-economic fundamentals. I discuss an alternative possible indicator for monetary policy: the term structure of interest rates. I make the obvious point that the monetary authorities would be well advised to look at many available indicators simultaneously. However, I emphasize the advantages of announcing a single *intermediate target* as opposed to relying on a single indicator to attain the target. It is concluded that, of the alternative intermediate nominal targets that have been proposed, nominal GNP may be the best. This is all the more true in the international context, where I have called the proposal international nominal targeting.

RECENT LIBERALIZATIONS: DIMINISHING 'COUNTRY BARRIERS', AS INDICATED BY COVERED INTEREST DIFFERENTIALS

A number of different criteria for measuring the degree of international capital mobility have been proposed and have been reviewed elsewhere.[1] If the aim is to measure the extent of 'country barriers' – capital controls, transaction costs and other barriers to the integration of national financial markets across political boundaries – then the best measure is the covered or 'closed' interest differential, i.e. the difference between offshore and onshore interest rates, hedged so as to eliminate exchange risk.[2] The virtues of this measure are well illustrated by three major liberalization episodes of the 1970s: Germany in 1973–4, the UK in 1979 and Japan in 1979–80.

In the early 1970s, Germany had stringent capital controls in place, designed to discourage the acquisition of German assets by foreign residents. The government essentially prohibited the payment of interest to non-residents on large bank deposits, taxed any new credits by non-residents to German banks and prohibited non-residents from buying German bonds. Most of these controls were removed in late 1973 and 1974. Figure 16.1 illustrates the episode. The lower two lines are the Euro-mark interest rate and the covered Euro-dollar interest rate in London, which are always virtually identical because covered interest parity always holds within the London Euromarket. During most of 1973, these Euro-rates lay far below the German interbank rate, indicating that the controls were indeed effectively preventing foreign residents from obtaining assets within Germany. As the figure shows, the gap narrowed at the end of 1973 and disappeared in the course of 1974, confirming the removal of controls.[3]

Japan maintained stringent controls on capital inflows through most of the decade. Foreign residents were prohibited outright from holding many kinds of assets in Japan. (Until 1979, the Japanese, like the Germans earlier, were concerned about excessive capital inflows and appreciation of the yen.) The Ministry of Finance removed the prohibition against foreign investment in April 1979 and formalized the liberalization in December 1980. Further liberalization measures followed, relaxing controls against both inflows and outflows, notably the yen–dollar agreement between the Ministry of Finance and the US Treasury in May 1984.

Figure 16.2 illustrates the Japanese case. During the period January 1975 to April 1979, the differential between the Gensaki interest rate (a three-month rate) in Tokyo and the Euro-yen interest rate in London averaged 1.84 per cent, showing the efficacy of the controls on capital inflow. During the period May 1979 to November 1983, the differential fell sharply to −0.26 per cent. The fact that the differential was actually somewhat negative during this period is evidence that the controls that remained were working to discourage outflow more than inflow. In the period 1985–8, the differential was essentially zero, showing evidence of complete liberalization.[4]

A third liberalization took place in Britain in 1979. The incoming Thatcher government removed the restrictions requiring British banks to keep their 'offshore' accounts separate from their domestic accounts. The onshore and covered offshore pound interest rates are shown in Figure 16.3. In 1978, the three-month Euro-pound interest rate averaged 1.43 per cent per annum higher than the UK interbank interest rate, indicating effective controls against capital outflow. The differential fell to 0.29 per cent per annum in 1979 and to zero soon thereafter.[5]

The liberalization trend spread more widely in the 1980s. Australia began to liberalize early in the decade and New Zealand followed suit. France, which strengthened controls on outflow when the Socialists came to power in 1981, began to remove the controls in the late 1980s. France and Italy are both expected to meet a mid-1990 deadline for full liberalization among the twelve members of the EC. In the enlarged EC, only Spain, Portugal, Greece and Ireland are expected to need later deadlines. Most tests of covered interest parity

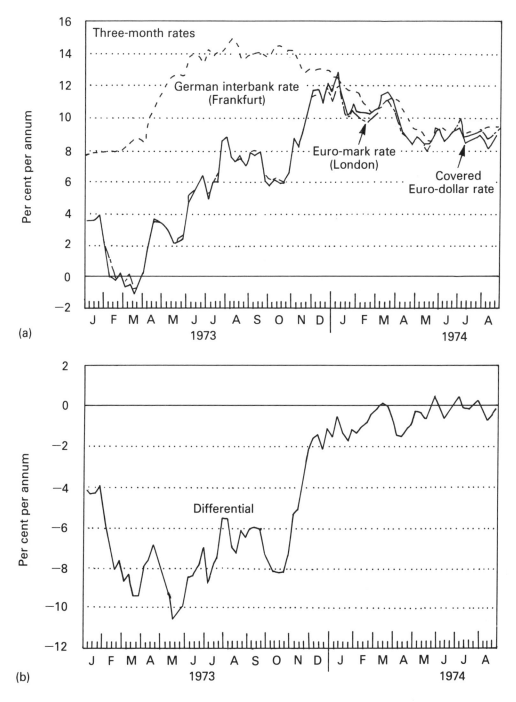

Figure 16.1 Financial liberalization in Germany: German and Eurocurrency interest rates. Data are Wednesday quotations. The covered Euro-dollar rate is calculated using the three-month forward premium for the deutsche mark–dollar exchange rate. Positive values in part (b) indicate a differential in favour of offshore assets

335

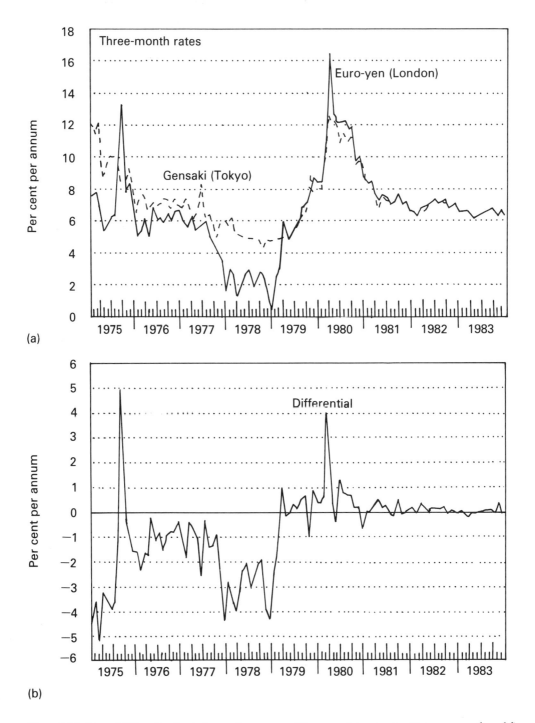

Figure 16.2 Financial liberalization in Japan: Japanese and Euro-yen interest rates. Data are month-end figures. Positive values in part (b) indicate a differential in favour of offshore assets

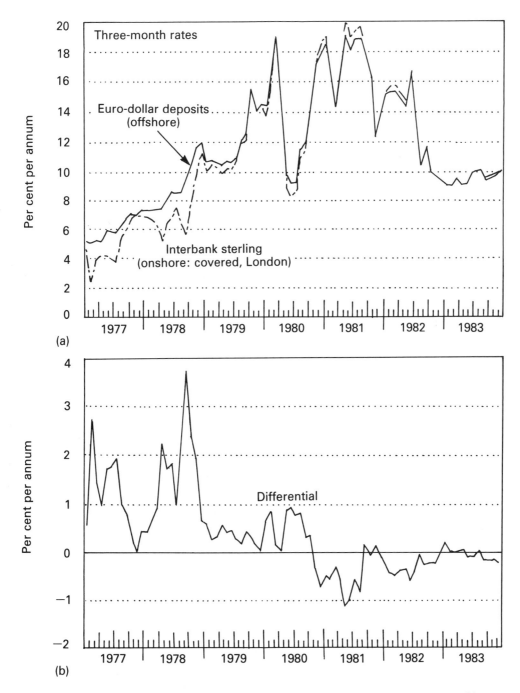

Figure 16.3 Financial liberalization in the UK: UK and Euro-dollar interest rates. Data are monthly averages of weekly (Wednesday) observations. The covered interbank sterling rate is calculated using the three-month forward premium on the sterling–dollar exchange rate. Positive values in part (b) indicate a differential in favour of offshore assets

Table 16.1 Regressions of absolute covered interest differential against constant and trend, monthly data, September 1982–April 1988

Country	Number of observations	Constant[a]	Trend[a]	R^2
		Coefficients		
Australia	68	2.01 (0.43)	−0.03 (0.01)**	0.11
Austria	65	0.20 (0.09)	0.00 (0.00)	0.00
Belgium	68	0.14 (0.05)	0.00 (0.00)	0.05
Canada	68	0.13 (0.04)	0.00 (0.00)	0.03
Denmark	68	4.72 (0.35)	−0.03 (0.00)**	0.19
France	68	3.98 (0.58)	−0.06 (0.01)**	0.23
Germany	68	0.66 (0.04)	−0.01 (0.00)**	0.57
Greece	58	9.78 (1.46)	−0.00 (0.04)	0.00
Hong Kong	68	0.12 (0.06)	0.00 (0.00)	0.03
Italy	68	2.11 (0.37)	−0.03 (0.01)**	0.12
Japan	68	0.25 (0.03)	−0.00 (0.00)**	0.06
Malaysia	63	1.04 (0.31)	0.01 (0.01)	0.05
Mexico	43	26.34 (3.23)	−0.44 (0.13)**	0.22
Netherlands	68	0.36 (0.02)	−0.00 (0.00)**	0.47
New Zealand	68	3.50 (0.46)	−0.04 (0.01)**	0.16
Norway	50	1.09 (0.22)	−0.00 (0.01)	0.00
Portugal	61	19.15 (1.89)	−0.33 (0.05)**	0.42
Bahrain	64	2.28 (0.26)	−0.00 (0.01)	0.00
Singapore	64	0.37 (0.06)	−0.00 (0.00)	0.00
South Africa	67	2.05 (2.32)	0.00 (0.06)	0.00
Spain	67	5.32 (0.76)	−0.07 (0.02)**	0.19
Sweden	68	0.50 (0.09)	−0.00 (0.00)*	0.05
Switzerland	68	0.61 (0.05)	−0.01 (0.00)**	0.22
UK	68	0.13 (0.03)	0.00 (0.00)**	0.14

Notes: Covered interest differential is the interest differential less the corresponding forward premium or discount. Forward data are generally from Barclays Bank. Interest rates are onshore rates taken from various country sources.

[a] Standard errors in parentheses.

* Trend coefficient differs from zero at the 5 per cent significance level.

** Significant at the 1 per cent level.

have somewhat artificially tested the hypothesis of 'perfect' capital mobility; these tests, however, generally provide little indication about the degree of capital mobility because the covered interest differential is never *exactly* zero.[6] Furthermore, most tests have been confined to small subsets of the G10 countries, as theirs are the only currencies that have well-developed Euromarkets. However, it has recently become possible to obtain London forward rate quotes for more countries for the period since September 1982. These data used together with local interest rates are ideal for studying the extent of integration in the 1980s. Frankel (1989) examined the magnitude and

variability of the covered interest differentials over the *average* of the period. Here we examine the *trend* for each of twenty-three countries in order to look for evidence of liberalization taking place within the sample period 1982–8.[7]

Table 16.1 presents the results of regressions of the absolute covered interest differential against time. Twelve countries show statistically significant downward trends (at the 95 per cent level). The seven with the most rapid estimated trend, listed in descending order, are as follows: Portugal, Spain, France, New Zealand, Denmark, Australia and Italy. This is precisely the list that one would have expected for countries liberalizing in the

1980s. The other five countries with significant downward trends are as follows: Germany, Switzerland, the Netherlands, Sweden and Japan. This groups already had small differentials at the beginning of the sample period anyway. The same is true of six of the ten countries with statistically insignificant trends in Table 16.1: Austria, Belgium, Canada, Hong Kong, Norway and Singapore. Only one country appears to have a statistically significant *upward* trend in the magnitude of its covered interest differentials during the sample period, namely the UK, which was starting from the third lowest position of any of the twenty-three countries (after Hong Kong and Canada). The implication is that there are only four countries in the sample that by 1988 had still made little effort toward liberalization: Greece, Bahrain, Malaysia and South Africa. (Needless to say, most countries with large barriers are not in the sample, because their currencies do not have forward rates quoted offshore.)

The USA is not in the Table 16.1 sample because the dollar is the currency relative to which the forward rates of the other currencies are measured. But for the USA as well, the differential between the offshore interest rate and the domestic rate has fallen over time, perhaps as the result of innovation in the Euromarkets. Reinhart and Weiller (1987: 16–18) find that the Euro-dollar–US CD differential had a statistically significant downward trend over the period 1971–87 and that 'the initial gap is all but eliminated by the end of the period'. In particular, the differential was smaller after 1983 than during the period 1978–82.[8]

All the preceding results, and most of the tests of closed interest parity that others have done in the past, apply only to international arbitrage among short-term deposits. Feldstein and Horioka (1980) surmised that international arbitrage does not work as well for long-term bonds. As Akhtar and Weiller (1987) point out, there is a need to test closed interest parity at the longer end of the maturity spectrum. Recently, a few studies have attempted to extend the tests to long-term bonds. The differential between long-term interest rates in

the USA and in the Euro-dollar bond market can be seen to have declined in the course of the 1980s.[9] Popper (1990), using currency swap data, finds that the differential between swapped Japanese and US government bonds by 1986 was as small as the differential between short-term assets.[10] The (tentative) conclusion is that bonds issued by different major industrialized countries, when otherwise similar in nature, have in fact become relatively close substitutes in the course of the 1980s.[11]

'CURRENCY BARRIERS': DECOMPOSITION OF THE FORWARD DISCOUNT INTO THE EXCHANGE RISK PREMIUM AND EXPECTED DEPRECIATION

It is well known that the elimination of barriers to the movement of capital across national boundaries as reflected in covered interest differentials is not enough to equalize interest rates across countries. Let i be the US interest rate and i^* be the foreign interest rate. The interest differential $i - i^*$ can be tautologically decomposed as follows:

$$i - i^* = (i - i^* - \text{fd}) + (\text{fd} - \Delta s^3) + \Delta s^e \tag{16.1}$$

where fd is the annualized forward discount and Δs^e is the annualized expected rate of depreciation of the dollar against the local currency. The first term, the covered interest differential, is associated with the country or political jurisdiction in which an asset is issued, not with the currency in which it is denominated. We have already seen that liberalization sharply reduced the differential in 1979 in the cases of Japan and the UK and gradually reduced it in the 1980s in the cases of France and other countries. The second and third terms, which are the exchange risk premium and expected depreciation respectively, are associated with the currency of denomination, not with the political jurisdiction. Given the high volatility of floating exchange rates, it is quite possible that the latter terms have increased in size and variability in the 1980s rather than decreased.[12]

The conventional wisdom among economists is that the expected depreciation term is small in magnitude and variability, and the risk premium term larger in both magnitude and variability. This conventional wisdom emerges from the rational expectations methodology. The rational expectations methodology infers what investors must have expected *ex ante* from what actually happened *ex post*. The common application in international finance is the interpretation of findings of bias in the forward discount. The standard regression equation is

$$\Delta s_{t+1} = a + b\mathrm{fd}_t + u_{t+1}, \qquad (16.2)$$

where u_{t+1} is a random error that should be uncorrelated with the forward discount at t if expectations are rational. The null hypothesis of unbiasedness is represented by $b = 1$: all the variation in the forward discount would be explained as variation in expected depreciation rather than as variation in the risk premium. (Sometimes the null hypothesis is also interpreted as implying $a = 0$. But usually the focus is on the *time-varying* component of the bias, rather than on the constant term.[13])

The standard finding is that the coefficient b is in fact significantly less than unity. Often it is close to zero (or even negative). Under the rational expectations methodology, this rejection of the null hypothesis is interpreted as evidence of an exchange risk premium that varies over time with the forward discount. When results show an estimate of b that is insignificantly different from zero – an instance of the popular random walk findings – the rational expectations methodology interprets it as evidence that there is no variation in expected depreciation (the third term in equation (16.1)) and that all the variation in the forward discount represents variation in the exchange risk premium (the second term in the equation).[14] Fama (1984) and Hodrick and Srivastava (1986) have argued that, when b is found to be significantly less than one-half, this is evidence that the variation in expected depreciation (even if not zero) is smaller than the variation in the risk premium.[15]

The alternative interpretation argues that one cannot reliably infer *ex ante* expectations from movements that are observed *ex post*, even when the systematic component of the movement appears statistically significant by standard criteria. The rational expectations methodology could fail either because agents do not act rationally or because distributional difficulties associated with the 'peso problem' invalidate the test statistics in conventional sample sizes. The proposition that observed patterns of movement in the exchange rate reflect investors' expectations is a proposition that one would like to be able to test rather than impose *a priori*.

In recent years, a number of researchers have begun to use survey data as an alternative method of measuring investors' expectations.[16] A measure of expected depreciation based on survey data is exempt from some of the problems that plague conventional measures and can be used to test propositions such as a constant risk premium and the validity of the rational expectations methodology itself. Of course, the survey data undoubtedly have problems of their own; their measurement of market participants' expectations may be subject to error. Nevertheless, even allowing for the possibility of measurement error, one can learn much from this approach.

Most of these papers so far have used data that only went up to 1985. One might wonder whether the results changed in any way in the late 1980s, as a result of either the continued process of financial integration documented in the first section, a new era in the history of the dollar[17] or new forecasting techniques used by participants in the foreign exchange market. Furthermore, because these data sets are so new, three additional years of data are of interest in that they can increase the sample size by one-half.

Table 16.2, taken from Frankel and Froot (1990b), reports an update of one of the earlier tests to include data through 1988. It is a regression of the expected depreciation of the currency against the forward discount. For two out of the three terms studied, the coefficients are even closer to unity than they were in the 1981–5 results (see Froot and Frankel 1989). The results support the

Table 16.2 Test for time-varying risk premium, ordinary least squares regression of expected depreciation on forward discount, June 1981–August 1988

	Term		
	Three-month	*Six-month*	*Twelve-month*
Estimated slope coefficient (*b*)[a]	1.12 (0.20)	1.11 (0.15)	1.00 (0.18)
Hypothesis test statistic:			
b = 0	5.73*	7.61*	5.44*
b = 0.5	3.18*	4.20*	2.73*
b = 1	0.63	0.77	0.03
a = 0, *b* = 1	20.9*	41.8*	–[b]
*R*²	0.36	0.58	0.53
Durbin–Watson statistic (lower bound)	1.60	1.29	0.90

Source: Frankel and Froot 1990
Notes: Estimated equation is:

$$\Delta \hat{s}^e = a + b\,\mathrm{fd}_t + e_t,$$

where $\Delta \hat{s}^e$ is survey of the expected depreciation of the dollar over the given horizon and fd is the corresponding forward discount on the dollar for that horizon. Separate constant terms were estimated for each currency, but, to save space, they are not reported. The five currencies are the pound, mark, Swiss franc, yen and French franc.
[a] Reported standard errors in parentheses are calculated using the generalized method of moments. Although overlapping observations are not an issue because *ex post* spot rate changes do not enter in, pooling across currencies creates a correlation across exchange rates. (The reported test statistics assume homoskedasticity; correcting for possible heteroskedasticity makes little difference.)
[b] The F statistic is not reported, because the GMM covariance matrix is not positive definite.
* Indicates rejection of the null hypothesis at the 95 per cent significance level.

view that the variation in expected depreciation is large and the variation in the risk premium is small – precisely the reverse of the conventional wisdom – even more strongly than did the earlier results.

Three null hypotheses are relevant: $b = 0$, $b = 0.5$ and $b = 1$. The first null hypothesis would represent the view that none of the variation in the forward discount represents variation in expected depreci-

ation; it is easily rejected at the 99 per cent level of significance. The second represents the middle-of-the-road case where the variance of expected depreciation is equal to the variance of the exchange risk premium; it is also rejected at conventional significance levels in favour of the hypothesis that expected depreciation is more variable than the risk premium. The third hypothesis represents the view that *all* the variation in the forward discount represents variation in expected depreciation and *none* represents variation in the risk premium; the results by a wide margin do not reject this hypothesis.

These findings do not imply that the risk premium is zero. A majority of the *t* ratios, when computed for the five individual currencies, show statistically significant constant terms, part of which could be due to constant risk premiums (as opposed to the convexity term).[18] Moreover, the results do not even imply that the risk premium is necessarily constant.[19] However, the finding does suggest that variation in the forward discount does not reflect variation in the exchange risk premium as conventionally thought.

The sum of the covered interest differential, the first term in equation (16.1), and the exchange risk premium, the second term in equation (16.1), is the uncovered interest differential, or the expected difference in rates of return across countries:

$$i - i^* - \Delta s^e = (i - i^* - \mathrm{fd}) + (\mathrm{fd} - \Delta s^e). \tag{16.3}$$

In view of the evidence that the magnitude and variability of the first term $(i - i^* - \mathrm{fd})$ have been small in the 1980s and that the magnitude and variability of the second $(\mathrm{fd} - \Delta s^e)$ have also been small (relative at least to what is conventionally inferred on the basis of the rational expectations methodology), one might expect that the same is true of the uncovered interest differential.[20] Reinhart and Weiller (1987: 10–15), using the survey data to measure expected depreciation, find that this is indeed the case: for the sample period October 1984 to June 1986, the average uncovered interest differential between Japan and the USA is opposite in sign to, and less than one-twentieth the size in absolute magnitude of, the differential inferred by the rational expectations methodology on the basis of the difference in *ex post* rates of return, even though this differential appears statistically significant at the 99 per cent level.

HOW RETURN CORRELATIONS ACROSS GERMANY, JAPAN, THE USA AND THE UK CHANGED IN THE 1980s

In this section, we look at how correlations across the four countries that are the most important financially changed in the 1980s. We start the sample in March 1973, with the beginning of generalized floating, and go up to February 1989. We divide the sample at 1979, the year of the initial Japanese and British liberalizations. We choose October 1979 as the precise breaking point because we shall need to take account of the fact that US interest rate and exchange rate volatility increased in the 1980s, and the increase can be dated from the October change in operating procedures on the part of the Federal Reserve.

The variances reported in Table 16.3 show that short-term interest rates did indeed become more volatile in the 1980s in the UK and the USA, and long-term interest rates did so in all four countries. The variability of the dollar–pound, dollar–mark and dollar–yen exchange rates also increased in the 1980s. In the case of the pound, the increase in variability only occurred in the early 1980s; during the four-year period beginning March 1985, the variance was not much higher than in the 1970s. Stock markets also became more volatile in all four countries in the 1980s (though in the UK case the stock market variance fell in the *early* 1980s).

How would we expect the correlation of interest rates across countries to have changed in the 1980s? On the one hand, the results of the first section show that the covered interest differential, the first term in equation (16.1), virtually disappeared in the course of the 1980s. Thus one might guess that the variability of the interest differentials fell and the correlation of interest rates across countries increased in the 1980s.[21]

On the other hand, the evidence from the second section of this chapter suggests that although the variance of the exchange risk premium, the second term in equation (16.1), may have been small in the 1980s, the variance of expected depreciation, the third term, was large. This suggests that the correlation of interest rates across countries may have fallen rather than risen. Indeed, Kasman and Pigott (1988: 33) find that the association among major countries' nominal interest rates became looser in the 1980s than it had been in the 1960s or 1970s. Specifically, they find a decline in the correlation between US short-term interest rates and those of Germany, Japan

Table 16.3 Increased variances in the 1980s

Variable	Sample	USA	UK	Germany	Japan
Overnight interest rates	March 1973–April 1974	5.49	4.88	9.17	8.98
	October 1979–April 1989	12.03	8.50	6.26	4.88
Bond yields	March 1973–September 1979	0.47	2.42	2.68	1.44
	October 1979–April 1989	4.66	4.03	2.20	3.28
Stock market price indices[a]	March 1973–September 1979	0.01	0.11	0.01	0.02
	October 1979–October 1989	0.11	0.25	0.14	0.30
Exchange rates[a]	January 1973–October 1979		0.02	0.02	0.02
	November 1979–October 1989		0.04	0.04	0.06

Notes: [a] Stock market indices are expressed in logarithms. Exchange rates are the logarithms of the dollar price of the foreign currency.

Table 16.4 Correlations among interest rates and stock prices, monthly data

	Overnight interest rates		Long-term interest rates		Stock prices	
	1970s	1980s	1970s	1980s	1970s	1980s
USA versus:						
UK	0.03	0.36	0.07	0.76	0.73	0.98
Germany	0.54	0.87	−0.37	0.91	0.67	0.93
Japan	0.22	0.60	−0.25	0.79	0.66	0.97
Japan versus:						
UK	0.16	0.48	0.69	0.86	0.91	0.97
Germany	0.44	0.71	0.72	0.87	0.70	0.89
Germany versus:						
UK	−0.35	0.48	0.29	0.88	0.81	0.94

Notes: For definitions of interest rates and stock prices, see Table 16.3. The sample period for the 1970s extends from March 1973 to September 1979. The sample period for the 1980s extends from October 1979 to April 1989 for the interest rates and October 1979 to February 1989 for the stock prices.

the UK and Canada (though the correlations of long-term interest rates increased sharply). The dispersion across the five countries' interest rates also increased sharply after 1972 (mean absolute deviation of countries' rates, whether short term or long term) and increased somewhat further after 1979 when German and Japanese interest rates failed to rise as much as the rates of the other countries.

Table 16.4 shows cross-correlations among UK,

Table 16.5 Forecasting the inflation spread (twelve-month minus three-month) from interest rate term spreads, monthly observations, January 1955–December 1988

Interest rate term spread	Mishkin approach, twelve-month minus three-month	Alternative approach, five-year minus overnight federal funds
Constant term	−0.39	−0.25
t statistic:		
corrected[a]	−1.93	−1.70
uncorrected	−3.32	−3.01
Coefficient of term spread	0.68	0.34
t statistic:		
corrected[a]	2.26	4.02
uncorrected	3.71	6.62
Adjusted R^2	0.030	0.095

Source: Frankel and Lown 1990

Notes: Regression is $infs_t = a + b\,ints_t + u_t$, where infs is the difference between the twelve-month and three-month (realized) inflation rates from *t* forward, and ints is the interest rate spread at time *t* (twelve-month minus three-month, or five-year minus overnight federal funds rate, as the case may be).

  [a] *t* statistics corrected for the moving-average error process (introduced by overlapping monthly observations of year-ahead forecasts). The uncorrected *t* statistics are biased upwards.

German, Japanese and US money market interest rates. All six correlations have increased in the period since October 1979.[22] As Table 16.5 shows, all six cross-correlations among these countries' long-term interest rates also increased, as did the correlations among the changes in interest rates. Evidently, the high variability of expected depreciation in the 1980s was not enough to overcome the low variability in covered interest differentials and exchange risk premiums.

Table 16.4 reports statistics for stock prices as well (though the logic of the decomposition in equation (16.1) does not apply because stock prices are not the same thing as stock returns). Again, all six cross-correlations increased in the 1980s.[23] (When changes in stock prices are computed, however, three of the six correlations fall rather than rise in the second period.)

Although not reported in the table, the correlations among the four long-term interest rates increase both in the October 1979 to June 1984 and July 1984 to April 1989 subperiods. The same is true of the correlations of the stock markets, except that the three correlations with the German stock market decline in the period from July 1984 to February 1989. The pattern among the money market rates is more varied. To sum up the overall evidence on return correlations, it is consistent with the view that the degree of international capital mobility increased in the 1980s.

INDICATORS FOR MONETARY POLICY

The October 1979 change in Federal Reserve operating procedures represented an acknowledgement that nominal interest rates were not a useful indicator of whether monetary policy was tight or loose, in part because of the difficulty of distinguishing changes in the nominal interest rate from changes in the real interest rate. Since 1982, however, it has become widely acknowledged that M1 and other monetary aggregates are also not reliable indicators, because of large and lasting shifts in velocity. Thus there has been a search for new indicators.

One indicator/guide for monetary policy that has been suggested is the exchange rate (see, for example, Williamson 1985; McKinnon 1984). Theory tells us that when exchange rates are fixed and capital mobility is low, monetary policy is primarily reflected in interest rates, but that, under modern conditions of floating exchange rates and high capital mobility, changes in monetary policy should be reflected primarily in exchange rates.

There is evidence that exchange rates do indeed contain useful information about market expectations regarding future monetary policy. One example comes from the period in the late 1970s and early 1980s when unexpectedly high weekly money announcements would regularly cause nominal interest rates to jump significantly upward. Clearly, during this period, market participants were using the news in the announcements to revise their expectations regarding the ease of future monetary policy. The question was whether an observed increase in the nominal interest rate was an increase in the real interest rate, signifying the expectation of tighter monetary policy in the future, or an increase in the expected inflation rate.

The foreign exchange market contains the answer. In the late 1970s, positive money surprises were associated with increases in the price of foreign exchange, indicating that the increases in the nominal interest rate were increases in expected inflation. In the period July 1980 to November 1982, the reverse was true. Positive money surprises were associated with decreases in the price of foreign exchange, indicating that the increases in the nominal interest rate were increases in the real interest rate (in the expectation that the Federal Reserve would act to bring the money supply back toward its intended path).[24]

Another indicator/guide for monetary policy that has been suggested is the price of gold and other basic mineral and agricultural commodities. There is similar evidence that such prices contain useful information about market expectations regarding future monetary policy. In the period July 1980 to November 1982, positive money surprises were associated with decreases in the prices of commodities, indicating again that the increases in the nominal interest rate were increases in the real interest rate and were signs of a tighter, rather than looser, expected future monetary policy.[25]

Note, however, that the usefulness of the exchange rate or commodity prices as immediate indicators of the perceived stance of monetary policy does not mean that it would be wise for the authorities to pre-commit to targets for these prices, any more than to M1. There are large disturbances in the demand for foreign exchange, the demand for gold and the demand for M1. Committing to a fixed number or target range for any of these three magnitudes would mean that the disturbances would be more fully transmitted to the level of real GNP and the general price level.[26]

Yet another possible indicator of the expected future ease of monetary policy, which has received increased attention since it was cited in a speech by Federal Reserve Vice Chairman Manuel Johnson (1988), lies in the term structure of interest rates.[27] The idea is that, when the yield curve becomes steeper, this is a sign that the market expects inflation to increase in the future, and when its slope falls, a sign that the market expects inflation to decrease. A simplistic interpretation of this idea would assume that the real interest rate is constant, from which it follows that the term spread is equal to the difference between the inflation rate expected in the long term and the inflation rate expected in the short term.[28]

A more realistic model would allow for the fact that the short-term real interest rate is not constant in the short run, but would assume that there is a tendency for it to approach a constant gradually over time (as would be true in a model with goods prices that are sticky in the short run). Let us assume further the expectations hypothesis of the term structure: that the long-term interest rate is the average of the expected short-term interest rates over the relevant maturity, up to a possible (but constant) term premium. Then it is easy to show that the expected inflation rate can be expressed (up to a constant term) as a linear combination of the long-term and short-term

interest rates (with weight greater than unity on the former and negative weight on the latter, so that the linear combination is extrapolating out along the yield curve) (Frankel 1982). It then follows that the difference between any expected long-term inflation rate and any expected short-term inflation rate is proportional to the spread between any long-term interest rate and any short-term interest rate. But the constant of proportionality is not unity, as in the case of a constant real interest rate, and investigators need not use interest rate maturities that correspond to the horizon over which they wish to forecast inflation.

Table 16.5, taken from Frankel and Lown (1991), reports some preliminary evidence on this topic. The first column shows regressions in which the terms of the interest rates used in the forecast match the terms of the inflation rates to be forecast, as would be required under the theoretical framework that assumes that real interest rates are constant. The estimate for the coefficient on the interest rate spread is greater than zero and less than unity. This finding suggests that, on the one hand, there may indeed be forecasting power in the term structure, but that, on the other hand, the real interest rate does not appear to be constant. Thus far, the results match those obtained by Mishkin (1988, 1989). But the practical advantage of the alternative theoretical framework allowing for short-term variation in the real interest rate is that it allows one to use a more reliable estimate of the slope of the yield curve, rather than being restricted to a narrow term spread that matches the inflation rates to be forecast. In the second column of Table 16.5, we use the spread between the five-year interest rate and the overnight federal funds rate, even though we wish to forecast the one-year/ three-month change in the inflation rate. As indicated by either R^2 or significance levels, the ability to predict changes in the inflation rate is greater than when the one-year/three-month term spread was used. The conclusion is that the alternative framework may be more useful for forecasting the future movement of inflation, reinforcing the theoretical desirability of allowing for variation in the real interest rate.[29]

THE RELATIONSHIP BETWEEN THE EXCHANGE RATE AND SHORT- AND LONG-TERM INTEREST RATES

The Dornbusch (1976) model of overshooting when capital is perfectly mobile and goods prices are sticky, which entails a positive relationship between the real exchange rate and the real interest differential, is by now fifteen years old. Some may regard it as old fashioned because investor behaviour is not 'rigorously derived from first principles of intertemporal optimization'. Yet there is at least one sense in which the Dornbusch model arrived before its time. As we have seen, the assumption of perfectly integrated world financial markets was less true in the 1970s than in the 1980s. (Also, real interest differentials did not show as much variability in the 1970s as they did in the 1980s.) Thus, one might expect that the relationship between the real exchange rate and the real interest differential would have become stronger in the 1980s. This section presents some results on the changing relationship between the exchange rate and the interest differentials. The results should perhaps be viewed more as descriptive correlation statistics than as estimates of any structural system. Nevertheless, it is appropriate to consider further what relationships between the exchange rate and interest rates would be expected under alternative possible models.

In the old-fashioned flow approach (with no role for expectations), the short- and long-term interest differentials each had positive effects on a country's balance of payments, via the short- and long-term capital accounts respectively; thus under floating rates each had a positive effect (along with determinants of the trade balance) on the demand for domestic currency and on the foreign exchange value of the currency. In the monetarist approach of the early 1970s, by contrast, only the short-term interest differential mattered (assuming that the short-term interest rate was the rate of return relevant for money demand), and it had a *negative* effect on the value of the currency. The reason was that a high nominal interest rate necessarily reflected a high expected inflation rate. Because the currency was expected to lose value in the future, investors had a low demand for it today.

For the overshooting model, let us combine the no-risk-premium assumption with a regressive model of exchange rate expectations:

$$\mathrm{fd} = \Delta s^e \qquad (16.4)$$

$$\Delta s^e = -\theta(s - \bar{s}) + (\Delta p^e - \Delta p^{*e}), \quad (16.5)$$

where s is the log of the spot exchange rate, $\bar{s}$ is its value in long-run equilibrium, Δp^e and Δp^{*e} are the domestic and foreign expected inflation rates respectively and θ is a 'speed of adjustment' parameter relating the expected exchange rate change to the current 'overvaluation' of the currency. Solving for the exchange rate,

$$s = \bar{s} - \frac{1}{\theta} [\mathrm{fd} - (\Delta p^e - \Delta p^{*e})]. \quad (16.6)$$

Now, on the assumption of complete integration of financial markets, add the assumption of covered interest parity, $\mathrm{fd} = i - i^*$:

$$s = \bar{s} - \frac{1}{\theta} [i - i^* - (\Delta p^e - \Delta p^{*e})]. \quad (16.7)$$

An increase in the nominal interest rate has a positive effect when expected inflation is held constant (as in the flow approach), while an increase in the expected inflation rate has a negative effect (as in the monetarist approach).[30]

In the sticky price model, the expected inflation rate should be related to the difference between the long-term and short-term interest rates (as explained in the section on indicators for monetary policy). There probably exist better predictors of inflation than the term spread. Possible measures of expected inflation include distributed lags on past inflation, forecasts of larger econometric models and surveys of expectations of market participants. But the subject at hand is the relationship among exchange rates, short-term interest rates and long-term interest rates. The sticky price model suggests that in a regression of the exchange value of domestic currency against the short-term nominal interest differential and the differential in term spreads, we should look for a negative sign on the latter.[31]

Some of our regressions include the covered interest differential as an additional explanatory variable in order to embody a role for the degree of financial market integration. If the covered interest differential is thought to constitute a non-negligible gap between the interest differential and expected depreciation, then in place of covered interest parity we substitute the covered interest differential, $\text{cid} = i - i^* - \text{fd}$, into equation (16.4):

$$s = \bar{s} - \frac{1}{\theta}[i - i^* - \text{cid} - (\Delta p^e - \Delta p^{*e})]. \tag{16.8}$$

So we expect the covered interest differential to have a coefficient $(1/\theta)$ that is opposite in sign to that of the nominal interest differential.

Finally, the expected inflation differential at time t can be proxied by the spread between the long-term interest differential $i_1 - i_1^*$ and the short-term differential $(+s_d)$, which is the differential in term spreads. Thus the general estimating equation is

$$s_t = \bar{s} + b(+s_d)_t + c(\text{cid})_t + d(i_1 - i_1^*)_t + u_t \tag{16.9}$$

When the regressions are run on levels of the nominal exchange rate, the model is supported (though the results are omitted to save space). For all three currencies – pound, yen and mark – the coefficients on the three-month interest differential, the term premium and covered interest differential are generally as hypothesized (positive, negative and negative, when the dependent variable is the log of the value of the local currency in terms of dollars) and generally appear statistically significant. In addition, the logarithmic difference in stock market price indices, when included to try to capture 'safe-haven' shifts between countries in portfolio preferences, appears

to have a positive and highly significant effect on the demand for and value of the local currency.[32] However, low Durbin–Watson statistics indicate the presence of serial correlation.

When the regressions are run on first differences, statistical significance disappears. The exception is that, for the case of the dollar–pound exchange rate, an increase in the differential between the UK and US short-term interest rates is associated with a statistically significant effect of the reverse sign. Such findings are an old problem in exchange rate regressions, a problem generally attributed to simultaneity: when a disturbance causes the pound to depreciate, the Bank of England raises British interest rates in response. In the present instance, attempts to address the simultaneity problem with instrumental variables were unsuccessful. Further details and related results are given in an Appendix (page 352).

CHARTISTS, FUNDAMENTALISTS AND TRADING IN THE FOREIGN EXCHANGE MARKET

The conclusion from the preceding section is that even though the standard macroeconomic theories of exchange rate determination draw some empirical support from observed reactions to news (such as the money announcements discussed in the fourth section), and even though real interest differentials appear to have explanatory power for exchange rates on *levels*, the ability to predict *changes* in the exchange rate is close to nil.

Figure 16.4 illustrates the problem. During most of the period since 1973, the real value of the dollar has been highly correlated with the differential in real interest rates between the USA and trading partners, as equation (16.6) says it should be. At times, however, the dollar departs from the path dictated by macroeconomic fundamentals. The most notable episode is the period from mid-1984 to February 1985, when the dollar continued to appreciate at an accelerated speed despite the fact that the real interest differential – and virtually all other measures of macroeconomic fundamentals as well – was moving in the opposite direction. Some

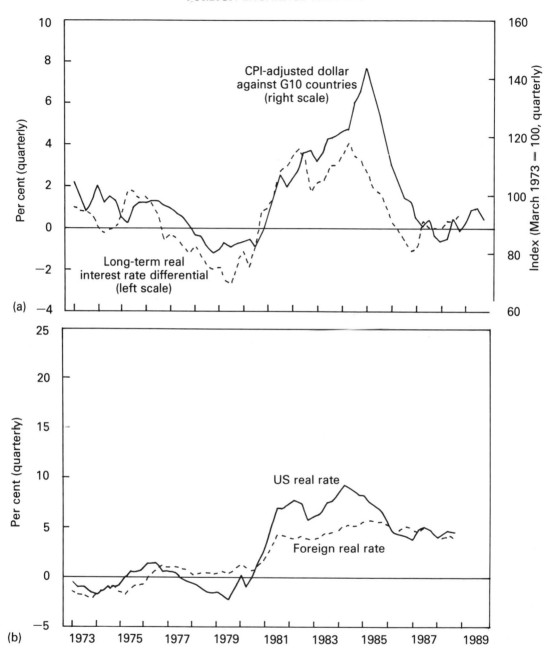

Figure 16.4 (a) The dollar and real interest rates; (b) US and foreign (G10) interest rates. The CPI-adjusted dollar is a weighted average index of the exchange value of the dollar against the currencies of the foreign G10 countries plus Switzerland, where nominal exchange rates are multiplied by relative levels of consumer price indices. Weights are proportional to each country's share of world exports plus imports during 1978–83. The long-term real interest rate differential is the long-term real US interest rate minus the weighted average of long-term real foreign-currency interest rates

Source: Federal Reserve Board of Governors

have suggested that the appreciation of the dollar in 1988–9 may have been of a similar nature. Ken Froot and I have suggested that such episodes may be examples of speculative bubbles, and that they are best described by models in which market participants are *not* necessarily assumed to agree on the correct model for forecasting the exchange rate (Frankel and Froot 1990a).

Let us begin with the tremendous volume of foreign exchange trading. The Federal Reserve Bank of New York (1989) has just released its triennial count of transactions in the US foreign exchange market. It showed that in April 1989 foreign exchange trading (adjusted for double counting) totalled $110.5 billion among banks (an increase of 121 per cent from March 1986) and $18.4 billion among non-bank financial institutions (an increase of 116 per cent).

What is the importance of trading volume? There are three possible hypotheses. First, the higher the liquidity of the markets, the more efficiently is news regarding economic fundamentals processed and the smaller is 'unnecessary volatility' in the exchange rate. Second, the foreign exchange market is already perfectly efficient, so trading volume is irrelevant and uninteresting. Third, much trading is based on 'noise' rather than 'news', and leads to excessive volatility. Choosing convincingly among these three hypotheses is far too large a task to accomplish here.

There is evidence that trading volume, exchange rate volatility and the dispersion of forecasters' expectations (as reflected in the survey data) are all positively correlated (see Frankel and Froot 1990b; or Ito 1990). The direction of causality has not yet been definitively established. But Granger-causality tests show that the degree of dispersion has strong effects on the market. Dispersion Granger-causes volume at the 90 per cent level in three currencies out of four. Dispersion also Granger-causes volatility. Frankel and Froot (1990b) also find that the contemporaneous correlation between volume and volatility is high. One interpretation of these results is that the existence of conflicting forecasts leads to noise-trading – the causation runs from dispersion in expectations to

the volume of trading, and then from trading to volatility – though there probably exist other interpretations as well.

In a study of minute-by-minute foreign exchange market data, Goodhart and Figliuoli (1991: 31) find 'no signs at all of sudden major jumps on the receipt of "news"'. For the most part, foreign exchange markets in a given country are open during exactly the same hours that news is released, so that it is difficult to do a study of noise trading and volatility such as that carried out by French and Roll (1986) for the stock market. However, Goodhart and Giugale (1988) find some evidence in hourly data that could be interpreted as supporting the view that spot rate movements occur in response to trading volume and not just to news. The variance of changes over the weekend is small, even though a lot of news relevant to the foreign exchange market comes out over the weekend. Moreover, each Monday morning the volatility for each European currency is high in the first hour of trading in the geographical market where that particular currency has the highest trading volume, even when other markets open earlier in the day and could in theory have been just as able to process any weekend news. Finally, trading volume in London and volatility both reach daily low points during the lunch hour, even though news is still coming out then.

Interestingly, the banks in the 1989 New York survey reported that only 4.9 per cent of their trading was with a non-financial firm; the corresponding figure reported by the non-banks was only 4.4 per cent. In other words, more than 95 per cent of the trading takes place among the banks and other financial firms, rather than with customers such as importers and exporters. If the 1986 data are a guide, similar proportions apply in London (still the world's largest foreign exchange market). Clearly, trading among themselves is a major economic activity for banks. Schulmeister (1987: 24) found that in 1985 twelve large US banks earned a foreign exchange trading income of $1.165 billion. In every year that he examined, every single bank reported a profit from its foreign exchange business.

Goodhart (1988: 25, Appendix D) has surveyed banks that specialize in the London foreign exchange market: 'Traders, so it is claimed, consistently make profits from their position-taking (and those who do not get fired), over and above their return from straight dealing, owing to the bid/ask spread' (1988: 59). Apparently they consider the taking of long-term positions based on fundamentals, or of any sort of position in the forward exchange market, as too 'speculative' and risky. Bankers recall the Franklin National crisis and other bank failures caused by open foreign positions that were held too long. But the banks are willing to trust their spot exchange traders to take large open positions, provided the traders close most of them out by the end of the day, because these operations are profitable in the aggregate. According to Goodhart and others, a typical spot trader bases decisions to buy and sell not on any fundamentals model but on the knowledge of what deals other traders are offering at a given time and a feel for what their behaviour is likely to be later in the day.

The theory of speculative bubbles developed in Frankel and Froot (1990a) says that over the period 1981–5 the market shifted weight away

Table 16.6 Techniques used by exchange rate forecasting services

Year	Number of services surveyed	Number using technical models	Number using fundamental models	Number of both models	Average maximum time horizon	Average minimum time horizon
Counting each firm separately						
1978	22	2	18	1	4 years	22 weeks
1979						
1980						
1981	13	1	11	0	1.23 years	
1982						
1983	10	7	0	2		
1984	13	9	0	2		2.6 days
1985	20	12	1	6	8 months	1.6 days
1986	25	13	0	12		
1987	25	10	0	11		
1988	27	12	1	12		
Counting each service separately [a]						
1978	23	3	19	0		
1979						
1980						
1981	13	1	11	0		
1982						
1983	11	8	1	1		
1984	13	9	0	2		
1985	24	15	5	3		
1986	34	20	8	4		
1987	31	16	6	5		
1988	31	18	7	6		

Source: *Euromoney*, August 1978–August 1988 issues

Notes: [a] Each firm is allowed to offer more than one service. If one or more services did not indicate the nature of their models, the number of services for a given year will not add up to the total in the second column. Empty cells in the sixth and seventh columns indicate a lack of meaningful data.

from the fundamentalists and toward the technical analysts or 'chartists', this shift being a natural response to the inferior forecasting record of the former group; the shift in the weighted-average forecast of future changes in the value of the dollar in turn shifted the demand for dollars and therefore its price in the foreign exchange market.

Is there any sort of evidence for such a theory? *Euromoney* magazine runs a yearly August review of between ten and twenty-seven foreign exchange forecasting services. Summary statistics are reported in Table 16.6. The trend is very clear. In 1978, eighteen forecasting firms described themselves as relying exclusively on economic fundamentals, and only two on technical analysis. By 1985, the positions had been reversed: only one firm reported relying exclusively on fundamentals, and twelve on technical analysis. (There are no signs of a 'fundamentalist revival' in more recent years.)

As the table indicates, a number of firms combine the two approaches or offer a separate service of each kind. In this case, technical analysis is typically used for short-term forecasting and fundamentals for long-term forecasting.[33] This pattern matches up well with the results from surveys of market participants' exchange rate expectations, described in Frankel and Froot (1990a, b): at horizons of one week and one month, respondents tend to forecast by extrapolating recent trends, while at horizons of three, six and twelve months they tend to forecast a return to a long-run equilibrium such as PPP.[34]

In short, it may indeed be the case that shifts over time in the weight given to different forecasting techniques are a source of change in the demand for dollars and that large exchange rate movements may take place with little basis in macroeconomic fundamentals.

CONCLUSIONS

This chapter has touched on many disparate points. It is now necessary to draw the unifying conclusions and, in particular, to draw the implications for the making of monetary policy.

In the first section we saw tangible evidence that low transaction costs and low government controls have brought about a highly integrated world financial market, and in the sixth section we saw that the volume of transactions in the foreign exchange market is indeed tremendous. In theory, a world of floating exchange rates and high capital mobility should be a world in which the exchange rate is a very good indicator of whether monetary policy is loose or tight. In practice, although the exchange rate does often contain valuable information on the perceived stance of monetary policy, at other times it undergoes large movements for reasons that appear to have no connection with macroeconomic fundamentals but rather to stem from the internal dynamics of foreign exchange market trading.

A number of implications follow regarding exchange rate volatility. First, because expectations of exchange rate changes can be large, there is no reason to expect *real* interest rates to be equalized across countries, even when arbitrage does equalize interest rates expressed in a common currency. Second, speculative bubbles may mean that exchange rate volatility is 'excessive'.

Several further points on the idea of 'excess' volatility should be noted. On the one hand, speculative bubbles need not be 'irrational' on the part of market participants in order to constitute an additional source of variation in the exchange rate. On the other hand, if the bubble component of the exchange rate happened to be negatively correlated with the fundamentals component, it is conceivable that total variability could be smaller with the bubbles than without them. More generally, it is difficult to make firm statements regarding the implications for economic welfare. Using monetary policy to suppress variability in the exchange rate may mean creating more variability elsewhere in the economy. Even if it can be established that exchange rate volatility is needlessly large, it is not clear that the monetary authorities can do anything to eliminate speculative bubbles. The Williamson–Miller proposal assumes that speculative bubbles would disappear if the government announced target zones, but this is only a hope and an assertion.[35]

If exchange rate movement is not always tied to macroeconomic fundamentals, then it also follows that exchange rates are not by themselves reliable indicators of monetary policy. Indeed, no single monetary indicator is sufficient in itself. Exchange rates, commodity prices and the term structure of interest rates all contain useful information, but they should be used in conjunction with each other (as Manuel Johnson suggested) and with other indicators as well. This conclusion is a familiar principle. But it should not be confused with the claim that the monetary authorities can always do better by simultaneously pursuing multiple *targets* (the goals such as output, inflation and the trade balance that the country cares about) than they can by publicly announcing a single (intermediate) target variable. For important reasons which are by now well known, it is optimal for the authorities to have at least *some* degree of pre-commitment to a nominal target. To try to obtain the advantages of reduced expectations of inflation in the wage-setting process, monetary authorities often declare a commitment to refrain from over-expansion; for such declarations to be credible, it helps for the authorities to announce a specific nominal intermediate target by which the public can evaluate the genuineness of the commitment.[36] Similarly, to try to obtain the advantages of international co-ordination, the G7 holds regular meetings; for substantive co-ordination agreements to be enforced, it would help for the governments to set specific intermediate targets by which they could evaluate the genuineness of each others' commitment.

What variable should be the intermediate target to which authorities express some degree of commitment? Three candidates that have been proposed are the exchange rate, the price of gold and other commodities, and the money supply. While these three variables do contain useful information about the stance of monetary policy, they are not good candidates for intermediate targets because they are only distantly related to ultimate objectives such as output and inflation. Failure to accommodate disturbances in the demand for money, the demand for gold or the demand for foreign exchange would needlessly transmit these disturbances to the rest of the economy.

It has been argued by many that the optimal intermediate target to which the monetary authorities should publicly declare a degree of commitment is nominal GNP. Under a nominal GNP target, demand disturbances such as shifts in velocity are completely offset, while little is given up in the case of supply disturbances.[37] It can be shown that a nominal GNP target is in general better than an exchange rate or M1 target at minimizing a quadratic loss function in output, inflation and the exchange rate. The only exceptions arise if (1) an unexpected 10 per cent fluctuation in the exchange rate is considered much worse than an unexpected 10 per cent fluctuation in the price level, or (2) under a floating exchange rate regime, there are large disturbances in the demand for domestic currency that would disappear under an exchange rate target regime. Frankel (1989) offers a proof, gives further references and further develops the argument for nominal GNP targeting in the specific context of international co-ordination of monetary policy.[38]

APPENDIX: EXCHANGE RATE REGRESSIONS FOR THE 1970s AND 1980s COMPARED (USING MONEY MARKET INTEREST RATES)

In this appendix, we consider how exchange rate regression results differ between the 1970s and the 1980s.

Even in the golden days of exchange rate regressions (1976–80), the endogeneity of the interest rates (and money supplies) was a serious problem, in practice as well as in theory. Central banks often reduce the money supply or raise interest rates in response to a depreciation in their currencies. It was difficult to control for this source of simultaneity. As a result, the money supply and interest rate often showed up with the wrong sign in an exchange rate regression.

Econometrics has grown more cynical during

Table 16A.1 Exchange rate regressions

Nominal currency	Sample period	Constant	Short-term interest differential	Term spread	Durbin–Watson statistic	R^2
Levels						
Pound	March 1973–September 1979	5.24 (0.05)	−0.01 (0.01)	−0.01 (0.01)	0.07	0.17
	October 1979–April 1989	5.08 (0.16)	0.06* (0.01)	−0.08* (0.10)	0.16	0.35
Yen	March 1973–September 1979	−0.96 (0.01)	0.08* (0.01)	0.07* (0.01)	0.33	0.88
	October 1979–April 1989	−0.65 (0.08)	0.01 (0.02)	−0.00 (0.02)	0.01	0.01
Mark	March 1973–September 1979	3.73 (0.01)	−0.05* (0.00)	−0.03* (0.01)	0.46	0.68
	October 1979–April 1989	4.13 (0.05)	0.10* (0.01)	−0.13 (0.02)	0.19	0.38
First difference						
Pound	April 1973–September 1979	−0.13 (0.00)	−0.01 (0.01)	0.01* (0.00)		0.15
	October 1979–February 1989	−0.00 (0.00)	−0.01 (0.01)	(0.01)		0.01
Yen	April 1973–April 1979	−0.00 (0.00)	−0.02* (0.01)	0.02* (0.01)		0.07
	October 1979–April 1989	0.00 (0.00)	0.00 (0.01)	0.00 (0.01)		0.04
Mark	April 1973–September 1979	0.01* (0.00)	0.02 (0.01)	−0.01 (0.01)		0.03
	October 1979–April 1989	−0.00 (0.00)	0.00 (0.01)	0.00 (0.01)		0.04

Notes: The short-term interest differential is the difference between the US and foreign three-month money market rates. The term spread is the difference between the long-term government bond yield and the three-month rate. Exchange rates are expressed as foreign currency per dollar.
* Statistically significant at 95 per cent level.

the ten years since the days when we merrily ran exchange rate regressions. The error term, which we used to think of as a small residual that is left over after the equation's macroeconomic fundamentals have explained most of the variation in the exchange rate, has grown in importance far beyond its traditional bounds. Today it is considered noteworthy if the fundamentals explain *any* part of the movement in the exchange rate; the error term has taken over virtually everything.[39]

Regardless how one chooses to think of the origins of the error term (the two leading candidates at this point are unidentified mysterious shifts in the equilibrium real exchange rate and speculative bubbles or fads), the choice has major implications for the econometrics. If one accepts that the increased variability of the exchange rate in the 1980s is in part due to an increase in the variability of the error term and that the reaction function of the monetary authorities is a prime channel of endogeneity of the interest rate, then one might be *less*, rather than more, hopeful of finding a positive relationship between the exchange value of the currency and the interest differential in the 1980s.

The data on three-month interest differentials and covered interest differentials that we used for the period 1982–8 are not available before then. Thus, we use money market interest rates instead of the regular three-month rates. Some of the results for nominal exchange rates are shown in Table 16A.1. When the regressions are run on levels, passing from the time period 1973–9 to the time period 1979–89 changes the coefficient from negative to positive for each of the three currencies; in the case of the mark and pound, the coefficient appears significantly positive. But one cannot claim much evidence in favour of the overshooting model, because the Durbin–Watson statistics indicate high serial correlation. When the regressions are run on first differences, all statistical significance is lost. The results are no better when the real exchange rate is used for the dependent variable, or when instrumental variables are used.

NOTES

1 The four principal measures of barriers to mobility are saving–investment correlations (the Feldstein–Horioka definition), real interest differentials, uncovered interest differentials and covered interest differentials. For an exposition of how the four criteria relate, tests on recent data and extensive references, see Frankel (1989). Other guides to the literature on capital mobility include Caramazza *et al.* (1986) and Akhtar and Weiller (1987).

2 Covered interest parity could hold perfectly and yet many types of assets could be imperfectly substitutable across countries. For example, even if a yen bond in London is a perfect substitute for a yen bond in Tokyo, yen bonds may be imperfect substitutes for dollar or pound bonds because of exchange risk.

3 The German episode is analysed by Dooley and Isard (1980). See also Marston (1988).

4 Frankel (1984) examines the Japanese episode and gives further references.

5 The statistics are from Frankel (1988). The British liberalization is examined in Artis and Taylor (1990). See also Frenkel and Levich (1975, 1977).

6 For example, see Frenkel and Levich (1975, 1977). Akhtar and Weiller (1987) point out the need for measuring changes in the degree of capital mobility, as opposed to the usual artificial tests of perfect capital mobility.

7 Most of the forward rate data come from Barclays Bank. We have eliminated Mexico from the earlier sample because no forward rate data have been available since early 1986, and we have eliminated Ireland because, though rate data from early 1986 to early 1988 were quoted at one time, they appear to have been incorrect.

8 The statistics are in Frankel (1988: 587–81). On the magnitude of the differential at the start of the 1980s, see also Kreicher (1982).

9 Frankel (1988). A contributing factor was a step taken by the US Treasury to facilitate borrowing from abroad: the abolition of the withholding tax on interest paid to foreigners. On the proposition that US corporations in the early 1980s could borrow more cheaply in the Eurobond market than domestically, see also Kim and Stulz (1988) and Marr and Trimble (1988).

10 Reinhart and Weiller (1987: 11, Table 2) claim a similar finding for three-month holding period yields on long-term government bonds (and also equities), using forward premia (apparently constructed from the three-month Eurocurrency interest rates in the Appendix) to cover the exchange risk. However, the relation tested is apparently not an arbitrage condition because the risk of capital gains and losses remains.

11 It no doubt remains true, however, that such assets as real estate and business plant and equipment are neither perfect substitutes across countries nor perfect substitutes for bonds issued within their own countries.

12 Papers that focus on the decomposition of interest differentials into country components and currency components include Frankel (1989), Frankel and MacArthur (1988) and Kasman and Pigott (1988). The conclusion, that the currency component is now large even though the country component is now small, could be interpreted as supporting the view of McKinnon (1987), who attributes the difference to the floating exchange rate regime.

13 One reason to allow for a constant term is to allow for the possible role of the convexity term that can

emerge from Jensen's inequality.

14   Bilson (1985) in this context refers to the random walk case as a 'new empirical paradigm'.

15   Koedijk and Ott (1987) claim to weigh the two alternative interpretations of the standard forward bias regression. But in fact the article imposes the rational expectations methodology, thereby ruling out the alternative interpretation *a priori*, just as Fama and Hodrick and Srivastava do.

16   They include Dominguez (1986), Frankel and Froot (1987), Froot and Frankel (1989) and Froot and Ito (1989).

17   The history of the early 1980s was dominated by the large appreciation of the dollar and characterized by a non-interventionist policy on the part of the US government. Since 1985, the dollar has moved both down and up, and the USA has co-operated with other G7 countries to intervene in the foreign exchange market. For the period before 1980, only a few yearly observations are available (from a survey that used to be conducted by American Express Banking Corporation; see Frankel and Froot (1987)).

18   Kasman and Pigott (1988: 37) use our survey data to compute average foreign exchange risk premia for the dollar against the mark, yen and pound, and find them in the range 2.9–7.8 per cent. Such risk premia would be smaller and more plausible than the differences in *ex post* rates of return across currencies; they point out that the latter typically exceed the differences between yields on very-high-risk junk bonds and AAA-rated bonds.

19   It is possible that part of the variation in the regression error term could be attributed to a (time-varying) risk premium. The preferred interpretation in Frankel and Froot (1990a)is that the regression error represents (random) measurement error in the survey data. But results in Dominguez and Frankel (1990) suggest that the risk premium (as estimated by the survey data) does vary significantly with central bank intervention in the foreign exchange market and with the variance of the exchange rate, in the way that the portfolio balance model says it should.

20   An early and typical application of the rational expectations methodology to the measurement of the uncovered interest differential is Cumby and Obstfeld (1981).

21   Akhtar and Weiller (1987: 45–9) review several studies that generally find an increase in the correlation of interest rates among the USA and other countries since the 1970s.

22   I do not know how to reconcile these findings with the statistics reported by Kasman and Pigott (1988: 34) showing that the correlations of US short-term interest rates with those in Germany, Japan and the UK *decreased* from the 1970s to the period between 1980 and the second quarter of 1988. (It might help that when the correlations of Table 16.4 are recomputed on changes, two of the six turn out to fall in the 1980s.) In any case, I agree with their central conclusion that, despite the fall in covered interest differentials, differences among interest rates remain large because of expected currency changes.

23   Of course, the correlation of world stock market prices was particularly high in the crash of October 1987. See Bertero and Mayer (1989) and Von Furstenberg and Nam Jeon (1989).

24   Cornell (1982) and Engel and Frankel (1982). Further evidence that market participants regarded the M1 surprises as unintended deviations from Federal Reserve targets in the early 1980s lies in their quite different reactions to announcements of the monetary reserves; see Hardouvelis (1984).

25   The commodities are corn, feeders, gold, live cattle, soybeans, wheat, cocoa, silver and sugar. See Frankel and Hardouvelis (1985) and Grubaugh and Sumner (1989).

26   The policy problem is considered further in the concluding section of this chapter.

27   Johnson suggested that the Federal Reserve might look at three indicators together, the term structure and the first two measures mentioned above: the price of foreign exchange and the price of gold and other commodities. See Lown (1989).

28   For example, see Mishkin (1988, 1989), who finds that the spread between long-term and short-term interest rates does contain information useful in predicting future inflation rates. Unfortunately, his paper offers only a restrictive model that assumes that the real interest rate is constant. (It is ironic that such a simplistic interpretation is being placed on the term structure indicator after a decade in which the evidence of time variation in the real interest rate has been overwhelming (much of the evidence having been presented by Mishkin (1984a, b) himself).)

29   The question arises how to get an optimal estimator by using the entire term structure, rather than just two points. Further work will aim for even better inflation forecasts by using non-linear regression at each point in time to estimate the slope of the yield curve for that observation.

30   If the dependent variable is the real exchange rate, then the coefficient on the expected inflation differential should be the negative of the coefficient on the nominal interest differential (such as $1/\theta$ in the equation). If the dependent variable is the nominal exchange rate, then the absolute magnitude of the

coefficient on the expected inflation differential should be larger (by an additive factor λ, the semi-elasticity of money demand with respect to the interest rate), because of the effect on the equilibrium nominal exchange rate $\bar{s}$.

31 In Frankel (1979), the long-term interest differential was used as one of the proxies for the expected inflation differential in econometric estimation of the Dornbusch overshooting model. If the expected inflation rate is proxied by the term spread, then its coefficient will be altered because we saw in the third section that the factor of proportionality is not unity.

32 Bhandari and Genberg (1989) find that the correlation of stock prices and exchange rates changes sign over time, and in theory depends on the relative importance of real and monetary shocks.

33 A recent study by Allen and Taylor (1989: 4–5) confirms that chartism is most widely used at short horizons. Out of more than 200 questionnaires returned to the authors by chief foreign exchange dealers in the London market, 60 per cent judged charts to be at least as important as fundamentals in their forecasts at horizons of one week or less, while 85 per cent judged fundamentals to be more important than charts at horizons of one year or longer. Seventy-four per cent of the respondents reported that the source of their chartist input was on-line commercial services.

34 Notice in the table that as the relative weight of technical analysis rises between 1978 and 1985, the horizon of the forecasts offered by the services grows shorter.

35 The presumption that the government is in practice capable of 'beating the market at its own game' should be no more automatic when it comes to foreign exchange than in many aspects of the real economy.

36 The formalization of the argument for rules rather than pure discretion has been made by Kydland and Prescott (1977), Barro and Gordon (1983) and Rogoff (1985).

37 Supply disturbances are taken half as changes in output and half as changes in inflation. While this outcome will not correspond perfectly to the split that would be chosen under full discretion (unless the objective function happens to put equal weight on each), full discretion gives up the benefits of reducing inflation expectations through pre-commitment to a nominal target.

38 The argument for nominal GNP targeting in the context of international co-ordination includes, in addition to uncertainty regarding future disturbances, uncertainty regarding the proper model. One of the obstacles to co-ordination as conventionally conceived, where policy-makers bargain over M1 money supplies, is that the existing models completely disagree about whether a monetary expansion in one country has a positive or negative effect on its trading partners' economies. But if ministers in G7 meetings commit to joint expansion (or joint contraction, as the case may be) in terms of nominal GNP rather than M1, the presence of exchange rate stability as a goal will encourage each country to fulfil its nominal GNP commitment in part through fiscal policy or other instruments, and not solely through monetary policy. As a result, there may be less uncertainty that transmission from each country to the next will be positive. For more on the implications of uncertainty for co-ordination, see Frankel (1989), Ghosh and Masson (1988), Kenen (1990) and Holtham and Hughes Hallett (1987).

39 In recent years, the error term has not even been content with its traditional role of reminding us of the extent of our ignorance. Rather, it now masquerades as a 'theory' of its own, under the name of the 'random walk model'. Proud claims to have found that a particular variable follows a random walk are what I have in mind when I speak of the cynicism of modern econometrics. They are in truth a statement by the investigator that he has found nothing to say about what causes the variable to change.

BIBLIOGRAPHY

Akhtar, M. A. and Weiller, K. (1987) 'Developments in international capital mobility: a perspective on the underlying forces and empirical literature', Research Paper 8711, in *International Integration of Financial Markets and U.S. Monetary Policy*, Federal Reserve Bank of New York, December.

Allen, H. and Taylor, M. (1989) 'Charts, noise and fundamentals: a study of the London foreign exchange market', Discussion Paper 341, Centre for Economic Policy Research, London.

Artis, M. and Taylor, M. (1990) 'Abolishing exchange control: the UK experience', in A. S. Courakis and M. P. Taylor (eds) *Private Behaviour and Government Policy in Interdependent Economies*, Oxford: Clarendon Press, pp. 129–58.

Barro, R. and Gordon, D. (1983) 'A positive theory of monetary policy in a natural rate model', *Journal of Political Economy* 91 (4): 589–610.

Bertero, E. and Mayer, C. (1989) 'Structure and performance: global interdependence of stock markets around the crash of October 1987', Discussion Paper 307, Centre for Economic Policy Research, London.

Bhandari, J. and Genberg, H. (1989) 'International interdependence of stock markets and exchange rate movements', International Monetary Fund.

Bilson, J. (1985) 'Macroeconomic stability and flexible exchange rates', American Economic Review 75: 62–7.

Caramazza, F., Clinton, K., Côté, A. and Longworth, D. (1986) 'International capital mobility and asset substitutability: some theory and evidence on recent structural changes', Technical Report 44, Bank of Canada.

Cornell, B. (1982) 'Money supply announcements, interest rates, and foreign exchange', Journal of International Money and Finance 1 (August): 201–8.

Cumby, R. and Obstfeld, M. (1981) 'Exchange rate expectations and nominal interest differentials: a test of the Fisher hypothesis', Journal of Finance 36: 697–703.

Dominguez, K. (1986) 'Expectations formation in the foreign exchange market: new evidence from survey data', Economic Letters.

Dominguez, K. and Frankel, J. (1990) 'Does foreign exchange intervention matter? Disentangling the portfolio and expectations effects for the mark', Working Paper 3299, National Bureau of Economic Research, May.

Dooley, M. P. and Isard, P. (1980) 'Capital controls, political risk, and deviations from interest-rate parity', Journal of Political Economy 88 (2): 370–84.

Dornbusch, R. (1976) 'Expectations and exchange rate dynamics', Journal of Political Economy 84 (December): 1161–74.

Engel, C. and Frankel, J. (1982) 'Why money announcements move interest rates: an answer from the foreign exchange market', Working Paper 1049, National Bureau of Economic Research, in Journal of Monetary Economics 13 (January): 31–9.

Fama, E. (1984) 'Forward and spot exchange rates', Journal of Monetary Economics 14: 319–38.

Federal Reserve Bank of New York (1989) 'Summary of results of U.S. foreign exchange market survey conducted April 1989', Press release, 13 September.

Feldstein, M. and Horioka, C. (1980) 'Domestic saving and international capital flows', Economic Journal 90: 314–29.

Frankel, J. (1979) 'On the mark: a theory of floating exchange rates based on real interest differentials', American Economic Review 69 (4): 601–22. Reprinted in R. MacDonald and M. Taylor (eds) Exchange Rate Economics, vol. I, International Library of Critical Writings in Economics, Cheltenham: Edward Elgar.

—— (1982) 'A technique for extracting a measure of expected inflation from the interest rate term structure', Review of Economics and Statistics 64 (1): 135–41.

—— (1984) 'The yen/dollar agreement: liberalizing Japanese capital markets', Policy Analyses in International Economics 9, Washington, DC: Institute for International Economics.

—— (1988) 'International capital flows and domestic economic policies', in M. Feldstein (ed.) The United States in the World Economy, Chicago, IL: University of Chicago Press.

—— (1989) 'International nominal targeting (INT): a proposal for overcoming obstacles to policy coordination', in J. McCallum and R. Mundell (eds) Global Disequilibrium in the World Economy, special issue of Rivista di Politica Economica 79 (12): 257–94, Rome, December.

—— (1991) 'Quantifying international capital mobility in the 1980s', in D. Bernheim and J. Shoven (eds) National Saving and Economic Performance, Chicago, IL: University of Chicago Press, pp. 227–60.

Frankel, J. and Froot, K. (1987) 'Using survey data to test standard propositions regarding exchange rate expectations', American Economic Review 77 (1).

—— and —— (1990a) 'Chartists, fundamentalists, and the demand for dollars', in S. Courakis and M. Taylor (eds) Private Behaviour and Government Policy in Independent Economies, Oxford: Clarendon Press, pp. 73–126. Also in Greek Economic Review (1988) 10 (1): 49–102.

—— and —— (1990b) 'Exchange rate forecasting techniques, survey data, and implications for the foreign exchange market', Working Paper 90/43, International Monetary Fund, May.

Frankel, J. and Hardouvelis, G. (1985) 'Commodity prices, money surprises and Fed credibility', Journal of Money, Credit, and Banking 17 (4): 425–38.

Frankel, J. and Lown, C. (1991) 'An indicator of future inflation extracted from the steepness of the interest rate yield curve along its entire length', NBER Working Paper 3751 and Federal Reserve Bank of New York Research Paper 9122, June.

Frankel, J. and MacArthur, A. (1988) 'Political vs. currency premia in international real interest differentials: a study of forward rates for 24 countries', European Economic Review 32 (June): 1083–121. Reprinted in R. MacDonald and M. Taylor (eds) (1992) Exchange Rate Economics, vol. II, International Library of Critical Writings in Economics, Cheltenham: Edward Elgar.

Frankel, J. and Rockett, K. (1988) 'International macroeconomic policy coordination when policymakers do not agree on the true model', American Economic Review 78 (3): 318–40.

French, K. and Roll, R. (1986) 'Stock return variances: the arrival of information and the reaction of traders', Journal of Financial Economics 17 (1): 5–26.

Frenkel, J. and Levich, R. (1975) 'Covered interest arbitrage: unexploited profits?', *Journal of Political Economy* 83 (2): 325–38.

—— and —— (1977) 'Transaction costs and interest arbitrage: tranquil versus turbulent periods', *Journal of Political Economy* 85 (6): 1209–26.

Froot, K. and Frankel, J. (1989) 'Forward discount bias: is it an exchange risk premium?', *Quarterly Journal of Economics* 104 (416) issue 1 (February): 139–61. To be reprinted in R. Thaler (ed.) *Advances in Behavioral Finance*, New York: Russell Sage Foundation.

Froot, K. and Ito, T. (1989) 'On the consistency of short-run and long-run exchange rate expectations', *Journal of International Money and Finance* 8 (4): 487–510.

Ghosh, A. and Masson, P. (1988) 'International policy coordination in a world with model uncertainty', *IMF Staff Papers* 35 (2): 230–58.

Goodhart, C. (1988) 'The foreign exchange market: a random walk with a dragging anchor', *Economica* 55 (November): 437–60.

Goodhart, C. and Figliuoli, L. (1991) 'Every minute counts in financial markets', *Journal of International Money and Finance* 10: 23–52.

Goodhart, C. and Giugale, M. (1988) 'From hour to hour in the foreign exchange market', Financial Markets Discussion Paper 33, London School of Economics, September.

Grubaugh, S. and Sumner, S. (1989) 'Commodity prices, money surprises, and Fed credibility: a comment', *Journal of Money, Credit, and Banking* 21 (3): 407–8.

Hardouvelis, G. (1984) 'Market perceptions of federal reserve policy and weekly monetary announcements', *Journal of Monetary Economics* 15 (September): 225–40.

Holtham, G. and Hughes Hallett, A. (1987) 'International policy coordination and model uncertainty', in R.C. Bryant and R. Portes (eds) *Global Macroeconomics: Policy Conflict and Cooperation*, London: Macmillan.

Ito, T. (1990) 'Volatility, volume of trade, and heterogeneity', paper presented at the American Economics Association Meetings, December.

Johnson, M. (1988) 'Current perspectives on monetary policy', *Cato Journal* 8 (Fall): 253–60.

Kasman, B. and Pigott, C. (1988) 'Interest rate divergences among the major industrial nations', *Federal Reserve Bank of New York Quarterly Review* 13 (3): 28–44.

Kenen, P. (1987) 'Exchange rates and policy coordination', Brookings Discussion Paper 61, Washington, DC: Brookings Institution, October.

—— (1990) 'The coordination of macroeconomic policies', in W. Branson, J. Frenkel and M. Goldstein (eds) *International Policy Coordination and Exchange Rate Fluctuation*, Chicago, IL: University of Chicago Press.

Kim, Y.-C. and Stulz, R. (1988) 'The Eurobond market and corporate financial policy: a test of the clientele hypothesis', *Journal of Financial Economics* 22: 189–205.

Koedijk, K. G. and Ott, M. (1987) 'Risk aversion, efficient markets and the forward exchange rate', *Federal Reserve Bank of St Louis Review* 69 (10): 5–13.

Kreicher, L. (1982) 'Eurodollar arbitrage', *Federal Reserve Bank of New York Quarterly Review* 7 (2): 10–12.

Kydland, F. E. and Prescott, E. C. (1977) 'Rules rather than discretion: the inconsistency of optimal plans', *Journal of Political Economy* 85 (June): 473–91.

Lown, C. (1989) 'Interest rate spreads, commodity prices, and the dollar: a new strategy for monetary policy?', *Federal Reserve Bank of Dallas Economic Review*, July.

Marr, M. W. and Trimble, J. (1988) 'Domestic versus Euromarket bond sale: a persistent borrowing advantage', Tulane University.

Marston, R. (1988) 'Exchange rate coordination', in M. Feldstein (ed.) *International Economic Cooperation*, Chicago, IL: University of Chicago Press.

McKinnon, R. (1984) *An International Standard for Monetary Stabilization*, Policy Analyses in International Economics 8, Washington, DC: Institute for International Economics.

—— (1987) 'Monetary and exchange rate policies for international financial stability: a proposal', Stanford University, Stanford, CA.

Mishkin, F. (1984a) 'Are real interest rates equal across countries? An empirical investigation of international parity conditions', *Journal of Finance* 39: 1345–58.

—— (1984b) 'The real interest rate: a multi-country empirical study', *Canadian Journal of Economics* 17 (2): 283–311.

—— (1988) 'What does the term structure tell us about expected inflation?', Working Paper 2626, National Bureau of Economic Research.

—— (1989) 'The information in the longer-maturity term structure about future inflation', Columbia University, Graduate School of Business, March.

Popper, H. (1990) 'International capital mobility: direct evidence from long-term currency swaps', *International Finance Discussion Papers 386*, Federal Reserve Board, September.

Reinhart, V. and Weiller, K. (1987) 'Increasing capital mobility: evidence from short-term and long-term markets', in Federal Reserve Bank of New York, *Research Papers on International Integration of Financial Markets and U.S. Monetary Policy*, December.

Rogoff, K. (1985) 'The optimal degree of commitment to an intermediate monetary target', *Quarterly Journal of Economics* 100 (November): 1169–89.

Schulmeister, S. (1987) 'An essay on exchange rate dynamics', Research Unit Labor Market and Employment Discussion Paper 87–8, Wissenschaftzentrum Berlin für Sozialforschung.

Taylor, M. and Allen, H. (1992) 'The use of technical analysis in the foreign exchange market', *Journal of International Money and Finance* 11 (3): 304–14.

Von Furstenberg, G.M. and Nam Jeon, B. (1989) 'International stock price movements: links and messages', *Brookings Papers on Economic Activity* 1: 125–80.

Williamson, J. (1985) *The Exchange Rate System*, Policy Analyses in International Economics 5, Washington, DC: Institute for International Economics.

Williamson, J. and Miller, M. (1987) *Targets and Indicators: A Blueprint for the International Coordination of Economic Policy*, Policy Analyses in International Economics 22, Washington, DC: Institute for International Economics.

17

FOREIGN EXCHANGE RATE EXPECTATIONS

Micro survey data

Takatoshi Ito

As rational expectations have become a popular benchmark for thinking about financial and macroeconomic hypotheses, many economists have become more interested in directly measuring the expectations of market participants. Although survey data for many domestic variables, including interest rates and inflation rates, have been frequently analysed by many investigators (see, for example, Mishkin 1983: ch. 4), it is only recently that survey data on foreign exchange rates have become available and been analysed. Dominguez (1986) and Frankel and Froot (1987a, b) have exploited the survey data made available by the Money Market Service (MMS), the *Amex Bank Review* and the *Economist Financial Report*.[1]

In the surveys that were investigated by Dominguez and by Frankel and Froot only the median responses were reported. Heterogeneity among market participants, if it exists, had been aggregated out. If the market consists of homogeneous agents that share the same forecasting model with common beliefs (priors) and information, then the median response will describe the market sufficiently well in terms of forecasts. However, if market participants differ in the forecasting characteristics, then focusing on the median misses the most interesting questions, such as whether the differences persist or are temporary, whether the differences are correlated with the participant's traits and whether a rationality hypothesis is more likely to be rejected in individual data. Only individual responses of survey data can answer these questions.

In this chapter, I shall use the survey data collected by the Japan Center for International Finance (JCIF) in Tokyo, which allows me to investigate the individual responses in the survey. In particular, the JCIF data set has two distinct advantages over the data used by Dominguez and by Frankel and Froot. First, the JCIF data consist of individual responses with no missing observations. This is the first attempt to study the individual responses of exchange rate expectations, although individual responses of inflation expectations have been studied by Figlewski and Wachtel (1981). Second, not only financial institutions but other companies as well are polled in the JCIF survey. Therefore there is a chance to associate possible heterogeneity with the traits of the forecasters' industry.

There are four major findings in this chapter. First, market participants are found to be heterogeneous. There are significant 'individual effects' in their expectation formation. Second, the individual effects have characteristics of 'wishful expectations': exporters expect a yen depreciation (relative to others) and importers expect a yen appreciation (relative to others). Third, many institutions are found to violate the rational expectations hypothesis. Most of them underestimated the degree of yen appreciation. Fourth, forecasts with long horizons showed less yen appreciation than those with short horizons. Put differently, market participants appear to have a 'bandwagon' expectation in the short run, but a 'stabilizing' one in the long run. The 'twist' in forecast term structure could be 'consistent' (in the sense of Froot and Ito (1989)) if an iterated substitution of a short-term forecast yields a long-term forecast. However, cross-equation constraints implied by the consistency are strongly rejected.

DATA SUMMARY

The data description

The JCIF has conducted telephone surveys twice a month, in the middle and at the end of the month, on Wednesdays, since May 1985. Forecasts of the yen–dollar exchange rate for the one-, three- and six-month horizons are obtained from foreign exchange experts in forty-four companies, including fifteen banks and brokers, four securities companies, six trading companies, nine export-oriented companies, five life insurance companies and five import-oriented industries.[2] Each respondent is asked to give a point forecast for each horizon. In this chapter I assume that reported forecasts are the subjective means of respondents. We do not have any data on the subjective variance or range. The survey is meticulously arranged so that all forty-four companies on the permanent list respond every week.

When a data set is analysed as panel data, the mean across individuals and the mean across time should not be confused. In the following, the mean across forty-four individuals at a time will be referred to as the (cross-section, total) average; the mean across individuals at a time in an industry group will be referred to as the group average. The mean across time of an individual, of a group or of the 'average' will be referred to as the (time) mean of the individual, of the group or of the average, respectively.

The JCIF calculates the total average, the standard deviation, the maximum and the minimum of the forty-four responses and also the industry group averages and the group standard deviations. On the day after the survey, the JCIF informs its subscribers, including those who are polled, of the summary statistics. The total average is also released to the press and other media.

I shall use, in addition to the panel data of the forty-four companies, the public information part of the survey, the cross-section average (AVE) and the group averages for the different industries: banks (BAN), securities companies (SEC), trading companies (TRA), companies in the export industries (EXP), insurance companies (INS) and companies in the import industries (IMP). The unit is yen per US dollar, so that a negative movement indicates a yen 'appreciation'. The spot exchange rate $s(t)$ is measured at the closing quote in Tokyo on Wednesday of the survey week.

Overview

Table 17.1 shows the time means of (unconditional) expected changes (in per cent) from the spot rate at the time of the survey for the cross-section total average and the group averages, and Table 17.2 shows the same for each individual. For the purposes of discussion, the actual (ex post) changes of the spot exchange rate (ACT) for each horizon are reported in the same table. For each horizon and each individual or group, subtracting the actual changes from the forecasts produces the forecast errors.

In the one-month horizon, the (total) average on a typical week showed an expected 1.4 per cent yen appreciation. The group averages ranged from a 0.8 per cent to a 2 per cent appreciation. Relative to the total average, the export industry was the most biased towards a yen depreciation, and the trading companies and the import industries were the most biased towards a yen appreciation. Looking at individual data, one extreme predicted a 1.4 per cent depreciation of the yen, while the other extreme predicted a 3.1 per cent appreciation. The distribution of individual forecasts has a nice unimodal distribution. The average expected appreciation of the yen in the three-month horizon was 1.4 per cent, about the same as in the one-month horizon. (Note that no adjustment is made with respect to the length of horizon.)

As in the one-month horizon, the export industry shows a yen depreciation bias (from the total average) and the trading companies show a

Table 17.1 Time mean of $s_j^e(t, k) - s(t)$,[a] May 1985–June 1987 (number of observations, 51)

Horizon	1 month	3 month	6 month
AVE	−1.420	−1.431	−0.044
BAN	−1.404	−1.658	−0.957
SEC	−1.097	−0.834	+0.621
TRA	−1.956	−2.453	−0.948
EXP	−0.775	−0.137	+1.736
INS	−1.746	−2.309	+0.302
IMP	−1.937	−1.536	−0.430
ACT	−2.064	−5.970	−11.987

Note: [a] Mean of the (unconditional) expected changes (in per cent). Not annualized or adjusted for k.

yen appreciation bias in the three-month horizon. A wide disagreement among individuals begins to appear in the three-month forecasts. It becomes a bimodal distribution: one group believes that the yen depreciates from the one-month to three-month forecast horizon, while the other believes that the yen continues to appreciate.

For the six-month horizon, the total average shows that the market expects the yen to return to nearly the prevailing level at the time of forecast. This is a sharp turnaround from the forecast of a 1.4 per cent yen appreciation in three months. In fact, each of the group averages indicates that the group anticipates less yen appreciation in the six-month horizon than in either the one-month or the three-month horizon.

The findings of this subsection can be summarized and related to the contents of the rest of this chapter. First, the findings are highly suggestive of heterogeneous market participants. A rigorous analysis and interpretation of the heterogeneity will be provided in the section on rationality of expectations. Second, large forecast errors were recorded during the intermittent waves of yen appreciation after September 1985. Econometric tests on various forms of the rational expectation hypothesis will be conducted in the penultimate section. Third, the total average and most of the group averages have a 'twist' in their forecasts, a yen appreciation in the short horizon and a yen depreciation in the long horizon. The final section

Table 17.2 Unconditional expected change, distribution among individual respondents of the time mean of forecasted changes in the exchange rate over the specified horizon

Horizon 1 month	3 month	6 month
per cent +5.0		
		×
		××
	×	
		××××
	×	××××
×		×
	××	××××
0.0 ×	××	××××
××	×××	××××
××××	×××××××××	×××××
×××××××××××××××	×	××××××
×××××××××××	×××××××	×
×××××××	×××××××	××
××	××××	×
×	××	××
	×	×
	××	
	×	×
−5.5		×
max 1.41	max 3.25	max 4.62
min −3.10	min −4.76	min −5.20

Note: ×, one respondent.

investigates whether such twists in expectations are internally consistent.

WISHFUL EXPECTATIONS AND HETEROGENEITY

Econometric issue – a special case of panel data

Recall that our micro survey data set consists of forty-four individuals and fifty-one observations. Suppose that an individual forecast formation at time t consists of a common structural part based on public information, $f[I(t)]$, and an individual effect, g_j. For a given forecast horizon k (suppressed notation) the expected exchange rate for individual j, $j = 1, \ldots, J$ (where in this chapter $J = 44$) is

$$s_j^e(t) = f[I(t)] + g_j + u_j(t), \qquad (17.1)$$

where $s_j^e(t)$ is a k-step-ahead forecast of the spot exchange rate at time t by individual j and $u_j(t)$ is a pure random disturbance (with respect to j and t) representing, for example, a measurement or a rounding error. The cross-section average of individual forecasts $s_{AVE}^e(t)$ is defined as

$$s_{AVE}^e(t) = f[I(t)] + g_{AVE} + u_{AVE}(t) \quad (17.2)$$

where $x_{AVE}(t) = E x_j(t)/J$ with $x = s^e$, g and u. Assume that $f[I(t)]$ contains a constant term so that normalization, $g_{AVE} = 0$, is possible. Then subtracting each side of (17.2) from the corresponding side of (17.1) we obtain

$$\begin{aligned} &s_j^e(t) - s_{AVE}^e(t) \\ &= g_j + [u_j(t) - u_{AVE}(t)]. \end{aligned} \qquad (17.3)$$

The estimator of the individual effect g_j can be obtained by regressing the left-hand side of (17.3) on a constant over the sample period (across time). This procedure is simple and robust. It is unnecessary for the econometrician to know the exact structure of $f[I(t)]$ as long as it is common to everybody for every survey date.

If the difference in the individual effects of two individuals is to be estimated, a similar method can be employed.

$$\begin{aligned} s_j^e(t) - s_h^e(t) = g_j - g_h + [u_j(t) - u_h(t)], \\ h \neq j. \qquad (17.4) \end{aligned}$$

A (composite) disturbance term in equations (17.3) and (17.4) has mean zero and no serial correlations if $u_j(t)$ is serially and cross-sectionally uncorrelated and $f[I(t)]$ is exactly common to all individuals.

If the difference in individual beliefs extends to 'idiosyncratic' coefficients on publicly available information in the structural part $f[I(t)]$, the above procedure needs to be modified but is still applicable. Suppose, for example, that the forecast is in an extrapolative form:

$$\begin{aligned} s_j^e(t) - s(t) &= a_j + b_{1j}[s(t-1) - s(t)] \\ &\quad + b_{2j}[s(t-2) - s(t-1)] \\ &\quad + u_j(t), \end{aligned}$$

$$(17.5)$$

where g_j is the difference in a_j. Then the idiosyncratic individual coefficients can be estimated by regressing the following equation for all j:

$$\begin{aligned} &s_j^e(t) - s_{AVE}^e(t) \\ &= a_j - a_{AVE} \\ &\quad + (b_{1j} - b_{1AVE})[s(t-1) - s(t)] \\ &\quad + (b_{2j} - b_{2AVE})[s(t-2) - s(t-1)] \\ &\quad + u_j(t) - u_{AVE}. \end{aligned} \qquad (17.6)$$

The above procedure parallels the technique in the panel data analysis, although in the usual examples of panel data analysis the right-hand side variables take different values for different individuals. Instead, it is reasonable here to assume that the structural part and the values of regressors (i.e. the past values of the exchange rates) in exchange rate forecasts are identical for all individuals, but with possibly different coefficients.

Heterogeneous participants in the Tokyo market

In search of hard evidence for (or against) heterogeneity among market participants, I estimate forty-four individual effects g_j and 'group effects'. In detecting the group effect, a group average forecast calculated by the JCIF is treated as an individual j, and then the total average (or another group average) is subtracted.[3]

The individual (or group) effects g_j, estimated using equation (17.3), are reported in Tables 17.3 and 17.4.[4]

From Table 17.3 we learn that, for any horizon, group effects are significant for the export industry, with a depreciation bias, and for the trading companies, with an appreciation bias. A significant appreciation bias was also detected for the import industry for the one-month horizon, for

Table 17.3 Group deviations from the total average, for each horizon

	1 month		3 month		6 month	
	a	DW or ρ	a	DW or ρ	a	DW or ρ
BAN	0.017	0.284	−0.228	0.530	−0.941	0.371
t statistic	(0.25)	(2.04)	(−1.28)	(4.29)	(−5.74)[a]	(2.81)
SEC	0.305	0.438	0.561	0.421	0.743	0.446
t statistic	(1.25)	(3.38)	(1.62)	(3.14)	(1.47)	(3.49)
TRA	−0.536	DW = 2.13	−1.022	DW = 1.61	−0.908	0.467
t statistic	(−4.98)[a]		(−7.56)[a]		(−2.57)[a]	(3.61)
EXP	0.645	DW = 2.07	1.294	DW = 1.62	1.832	0.435
t statistic	(8.55)[a]		(12.68)[a]		(6.11)[a]	(3.41)
INS	−0.326	0.474	−0.815	0.645	0.301	0.661
t statistic	(−1.54)	(3.72)	(−1.93)[a]	(5.86)	(0.54)	(5.99)
IMP	−0.517	DW = 1.47	−0.079	0.301	−0.434	0.422
t statistic	(−3.76)[a]		(−0.29)	(2.17)	(−1.39)	(3.27)

Notes: DW, Durbin–Watson coefficient.
  [a] Value indicates the 'heterogeneous' group at the level of 1 per cent.

the insurance industry for the three-month horizon and for the banking sector for the six-month horizon.

The distinctive effect of exporters in contrast to importers or to trading companies can be highlighted by measuring the difference in individual effects directly, as in equation (17.4). (This is not reported here; see Ito (1988b).) Exporters have a depreciation bias in their expectation formation compared with importers and trading companies for any horizon. Table 17.4 shows that, for any horizon, about half of the forty-four individuals have a significant bias in their forecasts. The deviations are sometimes very large.

One might object to a formulation of the individual effects in the form of biases in the constant term. They could have different models. Since it is not likely that the JCIF or the econometrician could persuade each forecaster to justify the forecast with a model every week, we have to guess the form, assuming that each market participant has a common autoregressive forecasting model but with different coefficients on the lag terms (possibly because of differences in their prior beliefs). As discussed above, idiosyncratic coefficients can be estimated from equation (17.6). The results are shown in Table 17.5.

Table 17.4 Wishful expectations, distribution of individual effects

	Horizon		
	1 month	3 month	6 month
per cent +5.0		✕	✕
			✕✕
		✕	✕
			✕
	✕		✕o
		✕✕	o
	✕	✕✕o	✕o
	✕		✕✕oo
	✕✕✕oo	oooooooooo	ooo
0.0	✕oooooooooooo	o	ooo
	✕ooooooooooo	ooooooo	ooooo
	✕✕✕ooo	oooooooo	ooooo
	✕✕✕✕	✕✕✕o	✕✕oo
	✕	✕o	✕o
		✕	✕o
		✕✕	✕
		✕	✕✕
		✕	
−5.5			o
			✕✕

Notes: ✕, significant individual effects; o, insignificant individual effects.

Table 17.5 Idiosyncratic effects: extrapolative form

$$s_j^e(t) - s_{AVE}^e(t) = a_j - a_{AVE} + (b_{1j} - b_{1AVE})[s(t-1) - s(t)] + (b_{2j} - b_{2AVE})[s(t-2) - s(t-1)] + u_j(t) - u_{AVE}$$

	1 lag ($b_2 = 0$)						2 lags					
	1 month		3 month		6 month		1 month		3 month		6 month	
	H0	H1	H0	H1	H0	H1	H0	H1	H0	H1	H0	H1
BAN F	0.122	0.103	2.51	2.48	2.34	18.19	0.433	0.338	2.60	3.13	0.732	17.3
sig	0.729	0.903	0.120	0.095	0.133	0.00*	0.651	0.798	0.086	0.035	0.487	0.00*
SEC F	0.815	1.37	0.037	1.41	0.000	1.03	0.699	1.51	0.281	1.32	0.032	0.740
sig	0.371	0.265	0.847	0.253	0.984	0.367	0.502	0.224	0.756	0.280	0.968	0.533
TRA F	0.461	21.0	0.390	24.6	0.652	5.16	1.69	16.76	1.91	18.0	0.583	4.01
sig	0.500	0.00*	0.535	0.00*	0.423	0.009*	0.196	0.00*	0.161	0.00	0.562	0.013
EXP F	4.28	40.5	2.16	66.44	0.557	18.33	2.29	52.1	2.88	64.8	0.186	18.6
sig	0.044	0.00*	0.148	0.00*	0.459	0.00*	0.113	0.00*	0.067	0.00*	0.831	0.00*
INS F	0.429	2.12	2.29	3.56	3.49	1.89	0.347	1.68	1.12	2.71	1.46	1.14
sig	0.516	0.132	0.317	0.037	0.068	0.162	0.708	0.186	0.335	0.056	0.242	0.345
IMP F	3.68	7.70	1.36	0.726	1.29	2.31	1.73	5.41	1.08	0.763	1.07	1.93
sig	0.061	0.001*	0.249	0.489	0.262	0.110	0.188	0.003	0.347	0.521	0.352	0.139

Notes: F, F statistics; sig, significance level; H0, no idiosyncratic coefficient effects, $b = 0$ (allowing for individual effect of a constant bias); H1, no idiosyncratic coefficient of individual (constant) effect, $a = b = 0$.

Table 17.5 once again shows that exporters and trading companies are significantly heterogeneous for each of the three horizons. However, the differences come from the biases in the individual (constant-term) effects, not from the idiosyncratic coefficients of the lagged variables. Importers for the one-month horizon and banks for the six-month horizon also show the individual (constant) effect, as in Table 17.3, but fail to show the idiosyncratic coefficients on the lagged variables. Therefore, the heterogeneity is more like a constant bias rather than the differences in reacting to the recent changes in the exchange rate. Tables 17.3–17.5 show solid evidence for heterogeneous expectation formations among market participants.

Discussion: heterogeneity and rational expectations

Most of the modern theory of finance and macroeconomics assumes the existence of a representative agent whose decision is an aggregate of those of market participants. In fact, the hypothesis of rational expectations would require that market participants be homogeneous in their formation of expectations since the true stochastic process is unique. Therefore, findings of heterogeneity in this section cast some doubts on the homogeneous agent framework commonly used in finance and macroeconomics.

One might argue that, if agents have private information that econometricians do not observe, the existence of individual effects may not be inconsistent with rational expectations. However, important news and variables in the foreign exchange market are generally common knowledge. In fact, even if the individual information sets are different, the difference in expectations conditional on a common (i.e. intersection) information set should be unbiased. The constant term, which detects individual effects, is certainly contained in the common information set. Thus, the finding of significant individual biases rejects rational expectations.[5]

Put differently, under the assumption of rational expectations but private information, the forecast differences across individuals, i.e. the dependent variables in equations (17.3) and (17.4), must be serially uncorrelated, contrary to our findings, provided that lagged group average forecasts are part of the common information set (which is the case in the JCIF survey as explained in the first part of this section).

One possible explanation of heterogeneity consistent with rational expectations would be a slow learning process due to a strongly biased prior. However, one has to model a learning process to assert this. Then we would be able to discuss how biases can be related to individual priors and learning processes. This is beyond the scope of this chapter.

Discussion: wishful expectations

Having established heterogeneity, a discussion of why certain market participants have depreciation or appreciation biases is in order. From Tables 17.3 and 17.4 we notice some regularity in the group effects: in the one-month-ahead forecasts, exporters have a depreciation bias while importers have an appreciation bias. The exporters' forecasts show a continuing deviation from the mean, significantly biased toward a yen depreciation, as the forecast horizon lengthens. In the three-month-ahead and six-month-ahead predictions, trading companies, as opposed to importers, show a bias towards appreciation.

Exporters tend to be long in dollars and importers short in dollars. It is difficult to cover the exposure to the foreign exchange risk completely since the forward markets exist only up to a one-year horizon and timings of trade and financial transactions cannot be matched exactly.

Therefore exporters wish that the yen will depreciate in the future, enabling their profit margins to increase and their products to compete better in the foreign markets. (This argument rests on an assumption of incomplete 'pass-through', which is documented, for example, by Krugman (1987) and Ohno (1988).) Their responses, being biased towards a yen depreciation relative to the average, seem to agree with their wishes.

In contrast, importers' responses reflect their wish for a stronger yen so that their import costs will decrease given incomplete pass-through. Note

that the group effect of trading companies behaves like that of import industries. One might think that the change in the exchange rate would be neutral for trading companies, since they are just intermediaries of imports and exports. However, the leading Japanese trading companies handle more imports than exports. In 1983, the revenues of the leading nine trading companies were derived from export-oriented activities for 20.0 per cent, import-oriented activities for 23.6 per cent, domestic activities for 40.3 per cent and trade between foreign countries for 16.1 per cent (Shinohara 1986: 164).

Hence, the findings show that market participants apparently form 'wishful expectations'. (A 'Chicago test' for the validity of survey data would be to check whether money is where the mouth is. But the result here shows that people 'put the mouth where the money is'.) These 'wishful expectations' – or an 'optimist' view in Hey's (1984) sense – may be a reflection of non-rational honest mistakes in expectation formation. A straightforward interpretation would be for respondents to mix wishful thinking with objective forecasts.[6] However, there are a few deeper explanations of wishful expectations.[7]

The Japanese manufacturing and trading companies usually set an in-house exchange rate for internal accounting, and the rate can be used for co-ordinating the sales department with the other departments. It is possible that these in-house rates are heterogeneous, and moreover are slightly biased so that the sales department is encouraged. The survey responses from these companies may be influenced by the biased in-house exchange rate, although the respondent is not from the sales department.

If the announcement of the JCIF survey is very influential on the market, the respondent may be induced to try manipulating the announced survey result by answering with biased forecasts. Exporters respond to the JCIF by announcing a depreciated rate, but only slightly depreciated so as to avoid obvious detection, in the hope that the survey mean is biased towards depreciation. Exporters hope that the mean expectation with an 'unexpected' depreciating bias could cause others to start selling yen, thus creating a self-fulfilling prophecy; if importers understand that exporters have incentives to lie, then importers would counter by manipulating their announcements, and vice versa. Thus, as a Nash equilibrium, the mean may not be biased after all, although exporters and importers are biased.

Despite its appeal to economists who are trained to think seriously about expectation and manipulation, this story of a manipulative motive has a few shortcomings. First, the size of survey, i.e. forty-four respondents, is large enough that a manipulation by one respondent is insignificant unless the bias is large enough to be easily detected by the JCIF. Second, if other participants understand that exporters and importers have incentives to lie, then they would not take the JCIF survey seriously, thereby removing the incentive to lie. It may be the case that market participants are simply naive in forming wishful expectations.

RATIONALITY OF EXPECTATIONS

Tests of unbiasedness and orthogonality

In this section I shall apply standard tests of rational expectations to these survey data.[8] First, if the forecasts are rational, the forecast errors should be random. In other words, survey forecasts should be unbiased. Second, given rational expectations, forecast errors should be uncorrelated with (orthogonal to) any information available at the time the forecast is made. Otherwise, the variable correlated with the *ex post* error could have been exploited to make a better forecast.

Under the null hypothesis of rational expectations, the realized spot rate is the sum of a forecast and a forecast error:

$$s(t + k) = s^e(t, k) - h(t, k), \quad (17.7)$$

where $h(t, k)$ is the mean zero forecast error, uncorrelated with any variables available at t. It is well known that forecast errors are serially correlated if the forecast horizon is longer than the

observational frequency, i.e. $k > 2$. Therefore, rational expectations imply that $a = 0$ and $b = 1$ in the following regression:

$$s(t + k) - s(t)$$
$$= a + b[s^e(t, k) - s(t)] + u(t). \quad (17.8)$$

The test statistics are calculated using the generalized method of moments to take care of the serial correlations of $u(t)$. Results of this unbiasedness test are reported in Table 17.6(a).

Unbiasedness is rejected for trading companies and insurance companies for the one-month horizon, for securities and import companies for the three-month horizon and for all groups except banks and import industries for the six-month horizon. These rejections are evidence for rejecting a rational expectations hypothesis in that market participants had unbiased forecasts. We would miss some rejections if we were only to look at the average of the forty-four participants since, for the one-month and three-month horizons, rejections by some groups are not detected in the average for all participants.[9]

The second implication of rational expectations is orthogonality: under the null hypothesis, forecast errors $h(t, k) = s^e(t, k) - s(t + k)$ are uncorrelated with any information $z(t)$ at time t. In the literature, the past forecast errors $s^e(t - k, k) - s(t)$, the forward premium $f(t, k) - s(t)$ or the recent actual change $s(t - k) - s(t)$ have been popular candidates for variables in the information set. I shall follow the standard procedure by regressing the *ex post* forecast errors on these candidate variables:

$$s^e(t, k) + s(t + k)$$
$$= a + b[z(t) - s(t)] + e(t), \quad (17.9)$$

where $z(t) = s^e(t - k, k), f(t, k), s(t - k)$. Rational expectations (orthogonality) is a null hypothesis of $a = b = 0$. Results of the estimation of equation (17.9), with $z(t) = s(t - k)$, and the test of the null hypothesis are reported in Table 17.6(b). (Results for other cases of $z(t)$ are essentially the same and are

Table 17.6 Tests of rational expectations

	Estimates and standard errors of a and b; χ^2 and significance level for AVE			Number of cases in group data			Number of cases in micro data		
	1 month	3 month	6 month	1 month	3 month	6 month	1 month	3 month	6 month
(a) Unbiasedness									
a	−0.028 (0.017)	−0.043 (0.034)	−0.119 (0.041)						
b	−0.485 (0.969)	1.167 (1.167)	0.908 (0.741)						
χ^2	2.59 (0.274)	5.21 (0.074)	10.09 0.006*						
Fail to reject H (at 1 per cent)				4	4	2 (IMP, BAN)			
Reject H (at 1 per cent)	−			2 (TRA, INS)	2 (SEC, IMP)	4			
(b) Orthogonality, past exchange rate movement, with 1 lag									
a	0.004 (0.010)	0.042 (0.025)	0.114 (0.036)						
b	0.166 (0.203)	0.306 (0.225)	0.227 (0.358)						
χ^2	3.883 0.144	9.504 0.009	18.908 (0.000)						
Fail to reject H (at 1 per cent)				5	3	0	37	26	11
Reject H (at 1 per cent)				1 (EXP)	3 (SEC, EXP, IMP)	6	7	18	33
(c) Orthogonality, past exchange rate movement, with 2 lags									
a	0.007 (0.011)	0.043 (0.025)	0.112 (0.034)						
b	0.247 (0.185)	0.330 (0.220)	0.183 (0.299)						
c	−0.323 (0.207)	−0.095 (0.093)	0.174 (0.342)						
χ^2	38.29 (0.000)	14.35 (0.002)	21.75 (0.000)						
Fail to reject H (at 1 per cent)				0	2 (BAN, TRA)	1 (BAN)	11	22	21
Reject H (at 1 per cent)				6	4	5	33	22	23

not reported here. See Ito (1988b).) There are only a few instances of rejections of the one-month and three-month horizons. However, for the six-month horizon the rejection is unanimous. This is consistent with the results of unbiasedness tests. So far, there is little evidence rejecting the rational expectations hypothesis for the shorter horizons.

Variables in the information set are not restricted to those tested above. When the second lagged term is added, the number of rejection cases increases dramatically. The results of estimating the following equation are reported in Table 17.6(c):

$$s^e(t, k) - s(t + k) = a + b_1[s(t - k) - s(t)]$$
$$+ b_2[s(t - k - 1)$$
$$- s(t - 1)] + e(t).$$
$$(17.10)$$

Table 17.6(c) shows rejections for most groups in all horizons. Even if the orthogonality test is conducted at the individual level, about three-quarters of the individuals are judged to be irrational.

Discussion: peso problem and bubbles

Failure of the rationality test in small samples may not imply that expectations are formed irrationally, in view of the often involved caveats of peso problems and bubbles.[10] (See Obstfeld (1987) and Evans (1986) and references therein for discussions of these issues.) Suppose that conditional forecasts were formed rationally taking into account a small probability of a 'crash', but that the crash did not occur in the (small) sample. Then forecasts appear to have been biased when judged from *ex post* forecast errors. This is known as the peso problem. The sample size of this study is admittedly small (about two years), and this could be a reason for a rejection of rationality.

However, the sample period for this study includes a volatile period after the Plaza Agreement of September 1985. (See Ito (1987) for a news analysis of the exchange rate volatility after the Plaza Agreement.) The process of the sharp yen appreciation after the Plaza Agreement can be

regarded as a long-awaited 'crash' of the dollar value. However, market expectations underestimated the magnitude of this crash.[11]

In summary, this section shows that most of the market participants violate necessary conditions of the rational expectations hypothesis. However, these results should be interpreted with caution because they could be a case of a peso problem.

EXPECTATIONAL TWIST

Introduction to twist and consistency

In this section, the consistency of expectation formation of short- versus long-term expectations, as discussed in Froot and Ito (1989), is explored. Frankel and Froot (1987b) showed that the short-term expectations are of the bandwagon type, while the long-term expectations show some regressive characteristics.[12] Thus, I shall first replicate their regressions and then raise the question of how to interpret a 'twist' found in the data.

However, Frankel and Froot (1987b) ignored the consistency issue of short- and long-term expectations formation: if expectations formation is internally consistent, a long-term forecast should be identical to the results of sequential substitutions of short-term forecasts, given a function of expectations formation. The consistency becomes a testable hypothesis in the form of cross-equation constraints on the coefficients of the short- and long-term forecast equations. This consistency problem is parallel to the cross-equation constraints implied in the context of the interest rate term structure (Sargent 1979) and in the context of uncovered interest parity (Ito 1988a; Ito and Quah 1989). Froot and Ito (1989) have applied the test of consistency to the data collected by the MMS for one-week and one-month-ahead forecasts and the *Economist Financial Report* for three-, six- and twelve-month forecasts. They also used the averages from the JCIF data. In this chapter, the same test is applied to the group means of the JCIF data, where one-, three- and six-month forecasts are available.

Table 17.7 Expectation formation, extrapolative expectation with one lag

$$s_j^e(t, k) - s(t) = a + b[s(t-1) - s(t)] + E(t)$$

	1 month			3 month			6 month		
	a	b	χ^2	a	b	χ^2	a	b	χ^2
AVE	−0.015	−0.011	49.42	−0.017	0.137	9.60	−0.002	0.220	5.49
	(0.002)	(0.035)	0.000	(0.005)	(0.050)	0.000	(0.009)	(0.066)	0.002
BAN	−0.014	−0.008	62.85	−0.019	0.087	6.75	−0.011	0.134	2.06
	(0.001)	(0.044)	0.000	(0.005)	(0.056)	0.003	(0.009)	(0.077)	0.139
SEC	−0.011	−0.058	8.05	−0.011	0.149	2.46	0.006	0.224	1.69
	(0.003)	(0.061)	0.001	(0.005)	(0.108)	0.097	(0.009)	(0.141)	0.195
TRA	−0.020	−0.029	69.67	−0.027	0.067	21.42	−0.011	0.194	2.41
	(0.002)	(0.068)	0.000	(0.004)	(0.096)	0.000	(0.006)	(0.120)	0.101
EXP	−0.009	0.061	18.82	−0.004	0.168	3.19	0.016	0.304	6.77
	(0.001)	(0.039)	0.000	(0.004)	(0.068)	0.050	(0.010)	(0.095)	0.003
INS	−0.018	0.015	17.20	−0.027	0.237	18.42	−0.001	0.376	5.79
	(0.003)	(0.067)	0.000	(0.005)	(0.068)	0.000	(0.010)	(0.111)	0.006
IMP	−0.018	−0.134	28.43	−0.019	0.285	6.95	−0.008	0.288	3.60
	(0.003)	(0.075)	0.000	(0.006)	(0.108)	0.002	(0.008)	(0.110)	0.035

Number of cases in micro data

	1 month	3 month	6 month
$b \gg 0$ sig.	3	8	10
$b > 0$ insig.	18	29	31
$b < 0$ insig.	20	7	3
$b \ll 0$ sig.	3	0	0

Notes: Cases: $b < 0$, belief in a bandwagon effect; $b = 0$, belief in constant appreciation; $b > 0$, distributed lag form; H: $= b = 0$, belief in random walk. Estimates of a and b and their (standard errors); χ^2 for hypothesis H: χ^2(df = 2) and (significance level). AR1 process on E is assumed. ρ is not reported here.

An example of extrapolative expectation with one lag

First, let us consider, following Frankel and Froot (1988), the extrapolative expectation with one lag:

$$s^e(t, k) - s(t)$$
$$= a + b[s(t-1) - s(t)] + e(t). \tag{17.11}$$

In (17.11), $b < 0$ implies a (destabilizing) bandwagon effect, while $b > 0$ implies a stabilizing expectation formation. Results are reported in Table 17.7 which shows that the 1 per cent yen appreciation would make the average individual expect a further 0.01 per cent appreciation in one month. However, the table also implies that the shock would make the same individual form an expectation of a 0.13 per cent depreciation in three months and 0.22 per cent depreciation in six months. Although different groups have different biases, the pattern of coefficients,

$$b(\text{one month}) < b(\text{three months})$$
$$< b(\text{six months}),$$

is almost unanimously observed. Hence, we may draw a conclusion, similar to that of Frankel and Froot (1987b), that the long-term expectation is more stabilizing than the short-term expectation.

370

Table 17.8 Consistency tests

One-month vs three-month expectations

$s_j^e(t, 1) - s(t) = d_1 + a_1 s(t) + b_1 s(t-1) + c_1 s(t-2)$
$s_j^e(t, 3) - s(t) = d_3 + a_3 s(t) + b_3 s(t-1) + c_3 s(t-2)$

H: consistency restrictions
$d_3 = [2 + a_1 + b_1 + (1 + a_1)^2] d_1$
$a_3 = c_1 - 1 + 2(1 + a_1)b_1 + (1 + a_1)^3$
$b_3 = (1 + a_1)c_1 + b_1^2 + b_1(1 + a_1)^2$
$c_3 = c_1(1 + a_1)^2 + b_1 c_1$

Estimates
AVE, one-month (OLS)
d_1	−0.0261 (0.0050)
a_1	0.0008 (0.0001)
b_1	0.0001 (0.0002)
c_1	−0.0003 (0.0001)

AVE, three-month (GMM)
d_3	−0.0254 (0.0071)
a_3	−0.0008 (0.0071)
b_3	0.0005 (0.0001)
c_3	0.0003 (0.0001)

AVE, H
χ^2	2,182.1 (0.000)

Three-month vs six-month expectations

$s_j^e(t, 3) - s(t) = d_3 + a_3 s(t) + b_3 s(t-3) + c_3 s(t-6)$
$s_j^e(t, 6) - s(t) = d_6 + a_6 s(t) + b_6 s(t-3) + c_6 s(t-6)$

H: consistency restrictions
$d_6 = (2 + a_3)d_3$
$a_6 = (1 + a_3)^2 + b_3 - 1$
$b_6 = (1 + a_3)b_3 + c_3$
$c_6 = (1 + a_3)c_3$

Estimates
AVE, three-month (OLS)
d	0.0218 (0.0220)
a	−0.0009 (0.0003)
b	0.0004 (0.0003)
c	0.0002 (0.0002)

AVE, six-month (GMM)
D	0.0508 (0.0285)
A	−0.0019 (0.0003)
B	0.0006 (0.0002)
C	0.0008 (0.0001)

AVE, H
χ^2	570.1 (0.000)

Notes: Standard errors are given in parentheses. In the group data, H is rejected for all six groups in both cases. In the micro data, H is rejected for forty-two out of forty-four individuals in both cases.

It is easy to show that so long as the extrapolative expectation with one lag is assumed, a twist, i.e. an appreciation in the short run and a depreciation in the long run, in expectation is impossible. Put differently, the assumed formulation is not rich enough for the observed twist to be consistent.

Consistency tests

Next, we adopt a distributed lag expectation formulation with more than two lags, a formulation rich enough to produce a twist in expectation. Consider estimating the following k-month ($k = 1, 3, 6$) expectation formations:

$$s^e(t, k) = d_k + (1 + a_k)s(t) + b_k s(t-1)$$
$$+ c_k s(t-2) + u_k(t), \qquad (17.12)$$

where $u_k(t)$ are independent random variables representing observation errors. After substitution using the iterated projection (see Froot and Ito 1989), the consistency restrictions as cross-equation constraints are derived (Table 17.8).

Each of two sets of cross-equation restrictions, one-month versus three-month and three-month versus six-month, is tested separately and the results are reported in Table 17.8. The consistency is overwhelmingly rejected in this formulation, too.

Discussion: inconsistency

I hasten to add a caveat. If we misspecify the expectation formation, then the results in this section are not valid. For example, if a policy switch, such as a monetary tightening, is expected to occur around the second month from the point of forecasting, it is 'consistent' to have a twist, although the test in this chapter would not capture it.

One might think that people use different economic variables for forecasting the future spot rate with different horizons. For example, chart (technical) analysis, which is a special case of (univariate) distributed lag expectation formations, is used for the short-term horizon, but other factors come into consideration for the long-term horizon. A list of other factors includes trade balances, inflation rate differentials, interest rate differentials, fiscal deficits and policy switches. However, if these factors are relevant in the long run, they should be relevant in the short run, although the effect may be small in the short run.[13]

CONCLUDING REMARKS

In this chapter, newly available survey data on the expected exchange rate in the Tokyo market were used to test several hypotheses regarding expectation formations. The JCIF data set is better than the data sets previously used by Frankel and Froot (1987a, b) in that the survey includes the expectations of different industries, not only of banks and financial institutions but also of exporters and importers. Moreover, individual responses can be used to avoid the aggregation problem altogether.

The following are the major findings of this chapter. First, market participants are heterogeneous, with constant-term biases in their expectation formations. Second, 'wishful expectations' were found: exporters (importers) are biased towards yen depreciation (appreciation) relative to others. Third, when the usual rationality tests were applied among different groups, the unbiasedness of expectation was rejected in a few instances for shorter horizons and unanimously for the six-month horizon. Orthogonality was soundly rejected. We can conclude that we have strong evidence against rational expectation formation in the Tokyo foreign exchange market. Fourth, consistency is overwhelmingly rejected given that the expectation formation is a distributed lag structure with two lags.

The present chapter suggests that it is important to consider a model with heterogeneous agents for the international financial market. I hope that this chapter stimulates research in this direction.

NOTES

1 Dominguez (1986) used the MMS data from 1983 to 1985 to test a rational expectations hypothesis. Unbiasedness and the independence of forecast errors from the forward premium were tested. She found that survey forecasts were no better than the spot rate in predictive power and that rationality was in general rejected. In addition to the MMS data, Frankel and Froot (1987a, b) exploited the survey data collected by Amex Financial Service and also *The Economist*, which have longer sample periods and different forecast horizons. They found that expectations do respond to exchange rate changes. Moreover, short-term forecasts are more 'destabilizing' than long-term forecasts; i.e. the response to the degree of forecasted appreciation in response to appreciation is larger in the short-term horizon than in the long-term horizon.

2 The first few surveys were conducted not on Wednesdays but on the middle and last business days of the month. However, the survey date was fixed on Wednesday after the fourth observation. A twice-a-month survey means that observations are usually fortnightly, with a couple of exceptions in a year. That is, there are twenty-four instead of twenty-six observations in the JCIF data in fifty-two weeks. It is unfortunate that the interval is not fixed. In the following, I disregard the problem arising from a mix of two- and three-week intervals. The survey started with forty-two companies and expanded to the current forty-four after the fourth survey in July 1985.

3 Since the micro panel data set was made available on the condition that the anonymity of the source should be honoured, it is impossible to aggregate the individuals into groups.

4 For some cases, an allowance had to be made for AR(1) serial correlation in $u_j(t) - u_{\text{AVE}}(t)$, or in $u_j(t) - u_b(t)$, contrary to the assumptions mentioned earlier. This may be due to either serial correlation in u_j or deviations in $f[I(t)]$ among individuals. However, many rejection cases (i.e. confirming heterogeneity) are found without AR(1) disturbances.

5 I owe the observation in this paragraph to an anonymous referee. There have been some investigations examining whether diverse expectations can be rational depending upon agents' information sets (see, for example, Feldman (1987), Marcet and Sargent (1989) and Frydman (1982, 1987)).

6 One might think that intelligent people like professional traders and dealers can separate wishful thinking from scientific forecasts. However, there is some evidence in the psychology literature, kindly

suggested by Kenneth J. Arrow, that wishful thinking is rather common in social cognition and views of the self.

> Theories of the causal attribution process, prediction, judgments of covariation, and other tasks of social inference incorporated the assumptions of the naive scientists as normative guidelines with which actual behavior could be compared.
>
> It rapidly became evident, however, that the social perceiver's actual inferential work and decision making looked little like these normative models. Rather, information processing is full of incomplete data gathering, shortcuts, errors, and biases. In particular, *prior expectations and self-serving interpretations* weigh heavily into the social judgment process.
>
> (Taylor and Brown 1988: 194, my italics)

7 One might think that there may be self-selection among entrepreneurs and dealers: those who are optimistic about the yen appreciation (depreciation) develop import (export) business. However, the JCIF polls include only leading companies, so that it is difficult to imagine that they change their types of business because of exchange rate expectations. Those who are in charge of foreign exchange expectations and trades in those companies are usually in-house staff, who are subject to a lifetime employment practice. It is hardly the case in Japan that foreign exchange professionals hop companies according to their biases in expectations.

8 For the aspects of econometrics, see Mishkin (1983). The same procedure has been applied to the MMS data by Dominguez (1986). In this chapter, I assume that reported forecasts in the survey are the subjective means of respondents. However, if agents were reporting the medians of a skewed subjective distribution then the results of rationality tests could be affected.

9 However, Muth (1961) originally interpreted rational expectations as applying only to aggregate expectations.

10 If the forward rate is used in place of the expectation of survey data, as is the case in papers other than those with survey data, risk aversion is another source of bias in forecast errors.

11 In that sense it may seem inappropriate to invoke the peso problem explanation in the usual sense for this period. The biased forecast errors resulting from the underestimation of the magnitude of a crash could be called the 'Plaza problem'. Both 'peso problems', which arise when an infrequent

crash did not happen, and 'Plaza problems', which occur when an infrequent crash did happen, are small-sample problems. Moreover, the latter is a special case of a peso problem: a policy switch, including interventions, could halt a dollar decline and reverse the movement with a small probability. That did not happen in the small sample.

12 Frankel and Froot (1987b) showed, using the MMS, *The Economist* and the AMEX data sets, that short- and long-term expectations seem to have different characteristics. The data set with the short-term horizon yields the estimates indicating a bandwagon type (extrapolative) effect, while the data set with the long-term horizon yields results with a more regressive nature. However, the direct comparison of the short-term and long-term horizons is limited in their study because of the spread of horizons across different data sets and different sample periods.

13 Suppose that uncovered interest parity (no risk premium) holds. An interest rate differential of 6 per cent implies that the exchange rate changes by approximately 3 per cent in six months, a significant and easily detectable change. However, it predicts only a 0.5 per cent change in one month, a change that is small and may escape detection.

REFERENCES

Dominguez, K. M. (1986) 'Are foreign exchange forecasts rational?', *Economics Letters* 21: 277–81.

Evans, G. W. (1986) 'A test for speculative bubbles in the sterling–dollar exchange rate: 1981–84', *American Economic Review* 76 (September): 621–36.

Feldman, M. (1987) 'An example of convergence to rational expectations with heterogeneous beliefs', *International Economic Review* 28 (October): 635–50.

Figlewski, S. and Wachtel, P. (1981) 'The formation of inflationary expectation', *Review of Economics and Statistics* 63 (February): 1–10.

Frankel, J. A. and Froot, K. A. (1987a) 'Short-term and long-term expectations of the yen/dollar exchange rate: evidence from survey data', *Journal of the Japanese and International Economies* 1 (September): 249–74.

—— and —— (1987b) 'Using survey data to test standard propositions regarding exchange rate expectations', *American Economic Review* 77 (1): 133–53.

Froot, K. A. and Ito, T. (1989) 'On the consistency of short-run and long-run exchange rate expectations', *Journal of International Money and Finance* 8 (December): 487–510.

Frydman, R. (1982) 'Towards an understanding of market processes: individual expectations, learning, and convergence to rational expectations equilibrium', *American Economic Review* 72 (September): 652–68.

—— (1987) 'Diversity of information, least squares learning rules and market behavior', mimeo, New York University, Department of Economics.

Hey, J. D. (1984) 'The economics of optimism and pessimism: a definition and some applications', *Kyklos* 37: 181–205.

Ito, T. (1987) 'The intradaily exchange rate after the Group of Five agreement', *Journal of the Japanese and International Economies* 1 (September): 275–98.

—— (1988a) 'Use of (time-domain) vector auto-regressions to test uncovered interest parity', *Review of Economics and Statistics* 70 (May): 296–305.

—— (1988b) 'Foreign exchange rate expectations: micro survey data', Working Paper 2679, National Bureau of Economic Research, August.

Ito, T. and Quah, D. (1989) 'Hypothesis testing with restricted spectral density matrices, with an application to uncovered interest parity', *International Economic Review* 30 (February): 203–15.

Krugman, P. (1987) 'Pricing to market when the exchange rate changes', in S. W. Arndt and J. D. Richardson (eds) *Real-Financial Linkages Among Open Economies*, Cambridge, MA: MIT Press.

Marcet, A. and Sargent, T. J. (1989) 'Convergence of least squares learning in environments with hidden state variables and private information', *Journal of Political Economy* 97 (December): 1306–22.

Mishkin, F. S. (1983) *A Rational Expectations Approach to Macroeconometrics*, Chicago, IL: University of Chicago Press.

Muth, J. F. (1961) 'Rational expectations and the theory of price movements', *Econometrica* 29 (July): 315–35.

Obstfeld, M. (1987) 'Peso problems, bubbles, and risk in the empirical assessment of exchange-rate behavior', Working Paper 2203, National Bureau of Economic Research, April.

Ohno, K. (1988) 'Export pricing behavior of manufacturing: a U.S.–Japan comparison', mimeo, International Monetary Fund, June.

Sargent, T. (1979) 'A note on maximum likelihood estimation of the rational expectations model of the term structure', *Journal of Monetary Economics* 5: 133–43.

Shinohara, M. (ed.) (1986) *Lectures on the Japanese Economy* (in Japanese), Tokyo: Keizai Shinpo Sha.

Taylor, S. E. and Brown, J. D. (1988) 'Illusion and well-being: a social psychological perspective on mental health', *Psychological Bulletin* 103: 193–210.

18

DETECTING STRUCTURAL CHANGES IN THE SPOT AND THE FORWARD FOREIGN EXCHANGE MARKETS

From January 1974 to September 1986

Hiroya Akiba and Tomoki Waragai

INTRODUCTION

In this chapter[1] we focus on one central question – the exact point in time when significant structural changes occurred in the foreign exchange markets. We also examine an empirical issue, i.e. whether the link between the spot and the forward exchange rate is strong, in the sense that the level of (or change in) the future spot rate 'fully reflects' available information, i.e. the level of (or change in) the forward rate. Thus, the issue should be treated in a broader concept of the efficiency hypothesis in international finance. However, our approach is indirect and clearly different from the traditional approaches in this respect.

It has been widely recognized from accumulated evidence that the forward exchange rate is an unbiased predictor of the corresponding future spot exchange rate. However, it is also well known that the forward exchange rate is approximately the best available predictor of the corresponding future spot exchange rate, although it is not a very good predictor.[2]

Aside from this issue of prediction, it has been observed from all data that, in general, spot and forward exchange rates move together. That is, although there is a small difference between the spot rate and the forward rate, the difference is relatively constant and is small in comparison with changes in both the spot and forward rates.[3]

From these two empirical 'regularities' it can be inferred that the spot rate and hence the forward rate follow approximately a random walk process.[4] This is consistent with an empirical conclusion of Meese and Rogoff (1983a, b) that a random walk model turned out to predict the future spot rate as well as did any estimated asset market model of the dollar–mark, dollar–yen, dollar–pound and trade-weighted dollar exchange rates up to twelve-month forecast horizons. The relative efficiency of the random walk model, however, diminishes as the forecast horizon approaches one year.[5] Nevertheless, the evidence provided by Meese and Rogoff seems particularly damaging to the asset market models since the forecasts of the exogenous variables use actual realized values and hence are free from uncertainty.[6,7]

However, as Meese and Rogoff (1983a) also indicate, while a random walk model outperforms the out-of-sample forecast for up to twelve months, it is by no means a good predictor. Because some structural models outperform the out-of-sample forecast for longer horizons, the results of Meese and Rogoff are not evidence to reject the asset market approach itself.[8] Their results could be interpreted that, while the short-run movement of exchange rates is dominated by 'news' (Frenkel 1981), structural factors exert stronger effects in the longer run. It should be stressed, however, that the way such structural factors affect the exchange rates would also be altered by structural changes. Thus, an investigation of structural change is inevitable since structural models would not make sufficiently accurate statistical forecasts because of structural changes.

Meese and Rogoff merely suggest that possible causes of the poor performance of the structural models should be found in such factors as the instability of the money-demand function or the inadequate modelling of expectations formation etc. This suggests specification errors. A particular specification error may arise if the foreign exchange market undergoes structural changes.

The purpose of this chapter is twofold. The first purpose, which is our main concern, is to ascertain the particular point in time when structural change occurred in the forward exchange markets for five major forward exchange rates *vis-à-vis* the US dollar in the recent floating period. (The actual samples used are the forward premia – see the third section.) The second purpose is to compare the results with those of our previous investigations of the spot exchange rates for the same five currencies. If there were a strong link between the spot and the forward rate, in the sense that the spot rate n periods in the future fully reflects the current n-period forward rate, then it could reasonably be expected that the points in time of structural change for the two exchange rates should be different by exactly n periods.[9] In this sense, our present investigation would be classified as another, although indirect, test of the efficiency hypothesis in international finance.[10] On the other hand, if both spot and forward rates move together, then the points in time of structural change for the two exchange rates should coincide. Since there are several novelties in our analysis, they should be explained briefly.

First, we employ a time-series model, in particular an autoregressive (AR) model, that is normally used for predictions in economics, in order to identify structural changes. It is natural to focus first on the movement of data for examining the qualitative characteristics. An AR model has another desirable feature in that it is free from the problem of arbitrariness arising from the choice of explanatory variables in any regression models to test structural changes.[11, 12]

Second, the MAIC method (minimization of Akaike's information criterion (AIC)) is employed to identify structural changes, as well as to select the order of the AR model. Since the MAIC method implies minimization of the Kullback–Leibler information measure, it can serve as a powerful alternative to the test of the hypothesis method which inherently has an arbitrariness in the determination of the significance levels.[13] Here, however, we apply the MAIC method one step further to the analysis of structural change. In identifying structural changes our method is a superior alternative to the traditional methods, such as the Chow test etc. These depend on some arbitrariness in selecting the significance levels.

In our analysis, monthly observations from January 1974 through September 1986 (153 samples) for spot–forward spreads of the pound sterling, the deutsche mark, the Swiss franc, the French franc and the Japanese yen *vis-à-vis* the US dollar are used. It is shown statistically that the sample spot–forward spreads underwent structural changes. The most significant structural changes occurred in (1) June–July 1982 for the pound sterling, the deutsche mark and the Swiss franc, (2) February–March 1981 for the French franc and (3) December 1974 to January 1975 for the Japanese yen. These results for the spot–forward spreads are compared with those for the spot rates (Waragai and Akiba 1987a) in order to examine statistically whether there exists a strong link between spot and forward rates, as the efficiency hypothesis asserts.

The organization of the chapter is as follows. In the following section the formulation of our experiment is outlined in some detail. The third section is devoted to presenting our calculation results and to identifying the point in time when each exchange rate underwent structural changes. In the fourth section we briefly discuss some problems of our technique and each point in time of structural change by going into the historical background of foreign exchange markets. The points in time are compared with those obtained for the spot exchange rates in our previous work (Waragai and Akiba 1987a). The final section summarizes our analytical method and conclusions.

FORMULATION OF THE EXPERIMENT

The technique we employ in this chapter is explained in some detail in this section.[14] The method is called the MAIC method and can be used to detect the particular point in time when a structural change occurred.

Suppose there is a set of random data $\{x(t)\}$ of the random variable $X(t)$, which is a time history of the forward exchange rate of each currency vis-à-vis the US dollar.[15] In order to eliminate the time trend components from the data, it is simply assumed that $\{x(t)\}$ has a trend factor $\mu(t) = \alpha + \beta t$. Parameters α and β are estimated by the least squares method:

$$\min \sum [x(t) - \mu(t)]^2. \qquad (18.1)$$

Next, let us define $z(t)$ as

$$z(t) = x(t) - \hat{\mu}(t) \qquad (18.2)$$

where $\hat{\mu}(t) = \hat{\alpha} + \hat{\beta}t$ ($\hat{\alpha}$ and $\hat{\beta}$ are the least squares estimators). It is assumed that the random process $\{z(t)\}$ could be generated from an AR model

$$z(t) = \sum_{i=1}^{p} a_i z(t-i) + u(t) \qquad (18.3)$$

where p is the order of the AR model, a_i are the coefficients and $u(t)$ is white noise, $N(0, \sigma^2)$. Both the Yule–Walker equation and the AIC can be utilized for estimation of the a_i and determination of the order p. We used the AIC which is given by the following equation without a common term:

$$\text{AIC} = N \log \hat{\sigma}^2 + 2p \qquad (18.4)$$

where

$$\hat{\sigma}^2 = -\sum_{k=0}^{p} \hat{a}_k \, \hat{\gamma}_k \qquad a_0 = -1 \qquad (18.5)$$

$$\hat{\gamma}_j = \sum_{k=1}^{p} \hat{a}_k \, \hat{\gamma}_{k-j} \qquad j = 1, \ldots, p \qquad (18.6)$$

$$\hat{\gamma}_k = \sum_{i=1}^{N-k} \frac{z(i)z(i+k)}{N} \qquad (18.7)$$

The model given by minimizing AIC can be considered the AR model best fitted to the data $\{z(t)\}$.

The method employed up to now is the identification procedure of a stationary random process. If we are to detect structural changes utilizing the AR model, it is necessary to fit an AR model in non-stationary situations. To detect non-stationarity Osaki and Tong (1975) employed the AIC method. In the rest of this section we outline (hinted at in Ozaki and Tong's work) how to apply the AIC method to detect a structural change in $\{z(t)\}$.[16, 17]

A random process with a structural change can be considered non-stationary for the whole process, i.e. before and after the structural change. However, each process before and after the structural change may be considered a stationary process. Figure 18.1 illustrates our application of the AIC method for detection of a structural change.

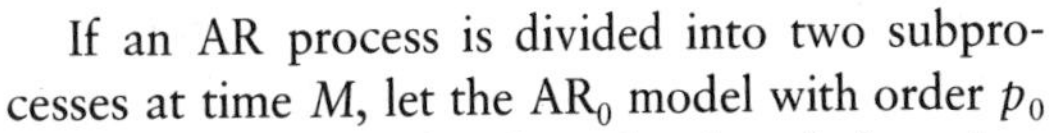

Figure 18.1 Application of the AIC method for the detection of a structural change

If an AR process is divided into two subprocesses at time M, let the AR_0 model with order p_0 and AIC_0 be best fitted to the data before time M,[18] and the AR_1 model with order p_1 and AIC_1 best fitted to those after M. Then, the AIC_M throughout the process is defined as

$$\text{AIC}_M = \text{AIC}_0 + \text{AIC}_1.$$

Since the AIC is an information measure that indicates the poorness of fit, it is the time M^* defined by

$$\text{AIC}_{M^*} = \min \text{AIC}_M$$

377

Table 18.1 The UK: three-month spot–forward spreads

	12.74	6.75	12.75	6.76	12.76	3.77
AIC_0	24.566	25.655	26.497	34.861	53.954	59.455
AIC_1	125.100	123.336	123.308	124.077	110.214	89.108
AIC_M	149.666	148.991	149.805	158.938	164.168	148.563
	6.77	7.77	12.77	1.78	6.78	9.78
AIC_0	63.014	64.945	69.535	68.820	67.038	68.209
AIC_1	80.496	79.157	75.434	75.279	75.216	70.498
AIC_M	143.510	144.102	144.969	144.099	142.254	138.707
	12.78	2.79	6.79	8.79	10.79	12.79
AIC_0	71.060	72.632	75.418	75.297	76.771	78.080
AIC_1	71.873	67.976	71.820	66.100	65.218	68.917
AIC_M	142.933	140.608	147.238	141.397	141.989	146.997
	6.80	12.80	2.81	6.81	9.81	12.81
AIC_0	99.842	108.504	109.260	113.214	112.244	117.311
AIC_1	68.758	12.909	12.846	12.796	1.727	−7.402
AIC_M	168.600	121.413	122.106	126.010	113.971	109.909
	1.82	5.82	6.82	12.82	6.83	12.83
AIC_0	116.698	117.478	119.100	123.314	125.136	125.513
AIC_1	−10.435	−8.158	−13.261	1.104	−7.592	−1.215
AIC_M	106.263	109.320	105.839	124.328	117.544	124.298
	6.84	12.84	6.85	9.85	12.85	
AIC_0	125.655	134.976	147.885	145.530	147.197	
AIC_1	−10.318	−21.749	−18.700	−13.665	−5.042	
AIC_M	115.337	113.227	129.185	131.865	142.155	

that can be considered to divide the whole process best into two subprocesses.[19] In other words, it would be possible to consider that a structural change occurred at time M^*.[20]

COMPUTATION RESULTS OF AKAIKE'S INFORMATION CRITERION

The data are monthly observations (taken at the end of the month) of the three-month forward foreign exchange rates for five major currencies vis-à-vis the US dollar, expressed as the percentage (per annum) spread.[21, 22] The data of the six-month

spot–forward spread for the Japanese yen are also used. The sample period covers the recent floating period since early 1973, but for our calculation of the time period M^*, January 1974 was selected as the starting period because it ensures stability of the estimators.[23]

In order to avoid any arbitrariness and to increase the accuracy as much as possible, we set the following criteria: (1) for every currency the data were divided by every six months in principle and (2) the data were divided on the occasion when the exchange rates of European currencies were realigned and when structural changes were suspected from data observation.

Table 18.2 France: three-month spot–forward spreads

	12.74	6.75	12.75	6.76	12.76	3.77
AIC_0	26.828	32.439	36.114	46.322	55.580	55.103
AIC_1	271.529	265.377	258.004	251.811	245.892	241.035
AIC_M	298.357	297.816	294.118	298.133	301.472	296.138
	6.77	7.77	12.77	1.78	6.78	9.78
AIC_0	55.983	57.936	65.219	65.148	70.434	71.936
AIC_1	238.108	234.894	228.951	227.085	217.310	213.383
AIC_M	294.091	292.830	294.170	292.233	287.744	285.318
	12.78	2.79	6.79	8.79	10.79	12.79
AIC_0	77.609	79.416	79.820	80.189	81.385	81.461
AIC_1	209.848	207.524	200.556	198.108	195.371	193.127
AIC_M	287.457	286.940	280.376	278.297	276.756	274.588
	6.80	12.80	2.81	6.81	9.81	12.81
AIC_0	98.062	105.258	105.406	130.664	159.963	155.120
AIC_1	179.811	173.544	161.637	147.663	135.637	130.743
AIC_M	277.873	278.802	267.043	278.327	295.600	285.863
	1.82	5.82	6.82	12.82	6.83	12.83
AIC_0	157.070	200.779	199.247	240.892	247.862	254.691
AIC_1	127.946	104.770	97.343	78.969	40.739	38.741
AIC_M	285.016	305.549	296.590	319.861	288.601	293.432
	6.84	12.84	6.85	9.85	12.85	
AIC_0	264.490	270.230	276.129	281.790	287.966	
AIC_1	31.178	28.904	23.480	18.739	14.605	
AIC_M	295.668	299.134	299.609	300.529	302.571	

The computation results are summarized in Tables 18.1–18.5.[24] From the purely statistical point of view, i.e. according to the MAIC method, the following conclusions were derived from the tables.[25]

The UK (Table 18.1 and Figure 18.2)

The forward exchange rate of the pound sterling underwent the most significant structural change in June–July 1982. The AR_i selected by the MAIC method are[26]

$$AR_0 \qquad z(t) = 0.80941z(t - 1)$$

$$AR_1 \qquad z(t) = 0.84584z(t - 1)$$

France (Table 18.2 and Figure 18.3)

The point in time of the structural change for the forward rate of the French franc was February–March 1981. The AR_i selected by the MAIC method are

$$AR_0$$
$$z(t) = 0.84444z(t - 1) - 0.15465z(t - 1)$$

$$AR_1$$
$$z(t) = 0.48797z(t - 1)$$

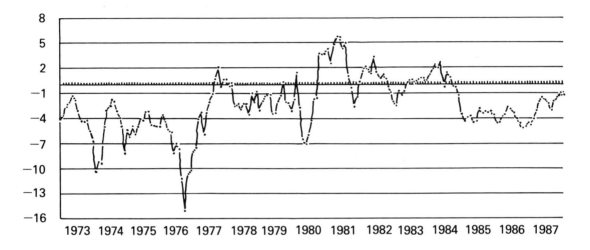

Figure 18.2 Monthly observations of spreads between the three-month forward rate and the spot rate (per cent per annum) of the pound sterling

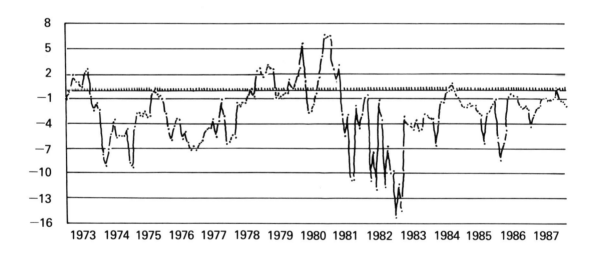

Figure 18.3 Monthly observations of spreads between the three-month forward rate and the spot rate (per cent per annum) of the French franc

Table 18.3 West Germany: three-month spot–forward spreads

	12.74	6.75	12.75	6.76	12.76	3.77
AIC_0	10.754	10.916	9.839	6.755	7.817	5.160
AIC_1	14.874	6.273	14.565	20.480	25.882	27.822
AIC_M	25.628	17.189	24.404	27.235	33.699	32.982
	6.77	7.77	12.77	1.78	6.78	9.78
AIC_0	2.368	1.850	7.108	1.753	−0.471	−2.908
AIC_1	15.402	16.181	4.843	4.728	7.320	8.862
AIC_M	17.770	18.031	11.951	6.481	6.849	5.954
	12.78	2.79	6.79	8.79	10.79	12.79
AIC_0	4.377	−2.525	−5.356	−8.527	−7.776	−8.649
AIC_1	2.200	2.472	2.943	7.272	4.725	5.940
AIC_M	6.577	−0.053	−2.413	−1.300	−3.051	−2.709
	6.80	12.80	2.81	6.81	9.81	12.81
AIC_0	35.489	25.217	46.414	34.835	33.405	40.064
AIC_1	1.761	−3.423	−20.921	−38.280	−36.386	−46.873
AIC_M	37.250	21.794	25.493	−3.445	−2.981	−6.809
	1.82	5.82	6.82	12.82	6.83	12.83
AIC_0	38.141	35.096	35.277	41.591	38.405	36.508
AIC_1	−48.351	−37.086	−56.749	−46.767	−50.727	−32.534
AIC_M	−10.210	−1.990	−21.472	−5.176	−12.322	3.974
	6.84	12.84	6.85	9.85	12.85	
AIC_0	31.005	32.550	35.117	29.529	30.369	
AIC_1	−28.289	−26.884	−32.488	−24.075	−25.969	
AIC_M	2.716	5.666	2.629	5.454	4.400	

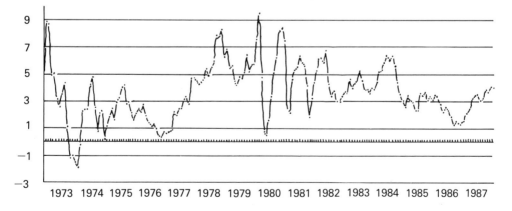

Figure 18.4 Monthly observations of spreads between the three-month forward rate and the spot rate (per cent per annum) of the deutsche mark

Table 18.4 Switzerland: three-month spot–forward spreads

	12.74	6.75	12.75	6.76	12.76	3.77
AIC_0	5.575	−2.843	−0.434	−8.280	−8.090	−2.951
AIC_1	43.852	46.123	30.773	33.974	37.948	55.986
AIC_M	49.427	43.280	30.339	25.694	29.858	53.035
	6.77	7.77	12.77	1.78	6.78	9.78
AIC_0	−5.764	−8.093	−9.705	−9.375	−15.445	−14.586
AIC_1	47.786	40.764	25.578	17.446	21.812	7.763
AIC_M	42.022	32.671	15.873	8.071	6.367	−6.823
	12.78	2.79	6.79	8.79	10.79	12.79
AIC_0	1.328	−4.614	−12.196	−14.565	−12.355	−10.616
AIC_1	5.403	4.717	6.464	9.250	5.813	8.724
AIC_M	6.731	0.103	−5.732	−5.315	−6.542	−1.892
	6.80	12.80	2.81	6.81	9.81	12.81
AIC_0	33.833	18.817	35.999	28.658	42.034	50.090
AIC_1	11.656	−0.310	−21.607	−21.183	−17.505	−23.017
AIC_M	45.489	18.507	14.392	7.475	24.529	27.073
	1.82	5.82	6.82	12.82	6.83	12.83
AIC_0	43.594	39.462	40.267	53.479	55.303	49.900
AIC_1	−35.276	−27.599	−57.031	−56.887	−47.747	−34.912
AIC_M	8.318	11.863	−16.764	−3.408	7.556	14.988
	6.84	12.84	6.85	9.85	12.85	
AIC_0	41.419	55.798	62.361	54.799	49.511	
AIC_1	−24.033	−26.592	−22.131	−16.299	−10.907	
AIC_M	17.386	29.206	40.230	38.500	38.604	

West Germany (Table 18.3 and Figure 18.4)

The forward exchange rate of the deutsche mark experienced the most significant structural change at the same point in time as the pound sterling, i.e. June–July 1982. The AR_i selected by the MAIC method are

AR_0
$$z(t) = 1.00520z(t-1) - 0.34765z(t-2)$$

AR_1
$$z(t) = 0.84502z(t-1)$$

Switzerland (Table 18.4 and Figure 18.5)

The point in time of structural change for the forward rate of the Swiss franc was the same as for the pound sterling and the deutsche mark, i.e. June–July 1982. The AR_i selected by the MAIC method are

AR_0
$$z(t) = 1.11070z(t-1) - 0.32799z(t-2)$$

AR_1
$$z(t) = 0.91420z(t-1) + 0.20319z(t-2)$$
$$- 0.31295z(t-3)$$

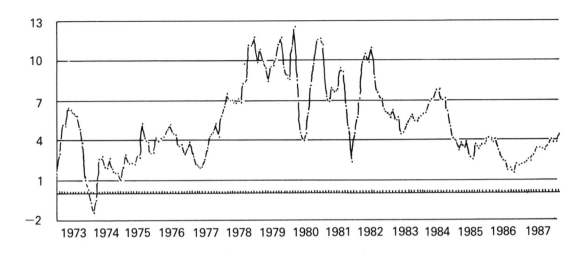

Figure 18.5 Monthly observations of spreads between the three-month forward rate and the spot rate (per cent per annum) of the Swiss franc

Japan

The three-month forward exchange rate of the Japanese yen (Table 18.5(a) and Figure 18.6(a)) experienced the most significant structural change in the period from December 1974 to January 1975. The AR_i selected by the MAIC method are

$$AR_0 \quad z(t) = 0.44578z(t-1)$$
$$AR_1 \quad z(t) = 0.91726z(t-1)$$

The point in time of structural change for the six-month forward rate (Table 18.5(b) and Figure 18.6(b)) turned out to be the same as that for the three-month rate, i.e. December 1974 to January 1975. The AR_i selected by the MAIC method are

$$AR_0 \qquad z(t) = 0.54890z(t-1)$$
$$AR_1$$
$$z(t) = 1.04939z(t-1) + 0.01402z(t-2)$$
$$- 0.14783z(t-3)$$

Since the point in time M^* that optimally cuts off $\{z(t)\}$ for five major currencies is determined by a purely statistical technique – the MAIC method – we briefly discuss each point in time of structural change by reviewing the historical background of

each forward exchange rate in the next section. These points in time are compared with those obtained for the spot exchange rate in our previous work (Waragai and Akiba 1987a). Some technical comments are also given in some detail.

DISCUSSION

First, a comparison is made between the points in time of structural change in the five spot rates (in Waragai and Akiba 1987a) and in the forward rate for the same five currencies in the present investigation.

In Table 18.6, there is no currency that showed a systematic relationship between the points in time of structural change for the spot rate and the spot–forward spreads. Thus, we can infer that the points in time of structural change in the spot–forward spreads are caused by changes in the forward rates for these currencies.[27]

If there is a strong link between these two rates, i.e. the spot and the forward rates, the points in time in the two studies should either (1) coincide, if both rates have moved together ('an empirical regularity', e.g. Mussa (1979), or (2) be earlier by exactly three (or six) months for the forward rates than for the spot rates (the forward market effi-

Table 18.5(a) Japan: three-month spot–forward spreads

	12.74	6.75	12.75	6.76	12.76	6.77
AIC_0	50.124	65.301	81.110	93.163	105.250	115.224
AIC_1	83.165	78.217	53.317	60.415	64.992	67.306
AIC_M	133.289	143.518	134.427	153.578	170.242	182.530
	12.77	6.78	9.78	12.78	6.79	12.79
AIC_0	124.608	132.896	136.922	142.235	151.489	160.404
AIC_1	46.398	32.225	34.982	31.370	30.063	23.439
AIC_M	171.006	165.121	171.904	173.605	181.552	183.843
	6.80	11.80	12.80	6.81	12.81	6.82
AIC_0	180.635	183.479	184.485	191.801	200.784	207.228
AIC_1	72.147	−9.420	−8.640	5.100	−34.577	−44.899
AIC_M	252.782	174.059	175.845	196.901	166.207	162.329
	12.82	6.83	12.83	6.84	12.84	6.85
AIC_0	221.931	229.785	237.186	241.962	251.670	260.202
AIC_1	−47.717	−46.789	−32.391	−22.330	−25.526	−18.307
AIC_M	174.214	182.996	204.795	219.632	226.144	241.895
	9.85	12.85				
AIC_0	263.555	267.703				
AIC_1	−15.088	−14.001				
AIC_M	248.467	253.702				

ciency hypothesis).[28] Thus, it could be argued that the link between the two rates is not strong enough.[29] We could conclude that the two rates have not moved together from the statistical point of view and that the spot rate three months (six months) in the future did not fully reflect the current three-month (six-month) forward rate, as the advocates of the efficient market hypothesis have asserted.[30]

The foregoing conclusion is reinforced with a comparison of the points in time of a structural break between the spot and the forward rates, obtained from our previous investigation. The points in time of a structural break shown in Table 18.7 are calculated with a shorter sample period, January 1974 to August 1985. The end point was deliberately selected in order to avoid any structural changes that might have been caused by the

effect of the co-ordinated (but anticipated) intervention by the G5 nations in the fall of 1985. All the exchange rates except the pound sterling rate also show the different points in time of the structural break.

As we have argued elsewhere (Waragai and Akiba 1987b, 1989b), the spot rates were very sensitive to the co-ordinated (but anticipated) intervention by the G5 nations. However, as Table 18.8 makes clear, the forward rates are not sensitive to those anticipated interventions. In fact, three out of a total of five forward exchange rates exhibit the same points in time of structural break.[31] This fact is not totally unexpected, because the forward rates could not fully anticipate the point in time of the co-ordinated intervention by the G5 nations. Thus, only the spot rates were affected strongly by those interventions, while the

Table 18.5(b) Japan: six-month spot–forward spreads

	12.74	6.75	12.75	6.76	12.76	6.77
AIC_0	35.485	42.215	51.238	56.476	62.202	65.261
AIC_1	14.824	16.905	10.285	23.049	27.993	34.204
AIC_M	50.309	59.120	61.523	79.525	90.195	99.465
	12.77	6.78	9.78	12.78	6.79	12.79
AIC_0	68.955	69.637	70.190	74.809	76.972	79.640
AIC_1	8.246	6.664	6.831	6.669	7.826	3.116
AIC_M	77.201	76.301	77.021	81.478	84.798	82.756
	6.80	11.80	12.80	6.81	12.81	6.82
AIC_0	103.822	95.955	96.094	98.970	105.268	106.483
AIC_1	47.732	−19.848	−21.217	−11.831	−40.889	−43.225
AIC_M	151.554	76.107	74.877	87.139	64.379	63.258
	12.82	6.83	12.83	6.84	12.84	6.85
AIC_0	124.144	125.782	128.598	126.362	134.872	142.185
AIC_1	−44.741	−45.449	−29.587	−23.290	−24.660	−20.461
AIC_M	79.403	80.333	99.011	103.072	110.212	121.724
	9.85	12.85				
AIC_0	143.291	145.419				
AIC_1	−15.932	−16.108				
AIC_M	127.359	129.311				

Table 18.6 Comparison of points in time of structural change, January 1974–September 1986

Exchange rate	Spot rate	Forward rate[a]
Pound sterling	September–October 1985	June–July 1982
French franc	December 1980–January 1981	February–March 1981
Swiss franc	December 1974–January 1975	June–July 1982
Deutsche mark	September–October 1985	June–July 1982
Japanese yen	September–October 1985	December 1974–January 1975[b]

Source: Waragai and Akiba 1987a

Notes: [a] Spreads between the three-month forward and the spot rates (per cent per annum).
[b] Both the three-month and the six-month spot–forward spreads (per cent per annum).

forward rates adjusted themselves, though not fully, to such changes in the spot rate as a given condition. The evidence seems to manifest an interesting feature of the forward exchange rates.

Second, technically speaking, we are concerned only with an AR model in this chapter. If $u(t)$ in equation (18.3) is not white noise, we could have used an autoregressive moving-average (ARMA) model. For our present investigation, however, we employed an AR model rather than an ARMA model. The reason for this lies in the fact that the moving-average part of the ARMA model cannot be interpreted easily from an economic point of view and also, practically speaking, an ARMA model cannot always assure a better estimation than an AR model.[32]

Third, our method (which is just an application of the AIC one step further) can identify whether and when one structural change occurred within a

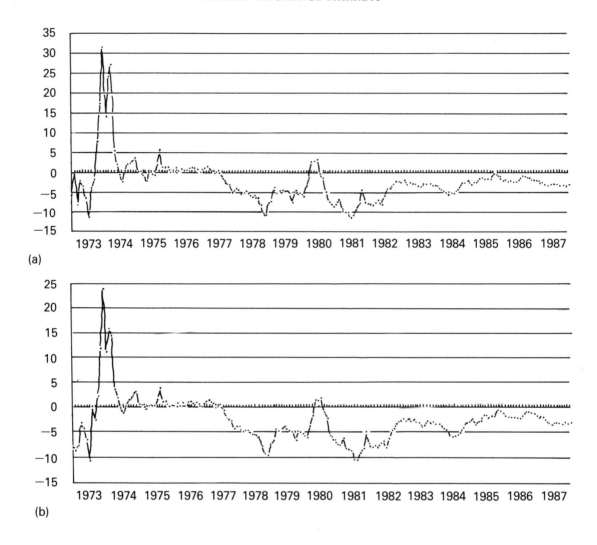

Figure 18.6 Monthly observations of spreads between (a) the three-month forward rate and the spot rate (per cent per annum) and (b) the six-month forward rate and the spot rate (per cent per annum) of the Japanese yen

process. If there are several structural changes in a process, we can use another application method proposed by Waragai (1987; see also Waragai and Akiba 1989c).[33] The application method of the AIC employed in this chapter was devised by us in order to identify a turning point within a process, and it is the most useful method if the process is divided into two subprocesses with different characteristics.

The next point is in a sense more subtle. Even though we could conclude that each forward foreign exchange rate for the five major currencies underwent a structural change at time M^*, it is not so clear from which side of the forward exchange rate the structural change occurred. In other words, since the exchange rate is just a relative price of two monies, a structural change of the dollar–pound forward rate, for example, occurs

Table 18.7 Comparison of points in time of structural change, January 1974–August 1985

Exchange rate	Spot rate	Forward rate[a]
Pound sterling	January–February 1982	January–February 1982
French franc	December 1980–January 1981	February–March 1981
Swiss franc	August–September 1979	September–October 1978
Deutsche mark	October–November 1979	June–July 1982
Japanese yen	June–July 1980	December 1974–January 1975[b]

Source: Akiba and Waragai 1989b: Table 6; spot rates from Waragai and Akiba 1986

Notes: [a]Spreads between the three-month forward and the spot rates (per cent per annum).
[b]Both the three-month and the six-month spot–forward spreads (per cent per annum).

Table 18.8 Comparison of points in time of structural change, forward rate[a]

Exchange rate	Sample period	
	January 1974–August 1985	January 1974–September 1986
Pound sterling	January–February 1982	June–July 1982
French franc	February–March 1981	February–March 1981
Swiss franc	September–October 1978	June–July 1982
Deutsche mark	June–July 1982	June–July 1982
Japanese yen	December 1974–January 1975	December 1974–January 1975

Notes: [a]Spreads between the three-month forward and the spot rates (per cent per annum), August 1985.
[b]Both the three-month and the six-month spot–forward spreads (per cent per annum).

either with the pound sterling or with the US dollar, or with both. However, since the point in time M^* when each forward rate experienced a structural change differs, we could safely interpret either that structural changes occurred in each of the five countries (not in the standard country, i.e. the USA), or that structural changes for the five currencies outweighed that for the USA.

Finally, the background in the real-world foreign exchange markets around the time when the AIC showed a minimum is briefly reviewed. It should be stressed that we merely point out what was happening at M^* for each forward exchange rate and have no intention of suggesting any possible cause of structural changes.

The dollar–pound sterling forward rate experienced the most significant structural change from early to mid-1982, according to the AIC_M. The spot exchange rate of the pound sterling began to depreciate from late 1981 as interest rates decreased. Owing mainly to the slowdown of the rate of inflation below the average for OECD countries, the rate of interest showed a continuous fall in 1982 and the spot rate kept depreciating rapidly. In fact, the lending rates were lowered three times: on 8 June, 14 July and 30 July. Our calculation of AIC_M showed that the dollar–pound forward rate experienced the most significant structural change around this time.

In the period from February to March 1981, when the French franc–dollar forward rate experienced the most significant structural change, the spot rate was depreciating. However, backed by the relatively high interest rate, the spot rate was changing steadily. The French franc was dealing at around the upper limit amongst the EMS currencies. In mid-February, the deutsche mark rate recovered rapidly as the German authorities adopted restrictive monetary policies. As a consequence, the French franc fell below the deutsche mark in rank among the EMS currencies. It could be argued, judging from the movement of the French franc–dollar spot rate, that the forward rate experienced a structural change in mid-1981 when the Socialist party took power (10 May 1981). However, according to the AIC_M, the M^* for the forward rate was earlier by three months than the time of change of the government.

In early 1982 Switzerland also experienced a slowdown in the rate of inflation. However, there was a sufficient amount of liquidity by currency swaps because of a fear of a cooling down of the economy. This made the rates of interest fall, and correspondingly the discount rate was cut by a $1/2$ per cent on 19 March. The fall in the rate put further downward pressure on domestic rates of interest, and in May the interest rate differential for three months was about 10.5 per cent in favour of the US dollar and about 6 per cent in favour of the deutsche mark. Thus, capital outflowed in a substantial amount that put selling pressure on the Swiss franc, and the spot rate actually depreciated suddenly from June. Our calculation of AIC_M showed that the Swiss franc–dollar forward rate experienced the most significant structural change around this time.

The deutsche mark–dollar spot rate showed a falling tendency, while the mark rate against the other currencies showed a rising tendency during 1982. In June, the differences in opinion in the coalition cabinet were intensified on the draft budget for the fiscal year of 1983. The mark–dollar spot rate began to depreciate again because of this political crisis and because of the rapid increase in the demand for the dollar in the foreign exchange markets due to a worsening of the situation in the Middle East. On 14 June there was another realignment of the EMS currencies and both the deutsche mark and the Dutch guilder appreciated by 4.25 per cent, while the French franc depreciated by 5.75 per cent and the Italian lira by 2.75 per cent. Our calculation of AIC_M showed that the deutsche mark–dollar forward rate experienced the most significant structural change around this time.

In the period from December 1974 to January 1975 when the Japanese yen–dollar forward rate experienced the most significant structural change, the yen was appreciating. It is well documented that this appreciation of the yen from December 1974 reflected capital inflows (both long term and short term). It has also been asserted that those

capital movements were caused mainly by the interest rate differentials between the USA and Japan. It should also be pointed out that 1974 was characterized as the year of both regulation and deregulation of foreign exchange control by the Japanese government. However, they deregulated inflows of foreign capital and such arrangements were made in particular during the second half of the year.

CONCLUSIONS

The main purpose of this chapter was to find the particular point in time when the forward exchange rate of five major currencies *vis-à-vis* the US dollar underwent a structural change in the recent floating period. Our calculation results of the particular point in time when the forward exchange rates experienced structural changes are reported in Tables 18.1–18.5 and are discussed in some detail in the previous section.[34] The second purpose was to compare the results for the forward rates with those for the spot rates in our previous investigation.

Technically speaking, our approach (the MAIC method) has two distinct advantages over traditional approaches. First, we can avoid any arbitrariness in two areas: (1) arbitrariness in the determination of the significance levels, since the MAIC method is a powerful alternative to the test of the hypothesis method, and (2) arbitrariness arising from the specification of regression models, since only a time-series model is employed. Second, since the MAIC method has been employed extensively in time-series analyses, our method is a straightforward application which brings it one step further towards detecting structural changes.

Although it was possible to ascertain the particular point in time of structural change for each forward rate, the method was unable to confirm a strong relationship between the forward and the spot rates. Furthermore, the points in time of structural change for the spot and the forward rates are not systematically different for the five currencies. Thus, although our method is in a sense indirect, the evidence explored in this chapter serves as another indication that the efficient market hypothesis does not hold, at least not for our sample period.

In economics it is important to make a clear distinction between transitory (or fluctuating) factors and semi-permanent (or relatively constant) factors. Economic analysis of the former factors would be difficult (or impossible) if structural changes were ignored, since the 'structure' is essentially a semi-permanent factor. This point was emphasized by Keynes some fifty years ago:

> Economics is a science of thinking in terms of models.... The object of a model is to segregate the semi-permanent or relatively constant factors from those which are transitory or fluctuating so as to develop a logical way of thinking about the latter, and of understanding the time sequences to which they give rise in particular cases.
>
> (1973: 296–7)

Since the particular points in time of structural change are identified for all currencies, such information should be given special attention when regressing structural models.

NOTES

1 This chapter continues past work by the authors on structural change in the foreign exchange markets. The previous work utilized different data: (1) spot rate – 140 samples (Waragai and Akiba 1986), 153 samples (Waragai and Akiba 1987a; revised in Waragai and Akiba 1989a) and divided samples (Waragai and Akiba 1987b; shortened in Waragai and Akiba 1989b), and (2) forward rate – 140 samples and three-month forward premia (Akiba and Waragai 1988), 153 samples and three-month forward premia (Akiba and Waragai 1989a) and 140 samples and three- and six-month forward premia (Akiba and Waragai 1989b). The present investigation deals with the forward rate of three- and six-month premia (the Japanese yen rate) for the period from January 1974 to September 1986 (153 samples), to be comparable with Waragai and Akiba (1987a) and Akiba and Waragai (1989a).

2 See, for example, Mussa (1979), Levich (1979, 1984), Stein (1980), Isard (1987) and Boothe and Longworth (1986), among many others.

3 See, for example, Mussa (1979), Boothe and Longworth (1986) and Frenkel (1981), among others.

4. See, for example, Frenkel (1981), Mussa (1979), Huang (1984) and Park (1984) to name a few. For an empirical issue of the out-of-sample forecast, see, for example, Meese and Rogoff (1983a, b).

5 In fact, Meese and Rogoff (1983a) show that some structural models outperform the random walk model for a thirty-six-month forecast horizon.

6 In Meese and Rogoff (1983b) the same conclusion as with the superior forecasting power of the random walk model up to a twelve-month forecast horizon is confirmed by a 'grid search' technique that imposes some theoretical coefficient constraints.

7 Lafranc and Racette (1985), based on their *estimation*, concluded that Meese and Rogoff's results (1983a, b) are premature. It is clear, however, that the former misunderstood the latter; the latter simply asserts that the structural models do not perform better than a random walk model for the *out-of-sample forecast*.

8 For empirical studies of a random walk process for the out-of-sample forecast, see, for example, Finn (1986), Somanath (1986), Hakkio (1986) and Ahking and Miller (1987).

9 Here it is implicitly assumed that changes in the forward rate are independent and are not affected by those in the spot rate.

10 As often commented (e.g. Levich 1979, 1984), the test in the literature presupposes, implicitly or explicitly, the rational expectations hypothesis.

11 As Meese and Rogoff (1983a, b) indicate, a univariate time series or a vector time-series model has some predictive power. Furthermore, such time-series models have another desirable character in that they do not depend on any particular economic theory. Since regression models are in general based on and are supposed to test some economic hypothesis, it is hoped that these two models, i.e. time-series models and regression models, serve as complements to each other.

12 There are other time-series models that could be alternatives to an AR model: an AR model with a moving-average process or an ARIMA model in which the time trend can be handled. We used an AR model because (1) much more data are needed for ARMA or ARIMA models and (2) interpretation is easier for an AR model. It should be emphasized that 'structural changes' also include changes in a trend factor. For the procedure of eliminating a trend factor from each divided subprocess, see the second section (note 18).

13 The MAIC method has been employed in econom-

etric works to select the order of AR models. Here we also apply the MAIC method to select the order of an AR model in order to avoid any arbitrariness.

14　The basic idea was developed in Waragai (1986).

15　The sample forward exchange rates (spot–forward spreads) are explained in the next section. For randomness of exchange rates, see note 4.

16　The term 'structural' change should be interpreted as having a purely statistical meaning, although a statistical meaning would include economic meanings.

17　Kitagawa and Akaike (1978) is a generalization of Ozaki and Tong (1975). However, we adopt a different procedure here from Kitagawa and Akaike, deliberating special features (uncertainty and small size of samples) of economic data. Our procedure is also useful in handling more than two structural breaks (Waragai 1987; Waragai and Akiba 1898b). See also notes 18 and 26.

18　It should be pointed out that the procedure of equations (18.1) and (18.2) for eliminating a trend factor is applied to each divided subprocess of $\{x(t)\}$ for (t_0, M) and for (M, t_N). This means that changes in the trend factor are taken into consideration before and after M.

19　Here it is assumed that there exists only one breakpoint in a whole process. Perhaps one should ask (1) whether a structural change has occurred at all, and (2) whether two or more changes have occurred. The first question is resolved by comparing the AIC_M with the AIC_A (for all data assuming no structural change), as we do in note 34, and by invoking an empirical criterion that the difference between $AR(A)$ and $AR(M)$ is significant if $|AIC_A - AIC_M|$ is greater than 1 or 2 (the second remark of Sakamoto et al. (1986: 63)). The second question can also be resolved by utilizing this second remark: If there is (are) other point(s) $M^{*\prime}$ such that $|AIC_{M^{*\prime}} - AIC_{M^*}| < 1$ (or 2) (which means that the difference is not sufficient, i.e. the process could be divided into at least three subprocesses), more than two breakpoints are suspected and the whole process is divided into several subprocesses. Then, one can apply the MAIC method and calculate the AIC to identify the true M^* for each subprocess. Here, applying this method to the calculated AIC in Tables 18.1–18.5, it is judged and assumed that there is one breakpoint for each forward premium. (However, see note 26 for the pound sterling rate.) For more detail, see, for example, Waragai (1987). Because the application method in this chapter was devised in order to identify a turning point within a process, the second question should be further examined from statistical and economic viewpoints.

20　According to Dr W.S. Chow, it may be possible to summarize roughly that Osaki and Tong (1975) is closer to the t test in spirit, while our new application is closer to the F test.

21　The actual values of AIC were calculated by AIC = $N \log \hat{\sigma}^2 + 2(p + 2)$ instead of equation (18.4) because of an implicit assumption of the normal distribution (see Ozaki and Tong 1975). If, because of eliminating the time trend from $z(t)$ (see equation (18.2)), an increase in parameters is also taken into consideration, the last term of equation (18.4) should be $2(p + 4)$. However, such modification will only make AIC greater by either 2 or 4, and will not alter the final conclusion.

22　Data for the European currencies are from *Gaitame Nenkan* (Gaikoku Kawase Joho-sha), 1974–87. Data for the Japanese yen were kindly provided by the Bank of Japan.

23　September 1986 was selected as the end point because of the data availability at the time of estimation for Waragai and Akiba (1987a). For comparison purposes we select the same sample period for the present study.

24　The data are shown in Figures 18.2–18.6 for the period January 1973 to December 1986. However, as mentioned earlier, AIC is calculated from January 1974. See also note 23 for the end point.

25　In these tables, the first line is a possible point in time M (month and year) of the structural break, the second line is the calculated AIC for (t_0, M) (i.e. AIC_0), the third line that for (M, t_N) (i.e. AIC_1) and the last line the sum, i.e. $AIC_M = AIC_0 + AIC_1$. According to the MAIC method, the point in time M^* that minimizes AIC_M should be chosen. Details of the calculation results are available from the authors on request.

26　It is literally true that the AIC took its minimum value (105.839) at this point in time (see Table 18.1). However, it took the second minimum value (106.263) in January–February 1982. Sakamoto et al. (1986: ch. 4) remarked that the difference in AIC can be considered as significant if the difference is more than 1 or 2. Because the actual difference is less than unity, it would be possible to conclude that there exist two distinct points in time of structural change for the forward rate of the pound sterling during this sample period. This is also true for the forward rate of the pound sterling in Akiba and Waragai (1988). For an analysis of two different points in time of structural change for the spot exchange rates, see also our previous work (Waragai 1987; Waragai and Akiba 1987b, 1989b).

27　It should be recalled that this inference holds with the implicit assumption made in note 9.

28　The sample period is exactly the same in both

Waragai and Akiba (1987a) and the present study.

29 This conclusion is also based on the implicit assumption made in note 9.

30 It should be recalled that the spread (per cent per annum), not the forward rate itself, was used in the present study. Furthermore, our conclusion should be taken as tentative in that it is based on the MAIC method and did not consider several key assumptions that the efficient market hypothesis holds strictly. For such assumptions, see, for example, Hansen and Hodrick (1980: 830) or Evans (1986: 622).

31 Because the point in time of structural break of the pound sterling rate can be regarded as identical in our two studies (as remarked in note 26), four out of a total of five forward exchange rates actually exhibit the same points in time of structural break.

32 See note 12 which also explains a technical reason for fewer data for an AR model.

33 Several points in time of structural change could be identified by the piecewise method (see Ozaki and Tong 1975). However, such a method would violate the essential requirement of having a sufficient number of observations to estimate an AR model because of fractionizing data. See also note 19.

34 We also consider the case where there is no structural change in our sample period and calculate its AIC. The AIC_{M^*} is compared with AIC_A (with all data, assuming no structural change) as follows:

		AIC_A		AIC_{M^*}
(a)	Three-month spot–forward spread			
	West Germany	29.272	>	−21.472
	Japan	276.993	>	133.289
	France	300.661	>	267.043
	Switzerland	53.723	>	−16.764
	UK	151.929	>	105.839
(b)	Six-month spot–forward spread			
	Japan	147.780	>	50.309

Thus, we can reject a hypothesis that there exists no structural change within the sample period.

BIBLIOGRAPHY

Agmon, T. and Amihud, Y. (1981) 'The forward exchange rate and the prediction of the future spot rate: empirical evidence', *Journal of Banking and Finance* 5: 425–37.

Agmon, T. and Arad, R. (1983) 'Currency-related risk and risk premium in the world's currency market', *European Economic Review* 22: 257–64.

Ahking, F. W. and Miller, S. M. (1987) 'A comparison of the stochastic processes of structural and time-series exchange-rate models', *Review of Economics and Statistics* 67 (3): 496–502.

Akaike, H. (1973) 'Information theory and an extension of the maximum likelihood principle', in B. N. Petrov and F. Kaski (eds) *2nd International Symposium on Information Theory*, Budapest: Akademiai Kiado.

—— (1974) 'A new look at the statistical model identification', *IEEE Transactions on Automatic Control* AC–19–6: 716–23.

Akiba, H. and Waragai, T. (1988) 'Fluctuation of forward exchange rates and structural changes in the foreign exchange markets: January, 1974 through August, 1985', presented at the Annual Meeting of the Southern Economic Association in San Antonio, Texas, 20–2 November.

—— and —— (1989a) 'Forward foreign exchange rates and structural changes: an application of AIC to five major currencies; January, 1974 through September, 1986', presented at the Spring Meeting of the Japan Association of Monetary Economics, 27–8 May.

—— and —— (1989b) 'An econometric analysis of detecting structural changes in the forward foreign exchange markets with MAIC method', March.

Backus, D. (1984) 'Empirical models of the exchange rate: separating the wheat from the chaff', *Canadian Journal of Economics* 17 (4): 824–46.

Bilson, J. F. O. (1981) 'The "speculative efficiency" hypothesis', *Journal of Business* 54 (3): 435–51.

Boothe, P. and Longworth, D. (1986) 'Foreign exchange market efficiency test: implications of recent empirical findings', *Journal of International Money and Finance* 5: 135–52.

Cornwell, W. B. (1977) 'Spot rates, forward rates and exchange market efficiency', *Journal of Financial Economics* 5: 55–65.

Cornwell, W. B. and Dietrich, J. K. (1978) 'The efficiency of the market for foreign exchange under floating exchange rates', *Review of Economics and Statistics* 62: 111–20.

Engel, C. M. (1984) 'Testing for the absence of expected real profits from forward market speculation', *Journal of International Economics* 17: 299–308.

Evans, G. W. (1986) 'A test for speculative bubbles and the sterling–dollar exchange rate: 1981–84', *American Economic Review* 76 (4): 621–36.

Fama, E. (1976) 'Forward rates as predictors of future spot rates', *Journal of Financial Economics* 3: 361–77.

Finn, M. G. (1986) 'Forecasting the exchange rate: a monetary or random walk phenomenon?', *Journal of*

International Money and Finance 5: 181–93.

Frankel, J. A. (1979) 'The diversifiability of exchange risk', *Journal of International Economics* 9: 379–93.

—— (1982) 'A test of perfect substitutability in the foreign exchange market', *Southern Economic Journal* 49 (2): 406–16.

—— (1982) 'In search of the exchange risk premium: a six-country test assuming mean–variance optimization', *Journal of International Money and Finance* 1: 255–74.

Frenkel, J. A. (1981) 'Flexible exchange rates, prices, and the role of "news": lessons from the 1970s', *Journal of Political Economy* 89 (4): 665–707.

Frenkel, J. A. and Razin, A. (1980) 'Stochastic prices and tests of efficiency of foreign exchange markets', *Economics Letters* 6: 165–70.

Fukuda, T. (1979) 'A method of rapid malfunction diagnosis of random processes by formulation of autoregressive modelling', *Theoretical and Applied Mechanics* 27: 461–70.

Gregory, A. W. and McCurdy, T. H. (1984) 'Testing the unbiasedness hypothesis in the forward foreign exchange market: a specification analysis', *Journal of International Money and Finance* 3: 357–68.

Hakkio, C. S. (1986) 'Does the exchange rate follow a random walk? A Monte Carlo study of four tests for a random walk', *Journal of International Money and Finance* 5: 221–9.

Hansen, L. P. and Hodrick, R. J. (1980) 'Forward exchange rates as optimal predictors of future spot rates: an econometric analysis', *Journal of Political Economy* 88 (5): 829–53.

Hodrick, R. J. and Srivastava, S. (1984) 'An analysis of risk and return in forward foreign exchange', *Journal of International Money and Finance* 3: 5–29.

Huang, R. D. (1984) 'Some alternative tests of forward exchange rate as predictors of future spot rates', *Journal of International Money and Finance* 3: 153–67.

Isard, R. (1987) 'Lessons from empirical models of exchange rates', *IMF Staff Papers* 34 (1): 1–28.

Keynes, J. M. (1973) *The Collected Writings of John Maynard Keynes*, vol. XIV, London: Macmillan.

Kitagawa, G. and Akaike, H. (1978) 'A procedure for the modelling of non-stationary time series', *Annals of the Institute of Statistical Mathematics* 30: 351–63.

Kraats, R. H. V. and Booth, L. D. (1983) 'Empirical tests of the monetary approach to exchange-rate determination', *Journal of International Money and Finance* 2: 255–78.

Krasker, W. S. (1980) 'The "peso problem" in testing the efficiency of forward exchange markets', *Journal of Monetary Economics* 6: 269–76.

Lafrance, R. and Racette, D. (1985) 'The Canadian–U.S. dollar exchange rate: a test of alternative models for the seventies', *Journal of International Money and Finance* 4: 237–52.

Leventakis, J. A. (1978) 'Exchange rate models: do they work?', *Weltwirtschaftliches Archiv* 123 (2): 363–76.

Levich, R. M. (1979) 'On the efficiency of markets for foreign exchange', in R. Dornbusch and J. A. Frenkel (eds) *International Economic Policy: Theory and Evidence*, Baltimore, MD: Johns Hopkins University Press, pp. 246–69.

—— (1984) 'The efficiency of markets for foreign exchange: a review and extension', in G. D. Gay and R. M. Kolb (eds) *International Finance: Concepts and Issues*, Reston, VA: Reston Publishing, pp. 397–428.

Meese, R. A. and Rogoff, K. (1983a) 'Empirical exchange rate models of the seventies: do they fit out of sample?', *Journal of International Economics* 14: 3–24.

—— and —— (1983b) 'The out-of-sample failure of empirical exchange rate models: sampling error or misspecification?', in J. A. Frenkel (ed.) *Exchange Rates and International Macroeconomics*, Chicago, IL: University of Chicago Press.

—— and —— (1985) 'Was it real? The exchange rate–interest differential relation, 1973–1984', International Finance Discussion Paper 268, August, Federal Reserve System.

Mussa, M. (1979) 'Empirical regularities in the behavior of exchange rates and theories of the foreign exchange market', in K. Brunner and A. H. Meltzer (eds) *Policies for Employment, Prices, and Exchange Rates*, Carnegie-Rochester Conference Series on Public Policies, vol. 11, Amsterdam: North-Holland.

Overturf, S. F. (1982) 'Risk, transactions charges, and the market for foreign exchange services', *Economic Inquiry* 20 (2): 291–302.

Ozaki, T. and Tong, H. (1975) 'On the fitting of non-stationary autoregressive models in time series analysis', *Proceedings of the 8th Hawaii International Conference on System Sciences*, North Hollywood, CA: Western Periodicals.

Park, K. (1984) 'Tests of the hypothesis of the existence of risk premium in the foreign exchange market', *Journal of International Money and Finance* 3: 169–78.

Sakamoto, Y., Ishiguro, M. and Kitagawa, G. (1983) *Johoryo Toukeigaku*, Tokyo: Kyoritsu Shuppan (English translation, *AIC Statistics*, Dordrecht: D. Reidel, 1986).

Schinasi, G. S. and Swamy, P. A. V. B. (1987) 'The out-of-sample forecasting performance of exchange rate models when coefficients are allowed to change', International Finance Discussion Paper 301, January, Federal Reserve System.

Somanath, V. S. (1986) 'Efficient exchange rate forecasts: lagged models better than the random walk', *Journal of International Money and Finance* 5: 195–220.

Stein, J. 'The dynamics of spot and forward prices in an efficient foreign exchange market with rational expectations', *American Economic Review* 70 (4): 565–83.

Waragai, T. (1986) 'Jikeiretsu ni motozuku Kouzou Henka no Kenshou', *Chochiku Keizai Riron Kenkyukai Nenpou* 2 (July): 131–48 (in Japanese).

—— (1987) 'Der Einfluß von Reorganisationen auf die Unternehmensentwicklung: Eine ökonometrische Analyse', Discussion Paper D-19, Universität Bonn.

Waragai, T. and Akiba, H. (1986) 'Structural change and time series exchange rates: application of AIC to seven major exchange rates; January, 1974 through August, 1985', mimeo.

—— and —— (1987a) 'Structural changes in the foreign exchange market: an application of AIC to seven major exchange rates; January, 1974 through September, 1986', presented at the 1987 European Meeting of the Econometric Society in Copenhagen, Denmark.

—— and —— (1987b) 'Structural changes in the foreign exchange market: an application of AIC to seven major exchange rates', presented at the International Conference of Economists on Economic Development and the World Debt Problem, Zagreb, Yugoslavia.

—— and —— (1989a) 'An econometric analysis of detecting structural changes in the seven major exchange rates with MAIC method; January, 1974 through September, 1986', *Journal of International Economic Integration* 4 (1): 27–58.

—— and —— (1989b) 'An analysis of structural changes in the seven major exchange rates', in H. W. Singer and S. Sharma (eds) *Growth and External Debt Management*, London: Macmillan, pp. 146–59.

—— and —— (1989c) 'An arbitrariness-free method of detecting structural changes', *Economics Letters* 29 (1): 27–30.

19

THE PURCHASING POWER PARITY CRITERION FOR STABILIZING EXCHANGE RATES

Kenichi Ohno

INTRODUCTION

The naive expectation that a floating exchange rate system would provide an automatic trade adjustment mechanism gave way to dismay during the 1980s as the world witnessed large swings in exchange rates, which were inexplicable by macroeconomic fundamentals, accompanied by huge and persistent trade imbalances among developed economies. Mainstream economists and policy-makers have come to the view that exchange rates need to be managed. The Plaza Agreement of 1985, the Louvre Accord of 1987 and routine G7 statements on the joint commitment to stabilize exchange rates indicate that a continuous process of international monetary reform has now been institutionalized. Within Europe, regional integration is likely to accelerate as arrangements under the EMS are extended and intensified.

As the effort to regulate exchange movements gathers momentum, it is important to prepare a blueprint for an ideal system to which incremental reform measures are supposed to take us ultimately. One such proposal has been advanced by Williamson (1985) and Williamson and Miller (1987). The Williamson proposal envisages adjustable target zones with the objective of balancing current accounts in the medium term (except for relatively small capital flows which are consistent with intertemporal optimization).

This chapter presents another, quite different argument for stabilizing nominal exchange rates based on the normative interpretation of PPP. This proposal, advocated most strongly by McKinnon (1984, 1988), aims at ensuring long-term price stability in an increasingly integrated world. The serious defect of fixed exchange rate systems in the past – including the classical gold standard and the post-war Bretton Woods system – was the lack of a built-in mechanism to avert global inflation and deflation. The McKinnon proposal explicitly introduces such a mechanism in the form of trilateral monetary co-ordination with a nominal anchor consisting of a basket of tradeable goods.

Progress towards exchange rate stability requires re-examination of the old prejudice against fixity of exchange rates. As long as people continue to believe that stable exchange rates must be traded off against stable domestic prices, there will be no broad political support for a fixed exchange rate system, and transition to such a system, even if tried, is unlikely to succeed. This is because exchange rate stability requires regressive expectations which can be achieved only if people have confidence in the newly proposed system.

The chapter is organized as follows. The following section reviews different interpretations of PPP and introduces the McKinnon proposal as a distinct interpretation. The third section discusses policy implications of the McKinnon proposal, while its operational rules are presented in the fourth section. The fifth section discusses the need for a regime change in transition from a floating exchange rate system to a fixed exchange rate system. The sixth section re-examines the cheap dollar policy of the USA in the last two decades.

Finally, the last section briefly discusses estimation of PPP.

PURCHASING POWER PARITY TODAY

The modern concept of PPP originated with the writings of Gustav Cassel (1918, 1921, 1922) in the unsettling monetary aftermath of the First World War. It is well to remember that his exposition of the PPP doctrine included both normative and positive statements: (i) the PPP exchange rate, at which purchasing powers of different national currencies were equalized, was the only *equilibrium* or *desirable* rate; and (ii) the actual nominal exchange rate would *tend towards the PPP level* over time, provided the government did not intervene to prevent it.[1]

Since Cassel's time, economists have long been fascinated with various aspects of the PPP doctrine. PPP has many interpretations and applications and different people often mean different things when they invoke PPP and its derivative concepts. At the outset, it is useful to devote some space to reviewing the popular current uses of the PPP doctrine, for the validity and usefulness – and even the estimation technique – of PPP cannot be evaluated independently of the way it is put to use.

Theory of exchange rate determination

The first, and perhaps the most traditional, version of the PPP doctrine is a purely empirical proposition. It is the theory of exchange rate determination where the nominal exchange rate is predicted to move so as to offset differential inflation rates across countries.[2] This view is often (but not necessarily) combined with the monetary theory of inflation, where a typical causal link runs from money to prices and to the exchange rate. This interpretation of PPP with unilateral causation was dominant until the 1970s.

Correlation between domestic inflation and the nominal exchange rate has been well documented for countries with hyperinflation. However, for low-inflation countries, serious doubt has been thrown on the validity of PPP as a theory of exchange rate determination. Empirically, PPP does very poorly in the short to medium run as far as major currencies in the 1970s and the 1980s are concerned (Frenkel 1981). More recently, however, attention is being directed to the statistical verification of a long-run correlation between prices and nominal exchange rates – in other words, whether there is a notable mean-reverting component in the low frequencies of real exchange rates (Huizinga 1987; Mecagni and Pauly 1987; Ohno 1989). While researchers are yet to arrive at a definitive conclusion, it appears that the predictive power of PPP is much higher at low frequencies (typically long-run trends) than at high frequencies (month-to-month or even year-to-year fluctuations), suggesting cointegration of prices and the exchange rate.

However, one point must be recalled: statistical correlation does not necessarily reveal causality. Mean reversion of real exchange rates can occur either because exchange rates adjust to prices or because prices accommodate exchange rate movements. In the first case, PPP is truly a theory of exchange determination. In the second case, PPP becomes a theory of price determination via commodity arbitrage, with the exchange rate as one of the forcing variables. As far as the yen–dollar exchange rate is concerned, causality seems mutual (Ohno 1989).

In the discussion of PPP as a theory of exchange rate determination, from Keynes (1923a) to Samuelson (1964) and to Dornbusch (1987), much (perhaps too much) attention has been paid to the fact that nationally compiled price indices have different weights. The PPP doctrine is often discredited because, even in an ideal situation where the law of one price holds for every individual good, PPP calculated using these imperfectly comparable indices will diverge from the actual exchange rate unless relative prices among individual goods remain the same – an unlikely proposition. Many formulae for measuring PPP disparity due to relative price changes have been invented and taught at universities as if this were the essence of the PPP doctrine. While practically important, the purely statistical problem of constructing a standard commodity basket should not detract from other important aspects of PPP.

The concept of long-run equilibrium

Quite apart from the empirical validity of PPP, theorists accept PPP as one of the building blocks for constructing various models of exchange rate determination. The two standard theories of exchange rates – the Dornbusch overshooting model and the portfolio-balance model – as well as many other models contain PPP as the long-run equilibrium rate toward which people expect the actual exchange rate to gravitate after an initial shock. For the purpose of theory, whether PPP accurately predicts the movement of exchange rates empirically and *ex post* is less important than the assumption that, *ex ante*, people do expect exchange rates to follow the paths implied by PPP in the long run.

PPP as a (very) long-run equilibrium is an appealing concept, since the international goods market can hardly be considered in full equilibrium unless the law of one price prevails. It is true that many manufactured goods are imperfect substitutes for each other and that commodity arbitrage usually takes a considerable amount of time. Nonetheless, these qualifications only widen the margin within which the law of one price is deemed to hold. If proper account is taken of transportation costs and quality changes, indefinite and persistent divergence from the law of one price is inconsistent with the notion of long-run equilibrium in the goods market under largely free trade.

Conversion factor for income comparison

PPP is also used for a quite different purpose, namely for comparing income and living standards of countries with dissimilar economic characteristics. International economic organizations have a practical need to determine and rank (say) per capita incomes of its member countries, according to which their lending and other policies might be set. Such comparison requires that all local-currency values be converted to a common unit, typically the US dollar.

However, there is a well-known problem in using the actual exchange rate as the conversion factor. Some LDCs have grossly overvalued exchange rates which makes the comparison of living standards unrealistic. Other LDCs have multiple exchange rates, where the appropriate rate for conversion is not obvious. For developed countries, the problem is different but equally serious. When there are large swings in the exchange rates among major currencies, GNP, per capita income, cost of living and so on of one country versus another are changed dramatically, although productivity, resource endowment and living conditions remain virtually the same within each country.

In order to avoid biases and spurious changes in the measurement of national income, both the World Bank and the OECD compute more realistic conversion factors based on the principle of absolute PPP (Ward 1985; Kravis 1986). Every five years they collect the local-currency price data of major categories of national expenditure and use them to update the conversion factors for international comparison. Naturally, their commodity baskets contain many non-tradeable goods and services as well as tradeables. In addition, their price data are evaluated at market price, i.e. they include net indirect taxes. Although these choices are reasonable given the purpose of their exercise, these PPP estimates are not directly transferable to other applications of the PPP doctrine. For instance, there is no reason to believe that actual exchange rates would converge to the OECD or World Bank estimates of PPP which include prices of non-tradeables. Nor would one regard the estimated conversion factors as proper target zones for stabilizing exchange rates.

Normative policy criterion

Finally, there is another important aspect of PPP, which serves as the normative benchmark for guiding monetary and exchange rate policies.

For an LDC wishing to expand and diversify the

export base, it is important to have a 'realistic' exchange rate which allows the tradeable sector to compete effectively with foreign products. More often than not, however, countries with a lapse in fiscal and monetary discipline permit high domestic inflation to develop and eventually price themselves out of international competition. When this occurs, devaluation of the home currency is necessary to restore the lost price competitiveness. In the absence of detailed price data, one would normally take the most recent period prior to a bout of inflation as the base, and use relative price indices to calculate the required amount of corrective devaluation.[3]

For developed countries, the idea of using PPP as a policy criterion is proposed by Ronald McKinnon. The remainder of this chapter is devoted to this particular interpretation of PPP. The industrial world has become integrated economically not only through trade but also financially to such an extent that McKinnon contends the only practical way to ensure global price stability is through co-ordination rather than through independent and inward-looking policies of individual countries. While an internationally common currency is unlikely to emerge and replace national currencies in the foreseeable future, McKinnon believes that the major industrial economies can simulate the situation under a common monetary standard by means of monetary co-operation.

The policy co-ordination that McKinnon proposes is a unique one. It is basically a *monetary* proposal, rather than a broad mixture of fiscal, monetary and structural recommendations as in the 'indicators' approach. Its primary objective is to attain long-term price stability among major industrial countries. The key ingredients of his proposal are (i) commitment to permanently fixed nominal exchange rates; (ii) use of the price of a broad basket of internationally tradeable goods as the nominal anchor of the system; and (iii) relative-price adjustment mechanisms based on divergent price movements of various non-tradeable goods. At the operational level, McKinnon proposes a few basic rules that the

central banks of the USA, Japan and Germany (or a European central bank in the future) should abide by. This version of PPP encompasses a sweeping reform of the international monetary system as well as a radical change in the way macroeconomic policies are conducted in each country. In the following sections, various aspects of the McKinnon proposal will be examined in some detail.

PURCHASING POWER PARTITY AS A POLICY CRITERION

According to the PPP criterion for stabilizing exchange rates, nominal exchange rates should be set at levels where the prices of a common broad basket of internationally tradeable goods in different countries are equalized when converted to a single currency unit using these exchange rates.

Under a system of permanently fixed exchange parities and free trade, PPP in tradeable goods is a trivial proposition because it is always satisfied, for there will be ample time for international commodity arbitrage to assert itself. Under a floating exchange rate regime, however, PPP in tradeable goods is far from trivial. Prices of most tradeable goods (with the exception of precious metals and certain primary commodities which are traded in efficient international markets) are sticky, while exchange rates can change rapidly. As a consequence, violation of the law of one price becomes the rule rather than the exception, especially for manufactured goods. Under such circumstances, PPP in tradeables will not hold unless the exchange rate happens to be at the 'correct' level. One problem that must be addressed is how the 'correct' level can be estimated so as to make the transition from the present regime to a new regime of fixed exchange rates as smooth as possible.

However, the PPP criterion goes beyond estimating the 'correct' starting values for a new regime and includes important policy implications. Its most important policy implications are discussed below.

Commitment to permanently fixed exchange rates

The microeconomic costs of exchange rate instability are by now well known. Although some economists view the exchange rate as just another asset price which merely transmits information emanating from other sectors of the economy, the exchange rate is different from other asset prices because it is the relative price of *numeraires*. Unlike prices of gold, crude oil or wheat, the exchange rate affects relative positions of *every* price and contract denominated in different currencies. Unstable standards of value not only distort internal relative prices between tradeables and non-tradeables but also induce unnecessary macroeconomic instability through imported inflation and deflation. These adverse, across-theboard effects of exchange changes would be less troublesome if all internal prices adjusted immediately and proportionately to any change in the exchange rate. In reality, however, the incidence of a fluctuating exchange rate is far from uniform.

Fixing nominal exchange rates among major industrial countries implies that these countries will lose independence in monetary policy and subject themselves to a common monetary policy of the whole system. The money supply of each country will be endogenized through the obligation to maintain official parities, and interest rates will also converge internationally. Furthermore, each member country of the system will tend to have the same rate of inflation in tradeable goods through international commodity arbitrage.

This will provide an environment of long-term monetary stability in which national economies become ever more integrated through trade and finance, as if they were regions of a single country. McKinnon considers lasting stability in the conversion rates of national currencies as the prerequisite for promoting growth and efficiency of the world economy. Furthermore, he believes that industrial economies became highly interdependent during the 1970s and the 1980s, that most macroeconomic shocks of these decades had international origins and that authorities' outmoded obsession for independent monetary action is not only unattainable but positively harmful in its consequences.

Nominal anchor

Then there is the famous $N - 1$ problem. To fix exchange rates among N countries, only $N - 1$ independent actions are necessary. How to allocate the remaining one degree of freedom among member countries has been a major sticking point in designing a system of fixed parities. McKinnon's answer is to assign it to anchoring the common price level.

The PPP criterion adopts the common price level of internationally tradeable goods as the *nominal anchor* for the new international monetary system. Generally speaking, a nominal anchor is something – often some reference index – which serves as an 'anchor' to prevent instability of various nominal variables in the system, and especially the general price level. Ideally, the authorities are obliged to adjust their policies systematically so as to stabilize this index over time.[4] It can arguably be said that none of the international monetary systems in the past had an effective nominal anchor. The world-wide price trend under the nineteenth-century gold standard was at the mercy of supply and demand conditions of gold, over which the authorities had little control. The Bretton Woods system contained the undesirable mechanism by which inflationary pressure in the USA was amplified and transmitted abroad through the unilateral obligation to intervene by the others. The current managed float, where each country mainly minds its own domestic price trends, lacks an enforceable mechanism to prevent world-wide inflation or deflation.

For the success of any international monetary system, it is imperative that an explicit provision is made for a workable nominal anchor. McKinnon's PPP criterion proposes that the price of a broad basket of tradeable goods, including both primary commodities and manufactured products, be such an anchor. The advantage of this is twofold.

First, it strikes a proper balance between *rele-*

vance and *controllability* which are two requirements for a good nominal anchor. On the one
hand, while nominal GNP and GNP deflators are
highly relevant for economic well-being, they are
announced with long lags and frequent revisions.
On the other hand, gold and other primary
commodity prices are reported daily with precision
but have only remote consequences for national
welfare. The price of a broad basket of tradeable
goods (something like producer or wholesale price
indices) is more desirable because it is both
economically meaningful and readily available
with only a short delay.

Second, it is a natural, and in fact the only
consistent, nominal anchor in a system based on
economic integration and fixed parities. When
relative prices change within each country, it is
obviously impossible to stabilize *all* prices.
Suppose there is a tendency for tradeable prices to
fall relative to non-tradeable prices because of a
sectoral productivity differential. Suppose further
that each country has a different degree of internal
price divergence.[5] In such a situation, if each
country attempted to stabilize non-tradeable prices
(or a combination of tradeable and non-tradeable
prices), PPP in tradeables would require that
nominal exchange rates be adjusted over time.
This is inconsistent with maintenance of fixed
exchange rates. Worse, once parities were allowed
to change, expectations about future realignment
would be unleashed and foreign exchange markets
would soon be dominated by 'news'. Orderly and
gradual adjustment in exchange rates under free
capital mobility is very difficult to implement, as
was learned in the 1980s and will be further
discussed in the fifth section.

Adjustment mechanism

How should adjustment be made when there is a
real shock – say, a shift in demand, a bout of
technological breakthroughs or a discovery of
mineral resources – under a fixed exchange rate
regime? A successful international monetary
system must surely have an adjustment mechanism
which can smoothly absorb these (mostly country-

specific) real shocks. An ideal floating exchange
rate system was supposed to provide exactly such a
mechanism. But its actual working has been
plagued with overshooting and misalignment.

Contrary to the popular belief, McKinnon
argues that adjustment will be smoother under a
fixed exchange rate system than a floating
exchange rate system, given an exogenous real
shock and required changes in relative prices and
resource reallocation. This is particularly so if the
economy is highly integrated with the rest of the
world. As striking historical examples, McKinnon
points to the experiences of the Dutch and the
British:

With the worldwide increase in the price of
oil in 1979, and Britain's emergence as a
major oil exporter, investors projected that
U.K. foreign exchange earnings would be
greater in the future.... This was immediately registered in the foreign exchange
market by a large increase in the demand for
spot sterling in 1979. Thus, the nominal (and
real) foreign exchange value of sterling rose
sharply, precipitately deflating the British
economy and reducing international competitiveness so as to wipe out a large chunk
of British manufacturing in 1980–81....

The Dutch experience with the discovery
and development of large natural gas fields
in the early 1960s is an instructive comparison. Because everyone knew that under
the old Bretton Woods system the guilder's
foreign exchange value was fixed in dollar
(and mark) terms throughout the 1960s, no
immediate international rush into guilder
assets took place – and there was no precipitate exchange appreciation and deflation
of the Dutch economy. To be sure, as the
natural gas sector expanded and the tax
revenues were spent for domestic goods and
services thus bidding up wages, other Dutch
tradable goods industries inevitably declined
– the well-known phenomenon called the
'Dutch Disease.' But this decline was
gradual. The fixed exchange rate avoided

sharp appreciation and deflation – accompanied by heavy unemployment – of the kind that Britain was to suffer a decade later.

(McKinnon 1988: 87–8)

It should be noted that the relative price of concern here is not the price ratio of tradeable goods in country A versus tradeable goods in country B, but the price ratio between tradeable goods and non-tradeable goods within a country. It is the latter price ratio that directly affects an economy's resource allocation and trade flows.

If the McKinnon proposal is successfully launched, the world economy will have a common and stable price level of tradeable goods. Relative price adjustment under this regime would be effected by letting individual prices of both tradeable and non-tradeable goods adjust freely, while keeping the average price of well-defined tradeable goods constant in every currency.[6] Diverging internal prices have been a focus of many international trade theories, and also provide the core concept for the Scandinavian model of inflation. Empirically, such tendencies have been identified in many studies, classically by Balassa (1964) and more recently by Marston (1987).

Suppose the monetary authorities of major industrial countries had succeeded in (i) fixing nominal exchange rates at the PPP level defined by tradeable goods and (ii) stabilizing the common tradeable price level over a long period of time. How would various domestic prices – consumer prices, unit labour cost, GNP deflators, nominal wages – behave in such a hypothetical world?

Figures 19.1–19.3 give us a clue.[7] Each figure shows, respectively for the USA, Japan and Germany, various domestic prices deflated by domestic tradeables prices (i.e. the producer price index) for the period 1960–89. This simulates – counterfactually – continuous stability in exchange rates and tradeables prices using the data which were in fact characterized by price instability especially in the 1970s and 1980s. The contrast between the USA and Japan is immediately clear. Japan had greatly diverging internal relative prices as its tradeable sector far outstripped its non-tradeable sector in productivity growth. No such long-term trends are apparent in the US data.

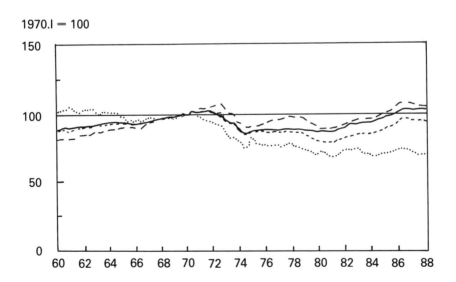

1970.I = 100

Figure 19.1 USA: internal price movements, 1960–88 (simulated with unchanging producer prices). The series on producer prices is simply subtracted from those on wages, consumer prices, GNP deflator and unit labour costs: ———, CPI;·   ----, GNP deflator;   ....., unit labour cost;   ---, wages

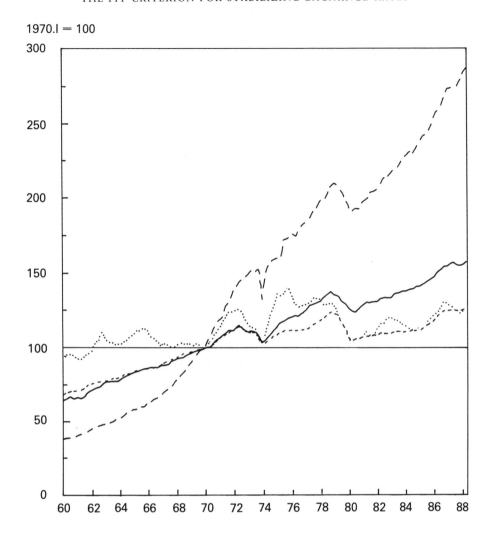

1970.I = 100

Figure 19.2 Japan: internal price movements, 1960–88 (simulated with unchanging producer prices). The series on producer prices is simply subtracted from those on wages, consumer prices, GNP deflator and unit labour costs: ———, CPI;   ----, GNP deflator;   · · · · ·, unit labour cost;   ---, wages

Germany is an intermediate case where internal relative wages changed moderately over time. Another salient feature of these figures is the downward spikes corresponding to the two so-called 'oil shocks' in the 1973–4 and 1979–80. During these periods, tradeable prices rose faster than non-tradeable prices and caused irreversible change in relative prices. Except for unit labour costs which are affected by business cycles, all three figures reveal a sharp contrast between the

Bretton Woods period where internal relative price movements were highly stable and predictable and the subsequent floating rate period where the long-term trends were frequently disturbed. However, notwithstanding these disturbances in the 1970s and the 1980s, the general trends in internal relative prices since the 1960s have continued.

Of these internal price movements, further consider nominal wages. Under the McKinnon proposal, the average tradeable price is anchored

401

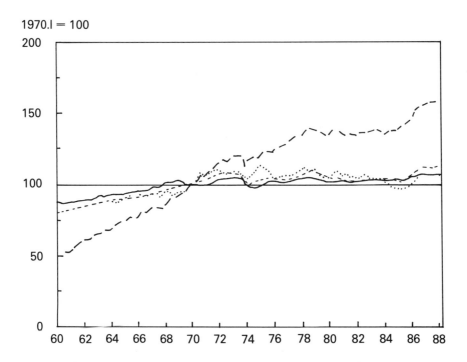

1970.I = 100

Figure 19.3 Germany: internal price movements, 1960–88 (simulated with unchanging producer prices). The series on producer prices is simply subtracted from those on wages, consumer prices, GNP deflator and unit labour costs:
————, CPI;   ----, GNP deflator;   ·····, unit labour cost;   ———, wages

while non-tradeables' prices are free to change. Nominal (and real) wages may respond to domestic aggregate demand in the short run, but as the time scope lengthens the change in nominal wages will reflect mostly the change in labour productivity. One of the important objectives of the PPP criterion is to restore nominal prices (whether in dollar or yen) as indicators of economic scarcity. By contrast, under the current system the movement of nominal wages is mostly dominated by monetary disturbances including inflation and exchange misalignment, and it is difficult to extract real signals from such a noisy price. Scrambled signals confuse economic agents and hamper real adjustment when it is actually required.

The phenomenon of diverging non-tradeable prices and stable tradeable prices under fixed exchange parities is not historically unprecedented. The Bretton Woods system offers one example.

Throughout the 1960s, Japanese nominal wages rose at the annual rate of 11.3 per cent while US wages increased only at 3.8 per cent per year – because of differential labour productivity growth in the two countries. All this while, the nominal yen–dollar rate was fixed at 360 and producer prices in both countries were virtually unchanged, rising only 1.2 per cent in Japan and 1.5 per cent in the USA annually. In addition, Japanese money supply was largely endogenous to the commitment to the fixed parity – and ultimately to US monetary policy. Money in Japan necessarily increased much faster than in the USA in order to prevent imbalance in the balance of payments.

By the early 1970s, however, the common monetary standard of the Bretton Woods system broke down and money supply no longer followed productivity change or real growth. Between 1975 and 1986, US nominal wages exactly doubled and Japanese wages increased by 90 per cent.

However, had wages reflected productivity changes as in the 1960s, they would have risen only 17 per cent in the USA and 52 per cent in Japan. Under the current regime, nominal wages no longer reflect productivity and are biased upwards due to world-wide inflation.

Trade imbalance and the exchange rate

In 1987 – the year of the Louvre Accord and the Wall Street crash – economists had an intense debate in the press on correlation between the dollar exchange rate and the US trade deficit. Feldstein, Dornbusch, Krugman and many others took the position that a further significant depreciation of the dollar was unavoidable and indeed desirable if the trade imbalance was to be corrected. These economists viewed the trade problem essentially as that of the wrong real exchange rate, defined as the relative price of country A's tradeables against country B's tradeables. To them, reducing the fiscal deficit was not central to correcting the trade imbalance, and it mattered only to the extent that fiscal tightness lowered interest rates which tended to depreciate the dollar. This view can be termed the 'balanced trade criterion' for managing exchange rates.

In contrast, the PPP criterion for stabilizing exchange rates embraces a fundamentally different view based on the absorption principle. McKinnon, Mundell, Modigliani and others argued that the US trade deficit in the 1980s was primarily an aggregate demand problem. As long as the federal government continued to overspend its revenue while private sector savings continued to stagnate, no adjustment in the nominal or real exchange rate could significantly narrow the resulting enormous savings–investment gap. As the vehicle currency country, the US government is able to preemptively issue Treasury securities in international financial markets, thereby forcing foreign economies to generate net savings which are used to finance US dissavings – without having to formally arrange official or commercial loans with foreigners.

These economists seriously question the validity of the traditional argument that a cheap dollar can improve the US trade balance when the world economy is integrated. An exchange rate depreciation *may* have a favourable effect on the home country's competitiveness, but – if the economy is highly open – it also stimulates investment in the tradeable sector and other components of absorption which has an adverse effect on the trade balance, with an uncertain net impact. For example, the co-ordinated policy to drive up the yen against the dollar caused a recession in the tradeable sector of Japan in 1987–8 and depressed Japanese import demand so that the trade imbalance remained substantial despite a large change in the real yen–dollar exchange rate.

According to the PPP criterion, exchange rate policy should not be used for balancing or in any way affecting the trade balance. This is because exchange rate policy does not have the comparative advantage in achieving external balance – it is fiscal and other aggregate demand policies that will be most effective for that purpose. Instead, consistent with the PPP criterion, the objective of exchange rate policy (supported by appropriate monetary co-ordination) should be confined to stabilization of the common price level. McKinnon (1988) notes that the similar size of the US fiscal deficit and the US trade deficit during the 1980s was not accidental. US external balance should be restored not by manipulation of the dollar but by decisive policy actions on the budget deficit and the promotion of private savings.

Some critics of McKinnon – notably Krugman and Baldwin (1987) – purport to show that a fixed exchange rate is inconsistent with real adjustment. They argue that, in order to eliminate undesirable trade imbalance, a change in relative price is necessary. Since their model has only one relative price (exchange rate) by construction, it follows that the exchange rate must change if one wishes to change the trade balance. However, their mono-product model cannot refute the McKinnon proposal which assumes a more complex and realistic economic structure. As soon as the existence of non-tradeable goods in addition to tradeable goods is considered, adjustment of the nominal exchange rate is no longer necessary in order to change the internal relative price. The literature on the transfer problem also tells us that, in general, there is no presumption that the terms of trade of a capital-receiving country (i.e. country with a trade deficit) have to improve or worsen. The relationship between the exchange rate and the trade balance is not a simple one in an open, large economy.

OPERATIONAL RULES

Operationally, the McKinnon proposal consists of a few simple monetary rules.[8]

First rule: establishing exchange parities

The key element of the McKinnon proposal is the establishment of fixed exchange rates among the three countries: the USA, Japan and Germany (or the EMS). The first basic task for policy-makers is to calculate the starting exchange rates based on PPP in tradeable goods. Once determined, these parities will be irrevocable as long as the system survives.

Technical problems in the estimation of these initial values will be discussed further in the final section. Here it suffices to say that estimation of PPP can be performed with scientific accuracy and estimated PPP exchange rates using different methods are quite similar to each other, as will be seen below.

Aside from technicalities in estimating PPP, there are two practical issues that have to be considered in the transition from a floating exchange rate system to a fixed exchange rate system. The first is concerned with inflation momentum and the second with credibility of the new system.

New parities should be set at levels such that tradeable prices of individual countries will converge to a common level most smoothly. This requires that the new parities be sufficiently close to current PPP levels to avoid unnecessary inflation or deflation during the transition. However, current PPP exchange rates may not be exactly the right rates for the following reason. Under the current regime, exchange rates are almost always misaligned (by the PPP criterion), exerting different price pressures on individual economies. For example, following the Plaza Agreement and during the second half of the 1980s, the yen was continuously overvalued against the dollar and as a consequence Japanese inflation was consistently lower than US inflation. At the end of 1988, wholesale prices were rising by an annual 4.0 per cent in the USA compared with −1.1 per cent in Japan – a difference of more than 5 per cent. Such inflation momentum does not disappear immediately under the new system but will continue at least for a few quarters and perhaps longer. Thus McKinnon recommends that starting parity values for the new system should be the estimated PPP rates adjusted for such drifts.

Next is the concern that people may have less than full confidence on the effectiveness of the newly proposed system. This is a serious matter because the survival of a fixed exchange rate system requires regressive exchange rate expectations, and the success of the system thus depends on how quickly credibility of the new system is established. Convincing the populace mainly belongs to the realm of statesmanship rather than economics, but three necessary conditions for persuasion should be recognized. First, the secrecy which characterizes the current G7 co-ordination should be abandoned and the new parities should be officially announced. These parities should be permanent as the McKinnon proposal prescribes. Second, the adjustment mechanism under a fixed exchange rate system and its feasibility (see the third section) should be understood thoroughly by policy-makers and propagated to the general population. If people are indoctrinated that price stability is incompatible with a fixed exchange rate system, no support for it will emerge. Third, recognizing that credibility may not be gained overnight, the initial band for allowable exchange fluctuation could be somewhat broad, say 5 per cent of the new parities. As experience gathers and confidence solidifies in the new system, the band could be narrowed. The margin of 1 per cent around the parity, the same as in the Bretton Woods system, is suggested by McKinnon.

Second rule: symmetry in monetary adjustment

After the parities are set, how can actual exchange rates be guaranteed to stay close to the parities? – by symmetric monetary adjustment. Specifically, monetary authorities of the USA, Japan and Germany (or the EMS) are required to adjust their *relative* policy stance to maintain the exchange parities, using two of the three degrees of policy freedom which are available to them.

Suppose pressure developed to push up the yen against the dollar beyond the band of allowable fluctuations. The Bank of Japan would be required immediately to ease monetary policy from the prescribed position (see the third rule) and at the same time the US Federal Reserve would be required to tighten relative to its prescribed position. This could normally be achieved by daily fine-tuning of short-term interest rates through open market operations. If necessary, such operations could be supported by changes in discount rates.

Direct intervention in the foreign exchange market would not be called for except in an emergency in which confidence in the system deteriorated. But if such an emergency unfortunately arose, intervention must be *symmetric, non-sterilized and without limit*. Expectations would become stabilizing only if domestic monetary policies were adjusted in the appropriate way. Intervention would be effective mainly as a signal of authorities' firm commitment that the monetary base would decrease in a weak-currency country and increase in a strong-currency country, and that this would continue until pressure on the exchange rates disappeared. The need actually to resort to interest rate adjustment or intervention is inversely related to people's confidence in the stability of exchange rates.

Third rule: nominal anchor

In a fixed exchange rate system tradeable price levels in the USA, Japan and Europe would converge. The last degree of freedom in the triumvirate monetary policy should be used to ensure that the common inflation in tradeable goods would be zero in the long run (see the third section).

The three monetary authorities are required to do the following. First, they need to monitor the price trend of tradeable goods in each currency constantly. Ideally, a unique 'international tradeable price index' representing the production structure of major industrial countries should be constructed and used as the nominal anchor of the system. Until such an index is devised, existing producer price indices or wholesale price indices which are compiled somewhat differently from country to country could be used. Bias arising from different weights of these national indices would, as a practical matter, be quite small.

Second, if global inflation or deflation is detected, the three monetary authorities are required to adjust policy stance simultaneously – typically by accelerating or decelerating money supply growth. Unless centrifugal pressure exists in the foreign exchange market, their *relative* policy stance should remain unchanged. Under this system, relative monetary policy is assigned to stabilizing prices. Because judging price movements is difficult, stabilizing the nominal anchor may not always succeed in the short run. But as long as *long-term* stability of tradeable prices is ensured, policy-makers need not be very concerned about short-term price fluctuations. If producers, consumers and investors are assured that the international purchasing power of their national currency will remain virtually the same in ten or twenty years' time, annual ups and downs in the price level will do little harm to economic efficiency.

Lastly, as a long-term norm, it is useful to calculate the normal growth rate of money supply for each country in the absence of exchange rate pressure or global price pressure. The normal growth rate of money would depend on the potential growth rate of output as well as the trend in velocity. Technical problems in defining money and predicting these trends will still remain, but they are not unique to the McKinnon proposal. Moreover, long-term exchange rate and price stability would minimize the uncertainty surrounding these forecasts.

Is a common currency necessary?

McKinnon argues that the benefits of a common monetary standard concerning economic stability and efficiency can be achieved even without a unified currency, and the existence of many national currencies is compatible with these benefits. During the nineteenth-century gold standard years and also the Bretton Woods years, despite lack of monetary independence the monetary authority could (and did) control and regulate the banking sector in each country more or less independently from those of other countries. If a financial crisis broke out, each central bank had the right and the obligation to assume the role of the 'lender of last resort' within each country. Thus the policy of each central bank did matter institutionally although money supply was not independent in the macroeconomic sense.

To promote international monetary co-ordination, the scope of co-ordination should not be broadened unnecessarily. To implement the McKinnon proposal, all power over monetary and financial matters could still be decentralized so long as the three rules presented above are observed. McKinnon would rather not see the hasty establishment of a World Central Bank or the issuance of a common currency which would obscure the responsibility of protecting the financial system against banking crises. Fixed exchange rates will function well even if national currencies continue to circulate and monetary authorities' supervisory responsibilities remain within national boundaries.

Thus the McKinnon proposal does not require any substantive reorganization in the existing monetary and financial institutions. It is in the behavioural pattern of major central banks that a bold reform is called for.

REGIME CHANGE

One criticism often raised against restoration of fixed exchange rates points to the fact that private capital flows are much larger than the foreign exchange reserves which could be mobilized by monetary authorities. This leads to the concern that governments might not be able to manage – let alone fix – exchange rates against market trends. This argument, while apparently plausible, needs to be reassessed with historical facts and more careful thinking.

Historically, there has been no simple correlation between private capital movement and stability in exchange rates. Even with tight capital control and little portfolio capital movement, people will use all possible ways – legal and illegal – to move funds once destabilizing expectations are formed, leading to an eventual collapse of fixed parities. The Bank of England was unable to prevent such destabilizing speculations in the 1960s. Despite massive intervention, the Bank of Japan and the Bundesbank were equally powerless to support their dollar parities at the end of the Bretton Woods period and the subsequent Smithsonian rates. In contrast, the full-fledged international gold standard of 1880–1913 had absolutely no parity realignment for over three decades, although private capital flows were a few to several percentage points of each country's GNP and the gold reserve of the Bank of England was minuscule compared with these capital flows. Sustainability of a fixed exchange rate system mainly depends not on the size of capital flows or foreign exchange reserves but on the stability of exchange rate expectations.

Assuming that people are rational, regressive exchange rate expectations require that actual exchange rates do revert to previous levels after each temporary shock. The necessary condition for this is that monetary policy is not prone to excessive expansion or contraction (relative to the world norm) which will necessitate depreciation or appreciation. A country whose macroeconomic policy is constrained by the commitment to a fixed exchange rate satisfies this condition because its money supply is endogenously determined to align domestic inflation with world inflation. Furthermore, fixed exchange rates reduce exchange risk to a negligible level. On the other hand, under a floating exchange rate system information required of international businessmen and investors is far greater. A country with a floating exchange rate or which retains the right to change the exchange rate under certain conditions (crawling peg, adjustable peg and adjustable target zone) is unlikely to have stabilizing expectations because of the high degrees of uncertainty about when, in which direction and by how much the right is exercised.

Stabilizing regime

There are two stable *systemic* equilibria with regard to stability of expectations and commitment to fixed parities – stable in the sense that the initial state of affairs, whether turbulent or tranquil, will return after each shock. One systemic equilibrium is characterized by strong commitment by the authorities to defend the existing fixed exchange rates unconditionally and indefinitely using all policy instruments. If the authorities' commitment is credible, expectations become stabilizing which ensures that actual exchange rates will not deviate from the prescribed bands. This in turn facilitates the implementation of the official commitment – and the virtuous circle begins.

When nominal exchange rates have been constant for a number of years, people may forget that exchange rates are what they are because of monetary policy. A myth will be born that exchange rates are immutable, and one dollar must inherently be equal to (say) 360 yen as one mile must necessarily be equal to 1.609 kilometres. Under these circumstances, monetary authorities will be able to maintain fixed parities without moving a finger, enhancing the myth and dispelling the remaining doubt about sustainability of the parities. History proves that this is not a fantasy. After the Civil War the USA was naturally expected to return to the gold standard at the pre-war parity, and it did. Severe financial crises of the

late nineteenth century did not leave any trace in the nominal exchange rates of principal countries. More recently, few Japanese imagined that a dollar could be anything other than 360 yen until the Bretton Woods system collapsed before their eyes.

Destabilizing regime

The second systemic equilibrium obtains when the authorities support exchange rate flexibility, allow actual exchange rates to move beyond any specific targets and pledge that domestic monetary policy will not be subjugated to exchange rate stabilization. Under *laissez-faire* exchange rate policy, formation of people's expectations will be completely different from the first case. In the absence of expectational anchors (i.e. official parities), developments in the foreign exchange market will be dominated by market psychology leading to a situation (which Keynes called the beauty contest) where people attempt to guess other people's guesses about what others think, *ad infinitum*. Daily volatility, medium term misalignment and unpredictability from currently available information are well-documented features of exchange rates under such a system. The dominant driving force of exchange rates is news, and fundamentals matter only to the extent that they appear on the Reuters screen. News unrelated to fundamentals also hits the market. Fashionable news constantly shifts, from US M1 and short-term interest rates in the early 1980s to monthly trade statistics in the mid-1980s, and now to Eastern European and Middle Eastern situations. Once out of favour, some news (e.g. US monetary and trade news) is almost completely ignored. Other irregularities include alternating calm and turbulent periods in the foreign exchange market and shifting currencies in the spot light. These shifts cannot be explained by fundamentals which do not move in such a discontinuous manner.

In such a world, capital which would otherwise stay within a country for a long time is forced to make intra-daily trips between different currencies in pursuit of exchange gain. The volume in the foreign exchange market grows disproportionately to savings and investment flows and the authorities are no longer able to stem the swollen tide. Policy to permit instability of exchange rates actually encourages destabilization of expectations and exchange rates – and the self-fulfilling prophecy is realized. This is what the world witnessed in the 1970s and the 1980s.

The fallacy in Friedman's classical argument (1953) that speculation would be stabilizing under a floating exchange rate system is now clear. And the debate which was stimulated by his argument over stability or instability of exchange rate expectations was futile because it did not recognize the crucial dependence of expectations on the international monetary system. Expectations are stabilizing in a successful fixed exchange rate system and destabilizing in a floating exchange rate system, and in either case consistent with the perpetuation of the existing order. McKinnon is proposing that the world economy make a transition from a destabilizing regime to a stabilizing regime. The fact that speculation is destabilizing under the current system does not provide any proof that it will also be destabilizing under the proposed regime.

Bretton Woods revisited

It is useful to compare the McKinnon proposal with different exchange rate systems from the viewpoint of regime change. The first comparison is with the Bretton Woods system. The McKinnon proposal differs from the Bretton Woods system in the following three important respects. First, exchange rates would be *permanently* fixed and no realignment for the reason of 'fundamental disequilibrium' would be permitted. Under the Bretton Woods system, the deutsche mark and the pound sterling underwent disruptive processes of parity adjustment, although the yen was spared such distress. Second, a nominal anchor consisting of a common tradeable goods basket would be in place. The nominal anchor of the Bretton Woods system was officially gold, but global price stability depended in effect on US monetary policy. This turned out to be an undependable mooring espe-

cially after the late 1960s when the official linkage between the dollar and gold was removed. Third, symmetric co-ordination among the USA, Japan and Europe would be institutionalized. If implemented, this would be the first multilateral attempt to control global liquidity. In contrast, the Bretton Woods system was characterized by asymmetry between a benign neglect of the centre country and a unilateral obligation to intervene by all other countries. It lacked a mechanism to prevent US inflation from being transmitted to the rest of the world.

The McKinnon proposal is a far more stabilizing regime than the Bretton Woods system because it explicitly provides irreversibility of exchange rate parities and an arrangement for avoiding global monetary instability that could lead to a collapse of the system.

Williamson proposal

The Williamson proposal advocates adjustable target zones. Under his proposal, actual exchange rates would have to be confined to the vicinity of what he terms the 'fundamental equilibrium exchange rates' (FEERs). The FEER is defined as 'that which is expected to generate a current account surplus or deficit equal to the underlying capital flow over a cycle, given that the country is pursuing "internal balance" as best as it can and not restricting trade for balance of payments reasons' (Williamson 1985: 14). Clearly, the main objective of the Williamson proposal is to manage trade flows using exchange rate policy, differing fundamentally from the McKinnon proposal based on the PPP criterion for stabilizing exchange rates. Williamson's 1985 book shows how to estimate FEERs step by step. His 1987 book co-authored with Miller extends the original proposal by proposing a unique policy mix: assign *relative* short-term interest policy to exchange rate targets and the *absolute* level of short-term interest rates to aggregate demand management on a global scale. In addition, fiscal policy should be used to fine-tune aggregate demand within each country. A large econometric model (MCM model) is simulated to demonstrate the superiority of the Williamson–Miller blueprint over other proposals, including McKinnon's.

One may be puzzled at the peculiar assignment of monetary policy to external balance and fiscal policy to price stability. However, the more serious problem of the Williamson proposal is the suggestion that FEERs and the target zones around them need to be adjusted over time as various real shocks hit the system. Although the authors assert that expectations would be supportive of target zones when their revisions are gradual and foreseen, they lack the argument to substantiate their claim. Unlike the McKinnon proposal, the Williamson proposal contains a systemic dilemma: on the one hand, there is no commitment to long-term stability of exchange rates; and on the other hand, maintenance of target zones requires regressive expectations. Since the formula for FEERs is publicized, anyone who follows macroeconomic news would know the direction of the next target zone adjustment. As soon as it was known, could an investor with an international portfolio resist reshuffling his assets? Or could the market ignore a rumour – however groundless – that the US trade deficit announced next week would be larger than previously anticipated?

The Williamson proposal is an unstable regime from the viewpoint of systemic stability. Such a system is likely to degenerate either to a *de facto* fixed exchange rate system where – despite the avowed flexibility – realignment becomes less and less frequent, thereby promoting regressive expectations (examples are the Bretton Woods system and the EMS), or a *de facto* floating exchange rate system where news dominates the foreign exchange market and target zones are adjusted passively to more or less independent movements of exchange rates (an example is the current system of G7 co-ordination based on clandestine reference ranges).

REAPPRAISAL OF CHEAP DOLLAR POLICY

The USA adopted cheap dollar policy intermit-

tently during the 1970s and the 1980s. Did the policy achieve its objective of improving the international competitiveness of US industry in the long run?

It was argued in the third section that manipulation of nominal exchange rates was unlikely to affect trade flows among financially open industrial countries systematically. This was because depreciation induced macroeconomic repercussions which partially or totally offset the desirable relative price effect. The argument, however, did not deny the presumption that a dollar depreciation did improve price competitiveness of US industry. It is now asked whether cheap dollar policy has a favourable effect on US competitiveness in the long run as well.

Before presenting the main argument, two clarifications are in order. First, simple trade theory equates an exogenous change in the nominal exchange rate with a change in relative tradeable prices between the home country and abroad. This is so because 'all other things' including the stance of monetary and fiscal policies and the domestic price level are assumed given. However, this assumption is not permissible in analysing the consequence of cheap dollar policy; at issue is how these other things are systematically affected by such a policy, and thus partial equilibrium of the simple trade theory is of no use. Second, two devaluation policies should be distinguished. The one is a once-for-all devaluation within a comprehensive macroeconomic stabilization programme, and its objective is retroactively to restore the competitiveness of domestic industry which was lost by the past surge in domestic inflation. The other is an attempt to improve the trade balance by actively and continuously driving down the home currency and thereby helping domestic industry, although inflation differential did not exist initially. It is the second case which is discussed here.

Last forty years

Under the Bretton Woods system, and particularly between 1950 and 1969, the yen–dollar rate was

1951 = 100

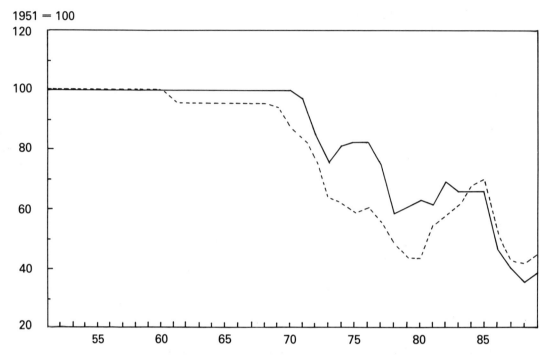

Figure 19.4 Nominal yen–dollar (———) and mark–dollar (---) rates

1951 = 100

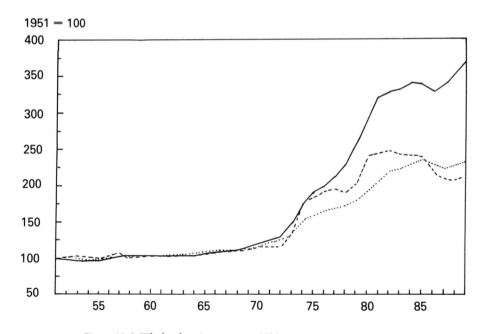

Figure 19.5 Wholesale prices: ———, USA; ---, Japan; ····, Germany

never adjusted and the mark–dollar rate was adjusted only once in 1961 by revaluing the mark by 5 per cent (Figure 19.4). Until the mid-1960s the USA was acting responsibly as a nominal anchor of the system which McKinnon calls the 'international dollar standard'. Glancing at Figure 19.5, one is struck by the fact that tradeable prices of the USA, Japan and Germany not only stayed close to each other but also very stable for as long as twenty years. During these years, the Bretton Woods system was more successful than the classical gold standard in providing global price stability.

However, this regime started to crumble as the USA became increasingly permissive of inflation in the second half of the 1960s and ended when fixed parities were abandoned altogether in the early 1970s. Since then, the yen–dollar and mark–dollar rates have had a long-term upward (i.e. dollar depreciation) tendency apart from irregular short-term fluctuations (Figure 19.4). In the meantime, tradeable prices in the three countries diverged and world-wide inflationary pressure surfaced (Figure 19.5).

It is an indisputable fact that the USA had a higher inflation rate and a weaker currency relative to Japan and Germany after 1973. Two hypotheses are consistent with this fact (McKinnon 1989). The first hypothesis is that the desire to achieve higher output and lower unemployment along the Phillips curve imparted an inflationary bias to US monetary policy, and the resulting higher US inflation depreciated the dollar. The second hypothesis is that every several years political pressure in Congress to depreciate the dollar in the face of a huge trade deficit forces the Federal Reserve to adopt a more relaxed policy stance than it would otherwise take, which fuels domestic inflation with a long and variable lag. McKinnon supports the second interpretation.

Consequences of driving down the dollar

Figure 19.4 shows that weakening of the dollar did not occur gradually throughout the two decades but came in three distinct waves of rapid deprecia-

tion: 1971–3, 1977–8 and 1985–7. These coincided with periods during which a large US trade deficit and protectionism in the US legislature emerged. Each time, a group of influential economists advocated devaluation of the dollar as a cure for lost competitiveness, which was eventually adopted as the official policy of the US administration. However, much more than talk is needed to drive down the dollar over the medium term; it is necessary that US monetary policy be systematically expansionary relative to its major trading partners, by keeping money supply above the desired money demand. This can be achieved by (as the domestic monetarist would invariably argue) injecting too much money into the economy or by a reduction in demand for dollars and dollar-denominated financial assets under financial openness.

This does not imply that members of the FOMC intentionally pursued inflationary policy. In all likelihood, such a disgraceful idea was the last thing on their mind. Inflationary bias of US monetary policy was more subtle and emerged as a result of genuine policy dilemma where the FOMC was inhibited from taking early decisive action against domestic overheating because it would have an adverse effect on the foreign exchange market. Their response therefore was a little too late and a little too modest.

Intentionally or not, intermittent attempts to depreciate the dollar caused US domestic inflation with a lag. While empirical correlation between depreciation and higher inflation is well recognized, the reason for such correlation may not be correctly understood for the USA. One channel is through passthrough of foreign prices. However, many empirical studies conclude that the pass-through effect of depreciation is quantitatively insignificant for the USA. The more important channel is through the signal effect of the exchange rate by which news of expansionary domestic monetary policy immediately depreciates the dollar because people have rational expectations. The dollar leads inflation in time but it does not cause inflation in the true sense.

This points to the possibility that the pursuit of

cheap dollar policy may be highly counterproductive. The long-term consequence of such a policy may well be higher inflation with little gain in competitiveness in real terms. If the ultimate objective of improving competitiveness is to raise the economic welfare of US citizens, artificial manipulation of nominal variables such as the exchange rate is not, in the end, the best policy to improve per capita real GNP and the potential growth rate significantly. To challenge Japanese and European rivals and maintain the industrial base worthy of the leading nation of the world, what is mostly required is a combination of hard work and thrift, leadership in science as well as product development, obsession with quality and customer satisfaction, organizational flexibility to cope with a changing environment, government policies supportive of competition and entrepreneurship, and other *real* efforts. Permanently fixed nominal exchange rates would leave no room for money illusion and would make clear to people what really drives the economic well-being of a country. In contrast, floating exchange rates breed the fallacious view that domestic industry can be invigorated, even without productivity gain, by readjusting artificial conversion rates of paper money. Perhaps we should go back to the old-fashioned idea that a weak currency is an indication of a weak economy, and not a strong one.

ESTIMATING PURCHASING POWER PARITY

Estimating PPP exchange rates under a floating exchange rate system poses a number of technical problems. First, if price indices (rather than local-currency price data) are used to calculate PPP, the 'base-year' problem arises because the ratio of two countries' prices is correct PPP only up to a positive multiplicative factor. This factor must somehow be estimated. Second, PPP exchange rates are not constant but drift over time if one country adopts expansionary monetary policy relative to another and thus allows higher inflation. Third, even among tradeable goods, deviation from PPP and the speed with which prices

adjust to new exchange rates differ depending on the tradeability of each commodity. Thus, there is no single PPP exchange rate that would align all tradeable prices individually, and the exact specification of the commodity basket becomes important.

Despite these problems, there are several different methods to estimate PPP and estimates derived from them are closely bunched together. Table 19.1 reports estimates for yen–dollar and mark–dollar PPP exchange rates defined in terms of tradeables (the producer price index, including manufactured goods) and other price indices where available, as of the first quarter of 1990. Alternative estimation methods are briefly described below.

Cassel–Keynes method

The methodology used by Cassel (1922) and Keynes (1923a) is still practised widely. To estimate PPP exchange rates after the First World War, they chose a 'base-year' when it could reasonably be assumed that PPP had actually held and then updated the base-year exchange rate using subsequent relative price movements.[9] The validity of this method obviously depends on the certainty of PPP in the base-year. The base-year selected by these economists was 1913, the year before the war broke out. The assumption that PPP held in 1913 is justifiable because of the unparalleled exchange rate stability and openness of principal economies under the gold standard. However, this method is much less suitable in the 1990s when no one is certain about the base-year and different choices of the base-year yield a distressingly wide dispersion of estimates.

Long-run averaging

To circumvent this problem, one could use the long-run average of past relative prices, rather than a single base-year, as the benchmark for estimation. This methodology can be used if PPP is assumed to hold in the long run and there are short-run dynamics which narrow the deviation

Table 19.1 Purchasing power parity estimates for 1990.I

Method and base period	Yen–dollar				Mark–dollar			
	PPI	ULC	CPI	GNP deflator	PPI	ULC	CPI	GNP deflator
Long-run averaging with base 1975.I–1990.I	175	195	180	179	2.03	2.27	1.90	2.01
Long-run averaging with base 1980.I–1990.I	172	188	174	174	2.14	2.32	2.02	2.11
Morrison–Hale method with base 1985, updated[a]	200	–	–	–	2.33	–	–	–
Price survey by Japan's economic planning agency[b]	169	–	–	–	2.03	–	–	–
Price pressure method with sample period of 1975.I–1988.II updated using PPI or ULC	170	186	–	–	2.04	2.19	–	–

Notes: Unless otherwise noted, indices used are producer prices (PPI), unit labour costs (ULC), consumer prices (CPI) and GNP deflator, all taken from OECD *Main Economic Indicators*. Exchange rates are from IMF *International Financial Statistics*. See text for explanation of each methodology.
[a] Estimation in September 1989, further updated using PPI to 1990.I.
[b] Published in October 1989 in the form of living cost comparison. The estimates shown are rearranged results for durable goods.

from PPP (technically, this condition is called cointegration of relative prices and the nominal exchange rate). While the question remains of how far back one should look to calculate long-run averages, the bias arising from different base periods appears small. Estimates using two sets of long-run averages in Table 19.1 are similar, especially for the yen–dollar rate.

Morrison–Hale method

Based on the methodology of absolute PPP (i.e. using local-currency price data rather than price indices), the OECD estimates PPP exchange rates among major industrial countries every five years. The price data from which the OECD estimates are derived contain many non-tradeable components. Morrison and Hale (1987) and Hale (1989) revaluated the OECD data by purging non-tradeables and using a new set of weights reflecting the trade patterns of the USA, Japan, Germany and the UK

to estimate PPP in *tradeable* goods. One drawback of the Morrison–Hale method is inclusion of net indirect taxes in the OECD data. Some tradeable goods, notably energy-related goods, have greatly different tax and tariff structures across countries. Since energy is more heavily taxed in Japan and Germany than in the USA, the Morrison–Hale estimates are biased upward and are higher than other estimates.

Price survey

In 1989, a number of Japanese ministries and agencies sampled prices in Japan and its trading partners in response to a criticism that Japanese prices were too high. The result was cost of living indices for individual countries evaluated at *actual exchange rates*. The methodology is essentially that of absolute PPP over a limited number of goods and services, and it is quite easy to rearrange the results as such. Using the data reported in the

413

Economic Planning Agency's *Bukka [Price] Report '89* (October 1989), implied PPP yen–dollar and mark–dollar rates are shown in Table 19.1.

Price pressure method

Instead of guessing which base-year would be reasonable, the multiplicative factor in relative PPP can be statistically estimated by using information contained in the entire sample period and assuming a structural model of relative price and relative cost movements. The price pressure method takes advantage of differential speeds of adjustment to exchange rate shocks in a model with two types of goods: tradeable output (mainly manufactured goods) and non-tradeable input (labour). When the nominal exchange rate deviates from PPP, the price of output adjusts more quickly than the price of input. Because of these divergent price movements, firms experience variation in profitability – excess profit when the home currency is undervalued and profit squeeze or even loss when it is overvalued. This relationship is captured by the two basic equations: the relative price equation and the relative cost equation. The PPP exchange rate is estimated as the path of the exchange rate that would have exerted no price pressure on either the home or the foreign economy. Details of estimation are discussed in Ohno (1990).

In sum, PPP estimation, while not a trivial exercise, can be performed with scientific accuracy and thus agnosticism about PPP exchange rates should be dispelled.

NOTES

1   The two sides of Cassel's concept of PPP can be seen in the following passages: positive, 'Given a normal freedom of trade between two countries, A and B, a rate of exchange will establish itself between them and this rate will, smaller fluctuations apart, remain unaltered as long as no alteration in the purchasing power of either currency is made and no special hindrances are imposed upon the trade' (1921: 36); normative, 'The purchasing power parities represent the true equilibrium of the exchanges, and it is, therefore, of great practical value to know these parities' (1921: 38).

2   In *The New Palgrave Dictionary of Economics*, Dornbusch opens the discussion of PPP thus: 'Purchasing Power Parity (PPP) is a theory of exchange rate determination. It asserts (in most common form) that the exchange rate change between two currencies over any period of time is determined by the change in the two countries' relative price levels' (1987: vol. III, 1075).

3   This is the Cassel–Keynes method of estimating PPP. See the last section.

4   This is not a new idea. As Keynes put it,

> it would promote confidence, and furnish an objective standard of value, if, an official index number having been compiled of such a character as to register the price of a standard composite commodity, the authorities were to adopt this composite commodity as their standard of value in the sense that they would employ all their resources to prevent a movement of its price by more than a certain percentage in either direction away from the normal.
>
> (1923b)

5   Between 1975 and 1985, consumer prices (which contain many non-tradeable prices) rose 19.9 per cent relative to wholesale prices (mostly tradeable prices) in Japan. Corresponding figures for the USA and Germany are 6.9 per cent and −0.5 per cent, respectively.

6   Needless to say, stability in the *average* tradeable prices is perfectly consistent with variability in the prices of individual tradeable goods. If an innovation occurs in the production of integrated circuits, their absolute (hence relative) price will decline in dollar, yen and mark. It is also conceivable that the relative price between primary commodities and manufactured goods will steadily change while the overall tradeable price level remains constant.

7   Price data are from OECD's *Main Economic Indicators*; exchange rate data are from IMF's *International Financial Statistics*.

8   McKinnon (1989) himself presents four rules. However, since his second rule (symmetric monetary adjustment) and his third rule (non-sterilization) are closely related, they are combined in this presentation.

9   'When two currencies have been inflated, the new normal rate of exchange will be equal to the old rate multiplied by the quotient between the degrees of inflation of both countries' (Cassel 1921: 37).

BIBLIOGRAPHY

Balassa, B. (1964) 'The purchasing power parity doctrine reexamined: a reappraisal', *Journal of Political Economy* 72: 584–96.

Cassel, G. (1918) 'Abnormal deviations in international exchanges', *Economic Journal* 28 (112): 413–15.

—— (1921) *The World's Monetary Problems*, New York: E.P. Dutton.

—— (1922) *Money and Foreign Exchange After 1914*, New York: Macmillan.

Dornbusch, R. (1987) 'Purchasing power parity', in J. Eatwell, M. Milgate and P. Newman (eds) *The New Palgrave: A Dictionary of Economics*, vol. III, New York: Stockton Press, pp. 1075–85.

Frenkel, J. A. (1981) 'Flexible exchange rates, prices, and the role of "news": lessons from the 1970s', *Journal of Political Economy* 89 (4): 665–705.

Friedman, M. (1953) 'The case for flexible exchange rates', in M. Friedman (ed.) *Essays in Positive Economics*, Chicago, IL: University of Chicago Press, pp. 157–203.

Hale, J. (1989) *Dollar Exchange Rates – Powering Their Way to Purchasing Parity*, London: Goldman Sachs.

Huizinga, J. (1987) 'An empirical investigation of the long run behavior of real exchange rates', paper presented at the Conference on the Dynamic Behavior of PPP Deviations, Cambridge, MA, August.

Keynes, J. M. (1923a) *A Tracton Monetary Reform*, New York: Macmillan.

—— (1923b) 'Positive suggestions for the future regulation of money', reprinted in J. M. Keynes (1931) *Essays in Persuasion*, New York: Macmillan.

Kravis, I. B. (1986) 'The three faces of the international comparison project', *The World Bank Observer* 1 (1): 3–26.

Krugman, P. and Baldwin, R. E. (1987) 'The persistence of the U.S. trade deficit', *Brookings Papers on Economic Activity* 1: 1–43.

Marston, R. (1987) 'Real exchange rates and productivity growth in the United States and Japan', in S. W. Arndt and J. D. Richardson (eds) *Real-Financial Linkages among Open Economies*, Cambridge, MA: MIT Press.

McKinnon, R. I. (1984) *An International Standard for Monetary Stabilization*, Washington, DC: Institute for International Economics.

—— (1988) 'Monetary and exchange rate policies for international financial stability: a proposal', *Journal of Economic Perspectives* 2 (1): 83–103.

—— (1989) 'Toward a common monetary standard through the regulation of exchange rates', paper presented at the Conference on Global Disequilibrium, McGill University, Montreal, May.

McKinnon, R. I. and Ohno, K. (1989) 'Purchasing power parity as a monetary standard', in O. F. Hamouda, R. Rowley and B. M. Wolf (eds) *The Future of the International Monetary System: Change, Coordination or Instability*, Aldershot: Edward Elgar, chapter 7.

Mecagni, M. and Pauly, P. H. (1987) 'Recursive band spectrum analysis of purchasing power parity', paper presented at the Conference on the Dynamic Behavior of PPP Deviations, Cambridge, MA, August.

Morrison, D. and Hale, J. (1987) 'The search for equilibrium exchange rates', *The International Economics Analyst*, London: Goldman Sachs.

Ohno, K. (1989) 'Testing purchasing power parity and the Dornbusch overshooting model with vector autoregression', *Journal of the Japanese and International Economies* 3 (2): 209–26.

—— (1990) 'Estimating yen/dollar and mark/dollar purchasing power parities', *IMF Staff Papers* 37 (3): 700–25.

Samuelson, P. A. (1964) 'Theoretical notes on trade problems', *Review of Economics and Statistics* 46: 145–54.

Ward, M. (1985) *Purchasing Power Parities and Real Expenditures in the OECD*, Paris: OECD.

Williamson, J. (1985) *The Exchange Rate System*, revised edn, Washington, DC: Institute for International Economics, June.

Williamson, J. and Miller, M. H. (1987) *Targets and Indicators: A Blueprint for the International Co-ordination of Economic Policy*, Washington, DC: Institute for International Economics, September.

20

WAS THERE A TARGET ZONE?

Takatoshi Ito

INTRODUCTION

A target zone as an alternative monetary system has been advocated by many economists and policy-makers.[1] Advantages, shortcomings and feasibility of the target zone proposal have been examined in detail.[2] It seems that the world is ready to conduct a target zone experiment. In fact, many participants in the foreign exchange markets believe that the monetary authorities of the G7 nations, especially Japan and the USA, have a reference range, or a target zone, in mind for their management of the exchange rate movement, although government officials have always denied the existence of a target zone.[3] Denials by government officials do not necessarily mean that there has been no target zone. A (quiet) target zone could have been introduced without an announcement to the outside world. Was there a target zone?

In this chapter, I shall claim that a target zone *did* exist. The secret testing of a target zone probably started at the same time as the Baker–Miyazawa joint press release of 31 October 1986, but ended soon after the Black Monday of October 1987.

Although government officials on both sides of the Pacific have repeatedly denied the existence of a target zone, there are pieces of evidence that economic policy has been conducted with an intention to keep the yen–dollar exchange rate in a certain range. Until the official policy changes from a 'quiet zone' to a 'loud zone', outsiders have to rely on indirect evidence such as how market

participants perceive the policy, when interventions are conducted, how the domestic policy is conducted and what intentional or unintentional news leaks suggest the existence of a target zone. Moreover, the end of a target zone is almost always accompanied by a large jump away from the boundary of the target zone. When all the pieces are put together, a 'target zone' emerges.

I shall argue that there were five different phases after the Plaza Agreement of September 1985: (i) the Plaza Agreement aiming the yen–dollar rate at 200; (ii) a discord between the USA and Japan; (iii) a target zone experiment starting October 1986; (iv) a breakdown after the Black Monday; and (v) a (possible) re-establishment of a target zone in December 1987.

Figure 20.1 shows the daily movement of the yen–dollar exchange rate in relation to these five phases. The existence of the range of the latest phase is not clear cut.

FROM THE PLAZA AGREEMENT TO A TARGET ZONE

The Plaza Agreement symbolizes a change in US policy from non-cooperation to co-operation with regard to exchange rate management. In the Plaza Agreement, the G5 agreed to use the policy tools necessary to push down the value of the dollar. Just prior to the Plaza Agreement, the yen–dollar exchange rate was near 240. They aimed at the level of 200, although there was no explicit zone around the target. The initial impact of the Plaza Agreement along with forceful interventions by

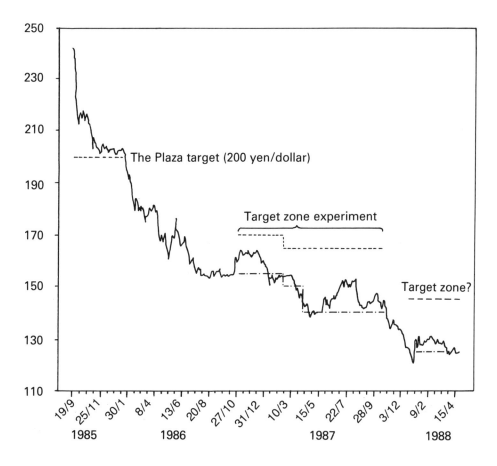

Figure 20.1 Yen–dollar rate in relation to five phases after the Plaza Agreement

central banks pushed the yen–dollar exchange rate down to 215 by mid-October. With a target of 200 in mind, the Bank of Japan decided to help yen appreciation by raising the interest rate in late November. The Bank of Japan used the interest rate to bring the exchange rate near 200 and keep it there.[4]

The second phase, which extends from February to October 1986, was marked by disagreement between the USA and Japan over an appropriate level for the yen–dollar rate. With oil prices declining, there was building pressure for further yen appreciation. After meeting with Secretary Baker, Finance Minister Takeshita announced that he would allow the yen to go

below 200. The yen quickly appreciated toward 190. When the yen went below 180 in mid-March, the Bank of Japan reversed the direction of intervention, from selling the dollar to buying the dollar. The Japanese authorities, worried about damage to its export industries and a weak economic prospect, tried to stop a steep yen appreciation. This was a clear switch in the Japanese position. In the spring of 1986, few people in Japan predicted that the yen would soon reach and stay around 150. However, the US authorities, with trade deficits showing no sign of a turnaround and a weak economy, did not mind further dollar depreciation. Much to the dismay of the Japanese government and export industries, the yen appreciated to near 150 in late July and stayed between 150 and 155 until mid-October.

TARGET ZONE EXPERIMENT

The third phase was a period of a (quiet) target zone, initiated with a joint press release of the Miyazawa–Baker agreement of 31 October 1986. In the agreement, the exchange rate at the time, 160, was considered to be near the level that is consistent with its fundamentals. However, in a press conference, Finance Minister Miyazawa denied the existence of a target zone.

The range set by the Baker–Miyazawa agreement is believed to have been from 155 to 170, or approximately ±8 yen (5 per cent) of the rate of the time, i.e. 161.5 at the close of the Tokyo market on 31 October. The timing of setting up the target zone was ideal. By October, the expectation in Japan was adjusted to the reality that the appreciated yen, say 155–70, was going to stay. It happened that the yen suddenly depreciated from 155 to 160 within three days in late October (from the 21st to the 24th, responding to the favourable news of the US durables goods orders in September).[5] The Japanese authority must have calculated that it was acceptable, if the USA agreed, to keep the exchange rate around the 'current level'. The US authority, fearing that the yen might further depreciate, agreed to put a ceiling on how much the yen should appreciate in return for a promise that the Japanese government did not want the yen to depreciate further. Thus, I conjecture that Japan insisted on an appreciation limit of 155, slightly above the record high back in August, and wished to push it back to 170, while the USA insisted on not reversing the yen appreciation trend.[6]

Although the range 155–70 is considered to be a reasonable guess by many experts, it is possible that the Baker–Miyazawa agreement intended a different one. One possibility is that the range was as wide as 150–70. Another scenario is that the two finance ministers agreed that the current yen–dollar level was consistent with the fundamentals, but failed to specify the exact range or had different ranges in their minds.

Immediately after the announcement, market participants, guessing what was agreed between Baker and Miyazawa, thought that the range was a narrow one, which confined the movement of the yen in the range 160–5 for November. However, the US authorities did not take significant steps when the yen went into the 150s. The real test came in early January 1987, when the yen appreciated from the high 150s to the low 150s very quickly. Finance Minister Miyazawa flew to Washington to consult with Treasury Secretary Baker, presumably to reaffirm the two-month-old target zone.

The Bank of Japan also heavily intervened as the rate approached 150. On 7 January 1987, an intervention started for the first time since the target zone came into effect. The Bank of Japan, in concert with Germany and France, intervened in support of the dollar at around 158 (*Nihon Keizai Shinbun*, 8 January 1987). It seemed that this gave an impression that the Bank of Japan was signalling that 158 was the defence line. However, the yen appreciated further, as Treasury Secretary Baker made a statement on 8 January to the effect that the dollar depreciation was a logical consequence. On 14 January, the yen appreciated from 155.5 at the opening to 153.8 at the closing of the Tokyo market, in spite of the intervention by the Bank of Japan.

Thus, in mid-January the market received mixed signals. The Japanese government, which made it clear that it did not want further yen appreciation, resorted to strong intervention. It was reported that the Bank of Japan bought about $8 billion in the first two weeks of January 1987 (*Nihon Keizai Shinbun*, 15 January 1987). This rather heavy intervention, triggered at the level of 158, supports the guess that the lower bound was 155.

However, several US officials, including the Treasury Secretary, were making comments to the effect that the US government wanted further dollar depreciation. Moreover, the Federal Reserve did not intervene in support of the dollar. The wave of yen appreciation stopped without breaking the 150 barrier, when Finance Minister Miyazawa flew to Washington on short notice and reaffirmed the October agreement with the Treasury Secretary.[7] Japan promised to lower the discount rate and Treasury Secretary Baker testified on 22 January that a sudden depreciation of the dollar has an adverse effect. Finance Minister Miyazawa also suggested in an interview upon his return to Japan that a concerted intervention would take place if the yen appreciated toward 150 (*Nihon Keizai Shinbun*, 25 January). On 28 January, the Federal Reserve did intervene in the market (at 150–1). This last piece of evidence suggests the possibility of a scenario other than the target zone of 155–70. In particular, it is possible that 150, rather than 155, might have been the floor for the dollar, or that there was a discrepancy in interpretation between the USA and Japan about exactly what was the range 'consistent with the fundamentals'. With this account of events in January, my conjecture on what had happened is the following. The Miyazawa–Baker agreement of October 1985 had set the target zone of 155–70. However, the market thought that the range was even narrower than that, such as 160–5, and stayed in that range for more than two months. Without confirming or denying the existence of the target zone, the central banks took advantage of the misperception because it contributed to a stable market. However, when the suspected barrier of 160 was broken, there was a difference in reaction between Japan and the USA; the latter let the dollar depreciate and the former resisted. This gave the impression that the October agreement was not in force, or that the USA and Japan had different interpretations of the same agreement. This confusion caused the market to become too sensitive to officials' statements, adding to the volatility of the exchange rate. This continued until Miyazawa went to see Baker in late January.

In February 1987, there were news leaks to the effect that the USA proposed to establish a reference range of the exchange rate in preparatory discussions toward a G7 meeting.[8] The G6 (Italy being absent) reaffirmed in Louvre their willingness to stabilize the exchange rate around the (then) current rate, since it was consistent with underlying fundamentals, but avoided mentioning any specific numbers for the range, if one existed. In the market at the time the Louvre Accord was interpreted as a target zone of 150–60 (*Nihon Keizai Shinbun*, 23 February 1987). A study based on interviews contends that the Louvre Accord had 153.50 as the yen–dollar central rate with 2.5 per cent and 5 per cent as soft and hard bands around the central rate (Funabashi 1988: 186).

I have argued that the target zone established in October 1986 was 155–70, with the possibility of it being 150–65. Was there a change in the upper (yen depreciation) limit? We would not know this because the upper limit was not tested in the coming months. Was there a change in the lower limit? I tend to think so because the market successfully broke the limit in January. In this chapter, I take the position that the target zone changed from 155–70 (effective in October 1986) to 150–65 (effective at the time of the Louvre Accord) in February. However, I would not dismiss the possibility that there was one consistent range of 150–65 from October 1986 to April 1987 (especially in the minds of the US policy-makers).

The next test of the target zone came in late March. On Monday, 23 March, the yen went under 150 in the New York market. The Federal Reserve intervened, but only by several million dollars. The yen appreciation continued on 24 March. In the Tokyo market, the Bank of Japan intervened by buying $1.7 billion on 24 March. The Federal Reserve also intervened on its own account, as opposed to being just an agent for other central banks, with about $0.7–0.8 billion on 24 March (*Nihon Keizai Shinbun*, 26 March 1987). These figures showed that the lower (yen appreciation) limit set in the Louvre Accord was indeed 150. During the rest of the week, the market forces, which saw that the yen had to appreciate in order to help avoid protectionist legislation in the USA, made the yen appreciate further, despite the massive intervention by central banks. On 27 March, the yen closed at 149 in the Tokyo market where the Bank of Japan bought $2 billion, and the yen appreciated to 147 in the New

York market on the same day, prompting the New York Federal Reserve to intervene for five straight days.

The G7 met again on 8 April 1987. Since there was no new content in the announcement, the yen appreciated from 145.6 (Thursday, 8 April, Tokyo closing) to 142.5 (Monday, 13 April, Tokyo closing).[9]

At the G7 meeting of April 1987, or sometime around it, the target zone must have been changed to reflect a new reality. When interventions cannot prevent the appreciation and when no drastic change in the fundamentals, such as the interest rate, is possible, the target zone should be changed. I conjecture that the new range was 140–60.[10] (It could have been 140–55.) When the yen gradually depreciated to 150 in July, there were no signs of intervention in support of the yen. Clearly the range was much broader than 150.

On Friday, 14 August, the USA announced the trade deficit for the month of June as $15.7 billion, which was much larger than expected. It was also revealed that the January–June 1987 trade deficits were higher than those of 1986. After this news, the yen appreciated from 152.4 (Friday, 14 August, Tokyo closing) to 143 (21 August 1987, Tokyo closing) without much intervention or other signals from the monetary authorities. It was clearly within the target zone.

As the yen approached the lower limit of 140, there were several signals implying the existence of a limit. As mentioned above, the existence of the target zone was revealed (leaked?) on the front page of the paper on 20 August. There were several occasions, for example on 19, 26 and 27 August, when the Bank of Japan intervened in support of the dollar (reported in *Nihon Keizai Shinbun*, 21 and 28 August) at around 144. The Federal Reserve joined with the Bank of Japan on 27 August and 1 September at around 141. These facts support the conjecture that there was in fact a target zone with 140 as a lower (appreciation) bound for the yen. Since the yen was stabilized above 140 for the month of September and most of October, the signal sent by the authorities seems to have worked this time.

The target zone was abandoned, or at least temporarily shelved, soon after the Black Monday of October 1987. The G7 announcement on 27 September again reconfirmed that the exchange rate was consistent with underlying fundamentals. It was widely believed that the range established in the Louvre Accord was not changed.

At the beginning of October, there were many signs that the Bank of Japan and the Federal Reserve wanted to guide the interest rate higher as a precautionary measure against possible inflation. However, the (near) crash of the New York stock market prompted the Federal Reserve to pump in liquidity to prevent a panic. When it became clear that the stock price would not recover promptly, and the lower interest rate would prevail to give a lift to the stock market and the economy in the USA, expectations in the exchange market changed drastically.

The lower limit of 140 was broken on 28 October in the New York market without much resistance from the monetary authorities. In the following two weeks, many reports and interviews came from the USA suggesting that the Louvre Accord had been abandoned and that the USA would put a higher priority on easing monetary policy. This news convinced the market that the target zone had gone and the yen appreciated to a level of 133–4.

The yen appreciated to below 130 on 10 December after the announcement of the large US trade deficit for the month of October ($17.6 billion). Although central banks, including the Bank of Japan and the Federal Reserve, intervened, the selling pressure was strong. At this point there was no mention or reference to a target zone. Clearly no target zone was in effect at this time.

IS THERE A NEW TARGET ZONE NOW?

In the G7 announcement of 23 December, there was no indication that there was a target zone. Although the announcement declared that a further dollar depreciation would have an adverse effect, it was not received by the market as a strong commitment to defend a particular range (*Nihon Keizai Shinbun*, 24 December 1987). However, a new wave of yen appreciation pushed the yen–dollar rate to near 120 on 4 January, and the Federal Reserve, along with the Bank of Japan, intervened in support of the dollar. This pushed the yen back to 125 the following day.

On 7 January, a Japanese newspaper reported on the front page that there was a new range, the high 120s to the high 140s, as the target zone, which had been established since the December G7 meeting. This was either a change in policy from a quiet target zone to a loud target zone or a deliberate leak in order to prevent the yen appreciating again.

From these facts, I would consider that a new target zone was established in the December G7 meeting. However, subsequent events would cast some doubts about the existence of a revised range for a target zone in 1988.

When the yen appreciated below 125 in late March, there was no sign of strong resistance either from the Bank of Japan or the Federal Reserve. If a target zone, such as the one in existence between October 1986 and October 1987, was in effect with a revised range, 125–45, there would have been more intervention and Gyosei Shidou to stop the yen from breaking 125. One could only speculate that the USA had long abandoned (or shelved) the target zone, while the Japanese authority wished to make the market believe that one existed.

With an announcement on 15 January of a reduced trade deficit for the month of November 1987, the yen depreciated above 130. Since then, the yen has been fluctuating most of the time between 124 and 130. Only time will tell whether a new target zone was in effect in the first half of 1988.

A LESSON FROM THE TARGET ZONE EXPERIMENT

As I explained above, the target zone of October 1986 was introduced at a very good time. Both sides could agree that the current level was a good place to stay.

Is the target zone effective? Since one of the virtues of the target zone proposal is its flexible and discretionary aspect about changing the range freely in response to changes in the economic fundamentals, one cannot judge the success or failure of a target zone by looking at the duration of a particular range. The effectiveness should be measured by the volatility of the exchange rate compared with a situation where there was no such thing. If the existence of a range is likely to make investors take profit earlier than otherwise and loss later than usual, then this would contribute to relative stability. A market perception of the target zone has a stabilizing effect (as Krugman (1988) illustrated using a theoretical model). Reading through reports from the market, this seemed to be the case when the exchange rate was inside the target zone (this could be a Krugman (1988) effect).

The problem occurs when the range is challenged. If the central banks tried to defend an unrealistic rate, it would create strong speculation against the central banks and result in a sudden change in the exchange rate after the defence line was broken. This only creates additional volatility. Therefore, the key to the success is determining how wide the range should be, how much resistance should be applied to defend the range and when the range should be revised.

A one-year-long target zone from late October 1986, with revisions to the range, was successful in that the exchange rate was contained in the range without too much distortion in domestic policies and that the movement within the range was rather stable (the Krugman effect). The problem was the timing of the range changes. With hindsight, the abandonment of the former zone could have been made more easily and earlier, especially as Gyosei Shidou by the Ministry of Finance in an attempt to distort capital flows was both undesirable and ineffective.

Should the target zone be announced? Immediately after the Baker–Miyazawa announcement, market participants were guessing what the US and Japanese monetary authorities had agreed upon. They sensed that there was a target range but they did not know the ceiling and floor numbers. This made the market quite nervous and sensitive to any news, or even a rumour, about the range,.[11] Another example was in January 1987 when the market received conflicting signals from the Japanese and US governments. This confusion made the market too sensitive to officials' statements which added to the volatility of the exchange rate. The sensitivity to statements by government officials in order to guess the range increases the volatility of the exchange rate. In this case, being secretive about the range creates a destabilizing effect.

There are several possible reasons for having a quiet target zone. First, if a market happened to believe that the range is narrower than the actual range, which was the case in November and December of 1986, there is an added bonus to the Krugman effect. Second, being quiet about a target zone would avoid loss of face when the range had to be adjusted. Theoretically, the authorities could even change the range without being detected at all. However, the former event could only happen in an exceptional case and would have just a temporary effect, and the latter would conflict with the primary purpose of the target zone. In order to have a positive Krugman effect, the authority must convince the market about the existence of a range.

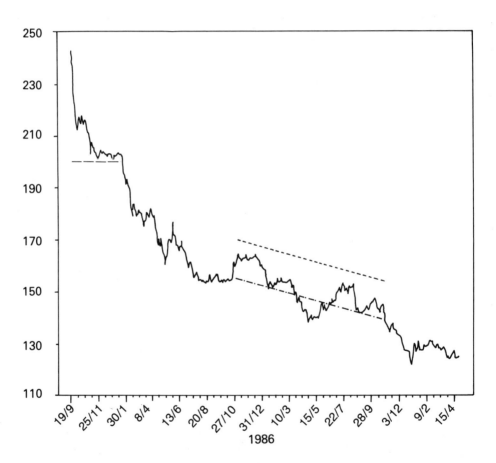

Figure 20.2 Sliding zone experiment: ———, yen–dollar exchange rate; — — —, ¥200; ----, upper limit; –·–·–·–, lower limit

You cannot have effects from a reputation without risking a reputation, at least sometimes. By reserving the right to change a range at any time, changing a zone would not necessarily damage the reputation. The benefit of a loud target zone seems to outweigh that of a quiet target zone.

A PROPOSAL FOR A MOVING TARGET ZONE

Shooting a moving object may be more difficult than shooting a still object. However, there is good reason to believe that a target zone should be moving, like a snake. If a significant (nominal or real) interest rate differential exists, or if a significant current account imbalance exists, then the market expects that the exchange rate should be adjusted in the long run. So long as the market expects a long-run depreciation of the dollar, it is a mistake to set a fixed band. The target range has to be adjusted from time to time. However, the change in range is always accompanied by a speculative attack. In order to avoid this, the sliding floor and ceiling should be announced. According to some prescribed formula the target zone could be adjusted every month. On this line of thought, the ceiling and floor of a target zone can be indexed to various indicators.

A sliding target zone would eliminate the difficult task of deciding when to change the range, and save the reputation of the authorities when doing so. If a moving target zone can contain the movement of the spot rate within it, the sudden jump at the collapse of the target zone is also eliminated.

Figure 20.2 indicates such an experiment. In this figure, the target zone was set to slide from [155, 170] to [140, 155] in the year following the Miyazawa–Baker agreement of October 1986. Most movement during the year is contained within the range. In a more sophisticated proposal, a set of indicators to which the ceiling and floor is indexed should be considered. This should be the topic of future research.

NOTES

1 Most notable and influential proposals have come from the Institute of International Economics: see Williamson (1985) and Williamson and Miller (1987). See also Alogoskoufis (1987) and Currie and Wren-Lewis (1988). See Funabashi (1988) for establishing evidence for the target zone through interviews of policy-makers.

2 For an academic enquiry from a neutral viewpoint, see Frenkel and Goldstein (1986). Krugman (1988) provides an interesting example in which the exchange rate movement *inside* the band is stabilized.

3 Whether it was called a 'target zone' or a 'reference range' was based on political considerations (see Funabashi 1988: 198). Since the difference is not established in the academic literature, I use the words interchangeably in this chapter.

4 This is a very simplified account of what happened right after the Plaza Agreement. For a careful detailed account of the events after the Plaza Agreement, see Ito (1987). In addition, there is direct evidence. In an interview for *Toyo Keizai* magazine (special issue, 22 May 1987), Mr. Tomomitsu Oba confirmed that 200 was the target at the time of the Plaza Agreement. See also Funabashi (1988: 18) for a quote of 200 as the target by the then Finance Minister Takeshita.

5 A conspiracy theory contended that the Ministry of Finance leaked information just before the agreement to manipulate the base of the exchange rate (see Funabashi 1988: 162).

6 Funabashi (1988: 163) reports that the Japanese side was aiming to push the yen–dollar rate back to 170 at the time.

7 'The Ministers expressed their view that during most of the period since October 31, 1986, the yen–dollar exchange rate has been broadly consistent with underlying fundamentals, although there were recent instances of temporary instability in exchange markets. Accordingly, the Ministers reaffirmed their willingness to cooperate on exchange market issues' (*Nihon Keizai Shinbun*, 25 January 1987).

8 Leaks were reported in *Nihon Keizai Shinbun* (11 February, 14 February, 20 February, 1987). It was reported that the US authority judged that the yen and the German mark had appreciated enough and a reference range would be a target for policy co-ordination (*Nihon Keizai Shinbun*, 20 February 1987). The following report suggested that Japan was reluctant about the idea of the reference range (*Nihon Keizai Shinbun*, 21 February 1987). About

six months later, a news report came out to confirm that the target zone was established at the Louvre meeting. The report did not specify numbers for the range (*Nihon Keizai Shinbun*, 20 August 1987). After the G7 meeting of September 1987, there was a report that the range established in the Louvre was 140–60 (*Nihon Keizai Shinbun*, 28 September 1987).

9 During the week before the G7 meeting, when the yen appreciated from 149 to 145, the Ministry of Finance and the Ministry of International Trade and Industry were applying pressure, in various forms (Gyosei Shidou), to institutional investors and exporters not to sell dollars. I am not sure that these Gyosei Shidou had to be a part of a target zone.

10 Funabashi (1988: 189) reports that Baker suggested rebasing the yen–dollar central rate to the current rate of 146 with 2.5 per cent and 5 per cent bands around it.

11 For example, on 6 November a rumour swept through the market that an appropriate level was 154–60, which brought the yen from 164 to 161 in an hour (*Nihon Keizai Shinbun*, 7 November 1986).

REFERENCES

Alogoskoufis, G. (1987) 'On optimal world stabilization and the target zone proposal'. Discussion Paper 214, Center for Economic Policy Research, December.

Currie, D. and Wren-Lewis, S. (1988) 'Evaluating the extended target zone proposal for the G3'. Discussion Paper 221, Center for Economic Policy Research, January.

Frenkel, J.A. and Goldstein, M. (1986) 'A guide to target zones'. *IMF Staff Report* 33: 633–73.

Funabashi, Y. (1988) *Managing the Dollar: From the Plaza to the Louvre*, Institute for International Economics, May.

Ito, T. (1987) 'The intradaily exchange rate dynamics and monetary policies after the Group of Five agreement', *Journal of the Japanese and International Economies* 1: 275–98.

Krugman, P. (1988) 'Target zone and exchange rate dynamics', Working Paper 2481, National Bureau of Economic Research, January.

Williamson, J. (1985) *The Exchange Rate System*, 2nd edn, Washington, DC: Institute for International Economics.

Williamson, J. and Miller, M.H. (1987) *Targets and Indicators: A Blueprint for the International Co-ordination of Economic Policy*, Institute for International Economics, September.

21

WHY FLOATING EXCHANGE RATES FAIL

A reconsideration of the liquidity trap

Ronald McKinnon

How well do interest rates on bonds denominated in different currencies register international risk? I shall argue that, under floating exchange rates, short-term interest rates are pinned down in each separate national money market. Thus, in the short run when investor perceptions of international risk can change sharply, short-term interest rates fail to act as shock absorbers for offsetting that risk. The result is overshooting or 'excess' volatility in spot exchange rates, changes in which must bear the brunt of keeping asset portfolios in balance.

In addition, because short-term interest rates are caught in national liquidity traps, open interest parity fails when the system is disturbed by 'news'. Under floating, neither short-term interest differentials nor premia or discounts in the forward exchange market reflect observed short-run changes in exchange rates. Why, among the major industrial economies, the forward exchange rate contains no useful information on subsequent short-term movements in the spot exchange rate is a puzzling phenomenon explored in great empirical detail by Goodhart (1988).

In effect, the international capital market is inherently inefficient in adjusting for risk when, on the one hand, international flows of goods and interest-bearing financial capital are quite free, while, on the other hand, there is no common monetary standard under which this massive interchange of goods and financial assets takes place.

SEPARATE CURRENCY DOMAINS: SOME STYLIZED FACTS

The relevant world economy is divided into several distinct currency domains separated by floating exchange rates. The monetary authority in each country (domain) fixes its national money supply (or domestic rate of money growth) independently of pressure for or against its currency in the foreign exchanges. However, international investors choose portfolios of bonds, equities and real assets across countries (blocs) without restraint, and the economies in question are integrated in commodity trade.

As with the industrial economies today, such separate currency domains imply the following.

1 Within each country, domestic currency prices are 'sticky': they are not immediately sensitive to exchange rate changes.
2 Domestic transactors hold virtually all of the supply of (narrow) money – coin and currency, chequing accounts and so on – within each country. Foreigners might hold domestic bonds and equities, but not significant transactions balances in the domestic currency.[1]

(1) and (2) are complementary. In market economies, firms producing brand-name goods and services find it convenient to fix invoice prices in the domestic currency for weeks or months at a time.[2] And such Hicksian 'fix price' goods and services constitute the bulk of consumption and production in the industrial economies. Thus only domestic transactions generate demand for the national money narrowly defined. Should the need arise for foreign exchange, this is intermediated by banks – thus making direct holdings of foreign transactions balance by domestic nationals

unnecessary (or negligibly small).

Although the domestic price level in each industrial country remains rigid – at least for finite periods of time – exchange rates are highly flexible as international investors switch their preferences between foreign and domestic securities. Unlike the situation when a common monetary standard prevails – as with the classical gold standard before 1914 or the calmer periods under the Bretton Woods system of fixed official exchange parities from 1950 to 1970 – each investor must continually guess the course of each country's exchange rate and compare it with the differing interest yields on dollar, mark, yen or sterling assets. The spot exchange rate behaves as a forward-looking asset price that is extremely sensitive to 'news' regarding, say, how much the future money supply in country A might be expanded *vis-à-vis* country B, or how future taxes on assets in A might be levied, or how A's prospective terms of trade and future foreign exchange earnings might change and so on (Frenkel and Mussa 1980). Thus, the exchange rate appears to fluctuate randomly; it cannot be predicted on the basis of past information on money growth, trade deficits, GNP growth and so on (Meese and Rogoff 1983).

One important casualty of this turbulence on the foreign exchange markets is the 'law of one price'. Because similar (or even the same) brand-name goods are invoiced for discrete periods of time in the national currency for each country, they will be more or less always out of alignment with each other as the exchange rate fluctuates. Producers in country A find that they are continually subject to exchange risk in selling to country B – risk against which it is impossible to hedge fully (McKinnon 1988a). At a more macroeconomic level, continual price-level misalignments will develop. For example, the devaluation of the dollar from 1986 to 1988 drove the American price level (for tradeable goods) far below its European and Japanese counterparts.

In the much longer run, however, arbitrage in international goods markets tends to restore PPP – although many years might elapse before the price level in the country with the undervalued currency

increases sufficiently (McKinnon and Ohno 1989). For example, the greater US price inflation in 1990 compared with hard currency Europe and Japan is a consequence of the earlier undervaluation of the dollar. But new 'exogenous' exchange rate fluctuations will prevent complete price-level alignment from finally occurring. Slow-to-adjust goods markets are always more or less out of equilibrium while exchange rates swing around to balance rapidly shifting asset preferences.

THE MODEL

Our model of the liquidity trap, showing the failure of open interest parity and excessive exchange rate volatility, is confined to a single industrial country such that the rest of the world remains passive. Nevertheless, the principles involved easily generalize to mutual (non-) adjustment of short-term interest rates across many countries.[3]

Although holdings of narrow money M1 by non-banks are confined to nationals of the country in question, let us assume 'perfect' capital mobility in the international bond market. No exchange controls impede international capital movements and default risk on the chosen short-term instruments at home and abroad is assumed to be negligible. Domestic nationals *and* foreigners shuffle freely between domestic and foreign (short-term) bonds so that covered interest parity always holds:

$$i - i^* = f = \frac{F - S}{S} \qquad (21.1)$$

where i is the domestic (short-term) interest rate, i^* is the equivalent foreign interest rate, S is the spot exchange rate (domestic currency/foreign currency), F is the forward exchange rate and f is the forward premium on foreign exchange with the same term to maturity as i and i^*. Because this covered interest arbitrage is risk free, the empirical robustness of equation (21.1) for Eurocurrency deposits is well established (Aliber 1973; Goodhart 1988).

Nevertheless, in our 'forward-looking' asset

portfolios, foreign and domestic bonds are *not* perfect substitutes. i need not be equal to i^* nor need $i - i^*$ equal the expected change in the spot exchange rate. Currency risk and political uncertainty combine to drive a wedge between domestic and foreign interest rates – a wedge that varies through time. To capture this effect, let us complete our basic model by using a set of equations provided by Schroder (1990) simplifying an earlier model of McKinnon (1983), which is a generalization of an approach pioneered by Dornbusch (1976). Except for i, lower case letters denote logarithms.

$$\dot{p} = \delta(s - p - k) \qquad \text{with } \delta > 0$$
$$\text{goods market} \qquad (21.2)$$

$$m - p = \eta y - \varepsilon i > 0 \qquad \text{with } \eta, \varepsilon > 0$$
$$\text{money market} \qquad (21.3)$$

$$i = i^* + \theta(\bar{s} - s) + z \qquad \text{with } \theta > 0$$
$$\text{bond market} \qquad (21.4)$$

For our small open economy, $s - p - k$ in equation (21.2) is the deviation of the real exchange rate $s - p$ from PPP. If the foreign price level P^* is unchanging, then k can be considered a constant. Also, assume the domestic real output y is given at the full employment level. Financial shocks affect domestic absorption *ex ante* (the demand for goods and services) and thus the domestic price level p but not real output.

In response to exogenous shifts in s, the co-efficient δ in equation (21.2) gives the speed of adjustment of the domestic price level p in restoring PPP at $s - p = k$. The greater the deviation of the real exchange rate from k, the greater the pressure on domestic prices to adjust. Being part of the same forward-looking process by which the exchange rate is determined, the prices of tradeable and non-tradeable goods are presumed to adjust at the same rate. For example, an inflationary scare, which suddenly depreciates the domestic currency (increases s), will set in motion a broad price inflation across all sectors of the domestic economy.[4]

In equation (21.3), the money demand function is narrowly defined. Direct currency substitution between domestic non-interest-bearing money and foreign cash balances or foreign bonds is initially ruled out – although that possibility is considered later. Neither $\dot{s}^e$ (the expected change in the exchange rate) nor i^* (the foreign interest rate) affect domestic liquidity preference – which is wholly determined by the domestic (short-term) rate of interest i as long as y is given. This simplifying assumption of no direct currency substitution will be relaxed later.

In equation (21.4), the parameter z introduces risk explicitly into the international bond market. When 'news' arrives about, say, an increased threat of future inflation at home or higher future taxes on holders of domestic assets, the index z increases as international investors switch their asset preferences from domestic to foreign bonds. z is a measure of the risk premium, or the increased yield, that international investors require to hold the now riskier domestic bonds into the indefinite future. Thus, if the exchange rate remains unchanged when news arrives, portfolio balance in the international bond market requires that

$$i = i^* + z. \qquad (21.5)$$

Only if (21.5) holds continuously through time as z varies will relative interest rates do their job as shock absorbers for balancing international bond portfolios. Indeed, as we shall see, (21.5) is the 'long-run' equilibrium condition for determining short-term interest rates in the international bond market for any given information set available to international investors.

THE LIQUIDITY TRAP

Under floating exchange rates, however, (21.5) does not hold in the short run. Rather, i is 'trapped' by the unchanging domestic liquidity preference function, and unchanging national money supply, shown in equation (21.3). Because p and y are also sticky (do not jump) when news arrives, i is the only endogenous variable in equation (21.3).

427

For example, suppose we start from a portfolio equilibrium where foreign and domestic bonds are equally risky, i.e. $z = 0$ and $i = i^*$, and the exchange rate is not expected to change. The international bond market is in balance. Now suppose that news arrives that raises z, i is still fully determined by equation (21.3): it remains pegged at i^*. Thus, in the short run

$$i < i^* + z \qquad (21.5a)$$

even though domestic bonds are now perceived to be riskier.

Similarly, if the model were generalized to two or more countries, foreign interest rates would be pinned down in foreign money markets by each national liquidity preference function. This Keynesian-type problem of non-adjusting short-term interest rates arises because the domains of circulation for narrow monies are separated by national boundaries. Under floating exchange rates, narrow money cannot leave that country whose assets are perceived to be riskier, thus preventing its short-term interest rates from rising; nor is the supply of narrow money in safer countries naturally increased in order to permit its short-term interest rates to fall.[5]

In developing an argument for the non-adjustment of short-term interest rates to international 'news', domestic monetary policy under floating exchange rates was defined simply as keeping the national money supply M fixed. Then, with an unchanging national money demand function, i.e. given the parameters in equation (21.3), short-term rates of interest were caught in a national liquidity trap. In practice, short-term interest rates could still fluctuate with the demand or supply of the national money. However, these interest rate fluctuations are not responses to changes in perceived risk in the international bond market.

Alternatively, national monetary authorities could choose to exercise their independence under floating by keying domestic open market or discount operations on some principal short-term interest rate in the national money market. Through much of its history, the US Federal

Reserve System has chosen to smooth short-run fluctuations in either the Treasury bill rate or – in more recent times – the interest rate on federal funds (the rate at which banks borrow or land reserves to each other) irrespective of pressure on the dollar in the foreign exchange market.[6] Then, even if the national money demand function does shift when news arrives and is digested by investors in the international bond market, domestic short-term interest rates will still fail to respond.

EXCHANGE RATE EXPECTATIONS AND 'NEWS'

So far, the idea of the liquidity trap has been developed without modelling how exchange rates respond to new information. And the basic idea of non-adjusting interest rates in the very short run remains valid for a variety of possible movements in the exchange rate – some of which we shall now consider.

When news arrives as indicated by an increase in z, s and possibly $\bar{s}$ jump discretely – even though the short-term interest rate is immobile. $\bar{s}$ is the 'long-run' equilibrium value for the exchange rate (in the minds of international investors) towards which s then subsequently gravitates smoothly – as described by the adjustment parameter θ in equation (21.4). But the nature of this long-run equilibrium is highly dependent on the qualitative nature of the new information. Is the change in z permanent or transitory? Does it reflect an expected change in domestic monetary policy, in future taxes or in the country's terms of trade?

Rather than give a complete taxonomy of all possible forms that news might take, let us explore a few leading examples where the news itself is fairly transparent to international investors. Bubbles or bandwagon effects – where individual investors project that the exchange rate will continue moving in the same direction perhaps because they believe others are privy to information they do not have – are presumed to be absent. In practice, however, bandwagon effects seem to have been important in explaining both short- and intermediate-term movements in the dollar exchange rate in the 1970s and 1980s (Frankel and Froot 1986; Woo 1987).

However, in assessing whether floating exchange rates are inherently excessively volatile, I shall take the conservative course of omitting bandwagon effects from the former analysis. If floating rates are shown to be excessively volatile in the absence of bandwagon effects, then the situation can only be worsened if such effects are present.

Once bandwagon effects are ruled out, purely transitory shocks to z would seem to have no great economic significance for exchange rate movements. Let us therefore confine our analysis to 'permanent' changes in the riskiness of domestic bonds: news that increases z which international investors believe will persist indefinitely and which eventually forces an increase in domestic interest rates. In case I,[7] we shall analyse a representative non-monetary shock – a change in taxation – which leads to once-and-for-all changes in $\bar{s}$ and $\bar{p}$ as people move from domestic to foreign bonds. In case II, we consider more general 'country' risk where concern for future inflation or political stability induces people to shift out of both domestic money and bonds.

Case I: Increased domestic taxation of foreign investments

Start again from a stationary equilibrium where $i = i^*$ and $\dot{p}^e = \dot{s}^e = 0$. Let z_1 denote an increase in risk which is not monetary in origin. For example, a threat to increase future taxes on domestic investments owned by foreigners – say, a domestic withholding tax on interest and dividends flowing abroad – would increase z_1. In the short run, international investors now shift their preferences away from domestic to foreign assets, thus depreciating the domestic currency until effective yields – interest rates plus expected change in the exchange rate – compensate for the higher taxes on domestic bonds. Rewriting equation (21.4), we have

$$i = i^* + \theta(\bar{s} - s) + z_1. \qquad (21.4a)$$

First consider the economy's new long-run equilibrium associated with exchange rate depreciation and inflation, and then work backwards to look at the short and intermediate runs. Because the nominal money supply remains, and is anticipated to remain, anchored, the exchange rate and the domestic price level are stationary in the long run:

$$s = \bar{s} \qquad (21.6)$$
$$p = \bar{p} \qquad (21.7)$$
$$\dot{p} = 0. \qquad (21.8)$$

Substituting (21.6)–(21.8) into (21.2), (21.3) and (21.4a) gives the new long-run values of the interest rate, the price level and the exchange rate when the system is again at rest. Substituting (21.6) into (21.4a) determines the long-run interest rate.

$$\bar{i} = i^* + z_1 \qquad \text{and} \qquad \frac{d\bar{i}}{dz_1} = 1.$$

$$(21.5b)$$

The domestic interest rate eventually increases by the full amount of the perceived increase in risk.

Then substituting (21.7) and (21.5b) into (21.3) yields the price level in long-run equilibrium:

$$\bar{p} = m - \eta y + \varepsilon(i^* + z_1) \qquad (21.9)$$

where

$$\frac{d\bar{p}}{dz_1} = \varepsilon. \qquad (21.9a)$$

After z increases, price inflation ensues until real cash balances are reduced sufficiently to release i from its liquidity trap. Only after rising to $\bar{i}$ does i fully reflect the greater risk of holding domestic bonds. Through this inflation process, there has been *indirect currency substitution* (McKinnon 1985). Real cash balances have been reduced, in favour of domestic bonds, by an increase in the price level.

Finally, substituting (21.6), (21.7) and (21.8) into (21.2) yields

$$\bar{s} = \bar{p} + k. \qquad (21.10)$$

Because the real exchange rate remains unchanged when PPP is restored, the long-run equilibrium value for the nominal exchange rate depreciates proportionately to the increase in the price level:

$$\frac{d\bar{s}}{dz_1} = \frac{d\bar{p}}{dz_1} = \varepsilon. \quad (21.10a)$$

The path the economy takes towards this new equilibrium is portrayed in Figure 21.1. Because the price level, real money stock and nominal short-term interest rate do not jump when news arrives, the exchange rate must depreciate sufficiently sharply to keep the international bond market in balance. Figure 21.1 shows the exchange jumping immediately from a to b and overshooting its long-run equilibrium at c. Regressive expectations are thereby established for subsequent (slow) appreciation from b down to c. Note that the zero

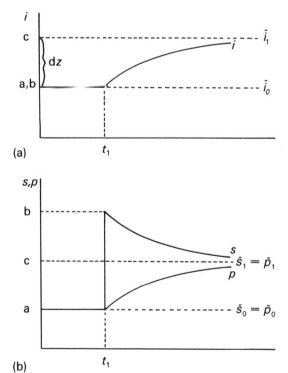

(a)

(b)

Figure 21.1 Exchange rate overshooting with the interest rate immobile in the short run

interest differential $i - i^*$ at b does *not* reflect this expected movement in the exchange rate. Because i is immobilized in the domestic money market, open interest parity fails: the forward rate does not equal the expected future spot exchange rate.[8]

The exchange rate's initial jump from a to b (Figure 21.1) can be calculated by substituting (21.10a) into (21.4a) to get

$$\frac{ds}{dz_1} = \varepsilon + \frac{1}{\theta}. \quad (21.11)$$

For a given increase in the risk premium z_1, the exchange rate jumps according to the elasticity of the demand for money and inversely to the perceived speed of adjustment θ: the rate at which s approaches $\bar{s}$. And, in turn, θ will depend on the rate of increase in domestic prices and thus on the speed with which the domestic nominal interest rate is released from its liquidity trap – as shown in Figure 21.1(a).

Although not necessary for the overshooting argument, suppose that the price level – in increasing from $\bar{p}_0$ to its new long-run equilibrium at $\bar{p}_1$ – adjusts at the same rate as the exchange rate regresses (appreciates) from its short-run equilibrium at b to its new long-run equilibrium at $\bar{s}_1$: in equations (21.2) and (21.4), the adjustment parameters are such that $\delta \approx \theta$. Then, from the geometric symmetry in Figure 21.1(b), we see that the degree of exchange rate overshooting cb is about the same as the jump ac in the long-run equilibrium of the exchange rate (and price level).

Apart from the high degree of volatility in the exchange rate, however, the domestic price level has been destabilized by a *non-monetary* shock that happened to change international asset preferences. Because the national central bank remained passive in the face of a depreciating currency, the (threatened) withholding tax on foreign investors forced an increase in the domestic price level as an alternative means whereby domestic short-term interest rates could increase. And other 'non-monetary' shifts in international asset preferences – say, because of some perceived shift in a country's terms of trade – can similarly destabilize the domestic price level when exchange rates are left free to float.[9]

Case II: Generalized country risk

Changes in risk were confined to the international bond market in case I: a threatened increase in the withholding tax on foreign investors did not directly affect the demand for money by domestic transactors (equation (21.3)).

However, more generalized political risk in any one country could induce domestic bond holders *and* money holders to alter their international asset positions (Schroder 1990). The emerging threat of a new, more populist government could make domestic wealth owners uneasy about future exchange controls, or higher wealth taxes, or higher price inflation and so on. Although not knowing which of these possibilities is most likely, wealth owners could shift away from domestic money and bonds into foreign exchange assets.

Start again from zero inflation where domestic prices and interest rates are aligned internationally. Suppose news arrives that country-specific political risk has increased. Investors now demand the risk premium z_2 on domestic financial assets. In any new long-run equilibrium, with an unchanging nominal exchange rate, the domestic interest rate must increase by z_2 to keep the international bond market in balance:

$$\bar{i} = i^* + z_2, \qquad (21.5c)$$

similar to case I. Before this final equilibrium is reached, continuous bond market equilibrium still requires

$$i = i^* + \theta(\bar{s} - s) + z_2. \qquad (21.4b)$$

Equilibrium in the national money market, however, differs from case I. To incorporate this country-specific political risk, let us replace equation (21.3) with (21.3a) to get

$$m - p = \eta y - \varepsilon i - \gamma z_2 - \gamma[\theta(\bar{s} - s) + i^*]. \qquad (21.3a)$$

In equation (21.3a), the behaviour of money holders has been internationalized in two closely related respects. First, domestic transactors directly respond to political news by reducing their demand for (domestic) money by γz_2. Such direct currency substitution out of domestic money into foreign exchange breaks down the previously assumed insularity of the national money demand function. Second, logical consistency requires that domestic transactors also respond to the foreign interest rate and to expected changes in the exchange rate. Thus the far right-hand term in (21.3a) is also modified by the parameter γ.

Because money holders are mainly concerned with making payments for goods and services invoiced in the domestic currency, they are *less* prone to switch into foreign exchange than are yield-seeking foreign or domestic holders of the country's bonds. Thus we impose the condition that $\gamma < \varepsilon$. Money holders remain somewhat insular: the demand for money is more strongly influenced by changes in i (the return on bonds denominated in the same currency) than by i^*, or by expected exchange rate changes.[10] Algebraically, case I is case II taken to the limit where $\gamma \to 0$.

For case II where $p = \bar{p}$ and $s = \bar{s}$, the price level and exchange rate may be solved by substituting (21.5c) into (21.3a) to get

$$\bar{p} = m - \eta y + (\varepsilon + \gamma)(i^* + z_2). \qquad (21.12)$$

Noting that $\dot{p} = 0$ in final equilibrium, equation (21.2) then yields equation (21.10):

$$\bar{s} = \bar{p} + k.$$

For any change in generalized country risk, the corresponding changes in the long-run values of the interest rate, price level and exchange rate are

$$\frac{d\bar{i}}{dz_2} = 1 \qquad (21.13)$$

$$\frac{d\bar{p}}{dz_2} = \varepsilon + \gamma \qquad (21.14)$$

$$\frac{d\bar{s}}{dz_2} = \varepsilon + \gamma. \qquad (21.15)$$

The domestic price level increases – and the exchange rate depreciates – by more than ε. Country risk in case II induces an additional decline in demand for domestic money – as measured by γ. The increase in the price level and exchange rate is represented in Figure 21.1(b), but now the distance ac – the increase in prices and the exchange rate in long-run equilibrium – is $\varepsilon + \gamma$ rather than just ε as in case I.

When the monetary authority leaves the national money supply m unchanged in the face of increased country risk (case II), price inflation will be generated by the eventual risk-adjusted increase in the nominal interest rate and by direct currency substitution. The more elastic is the demand for domestic money from either effect, the greater this price inflation will be. In comparison with a financially closed economy, the presence of foreign portfolio alternatives magnifies these elasticities – thus accentuating the inflationary impact of heightened domestic political risk.

Although the long-run price level and exchange rate increase more in case II than in case I, exchange rate 'overshooting' in the short run remains proportionally the same because the underlying equations for the goods, money and bond markets are logarithmic. To see this, remember that m and y are fixed and p is unchanging when news arrives. Then differentiate the bond market equation (21.4b) and the money market equation (21.3a) with respect to z_2, and solve simultaneously to get

$$\frac{di}{dz_2} = 0 \qquad (21.16)$$

and

$$\frac{ds}{dz_2} = \varepsilon + \gamma + \frac{1}{\theta}. \qquad (21.17)$$

Because the interest rate remains caught in its liquidity trap in the short run, the degree of exchange rate overshooting is again determined by $1/\theta$ – as in case I. Although the direct substitution

away from domestic money now tends to reduce i, the expected exchange appreciation arising out of the overshooting tends to increase i. The two effects cancel to leave the domestic interest rate unchanged when news arrives – as in Figure 21.1(a). Presuming again that the price level and the exchange rate subsequently adjust at the same speed, the symmetrically proportionate overshooting of the exchange rate in class II can also be represented by the distance cb in Figure 21.1(b) – with its absolute magnitude now greater because of the presence of direct currency substitution.

PERVERSE CHANGES IN SHORT-TERM INTEREST RATES AND AGGRAVATED OVERSHOOTING IN THE FOREIGN EXCHANGES

In response to some sudden change in international risk, whether similar to case I or to case II, are there plausible circumstances when short-term interest rates could adjust the 'wrong' way – and thus aggravate exchange rate volatility?

Even if domestic money holders do not see foreign exchange assets as a convenient portfolio alternative, i.e. $\gamma \to 0$, they could well be sensitive to expected future domestic price inflation signalled by a discrete devaluation of the exchange rate. Being in direct contact with goods markets, cash-balance holders could move out of domestic money into (inventories of) commodities. As long as the price inflation was expected to continue, the demand for domestic money could be substantially reduced.

The actual rate of price inflation is determined by the deviation of the spot exchange rate from PPP – as per equation (21.2). Let us presume that expected inflation, π, is equal to actual inflation:

$$\pi(s) = \dot{p} \qquad (21.18)$$

where $d\pi/ds = \delta > 0$ from equation (21.2). Combining the approach of Schroder (1990) with that of Sung (1988), the money demand function is rather generalized to

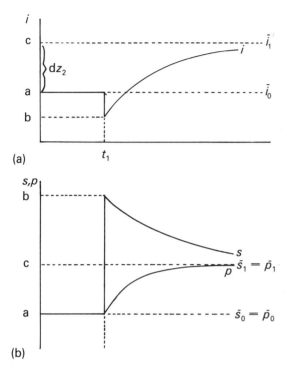

Figure 21.2 Aggravated exchange rate overshooting with a perverse short-run adjustment in the interest rate

$$m - p = \eta y - \varepsilon i - \alpha \pi - \gamma[z_2 + \theta(\bar{s} - s) + i^*]$$
$$(21.3b)$$

where α denotes the direct elasticity of money demand with respect to anticipated domestic inflation. Tanzi (1982) shows that expected inflation directly influences the demand for money in the USA – although his empirical analysis does not use the exchange rate as a forward signal.

Let arriving news of general country risk again be denoted by z_2. Because subsequent domestic price inflation is confined to the intermediate run, long-run increases in the domestic price level, exchange rate and interest rate remain as described in equations (21.13)–(21.15) for case II.

However, the short-run response of the interest rate to an increase in z_2 is now very different. From the immediate depreciation of the domestic currency, inflationary expectations rise – possibly quite sharply. People reduce their demand for

money according to the parameter α. But, in the short run, real cash balances cannot change because the price level is sticky and the stock of nominal money is given. To keep the domestic money market in balance in the face of excess liquidity, therefore, i must fall immediately when z_2 increases – which accentuates capital flight into foreign bonds. This initially perverse movement in the short-term interest rate, when news arrives, is shown in Figure 21.2(a).

This perverse movement in the short-term interest rate then aggravates the overshooting (depreciation) of the exchange rate above its long-run equilibrium value. To see this algebraically, differentiate the bond market equation (21.4b) and money market equation (21.3b) with respect to z_2, insert the new long-run equilibrium values for $\bar{i}$, $\bar{p}$ and $\bar{s}$ and then solve simultaneously for the short-run impacts on the exchange rate and interest rate:

$$\frac{di}{dz_2} = -\frac{\alpha\delta}{\varepsilon + \alpha}\frac{ds}{dz_2} < 0 \text{ if } \frac{ds}{dz_2} > 0 \quad (21.19)$$

$$\frac{ds}{dz_2} = \frac{\varepsilon + \gamma + 1/\theta}{\Delta}$$

where

$$\Delta = 1 - \frac{\alpha\delta}{\theta(\varepsilon + \gamma)} \quad (21.20)$$

When news arrives, equation (21.19) shows how the domestic interest rate falls as the exchange rate depreciates. Moreover, with inflationary expectations now influencing money demand directly, a stable short-run equilibrium for the exchange rate might not exist. Additional capital flight from the falling interest rate may induce a 'vicious circle' of exchange depreciation, a rising price level and increasing inflationary expectations (Sung 1988).

Although such vicious circles may be economically plausible in some circumstances, let us rule them out in our formal model. To ensure that the system will come to rest at its long-run equilibrium values defined by equations (21.13)–(21.15), let us impose the stability condition that $0 < \Delta < 1$.

This requires

$$\frac{\alpha\delta}{\theta(\varepsilon + \gamma)} < 1. \qquad (21.21)$$

If condition (21.21) holds, the short-run exchange depreciation – the increase in s – is bounded. To further understand the meaning of (21.21), again suppose that $\delta \approx \theta$: the pressure on the exchange rate to converge to its long-run equilibrium is similar to that on the price level. Then, the jump in the short-run exchange rate varies directly with α; and, indeed, the stability condition reduces to $\alpha < \varepsilon + \gamma$. This condition could be violated if the domestic money demand function remains insular with $\gamma \rightarrow 0$ and its interest elasticity ε is small. However, α is almost certain to be less than ε because the domestic bonds are usually a more convenient alternative to holding money than are commodity inventories. Thus, unless bandwagon effects or bubbles are present, a vicious circle can be ruled out.

Nevertheless, perverse adjustments in short-term interest rates greatly increase the volatility of 'equilibrium' movements in the exchange rate – whether responding to changes in tax risk (case I) or to generalized country risk (case II). This 'exaggerated' overshooting of the exchange rate is plotted in Figure 21.2(b) where the vertical distance cb now exceeds ac. The erratic path for the short-term interest rate – first falling sharply and then rising gradually as inflation reduces real cash balances – can be seen in Figure 21.2(a).

OPTIMAL MONETARY POLICY IN THE FACE OF DIRECT AND INDIRECT CURRENCY SUBSTITUTION

In a 'free float', monetary policy is not used to smooth fluctuations in the exchange rate. Implicitly, the central bank has other, more purely domestic goals – traditionally the most important being to stabilize the domestic price level.

Let us accept this traditional objective in its own right. In a hypothetical social utility function, suppose that reducing exchange rate volatility *per se* is given no weight. However, the authorities aim to stabilize the average level of domestic-currency prices.

Then, the central bank's technical mandate is to balance the (possibly) fluctuating demand for the domestic money by varying its supply so that the national price level remains fairly constant. But changes in the *ex ante* demand for domestic money are difficult to measure; and the consequences of getting the balance wrong are evident only with a lag – perhaps after price inflation develops and is hard to stop. Thus, to gauge whether or not the current demand for domestic money is shifting, central bankers often look to immediately available prices in auction markets – interest rates, foreign exchange rates, primary commodity prices and so on – for guidance.[11]

Suppose our economy is too small to influence primary commodity prices on a world-wide basis. The preferred monetary indicator then boils down to a choice between the domestic short-term rate of interest and the foreign exchange rate(s) against some 'hard' foreign currency(s). Can the model developed above then throw light on which more accurately indicates whether current monetary policy is too tight or too easy?

In both cases I and II, the news that shifted portfolio preferences was 'expectational' or 'forward looking': the perceived increase in future risk required an eventual increase in the interest rate on domestic bonds in order to rebalance international asset portfolios. Once long-run equilibrium was re-established with a higher price level, the reduction in the real stock of money finally permitted the necessary increase in interest rates.

Suppose now that the central bank had chosen to key on the short-term domestic interest rate as its monetary indicator. In the traditional manner, the monetary authority expands the domestic money supply when facing (incipient) upward pressure on the interest rate – and vice versa. For either case I or case II, the central bank would be resisting the natural increase in the interest rate on domestic bonds needed to offset the higher domestic risk – as shown in Figure 21.1(a). If the domestic money supply began to increase after news arrived, the exchange rate would depreciate even more sharply. Stronger and more immediate inflationary pressure would develop in the domestic economy. As long as the central bank tries to prevent the interest rate from increasing, no long-run equilibrium for the price level or for the exchange rate would be sustainable.

Suppose the interest rate initially moved 'perversely', i.e. it fell when international risk increased as shown by the movement from a to b in Figure 21.2(a). At first, the monetary authorities would be induced to contract the money supply. But this correct response would be overridden some weeks or months later when the interest rate rose above a en route to its new long-run equilibrium at point c. Targeting the domestic interest rate, when international risk premia change continually, is too treacherous.

In contrast, suppose that the central bank keyed on the exchange rate itself – provided that a rate close to PPP with a 'hard' currency trading partner(s) was properly selected (McKinnon and Ohno 1989). Then changes in the nominal money supply could allow the short-term interest rate to compensate directly for perceived changes in international risk – without disturbing the exchange rate or the price level.

To see this, consider again the country risk case where z_2 suddenly increases. From equation (21.4b), the exchange rate would stay constant if the interest rate immediately rose to

$$di = dz_2. \qquad (21.18)$$

Following Schroder (1990), the necessary monetary contraction for satisfying (21.8) is found by totally differentiating equation (21.3a) to get

$$dm = -(\varepsilon + \gamma)\, dz_2 < 0. \qquad (21.19)$$

The supply of nominal money is reduced to match the fall in the 'effective' demand for real money. And this fall in effective demand can be partitioned into *direct* currency substitution, as indicated by the parameter γ for case II, and *indirect* currency substitution through the impact of the increased domestic interest rate, as indicated by the semi-elasticity ε for both cases I and II. One way or another, such currency substitution will eventually take place. If the nominal stock of money is not immediately decreased, then we have seen how price inflation will ensue so as to reduce the real stock.

However, this necessity of reducing the real money stock as z_2 increases is more neatly accomplished by following a fixed exchange rate rule. As the exchange rate tends to depreciate, the central bank will reduce the nominal (and real) stock of money directly by selling off foreign exchange reserves or by open market sales of bonds. Either approach satisfies equation (21.19) – thus leaving higher short-term interest rates without otherwise disturbing the economy's macroeconomic equilibrium.

The beauty of so targeting the exchange rate is that the authorities need not have good estimates of ε or γ – or know how much the interest rate must increase in final equilibrium. They may not be able to distinguish between case I and case II as the source of the financial disturbance. Nevertheless, by simply reducing the money supply and raising short-term interest rates by whatever is necessary to defend the exchange rate, they succeed in reducing the (real) stock of money in line with the reduced demand for it while leaving the domestic price level undisturbed.

A CONCLUDING NOTE ON THE PREVALENCE OF INTERNATIONAL RISK

By stabilizing the exchange rate, the monetary authorities free the domestic short-term interest rate to reflect shifting assessments of international risk better. The liquidity trap, or perverse short-run movements in interest rates, are avoided. Therefore, the international bond market works more efficiently when the exchange rate is fixed than when it is floating.

In contrast with the above analysis that took (shifting) risk premia to be exogenously determined, the *prevalence* of this expectational risk –

the frequency and magnitude of shifts in the parameters z_1 and z_2 – itself may depend on the nature of the exchange rate regime in place.

The probability of experiencing 'non-monetary' shocks, such as the tax changes analysed in case I, could well be independent of whether the exchange rate was fixed or floating. That is, such shocks are no more or less likely to occur under fixed compared with floating exchange rates. Nevertheless, under a fixed exchange rate they are much less likely to destabilize the domestic price level when they do occur.

However, the probability of shocks in the form of 'country risk' – as per case II – would seem to be much less likely once the exchange rate was known to be safely fixed in the context of a generally accepted common monetary standard (McKinnon 1988a). Then, the domestic rate of price inflation would be constrained to that prevailing in the 'hard currency' outside world. Because people no longer need fear that the exchange rate twenty years from now will differ much from today's, their international portfolio preferences would be less volatile in the face of current changes in the domestic political scene.

NOTES

1 In practice, 'direct' currency substitution between the narrow monies of the industrial countries is minimal. For transactions purposes, Americans hold few yen and Japanese few dollars. Within some LDCs, on the other hand, foreign currencies circulate in parallel with the national one – with highly destabilizing consequences for the domestic price level (McKinnon 1985).

2 See McKinnon (1979: ch. 4) for a detailed analysis of why this invoicing is economically rational.

3 A more serious analytical simplification is the omission of long-term interest rates, which are not tied down by each national money market. Under floating exchange rates, long-term interest rates have been exceedingly volatile compared with the gold standard before 1914 and the fixed exchange rate dollar standard of the 1950s and 1960s. But analysing excess volatility in long-term interest rates is a story for another time (McKinnon 1990b).

4 Possibly consistent with John Taylor's (1980)

model of staggered labour contracts – although the labour market is not explicitly modelled in this chapter. Note that these inflationary consequences do not depend on an increase in the trade surplus. Indeed, there is no predictable relationship between such a devaluation and the net trade balance (McKinnon 1990a). Hence, I have chosen to omit the details of net trade flows from the model.

5 Under a symmetrical fixed exchange rate regime maintained by non-sterilized intervention in the foreign exchanges or by 'equivalent' domestic open market operations, the money supply would automatically contract in the riskier country (allowing its short-term interest rate to rise) and would rise in the country seen to be a safe haven – thus allowing its short-term interest rates to fall.

6 From October 1979 to the summer of 1982 was the only time that the Federal Reserve Bank attempted to execute American monetary policy without targeting – or trying to smooth – some short-term interest rate (Heller 1988). Instead, they aimed, not very successfully, for a fixed rate of growth in M1. But this resulted in such extreme volatility in short-run interest rates that the policy was subsequently discontinued.

7 The algebraic development of case I follows that suggested by Schroder (1990).

8 In Dornbusch's (1976) model, where shocks are confined to the national money market rather than the international bond market, open interest parity holds after the exchange rate overshoots and regressive expectations set in.

9 For example, a permanent fall in the price of oil could induce exchange depreciation and a severe price inflation in an oil-exporting country – although the precise analytics might differ from the above analysis of a withholding tax on foreign interest and dividends. Indeed, equation (21.2) representing the goods market would have to be altered to distinguish between tradeable and non-tradeable goods – in order to represent the impact of changes in the equilibrium 'real' exchange rate properly.

10 Schroder (1990) has a very similar, although not identical, formulation for the demand for money in (21.3a). He allows γ to take on different values according to whether it modifies z_2 or $\theta(\bar{s} - s) + i^*$. However, the foreign exchange risk margin seems similar for both terms. Being hard pressed to come up with any intuitive argument on why they should differ, I adopt the simpler notation – the single parameter γ – which presumes they do not.

11 The position of a pure domestic monetarist is somewhat different. In this view, the demand for money is subject to small, unpredictable random fluctua-

tions but is otherwise fairly stable through time. In particular, major expectational shifts in international asset preferences do not significantly impact the demand for the national money. Thus, in order to minimize volatility in inflationary expectations, the central bank does its best to keep domestic money growth within a prespecified narrow range.

REFERENCES

Aliber, R. (1973) 'The interest-rate parity theorem: a reinterpretation', *Journal of Political Economy* 81 (6): 1451–9.

Dornbusch, R. (1976) 'Expectations and exchange rate dynamics', *Journal of Political Economy* 84: 1161–76.

Frankel, J.A. and Froot, K. (1986) 'Understanding the U.S. dollar in the eighties: a tale of chartists and fundamentalists', *Economic Record*, special issue: 24–38.

Frenkel, J. and Mussa, M.L. (1980) 'The efficiency of foreign exchange markets and measures of turbulence', *American Economic Review* 70: 374–81.

Heller, R. (1988) 'The making of U.S. monetary policy', Seminar for Economic Policy, The University of Cologne, Germany, April.

Goodhart, C. (1988) 'The foreign exchange market: a random walk with a dragging anchor', *Economica* 55 (220): 437–60.

Keynes, J.M. (1936) *The General Theory of Employment, Interest and Money*, London: Macmillan.

—— (1937) 'The *ex-ante* theory of the rate of interest', *Economic Journal* 47: 663–9.

McKinnon, R.I. (1979) *Money in International Exchange: The Convertible Currency System*, New York: Oxford University Press.

—— (1983) 'Why floating exchange rates fall',

Working Paper E-83-12, Hoover Institution, Stanford University.

—— (1985) 'Two concepts of international currency substitution', in M.B. Connolly and J. McDermott (eds) *The Economics of the Caribbean Basin*, London: Praeger, pp. 101–18.

—— (1988a) 'Monetary and exchange rate policy for international financial stability: a proposal', *Journal of Economic Perspectives* 2 (1): 83–103.

—— (1988b) 'An international gold standard without gold', *The Cato Journal* 8 (2): 351–74.

—— (1990a) 'The exchange rate and the trade balance: insular versus open economies', *Open Economies Review* 1 (1): 17–38.

—— (1990b) 'Interest rate volatility and exchange risk: new rules for a common monetary standard', *Contemporary Policy Issues* 9 (2).

McKinnon, R.I. and Ohno, K. (1989) 'Purchasing power parity as a monetary standard', in O. Hamouda, R. Rowley and B. Wolf (eds) *The Future of the International Monetary System*, Aldershot: Edward Elgar, pp. 42–67.

Meese, R. and Rogoff, K. (1983) 'Empirical exchange rate models of the 1970s: do they fit out of sample', *Journal of International Economics* 14: 3–24.

Schroder, J. (1990) 'International risk and exchange rate overshooting', *Journal of International Money and Finance*, forthcoming.

Sung, L.M. (1988) 'Exchange-rate expectations and interest rates in financially integrated economies', Ph.D. Dissertation, Stanford University.

Tanzi, V. (1982) 'Inflationary expectations, taxes and the demand for money in the U.S.', *IMF Staff Papers* 29 (2).

Taylor, J. (1980) 'Aggregate dynamics and staggered contracts', *Journal of Political Economy* 88: 1–23.

Woo, W.T. (1987) 'Some evidence on speculative bubbles in the foreign exchange market', *Journal of Money, Credit and Banking* 19 (4): 499–514.

22

THE DEBT DENOMINATION DECISION

Robert Z. Aliber

The key decision in international financial management is the debt denomination decision. When borrowing, managers of firms must decide whether to sell new debt and bank loans denominated in their domestic currency or in a foreign currency. Domestic currency, for all practical purposes, is the currency in which the firm reports its income to its stockholders, or to its owners. For most purposes the relevant foreign currency is either the currency of one of the foreign countries in which the firm sells or produces, or the currency of one of the small number of countries in which the firm can borrow readily. The choice of currency for the denomination of debt and bank loans affects both the level and the variability of the firm's income because it impacts on net interest payments and foreign exchange gains and losses.

The key elements in the debt denomination decision can be grouped into two sets. First, the market factor set includes the interest rates on bonds and bank loans denominated in the domestic currency, the interest rates on comparable bonds and bank loans denominated in one of several foreign currencies and the anticipated change in the exchange rate for each of these foreign currencies in terms of domestic currency. Second, the firm-specific factor set includes the foreign exchange exposure associated with the various components of the firm's income statement and its balance sheet, the risk associated with individual foreign currencies, the risk of a portfolio of various foreign currencies and the relation between the firm's total income and capital gain (or loss) from a change in the exchange rate at a time when the firm has a foreign exchange exposure.

The central decision for the firm is whether the currency denomination of its debt and its bank loans should be managed to reduce or fully neutralize the foreign exchange exposure of its income statement or whether the currency denomination of its debt and bank loans should be managed to increase its net income, either by reducing its borrowing costs or by increasing its foreign exchange gains – at least in an anticipated sense. The inputs to this decision include both the market factors (the relation between the interest rates on comparable bonds denominated in different currencies and the anticipated change in exchange rates) and the firm-specific factors (the firm's attitude toward risk and the relation between the income associated with changes in the firm's foreign exchange exposure and its total income). An individual firm might, and should, have different postures toward maintaining foreign exchange exposures in different groups of currencies, because the market factors associated with each of these groups of currencies might differ. Two firms involved with the same group of foreign currencies may follow quite different policies when making the debt denomination decision because of differences in their attitudes toward risk.

The debt denomination decision for the firm is the mirror image of the portfolio decision of the investor. The key elements in the portfolio decision are all present in the debt denomination decision – the interest rates on comparable assets denominated in various foreign currencies and in the domestic currency, the anticipated change in the exchange rate for each of these currencies in terms of domestic currency, the investor's attitude toward risk and the risk associated with a portfolio of foreign currencies. The debt denomination decision has one element not usually associated with the portfolio decision – the firm may have revenues and costs in individual foreign currencies and hence income or profits in these currencies. Similarly, to the extent that the firm's profits on its domestic production or sales are sensitive to changes in exchange rates, the firm has an income-statement exposure. Paradoxically, the firm may have an income-statement exposure even though it is not engaged in importing or exporting or any other international activities.

The measurement of the exposure of the firm's income statement is discussed in the next section of this chapter. Then the market factors are analysed; the techniques for altering the foreign exchange exposure of the firm's balance sheet and the comparative costs of each technique are reviewed. Next, the firm-specific factors are evaluated. Each of several strategies that a firm might adopt toward its foreign exchange exposure is evaluated.

THE FOREIGN EXCHANGE EXPOSURE OF THE FIRM'S INCOME STATEMENT

The key question for the firm involves whether the currency denomination of debt and bank loans should be managed to neutralize the foreign exchange exposure of the income statement. Hence, the first element in the debt denomination decision involves estimating the exposure of several components of its income statement and the sensitivity of the firm's income in domestic currency to changes in exchange rates. Changes in exchange rates may lead to changes in the domestic income associated with royalties and licence fees from foreign firms and the firm's foreign subsidiaries, the domestic income equivalent of the profits of the firm's various foreign subsidiaries as reported in the currencies of the

countries in which these subsidiaries are organized and the domestic income on its export activities. Similarly, changes in exchange rates may lead to changes in the domestic income of its domestic production and sales. Moreover, the profits of the firm's foreign subsidiaries – as reported in the currencies of the countries where they are organized – may be significantly affected by changes in exchange rates.

The measurement of the foreign exchange exposure of these several activities is considered in turn. Consider the foreign exchange exposure of the firm's royalty and licensing income, initially under the assumption that the payment of royalties and licence fees is in the domestic currency and subsequently in a foreign currency. If the firm contracts to be paid royalty and licensing income in its domestic currency, it might seem that the firm does not have a foreign-currency exposure – instead the payor has a foreign exchange exposure. If, however, the change in the exchange rate would cause the payor to go bankrupt or to become financially distressed so that it could not make its contractual payments, then the firm has a foreign exchange exposure.[1] If the firm contracts instead to receive payment in a foreign currency, then the domestic-currency equivalent of the scheduled receipts in the foreign currency will change whenever the exchange rate changes. The foreign exchange exposure of a projected stream of receipts in each of several foreign currencies can be measured as the discounted present value of the anticipated receipts in each of these foreign currencies.[2]

Consider the exposure of the income on exports to various foreign countries. These export sales may be invoiced in the currency of the buyer or the currency of the seller. If the exports are invoiced in the currency of the buyer and the buyer's currency depreciates, the firm incurs a foreign exchange loss and the domestic income attached to export sales declines. As a result, the unit volume of exports may decline as the price of these goods in the buyer's currency is increased relative to the price of similar or competitive goods produced in the buyer's country, or the profits per unit of export sales decline because the price in the buyer's currency is not increased by as much in percentage terms as the change in the exchange rate. In most cases, both export volume and profits per unit of export decline. Indeed, the firm has a foreign exposure on its exports unless the firm is able to increase its selling price in the foreign country by the same percentage amount as the change in the exchange rate and still maintain the volume of its sales. And the economic condition for being able to raise selling prices is that the firm has no effective competitors in the various foreign countries to which it exports.

If export sales are denominated in the firm's currency, it might seem that the firm does not have a foreign exchange exposure on these sales, but that the importer has the foreign exchange exposure. However, the volume of the importer's purchases is likely to decline as the importer has to pay a higher price in its own currency for imports; the importer's sales may decline and its profits per unit of sales may also decline. Hence, the factors that lead to a foreign exchange exposure when the exports are denominated in the firm's currency are the same as those when the exports are denominated in the importer's currency. In both cases, the exporter's exposure is the anticipated revenues in the foreign currency discounted to the present.[3]

The firm's foreign exchange exposure on its export sales is the anticipated revenues in the foreign currency or, more precisely, the discounted present value of these revenues.[4] The appropriate interest rate is the market interest rate in the country in which the exports are sold.

Consider the exposure of the projected income of the firm's foreign subsidiaries. Initially, this income is estimated in the currency of the country in which the subsidiary is located, and then the domestic-currency equivalent is determined on the basis of the anticipated exchange rate. If the foreign currency depreciates more rapidly than anticipated, the domestic-currency equivalent of the subsidiary's income is smaller than anticipated. The anticipated income of these subsidiaries can be estimated under a number of assumptions about exchange rates at various future dates: the firm's

exposure in each of these foreign currencies is the present value of the anticipated income in these currencies. The exposure of the income of the foreign subsidiaries differs from the exposure of royalty and licensing income in foreign currencies of the parent in one significant way – the income in each of the foreign currencies may vary as the foreign exchange value of the currencies of the countries in which the subsidiaries are located varies. Thus, each of the foreign subsidiaries has its own foreign exchange exposure and its income is sensitive to changes in the exchange rate.[5] The firm's exposure in each currency is the domestic-currency equivalent of the anticipated profits of each of the foreign subsidiaries.

The firm may have an exposure on its income statement even though the firm does not participate in international trade. The income statement is exposed if profits on domestic sales are sensitive to changes in exchange rates, perhaps because the firm's products are competitive with imported goods or because one of the components to domestic production is imported. Changes in the exchange rates might lead to changes in the volume of domestic sales or to changes in the price and hence unit profit of domestic sales. The foreign exchange exposure of export sales provides this analogy: if one or several foreign currencies should depreciate, then the domestic demand for imports may increase and the firm may lose sales in its domestic market. If the firm responds to the loss of its market share by cutting prices, then its profits per unit of sales decline. The foreign exchange exposure of domestic sales and revenues is measured as the foreign-currency equivalent where the foreign currency is that in which the sales are sensitive.

Each of the components in the foreign exchange exposure of the income statement can be expressed in present value terms. Two factors complicate the estimation of the foreign exchange exposure in these terms. The first is the estimation of the revenues associated with each of the activities. The second is the choice of the interest rate used in the present value calculation. The complication is that estimates of some of the components are less certain than estimates of others. (Despite the uncertainty, the firm's confidence in its ability to develop estimates of its future sales is likely to be greater than its confidence in its ability to develop estimates of future exchange rates.)

The firm may have an income-statement exposure in a number of foreign currencies. Eventually, the firm's managers view its foreign exchange exposures in a portfolio context. Managers might group income-statement exposures in various foreign currencies; or instead they may determine that the firm's aggregate foreign income-statement exposure is the sum of its income-statement exposures in individual foreign currencies. To the extent that the foreign exchange values of different national currencies are highly correlated, the income-statement exposures in these currencies can be grouped.

MARKET FACTORS AND THE CURRENCY DENOMINATION OF A FIRM'S DEBT

Changes in the currency denomination of the firm's debt and bank loans can reduce or fully neutralize the exposure of its income statement. Alternatively, the currency denomination of the firm's debt and bank loans can be managed to increase the firm's foreign exchange exposure to profit from anticipated changes in exchange rates. Moreover, efforts to arrange the currency denomination of a firm's debt and bank loans to reduce its net interest costs can alter its foreign exchange exposure.

A firm with a foreign exchange exposure increases the sensitivity of its income or its net worth and, perhaps, its market valuation to changes in exchange rates. Because many firms seek to minimize the variance in their income, managers may attempt to reduce their foreign exchange exposures – if other things are equal. But other things are rarely equal – altering the foreign exchange exposure may incur various costs. For the firm, the relevant trade-off is between the cost of reducing (or increasing) its foreign exchange exposure and the benefits of having a smaller

foreign exchange exposure – or of not having any foreign exchange exposure.

The firm can alter its foreign exchange exposure through a variety of now traditional techniques, including leading-and-lagging, forward exchange contracts, futures contracts in foreign exchange, options on foreign exchange and foreign exchange swaps. And some more esoteric techniques are available and may be used when the traditional techniques are not available – these techniques include the pricing of commodity sales transactions, speculation in inventories or real assets and various non-market swaps.

Consider a firm that alters its foreign exchange exposure through the purchase of a three-month forward exchange contract. This transaction may reduce or fully neutralize the firm's exposure on its income statement or increase the firm's exposure. The cost of the purchase of a three-month forward contract is the difference between the amount of domestic currency in settlement of the forward contract and the amount of domestic currency realized when the foreign currency which is taken in delivery in the settlement of the forward contract is immediately sold for domestic currency. This 'cost' can be negative or positive. It is closely approximated as the difference between the exchange rate in the forward contract and the spot exchange rate on the date when the forward contract matures.[6] Computation of this cost always involves a comparison between the exchange rate used to effect a change in the firm's foreign exposure with the spot exchange rate at some future date, usually on the date when the forward exchange contract matures. If the forward exchange rate and the spot exchange rate at the maturity of the forward exchange rate are not significantly different, there is no cost to altering the firm's foreign exchange exposure by altering the currency denomination of its debt. And the flip-side of this statement is that there is no anticipated gain from altering the firm's foreign exchange exposure in anticipation of a profit from an anticipated change in the spot exchange rate.

That the firm can alter its foreign exchange exposure without cost may seem surprising and comparable with the proverbial free lunch, for even though firms would be willing to pay for the lunch, they are not required to do so. The story is that transactions of US firms to hedge a long foreign exchange exposure in the German mark and of German firms to hedge their foreign exchange exposures in the US dollar tend to be offsetting. Hence, both groups of firms may be able to reduce their foreign exchange exposures in their transactions with each other – and conceivably at no net cost. An insurance analogy is inappropriate because there is no intermediary in the forward exchange market that shares in the risk-reduction activity; instead, the banks act as brokers in the forward exchange market and marry the transactions of the US firms with those of the German firms at a very modest charge – essentially the difference between their buying and selling rates for forward exchange contracts with the two parties.

Similarly, assume managers alter the firm's foreign exchange exposure through leading-and-lagging; the firm borrows in a foreign currency, converts these borrowed foreign funds into domestic currency and uses the domestic funds to repay its domestic loans. As the firm's interest payments increase in one currency, and its interest payments decline in the second currency, there is likely to be an increase in its interest payments. Moreover, there is a change in the timing of the firm's foreign transactions – the firm enters into a spot exchange transaction today rather than in three or six months. The cost of leading-and-lagging is the difference between the interest payments during the term of the loan and the amounts of foreign exchange realized on the date when the borrowed funds are converted and on the date when the borrowed funds are repaid. This amount can be approximated as the difference between the interest rate differential and the realized change in the exchange rate over this same interval. If the interest rates on the two loans are not significantly different from the change in the exchange rate in percentage terms, there is no cost to altering the firm's exposure. Again the free lunch question arises, and again the answer

involves the impact of the hedging transactions of the US firm and of the German firm on current exchange rates and interest rates. The mirror image of this proposition is that there is a cost to altering the firm's foreign exchange exposure only to the extent that there is a difference between the two interest rates and the percentage change in the exchange rate. And if the US firm incurs a cost in altering its foreign exchange exposure, the German firm alters its exposure and at the same time realizes a profit – a free lunch.

Because exchange rate movements are volatile, individual forward contracts are poor predictors of the spot exchange rate on the dates when the forward exchange contracts mature. The central question is whether, for a large number of forward exchange contracts in each foreign currency, the forward exchange rate is a biased or an unbiased predictor of the future spot exchange rate. If the forward exchange rate is an unbiased predictor, then the forecast errors on one side of the spot exchange rate and the forecast errors on the other side of the spot exchange rate more or less cancel each other out. The alternative result is that the forecast errors on one side of the spot exchange rate are substantially larger than the forecast errors on the other side of the spot exchange rate. If the alternative result is valid, the interpretation might be that investors demand, and receive, a risk premium.

The concept for estimating the costs of altering the firm's exposure is known as Fisher Open; it involves the relationship between interest rates on comparable asserts denominated in different currencies and the realized change in the exchange rate over this same holding period. An alternative version is that the Fisher Open involves the relationship between the forward exchange rate and the spot exchange rate on the date of the maturity of the forward exchange contracts. (These two versions would prove identical in measured costs if domestic and foreign assets were not significantly different in political risk.)

The residual or difference between the two versions can be considered a risk premium, a forecast error or some combination of both. The forecast error reflects that predicting changes in exchange rates is a risky activity because the movements in spot exchange rates form one period to the next and from one month to the next may be volatile. Investors do their best to forecast the next period's exchange rate, but frequently they are overwhelmed by unanticipated events and the resulting very large unanticipated movements in the spot exchange rate. Some investors may be willing to increase their exposure to foreign exchange risk only if they receive an additional payment – a risk premium – for incurring the risks associated with cross-border finance. The economic situation is that, the larger the unanticipated movements in the exchange rate, the larger the forecast error and the larger the minimum required risk premium. In a world characterized by a variety of monetary and structural disturbances, there are likely to be large deviations from Fisher Open on a monthly or quarterly basis, with the result that any firm or investor maintaining an exposed position in foreign exchange is likely to realize a significant loss – or gain.

Firms and investors may seek to reduce or minimize their exposure to loss from changes in exchange rates because they believe the cost of the loss dominates the benefits of the gain – even if both are equally probable. Firms and investors would increase their exposure to loss from changes in exchange rates only if they anticipate a large gain in an expected value sense, or at least a savings in interest costs on borrowed funds from maintaining an exposed position in foreign exchange and carrying the associated risk. The implicit proposition is that the cost of reducing or eliminating the exposure is too high relative to the anticipated loss from maintaining an exposed position in foreign exchange and bearing the uncertainty associated with possible changes in the exchange rate. In effect, the firms and the investors carrying foreign exchange exposures self-insure – they believe that the additional income from the savings in interest payments associated with maintaining a foreign exchange exposure is adequate to compensate for the occasional foreign exchange losses and for carrying the uncertainty associated

with changes in exchange rates.

Fisher Open has been subjected to many tests, especially in the form of the proposition that the forward exchange rate should be considered an unbiased (or a biased) predictor of the future spot exchange rate. To a lesser extent, studies have been undertaken to assess the relationship between the difference in interest rates on comparable assets denominated in different currencies and the observed change in the exchange rate. (If the interest rates are those on Eurodeposits, then the second test is identical with the first.) The general thrust of these studies is that on average forward rates are very close to being unbiased predictors of future spot exchange rates. The economic rationale for this conclusion is that the firms in each of several countries use foreign exchange contracts as a way to reduce their foreign exchange exposures – and the sales of the German mark in the forward market by US firms and the sales of US dollars in the forward market by German firms tend to' be offsetting.

The empirical observation that forward exchange rates are unbiased predictors of future spot exchange rates must be reconciled with the observation that there is a substantial difference among countries in real interest rates. The countries with low real interest rates are the capital-rich countries, while the countries with high real interest rates are the capital-poor countries. The difference in real interest rates can be thought of as the return required for the marginal investor for taking on a foreign exchange exposure.

The combination of competition among the suppliers of these different financial instruments and arbitrage by firms and investors among those for altering exposure ensures that the costs to the firm or investor of using one of these techniques is not likely to differ by a large amount from the costs of some other technique. The cost of altering foreign exchange exposure through the use of forward contracts and through the use of futures contracts is likely to be less than 0.1 per cent in a major currency, and perhaps closer to 0.02 or 0.03 per cent. Similarly, the cost of forward contracts and the cost of leading-and-lagging are not likely to differ by more than several tenths of 1 per cent. Any difference between the cost of these two techniques means that there is a deviation from the interest rate parity theorem and, since this concept is based on arbitrage, any observed deviation implies that the financial assets or liabilities used for this comparison are less than perfect substitutes for each other.[7] Arbitrage may be constrained because of exchange controls. Or tax considerations may favour one technique for altering exposure rather than another.

The cost of each of the techniques for altering exposure is an opportunity cost. Hence, the cost of altering the firm's exposure can only be calculated after the end of the investment period, when the spot exchange rate is known. The cost of altering the firm's exposure is the return for maintaining the exposed position during the period when the exchange rate changes.[8]

The costs of each technique for altering exposure may be compared in a present value analysis. For example, assume a US firm wants to pay £10 million in two years. The US firm can buy British pounds today for delivery in two years; in two years, the firm is obliged to deliver $3.5 million (on the assumption that the forward exchange rate is $1.75 = £1.00). The present value of $3.5 million in two years can be obtained by using the firm's marginal cost of dollar funds as the interest rate. Alternatively, the firm might lead-and-lag; in this case, the firm uses present value analysis to determine the amount of British pounds that must be acquired today to compound to £2 million in two years; here present value analysis is applied to the British pound investment.

FIRM-SPECIFIC FACTORS AND THE CURRENCY DENOMINATION OF DEBT

If the managers of a firm were confident that Fisher Open would remain continuously valid, they would be indifferent about the currency denomination of its debt. The firm might have an income-statement exposure, but the managers would not be able to alter its aggregate foreign exchange exposure by altering the currency denomination of its bank loans and debt. The managers of the firm are concerned about the currency denomination of its debt because they believe there are non-trivial differences from Fisher Open in an *ex ante*, or anticipated, sense. The inputs to the debt denomination decision include the risk aversion of the firm, the risk the firm associates with particular foreign currencies, the distribution of the firm's income-statement exposure by currency and the significance of the potential foreign exchange gains and losses to the firm's income, net worth and market valuation.

Risk aversion

Individual investors can be ranked by the risk premium that each requires for acquiring or maintaining exposure to loss – and to gain – from unanticipated changes in exchange rates. Similarly, individual firms can be ranked according to their willingness to bear the various cross-border risks.[9] The cliché that is the cornerstone of one view is that 'we specialize in producing shoes or machine tools, not in speculating in the foreign exchange'. This statement is a cop-out. Almost every firm that takes this view is implicitly speculating in foreign exchange because it has failed not only to devote any resources to measuring its foreign exchange exposure but also to arrange the currency denomination of its debt so that its income statement is not exposed.

For the managers of the firm, the key question is how their risk aversion compares with the risk aversiveness of investors as a group and of firms as a group. In this context, risk aversion is firm specific and should be distinguished from the risk that each firm encounters because of the set of currencies in which the firm has an income-statement exposure.

For firms and for investors, the relevant risk is that of a portfolio of foreign currencies rather than an individual foreign currency. The less strong the correlation among the changes in the exchange rates of these several foreign currencies, the greater the likelihood that some firms and investors acquire or maintain exposures in each of several different foreign currencies. For these firms and investors, maintaining exposure in a group of foreign currencies leads to a disproportionate increase in the returns relative to the risk; for the firm, the increase in the return is a result of the reduction in interest costs; for the investor, the increase in the return is a result of higher interest income. And by extension, the risk of exposures in various foreign currencies can be grouped with a variety of other financial and non-financial risks, on the basis of the same proposition that there is an unusually large increase in the returns relative to the increase in risk as long as the changes in the price of these assets is less than perfectly correlated.

Some firms may manage the currency denomination of their bonds and bank loans to reduce their exposure to foreign exchange risk. In contrast, other firms may manage the currency composition of their debt so that the effect is an increase in their foreign exchange exposure and increased sensitivity to gain and loss from changes in the exchange rates.

One difference among firms that affects their willingness to maintain a foreign exchange exposure is that their risk aversion may differ. The greater the risk aversion, the less likely is the firm to knowingly maintain a foreign exchange exposure.

National domicile

Firms headquartered in different countries may have somewhat similar exposures of their income statements. Consider a US firm with an income-statement exposure in the Canadian dollar and a Canadian firm with an income-statement exposure in the US dollar. Assume the size of each income-statement exposure is similar. Both the US firm and the Canadian firm are concerned about the debt denomination decision. The Canadian firm could reduce its foreign exchange exposure by borrowing US dollars, at least to the extent that the increase in the volume of US dollar-denomin-

ated loans or borrowings offsets the US dollar exposure of its income statement. The Canadian firm might increase its US dollar borrowings so that they exceed the volume of its exposure on its income statement to reduce interest costs; at the same time the firm can reduce both its exposure and net interest costs by borrowing US dollars. In contrast, if the US firm seeks to reduce the exposure of its income statement by borrowing Canadian dollars, it increases its net interest payments. The asymmetry reflects that the difference in interest rates on comparable assets is large relative to the anticipated change in the exchange rate.

Risk of particular foreign currencies and the portfolio effects

Individual foreign currencies can be ranked by their riskiness. Risk might be measured by the volatility of the movement of the foreign exchange value of individual foreign currencies, where the volatility might be measured as the range of movement or the standard deviation. Alternatively, the risk might be measured as unanticipated movement in the exchange rate, and either the range or standard deviation of the actual movement about the unanticipated movement.

The firm's attitude toward its exposure might be a function of the riskiness of particular currencies and the cost of altering its exposure. The algorithm is that the firm might maintain exposure in those currencies where the risk is low, and reduce its exposure in those currencies considered very risky. Moreover, this posture toward exposure in particular foreign currencies should be viewed in the context of a portfolio of currencies.

One implication of the portfolio argument is that the larger the firm and the more diverse the array of its foreign exchange exposures, the stronger the case for maintaining these exposures for any given posture toward risk aversion. The rationale is that as the number of currencies in which the firm has income-statement exposures increases, the larger the impact of the inclusion of each additional currency on the firm's income relative to the impact on the riskiness of the firm's portfolio of currencies. The commonsense interpretation is that those firms with income-statement exposures in a diverse group of foreign currencies are best positioned to carry these exposures and 'collect' the risk premium in the foreign exchange market.

Materiality

One principle of personal finance is that individuals can increase their incomes by carrying small risks rather than buying insurance against these risks. Thus, individuals may buy automobile and homeowner's insurance with large deductibles; the principle is that they minimize the total cost by self-insuring for small risks. Similarly, individuals may buy major medical insurance and self-insure the cost of smaller medical expenses. The implication is that firms might carry small or modest exposures to their income statements and hedge any exceptionally large exposures. The distinction between large and small is arbitrary and firm specific; for each firm the question becomes how large a foreign exchange loss it could accept during a quarter or a year without having an unusual impact on its reported income or its market. The larger the firm, the larger the foreign exchange exposure it might carry.

CONCLUSIONS

The key decision in the debt denomination decision is whether the firm should denominate its debt and bank loans in its domestic currency or in a foreign currency. The managers of the firm must decide whether the denomination of debt and bank loans should be managed to increase or reduce the foreign exchange exposure of its income statement. Hence, they must first measure the components of the foreign exchange exposure associated with royalty and licensing income, and the income of the firm's foreign subsidiaries, exports and domestic sales. Then the managers must address the market factors associated with exchange risk and decide whether they believe that

risk premia are evident in the foreign exchange market. The less convinced they are that risk premia exist, the stronger the case for hedging the firm's foreign exchange exposure. The flip-side of this statement is that the more evident the risk premia, the larger the possible cost of hedging exposure and the greater the return from carrying the exposure.

Several firm-specific factors affect the firm's posture toward carrying or hedging foreign exchange exposure. A central one is its own attitude towards risk aversion. Moreover, the larger the array of currencies in which the firm has income-statement exposures, the more likely it is to view these exposures in a portfolio context. The firm might hedge only those exposures so large that the foreign exchange losses could have a significant impact on earnings and market value.

NOTES

1   The analogy is the foreign exchange exposure of the major international banks on their loans to Mexico, Brazil and Argentina. These loans were denominated in US dollars, German marks or Japanese yen; the borrowers acquired the foreign exchange exposure. But when the currencies of Mexico, Brazil and Argentina depreciated sharply, the debt-servicing burden of the borrowing countries increased significantly and many went bankrupt.

2   The interest rate used in the present value calculation is likely to be the host-country interest rate or to be based on this interest rate.

3   A distinction must be made between the income-statement exposure on anticipated foreign sales and the balance-sheet exposure on sales-financing loans to the importers.

4   The firm's foreign exchange exposure on its export sales is not independent of whether export sales are invoiced in the firm's currency or the importer's currency. The rationale is that the volume of exports may decline more rapidly if the importer acquires the foreign exchange exposure than if the exporter does.

5   To some extent, the foreign exchange exposure of the foreign subsidiaries and of the parent may be offsetting.

6   The difference between the cost computed from payments and receipts and the approximation based on the exchange rate in the futures contract

and the spot exchange rate on the date when the forward contract matures is a set of transactions costs.

7   There may be a difference between the cost of forward contracts and the cost of leading-and-lagging because the financial instruments denominated in different currencies used in leading-and-lagging are less than perfect substitutes for each other in terms of sensitivity to default or the exchange controls.

8   An alternative – and incorrect – approach to measuring the cost of altering the firm's exposure involves a comparison between today's forward exchange rate and today's spot exchange rate. This approach confuses the costs of two different techniques for altering foreign exchange exposure.

9   Finance theory stipulates that the managers of the firm should ignore risk in their borrowing and lending decisions. Individual investors can as a group neutralize the risk they associate with particular firms.

BIBLIOGRAPHY

Aliber, R.Z. (1978) *Exchange Risk and Corporate International Finance*, London: Macmillan.

Huizinga, J. and Miskin, F. (1984) 'Inflation and real rates on assets with different risk characteristics', *Journal of Finance*, July: 699–714.

Levi, M.D. (1983) *International Finance: Financial Management and the International Economy*, New York: McGraw-Hill.

Levich, R.N. (1979) *The International Money Market*, New York: JAI Press.

Makin, J.H. (1978) 'Portfolio theory and the problem of foreign exchange risk', *Journal of Finance*, May: 517–34.

Oxelheim, L. (1985) *International Financial Market Fluctuations*, Chichester: Wiley.

Papadia, F. (1981) 'Forward exchange rates as predictors of the future spot rates and the efficiency of the foreign exchange market', *Journal of Banking and Finance*, June: 217–40.

Wihlborg, C. (1977) *Currency Risks in International Financial Markets under Different Exchange Rate Regimes*, Stockholm: Institute for International Economics.

Part V

INTERNATIONAL DEBT ISSUES

The decade of the 1980s will be remembered as the decade of debt. By the early 1990s, the severity of the crisis had abated somewhat. This was the result of the Brady initiative, the easing of terms on Paris Club reschedulings, the continuation of other programmes of debt relief and restructuring and the strong export performance of some debtor countries. Since the Brady plan was launched in 1989, five Latin American LDCs have reached debt reduction agreements with their bank creditors. Yet, their burden is heavy. Debt servicing averaged 30 per cent of their export earnings in 1991. To be sure, debt indicators improved and so did flows to LDCs. However, a problem not addressed by the Brady initiative is the heavy burden of official debt and debt service in some LDCs. The cumulative burden of higher oil prices, arrears and heavy official debt burdens is acute in severely indebted low-income countries where actual debt service has been about 40 per cent of scheduled debt service in the early 1990s. A favourable development is the ongoing economic reforms and structural objectives in many indebted LDCs. They lift the burden of debt far more effectively than debt forgiveness.

The first chapter in this part introduces the reader to the concept of country risk. Although the terms country risk and sovereign risk are often used interchangeably, their implications are different. The former arises when debt servicing is dependent on the actions of government. Sovereign risk is a subset of country risk and arises when the ultimate obligator is the sovereign, i.e. the government or one of its agencies. From the perspective of the creditor, this distinction is inconsequential because for him what matters is the source of repayment which, in turn, is the same in both cases, namely, the foreign exchange earning of the country. If there is an economic crisis causing shortfall in foreign exchange earnings, the sovereign will be unable to discharge its external obligations. Under these circumstances, the private sector obligator will also fail to service debt, although it suffers from no liquidity or cash-flow snags in its operations and its creditworthiness is intact. Country risk has differing incidence across assets and investors which results in comparative advantage of different agents. Lessard identifies certain steps that would reduce some of the most costly effects of country risk. In the next insightful chapter, Kenen makes an impassioned case for debt relief and the creation of an International Draft Discount Corporation. He argues that it will serve the interests of both the LDCs and commercial banks best. Max Corden in the third chapter proposes an identical plan of an international debt facility to buy the debt of developing countries at a discount and mark down its contractual value. This chapter also considers the central question of how the debtor countries, creditor banks and owner of the facility will be affected. It analyses the distribution of gains and losses among them. Max Corden also attempts to separate 'market price effect' from the 'ceiling effects'.

The alternative schemes for resolving the debt crisis have received great attention, and in the fourth chapter Lessard presents his own and discusses the merits and demerits of others. Debt–

equity swaps and other variants that combine debt buybacks with alternative forms of finance were held out as the leading methodologies by institutional observers, bankers and private sector groups in LDCs. However, such exchanges were considered inconsequential or even damaging to the economic interests of LDCs by many academics and LDC governments. Lessard first deals with the spurious dichotomy between debt conversion and debt reduction and then proposes a plan of action for the various economic agents in resolving the debt crisis.

While discussing the international debt issues, too often the largest debtor country in the world, the USA, gets ignored. The outstanding US debt was more than $2.5 trillion in the early 1990s, which is more than twice the level of the LDC debt. The fifth chapter by Fieleke deals with that very issue. He talks about the reasons behind the massive twin deficits and the debt in an international context, as well as discussing how the US economy performed while in debt and why despite all apprehensions the dollar did not hard land. The US economy lost little competitiveness for supply-side reasons and, contrary to widespread expectation, the labour productivity gains were virtually as great as those in other industrial nations. He foresees a continuation of depreciation of the dollar and shrinking of the trade deficit in the medium term. However, painful demand-side adjustments are unavoidable and the USA will be obliged to consume less than it otherwise would.

With large household savings and recurrent current account surpluses, Japan became the largest lender to the USA. In the sixth chapter in this section, Frankel focuses on how this process worked. Financial liberalization in Japan, its low interest rates and the 'safe haven' hypothesis made the USA an attractive proposition for Japanese foreign investment. The post yen-appreciation financial developments in this context are also significant and have been discussed by Frankel. This chapter ends by assessing the implications of the US debt for the Japanese economy.

The last chapter in this section relates to management decisions and addresses one of the key decisions in international financial management, namely the debt denomination decision. This aspect of debt is important for the manager of a borrowing firm as well as for a borrowing country. If a firm decides to borrow in a foreign currency, it must realize that the choice of currency affects both the level and variability of the firm's income because it impacts on net interest payments and foreign exchange gains and losses. Aliber separates the key elements in the debt denomination decisions into two sets: first, the market factor set, and second, the firm-specific factor set. Managers must methodically measure the various components of exposure and juxtapose them against the risk premia; if the possibilities of risk premia are not convincing, a strong case emerges for hedging the exposure.

23

COUNTRY RISK AND THE STRUCTURE OF INTERNATIONAL FINANCIAL INTERMEDIATION

Donald R. Lessard

Country risk stands out in today's global financial system for several reasons. It is perceived to be a major threat to the system's stability, more so than virtually any other single category of risk. It is also perceived to follow different rules from most other types of risk, and hence to require different institutional approaches. This is reflected in the specialization of particular institutions in bearing country risk, the important risk-mitigating role of multilateral institutions or arrangements, including the IMF, the World Bank and the Paris Club, and the lack of specialized markets for laying off this risk.

A major distinction between finance in a single country and finance in an international context is that various assets are denominated or determined in different currencies and hence are subject to differing currency risks. An even more important distinction, though, is that the cash flows associated with various assets are generated in different countries. As a result, assets are subject to different tax regimes, to different political and regulatory risks and to different actual or potential restrictions regarding their convertibility and remittability. In general, these *jurisdiction-specific* factors have two effects:

1 they alter the expected net of tax cash flows that any investor can appropriate;

2 they cause divergences in appropriable returns among investors located in different jurisdictions and, as a result, lead them to skew their portfolios away from the 'world market portfolio' toward assets for which they have

resulting comparative advantage. This, in turn, alters the risk premium demanded on various assets in equilibrium and reduces the efficiency of resource allocation.

This chapter raises several issues regarding country risk and offers some views on how these issues might be incorporated in a more comprehensive perspective. The issues raised include the following.

- What is country risk?
- How do its effects differ across assets or investors?
- Who has comparative advantage in bearing it?
- How does it change the pattern of financial intermediation?
- How does it affect the efficiency of resource allocation?
- What can be done about it?

Clearly, this is far too large a range of issues on which to provide definitive explanations, models or prescriptions. Instead, an attempt will be made to link various aspects of the phenomena that have been discussed in the literature. In examining the impact of country risk on the structure and efficiency of international financial intermediation, I focus on two salient features of the current structure: (1) the home bias in risky asset holdings among financially developed countries, and (2) the apparent crowding out of domestic claims and cross-border risk-bearing claims by sovereign borrowing in the case of LDCs.

This chapter is organized in four sections. The first section focuses on the definition of country risk with particular attention to its sources and incidence across classes of assets and investors. The second section develops the concept of comparative advantage in bearing county risk. The third section examines the impact of country risk on the valuation of assets and capital market equilibrium and its consequent implications for the efficiency of international financial intermediation. The fourth section concludes with an exploratory discussion of policy measures that might address some of the most critical undesired effects of country risk.

WHAT IS COUNTRY RISK?

Country risk, broadly defined, comprises those risks associated with claims against (economic agents in) a particular country, including but not limited to claims on the government of that country. In the financial press and academic journals, it is typically associated with the risks of loans by commercial banks to LDCs. However, it encompasses a much wider range of uncertainties in returns on various types of claims held against a country or economic agents within a country either by foreign or domestic claimants. In the cases of loans to sovereign borrowers, for example, it refers to the possibility of non-performance in the form of default or delayed repayment. In contrast, in the case of direct foreign investment claims, for example, country risk not only includes the risks associated with aggregate payments crises – typically termed transfer risks – but also may include a variety of other fiscal and policy risks as well as risks of outright expropriation typically included under the heading of political risk.

An understanding of the issues associated with country risk is complicated by differences in the definitions employed in the existing literature. In the literature on international lending, the terms *country* or *sovereign risk* typically refer to the risk of rescheduling or outright default resulting from external payments crises (e.g. Eaton and Gersovitz 1981; Walter 1981; Eaton *et al.* 1986). These crises are viewed as stemming from either bad luck, bad faith, mismanagement or, more typically, an indistinguishable mix of the three. *Transfer risk* applies to the exposure of claims against domestic corporations or projects to various policy responses to aggregate exchange crises. In contrast, in the literature on direct foreign investment, *political risk* typically is viewed as the risk of political discontinuities resulting in losses through expropriation or major policy shifts (see, for example, Kobrin 1979). In the case of portfolio equity investment, in turn, *country risk* is defined as the common variability in returns of shares of firms based in or operating in a given country (e.g. Agmon 1973; Solnik 1973; Lessard 1976). Finally, with reference to the international interaction of money markets, *political risk* is typically viewed as the risk of imposition of exchange controls (e.g. Aliber 1973, 1978; Dooley and Isard 1980).

These risks have several traits in common. First, they all apply to claims on governments of or activities within particular jurisdictions. Second, most of them involve elements of policy choice as well as chance. Third, many of them have different impacts across classes of claims or claimants.

Before trying to provide a more general definition, I illustrate risks that might be considered country risks in order to explore the extent that these risks are the result of chance, choice or some interaction of the two as well as the extent to which the impacts of the risks are general or are specific to particular classes of claims or claimants, since country risk is a factor that changes the probability of a particular set of actions with particular impacts on the distribution of payoffs to various classes of assets and/or investors.[1]

Sources of country risk

Country risks can result from exogenous shocks (chance), endogenous behaviour (choice) or the interaction of the two. Extreme exogenous economic events, such as the collapse of external markets for a country's key exports, clearly can lead to non-performance on most of its obligations. Similarly, extreme political events, such as wars or coups, may result in the repudiation of all claims. In most cases, though, country risks will be the result of sequences of events and policy responses that may be initiated either by shifts in political values or by changes in economic circumstances.

Economic circumstances are strongly influenced by world economic circumstances, but also reflect the success of existing domestic policies. Political values can shift as a result of discontinuities in power relationships such as coups or revolutions, but also from 'normal' political processes, including elections or evolving values within the ruling groups. These sources of country risk, ranging from microeconomic and micropolitical to macrointeractive, are depicted in Table 23.1.

In the case of countries with relatively stable political regimes, most country risks will result from the interaction of policy responses and exogenous events. At a macroeconomic level, external shocks and internal power realignments can lead to overall distress. At a microeconomic level, changes in circumstances may facilitate changes in underlying political forces, but policies may also respond directly to circumstances with no change in the underlying policy frames, especially

in seeking to capture windfalls earned by particular sectors, firms or investors, and in preserving firms or activities that themselves are in distress because of changing circumstances. LDCs, given their typical relatively undiversified economic structures, dependence on external finance and internal rigidities, are particularly vulnerable to external shocks, such as swings in world economic activity or variations in world interest rates. In addition, they typically display less political stability than industrialized countries, at least in part because of their external economic vulnerability.

The distinction between exogenous and endogenous risks closely parallels the distinction drawn in the literature on sovereign debt between a country's ability and its willingness to pay. Since the ability to pay at any point in time reflects previous strategic choices as well as choices about the future, it is often difficult or impossible after the fact to distinguish chance outcomes and policy choices. The same difficulty applies to contracts at the project or enterprise level and acts as a major barrier to writing enforceable contracts across borders. This mixture of choice and chance has major implications for the structure of international financial intermediation, which is

Table 23.1 Sources and dimensions of country risks

Nature of exogenous risk factors[b]	Nature of endogenous risk factors[a]		
	Not significant	Specific	General
Not significant	No risk	*Micropolitical* Targeted expropriation, shift in regulation	*Macropolitical* Blanket expropriation, breakdown in public order
Affecting particular sectors	*Microeconomic* Firm-specific commercial losses	*Microinteractive* Windfall taxes	More of same
Affecting general economy	*Macroeconomic* Commercial losses	*Macrointeractive* Commercial losses, transfer losses	Total loss

Notes: [a] For example: *public order* – wars, coups, violence; *policy shifts* – change of party, change of government, change of minister, change of priorities; *macroeconomic policy* – level of public expenditure, real exchange rates, exchange controls, credit conditions, commercial policy, labour market policy etc.; *management* – efficiency, honesty.
[b] For example: *trade* – protectionism, reduced global demand, shifting, terms of trade; *financial* – increased interest rates, loss of access to markets or institutions.

discussed in later sections. In particular, it gives rise to comparative advantage in managing international risks, the subject of the second section, since risk mitigation, in this case the ability to deter opportunistic behaviour at the country or firm level, takes on paramount importance. And it contributes to the skewing of the structure of external financing for LDCs, which is discussed in the third section.

Factors influencing policy choices

A country's choice of strategic actions will depend on its economic circumstances, its political values and the internal and external consequences of various actions. The domestic consequences include the impact on future savings as the result of actions that jeopardize particular classes of claims and the distributional effect of these actions. The external consequences of a given action involve both the avoidance of the current onerous obligations and the loss of the future benefits associated with continued compliance. In the case of outright default on foreign obligations, for example, the current gain – the obligations that are avoided – must be traded off against the sanctions, including reduced access to future trade and finance, that will be imposed by the lender and other countries that recognize the validity of its claims.

In the absence of an effective supranational legal framework for enforcing cross-border claims, a contract's self-enforceability, i.e. the extent to which the benefits of continued compliance outweigh those of default, becomes a critical consideration in this regard. Both internal and external considerations contribute to self-enforceability. Further, self-enforceability is increasingly buttressed by legal sanctions that apply to transactions of a commercial nature even if one party is a sovereign and by institutional enforcement provided by collective entities including the IMF and the World Bank.

In the case of an industrialized country with a democratic government, domestic considerations are likely to play a major role in the enforcement of any particular class of claims. Foreign investors,

especially if they cannot be effectively singled out, become free-riders on these domestic forces. Thus, the risk of strategic actions is likely to be a function of the magnitude of claims held by foreign investors relative to those held by their domestic bedfellows. Further, the complex and pervasive commercial interactions of local firms and foreign-owned multinational firms, as well as of the government with foreign-owned multinationals and financial institutions, imply that substantial legal sanctions would apply in the case of any across-the-board action resulting in non-performance on specific claims. These legal sanctions, coupled with the existence of politically influential local bedfellows, can be expected to make external financial non-performance more costly and hence less likely. Nevertheless, cross-border claims are still likely to differ from claims issued within the home jurisdiction, especially when the concept of country risk is extended to include a lesser likelihood of government interventions on behalf of foreign investors relative to domestic investors as well as to a greater likelihood of prejudicial government actions against foreigners.

In the case of LDCs, with shallow domestic financial markets, the bedfellow effect is much less important. External sanctions play a greater role, with the usual conclusion being that the 'best credit risks' are those countries that would suffer most if they were forced to become commercially or financially autarkic.

Relative importance of chance and policy choice

Generalized macroeconomic or macropolitical risk factors are common to most claims against a given country. Some are the result of exogenous shocks to the national economy, others of the country's policy choices, which may or may not represent a response to exogenous events. For a country such as Canada, for example, with close trade and investment links with the USA and other OECD countries and significant concentration of activity in the natural resource sector, major exogenous forces will be variations in world economic activity, interest rates and commodity prices.

Policy risk variables involve the array of monetary, fiscal and regulatory choices available to Canada for influencing overall economic activity and for shifting economic benefits among various groups. An LDC such as Mexico faces a similar set of exogenous forces, albeit with a far greater negative exposure to fluctuations in world interest rates. Further, its range of possible policy responses is quite different, especially if one includes the possibility of a major change in political regimes as well as the substantial variations that can occur within the 'institutional revolution'.

If all claims on Canada or Mexico were shares in Canada or Mexico Inc., respectively, and if government policies did not result in any transfers among claimants, then the country risk in each case would be the risk of variations in the value (permanent income) of national assets. However, given the complexity of the claims structure, as well as the array of mechanisms available to either sovereign to affect transfer between labour and capital, various regions of the country, the employed and unemployed and so forth, the country risk of any particular claim will depend to a considerable extent on policy choices as well as potential exogenous shifts in national wealth. This is likely to be even more marked in the case of Mexico, given the greater potential for conflict between external and internal claimants.

Incidence of country risk

The possibility of extreme shifts in a country's economic or political circumstances gives rise to generalized country risks that have the same effect on all classes of claims and claimants. Such 'all or nothing' risks, which include extreme cases of sovereign risk (the risk of non-performance on sovereign claims) and transfer risk (the risk of non-availability of foreign exchange to cover private foreign obligations), are for most countries much less likely than asset-specific or investor-specific risks (risks whose incidence differs across classes of claims and, perhaps, claimants.

Consider the case of an LDC experiencing a balance-of-payments crisis. The usual prescription applied by the IMF is a reduction in the deficit and devaluation of the currency. Government deficit reduction may be achieved by tax increases or expenditure reduction. This typically is accompanied by limits on the expansion of the money supply or on bank credit. The object is to squeeze the domestic economy enough to re-establish foreign balance by reducing import demand. Other instruments used to ameliorate payments crises include export subsidies, special import levies, interest rate policies, additional government borrowing or, alternatively, foreign exchange controls. While many of these steps are associated with LDCs, steps taken by the recent socialist government of France serve as a reminder that most industrialized countries have at one time or another resorted to such measures.

The exposure of particular types of claims to various policy responses to a payments crisis is illustrated in Table 23.2. The risk of repudiation of foreign claims applies directly only to sovereign claims, but in practice it is likely to coincide with the imposition of exchange controls or other measures that affect other classes of claims. A moratorium on all external payments will affect all obligations but, in most cases, will result in a larger loss on fixed income claims than on equity claims where the value of income not remitted can be protected more easily. A devaluation, in contrast, will have no direct negative effects on foreign-currency-denominated claims, but it will result in a loss on domestic-currency-denominated claims. Indirectly, it may enhance the value of foreign-currency-denominated claims by reducing the value of other competing claims. However, it may also lead to losses on foreign-currency-denominated debt if it results in a worsened financial situation of borrowing firms. Its effects on portfolio or direct equity investment will be only indirect, will depend on the operating and financial exposure of the firms in question and may be positive, negative or neutral. The choice of measures and consequently the degree of loss to various classes of claims and claimants will depend on many factors including the relative bargaining power of the various parties as well as the degree of

Table 23.2 Incidence of country risk by type of claim

	Type of external claim					
Type of risk	*Foreign currency government debt*	*Home currency government debt*	*Foreign currency debt of private firms*	*Home currency debt of private firms*	*Portfolio equity in local private firm*	*Direct equity in foreign controlled local firm*
Government default on external claims	×	×	×	×	×	×
Exchange controls		×	×	×	×	×
Inflation/devaluation		×	×[a]	×[b]	×[a]	×[a]
Adverse changes in fiscal policy		×	×[a]	×[a]	×[b]	×[b]
Credit controls				×[a]	×[a]	×[a]
Changes in limits on foreign ownership					?	×
Limits on behaviour of foreign controlled firms						×

Source: Lessard *et al.* 1983
Notes: [a] Indirect effect via impact on borrowing firm's cash flows.
[b] Direct and indirect effect.

self-enforceability of each financial arrangement.

In general, asset-specific and investor-specific risks can result from the differing incidence of general policy measures, from selective responses to changes in general economic or political circumstances, from selective policies oriented toward goals such as limiting foreign ownership and from policies triggered by either windfall profits or financial distress of specific firms. Examples of some of the possibilities are presented below.

General policy measures with differing incidence

Not only will different events give rise to different actions, but the incidence of various event–action–effect chains will differ across classes of claims and, perhaps, classes of claimants holding particular types of claims. Only an extreme loss of wealth due to external changes or a radical political shift resulting in a severing of all existing external trade and financial linkages is likely to result in a total loss on all foreign claims. Such a zero–one view of country risk is not valid even for the foreign-currency-denominated sovereign debt of most LDCs, and certainly not for the wider range of claims held against more advanced countries by local and foreign investors. Because of their differing political values as well as the internal and external constraints they face, different nations are likely to respond to macroeconomic distress leading to problems with foreign obligations through different mixes of general fiscal, monetary and regulatory measures rather than through explicit non-performance on any particular class of claim, although the use of foreign exchange restrictions has been quite common. Macroeconomic crises typically are the result of both exogenous economic circumstances and endogenous policy choices. Further, given a state of crisis, a country's response and its implications for various classes of claims and claimants is to a large extent a strategic choice and not merely a mechanical passing through of the existing state of affairs to external claimants.

Selective response to general circumstances

In addition to general measures with differing incidence, a government can respond to changes in political or economic circumstances through selective measures. Examples include price controls, performance requirements or taxes imposed on specific sectors of the economy. Such selective measures are particularly likely in response to macropolitical shifts that change the values and/or constraints faced by the state. Examples of selective measures in response to a general economic crisis coupled with political shifts include the imposition of limits on foreign travel for local residents by France and the adoption of dual exchange rates by Mexico.

Selective measures in response to specific policy objectives

Asset-specific and investor-specific risks often result from the possibility of selective measures oriented toward specific policy goals. A common case is the attempt by government to maintain or increase indigenous control of economic institutions. In the mid-1970s, for example, Canada enacted the National Energy Policy (NEP) and the Foreign Investment Review Act (FIRA), both of which discriminated directly or indirectly against foreign investors, and it enacted programmes in the high-technology sector to benefit Canadian-owned firms. Germany integrated its personal and corporate income taxes in a way that imposes a substantially higher tax on foreign shareholders than on domestic ones, and many countries, including Japan and Switzerland, maintain restrictions on foreign ownership of shares.

In addition to these direct specific policies, policies with similar indirect effects are common. A case in point is Canada's preferential tax treatment of the manufacturing sector. Because of the interactions with the US tax system, this measure results in higher effective tax rates on US-owned manufacturing facilities than on Canadian-owned manufacturing facilities. Measures to integrate corporate and investor taxation often have similar effects.

Selective measures triggered by circumstances of specific firms or sectors

A final category of policies that give rise to asset-specific and investor-specific risks are interventions to limit or tax windfall profits or to support firms or sectors encountering financial distress.

Virtually all governments of industrialized natural-resource-producing countries imposed some form of price regulation or windfall profit tax to recover a share of the rents accruing to oil production resulting from the first and second oil shocks. Clearly, this is an asset-specific risk. However, it is also an investor-specific risk to the extent that the likelihood or severity of the tax depends on the nationality of the owners. Canada, through its NEP, attempted to ameliorate the impact of provincial and federal taxes and price controls in Canadian firms, thus signalling that there was a risk of differential treatment in the energy sector.

Another asset-specific risk that is likely to be investor specific to the prejudice of foreigners is the uncertainty regarding the extent to which the local government will intervene on behalf of financially distressed firms or act as lender of last resort to local financial institutions. Most governments, regardless of their professed belief in markets, from time to time intervene to rescue distressed firms. While such interventions typically are motivated by the desire to maintain employment or a significant technological capacity, they often benefit lenders or bondholders, and in some cases even shareholders. If these interventions are less likely when the owners or lenders are foreign, they are a source of cross-border investment risk. Such was the case with the refusal of the Italian authorities to take responsibility for the liabilities of Banco Ambrosiano's foreign subsidiaries. Of course, the opposite may occur at times because of the greater leverage of foreign lenders. Chile, for example, was forced to assume the external obligations of its private banks.

Toward a general definition

While the various types of risks described vary

greatly in their sources and incidence, a common feature of virtually all of them is that they involve some element of policy choice on the part of a sovereign. Therefore, country risk can be defined as the risk of changes in an asset's value due to sovereign policy responses that involve general or selective default on, confiscation of or taxation of claims in response to circumstances under which either or both the ability and willingness of the sovereign to meet all the claims placed on it is impaired. Clearly, these risks can apply to assets within a single jurisdiction as well as to claims across jurisdictional boundaries. Therefore, the most restrictive term *cross-border risk* should be applied to those risks affecting only cross-border claims.

WHO HAS COMPARATIVE ADVANTAGE IN BEARING COUNTRY RISK?

Comparative advantage in bearing or managing risk can arise in any stage of the risk management process including identification, analysis of consequences, mitigation, and allocation and diversification. Some parties will be better than others at identifying risks and assessing their impacts on particular contracts or undertakings. This depends in large part on a party's prior experience and scope of activities. To the extent that the risks in question entail an element of choice, comparative advantage in mitigation will reflect various parties' leverage or bargaining power, which in turn reflects the direct or indirect sanctions it can bring to bear on the non-performing party. Comparative advantage in risk allocation, in contrast, will reflect the parties' appetite for risk and, more importantly, the diversity of its exposures and hence its ability to ameliorate risk through diversification. These sources of comparative advantage are summarized in Table 23.3.

In some cases these functions are separable, and optimal risk management will involve specialization by function as well as by type of risk. In other cases, one function may not be separable from another and comparative advantage will reflect

Table 23.3 Sources of comparative advantage in international risk management

Identification	Superior information: experience, scope, access
Analysis of incidence	Superior information: experience, scope, access
Mitigation	Leverage: ability to monitor behaviour and to impose sanctions, seniority, perception of legitimacy on part of debtor and other creditors
Allocation/ diversification	Diversification: degree of exposure to same or related risks

some averaging of the various functions. Consider the case of commercial banks lending to LDCs. They have an advantage in risk mitigation relative to most other potential lenders because of their relatively high degree of bargaining power *vis-à-vis* LDCs, but a disadvantage in risk allocation given their relative over-exposure to LDC credits.

Application to country risks

The concept of comparative advantage in risk management is a general one. However, the strength of this comparative advantage in terms of each of the risk management functions and the relative importance of the functions will depend on the type of risk being addressed.

The dimensions of risk affecting international contracts can now be related to the sources of comparative advantage in different risk management functions in order to judge the comparative advantage of different classes of institutions in managing particular aspects of country risk. Table 23.4 focuses on three functions: a combination of risk identification and analysis of incidence, risk mitigation and risk allocation. While admittedly subjective, this table suggests that exploiting comparative advantage requires an unbundling of macro and micro risks as well as some specialization by institution in terms of the functions they perform.

Table 23.4 Comparative advantage in international risk management

Risk management function 2	Institution				
	Official lenders	Commercial banks	Institutional investors	Direct investors	Local investors
Macro risks					
Assessment	++	++	0	0	+
Mitigation	++	++	0	−	−
Diversification	0	−	+	0	−
Micro risks					
Assessment	+	0 to +[a]	−	++	++
Mitigation	+ to −[b]	+	−	++	++
Diversification	+	0	+	0[c]	−

Notes: [a] ++ if allowed to have significant local operations.
[b] Multilateral financial institutions appear to have an advantage in influencing micro level policy choices such as output pricing as limiting diversion of funds in capital goods purchasing. However, they appear to be at a disadvantage in monitoring management performance and limiting the diversion of proceeds in commercial ventures. The International Finance Corporation, for example, a significant lender and investor in third world enterprises, finds that it shares joint ownership of many 'poor projects' with local owners who are doing extremely well.
[c] Depends on whether micro risk is country specific or project specific or if it is specific to the industry on a world-wide basis.

Official lenders, such as the World Bank, have an advantage in the assessment and mitigation of endogenous macro level risks, given their access to policy-makers, the sanctions they can exert if their suggestions are not followed and the seniority of their claims in case of rescheduling. However, their capacity and willingness to take on various exogenous risks inherent in specific LDC economic undertakings are quite limited. Typically, they lend only on a general obligation basis and thus do not bear specific risks such as shifts in commodity prices or the commercial failures of sectoral programmes or specific projects. Further, because of their senior creditor status, they are able to shift many of the remaining risks to less senior claimants.[2] At the micro level, they have substantial advantages in mitigating risks associated with the selection and execution of standard types of projects. However, they lack the commercial knowledge and profit incentives necessary to monitor more entrepreneurial activities.

Commercial banks, because of their demonstrated ability to act collectively, also have strong leverage at the macro level. However, the current spotlight on their precarious capital positions makes it painfully clear that they are over-exposed to such risks. At the micro level, they may be advantaged or disadvantaged depending on whether they operate extensively within the local economy and are allowed to bring full sanctions to bear on local borrowers in the case of nonperformance.

Institutional investors, including insurance companies and pension funds, have little or no leverage over macro or micro risks but could diversify various LDC risks to a much greater extent than the much more highly exposed banks and credit agencies. Direct investors clearly have greater expertise in managing micro level risks, but typically are at a disadvantage in terms of mitigating macro level risks.

Local investors presumably have information advantages at the micro level, but they may or may not have advantages in terms of mitigating particular risks or the incidence of those risks. With regard to risk of loss resulting from changes in government policy, locals could conceivably have more or less leverage than foreign governments, banks or firms. In those cases where foreign borrowing is accompanied by capital flight, though, it would appear that foreign entities have the upper hand. Local investors may also differ in the impact of particular measures, particularly those associated with foreign exchange transfer. Since they value local expenditures more highly than do foreign investors, they have an option to switch their expenditures to the local goods that foreigners do not.[3]

COUNTRY RISK AND THE STRUCTURE AND EFFICIENCY OF INTERNATIONAL FINANCIAL INTERMEDIATION

A complete model of the effects of country risk on the structure of international financial intermediation lies beyond the current frontier of financial economics, and certainly beyond the scope of this review. Substantial insights regarding the nature and impact of country risk, however, can be gained by observing, *grosso modo*, departures of asset holdings from idealized patterns and assessing the extent to which these departures might be attributable to various aspects of country risk.

In an idealized world capital market as characterized by the CAPM, the introduction of generalized country risk – where all claims on a given country regardless of who holds them are subject to the same risk – would have little or no effect on the optimal pattern of asset holdings by different investor groups.[4] In such a market, with no barriers to cross-border investment, no differences in consumption preferences and no asset-specific or investor-specific country risks, optimal asset holdings for all investors would consist of a universal portfolio of risky assets combined with varying proportions of a minimum risk portfolio depending on the investor's risk aversion.[5]

The structure of international financial intermediation that we observe differs substantially from this idealization. Among industrialized countries, the pattern of financial intermediation differs considerably from that within single representative jurisdictions. Both gross and net cross-border claims represent a small fraction of domestic financial claims on either a gross or a net basis. Further, the pattern of cross-border claims is quite skewed, with relatively larger proportions of cross-border holdings taking the form of sovereign claims (Treasury bills, bonds etc.), private debt and direct investment instead of portfolio investment in risky equity claims than the fractions of total financial claims represented by each class of claim. This is ironic, since risky claims provide the prime benefits of international diversification, while investors could be expected to hold relatively home-biased portfolios of less risky claims such as bonds in order to match their differing consumption patterns. As a result, cross-border risks with relatively small associated costs would eliminate international holdings of (nearly) riskless claims, but the costs required to justify holding only domestic risk assets would be much larger. Cooper and Kaplanis (1986b), for example, using historical return covariances and market risk premia, estimate that the cross-border 'penalty' required to explain the difference between the observed holdings of a US investor and the fully diversified world portfolio is less than 3 per cent per annum, the same order of magnitude as real interest rates and risk premia; but this required penalty would have to be considerably higher to explain investor behaviour in some other countries, ranging up to 40 per cent for Italy!

In the case of LDCs, especially those in external financial difficulty, the pattern is even more extreme. Virtually all external claims against the major borrowers are in the form of sovereign borrowings or private borrowings that are implicitly or explicitly guaranteed by the sovereign, and a majority of them are in the form of floating rate loans from commercial banks. Further, in some cases these external claims exceed total internal claims.[6]

The features of country risk that may account for these divergences in patterns of international intermediation from CAPM idealizations include its asset and investor specificity, its element of moral hazard and the resulting information asymmetry between various agents. I begin with a general discussion of the impact of country risk on asset holdings and prices. I then explore the extent to which it may account for (1) the home bias in risky asset holdings among financially developed countries and (2) the apparent crowding out of domestic claims and cross-border risk-bearing claims by sovereign borrowing in the case of LDCs.

Country risk and asset evaluation

If country risks were simply the passing through of exogenous risks faced by countries, they would have no unique effects on the structure of asset holdings and prices. Of course, they would be reflected in asset values through their impact both on expected cash returns (cash flow effects) and on the (co)variability of future returns (risk premium effects), but these effects would be no different from those of the exogenous risks. It is the discretionary policy choice element of country risk and the ensuing information and enforcement issues that give rise to its stylized special effects: an uneven impact across assets and investors, with a virtual elimination of particular types of financial contracting and non-price clearing for others.

Consider the simplest case of sovereign borrowings in foreign currencies. A risk that the sovereign will be unable to pay owing to external circumstances, if recognized by both borrower and lender, will result in an adjusted promised rate that maintains the expected rate of return at the riskless level as long as the risk of default is uncorrelated with undiversifiable external factors.[7] If the risk of non-performance is systematic in the sense that it is related to, say, the world business cycle, the equilibrium expected return will include a risk premium reflecting the contribution of this asset to the variance of investors' portfolios. In either case, the borrower, if small, will face an elastic supply of credit at the risk-adjusted promised rate.[8]

If the risk of non-performance includes an element of policy choice, the claim becomes unenforceable when the cost in terms of borrower utility of meeting its obligations exceeds penalties associated with non-performance, also measured in terms of the borrowers' utility. Therefore, the total amount of credit must be limited and, in general, some structure of penalties must be imposed to provide the borrower with the incentive to honour its obligation. Many variations on this theme have been developed, with most attention being focused on optimal default strategies and their effect on the price of debt and on borrowers' growth while the nature of the penalties of default and the mechanisms by which lenders can credibly impose these penalties have been simply assumed.[9]

When the analysis is extended to other types of claims, the range of situations that can be termed non-performance becomes much broader, the potential cash flow and risk premium effects become more complex and the problems of enforcement/incentives for performance become more problematic. In the case of obligations denominated in the national currency, non-performance encompasses not only explicit default, but implicit default in the form of opportunistic inflation and, if the claims are held by foreigners, the imposition of exchange controls and other measures that may partially or totally preclude the foreigner from realizing the value of the claim. In the case of credit or equity claims against private entities within the country, non-performance is further extended to include a whole host of policies, including tax policies, price control policies, competitive policies and labour market policies, that may affect the ability of a firm to meet its obligations and the ability of the lender or investor to appropriate its claim, as well as the ability of the sovereign to alter the internal or external purchasing power represented by the claim.

The cash flow effects of the various non-performance risks can be traced for any specific claim, although in most cases the possibility of non-performance will transform the pay-off into a non-linear function of the underlying risk factors, thus requiring a more complex contingent claims analysis. The risk premium effects will depend primarily on whether the risks of non-performance enhance or mitigate the systematic risk of the underlying claim.

The enforcement/incentive aspects of country risk associated with these more penetrating claims are particularly problematic. Since most non-performance here involves violation of implicit claims with widely varying incidence across asset and investor groups, the concerted imposition of external sanctions is less likely than in the case of non-performance on explicit external contracts and the strength of domestic claimants will depend on the voice in the political system and the credibility of their threat to shift assets elsewhere, transforming themselves into external claimants.

Country risk and cross-border asset holdings

Since country risk differs in incidence across both assets and investors, it can be expected to alter the structure of asset holdings in equilibrium. The possible role of country risk in explaining two observed departures from world-wide diversification – the home bias of investors' risky asset holdings in industrialized countries and the virtual absence of explicitly risk-shifting cross-border claims on LDCs – is examined below.

Country risk as a barrier to cross-border investment in risky assets

It is plausible that the risk of violations of the various implicit contracts that give value to equity claims would increase with the degree of foreign ownership of equity claims. At significant levels of foreign ownership, the ever-present conflict between the interests of capital, labour and other stakeholders would be transformed into a conflict among domestic and foreign interests and the behaviour of the state in mediating these claims would be fundamentally altered. Foreign investors would no longer be able to rely on domestic bed-fellows for political representation, and unless they could exercise similar power directly, they would be forced to rely on other enforcement mechanisms that typically would require absolute control of local firms and would involve substantial costs. If capital markets were globally integrated and all investors held similar portfolios of risky assets, as

the CAPM implies they should, the degree of foreign ownership of equities in most countries would be overwhelming: foreign investors would hold 95 per cent of Swiss assets, 90 per cent of UK assets, 80 per cent of Japanese assets, 50 per cent of US assets and so on.

The problem with this story is that there is no plausible mechanism by which individual foreign investors would jointly agree to limit their holdings of equities in a particular country to the optimal level given country risk. Individual investors could improve their risk–return frontiers by increasing local holdings, thus imposing a cost on other holders of such claims. Many countries, though, have regulations in place that serve the same purpose. Whether this is a politically rational response to the risk diversification–enforceability dilemma or an effort to preempt actions by foreigners with a significant stake in that country, though, is an open question. Foreign ownership of shares either is restricted to an acceptable proportion of shares (e.g. in Japan), limited to non-voting shares (e.g. in Switzerland) or discouraged through discriminatory taxation (e.g. in Germany).

Country risk and sovereign subordination

While country risk appears to be a factor in the home-biasedness of investor portfolios in industrialized countries, especially in the case of risky holdings where the greatest gross cross-border holdings should occur, it appears to have a radically different effect on LDCs in extreme financial difficulty. In these countries, country risk in the form of a significant probability of a government credit crisis appears to drive out not only cross-border risky flows but also domestic financial intermediation. The result is the substitution of cross-border sovereign claims that represent explicit, general obligations of the state for its implicit, domestic claims as well as for 'more penetrating' claims whose value depends on outcomes of specific projects or enterprises, but also on implicit claims on the sovereign.[10]

The mechanism for this crowding out of private foreign claims and virtually all domestic claims by external sovereign claims is the effective subordination of these other claims to sovereign obligations.[11] Recall that the enforceability of any particular claim depends on the trade-off between the benefits of default and the sanctions that will apply in such a case. A default on foreign obligations is likely to trigger collective action imposing partial or total real and financial autarky, while a default on implicit domestic obligations, depending on its impact on expectations of future behaviour, will result in further capital flight and a consequent reduction in domestic capital formation.

With hindsight, severe debt problems in LDCs have involved a slippery slope whereby

1 to increase or maintain domestic absorption in the face of external shocks and/or increase the power of the state in allocating resources, the sovereign has borrowed abroad, increasing its future fiscal and foreign exchange requirements;

2 in reaction to some internal or external shock, the state absorbs a significant proportion of the external obligations of the private sector to prevent failures that would reduce domestic confidence and/or violate its implicit or explicit guarantees to foreign lenders, thus increasing its fiscal and foreign exchange burdens;[12]

3 private claimants, recognizing their subordination to increased foreign claims on the sovereign, often as the result of the violation of some implicit contract by the increasingly pressed sovereign, seek to transfer assets to other jurisdictions;

4 in the absence of a securities market where such attempted transfers depress asset prices and hence face an implicit penalty, these attempted transfers create a run on foreign exchange reserves, forcing either further foreign borrowing (and subordination of private claims) or some form of default on existing claims.

Variations on this theme have occurred in most Latin American countries.

Country risk and the efficiency of international resource allocation

Country risk affects the efficiency of resource allocation through international capital markets in several ways. First, it reduces the completeness of financial markets both within and across jurisdictions, reducing the potential for bridging differences in time and risk preferences among different agents and reducing the impact of risk through diversification or pooling, which, in turn, alters required returns for various activities and shifts patterns of real investment. Second, it creates divergences between public and private returns or costs, reducing the social efficiency of private choices. Investment in exposed assets, for example, is reduced to a socially suboptimal level.[13] Third, by altering the structure of financial claims, it also alters incentives. In particular, it reduces the role of private agents in allocating funds within countries with the consequent loss of efficiency if such involvement provides important roles in project selection and management. Each of these is discussed briefly.

Changes in required private returns

To the extent that country risks increase contracting costs and/or that their incidence differs between groups of investors, they will change the extent to which claims are exchanged among agents and hence the extent to which differences in time and risk preferences are bridged and various risks are diversified. In the case of cross-border risks, for example, real interest rates in net borrower countries will remain above the general world level while those in net lender countries will be below that level. Further, to the extent that cross-border exchanges of risky assets are limited, domestic investors will choose to bear some potentially diversifiable exogenous risks. The cost of this incomplete diversification will be reflected in derived risk premia (described below), which may be substantial in the case of risky claims (equity, risky debt etc.) with little systematic risk within a fully diversified world portfolio but substantial systematic risk within the resulting local portfolio.

Costly contracting

Risks with a strategic element are likely to result in deadweight costs, i.e. costs to one party in the form of a loss in efficiency or a 'leakage' to third parties rather than a transfer between the parties to the contract. If borrowers are price-takers, these deadweight costs increase their cost of funds. Several alternative reasons for such divergences between the expected cost of funds to the borrower and the required expected return to investors have been identified, including uninformed equilibria, non-price market clearing, enforcement costs, efficiency costs of self-enforcing contracts and costs of financial distress.

Uniformed market equilibria refers to conditions under which a borrower pays a higher rate than it should given the objective probability of non-performance because of some type of information market failure. Several alternative versions involving sovereign borrowing have been articulated in the literature. Harberger (1976) argues that foreigners will persistently over-estimate the risks of non-performance by a particular nation and hence demand too high a promised rate of interest. While possible, this version is implausible since it relies on persistent information asymmetries but does not explicitly incorporate the moral hazard aspects of strategic country risks. Buiter (1983), in contrast, drawing on Ackerlof's 'lemons' analogy, suggests that lenders may not be able to distinguish good from bad borrowers *ex ante* and therefore set a promised rate that incorporates the average risk of non-performance. Aizenman (1985) relies on the uncertainty regarding the penalties of default to reach a similar result.

Monitoring and enforcement costs refer to costs borne by lenders or investors to monitor performance and penalize non-performance without necessarily obtaining the desired performance. Such costs include the costs of gathering information on borrowers' performance, losses of gains from trade if trade is cut off as the result of a breach of a particular contract or legal fees incurred by private or public claimants.

Derived risk premia

Various authors, including Black (1972), Stulz (1981), Errunza and Losq (1985) and Cooper and Kaplanis (1986a), have modelled the effect of various types of risks or constraints to cross-border investment as 'taxes' on cross-border investment.[14] While the specifics of each model differ, the main conclusions, not surprisingly, are that in each country all investors hold the same portfolio of risky assets, but the world portfolio is inefficient; i.e. nobody would hold the world portfolio as his sole risky investment. In consequence, the traditional relation between systematic risk (β) with respect to the world market portfolio and expected return does not hold.

Consider the case of a small-country government that imposes a linear tax θ on foreign holdings of asset i. If the asset should be held by both foreign and domestic investors, its gross of tax return R_i must lie on the domestic security market line (SML) and its net of tax return $R_i - \theta$ must lie on the foreign SML. The tax on foreign holdings induces two effects.

1 Because domestic and foreign investors now face different opportunity sets, the SMLs will not be identical and, given the assumption that the tax applies only to foreign investors, the domestic price of risk will be higher.

2 By shifting away from asset i, foreign investors reduce its systematic risk (covariance with their portfolio), while by shifting into this asset domestic investors increase its systematic risk from their perspective, thus further increasing the required return on this activity.

Figure 23.1 shows the 'knife-edge' case where the difference in systematic risk from the perspective of the two classes of investors just offsets the difference in return (θ) between the two groups. In many cases, though, it is unlikely to fall exactly on both SMLs. If the aggregate value of the 'taxed'

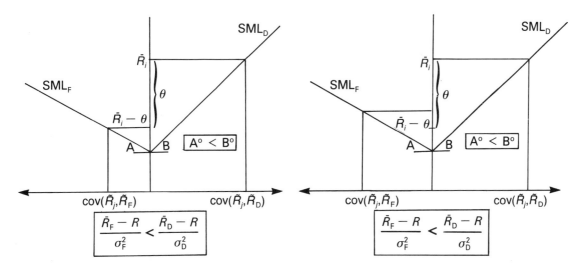

Figure 23.1 Impact of country risk on the risk premium: asset traded domestically and internationally

Figure 23.2 Impact of country risk on the risk premium: asset held exclusively by domestic investors

asset is large and it has substantial covariance with other assets, for example, the result of the tax would be a relatively small movement along the domestic SML, with the resulting change in expected returns being too small to induce foreigners to hold that asset, as shown in Figure 23.2.[15]

Divergences between private and social returns or costs

Many aspects of country risk are similar to taxes in that they involve a taking by the state. In such cases, of course, the social returns of a given activity will exceed its private returns and the efficiency of private choices will be reduced.

Country risk will result in a further wedge between private and social returns to the extent that it results in a supply curve of external finance to a country which will be upward sloping (in terms of expected and not just promised rates) and, eventually, vertical as credit is rationed. Buiter, for example, argues that, in order not to reveal their hand, 'dishonest' borrowers will restrict their borrowing and 'honest' borrowers will limit their borrowing both because of the deadweight cost

they bear and because to seek increased loans would signal 'dishonesty' and thus preclude them from the market. Various authors, including Sachs (1984) and Aizenman (1985), in contrast, show that credit rationing will result from creditors seeking to limit total lending to a level that will not induce non-performance on the part of the borrower. Bollier (1986) shows that in an uncertain environment a sovereign agent would also face an upward-sloping supply of debt and that at optimal levels of borrowing this debt would be both risky and priced accordingly.

With an upwardly sloping supply curve and/or credit rationing, of course, the social cost of borrowing will exceed the private cost by its contribution to the movement of the country along the curve. This result forms the basis for suggestions by Harberger, Aizenman and others that private foreign borrowing be limited or taxed. However, the same phenomenon also implies that private returns on activities that contribute to a country's ability credibly to commit to meet its obligations will be less than their social return and hence they should be subsidized! I return to this point in my concluding remarks.

Reduced role of market incentives in resource allocation

A final efficiency cost of country risk is that in many cases it reduces or eliminates the role of market forces in the allocation of resources within the economy in question. The reason for this, as discussed above, is that, when country risk is significant, sovereign finance or, at a minimum, finance with an implicit sovereign guarantee dominates unguaranteed lending, equity investment and other forms of finance that link the lenders' fortunes to those of a specific project or enterprise. As a result, lenders will have a stake only in aggregate national outcomes and will have little or no incentive or ability to involve themselves in the selection or management of specific economic activities. While this may be attractive to the sovereign in that it minimizes foreign interference in the economy, it also eliminates the potential benefits of foreign expertise and places the full burden of micro level allocation and management on the local bureaucracy. The minister of finance of Mexico or Brazil, for example, plays a much larger role in micro level allocation than the ministers of finance in the USA, the UK or even Japan.

CONCLUDING REMARKS

Country risk is a much broader and more complex phenomenon than the risk of default on external borrowings by sovereigns. It encompasses the full range of discretionary sovereign behaviour in response to payments crises, which themselves are at least in part the result of previous policy choices. It affects domestic as well as foreign investors, curtailing domestic private finance as well as foreign lending or investing. Given its differing incidence across assets and investors and the resulting comparative advantage of different agents in bearing this risk, it appears to have contributed to a substantial skewing of patterns of international financial intermediation relative to those typical within countries. While we are far from a complete understanding of the mechanisms

and effects of country risk, it is possible to identify certain steps that would reduce some of its apparently most costly effects.

Clearly, there remain many more questions than answers. It remains to be established that country risk is in fact a significant factor in limiting the diversification of risky assets across national boundaries. In contrast, there seems to be little question that, in the case of LDCs, it has contributed to a crowding out in favour of sovereign financing of both domestic financing and penetrating foreign finance, but the precise mechanisms of this crowding out are not well understood.

Given this far from complete understanding of the mechanisms and effects of country risk, it might be argued that no policy conclusions should be drawn. However, the literature is replete with normative results derived from models that focus only on sovereign borrowing or, perhaps, sovereign borrowing and a single category of private foreign borrowing. Many recommendations for dealing with the LDC debt crisis, for example, ignore possible implications of domestic financial intermediation and various types of penetrating cross-border claims.

Recommendations that private foreign borrowing be taxed or restricted because of its negative externalities, for example, should be accompanied by mechanisms for encouraging activities that through their net foreign exchange earnings generate positive externalities. Further, it should be recognized that such restrictions will create an advantage to domestic or foreign-based multinational firms relative to purely local firms since the former will be able to circumvent the restrictions via offshore borrowing accompanied by local investment.[16] The difficulty of implementing the resulting complex system of taxes and subsidies, though, suggests a greater reliance on market judgements, where firms are allowed to borrow abroad only to the extent that they can do so without explicit or implicit government guarantees. This would require credible mechanisms to protect sovereigns from being forced to assume the respective private obligations as happened in Chile and elsewhere. Ideally, the IMF would play this role, taking responsibility for the efficiency of international financial transactions rather than acting primarily as an enforcer of creditor claims.

What is needed is a much greater focus on institutional arrangements that would either reduce country risk or reduce its inhibiting effect on the functioning of financial markets. I suggest a few ideas as points of departure for further analysis.

Among industrialized capitalist countries, foreign claims are rendered enforceable largely by their free-rider status *vis-à-vis* domestic claims coupled with the sanctions provided by the commercial and financial interpenetration of the various economies. Nevertheless, a movement toward greater global diversification by investors and/or an increase in net cross-border flows, especially those involving risky equity claims, would appear to threaten existing mechanisms that determine the distribution of rents among labour, capital and government. Perhaps as a result, many governments limit foreign ownership of corporate equity. This, of course, results in an inefficiency in the bearing of macroeconomic and commercial risks. These limits on cross-border diversification can be relaxed to some extent by mechanisms that separate risk sharing from corporate governance, including institutional investment channels where governance is reserved for domestic players and futures and options markets that leave the underlying assets in the hands of domestic players while shifting the investment risks to others.

Sovereign risk as a barrier to cross-border investment will be eliminated only by limits on sovereign intervention, in return for regional or global rules regarding corporate governance. The snail's pace movement in this direction within the EC suggests that such a step will be a very long time coming across more diverse and less intertwined national economies, especially the USA and Japan.

The more pressing issues with regard to country risk, though, lie with the LDCs. Many current discussions of the LDC debt problem suggest that the major issue in international risk management is the mitigation and avoidance by lenders of risks of

non-performance by LDCs. However, another equally important dimension is the appropriate allocation among various lenders and investors of risks faced by LDCs. To solve only the first problem is analogous to addressing moral hazard by eliminating all fire and casualty insurance.

When viewed in terms of comparative advantage in risk bearing, the management of international risks inherent in the current structure of financing for LDCs is woefully inadequate and there is great room for improvement. While the existing structure is inefficient along many dimensions, there are a few key areas where a great deal of improvement is possible. These include a shift toward general obligation financing whose terms more closely match the borrowers' ability to pay, such as floating rate financing coupled with interest or currency swaps, price-level index or commodity-price-linked bonds; increased standalone finance where lenders/investors would be exposed to the commercial risks of projects or enterprises; and increased risk capital in the form of portfolio investment in equities and quasi-equities as well as direct foreign investment.

Many of these innovations involve the transfer of micro level (commercial) risks to private, foreign or domestic investors, lenders or providers of services. Typically, this involvement will be by parties with a comparative advantage in managing such risks by virtue of their knowledge of specific industries, their ability to manage specific activities and/or their relative ability to diversify away certain key risk elements.

However, these same parties – direct foreign investors, firms with alternative commercial linkages to specific projects such as licensing or other sales or service contracts involving contingent compensation, foreign institutional suppliers of risk capital and local investor groups – typically are at a disadvantage in coping with macro level non-commercial risks. Multilateral institutions, commercial banks and national export credit agencies are natural parties to unbundle these two types of risks. For example, they could simultaneously insure some of these macro risks and 'take a place at the table' to exert leverage on behalf of these claims. They could also exert leverage within the international financial community, especially the World Bank (and the other multinational development banks) and the IMF, to accord at least equal treatment to project-specific claims whether these are outright credits or contracts contingent on the success of specific projects.[17] All these steps would have the additional advantage of helping to create the conditions necessary for a viable private market in pure country risks.[18]

In addition to taking on more of the macro (non-commercial) risks faced by other parties, official financial agencies could also reduce their own exposures to adverse selection by exporters of capital goods or services by requiring (or encouraging through more favourable rates) that contracts be written in such a way as to transfer identifiable commercial risks to these firms. Such steps would go a long way to reintroducing appropriate micro level risk management while maintaining or improving the management of macro level risks.

NOTES

1 This distinction between action and effect depending on the nature of the asset is introduced by Kobrin (1979).

2 See Gennotte *et al.* (1986) for further discussion of this point.

3 This point is developed by Eldor *et al.* (1986).

4 Even in this idealized setting, though, country risk would have the same effects as a tax, driving a wedge between private and social returns and hence distorting resource allocation.

5 Even with variations in real exchange rates and differing consumption preferences, all investors would continue to hold a common portfolio of risky assets, although each (national) consumption group would also hold a unique minimum variance portfolio as well as a portfolio hedging away the consumption risk specific to them in a universal risky asset portfolio.

6 In the case of Mexico, for example, by 1985 external obligations were of the order of $100 billion, roughly double the value of domestic primary financial assets (M1 + M2).

7 In the literature on international bank lending, the term 'country-risk premium' refers to the spread between the base rate (e.g. LIBOR or prime) and the lending rate for a particular country. It is an adjustment to the promised rate, but it does not necessarily imply a risk premium in terms of expected costs. In contrast, in the financial economics literature, a risk premium is defined as an adjustment to the expected rate of return to compensate for the costs of risk bearing.

8 The risk-adjusted promised rate, of course, may rise with the level of borrowing, since there will be an increased probability that the borrower will be unable to pay and the supply of credit (the present value of the expected payment) can decline quickly to zero as the promised payment is increased beyond a critical level.

9 With regard to the costs of default, two major strands are represented by Eaton and Gersovitz (1981), who stress the utility loss from not being able to employ external finance to smooth consumption, and Sachs (1984), who stresses the loss of productivity of assets through reduced trade. Bollier (1986) combines the two in a continuous-time utility-maximizing model. With regard to the credibility of penalties, most researchers simply assert them, though some are beginning to explore conditions under which a unitary lender would actually impose them after the fact and others, e.g. Sundaram (1986), examine the case where atomistic lenders would co-operate to impose them.

10 For an excellent discussion of the relative risk of a sovereign's explicit foreign obligations and its implicit domestic obligations, see Protopapadakis (1985).

11 For a rigorous development of this argument, see Ize and Ortiz (1983) and Eaton (1986).

12 This point is developed by Frieden (1981).

13 This also implies that the social cost of foreign borrowing may exceed the private cost, a point made by Harberger (1976) and further developed by Aizenman (1985).

14 A constraint on cross-border investments, imposed to mitigate particular policy risks that would increase with foreign ownership, can be modelled as a tax as well. In this case, the 'tax' on cross-border investment would be a shadow price of the constraint.

15 For numerical illustrations of the magnitude of cross-border taxes or barriers required to induce degrees of home-biasedness in portfolio holdings, see Cooper and Kaplanis (1986b).

16 This point is developed in Agmon and Lessard (1976).

17 The proposed MIGA would play precisely this role.

18 By pure country risks, I refer to losses on scheduled general obligations. These would serve as a proxy

for the transfer risk elements inherent in more penetrating contracts.

BIBLIOGRAPHY

Agmon, T. (1973) 'The significance of the country risk factor for share price movements', *Journal of Business*, January: 24–32.

—— (1985) *Political Economy and Risk in World Financial Markets*, Lexington, MA: Lexington Books.

Agmon, T. and Lessard, D. (1976) 'The multinational firms as vehicles for international diversification: implications for capital importing countries', *Revista Brasileira de Mercados de Capitais*, December.

Aizenman, J. (1985) 'Country risk, incomplete information and taxes on international borrowing', paper presented at the Conference on Research in International Finance, 19–20 June, Centre HEC-ISA, Jouy-en-Josas, France.

Aliber, R.Z. (1973) 'The interest rate parity theorem: a reinterpretation', *Journal of Political Economy* 81 (6): 1451–9.

—— (1978) 'The integration of national financial markets', *Weltwirtschaftliches Archiv*.

Barnea, A., Haugen, R. and Senbet, L. (1985) *Agency Problems and Financial Contracting*, Englewood Cliffs, NJ: Prentice Hall.

Black, F. (1972) 'Capital market equilibrium with investment barriers', *Journal of Business*, July.

Bollier, T. (1986) 'International debt repudiation and opportunistic behavior in an uncertain environment', Ph.D. dissertation, Massachusetts Institute of Technology, Cambridge.

Buiter, W. (1983) 'Implications for the adjustment process of international asset risks: exchange controls, intervention policy, and sovereign risks', in R. Hawkins (ed.) *The Internationalization of Financial Markets and National Economic Policy*, Greenwich, CT: JAI Press.

Cooper, I. and Kaplanis, E. (1986a) 'Costs to cross-border investment and international equity market equilibrium', in Edwards *et al.* (eds) *Recent Advances in Corporate Finance*, forthcoming.

—— (1986b) 'Estimation of barriers to international investment', Working Paper IFA-91-86, London Business School.

Dooley, M. (1986) 'Capital flight: a response to differences in risks', *IMF Staff Papers*.

Dooley, M. and Isard, P. (1980) 'Capital controls, political risk, and deviations from interest rate parity', *Journal of Political Economy* 88 (2): 370–84.

Eaton, J. (1983) 'Country risk: an economic perspective', in R. Herring (ed.) (1985) *Managing International Risk*, Cambridge: Cambridge University Press.

—— (1986) 'Public debt guarantees and private capital flight', unpublished working paper, The World Bank, August.

Eaton, J. and Gersovitz, M. (1981) *Poor Country Borrowing in Private Financial Markets and the Repudiation Issue*, Princeton Studies in International Finance 47.

Eaton, J., Gersovitz, M. and Stiglitz, J. (1986) 'The pure theory of country risk', *European Economic Review* 39 (June): 481–513.

Eldor, R., Pines, D. and Schwartz, A. (1986) 'Productivity shocks and home asset preference', mimeo, Boston University.

Errunza, V. and Losq, E. (1985) 'International asset pricing under mild segmentation: theory and test', *Journal of Finance*, March: 105–24.

Frieden, J. (1981) 'Third World indebted industrialization: international finance and state capitalism in Mexico, Brazil, Algeria and South Korea', *International Organization* 35 (2): 407–31.

Gennotte, G., Kharas, H. and Sadeq, S. (1986) 'A valuation model for LDC debt with endogenous reschedulings', *World Bank Economic Review*, forthcoming.

Harberger, A. (1976) 'On country risk and the social cost of foreign borrowing by developing countries', mimeo.

—— (1980) 'Vignettes on the world capital market', *American Economic Review* 70: 331–7.

Herring, R. (ed.) (1985) *Managing International Risk*, Cambridge: Cambridge University Press.

Ize, A. and Ortiz, G. (1983) 'Fiscal rigidities, public debt, and capital flight', unpublished working paper.

Kobrin, S. (1979) 'Political risk: a review and reconsideration', *Journal of International Business Studies*, Spring/Summer.

Lessard, D. (1976) 'World, country and industry factors in equity returns', *Financial Analysts Journal*, January–February: 32–8.

Lessard, D. and Williamson, J. (1985) *Financial Intermediation Beyond the Debt Crisis*, Washington, DC: Institute for International Economics.

Lessard, D., Eckaus, R., Bollier, T. and Kahn, R. (1983) 'Country risk, capital market integration, and project evaluation: a Canadian perspective', unpublished report prepared for the Corporate Finance Division, Canada Finance.

Protopadakis, A. (1985) 'An analysis of government credit "crises"', Working Paper 85-14, Federal Reserve Bank of Philadelphia.

Sachs, J. (1984) *Theoretical Issues in International Borrowing*, Princeton Studies in International Finance 54.

Solnik, B. (1973) *European Equity Markets*, Lexington, MA: Lexington Books.

Stulz, R. (1981) 'On the effects of barriers to international investment', *Journal of Finance*, September: 923–34.

—— (1985) 'Pricing capital assets in an international setting: an introduction', *Journal of International Business Studies*, Spring.

Sundaram, A. (1986) 'Syndications, debtors' cartels and equilibria in international lending to LDCs', paper presented at the Conference on Research in International Finance, 19–20 June, Centre HEC-ISA, Jouy-en-Josas, France.

Vernon, R. (1985) 'Organizational and institutional response to international risk', in R. Herring (ed.) *Managing International Risk*, Cambridge: Cambridge University Press.

Walter, I. (1981) 'Country risk, portfolio decisions, and regulation in international banking', *Journal of Banking and Finance*, March.

24

ORGANIZING DEBT RELIEF

The need for a new institution

Peter B. Kenen

When Mexico suspended debt service payments in August 1982, creditor countries, led by the USA, responded promptly. Animated by concern about confidence in the banking system, not mere solicitude for the banks, they extended large short-term credits to Mexico and then put pressure on the banks to reschedule Mexican debt and lend more to Mexico, once the IMF had endorsed the policies that Mexico would follow to deal with its problems. This was the birth of the case-by-case approach to the debt problem. It was predicated implicitly on the belief that debtors faced a short-term problem arising from an unusual combination of world-wide recession and high interest rates brought on by a shift in the policy stance of the major industrial countries. On this view, it was eminently sensible for debtors to take on more debt temporarily in order to pay interest on their existing debts.[1]

The problem was still with us three years later, however, and the case-by-case approach was in trouble. The world economy was growing again and interest rates had fallen, but the debtor's export earnings were not growing and their governments were increasingly reluctant to deal with the IMF, which was asking for more austerity but providing less Fund credit. The banks were willing to reschedule larger amounts of debt for longer intervals but would put up new money only for the largest debtors.

THE BAKER AND BRADY PLANS

In October 1985, at the annual IMF–World Bank meeting in Seoul, the US Secretary of the Treasury, James Baker, proposed a three-part 'program for sustained growth' to deal with the debt problem:

First and foremost, the adoption by principal debtor countries of comprehensive macroeconomic and structural policies, supported by the international financial institutions, to promote growth and balance of payments adjustment, and to reduce inflation.

Second, a continued central role for the IMF, in conjunction with increased and more effective structural adjustment lending by the multilateral development banks . . . .

Third, increased lending by the private banks in support of comprehensive economic adjustment programs.

Austerity would fight inflation and produce the trade surpluses needed by the debtors to make their debt service payments. Structural reforms and new lending would generate the growth needed to reduce the burden of those payments. Secretary Baker went on to ask that the multilateral institutions and commercial banks adopt specific targets for new lending to the fifteen highly indebted countries listed in Table 24.1.

The banks fell far short of those targets, however, and actually reduced their claims on some debtor countries. In mid-1987, moreover, major US banks, led by Citicorp, set aside larger loan-loss reserves against their exposure to the debtor countries.[2] Secretary Baker came back to the banks in 1987 to ask that they develop a 'menu' of new instruments and methods to step up

Table 24.1 Discounts on the debts of fifteen heavily indebted countries

Argentina	82½	Ecuador	86½	Peru	97
Bolivia	89	Ivory Coast	94	Philippines	50½
Brazil	70½	Mexico	58½	Uruguay	45
Chile	35½	Morocco	56½	Venezuela	62¼
Colombia	43	Nigeria	76½	Yugoslavia	49

Source: Salomon Brothers, July 1989
Note: Discounts are for cash bids.

their lending. But the whole debt strategy began to change in 1988, even as the banks were adopting the menu approach, most notably in a new agreement with Brazil.[3]

At the economic summit in Toronto, the seven major industrial countries had agreed to grant debt relief to low-income countries, mainly in Africa, but had pointedly excluded middle-income debtors, mainly in Latin America. At the IMF–World Bank meeting in Berlin, however, the IMF Interim Committee proposed that the menu approach be broadened to include 'voluntary market-based techniques which ... reduce the stock of debt without transferring risk from private lenders to official creditors'. The aim of the menu approach was shifted from raising to reducing debt: a late but fundamental change in the official interpretation of the debt problem.

In March 1989, the new US Secretary of the Treasury, Nicholas Brady, endorsed the change in strategy, calling for a three-year waiver of clauses in existing loan agreements that stand in the way of debt reduction 'to accelerate sharply the pace of debt reduction and pass the benefits directly to the debtor nations', and called on the IMF and World Bank to use some of their policy-based lending to aid the debt-reducing process; some of it could be used to collateralize debt-for-bond exchanges at significant discounts and replenish reserves following cash buybacks of debt, and some could be used to underwrite the interest payments on new or modified debt contracts.

Events moved rapidly thereafter. The IMF and World Bank adopted guidelines to implement the Brady plan and the IMF extended new credits to

Mexico, Costa Rica and the Philippines in accordance with those guidelines. Japan agreed to provide $4.5 billion in supplementary lending (and has recently raised its pledge to $10 billion). Commercial banks began to negotiate an agreement with Mexico which would reduce its interest payments to the banks by as much as 35 per cent if every bank participated fully.[4]

Is there anything left to argue about? Unhappily, yes. Some economists, such as Bulow and Rogoff (1988, 1989), argue that debtors are wrong to use reserves or borrow to buy back debt, even at large discounts. Advocates of debt relief, such as Sachs (1989a) and myself, maintain that the Brady plan will not go far enough. It relies too heavily on debtors and creditors to strike mutually beneficial bargains; it does not provide enough resources to generate the deep debt reductions that debtors need to solve their problems; and it does not shift risk forthrightly enough from private lenders to official creditors. I would correct the defects of the Brady plan by creating a new international institution to manage and finance the debt-reducing process or assign the task to an existing institution but give it enough resources to get the job done.

THE CASE FOR DEBT RELIEF

Krugman (1989) argues that debt reduction can raise economic efficiency in a heavily indebted country, and thus raise the debtor's real income, reducing the probability of default. Therefore, a debt buyback can raise the present value of the remaining debt and can raise it sufficiently to compensate creditors for selling debt on terms that benefit the debtor. Even outright debt forgiveness can benefit both parties.

A large debt overhang reduces economic efficiency in two ways. First, high debt service payments require high tax rates that discourage capital formation and the repatriation of flight capital (see Sachs 1988, 1989b; Krugman 1989). Second, the government is the main maker of debt service payments in most of the heavily indebted countries and its payments figure in its budget.

Hence, they can prevent a devaluation from improving the trade balance because a devaluation raises the domestic-currency cost of servicing foreign-currency debt, increasing the budget deficit, raising the growth of the money supply and raising the inflation rate (see, for example, Dornbusch 1988). Therefore debtors must use less efficient methods to produce the trade surpluses required to make debt service payments.

When these and other inefficiencies are powerful, creditors confront what Krugman calls the debt relief Laffer curve (DRLC) – an apt but unfortunate name, because it should be taken more seriously than its namesake. If a debtor's obligations get very large, their expected value begins to fall. The income-depressing effects of the debt make it more likely that the debtor will default when an adverse shock arrives. By reducing that vulnerability, debt relief raises the expected value of the debt. The debtor is better off in 'good stages' because it keeps the incremental income produced by debt reduction, but creditors are better off in 'bad states' because the debtor is more likely to meet its obligations.

Krugman believes that the small debtor countries are on the downward-sloping side of the DRLC. He is less sure about large debtors. But he understates the strength and generality of the case for debt relief, which may apply most aptly to large debtors. Use of the conventional stochastic framework, with good and bad states, makes the shape of the DRLC depend entirely on the strength of the inefficiencies associated with a big debt overhang. Use of a different framework frees it from that limitation.[5]

Consider the framework used by Eaton and Gersovitz (1981), where repudiation is voluntary and can benefit the debtor unambiguously. This is the most appropriate framework for analysing the behaviour of a sovereign debtor, which never faces insolvency in a strict balance-sheet sense but must weigh the costs of continuing to service its debt against the costs of repudiation.

When a country can look forward to borrowing and growing, it is apt to reject repudiation. When it cannot expect to borrow more, its decision will depend on the advantages of halting debt service payments and the strength of the inefficiencies examined earlier, compared with the size of the penalties that creditors and their governments are likely to impose if the debtor repudiates. These may include the seizure of reserves, the penalty stressed in the current literature, but the debtor must also disguise its exports to keep creditors from seizing them and must pay for its imports with cash when trade-credit lines are cut. In effect, it can experience a deterioration in its terms of trade.

Repudation will be beneficial to the debtor when its debt is large compared with the present value of the penalties. By implication, debt reduction can be mutually beneficial, because it reduces the debtor's obligations but raises the expected value of the creditors' claims by reducing the debtor's incentive to repudiate. The DRLC comes into being not because of the inefficiencies produced by a debt overhang but because debt reductions can tilt the debtor's cost–benefit calculation against repudation.

There is no way to know *a priori* whether a particular country is on the downward-sloping side of the curve. That will depend in part on the nature of the penalties that creditors can be expected to impose. But these may not vary across countries in proportion to their debts, which means that large debtors are more likely to be on the downward-sloping side.

Unfortunately, large debtors are least likely to receive outright debt forgiveness. Their creditors are reluctant to accept the large accounting losses involved in reducing substantially the face value of their claims on Mexico, Brazil and Argentina. And though they would have to reduce them by less than the amount of debt forgiveness, because it would raise the expected value of their remaining claims, it is hard to persuade accountants, regulators and securities analysts that lower book values can mean larger economic values. When Citicorp and other US banks set aside larger loan-loss reserves, their stock prices rose; investors were ready to reward the banks for being more realistic. But investors who were eager to accept the tax-policy implications of the original Laffer curve are less eager to accept the more valid implications of the DRLC.

THE MECHANICS OF DEBT RELIEF

There is a secondary market for sovereign debt in which it can be shifted from bank to bank or to other institutions. Most countries' debts sell there at large discounts, reflecting the creditors' belief that debtors will not meet their obligations fully. Representative discounts are shown in Table 24.1. When the Interim Committee endorsed voluntary, market-based debt reduction, it had in mind transactions based on these discounts.

Such transactions can involve purchases of debt with currently available resources or purchases with future resources made by exchanging new debt for old. The second method is known as defeasance (which sounds pejorative, but isn't). Their benefits and costs depend in part on the values that debtors and creditors attach to the existing debt – which need not coincide precisely with those represented by the discounts quoted in the secondary market.[6]

Purchases with currently available resources have taken two forms: buybacks with cash and debt–equity swaps, which may be deemed to represent an exchange of debt for an entrepreneurial opportunity. Buybacks with cash have been debated extensively, and I have already reviewed the main issues, but these transactions have been rare. Debtor countries do not have the cash needed to buy back their debts, even at deep discounts. The Bolivian example is cited frequently but was very special; the money was provided by official donors expressly for the purpose of debt reduction.[7]

Several debtor countries have experimented with debt–equity swaps, but Chile is the only one that encouraged them enthusiastically. Difficulties arise on three fronts. First, many debtor countries are ambivalent about foreign direct investment of any sort. Second, they wonder whether they are attracting additional investments or merely subsidizing what would take place anyway on normal commercial terms. Third, they worry about inflationary side effects, because external debt must be exchanged for domestic currency before it can be used for equity investment, and the domestic currency is usually supplied by the central bank, expanding the money supply, as the government is usually running a budget deficit and cannot put up the money.

This brings us to the use of future resources to buy back debt. What can be done by defeasance? A small number of governments have offered 'exit bonds' to small and medium-sized banks interested in opting out of debt reschedulings and concerted lending. The problem of subordination, discussed below, does not arise in connection with these issues; the bonds do not take precedence over other obligations but were thought to be potentially attractive because buyers would not have to increase their exposure. Hence, the holders of old debt would not be adversely affected financially, and were expected to benefit indirectly, because the creditors' coalition would become more compact and cohesive.

Yet experience has not been encouraging. Argentina tried to issue exit bonds in 1987, but the terms were not attractive. Mexico was somewhat more successful in 1988, but it used reserves to guarantee its promise to repay. It bought zero-coupon US Treasury securities, which were used to back the principal of the Mexican bonds issued in exchange for Mexican debt. Yet Mexico's sales were smaller than expected, presumably because the interest payments were not guaranteed, and the promise to pay interest on the bonds was not more credible than the promise to pay interest on the debt. Exit bonds appeared in the menu of financial options listed in the 1988 agreement between Brazil and its bank creditors. Although they were not guaranteed, Brazil sold more than £1 billion to more than a hundred banks (Rhodes 1988), but it has not reached its £5 billion target.

It is sometimes suggested that debtors should subordinate old debt to new, to market the new debt successfully. But that cannot be done without the unanimous consent of those who hold the old debt, and this produces a paradox. If enough new debt is issued to retire much of the old debt, those who continue to hold the old debt may not accept subordination, even if the exercise sharply reduces the debtor's obligations and thus raises the expected value of the whole debt; the buyers of the new debt will be seen to appropriate most of the gain. But if the issue is cut back to reduce the redistribution of rights from holders of old debt to holders of new debt, the exercise will not reduce the debtor's obligations by enough to make subordination meaningful – to raise the value of the whole debt by enhancing the debtor's ability and willingness to service it.

When the problem of defeasance is viewed this way, the function of a new institution becomes very clear. It would guarantee new debt, whether by issuing its own obligations or by backing new bonds issued by the debtor countries.

THE FUNCTIONING OF A NEW INSTITUTION

I suggested the creation of a new institution soon after the debt crisis erupted (Kenen 1983).[8] An International Debt Discount Corporation (IDDC) would be established by the governments of the major industrial countries. It could be an independent entity or an affiliate of the IMF or World Bank. Its capital would be subscribed by its sponsors and used exclusively to guarantee its own obligations. Subscriptions might be made in proportion to the sponsors' shares in the capital of the World Bank or quotas in the IMF. The IDDC would issue its own long-term obligations to commercial banks in exchange for their claims on developing countries. (The claims would be those issued or guaranteed by debtor governments, not those of private entities, and limited to those having an original maturity longer than one year.)

In 1983, when my plan appeared, there was no secondary market for sovereign debt. That is why I did not suggest that the IDDC might buy up debt at market prices. Nevertheless, that approach raises some serious problems. Market rates would begin to reflect expectations about IDDC operations even before it came into being, and they

would cease to serve as independent benchmarks (Fischer 1989). Furthermore, debtors should not be given incentives to threaten repudiation – explicitly or by following imprudent policies – to force down the prices at which the IDDC could buy up their debts in the market and thus raise the amounts of debt relief that it would pass on to them (Corden 1988b). Hence, the IDDC should choose in advance the rate at which it will discount debt, say 40–50 per cent. A case can be made for using several discount rates and letting each debtor choose the one for its own obligations. This would be particularly sensible if larger discounts were linked to tighter policy conditions.

Commercial banks would not be required to do business with IDDC, but those that did would be subject to certain restrictions. First, banks should not be allowed to sell their claims on some debtors and keep their claims on others; a bank wanting to discount claims on any debtor country doing business with the IDDC should be required to discount a uniform fraction of its total claims on all such countries. Second, banks would have only a limited period, perhaps six months to a year, to decide whether they will turn to the IDDC.

Debtor countries would not have to deal with the IDDC either, and it would deal only with those countries that agreed to enter into suitable arrangements with the IMF and World Bank concerning the debtors' policies. During the time that banks are deciding whether they will sell to the IDDC, the debtor governments would have to decide whether they will do business with the IDDC; the discount window would be opened at the end of that period.

Sponsoring governments would agree to make changes in their banking laws and regulations if such changes are required for their banks to deal with the IDDC. Furthermore, they would permit their banks to amortize gradually some of the losses incurred by discounting debt with the IDDC. Bonds issued by the IDDC might be amortized over a thirty-year period, starting five years after issue, and bear an interest rate slightly higher than the then-current rate on long-term US government bonds. The bonds should be marketable, and the

IDDC should encourage the development of a secondary market for them. Furthermore, it should be empowered to redeem them by issuing new ones to holders of maturing bonds and in the open market.

Claims discounted by the IDDC would be converted into long-term debt at or slightly above the discounted value of those claims. The difference between the face value of the new debt and the discounted value of the old would yield a 'profit' that the IDDC might hold as a reserve or use for selective interest rate relief. Debt to the IDDC might be amortized over a twenty-five-year period, after a five-year grace period. It should bear an interest rate 50 basis points above the average rate on the IDDC's own bonds.

Many permutations of this plan have appeared recently. The boldest is by Robinson (1988), in which the new institution would issue consols. In that case, of course, it would be guaranteeing interest payments rather than principal, which would be eminently sensible. The present value of the institution's obligations would be the same whether its bonds were amortized or not, but its exposure to cash flow problems would be reduced.

Another variant would use the new institution to guarantee bonds issued directly by the debtors, rather than its own.[9] This option has one disadvantage. It would produce a large number of new bonds, each with its own market, rather than one issue by the IDDC with a single market, and the latter would probably function more efficiently. Furthermore, the terms of existing debt contracts allow banks to block bond issues by debtors, but they could be invoked as easily to block bond issues by the IDDC. The point is important because the success of the debt conversion exercise will depend on the ability of the IDDC to make banks an offer they cannot refuse or block.

ANSWERING THE CRITICS

Critics of an international agency invoke a litany of difficulties – adverse selection, moral hazard and the free-rider problem.

The first says that the IDDC will gather in the debt that is least likely to be honoured. This problem is minimized by the requirement that banks sell baskets of debt to the IDDC, offering some or all of their claims on all participating debtor countries. The problem could be eliminated by requiring all debtor countries to participate, but that would be impractical and unfair. Some debtor countries, like Korea, have worked hard to preserve their creditworthiness; they should not have to damage it.

The moral hazard argument says that the scheme would invite debtor countries to pursue irresponsible policies and would lead eventually to a new round of overborrowing.

The first part of this assertion says that debtor governments would be less concerned to achieve domestic stability and promote economic growth if their debts were reduced. In other words, it rejects the main rationale for debt relief, that debtors have failed to achieve their policy objectives because the debt overhang prevents them from doing so. (Alternatively, it may say that the debtors would take their obligations to the IDDC less seriously than their obligations to the commercial banks. That is unlikely. No country has kept up its debt service payments to the banks but suspended its payments to the IMF or World bank, but several have done the opposite.)

The second part of the assertion predicts that debt relief will cause another debt crisis by removing reminders of this one. There may be another debt crisis eventually, but its timing is less likely to reflect the manner of settling this one than the speed at which institutional memories fade. Many governments that strive today to meet their countries' obligations are not the ones that took them on, and they will not be around at the start of the next century to make new mistakes. Furthermore, the IDDC will not 'bail out' the banks, though the banks are likely to do better than by letting the debt problem drag on.

The free-rider problem needs to be taken more seriously. If one bank believes that the rest will grant debt relief, bilaterally or through an IDDC, improving the debtor's ability to meet its remaining obligations, it has an incentive to hang back. The obvious solution, mandatory participation by the banks, is not politically feasible. It is hard enough to shift risk from private to official creditors, let alone to shift from voluntary to mandatory debt reduction. But the problem may be less serious than commonly supposed.

Although debt reduction will raise the debtors' ability to meet their remaining obligations, some of the benefits will accrue to the IDDC. In fact, banks that hang back may be hurt, because debtor governments may be less concerned to meet their obligations to those banks than to the IDDC, and the governments sponsoring the IDDC will not be particularly interested in upholding the claims of banks that decline to do business with it. In other words, it may be possible to subordinate old debt to new debt when the new debt is owed to the IDDC, not formally by abrogating existing debt contracts, but informally by casting doubt on the likelihood that those contracts will be honoured.

Finally, the sponsors of the IDDC can limit the free-rider problem by offering incentives for banks to participate and penalizing those that do not. Participants can be allowed to amortize their losses, as proposed above. Non-participants can be required to mark remaining debt to market and thus acknowledge larger losses.[10] In short, the sponsors and debtors can make sure that the IDDC appropriates most of the increase in the value of the debt resulting from debt relief and thus reduce the value of the old debt still outstanding.

Critics have been slow to spot another problem. They endorse the view that participating debtors be subject to some form of conditionality – that they have a bargain with the IMF or take structural adjustment loans from the World Bank. It may be very hard, however, to condition debt relief. IMF drawings and World Bank structural adjustment loans are disbursed in tranches, not in a lump sum, and disbursements can be halted if policy commitments are not met. It is rather difficult to do this with debt relief. It would be foolish, indeed, to withdraw debt relief from governments that fail to meet their policy commitments, as that would merely make it harder for them to do so. It may

make sense, however, for the IDDC to grant relief provisionally and modestly at first, so that debtors are made to meet their policy commitments to qualify for permanent, full-scale relief. This argues for providing provisional relief by reducing the interest rate payable to the IDDC, and then moving to permanent relief by writing down the claims themselves by more than the counterpart of the initial interest rate reduction.

Two questions remain. Would the creation of an IDDC interfere with the resumption of voluntary lending? Why should the US taxpayer get involved?

The first is easily answered. Most of the numbers suggest that the heavily indebted countries are farther from returning to creditworthiness than they were at the start of the debt crisis. There has been no concerted lending to small debtors for some years, and the large debtors have continued to qualify only because banks have been reluctant to acknowledge the losses they would face if Argentina, Brazil and Mexico could not borrow enough to keep on paying interest. If the IDDC can facilitate large-scale debt relief, the debtors will be able to manage their economies more effectively, and this will hasten, not delay, the return to creditworthiness.

The second question has two answers. FIrst, the risks assumed by the sponsoring countries and their taxpayers are not large in so far as debtors lie on the downward-sloping side of the DRLC. Debt relief reduces the risk by raising the value of the debt. Second, taxpayers are already involved. They take on risks directly whenever the World Bank makes another loan to one of the heavily indebted countries, and they take them on indirectly whenever the commercial banks engage in additional concerted lending. But there are larger issues. The taxpayers are involved because the debt problem impinges on foreign policy, the prospects for democracy in the debtor countries and the outlook for reducing imbalances in the world economy. Much has been said about the need for the newly industrialized countries of Asia to liberalize their trade regimes and thus help to reduce the US trade deficit. The debtor countries could make an equally important contribution if their foreign exchange earnings were not eaten by their interest payments and their economies could grow more rapidly.

NOTES

1 This view is best represented in Cline (1984). The literature on debt is vast and space in this book is precious, so I do not cite all the relevant sources. Good bibliographies are found in Cohen (1989) and Dornbusch (1988), which also supplies a compact history of the debt problem; the theoretical literature is surveyed by Eaton et al. (1986).

2 For reasons and possible results, see Guttentag and Herring (1988).

3 On the early evolution of the menu approach, see World Bank (1988); on the Brazilian agreement, see Lamdany (1988a).

4 Under the agreement announced in July 1989, banks will have three main options: (1) to swap Mexican debt for long-term bonds at a 35 per cent discount; Mexico will buy zero-coupon US Treasury securities to guarantee the principal; (2) to switch from floating-rate debt, paying about 10 per cent when the agreement was announced, to new fixed-rate debt paying $6\frac{1}{4}$ per cent, without any change in face value; the interest rate will rise after 1996 if higher oil prices raise Mexico's oil revenues in real terms; (3) to retain their present claims but make new loans to Mexico over the next four years by enough to raise those claims by 25 per cent; they will thus capitalize some of Mexico's debt service payments. Interest payments under the first two options will be covered by a rolling eighteen-month guarantee, backed by Mexican deposits in escrow accounts. The agreement has to be ratified by individual banks, and some time will pass before we know how much of Mexico's debt will be covered by each option. Bankers forecast that those holding about 60 per cent of the debt will take the first option, with the rest divided evenly between the other two. In the light of experience with earlier debt-for-bond swaps, cited later in this chapter, the 60 per cent figure seems high. Even if the forecast is accurate, however, the whole package will reduce the face value of the debt by just 16 per cent (the 35 per cent reduction in face value multiplied by a 60 per cent participation *less* the 25 per cent increase in exposure multiplied by a 20 per cent participation), and it will reduce the present value of the debt by only 23 per cent (if the interest rate cut on the other 20 per cent is treated as being roughly equivalent to a 35 per cent reduction in face value).

5 The argument that follows is based on the model in Kenen (1989). A similar argument is made by Corden (1988a). The analysis depends crucially on one assumption. The penalties imposed when a debtor repudiates get weaker if they are delayed. Otherwise, the debtor would repudiate sooner rather than later. The use of the framework developed in the text also helps to answer the objections raised by Bulow and Rogoff (1988, 1989). Their case against debt buybacks is based on two premises: (1) debtors and creditors hold identical views about the future, so that prices prevailing in the secondary market represent debtors' valuations of their obligations, as well as creditors' valuations of their claims – under this assumption, a buyback at the market price cannot benefit a debtor unless the debtor can expect to raise its real income by reducing the inefficiencies associated with a large debt overhang; (2) if those inefficiencies reflect unexploited investment opportunities, a debtor would do better to use its scarce resources for capital formation than for debt reduction. In Kenen (1989), however, valuations by debtors and creditors differ, because the costs of repudiation borne by debtors do not directly raise the value of the creditors' claims, and I go on to show that a buyback at the market price can be mutually beneficial even under conditions resembling those embodied in the Bulow–Rogoff model. It can raise the debtor's income even when the opportunity costs of using scarce resources to buy back debt are larger at the margin than the costs of being in debt, including the income-depressing effects of a large debt overhang.

6 There are at least two reasons for differences between the market's valuations and those at which debtors and creditors will do business with each other. (1) If creditors believe that they can seize the debtor's assets in the event of default or repudiation, the market price will reflect the present value of the gross debt plus the value of the assets that creditors can seize in the event of repudiation – and the debtor's assets do not change when creditors swap debt in the secondary market. But the debtor's assets fall when it uses some of its assets to buy back debt, and creditors will want to be compensated for the fall in the stock of assets that they can expect to seize if the debtor repudiates the rest of its debt (Froot 1989; Kenen 1989). (2) The price at which the debtor can buy back debt for cash or trade it for new debt depends on both parties' expectations, whereas the market price depends on the creditors' expectations. All creditors do not have the same expectations, which is

indeed one reason for the existence of a secondary market. Corden (1988b) studies the implications of differences between debtors' and creditors' expectations; Williamson (1989) examines the implications of heterogeneity in the creditors' expectations.

7   Lamdany (1988b) points out, however, that some of the money was official aid earmarked for Bolivia, so the Bolivians had to act as though they were using their own resources. Sachs (1988) reports that banks agreed to a very large discount in the Bolivian case only under pressure from US regulators. (It should perhaps be noted that Mexico may have to lay out some $7 billion to implement its new agreement with the banks – $3 billion for zero-coupon bonds to guarantee principal and $4 billion more to fund the escrow accounts that back up the rolling interest-payment guarantee. These figures reflect the assumption in note 4 that banks holding 80 per cent of Mexico's debt will take the debt-reducing options and thus cut the present value of their claims on Mexico by 35 per cent. To buy back 80 per cent of the debt at a 35 per cent discount, Mexico would have to lay out some $28 billion. Buybacks are expensive.)

8   The proposal was introduced earlier (Kenen 1982), but so was its main rival. Felix Rohatyn published a similar plan early in 1983, but an early version appeared some months before (Rohatyn 1982, 1983). Credit or blame may really belong to G. C. Rodney Leach, then General Manager of the Trade Development Bank in London, whose proposal appears in a letter circulated late in 1982, and his plan had some features that have come up again. Banks would be shareholders in his institution, as in the one proposed by Robinson (1988). A revised version of my own plan was circulated privately in 1985 and another revision was published in Kenen (1988); this is the one described in the text.

9   The newest version of this variant comes from L. William Seidman, chairman of the Federal Deposit Insurance Corporation, who would elicit the required capital from the IMF, the World Bank, governments and commercial banks, but would charge the banks an annual premium to insure their holdings of the debtor's bonds (The New York Times, 10 July 1989). An earlier version by Rotberg (1988) was designed initially to encourage new bank lending but could be adapted to insure bond issues by the debtors.

10   Corden (1988b) makes the same suggestion, and it is my reason for reversing the position I took in earlier presentations that banks should not be made to write down their remaining claims.

REFERENCES

Bulow, J., and Rogoff, K. (1988) 'The buyback boondoggle', Brookings Papers on Economics Activity 2: 675–98.

—— and —— (1989) 'Sovereign debt repurchases: no cure for overhang', Working Paper 2850, Cambridge, MA: National Bureau of Economic Research, February.

Cline, W. R. (1984) International Debt: Systemic Risk and Policy Response, Washington, DC: Institute for International Economics.

Cohen, B. J. (1989) 'LDC debt: a middle way', Essays in International Finance 173, Princeton, NJ: International Finance Section, Princeton University.

Corden, W. M. (1988a) 'Debt relief and adjustment incentives', IMF Staff Papers 35: 628–43.

—— (1988b) 'An international debt facility?', IMF Staff Papers 35: 401–21.

Dornbusch, R. (1988) 'Our LDC debts', in M. Feldstein (ed.) The United States in the World Economy, Chicago, IL: University of Chicago Press for the National Bureau of Economic Research.

Eaton, J. and Gersovitz, M. (1981) 'Debt with potential repudiation', Review of Economic Studies 48 (March): 289–309.

Eaton, J., Gersovitz, M. and Stiglitz, J. E. (1986) 'The pure theory of country risk', European Economic Review 30 (June) 481–513.

Fischer, S. (1989) 'Resolving the international debt crisis', in J. Sachs (ed.) Developing Country Debt and Economic Performance, Chicago, IL:, University of Chicago Press.

Froot, K. A. (1989) 'Buybacks, exit bonds, and the optimality of debt and liquidity relief', International Economic Review 30 (February): 49–70.

Guttentag, J. and Herring, R. (1988) 'Provisioning, charge-offs, and the willingness to lend', Essays in International Finance 172, Princeton, NJ: International Finance Section, Princeton University.

Kenen, P. B. (1982) 'National economic policy, international adjustment, and exchange rates', Foreign Exchange Service Conference Proceedings, Philadelphia, PA: Wharton Econometric Forecasting Associates, Fall.

—— (1983) 'Third-world debt: sharing the burden. A bailout plan for the banks', The New York Times, 6 March.

—— (1988) 'A proposal for reducing debt burdens for developing countries', in D. B. H. Denoon (ed.) Changing Capital Markets and the Global Economy, Philadelphia, PA: Global Interdependence Center.

—— (1989) 'Debt buybacks and forgiveness in a model with voluntary repudiation', Working Paper 89-1, Princeton, NJ: International Finance Section,

Princeton University, July.

Krugman, P. R. (1989) 'Market-based debt reduction schemes', in J. A. Frenkel, M. P. Dooley and P. Wickham (eds) *Analytical Issues in Debt*, Washington, DC: International Monetary Fund.

Lamdany, R. (1988a) 'The Brazil financing package: main components and lessons for the future', unpublished manuscript, September.

—— (1988b) 'Bolivia, Mexico, and beyond ...', unpublished manuscript, June.

Rhodes, W. R. (1988) 'An insider's reflection on the Brazilian debt package', *The Wall Street Journal*, 14 October.

Robinson, J. D. (1988) 'A comprehensive agenda for LDC debt and world trade growth', Amex Bank Review Special Papers 13, London: American Express Bank, March.

Rohatyn, F. G. (1982) 'The state of the banks', *New York Review of Books*, 4 November.

—— (1983) 'A plan for stretching out global debt', *Business Week*, 28 February.

Rotberg, E. H. (1988) *Toward a Solution to the Debt Crisis*, New York: Merrill Lynch, May.

Sachs, J. (1988) 'Comprehensive debt retirement: the Bolivian example', *Brookings Papers on Economic Activity* 2: 705–13.

—— (1989a) 'Making the Brady Plan work', *Foreign Affairs* 68: 87–104.

—— (1989b) 'Conditionality, debt relief, and the developing country debt crisis', in J. Sachs (ed.) *Developing Country Debt and Economic Performance*, Chicago, IL: University of Chicago Press.

Williamson, J. (1989) 'Voluntary approaches to debt relief', *Policy Analyses in International Economics 25*, revised edn, Washington, DC: Institute for International Economics.

World Bank (1988) *Market-Based Menu Approach*, Washington, DC: World Bank Debt Management and Financial Advisory Services Department, September.

25

AN INTERNATIONAL DEBT FACILITY?

W. Max Corden

A common proposal designed to deal with the developing countries' debt problem is that there be set up an 'international debt facility' that would buy debt at a discount and then mark down its contractual value, hence providing debt relief. This facility could be envisaged either as a major scheme that, over a period, would deal with most or all outstanding commercial debt owed or guaranteed by governments, or as a more modest arrangement dealing with only small portions of debt, possibly only that which is owed by the governments of particular countries.

Many such proposals have been advanced. They vary in their details[1] and there are many difficulties, some major. Nevertheless, the frequency with which such proposals are made makes it worth examining them carefully in their many permutations.

MAIN ISSUES

There are three principal parties to the proposed transaction – the debtor governments, the creditor banks and the 'owners' of the facility. The central question is how the costs and benefits would accrue to various parties. Is there an element of 'foreign aid' or of a 'bank bail-out'? Alternatively, would the banks give up something? Could all three parties gain or, at least, could some gain without the others losing significantly, if at all? In other words, is there some systemic benefit?

The proximate redistributive effects – and possibly also the systemic effects – will depend crucially on three prices: the price at which the debt is bought, the price or value to which it is marked down and the price or perceived value to which remaining debt that is retained in the private sector moves as a result of the whole operation. The full economic effects will depend, of course, on how the various parties react to or deal with the proximate gains or losses.

In considering the details of such a scheme there are many choices to be made.

- The debt might be bought by the facility at the minimum price required for the banks to part with it voluntarily; it might be bought at current market prices; it might be bought at the market prices that existed at some earlier 'cut-off' date; or it might be bought at some other set of prices representing discounts on the contractual value. Conceivably it might even be bought at its contractual value.

- Purchased debt might be marked down to the cost at which the facility bought it, or to a higher or lower value than cost.

- The debt that is not sold by banks might maintain its present contractual status; it might be subordinated to the debt that the debtor countries will now incur to the facility; or it might be marked down by the debtors to an extent that would force the banks to sell all their debt to the facility.

A crucial question is how the facility would be financed. Here, also, there are differences among the various proposals, and the possibilities will be discussed shortly.

A SIMPLE SCHEME

Let us suppose that the scheme applies to any one debtor country. The facility goes into the market and offers to buy given amounts of debt. In the detailed example spelled out below, it will be assumed that the facility offers to buy half the stock of debt. Of course debt is not homogeneous, so that various decisions would have to be made on which debt to buy. It is quite likely that the facility would have to pay more than the initial market price, but one can assume that the facility would buy debt at a discount from the contractual value. The important question of what would determine the price, and in which direction it would move, will be taken up later.

The facility pays for the purchased debt with new bonds guaranteed by its owners. The banks are thus able to dispose of debt with the original contractual value that is subject to default risk in exchange for debt of a lower contractual value that is subject to much lower, possibly zero, default risk. One's first thought is that those that sell could not be worse off as a result. After all, selling is voluntary; there is no compulsion in this scheme. This conclusion is not necessarily true, and will have to be looked at again in the fourth section.

The facility would then mark down the contractual value of the debtor country's debt that it has acquired. It marks the debt down to the cost price to it – i.e. the contractual value of the new bonds it has issued to the banks. No funds are thus required from the owners of the facility – i.e. the governments that have underwritten the facility. But, of course, the facility's new assets are somewhat risky and, because of the guarantees on the bonds it has issued, this risk has been taken over by the facility's owners. Given this risk, there will be a potential need for funds from the owners, who may actually wish to finance contingency reserves specifically to allow for the risk. A major, and possibly overwhelming, obstacle to the establishment of a facility is the reluctance of governments to assume such risks. A question to be discussed below is whether this risk can be reduced or eliminated.

The debtor country apparently benefits because the contractual value of its debt has been reduced. But the gain to it will not necessarily be as great as it might seem at first. One possible view is that the market's perception of default risk, which led to the initial discount, was justified in the sense that this represented the true probability of default. In other words, there was a good chance in any case that the country would not repay the full contractual value of its debt. Reducing the contractual value as a result of the operation of the facility would not necessarily reduce actual payments (or the probability of actual payments expected to be made) to the same extent. Indeed, one might ask whether there is likely to be any gain to the debtor country at all.

HOW DEBTOR AND BANKS MAY GAIN

This matter of the possible gain to the debtor, and also to the banks, can be analysed more precisely if the concept of the debtor's 'capacity to pay' is introduced. This is defined as the ability to make resource transfers abroad to cover interest payments and repayment of principal. It depends on the country's output over a period of time, on its minimum consumption level and on its ability to transform output into tradeables (exports and import-competing products) required to generate the transfer. It also depends on the terms of trade.

It will be supposed at this stage that capacity to pay can vary as the result of various exogenous, uncertain events – such as terms-of-trade developments – but does not vary because of changes in the policies of the debtor country itself, which are simply taken as given. This is the assumption of 'exogeneity'. It will also be assumed for the moment that expectations about capacity to pay are the same among market participants, debtor countries and the decision-makers of the facility. This is the assumption of 'uniformity of expectations'. These two simplifying assumptions are important for the analysis of gains and losses from the establishment of a facility and therefore will be reconsidered in the seventh section.

There are two steps in the analysis. First I show why the banks might gain at the expense of the facility, and then I show why the debtor might gain. The second effect depends crucially on uncertainty.

Gain to the banks

To begin with, there is the 'market price effect'.[2] It can be shown that the banks will gain at the expense of the facility provided that the debt that they retain is not subordinated to the marked-down debt that the facility now holds. The reason is that the market price of the debt will rise (the discount will fall). The argument is quite simple when there is complete certainty about the capacity to pay (or repay).

Let us suppose that the contractual debt is $1,000 and the capacity to pay is $600. Assume at this stage that the latter is fixed. Hence the debtor country will neither gain nor lose; whatever happens, it pays $600. This is thought of as a single sum paid in a single future period, the sum consisting of principal and interested combined. Given the initial contractual debt, default or debt relief is then inevitable. The 'default ratio' would be 40 per cent.

The facility then offers to buy a proportion of the $1,000 in contractual debt from the banks at a discounted price. Here it will be assumed that it buys half the debt ($500) and that the price it pays is 80 cents to the dollar. Hence the facility pays $400 and marks the debt it has acquired down to its cost price. The contractual value of the total debt owed by the debtor country is thus reduced to $900. With the same capacity to pay as before, the default ratio becomes 33.3 per cent. The facility will finally get 66.7 per cent repayment of the debt it holds, thus making a loss of $133. The banks will get $333 for the debt they have retained (with a contractual value of $500), and when this is combined with the $400 they received from the facility they end up with $733, which is an improvement of $133 on what they would have received if the facility had not bought and marked down some of the debt. The discount on debt held by the banks has fallen from 40 per cent to 33.3 per cent.

In this example the facility's purchase price is 80 cents but the market price has risen only from 60 cents to 67 cents. The purchase price could therefore be reduced, leading to a bigger decline in the contractual value and hence to a further rise in the market price. The equilibrium price (where purchase and market prices are equal) would actually be $70\frac{1}{2}$ cents when the facility buys half the debt. If it bought a greater proportion, the price would be higher. These results can be derived as follows:

$$C_2 = C_1(1-q) + C_1qp \qquad (25.1)$$

$$p = R/C_2, \qquad (25.2)$$

where C_1 is the initial contractual value, C_2 is the contractual value after debt relief, q is the proportion of debt bought by a facility, R is the capacity to pay and p is the purchase price (equal to the market price after purchase) as a proportion of the initial contractual price. From equations (25.1) and (25.2)

$$\frac{R}{C_1} = (1-q)p + qp^2. \qquad (25.3)$$

From equation (25.3),

$$p = \frac{-(1-q) + [(1-q)^2 + 4qR/C_1]^{\frac{1}{2}}}{2q}.$$

There has been a pure transfer from the facility to the banks. All this will be reflected in the market price rising (discount falling) when the facility enters the market. It has to pay a higher price than the initial price to induce the banks to sell any debt to it. The banks will foresee that debt not sold will rise in value when some marking down takes place, and hence they will only sell at a sufficiently higher price. The price would not necessarily rise to its equilibrium value immediately, and could also overshoot, since banks and others in the market would not be able to predict this equilibrium in advance. The account given here, with its impression of precision, merely indicates likely tendencies.

The essential point can be restated as follows. When the contractual value of the total debt is reduced while total capacity to pay stays constant, each dollar's worth of contractual debt must be worth more in the market than before, provided that all dollars of contractual debt would be treated equally if there were some default.

Gain to the debtor

Uncertainty about capacity to pay and the 'ceiling effect' can now be introduced.[3] The mean expected repayment might be $600, but it could also be greater, up to a ceiling of complete repayment of $1,000, and it could be less, with a floor of zero. There is thus both upside and downside risk, and this will be taken into account in the market price. If the contractual value of the debt is reduced, say to $900, the ceiling will be lowered to $900. If the terms of trade, for example, turn out to be quite favourable, so that capacity to pay is actually $950, the actual payment will be $50 less than if the contractual value had stayed at its initial level. Thus the debtor gains at the expense of creditors from a markdown of the contractual value because the downside risk remains as before, whereas the offsetting upside risk (or gain) becomes less.[4]

SUBORDINATION: CAN A GAIN TO THE BANKS BE AVOIDED?

An interesting question is whether a gain to the banks at the expense of the facility – i.e. a 'bank bail-out' – can be avoided. The key here is subordination of the debt retained by the banks relative to the debt now owned by the facility.

When one talks about a gain to the banks, one means a gain relative to the initial situation when there was already a discount in the market. Earlier, of course, the banks incurred a loss once the probability of some default or forced debt relief was perceived by them or the market. Presumably, as

long as the bank gets less then $1,000 they will have incurred some loss as normally defined, even though the margin above the LIBOR that they charged originally must have taken into account the possibility of some default or of heavy pressure to provide some relief.

Suppose that, again, the facility buys half the debt and marks it down to cost. It buys it at 80 cents per dollar and so pays $400, total contractual debt being thus marked down to $900 as before. One now proceeds in two stages. First, let us assume that there is no doubt at all that the capacity to pay will be at least $400.

If it could be firmly established that, whatever is the capacity-to-pay outcome above $400, the debt held by the facility would always be paid first – i.e. would be 'senior' debt – then the facility would not make a loss and its owners would run no risk. But the banks would lose potentially, and the debtors gain, because the 'ceiling payment' has been reduced. Previously the maximum payment the banks could have received was $1,000, whereas now it is $500 for the debt they have retained plus the $400 they have already received from the facility. If capacity to pay turned out to be $950, previously the banks would have received $950, but now they can only receive $900. In contrast, the minimum they can receive remains $400.

Subordinating debt retained by the banks to facility-held debt thus ensures that the facility neither loses nor gains, taking on no risk, while the debtor countries gain potentially at the expense of the banks because of the ceiling effect. The expected loss to the banks would be reflected in a decline in the market price.[5]

If it were desired for some of the loss to the banks to be shared with the facility, the latter could mark down the debt by more than the discounted purchase price, hence making a clear loss now. Alternatively, only part of its debt might be given seniority. Here there is scope for many variations in the details of such a scheme, and these may have significant effects on the gains or losses for the banks and the facility. The key point is that the banks and the facility combined must make a potential loss – i.e. forgo the benefits of a very favourable capacity-to-pay outcome. The risk of an unfavourable outcome has not been eliminated, but the possibility of a very favourable return (above $900) has.

The second stage of the analysis is to assume that capacity to pay could be less than $400. In that case there would be some possibility that even debt given senior status would not be fully repaid. Hence risk for the facility would not be completely eliminated. The conclusion that subordination of debt retained by the banks to the debt owned by the facility would eliminate all risk for the facility hinges completely on the assumption that some minimum total payment – equal to the value of the debt that the facility has bought ($400 in the example) – is utterly assured. But the larger the proportion of the initial total debt that the facility takes over and marks down, the less likely it is that all risk for the facility would be eliminated by giving the debt it holds senior status. If the facility had bought up all the debt, no one but the facility could assume the risk.

There can never be utter certainty about prospective capacity to pay, so that some risk for the facility is inherent in the scheme. This implicit risk is particularly relevant for proposals that would have the facility take over a large part of the foreign debt of a country. The inevitable risk helps to explain the reluctance of governments of creditor countries to support proposals for such a facility.

REDUCTION OF UNCERTAINTY

Another possibility, worth exploring carefully because it is implicit in some proposals, can now be considered. The suggestion is that the Fund or World Bank may be able to increase or ensure certainty of payment at the new, marked-down value of the debt. The assumption maintained so far – that the actual repayment outcome depends only on exogenously determined capacity to pay, subject to the 'ceiling' imposed by the contractual value – is relaxed. Repayment can also depend on policies.

Suppose that initially the mean expected

capacity to pay was $600, with a probability of creditors getting more or less. If the total debt were marked down to $600, there would then be a $600 ceiling to the repayment. In addition, suppose that the Fund or World Bank were able to ensure that $600 also became the minimum repayment. This assurance might have been obtained with the aid of conditionality. Given this arrangement, there is no longer a necessary loss to the banks and the facility combined from the imposition of a reduced ceiling because that ceiling is associated with the imposition of a raised floor. Upside and downside risk have both been eliminated. Certainty has been obtained – or at least uncertainty has been reduced.

Certainty represents a net gain for the banks and the facility combined, given that they are risk averse. With subordination, the whole of this gain from certainty would go to the banks in the first case just discussed, in which a minimum repayment sufficient to cover the debt held by the facility was in any case ensured. But in the more general case, in which the facility has carried some of the risk previously (whether because no minimum was ensured or because there was no subordination), the gain would go partially to the facility.

It is often implied in debt relief proposals that the marked-down value of debt would have no more risk attached to it (or very little risk) because it would be close to the expected capacity to pay. It is doubtful whether this assumption is realistic. The implication is that willingness to repay – and the resolve to make the necessary adjustments – is not exogenous but rather can be made more 'certain' in return for debt relief. Perhaps a commitment that would successfully reduce perceived default risk could be obtained from the debtor country in some way or other. Debtor governments could make certain policy commitments. No doubt the Fund's conditionality procedures can play a role here. Conditionality can conceivably reduce uncertainty and default risk, although it can surely not eliminate them.

A reduction in uncertainty of repayment without necessarily any net change in the mean expected repayment is clearly a gain to the banks and the facility. But it is not necessarily a gain for the system as a whole. If uncertainty in the capacity to pay – for example, uncertainty in terms of trade movements – could be reduced, that would be a net gain. But if uncertainty in capacity to pay continues while repayment becomes more certain owing to conditionality, there has simply been a transfer in the burden of uncertainty toward the debtor country. For example, if the terms of trade turned out to be particularly adverse, the country would have to bear the whole burden instead of sharing it with the banks or the facility through some degree of default or debt relief.

This approach assumes that the mean expected capacity or willingness to pay stays unchanged but that the floor is raised and the ceiling lowered. There are also two other possibilities.

The first is rather similar to the one just discussed. Conditionality may raise the mean without raising the floor: it may raise expected capacity to pay through bringing about an improvement in policies. Although the banks lose through the ceiling effect, they may then nevertheless gain.

The other quite contrary possibility is that the probability of repayment is actually reduced when the facility takes over debt. As just noted, it is usually argued that, through associating conditionality with the establishment of a facility, the certainty of repayment can be improved. But a contrary view is that a facility that is subject to political pressure and that has no strong penalties available to it may be a less effective debt collector than private banks, which can threaten the withdrawal of trade credit as a potential penalty.

INTERESTS OF THE DEBTOR COUNTRIES AND MORAL HAZARD

There are several ways in which the debtor country might gain from the arrangement. Some have already been referred to, but they will now be brought together.

Reducing the default ratio

A gain that seems obvious at first sight but turns out to be primarily cosmetic is the reduction in the default ratio. The default ratio D equals $1 - R/C$, where R is the actual debt repayment made – i.e. the resource transfer – and C is the contractual value of the debt. D is reduced when the contractual value is marked down, even though the actual payment (which has been assumed to be exogenous so far) does not change.

Does it really matter if this default ratio falls, possibly to zero, when the resource transfer remains unchanged? One might say that the effect is purely cosmetic. If an emperor has few clothes, is it really necessary to proclaim the fact? Against this it can be argued convincingly that debt relief voluntarily provided by the creditors is always better than default.

There would clearly be a preference on the part of the debtor country for debt relief over default if penalties were associated with default. Even in the absence of current penalties, reputation – and hence future creditworthiness – may be influenced by whether there has been formal default rather than debt relief. Note that it has been assumed here that default depends purely on exogenous capacity to pay; hence penalties related to the default ratio would seem less likely or reasonable. Because capacity to pay completely determines actual repayments, there would be no point in the creditors imposing penalties.

Lowering the ceiling

The debtor country gains owing to the 'ceiling effect'. As has been pointed out, if capacity to pay turns out to be particularly favourable – above the new contractual value – the gain would go to the debtor rather than to the creditors because the ceiling for potential repayments has been lowered. This benefit to the debtor might disappear (and could even turn into a loss) if conditionality manages also to raise the floor for the repayment, shifting more of the risk toward the debtor country.[6]

Marking debt down below cost

The facility might mark the debt down by more than the cost price to it – possibly by much more – and the contractual value might then fall below the capacity to pay, even when the capacity to pay turns out to be quite low. At the limit, the debt might be marked down to zero. This would represent a straightforward transfer from the owners of the facility to the debtor countries – a case of foreign assistance. It is equivalent to the owner countries donating funds to the debtor country to buy back its debt.

Asymmetric expectations

A fourth kind of gain has not been referred to so far but is implicit in much advocacy of debt relief and could be important. The markets, specifically the banks, may be pessimistic and believe that there is some probability of default. Hence there is a market discount on the debt. But the government of the debtor country may have no intention of defaulting. There are 'asymmetric expectations'. Capacity to pay, after all, is not something clear cut. The government foresees difficulties and adjustment problems and seeks debt relief but – possibly for fear of penalties – does not intend ever to default, even though it has not succeeded in convincing the market of this. The issue of asymmetric expectations will be discussed further below. Here it can be noted that, if the government of the debtor country has no intention at all of defaulting, the whole of the fall in the contractual value of the debt brought about by debt relief through the operation of the facility or in some other way would represent a clear-cut gain to the debtor country in reduced prospective resource transfers.[7]

The creditors, however, having different expectations, do not perceive this reduction in the contractual value – or all of it – as a loss to them. They may expect to lose through the ceiling effect but also see some virtue in an explicit recognition of what they believe to be realities – that the country has limited capacity or willingness to pay,

that the emperor has fewer clothes than the initial contract specified.

Moral hazard

For three of the four reasons given here (other than the third, marking debt down below cost), the debtor country would want the price at which the facility buys debt from the banks to be as low as possible. The lower the price, the greater is the decline in the contractual value; hence, the lower the default ratio, the lower is the ceiling applying when events turn out favourably, and the lower are actual repayments if default is never intended.

If this purchase price is equal to or closely related to the market price, the debtor country therefore has an incentive to get the market price down. This can be done by making 'default noises' – just a hint here, a threat there – and the banks will be glad to sell at a low price, in the extreme case at any price above zero. This is the familiar 'moral hazard' problem.

A possible solution from the point of view of creditors seems to be for the facility's purchase price not to be determined by the market price, or at least by the market price ruling once the likelihood of such a facility being established has become serious. Market prices at some earlier 'cut-off' date might be taken. If the banks are to sell voluntarily, the purchase price will have to be no lower than the current market price. But it could be higher.

The problem is to fix a price that does not give a gain, or an undue gain, to the banks; otherwise there would be a bail-out. But what is a gain? Given the expectations created by their anticipation of the debtor country's capacity to pay, combined with the default noises made by the debtor government or others in that country, a sale of the debt to the facility at a very low price may still seem to be a gain to the banks. This is true even though the price is likely to represent a loss relative to the expectations at the time the loans were originally made. Presumably the facility should aim to avoid either gain or loss to the banks relative to the situation at some 'pre-discussion-of-facility' date – i.e. an appropriately early cut-off date.

Most proposals for a facility do not pursue in detail the critical question of how the price at which debt is to be purchased is to be determined, given that there is a moral hazard problem and that there must presumably be a separate price (discount) for each country. It is at this point that the greatest practical problems arise. Sometimes elaborate calculations, which are essentially estimates of capacity to pay, are proposed, but the political difficulties that such estimates would involve cannot be ignored. Given the thinness of existing markets, actual market prices, whether current or at some earlier cut-off date, may not be adequate guides.

TWO ASSUMPTIONS RECONSIDERED

At the beginning of this chapter two crucial assumptions were made: that the debtor's capacity to pay was exogenously determined – for example, by the terms of trade – and that expectations about the capacity to pay were the same among all the relevant parties. Given these assumptions, a fairly straightforward analysis followed that showed that a facility would yield a gain to the banks because of the market price effect and a gain to the debtor because of the ceiling effect. These gains would be at the expense of the facility, which would be taking over a risk. It was further assumed that debt owed to the facility would not be given seniority over debt retained by the banks. If the latter were subordinated, a gain to the banks and loss to the facility might be avoided.

Subsequently, the two initial assumptions have been removed in particular ways. In the fifth section the possibility was explored that the facility (or the World Bank or Fund acting on its behalf) could actually affect the debtor's policies so that capacity to pay would be improved to ensure certainty of repayment of the marked-down value of the debt. In other words, capacity to pay might no longer be exogenous. In the last section, one case of asymmetric expectations was noted. The

debtor government may have no intention of defaulting, but the market may not be convinced of this. In addition, moral hazard was introduced. Prospective repayment may depend not only on capacity to pay but also on willingness to pay (for given capacity), and threats of reduced willingness would affect the market price.

These complications to the initial approach are really special cases, but there are further cases that analysts of these issues sometimes have in mind. A more systematic approach is therefore needed.

First, the concept of expected capacity to pay determined by exogenous factors could be redefined as 'expected total repayment' determined both by expected capacity to pay and by expected willingness to pay.[8] Both would be influenced, or even determined, by policies. When the original concept of capacity to pay is broadened in this way, it becomes more plausible. If the redefined concept is to apply to the initial analysis in this chapter, it has to be assumed that expected policies are exogenous in the sense of not being expected to change as a result of the establishment of the facility or its activities.

The next step is to allow for endogenous policies affecting capacity and willingness to pay. The endogeneity of policies is central to many debt-strategy proposals. As noted in the fifth section, the basic idea is that the benefit to the debtor from debt relief provided through the intermediation of the facility would be reciprocated by improvements in the debtor's policies, and that some kind of assurance about these policies can be obtained, perhaps with the help of conditionality. In this way more certainty of repayment can be ensured.

With regard to endogenous willingness to pay, two points are usually made. The first, as noted above, is the moral hazard problem: threats of reduced willingness to pay can bring the market price down. A second idea not mentioned so far is that, when the contractual value of the debt is partially forgiven so that it is brought down to a more realistic level, the debtor government may have a greater willingness to repay the remainder. If the contractual debt was $1,000 and capacity to pay was $600, some default would be inevitable. It has then been argued that a large default is as bad as – and incurs similar penalties to – a more modest default, so that willingness to pay in that case might fall to zero. But if the contractual debt were marked down to $600, there would be a good chance that default could be avoided, and willingness to pay might become 100 per cent.

As regards asymmetric expectations about the capacity and willingness to pay, there are several possibilities worth noting. First, as already mentioned, the debtor may not intend, and hence not expect, to default while the market contrarily believes that there is a positive probability of default, thus explaining the market discount. In that case the debtor government will believe it would gain from any debt relief, whereas the creditors – selling their debt voluntarily on the market (and assuming no subordination) – will not expect to lose. If the facility paid the banks a price above the initial market price – still with a discount – the banks may believe that they would actually gain, even though, if the debtor government's expectations were correct, the banks would actually have lost by selling.

A scheme could conceivably be worked out whereby the facility pays, for example, $400 for debt with a contractual value of $500 and marks that debt down to only $450, with the margin of $50 adequately compensating the facility for the risk it incurs so that it neither gains nor loses. In this case the creditors believe that they gain through the market price effect, the debtor government believes that it gains because there is some reduction in the contractual price, and the facility neither gains nor loses.

This scheme leads into the second possibility, whereby the facility actually makes a profit or at least is expected to do so by its owners or managers. The market may have an unduly pessimistic view of the debtor's prospects, and hence there may be a large market discount. But the facility only marks the debt down by a little, so that the contractual value of the marked-down debt it holds stays well above the cost price and there is a high degree of certainty that there will be

low or zero default. All this depends on confidence in the ability to get the debtor's policies improved sufficiently to disprove the market's pessimistic expectations.

Finally, it has been argued in the main analysis here that the market price effect represents a benefit for the banks, at least relative to the situation after the debt crisis and the discount developed. But there may be some holders of debt who do not sell to the facility because – contrary to the expectations of marginal holders – they do not believe that the probability of default is high at all. They may value the debt they hold at the contractual value, not near the market price. They may have made a more optimistic assessment of capacity or willingness to pay. If they feel assured that there will be full repayment in any case, it would make no difference to them if the total contractual claims are reduced through the operation of the facility. But if they really believed that the debt is worth more than its market price, the question then arises why they did not buy up the debt held by others and so bring the price up to their optimistic expectations. The argument assumes that the market is, in some sense, imperfect.

WOULD NEW INVESTMENT INCREASE AS A RESULT OF THE FACILITY?

There are three parts to the answer to this question. If the debt of the facility is given senior rights the answer is not clear; it is possible that new investment would actually be discouraged.

First, the analysis has shown that for various reasons there may be an actual reduction in resource transfer from the debtor country as a result of the facility – i.e. the debtor country may actually gain something. Indeed, in the view of some this is the primary objective of the exercise. An expectation of such a gain would lead also to an expectation of lower taxation than otherwise – including taxation of profits and capital – and this may well encourage new investment.

Second, if the debt held by the facility does not

acquire senior rights, so that the discount in the market falls as described earlier, there should indeed be a tendency for investment inflows to resume or to increase. The facility will have assumed some of the burden of potential default on the existing debt, and new investors will have a lesser burden to bear than before.

Finally, the matter is not so simple if the existing debt is subordinated to the facility's debt. The question then is whether new debt incurred in the market would also be subordinated, or whether it would acquire seniority over the facility's debt. The reasonable assumption is that the facility would enjoy complete seniority. As noted above, in the absence of increased certainty, subordination would actually reduce the market price (raise the discount) owing to the 'ceiling effect'; hence new investment would be further discouraged. If all old debt had been sold to the facility, in effect new debt would then be completely subordinated to old debt.

IS THERE REALLY NEED FOR AN INTERNATIONAL FACILITY?

A central question remains. One might grant the desirability of a reduction in the contractual value of the debt but still wonder why an intermediary in the form of a facility along the lines proposed would be needed.

Although banks can sell the developing countries' debts in the market at a discount, bank managements may not feel free to grant outright relief in the form of reduction of the contractual value, possibly because of legal obstacles. In practice, however, relief in the form of long-term debt rescheduling and various debt transformations can be and has been granted – although such arrangements are different from reducing contractual value. One could also argue that there is no incentive for any private holder to grant relief because of the ceiling effect. There is always the possibility that the full contractual value will be repaid, so why forgo this possibility? Incentive for relief may be created, however, by the threat of more severe default.

One can think of three arguments in favour of the establishment of a facility from the points of view of the banks and the debtor countries involved.

A channel for resource transfer

The most obvious argument from the point of view of both parties is that the facility could act as a channel for the transfer of current resources (i.e. aid) from the countries that underwrite it, or for the possible transfer of future resources if some default risk is perceived. This, of course, is also an argument *against* a facility from the point of view of its potential owners if they are not interested in providing aid either in general or specifically to the debtor countries. This point will be taken up again below.

If foreign aid to the debtor countries is indeed intended, one alternative could be for the parties to negotiate debt relief contracts bilaterally and then for some or all of the industrial countries to guarantee the marked-down debts in part or in full. This arrangement would give particular industrial countries an opportunity to help those debtors that are of special interest to them. The familiar difficulty here is that the banks are not a single 'party', as the problems of organizing concerted lending have shown.

For the debtor countries the other alternative is to receive direct bilateral aid. The aid could be used by the debtor country to buy back some of its own debt. Again, there would be an opportunity for industrial countries to discriminate in favour of particular debtor countries. But the fundamental question is highlighted in that case: are funds received in aid best spent in buying back debt? They could perhaps be better used to finance extra investment.

A more orderly process

It could be argued that, if world economic conditions turned adverse, the alternative to the operation of such a facility would be a decentralized process of debt restructuring with relief. In that situation numerous bilateral arrangements – with the banks represented by committees that have difficulty in getting support from sufficient banks – could get rather disorderly. The facility could be an intermediary that would bring more orderliness to the process. An element of automaticity and consistency across countries and kinds of debt in the choice of purchase prices, the extent of relief and so on could smooth the restructuring and debt relief process. The facility might thus avoid default crises that could lead to political difficulties and disruption of trade flows.

Greater realism and certainty

A key feature of such proposals is that very uncertain obligations, with contractual values well above what is expected to be paid on a probability basis, would be replaced by more realistically valued debt that (in the view of proponents) would be more certain to be repaid and, ideally, would be free of serious default risk.

It might be argued that the increase in certainty (if it could be obtained) is in general desirable even though, to an extent at least, it does shift the burden of exogenous uncertainty (for example, in the terms of trade) back toward the debtor countries. This is possibly a gain because some uncertainty is believed to be endogenous – a result of the lack of firm political will by debtor governments rather than capacity-to-pay uncertainty. Then there is a role for conditionality and, hence, for the Fund or the World Bank. This does not necessarily mean that the two institutions or their owners should, through the facility, take on the remaining risks.

One negative point is also important. It refers not to the actual operation of a facility but to the effects of expectations that it might come into operation. It concerns a moral hazard problem. If the banks and the debtor countries believe that there is some chance that an institution such as the facility might be established to take over some of the risks, they will have less incentive to arrive at debt relief agreements directly or without disruption. The threat of disruption, particularly of trade flows, could be an inducement leadig the international community to establish such a facility. But if such an institution were never seen as being even a possibility, the parties directly involved would have an incentive to arrive at agreements. They would try to avoid prolonged uncertainty and disruption because it is damaging to them all.

IS ANY COMPULSION INVOLVED?

To what extent would such a scheme be voluntary? I first consider the debtor country and then the creditors.

On the debtor

On the one hand, if conditionality were not involved, a debtor country would have nothing to lose in the short run from debt relief through the medium of the facility. But in the long run it might lose some creditworthiness, since future creditors may well think that what has happened once can happen again. Therefore a debtor government, confident that it will be able to repay the full contractual value of its debt and wanting to take a long view, may benefit from staying out of the scheme. This is true even though there may be a market discount on its debt that suggests that, so far, the debtor country has not been able to convey its confidence to the market.

On the other hand, if conditionality were part of the scheme, then each debtor country could decide whether it preferred to accept the burdens of conditionality and get debt relief through the facility or whether it preferred to stay out. There would not need to be any compulsion.

On the creditor

Each bank could be free to sell or to keep as much as it liked of the debt it holds at present. Sales of debt need not be compulsory. As described here, the facility would operate in the market, even though this is not a feature of all proposals. But this freedom of the banks to sell or not to sell could be somewhat illusory. The willingness to sell will be influenced by the debtors' actions. A decision by the debtor government to subordinate debt that is not sold would lower the market price – as would threats of, or actual, default. Furthermore, changes in bank regulations in creditor countries that reduced the attractiveness to banks of holding on to debt could also increase the willingness to sell to the facility.

CONCLUDING REMARKS

From the viewpoint, first, of a debtor country, the availability of an international debt facility cannot be harmful to it because it cannot be compelled to participate and, if use of the facility is associated with conditionality, as is usually proposed, it may choose not to. But, for the reasons given in the sixth section, a debtor country is quite likely to gain from participation.

From the viewpoint of creditors, the banks would gain if sales of debt to the facility were truly voluntary, if there were no subordination of debt that is not sold to the facility, and if the moral hazard problems discussed in the sixth section were overcome. Otherwise the banks could lose. It has been noted that the moral hazard problem might be overcome by determining purchase prices of debt on some objective basis or on the basis of market prices at an early 'cut-off' point. But this can present some of the most difficult practical problems involved with the establishment of a debt facility.

Finally, and most crucial, there are the interests of the potential owners or underwriters of the facility to consider. If the facility would purchase a significant part of the commercial debt of all the developing countries that currently have problems – as is suggested in many of the proposals – a large transfer of risk internationally from private banks to the underwriting governments or multilateral institutions would take place. The extent of the transfers would depend on the detailed arrangements that have been discussed here. Of course a facility could operate on a small scale, but then it would only make a small impact on the world debt situation.

The potential owners may see some benefit in increasing certainty (which might be brought about by the debt relief process combined with conditionality) and in avoiding a disorderly process of debt restructuring, default and so on (as discussed in the ninth section). Furthermore, the owners may wish to provide aid to particular debtors or assistance to particular banks, although a generalized facility is not the best way of doing this. But it is inevitable that, by underwriting the obligations that the facility issues, the owner governments would assume some risk even when the debt not sold to the facility is subordinated to that held by the facility, and even more so without subordination.

NOTES

1 As far as I am aware, the first proposals of this general kind were advanced by Felix Rohatyn in *Business Week* (28 February 1983) and by Peter Kenen in *The New York Times* (6 March 1983). The proposal has been made by Sachs and Huizinga (1987) and by Percy Mistry, formerly of the World Bank (in *The Banker*, September 1987). In 1988 proposals of this general nature were made by Dr Sengupta, an Executive Director of the Fund, and by James Robinson, Chairman of American Express. There is an analysis of this kind of proposal in Feldstein and others (1987). The Omnibus Trade and Competitiveness Act of 1988, passed by both houses of the US Congress, included a provision for the Secretary of the Treasury to 'study the feasibility and advisability' of establishing an 'International Debt Management Authority'.

2 This discussion builds on Dooley (1988).

3 In several papers Paul Krugman has discussed the uncertainty aspects; see especially Krugman (1985).

4 The example that has been used is quite simplified, although sufficient to make the main points. As noted earlier, repayment is thought of as a single sum ($600, when there is certainty) paid in a single future period, the sum consisting of principal and interest combined. The analysis could be elaborated to allow for a stream of interest and amortization payments over time, in which case the sum should be thought of as the present value. There is then scope for changes in the time profile of payments. In that case a distinction between interest and

principal would have to be made. Debt relief may have an immediate effect in reducing interest payments, even though, if capacity to pay in total is really fixed, interest or amortization payments will increase later. Changes in the time profile of either interest or amortization payments that do not alter the present value leave the analysis presented above unchanged. The market discount is caused not only by the probability of default or forced debt relief as usually understood but also by the probability of forced rescheduling, pressures to participate in new money packages and so on. These are all ways of changing the time profile and reducing the present value of repayments.

5 An issue that is clearly important for the various proposals is whether it would be legally possible for existing debt that is retained by the banks to be subordinated to that acquired by the facility. Of course there would be no difficulty in such subordination if it were done with the agreement of the banks.

6 There may be a touch of perversity in the ceiling effect brought about by debt relief. Whenever capacity to pay improves exogenously – owing, for example, to a terms-of-trade improvement – some of the gains inevitably go to the debtor even before debt relief (i.e. when the ceiling is high). Similarly, some of the losses from a deterioration would be borne by the debtor, and not wholly by the creditors. In that case, lowering the ceiling as a result of debt relief increases the gains for the debtor when events, such as the terms of trade, turn out well but does not help when events turn out badly.

7 There is an important qualification to this argument. If the debtor country's government takes the long view, it will realize that debt relief through the facility or otherwise – even though entirely voluntary on the part of the creditors and in no way associated with actual default – could still have an adverse effect on its country's future creditworthiness. After all, when investors look back they will see that a $1,000 loan finally turned out to be worth less, for whatever reason. The government will never have the opportunity to show that it would have paid the full initial contractual value.

8 All this should be thought of in present value terms. See note 4.

REFERENCES

Dooley, M. P. (1988) 'Buy-backs and market valuation of external debt', *IMF Staff Papers* 35 (June): 215–29.

Feldstein, M. and others (1987) 'Restoring growth in the debt-laden Third World: a task force report to the Trilateral Commission', Triangle Papers, Report 33, New York: The Trilateral Commission.

Krugman, P. R. (1985) 'International debt strategies in an uncertain world', in G. Smith and J. Cuddington (eds) *International Debt and the Developing Countries*, pp. 79–100.

Sachs, J. and Huizinga, H. (1987) 'U.S. commercial banks and the developing country crisis', *Brookings Papers on Economic Activity* 2: 555–601.

26

BEYOND THE DEBT CRISIS
Alternative forms of financing growth
Donald R. Lessard

As the debt crises of developing countries continue with no end in sight, the structure and aggregate amount of these countries' obligations are receiving increasing attention. A structure of obligations dominated by general-obligation floating rate borrowing is far from ideal (Lessard and Williamson 1985; Krugman 1988) and has contributed to the severity of the crisis. The alternatives in resolving the crisis are receiving even greater attention, but with much less agreement. Debt–equity swaps and other variants that combine debt buybacks with alternative forms of finance, typically voluntary exchanges, are held out as the leading way out of the crisis by institutional observers, bankers, private sector groups in developing countries and a few academics (see, for example, Ganitsky and Lema 1988; Regling 1988). But such exchanges are typically depicted as inconsequential or even damaging to the interests of developing countries by many academic economists and developing-country officials (see, for example, Bulow and Rogoff 1988; Dornbusch 1988; Krugman 1988; Froot 1989).

Much of this debate rests on the false premise that one must choose between debt conversion and debt reduction. It is true that the champions of conversion programmes include banks that seek to maintain the value of their claims (see, for instance, Institute of International Finance 1989) and that much of the opposition to such programmes comes from developing countries and others who believe that substantial debt reduction is in order. But there is no logical or institutional reason that a reduction in debt should not be

accompanied by improved efficiency of the claims structure or that conversion somehow precludes reduction. Although the conversion of developing-country general obligations into alternative forms can take place through voluntary debt conversions, it can also occur through negotiated exchanges involving all lenders and through separate new-money packages. Therefore, it is inappropriate to associate the potential shortcomings and abuses of voluntary exchanges with alternative forms of finance.

This chapter therefore focuses on the alternatives to general-obligation finance in the inevitable restructuring of Latin American countries' obligations, whether or not this restructuring includes much debt reduction.

WHAT IS 'ALTERNATIVE' FINANCE?

Commercial alternatives to general-obligation finance are defined here as finance that involves *ex ante* risk sharing in particular projects or enterprises or in the borrowing country's portfolio and, in many cases, a corresponding sharing of responsibility and control. Although this broad definition includes modes of finance ranging from non-recourse project lending to direct foreign investment, it is narrower than commercial finance that includes all modes of finance that bear commercial terms (i.e. everything but concessional finance) or that involve a private lender, a private borrower, or both.

This definition excludes many types of financing that private lenders can provide on commercial terms. The types excluded are most forms of general-obligation financing, including traditional LIBOR-linked floating rate debt and fixed interest rate bonds, note issuance facilities and so on, whose service does not depend directly on outcomes within the borrowing country. But the definition does include contingent general obligations with terms indexed to factors that influence the borrowing country's ability to pay, like commodity prices or indices of external economic activity or industrial production in industrial countries.

The analysis emphasizes alternatives that provide gains to creditors and debtors, in contrast with those that simply shift the burden from one group to the other. In technical terms, this implies an emphasis on completing markets that currently function poorly or not at all. This emphasis calls for an assessment of why markets currently are not complete along the relevant dimensions – in particular, which political and institutional factors act as obstacles to various alternative financing modes.

WHY CONSIDER ALTERNATIVE FINANCE?

Alternatives to general-obligation borrowing are sought because these resources simply will not be sufficient to meet developing-country needs. But developing countries' financial problems are not because of limitations on the supply of international finance. Instead, they reflect the limited ability of particular developing countries to contract credibly for sufficient external finance, especially given the already substantial debt overhang that many countries face.[1]

The financing requirements of developing countries are small relative to the world capital markets. Even an ambitious figure of $20 billion a year is less than 10 per cent of the current net debt financing provided by the OECD markets and institutions. Individual countries face a virtually elastic supply on the condition that they make credible commitments to meet the terms of their obligations.[2] Therefore, tapping new funds should not be expected to increase greatly the supply of

funds to a particular country. A country can increase its actual supply of funds (or reduce the degree of debt relief required to put it back on a current basis), however, by recontracting in a way that shifts the promised payments across future circumstances and therefore expands the commitments it can back with credibility. So, the focus here is not the size of external financial markets or these markets' appetite for developing-country assets; instead it is how commercial alternatives to general-obligation finance can increase the actual funds to these countries, reduce the burden of external financing and improve the performance of the assets financed.

The goal of restructuring a country's obligations and recapitalizing its economy is to restore acceptable growth in the short run and provide the basis for dynamic long-run development involving domestic and foreign private interests. The main reasons for changing the amount and the structure of financing are as follows:

1   to reduce the 'overhang' of senior obligations (official and commercial bank debt) that distort public and private economic incentives within the country and preclude new, junior claims (project financing, direct investment, local equity investment) and that limit the explicit and implicit costs to debtors of current or potential future non-compliance;

2   to match more closely countries' obligations with their ability to pay (e.g. commodity prices and interest rates), thereby increasing the potential value of their obligations (and the costs of non-compliance); and

3   to rearrange the allocation of risks, rewards and responsibilities among agents to increase diversification and participation.

MODES OF ALTERNATIVE COMMERCIAL FINANCING

The many alternatives to general-obligation borrowing for obtaining external finance can be classified in three ways: expected cost, degree of risk sharing or hedging and degree of managerial participation in financed enterprise.

The expected cost has three components: the required expected return to investors, which may be substantially less than the promised rate in risky obligations; the deadweight cost or penalty in non-performance; and the monitoring and control costs associated with particular forms of finance. The required expected return to investors is determined by an international CAPM in which the risk premium is an increasing function of the covariance of this cost or return with aggregate world consumption; i.e. a world consumption β.[3] Therefore, short-term floating rate obligations or price-level-indexed obligations, with returns largely independent of variations in aggregate output, will command minimal investor risk premia.[4] But copper-linked bonds that have a significant positive covariance with aggregate output will require a substantial risk premium. A broadly diversified portfolio of local equities, though, will command only a slightly higher cost than floating rate debt since empirical analyses show that they are close to zero-β assets with respect to external factors.

The enforceability of sovereign credit depends on the lenders' ability to impose penalties for non-performance (see, for example, Eaton et al. 1986). These penalties generally result in deadweight costs, since the cost to borrowers is not offset by a corresponding gain to lenders. But there is no similar accepted model of deadweight costs associated with non-performance, nor are there any estimates of its magnitude.[5] It is assumed that expected deadweight costs depend on two factors: the expected non-performance and the ability of lenders to distinguish between bad luck and bad faith on the part of borrowers from meeting their commitments on particular claims. Therefore, these deadweight costs will be highest for non-contingent general obligations, especially floating rate obligations that enhance the probability of default through adverse interest rate movements.

Monitoring costs depend on the amount and frequency of information and influence required to enforce claims. At this stage it is assumed only that the costs are equal for all general obligations and higher for claims that penetrate the economy and thus may require information and influence at the level of firms or projects.

Risk sharing refers to the extent to which the contractual obligation is linked explicitly to some aspect of the borrower's economic situation and thus shifts risks in the domestic economy to the world economy. Equity investment, for instance, entitles the investor to a pro rata share of the profits of a particular firm, while commodity-linked bonds or export participation notes perform the same role for the whole economy. This attribute is most valuable to a borrower when the risks that are shifted contribute significantly to the variability of income or the availability of foreign exchange, or both – in other words, risks that are systematic at a local level. Outstanding examples are countries whose exports are dominated by one or two primary products, like Chile (copper), Malaysia (tin, palm oil) or Mexico, Nigeria and Venezuela (oil). Whether a particular contingent obligation provides national risk sharing depends on its covariance with national aggregate consumption or overall net foreign exchange transfers.[6]

Hedging is accomplished when financing terms are selected to minimize the borrower's exposure to adverse fluctuations in finance resulting from shifts in external economic variables, such as interest rates and exchange rates. Hedging can occur by purchasing options or by swap contracts. Using either of these instruments, the borrower can manage risk independently of the supply of capital.

Managerial participation or control refers to the extent of private agents' participation in the selection of investments and their management. With the exception of the World Bank, this participation is almost non-existent for general-obligation lenders. It will be greatest when there are claims contingent on the outcomes of particular projects or firms such as equities, quasi-equities, commercial bonds or project loans.

The positions along these dimensions of various alternatives, including general-obligation financing, direct foreign investment, portfolio equity investment (both in individual shares and in national funds), quasi-equity investment and project lending, are shown in Figure 26.1.

General-obligation financing, at the origin, provides the benchmark for the analysis. On an *ex ante* basis it offers the lowest cost, but it also involves no *ex ante* risk sharing or managerial involvement. Direct foreign investment typically has a higher expected cost, but it also combines risk sharing with managerial control of investments and, often, a substantial international integration of operations. Other alternatives typically are more focused in the dimensions that they provide. Commodity bonds, for instance, provide risk sharing but no managerial involvement, but portfolio equity and quasi-equity investment – where the lender is entitled to an income stream that depends in some well-defined way on the success of the project but with a narrow claim to participate in ownership or control – shares risks and responsibilities but over a narrower range of outcomes than direct investment.

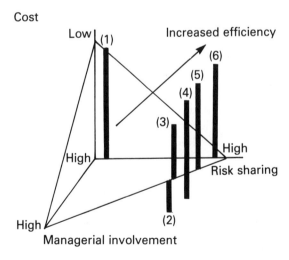

Figure 26.1 Modes of commercial finance: (1) general obligation; (2) direct foreign investment; (3) portfolio foreign investment (individual shares); (4) quasi-equity; (5) portfolio foreign investment (country fund); (6) commodity bond

ALTERNATIVE FINANCIAL INSTRUMENTS

Direct investment, the traditional alternative to sovereign borrowing, entitles the investor to a pro rata share of the distributed profits of the firm. It is typically motivated by the return the parent company expects to earn by using its existing know-how in a local operation and by incorporating the local operation in its global production and marketing network. Thus it responds largely to firm-specific, microeconomic factors and to macroeconomic prospects in the host country. In some cases, however, direct investment also overcomes limits to the enforceability of other cross-border claims posed by country risk or without the necessary local institutions.

Portfolio investment in equities quoted on public stock markets, like direct investment, entitles the investor to a share in the profits of private enterprise. Unlike the direct investor, however, the equity investor typically is seeking only a share of profits and not the responsibilities of control. Many equity investors deliberately restrict their holdings to a small percentage of the total stock (less than 5 per cent) to maintain liquidity and avoid being forced to take responsibility for saving the firm if they lose confidence in its management.

Portfolio equity investment can involve varying penetration of the domestic economy. The least penetrating mode, popular in many developing countries, is the offshore investment trust (closed-end fund) that invests in a broadly diversified portfolio of domestic shares. Other more penetrating modes involve investments in individual shares, either through offshore listings of developing-country firms or local purchases of locally listed shares. Although portfolio investment is typically defined as involving little or no managerial control, this can vary substantially. A national index fund may or may not participate in the governance of the firms in which it invests. But if it does, the general practice is to separate the nationality of ownership and control by appointing a local investment management firm to represent shareholder interests.

As opposed to direct investment, quasi-equity investments allow for separation of risk sharing and managerial control. These new forms of international investment include joint ventures, licensing agreements, franchising, management contracts, turnkey contracts, production sharing and international subcontracting.[7] They permit the host country to single out the particular features controlled by the foreign enterprise that cannot economically be obtained elsewhere and to contract for those without allowing foreign control of the domestic operation.

Non-recourse project or stand-alone finance provides another way to shift risks and responsibility to foreign investors by linking borrowing to particular enterprises or projects without a general guarantee. In such cases, the lender is exposed to the downside risks of the undertakings being financed, but in contrast to equity or quasi-equity claims, does not share in the upside potential. From the borrower's perspective, such financing can be thought of as borrowing at a rate that is independent of the project's success and purchasing insurance to service the debt if the project fails. It may also involve earmarking project revenues for servicing the project borrowing. Therefore, the lender would require a higher promised interest rate on such loans than on general obligations.[8]

Just as equities or quasi-equities linked to particular projects or firms transfer some or all of the risks of those undertakings to investors, contingent general obligations do the same for the country. A country that is heavily dependent on, say, oil or copper revenues could issue commodity-linked bonds. With such bonds, debt service would remain a sovereign obligation with the implied enforcement leverage, but the debt service under any circumstances would be determined by the commodity's price.

POTENTIAL BENEFITS OF ALTERNATIVE FINANCE

Since most alternative modes of finance involve somewhat higher expected costs than floating rate,

general-obligation borrowing, why should borrowers prefer them? The key reasons are that these alternatives are often more attractive in terms of their distribution of costs over time and across circumstances and in terms of their incentive effects and interactions with local financial markets. In contrast to expected cost, which by definition is a zero-sum game between lenders and borrowers, these dimensions can give rise to positive-sum combinations.[9]

Time profile of debt service

Other things being equal, a borrowing country will prefer financial instruments with a time profile of repayment obligations matching the profile of resources available for debt service. The rule of thumb is that long-term projects should be financed by loans with equivalent maturities, while current trade activities can be financed with short-term obligations. But for countries, the matching should be in terms of ability to pay at the aggregate level, which has little to do with the maturity of the assets being financed. In practice, the matching of the time profile of obligation with that of debt-servicing capacity requires spreading debt service equally over periods where foreign exchange surpluses or ready access to new financing (or both) are anticipated. It requires, in particular, avoiding the bunching of maturities. Debt rescheduling has transformed the obligations of most developing countries into perpetuities, leaving little room for further gains on this dimension. The time matching of developing countries' obligations could still be improved by recontracting on a price-level-indexed basis, thus transforming a nominal annuity into a real one. Automatic capitalization of the inflation portion of the nominal interest rate would serve roughly the same purpose.[10]

Profile of costs across circumstances

All investment involves risk taking. When a developing country finances an investment project by incurring debt, it implicitly accepts all the risks of the activity being financed. Losses can be passed on to the lender only by default or the threat of default – a strategy that typically involves deadweight costs.

An oil-producing country, for instance, might consider financing its needs either with general-obligation borrowing or with a share of its oil income. With general-obligation borrowing it would be committing itself to repay foreign exchange that is independent of the condition of the domestic economy.[11] Thus, the same debt service will be due when foreign exchange is scarce as when it is not. In general-obligation bank borrowing or floating rate notes, the borrower promises to pay a specified spread over short-term market rates regardless of circumstances. When the upswings in interest rates and thus debt service coincide with a deterioration of the borrower's overall foreign exchange situation (either because the factors giving rise to these swings tend to coincide with factors depressing demand for its exports or because of its other interest-bearing foreign obligations), such financing will involve large payments when foreign exchange is scarcest. In contrast, if servicing obligations take the form of a share of net foreign exchange earnings, repayments will be smallest when foreign exchange is scarcest, and vice versa. Obligations keyed to a country's capacity to pay are less costly in terms of its well-being, and thus the country should be willing to pay a somewhat higher expected cost for such financing.

Borrowing with an interest rate cap might be more costly, since lenders would charge a risk premium for the interest rate insurance implicit in the cap. But it might have less impact on the borrowing country, since payments would be limited in periods where market rates are very high and, as a result, the borrower is under great financial pressure. The expected cost of financing a particular activity with equity will probably be even higher, but its *ex ante* 'cost' to the borrowing country might be comparable or lower than the cost of bank credit since the largest payments would probably be due when times are good for the borrowing country. Over the past decade, the cumulative return to investors on private equity holdings in many highly indebted countries, including Brazil and Mexico, has been substantially less than that of general-obligation loans.[12]

Because borrowing countries and investors who participate in world capital markets are exposed to different risks, they will possess comparative advantage in bearing particular risks. The economies of Mexico, Indonesia and Nigeria, for instance, are much more vulnerable to shifts in energy prices than the world economy is. This comparative advantage will be reflected in the premium demanded by world investors for bearing oil price risks. It will be substantially lower than the premium that oil exporters should be willing to pay to avoid the risks. Thus these oil exporters can gain by reducing some of the risks through financing arrangements. In contrast, oil importers such as Brazil or the Republic of Korea would benefit from financing arrangements that relate debt service inversely to oil prices.

Because of domestic rigidities, developing countries can find themselves short of foreign exchange, which gives them a greater effective exposure to variations in real and nominal interest rates than industrial country borrowers or lenders.[13] This exposure will be reinforced since variations in world interest rates or the exchange rates of borrowed currencies accentuate the volatility of their foreign exchange earnings before debt service. As a result, developing countries, other things being equal, will benefit from financial terms that limit their exposure to such variations.

Once the question of cost is extended to one of how the costs are distributed across circumstances, appropriate terms for borrowing vary with the specific conditions of countries. The general rule is that a particular country should finance itself on terms that balance its existing external exposures. For example, a country where a few commodities make up a significant fraction of GNP or exports – relative to the role of these commodities in the world economy – should seek to shift the risks of these commodities to world financial markets. A country that has a high negative exposure to short-term interest rates because of heavy borrowing should seek forms of financing with fixed or capped interest rates.

Performance incentives

In addition to shifting risks, and thus stabilizing a borrower's net income (and wealth), finance with costs linked to specified circumstances may have important macro or micro level incentive effects that can increase a country's income or reduce its variability. Most debt literature focuses on incentive effects of external borrowing on the macroeconomic choices of the borrowing country. A large debt overhang, for example, makes the country less willing to forgo current consumption to invest, since it will suffer the full current loss but will capture only a fraction of the potential future benefits. These effects can be either exacerbated or ameliorated by alternative modes of finance. They are most important when there is a large debt overhang.

Incentives also apply to lenders, often whether or not there is a debt overhang. When financing takes the form of a general obligation, the lender has little stake in the success of the project financed and thus has little motivation for intervening in its design or management. In contrast, when debt service obligations are linked to the outcomes of specific projects or undertakings, with limited recourse to a country's general credit, foreign lenders or investors obtain a stake in the success of the project. This linkage can improve performance and reduce risk when lenders or investors have some control over variables crucial to a project's success. For example, if all or part of the yield on an obligation is tied to the performance of the project financed, the lender–investor has a greater interest in seeking appropriate project design with satisfactory management. Similarly, if the obligations of a borrowing country are linked to its volume of manufactured exports, lenders will have a greater interest in assuring that country's continued access to markets for its products. But if the potential lenders do not have control over variables relevant to the project's success, the main incentive impact of linking debt service obligations

to outcomes is an improvement in the credit analysis undertaken before the loan is made. In the extreme case where the project will not generate returns sufficient to service the debt, lenders will not provide any finance on a project basis, and thus the project will be killed.

The incentive effects on investors of any financial contract depend on its specificity. Because an equity share is specific to a particular firm, it gives investors an incentive to prove that firm's success. Because a production-share or risk-service contract (typically employed on oil and gas projects) links investor returns to a narrower measure of project success, it focuses incentives on managing those dimensions appropriately. General-obligation borrowing, in contrast, is not linked to any particular project or risk dimension and so provides lenders with a stake only in a country's overall foreign exchange situation.

When a foreign investor can enhance the value of an undertaking through its knowledge base or access to markets, some stakeholding will be beneficial. But in cases where domestic policy choices are the primary determinant of project success or failure, foreign participants will be exposed to opportunistic behaviour by the host government. Self-serving government policies will tend to confound the incentives facing the foreign investor and reduce the contract credibility. Since most activities involve both types of risks, it can be beneficial to separate them in contracting.

Impact on local financial markets and domestic savings

International finance can never be more than a complement to domestic savings. It will be available on the best terms, and employed most effectively, when it is accompanied by healthy domestic capital formation. A major problem in many developing countries is insufficient capital formation. Capital flight has been a principal contributor to a number of countries' external financial crises. This poor record reflects unattractive climates for domestic savings, including poor macroeconomic prospects, high taxes and regulations limiting investment; discrimination against domestic savings such as repressed interest rates and the threat of changes in inflation or other forms of default on implicit financial contracts; and macroeconomic policy distortions, especially in foreign exchange markets. It also reflects underinvestment, in many cases, in the institutional infrastructure required for financial deepening.

International finance in the form of general-obligation borrowing has allowed developing-country governments to bypass local financial markets. As a result, many of the policy measures necessary to stimulate domestic capital formation have been neglected. Certain forms of international finance, in contrast, especially portfolio investment in corporate equities and bonds, rely on domestic markets and therefore will be successful only as these markets flourish. If such claims are held by both foreign and domestic investors, each will provide the other with leverage in their respective policy contexts, increasing the security of these claims.

Completeness of local markets and potential benefits of external finance

Optimal external finance depends to a large extent on the completeness of a country's internal capital markets and the interaction between the structure of finance and micro or macro level economic outcomes. The simplest case exists when the domestic market is complete because it provides for full diversification of risks within the local economy – i.e. all risks are spread proportionally among all investors – and either the structure of finance has no micro level incentive effects or they are dealt with optimally within the national market. In this case, the sole benefit of international finance will be to align real interest rates with world rates and to diversify national risks. The risk-sharing benefit can be obtained through the issue of shares in a national index fund and does not require alternatives that penetrate the domestic economy.[14]

The more realistic case is where the domestic market is not complete and where the trade-off

between risk diversification and incentives is far from optimal. In this case, foreign commercial finance can serve to complete the local market and to create appropriate micro level incentives. The precise benefits depend on the departure from this ideal and the costs involved in terms of unnecessary risks that are borne, inefficiencies in project selection and management and socially profitable transactions that are not undertaken as a result of these departures.

OBSTACLES TO ALTERNATIVE MODES OF FINANCE

Even if alternative modes of finance are desirable for economic efficiency, they are not necessarily feasible. They generally are harder to enforce across national boundaries than general obligations and require specific domestic legal and institutional infrastructure. An obligation to pay a share of foreign exchange earnings, for instance, is ideal in matching a country's payments with its capacity to pay. But because foreign exchange earnings are both hard to define and subject to the borrowing country's actions, this kind of contract presents moral hazard of a degree that makes it unlikely that finance would be available. Similarly, when portfolio equity shifts firm-level risks to investors, it is an open-ended contract that relies on a body of company and securities law that few developing countries possess to protect minority investors against conveyance by insiders. Further, when alternative modes of finance penetrate the national economy they can impair national sovereignty, reduce the role of the state and, perhaps, reduce the rents of privileged domestic capital suppliers. Thus they will probably be opposed by various national constituencies.

Country risk

Financial contracts across national boundaries face a risk hierarchy. All contracts, except those involving a legal set-aside of specified foreign exchange earnings, are exposed to transfer risk – the risk that the country will not have or make available the foreign exchange to service the debt. Equity investments or loans to specific companies or projects are also subject to the commercial risks of the firm or project and country-policy risks. These commercial risks include changes in market conditions, costs and technology, and elements at least partly under managerial control. Policy exposures include measures that the country can adopt in managing its economy or policy measures of other countries. Examples are the austerity measures adopted by developing countries in response to their debt crises, which have thrown many local firms into severe financial crises. Protectionist policies also threaten export markets. Thus, in many cases, there is no clear dividing line between country and commercial risks.[15]

The greater exposure of alternative modes of finance to various country risks is a result of at least four factors. First, since they are subject to a wider variety of policy impacts, non-performance is significantly harder to define than with general obligations. Second, since they typically create divergent risk–return profiles among investors, they undermine the formation or functioning of lender cartels that underlie the enforceability of cross-border contracts. Third, in part because of the second factor, they typically are implicitly subordinated to general-obligation claims, exacerbating the conflict among various classes of claimants. Fourth, because of this conflict, they face an increased likelihood of opportunism by the borrowing country.

Because of these heightened exposures to country risks, investors in alternative obligations will seek to protect the obligations against transfer risk and give them the same status as those of scheduled creditors. Some export-oriented projects protect the export proceeds by putting them in escrow. In some cases this could even enable a country to borrow on better terms for a stand-alone project than would be possible for general obligations, despite the fact that the lender would be accepting the commercial risk of the project. This will generally be opposed by other creditors and violates the principle of not pledging specific assets or revenues to strengthen general obligations.[16]

Market-oriented projects that do not generate direct export revenues present a more complex problem. Even if financed on a limited recourse basis, they remain subject to transfer risk and, in many cases, to other risks emanating at least in part from domestic policy choices such as output pricing. These risks often inhibit financing from lenders who have the expertise to take on the commercial risks. Further, except in those cases where enforcement can be transferred to another jurisdiction through escrow mechanisms, there is a 'Catch 22' – the same factors that create these heightened exposures undermine the credibility of most steps that might be taken by the borrowing country to ameliorate them.

Most of these points apply to domestic and to foreign investors. If anything, domestic investors with their typically larger proportional exposures to the national economy are more subject to country risks than foreigners, a major factor in explaining the substitution of foreign for domestic capital accompanying capital flight.

Institutional preconditions

Most alternative modes of finance that penetrate the borrowing economy have institutional preconditions. First, the domestic legal system must provide effective enforcement of contractual terms, and private investors, especially foreign ones, must have access to that system and the sanctions it imposes. Portfolio equity investment, for instance, depends on the existence of a body of corporate and securities laws and practices that provide arm's-length minority shareholders with something like a pro rata participation in the benefits of the firms in which they invest.[17] These institutions, in turn, will only develop and function if the tax and regulatory environment does not discriminate against share ownership as opposed to direct investor control of enterprises. And to attract foreign investors, the country must be willing to allow them access to the country's market and to allow them to withdraw their funds when they feel that opportunities are better elsewhere.

The fact that new developing-country equity

funds have been launched over the past two years for many developing countries, including China, India, Malaysia, the Philippines, Korea, Thailand and Turkey, suggests that these obstacles can be overcome, and their market acceptance supports the view that the primary limiting factor is credible supply rather than demand. A further positive factor is that the steps required to attract foreign portfolio investment also improve the context for local equity investment.[18]

Direct investment, even in the form of cross-border joint ventures, typically does not rely to the same degree on local company law and is unaffected by securities legislation because of the linkages it creates through technology and product transfers. But direct investment remains exposed to policy risks, including steps that limit the parent company's discretion over local operations or constrains its ability to remit profits.

Quasi-equity contracts, since they are narrower and more explicit than equity contracts, may overcome some of these obstacles. They do not typically require the same sophisticated, capitalist, institutional infrastructure in the host country, and, since they generally expose investors only to certain relatively well-defined risks, they may be credible even when the investor has little or no control over the activity.

To see these differences, consider alternative arrangements that may be used for financing the development of oil reserves in a developing country. The key commercial risks in such an investment are the uncertainties regarding recoverable reserves, the price of oil in world markets and the operating costs of the field. But many risks involving the distribution of the gains between the two parties may make it difficult, if not impossible, to arrive at mutually agreeable contract terms. Such risks include obvious ones faced by the foreign producer of expropriation or some after-the-fact windfall profits taxes, but they also include risks faced by the host country like reservoir stripping or, perhaps, underproduction, and a boycott of output if a dispute occurs. Risks also expose the profitability of oil production of either party to general policy measures of the other (or, in the case of foreign investors, by their home country). These risks include exchange controls and changes in general tax policies.

With traditional direct or portfolio equity investment, the foreign investor faces the whole spectrum of these risks. This arrangement will be inefficient if such investors do not possess a comparative advantage relative to the host country in bearing those risks, either because investors' exposures to such risks are greater or because the risks involve a substantial element of moral hazard – i.e. the possibility that the host government will influence outcomes to its benefit but to the detriment of the foreign investor. The inefficiency and therefore the benefit of a more narrowly drawn risk contract naturally depend on the specific circumstances of each investment. Again, these arguments apply to domestic as well as foreign investors.

Political considerations

As with equity investment, many obstacles to increased quasi-equity flows lie in the policies of the developing countries. In many cases, alternatives have been spurned because of their perceived high cost. Although this may, in part, be justified because the supply of alternatives is not competitive, it also appears that many countries have underestimated the cost of the downside risks they have retained by financing projects with general-obligation borrowing.

That penetrating alternatives typically bypass the state, and so reduce its control over the internal allocation of resources, is another factor that has led borrower countries to resist them or at least favour general-obligation borrowing. As Frieden (1981) and others point out, increased state control over resources provided by sovereign borrowing was a major factor favouring its use. The same elements appear today in the debate over who should control the allocation of local resources should any portion of interest payments on sovereign debt be made in local currency.

Finally, of course, certain local private interests may also benefit from restrictions on inflows of penetrating finance. This is most probable when certain local groups have access to offshore markets on their own, while most firms are cut off form such flows.

Investor-country obstacles

Although most obstacles to alternative modes of finance lie in the policies and institutions of developing countries, significant obstacles have also been created through the policies and institutions of industrial countries. Tax laws and foreign investment insurance schemes in investor countries, for instance, favour direct investment over more limited contractual involvement, although the Overseas Private Investment Corporation (OPIC) and several European insurance schemes extend to contractual schemes that do not involve ownership. The World Bank confines itself exclusively to lending rather than taking risk positions, but it is now considering commodity-price-linked financing and cofinancing that support quasi-equity investment. The IFC has made quasi-equity investments in mining and forest products, but because of its mandate to finance only private sector undertakings these deals have typically been small.

ALTERNATIVE FINANCE WITH AN EXISTING DEBT OVERHANG

So far, we have focused on how a country should structure its external obligations if it were starting with a clean slate. But what about the desirability and feasibility of alternative modes of finance for countries with a debt overhang, where the current market value of their obligations is discounted from face value and access to new, voluntary financing is limited or non-existent? The presence of this overhang clearly complicates the analysis. It raises the tantalizing possibility of 'capturing' some of the discount, but at the same time it exacerbates the conflicts among various classes of claimants and changes borrowers' incentives on the overall structure of their obligations.[19]

Benefits of recontracting

The benefits of recontracting in ways that shift the circumstances under which payments are due and, possibly, the responsibility for specific activities can be examined in the context of the 'debt relief Laffer curve' that illustrates the trade-off between the face value of a country's obligations and their (discounted risk-adjusted) market value.[20] The debt relief Laffer curve (DRLC) in Figure 26.2(a) comprises two effects: the value of the debt assuming no incentive effects (DRLC*) that diverges from the 40° line as the possibility of non-payment increases, and an 'incentive wedge' that is responsible for the decline in the curve. This incentive wedge, in turn, reflects several effects. First, when the debt burden is large, a country has less incentive to make current sacrifices to improve its situation since a large part of the new income or resources generated will be captured by creditors. Second, a country is more likely to resort to 'taxes' on subordinated creditors, typically domestic

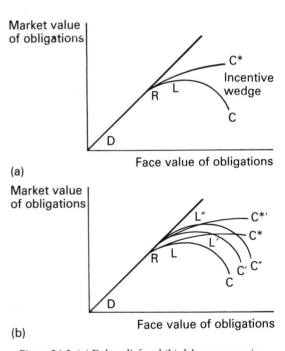

Figure 26.2 (a) Debt relief and (b) debt recontracting

504

depositors, bond holders and investors, to meet the claims of external senior creditors, and thus it acts to reduce their investment (see, for instance, Eaton 1987). Third, when the burden is large, a country is more likely to walk away from current obligations, implicitly choosing to relinquish some future international trade and finance possibilities.

The shape of the DRLC, however, is not independent of the way debt is structured. If, for example, debt is indexed to some exogenous variable that is positively related to a country's ability to pay, the 'no incentives' curve will shift up to DRLC*' (see Figure 26.2(b)) since a higher proportion of promised future payments will fall due under circumstances where the country can pay, and so the expected degree of non-payment will be smaller. Combined with the new incentive wedge, which will depend on the relative incentive effects of higher payments in good periods compared with lower ones in poor periods, this will yield a new overall curve, DRLC'.[21] Finally, if providing creditors (investors) with a direct participation in the risks and responsibilities of particular investments improves the selection and operation of these assets, restructuring to increase participation will lead to a further shifting of the curve to DRLC''.

If a debtor country could recontract by exchanging an efficient package of alternative obligations for all its existing general obligations with identical (pre-exchange) market values, it clearly would gain, and creditors would be indifferent. This is important, since without such an exchange, in moderately overhung countries there are no options to 'capture' discounts that are mutually desirable to creditors and debtors (Krugman 1988). And, if the exchange covers only some existing obligations, the benefit of the shifting DRLC would accrue to existing creditors and the country might actually be worse off.[22]

Concerted recontracting

A very strong case exists that borrowers and creditors would benefit from concerted recontracting that incorporates efficient alternatives to

floating rate general obligations. Mexico's 1986 proposal that would have linked some payments to oil prices, for example, would have benefited both parties if it could have been incorporated at a price that yielded lenders the same *ex ante* market value as the package they actually obtained. Under current circumstances, it is more probable that Mexico can achieve its desired reduction of current debt service and the desired face value of its obligations if it agrees to allow banks to recapture some of the concession if oil prices rise and to recycle some of the interest they forgo in the local currency to be invested or lent as they see fit. A possible mutual gain, of course, does not mean that recontracting will be easy because of the myriad conflicts and gaming behaviours present in the debt situation. In particular, creditors would have to grant the borrower some breathing space relative to the current debt service they would otherwise obtain to induce a borrower's commitment to greater payments than those implied by traditional obligations.

Voluntary recontracting

Voluntary recontracting can take two forms: exchanges of existing assets for penetrating financial claims (typically equity) with rights to the management and profits of particular assets; and exit bonds. Much of the apparent magic of debt–equity swaps (or exchanges involving any other alternative claim) disappears when they are broken down into their two component parts: a buyback of debt and a sale of equity with at least part of the secondary market discount being retained by the private parties to the transaction. The benefits of marginal buybacks (even at the secondary market price) are the subject of considerable dispute, with the conclusion that they are limited at best.

The wisdom of offering discounts on equity purchases depends primarily on whether they improve the aggregate investment base by encouraging new, economically beneficial investments that would not occur otherwise or by improving the efficiency of existing assets. Equity investors with strategic stakes in local firms will have incentives to improve their performance, and the improvement may be significant if the investors also bring the relevant expertise. This effect is likely to be greatest in cases where the conversion involves firms that have been controlled directly or indirectly by the local government. This benefit is not limited to takeovers by foreign firms. Domestic private investors may be able to do as well, with the additional benefit that they will add to the domestic political constituency for allowing a greater role for market forces.

Granting a discount also may be desirable if the exchange alters the aggregate structure of obligations in such a way as to induce an investor, for example, to accept a subordinated claim that will pay dividends only when, for instance, transferring some or all of the current debt discount to the new investment may be justified.[23] It must be recognized, however, that many debt–equity exchanges merely shuffle the asset ownership among investors and have no such potentially beneficial aggregate effects. Debt–equity exchanges also often result in such abuses as round-tripping. Nonetheless, debt–equity swaps can have indirect benefits by breaking the existing financial log-jam and focusing financial market interest on the country.

Many past debt–equity conversions seem to make little sense, even when converted through open auctions that recapture as much of the discount as possible. Foreign purchases of public utilities, in which there is no technology transfer by the new owners, little or no beneficial risk shifting and the possible increased conflicts between investors and the consuming public, appear to add little.[24] And the risk shifting and even incentive benefits do not require the full sale of assets in many cases. Intermediate quasi-equity investments will probably both improve the structure of a country's obligations and bring in foreign expertise when needed and will avoid some inevitable conflicts of foreign ownership.

Exit bonds and new financing

The key issue with exit bonds and new senior financing is that existing creditors will not typically grant the necessary waivers, since such waivers are tantamount to forgiving part of the debt. There are at least two cases in which the linkage of a buyback and the issuance of a new security can be mutually beneficial and thus overcome this obstacle. One is a buyback coupled with new project-linked finance; the other is a buyback coupled with the issuance of indexed exit bonds. For project financing, consider a country whose creditworthiness is too weak to sustain new general-obligation borrowing but which has a highly promising, export-oriented project whose development would be impossible without foreign finance. With stand-alone project financing (where project earnings are put in escrow to cover debt service), the project would go ahead and, at worse, the country would have no less free foreign exchange than it otherwise would have had, leaving the position of existing creditors unaffected. But if the project were successful, it would add to the supply of free foreign exchange and thus benefit the existing creditors. So the general creditors might waive their 'overhanging' senior claim to the project revenues to obtain the residual benefits.

The case with indexed debt is similar. Consider, for instance, bonds with substantially below-market interest rates offset by commodity-price-linked options. Such options could be sold successfully to non-bank third parties typically interested in such commodity plays only if they were senior to general-obligation debt. Because of the reduction in required debt service in 'bad' times, banks might grant such waivers, but they would not grant waivers to an equivalent new issue that did not involve a reduction in current debt service.

CONCLUSIONS: HOW TO GET THERE FROM HERE

Alternative modes of finance for developing countries including equity, quasi-equity and indexed general obligations offer major advantages of risk sharing and managerial participation over floating rate, general-obligation borrowing. The limited role they currently play in these countries' external financing shows a lack of awareness of these benefits, an assertion of state power and a series of obstacles to their issuance, including country risk and inadequate domestic institutional infrastructure. The debt crisis has underscored many of the benefits of alternatives, but little has been done to change the developing countries' financial structures because of the loss of access to voluntary finance, the preoccupation of banks and international institutions with maintaining the appearance of compliance with existing debt terms, the perverse borrower incentives created by the debt overhang and the heightened conflicts between classes of existing and prospective claimants.

After a review of the benefits and obstacles to alternative finance for a country that is starting with a clean financial slate, the general conclusions are as follows.

1 Any concerted refinancing arrangements should include recontracting along more efficient lines.
2 Despite the difficulties of marginal, voluntary exchanges in debt overhangs, carefully designed and managed programmes can result in significant mutual benefits.

In the case of concerted exchanges, the inclusion of alternative forms of finance that shift payments across circumstances can significantly close the gap between politically feasible levels of debt service and those that banks will demand. Voluntary exchanges should include debt–equity swaps and exchanges of existing government obligations for new obligations that are indexed to external variables (like commodity prices) or to some formula of profitability of domestic assets (like revenue bonds for fee-generating infrastructure).

Because of the obstacles to alternatives that existed before the debt crisis, this recontracting will not occur without significant changes in policies by creditor-country regulatory agencies, international financial institutions (IFIs), and the developing countries themselves.

Regulatory agencies

Restructuring through concerted new-money packages is largely the result of an accounting and regulatory system for US banks that allows them to operate with capital impaired by economic losses on developing-country loans – as long as banks do not 'realize' these losses through sales or swaps into alternative types of claims. Thus, the US government, through the deposit insurance and bank regulatory system, implicitly shares some of these banks' losses as long as they continue to hold the original obligations or their restructured equivalents. A step toward more efficient recontracting would be to allow banks to obtain similar benefits if they exchanged their holdings for alternative instruments. Creditor-country governments also apply much of the leverage required to put financing packages together, contending with conflicts and free-ridership among banks and opportunism on the part of borrowers. This leverage can and should be applied to support alternative approaches.

International financial institutions

International financial institutions, especially the IMF and the World Bank in its structural adjustment role, have worked in concert with holders of general obligations, often at the expense of foreign and domestic holders of alternative claims. Changing this role could be particularly useful in promoting quasi-equity investments and project lending that represent a middle ground between arm's-length and fully penetrating foreign finance. For example, with quasi-equity investments, the World Bank might extend its cofinancing programme to cover such operations. Alternatively, the IFC mandate might be broadened to allow it to take quasi-equity positions in government-sponsored projects that could be structured on a commercial, stand-alone basis. In addition, the World Bank or regional IFI might assist risk unbundling by enhancing such claims against transfer risk, perhaps by assigning some fraction of its net transfers to a country to a credit enhancement facility for designated claims.[25] This implicit shift of the benefits of such future financing from existing creditors to the new obligations would create a *de facto* seniority for these new claims without violating existing agreements. Thus, without a true risk-bearing capacity for the IFIs, they are not precluded from playing a role in supporting quasi-equity investments. Instead, the IFIs' strengths, and their preferred creditor position, make them ideal for bearing and mitigating transfer risk that can easily prevent such transactions from occurring.

For domestically oriented projects that provide no direct foreign exchange and that entail 'political performance risks', IFIs and investment guarantee authorities could do much to relieve this problem. An IFI, for instance, could include as project covenants the features and performance requirements that lenders need. Similarly, an IFI or a guarantee authority such as OPIC or the MIGA could provide guarantees against transfer risks. Such guarantees could be much narrower than those extended by the World Bank under its current cofinancing programmes and thus would allow greater specialization in risk taking.

Borrower governments

The first step for borrower governments is to recontract their debt and obtain relief through rescheduling, interest rate reductions or outright forgiveness. This may present them with a conflict, since moving to a more efficient structure of liabilities will reduce their bargaining power for relief. Thus they probably will not be the first to propose such recontracting, but they should be ready to make it a key element in their subsequent negotiations.

NOTES

1 This is not to deny that many developing countries, including the poorest countries in Latin America, face a debt relief and aid crisis where, regardless of how restructured, their obligations outweigh their ability to repay and voluntary external finance will not enable them to grow.

2 This result is from theoretical modes (see, for example, Eaton *et al.* 1986) and is supported by the fact that newly industrialized countries have been able to achieve very rapid growth in external financing in line with the growth of their economies.

3 Stulz (1981) derives an explicit international CAPM that links returns to assets' consumption βs.

4 Risk premia are defined here as in the financial econmics literature as increments in the expected return on an asset relative to the expected return on a zero-β asset, not as adjustments in promised rates to reflect anticipated defaults, as is common in the developing-country debt literature.

5 There is much uncertainty about the penalties a country will face when it does not meet its obligations. Most formal models assume that it will be relegated to financial and commercial autarky for at least some period. Many observers, though, argue that these penalties are much smaller (see, for example, Kaletsky 1985). Eichengreen and Portes (1989) infer from data from the 1920s through the 1950s that the differential impact of default on subsequent access to credit is small, but this inference is questionable since in the later period all developing countries went into commercial and financial autarky because of the world depression and the associated collapse of the international commercial and financial system.

6 A country's 'utility' will be a function of the level and variability of its overall consumption, assuming no distributional considerations. The impact of a particular obligation on this utility will depend on its contribution to the level and variability of net foreign transfers that influence consumption.

7 For a description of these instruments, see Lessard and Williamson (1985) and Oman (1984).

8 The exception would be where the lender is shielded from transfer risk by escrow arrangements that provide for debt service payments out of export proceeds before those are remitted to the host country.

9 The exception would be where a reduction in current interest rates, by reducing the probability of default, would increase the present value of lenders' claims.

10 Price-level-linked financing locks in a real interest rate, but inflation-adjusted nominal financing does not.

11 Floating rate borrowing, in fact, is likely to be more perverse since debt service will be greatest when nominal rates are highest, which is likely to coincide with periods of economic distress for developing countries.

12 Unpublished results provided by Vihang Errunza of McGill University.

13 This is equivalent to assuming that the country has a greater degree of risk aversion than the representative capital market agent.

14 To the extent that this diversification requires that a majority of risky assets be owned by foreign interests, the governance of these assets might be called into question. See Lessard (1988) for more on this point.

15 For a discussion of the nature and effects of country risk on general obligations, see Eaton *et al.* (1986). Lessard (1988) extends the analysis to alternative modes of finance.

16 There is an important difference between linking a claim to a specified outcome such as export proceeds and pledging such proceeds to back a non-contingent claim. Pledging assets presents the borrower with the worst of both worlds: the revenues of successful projects are encumbered and so not fully available to the national Treasury, whereas unsuccessful projects represent a drain on the Treasury. To set aside substantial components of foreign exchange earnings reduces a government's flexibility in difficult times and thereby reduces its overall creditworthiness.

17 A securities market is required as well. But the 'market' could be in a developed country, not where the firm is domiciled.

18 Even when portfolio equity is attracted by an offshore listing of a local firm's shares, the accounting and governance requirements of listings in major markets are likely to increase the quality of disclosure. But this mode may also divert trading volume to foreign markets, thus reducing the scale and depth of domestic institutions.

19 See Krugman (forthcoming) for a discussion of financing and forgiving.

20 This concept was first applied to the debt issue by Krugman (forthcoming) and subsequently has been elaborated by Krugman (1988), Froot (1989) and Claessens and Diwan (1989).

21 Krugman's (1988) example would suggest that this would not happen. He assumes, however, that a country is badly 'overhung' to the point that it uses all of its foreign exchange even in good periods. If one assumes there is headroom in good periods, Pareto efficient recontracting will be possible.

22 This point parallels the debate on the benefits of buybacks, with added gains resulting from efficient recontracting. For differing views on the benefits to borrowers of buybacks, from most pessimistic to most optimistic, see Bulow and Rogoff (1988), Krugman (1988), Dooley (1988) and Williamson (1988).

23 Elhanan Helpman's (forthcoming) negative conclusion on debt–equity exchanges is, in part, because of his assumption that they create new claims that are, *de facto*, senior to general obligations. The common argument that a country should not adopt 'dual exchange rates' for some investments overlooks that the debt overhang is not neutral in its impact on the value of different types of obligations, and that the same factors that led to a discount on the existing debt may justify a similar discount on other claims subject to the same country risk.

24 The profitability of such investments will depend on world energy prices and local levels of aggregate activity. It will usually be efficient to shift risks tied to aggregate output to foreign investors. Thus the desirability of international risk sharing will depend primarily on the country's net exposure to energy prices.

25 Several such proposals have been made within the IFIs in recent months.

REFERENCES

Bulow, J. and Rogoff, K. (1988) 'The buyback boondoggle', *Brookings Papers on Economic Activity* 2: 675–704.

Claessen and Diwan (1989) in I. Husain and I. Diwan (eds) *Dealing with the Debt Crisis*, Washington, DC: World Bank.

Dooley, M. P. (1988) 'Analysis of self-financed buybacks and asset exchanges', *IMF Staff Papers* 35(4): 714–22.

Dornbusch, R. (1988) 'Our LDC debts', in M. Feldstein (ed.) *The United States in the World Economy*, Chicago, IL: University of Chicago Press.

Eaton, J. (1987) 'Public debt guarantees and private capital flight', *World Bank Economic Review* 1 (May): 377–95.

Eaton, J., Gersovitz, M. and Stiglitz, J. (1986) 'The pure theory of country risk', *European Economic Review* 30 (June): 481–513.

Eichengreen and Portes (1989) in I. Husain and I. Diwan (eds) *Dealing with the Debt Crisis*, Washington, DC: World Bank.

Frieden, J. (1981) 'Third World indebted industrialization: international finance and state capitalism in Mexico, Brazil, Algeria, and South Korea', *International Organization* 35 (Summer): 407–31.

Froot, K. (1989) 'Buybacks, exit bonds and the optimality of debt and liquidity relief', *International Economic Review* 30 (January): 49–70.

Ganitsky, J. and Lema, G. (1988) 'Foreign investment through debt–equity swaps', *Sloan Management Review* 29 (2): 21–9.

Helpman, E. (forthcoming) 'The simple analytics of

debt–equity swaps and debt forgiveness', in J.A. Frenkel (ed.) *Analytical Issues in Debt*, Washington, DC: International Monetary Fund.

Institute of International Finance (1989) 'The way forward for middle-income developing countries', Report by the Board of Directors of the Institute of International Finance, Washington, DC, January.

Kaletsky, A. (1985) *The Costs of Default*, New York: Twentieth Century Fund.

Krugman, P. (1988) 'Market-based debt reduction schemes', NBER Working Paper 2587, Cambridge, MA: National Bureau of Economic Research.

—— (forthcoming) 'Financing vs forgiving a debt overhang', *Journal of Development Economics*.

Lessard, D. R. (1988) 'Country risk and the structure of international financial intermediation', in C. Stone

(ed.) *Financial Risk: Theory, Evidence and Implications*, Boston, MA: Kluwer.

Lessard, D. R. and Williamson, J. (1985) *Financial Intermediation beyond the Debt Crisis*, Washington, DC: Institute for International Economics.

Oman, C. (1984) *New Forms of International Investment for Developing Countries*, Paris: OECD.

Regling, K. (1988) 'New financing approaches in the debt strategy', *Finance and Development* 25 (March): 6–9.

Stulz, R. (1981) 'A model of international asset pricing', *Journal of Financial Economics* 9 (4): 383–406.

Williamson, J. (1988) *Voluntary Approaches to Debt Relief*, Washington, DC: Institute for International Economics.

27

THE USA IN DEBT

Norman S. Fieleke

When the US deficit on current international transactions soared to record levels during the mid-1980s, some observers perceived a grave loss of US competitiveness that was 'deindustrializing' America. Others warned of an imminent international financial crisis, predicting that the deficits would undermine confidence in the US dollar (and in dollar-denominated assets) and induce a sharp drop in the dollar's foreign exchange value and a sharp rise in US interest rates. The heightened interest rates would precipitate a US recession that would become world-wide – a 'hard landing'.[1]

Thus far, the landing has been far from hard. To be sure, the weighted average foreign exchange value of the dollar did decline fairly steadily and significantly in real terms (adjusted for US minus foreign inflation) during the years 1985–7. But US interest rates also generally declined, rather than rose, between the beginning and the end of this period, and both the US and the world economies grew at a healthy pace. Between the end of 1987 and this writing, the foreign exchange value of the dollar has changed relatively little, in spite of continued large US current account deficits; in fact, several central banks have on occasion sold large volumes of dollars in an effort to prevent the dollar from *rising* in the foreign exchange markets! The economic expansion has continued and the spectre of a hard landing is invoked much less frequently in economic discourse.

The non-occurrence to date of a hard landing does not prove that one will not take place. And even without a hard landing, the increasing US indebtedness generated by the nation's current account deficits will impose a growing burden on the US economy. This chapter examines the growth of US indebtedness to the rest of the world and the underlying causes, as well as the consequences and some proposed remedies.

THE MAGNITUDE OF US INDEBTEDNESS

As can be seen in Table 27.1, as recently as 1983 the USA was a net creditor in the community of nations, with assets abroad amounting to $89 billion more than foreign assets in this country. The transition from creditor to debtor status was swift and dramatic. The nation had attained its peak as a creditor in 1981, with a positive net international investment position of $141 billion. By the end of 1985 net indebtedness amounted to $117 billion, and by 1989 to $664 billion.

The change in the international investment position is attributable partly to asset purchases and sales (i.e. capital flows) and partly to changes in the value of the assets that are held. To illustrate, Table 27.2 shows that capital flows comprised by far the largest component of the change in the US position during 1989; foreigners loaned or invested about $215 billion in the USA, $88 billion more than US residents invested in foreign countries. Aside from such capital flows, rising securities prices increased the value of stocks and bonds held both in the USA and abroad, with foreign assets in the USA increasing by $53 billion more than US assets abroad on this count. Also, changes in the dollar exchange rates of other

511

Table 27.1 International investment position of the USA at year-end, 1970–89 (billions of dollars)

Year	US assets abroad	Foreign assets in the USA	Net international investment position of the USA (column 2 less column 3)
1970	165.4	106.9	58.5
1971	179.0	133.5	45.5
1972	198.7	161.7	37.0
1973	222.4	174.5	47.9
1974	255.7	197.0	58.7
1975	295.1	220.9	74.2
1976	347.2	263.6	83.6
1977	379.1	306.4	72.7
1978	447.8	371.7	76.1
1979	510.6	416.1	94.5
1980	607.1	500.8	106.3
1981	719.6	578.7	140.9
1982	824.8	688.1	136.7
1983	873.5	784.5	89.0
1984	895.9	898.1	−2.2
1985	949.7	1,066.9	−117.2
1986	1,073.4	1,347.1	−273.7
1987	1,175.9	1,554.0	−378.1
1988	1,265.6	1,796.7	−531.1
1989[a]	1,412.5	2,076.3	−663.7

Source: *Survey of Current Business* 66 (June 1986): 28; 69 (June 1989): 43; 70 (June 1990): 59
Notes: Detail may not add to totals shown because of rounding.
[a] Preliminary.

currencies somewhat altered the dollar value of foreign-currency-denominated stocks and bonds.

This measurement of the US position may be substantially in error, as the Commerce Department, the source of the data, points out. On the one hand, some US claims on foreigners are understated because of certain measurement conventions or difficulties. For instance, US official gold holdings – deemed, like US holdings of foreign currency, to be a claim on foreigners – are valued at a most conservative $42.22 per ounce. Revaluing this gold stock at $360 per ounce – roughly the market price at this writing – would raise the reported value of US assets abroad at year-end 1989 by more than $83 billion. Similarly, US direct investments abroad are carried at their original book value rather than at their higher current market value.

On the other hand, other measurement problems probably result in an understatement of the value of foreign assets in the USA. In particular, for years the USA has been receiving from abroad very large net receipts that cannot be traced to specific transactions – the so-called 'statistical discrepancy' in the balance of payments. Some, perhaps most, of these net receipts – which totalled $22 billion in 1989 – may well have been generated by 'capital account' transactions, particularly by foreign investment in the USA. Thus,

Table 27.2 The US net international investment position: summary of changes during 1989 (billions of dollars)

	US assets abroad	Foreign assets in the USA	Net international investment position of the USA (column 2 less column 3)
Position at end of 1988	1,265.6	1,796.7	−531.1
Changes in 1989 attributable to:			
Capital flows	127.1	214.7	−87.6
Price changes	13.3	66.7	−53.4
Exchange rate changes	−2.3	−1.3	−1.0
Other changes	8.9	−0.5	9.4
Total changes	146.9	279.6	−132.7
Position at end of 1989[a]	1,412.5	2,076.3	−663.7

Source: *Survey of Current Business* 70 (June 1990): 55
Notes: Detail may not add to totals shown because of rounding.
[a] Preliminary.

some understatement of foreign assets in the USA seems likely. Such an understatement would, of course, tend to lower the reported net indebtedness of the USA below its true value, while the likely understatement of US assets abroad would have the opposite effect.[2] On balance it is hard to say whether the published measure of the US net international investment position is significantly in error. Some considerations suggest an understatement, others an overstatement.

The transition of the USA from creditor to debtor status is not to be explained by transactions with a particular country or region. On the contrary, the US position turned more negative (or less positive) in all major areas for which US data are regularly published. As shown by Table 27.3, through 1988 the biggest swing was with Western Europe.

If the USA has become a sizeable net debtor, which countries are the creditors? Unfortunately, data on net international investment position – or 'net external assets', as the measure is generally called outside the USA – are officially published by only a few countries, and the comparability of

Table 27.3 Net international investment position of the USA by area at year-end, 1981 and 1988 (billions of dollars)

Area	1981	1988[a]	Change
Western Europe	−51.8	−436.9	−385.0
Japan	−1.7	−128.5	−126.8
Canada	66.9	53.5	−13.4
Latin American Republics and other Western Hemisphere	99.3	−23.6	−122.9
Other	28.3	2.9	−25.4
Total	140.9	−532.5	−673.5

Source: *Survey of Current Business* 69 (June 1989): 42; US Commerce Department staff

Notes: At this writing, data for the geographic areas listed are not available for 1989. The data shown were obtained in 1989 and the total in the column for 1988 differs somewhat from the total shown in Tables 27.1 and 27.2, which could be compiled from a 1990 source. In addition, detail may not add to totals shown because of rounding.

[a] Preliminary.

these national measures is doubtful. Some data published by the IMF for the major seven industrial democracies suggest that Japan, Germany and the UK have large net creditor positions (IMF 1988). Other major net creditors probably include Switzerland and some members of the OPEC, especially Saudi Arabia and Iraq (Deutsche Bundesbank 1986).

Once the USA became a net debtor, it became fashionable to compare its indebtedness with that of the LDCs. US indebtedness, it was widely reported, had come to exceed the indebtedness even of Brazil, the leading debtor among the developing nations. The comparison, however, was not valid. For one thing, the gross debt of the LDCs was being compared with US debt net of US assets abroad. Such comparison is sometimes defended on the grounds that the external assets of developing countries typically are relatively small or, when privately owned, are beyond the control or influence of developing-country governments. The argument has merit, but to ignore all such assets is extreme.[3]

If measured gross, on roughly the same basis as LDC debt is measured, the US external debt came to $753 billion at the end of 1985, the year during which the nation became a net debtor. This amount greatly exceeded the gross external debt of any LDC. Indeed, the total external debt of all the capital-importing developing countries then amounted to only about 1¼ times the US debt.[4]

In any event, by any conventional measure US indebtedness increased dramatically. We shall examine some explanations for the US external deficit and then consider the possible consequences of the deficit. Explanations can be classified into those that emphasize 'supply-side' factors, 'demand-side' factors, or both.

SUPPLY-SIDE EXPLANATIONS: PRICE COMPETITIVENESS

The large trade and current account deficits that have ballooned US net debt (Table 27.4) are often taken to signify a loss of US 'competitiveness'. What is meant by competitiveness is seldom

Table 27.4 US balances on selected components of international current account transactions, 1970–89
(billions of dollars)

Year	Balance on merchandise trade	Balance on services and income	Balance on unilateral transfers	Balance on current account (columns 2+ 3+4)
1970	2.6	5.9	−6.2	2.3
1971	−2.3	8.2	−7.4	−1.4
1972	−6.4	9.2	−8.5	−5.8
1973	0.9	13.1	−6.9	7.1
1974	−5.5	16.7	−9.2[a]	2.0
1975	8.9	16.3	−7.1	18.1
1976	−9.5	19.4	−5.7	4.2
1977	−31.1	21.8	−5.2	−14.5
1978	−33.9	24.3	−5.8	−15.4
1979	−27.5	33.1	−6.6	−1.0
1980	−25.5	34.9	−8.3	1.1
1981	−28.0	43.2	−8.3[b]	6.9
1982	−36.4	40.3	−9.8	−5.9
1983	−67.1	36.9	−10.0	−40.1
1984	−112.5	26.1	−12.6	−99.0
1985	−122.1	15.3	−15.5	−122.3
1986	−145.1	15.7	−16.0	−145.4
1987	−159.5	11.8	−14.6	−162.3
1988	−127.0	13.1	−15.0	−128.9
1989	−114.9	19.6	−14.7	−110.0

Source: *Survey of Current Business* 70 (June 1990)· 75– 6
Notes: Detail may not add to totals shown because of rounding.
    [a] Includes extraordinary US government transactions with India.
    [b] Break in series. Beginning with data for 1981, private remittances to foreign students in the USA are included.

spelled out, but the concern is commonly with factors that underlie the aggregate supply of US goods – factors such as technology, capital formation, research and development, and the quality of management and the labour force. Thus, to enhance US competitiveness, action has often been proposed to upgrade the education of the workforce (especially in mathematics and science), to grant more favourable tax treatment to investment in capital equipment, to relax the antitrust laws so that firms could pool their research efforts, to provide better patent protection for new inventions, and so on.

Analyses of supply-side competition, or of competition among suppliers, commonly divide it into two broad categories: price competition and non-price competition. Price competition is the subject of this section.

Arguably the best single index of a nation's changing overall price competitiveness is the change in its real exchange rate, i.e. the change in its average price level relative to the average foreign price level after taking into account the change in the average foreign-currency price of its currency. Thus, a nation's price competitiveness will be impaired by a rise in its domestic prices relative to foreign prices unless an offsetting decline occurs in the foreign-currency price of its currency.

Although analysts differ on precisely how to measure the real exchange rate, all widely used measures show big swings in US price competitiveness during the period of deterioration in the US trade and current account balances. In general, the indices suggest that the USA lost much price competitiveness between 1980 and 1985, but then rapidly regained the lost ground. For example, the index plotted as a solid line in Figure 27.1 shows a rise in US relative prices of 37 per cent (after incorporating nominal exchange rate change) from 1980 to 1985, followed by a decline to approximately the 1980 level by the end of 1987. The 'nominal' index plotted in the chart represents only the change in the foreign-currency price of the dollar. Clearly, it was this nominal exchange rate change, rather than changes in domestic or foreign

prices, that accounted for most of the large swings in US overall price competitiveness over this period.

It is widely agreed that the loss of US price competitiveness between 1980 and 1985 contributed substantially to the increase in the US trade deficit. But what caused the loss of price competitiveness? A number of factors could be responsible, not all of them supply side in nature. Here a supply-side factor – productivity change – is considered; other factors are discussed in a following section.

Changes in the productiveness of a country's resources can have an important influence on the

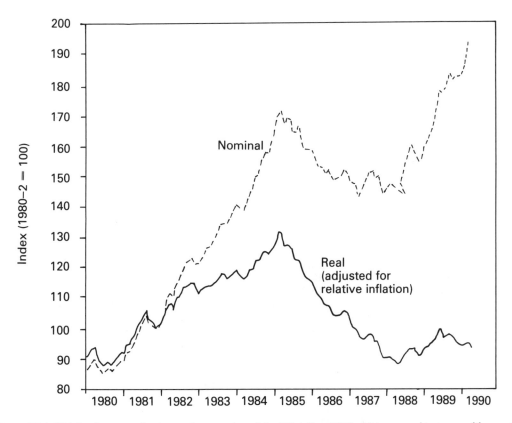

Figure 27.1 Weighted average foreign exchange value of the US dollar, 1980–90 (measured in terms of forty other currencies weighted according to manufactures trade; based on monthly averages of daily rates). Inflation is measured in terms of wholesale prices in manufactures excluding food and fuel

Source: Morgan Guaranty Trust Company

country's price competitiveness. If productivity rises, other things remaining equal, the money cost and price of a unit of output can fall. In evaluating overall productivity, one should consult a measure of the output yielded by a unit of all productive factors combined, including labour, land and capital. But such measures of total factor productivity are extraordinarily difficult to construct. Consequently, international productivity comparisons are commonly based on indices of output per input of labour in manufacturing, such as those in Table 27.5.

Do these indices suggest that lagging productivity growth was responsible for the decline in US price competitiveness between 1980 and 1985? Among the 'Big Seven' countries listed individually, the USA ranked in the middle in productivity performance over this period, surpassing Canada, France and West Germany but lagging behind Japan, Italy and the UK. But how did the USA perform by comparison with its major industrial competitors as a group? As shown in the last column, eleven foreign industrial countries achieved an average increase of about 25 per cent

Table 27.5 Output per labour hour in manufacturing in selected industrial countries, 1970–88 (indices: 1980 = 100)

Year	Country							
	USA	Canada	Japan	France	West Germany	Italy	UK	Eleven countries[a]
1970	78.9	77.0	52.8	64.6	65.6	57.2	78.8	64.0
1971	83.2	82.4	55.9	68.1	68.1	58.2	82.6	67.5
1972	86.4	86.5	61.4	71.0	72.7	63.1	87.2	72.2
1973	91.1	92.0	67.7	75.8	77.3	68.3	93.6	78.0
1974	88.8	93.4	70.5	77.4	80.5	73.1	95.2	80.7
1975	91.1	90.2	71.5	80.2	83.0	70.6	93.1	80.8
1976	95.4	96.5	76.9	85.4	88.8	80.2	97.3	86.5
1977	98.3	101.8	81.5	90.4	92.1	81.9	98.1	90.3
1978	99.9	103.0	88.0	94.6	94.9	87.2	99.5	94.2
1979	99.9	103.9	93.6	99.2	99.6	95.5	100.6	98.3
1980	100.0	100.0	100.0	100.0	100.0	100.0	100.0	100.0
1981	102.3	104.8	103.7	103.0	102.2	102.7	105.1	103.7
1982	104.8	100.1	110.0	110.3	103.7	105.2	111.4	106.6
1983	110.3	107.3	116.0	113.1	109.8	110.8	120.8	113.2
1984	116.2	116.5	124.3	115.3	113.9	121.9	127.5	120.2
1985	121.4	119.5	131.3	120.0	118.2	128.4	131.6	125.1
1986	126.1	119.9	133.4	122.2	118.1	129.6	136.0	126.6
1987	130.7	122.7	143.8	123.7	119.6	132.9	144.8	131.9
1988	133.7	126.6	154.8	130.3	125.1	136.9	152.0	138.6

Source: *Monthly Labor Review* 13 (April 1990): 98; staff of US Bureau of Labor Statistics

Notes: The data relate to all employed persons, including the self-employed, in the USA and Canada, and to all employees (wage and salary earners) in the other countries. Although the indices relate output to the hours of persons employed in manufacturing, they do not measure the specific contribution of labour as a single factor of production. Rather, they reflect the joint effects of many influences, including new technology, capital investment, capacity utilization, energy use and managerial skills, as well as the skills and efforts of the work force.

[a] A trade-weighted average of Canada, Japan, France, West Germany, Italy, the UK, Belgium, Denmark, the Netherlands, Norway and Sweden, but excluding in 1988 Belgium and the Netherlands, for which data are not available at this writing. The weights reflect the relative importance of each country as a US manufacturing trade competitor as of 1980.

over the years 1980–5, compared with an increase of nearly 21½ per cent in the USA. This differential of some 3½ per cent falls far short of accounting for the 37 per cent deterioration in overall US price competitiveness over this period.

In fact the US lag in labour productivity growth was far greater during the 1970s than during the 1980s when the US trade deficit increased so greatly. Between 1970 and 1975 labour productivity in manufacturing rose by 15 per cent in the USA and by 26 per cent in the eleven foreign industrial countries. And between 1975 and 1980 the increase was only 10 per cent in the USA and 24 per cent in the eleven other nations.

It is clear that the loss of US price competitiveness during 1980–5 should not be attributed to the relative US record on labour productivity in manufacturing over these years. To be sure, higher US productivity growth could, in principle, have yielded lower US inflation and, other things being equal, a smaller rise in the US real exchange rate than that shown in Figure 27.1. The relative US record on labour productivity in manufacturing, however, was extremely good during 1980–5 by comparison with the previous decade.

SUPPLY-SIDE EXPLANATIONS: NON-PRICE CONSIDERATIONS

Supply-side explanations of the US trade and current account deficits relate not only to the price competitiveness of US suppliers but also to non-price competition. US firms were often said to have lost competitiveness because their products had become inferior in quality to foreign brands. Automobiles provide a good illustration. During the 1980s, surveys showed that US consumers and engineers both considered foreign-brand cars generally to be of higher quality than US cars. Consumers buying foreign cars were more likely to be satisfied with their purchase and to report a low frequency of repairs than were the buyers of US cars (US Department of Commerce 1988; *Consumer Reports*, various issues evaluating automobiles). In addition, US firms were criticized for failing to tailor products to the preferences of foreign purchasers and for failing to mount aggressive, long-term marketing efforts in foreign lands.

Because such reports are so common, it may well be that US competitiveness did lag in terms of quality and other non-price considerations. How much weight to attach to these various non-price dimensions is impossible to quantify with any precision. However, other evidence suggests that, whatever the shortcomings of US firms, the worldwide performance of US management did not degenerate as the US trade deficit began to mushroom early in the 1980s.

Some of the most revealing evidence on the relative performance of US management has to do with the record of multinational firms headquartered in the USA. By and large, management has more scope to influence the operations of a multinational firm than a national firm. With activities in more than one country, the multinational firm is not chained to local customs, regulations or labour force. Over time management can shift activities of the firm from one nation to another as circumstances warrant, taking advantage of the best that each nation has to offer for the overall success of the firm. Thus, one may gain more insight into the international competitiveness of US management by examining the performance of US-based multinationals than by examining only the performance of US firms.

Summary data on performance in export markets for manufactures are presented in Table 27.6. As shown by the bottom line, the overall share of US-based multinationals – including exports by US parents as well as by their majority-owned foreign affiliates (MOFAs) – increased somewhat between 1966 and 1984, the latest year for which data are available at this writing. From these numbers, one might argue that US management was holding its ground in the international arena. By comparison, the first line shows that all US manufactured exports, expressed as a share of the world total, declined from 1966 to 1977, rose from 1977 to 1982 and then declined slightly between 1982 and 1984 (a period when the US trade deficit also increased sharply). Thus, the USA as a nation experienced some loss in competitive-

Table 27.6 Shares (as a percentage) in value of world manufactures exports[a]

	1966	1977	1982	1983	1984
USA	17.5	13.3	14.3	13.7	14.0
US Multinationals					
Parents	11.0	9.2	9.5	9.1	9.2
MOFAs[b]	8.2	9.7	9.7	9.9	10.3
Parents and MOFAs	17.7	17.6	17.7	17.7	18.1

Source: Lipsey and Kravis 1987

Notes: [a] The 'world' here is defined as all market economies.
[b] Exports by majority owned foreign affiliates (MOFAs) as per cent of exports by all countries except the USA.

ness by this indicator between 1982 and 1984, but the rising market share of US multinationals tends to exonerate US management. It is especially interesting that the US multinationals maintained their market share between 1982 and 1984 by raising the share of their MOFAs to compensate for a decline on the part of the US parents.

COMPETITIVENESS AND AGGREGATE SUPPLY

Perhaps the best summary indicator of a nation's overall supply-side competitiveness is the share of world output that the nation supplies. Measures of this share are not precise; it is difficult to construct accurate comparisons of the outputs of different countries, partly because the composition and price structure of output vary from country to country. Nonetheless, such comparisons are regularly made by the OECD, whose membership includes twenty-four countries, nearly all of them industrialized.

In Table 27.7, which draws on the OECD data, it can be seen that the USA held its own with respect to gross output between 1981 and 1987, a period during which the US trade balance registered a huge decline. Thus, at least by comparison with other countries, the USA did not display a serious aggregate 'supply-side' problem during these years of deterioration in its trade balance.

Table 27.7 US and OECD GDP and US trade balance, 1981–9

Year	US GDP as per cent of OECD GDP		US merchandise trade balance (billions of dollars; balance-of-payments basis)
	At current prices and exchange rates	At 1985 prices and exchange rates	
1981	38	45	−28.0
1982	40	44	−36.4
1983	42	44	−67.1
1984	44	45	−112.5
1985	45	45	−122.1
1986	39	45	−145.1
1987	36	45	−159.5
1988	35	45	−127.0
1989	36	45	−114.9

Source: *Survey of Current Business* 70 (June 1990): 76–7; OECD (1990) *National Accounts, 1960–88*, vol. I, Paris: OECD, pp. 123, 127 and 131; and *Main Economic Indicators* 90 (April 1990): 172

If the supply side cannot be held responsible for the US external deficits, what is to blame? After all, it is clear that the nation lost overall price competitiveness as the deficits began to increase. The answer may lie in the relationship between aggregate US supply and demand and, more precisely, in the forces that influence that relationship.

AGGREGATE SUPPLY AND DEMAND

If the residents of a nation demand, or absorb, more output than the nation is supplying, the gap is filled by net imports from abroad. Although the output supplied by the nation may be growing rapidly, total demand within the nation may be growing even faster, so that the nation's trade and current account deficits with the rest of the world expand (unless there are offsetting price changes, such as import price reductions). To stem the growth of the deficit, the nation must retard the growth of its demand (i.e. its absorption or expenditure) or accelerate the growth of its output.

The USA in the mid-1980s was such a nation. The data in Table 27.8 confirm that domestic demand grew faster than GNP in the USA in every year from 1983 through 1986, a period during which dramatic increases occurred in the country's deficits on international trade and current account. Note that during most of this period US output grew faster than output in other OECD countries as a group; however, US demand grew even faster by comparison with demand in other OECD countries.

It seems, then, that the US external deficits are not attributable to 'supply-side' problems, certainly not supply-side problems alone. Demand, or more precisely, the changing relationship between demand and supply, seems a more promising subject for analysis. In what follows, some explanations involving both demand and supply are considered. Foreign as well as US demand and supply are relevant, since some of what the USA supplies goes to satisfy foreign demand, while some of US demand is satisfied by foreign supply.

UNFAIR FOREIGN TRADING PRACTICES

One explanation often advanced for the US trade deficit is unfair foreign trading practices; the playing field is said to be 'tilted' against the USA. This explanation involves references to both demand and supply. Although it is foreign rather than US demand and supply that have allegedly been manipulated, the impact would have been to increase US net imports. On the supply side, other nations have been charged with subsidizing or 'dumping' their exports in world markets, thus lowering their supply prices and stealing both US and foreign markets from US suppliers. On the demand side, other nations are accused of imposing barriers against US exports, thereby reducing demand for them.

To be sure, unfair trading actions do occur, and national governments, including the US government, commonly undertake to shield firms within their borders against injury from such practices. In the USA, the law provides US industries with remedies against import competition from dumped

Table 27.8 Real GNP and real domestic demand in the USA and other OECD countries, 1981–9

	Real GNP				Real domestic demand			
	Level (1980 = 100)		Per cent change from preceding year		Level (1980 = 100)		Per cent change from preceding year	
Year	USA	Other OECD	USA	Other OECD	USA	Other OECD	USA	Other OECD
1981	101.9	101.5	1.9	1.5	102.2	100.0	2.2	0.0
1982	99.3	102.8	−2.5	1.3	100.3	101.0	−1.9	1.0
1983	102.9	105.1	3.6	2.2	105.4	102.5	5.1	1.5
1984	109.9	108.9	6.8	3.6	114.5	105.5	8.7	2.9
1985	113.5	112.6	3.4	3.4	118.9	108.7	3.8	3.1
1986	116.7	115.6	2.7	2.6	122.9	112.9	3.3	3.8
1987	120.9	119.6	3.7	3.5	126.8	117.7	3.2	4.4
1988	126.3	124.9	4.4	4.4	131.0	124.3	3.3	5.4
1989	130.0	129.8	3.0	3.9	134.1	129.6	2.4	4.3

Sources: OECD Economic Outlook 47 (June 1990): 181 and 188; and OECD Economic Outlook 47, Statistics on Microcomputer Diskette June 1990

or subsidized merchandise, as well as against other practices deemed unfair. Dumping is defined as the sale of foreign merchandise at prices below those charged in the foreign producers' home market, or below the foreign cost of production. The anti-dumping statutes provide for the imposition of antidumping duties to offset such price-cutting when a determination is made that a domestic industry is being materially injured – or threatened with such injury – by the dumped imports, or that the establishment of the industry is being materially retarded by such imports. Similarly, 'countervailing' duties are imposed to offset foreign subsidies upon a determination by US authorities that, because of subsidized import competition, a US industry is being materially injured – or threatened with such injury – or that the establishment of the industry is being materially retarded.[5]

During 1987, when the USA incurred its largest trade deficit ever, the nation imposed new anti-dumping duties on fifteen products from twenty-six countries, and imposed new countervailing duties on seven products from twelve countries. Other actions were taken against practices that the USA deemed unfair on grounds other than those covered under the antidumping or countervailing duty laws (US International Trade Commission 1988). Therefore, while unfair foreign trading practices may have operated to increase US imports, it is plain that US firms availed themselves of the provisions of US law in order to stem such increases. The burden of proof rests with those who suggest that US imports were bloated by unfair foreign trading practices in spite of the legal remedies that US firms can invoke against such practices. Unfair foreign trading practices were to be found long before the US trade deficit began to surge in the early 1980s, and it remains to be shown that those practices intensified so as to contribute substantially to the deficit.

Another difficulty with attributing the increased US deficit to unfair foreign trading practices is that the increase was distributed widely across both commodity categories and geographic areas. This fact is documented in Tables 27.9 and 27.10. It

Table 27.9 US merchandise trade, by major trading partners or areas, 1980 and 1987 (billions of dollars)

Country or area	1980	1987 Actual	1987 Allocated on basis of 1980 shares[a]
Canada			
US exports	41.6	62.0	46.5
US imports	42.9	73.6	70.4
Balance	−1.3	−11.6	−23.9
Japan			
US exports	20.8	27.6	23.2
US imports	31.2	84.6	51.2
Balance	−10.4	−57.0	−28.0
West Germany			
US exports	11.4	11.5	12.8
US imports	11.7	26.9	19.2
Balance	−0.2	−15.4	−6.4
Mexico			
US exports	15.2	14.6	17.0
US imports	12.6	20.3	20.6
Balance	2.7	−5.7	−3.6
UK			
US exports	12.8	13.8	14.3
US imports	9.8	17.2	16.1
Balance	3.0	−3.5	−1.8
OPEC			
US exports	17.4	10.7	19.4
US imports	55.6	24.4	91.2
Balance	−38.2	−13.7	−71.8
Rest of the world			
US exports	105.1	110.1	117.1
US imports	86.0	162.7	141.0
Balance	19.1	−52.6	−23.8
Total, all areas			
US exports	224.3	250.3	250.3
US imports	249.8	409.8	409.8
Balance	−25.5	−159.5	−159.5

Source: *Survey of Current Business* 70 (June 1990): 86–8
Notes: Detail may not add to totals shown because of rounding.
[a] Each area is allocated the same fraction of total 1987 US exports and imports as in 1980.

seems most unlikely that virtually all major trading partners of the USA would simultaneously have intensified unfair practices in their trade with the nation.

Table 27.9 presents aggregate data on trade

Table 27.10 US merchandise trade, by major end-use category, 1980 and 1987 (billions of dollars)

End-use category	1980	1987 Actual	Allocated on basis of 1980 shares[a]
Food, feeds and beverages			
Exports	36.4	25.3	40.6
Imports	18.5	24.8	30.4
Balance	17.9	0.4	10.2
Industrial supplies and materials			
Exports	72.3	70.0	80.7
Imports	132.3	113.7	217.0
Balance	−60.0	−43.8	−136.3
Capital goods, except automotive			
Exports	76.3	92.4	85.1
Imports	31.4	85.1	51.6
Balance	44.8	7.2	33.5
Automotive vehicles, parts and engines			
Exports	17.4	28.1	19.4
Imports	28.1	85.2	46.0
Balance	−10.7	−57.0	−26.7
Consumer goods (non-food), except automotive			
Exports	17.7	20.3	19.7
Imports	34.2	88.8	56.1
Balance	−16.5	−68.5	−36.4
All other, including balance-of-payments adjustments			
Exports	4.2	14.3	4.7
Imports	5.2	12.1	8.6
Balance	−1.0	2.2	−3.9
All categories			
Exports	224.3	250.3	250.3
Imports	249.8	409.8	409.8
Balance	−25.5	−159.5	−159.5

Source: *Survey of Current Business* 70 (June 1990): 90–2
Notes: Detail may not add to totals shown because of rounding.
[a] Each category is allocated the same fraction of total 1987 US exports and imports as in 1980.

between the USA and each of its five leading trade partners, listed in order of magnitude of total US trade with them in 1987. Similar data are shown for OPEC and for the rest of the world. Together, the five leading trade partners accounted for 53 per cent of US international trade (exports plus imports) in 1987; if OPEC is added, that share rises to 59 per cent. Clearly, the US trade balance deteriorated markedly from 1980 to 1987 with every listed area but OPEC, from which US imports of petroleum declined dramatically.

To identify the areas with which the US trade position deteriorated more than proportionately, the last column of the table shows what the value of US exports and imports with each area would have been in 1987 if each area had retained the same percentages of total US exports and imports as in 1980. Comparison of the last two columns reveals that the US trade balance worsened not only actually but disproportionately (the 1987 'actual' exceeds the 'allocated') with all listed areas except OPEC and Canada. While the greatest actual deterioration was with the 'rest of the world', the greatest disproportionate deterioration, amounting to $29 billion, was with Japan, with the rest of the world a very close second.

The deterioration in the US trade balance was distributed widely across commodity categories as well as across geographic areas. As indicated in Table 27.10, aside from the 'all other' category, the balance worsened between 1980 and 1987 in every major commodity category except industrial supplies and materials, a category influenced by the decline in oil imports. More than proportionate deteriorations occurred in foods, feeds and beverages, in capital goods, in automotive vehicles and parts and in consumer goods, as the actual 1987 deficit was larger for each category (or the actual 1987 surplus was smaller) than it would have been if the category had accounted for the same percentage of total exports and imports as in 1980. (See the last two columns of Table 27.10.)

Thus, the pervasiveness of the deterioration in the US trade balance makes it unlikely that unfair foreign trading practices played a major role. Does this conclusion hold even for US trade with Japan?

The issue is raised most often with regard to Japan, partly because the US deficit with that nation increased so sharply and amounted to more than two-fifths of the total US deficit in 1989. While precise explanation of trade flows is very difficult, quantitative studies have concluded that the increase in the US deficit with Japan was attributable mainly, or perhaps fully, to factors such as changes in prices, incomes and the yen–dollar exchange rate. Any impact of unfair trading practices was adjudged to be decidedly secondary (Bergsten and Cline 1985; Bergstrand 1986).

Japan's record is not without blemish, however. In particular, evidence has been marshalled that Japan has offered some formidable 'invisible' barriers to international trade. An invisible barrier is a system or regulation that applies to both domestic and foreign producers but that works, perhaps unintentionally, to reduce the share of imports in domestic consumption. Government procurement policies, the wholesale and retail distribution systems, the setting of product standards and the testing of products against these standards have commonly been alleged to constitute formidable invisible barriers in Japan. According to one investigation, if Japan's invisible barriers had been reduced to levels corresponding to those in the USA and the EEC in the early 1980s, Japan's manufactured imports might have increased by 27 per cent (equivalent to a rise of 7 per cent in the country's total imports), with at least half of the increased imports coming from the USA. At the same time, the investigation points out that such an increase would be far too small to eliminate the US trade deficit with Japan. Thus, the conclusion remains that the deficit was generated mainly, if not totally, by causes other than unfair trading practices (Christelow 1985–6).

If unfair foreign trading practices are an improbable explanation of the US trade and current account deficits, what other explanations might be more convincing?

PROBABLE CAUSES OF THE US TRADE AND CURRENT ACCOUNT DEFICITS

In its 1985 annual report, the Council of Economic Advisers identified three factors as the *immediate* causes of the US trade deficit: (1) the appreciation of the dollar in the foreign exchange markets after mid-1980; (2) the more rapid expansion of real income and demand in the USA than in the rest of the world after 1982; (3) the reduced demand for imports by the LDCs that began to experience severe difficulty in servicing their debt and in obtaining new loans after mid-1982 (US President 1985). Subsequent analyses have commonly cited the same factors. The weight of the evidence suggests that the first of these three factors accounted for more than half of the increased deficit, with the second factor accounting for perhaps one-third and other factors accounting for the balance (Hooper and Mann 1987).

The roles played by dollar appreciation and by rapid US demand growth have already been described. But what explains these factors themselves?

The dollar's value will rise in the foreign exchange markets if the demand for dollars exceeds the supply at prevailing exchange rates. During the early 1980s, one important development that led to increased demand for dollars, relative to the supply, was an increase in net borrowing from abroad by US residents. Foreign currency balances were exchanged into dollar balances to accommodate this increase in US borrowing, thereby bidding up the price of the dollar. The increased US borrowing was caused largely by changes in federal fiscal policy, especially the shift toward deficit in the budget, which occurred at a time when US monetary policy was relatively restrictive.

The key role played by government fiscal policy in inducing borrowing from abroad is suggested by an important accounting relationship: private domestic investment can be funded out of either the country's private saving or government saving, or out of funds loaned by foreigners. If government saving decreases without a compensating increase in private saving, private investors must tap foreign saving more heavily if they are to sustain their outlays.

The relative magnitudes involved in this accounting relationship for the USA are shown in Table 27.11, where private domestic investment in the fourth column is equal to the sum of its sources of financing, itemized in the first three columns. A negative number in one of the first three columns means that saving is being absorbed, on balance, rather than being made available for private domestic investment. Thus, in 1975 foreigners borrowed from current US saving, rather than lending out of their own saving. Government in the USA also borrowed to finance a deficit in 1975; consequently, out of private saving amounting to

19 per cent of GNP, only 13.7 per cent was left for private investment within the USA (after adjustment for problems of measurement, known as the statistical discrepancy).

In 1982 the government deficit increased sharply in relation to GNP and then remained large by historical standards through the remainder of the 1980s (especially through 1986). Over the same period, private saving as a percentage of GNP declined, rather than rising to compensate for the greater government dissaving. Thus, from 1982 through 1987 private investment was increasingly financed by US borrowing from abroad, as can be seen in Table 27.11. Such borrowing from abroad allowed total US demand, or spending, to increase faster than US output.

This net borrowing from abroad, it should be

Table 27.11 Major categories of saving and investment as a percentage of GNP for the USA, 1970–90

Year	Gross private saving	Government saving	Net investment (lending) by foreigners	Gross private domestic investment (columns 2+3+4)
1970	16.2	−1.0	−0.5	14.7
1971	17.3	−1.8	−0.1	15.6
1972	16.8	−0.3	0.2	16.7
1973	18.0	0.6	−0.6	17.6
1974	17.3	−0.3	−0.4	16.3
1975	19.0	−4.1	−1.4	13.7
1976	18.0	−2.2	−0.5	15.6
1977	17.8	−1.0	0.4	17.3
1978	18.2	0.0	0.5	18.5
1979	17.8	0.5	−0.1	18.1
1980	17.5	−1.3	−0.5	16.0
1981	18.0	−1.0	−0.3	16.9
1982	17.6	−3.5	0.0	14.1
1983	17.4	−3.8	1.0	14.7
1984	17.9	−2.8	2.4	17.6
1985	16.6	−3.3	2.8	16.0
1986	15.8	−3.4	3.2	15.6
1987	14.7	−2.4	3.3	15.5
1988	15.1	−2.0	2.4	15.4
1989	15.4	−2.0	1.8	14.8
1990.I	15.3	−2.5	1.5	13.9

Source: US Board of Governors of the Federal Reserve System, Fame Data Base
Note: Detail may not add to totals shown because of statistical discrepancy.

noted, is essentially the same as the current account deficit in the US balance of payments. Although the government deficit and the current account deficit are thus related in an accounting sense, the sizes of the two deficits can still vary independently of each other, and on occasion inverse variation takes place. For example, from 1971 to 1972 the government deficit diminished while net borrowing from foreigners (the current account deficit) expanded.

Such inverse variation is not likely when the government deficit changes dramatically in response to a change in government policy, as was the case in the USA in 1982, a year when a major federal tax reduction began to take effect even as spending on federal programmes was accelerating. While views differ regarding the short-run impact of government deficits, the dominant theory is that such a policy-induced surge in government borrowing in a country will put upward pressure on interest rates (adjusted for expected inflation) in that country, thereby attracting foreign investment. As foreign investors acquire the country's currency in order to invest there, they bid up the price of that currency in the foreign exchange markets. The higher price of the country's currency will discourage foreigners from purchasing its goods but will encourage residents of the country to use their now more valuable currency to purchase foreign goods, so that the country's current account will move toward deficit (or toward a larger deficit). In addition, any increase in the country's total spending resulting from the enlarged government deficit will go partly for imports and for domestic goods that would otherwise be exported, also worsening the current account balance. Again, to return to one of our central themes, we can see from this brief description that the deterioration of the current account balance is associated with an increase in the country's total demand relative to the country's output.

Figure 27.2 supports the view that an increase in the government deficit tends to increase the current account deficit at least over the medium run.[6] The government deficit represented in this figure has been adjusted to exclude the effects of the business cycle; for example, any declines in tax revenues occurring because of recessions have been added back to the recorded level of government receipts, reducing the recorded deficit. Such adjustments are warranted because our interest is in deficits that tend to add to the pre-existing level of borrowing and spending, rather than in deficits that merely offset a decline in aggregate borrowing and spending elsewhere in the economy. Since cyclically adjusted data are not available for state and local government deficits, Figure 27.2 uses data for the federal deficit, which has been the focus of concern. Also, the federal deficit for each year is matched with the current account deficit for the following year, on the assumption that some time is required for an increase in the federal deficit to influence the current account deficit.

As noted above, a change in the federal deficit is presumed to affect the current account deficit partly through its impact on the dollar price of foreign exchange. Figure 27.3 suggests that the hypothesized relationship between the government deficit and the exchange rate did indeed prevail over the period 1973–85, although the relationship is rather loose. In this case, the government deficit for each year is paired with the exchange rate for the same year, with no lag, on the common assumption that exchange rates react promptly to stimuli, or even anticipate them (but then affect the current account with a lag). Also, the dollar price of foreign exchange, rather than the foreign exchange price of the dollar, is plotted; therefore, a downward movement signifies appreciation of the dollar.

Although Figures 27.2 and 27.3 are suggestive, strong conclusions should not be drawn from them alone. The exchange rate and the current account are influenced not just by the government deficit but by other factors as well.[7] Other factors likely to have contributed significantly to the dollar's appreciation during the early 1980s – and thus to the current account deficit – were an anti-inflationary US monetary policy, US tax law changes and deregulation that enhanced the after-tax profitability of investing in the USA, the easing of restric-

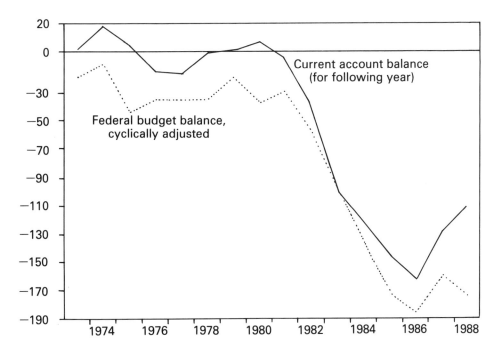

Figure 27.2 The current account and Federal budget deficits of the USA. The cyclically adjusted Federal budget balance is based on 6 per cent unemployment GNP trend

Sources: Survey of Current Business, various issues, and staff of the Department of Commerce, Bureau of Economic Analysis

tions over capital outflows from Japan and more restrictive government fiscal policies in some major foreign industrial countries (Feldstein 1985; McCulloch and Richardson 1986; Helkie and Hooper 1988). The net flow of capital into the USA was also fostered by the loss of investment appeal on the part of the LDCs that could not meet interest payments on their debt.

If net capital flows into the USA became so large during the 1980s, what form did these inflows take? As shown in Table 27.12, privately owned capital generally accounted for the great bulk of the inflows; foreign net purchases of US securities, foreign direct investment and inflows through US banks all made substantial contributions. From 1986 through 1988, the private inflows were substantially augmented by inflows of officially owned capital, as 128 billion of dollar holdings in the USA were acquired by foreign monetary authorities, some of whom had sold

their own currencies in exchange for dollars in an effort to limit their currencies' appreciation in the foreign exchange markets.

If in this section we have correctly identified the leading causes of the US external deficits, we are confronted with a puzzle: if the increase in the deficits was due primarily to the appreciation of the dollar and the relatively rapid growth of US total demand (as immediate causes) during the first half of the 1980s, why in subsequent years did the deficits decrease so little (Table 27.4) as the dollar depreciated so greatly (Figure 27.1) and as US demand grew more slowly (Table 27.8)?

Various explanations have been advanced. One of the more plausible is that responses to the dollar's depreciation are taking longer than did the responses to the appreciation. In particular, some foreign exporters, having just invested in gaining a larger share of the US market in response to the appreciation, may have been loath to give up their

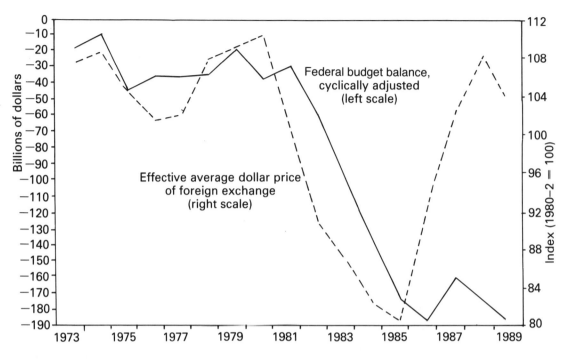

Figure 27.3 The real exchange rate and the Federal budget deficit of the USA, 1973–89

Sources: *World Financial Markets*, various issues, and staff at Morgan Guaranty Trust; *Survey of Current Business* 70 (March 1990) 19, and staff at the Bureau of Economic Analysis

market gains immediately and instead may have been sacrificing profits in order to retain most of their price competitiveness for the time being in spite of the dollar's depreciation. Another explanation is that factors other than changes in exchange rates and in total demand have an appreciable influence on the external deficit. For example, some studies have concluded that demand for imports grows relatively faster in response to income growth in the USA than it does in the rest of the world, so that the US trade balance will deteriorate unless US income grows much slower than income abroad, other things being equal (see especially Houthakker and Magee 1969). Some more recent research maintains that such a difference in the 'income elasticity of demand for imports', if it exists at all, is not so important in sustaining the US trade deficit as another factor, namely the continuing introduction

by foreign producers of new product lines that capture the fancy of American consumers (Helkie and Hooper 1988).

In any event, the US current account deficit remains large, and US external indebtedness continues to mount. Having considered the causes of the US deficit, we turn now to the consequences. These can be divided into two categories: past and future. Our chief concern is with consequences for the USA rather than for the rest of the world.

THE CONSEQUENCES TO DATE

To some observers, the large US external deficits connote something more alarming than reduced US competitiveness; they connote the 'deindustrialization' of America. According to this school, US manufacturing not only has lost ground in export markets, but has been in retreat before a flood of

Table 27.12 Capital transactions in the US balance of payments, 1980–9 (billions of dollars)

Type of transaction	1981	1982	1983	1984	1985	1986	1987	1988	1989[a]
Private capital, net	−22.6	−23.2	29.1	77.0	110.1	95.7	100.2	98.7	102.9
Securities, net	4.1	5.1	10.1	30.8	63.9	70.5	29.2	38.7	47.6
Foreign net purchases	9.8	13.1	16.9	35.6	71.4	74.8	34.5	46.6	69.5
US Treasuries	2.9	7.0	8.7	23.0	20.4	3.8	−7.6	20.2	30.0
US corporate bonds	2.1	2.8	2.2	13.9	46.6	53.8	26.5	26.8	33.0
US corporate stocks	4.8	3.3	6.0	−1.3	4.3	17.2	15.6	−0.5	6.6
US net purchases of foreign securities	−5.7	−8.0	−6.8	−4.8	−7.5	−4.3	−5.3	−7.8	−21.9
Direct investment, net	15.6	12.8	5.3	13.8	5.9	15.4	15.8	42.2	40.5
Foreign direct in USA	25.2	13.8	11.9	25.4	19.0	34.1	46.9	58.4	72.2
US direct investment abroad	−9.6	−1.0[b]	−6.7	−11.6	−13.2	−18.7	−31.0	−16.2	−31.7
Net flows reported by US banks	−42.0	−45.4	20.4	22.7	39.7	19.8	46.9	13.9	10.5
Other	−0.2	4.2	−6.6	9.7	0.6	−10.0	8.2	3.8	4.3
Official capital, net	−5.3	−7.5	−0.4	−5.5	−7.8	33.9	55.4	38.6	−15.3
Total reported capital flows, net	−27.9	−30.7	28.8	71.6	102.3	129.7	155.5	137.3	87.6
Statistical discrepancy	19.9	36.6	11.4	27.5	20.0	15.8	6.8	−8.4	22.4
Current account balance	6.9	−5.9	−40.1	−99.0	−122.3	−145.4	−162.3	−128.9	−110.0

Sources: *Survey of Current Business* 69 (June 1989): 79; 70 (June 1990): 72, 76, 77 and 97; and US Department of Commerce staff

Notes: Minus sign indicates an outflow.
 [a] Preliminary.
 [b] Break in series.

competing imports. Strong action has therefore been recommended to preserve the viability of domestic industry.

To be sure, total US output and employment would have been higher if exports had been greater, or competing imports smaller, other things being equal. But once this point is granted how did the US economy in fact perform under the intensified foreign competition?

The answer is perhaps best conveyed by aggregative data on the production of goods and services. Because goods are generally more transportable than services, firms that produce goods usually are subject to more foreign competition than are firms that produce services. According to the data in Table 27.13, the production of US goods grew faster than either US GNP or the

production of US services after the 1981–2 recession, and the growth of goods production over this period compares favourably with that during previous recent expansions. By this measure, then, US goods producers did well, even with the heightened foreign competition; evidently, the growth of total US demand was rapid enough to accommodate a substantial rise in US production as well as in US imports. (During recessions, of course, goods output actually declines, while services output usually continues to grow.) While it would be a mistake to describe the performance of US industry in superlatives, it is an even greater exaggeration to speak of the deindustrialization of America.

Although the US external deficits have not been destroying American industry, they have exercised

Table 27.13 Percentage changes in US real output during recessions and the succeeding expansions, 1969–90

Period (year and quarter)	Percentage change			
	Goods	*Services*	*Structures*	*Total GNP*
1969.IV–1970.IV (recession)	−3.3	1.6	2.4	−0.4
1970.IV–1973.IV (expansion)	17.6	12.0	12.7	14.5
1973.IV–1975.I (recession)	−7.8	3.0	−18.9	−4.3
1975.I–1980.I (expansion)	25.2	18.7	28.1	22.4
1980.I–1980.III (recession)	−3.6	0.8	−10.4	−2.3
1980.III–1981.III (expansion)	5.8	1.3	2.5	3.3
1981.III–1982.IV (recession)	−7.3	1.2	−6.3	−3.2
1982.IV–1990.I (expansion)	41.2	27.3	24.3	32.7

Source: US Board of Governors of the Federal Reserve System, Fame Data Base

a moderating influence. As already noted, US output would have grown even more rapidly in the absence of those deficits; the result might well have been an overheated economy, with appreciably higher inflation and interest rates.

This conclusion is supported by the data in Table 27.8. The growth rate of US real domestic demand in the years 1983–6 was high by historical standards – and extraordinarily high in 1983 and 1984, the two years of greatest increase in the US trade and current account deficits. Indeed, the 8.7 per cent growth in US domestic demand in 1984 was the highest since 1951. Had the USA been unable to acquire additional goods and services from abroad to help satisfy this surging demand, the nation could have experienced 'bottlenecks' – if not more general shortages – as well as an acceleration of inflation. Even with the huge increase in its net imports, the US economy expanded its output in 1984 by 6.8 per cent, which, again, was the fastest rate of growth since 1951.

Partly because of the availability of imported goods, this rapid expansion took place without any rise in overall inflation as measured by the GNP deflator. To be sure, the nation's high rate of unemployment – 7.4 per cent in 1984 – also militated against rising inflation. But the unemployment rate did fall steadily after 1983, and by the end of 1986, according to some authorities, was at or near the level at which it would no longer serve to restrain inflation (Wachter 1986). This level would have been reached much sooner without the increase in net imports.

It also seems clear that interest rates would have been higher in the USA had the nation been foreclosed from borrowing abroad. As reported in Table 27.11, gross private saving in the USA declined markedly as a share of GNP from 1981 to 1989 even though government dissaving during the 1980s was at unusually high levels; the nation stepped up its foreign borrowing to help offset these developments. Without the availability of foreign financing, US interest rates would have risen so as to choke back the level of private domestic investment to the lower level of financing provided from domestic sources alone. Even with the net inflow of foreign capital, US interest rates, both short and long term, reached record heights in the early 1980s (US Bureau of the Census 1975, 1986).

Thus, the near-term consequences of its external deficits seem to have been rather beneficial for the USA. What about the longer term?

MUST THE DEFICIT BE REDUCED?

Both common sense and experience testify that neither individuals nor nations can incur debt without regard to ability to repay. But it would be a gross exaggeration to suggest that the USA has been threatened with an imminent debt crisis. By no conventional statistical indicator is the nation in such desperate straits.

In this kind of analysis, it is common to distinguish between liquidity and solvency risk. Although countries do not declare bankruptcy, a country is insolvent if it is unable, for either economic or political reasons, to meet its debt obligations over the long term. By contrast, illiquidity means that a country cannot meet its obligations coming due in the near term, but can discharge those obligations, with accrued interest, in the longer run, along with the rest of its obligations.

To assist in evaluating such risk, analysts have developed various indicators of the burden of international indebtedness. Although these indicators are crude, they can help to signal emerging distress. Some widely used indicators focus on the share of a country's output or income that is owed to its creditors. Others focus on the share of export earnings that is absorbed by payments to creditors, recognizing that some significant fraction of those earnings must remain to pay for imports.

Table 27.14 contains data for some of these indicators that were readily available for a sample of diverse countries. At the end of 1989 gross external debt as a percentage of GNP was lower for the USA than for any of the other countries; no alarm was being sounded by this indicator. Nor was gross external debt as a percentage of exports high by comparison with the typical country listed. Somewhat less reassuring was the percentage of US export receipts consumed by debt service payments to foreign creditors. On balance, one could hardly make the case from such indicators that the USA was facing a debt crisis, especially since the indicators fail to take into account the relatively large foreign assets held by US residents.

One key difference between the USA and the countries that have suffered debt repayment problems in recent years is that the great bulk of US external debt has been denominated in US rather than foreign currency. Unlike debtors in these other countries, US debtors generally have not had to acquire foreign exchange with which to service their external debts. Were this practice to continue, US debtors would be unlikely to experience more difficulty in meeting their external obligations than in meeting their obligations to domestic creditors. In other words, any debt crisis encountered by the USA would be a general crisis, imperilling resident as well as foreign creditors, rather than an exclusively international crisis. Only

Table 27.14 Selected debt burden indicators for the USA and other countries, 1989

	Gross external debt as per cent of		Debt service on gross external debt as per cent of exports of goods, services and private transfers
	GNP or GDP	*Exports of goods, services and private transfers*	
USA	14.1	123.3	72.0
Canada	39.8	144.7	55.5
Germany	25.0	68.9	45.0
Denmark	72.0	175.0	117.5
Argentina	117.0	506.4	89.8
Brazil	38.9	304.3	103.2
Mexico	54.4	269.5	90.3

Source: Morgan Guaranty Trust Co.
Note: Data are partly estimated.

a most unlikely development, such as systematic lending by foreigners to unsound US businesses or limitations by the US government on US payments to foreign creditors, would generate a peculiarly international problem. On the other hand, should US external debt come to be denominated largely in foreign currencies, a depreciation of the dollar against those currencies would, of course, increase the number of dollars that US debtors were obligated to repay; and a sharp depreciation could provoke a debt crisis that was initially concentrated in the international sector.

The fact that US external debt is owed overwhelmingly in dollars does not mean that the debt imposes no burden, nor does the improbability of an external debt crisis mean that the USA could continue along the path set upon a few years ago. Even if a nation were inclined to borrow without limit, others generally would not lend to it beyond its perceived capacity to service its debt. The moral for the USA is that it would be unable to continue incurring such relatively large current account deficits in the long run, even if its government deficit remained large.

The long run, however, could be rather long. Some elementary computations are illuminating. In 1987 the US current account deficit attained a peak of 3.6 per cent of US GNP, with GNP at $4.5 trillion. Suppose that the current account deficit were to run at 3.5 per cent of GNP, and that nominal GNP were to increase by 6 per cent each year, a fairly modest rate by recent historical standards. Also suppose that the average interest rate, or more generally the average rate of return, earned by foreigners investing in the USA were 8 per cent per annum. Finally, since the USA reportedly received nearly as much in interest and other income payments from foreigners as it made to them in 1989 (even though the data showed the nation then to be a sizeable net debtor), we shall suppose that the USA did not in fact become a net debtor until this writing.

On these assumptions, the fourth column of Table 27.15 shows how net interest earned by foreigners would rise as a percentage of US GNP over a fifty-year period. After a half-century, this interest burden would amount to about 4.7 per cent of US GNP. More likely, if US net debt did rise markedly in relation to GNP, foreigners would demand higher interest rates to compensate for the reduced creditworthiness of the nation (for the seemingly greater risk of lending to it). Thus, the percentages in the fourth column would climb initially at a faster pace than shown, and then at a slower pace as foreigners became reluctant to extend additional loans. Indeed, to contemplate a net foreign debt of the USA amounting to more than half its GNP, as this scenario does, might seem beyond the realm of reason. As the data in Table 27.14 suggest, such ratios did obtain for gross (and presumably net) external debt at the end of 1988 for some countries, but most were less developed, with much smaller economies, than the USA. Moreover, net interest ratios approaching the highest levels shown in the fourth column of Table 27.15 would probably translate into something like two-fifths of US exports of goods and services. In any event, our calculations are merely illustrations, not forecasts.

An interesting alternative is to assume that the US current account deficit did not rise with GNP but continued at an annual rate of about $150 billion (a rate somewhat exceeded during mid-1987) and to retain the other assumptions underlying the preceding computations. In this case, the net interest burden as a percentage of GNP would move upward for many years, as shown by the last column in Table 27.14, but would then decline (beginning with the eighteenth year, not shown in the table). This scenario seems much less threatening.

Variations in the underlying assumptions would, of course, yield different hypothetical outcomes. What seems clear from the calculations presented is that the US current account deficit could not remain so high *in relation to GNP* as it was in 1987. And in fact the deficit has decreased not only in relation to GNP but in absolute magnitude, amounting to $110 billion, or 2.1 per cent of GNP, in 1989. It is not so immediately obvious that the deficit must be reduced still further. As illustrated in Table 27.15, even with a continuing

Table 27.15 Net US interest burden from external debt under differing assumptions
(billions of dollars, unless otherwise noted)

Year	Nominal GNP	Annual current account deficit assumed to be 3.5 per cent of GNP			Annual current account deficit assumed to be $150 billion		
		Cumulative current account deficit	Net interest on cumulative deficit	Net interest as per cent of GNP	Cumulative current account deficit	Net interest on cumulative deficit	Net interest as per cent of GNP
1	4,500	157.5	12.6	0.28	150	12	0.27
2	4,770	324.5	26.0	0.55	300	24	0.50
3	5,056.2	501.4	40.1	0.79	450	36	0.71
4	5,359.6	689.0	55.1	1.03	600	48	0.90
5	5,681.1	887.8	71.0	1.25	750	60	1.06
6	6,022.0	1,098.6	87.9	1.46	900	72	1.20
7	6,383.3	1,322.0	105.8	1.66	1,050	84	1.32
8	6,766.3	1,558.8	124.7	1.84	1,200	96	1.42
9	7,172.3	1,809.9	144.8	2.02	1,350	108	1.51
10	7,602.7	2,076.0	166.1	2.18	1,500	120	1.58
20	13,615.2	5,793.7	463.5	3.40	3,000	240	1.76
30	24.382.7	12,451.7	996.1	4.09	4,500	360	1.48
40	43,666.7	24,375.0	1,950.0	4.47	6,000	480	1.10
50	78,198.7	45,727.9	3,658.2	4.68	7,500	600	0.77

Notes: Nominal GNP is assumed to increase by 6 per cent annually. Interest rate is assumed to be 8 per cent and is applied to the net debt outstanding at the end of each period, which is taken to be zero prior to year one.

annual deficit as great as $150 billion, US GNP presumably would eventually increase more rapidly than US net indebtedness (the accumulated deficit), so that the net interest burden would begin to decline in relation to GNP well before reaching the level of 2 per cent.

To suggest that the USA might continue to incur a sizeable current account deficit is not to imply that the nation can avoid any adjustment in its external accounts. As US net interest payments to foreigners increase with US net indebtedness, the nation will have to generate increasing net surpluses (or smaller net deficits) on other current account transactions – essentially merchandise trade – in order to limit expansion of the overall current account deficit. How this adjustment takes place is the topic of the next section.

THE NATURE OF THE ADJUSTMENT

The point has been made that total US demand, or spending, increased faster than US output during most of the 1980s, and that the nation is absorbing foreign saving to finance the gap. To reduce the imbalance, or to prevent it from rising as interest payments to foreigners go up, the USA must raise the growth rate of its output or reduce the growth rate of its spending. As can be seen in Table 27.8, the nation did succeed in lowering the growth rate of demand relative to that of GNP during the latter part of the 1980s. However, the rate of inflation, as measured by the GNP deflator, rose from 2½ per cent in 1986 to 4¼ per cent in 1989, implying that the nation's productive capacity was being strained beyond the point at which prices could be held relatively stable.

For the future, reducing the current account deficit while restraining inflation will require that total demand grow more slowly than in recent years. Efforts to sustain output growth at the rate of the mid to late 1980s would court a marked rise in the rate of inflation. Of course, measures that raised output by raising productivity would not invite higher inflation. But raising the productivity of capital would tend to attract more investment from abroad and, as we have seen, investment from abroad works to enlarge rather than diminish the current account deficit. Therefore, policies designed to raise the growth rate of output probably hold little promise for shrinking the external imbalances of the USA.

The alternative course, restraining total spending, is now under way. Slowing the growth of *consumption* spending, private or government, would, of course, be equivalent to accelerating the pace of saving, unless output growth slowed to the same degree. Alternatively, if the course of saving were left unchanged, the economy could cut back on the growth of its private *investment* spending. Cutting back on investment in plant and equipment, however, would reduce the nation's future output.

The government might well step up the rate of saving by contracting the budget deficit, either by cutting back its own spending programmes or by raising taxes so that households would lower their consumption spending.[8] If reduction of the budget deficit – and of the economic stimulus the deficit provides – took place at a moderate pace, a recession need not ensue, since a goal of the deficit reduction would be to allow US net exports, another stimulus, to expand more rapidly. One way that such deficit reduction could boost US net exports would be by generating a depreciation of the dollar's foreign exchange value, just as enlargement of the deficit had generated an appreciation.

Thus, if US spending must be constrained, cutting the federal budget deficit seems a relatively appealing strategy for cutting the international trade deficit. But are alternative or supplementary strategies available that do not rely on such direct attacks on spending? This economist is tempted to reply that there is no free lunch.

One alternative government strategy would be to do nothing at all – to take no action designed specifically to shrink the US trade deficit, even in relation to GNP. As US indebtedness mounted in relation to US exports and GNP, investors would become more reluctant to lend to, or acquire net claims on, the USA, thus putting upward pressure on US interest rates and downward pressure on the foreign exchange value of the dollar. Indeed, this process seemed to be under way late in 1986 and at times during 1987, as some US interest rates rose sharply in relation to rates in some other industrial countries even as the dollar dropped in value (Figure 27.1) against the currencies of those countries. The higher US interest rates would discourage US builders and other businesses from investing in new structures and equipment, and this reduced spending would help to improve the US trade balance, albeit at the expense of future US growth. Trade balance improvement would also be fostered by the depreciation of the dollar.

Just how dollar depreciation improves the US trade balance is a matter of some debate. One conceivable route is via a reduction in the purchasing power of US money balances. A rise in the dollar price of foreign currency (dollar depreciation) tends to raise the dollar prices of foreign goods imported into the USA, as well as the prices of substitute goods produced within the country. Thus, the purchasing power of US residents could be somewhat diminished, discouraging spending and improving the balance of trade.

Dollar depreciation typically has another related price effect that also is helpful. The depreciation-induced rise in the dollar price of imports, and of exports, encourages US businesses to shift resources into the production of export goods and of goods that can substitute for imports, and away from the production of goods that do not move in international trade. The same price movements encourage US consumers to switch their purchases away from the goods that move in international trade and toward non-traded goods.

Again, the tendency is to improve the trade balance. And if the prices of non-traded goods decline, or rise more slowly than before the depreciation, the nation need not experience a marked rise in its overall rate of inflation.

Still another government strategy to reduce the trade deficit would be protectionism. Now, the US trade deficit has been very large, and any US import tariffs or quotas severe enough to have a sizeable initial impact on the deficit would certainly provoke foreign retaliation against US exports. Even in the absence of retaliation, tariffs or quotas would not be very effective in decreasing the trade deficit unless they somehow reduced total US spending. A tariff could reduce spending if the tariff revenue were used by the government to cut back on its budget deficit, but other taxes would offer the same opportunity without the cost of an international trade war. Protectionism, therefore, is not a promising approach to the problem.

Of the various strategies considered, then, the most desirable would be a combination of federal deficit reduction and tolerance of dollar depreciation. The adjustment process under way thus far has not been ideal. At this writing, significant federal deficit reduction is problematical and interest rates remain at levels relatively high by historical standards, tending to depress private investment. In this connection, Table 27.11 indicates that the unusually high level of US borrowing from abroad after 1982 was not accompanied by an unusually high level of private domestic investment. The implication is that the increased borrowing from abroad went mainly or entirely to finance increased consumption. Unlike sound investment, consumption generates no return with which to repay a loan. Thus, to service its foreign debt the USA will have to consume less than it otherwise would.

SUMMARY

After 1982 the US international investment position dramatically shifted from one of sizeable net creditor to much more sizeable net debtor, with

further huge, debt-augmenting deficits in the offing. This transformation occurred even though the USA may have lost little or no competitiveness for 'supply-side' reasons. In particular, during the years of rapid deterioration in the US trade balance, US labour productivity gains were virtually as great as those in other industrial nations; the performance of US-based multinational firms suggests that US management was maintaining its international competitiveness; and the USA did in fact maintain its share of world output.

Nor can unfair foreign trading practices explain much of the US external deficits. The deterioration in the US trade balance was distributed widely across commodity categories, as well as across geographic areas. It seems most unlikely that virtually all major trading partners of the USA would simultaneously have intensified unfair practices in trade with the USA in virtually all major commodity categories.

A more plausible explanation of the US external deficit focuses on (1) the more rapid expansion of real income and demand in the USA than in the rest of the world after 1982 and (2) the appreciation of the dollar in the foreign exchange markets after mid-1980, a development that reduced the price competitiveness of US goods. Both of these factors stimulated greater growth in US purchases of foreign goods than in foreign purchases of US goods; both factors were themselves a result largely of the world-wide blend of monetary and fiscal policies, including the huge increase in the US federal budget deficit. This increase in net federal spending boosted aggregate US demand. Moreover, the increase in US government borrowing associated with the budget deficit, coupled with an anti-inflationary US monetary policy, tended to push up US interest rates (adjusted for inflation), thus attracting investment by foreigners whose purchases of dollar-denominated securities served to bid up the value of the dollar in the foreign exchange markets.

Contrary to a widespread impression, the US trade deficits were not accompanied by a 'deindustrialization of America'. Following the 1981–2 recession, the production of goods grew faster than the production of services within the USA, and the growth of goods production compared favourably with that during earlier economic expansions. Thus, US goods producers fared relatively well despite the increased US trade deficit. Rather than destroying large segments of American industry, imports from abroad helped to satisfy the swiftly growing US demand, without the development of shortages and rising inflation.

Although the net foreign debt of the USA soared with the trade deficit, no crisis looms for the nation on indebtedness. Over the longer run, of course, foreigners would not be prepared to lend more and more to a nation whose indebtedness continued to rise in relation to its gross output and exports. Thus, the US current account deficit has to shrink in relation to the nation's output and exports, and the trade deficit in particular must diminish if the nation is to fund increasing net interest payments to its foreign creditors. The depreciation of the dollar that took place after February 1985 will contribute to this adjustment, as would further dollar depreciation and measures to reduce the federal budget deficit. The adjustment will not be painless for the USA, which will be obliged to consume less than it otherwise would.

NOTES

1   Perhaps the most articulate exponent of the hard landing scenario was Stephen Marris (1985, 1987).
2   While some part of the large unidentified receipts in the US balance of payments has surely taken the form of foreign investment in the USA, it would almost certainly be a mistake to attribute all of these net receipts to such capital account transactions. Much evidence exists that a significant portion of the receipts has been generated not by capital account but by current account transactions, such as the sale of US goods and services abroad or the charging of interest on US loans to foreigners. In so far as the unidentified receipts have resulted from current account transactions, the reported value of US net indebtedness requires no upward revision.
3   It should also be noted that the measure of the US position in Tables 27.1–27.3 includes equity as well as debt claims, while the customary measures

of the debt of LDCs do not include equity held by foreigners. For a discussion of these matters, see Herman (1987: 1–4).
4   Herman (1987: 1–2); also see the latest issue of IMF's *World Economic Outlook* for more recent data than Herman supplies on developing-country debt.
5   For an outline of US law and procedures relating to the imposition of antidumping duties and countervailing duties, see US International Trade Commission (1989).
6   After surveying the estimates yielded by a large number of multi-country models, John F. Helliwell concludes that 'the US fiscal policy of the first half of the 1980s was responsible for about half of the buildup in the external deficit ...' (1990: 17).
7   Among these factors are resource discoveries, changes in tastes and technology and differences in national growth rates. Changes in tastes and in technology, however, as well as growth trend differentials, generally exert their influence gradually over long periods and major resource discoveries are rare. From year to year, movements in the real exchange rate and current account are more powerfully influenced by business cycle fluctuations, by government controls and by government monetary and fiscal policy, including changes in the government deficit such as those depicted in Figures 27.2 and 27.3.
8   Considerable controversy exists within the economics profession over the impact of government revenues and spending on aggregate demand. For example, see Martin Feldstein and Douglas W. Elmendorf, 'Government debt, government spending, and private sector behavior revisited: comment'; Franco Modigliani and Arlie G. Sterling, 'Government debt, government spending, and private sector behavior: a further comment'; and Roger C. Kormendi and Philip Meguire, 'Government debt, government spending, and private sector behavior: reply and update', in *American Economic Review* 80 (June 1990): 589–617.

REFERENCES

Bergsten, C. F. and Cline, W. R. (1985) *The United States–Japan Economic Problem*, Policy Analyses in International Economics 13, Washington, DC: Institute for International Economics, pp. 45–6.

Bergstrand, J. H. (1986) 'United States–Japanese trade: predictions using selected economic models', *New England Economic Review*, May–June: 26–37.

Christelow, D. (1985–6) 'Japan's intangible barriers to

trade in manufactures', *Federal Reserve Bank of New York Quarterly Review*, Winter: 11–18.

Deutsche Bundesbank (1986) 'External assets of the Federal Republic of Germany in mid-1986', *Monthly Report of the Deutsche Bundesbank* 38 (October): 30.

Feldstein, M. S. (1985) 'The view from North America', in C. F. Bergsten (ed.) *Global Economic Imbalances*, Special Reports 4, Washington, DC: Institute for International Economics, p. 7.

Helkie, W. L. and Hooper, P. (1988) 'An empirical analysis of the external deficit, 1980–86', in R. C. Bryant, G. Holtham and P. Hooper (eds) *External Deficits and the Dollar: The Pit and the Pendulum*, Washington, DC: Brookings Institution, Table 2-17.

Helliwell, J. F. (1990) 'Fiscal policy and the external deficit: siblings, but not twins', Working Paper 3313, Cambridge, MA: National Bureau of Economic Research, April.

Herman, B. (1987) 'The United States as a debtor country: indicators of resource transfer and solvency', Working Paper 2, UN Department of International Economic and Social Affairs, February.

Houthakker, H. S. and Magee, S. P. (1969) 'Income and price elasticities in world trade', *Review of Economics and Statistics* 51 (May): 111–25.

Hooper, P. and Mann, C. L. (1987) 'The U.S. external deficit: its causes and persistence', International Finance Discussion Papers 316, Washington, DC: Board of Governors of the Federal Reserve System, pp. 41–2, 95–6.

IMF (1988) *World Economic Outlook, April 1988*, World Economic and Financial Surveys, Washington, DC: IMF, p. 89.

Lipsey, R. E. and Kravis, I. (1987) 'The competitiveness and comparative advantage of US multinationals, 1957–1984', *Banca Nazionale del Lavoro Quarterly Review* 161 (June): 151.

Marris, S. (1985) *Deficits and the Dollar: The World Economy at Risk*, Washington, DC: Institute for International Economics.

—— (1987) *Deficits and the Dollar Revisited*, Washington, DC: Institute for International Economics.

McCulloch, R. and Richardson, J. D. (1986) 'US trade and the dollar: evaluating current policy options', in R. E. Baldwin and J. D. Richardson (eds) *Current US Trade Policy: Analysis, Agendas, and Administration*, NBER Conference Report, Cambridge, MA: National Bureau of Economic Research, pp. 56–7.

US Bureau of the Census (1975) *Historical Statistics of the United States, Colonial Times to 1970*, Part II, Washington, DC: US Government Printing Office, pp. 1001–4:

—— (1986) *Statistical Abstract of the United States: 1987*, Washington, DC: US Government Printing Office, pp. 492–3.

US Department of Commerce (1983) *The US Automobile Industry, 1982*, Washington, DC: US Department of Commerce, pp. 49–51.

US International Trade Commission (1988) *Operation of the Trade Agreements Program, 1987*, Publication 2095, Washington, DC: USITC, ch. 5, pp. 4–11.

—— (1989) *Operation of the Trade Agreements Program, 1988*, Publication 2208, Washington, DC: USITC, pp. 140–2.

US President (1985) *Economic Report of the President*, February, Washington, DC: US Government Printing Office, pp. 102–3.

Wachter, M. L. (1986) 'Comment on Lawrence H. Summers's "Why is the unemployment rate so very high near full employment?"', *Brookings Papers on Economic Activity* 2: 390–1.

28

US BORROWING FROM JAPAN

Jeffrey A. Frankel

INTRODUCTION

The USA became a net debtor internationally in early 1985, for the first time since the First World War. By the end of 1987 it had accumulated a net debt of $368 billion on the books, making it by far the largest net debtor nation in the world.[1] The IMF estimates that the debt will exceed $700 billion by the end of 1989.[2] At the current rate of borrowing – $150 billion a year – the debt will pass the $1 trillion mark in 1991. Meanwhile, Japan has become the largest creditor nation, with a net foreign investment position predicted to rise from $266 billion at the end of 1987 to more than $400 billion by the end of 1989.

Generating particular concern in the USA politically is the component of foreign-held assets that consists of foreign direct investment, even though this is only 17 per cent of the total as of the end of 1987 ($262/$1,536 billion).[3] In the 1988 presidential campaign, the Democrats have cited statistics that 10 per cent of American manufacturing is in the hands of foreign investors, and that 40 per cent of the commercial real estate in Los Angeles, 30 per cent in Houston and 20 per cent in other large cities is owned by foreigners.

The first half of this chapter examines briefly the major factors that brought about the original shift to US borrowing in the 1980s and that will determine future developments. The second half examines the implications of US indebtedness to Japan for the economic and political futures of the two countries.

ORIGINS OF THE US BORROWING FROM JAPAN

The Japanese pool of savings

The story of the record capital flows begins with the large pool of savings in Japan. Japanese households save at a rate of 22.5 per cent of disposable income, compared with 5.1 per cent in the USA, with most European countries somewhere in between.[4] Others have discussed extensively the reasons for the high Japanese saving rate – the rapidly aging population, the high price of housing and the Japanese tax system. It will be interesting to see if the abolition of the *maruyu* system in April 1988 leads to a reduction in the level of saving in Japan. In view of the lack of evidence that the elasticity of saving with respect to the rate of return is high, or even positive, such a response seems unlikely. (Saxonhouse (1982) argues that Japanese are target-savers and thus may even *increase* saving in response to decreases in the after-tax rate of return.)

Also important for explaining the international capital flow is the fact that a high and increasing share of the Japanese pool of savings takes the form of portfolios held by insurance companies and trust funds. Managers of such funds are considered more ready to explore overseas outlets for their investments than are small individual savers or non-financial corporations, while even banks take only limited net open positions in foreign currency.

The Japanese saving rate has been high, and the

US rate low, for some time.[5] We must look at other factors to explain why Japanese residents elected to increase sharply their net claims on Americans in the 1980s.

Rates of return

Perhaps the most easily identified incentive for the Japanese to begin sending vast amounts of capital to the USA after 1980 was the increase in US rates of return.[6] US interest rates increased sharply between 1980 and mid-1982, especially long-term rates. Nominal interest rates declined subsequently, but because expected inflation was declining, long-term real interest rates did not peak until mid-1984. Real interest rates also rose in Japan and other trading partners, but not by as much. Thus the differential shifted in favour of US investments. Over this same period, the differential yield on equities also shifted in favour of the USA: the differential in dividend yields increased from 2.9 per cent at the end of 1980 to 3.7 per cent in mid-1984, and the differential in earnings–price ratios increased from 4.8 per cent to 6.3 per cent.[7]

While this shift in real rates of return in the early 1980s can explain the increased attractiveness of investing in the USA as opposed to Japan, two questions immediately follow. First, what caused the shift? Second, why did the demand for US assets continue to increase after mid-1984, when the real interest differential (and the equity yield differentials as well) began to decline?

To explain the US real interest rate, think of it as determined so that the funds needed for investment do not exceed the funds available from saving, the investment rate depending negatively on the real interest rate and the national saving rate also depending (presumably positively) on the real interest rate. (National saving is defined as private saving plus public saving, i.e. whatever private saving is left over after financing the budget deficit.) Then the increase in real interest rates could be due either to an upward shift in investment demand, a downward shift in the supply of national saving or some combination of the two.

The most popular explanation, and the one to which I subscribe, is that the enormous structural increase in the federal budget deficit reduced national savings and forced up the real interest rate. The budget deficit averaged less than 2 per cent of GNP in the 1970s, but climbed to 5 per cent of GNP following the 1981–3 tax cuts and defence build-up. According to some theories, there should have been an increase in private saving to offset the deficit. But US personal saving rates have been significantly lower in the mid-1980s than they were in the 1970s, not higher. Total net national saving – private plus public – has fallen from an average of 7 per cent of GNP in the 1970s (already down from the 1950s and 1960s) to less than 2 per cent of GNP in 1987.

At the same time that the USA was increasing its structural budget deficit, Japan took substantial steps to *reduce* its budget deficit, accentuating the differential in real interest rates and thereby providing further incentive for the flow of capital out of Japan and into the USA. Estimated structural changes in the central government budget deficit between 1980 and 1986 are +2.7 per cent of GNP for the USA and −1.8 per cent of GNP for Japan (IMF 1986).

An alternative explanation sometimes given for the increase in US real interest rates is that US investment demand increased in response to the more favourable treatment toward business fixed investment in the 1981 tax bill and to the generally pro-business climate of the Reagan Administration. There are several problems with this argument. In the first place, although the investment rate did rise rapidly in 1983–4, the investment rate always rises in expansions and this increase was not greater than the decline in the 1981–2 recession: by 1987 the US investment rate had at best only reattained the level of the 1970s.[8] In the second place, calculations of the benefits of the tax incentives suggest that they were smaller than the increase in real interest rates, so that the after-tax cost of capital was not reduced. In the third place, the Treasury tax reform plan of 1984 and the revised tax reform plan actually passed by Congress and signed by the President in 1986 raised corporate income taxes and undid the effects of the 1981 bill. An increase in investment thus seems less able to explain the US demand for funds than does the increase in the structural budget deficit.

International financial market liberalization

Before the present decade, one might not have expected shifts in fiscal policy to have such large effects on capital flows to or from Japan. In the 1970s the degree of international capital mobility was much lower, owing to controls by the Japanese government and less well-developed financial markets in Japan generally. Indeed a fiscal contraction such as that enacted by Japan in the early 1980s would have been predicted by the Japanese macroeconomic models of the time to result in a shift of international demand *toward yen*, as opposed to the shift toward dollars that in the event became apparent. In other words, these models featured a sufficiently low degree of international capital mobility that effects on the capital account from changes in interest rates were thought to be outweighed by effects on the trade account from changes in the level of income.

In 1979–80, the Japanese government removed most of the controls that had previously prevented foreign residents from buying assets in Japan. A number of studies have documented that the change in policy actually had the effect predicted by economic theory. From January 1975 to April 1979 there had been a substantial differential between the three-month *gensaki* interest rate that could be earned in Tokyo and the comparable three-month Euro-yen interest rate that could be earned offshore in London: 1.84 per cent. This differential was evidence that foreign investors had not been free to hold Japanese assets. Thereafter, the differential fell sharply (as Figure 28.1 shows). Indeed, it actually turned negative (−0.26 for the period May 1979 to November 1983), demonstrating that the controls that remained were, if anything, discouraging capital from *leaving* the country rather than from entering it.[9]

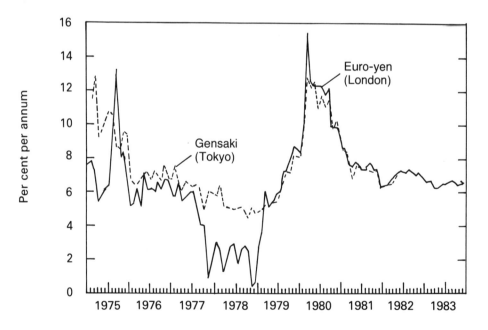

Figure 28.1 Interest rates on the yen

Source: Frankel 1984

538

A controversy arose in October 1983 when some American businessmen, alarmed by devastating competition from Japanese exporters, convinced top officials in the US Treasury Department, despite the evidence just cited, that the Japanese government was still using some form of capital market restrictions to keep the value of the yen lower than it would otherwise be. There followed a campaign by the US government to induce Japan to adopt a whole list of measures further liberalizing its capital markets. This campaign, which reinforced forces already under way within Japan, came to fruition in the May 1984 yen–dollar agreement between the Treasury and the Ministry of Finance.

The predictable result of the liberalization was an increase in net capital outflows from Japan, attracted by the higher rates of return available in the USA. The Japanese rate of acquisition of long-term assets abroad jumped from $32.5 billion in 1983 to $56.8 billion in 1984, the majority of it in the form of portfolio investment. The offshore–onshore interest differential disappeared altogether. Furthermore, the yen depreciated another 8 per cent against the dollar in 1984. In short, the yen–dollar agreement was successful at increasing Japan's integration into world financial markets, but not at the stated US goal of promoting an increase in the demand for Japanese assets. Indeed, the combination of the increase in US interest rates and the Japanese liberalization – which has proceeded steadily with further measures such as the liberalization of ceilings of foreign security holdings by Japanese insurance companies and trust banks – together explains most of the capital outflow.[10]

Country risk and the safe haven hypothesis

Another important determinant of international capital flows is country risk, the risk attaching to assets issued in a given country (as opposed to assets denominated in a given currency) that their value will be impaired by default, future capital controls etc. (as opposed to adverse movements in the exchange rate). It has been suggested in particular that the explanation for the enormous flows of capital to the USA in the 1980s is a decrease in investors' perceptions of country risk there relative to the rest of the world. This is the 'safe haven' hypothesis. Its proponents are mostly the same observers who would explain the increase in US real interest rates as an increase in investment demand. It is obvious that ever since August 1982 assets held in Latin America and other debt-troubled regions have been much less attractive than assets held in the USA, from the viewpoint of investors residing in those countries as much as banks residing in the creditor countries. It is much less clear that the perceived safety of assets held in the USA has increased relative to Japan or Europe. Indeed the Japanese financial liberalization just described should, if anything, have reduced country risk associated with Japan.

The tests of three-month onshore–offshore interest rate parity suggest that, not only do no important barriers remain to separate international investors from the portfolios they wish to hold, but furthermore Japanese assets and US assets (covered to eliminate foreign exchange risk) are close to perfect substitutes in investors' portfolios. Until now, these conclusions have only been established for short-term assets, however. It has been argued, for example by Feldstein and Horioka, that capital may be less mobile across national boundaries at longer-term maturities:

> It is clear from the yields on short-term securities in the Eurocurrency market and the forward prices of those currencies that liquid financial capital moves very rapidly to arbitrage such short-term differentials.... There are however reasons to be sceptical about the extent of such long-term arbitrage.
> (1980: 315)

Studies of international interest rate parity have been restricted by a lack of forward exchange rates at horizons going out much further than one year. But even without the use of forward rate data, there are ways of getting around the problem of exchange risk. Frankel (1987: 9.5.1) compares long-term interest rates on Euro-dollar bonds with rates on dollar bonds issued in the USA. In 1980–2, US corporations were able to borrow more cheaply in the Euromarket than by issuing bonds domestically. The differential apparently became as large as 3.3 per cent in July 1981.[11] It is not clear why US borrowers did not take greater advantage of the cheaper offshore rates than they did. The onshore dollar interest rate fell sharply in mid-1982 relative to the Eurobond rate, which is consistent with the hypothesis of a safe-haven shift into US assets at that one point in time. But it is also consistent with another hypothesis.

As late as 1982 there remained some frictions that prevented perfect arbitrage between the USA and Euromarkets. After US corporate bond rates rose to post-war record levels in 1980 and 1981, and after the LDC debt crisis undermined confidence in the banking system in 1982, a keener interest in issuing bonds directly in the Euromarket sprang up among US corporations. Such innovations as currency swaps, interest rate swaps, note issuance facilities and Eurocommercial paper developed rapidly in 1983 and 1984, making it easier for US corporations to use the Euromarket without the intermediation of banks. This was the international aspect of the well-known trend of 'securitization'. Securities-market facilities, as opposed to bank loans, rose from 26 per cent of total new lending facilities arranged in international financial markets in 1981 to 59 per cent in 1983 and 91 per cent in 1985, according to Bryant (1987: 56). In 1984, foreign purchases of US securities for the first time passed banking flows as the largest component of the US capital inflow, on either a gross or a net basis. Foreign net purchases of US corporate securities rose from $15 billion in 1982 to $48 billion in 1985, most of it through the Euromarket (*US Federal Reserve Bulletin*, May 1985, May 1986). Assisting in the increase in US corporate borrowing abroad was the July 1984 abolition by the US Treasury of the withholding tax on interest payments from US issuers to foreign residents.

Thus the hypothesis is that it simply took several years to arbitrage away the interest differential that opened up in 1980–2. What might at

first be regarded as a puzzlingly slow response could instead be viewed as a relatively rapid response in the light of the institutional innovations needed and the large shift in the quantity of Eurobond issues involved. The hypothesis that the last barriers to perfect international financial integration were broken down around 1982 can explain the sharp fall in the positive Euro–US differential at the long end of the maturity spectrum.

Even if one instead interprets the mid-1982 fall in the long-term interest differential as evidence of a safe-haven shift into US assets at that time, this factor cannot explain the continued increase in the demand for US assets thereafter. The differential was steady, or if anything rose a little, in 1983 and 1984.

Is it possible that changes in perceived country risk in Japan are a factor? Data on currency swap rates can be used in place of forward exchange rates to test the long-term version of interest rate parity. Popper (1987) finds that the swap-covered return differential on five-year US government bonds versus Japanese bonds averaged only 1.7 basis points from 3 October 1985 to 10 July 1986, and that the differential on seven-year bonds averaged only 5.3 basis points. The means mask a little variation in the differential. But a band of 46 basis points is large enough to encompass 95 per cent of the observations for the five-year bonds; the band is 34 basis points for the seven-year bonds. These differentials are small, relative not only to the equivalent differentials for the UK, for example, but relative even to the short-term differentials. Thus the results have two implications. The wider implication is to refute the Feldstein–Horioka conjecture that capital is less mobile for long-term assets than for short-term assets. The implication for the narrower question at hand is that by 1986 there appear to have been no significant country-risk factors rendering Japanese assets imperfect substitutes for Euromarket assets. The same was true of US assets by 1986. We evidently must look somewhere other than to country risk to explain the more recent Japan–USA capital flows.

Expected appreciation of the yen against the dollar

The dollar–yen interest differential declined substantially from 1984 to 1987, which should by itself have caused a reduced demand for dollar assets. But exchange rate expectations are an equally important determinant of the expected rate of return and therefore of the relative demand for dollar and yen assets. Simple notions of long-run PPP or exchange rate overshooting suggest that the 24 per cent appreciation of the dollar against the yen from 1978 to February 1985 (not to mention the consequent US trade deficit and Japanese surplus) should have generated expectations of future dollar depreciation back toward long-run equilibrium.

Indeed surveys of market participants over this period show an increase in the expected future rate of dollar depreciation. A survey conducted annually over the period 1981–4 by American Express Banking Corporation in London, for example, shows that expected year-ahead depreciation of the dollar against the yen averaged 9.25 per cent, up sharply from 1976–8 (Frankel and Froot 1985: Table 2). Similarly, a survey conducted every six weeks by the *Economist*-affiliated *Financial Report* shows that for the period June 1981 to December 1985 expected year-ahead depreciation of the dollar against the yen averaged 10.67 per cent (Frankel and Froot 1987: 254). Investors systematically expect the exchange rate to regress toward a long-run equilibrium such as PPP, at an estimated rate in the American Express data equal to 12 per cent of whatever the current gap is (Frankel and Froot 1987: 263).

The overshooting theory suggests that the 40 per cent depreciation of the dollar against the yen from February 1985 to February 1987, the time of the Louvre Accord to stabilize the exchange rate, should have brought the exchange rate much closer to its perceived long-run equilibrium – if not past it – and thus should have reduced the expected rate of future dollar depreciation. The *Economist* survey indeed shows expected year-

ahead dollar–yen depreciation declining to 4.0 per cent by 20 January 1987, and declining further to 1.6 per cent by 2 February 1988. This decline in expected depreciation furnishes one possible explanation of how international investors would have been willing to continue increasing their holdings of dollar securities after 1984 despite the decline in the nominal interest differential.[12]

Unfortunately for the overshooting theory, the regressive model of expectations does not at all fit the pattern of a shorter-term expectations survey of foreign exchange traders conducted weekly by Money Market Services (MMS). Over the period October 1984 to February 1986, when the dollar was high, the MMS respondents forecast dollar depreciation against the yen at a four-week horizon equal to 2.99 per cent per annum and at a one-week horizon of 5.40 per cent per annum (Frankel and Froot 1987: 254). But as of 6 February 1987, for example, when the dollar was much lower, the MMS respondents forecast depreciation at an even more rapid rate: 34.57 per cent per annum at the four-week horizon and 15.15 per cent per annum at the one-week horizon. The problem is that, at horizons of one week to three months, the MMS survey respondents forecast by extrapolating the most recent trend, rather than by a model of regression toward any long-run equilibrium. In a week when the yen appreciates 1 per cent, for example, the MMS respondents forecast a further appreciation of 0.24 per cent over the coming week (12 per cent per annum). Such estimates are statistically significant at the 99 per cent level (Frankel and Froot 1987: 263). Ito (1987) and Froot and Ito (1988) have found similar results using survey data collected from Japanese respondents by the Japan Center for International Finance.

Thus the problem of exchange rate determination is complicated by the fact that short-term 'speculators' do not appear to agree on a simple model of regression toward an equilibrium dictated by fundamentals. It is quite possible that their high-volume trading is based on ever-changing and diverse guesses as to what the current market trend is, and that excess volatility in the foreign exchange market is the result. Fortunately, for present purposes we are not trying to explain the yen–dollar exchange rate, but only the flow of capital from Japan to the USA.

The capital flow that we are trying to explain consists overwhelmingly of long-term securities. Indeed, more than 100 per cent of the Japanese capital outflow is long term: according to Japanese data, short-term capital has on net been flowing in the other direction since 1984 (through the first half of 1988).[13] Thus short-term expectations may be less relevant than long-term expectations for explaining the flow. Over 83 per cent of the long-term net capital flow from Japan to the USA in 1986 consisted of investment in securities, despite the recent growth of Japanese foreign direct investment (Frankel and Froot 1987: 16). Most consists of purchases of dollar-denominated bonds and is thus sensitive to exchange rate expectations. Out of the gross Japanese investment in foreign securities in 1986, only 1.9 per cent consisted of yen-denominated external bonds (Frankel and Froot 1987: 17). Only 6.9 per cent consisted of equities, even with the unprecedented growth in Japanese investment in the US stock market in 1986, and returns on foreign equity investment may anyway be as sensitive to exchange rate changes as are bond returns. Thus for most of the Japan–USA capital flow, long-term exchange rate expectations are probably an important determinant. The argument appears intact: the realized depreciation of the dollar since 1985 has reduced investors' expectations of *future* depreciation, and thus given them an incentive to continue buying dollar assets.

One might argue further, based on the MMS expectation survey results, that the observed flow of short-term capital *into* Japan during the recent three-year period of yen appreciation is due to speculators forming expectations of further yen appreciation by extrapolation of the recent trend. But this argument would itself be rather speculative. It would require that those individuals who engage in short-term speculation form expectations differently from those who buy and sell longer-term securities on the basis of economic fundamentals, though it is possible that a single bank or other institution does both simultaneously.[14]

An alternative explanation for the pattern whereby Japan at the short term is borrowing on net, while at the long term is investing abroad on net, is that Japan is providing the intermediation function of the World Banker, as did the USA in the 1960s. The importance of Japanese banks, and the magnitude of Japanese wealth more generally, would be enough to explain this World Banker role. But the intermediation pattern – borrowing short term and lending long term – could also be explained if the Japanese tend to have a longer time horizon in their planning than Americans. This hypothesis would match frequently heard criticisms of American managers, stockholders and speculators as focusing too much on short-term profits, compared with their Japanese counterparts who prosper over time because they are prepared to take short-term losses in order to make long-term gains.[15]

Diversification of exchange risk

One way of getting a handle on investors' demand for dollar assets versus yen assets is the theory of optimal portfolio diversification. Even in the absence of factors like capital controls of country risk (the second and fourth factors above, respectively), investors do not base their demands for yen versus dollars solely on expected returns (interest rates and expected currency depreciation, the third and fifth factors above, respectively), because they are also concerned about exchange rate risk. The observation that conditional exchange rate variances themselves vary over time has generated a great deal of research in the last few years. In the present context, Kawai and Okumura (1988: 13) find a negative effect of the yen–dollar standard deviation on the Japanese capital outflow for the period 1984.1–1987.9. Can variation in the risk premium explain variation in the Japanese demand for dollars?

Let x be the share of the portfolio allocated to dollar assets as opposed to yen. If an investor seeks to maximize a function of the mean and variance of end-of-period wealth, it can be shown that the optimal share is given by (Frankel 1986 or Fukao 1987, 1988)

$$x = A + B\,\mathrm{rp}$$

A is known as the 'minimum-variance portfolio' and the other term is the 'speculative portfolio', where $B = 1/RV$, rp is the risk premium (the dollar–yen interest differential minus expected dollar depreciation), R is the coefficient of relative risk aversion and V is the conditional variance of the exchange rate.

One can estimate the conditional variance in a number of ways (e.g. by the now-popular ARCH model or by extracting implicit variances from options prices). But existing studies of exchange risk have been hampered by the difficulty in knowing whether an increase in uncertainty should reduce the demand for dollar assets or should reduce the demand for the other currency. Kawai and Okumura presuppose that it should reduce the demand for dollars, and thus are puzzled by the fact that their uncertainty term appears with a significant positive coefficient for the period 1982.1–1983.12. But the theory says that if the stock of dollar assets x falls short of the share given by the minimum-variance portfolio A, at a point in time, then the risk premium on dollars will be negative and an increase in uncertainty V will indeed raise the demand for dollars. Given the rapid rate at which the US budget deficit has been pumping out dollar assets into the world portfolio, via the US current account deficit, it is possible that $x - A$ has gone from negative to positive since 1983, so that the sign of the risk relationship has flipped.

It may be worth trying some crude calculations. If we are willing to assume that the relevant measure of purchasing power is a basket with weight A' on goods whose price in the short run is set (non-stochastic) in terms of dollars and weight $1 - A'$ on goods whose price is set in terms of yen, then the minimum-variance portfolio turns out to be given by A'. For Japanese residents, we could measure A' by the share of imports in GNP, 0.064

in 1986.[16] Data in Kawai and Okumura show that the proportion x of the securities portfolios of Japanese financial institutions in the aggregate that was held as foreign securities was 3.13 per cent in 1980, 9.48 per cent in 1984 and 16.47 per cent as of March 1987. (If one measures the holdings as percentages of total assets rather than just securities, then the numbers are much smaller and would be still more so if one sought to include the holdings of small investors and non-financial institutions.) Thus it is indeed possible that the amount of dollar assets held by Japanese investors now exceeds the share dictated by the minimum-variance portfolio.

It is likely that Japanese investors, and probably investors residing in the USA as well, have in fact been less diversified internationally than mean-variance optimization says they should be. Whenever one looks behind the figures on net capital flows, one finds that Japanese investors are increasing their gross claims on the USA much more quickly than their net claims: US residents are simultaneously increasing their gross claims on Japanese residents. This suggests that one could explain the rapid 1980s increase in the share of Japanese portfolios allocated to dollars as a process of diversification taking place in the aftermath of financial liberalization. It is difficult to tell whether this process has run its course: the optimal portfolio calculation is extremely sensitive to small changes in the risk premium that is assumed.[17]

The yen value of the 1984 Japanese holdings of dollars has fallen by half, so that Japanese investors have had to buy the same amount of dollars all over again just to keep the share constant. The Japanese private sector faltered in 1987 in its appetite for US assets and the Bank of Japan stepped in as the major financing source of the US current account deficit.

In 1988 there appears to have been something of a renewal in the interest of Japanese and other investors in US assets. One reason is new increases in US interest rates. Another is the positive effect of trade developments on expectations as to the dollar's prospects: in 1988 the long-awaited improvement in the US deficit finally materialized, even in dollar terms, in (delayed) response to the preceding three years of dollar depreciation. This improvement had been forecast by standard economic models, but the foreign exchange market had grown tired of waiting for it and thus was taken by surprise.

The US trade balance will probably continue to improve through 1989. But it will take further depreciation of the dollar if the US current account and the corresponding need for foreign borrowing are to diminish in the 1990s. It is to be hoped that such developments will be the outcome of serious efforts by the new American President to reduce the US budget deficit. Otherwise, any improvement in the US trade balance would most probably come at the expense of US investment in plant and equipment.

IMPLICATIONS OF THE US DEBT TO JAPAN

One immediate implication of the new debtor status of the USA is that it will have to begin to service its debt, to pay interest to Japan and its other creditors. I say 'begin to' because, even though the records show that the US net foreign investment position became negative in early 1985, as recently as 1987 the investment income account – interest payments, dividends and repatriated earnings for overseas investments – still showed a surplus.[18] But from now on there will be a rising US deficit in investment income, perhaps as big as $50 billion in the early 1990s.

One possibility is that the USA could continue to borrow in order to make these interest payments, as the Latin American countries did until 1982. The other possibility is that the USA could eliminate its trade deficit, through some combination of lagged effects of the 1985–7 dollar depreciation, further depreciation in the future and belt-tightening (perhaps including a recession at some point). The country could even begin to run a trade surplus in order to earn the foreign exchange needed to service the debt; this is what most of the Latin American countries have been forced to do since 1982.

For at least the next few years, the USA will surely continue to borrow; a $150 billion trade deficit cannot be turned into a surplus overnight. But it is quite possible that the USA will gradually reduce its rate of borrowing over the next ten years or so, until it returns to current account balance. At this point it would be running a trade surplus, of the order of $50 billion or more. (It would be much harder for the country to begin reducing its outstanding debt, however, and there is virtually no chance that the USA will be able to pay off the debt and return to creditor status in this century.)

As the US trade deficit declines, the bilateral deficit with Japan is likely to decline in proportion. One might think that popular resentment against Japan would decline as a result, and that it would disappear entirely on the day when the USA begins to run a trade surplus with Japan. But the politics may evolve quite differently. By then, the Japanese would own a high proportion of the American capital stock, of the claims to American output. The money earned via the trade surplus would merely go to service the debt. As a recent book imagines the situation fifteen years from now, 'every single American works an entire month for no purpose than to pay off debts owed to Japanese and other foreign creditors' (Burstein 1988).

The Japanese would be resented by the American public as wealthy rentiers. It is already the case that total Japanese income per capita has surpassed American levels. Japanese wages, which were four and a half times as high as US wages in 1970, had almost caught up by 1988 when compared in common dollar terms. The Japanese standard of living has lagged behind their income. But it is rapidly catching up as well.

The implications of the US indebtedness to Japan fall into three areas: implications for the Japanese economy, implications for the US economy – in the short run, medium run and long run – and political implications.

Implications for the Japanese economy

As Japan runs a smaller trade surplus, it will have to substitute domestic demand for its goods in place of foreign demand. This will involve some major dislocations in the Japanese economy. But there is every indication that they are handling the transition relatively smoothly.

The Japanese economy has shown in its history a remarkable ability to adjust rapidly to each new shock that comes along. The first big adjustment after the war was the need to invest and export. The second big adjustment was the need to conserve energy (and to substitute government demand for corporate investment demand, while maintaining price stability) after the 1973 oil price shock. Substituting domestic demand for export demand is thus only the latest in a series of adjustments.

The two Maekawa reports released in 1986, which were received by jaded Americans as only the latest in a long series of packages of 'empty promises' to increase imports, were in fact a bold proposal to restructure the Japanese economy along the lines of substituting domestic demand for export demand.[19] The increased domestic demand could come from the government, the consumer, or both. We consider each briefly.

A major obstacle to increased spending from the government is the very strong belief on the part of the Ministry of Finance bureaucracy (particularly the more domestically oriented people in the Budget and Tax Bureaux) in the need to reduce the budget deficit, which was seen to have become out of control in the 1970s. In May 1987 the beliefs of the 'domesticists' in the Ministry of Finance were overcome by the 'internationalists', including the new Finance Minister Miyazawa, to the extent of a 6 trillion yen package of fiscal stimulus. In this episode, the internationalists used two key weapons: *endaka* and *gaiatsu*.

Endaka means 'big yen', and is the key to many changes that will take place in Japan from now on. By 1987 the yen had appreciated beyond the point where traditional export industries start complaining, and to the point where thought is given to phasing them out. It was thus clear that other sorts of activities would have to take their place.

Gaiatsu means 'foreign pressure', and has been

the key to many changes made in Japan in the past. For a number of years, and especially since James Baker became Secretary of the Treasury in 1985, the USA had been pressuring Japan to adopt a more expansionary fiscal policy.[20] In 1986 and 1987 the pressure took the form of a threat: if the Japanese and Germans did not enact sufficiently large fiscal expansions, then Secretary Baker would not abide by his promise to help keep the dollar from depreciating further. (The promise to stabilize the exchange rate at current levels was made in the Baker–Miyazawa Accord of November 1986 and the subsequent Louvre Accord of February 1987. 'Stabilize' meant both foreign exchange intervention in support of the dollar and, even more importantly, Baker refraining from 'talking down the dollar'.) Thus *endaka* and *gaiatsu* came together.[21]

Major obstacles to increased spending by consumers are the Japanese people's habits of long work-weeks and high saving, the inefficient retailing system and the exorbitant price of space.[22]

Of these obstacles, the length of the work-week appears to be giving way first, as a new generation of Japanese take to leisure and travel. Helping to get the saving rate down in the longer term is the fact that by the end of the century a higher proportion of the population will be retired. The high price of land is unlikely to change until Japanese land-use regulations are liberalized and until rice fields in and around urban areas lose some of their sacrosanct status. The rice farmers are sufficiently powerful that there is little prospect of Japan unilaterally giving up its virtual ban on rice imports in the near future. But the country may be prepared to bargain it away as part of a multilateral reduction of agricultural barriers in the Uruguay Round of trade negotiations.

Rice is the one sector in which American allegations of strong Japanese protection are still accurate (most government barriers in other sectors having been liberalized by now). Japan often raises a national security argument in answer to such allegations. The national security argument is not quite as absurd when raised in the context of Japanese agriculture as when raised, for example, by the US clothing lobby (or when raised in opposition to the purchase by a Japanese company of Fairchild, an electronics company that was already owned by a French firm). Japan *is* already dependent on imports for a high percentage of its food supply, and in 1973 Richard Nixon *did* embargo soybean exports to Japan with little regard for the consequences.

Implications for the US economy

The new US indebtedness has short-run implications for financial markets, medium-run implications for the American business cycle and long-run implications for the US standard of living on into the next century.

Many observers have been worried for some time that if Japanese investors reduce their demand for US assets, US interest rates might rise sharply (prices of US bonds and equities might fall), even as the dollar plummets against the yen. In April of 1987, nervous Japanese investors did indeed pull out of the Treasury securities market, sending bond prices down. The stock market followed suit in October 1987.

It could be argued that the question whether it is foreign residents or American residents that hold US assets is not relevant to the likelihood that there will be a sudden shift into foreign assets. In this regard, the fact that it is the USA that has been borrowing in the 1980s is less important than the greatly increased degree of international capital mobility that made such borrowing possible. The world-wide simultaneity of the October stock market crash is an illustration of this point. But there are two reasons why the US indebtedness makes financial markets particularly vulnerable. First, the persistent tendency of American politicians to postpone the day of fiscal reckoning further and further into the future throws into doubt the quality of US policy-making in the minds of investors around the world. Second, the character of public resentment against Japan in trade matters, and the early signs of its translation into similar xenophobia on investment matters, raise the danger that the USA at some point will enact populist penalties against foreign holdings. On both scores, Japanese and other investors have grounds for nervousness.

The implications for the US business cycle are equally disturbing. The foreign indebtedness does not particularly raise the probability that there will be a recession in, say, 1989. But sooner or later the USA will experience what will be its tenth recession since the Second World War. (Many believe that the fact that the US economy is now close to, or at, full employment and that inflationary pressures appear to be picking up *does* raise the probability that the recession will come sooner rather than later.) When it does come, it may be deeper than most Americans are expecting. The reason is that the public authorities will not be as free to use monetary or fiscal policy to moderate the recession as they have been in the past.

The authorities will not be as free to use monetary policy, i.e. to expand the money supply and reduce interest rates, because of the need to keep foreign (and domestic) investors from seeking to pull their money out of the country. It would be precisely at such a time that investors would be the most nervous, and monetary discipline and higher interest rates would be needed to reassure them.

Nor will the authorities feel free to use fiscal policy to counteract a recession, i.e. to raise government spending or to cut taxes. Tax receipts would plummet in a recession and the budget deficit would quickly soar back over $200 billion. Congress and the White House would at last see vividly the error in their fiscal ways. They would acquire the political will to resist spending increases and tax cuts, at precisely the first time in seven years when it is the inappropriate thing to do.

This loss of freedom to use macroeconomic policy to address domestic problems is a familiar one to many small debtor countries. But it will be a novel situation for Americans, and they will take some time to get used to it.[23] (Even securities-market analysts in the USA appear not yet to have learned the lesson that the Federal Reserve may no longer be free to lower interest rates in the event of an economic downturn.)

These implications for short-run financial market volatility and medium-term business cycle movements are necessarily somewhat speculative. They depend on the confidence of investors, which is always difficult to predict. But the longer-term implications for the US standard of living are inescapable. Just to service the international debt in 1992, Americans will have to cut back aggregate consumption by $50 billion a year relative to output, with the difference being transferred abroad.[24] To prevent the level of debt from continuing to rise as fast as it now is would require cutting back consumption more, and to prevent it from rising at all would require cutting back still more. If the country responds by postponing the adjustment farther into the future, this means that the ultimate adjustment required will be that much larger.

How can the USA accomplish the needed increase in the rate of national saving (judged by some as a need to hold the rate of growth of total consumption to 1½ per cent per year, or 1 per cent below the rate of growth of potential output)? GIven that private saving behaviour is not easily amenable to influence by government policy, this means a more serious effort to cut the federal budget deficit. Where to cut? I can think of a number of expenditures that need to be cut. But there are others that it seems to me need to be increased, such as education, which is an input into the stock of human capital and thus is key to getting our productivity back up. Everyone has their own priorities, but I haven't heard anyone explain how to balance the budget by cutting spending. (I'm not counting politicians, who think that uttering the words 'cut spending' is enough, and that it is not necessary to identify where they want to cut – either before or after they are elected.) Thus it seems that any solution is going to have as an important element an increase in taxes, as politically unpopular as that may be.

This does not necessarily mean an increase in income taxes. One of several alternatives would be a tax on energy. Imposing a federal tax on gasoline of the order of taxes in Europe and Japan (or Canada) could solve the budget deficit virtually at

one stroke.[25] It is estimated that every 12 cents a gallon would raise $12 billion in revenue (Congressional Budget Office 1988). Aside from the macroeconomic motivation, an argument for a substantial energy tax can be made on microeconomic grounds as well. The country has been losing billions of dollars' worth of time and expense to traffic congestion, accidents and pollution; and now we have the endangered ozone layer and the greenhouse effect, which are serious matters for concern. A national energy tax could thus be sold as a sort of 'user tax', to discourage over-use of the highways, the hospitals and the atmosphere. A national security argument could also be made, to reduce vulnerability to potential future OPECs.

Political implications

Political scientists and historians, as well as economists, have been quick to draw the inference that America's transformation from world's largest creditor to world's largest debtor will entail a loss of American political power as well as economic power. Paul Kennedy has elicited much response with his account of how past hegemons have lost their economic wealth by extending their military spending beyond their means, and as a result have lost their political and military preeminence as well.

So far, American policy-makers have shown no signs of having lost power in world affairs, or at least no signs of being aware of it. One example comes from the recent 'Miyazawa initiative' for dealing with the Third World debt problem. It is a sign that the Japanese have begun to respond to American calls for them to play a greater role in world affairs, commensurate with their economic status.

At a time when a majority of observers are arguing the need for a relatively radical alteration (generally involving debt reduction) in the US-fashioned debt strategy, the Japanese are arguing for what is essentially a version of the Baker Plan for continued lending. One would expect the US Treasury to welcome the Japanese proposal with open arms. After all, the Baker Plan has been missing the key ingredient, namely a source for the money, which the Japanese seem inclined to supply. Yet the Americans discouraged the Japanese from presenting the details of their proposal at the September 1988 IMF–World Bank meetings in West Berlin. Treasury Secretary Nicholas Brady went out of his way to record his displeasure, with the statement that the USA 'regards with skepticism proposals that may appear to conform to the basic principles of the debt strategy, but which in practice only produce an illusion of progress' (Silk 1988). Evidently the Treasury want Japan's participation to consist 100 per cent of putting up the money and 0 per cent of constructive suggestions, and is not satisfied with 98 per cent and 2 per cent.

American economic policy-makers should be passing some of the hegemonic burden on to multilateral institutions, for example considering a Japanese candidate for the next Managing Director of the IMF and supporting the integrity of the institution under its current Managing Director, Michel Camdessus. Instead, the Treasury has begun recently to treat the IMF as an agency of the US government. It evidently sought to override normal procedures on a recent Fund loan to Argentina, something the Treasury never tried to do even in the years of the Donald Regan autocracy.[26] (The Americans ignored entirely a statement at Berlin by Bank of Japan Governor Satoshi Sumita which was considered as important by Japanese economic policy-makers as the debt initiative: that they now favour an increased reserve-currency role for the yen in the international monetary system.)[27]

It is difficult to see what in the mechanics of international relations will force US policy-makers to accept a loss of power in the short term.

If one is in a fundamentally weak bargaining position but doesn't know it, one is not in such a weak bargaining position after all.

But the US government's financial inability to continue to spend so lavishly on defence, and the inability to incur new foreign aid expenditures or to acknowledge losses on existing loans to troubled debtors, is already forcing it to ask financial assistance from Japan. It is only a matter of

time before Americans learn to bow like a Japanese when making such requests.

NOTES

1 Indeed the *net* debt of the USA is roughly equal to the *gross* debt of all of Latin America.

2 $710 billion (IMF 1988).

3 The figures are from the US Department of Commerce. Stekler (1988) discussed the formidable measurement problems.

4 In 1985 (Frankel 1987).

5 Furthermore, the USA, like Japan, has seen an increasing share of its savings pass into portfolio funds that are more prone to invest overseas than individual investors would be acting on their own.

6 Recent econometric studies of the effect of interest rates on Japanese capital outflows include Amano (1986), Ueda (1987) and Kawai and Okumura (1988).

7 The source is *Capital International Perspectives*, New York: Morgan Guaranty.

8 Gross private domestic investment in 1987 was 15.7 per cent of GNP, down from 16.5 per cent in the 1970s. Net private investment (i.e. net of depreciation) in 1987 was 5.4 per cent of GNP, down from 6.2 per cent in the 1970s (and 7.0 per cent in the 1960s).

9 The source is Frankel (1984: 23). Other studies documenting this change include Otani and Tiwari (1981), Council of Economic Advisers (1984) and Ito (1986).

10 Ueda (1987) and Fukao (1988) are two econometric studies that find that the combination of interest rate differentials and the relaxation of Japanese portfolio restrictions explains most of the outflow in the early 1980s. Restrictions on the acquisition of foreign assets by insurance companies and trusts were liberalized in 1986 and 1987. See Fukao (1988: Appendix D).

11 The data are from Morgan Guaranty.

12 In the middle part of 1988, the dollar appreciated again against the yen: from 128 on 2 February to 134 on 30 August. During this interval the one-year expected rate of dollar depreciation also rose: from 1.6 per cent to 7.5 per cent as measured by the survey data. (The expected depreciation is thus somewhat higher than it was in January 1987, when the level of the dollar was higher (151). This is consistent with the finding in Frankel and Froot (1987) that, for the case of the yen, the regressive expectations model does not fit the survey data quite as well as adaptive or distributed-lag expectations.) The one-year forward discount rose from

3.2 per cent to 3.8 per cent.

13 The short-term capital flow figures include authorized foreign exchange banks' balances. The source is Bank of Japan data, as reported for example by the Economic Planning Agency. The US balance-of-payments statistics no longer recognized the short-term/long-term distinction.

14 Froot and Ito (1988) find in the survey data that the process whereby short-term expectations are formed is not consistent with the process whereby long-term expectations are formed, in that the former iterated forward differs significantly from the latter.

15 Hatsopoulos et al. (1988) identify such a difference between the two countries in corporations' horizons, and attribute it to higher after-tax cost of capital in the USA than in Japan.

16 This might understate the figure a little because some imports are denominated in other currencies (e.g. 3 per cent in yen), or overstate it to the extent that Japan produces some traded goods with prices determined on world markets.

17 The yen–dollar variance V is estimated at 0.01186 in Frankel (1986). Together with the parameter value $R = 2$, the equation implies that a change in the risk premium of 0.01 (100 basis points) is enough to change the demand for dollars by 0.01/0.02362 = 42.3 per cent of the portfolio!

18 The explanation for how the US surplus on investment income could linger three years after the loss of a net creditor status is as follows. US assets in other countries have a composition weighted to those that pay higher returns (foreign direct investment and bank loans, though in the latter case one might wonder whether all the interest payments that appear in the accounts since 1982 have been entirely genuine), while foreign holdings in the USA consist more of assets with lower returns (US Treasury securities and high-quality corporate bonds). There are some who argue that the lingering surplus in investment income is evidence that the net asset position must be better than reported, as a result of the (admittedly sizeable) statistical problems in measuring it. But this is incorrect; there is in fact little information in the investment income statistics that is not derived from the records on the asset position with the exception of the earnings on foreign direct investment.

19 Its boldness lay in part in the fact that the Maekawa Commission was Prime Minster Nakasone's way of circumventing the bureaucracy.

20 Baker's motive charitably interpreted was to accompany correction of the US budget deficit with expansion in Japan and Germany so as to avoid a world recession. The motive less charitably interpreted was to substitute foreign expansion for the needed US fiscal correction, thereby passing the blame for the US trade deficit onto foreigners. Either way, econometric estimates of the effects of expansion in Japan (or even expansion among all trading partners) in fact show small effects on the US trade balance.

21 These events are recounted in Funabashi (1988).

22 Housing is 65 per cent of saving in Japan, compared with 31 per cent in the USA.

23 It is ironic that public anxiety focuses so heavily on the foreign direct investment component rather than the portfolio investment component. Not only is the former much smaller than the latter, as noted at the outset of the chapter, but there is much less potential for destabilizing the American economy. It is likely that, in the event of a cyclical downturn, Japanese-owned factories and offices in the USA would be less prone to lay off workers than would their American-owned counterparts. For one thing, Japanese corporations have a tradition of not laying off workers. For another, the Japanese are especially sensitive to political concerns among the American public.

24 Furthermore, this transfer of resources must be accompanied by a deterioration in the US terms of trade for the transfer to be fully 'effected'. The 50 per cent depreciation of the dollar that we have already had (against the yen) has not yet been passed through into a corresponding increase in import prices.

25 One reason why the USA has not put a large federal tax on gasoline is that it would hurt the oil-producing states at a time when the local economy is already weak. On the other hand, it seems to me that a major reason why we have not put a large tariff on imported oil is that it would help the oil companies too much, at the expense of the northeast. Either kind of tax in isolation would be very difficult to enact on political grounds, and perhaps undesirable on redistributional grounds. But a possible solution would be an oil import tariff together with a tax on gasoline and other products, calculated in such a way as to avoid hurting the oil-producing states. A few years ago there were proposals for reform that would be revenue neutral with respect to taxes; this is a proposal that would be neutral with respect to Texas.

26 Much of the Treasury's motivation in steam-rolling over Sumita and Camdessus appears to have been to avoid in advance of the November election all mention in the newspapers of a deteriorating debt problem.

27 In the past the US Treasury has strongly urged a

reserve-currency role for the yen, alongside the dollar and the mark, but Japanese authorities have been reluctant out of a fear of increased monetary instability. The Bank of Japan has apparently changed its mind as a result of recent efforts to intervene directly in the market for marks. If all three currencies had equal status, then the Japanese and Germans could intervene directly in each other's currencies, rather than having always to go through the dollar as has been the case up to now.

REFERENCES

Amano, A. (1986) *Japan's External Imbalance and Exchange Rates*, Kobe University, March.

Bryant, R. (1987) *International Financial Intermediation*, Washington, DC: Brookings Institution.

Burstein, D. (1988) *Yen!*, New York: Simon and Schuster.

Congressional Budget Office (1988) 'Reducing the deficit: spending and revenue options', March: 346.

Council of Economic Advisers (1984) *Economic Report of the President*.

Feldstein, M. and Horioka, C. (1980) 'Domestic saving and international capital flows, *Economic Journal* 90: 314–29.

Frankel, J. (1984) *The Yen/Dollar Agreement: Liberalizing Japanese Capital Markets*, Washington, DC: Institute for International Economics.

—— (1986) 'The implications of mean–variance optimization for four questions in international macroeconomics', *Journal of International Money and Finance 5* (March): 553–75.

—— (1987) 'International capital flows and domestic economic policies', in M. Feldstein (ed.) *The United States in the World Economy*, Chicago, IL: University of Chicago Press.

—— (1988) 'The flow of capital from Japan to the United States in the 1980s', in M. Yoshitomi (ed.) *Correcting External Imbalances*, Tokyo: Economic Planning Agency. Also translated into Japanese and published in abbreviated form in *Kinyu Journal*, 1988.

Frankel, J. and Froot, K. (1985) 'Using survey data to test some standard propositions regarding exchange rate expectations', *American Economic Review*, 77 (March).

—— and —— (1987) 'Short-term and long-term expectations of the yen/dollar exchange rate: evidence from survey data', *Journal of the Japanese and International Economies* 1: 249–74.

Froot, K. and Ito, T. (1988) *On the Consistency of Short-run and Long-run Exchange Rate Expectations*, National Bureau of Economic Research, March.

Fukao, M. (1987) 'A risk premium model of the yen–dollar and DM–dollar exchange rates', *OECD Economic Studies 9* (Autumn): 79–104.

—— (1988) 'Balance of payments imbalances and long-term capital movements: review and prospects', in M. Yoshitomi (ed.) *Correcting External Imbalances*, Tokyo: Economic Planning Agency.

Funabashi, Y. (1988) *Managing the Dollar: From the Plaza to the Louvre*, Washington DC: Institute for International Economics.

Hatsopoulos, G., Krugman, P. and Summers, L. (1988) 'US competitiveness: beyond the trade deficit', *Science*, 15 July: 299–307.

IMF (1986) *World Economic Outlook*, October, p. 53.

—— (1988) *World Economic Outlook*, April, p. 89.

Ito, T. (1986) 'Capital controls and covered interest parity', *Economic Studies Quarterly* 37: 223–41.

—— (1987) 'Wishful expectations and expectational twists in the Euro-yen foreign exchange market', University of Minnesota, March.

Kawai, M. and Okumara, H. (1988) 'Japan's portfolio investment in foreign securities', Japan–US Consultative Group on International Monetary Affairs, January. Revised for *JCIF Policy Studies*, Series N. 9.

Otani, I. and Tiwari, S. (1981) 'Capital controls and interest rate parity: the Japanese experience 1978–81', *IMF Staff Papers*, December.

Popper, H. (1987) 'Long-term covered interest rate parity: two tests using currency swaps', University of California, Berkeley.

Saxonhouse, G. (1982) 'Japanese saving behavior: a household balance sheet approach', University of Michigan, Ann Arbor, November.

Silk, L. (1988) 'A strident US at IMF talks,' *New York Times*, 30 September.

Stekler, L. (1988) 'Adequacy of data for international policy coordination', in *International Policy Coordination and Exchange Rate Fluctuations*, NBER Conference, Kiawah Island, 27–9 October.

Ueda, K. (1987) 'Japanese capital outflows: 1970 to 1986', Osaka University, August.

Part VI

INTERNATIONAL CURRENCY MARKETS

Regional bias is not confined to trade in goods and non-factor services; it is also a characteristic feature of trade in financial services. For instance, foreign borrowing and lending in deutsche-mark-denominated assets is concentrated in Western Europe. Japan's yen-denominated imports and exports are concentrated in the Asian Pacific region, with a large majority of borrowers in the samurai, shibosai and Euro-yen markets also situated in the same region. The reason behind regional bias in trade in goods and in financial services is the same, namely lower transaction costs. Traits like market information, scale economies and consumer preferences further promote regional bias. However, there is a more important feature which underpins regional tendencies of trade in financial services and international currencies, i.e. risk. Currencies in an economic region usually form a zone and these currencies have lower exchange rate volatility with each other than with the currencies outside the zone. For this reason, West European investors or borrowers expose themselves to lower currency risk by lending or borrowing in the deutsche mark rather than in, say, the dollar. At present the dollar and deutsche mark zones are in full operation (Brown 1989). Both these zones are further subdivided into an inner zone and an outer zone. In the former, the exchange risk is extremely low. The inner zone of the dollar comprises the Canadian dollar while that of the deutsche mark comprises the Swiss franc, Dutch guilder, Austrian schilling and the Belgian franc. The outer zone of the dollar includes the Latin American currencies and those of the Asian newly industrializing countries. In the early 1990s, debate began on whether the currencies of the Asian newly industrializing countries are part of the yen zone. The currencies in the outer zone of the deutsche mark included the French franc, the lira and the pound.

Over the 1980s the asset and liability structure of the international financial markets underwent a sea change. By the middle of the decade Japan had emerged as the leading creditor country while the USA, hitherto the largest creditor, turned into the largest debtor economy. Black, in the first chapter, considers the question whether this will lead to the yen becoming a rival of the dollar as a reserve currency and vehicle currency in the foreign exchange market. *A priori* it is believed that it will because the evolution of the dollar as the dominant currency in the international financial markets occurred in a similar manner, and if history were to repeat, the answer to the above question would have to be yes. However, this line of logic tends to be simplistic. There will indeed be changes in the role played by major currencies with international traders, investors and borrowers changing their pattern of currency utilization. Also, the interbank and foreign exchange markets are bound to be affected. Thus, as the volume of dollar-based trade and investment flows drops back from dominance to mere *primus inter pares*, so will the dollar's role in the foreign exchange market. As for the reserve currency, the multi-reserve currency system is a reality to stay. With changes in the international financial markets, diversification in the mix of reserve currency is naturally to be expected. The effect of reserve diversification on exchange rate stability will depend on its effect on policy in the reserve centres. If diversification promotes discipline in the reserve centres, it will indeed have a stabilizing effect. Another important inference is that as intra-regional trade and investment grows, the regional currencies in Europe (the deutsche mark) and the Asian Pacific region (the yen) are gradually going to grow in importance. As alluded to above, the role of the deutsche mark is already substantial. However, whenever the idea of the yen bloc is raised in Asia, it is dismissed as premature – if not totally non-viable – but if one takes a look at the intra-trade and investment data in the region some kind of yen bloc has informally emerged. In the foreseeable future, the ASEAN countries with heavy export dependence on Japan may well strengthen their links with the yen. The East Asian newly industrializing economies have a heavier dependence on the USA for trade. But since they compete with Japan in international markets, they would naturally earn more from their exports if their currencies are pegged to the yen and the yen appreciates. In this process they will also not have lost any competitiveness *vis-à-vis* Japan.

During the recent period, apart from the deutsche mark, the Swiss franc is being used internationally with increased vigour. In the second chapter in this section, Tavlas discusses the use of the deutsche mark as an international currency. He first focuses on the theoretical criteria behind the emergence of an international currency and then relates them to the deutsche mark. He identifies several causes behind the expanding role of the deutsche mark during the 1980s. There has been some increase in the proportion of world trade denominated in the deutsche mark and its use in interbank trading has remained rather steady. To be sure, the dollar trading dominates the currency market but the deutsche mark and the yen are the currencies that are traded most against the dollar. Also, these two currencies are used as intervention

vehicles by the USA. In addition, an enhancement in the role of the deutsche mark has taken place with regard to its use in international capital markets and in official foreign exchange holdings.

The next chapter, by the editor of this collection, similarly traces the rise of the yen as an international currency. Since 1980, the yen has gradually internationalized. Although Japan's yen-denominated current account transactions have grown, the use of the yen in trade between third currencies has remained negligible. The deutsche mark is far ahead of the yen in this respect. In terms of the volume of currency traded on the foreign exchange markets, the yen is again well behind the dollar and the deutsche mark. However, going by the daily turnover, the importance of Tokyo in the foreign exchange markets is generally regarded as second after London. In the foreign exchange trade, likewise, the dollar–yen exchange rate is considered the second busiest after the dollar–deutsche mark rate. Recent growth of trading in the yen–deutsche mark rate has helped in the progress of the yen's internationalization. Internationalization of the yen has made further progress after its appreciation in 1985, but it will undoubtedly remain the third international currency in the foreseeable future.

The last chapter, by Mahler, traces a rather interesting recent development, namely internationalization of the Korean capital markets. It develops a concept called the 'internationalization windfall'. This experience will be useful in future to other developing countries that will move on the road to internationalizing their capital markets. Several of them have made some progress in this regard while others are waiting in the wings.

REFERENCE

Brown, B. (1989) 'Pattern of capital flows', in R. Z. Aliber (ed.) *The Handbook of International Financial Management*, Homewood, IL: Dow-Jones-Irwin, pp. 709–31.

29

THE INTERNATIONAL USE OF CURRENCIES

Stanley W. Black

INTRODUCTION

In the 1980s, major changes have taken place in the structure of international assets and liabilities. Japan has swiftly become the world's largest net lender, with net assets of $240 billion at the end of 1987. Her banks are now acting as international financial intermediaries, with Japan's short-term net liabilities of $169 billion balancing against long-term net assets of $410 billion. This position is analogous in some ways to that of American banks in the post-war period from 1945 to 1980 and by British banks in the nineteenth and early twentieth centuries, as bankers to the world, borrowing short and lending long. The British banks built up their intermediary position gradually over the nineteenth century, and by the turn of the century the gold standard had effectively become a key currency system based on the pound sterling (Lindert 1969). During the first half of the twentieth century culminating in the post-Second World War period, American banks replaced British banks as financial intermediaries to the world, based on the strong US external payments position. At the same time, the dollar gradually took over from the pound sterling the role of leading international currency, both as a reserve currency for monetary authorities and as a vehicle currency in private exchange market transactions. It is clear that Japanese banks are now the largest financial intermediaries internationally. The question underlying this chapter is whether under current conditions there are reasons to believe that a similar process of evolution will lead the

Japanese yen to rival the dollar as reserve currency and vehicle currency in foreign exchange markets.

Consideration of this question requires us to recall first the reasons for the existence of reserve currencies and vehicle currencies. Those steeped in neo-Walrasian general equilibrium theory often find the concept of international reserves to be mysterious, since the existence of perfect capital markets should enable the international extension of credit to fill any gaps between domestic income and expenditure with purchases or sales of goods and services to foreigners. To explain reserve currencies we must rely on the concept of *convertibility*, which is required for most external transactions in goods and services. Whenever international transactions involve residents of countries using different currencies, assets must usually be converted from one currency to another, either by importers or by exporters, in the process of making payments. In fact, a much larger proportion of goods and services is purchased from or sold to foreigners as part of the international division of labour than would appear from examination of current account imbalances alone. The weighted average share of foreign trade in OECD countries' GDP during 1960–80 was 14.4 per cent, while the average current account balance was 0.1 per cent.

That maintenance of convertibility is a non-trivial matter is illustrated by the fact that, in 1988, only fifty-one of the 151 members of the IMF had currencies which were freely convertible for current account transactions without special charges or restrictions. Of these fifty-one, only fifteen had currencies that were also freely convertible for capital account transactions. The reasons that convertibility is so difficult to maintain are much the same as the reasons why inflation is so hard to control in many countries. In fact, maintenance of convertibility can be regarded as giving a currency purchasing power over foreign goods and services, much as maintenance of price stability assures purchasing power over domestic goods and services. Political commitments to full employment and/or excessive monetary financing of government deficits are often pursued to the detriment of the internal and external value of the currency. Various strategems are then adopted to prevent residents from evading the inflation tax, usually involving some loss of convertibility of the domestic currency into other currencies. Under these conditions, central banks have found it essential to maintain a stock of reserve assets to ensure the maintenance of convertibility.

For countries with pegged exchange rates, the necessity for adequate stocks of international reserves to maintain the convertibility of their currencies is fairly obvious. A major surprise of the functioning of floating rates is the continued need for international reserves. Many central banks have continued to intervene frequently even in floating exchange markets for the purpose of reducing the degree of short-run fluctuation in exchange rates. Recent studies (Lizondo and Mathieson 1987) have confirmed the continued stability of demand functions for international reserves, particularly for industrialized countries but for developing countries as well. Few industrialized countries indeed have been willing to leave the determination of the exchange rate at which their currency is convertible entirely to market forces.

The choice of currency in which to hold reserves has been shown to depend on portfolio risk and return, international monetary agreements, political considerations and operational factors relating to the most useful currency for intervention purposes (De Macedo 1982; Heller and Knight 1978; Officer and Willett 1974). The extent of use of different currencies in the interbank market is a key determinant of the usefulness of a currency for intervention purposes. The turnover of currencies in the interbank market depends on customer demand, endogenous trading generated within the interbank market and the extent to which a currency is used indirectly as a *vehicle* for invoicing transactions between other currencies. The demand for a vehicle currency in turn rests on economies of scale, transactions costs and informational efficiencies in the interbank market for foreign currencies.

In this chapter we discuss the factors influencing the use of currencies as international reserve assets and vehicle currencies. The chapter is organized as follows. In the second section we discuss trends in the international use of currencies, based on recent data. In the third section we then analyse the choice of invoicing currency by exporters and borrowers in international markets. Given customer demands for currencies, in the fourth section we first discuss the interbank market and the determination of bid–ask spreads for different currencies. Based on the analysis of bid–ask spreads, we then discuss a model of the evolution of the use of vehicle currencies. The fifth section offers some conclusions.

TRENDS IN THE USE OF INTERNATIONAL CURRENCIES

International trade

Currencies may be used internationally as a means of payment, a store of value and a unit of account (Cohen 1971; cited in Hamada and Horiuchi 1987). Their use as a means of payment arises from international transactions in goods and services, as noted above. The extent of use of different currencies for payments is related both to the *volume* of trade of different countries and the currencies in which that trade is *denominated*. Table 29.1 indicates three patterns of currency denomination of trade flows among industrialized countries: a European pattern with roughly three-fourths of exports and about two-fifths of imports denominated in domestic currency, the Japanese pattern with three-fifths of exports and nine-tenths

Table 29.1 Currency distribution of world trade
(per cent)

	Exports		Imports	
	US dollar	National currency	US dollar	National currency
USA	98	98	85	85
Japan	60.9	33.8	93.0	2.0
Germany	7.2	82.3	33.1	42.8
UK	17	76	29	38
France	11.6	62.4	28.7	35.8
World total	54.8	–	54.3	–

Sources: NIESR, *National Institute Economic Review*; and
Bank of Japan, from Hamada and Horiuchi 1987

Notes: Figures for Japan's exports are for 1982 and Japan's
and Germany's imports are for 1980. Figures for the
UK and France are for 1979. Figures for the USA are
estimated.

yen has been rising. Thus Japan seems to be evolving in the direction of the European pattern, at least with respect to exports.

In addition, there is some indirect evidence that the share of US trade denominated in foreign currencies is rising. For example, the share of commercial liabilities to unaffiliated foreigners by US non-bank enterprises payable in foreign currencies rose from 6.8 per cent to 9.3 per cent from the end of 1984 to the end of 1988, while the share of their *total* liabilities payable in foreign currencies rose from 10.1 per cent to 17.0 per cent (*Federal Reserve Bulletin* 1989). Likewise, the share of bank liabilities to foreigners payable in foreign currencies has risen from 2.7 per cent to 9.9 per cent over the same period. However, unlike the figures for commercial liabilities of non-banking business enterprises, the external commercial *claims* of these firms (mostly trade receivables) remain overwhelmingly payable in dollars. The share of *banks'* claims on foreigners payable in foreign currencies has on the other hand risen from 2.9 per cent to 12.3 per cent, matching the increase in banks' liabilities in foreign currency.

of imports denominated in US dollars and the US pattern with most exports *and* imports denominated in dollars. Table 29.2 shows that the share of Japanese exports denominated in dollars has been falling over time, while the share denominated in

Table 29.2 Percentage of Japanese total trade invoiced in yen and other currencies, 1970–87

Currency	1970	1975	1980	1982	1983	1984	1987
Yen							
Export	0.9	17.5	29.4	32.2	34.5	33.7	34.7
Import	0.3	0.9	2.4	n.a.	n.a.	n.a.	11.6
Dollar							
Export	90.4	78.0	65.7	62.3	60.4	61.4	55.6
Import	80.0	89.9	93.1	n.a.	n.a.	n.a.	80.5
Pound sterling							
Export	7.1	1.9	1.1	1.4	1.0	0.9	1.0
Import	8.8	3.8	0.9	n.a.	n.a.	n.a.	n.a.
Mark							
Export	0.5	1.1	1.9	2.1	2.1	1.9	2.0
Import	2.8	1.5	1.4	n.a.	n.a.	n.a.	n.a.
Other							
Export	1.1	1.5	1.9	2.0	2.0	2.1	6.7
Import	8.1	3.9	2.2	n.a.	n.a.	n.a.	n.a.

Source: Ministry of Finance, *Annual Report of the International Finance Bureau* 1985, from Hamada and Horiuchi 1987 and
Tavlas and Ozeki 1991

Note: n.a., not available.

Table 29.3 Shares of world exports (per cent)

	1975	1980	1984	1987	1989
USA	13.2	11.7	12.3	10.8	12.5
Japan	6.8	6.9	9.6	9.8	9.4
Germany	11.0	10.2	9.7	12.5	11.7
UK	5.3	5.8	5.3	5.6	5.2
France	6.5	6.1	5.5	6.3	6.2
Oil-exporting countries	7.3	15.7	9.3	5.6	n.a.

Source: IMF, *International Financial Statistics*
Note: n.a., not available.

According to Table 29.3, the US share of world exports was declining until 1987, but has rebounded since then. The Japanese and German shares, which were rising, are now declining slightly. Since the relatively high Japanese share of exports denominated in dollars is declining, this strongly suggests that the share of world trade denominated in dollars has been declining, even without taking into account the drastic drop in the OPEC share of world exports, which is denominated entirely in dollars. At the same time, the share of world trade denominated in deutsche marks and yen has been rising.

Long-term capital

Turning to the use of international currencies as a store of value and unit of account in the international bond markets, we notice similar trends in Table 29.4. While the dollar remains the largest currency of issue at 45 per cent of the total in 1989, its share has declined by 11 percentage points, while the share of the yen has increased from 6 to 10 per cent. The increasing share of yen-denominated bonds appears to be due to the increasing willingness of Japanese borrowers to tap the Euro-yen bond market, as well as some increased use of the samurai bond market by foreigners. The liberalization of Japanese foreign exchange regulations has permitted these developments.

Short-term capital

The market for international bank loans and deposits is increasingly becoming a multi-currency market as well. A major factor here has been the increased foreign asset position of Japanese banks, as shown in Table 29.5. Of course, the 62 per cent increase in the dollar value of the yen from the end

Table 29.4 International bonds outstanding, by currency of issue (billions of US dollars)

	1982		1985		1987		1989	
US dollar	144.0	(56.5%)	316.7	(56.8%)	423.8	(43.2%)	567.7	(45.3%)
Yen	16.5	(6.5%)	42.7	(7.7%)	121.7	(12.4%)	125.0	(10.0%)
Swiss franc	43.0	(16.9%)	78.9	(14.2%)	157.0	(16.0%)	139.7	(11.1%)
Deutsche mark	31.0	(12.2%)	50.4	(9.0%)	98.5	(10.0%)	96.8	(7.7%)
Sterling	4.0	(1.6%)	19.2	(3.4%)	54.2	(5.5%)	74.0	(5.9%)
ECU	2.0	(0.8%)	16.5	(3.0%)	38.3	(3.9%)	51.4	(4.1%)
Other	14.5	(5.7%)	33.9	(6.1%)	87.8	(9.0%)	197.7	(15.8%)
Total	255.0	(100.0%)	557.4	(100.0%)	981.3	(100.0%)	1252.3	(100.0%)

Source: BIS, *Annual Report* 1990

Table 29.5 International bank assets by nationality of bank (billions of US dollars)

	1985		1987		1989	
Germany	191.2	(7.0%)	347.9	(7.9%)	435.8	(8.5%)
Japan	707.2	(26.1%)	1,552.1	(35.4%)	1,967.2	(38.3%)
UK	192.9	(7.1%)	253.9	(5.8%)	247.3	(4.8%)
USA	590.2	(21.7%)	647.6	(14.8%)	727.4	(14.1%)
Other	1,033.3	(38.1%)	1,579.8	(36.1%)	1,761.5	(34.3%)
Total	2,714.8	(100.0%)	4,381.3	(100.0%)	5,139.2	(100.0%)

Source: BIS, *Annual Report* 1990

Table 29.6 International bank assets by location of bank (billions of US dollars)

	Changes, excluding exchange rate effects				Stocks in 1989	
	1986	1987	1988	1989		
Germany	38.8	17.0	17.4	54.3	268.5	(5.3%)
Japan	126.6	166.6	166.7	152.5	842.0	(16.7%)
UK	87.5	89.1	33.9	55.1	924.0	(18.4%)
USA	50.3	29.4	50.7	45.0	599.3	(11.9%)
Offshore centres	122.5	147.2	97.7	133.0	512.1	(10.2%)
Other	91.6	118.5	58.6	150.7	1,884.9	(37.5%)
Total	517.3	567.8	425.0	590.6	5,030.8	(100.0%)

Source: BIS, *Annual Report* 1990

Table 29.7 The currency composition of banks' external assets (billions of US dollars)

	Changes, excluding exchange rate effects				Stocks in 1989	
	1986	1987	1988	1989		
US dollar	188.8	184.1	94.6	137.8	1,469.9	(64.3%)
Deutsche mark	0.9	31.1	31.3	29.5	341.9	(15.0%)
Swiss franc	7.9	−1.5	−4.8	2.7	113.8	(5.0%)
Yen	20.8	30.7	14.0	38.8	177.4	(7.8%)
Sterling	8.5	5.2	22.8	15.7	77.1	(3.4%)
ECU	6.2	8.2	15.6	16.4	104.9	(4.6%)
Total	233.1	257.8	173.5	240.9	2,285.0	(100.0%)

Source: BIS, *Annual Report* 1990

of 1985 to the end of 1987 plays some role in the doubling of the Japanese banks' foreign assets over the period. Table 29.6 examines the growth of international bank assets by market centre excluding exchange rate changes, indicating that the UK remains by far the largest individual market. But in the last few years, Japan has emerged as the second leading centre, followed by the USA and the various offshore centres. The increased financial clout of Tokyo and of Japanese banks has begun to influence the currency composition of the international assets of banks in industrialized countries. Table 29.7, which excludes the effects of exchange rate changes, shows that the US dollar retains the largest currency share at 64 per cent, but that the deutsche mark amounts to about 15 per cent and the yen 8 per cent.

The interbank market

Information on the use of currencies in the interbank market is available from surveys conducted by central banks in New York, London and Tokyo in March 1986 and in April 1989. The surveys summarized in Table 29.8 show that the interbank market in those centres remains a dollar-based market, but is becoming less so. Up to 9 per cent of trades reported by banks in London did not involve

the dollar, mostly between the mark and the pound. Cross-currency trading in New York is also growing significantly. Within these dollar-based markets, the share of the yen has increased substantially in recent years, up from 10 per cent in New York in 1980 to 25 per cent in 1989, while the deutsche mark share has remained roughly stable. According to Table 29.8, in Tokyo dollar–yen trading accounted for 77 per cent of interbank transactions in 1986, with the balance mainly in deutsche marks and Swiss francs.

According to information obtained from interviews in Milan, interbank trading in a typical smaller market centre in which there are exchange controls may only involve the domestic currency in about 25–30 per cent of the total volume, which is comparable with the sterling share in London shown in Table 29.8. In such markets, up to 70 per cent of volume would involve cross-currency trades from the point of view of the local currency. Thus the question of the use of a vehicle currency arises all the time. Information received in Milan suggested that the dollar share of such business has fallen sharply in the last few years, to the point where it is now roughly comparable with the deutsche mark share. Bid–ask spreads on the dollar–lira were quoted at 0.04 per cent, compared with 0.01 per cent on the mark–lira. The lower spread on the mark is presumably related to the

Table 29.8 The currency composition of banks' foreign exchange market turnover (per cent)

	New York		London		Tokyo
	March 1980	*April 1989*	*March 1986*	*April 1989*	*March 1986*
Deutsche mark	31.7	32.9	28	22	10.4
Yen	10.2	25.2	14	15	77.0
Sterling	22.8	14.6	30	27	3.4
Swiss franc	10.1	11.8	9	10	5.6
French franc	6.9	3.2	4	2	0.3
Canadian dollar	12.3	4.0	2	2	–
Other currency	6.0	4.7	10	13	3.3
Cross-currency	–	3.6	3	9	–

Sources: Federal Reserve Bank of New York; Bank of England, *Quarterly Bulletin* 1986: 379–82; *Kinyu Zaisei Jijou* September 1986: 38–9

558

existence of the EMS as well as to competitive pricing by German banks bidding for market share. In general, improved communications facilities such as video quote screens for the major currencies have reduced the need for vehicle currencies by reducing information costs. Where direct cross-currency quotations are not readily available in the local market, they can often be obtained by working with a correspondent bank in the market of one of the two currencies involved. For example, escudo–krone quotations could be obtained from either Copenhagen or Lisbon.

International reserves and central bank intervention

The shifting patterns of use of international currencies in private markets discussed above has its reflection in changing patterns of holdings and use of international reserves by central banks. Table 29.9 indicates that the share of the US dollar in official foreign exchange holdings of industrial countries has declined from 83.5 per cent to 60.2 per cent since 1979, while the share of the yen has risen from 2.6 to 7.9 per cent and the share of the mark has risen from 9.4 per cent to 19.3 per cent. There is little information available on the *use* of currencies in intervention by central banks, but Table 29.10 shows that the share of the dollar in interventions in the EMS has declined from 71.5 per cent during 1979–82 to 26.3 per cent during

1986–7. This is consistent with the indications that the dollar is playing a smaller role in private markets in Europe. Table 29.10 shows that yen intervention has become significant for the USA since the Plaza Agreement of 1985.

FACTORS AFFECTING THE CHOICE OF CURRENCY BY TRADERS AND BORROWERS

Choice of invoice currency

While the patterns of currency use in international trade shown in Table 29.1 have been known for some time (Grassman 1973; Page 1981), our understanding of the reasons for their existence and their evolution has been inadequate. McKinnon (1979) explained the European pattern as arising because exporters of industrial products desire to minimize risk in their home currency by denominating exports in the home currency. Bilson (1983) further pointed out that 'the importer's price risk is likely to be both larger and more highly correlated with the exchange rate than the exporter's cost risks. Hence, by accepting the foreign exchange risk, the importer obtains an important hedge against the price risk of the transaction.' Rao and Magee (1980) argued that if the exporting firm were free to set price it would be set so as to make the firm indifferent to exchange risk.

Recently, Bissaro and Hamaui (1988) have

Table 29.9 Share of national currencies of total identified official holdings of foreign exchange, end of year 1979–89 (per cent)

	1979	1981	1983	1985	1987	1989
Industrial countries						
US dollar	83.5	78.7	77.4	65.4	70.6	60.2
Pound sterling	0.7	0.7	0.8	2.1	1.5	2.7
Deutsche mark	9.4	12.8	12.8	19.4	16.5	19.3
French franc	0.6	0.4	0.3	0.5	0.8	1.3
Swiss franc	1.4	1.7	1.4	1.8	1.1	1.7
Netherlands guilder	0.6	0.8	0.5	1.0	1.1	1.1
Japanese yen	2.6	3.7	5.1	8.8	6.6	7.9
Unspecified currencies	1.2	1.2	1.7	1.1	1.8	5.8

Source: IMF, *Annual Report* 1990

Table 29.10 Currency distribution of foreign exchange intervention by countries in the European Monetary System exchange rate arrangements (per cent)

		1979–82	1983–5	1986–7
US dollars	P	17.2	15.1	20.9
	S	54.3	38.6	5.4
EMS currencies				
at the limits		11.2	10.5	15.2
intramarginal	P	5.8	19.7	22.2
	S	10.2	13.3	34.3
Others	P	0.1	2.2	0.9
	S	1.2	0.6	1.1
Total		100.0	100.0	100.0

Source: EMCF, BIS, from Mastropasqua *et al.* 1988
Notes: P, purchases; S, sales.

advanced understanding of these matters significantly by constructing a model of risk-averse firms that explains the setting of prices, the choice of invoice currency and the determination of the contract period. The key assumptions of the model are that (1) the exporter's risk on sales denominated in foreign currency increases with the length of the contract period as well as with the variability of exchange rates; (2) the importer's risk on sales denominated in the exporter's currency *decreases* with the length of the contract period while increasing with exchange rate variability; and (3) sales adjust gradually to changes in prices, following Phelps and Winter (1970). The longer settlement period reduces risk for the importer because it shortens the lag between payment and resale of the goods and also increases the chance of being able to prepay at a favourable exchange rate. It increases risk for the exporter who faces an increased risk of default or repayment at an unfavourable exchange rate.

The results of Bissaro and Hamaui imply that $p < ep^*$ as long as there is exchange risk, where p is the price in domestic currency and ep^* is the domestic currency equivalent of the price in foreign currency. Therefore pricing does respond by offsetting the effect of exchange risk to some extent. There is an optimal share of invoicing in

each currency, however, as long as neither risk aversion by both parties nor the expected change in the exchange rate are too large. The results show that the share of exports denominated in domestic currency declines with expected depreciation in the domestic currency and rises with an increase in variability. Thus the exporter seeks to avoid the effects of anticipated depreciation by shifting to the importer's currency in the first case and shifting increased risk to the importer in the second.

Utilizing this framework, Bissaro and Hamaui show that the share of Italian exports denominated in lire versus other currencies fluctuated over the period 1977–86 in accordance with expected depreciation and variability as implied by the model. Their results need to be replicated with other countries' data. But with that qualification, their model seems to explain the rise in the share of Japanese exports denominated in yen and the apparent rise in the share of US imports denominated in foreign currencies discussed in the second section above. Furthermore, it suggests further evolution in those trends, since the incentives for Japanese exporters to denominate in yen and the incentives for all exporters to the USA to denominate in their own currencies remain unabated. What about the incentives for US exporters to denominate in other currencies? During the last few years, as the dollar has trended downward, one would have expected a significant shift to have occurred. But the data on commercial claims by US non-banking enterprises on foreigners cited in the second section suggest no shift.

Choice of borrowing currency

Some writers on corporate finance have suggested that firms might be indifferent to the currency in which their debt is denominated if they are willing to rely on the uncovered interest parity condition that the interest differential just compensates for expected exchange rate changes (Aliber 1978: 137–9). Unfortunately the exact form of this condition and its equivalent, the unbiasedness of the forward exchange rate as a forecast of the future spot rate, have been pretty thoroughly rejected by the data, for reasons which are not completely understood (Hodrick 1987). Aliber suggests more active strategies for firms which seek to take advantage of apparently systematic deviations from uncovered interest parity. The share of bonds issued in domestic versus foreign currency would then depend directly on the differential expected return as measured by the uncovered interest differential (adjusted for the expected change in the exchange rate) and inversely on the variability of the exchange rate as a measure of exchange risk. Johnson (1988) has shown that the currency denomination of Canadian long-term corporate bonds over the period 1970–9 fluctuated in response to the uncovered interest differential. Areskoug (1980) has found a similar relationship between exchange risk and the currency denomination of Eurobonds.

These findings are not inconsistent with the evidence cited in the second section on the changing currency denomination of external bond issues and bank lending. However, the more significant factor affecting the rising share of yen-denominated bonds and bank loans appears to be the increasing wealth position of agents whose preferred currency habitat, in McKinnon's words, is the yen.

THE INTERBANK MARKET

There have been few attempts to model the interbank currency market. Krugman (1980) and Chrystal (1984) have each discussed the emergence of vehicle currencies in the interbank market based on transaction costs, using different models. Each assumes an underlying structure of payments based on transactions in goods and capital markets. Each assumes that transaction costs will be inversely proportional to volume in each bilateral currency market. Each then shows that a vehicle currency will emerge whenever *indirect* exchange costs through the vehicle are less than direct exchange costs between two non-vehicle currencies. In contrast with their work, in this chapter we *derive*

the structure of transaction costs. We then modify the approach of Chrystal, who used a model of uninformed traders based on the origin of currencies in barter exchange. In contrast, we use a model of liquidity traders who know exactly *where* to trade but who must rely on dealers and speculators to set the price at which they may trade.

Bid–ask spreads

The basic transaction cost in the interbank market is the bid–ask spread (Levich 1985). Banks which are active in the market quote bid and offer prices at which they are prepared to deal with each other and with (large) customers. Around 10–15 per cent of transactions reported by banks arise through dealings with non-bank customers; the rest arise through dealings with other banks, either directly or through brokers. The basic problem for the bank trader is to maximize trading profits without becoming over-exposed to risk in any one currency. Since banks are committed to trading at the prices they quote, their positions are continually becoming unbalanced via trades with each other and with customers. As this happens they seek to square up their positions by further transactions, thus generating additional volume in the market. Finally, banks will actively take positions by trading at what they regard as favourable prices, expecting to close out the position later at a profit.

Allen (1977) and Booth (1984) have discussed the determination of bid–ask spreads in the foreign exchange market, while Demsetz (1968) and more recently Cohen *et al.* (1986) have discussed bid–ask spreads in securities markets. Both Allen and Booth assume that the dealer is risk averse and analyse the problem as a type of portfolio choice. In Allen (1977), the portfolio choice variables are the bid and ask prices, which are assumed to influence the probabilities of transacting at those prices. The relationship between prices and probabilities seems intuitively plausible but empirically difficult to estimate. In Booth (1984), interaction between a risk-averse monopolistic dealer and risk-averse customers leads to a bid–ask spread which depends only on differences in the exchange rate expectations of customers on the buying and selling sides of the market, implausibly independent of degrees of risk aversion and of exchange risk.

The following analysis assumes random buy and sell orders placed by liquidity traders 'at the market' with a representative competitive risk-neutral dealer who then clears the market in deals with price-sensitive speculative traders. Let $\tilde{Q}_s$ and $\tilde{Q}_d$ be random sell and buy orders in a specific bilateral currency market from liquidity traders, each with mean $\bar{Q}$. Let P_b and P_a be the dealer's posted bid and ask prices. The actual price $\tilde{P}$ at which the dealer can close out his position is determined, after orders from liquidity traders have been received and accepted by interaction with price-sensitive traders, according to the equation

$$\tilde{Q}_s + b(\tilde{P} - \bar{P}) = \tilde{Q}_d - a(\tilde{P} - \bar{P}). \quad (29.1)$$

The representative dealer's profit can then be defined as

$$\tilde{\pi} = \tilde{Q}_d(P_a - \tilde{P}) + \tilde{Q}_s(\tilde{P} - P_b). \quad (29.2)$$

If we define the spread $t = P_a - P_b$ and the expected value of $\tilde{P} = \bar{P}$, then the expected value of the dealer's profit is

$$\bar{\pi} = \text{cov}(\tilde{Q}_s - \tilde{Q}_d)(\tilde{P} - \bar{P}) + \bar{Q}t. \quad (29.3)$$

Using (29.1) we can write (29.3) as

$$\bar{\pi} = -(a + b)\sigma_p^2 + \bar{Q}t. \quad (29.4)$$

The assumption of competitive risk-neutral dealers will force expected profit to zero (or to a level just sufficient to cover dealer costs). As a result we find

$$t = \frac{(a + b)\sigma_p^2}{\bar{Q}}. \quad (29.5)$$

The implication of this analysis is that spreads in the interbank market will vary directly with riskiness as measured by the variability of the exchange rate in the very short run and inversely

with the expected volume of transactions in the market. Thus wider spreads will be expected in low volume markets and narrower spreads in markets where the authorities enforce narrow bands of short-term fluctuation, as in the EMS. Imperfect competition would be reflected in wider spreads which would just tempt new entrants to reduce spreads to earn profits and gain market share. Where bank dealers expect to have multiple relationships with customers, price competition in the exchange market might be used to attract business that would bring profits in other areas.

The discussion so far relates to spreads quoted by bank dealers to customers. But Cohen *et al.* (1986) make clear that in securities markets observed *market* spreads will frequently be less than dealer spreads. Close observation of exchange market behaviour confirms their conclusion. In active markets dealers will be constantly changing quotes with the arrival of new information and new orders from customers. Overlapping quotes from different dealers each using the same spread will create a narrower *market* spread during periods of significant market activity. Thus observed market spreads will also vary from (29.5) inversely with the *current* volume of transactions.

Vehicle currencies

According to Krugman (1980) and Chrystal (1984), the use of vehicle currencies arises whenever indirect transaction costs through the vehicle are less than direct transaction costs between two non-vehicle currencies. Armed with the above analysis of transaction costs, let us now consider this question, following the approach of Chrystal based on Jones (1976).

$T = (t_{ij})$ is a matrix of transaction costs or bid–ask spreads between currencies defined by equation (29.5). Assume that

$$t_{ij} > t_{in} + t_{nj} \quad (29.6)$$

for some $i, j \neq n$.

$U = (u_{ij})$ is a matrix of the fraction of customers entering on a given day who wish to exchange currency i for currency j directly ($u_{ij} = 0$). For simplicity, assume that U is symmetric.

$u = (u_1, \ldots, u_n)$ is a vector of the row or column sums of U representing the fractions of customers wanting to transact in currency i directly.

$q = (q_1, \ldots, q_n)$ is a vector of customers who transact in currency i taking account of both direct and vehicle use of each currency.

s is the fraction of currency exchanges occurring indirectly through the medium of currency n. The second transaction is assumed to take place on the same day.

m is the number of individuals entering the market each day to make either direct or indirect transactions, assumed constant for the purposes of this analysis. Each individual transaction is assumed to be of equal size.

The number of customers demanding currency i on a given day is then mu_i if $i = 1, \ldots, n - 1$ and $mu_n + ms$ if $i = n$. Since the total number of participants is $m + ms$, we find q_i related to u_i as

$$q_i = \frac{mu_i}{m + ms} = \frac{u_i}{1 + s} \qquad (29.7)$$

for $i = 1, \ldots, n - 1$ and

$$q_i = \frac{mu_n + ms}{m + ms} = \frac{u_n + s}{1 + s} \qquad (29.8)$$

for $i = n$. Equations (29.7) and (29.8) can be written in vector form as

$$q = u + \frac{s}{1 + s} (e_n - u) \qquad (29.9)$$

where $e_n = (0, 0, \ldots, 0, 1)$.

The analysis, which differs up to this point only slightly from that offered by Jones and Chrystal, is completed by specifying s as the sum of u_{ij} over all i, j such that condition (29.6) holds. Consider a matrix U for which the matrix T indicates that at least one bilateral currency market is dominated in the sense of (29.6) by a vehicle. Then $s > 0$ and (29.9) indicates that q_i falls for all $i \neq n$ and rises for $i = n$. We can now see from (29.5) how this will

increase t_{ij} for all i, $j \neq n$ and reduce t_{in} and t_{nj}, through the changes in volume shown in (29.9). Further extension of the use of the vehicle is likely as transaction costs through it fall and costs of directing transactions through non-vehicle currencies rise.

There is nothing in this analysis to prevent the emergence of multiple vehicle currencies, especially if transaction costs rise in the dominant vehicle currency because of increased exchange rate variability or reduced transaction volume. Nor is there anything to prevent technological change in communications from reducing dealers' costs, omitted from (29.5), in such a way as to mitigate the need for vehicle currencies altogether.

The fact that evolution seems to be led by the private market rather than by official users should make it gradual. It would be interesting to pursue a stability analysis of the process described above to examine this question.

CONCLUSIONS

The evolution of the international monetary system has its roots in the response of participants in private markets to the changing properties of internationally convertible currencies and to the changing relative importance of different groups of participants. As we have seen, both changing trade patterns and changing patterns of currency denomination of trade have had an impact on the use of currencies in international trade. Continued evolution of currency denomination appears particularly likely, given the incentives faced by traders and the historical patterns which still exist. With respect to the use of currencies in the capital markets, while comparative risk-adjusted borrowing costs appear to be an important factor, the changing balance of external asset positions of borrowers with different currency habitats may be even more so. Further evolution in external asset positions are predictable on the basis of sluggish adjustment of current external imbalances, implying further evolution in the use of currencies in capital markets.

With international traders and investors

changing their use of international currencies, the interbank foreign exchange market is bound to evolve in the same direction. As the volume of dollar-based trade and investment flows drops back from dominance to merely *primus inter pares*, so will the dollar's role in the foreign exchange market. It seems quite likely that as intra-regional trade and investment links grow tighter within Europe, the EMS will further promote the use of European currencies in international trade already clear from Table 29.1. To some extent, similar developments may be expected within East Asia, but the absence of the European degree of political and economic integration will inevitably limit the development of EMS-type arrangements in Asia. But to the extent that Japan's exports to East Asia are significantly invoiced in yen, there will be a natural tendency for yen financing. Most of the other Pacific Basin currencies, however, are not completely convertible for current *and* capital transactions, thus limiting the potential for the development of an interbank foreign exchange market among East Asian currencies.

Beyond the question of regional use of specific international currencies lies the overall structure of international payments and the international monetary system. Inevitably, the evolution in the structure of payments discussed above will have its impact on the markets and on the institutions of the international monetary system. The multi-reserve currency system appears to be a reality, even if the data in Table 29.9 show the dollar still to be the dominant element in foreign exchange reserves. It has been suggested by some writers (Bergsten and Williamson 1983) that evolution towards a multi-reserve currency system, if led by official use of currencies, might be destabilizing. Others, such as Kenen (1981), have dismissed this possibility. Gyooten (1986) has suggested that the multi-reserve currency system will promote exchange rate stability if accompanied by policy co-ordination among the reserve currency countries.

My tentative conclusion is that the effect of reserve diversification on exchange rate stability will depend on its effect on policy in the reserve centres. If diversification promotes discipline in reserve centres, it will be stabilizing. If, however, reserve centres seek to avoid the consequences of their exposure to discipline by limiting access to their markets and reducing the convertibility of their currencies, it could lead to withdrawal of funds and destabilizing behaviour.

REFERENCES

Aliber, R. Z. (1978) *Exchange Risk and Corporate International Finance*, New York: Wiley.

Allen, W. A. (1977) 'A note on uncertainty, transactions costs and interest parity', *Journal of Monetary Economics* 3: 367–73.

Areskoug, K. (1980) 'Exchange rates and the currency denomination of international bonds', *Economica* 47: 159–63.

Bergsten, C. F. and Williamson, J. (1983) *The Multiple Reserve Currency System: Evolution, Consequences, and Alternatives*, Washington, DC: Institute for International Economics.

Bilson, J. F. O. (1983) 'The choice of an invoice currency in international transactions', in J. S. Bhandari and B. H. Putnam (eds) *Economic Interdependence and Flexible Exchange Rates*, Cambridge, MA: MIT Press.

Bissaro, G. and Hamaui, R. (1988) 'The choice of invoice currency in an inter-temporal model of price setting', *Giornale degli Economisti e Annali di Economia* 47: 139–61.

Booth, L. D. (1984) 'Bid–ask spreads in the market for foreign exchange', *Journal of International Money and Finance* 3: 209–22.

Chrystal, K. A. (1984) 'On the theory of international money', in J. Black and G. S. Dorrance (eds) *Problems of International Finance*, New York: St Martin's Press.

Cohen, B. J. (1971) *The Future of Sterling as an International Currency*, London: Macmillan.

Cohen, K. J., Maier, S. F., Schwartz, R. A. and Whitcomb, D. K. (1986) *The Microstructure of Securities Markets*, Englewood Cliffs, NJ: Prentice Hall.

De Macedo, J. B. (1982) 'Portfolio diversification across currencies', in R. N. Cooper (ed.) *The International Monetary System under Flexible Exchange Rates*, Cambridge, MA: Ballinger.

Demsetz, H. (1968) 'The cost of transacting', *Quarterly Journal of Economics* 83: 33–53.

Federal Reserve Bulletin (1989) September, 75 (9): Table 3.22.

Grassman, S. (1973) 'A fundamental symmetry in international payments patterns', *Journal of International Economics* 3: 105–16.

Gyooten, T. (1986) 'Internationalization of the yen: its implications for the US–Japan relationship', in T. Patrick and R. Tachi (eds) *Japan and the United States Today: Exchange Rates, Macroeconomic Policies, and Financial Market Innovations*, New York: Center on Japanese Economy and Business, Columbia University.

Hamada, K. and Horiuchi, A. (1987) 'Monetary, financial and real effects of yen internationalization', in S. W. Arndt and J. D. Richardson (eds) *Real-Financial Linkages among Open Economies*, Cambridge, MA: MIT Press.

Heller, H. R. and Knight, M. (1978) *Reserve Currency Preferences of Central Banks*, Princeton Essays in International Finance 131.

Hodrick, R. J. (1987) *The Empirical Evidence on the Efficiency of Forward and Futures Foreign Exchange Markets*, Chur: Harwood.

Johnson, D. (1988) 'The currency denomination of long-term debt in the Canadian corporate sector: an empirical analysis', *Journal of International Money and Finance* 7: 77–80.

Jones, R. A. (1976) 'The origin and development of media of exchange', *Journal of Political Economy* 84: 757–75.

Kenen, P. B. (1981) 'The analytics of a substitution account', *Banca Nazionale del Lavoro Quarterly Review* 139: 403–26.

Krugman, P. (1980) 'Vehicle currencies and the structure of international exchange', *Journal of Money, Credit, and Banking* 12: 513–26.

Levich, R. M. (1985) 'Empirical studies of exchange rates: price behavior, rate determination and market efficiency', in R. W. Jones and P. B. Kenen (eds) *Handbook of International Economics*, vol. II, Amsterdam: North-Holland.

Lindert, P. B. (1969) *Key Currencies and Gold*, Princeton Studies in International Finance 24.

Lizondo, J. S. and Mathieson, D. J. (1987) 'The stability of the demand for international reserves', *Journal of International Money and Finance* 6: 251–82.

Mastropasqua, C., Micossi, S. and Rinaldi, R. (1988) 'Interventions, sterilization and monetary policy in EMS countries, 1979–1987', in F. Giavazzi, S. Micossi and M. Miller (eds) *The European Monetary System*, New York: Cambridge University Press.

McKinnon, R. I. (1979) *Money in International Exchange*, New York: Oxford University Press.

Officer, L. H. and Willett, T. D. (1974) 'Reserve-asset preferences in the crisis zone, 1958–67', *Journal of Money, Credit, and Banking* 6: 191–211.

Page, S. A. B. (1981) 'The choice of invoicing currency in merchandise trade', *National Institute Economic Review* 85: 60–72.

Phelps, E. S. and Winter, S. G. (1970) 'Optimal price policy under atomistic competition', in E. S. Phelps (ed.) *Microeconomic Foundations of Employment and Inflation Theory*, New York: Norton.

Rao, R. K. S. and Magee, S. P. (1980) 'The currency of denomination of international trade contracts', in R. M. Levich and C. G. Wihlborg (eds) *Exchange Risk and Exposure*, Lexington, MA: Lexington Books.

Tavlas, G. S. and Ozeki, Y. (1991) 'The Japanese yen as an international currency', unpublished IMF Working Paper 91/2, Washington, DC.

30

THE DEUTSCHE MARK AS AN INTERNATIONAL CURRENCY

George S. Tavlas

INTRODUCTION

Since the move to a regime of managed floating exchange rates in 1973, the international monetary order has progrssed gradually toward a multi-currency system. To be sure, the system continues to be dominated by the US dollar, but other currencies – particularly the deutsche mark, yen and Swiss franc – are being employed internationally with increasing regularity.

In this chapter we discuss the use of the deutsche mark as an international currency. The chapter is divided into five sections including this introduction. The following section deals with the conditions underlying the emergence of an international currency; theoretical considerations suggest that several important factors contribute to a currency's international use. In the third section we discuss these contributory factors as they relate to the deutsche mark and identify trends in several of them that presage an expanding role for the mark. In the fourth section we describe recent developments that illustrate the growing international role of the deutsche mark during the 1980s. The fifth section provides concluding comments.

DETERMINANTS OF INTERNATIONAL CURRENCY USE

An international currency fulfils three basic functions in the international monetary system – it serves as a medium of exchange, a unit of account and a store of value (Table 30.1). As a *medium of exchange*, private agents use international currency in direct exchange and as a vehicle – i.e. in indirect exchange between two other currencies – in foreign trade and international capital transactions. Official agents use international currencies as vehicles for intervention and for balance-of-payments financing. As a *unit of account*, an international currency is used for invoicing merchandise trade and for denominating financial transactions. International currencies are also used by official agents in defining exchange rate parities. As a *store of value*, private agents hold international currencies as financial assets (e.g. in the form of bonds held by non-residents). Similarly, official agents hold international currencies and financial assets denominated in such currencies as reserve assets.

Two sets of factors are essential if a currency is to be used internationally. First, there needs to be confidence in the value of the currency and in the political stability of the issuing country. High and variable inflation rates – relative to those of other countries – generate nominal exchange rate depreciation and variability. These factors increase the costs of ascertaining information and performing efficient calculations about the prices bid and offered for tradeable goods and capital assets, thereby undermining the uses of a currency as an international unit of account, store of value and medium of exchange. Further, inflation increases the costs of holding a currency by eroding its purchasing power, debasing the currency as an international store of value and medium of exchange.

Table 30.1 The roles of an international currency

Function	Sector	
	Private	*Official*
Unit of account	Currency used for invoicing foreign trade and denominating international financial instruments	Currency used in expressing exchange rate relationships
Means of payment	Currency used to settle international trade and to discharge international financial obligations	Intervention currency in foreign exchange markets and currency used for balance-of-payments financing
Store of value	Currency in which deposits, loans and bonds are denominated	Reserve asset held by monetary authorities

In turn, the achievement of relatively low levels of inflation and inflation variability depends importantly on stable and consistent government policies. In this connection, a track record of sustained current account deficits in excess of normal private capital inflows – i.e. those capital inflows that exist in the absence of undue restrictions on trade or special incentives to incoming or outgoing capital – can lead to continuous exchange rate depreciation, eroding confidence in the currency.

Second, a country should possess financial markets that are substantially free of controls (such as trade restrictions and capital controls), broad (e.g. contain a large assortment of financial instruments) and deep (e.g. existence of well-developed secondary markets). It should also possess financial institutions that are sophisticated and competitive in offshore financial centres. In general, just as relatively low levels of inflation and inflation variability contribute to the *demand* for international currencies, well-developed financial markets facilitate the *supply* (as well as the demand) of such assets. Thus, the large financial markets of New York and London contribute to the use of the US dollar and sterling, respectively, as international currencies. On the other hand, restrictions aimed at discouraging the use of the deutsche mark as a reserve currency for many years restrained the international use of that currency.

The absence of financial market controls contributes to lower costs of transacting in a currency than would otherwise be the case. For example, restrictions on the convertibility of a currency result in higher transfer costs (e.g. a greater likelihood of illiquidity), impeding the use of a national money as an international currency. Correspondingly, a country that possesses financial markets that are broad and deep is in a position to serve as an international banking centre. Specifically, such a country can be expected to provide a high degree of efficiency in international liquidity transformation by accepting short-term liquid liabilities denominated in its own currency while making long-term less liquid loans abroad.

While the foregoing conditions are important determinants of international currency use, they do not fully explain why a currency emerges as a *dominant* international currency. In this regard, studies of invoicing practices between exporters and importers have shown that dominance of a nation's currency in its international role also appears to be directly related to the country's share of world exports, the proportion of its exports that are specialized manufactured products and the extent of its trade with developing countries. These observed behavioural patterns reflect the tendency for trade between developed countries typically to be denominated in the currency of the exporter since the market situation of the importer often provides a hedge against currency fluctuations; specifically, importers can often pass through the consequences of exchange rate changes by charging a higher price for their products in the domestic market. This course of action is most practical in small, open economies in which a large domestic import-competing industry does not exist and helps explain why trade between developed and developing countries is usually denominated in the currency of the developed countries. Further, to the extent that importers do bear some risk by denominating in the currency of the exporter, importers gain knowledge that helps them anticipate future exchange rate movements better than the average participant in foreign exchange markets. The profitability of this knowledge could offset the risk of exchange rate volatility.

On the other hand, exporters are more likely to find it difficult to cut factor payments that had been previously set via contract. This is particularly the case for exporters of manufactured products involving long production lags. Since unforeseeable exchange rate movements would have to be absorbed through lower profit margins, such exporters have an incentive to invoice in their own currency. Exporters can hedge, of course, but the

use of the forward market increases their costs. It is more expedient to pass the risk off to the importer who, in any event, often possesses a natural hedge against exchange rate risk.

The combination of all of the foregoing factors – relatively low inflation, broad and deep financial markets and pertinent trade patterns – fosters vehicle use and generates familiarity and confidence that encourage formation of primary-product and financial-asset currency blocs, further lowering transaction costs and reinforcing international currency use. What are the implications of these factors with regard to use of the deutsche mark as an international currency?

IMPLICATIONS FOR THE DEUTSCHE MARK

Inflation and the credibility of monetary policy

Since 1975 monetary policy in Germany has followed a medium-term orientation aimed at keeping the value of money stable. A medium-term anti-inflationary orientation for monetary policy

Table 30.2 Inflation and inflation variability[a]

Period	France	Germany	Italy	Japan	Switzerland	UK	USA
Inflation rate							
1970–4	7.6	5.6	9.1	10.7	7.1	9.6	6.1
1975–9	10.2	4.2	15.9	7.5	2.9	15.7	8.1
1970–9	*8.9*	*4.9*	*12.5*	*9.1*	*5.0*	*13.3*	*7.2*
1980–4	11.2	4.5	16.6	3.9	4.4	9.6	7.5
1985–90	3.5	1.5	6.3	1.5	2.7	6.0	3.9
1980–90	*7.0*	*2.9*	*10.9*	*2.6*	*3.5*	*7.6*	*5.5*
1970–90	*7.9*	*3.8*	*11.7*	*5.7*	*4.2*	*10.1*	*6.3*
Inflation variability							
1970–4	3.4	0.9	6.0	7.4	1.6	3.5	3.1
1975–9	1.2	1.2	3.5	3.3	2.4	5.8	2.2
1970–9	*2.6*	*1.5*	*5.6*	*5.9*	*3.2*	*5.6*	*2.8*
1980–4	2.4	1.5	3.8	2.2	1.6	5.2	3.9
1985–90	1.2	1.2	1.5	1.2	1.6	2.2	1.2
1980–90	*4.2*	*2.0*	*5.8*	*2.1*	*1.8*	*4.2*	*3.3*
1970–90	*3.7*	*2.0*	*5.9*	*5.3*	*2.6*	*5.6*	*3.1*

Source: IMF, *International Financial Statistics*

Notes: [a]Based on consumer price indices. Inflation variability is measured by the standard deviation using quarterly data for the indicated periods.

was also adopted in the 1970s by a number of other large industrial countries, including France, Italy, Japan, Switzerland, the UK and the USA. Underlying this medium-term approach is the view that in the short run monetary growth is an important determinant of nominal income growth and the balance of payments, and that over the medium term its primary impact is on inflation and the nominal exchange rate.

In comparison with these other major industrial countries, the medium-term orientation of Germany's monetary policy has been quite successful in maintaining a stable internal value of the deutsche mark. In fact, over 1970–90 Germany experienced the lowest average annual inflation rate (3.8 per cent) among these countries (Table 30.2). The Bundesbank's success with respect to inflation has procured credibility for Germany's monetary policy and has led to a situation whereby the mark serves as the nominal anchor for the other currencies participating in the exchange rate mechanism of the EMS. Other members of the ERM have effectively elected to use the deutsche mark as an official numeraire by pegging their currencies against the mark, thereby borrowing some of the Bundesbank's credibility as an unyielding foe against inflation. In turn, Germany's performance with respect to inflation and its participation in the ERM have provided benefits for Germany, including some retention of domestic monetary independence and decreased volatility of the nominal exchange rate against the currencies of its EMS partners.

German financial markets

During the period encompassing the late 1960s through the early 1980s, the Bundesbank attempted to moderate the international use of the deutsche mark. Underlying this approach – which emerged under the Bretton Woods fixed exchange rate regime – was the view that substantial swings in capital flows could impede domestic stabilization objectives. While the move to a floating exchange rate system increased the Bundesbank's control over domestic monetary conditions, the

gain in control may have been less for Germany than for other large developed countries in view of the relative openness of Germany's economy.

Consequently, in order to tighten its grip on domestic monetary conditions the Bundesbank extended relatively firm control over capital inflows. In this context, a 'gentleman's agreement' entered into by the Bundesbank and the German banks in 1968 stipulated that only German banks could lead syndicates for deutsche-mark-denominated bonds. The rationale underlying the agreement was that German banks would be more apt to follow the advice of the Bundesbank than would foreign banks and therefore could be more effectively controlled. A second important restriction concerned the kinds of bond issues that were allowed. Only the standard fixed rate issue was permitted. Innovative financial instruments – including floating rate notes, zero-coupon bonds and bonds linked to currency and interest rate swaps – were strictly prohibited.

These and other restrictions weakened the competitive position of German banks *vis-à-vis* foreign banks and led to innovations aimed at avoiding these regulations. For example, the upsurge and increased variability in inflation during the 1970s rendered fixed rate bonds less attractive than other more flexible instruments. Also, technological improvements (e.g. in data processing) lowered transaction costs, making it easier for regulated financial institutions to innovate in order to avoid the regulations. Consequently, in order to maintain the competitive position of the deutsche mark relative to other currencies, most financial market restrictions have been lifted in recent years.

Nevertheless, partly because of Germany's relatively late move to ease restrictions, the breadth and depth of German financial markets have lagged behind some other large financial centres, mostly notably those of London and New York. In this connection, a turnover tax on all secondary market dealings in bonds and equities has prevented the establishment of a market in short-term commercial paper and encouraged the switching of secondary trading in deutsche-mark-denominated paper to financial centres outside Germany. Also, the equity market is thin and narrow, and futures trading has only recently been allowed. While measures have recently been taken to enhance Germany's competitiveness in these areas, the fact that Germany has lagged other financial centres in several important respects has restricted Germany's relative efficiency in competing for international funds.

Trade patterns

Developments in Germany's trade patterns in recent years have generally been conducive to the international use of the deutsche mark on several accounts. First, Germany has become the world's largest supplier of exports to the world, surpassing the USA since 1986 and enhancing the potential role of the mark as an invoicing vehicle. Second, between 1980 and 1989 the share of specialized manufactured goods (primarily machinery and transport goods) in relation to total German exports rose from 38 to 47 per cent. It should be noted, however, that other key currency countries also experienced rising shares of exports comprising specialized manufactured goods over 1980–9. In this connection, the share of such goods in total exports for the USA rose from 32 per cent to 44 per cent; for Japan, the share of such exports rose from 52 per cent to 71 per cent.

Finally, a potentially mitigating factor with respect to the deutsche mark's international use is that Germany's trade with developing countries has decreased in recent years. Thus, German exports to developing countries as a share of total German exports declined from about 26 per cent in 1980 to 17 per cent in 1989, and German imports from developing countries as a percentage of total German imports declined from 29 per cent to 20 per cent. However, these declines have been more than offset by a rising proportion of German trade that has been directed toward other European countries. For example, about 70 per cent of German imports were from EC countries in 1989, compared with 62 per cent in 1980. Given that EC countries have in recent years invoiced a growing proportion of their exports in terms of deutsche marks, the decline in Germany's trade with developing countries need not imply an overall decline in the share of world trade denominated in deutsche marks. In addition, corresponding declines in trade shares with developing countries were experienced by most other large developed countries – including Japan and the USA – during the 1980s.

RECENT TRENDS

The preceding discussion suggests that the determinants of international currency use imply an expanding international role for the deutsche mark. In order to determine how these various factors have combined to influence the internationalization of the deutsche mark, the following discussion presents data pertaining to the use of the mark as a unit of account, medium of exchange and store of value.

Currency-invoicing patterns

The currency-invoicing patterns of German exports and imports during the 1980s are provided in Table 30.3. The data indicate that there has been little change in the currency denomination of German exports over 1980–7; specifically, the share of Germany's exports invoiced in deutsche marks has remained about 82 per cent. A substantial rise (about 10 percentage points) has occurred, however, in the share of German imports denominated in deutsche marks during 1980–8: this change has been mainly at the expense of US-dollar-denominated imports.

Several points are worth making in this regard. First, the declining proportion of German imports from developing countries – according to the inference drawn from the observed patterns of invoicing behaviour – would imply a corresponding decrease in imports denominated in deutsche marks. However, to the extent that developing country exports (i.e. mainly primary products) are denominated in US dollars, the decline that took place in US dollar import invoicing is at least partly

Table 30.3 Currency invoicing of German foreign trade[a]

	1980	1981	1982	1983	1984	1985	1986	1987	1988
Exports									
Deutsche mark	82.5	82.2	83.2	82.6	79.4	79.5	81.5	81.5	n.a.
US dollar	7.2	7.8	6.7	7.0	9.7	9.5	7.7	7.4	n.a.
Pound sterling	1.4	1.3	1.3	1.5	1.7	1.8	1.7	1.8	n.a.
French franc	2.8	2.8	2.8	2.8	2.8	2.7	2.7	2.5	n.a.
Swiss franc	0.5	0.5	0.5	0.5	0.5	0.5	0.5	0.6	n.a.
Japanese yen	–	–	–	–	0.3	0.4	0.4	0.5	n.a.
Other	5.6	5.6	5.5	5.8	5.7	5.7	5.5	5.7	n.a.
Imports									
Deutsche mark	43.0	43.0	44.6	46.1	47.0	47.8	51.7	52.7	52.6
US dollar	32.3	32.3	31.3	28.8	29.2	28.1	23.1	22.0	21.6
Pound sterling	3.4	3.7	2.5	2.7	2.4	3.0	2.3	2.5	2.4
French franc	3.3	3.0	3.4	3.5	3.6	3.8	4.1	3.9	3.6
Swiss franc	1.6	1.6	1.6	1.5	1.5	1.5	1.7	1.8	1.7
Japanese yen	–	–	–	–	–	1.8	2.6	2.5	2.5
Other[b]	15.4	16.4	16.6	17.4	16.5	14.0	14.5	14.9	15.6

Source: Deutsche Bundesbank

Notes: n.a., not available.
[a]Sum may not add to 100 due to rounding.
[b]Includes trade invoiced in ECUs, the share of which was less than 0.1 per cent of total imports in each year.

explainable by this fact. Second, the redirection of German trade has involved a higher proportion of trade with European countries. As noted, about 70 per cent of German imports were from EC countries in 1988, compared with 62 per cent in 1980.[1] Since the EC countries have in recent years invoiced a growing proportion of their exports in deutsche marks, this also helps explain the increase in the deutsche mark denomination of German imports and illustrates a regional process underlying the increased use of the mark.[2] Increased use of the deutsche mark as an international currency has been due in good measure to the importance of the mark as a key currency within Europe. In this regard, recent action taken to open trade and financial connections between Western and Eastern Europe should contribute to the wider use of the deutsche mark. For example, effective from 1 January 1990, the Yugoslav dinar was pegged to the deutsche mark.

Data pertaining to world invoicing patterns are presented in Table 30.3. The table utilizes data available in Page (1981) and Black (1989) relating the currency composition of exports and imports of each of the six largest industrial countries and of OPEC. However, Page and Black present data for 1980 and 1987, respectively, on the proportion of a country's exports and imports invoiced in a certain currency. The data in Table 30.3 adjust these proportions by incorporating a country's share of world trade. This adjustment is made in the case of Germany by noting that, in 1987, 82 per cent of German exports were denominated in deutsche marks while the share of world exports provided by Germany was 12.5 per cent; multiplying these two numbers together indicates that 10.2 per cent of world exports in 1987 were denominated in deutsche marks on account of Germany's contribution alone.

Performing similar calculations for the other countries and for OPEC yields the following results. In 1980, at least 34.5 per cent of world exports were denominated in US dollars. (Together, the six largest industrial countries and

OPEC accounted for 60.5 per cent of world exports in 1980 and 55.2 per cent in 1987.) Correspondingly, at least 10.2 per cent of world exports were denominated in deutsche marks. In 1987, the respective numbers were 24.8 per cent of world exports denominated in US dollars and 12.4 per cent in deutsche marks on account of the invoicing behaviour and trade involving these countries. In the absence of other relevant invoicing data and assuming that the export-invoicing behaviour of the rest of the world remained unchanged between 1980 and 1987, these numbers suggest that the share of world exports denominated in US dollars fell by 9.7 per cent over this period while the shares denominated in deutsche marks and in yen rose by 2.2 per cent and 1.5 per cent respectively.

The deutsche mark as a medium of exchange vehicle

Developments regarding the volume of currencies traded on foreign exchange markets suggest the relative importance of currencies as unit of account and medium of exchange vehicles. Data on the currency turnover in the interbank markets are available from surveys conducted by central banks in New York, London and Tokyo in March 1986,

April 1989 and at earlier dates in New York. These data, summarized in Table 30.4, indicate that the interbank markets continued to be dominated by transactions involving the US dollar. The share of the deutsche mark has been rather stable, while the share of the Japanese yen has increased.

Another measure of a currency's role as an international medium of exchange is its use in exchange market intervention by central banks. Table 30.5 provides data on the use of the deutsche mark as an intervention vehicle within the EMS from 1979 to 1989; both obligatory and intramarginal interventions are reported. The data show that a substantial increase in the level of deutsche mark intervention has occurred.

While these data show an increase in the absolute amount of deutsche mark intervention in the EMS, they do not provide information on the *share* of deutsche mark intervention. Table 30.6 reports data on the currency distribution of foreign exchange intervention in the EMS. The data are in part from Mastropasqua *et al.* (1988), who report the currency distributions of EMS intervention in three categories: US dollars, EMS currencies and other currencies; however, intervention in deutsche marks is not broken out separately. Mastropasqua *et al.* present intervention data for three periods: March 1979 through 1982, 1983 through 1985

Table 30.4 Currency composition of turnover in major foreign exchange markets (per cent of total turnover)

Currency	New York				London		Tokyo	
	March 1980	April 1983	March 1986	April 1989	March 1986	April 1989	March 1986	April 1989
Against US dollar								
Deutsche mark	31.8	32.5	34.2	32.9	28.0	22.0	10.4	9.7
Pound sterling	22.7	16.6	18.6	14.6	30.0	27.0	3.0	4.3
Japanese yen	10.2	22.0	23.0	25.2	14.0	15.0	77.0	72.1
French franc	6.9	4.4	3.6	3.2	4.0	4.0	0.3	0.2
Swiss franc	10.1	12.2	9.7	11.8	9.0	10.0	5.6	4.4
Canadian dollar	12.2	7.5	5.2	4.0	2.0	2.0	0.0	0.0
Other	6.1	4.6	5.8	8.3	10.0	11.0	3.3	3.2
Cross-currency	n.a.	0.2	n.a.	n.a.	3.0	9.0	0.0	6.1

Sources: Federal Reserve Bank of New York, Bank of England, Bank of Japan, press releases, 13 September 1989
Notes: Numbers are rounded and may not add up to 100. n.a., not available.

Table 30.5 Intervention in the European Monetary System in deutsche marks (purchases and sales in billions of deutsche marks)

Year	Obligatory	Intramarginal	Total
1979[a]	3.6	10.8	14.4
1980	5.9	6.9	12.8
1981	19.6	20.9	40.5
1982	3.0	22.2	25.2
1983	25.0	32.0	57.0
1984	4.7	37.8	42.5
1985	0.4	60.4	60.7
1986	23.1	109.6	132.7
1987	15.0	109.5	124.5
1988	0.0	43.1	43.1
1989	10.0	29.0	39.0

Sources: Deutsche Bundesbank, *Report of the Deutsche Bundesbank*, various issues, 1980–90
Note: [a]From March 1979.

and 1986 through the first half of 1987. Their data show that the share of US dollar intervention declined from 71.5 per cent in the first period to 26.3 per cent in the third period.[3]

To obtain a measure of the role of deutsche mark intervention within the EMS, the following procedure was adopted. Data pertaining to the

Table 30.6 Currency distribution of foreign exchange intervention (per cent of total intervention)

Currency	1979–82	1983–5	1986–8
EMS intervention			
US dollars	71.5[a]	53.7	26.3[b]
EMS currencies	27.2[a]	43.5	71.7[b]
(Deutsche marks)	(23.7)[a]	(39.4)	(59.0)[b]
Others[c]	1.3[a]	2.8	2.0[b]
US Federal Reserve and Treasury intervention			
Deutsche marks	89.7	67.9	57.5
Yen	10.3	32.1	42.5

Sources: Deutsche Bundesbank, *Report of the Deutsche Bundesbank*, various issues, 1980–90; Federal Reserve Bank of New York, *Quarterly Review*, various issues, 1980–9; Mastropasqua *et al.* 1988
Notes: Total intervention includes both purchases and sales.
     [a]From March 1979.
     [b]To June 1987.
     [c]From 1985, includes intervention in private ECUs.

periods used by Mastropasqua *et al.* were obtained from various issues of the Bundesbank's *Monthly Reports*. These data are available only in terms of deutsche mark denomination while Mastropasqua *et al.* report figures in terms of US dollars. Consequently, the Bundesbank's figures were converted into US dollars by using the average deutsche mark–dollar exchange rate for each subperiod. On this basis the share of intervention in deutsche marks was estimated. The decline in the share of US dollar intervention in the EMS was largely the counterpart of a substantial increase in the share of deutsche mark intervention.

Finally, Table 30.6 also reports the currency distribution of intervention by the US Federal Reserve and the US Treasury over three periods: 1979–82, 1983–5 and 1986–8. All intervention by the US authorities has been in terms of either the deutsche mark or the Japanese yen. Although the data show a decline in the deutsche mark's share, the mark nevertheless accounted for more than half of this intervention during 1986–8.

The deutsche mark as an investment currency

For purposes of exposition, foreign deutsche mark claims can be classified into three broad categories:[4] (i) claims held in Germany by non-residents – these claims can be on German banks, enterprises or the public sector and can be short or long term; (ii) claims held outside Germany by non-residents in the form of Euro-deutsche mark (short-term) deposits – the borrowers of such funds are typically foreign offices or subsidiaries of German banks; and (iii) claims held outside Germany by non-residents in the form of Euro-deutsche mark (long-term) bonds.

Data pertaining to each of these categories (denominated in deutsche marks) are presented in Table 30.7. Deutsche mark claims in Germany held by non-residents, which accounted for about 60 per cent of total claims in Germany by non-residents at the end of 1987 (Fröhlich 1988), more than doubled between 1980 and 1986. Approximately half of the increase took place in 1985 and 1986. This large increase has been attributed in

Table 30.7 Foreign deutsche mark claims[a] (billions of deutsche marks)

	1980	1981	1982	1983	1984	1985	1986	1987	1988	1989
Deutsche mark claims in Germany held by foreigners										
Total[b]	206	268	292	320	359	437	508	497	536	585
Of which:										
Per cent long term	(61.8)	(60.5)	(60.3)	(64.5)	(64.2)	(70.1)	(75.7)	(75.4)	(75.0)	(72.0)
Per cent short term	(38.2)	(39.5)	(39.7)	(35.3)	(35.8)	(29.9)	(24.3)	(24.6)	(25.0)	(28.0)
Held on:										
German banking system	(106)	(121)	(121)	(125)	(143)	(159)	(178)	(184)	(195)	(222)
Enterprises and individuals[c]	(69)	(86)	(86)	(96)	(107)	(149)	(164)	(127)	(149)	(165)
Public sector[d]	(31)	(61)	(85)	(99)	(109)	(128)	(166)	(186)	(192)	(198)
External deutsche mark claims held by foreigners[e]										
Euro-money markets	266	288	303	337	376	398	383	460	516	599
as per cent of all Euro-dollar, Euro-yen and Euro-deutsche mark deposits[f]	(n.a.)	(n.a.)	(12.3)	(11.8)	(10.8)	(12.5)	(12.3)	(14.6)	(13.7)	(14.2)
External deutsche mark bonds[g]	57	57	61	64	71	85	102	107	124	128
Memorandum item										
Net purchases (+) or sales (−) of domestic bonds by foreigners	0.3	−1.5	2.3	10.8	13.8	31.5	59.1	35.0	2.1	0.7

Sources: Bundesbank, Monthly Report, various issues; and H.P. Fröhlich 1988

Notes: [a] End-of-year data except for 1980, 1981 and 1989 which are mid-year.
  [b] Excluding direct investment, other equity holdings and real estate transactions. Does not include foreign claims in instruments denominated in other currencies.
  [c] Includes bond issues of the Federal Railways and Federal Post Office.
  [d] Includes deutsche mark notes held by foreigners (estimated).
  [e] Banks in the European reporting area and in Canada and Japan.
  [f] Dollar liabilities in the European reporting area (here including Germany), Japan and Canada, as well as of International Banking Facilities and certain offshore branches of US banks to depositors outside the USA, yen liabilities of banks in the European reporting ???.
  [g] Computed from data on the total outstanding (face value) and estimated domestic holdings.

part to the measures taken to deregulate the financial system at the end of 1984 and in 1985 (Reinhold and Oldenbourg 1986; Deutsche Bundesbank 1987; Thomas 1987). In particular, the abolition of the coupon tax on interest income received by non-residents from domestic bonds and the introduction of more flexible financial instruments in the capital market increased the attractiveness to foreigners of investing in the German financial system. In this context, net foreign purchases of domestic bonds by non-residents rose from DM 13.8 billion in 1984 to DM 59.1 billion in 1986 (see memorandum item in Table 30.7). External deutsche mark claims held by foreigners also rose between 1980 and 1986 but at a considerably slower rate than claims held in Germany (Table 30.7). Whereas in 1980 total external claims (Euromoney market claims and external deutsche mark bonds) amounted to about 1½ times foreign claims held in Germany, by 1986 the amount of foreign claims held in Germany had surpassed external claims. This development is also explained in part by the liberalization measures introduced in 1984 and 1985 which made foreign investment in Germany more attractive. As a result, there was a substitution of foreign lending towards deutsche mark investments in Germany. The announcement of the withholding tax in the fourth quarter of 1987 contributed to a substitution of foreign deutsche mark lending towards external investments and away from claims in Germany. As noted by Lipschitz et al. (1989: 48), it appeared that the major part of the proposed withholding tax was reflected in the relative yields of foreign and domestic deutsche mark bonds. The withholding tax decreased the demand for domestic instruments, thereby lowering the price of such instruments and raising their yields. Whereas the average yield on German public authority bonds was over 50 basis points lower than the average on issues by foreign public bodies in the first nine months of 1987, following the announcement of the withholding tax this differential almost entirely disappeared and by August 1988 foreign issues were trading about a ¼ percentage point lower than German issues

(Lipschitz et al. 1989: 48–9). Consequently, in 1987 external deutsche mark claims held by non-residents rose sharply (by 17 per cent) while foreign claims held in Germany declined.[5] Similarly, net purchases of domestic bonds by foreigners fell to DM 35.0 billion in 1987 from DM 59.1 billion in 1986.

In turn, the announcement of the abolition of the withholding tax in April 1989 contributed to a sharp increase in foreign deutsche mark claims held in Germany during the first half of 1989. During the same period, there occurred a further substantial rise in external deutsche mark claims held by foreigners. Over the entire period 1980 through the first half of 1989, the attractiveness of deutsche mark claims to non-residents is evident as such non-resident claims held in Germany increased by over 180 per cent and those held externally rose by 125 per cent.

Table 30.7 also shows that shares of deutsche mark claims in Germany held by non-residents have been predominantly long term. Further, the share of long-term claims rose during the 1980s. This reflects in part Germany's comparative disadvantage with regard to short-term financial instruments which, in turn, restricts the efficiency of the German financial market in international liquidity transformation.

In order to assess the performance of the deutsche mark vis-à-vis other currencies in international capital markets. Table 30.8 presents data on the use of the deutsche mark and other currencies as a store of value and unit of account in such markets over the period 1981–9. The data in the table classify the uses of currencies into three types of instruments: (i) external bank loans, which include foreign and international bank loans; (ii) external bond issues, which include foreign and international issues and special placements; and (iii) Eurocurrency deposits. These data have been compiled by the BIS; they differ from the data presented in Table 30.8 in that the BIS data include resident holdings in the definitions of external bond issues and Eurocurrency deposits. In general, the data indicate a growing role for the deutsche mark in international capital markets.

Table 30.8 Relative shares based on external capital market data[a] (per cent)

	1981–4 average[b]	1985	1986	1987	1988	1989	1990
Shares of currencies of external bank loans[c]							
Japanese yen	5.9	18.5	16.1	10.8	5.6	4.7	1.8
US dollar	83.3	62.5	67.0	65.1	69.9	75.0	64.6
Pound sterling	3.1	3.4	6.4	14.7	14.1	9.0	13.5
ECU	1.3	7.1	2.2	2.4	2.8	4.0	8.0
Deutsche mark	1.7	2.1	3.0	2.4	2.2	2.9	5.7
Swiss franc	1.2	3.0	2.1	0.7	0.3	0.3	0.1
Other	3.5	3.4	3.2	3.9	5.1	4.1	6.3
Total	100.0	100.0	100.0	100.0	100.0	100.0	100.0
Currency denomination of external bond issues[d]							
Japanese yen	5.7	9.1	10.4	13.7	8.4	8.3	13.3
US dollar	63.2	54.0	53.9	38.8	41.2	52.0	37.9
Swiss franc	14.7	11.3	10.7	12.9	11.1	7.5	9.4
Deutsche mark	6.3	8.5	8.0	8.0	10.1	6.3	7.4
Pound sterling	3.4	4.0	4.6	7.8	9.4	7.1	8.6
Canadian dollar	1.6	1.6	2.3	3.4	5.7	4.4	2.6
ECU	1.7	5.2	3.4	4.0	4.9	4.9	8.1
Australian dollar	–[e]	1.6	1.5	4.9	3.4	2.2	2.2
French franc	–[e]	1.1	1.7	1.3	1.3	2.1	3.8
Netherlands guilder	1.8	1.3	1.3	1.1	1.2	0.9	0.5
Other	1.6	2.3	2.2	4.1	3.3	4.3	6.2
Total	100.0	100.0	100.0	100.0	100.0	100.0	100.0
Currency denomination of Eurocurrency deposits							
Japanese yen	1.8	3.4	4.5	5.8	5.5	5.4	5.0
US dollar	74.0	67.9	63.5	58.2	60.1	57.9	53.0
Deutsche mark	11.4	11.4	12.8	14.2	13.3	15.3	16.5
Swiss franc	5.8	6.4	7.2	7.7	5.4	5.0	5.8
Pound sterling	1.4	2.0	2.1	2.8	3.4	3.1	3.9
French franc	0.9	1.2	1.2	1.4	1.3	1.3	2.2
ECU	5.1	2.6	2.6	2.8	3.0	3.5	4.6
Other[f]	4.3	5.0	6.0	7.0	7.9	8.5	9.0
Total	100.0	100.0	100.0	100.0	100.0	100.0	100.0

Sources: OECD, *Financial Market Trends*, various issues; BIS, *International Banking and Financial Market Developments*, various issues

Notes: [a]End-of-period data.
[b]The average of 1981–4 data are used since the 1980 data are not consistent with the 1981–4 data.
[c]Foreign and international bank loans, excluding loan renegotiations.
[d]Includes international issues, foreign issues and special placements.
[e]Included in other categories prior to 1983.
[f]Includes foreign currency position of banks in the USA for which no currency breakdown is available.

Table 30.9 Currency shares of official exchange holdings, 1980–9 (per cent)

Currency	1980	1982	1984	1986	1988	1989[a]
All countries						
Deutsche mark	14.9	11.7	11.6	13.7	16.0	19.6
US dollar	68.6	70.4	69.3	66.0	63.8	59.2
Pound sterling	2.9	2.3	2.9	2.6	2.8	2.8
Japanese yen	4.3	4.6	5.5	7.5	7.7	8.1
French franc	1.7	1.1	0.8	0.9	1.2	1.2
Swiss franc	3.2	2.4	2.0	1.9	2.0	2.0
Netherlands guilder	1.3	1.1	0.7	1.0	1.1	1.0
Unspecified currencies	3.1	6.1	7.0	6.4	5.4	6.0
Selected EC countries[b]						
Deutsche mark	12.0	10.3	16.6	14.9	20.3	23.4
US dollar	80.2	80.9	72.9	71.3	63.7	57.9
Pound sterling	1.0	0.8	1.4	1.7	1.3	0.7
Japanese yen	2.0	3.5	4.7	6.2	6.7	4.7
French franc	0.8	0.2	0.1	0.1	1.4	1.4
Swiss franc	1.0	1.6	1.8	2.1	2.2	2.1
Netherlands guilder	1.0	1.0	0.8	1.1	1.0	1.2
Unspecified currencies	1.9	1.8	1.8	2.8	3.4	8.7

Sources: IMF, *Annual Report*, various issues, 1978–90; and IMF staff estimates

Notes: Numbers are rounded and may not add up to 100.

[a]End-of-year data.

[b]Data are IMF staff estimates and are in some instances based on interpolation.

The importance of currencies as international units of account and stores of value can also be gauged from their use as official reserves. In this regard, Table 30.9 reports currency shares of official holdings of foreign exchange by all reporting countries and by selected EC countries from 1980 to 1989. With respect to holdings by all countries, the data show that the largest gain was registered by the deutsche mark (4.7 percentage points) as its share reached nearly 20 per cent in 1989. The data also show a more striking rise in the share of mark holdings by EC countries (11.4 percentage points); this rise was at the expense of the US dollar.

CONCLUSIONS

This chapter has investigated the theoretical factors underlying the international use of a currency, examined recent developments in those factors pertaining to the deutsche mark and presented data on the extent of the internationalization of the deutsche mark that occurred during the 1980s. The main findings of the chapter are as follows. Theoretical considerations indicate that several factors combine to propagate the internationalization of a currency: relatively low levels of inflation and of inflation variability, which are predominantly the result of credible government policies, and a relatively stable external value of a currency; open, deep and broad financial markets; and a country's share of world exports, the share of its merchandise exports comprising differentiated manufactured goods and (to a lesser extent) its developing-country trade links. In general, recent developments in these factors with respect to Germany were found to presage an expanding role for the deutsche mark as an international currency.

The data corroborated this expectation. The available evidence indicates that there has been some increase in the proportion of world trade denominated in deutsche marks. Regarding the role of the deutsche mark as a medium of exchange vehicle, usage of the deutsche mark in interbank trading has remained rather steady. The dollar continues to dominate the interbank market, but the deutsche mark and the Japanese yen are the currencies that are traded most against the dollar. Moreover, the deutsche mark together with the Japanese yen are the two currencies used as intervention vehicles by the USA. Finally, an increase in the role of the deutsche mark has taken place with regard to its use in international capital markets and in official foreign exchange holdings. Corresponding increases were registered by a number of other currencies – most notably the Japanese yen – at the expense of the US dollar.

In sum, the findings confirm the move to a multi-currency international monetary system and the deutsche mark's emergence as a key component of that system. The findings also confirm that the expanding international role of the mark has stemmed in substantial measure from the mark's importance as a key currency within Europe. Thus, an increase in deutsche mark invoicing by European countries has more than offset any lessening of deutsche mark invoicing that may have resulted from the declining share of Germany's trade conducted with developing countries. In addition, a striking increase has occurred in the use of the deutsche mark as an intervention vehicle within the EMS. Indeed, the role of German monetary policy has effectively led to the use of the deutsche mark as an official currency peg within the EMS. Likewise, contributing to the increase in the use of the mark in official foreign exchange holdings has been the rise in the share of such holdings by European countries.

Given the mark's role as the key currency in Europe, the move toward European economic and monetary integration is likely to further enhance its position as an international currency. In this connection, recent actions to peg the Yugoslav dinar to the deutsche mark (effective 1 January 1990) and to tie the Belgian franc more closely to the mark (effective June 1990) are indicative of this process. Eventually, European economic integra-

tion may culminate in the full centralization of monetary authority (a European central bank) and the use of a single European currency (the ECU). The introduction of a single currency would have several advantages relative to a system of national monies linked by fixed exchange rates. These advantages include the elimination of transaction costs and exchange rate risk and the attainment of complete financial market integration. The elimination of costs of information, search and uncertainty on intra-European transactions can be expected to contribute to the vehicle use of a single European currency. Consequently, European monetary union is likely to enhance the international (i.e. global) use of a new European currency, compared with the existing situation of national European currencies. If European monetary union does proceed in such a direction, it seems reasonable to infer that in large measure it is the reputation of the deutsche mark that will give credibility to the new currency.

NOTES

1   These data are from Data Resources Incorporated's World Trade Model.

2   In 1980, 9 per cent of French exports were denominated in deutsche marks; in 1987 the deutsche mark share was 10 per cent. For Italy, the share of deutsche-mark-denominated exports rose from 14 per cent in 1980 to 18 per cent in 1987. These data are from Black (1989).

3   Some of this decline could be due to valuation effects resulting from exchange rate changes. Nevertheless, these data are indicative of longer-term trends. This also applies to data on the investment uses of currencies presented below.

4   This categorization is used by the Deutsche Bundesbank. The Bundesbank defines deutsche mark claims held outside Germany narrowly and excludes claims outside Germany held by German residents. This definition differs from that used by the BIS (see below).

5   Although the announcement of the withholding tax did not occur until the fourth quarter of 1987, it had a marked impact on foreign claims held in Germany. Thus, such claims rose from DM 508 billion in December 1986 to DM 539 billion in June 1987; however, they fell to DM 497 billion in December 1987.

REFERENCES

Black, S. (1989) 'Transactions costs and vehicle currencies', IMF Working Paper WP/89/96, Washington, DC: IMF, November.

Deutsche Bundesbank (various issues) *Annual Report.*

—— (1987) 'Foreign deutsche mark assets and liabilities', *Monthly Report, Frankfurt* 39 (May): 13–23.

Fröhlich, H. P. (1988) 'Weltwährung D-Mark? Beiträge zur Wirtschafts- und Sozialpolitik, Institut der deutschen Wirtschaft, September.

Lipschitz, L., Kremers J., Mayer, T. and McDonald, D. (1989) *The Federal Republic of Germany: Adjustment in a Surplus Country*, Occasional Paper 64, Washington, DC: IMF, January.

Mastropasqua, C., Micossi, S. and Rinaldi, R. (1988) 'Interventions, sterilization and monetary policy in European Monetary System countries, 1979–87', in F. Giovazzi, S. Micossi and M. Miller (eds) *The European Monetary System*, Cambridge: Cambridge University Press.

Page, S. A. B. (1981) 'The choices of invoicing currency in merchandise trade', *National Institute Economic Review* 85 (March): 60–72.

Reinhold, R. and Oldenbourg, T. (1986) 'Auslandsbanken im Liberalisierten DM-Kapitalmarkt', *Deutsche Bundesbank, Auszüge aus Presseartikeln* 74, 3 November.

Thomas, K. (1987) 'DM-Auslandsanleihen und Innovationen am deutschen Kapitalmarkt', *Deutsche Bundesbank, Auszüge aus Presseartikeln*, March: 5–7.

31

THE INTERNATIONALIZATION OF THE YEN

Dilip K. Das

THE LARGEST CREDITOR STATUS

Riding on the domestic economy's long-running expansion, balance-of-payments surpluses and an appreciating yen and assisted by deregulation of the domestic banking and financial markets, Japan turned into the most solvent nation and the leading financial power of the latter half of the 1980s. Following the Murchison–Solomon report, there was a good deal of American pressure on Japan during the meetings of the *ad hoc* group on the yen–dollar exchange rate to internationalize the yen. It helped overcome the domestic conservative opposition which was eager to maintain the status quo for two ill-founded reasons. First, they thought that internationalizing the yen would amount to losing control over the monetary aspect of the domestic economy. They believed that internationalizing the yen would interfere with their control of money supply and therefore would increase the variability of the exchange rate. Second, they were firmly of the opinion that the time for a transition from an industrial economy to a post-industrial or service economy was not yet ripe.

Japan's rise as a financial superpower followed in tandem with its status as an economic superpower. The size of the economy determines its innate ability and attractiveness as a centre for international financial activity (Choi *et al.* 1986). Additionally, Japan's rise was based on a meticulously considered and well-orchestrated long-term strategy agreed between the financial community and the Japanese authorities, following the revision of the Foreign Exchange and Foreign Trade Control Law in 1980. The surge in Japan's status began with the expansion of foreign exchange trading by the Japanese banks in 1980, followed in 1982 by a building up and expansion in international yen securities trading. In 1984, Japanese banks began concentrating on the enlargement of their lending in international markets to non-Japanese corporate borrowers. After the yen appreciation, in 1986 they targeted the interbank market and, as we shall see, became a force to reckon with.

Hints of Japan's new status can be traced back to 1981, when its net international financial outflow was $9.7 billion. Little attention was paid at this point and it could not be taken as the beginning of a megatrend that may shape the years ahead because an asset ownership of this size was tiny in volume by international standards. The comparable figure for the USA was $140.7 billion. However, at this point it was obvious that the Japanese economy had swung from being a capital importer to a capital exporter. Its net overseas assets continued to rise monotonically, as did the activity of the Japanese financial institutions in the international capital markets. At the beginning of 1984, the US banks were lending and borrowing more than those of any other country, with a 27 per cent share of the international assets market. Japan stood second with 23 per cent of the total, followed by France, Great Britain and West Germany, each with a market share of between 5 and 10 per cent. However, the US banks and securities firms were on the wane and the Japanese

Table 31.1 International positions by nationality of ownership of international assets, 1985–90
(billions of US dollars)

Country	September 1985	December 1985	December 1986	December 1987	December 1988	December 1989	September 1990
Japan	639.6 (25.7)	706.2 (26.3)	1,119.3 (32.4)	1,553.9 (35.4)	1,765.4 (38.2)	1,967.4 (37.9)	2,071.5 (36.0)
USA	580.2 (23.3)	589.4 (21.9)	600.3 (17.4)	649.4 (14.8)	666.8 (14.4)	727.7 (14.0)	687.9 (11.9)
France	221.0 (8.8)	233.7 (8.7)	288.7 (8.4)	376.6 (8.6)	384.1 (8.3)	432.9 (8.4)	524.8 (9.1)
Germany	165.1 (6.6)	191.2 (7.1)	270.1 (7.8)	346.9 (7.9)	354.0 (7.7)	435.6 (8.4)	551.2 (9.5)
UK	181.7 (7.3)	191.8 (7.1)	211.5 (6.1)	253.9 (5.7)	239.1 (5.2)	247.1 (4.8)	267.2 (4.6)

Source: BIS, *International Banking and Financial Market Developments*, Basle, various issues
Note: Figures in the parentheses stand for the proportional share of the total international asset market (in per cent).

were expanding. In June 1985, their ownership of international assets was very close to that of the USA and, as seen in Table 31.1, by September 1985 they overtook the USA and Japanese banks became by far the largest nationality group in the international banking market. Japan became the world's leading creditor economy. Japanese banks surpassed the US banks as principal lenders to final borrowers in the international markets by a large margin. The BIS figures for the third quarter of 1985 showed Japanese banks owning 26 per cent of total international assets as opposed to 23 per cent for the US banks. The French banks stood in third position with 8.8 per cent while the British and German banks owned 7.3 per cent and 6.6 per cent respectively. Much of this growth was the result of interbank activity by Japanese banks. They had become the largest single players on the interbank markets as well as the largest lenders of new funds outside the interbank market. At this point, thanks to the balance-of-payments surpluses, the Japanese banks also forged ahead as the leading group of foreign currency lenders outside London. Thus, in a remarkably short time span Japan turned from a net capital exporter to the largest creditor in the world, investing its surplus liquidity in foreign securities, real estate and control of corporations.

A year later, at the end of December 1986, according to the BIS statistics Japanese banks had amassed almost a third (32.4 per cent) of all international banking assets worth $119 billion, a long way ahead of the USA which had $600 billion, or close to one-sixth (17.4 per cent). The French banks retained their third position with 8.4 per cent of the total assets, the German banks had 7.8 per cent and the British banks 6.1 per cent. The Japanese assets increased by 75 per cent *in nominal dollar terms* between September 1985 and December 1986, i.e. they nearly doubled. The US assets increased by 3.4 per cent over the same period, i.e. they stagnated. However, in yen terms the Japanese assets had increased only by 23 per cent. The appreciating yen allowed Japanese banks, with yen capital, to increase their dollar lending faster than the US banks. There was a strong exchange rate valuation effect on the rising proportion of Japanese international lending in yen. As Table 31.1 shows, after 1986 the Japanese banks' ownership of international assets always remained more than 35 per cent of the total. They touched their high water mark in 1988, with 38.2

per cent ownership of the total international assets. Their closest rivals, the American banks, have recorded a monotonic decline in their market share. However, they were not alone in the fall, with the banks in the UK also recording a declining trend. Conversely, the French and the German banks, which did not loom large in terms of volume, recorded increases in their market shares. In the first half of 1990, the international claims of Japanese banks declined by $52 billion. They had expanded by $230 billion in the latter half of 1989 (BIS 1990). The 1990 contraction is attributed to the collapse of the Japanese stock market and the depreciation of the yen.

Japanese banks and securities firms began to loom large in the international financial markets and fanciful sobriquets like 'behemoths' and 'juggernauts' came to be used for them. In 1985, the *Banker*'s list included five Japanese banks among the world's top ten, the Dai-Ichi Kangyo, Fugi, Sumitomo, Mitsubishi and Sanwa, respectively ranked second, third, fifth, sixth and eighth. The two US banks to survive were the Citicorp at the top and BankAmerica, fourth. After the yen's appreciation, the Japanese banks further moved up on the *Banker*'s league table and all the first five were Japanese in 1986, four with assets over the $200 billion mark. The Citicorp slipped to sixth. Out of the top ten banks in this list, seven were from Japan. The appreciating yen and pressure on the dollar had a dramatic impact on the relative rankings. Japanese securities firms played an active role in recycling Japan's trade surpluses and investing its surplus savings abroad, and in the process established themselves in the international financial markets. The so-called Big Four, namely Nomura, Daiwa, Nikko and Yamaichi, all more or less trebled their market capitalization in 1986. All the Big Four found themselves among the top ten lead managers. Nomura soon grew into a colossus and became six times larger than Salomon Brothers and nearly ten times larger than Merrill Lynch, the two largest non-Japanese securities houses by market capitalization. The Japanese banking system which essentially comprised twelve commercial banks, called the 'city' banks, seven trust banks and three long-term credit banks seemed invincible. Japanese financial institutions occupied the commanding heights of international finance. In terms of financial muscle, Japan was in much the same position as the USA was in the 1960s.

The 1990 pecking order – which was based on 1989 statistics – showed that all the six largest banks in terms of assets were Japanese, each having assets larger than $350 billion. The largest non-Japanese bank was Crédit Agricole, with assets worth $242 billion, which stood seventh on the *Banker*'s league table for 1990. At this point, fourteen of the twenty largest commercial banks in the world were Japanese. Of the top thirty-six banks, only the Citicorp was headquartered in the USA and even the second tier banks like Tokai and Mitsui (pre-merger) began to rival it in terms of assets. Thus, since the mid-1980s the strength of the Japanese financial institutions has grown dramatically. The financial statistics cited above amply manifest their awesome power as well as the change in the leadership in international commercial banking.

The growth of a country as an international banking power is closely correlated with the growth of its banks and securities firms. The larger they are, the greater is their impact on the international financial markets. The international presence of Japanese banks and securities firms grew *pari passu* with their size and therefore financial strength, and throughout the latter half of the 1980s they dominated the international financial stage. Their involvement in lending in the LDCs increased over the 1980s because they were the source of new lending, particularly for the Latin American debt restructurings. This was the period when the US and the European banks were downscaling their LDC exposures. Therefore, the Japanese banks' share of the total outstanding debt grew and by the late 1980s they became the second largest national group of bank creditors to LDCs after the USA. During the 1980s, the financial service industry experienced the same movement towards globalization that the goods-producing industries had experienced in the 1950s and

1960s. While internationalizing its operations – both geographically and functionally – the international financial community virtually concurred that the Japanese financial institutions will be the financial power of the 1990s (Myers 1989; Goldberg and Hanweck 1991).

PROGRESS IN INTERNATIONALIZATION

After 1980, extensive measures were taken to deregulate and liberalize Japanese financial markets. These endeavours were accelerated after 1986. The offshore market was established in the same year and definitive measures were taken to facilitate non-residents' use of the Euro-yen sector. Despite all this and despite Japan's status as the largest creditor nation, yen internationalization has so far made only modest progress. The yen has not displaced the deutsche mark as the second most important international currency. Notwithstanding the recent travails of the American economy, the dollar continues to be the most international currency because (a) it is a vehicle currency and the medium of exchange in the foreign exchange markets and large amounts in any pairs of currencies can be traded by going through the dollar, (b) central banks the world over use it as the intervention currency to manage exchange rates and the largest proportion of official international reserves are held in the dollar, and (c) in general, when neither party to the contract is American, commercial contracts are denominated in the dollar. The variables that facilitate and promote the international use of a currency include, first, confidence in the value of the currency supported by the economic strength and political stability of the country issuing the currency. Other than the volatility issue, high and variable relative inflation rates render a currency unfit for international use. Second, the domestic financial markets of the issuing country should possess a broad assortment of financial instruments and they should be deep in terms of secondary markets. These markets should be well developed, if internationalization is their objective,

Table 31.2 Yen invoicing of Japanese trade, 1975–89 (per cent)

	Yen denominated exports	Yen denominated imports
1975	17.5	0.9
1980	29.4	2.4
1983	40.5	3.0
1985	35.9	7.3
1986	35.5	9.7
1987	34.6	11.6
1988	34.3	13.6
1989	34.7	14.1

Source: Ministry of Finance, Kokusai Kin'yukyoku nenpo, Annual Report of the International Finance Bureau, Tokyo, various issues

and must not be overly regulated and controlled. Well-developed markets are necessary to support the supply and demand for such a currency. The existence of instruments like bankers' acceptance (BA) markets facilitates trade financing in that currency and leads to explanation of trade invoicing in it.[1] In addition, since the dollar has been the principal currency for international trade and investment, the dollar market for each currency is larger in volume and more active than the market between any other two currencies. It is axiomatic that, the larger the volume of transactions conducted in a currency, the lower is the transaction cost of using it. The other variable that impinges upon the transaction cost is exchange rate volatility, and therefore the exchange risk. From these perspectives, the dollar has had impeccable qualifications to be the leading international currency and little wonder that it has maintained its supremacy, although its international role contracted over the 1980s. Conversely, internationalization of the yen has grown – albeit gradually – since 1980.

On the inflation front, owing to a medium-term anti-inflationary monetary policy stance, the Japanese economy did well except for a bad patch in the first quinquennium of the 1970s. In absolute terms, the average inflation rate for the 1970s was higher than for the 1980s. The average for the former period was 9.3 per cent while for the latter it was 2.5 per cent. Comparative data for 1970–9 indicate that Japan experienced the third lowest inflationary rate in the industrial world. Switzerland and Germany were two better performers. But, if the inflationary rates are compared only for the 1980–9 subperiod, the Japanese economy turns out to be the best performer with the lowest average. The average for 1985–9 is as low as 1.0 per cent which is partly attributable to the price-steadying effect of the yen appreciation. These numbers silently speak for themselves and convey that the monetary policy succeeded in maintaining the internal value of the yen. This established its credibility which in turn contributed to the process of yen internationalization.

The current account transactions of Japan and the currency invoicing pattern of its trade are an important pointer to the yen internationalization. Table 31.2 shows that the yen-denominated trade transactions have grown over the years in an unbalanced manner. While they abound in the case of exports, their growth has been slow in the case of imports. The 1983 levels are as far apart as 41 per cent and 3 per cent for exports and imports respectively. During the latter half of the 1980s, the share of export transactions in yen declined and remained around 35 per cent. There are several reasons behind the lack of progress on this count. First, Japan's imports of primary goods and industrial raw materials are traditionally invoiced in the dollar and the pound sterling. Second, a substantial proportion of Japanese exports go to the USA. Third, although the market for BA was created in June 1985, it has remained depressed and the transaction costs are still considered high, which has proved to be an effective drag. This is a classic case of the egg and chicken riddle. The BA market is not growing because there is little growth in the yen invoicing of Japanese trade which, in turn, has been retarded because of the low volume of the BA market. About a third of the BAs had to be financed in New York because of the market constraints in Tokyo. Fourth, many Japanese firms prefer invoicing their exports in foreign currencies to enable them to absorb the initial shock of the currency appreciation, i.e. to control their pass-through in export prices. It helped them in maintaining the export prices, and hence the demand, at the pre-appreciation level.

Unlike exports, the proportion of import transactions in the yen has recorded a steady increase and doubled over the 1985–9 period. This reflects a rise in the share of manufactured imports from East and Southeast Asian developing countries, following the yen appreciation. Since Japan's trade structure has changed its axis from the vertical to the horizontal, the international division of labour will continue and so will the yen's share of import trade. The use of the yen in trade between third countries is negligible. The yen's share of total world trade was calculated at 4.2 per cent in 1988 (Sawai 1989). In 1989, it inched up to 4.3 per cent which shows the unattractiveness of the yen as an instrument of international trade. As opposed to the yen, the level of internationalization of the deutsche mark is higher. More than 80 per cent of Germany's (FRG) exports and over 40 per cent of its imports are invoiced in the deutsche mark (Sawai 1989). The deutsche mark's share of total world trade, in 1988, was estimated at 14 per cent (Tavlas 1990). Thus, it is easy to see that the role of the yen as an invoicing currency has not become significant as yet.

The volume of the yen traded on the foreign exchange market is another indicator of its relative importance as the unit of account and vehicle or medium of exchange currency. Data relating to the currency turnover in the interbank markets in New York, London and Tokyo show a sharp rise in the share of the yen in the New York market. The market share for the yen increased from 5.0 per cent to 12.5 per cent over 1980–9. In London, it chalked up only a marginal increase, from 7.0 per cent to 7.5 per cent. The Tokyo market recorded a marginal decline in the yen's share over this period (Tavlas 1990). As opposed to the yen, the market share of the deutsche mark remained steady in New York and Tokyo but fell marginally in London. The large capital outflows that enabled the Japanese economy to dominate the international financial markets, somewhat paradoxically, had a negative effect on the process of yen internationalization. The outflows required Japanese investors to sell yen in the foreign exchange markets in order to obtain dollars and other currencies to make foreign investment. This created a yen selling pressure in the markets which in turn weakened the position of the yen *vis-à-vis* the other SDR currencies.

The foreign exchange markets are the twenty-four-hour markets and London, Tokyo and New York together account for over two-thirds of total foreign exchange business. The three dominate dealings in their own eight-hour time slots. London is the major centre in the European time zone, Tokyo in the Asian Pacific time zone and New York in North America. Competition among them is intense. According to the last official survey, conducted by the BIS in 1989, the global net daily turnover was $640 billion, of which London accounted for $187 billion, New York for $129 billion and Tokyo for $115 billion. The remainder was divided between eleven other countries, with Switzerland, Singapore and Hong Kong taking significant slices of the foreign exchange business. Since then, London has maintained its dominance and remained the largest market for both interbank and corporate foreign exchange business. But Tokyo has caught up with and possibly overtaken New York as the second largest centre. The next survey is likely to confirm New York's relegation to third place (McCallum 1991). In the foreign exchange market, traders develop a range of different currency rates to deal in and, since the dollar has impeccable qualifications, the dollar exchange rates dominate the markets. The dollar–mark rate is the busiest exchange rate, closely followed by the dollar–yen rate. Dollar–sterling, dollar–Swiss franc and yen–mark rates take third, fourth and fifth ranks. The importance of the dollar–yen rate and the growth of the yen–mark rate have helped in the progress of internationalization of the yen and added to the importance of Tokyo.

In terms of the currency composition of international bank assets, the yen is at present positioned after the dollar and the deutsche mark. According to the statistics published by the BIS,

the volume of yen-denominated assets is far smaller than those denominated in dollars. Although the difference between the volume of assets in the yen and the deutsche mark is not large, the yen comes after the deutsche mark. Of the total international bank assets at the end of September 1990, 49.9 per cent were dollar denominated, 14.3 per cent were in the deutsche mark and 11.6 per cent in the yen (BIS 1991).

Use of a currency as a reserve currency is considered a barometer of its accepted international significance. In the early 1970s, use of the yen in foreign exchange reserves of countries was negligible. During the major part of the 1970s, over 75 per cent of the reserves were held in the dollar. The pound sterling was the second most important reserve currency in the first half of the decade but it was displaced by the deutsche mark in the latter half. Diversification of exchange reserves out of dollars into other currencies was modest until 1977. The sharp depreciation of the dollar over 1977–80 was accompanied by a decline in the share of the dollar in total foreign exchange reserves from 79 per cent at the end of 1977 to 69 per cent at the end of 1980. This was a logical reaction of the central bankers all the world over. There was a weak reversal in the diversification away from the dollar in the early 1980s when the dollar appreciated strongly relative to the other SDR currencies; the share of the dollar rose to 71 per cent in 1983 (Table 31.3). However, by 1985 it declined by 7 percentage points as the monetary authorities again diversified the currency composition of their exchange reserves, and the proportion of reserves denominated in the deutsche mark, the yen and, to a smaller extent, the pound sterling increased. The extensive foreign exchange market intervention by Japan, Germany and the USA after the Plaza Agreement led to a rise in the proportion of reserves held as dollar-denominated assets during 1986 and 1987. However, the share of the dollar fell sharply thereafter to 60 per cent at the end of 1989. The counterpart of this fall was a sharp increase in the share of the deutsche mark, which increased from 14 per cent to 19 per cent over 1987–9. Thus, almost a fifth of the total

Table 31.3 Currency breakdown of exchange reserves, 1980–9 (per cent)

	1980	1981	1982	1983	1984	1985	1986	1987	1988	1989
All countries										
US dollar	68.6	71.5	70.5	71.4	70.1	64.9	67.1	67.2	64.9	60.2
Pound sterling	2.9	2.1	2.3	2.5	2.9	3.0	2.6	2.4	2.8	2.7
Deutsche mark	14.9	12.8	12.4	11.8	12.7	15.2	14.6	14.4	15.7	19.3
French franc	1.7	1.3	1.0	0.8	0.8	0.9	0.8	0.8	1.0	1.3
Swiss franc	3.2	2.7	2.7	2.4	2.0	2.3	2.0	2.0	1.9	1.7
Netherlands guilder	1.3	1.1	1.1	0.8	0.7	1.0	1.1	1.2	1.1	1.1
Yen	4.4	4.2	4.7	5.0	5.8	8.0	7.9	7.5	7.7	7.9
Unspecified currencies	3.0	4.2	5.2	5.3	5.0	4.6	3.9	4.4	4.9	5.7
Industrial countries										
US dollar	77.2	78.4	76.6	77.1	73.5	65.0	69.4	70.3	67.8	59.4
Pound sterling	0.8	0.7	0.7	0.7	1.4	1.9	1.3	1.1	1.6	1.4
Deutsche mark	14.3	13.0	12.5	13.0	15.2	19.5	16.8	15.9	17.4	22.9
French franc	0.7	0.5	0.1	0.1	0.1	0.1	0.1	0.4	0.7	1.1
Swiss franc	1.7	1.7	1.7	1.5	1.5	2.1	1.7	1.6	1.7	1.5
Netherlands guilder	0.7	0.8	0.7	0.5	0.6	1.0	1.1	1.3	1.1	1.2
Yen	3.3	3.6	4.5	5.1	6.3	8.9	8.3	7.1	7.0	8.2
Unspecified currencies	1.3	1.3	3.2	2.1	1.4	1.5	1.4	2.3	2.7	4.4
Developing countries										
US dollar	59.9	64.4	64.2	65.4	66.6	64.8	63.5	60.4	58.1	62.1
Pound sterling	5.1	3.5	4.0	4.4	4.4	4.3	4.6	5.2	5.6	5.7
Deutsche mark	15.4	12.7	12.3	10.5	10.0	10.2	11.1	11.1	11.7	11.4
French franc	2.7	2.1	2.0	1.7	1.5	1.9	2.0	1.8	1.7	1.8
Swiss franc	4.8	3.8	3.8	3.4	2.6	2.7	2.6	2.7	2.6	2.4
Netherlands guilder	1.9	1.4	1.5	1.1	0.8	0.9	1.1	1.1	0.9	0.8
Yen	5.4	4.9	4.9	4.8	5.2	7.0	7.1	8.6	9.4	7.1
Unspecified currencies	4.8	7.3	7.3	8.7	8.8	8.3	7.9	9.0	9.9	8.7

Source: IMF, *Annual Report 1990*

exchange reserves were denominated in the deutsche mark at the end of the decade. Relatively, they increased from twice the volume of the yen reserves in 1985 to two and a half times the volume in 1989. The yen-denominated reserves did not expand after 1985 when they were 8.0 per cent of the total. They ended the decade virtually at the same level.

The industrialized countries evinced a clear preference for the deutsche mark over the yen. Close to a quarter of their total foreign exchange reserves were denominated in deutsche marks. Also, its proportion had increased by 8.6 per cent over the 1980–9 period. The corresponding increase of the yen reserves was only 4.9 per cent. The situation for the developing countries was the reverse. The deutsche mark was not their favoured reserve currency and its proportion in their total reserves recorded a decline over this period. The yen's share of their reserves increased to 9.4 per cent of the total in 1988 but declined somewhat the next year. This differential behaviour may be explained by (a) the differences in the relative exposure to yen liability of the two country groups and (b) the differences in the trade partners of the two sets of economies.

The weight of the yen has gone on increasing in the SDR currency basket since its inception. Yet, in the current SDR valuation basket it stands third after the dollar and the deutsche mark. The percentage weight of the yen was 7.5 at the time of the inception of the SDR in 1974. At the time of the

Table 31.4 Current valuation of the special drawing rights basket

Currency	Percentage weight	Currency unit
Dollar	42	0.452
Deutsche mark	19	0.527
Yen	15	33.400
French franc	12	1.020
Pound sterling	12	0.089

Source: IMF, *International Financial Statistics: 1990 Yearbook*

1981 recomposition of the SDR basket, the yen's weight increased to 13 per cent. When it was revised in January 1986, the yen's weight was further increased to 15 per cent. It gained by 1 per cent each at the expense of the French franc and the pound sterling. The proportional weights of different currencies in the current SDR basket are given in Table 31.4.

THE YEN IN THE INTERNATIONAL BONDS MARKET

The process of internationalization of a currency gains momentum when non-residents raise funds in it in the domestic financial markets or in Euro-markets. Raising of funds through international bonds by non-residents in the Japanese capital markets increased somewhat after 1980. All the early expansion was concentrated in syndicated loans and sales of yen-denominated foreign bonds. The instruments used included (1) samurai bonds or yen-denominated public placements by non-residents, (2) shibosai bonds or yen-denominated private placements by non-residents, and (3) the Euro-yen bonds. As seen in Table 31.5, regarding the samurai and the shibosai markets, the former was more active in the 1980s while the latter stabilized at a relatively low level. The samurai market was exclusively utilized by sovereign borrowers and supranational institutions like the

Table 31.5 Yen- and foreign-currency-denominated funds raised by non-residents (billions of yen)

	Samurai bonds		Shibosai bonds		Shogun bonds		Euro-yen bonds	
	Number	Amount	Number	Amount	Number	Amount[a]	Number	Amount
1970	1	6	–	–	–	–	–	–
1971	3	33	–	–	–	–	–	–
1972	6	85	1	10.69	–	–	–	–
1973	–	–	6	40.05	–	–	–	–
1974	–	–	–	–	–	–	–	–
1975	2	20	–	–	–	–	–	–
1976	6	65	–	–	–	–	–	–
1977	15	294	3	30.00	–	–	2	30
1978	29	722	11	105.00	–	–	1	15
1979	16	333	6	67.00	–	–	2	25
1980	14	261	–	–	–	–	4	55
1981	27	495	13	117.50	–	–	5	80
1982	37	663	30	193.00	–	–	6	95
1983	41	720	32	179.00	–	–	4	70
1984	37	915	34	199.50	–	–	13	227
1985	35	1,115	24	157.50	8	932.36	66	1,445.7
1986	21	590	21	195.00	10	956.39	141	2,551.5
1987	15	420	10	77.50	8	847.80	151	2,993.9
1988	22	635	19	162.20	1	100.00	224	2,213.0

Source: Ministry of Finance, *Kokusai Kin'yukyoku nenpo*, Annual Report of the International Finance Bureau, 1989–90, Tokyo
Note: [a] Millions of dollars.

ADB and government agencies. The samurai market has been important to Asian borrowers like China, India and Korea. These borrowers would have faced problems if they had tried to tap the Euromarkets. By the late 1980s, it was obvious that both these markets had reached their plateaux. The shogun bonds or foreign-currency-denominated foreign bonds were born in August 1985. This was another attempt to internationalize Japanese bonds markets and in the process internationalize the yen. Like the first two, this market also stagnated despite the low coupon rate. The yen-denominated syndicated loans fell sharply after 1985. Their weak performance was ascribed to the following market drawbacks. First, the secondary for this type of bond was considered underdeveloped. Although the Big Four securities firms undertook to maintain a secondary market in these issues in a bid to improve the liquidity, the move failed to improve the situation appreciably and a lack of liquidity is still considered a frailty of these markets. Second, the issuing procedures were cumbersome and included onerous rigmarole such as advance notification to the Ministry of Finance and a long drawn-out decision-making process for underwriters' issuing terms. In addition, the limit of smallest acceptable issue of 10 billion yen was too high for a developing-country borrower. Third, participants who made quick use of currency swaps faced several obstacles. Fourth, shibosai bonds were strictly controlled and the amount raised through them was limited to one-third of samurai bonds. Fifth, these markets were adversely influenced by the sharp appreciation of the yen which more than offset the low coupon incentive for most borrowers. Consequently, all three markets remained insignificant in size.

The Euro-yen markets operated in all large financial centres, London being the most important in this respect. Japanese banks have the largest share in the Euro-yen transactions; they cover over a half of the total market. The remainder is dealt with by foreign banks, foreign monetary authorities and non-financial institutions. These markets also remained thin until March 1985, when the Foreign Exchange Council

of Japan advocated the promotion of Euro-yen transactions as another important step towards the internationalization of the yen. To this end, several measures were recommended and implemented to facilitate the issuance of Euro-yen bonds, medium- and long-term Euro-yen loans for non-residents, short-term Euro-yen loans to residents and short-term Euro-yen CDs. The issuing controls were made less burdensome, the issuing procedure was streamlined and the terms of issue were made flexible. The Euro-yen bond market has enormous liquidity of the secondary market, which according to an estimate enabled the coupon for Euro-yen issues to be cut by around 0.5 per cent compared with the new issues coming in the samurai market (*Euromoney* 1987). Consequently, the Euro-yen bond issues became more popular than the samurai bonds and recorded strong growth after 1985. It is generally believed that the Euro-yen markets took the growth away from the samurai bond market. They soon overtook the samurai bonds in terms of number and volume of issue. The associated swap deals were made easier by allowing the Japanese and foreign securities firms to step in. It added a flavour of competition to this business. It was important because as much as 80 per cent of Euro-yen issues are swapped for other currencies (Thorn 1987). The recent expansion of the Euro-yen bond market is expected to lead to wider use of the yen by non-residents both for raising capital and for investment purposes. Of late, these bonds have found acceptance among international investors seeking to diversify their portfolios in terms of currencies. The diversity of borrowing participants has expanded with the growth in the volume of the market. The US residents are the largest group of borrowers in the Euro-yen markets. Others include Australians, Canadians, French and Swedes. The majority of borrowing entities are corporations from these countries or multinational corporations.

The international bond market has been dominated by the following three currency sectors: the dollar, the pound sterling and the yen. The statistics in Table 31.6 give a comparative picture of the fixed rate issues over 1986–90. Comparative data

Table 31.6 Currency structure of international bond issues, 1986–90 (per cent)

	Dollars	Yen	Pound sterling	Total[a]
1986	42.3	17.4	4.5	108.6
1987	15.5	26.7	11.9	68.9
1988	26.8	12.0	10.5	99.4
1989	29.1	16.2	12.4	89.0
1990 (September)	32.2	15.8	5.8	119.9

Source: BIS, *International Banking and Financial Market Development*, Basle, February 1991
Note: [a] Billions of dollars.

reveal that yen-denominated issues have not gained consistently relative to their dollar-denominated counterparts. They ranked second to dollar issues in each year except 1987 when they were the largest. Although comparable figures are not available for the years before 1986, the yen's share more than doubled between 1983 and 1985. Taking another dimension of international assets, namely the composition of foreign currency holdings of banks reporting to the BIS, Table 31.7 shows a continuous swing towards the yen in the recent past. The yen's share recorded a sharp rise from 10.7 per cent in 1985 to 28.0 per cent in

1988. This increase was at the cost of both the dollar and the deutsche mark. After 1988, the yen's share stabilized and it stayed around its 1988 level in 1990, when it was 27.8 per cent. Over the 1985–90 period the two rival currencies had lost ground in this respect; the dollar's position had slipped from 58.3 per cent to 34.3 per cent while that of the deutsche mark went from 10.1 per cent to 4.1 per cent. These two indicators are a pointer to the realization and recognition of the growing importance of the yen by international banking and financial communities.

It is apparent from the foregoing exposition that the yen is more widely used in capital account transactions than in current account transactions and that its internationalization has occurred faster in the long-term transactions than in the short-term ones. A statistical analysis relating to the capital account revealed that Japan's long-term capital outflows were predominantly in the form of securities. They were dominated by the US financial instruments ranging from Treasury securities to LBOs. A major part of the outflows were dollar denominated. The EC was a relatively smaller destination while the East Asian economies were even smaller. The composition of debt instruments and the direction of international capital flows had

Table 31.7 Currency composition of foreign currency holdings for the reporting banks of the Bank for International Settlements (billions of dollars)

Currencies	1985 December	1986 December	1987 December	1988 December	1989 December	1990 September
US dollars	401.6	444.7	459.9	491.1	535.7	493.2
Other currencies of which	287.2	453.7	703.5	737.0	831.8	942.9
Belgian francs	6.8	9.8	13.0	12.1	13.4	18.4
Deutsche marks	69.9	116.4	147.9	145.4	188.1	224.5
French francs	26.5	34.5	46.7	42.5	50.9	59.5
Guilders	15.6	19.8	23.5	21.4	29.5	34.1
Italian lire	2.7	5.9	4.7	3.4	12.8	9.6
Sterling	40.0	49.5	72.2	77.0	73.8	92.4
Swiss francs	35.4	59.5	80.0	66.1	58.4	69.2
Yen	73.8	137.9	288.5	344.4	372.7	399.3
Other	16.4	20.2	26.9	24.7	32.1	35.9

Source: BIS, *International Banking and Financial Market Developments*, Basle, February 1991

an undesirable impact on the internationalization of the yen. Because of this skewed pattern of capital flows, a large number of countries did not have any incentive or need to accumulate yen-denominated assets or balances to service their yen-denominated loans. This has proved to be detrimental to the yen internationalization process (Japan Economic Institute 1990). In addition, when the pound sterling and the dollar became international currencies, London and New York had highly developed financial markets which, in turn, were conducive to financial intermediation in terms of the pound sterling and the dollar respectively. As opposed to this scenario, Japan had tightly regulated financial markets until the early years of the 1980s and its financial intermediation was not predominantly yen denominated (Tavlas and Ozeki 1991). Furthermore, some segments of Japanese financial markets are still considered narrow and thin instead of broad and deep. The Euro-yen markets are still not totally deregulated. This state of affairs is considered a disincentive to those willing to hold short-term yen-denominated assets.

CONCLUSION

A long-sustained outstanding performance on the economic front, recent current account surpluses and an appreciating yen turned Japan into the most solvent nation and the leading financial power of the latter half of the 1980s. Japan was known to be a country of highly restricted financial markets. The surge in Japan's status as a leading creditor began with the financial deregulation and liberalization after 1980. By the mid-1980s, it had become the largest creditor nation in the world and the Japanese banks and securities firms became the largest in their respective categories.

Since 1980, the yen has gradually internationalized while the significance of the dollar has somewhat declined, although the latter is still the domineering international currency because it is impeccably suited to be the vehicle and intervention currency. Japan's yen-denominated current account transactions have grown a little over the 1980s but the use of the yen in trade between third countries is negligible. The deutsche mark is far ahead of the yen in this respect. In terms of the volume of currency traded on the foreign exchange markets, the yen is well behind the dollar and the deutsche mark. Going by the daily turnover, the importance of Tokyo in the foreign exchange markets is generally regarded as the second largest after London. In the foreign exchange trade, likewise, the dollar–yen exchange rate is considered the second busiest after the dollar–deutsche mark rate. Recent growth of trading in the yen–deutsche mark rate has helped in the progress of yen internationalization.

Japan's large capital outflows were largely in the dollar and their direction essentially was towards the USA, the EC and the East Asian developing countries, with the USA being the principal recipient. The composition of debt instruments and the direction of international capital flows from Japan had an undesirable impact on the internationalization of the yen. In terms of the currency composition of international bank assets, the yen is at present positioned after the dollar and the deutsche mark. Similarly, the yen is far behind the dollar and the deutsche mark as a reserve currency. The industrialized countries evinced a clear preference for the deutsche mark over the yen in their reserves, whilst the trend in the developing countries was just the opposite. Although the weight of the yen has gone on increasing in the SDR currency basket since its inception, it stands at third position there also.

The yen internationalization process did not receive a great deal of support from the samurai bonds, shibosai bonds and shogun bonds markets because all three of them stagnated despite a low coupon rate. Concerted attempts were made to develop the Euro-yen bond markets; consequently they recorded strong growth after 1985. It is expected to lead to wider use of the yen by non-residents both for raising capital and for investment purposes. Taking another dimension, namely the composition of foreign currency holdings of banks reporting to the BIS, there has been a continuous swing towards the yen in the recent past which indicates the growing importance of the yen in the international banking and financial community.

The yen has been more widely used in capital account transactions than in current account transactions and its internationalization has occurred faster in long-term transactions than in short-term ones. Although the process of yen internationalization has progressed, particularly after the appreciation, it is and is likely to remain the third international currency in the foreseeable future. This ranking is not incompatible with a high degree of internationalization of the Japanese financial system and Japan's status as the largest international creditor.

NOTE

1   A bankers' acceptance market allows a bank which has provided trade financing to a customer to resell his claim to a third party under his guarantee.

REFERENCES

BIS (1990) *International Banking and Financial Market Developments*, Basle, November, p. 16.

—— (1991) *International Banking and Financial Market Developments*, Basle, February.

Choi, S. P., Tschoelg, A. E. and Yu, C. M. (1986) 'Banks and the world's major financial centers 1970–1980', *Weltwirtschaftliches Archiv* 122: 48–64.

Euromoney (1987) 'Samurais battle it out', April: 47–53.

Goldberg, L. G. and Hanweck, G. A. (1991) 'The growth of the world's 300 largest banking organisations by country', *Journal of Banking and Finance* 15: 207–23.

Japan Economic Institute (1990) *JEI Report*, 5 October, p. 9.

McCallum, J. (1991) 'London, Tokyo and New York dominate in their time slots: big three battle it out', *The Financial Times*, 29 April.

Myers, H. F. (1989) 'Japanese banks are building a global role', *Asian Wall Street Journal*, 12 September.

Sawai, Y. (1989) 'Internationalization of the yen: a progress report', *Tokyo Financial Review*, November: 10–16.

Tavlas, G. S. (1990) 'On the international use of currencies: the case of the deutsche mark', Working Paper WP/90/3, Washington, DC: International Monetary Fund.

Tavlas, G.S. and Ozeki, Y. (1991) 'The Japanese yen as an international currency', IMF Working Paper WP/91/2, Washington, DC: IMF, January.

Thorn, R. S. (1987) *The Rising Sun*, Singapore: The Institute of Southeast Asian Studies, pp. 67–70.

32

INTERNATIONALIZATION OF THE KOREAN CAPITAL MARKET

Walter Mahler

INTERNATIONALIZATION OF THE KOREAN CAPITAL MARKET

In January 1981 the Korean government announced its first Capital Market Internationalization Plan, which specified four stages of gradual movement toward full integration of the domestic and foreign capital markets. These stages and the timing originally envisaged were as follows:

Stage 1 (1981–4) Allow foreign investors to invest indirectly in Korean securities. As a launching step, the government allowed two domestic securities companies to set up international investment trust funds in Europe and allowed a closed-end fund (the Korean Fund) to be established in the USA. In addition foreign securities firms were encouraged to establish representative offices in Korea, while domestic securities firms were encouraged to establish branches in foreign countries.

Stage 2 (from 1985) Allow limited direct foreign portfolio investment in domestic securities and the issuance and listing of Korean securities in foreign capital markets.

Stage 3 (late 1980s) Relax limits on direct foreign investment in domestic securities. Allow domestic firms to raise equity funds in external markets with the prior approval of the Ministry of Finance. Also allow foreign security firms to conduct security business in Korea and domestic security firms to conduct overseas business.

Stage 4 (early 1990s) Complete liberalization of the Korean capital market by allowing Korean investors to invest in foreign securities and foreign securities to be listed in the Korean capital market.

The plan for capital market internationalization was motivated by various considerations. First, it was in line with the Korean government's efforts in 1979 and 1980 to pursue substantial liberalization of foreign trade, foreign direct investment and foreign exchange transactions. It was part of the general effort to liberalize the economy to create a more competitive economic environment. It was believed that opening the capital market would help accelerate modernization of the domestic capital market by introducing foreign competition and new forms of financing to the security business. It was expected that permitting foreign portfolio investment in Korea would boost the demand for domestic securities, which had remained sluggish during 1979 and 1980. At the time that the capital market liberalization was announced, Korea was experiencing an extraordinarily high current account deficit, almost entirely financed by reliance on borrowing from foreign banks. Liberalization of the domestic capital market was considered to be a necessary condition for Korea to join the OECD of which, at that time, Korea expected to become a member country by the late 1980s.

The progress in capital market internationalization between 1981 and May 1988 is shown in Tables 32.1 and 32.2. There appeared to be two major concerns behind Korea's cautious internationalization of its capital market: to ensure, first, that domestic firms not be taken over by

Table 32.1 Korea: progress in capital market internationalization (in chronological order)

Year	Month	Name of entity established	Millions of US dollars
1981	11	Korea International Trust	25
1981	11	Korea Trust	25
1984	5	Korea Fund	60
1985	3	Korea Growth Trust	30
1985	4	Seoul International Trust	30
1985	4	Seoul Trust	30
1985	12	Korea Small Companies Trust	2
1985	12	Samsung Convertible Bond (CB) issued	20
1986	3	Korea Emerging Companies Trust	3
1986	5	Daewoo Heavy Industry CB issued	40
1986	6	Korea Fund capital base increased	40
1986	7	Yukong CB issued	20
1987	3	Korea Europe Fund	30
1987	8	Gold Star CB issued	30
1988	7	Korea Europe Fund capital base increased	30
1988	7	Saehan Media CB issued	30

Source: Ministry of Finance

foreigners, and second, that the scope of potential inward or outward capital flows not be so large as to disrupt the stability of the domestic capital market or the won exchange rate seriously. In the light of these concerns, it was considered desirable to proceed gradually with internationalization of the capital market.

The sharp improvement in Korea's current account balance in the second half of the 1980s was not envisaged at the time that the four-step internationalization plan was announced in 1981.[1] Hence, it was originally envisaged that the purchase of Korean shares by foreigners would be liberalized more quickly than the purchase of foreign shares by Koreans. It was originally

Table 32.2 Korea: investment by foreigners in Korean securities, 1981–8[a] (millions of US dollars)

International Trust Funds (7 funds)	145
Korea Fund	100
Korea Europe Fund	60
Convertible bonds issued abroad (5 issues)	140
Total	445

Source: Ministry of Finance
Note: [a]Value of the initial offerings, not present market value.

planned to have complete liberalization of inward flows of capital by the late 1980s and to remove restrictions on direct purchases of Korean shares by foreigners. However, because of the large current account surpluses and the accompanying problem of excessive money supply growth, the authorities have not allowed any direct portfolio purchases of Korean stocks except for the purchase of convertible bonds issued by four large Korean companies; moreover, only very modest indirect inflows of portfolio capital were permitted in 1986–8. In the light of the large current account surpluses the authorities have proceeded more slowly with the liberalization of inward flows of portfolio investment than had been originally envisaged. No plans have yet been announced to allow foreign firms to be listed on the Korea Stock Exchange (KSE) or to allow Korean firms to be listed on foreign stock exchanges. While the planned liberalization of the inflow of portfolio investment has been delayed, the planned outflow of foreign investment has been speeded up. In the second half of 1988, an investment trust was set up to facilitate indirect stock purchases in foreign markets by Korean institutional investors.

In early December 1988, Korea announced a

revised programme for internationalization of the securities market during the next four years.

1 The existing overseas funds for indirect foreign investment in the Korean stock market, including the Korea Fund, will be allowed to expand. The Korea Fund was allowed to increase its capital in 1989. Depending on the international capital market situation, there will also be an expansion of beneficiary certificates for foreigners issued by the Korean-managed international trusts.

2 Korean companies will be allowed to issue more convertible bonds abroad from 1989 and they will be allowed to issue bonds with warrants and depository receipts in 1989–90.

3 Foreigners who have bought convertible bonds in Korean companies will be able to convert them to equity, sell the equity and invest it in the Korean stock market beginning in 1991.

4 Starting in 1992, foreigners will be allowed to invest directly in the Korean stock market, although initially there will be limits on individual and total foreign purchases as well as on the foreign holdings of individual stocks.

5 Korean institutional investors will be allowed to expand investment in overseas securities markets from 1989, all business enterprises will be allowed to make such investments from 1990 and individual investors will be allowed to invest in foreign stocks from 1992.

6 Foreign brokerage firms will be allowed to own as much as 40 per cent of Korean securities firms starting in 1989, compared with the current limit of 10 per cent.

7 Foreign securities firms will be allowed to set up branches in the country and to form joint ventures with Korean securities firms starting in 1991.

These measures were in line with general expectations regarding the likely pace of internationalization. The extent of liberalization in 1992 has not been announced in detail, but it appears that complete liberalization will not take place until later in the decade.

Since June 1981, seven international trust funds for foreign investors have been set up with a total initial investment amount of $145 million. Foreigners can purchase beneficiary certificates in the trust funds, which are managed by Korean security investment trust companies. These are open-ended funds[2] which invest in Korean corporate shares and, in some cases, partially in bonds. While the beneficiary certificates are not listed on any stock exchanges, they are traded in informal markets arranged by a few foreign securities companies. Table 32.3 presents details of five of these investment trusts.

Two closed-end mutual funds[3] with foreign managers have also been established. The Korea Fund was established in August 1984 with an initial capital base of $60 million, which was increased by $40 million in May 1986. The Korea Fund is listed on the NYSE. The Korea Europe Fund was established in London in March 1987 with an initial capital base of $30 million, which was increased by $30 million in July 1988.

In addition to the above special funds, five Korean companies have been allowed to issue convertible bonds to foreign investors. The first convertible bond was issued by Samsung Electronics in December 1985. Table 32.4 gives details of three of these issues. In November 1985, the Ministry of Finance announced guidelines for allowing the largest Korean firms to issue bonds in the international bond market, which would be convertible into stock. The issuing companies were required to have assets of at least W 50 billion, to meet certain rating criteria of the Korean securities regulators and to have a share price corresponding to a complicated formula that sought to ensure that the company had had a strong performance in the recent past. The announced criteria limited the field of potential issuers to fourteen major companies. Foreign investors were to be restricted to not more than 15 per cent of the paid-in capital of the companies issuing convertible bonds, with a single foreigner allowed to hold up to 3 per cent of the paid-in capital.

Foreigners have not been permitted to make any direct purchases of either corporate bonds or government bond issues in Korea. While the internationalization of portfolio investment has proceeded slowly, the Korean authorities have taken a number of measures to liberalize direct foreign investment in Korea, as well as to facilitate direct investment by Korean firms in foreign countries. In 1985, three foreign securities companies were allowed permission to purchase up to 10 per cent of the equity of certain large Korean securities firms. The motivation for permitting such purchases was to facilitate staff training and managerial assistance from foreign securities companies and to increase the international business of the Korean securities companies.

The performance of foreign portfolio investment in Korea has been remarkable, with every type of investment yielding high returns (Table 32.5). In the light of this performance and that of the Korean economy, it is not surprising that considerable excess demand by foreigners for participation in the Korean capital market has emerged. The magnitude of this demand is clearly reflected in the extent to which the stock in the Korea Fund has traded at high premia over its net asset value. When they were initially issued in 1984, the Korea Fund shares traded at a premium in the 10–20 per cent range, which increased gradually to reach a remarkable 157 per cent at the end of August 1987,[4] before the stock market crash in New York in October 1987. No other country's closed-end fund (or any other kind of closed-end fund) had ever reached premia anywhere close to this level, with the exception of the Taiwan Fund, which reached an even higher premium at some points during 1987. Table 32.6 gives a comparison of the premia of all of the country open-end funds traded in the New York stock markets during 1988.

Although all the stock markets in the world that permit free capital flows dropped by 25–50 per cent in October 1987, the Korean stock market composite price index actually increased by 5 per cent. Although the KSE composite price index and the net asset value of the Korea Fund shares remained almost unchanged, the price of Korea Fund shares dropped sharply (even more than the Dow–Jones industrial average) so that the premium over net asset value was reduced to only 61 per cent by the end of October. In the subsequent year, the Korean stock market was one of the most buoyant in the world, with the composite price index increasing by about 81 per cent between end-October 1987 and end-December 1988. While the net asset value of the Korea Fund increased sharply, the price of Korea Fund shares increased slightly more, increasing the premium over net asset value to 66 per cent as of end-December 1988. This premium increased further to 120 per cent as of end-September 1989.

THE KOREA FUND AND KOREA EUROPE FUND PREMIUM

It is difficult to discern what determines the premium on the Korea Fund.[5] Most closed-end stock funds, including all of the country closed-end funds for countries with open capital markets, sell at a discount which typically ranges between 10 and 35 per cent (see Table 32.6).[6] This appears to reflect the fact that the shareholder has no way of redeeming his stock at its net asset value and the managers of the closed-end fund, who receive annual fees for operating the fund, have no incentive to liquidate the fund so that the shareholders can attain the difference between the share price and the net asset value. The annual managerial fees, as well as the initial underwriting charges, associated with the fund tend to lead to a discount equal to these fees as a percentage of the value of the portfolio of the fund. Since all new funds involve underwriting charges (typically 7 per cent), they all have to be sold at an initial premium over the net asset value (i.e. the cash left over after underwriting charges are deducted). However, these negative features should be at least partly offset by the fact that the holder of the shares obtains a diversified portfolio, as well as professional managerial expertise in choosing stocks in a foreign market, and avoids the foreign exchange conversion costs of direct purchases in a foreign market.

Table 32.3 Outline of international investment trusts

	Korea International Trust	Korea Trust	Korea Growth Trust	Seoul International Trust	Seoul Trust
Date of establishment	19 November 1981	29 November 1981	29 March 1985	19 April 1985	30 April 1985
Amount of establishment	US$15 million (1,500,000 units) Additional tranche of US$10 million (16 December 1983)	US$15 million (1,000,000 units) Additional tranche of US$10 million (12 January 1984)	US$30 million (3,000,000 units)	US$30 million (3,000,000 units)	US$30 million (3,000,000 units)
Objective	Long-term capital appreciation through investment in listed shares of Korean corporations	Long-term capital appreciation through investment in listed shares of Korean corporations	Long-term capital appreciation through investment in the securities and bond markets of Korea	Long-term capital appreciation through investment in the securities and bond markets of Korea	Long-term capital appreciation through investment in the securities and bond markets of Korea
Type of trust	Anon-shore, contractual type open-end fund	Anon-shore, contractual type open-end fund	Anon-shore, contractual type open-end fund	Anon-shore, contractual type open-end fund	Anon-shore, contractual type open-end fund
Investment policy	Achieve long-term capital appreciation Invest in securities, primarily equities, listed on the Korea Stock Exchange	Achieve long-term capital appreciation Invest in securities, primarily equities, listed on the Korea Stock Exchange	Achieve long-term capital appreciation Invest in securities, primarily equities, listed on the Korea Stock Exchange. A minimum bond content of 30 per cent was required initially, reduced to 20 per cent after 31 December 1985	Achieve long-term capital appreciation Invest in securities, primarily equities, listed on the Korea Stock Exchange. A minimum bond content of 30 per cent was required initially, reduced to 30 per cent after 30 June 1986	Achieve long-term capital appreciation Invest in securities, primarily equities, listed on the Korea Stock Exchange. A minimum bond content of 30 per cent was required initially, reduced to 20 per cent after 31 May 1986
Dividend policy	The trust intends to distribute its net current dividend and interest income Realized capital gains will not be distributed	The trust intends to distribute its net current dividend and interest income Realized capital gains will not be distributed	The trust intends to distribute its net current dividend and interest income Realized capital gains will not be distributed	The trust intends to distribute its net current dividend and interest income Realized capital gains will not be distributed	The trust intends to distribute its net current dividend and interest income Realized capital gains will not be distributed

Life of trust				
Payment of dividends will be made annually	Payment of dividends will be made annually	Payment of dividends will be made annually	Payment of dividends will be made annually	Payment of dividends will be made annually
Terminate in 2001	Unlimited	Terminate at the end of the accounting period on 31 March 2005	Terminate in the year 2005 unless extended	Terminate at the end of the accounting period on 30 April 2005

Source: Korea Stock Exchange

Table 32.4 Outline of convertible bond issuing terms and conditions

	Samsung Electronics	Daewoo heavy industries	Yukong
Bond type	Non-guaranteed convertible bonds	Non-guaranteed convertible bonds	Non-guaranteed convertible bonds
Issue amount	US$20 million	US$40 million	US$20 million
Issue date	5 December 1985	15 May 1985	7 July 1986
Denomination	US$5,000	US$5,000 bearer bonds, US$15,000 (minimum) plus multiples of US$5,000 registered bonds	US$5,000
Market for subscription	Euromarkets (public)	Euromarkets (public offering) and US markets	Euromarkets (public offering)
Coupon	5 per cent annually, in arrears	3 per cent annually, in arrears	3 per cent annually, in arrears
Maturity	15 years	15 years, 7 months	15 years
Conversion price	The arithmetic mean of (a) W 1,271 (the 'spot price') plus 30 per cent thereof; and (b) the average of the closing prices of the shares for the trading days in the 7 calendar day period immediately preceding the commencement of the conversion period	W 1,919; 50 per cent premium over base price of W 1,279. Base price is the arithmetic average of the closing prices on the KSE during the 6 business days immediately preceding the signing date	W 5,226; 55 per cent premium over arithmetic average of the closing prices of the shares for the trading days in the 7 calendar day period immediately preceding the signing date
Conversion period	On and after 19 October 1987 and prior to the close of business on 1 December 2000	Either on 23 November 1987 or from the date Korean authorities allow direct investment in shares by foreigners, whichever comes later	On and after 15 January 1988 and prior to the close of business 30 November 2001
Listing	Luxembourg Stock Exchange	Luxembourg Stock Exchange	Luxembourg Stock Exchange

The Korea Fund shares trade at a premium over their net asset value mainly because foreigners not resident in Korea cannot purchase Korean shares directly, and because the Korean stock market has been appreciating more rapidly than most stock markets and is expected to continue to do so. The extent of the premium would seem to depend on two major factors: first, the expectation of future increases in the value of shares in the Korean stock market relative to expected returns on investment in other capital markets and, second, the magnitude and duration of restrictions on direct purchases of Korean stocks. The premium would be expected virtually to disappear once complete internationalization of the Korean stock market takes place.

In the light of the long-term and recent performance of the Korean economy and the performance of the Korean stock market, it would be reasonable to expect the Korean stock market to have a superior performance in the future. Although Korean corporations' P/E ratios have increased sharply in recent years, they do not appear to be unreasonably high in the light of the superior

Table 32.5 Performance of portfolio foreign investment and convertible bonds (prices in US dollars)

Name and issue date	Issue price	End 1985	End 1986	End 1987	End May 1988	14 December 1988
Korea International Trust (11/81)[a]	9.94	–	21.5	34.4	43.9	59.2[b]
Korea Trust (11/81)[a]	14.95	–	27.8	40.4	51.3	67.5[b]
Seoul International Trust (4/85)[a]	9.95	–	17.6	26.0	32.1	42.0[b]
Seoul Trust (4/85)[a]	9.97	–	16.7	24.3	30.8	39.2[b]
Korea Growth Trust (3/85)[a]	9.94	–	16.4	25.1	31.6	40.5[b]
Korea Small Companies Trust (12/85)[a]	5.59	–	7.8	12.0	14.4	–
Korea Emerging Companies Trust (3/86)[a]	5.65	–	6.8	9.6	12.5	–
Korea Fund (5/84)[c]	12.7	17.6	34.0	55.1	80.0	81.4
Korea Europe Fund (4/87)[c]	10.71	–	–	19.0	29.5	–
Samsung (12/85)[c]	100	98.5	234.5	222.5	330.0	395.0
Daewoo (5/86)[c]	100	–	111.9	117.9	205.0	295.0
Yukong (7/86)[c]	100	–	101.0	122.5	185.0	195.0
Goldstar (8/87)[c]	100	–	–	92.5	105.0	125.0

Source: Ministry of Finance; and Ssongyong Investment and Securities Company Limited

Notes: [a]Net asset values.

[b]Market prices as of 14 December 1988 were approximately 45 per cent above the net asset values.

[c]Market prices.

performance of most Korean corporations. The Korean government clearly has modified its initial plan of capital market liberalization and, as indicated above, has announced a revised programme of liberalization during the 1989–92 period. However, the extent to which foreigners will be able to make direct purchases starting in 1992 has been left vague.

A third factor, of considerably less importance than the other two, contributing to a premium for the Korea Fund is the desire of international investors to further diversify their portfolios. Thus, there might be some willingness to pay a premium, even if the performance of the Korean stock market was expected to be equal to the rest of foreign investors' portfolios. However, it seems difficult to attribute the sharp reduction in the premium in the Korea Fund in the aftermath of the October 1987 stock crash, in most of the rest of the world, to changes in any of the above factors. It is possible that investors expected the stock market crash to lead to a reduction in the relative economic growth of the USA and Japan (Korea's main export markets) or to a general reduction in economic growth or world trade which would hurt Korea more than most countries.[7] However, the relative stability of the Korean stock market indicated that Korean investors did not envisage any serious consequences to the Korean economy from the external stock market declines. Whatever its reasons, this dramatically different response to the valuation of Korean stocks between foreign investors and Korean investors appears to justify the concern of government officials that significantly increased direct participation in the Korean stock market by foreigners might lead to increased rather than reduced volatility in the face of major disturbances. Both the general sharp stock price decline in the major markets and the change in the price of the Korea Fund relative to its net asset value call into question the widely believed efficiency of capital markets.

Table 32.7 reveals that there was a sharp reduction in the premium (or increase in the discount) in the price of the shares of other developing or developed country funds during October

Table 32.6 Premia or discounts of country mutual funds listed in stock exchanges in the USA (percentage difference between share price and net asset value)

Name of fund	27 May 1988	9 December 1988	16 June 1989
Brazil	−19	−34	−44
First Australia	−18	−20	−19
First Iberian	−10	−20	−
France	−11	−17	−9
Germany	−7	−9	−15
Helvetia	−12	−15	−13
Italy	−25	−18	−19
Korea	+84	+65	+100
Malaysia	−17	−26	−12
Mexico	−22	−34	−20
Taiwan	+58	−9ᵃ	−6
Thai	+42	+18	+15
UK	−22	−16	−16

Source: *Wall Street Journal*
Note: ᵃData for 2 December 1988.

1987, after the crash in all the major world markets. The buoyancy of US stock values seems to affect the premium of foreign country funds traded in the USA significantly. Just as investors are willing to support higher P/E ratios of US corporations during buoyant periods, so they are willing to pay higher premia for foreign country

funds. The premia on five of the six country funds shown in Table 32.7 increased between late October 1987 and late May 1988; the only exception was the Malaysia Fund where the discount became significantly larger, perhaps because of political factors.

It is worth taking a somewhat closer look at the evolution of the premium on the Korea Fund shares since it was formed in 1984. As indicated earlier, it is normal for closed-end funds to trade initially at a 7 per cent premium over net asset value, because of underwriting costs. Between its issue date in August 1984 and July 1985, the Korea Fund premium ranged between 10 per cent and 30 per cent; it has never traded at a discount (Table 32.8). During this period the KSE composite stock index remained almost stable. As indicated earlier, after a boom in 1972–8, the Korean stock market was lethargic during 1978–84. The only encouraging sign was an increase of about 10 per cent in the stock market index during the early months of 1984. In brief, the performance of the Korean stock market for a number of years until about November 1985 had been poor and gave little basis for a high premium for the Korea Fund shares. In fact, it was surprising that the premium remained in the 10–30 per cent range. However, between October 1985 and August 1986, the KSE

Table 32.7 Korea: comparison of country fund premia

	Difference between stock price and net asset value			Percentage change in price	
	9 October 1987	23 October 1987	27 May 1988	9 October– 23 October	9 October– 28 October
Korea	137	70	84		
Taiwan	35	12	58		
Malaysia	22	−4	−17		
Mexico	−29	−42	−22		
Italy	−13	−27	−25		
UK	−19	−34	−21		
Dow–Jones industrial average			−21	−26	
Korea Fund				−28	−48
Korea Stock Exchange Composite Index				+1	−1

share price index almost doubled, and the net asset value of the Korea Fund more than doubled. During this period, the Korea Fund premium ranged between 19 and 70 and averaged about 43. Between August and December 1986, there was little change in the KSE composite price index or in the net asset value of the Korea Fund, and the Korea Fund premium averaged about 47. The KSE share price index increased by 78 per cent during the first seven months of 1987. Even though the net asset value of the Korea Fund increased by only 40 per cent during this period, the premium of the Korea Fund increased to a peak of 157 at the end of August 1987. Not only had the Korean stock market performed well during this period, but stock markets throughout the world had also performed exceptionally well.

It was not surprising that the Korea Fund premium reached a peak following a period of sustained strong stock market performance in Korea as well as in most of the major world markets, although it is difficult to understand why the premium reached such a high level. Moreover, as indicated earlier, the sharp drop in the premium from 157 per cent at the end of August 1987 to 61 per cent at the end of October and 30 per cent in early December was surprising, given that the Korean stock market actually increased in value during this period. Not only was this change in the premium difficult to understand, but many other large month-to-month changes in the premium are equally difficult to explain by the fundamentals. Since there were no significant changes in the authorities' capital market liberalization policies until December 1988, this would not appear to be a factor causing month-to-month changes in the level of the premium. However, it was probably true that capital market internationalization progressed more slowly during this period than was generally expected, and this might have been one cause of the gradual increase in the level of the premium. The two other major factors I have mentioned – the performance of the Korean stock market, which is probably perceived as an indication of its future performance, and the performance of the stock markets in the USA and perhaps

other major markets – have both significantly affected the level of the premium. However, changes in the buoyancy of the US market appear to have been the dominant influence.

The performance of the Korea Fund relative to the changes in the KSE composite share price index does not appear to have much influence on the magnitude of the premium over the net asset value. The Korea Fund generally did better than the market index until 1986, but it significantly underperformed relative to the market index during 1987. During the six months before the premium reached a peak of 157 per cent in August 1987, the net asset value of the Korea Fund's shares increased by only 10 per cent, while the KSE composite share price index increased by 41 per cent.

THE INTERNATIONALIZATION WINDFALL

Despite the sharp increase in the prices of Korean stocks during the past three years and a sharp rise in the average P/E ratio, the hefty premium in the price of Korea Fund shares indicates a strong foreign interest in investing in the Korean stock market and suggests that, from an international viewpoint, Korean stocks are still significantly underpriced. There is no way to measure the extent of this underpricing because the premium of the Korea Fund reflects the combined effect of the very limited foreign access to the Korean market at present, the higher expected profits of Korean companies in the future, as well as an expectation that the market will remain at least partially closed to foreign direct portfolio investment for a number of years.

The concept of an internationalization windfall used in this chapter is defined as the total increase in the value of Korean shares that would occur if there were a quick, full internationalization of the Korean stock market. If the internationalization takes place over a longer period, the cumulative value of the internationalization premium will be larger but the present value of these future sums, appropriately discounted, should be about the

Table 32.8 Korea Fund and Korea Europe Fund data, 1984–9 (US dollars)

| End-month | Net asset value | Korea Fund | | Korean Europe Fund |
		Market price	Percentage market premium	Percentage market premium
1984.8	11.12	13.250	19	–
1984.9	11.21	14.375	28	–
1984.10	11.29	14.625	30	–
1984.11	11.39	14.625	28	–
1984.12	11.46	14.125	23	–
1985.1	11.57	13.000	12	–
1985.2	11.45	12.625	10	–
1985.3	11.38	14.000	23	–
1985.4	11.17	13.500	21	–
1985.5	11.24	14.250	27	–
1985.6	11.49	14.750	28	–
1985.7	10.95	15.000	45	–
1985.8	10.87	14.250	31	–
1985.9	10.83	13.500	31	–
1985.10	11.10	14.000	26	–
1985.11	12.13	16.750	38	–
1985.12	13.42	17.625	31	–
1986.1	14.40	17.125	19	–
1986.2	15.83	26.875	20	–
1986.3	17.89	28.625	32	–
1986.4	17.75	29.375	65	–
1986.5	21.76	32.250	48	–
1986.6	22.36	33.375	49	–
1986.7	24.26	33.500	38	–
1986.8	23.52	37.375	59	–
1986.9	23.11	36.750	59	–
1986.10	22.25	31.500	42	–
1986.11	24.01	32.500	35	–
1986.12	24.49	34.750	42	–
1987.1	28.62	44.000	54	–
1987.2	29.49	63.500	81	–
1987.3	33.48	63.500	90	–
1987.4	30.61	62.750	105	155
1987.5	31.94	65.750	106	157
1987.6	33.36	70.125	110	124
1987.7	34.22	85.750	151	149
1987.8	32.52	83.500	157	194
1987.9	32.56	74.875	130	162
1987.10	32.77	52.625	61	35
1987.11	32.30	45.000	39	42
1987.12	33.85	55.125	63	52
1988.1	37.61	63.000	68	79
1988.2	37.29	81.250	118	93
1988.3	37.48	71.500	91	100
1988.4	39.31	72.000	83	91

1988.5	41.57	76.500	84	87
1988.6	42.22	70.250	66	80
1988.7	42.02	74.875	78	60
1988.8	37.60	66.625	72	56
1988.9	37.60	60.000	60	49
1988.10	41.85	66.000	58	58
1988.11	13.80[a]	22.250[a]	61	54
1988.12	15.93	26.500	66	69
1989.1	16.45	26.500	61	72
1989.2	17.23	30.375	76	86
1989.3	18.87	35.500	88	109
1989.4	17.44	33.000	89	93
1989.5	17.66	34.625	96	108
1989.6	16.87	31.625	88	99
1989.7	16.40	33.625	105	96
1989.8	19.27	39.500	105	141
1989.9	19.13	42.000	120	137

Sources: Daewoo Research Institute; *Wall Street Journal*; International Finance Corporation
Note: [a] Data starting in November 1988 reflect a three-for-one split in Korea Fund shares.

same. This potential rise in the value of Korean stock represents hidden wealth of considerable magnitude.[8] This raises the difficult issue of who should receive this windfall and how complete capital market internationalization should be implemented. A quick liberalization of the stock market could be done in such a way as to give all the benefit to Korean stockholders, but a gradual liberalization would almost inevitably give a significant windfall to foreigners. While the total magnitude of the internationalization windfall cannot be measured, the part that goes to foreigners as a result of gradual liberalization can be fairly closely measured if liberalization takes the form of an expansion of closed-end funds[9] traded in foreign markets. For each new issue of closed-end shares, the windfall to foreign investors is the difference between the issue price (the net asset value plus the underwriting charges) and the initial market price in the foreign market. Thus, when $30 million worth of Korea Europe Fund shares were issued at a price of $10 a share in 1987 and the initial market price in London increased to $20 per share, the windfall to foreign investors was $30 million.

Once internationalization is complete, the premium over net asset value on Korea Fund type shares will disappear. This will be achieved by a combination of a bidding up of Korean stock prices and an increase in the volume of foreign holdings of Korean shares. While we do not know either of these magnitudes at present, it is worth making some assumptions in order to illustrate this phenomenon. As of December 1988, the total market value of all stocks listed on the KSE was about W 64 trillion, or $94 billion at an exchange of W 680 per US dollar. The value in the Korean market of foreign portfolio holdings as of December 1988 was roughly $2 billion, or about 2 per cent of the total share market value. If we assume that the total market value of listed stock will double by the time internationalization is completed, the market value at that time will be about $188 billion (assuming the exchange rate remains unchanged). If we assume that foreigners will then hold 10 per cent of the total shares outstanding,[10] valued at $18.8 billion, this means that holdings by foreigners would increase by $16.8 billion by the time internationalization is complete. We then wish to isolate the windfall that will go to foreigners as a result of new investments in foreign-held Korean funds, since the windfall on existing foreign-held Korean funds is already reflected in the premium of their prices over their net asset values. If we assume the value of the present holdings of foreigners doubles to $4.0 billion, this means that new foreign purchases will account for $14.8 billion. If we assume that the initial value of these shares when Korea Fund type issues are made is $9.7 billion and if we assume that the present premium over issue price is about 70 per cent and that this percentage will decline on a straight-line basis as the $9.7 billion worth of securities is purchased, the windfall to foreigners from further gradual internationalization will be about $1.78 billion ($14.8 − $9.7 billion = $5.1 billion × 35 per cent). This is clearly a rough guess as to the magnitude of the windfall that might go to foreigners and I do not wish the reader to get distracted by the weaknesses of such a calculation. The only important point that needs to be made here is that the magnitude of the potential windfall to foreigners is very large.

An even larger windfall will go to the direct domestic holders of Korean stocks. How the internationalization windfall is allocated could have a significant impact on Korea's wealth distribution, as well as on the wealth of the particular foreign investors who are given the valuable indirect right to invest in the Korean equity market in the period leading up to complete internationalization. If an announcement were made today that the Korean stock market would be completely international-ized one month from today, the average price of Korean shares would increase during this one-month period to a level that Korean investors believe foreign investors would be willing to pay when the market is internationalized.[11] The important point is that most (perhaps all) of the increase would occur before any additional foreigners could participate directly in the market. The net asset value of Korea Fund type shares would increase sharply, but this would be offset by the elimination of the premium over net asset value, so that there would probably be some net decline in the value of these shares. After the capital market was fully opened to foreigners, there would be a further adjustment in the price of Korean shares, either upward or downward, reflecting the difference between what Korean

investors expected foreign investors to be willing to pay for Korean stocks and what they were actually willing to pay. If the authorities were to announce today that there would be complete international-ization four years from now, there would be a sharp, but only partial, adjustment during the period after the announcement and then a gradual further adjustment (partly related to a higher level of uncertainty as to whether the authorities would carry out the announced plan after four years).

The authorities could proceed with a gradual internationalization in a number of ways. They could gradually expand the participation of foreign closed-end funds. Each infusion of foreign funds would presumably bid up the price of Korean securities and lower the premium over net asset value, with the price of the existing shares of foreign-owned closed-end funds adjusting to reflect these opposing forces. This process could be continued until the premium on the price of closed-end funds virtually disappeared or a discount emerged, at which point complete internationaliza-tion could be implemented. However, it will be explained shortly that the gradual expansion of closed-end funds would provide a larger immediate windfall to those foreigners permitted to make the additional indirect investments in Korea.

Given the present premium on the Korea Fund, how should expansions of this Fund or the issuance of similar funds be priced? As long as there is a significant premium over net asset value on the existing closed-end funds, any new similar funds issued at net asset value plus underwriting costs would be greatly oversubscribed, and the market price of such shares would be quickly bid up in the market after they were issued. Thus a windfall would go to whomever obtained the shares in the initial allocation. Giving this kind of windfall to foreigners would seem a questionable policy. This is precisely what happened when Korea issued the Korea Europe Fund. The premium on the Korea Europe Fund shares increased by more than 100 per cent before they were even placed on the market. It appears that this windfall went to the stockholders who received the initial allocation from the underwriters; however, the underwriters probably received a significant indirect benefit as well. In any case, investors who were able to purchase the shares at the issue price of $10.71 were able to sell them for $20 as soon as trading in the shares started and for $25 within a month. It is important to realize that the amount that is invested in the Korean stock market is only the original $10.71 a share minus the underwriting costs (usually 7 per cent of the share value). When a decision was made to add to the capital of the existing Korea Fund in 1986, it was decided to price the new shares at the existing market price which reflected a considerable premium over the net asset value of about 82 per cent. If the market is efficient, the average premium over net asset value should be only slightly lower for the now larger Fund. The premium over net asset value indicates the marginal value of indirect access to the Korean stock market.

A numerical example may help to explain this. Suppose that an existing fund has a market value of $60 a share and a total market value of $60 million, with a net asset value of $40 per share and a total net asset value of $40 million. Thus, the existing premium over net asset value is 50 per cent. Now assume that an additional $30 million worth of shares is issued at the market price of $60 a share, raising the total market value of the fund to $90 million. However, the net asset value also increases by $30 million, raising the total net asset value to $70 million and reducing the premium per share over net asset value to about 28.5 per cent. If the market is efficient, it should immediately bid up the price of the shares in the foreign market and the average premium so that the new average premium is close to the original premium of 50 per cent. It is likely to remain somewhat below 50 per cent, because the scarcity value of the limited foreign access to the Korean market should decline somewhat as the total foreign access increases (this represents an additional step toward internationalization). In practice, the price of the existing fund shares should be bid up as soon as the market hears the announcement that there will be a capital increase, thereby significantly raising the premium over net asset value. Then the market price, when the new shares are issued, should result in a premium over net asset value equal to that which existed before the announcement of the capital increase (ignoring the leakage in the form of under-writing costs).[12]

It is important to realize that just as much of the windfall goes to foreign investors in this case as in the case of the issuance of a new foreign fund, with shares priced close to the net asset value. But in this case, the windfall will go to the holders of the existing shares in the Fund, not to the purchasers of the new shares or to the underwriters. Infusion of capital in this form will yield the same amount for investment in the Korean stock market and will have the same impact on bidding up the price of Korean stocks. The magnitude of the windfall to foreign investors should also be the same, although the particular foreign investors receiving the windfall may be different.

It is difficult to devise a mechanism of gradual capital market liberalization that does not provide a significant windfall to foreigners, although an auction mechanism may provide the best solution. For instance, if the government were to auction the right to invest $100 million in Korean equities through a closed-end fund managed by a securities firm during 1990, with an assurance that no one else will be given this right in 1990, it is likely to receive a very substantial bid (close to the premium over net asset value on the existing closed-end funds). However, it might be difficult for the government to resort to a tax or auction mechanism without giving some clearer indication of the future course of internationalization of the capital market.[13] It is obvious that the value of being able to invest $100 million in the Korean stock market in 1990 depends on the course of internationalization in the future. It would be greatest if internationalization were to take place very slowly, and least if complete internationalization had already been announced and were to take place soon.

The use of an auction mechanism to decide which foreigners would have the right to make new investments in the Korean stock market might be enough to deter underwriters from making aggressive bids, since they may have little experience in assessing the risk of a change in the level of the premium over net asset value between the time when they make the bid and when they can actually distribute the fund shares.[14] But they should be able to lessen or eliminate this risk by obtaining commitments from investors to purchase the new stock at a specified price that would yield the underwriters a secure and adequate profit. While use of the auction mechanism would probably yield the highest return to the government for the planned new access by foreigners to the Korean market, close to the same result could be achieved by merely negotiating with a chosen group of underwriters. This would enable the authorities to continue to decide the country in which the new fund would be located as well as the specific underwriters, which have been important considerations to them. If the premium over net asset value of similar funds was 60 per cent, the government might offer the underwriter the normal 7 per cent underwriting fee and simply charge him slightly less than 60 per cent of the value of the new fund for the right to set up the new fund. The present procedure simply gives all this amount away as a gift.

An alternative to selling or auctioning off a specified magnitude of indirect investment opportunity in the Korean market each year until there is little or no auction premium paid would be to specify the level of a one-time tax on new indirect investment, say at 60 per cent for the first year, and accept any quantity of new funds by foreign investors willing to pay that level of tax. The tax level on new investment could then be reduced each year until it was eventually reduced to a level close to zero, at which point the market could be opened to direct foreign purchase of Korean stocks. Another alternative would be to seek to tax the capital gains on these foreign funds invested in Korean stocks, but this would be impracticable in so far as the funds are traded in foreign markets. Still another possibility would be to place a tax on the premium of the price of the closed-end funds over their net asset values. A wide variety of

mechanisms could be devised, but it would probably be best to levy a relatively small monthly tax of 1–2 per cent on the premium at the end of each month, rather than to levy a higher tax rate once a year. It might be even less disruptive to the market for these funds to pay the tax at a still lower rate on a weekly basis.[15] This tax would be paid by the managers of the fund out of its assets which, if the fund were fully invested, would require a small sale of the Korean stock holdings.

To summarize, the internationalization windfall that goes to foreigners goes entirely to the firm or individual given the right to purchase new shares at a price equal to the net asset value (plus underwriting charges) in the case of new closed-end funds, and to the present stockholders in the case of additions to the capital of the existing funds. The subsequent purchaser of such shares does not receive any windfall unless the government changes its policy to curtail international access to the Korean market for a longer period than implicitly assumed at the time the new shares are issued. It appears appropriate to consider capturing part of this internationalization windfall for the Korean people as a whole through an auction or tax mechanism.[16]

Besides foreign-managed closed-end funds, Korea has used two other mechanisms for internationalizing its capital market, namely domestically managed open-end investment trusts and convertible bonds sold in foreign markets. The next section explores whether these forms of internationalization also provide a windfall to foreigners.

While the international trust funds (open-end funds managed by Korean securities companies) were not set up to trade on foreign stock markets,[17] they have in fact been traded between foreign institutional investors at significant premia over their net asset value. At the end of July 1989 the premium on the beneficiary certificates issued by the international trusts was 72 per cent for each of the five largest trust funds, compared with about 94 per cent for the Korea Europe Fund and 105 per cent for the Korea Fund. The premium on the beneficiary certificates has consistently been less than for the closed-end funds, although the magnitude of the difference has varied widely. One reason for the lower premium on the beneficiary certificates is that they are less liquid because they do not trade on any stock exchange and the minimum size of transactions is relatively large.

While these trust funds have been set up as open-end funds that can be redeemed with the managers of the trust funds at their net asset value, as long as they can be traded abroad at a premium, there is obviously no incentive to redeem the beneficiary certificates. Thus, in practice the international investment trusts have been treated essentially like closed-end funds. Usually, shares in open-end funds cannot be traded and can be redeemed with the issuer only at their net asset value. The various Korean international trust funds provide the same access to the Korean securities market as the closed-end funds. The ability of foreigners to purchase such beneficiary certificates is a significant windfall, and they would be willing to pay much more than the net asset value for such investments. A similar use of an auction system or tax mechanism could be used in conjunction with any new issues of such international trust funds.

In the present circumstances of excess demand by foreigners to invest in Korean stocks, it does not make much difference whether Korea internationalizes its market through expansion of open-end or closed-end funds as long as they can both be traded abroad. Foreign investors are willing to pay a premium for either. In practice, foreign investors will not wish to redeem open-end funds because they are worth more than their net asset value. However, they would be willing to pay a higher premium for closed-end funds because they provide the same indirect access to the Korean stock market but have the advantage of being more liquid. Investors can easily sell these funds on the market and realize their full value at any time, while they can realize the full value of the open-end funds only by holding them until internationalization of the market is complete or by selling them in a less organized market.[18] Hence, if the government were to attempt to capture the premia foreigners were willing to pay, more revenue could

be obtained by auctioning closed-end funds or by taxing the premium on them.

The third method of internationalizing the Korean capital market, which has been used so far, is through the issuance of major Korean companies of convertible bonds in foreign markets. As can be seen in Table 32.4, the first four convertible bond issues had US dollar interest rates of 3–5 per cent and conversion premia of 50–5 per cent. So far, even though the stock of Samsung Electronics has appreciated enough to permit conversion, none has taken place because the price of the convertible bonds has increased to a level far above the present conversion value of the underlying stock. In other words, convertible bonds have become similar in nature to the Korea Fund shares and trade at a price far above the conversion value (or the net asset value of the stock).

New issues of convertible bonds could be priced in a way that captured most of the internationalization premium for the company that issued the bonds, which would benefit its shareholders. This was an extraordinarily attractive form of financing for the Korean companies that were declared eligible to issue convertible bonds, and it is remarkable that more companies did not issue them.[19] In 1988 convertible bonds could be issued with a lower interest rate and a higher conversion premium than was possible for the earlier issues. In September 1988, Saehon Media issued $30 million of convertible bonds with an interest rate of 1.75 per cent and a conversion premium of 65 per cent.[20]

If this method of internationalizing the capital market were used, little of the internationalization windfall would go to foreigners, but a major windfall would go to those companies deemed eligible. Just as future issues of Korea Fund type shares or investment-trust type shares could be auctioned or taxed, so could the right for Korean companies to issue any future convertible bonds in foreign markets. It is not practical to spread the windfall among all companies listed on the stock exchange because the amount of each foreign bond issue would be very small. Unless the windfall is fully taxed, the issuance of convertible bonds is less attractive than the other forms of internationalization, because it inevitably benefits particular companies, while the open- and closed-end stock funds potentially help the shareholders of all companies listed on the stock exchange. Once the Korean capital market has been fully internationalized, foreigners probably will not be willing to pay much premium for indirect access to the market, and a tax on such access would no longer be appropriate.

Although it will not be treated in this chapter, most of the discussion on the internationalization of the Korean stock market also applies to the opening up of foreign access to the government and corporate bond markets. As long as interest rates in Korea are higher than in the major capital markets and this differential is not fully offset by the perceived exchange rate risk, there will be high demand for access to such bonds, which can be subjected to various taxes.

Besides the question of who should receive the foreign component of the internationalization windfall, the issue arises as to whether the domestic component should be allowed to go completely to Koreans and foreign resident shareholders[21] or whether some of it should be captured for the good of the Korean people as a whole. It should be recognized that the option of allowing the present Korean stockholders to obtain all of the benefit of the share price increase that will accompany internationalization of the Korean market would probably make Korea's income and wealth distribution more unequal. Given the skewed pattern of share ownership, the relatively wealthy families would benefit more than the relatively poor.[22] This is especially true since Korea has no capital gains tax on the appreciation of financial assets.

The domestic component of the internationalization windfall cannot be isolated from other influences on share prices and, accordingly, cannot be taxed separately. It might be possible to isolate this component and tax it separately if the government were to announce a complete liberalization to take place in a short period and levy a 100 per cent temporary capital gains tax on the

increase in stock prices that occurred between the date of the announcement and, say, one month later, when the internationalization could be deemed largely completed. However, this would involve taxing unrealized capital gains and is not practical for a number of reasons. Still, the existence of the internationalization premium adds to the already good case for introducing a capital gains tax on the realized appreciation in the value of corporate shares.

CAPITAL GAINS TAXATION ON STOCKS AND BONDS

Both in the economic literature and in the practices in different countries, there is a wide divergence of views on whether, how much and in what form capital gains should be taxed. At present, the USA taxes fully both short- and long-term capital gains as part of its global personal income tax. Korea levies a high capital gains tax on real estate, but no capital gains tax on corporate shares or bonds. Japan also exempts capital gains on corporate shares from taxation unless an individual engages in enough trades to qualify him as a trader. During the early stages of capital market development, there is a strong case for not levying a tax on the capital gains in corporate shares. However, with the more than tenfold increase in the total market value of Korean stocks in the last five years, the Korean capital market can now be deemed matured enough to no longer need incentives.

The introduction of a capital gains tax on bonds and corporate shares is entwined with the issues of the continued acceptance of 'no-name' security accounts and the globalization of the personal income tax (combining all forms of personal income rather than taxing different forms of income separately, as under a schedular system). While it would be possible to introduce a flat rate, separate tax on capital gains of, say, 10 per cent, it would be better to eliminate 'no-name' securities, introduce a global income tax and include interest, dividends and capital gains as part of global income (perhaps with the capital gains component or all income indexed for inflation). Significant tax incentives for savings are no longer desirable in the new environment in which national savings exceed investment. Tax administration has also improved significantly so that enforcing a global income tax would not be too difficult. Increased concern about the horizontal and vertical equity of the tax system would also seem appropriate now that Korea's per capita income level puts it in the middle-income level. Taxing personal income on a global basis would improve the equity of income taxation.

The introduction of a capital gains tax raises a host of other issues, which I do not consider appropriate to discuss at length in this chapter. However, a few brief comments may be useful. There is considerable merit in adjusting the capital base through an appropriate index to take account of inflation and to ensure that only real gains are taxed. There is also a case for some mechanism to adjust for the bunching of gains realized in a one-year period that may have occurred over many years. Other issues include whether there should be different treatment of short- and long-term capital gains, whether the capital gains tax should be phased in gradually and whether different treatment should be given to capital gains from securities and to those from real estate.

There is some advantage to having a capital gains tax on securities in effect before additional capital market internationalization measures are fully implemented. The gradual introduction of the capital gains tax would probably lessen the risk of a severe adverse stock market response. While many countries give similar tax treatment to capital gains from real estate and securities, there may be a good case for maintaining a significant differential in treatment in favour of securities. Korea has managed to do a better job of discouraging real estate speculation than has Japan and a continuing effort to discourage real estate speculation is desirable and helps to channel savings into more productive investment.

It is not desirable to tax capital gains separately, even at progressive rates, because, if this form of income is not combined with other forms of income, wealthy taxpayers receive disproportionate benefits. At first, only 20 per cent of realized

capital gains might be treated as part of the total income of taxpayers, and over time this ratio could be increased to whatever ratio is deemed appropriate.

Although there is no capital gains tax on securities at present, there is a securities transfer tax, which was first introduced in 1963, but abolished in 1971 and then reintroduced in 1979. The tax is levied on the sales of stocks at a rate of 0.5 per cent of the sales value whether or not there is any capital gain. However, transactions of issues below par value are not taxed and sales resulting from newly issued securities at prices below the issue prices are not taxed if the sale takes place within one year of the public offering or before the record date for the first dividend after the exchange listing. The securities transfer tax was first established in lieu of a capital gains tax (Korea Securities Dealers Association 1987: 93). It would be possible to increase this tax to capture some of the increase in the value of stocks. However, this tax is much less equitable than even a flat rate capital gains tax on all sales, which would be applied to sales resulting in capital losses. It would probably be best to eliminate the securities transfer tax completely once any form of capital gains tax is implemented. While it might be continued as a means of discouraging short-run speculative behaviour resulting in rapid turnover, if this is the objective, perhaps there should be an exemption if the stock is held for a minimum period.

CONCLUSIONS

After briefly describing the recent evolution of the Korean market for corporate shares and bonds and the government's policy with regard to internationalization of the capital market, this chapter developed a concept called the 'internationalization windfall'. After establishing the existence of this economic rent, I discussed alternative policies by which the government could tax part of it. It is argued that the government's policy of gradual internationalization of the stock market inevitably provides a significant windfall to foreigners and to Korean shareholders and that this should be partially taxed for the benefit of the Korean people as a whole. It is also argued that the best mechanism for capturing the windfall would be to auction the right for any new indirect access by foreigners to the Korean capital market.[24] In order to concentrate on the form that internationalization should take, I do not attempt to address the issue of the optimum pace of internationalization or the benefits to be derived from internationalization. It is simply assumed that internationalization will take place gradually.

The Korean government is likely to open the stock market only gradually for a number of reasons. (1) There is a strong demand by foreigners to invest in Korea and this, if granted, would put pressure on the won to appreciate. At a time when there is a current account surplus, there is no need to attract foreign capital inflows. (2) There is a desire to avoid foreign purchase and control of Korean firms. (3) There is a concern that foreign investors would have a speculative, short-term focus, which might lead to destabilizing movements in and out of the Korean market, particularly during any periods of serious domestic unrest. (4) It is believed that Korean securities companies need more time to develop before they are in a position to compete with foreign securities firms.

NOTES

1 In 1980 the current account *deficit* was $5.3 billion (9.5 per cent of GNP), while in 1987 the current account *surplus* was $9.8 billion (8.0 per cent of GNP).
2 *Open-end funds*, commonly called mutual funds, are management investment companies that stand ready to redeem shares at or near the net asset value at all times. All such companies are open in at least one direction, since outstanding shares may be redeemed at the shareholder's discretion. Hence the number of shares outstanding tends to fluctuate from day to day, with corresponding changes in the fund's investment portfolio. *Net asset value* refers to the value per share of the investment fund's financial assets in the form of cash, bonds or stocks, valued in the local currency of the country of the investment and converted into the foreign currency

at the official exchange rate effective at the time of measurement.
3 *Closed-end funds* are investment companies that do not stand ready to redeem shares continuously. Hence, the total number of shares outstanding does not change from day to day. Shares of closed-end funds are traded through brokers (usually on organized stock exchanges) at prices agreed upon by the parties involved. There is no necessary relationship between the price of such a share and its net asset value. Since the fund does not stand ready to redeem shares or to buy them in the open market at the net asset value there is no obvious floor under the price, and since new shares cannot be purchased from the fund at the net asset value there is no obvious ceiling.
4 The Korea Europe Fund reached an even higher premium of 194 per cent at the end of August 1987.
5 Most of the discussion in this section will be based on the Korea Fund which has been in existence longer, but the nature of the issues raised is essentially the same for the Korea Europe Fund and the seven international trust funds.
6 In September–October 1989 after this chapter was written, closed-end country funds became the subject of an investment mania, which almost defies explanation and indicates that capital markets at times can be highly inefficient. As of 1 September 1989, the only closed-end country funds listed on American stock exchanges trading at a premium were Korea (105 per cent), Spain (23 per cent), India Growth (16 per cent) and Thai (15 per cent). On the same date the Germany Fund traded at a discount of 9 per cent and the Italy Fund at a discount of 18 per cent. At that point the premia on the Korea Fund and the Thai Fund were not unusual, but the 23 per cent premium on the Spain Fund was highly unusual in that no closed-end country fund for an open capital market had ever traded at a premium of this magnitude. However, this was just the start of the bizarre developments to follow. As of 6 October, a larger number of country funds were trading at premia as follows: Spain (145 per cent), Korea (120 per cent), Thai (48 per cent), First Iberian (Spain and Portugal, 49 per cent), Austria (38 per cent), Germany (27 per cent), India Growth (17 per cent), Italy (10 per cent), Malaysia (10 per cent) and Helveta (Swiss, 1 per cent). Press reports attributed the sharp increase in the premium of country funds to the recommendation of one or more Japanese brokerage firms to invest in the country funds of EC members (especially Spain which was also expected to

benefit from the Olympics in 1992) and certain emerging countries' markets (including Thailand and Malaysia). Given that it is possible for foreigners to purchase stock directly in Spain there appears to be no good reason to pay more than 10 per cent premium for the diversified portfolio and simplified transactions obtainable by purchasing shares in the Spain Fund. It was not surprising that as the premium reached unprecedented (and seemingly irrational) levels significant excess demand emerged to sell the Spain Fund short. The inability to execute orders to sell a stock short is highly unusual. (The supply of Spain Fund shares available to sell short was limited because relatively few shares were purchased on margin.) With the dramatic changes in Eastern Europe at the end of 1989 there was a second round of 'country-fund' mania especially in the neighbouring markets, again according to press reports based on Japanese brokerage firm recommendations. As of 12 January 1990, the following premia existed: Germany Fund (85 per cent), Korea Fund (75 per cent), Austria Fund (66 per cent), Thai Fund (66 per cent), Malaysia Fund (66 per cent) and India Growth Fund (48 per cent). The analysis in this chapter assumes that these high premia on country funds in open capital markets will not persist.

7 It is also possible that foreigners were more troubled by the political uncertainty resulting from the Presidential elections held on 16 December 1987. The low point in the Korea Fund premium of 30 per cent was reached on 4 December, shortly before the elections. However, the political uncertainty was already evident in August and September 1988, when the premium was very high and, if anything, the probability of the opposition gaining power diminished during October and November as it became increasingly clear that the main opposition parties would not be able to agree to support a single candidate.

8 It may be useful to provide an illustrative calculation, based on end-1988 data, of the possible magnitude of the internationalization windfall and of that portion that might go to foreigners. The Korea Fund and the Korea Europe Fund had a premium over net asset value of roughly 70 per cent, which can be interpreted as the upper limit of the internationalization windfall. For illustrative purposes we shall assume that the total value of Korean stocks would increase by 30 per cent if there were to be a complete internationalization of the capital market in a brief period. This potential rise in the value of Korean stocks represents hidden wealth of roughly W 19 trillion (30 per cent of end-

December 1988 market capitalization of W 64 trillion), equal to 15 per cent of 1988 GNP or more than 60 per cent of 1988 central government revenue collections.

9 This would also be true if it were to take the form of an expansion of open-end international investment trusts similar to the seven already in operation.

10 In 1985, foreigners held about 6 per cent of the total value of Japanese shares and about 14 per cent of the total value of Thai corporate shares; while foreigners may invest directly in the Thai stock market, there are limits (frequently 20 per cent) on the proportion that may be held directly by foreigners, which in a number of cases have been reached. See Rowley (1987).

11 The increase is likely to be less than the present premium over net asset value of Korea Fund type investments.

12 Assuming that any other factors that affect this premium are unchanged.

13 As it has now given such an indication, it could be argued that now is an appropriate time to introduce such a mechanism.

14 While the use of an auction mechanism for this purpose would be novel, this has been done in connection with import quotas to capture part of a similar form of economic rent.

15 Unlike the other mechanisms, which would seek to lessen or avoid the windfall to foreigners from new access to the Korean market, this mechanism could also be levied on the existing funds, although this might be deemed inappropriate. Unlike the other possibilities mentioned above, this would be an ongoing tax until the premium disappears, rather than a one-time tax.

16 The revenue derived from taxing this windfall that goes to foreigners and the domestic capital gains tax suggested later in this chapter could be used to meet the increased expenditure for social welfare that is likely to be an inevitable outgrowth of the sharp increase in per capita income in Korea and the more democratic government. I do not spell out the tactical considerations involved in introducing a tax auction mechanism on foreign access to the Korean stock market and how this issue might affect broader relationships regarding international trade.

17 While the Korean Growth Trust was set up to be listed on the Hong Kong Stock Exchange, it does not appear to have been traded on that exchange.

18 This chapter ignores the fact that different funds may have different values because of differences in the quality of their particular investment portfolio.

19 It is probable that there has been some restraint on the issuance of such bonds.
20 This company is generally considered a second-tier company without a secure profit situation; a first-rank corporation would presumably have been able to get even more favourable terms.
21 Foreigners who have been residents in Korea for six months or more are entitled to purchase shares in the Korean stock market.
22 At the end of 1987, 1 per cent of the shareholders owned 60 per cent of the total shares. See Korea Stock Exchange, various issues.
23 For a discussion of direct foreign investment, see Koo (1986).
24 The argument presented in this chapter is similar to that made for auctioning import quota licences rather than simply giving away quota rights. Both New Zealand and Australia have auctioned import quota licences. See Bergsten et al. (1987).

BIBLIOGRAPHY

Bergsten, C. F., Elliott, K. A., Schott, J. J. and Takacs, W. E. (1987) *Auction Quotas and United States Trade Policy*, Washington, DC: Institute for International Economics.

W. I. Carr (Far East) Limited (1988) *Korea Monthly Review*, August.

Cole, D. C. and Park, Y.-C. (1983) *Financial Development in Korea 1945–78*, Cambridge, MA: Harvard University Press.

The CT Guide to World Equity Markets 1988 (1988) London: Euromoney Publications.

International Finance Corporation (1988) *Emerging Stock Markets Factbook, 1988*, Washington, DC: International Finance Corporation.

Koo, B. (1986) 'The role of direct foreign investment in Korea's recent economic growth', in J. Kim (ed.) *Financial Development Policies and Issues*, Seoul, Korea: Korea Development Institute, pp. 189–236.

Korea Development Finance Corporation (1970) *Money and Capital Markets in Korea and the Potential for their Improvement*, Seoul, Korea.

Korea Securities Dealers Association (1988) *Securities Markets in Korea*, Seoul, Korea.

Korea Stock Exchange (various issues) *Stock*, Seoul, Korea.

Lee, Y. (1988) 'Internationalization of major financial sectors in Korea', paper presented at the Fourth KDI/CHIER Joint Seminar on Industrial Policies in the Republic of Korea and the Republic of China in Seoul, 8–9 February.

Lucky Economic Research Institute, *Korean Securities Market 1987*.

Rowley, A. (1987) *Asian Stockmarkets, The Inside Story*, Homewood, IL: Dow-Jones-Irwin.

Sakong, I. (1977) 'An overview of corporate finance and the long-term securities market', in C. K. Kim (ed.) *Planning Model and Macroeconomic Policy Issues*, Seoul, Korea: Korea Development Institute, pp. 228–62.

Tun Wai, U. and Hugh, T. P. (1973) 'Stock and bond issues and capital markets in less developed countries', *IMF Staff Papers*, July: 253–317.

Van Agtmael, A. W. (1984) *Emerging Securities Markets*, London: Euromoney Publications.

INDEX